Rick Steves'

MEDITERRANEAN
CRUISE PORTS

By Rick Steves with Cameron Hewitt

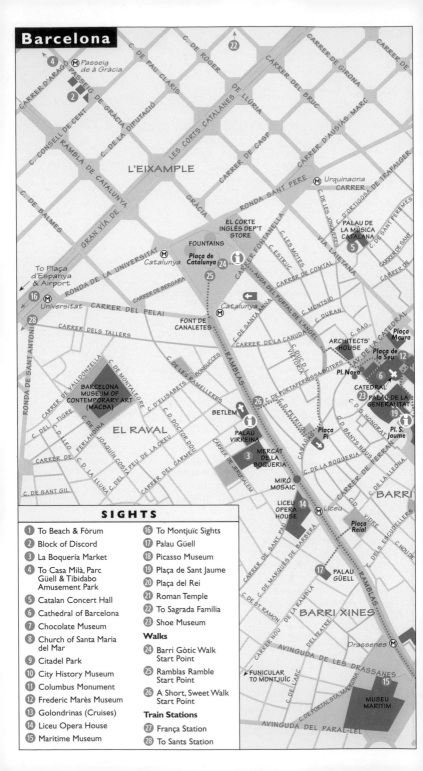

Barcelona

L'EIXAMPLE

Passeig de à Gràcia

C. DE PAU CLARIS

C. DE ROGER

CARRER DE GIRONA

CARRER DE

CARRER D'ARAGÓ

PASSEIG DE GRACIA

C. DE BALMES

C. CONSELL DE CENT

C. DE LA DIPUTACIÓ

RAMBLA DE CATALUNYA

LES CORTS CATALANES

CARRER DE CASP

CARRER DEL BRUC

CARRER D'AUSIAS MARC

GRAN VIA DE

GRÀCIA

RONDA SANT PERE

Urquinaona CARRER

RONDA DE LA UNIVERSITAT

D'ORTIGOSA DE TRAFALGER

Catalunya

EL CORTE INGLÉS DEP'T STORE

PALAU DE LA MÚSICA CATALANA

C. DE SANT PERE MÉS

CARRER DE SANT

To Plaça d'Espanya & Airport

Carrer de Bergara

FOUNTAINS

Plaça de Catalunya

VIA LAIETANA

C. DE LES JONQUERES

Universitat

CARRER DEL PELAI

AVDA DEL PORTAL DE L'ANGEL

Catalunya

C. LES MOTES

C. DE COMTAL

C. MONTSIÓ

CARRER DELS TALLERS

FONT DE CANALETES

C. DE SANTA ANNA

C. DURAN

C. SAG.

Plaça Maura

RONDA DE SANT ANTONI

C. DE VALLDONZELLA

C. DE MONTALEGRE

C. DE LES PONSBUGES

RAMBLAS

CARRER DE LA CANUDA

C. PUCA

VICTORIA

ARCHITECTS' HOUSE

AV. DE LA CATEDRAL

Plaça de la Seu

BARCELONA MUSEUM OF CONTEMPORARY ART (MACBA)

C. D'ELISABETS

C. DE LES RAMELLERES

C. DE PORTAFERRISSA

Pl. Nova

CATEDRAL

Plaça de la Seu

C. DEL TIGRE

C. FERLANDINA

C. DE JOAQUÍN COSTA

C. DOCTOR DOU

BETLEM

C. DE PETRIXOL

C. BOTERS

C. D. S. HONORAT

PALAU DE LA GENERALITAT

Pl. S. Jaume

EL RAVAL

C. DE LEÓ

C. PEU DE LA CREU

PALAU VIRREINA

Plaça Pi

C. BANYS NOUS

CARRER DE FERRAN

C. DE LA LLEONA

C. DE LA LLUNA

C. DEL CARME

CARRER DE JERUSALEM

MERCÁT DE LA BOQUERIA

CARRER DE LA BOQUERIA

BARRI

C. DE SANT GIL

MIRÓ MOSAIC

LICEU OPERA HOUSE

Liceu

Plaça Reial

C. D. DELS ESCUDELLERS

C. NOUDE

CARRER DE SANT PAU

C. DE MARQUÉS DE BARBERÁ

Drassenes

PALAU GÜELL

RAMBLAS

BARRI XINES

CARRER NOU DE LA RAMBLA

AVINGUDA DE LES DRASSANES

FUNICULAR TO MONTJUIC

MUSEU MARÍTIM

C. DE L'ARC

C. DE PORTAL STA. MADRONA

AVINGUDA DEL PARAL-LEL

SIGHTS

1 To Beach & Fòrum
2 Block of Discord
3 La Boquería Market
4 To Casa Milà, Parc Güell & Tibidabo Amusement Park
5 Catalan Concert Hall
6 Cathedral of Barcelona
7 Chocolate Museum
8 Church of Santa Maria del Mar
9 Citadel Park
10 City History Museum
11 Columbus Monument
12 Frederic Marès Museum
13 Golondrinas (Cruises)
14 Liceu Opera House
15 Maritime Museum

16 To Montjuïc Sights
17 Palau Güell
18 Picasso Museum
19 Plaça de Sant Jaume
20 Plaça del Rei
21 Roman Temple
22 To Sagrada Família
23 Shoe Museum

Walks
24 Barri Gòtic Walk Start Point
25 Ramblas Ramble Start Point
26 A Short, Sweet Walk Start Point

Train Stations
27 França Station
28 To Sants Station

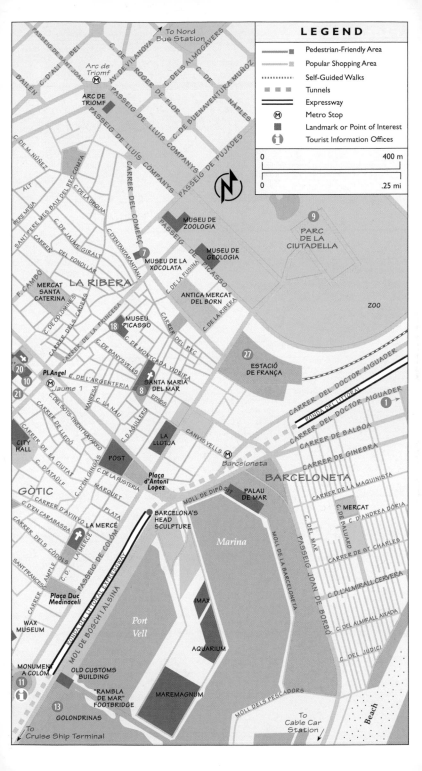

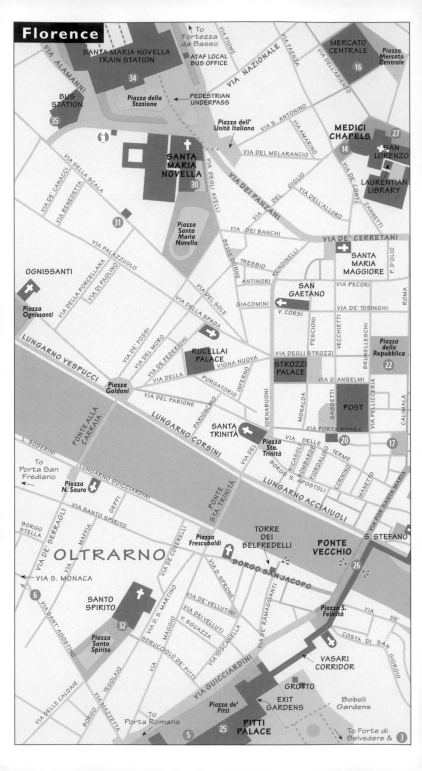

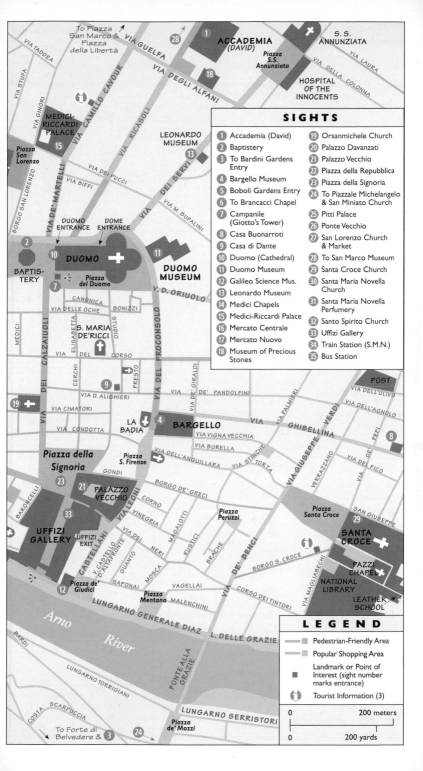

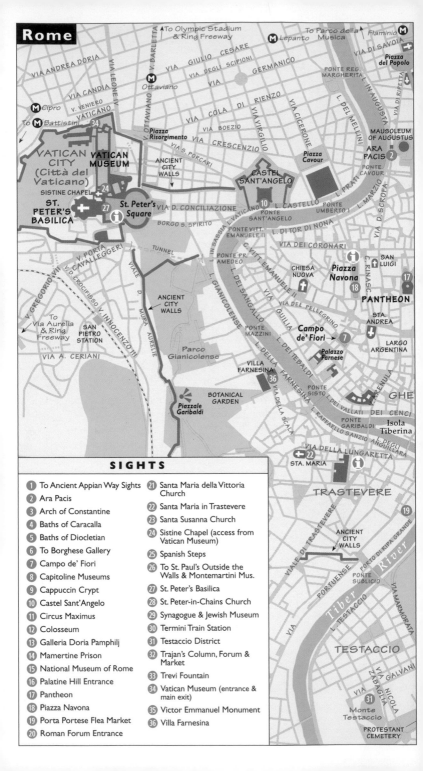

Rome

SIGHTS

1. To Ancient Appian Way Sights
2. Ara Pacis
3. Arch of Constantine
4. Baths of Caracalla
5. Baths of Diocletian
6. To Borghese Gallery
7. Campo de' Fiori
8. Capitoline Museums
9. Cappuccin Crypt
10. Castel Sant'Angelo
11. Circus Maximus
12. Colosseum
13. Galleria Doria Pamphilj
14. Mamertine Prison
15. National Museum of Rome
16. Palatine Hill Entrance
17. Pantheon
18. Piazza Navona
19. Porta Portese Flea Market
20. Roman Forum Entrance
21. Santa Maria della Vittoria Church
22. Santa Maria in Trastevere
23. Santa Susanna Church
24. Sistine Chapel (access from Vatican Museum)
25. Spanish Steps
26. To St. Paul's Outside the Walls & Montemartini Mus.
27. St. Peter's Basilica
28. St. Peter-in-Chains Church
29. Synagogue & Jewish Museum
30. Termini Train Station
31. Testaccio District
32. Trajan's Column, Forum & Market
33. Trevi Fountain
34. Vatican Museum (entrance & main exit)
35. Victor Emmanuel Monument
36. Villa Farnesina

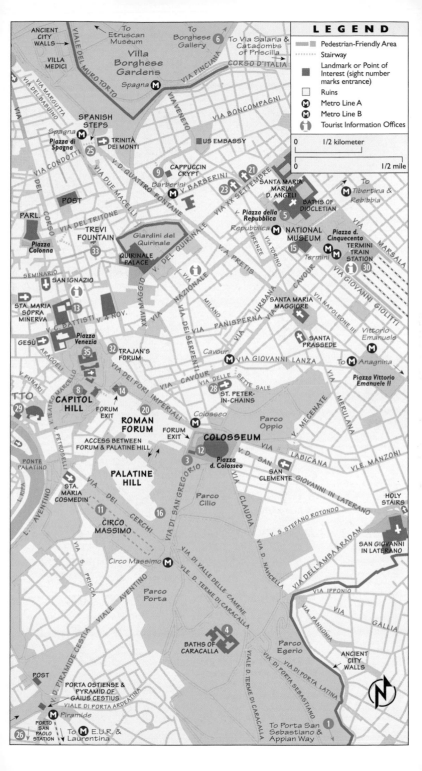

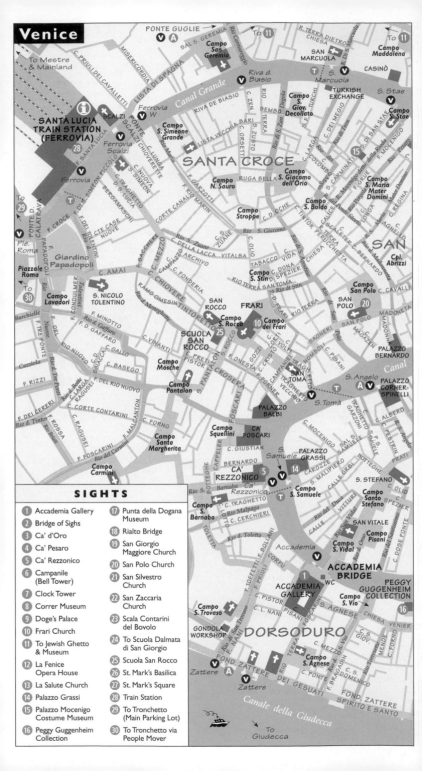

Venice

SIGHTS

1. Accademia Gallery
2. Bridge of Sighs
3. Ca' d'Oro
4. Ca' Pesaro
5. Ca' Rezzonico
6. Campanile (Bell Tower)
7. Clock Tower
8. Correr Museum
9. Doge's Palace
10. Frari Church
11. To Jewish Ghetto & Museum
12. La Fenice Opera House
13. La Salute Church
14. Palazzo Grassi
15. Palazzo Mocenigo Costume Museum
16. Peggy Guggenheim Collection
17. Punta della Dogana Museum
18. Rialto Bridge
19. San Giorgio Maggiore Church
20. San Polo Church
21. San Silvestro Church
22. San Zaccaria Church
23. Scala Contarini del Bovolo
24. To Scuola Dalmata di San Giorgio
25. Scuola San Rocco
26. St. Mark's Basilica
27. St. Mark's Square
28. Train Station
29. To Tronchetto (Main Parking Lot)
30. To Tronchetto via People Mover

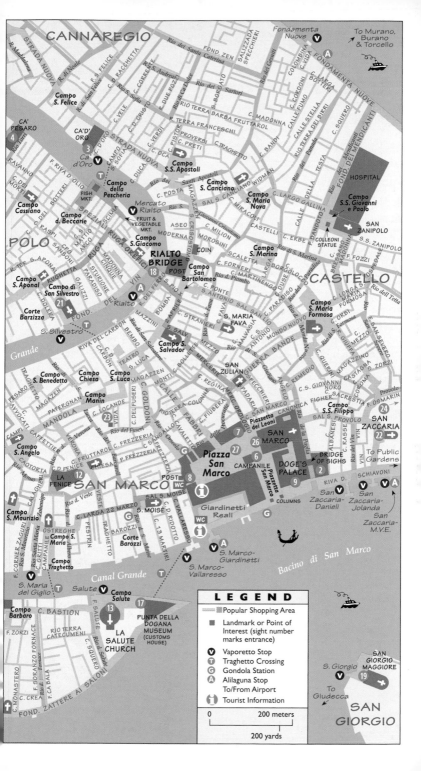

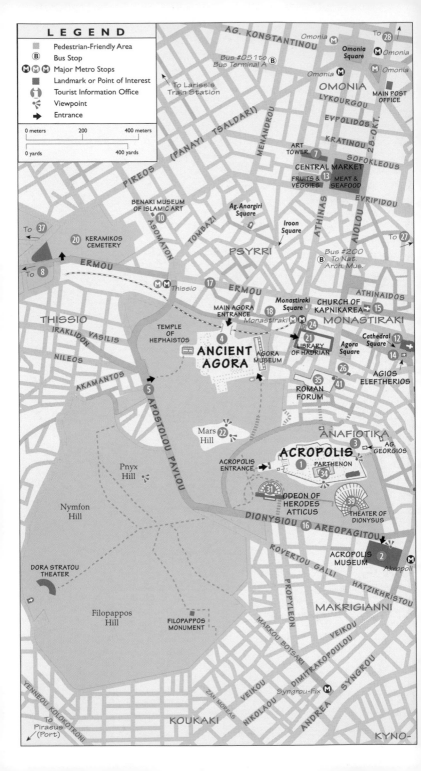

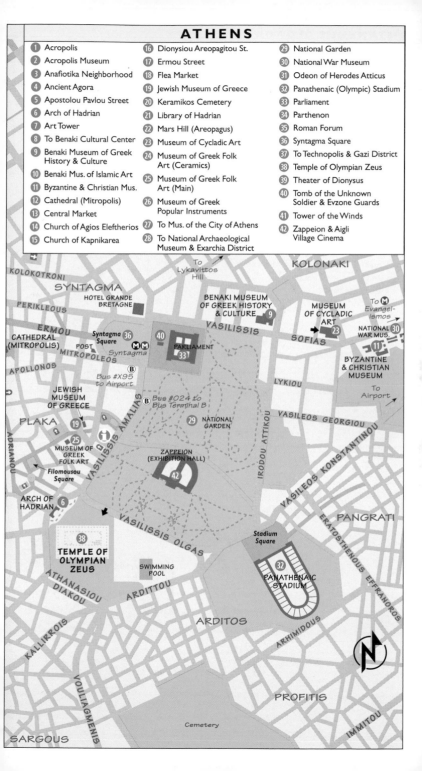

ATHENS

1. Acropolis
2. Acropolis Museum
3. Anafiotika Neighborhood
4. Ancient Agora
5. Apostolou Pavlou Street
6. Arch of Hadrian
7. Art Tower
8. To Benaki Cultural Center
9. Benaki Museum of Greek History & Culture
10. Benaki Mus. of Islamic Art
11. Byzantine & Christian Mus.
12. Cathedral (Mitropolis)
13. Central Market
14. Church of Agios Eleftherios
15. Church of Kapnikarea
16. Dionysiou Areopagitou St.
17. Ermou Street
18. Flea Market
19. Jewish Museum of Greece
20. Keramikos Cemetery
21. Library of Hadrian
22. Mars Hill (Areopagus)
23. Museum of Cycladic Art
24. Museum of Greek Folk Art (Ceramics)
25. Museum of Greek Folk Art (Main)
26. Museum of Greek Popular Instruments
27. To Mus. of the City of Athens
28. To National Archaeological Museum & Exarchia District
29. National Garden
30. National War Museum
31. Odeon of Herodes Atticus
32. Panathenaic (Olympic) Stadium
33. Parliament
34. Parthenon
35. Roman Forum
36. Syntagma Square
37. To Technopolis & Gazi District
38. Temple of Olympian Zeus
39. Theater of Dionysus
40. Tomb of the Unknown Soldier & Evzone Guards
41. Tower of the Winds
42. Zappeion & Aigli Village Cinema

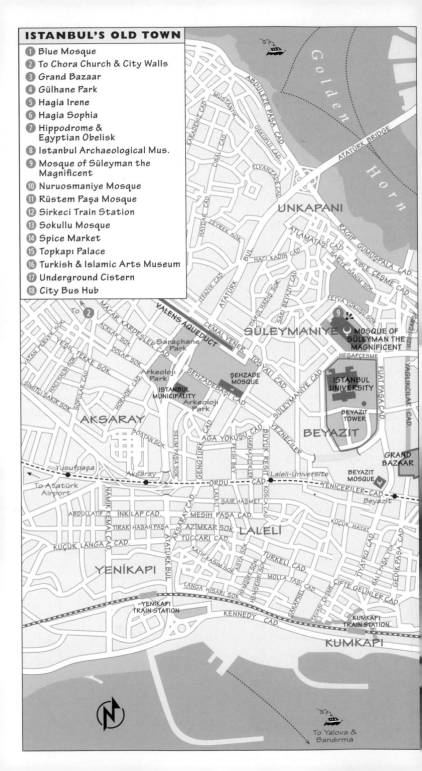

ISTANBUL'S OLD TOWN

1. Blue Mosque
2. To Chora Church & City Walls
3. Grand Bazaar
4. Gülhane Park
5. Hagia Irene
6. Hagia Sophia
7. Hippodrome & Egyptian Obelisk
8. Istanbul Archaeological Mus.
9. Mosque of Süleyman the Magnificent
10. Nuruosmaniye Mosque
11. Rüstem Paşa Mosque
12. Sirkeci Train Station
13. Sokullu Mosque
14. Spice Market
15. Topkapı Palace
16. Turkish & Islamic Arts Museum
17. Underground Cistern
18. City Bus Hub

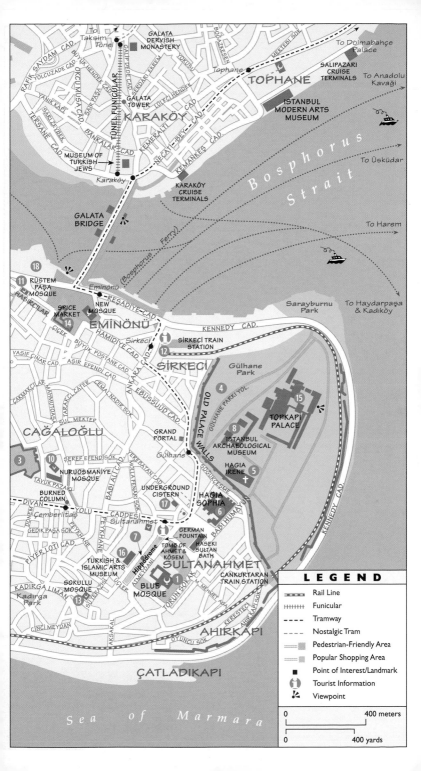

To
Taksim
Tünel

GALATA
DERVISH
MONASTERY

To Dolmabahçe
Palace

SALIPAZARI
CRUISE
TERMINALS

To Anadolu
Kavaği

Tophane

TOPHANE

RAFİK SAYDAM CAD.
YOLCUZADE CAD.
OKUMUŞ CAD.
BÜYÜK HENDEK CAD.
CATIP DEDE CAD.
SERDAR İ EKREM
YOKUŞU
BOĞAZKESEN
MEKTEBİ SOK.

GALATA
TOWER

KARAKÖY

ISTANBUL
MODERN ARTS
MUSEUM

TÜNEL FUNICULAR

YANIK KAPI CAD.
SARI PAŞA CAD.
BANKALAR CAD.
KEMERALTI
NEÇATİ BEY CAD.
KEMANKEŞ CAD.
LÜLECİ HENDEK CAD.

B o s p h o r u s

To Üsküdar

MUSEUM OF
TURKISH JEWS

Karaköy

KARAKÖY
CRUISE
TERMINALS

S t r a i t

GALATA
BRIDGE

To Harem

Ferry (Bosphorus)

18

11 RÜSTEM
PAŞA
MOSQUE

Eminönü

REŞADİYE CAD.

Sarayburnu
Park

To Haydarpaşa
& Kadiköy

HASIRCILAR
SPICE
MARKET

NEW
MOSQUE

14

EMİNÖNÜ

ÇİÇEK

HAMİDİYE CAD.

KENNEDY CAD.

Sirkeci

SİRKECİ TRAIN
STATION

12

VASİF ÇINAR CAD.

BÜYÜK POSTANE CAD.

AŞİR EFENDİ CAD.

ANKARA CAD.

EBUSSUUD CAD.

SİRKECİ

Gülhane
Park

4

ÇAKMAKÇILAR
MAHMUTPAŞA
TARAKÇILAR
CEMAL NADİR SOK.

GÜLHANE PARKI YOL.

OLD PALACE WALLS

15

TOPKAPI
PALACE

CAĞALOĞLU

ŞEREF EFENDİ SOK.

GRAND
PORTAL

8 ISTANBUL
ARCHAEOLOGICAL
MUSEUM

3

10

NURUOSMANİYE
MOSQUE

Gülhane

SOĞUKÇEŞME

HAGIA
IRENE

5

BABIÂLİ CAD.

YEREBATAN CAD.

MOLLA FENARİ SOK.

TAVUK PAZARI

BURNED
COLUMN

DİVAN
YOLU

Çemberlitaş

CADDESİ

Sultanahmet

UNDERGROUND
CISTERN

17

HAGIA
SOPHIA

6

BABIHÜMAYUN

KENNEDY CAD.

DÖNEM
PEYKHANE

GERMAN
FOUNTAIN

GEDİK PAŞA SOK.

7

TURKISH &
ISLAMIC ARTS
MUSEUM

16

Hippodrome

TOMB OF
AHMET &
KÖSEM

HASEKİ
SULTAN
BATH

CANKURTARAN
TRAIN STATION

PİYER LOTİ CAD.

ATMEYDANI

SULTANAHMET

KADIRGA LİMAN

SOKULLU
MOSQUE

13

1

BLUE
MOSQUE

TORUN SOKAK

M. MEHMET AĞ.

Kadırga
Park

AKSAKAL

İÇLER

M. MEHMET AĞ.

AHIRKAPI

CİNCİ MEYDANI

OYUNCU SOK.

AHIRKAPI SOK.

ÇATLADIKAPI

S e a   o f   M a r m a r a

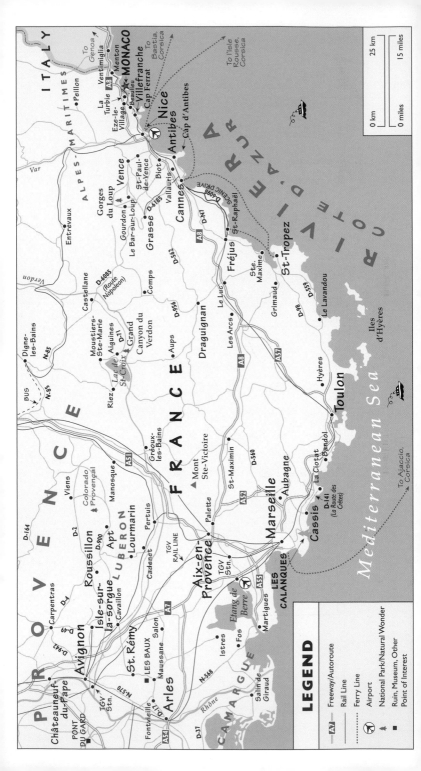

Rick Steves'®

MEDITERRANEAN CRUISE PORTS

AVALON
TRAVEL

CONTENTS

Rick Steves'

MEDITERRANEAN
CRUISE PORTS

AVALON
TRAVEL

CONTENTS

INTRODUCTION

Imagine yourself lazing on the deck of a floating city as you glide past the rooftops of Monaco, Venice, Mykonos, or Istanbul. Stepping off the gangway, you're immersed in the vivid life of a different European city each day. Tour some of the world's top museums, explore the ruins of an ancient metropolis, nurse a *caffè latte* while you people-watch from a prime sidewalk café, or take a dip in the Aegean at a pebbly beach. After a busy day in port, you can head back to the same cozy bedroom each night, without ever having to pack a suitcase or catch a train. As the sun sets and the ship pulls out of port, you have your choice of dining options—from a tuxedos-and-evening-gowns affair, to a poolside burger after a swim—followed by a world of nightlife. Plying the calm Mediterranean waters through the night, you wake up refreshed

in a whole new city—ready to do it all again.

Cruising the Mediterranean is more popular today than ever before. And for good reason. Taking a cruise can be a fun, affordable way to experience Europe—*if* you choose the right cruise, keep your extra expenses to a minimum...and use this book to make the absolute most of your time in port.

Unlike most cruising guidebooks, which dote on details about this ship's restaurants or that ship's staterooms, *Rick Steves' Mediterranean Cruise Ports* focuses on the main attraction: some of the grandest cities in Europe. Even if you have just eight hours in port, you can still ramble the colorful Ramblas of Barcelona, kick the pebbles that stuck in Julius Caesar's sandals at the Roman

Top Destinations

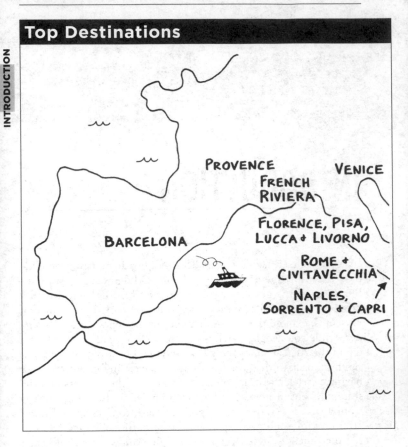

PROVENCE

FRENCH RIVIERA

VENICE

FLORENCE, PISA, LUCCA & LIVORNO

BARCELONA

ROME & CIVITAVECCHIA

NAPLES, SORRENTO & CAPRI

Forum, hike to the top of Athens' Acropolis, and hear the Muslim call to prayer warble across the rooftops from an Istanbul minaret. Yes, you could spend a lifetime in Florence. But you've got a few hours...and I have a plan for you. Each of this book's destination chapters is designed as a mini-vacation of its own, with advice about what to do and detailed sightseeing information for each port. And, to enable you to do it all on your own, I've included step-by-step instructions for getting into town from the cruise terminal.

For each major destination, this book offers a balanced, comfortable mix of the predictable biggies and a healthy dose of "Back Door" intimacy. Along with marveling at the Parthenon, Michelangelo's *David*, and Picasso's canvases, you'll perch on a bench alongside fisherfolk gazing out at the whitewashed harbor of a Greek island village. In each port, you'll get all the specifics and opinions necessary to wring the maximum value out of your limited time and money.

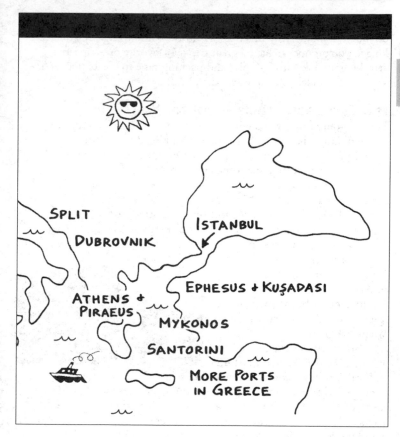

The best options in each port are, of course, only my opinion. But after spending half my adult life researching Europe, I've developed a sixth sense for what travelers enjoy.

About This Book

The book is divided into three parts: First, I'll suggest strategies for choosing which cruise to take, including a rundown of the major cruise lines, and explain the procedure for booking a cruise. Next, I'll give you a "Cruising 101"-type travel-skills briefing, with advice about what you should know before you go, and strategies for making the most of your time both on and off the ship. And finally, the vast majority of this book is dedicated to the European ports you'll visit, with complete plans for packing each day full of unforgettable experiences.

I haven't skimped on my coverage of the sights in this book—which is why it's a bricklike tome. Please don't hesitate to tear out just the pages that you need for each day in port. There's no point

INTRODUCTION

in hauling 60 pages on Barcelona for a day in Santorini. I won't be offended if you destroy this book (I do the same thing myself) as long as you promise to have a great trip. My favorite pre-trip ritual: attacking a book with a stapler and packing tape to create pocket-sized mini-guidebooks for each port of call.

Is a European Cruise Right for You?

I'm not going to try to convince you to cruise, or not to cruise. If you're holding this book, I assume you've already made that decision. But if you're a cruise skeptic—or even a cruise cynic—and you're trying to decide whether cruising suits your approach to experiencing Europe, I'll let you in on my own process for weighing the pros and cons of cruising.

I believe this is the first and only cruising guidebook written by someone with a healthy skepticism about cruises. When I was growing up, cruising was a rich person's hobby. I used to joke that for many American cruisers, the goal was not travel but hedonism: See if you can eat five meals a day and still snorkel when you get into port.

Since then, experiencing Europe's culture, people, and natural wonders economically and hassle-free has been my goal for three decades of traveling, tour guiding, and writing. And after all that time, I haven't found a more affordable way to see certain parts of Europe than cruising (short of sleeping on a park bench). For a weeklong Mediterranean cruise that includes room, board, transportation, tips, and port fees, a couple can pay as little as $100 per night—that's as much as a budget hotel room in many cities. To link all the places on an exciting one-week Mediterranean cruise on your own, the hotels, railpasses, boat tickets, taxi transfers, restaurants, and so on would add up fast. The per-day base cost for mainstream cruises beats independent travel by a mile. And there's no denying the efficiency of sleeping while you travel to your next destination—touring six dynamically different destinations in a single week without wasting valuable daylight hours packing, hauling your bags to the station, and sitting on a train.

And yet, I still have reservations. Just as someone trying to learn a language will do better by immersing themselves in that culture than by sitting in a classroom for a few hours, I believe that travelers in search of engaging, broadening experiences should eat, sleep, and live Europe. Good or bad, cruising insulates you from Europe. If the carpet merchants of Kuşadası are getting a little too pushy, you can simply retreat to the comfort of 24-hour room service, tall glasses of ice water, American sports on the TV, and a boatload of people who speak English as a first language (except, perhaps, your crew). It's fun—but is it Europe?

For many, it's "Europe enough." For travelers who prefer to tiptoe into Europe—rather than dive right in—this bite-sized approach can be a good way to get your feet wet. Cruising works well as an enticing sampler for Europe, to help you decide where you'd like to return and really get to know.

People take cruises for different reasons. Some travelers cruise as a means to an end: experiencing the ports of call. They appreciate the convenience of traveling while they sleep, waking up in an interesting new destination each morning, and making the most out of every second they're in port. This is the "first off, last on" crowd that attacks each port like a footrace. You can practically hear their mental starter's pistol go off when the gangway opens.

Other cruisers are there to enjoy the cruise experience itself. They enjoy lying by the pool, taking advantage of onboard activi-

ties, dropping some cash at the casino, ringing up a huge bar tab, napping, reading, and watching ESPN on their stateroom TV. If the *Mona Lisa* floated past, they might crane their neck, but wouldn't strain to get out of their deck chair.

With all due respect to the latter, I've written this book primarily for the former. But if you really want to be on vacation, aim for somewhere in the middle: Be sure to experience the ports that really tickle your wanderlust, but give yourself a "day off" every now and again in the less-enticing ports to sleep in or hit the beach.

Another advantage of cruising is that it can accommodate a family or group of people with vastly different travel philosophies. It's possible for Mom to go to the museum, Dad to lie by the pool, Sally to go snorkeling, and Bobby to go shopping...and then all of them can have dinner together and swap stories about their perfect days. (Or, if they're really getting on each other's nerves, there's plenty of room on a big ship to spread out.)

Cruising is especially popular among retirees, particularly those with limited mobility. Cruising rescues you from packing up your bags and huffing to the train station every other day. (Though be warned that once on land, accessibility for wheelchairs and walkers can vary dramatically.) A cruise aficionado who had done the math once told me that, if you know how to find the deals, it's theoretically cheaper to cruise indefinitely than to pay for a retirement home.

On the other hand, the independent, free-spirited traveler may not appreciate the constraints of cruising. For some, seven or eight hours in port is a tantalizing tease of a place where they'd love to linger for the evening—and the obligation to return to the ship every night is frustrating. If you're antsy, energetic, and want to stroll the cobbles of Europe at all hours, cruising may not be for you. However, even some seasoned globetrotters find that cruising is a good way to travel in Europe on a shoestring budget, yet still in comfort.

According to one cruise-activities coordinator, cruisers can be divided into two groups: Those who stay in their rooms, refuse to try to enjoy the dozens of activities offered to them each day, and complain about everything; and those who get out and try to get to know their fellow passengers, make the most of being at sea, and have the time of their lives. Guess which type (according to him) enjoys the experience more?

Let's face it: Americans have the shortest vacations in the rich world. Some people choose to dedicate their valuable time off to an all-inclusive, resort-style vacation in Florida, Hawaii, or Mexico: swimming pools, song-and-dance shows, shopping, and all-you-can-eat buffets. Cruising the Mediterranean gives you much the same hedonistic experience, all while you learn a lot about Europe—provided you use your time on shore constructively. It can be the best of both worlds.

Understanding the Cruise Industry

Cruising is a $30 billion-a-year business. Approximately one out of every five Americans has taken a cruise—about 12 million each year. But in adjusted dollars, the price of cruises hasn't risen in decades. This, partly, has sparked a huge growth in the cruise industry in recent years. The aging baby boomer population has also boosted sales, as older travelers discover that a cruise is an easy way to see the world. While the biggest growth has come from the North American market, cruise lines have also started marketing more internationally.

The industry has changed dramatically over the last generation. For decades, cruise lines catered exclusively to the upper crust—people who expected top-tier luxury. But with the popularity of *The Love Boat* television series in the 1970s and 1980s, then the one-upmanship of increasingly bigger megaships in the early 1990s, cruising went mainstream. Somebody had to fill all the berths on those gargantuan vessels, and cruise lines lowered their prices to attract middle-class customers. The "newlyweds and nearly-deads" stereotype about cruise clientele is now outmoded. The industry has made bold efforts to appeal to an ever-broader customer base, representing a wide spectrum of ages, interests, and income levels.

In order to compete for passengers and fill megaships, cruise lines offer fares that can be astonishingly low. In fact, they make little or no money on ticket sales—and some "loss-leader" sail-ings actually lose money on the initial fare. Instead, the cruise lines' main income comes from three sources: alcohol sales, gambling (onboard casinos), and excursions. So while cruise lines are in the business of creating an unforgettable vacation for you, they're also in the business of separating you from your money (once on the ship) to make up for their underpriced fares.

Just as airlines have attempted to bolster their bottom lines by charging more "pay as you go" fees (for food, checking a bag, extra legroom, and so on), cruise lines are now charging for things they used to include (such as "specialty restaurants"). The cruise industry is constantly experimenting with the balance between all-inclusive luxury and nickel-and-dime, à la carte, mass-market travel. (For tips on maximizing your experience while minimizing your expenses, see the sidebar on page 74.)

It's also worth noting that cruise lines are able to remain prof-itable largely on the backs of their low-paid crew, who mostly hail from the developing world. Working 10 to 14 hours a day (or more), seven days a week—almost entirely for tips—the tireless crew are the gears that keep cruises spinning. (For more, see page 68.)

Understanding how the cruise industry works can help you take advantage of your cruise experience...and not the other way around. Equipped with knowledge, you can be the smart consumer who has a fantastic time on board and in port without paying a premium. That's what this book is all about.

Traveling as a Temporary Local

Most travelers tramp through Europe as if they're visiting the cul-tural zoo. "Ooo, that Greek fisherman is mending his nets! Excuse me, could you do that in the sunshine with my wife next to you so I can take a snapshot?" This is fun. It's a part of travel. But a cam-era bouncing on your belly tells locals you're hunting cultural pea-cocks. When I'm in Europe, I try to be the best Greek or Spaniard or Italian I can be.

Europeans generally like Americans. But if there is a negative aspect to their image of us, it's that we are loud, aggressive, impolite, rich, superficially friendly, and a bit naive.

Even if you believe American ways are best, your trip will go more smoothly if you don't compare. Enjoy doing things the European way, and you'll experience a more welcoming Europe.

We travel all the way to Europe to enjoy differences—to become temporary locals. You'll experience frustrations. Certain truths that we find "God-given" or "self-evident," such as cold beer, ice in drinks, bottomless cups of coffee, and bigger being better, are suddenly not so true. One of the benefits of travel is the eye-opening realization that there are logical, civil, and even better alternatives. By immersing yourself in different cultures and experiencing different people and lifestyles, you'll broaden your perspective.

While Europeans look bemusedly at some of our Yankee excesses—and worriedly at others—they nearly always afford us individual travelers all the warmth we deserve. Judging from all the happy feedback I receive from travelers who have used my books, it's safe to assume you'll enjoy a great, affordable vacation—with the finesse of an independent, experienced traveler.

Thanks, and bon voyage!

Back Door Travel Philosophy
From *Rick Steves' Europe Through the Back Door*

Travel is intensified living—maximum thrills per minute and one of the last great sources of legal adventure. Travel is freedom. It's recess, and we need it. Experiencing the real Europe requires catching it by surprise, going casual..."Through the Back Door."

In many ways, spending a lot of money on sightseeing and excursions only builds a thicker wall between you and what you came to see. Europe is a cultural carnival, and, time after time, you'll find that its best acts are free and the best seats are the cheap ones. A tight budget forces you to travel close to the ground, meeting and communicating with the people, not relying on service with a purchased smile.

Connecting with people carbonates your experience. Extroverts have more fun. If your trip is low on magic moments, kick yourself and make things happen. If you don't enjoy a place, maybe you don't know enough about it. Seek the truth. Recognize tourist traps. Give a culture the benefit of your open mind. See things as different but not better or worse. Any culture has much to share.

Of course, travel, like the world, is a series of hills and valleys. Be fanatically positive and militantly optimistic. If something's not to your liking, change your liking.

Travel can make you a happier American as well as a citizen of the world. Our Earth is home to six and a half billion equally important people. It's humbling to travel and find that people don't have the "American Dream"—they have their own dreams. Europeans like us, but, with all due respect, they wouldn't trade passports.

Thoughtful travel engages us with the world. In tough economic times, it reminds us what is truly important. By broadening perspectives, travel teaches new ways to measure quality of life.

Globe-trotting destroys ethnocentricity, helping you understand and appreciate different cultures. Rather than fear the diversity on this planet, celebrate it. Among your prized souvenirs will be the strands of different cultures you choose to knit into your own character. The world is a cultural yarn shop, and Back Door travelers are weaving the ultimate tapestry. Join in!

PART I: CHOOSING AND BOOKING A CRUISE

CHOOSING A CRUISE

Each cruise line has its own distinct personality, quirks, strengths, and weaknesses. Selecting a cruise that matches your travel style and philosophy can be critical for the enjoyment of your trip. On the other hand, some cruisers care only about the price, go on any line that offers a deal, and have a great time.

Still, the more your idea of "good travel" meshes with your cruise line's, the more likely you are to enjoy your trip and your fellow passengers.

Gathering Information

Comparison-shopping can be a fun part of the cruise experience. Read the cruise-line descriptions in this chapter, then browse the websites of the ones that interest you. Ask your friends who've cruised, and who share your interests, about the lines they've used, and what they thought of each one. Examine the cruise lines' glossy brochures (view online, request them, or get them from your local travel agent)—how the line markets itself says a lot about what sort of clientele it attracts. Tune into the ubiquitous TV commercials for cruise lines. Photos of individual ships' staterooms and amenities—which you'll also find on the cruise lines' websites—can be worth a thousand words in getting a sense of the vibe of each vessel.

Once you've narrowed down the choices, read some impartial online reviews. The most popular site, www.cruisecritic.com, has reviews of cruise lines, specific ships, tips for visiting each port, and more. Other well-respected websites are www.cruisediva.com, www.cruisemates.com, and www.avidcruiser.com. If you feel that cruising is all about the ship, check www.shipparade.com, which delves into details about each vessel.

Many travel agencies that sell cruises have surprisingly informative websites. One of the best, www.vacationstogo.com, not only sorts different cruise options by price and destination, but also has useful facts, figures, and photos for each ship and port.

Most cruising guidebooks devote more coverage to detailed reviews of specific ships and their amenities than to the destinations—which makes them the perfect complement to this book. Look for *The Unofficial Guide to Cruises, Frommer's European Cruises and Ports of Call* (or other Frommer's titles), *Fodor's Complete Guide to European Cruises,* and others. (For destination-specific guidebooks, see the list on page 1234.)

As you compare cruises, decide which of the factors in the following section matter the most to you, then find a cruise line that best matches what you're looking for.

Cruise Considerations

In the next few pages you'll find a wide range of issues, big and small, to take into account when selecting your Mediterranean cruise. Of these, the three main factors—which should be weighted about equally—are **price, itinerary** (length, destinations, and time spent in each port), and **cruise line** (personality and amenities).

If you've cruised in the Caribbean, but not the Mediterranean, be aware that there are some subtle but important differences between these two destinations. In general, European cruises are more focused on the destinations, while Caribbean cruises tend to be more focused on the ship (passengers spend more time on the ship, and therefore the shipboard amenities are more important). People choosing between European cruises usually base their decision on the places they'll be visiting: Big cities or island villages? Ancient ruins or modern museums? Beach time or urban strolling? In contrast, on a Caribbean cruise, the priority is simply hedonistic fun in the sun.

Cruise Line

This chapter will give you a quick overview of some of the major lines to help you find a good match. For example, some cruise lines embrace cruising's nautical heritage, with decor and crew uniforms that really let you know you're on a ship. Others are more like Las Vegas casinos at sea. An armchair historian will be disappointed on a hedonistic pleasure boat, and a young person who's in a mood to party will be miserable on the *S. S. Septuagenarian.* Do you want a wide range of dining options on the ship, or do you view mealtime as a pragmatic way to fill the tank? After dinner, do you want to get to bed early, or dance in a disco until dawn?

While most US travelers opt for an American cruise line, doing so definitely Americanizes your travel experience. When you're on board, it feels almost as if you'd never left the good old U. S. of A.—with American shows on the TV, Heinz ketchup in the buffet line, and fellow Yanks all around you. If you'd rather leave North America behind, going with a European-flavored cruise line (such as Costa) can be an interesting cultural experience in itself. While Europeans are likely to be among the passengers on any Mediterranean cruise, they represent a larger proportion on European-owned cruise lines. Surrounded by Germans who enthusiastically burp after a good meal, Italians who nudge ahead of you in line, and French people who enjoy sunbathing topless, you'll definitely know you're in Europe.

Length

Mediterranean cruises can range in length from a few days to a few weeks. The typical cruiser sails for 7.2 days, but some travelers enjoy taking a 10-, 12-, or 14-day cruise, then adding a few days at either end to stretch their trip to two weeks or more. A cruise seven days or shorter tends to focus on one "zone" of the Mediterranean (Spain; Italy and France; Greek Isles); a longer cruise is more likely to provide you with a sampler of the whole area.

When to Go

Most Mediterranean cruises take place during a seven-month period of relatively warm weather, roughly between April and October. While July and August are popular times to cruise—with kids (and their teachers) on summer vacation—that also makes them the most crowded months, and the oppressive heat can make exploring the ports miserable. Shoulder season (May-June and September-October) usually has fewer crowds and better weather. Popular cruise ports are never really uncrowded, but they may be a little less jammed in shoulder season. And the weather, while potentially a bit chilly in May or October, is usually quite pleasant at the Mediterranean's southern latitudes. For a month-by-month climate chart that includes various ports, see page 1236.

Price

If you're on a tight budget and aren't fussy, look for the best deals. From the Mass-Market to the Ultra-Luxury categories, the per-person price can range from $100 to $700+ per day. Sales can lower those prices. (For more on cruise pricing, see page 36.)

While going with the cheapest option is tempting, it may be worth paying a little extra for an experience that better matches your idea of a dream cruise. If you're hoping for a glitzy ship with sparkling nightly revues, you'll kick yourself later if you saved $40 a day—but ended up on a musty ship with stale shows. If you want to maximize time exploring European destinations, it can be worth paying an extra $20 a day for an itinerary with two more hours at each port—that translates to just 10 bucks an hour, a veritable steal compared to the extra European experience it'll allow you to cram in. Don't be penny-wise and pound-foolish in this regard.

When evaluating prices and making a budget, remember to take into account all of the "extras" you might wind up buying from the cruise line: alcoholic drinks, meals at specialty restaurants, the semi-mandatory "auto-tip" (about $10-12 per day per person), shore excursions, and your gambling tab from the casino, just to name a few. (For more details on these hidden costs, see page 36.)

Ship Size and Amenities

When it comes to cruise ships, bigger is not necessarily better... although it can be, depending on your interests.

The biggest ships offer a wide variety of restaurants, activities, entertainment, and other amenities (such as resources for kids). The main disadvantage of a big ship is the feeling that you're being herded along with thousands of other passengers—three thousand tourists piling off a ship into a small port town definitely changes the character of the place.

Smaller ships enjoy fewer crowds, access to out-of-the-way ports, and less hassle when disembarking (especially when tendering—see page 110). If you're focusing your time and energy on the destinations anyway, a smaller ship can be more relaxing to "come home" to. On the other hand, for all of the above reasons, cruises on the smallest ships are typically much more expensive. Small ships also physically can't offer the wide range of eateries and activities as the big vessels; intimate, yacht-like vessels have no room for a climbing wall. And finally, on a small ship, you may feel the motion of the sea more than on a big ship (though, because of the stabilizers used by small ships, this difference isn't that dramatic).

Think carefully about which specific amenities are important to you, and find a cruise line that offers those things. Considerations include:

Food, both in terms of quality and variety (some cruise lines offer a wide range of specialty restaurants—explained on page 93);

Entertainment, such as a wide range of performers (musicians, dancers, and so on) in venues both big and small;

Athletic facilities, ranging from a running track around the deck, to a gym with equipment and classes, to swimming pools and hot tubs, to a simulated surf pool and bowling alley, to a spa with massage and other treatments;

Children's resources, including activities and spaces designed for kids, and a babysitting service;

Other features, including a good library, lecturers, special events, a large casino, wheelchair accessibility, and so on.

Some first-time cruisers worry they'll get bored while they're on board. Don't count on it. You'll be bombarded with entertainment options and a wide range of activities—particularly on a big ship.

Destinations

If you have a wish list of ports, use it as a starting point when shopping for a cruise. It's unlikely you'll find a cruise that visits every one of your preferred destinations, but you can usually find one that comes close.

Most itineraries of a week or more include a day "at sea": no stops at ports, just you and the open sea. These are usually included for practical reasons (most often, to connect far-flung destinations where there's no worthwhile stop in between, or on the final day of a cruise to backtrack all the way to your starting point). Because cruise ships generally travel at around 20 knots—that's only about 23 land miles per hour—they take a long time to cover big distances. For some cruise aficionados, days at sea are the highlight of the trip; for other passengers, they're a boring waste of time. If you enjoy time on the ship, try to maximize days at sea; if you're cruising mainly to sightsee on land, try to minimize them.

Time Spent in Port

If exploring European destinations is your priority, look carefully at how much time the ship spends in each port. Specific itinerary rundowns on cruise-line websites usually show the scheduled times of arrival and departure. Typical stops can range anywhere from 6 to 12 hours, with an average of around 8 or 9 hours. At the same port—or even on the same cruise line—the difference in port time from one cruise ship to another can vary by hours.

Most cruise lines want you on the ship as long as possible—the longer you're aboard, the more likely you are to spend money there (and for legal reasons, they can't open their lucrative casino and duty-free shops until they're at sea).

In general, the more expensive Luxury- and Ultra-Luxury-class lines offer longer stays in port. However, even if you compare cheaper lines similar in price, times can vary. For example, Norwegian, Costa, and MSC tend to have shorter times in port, while Carnival and Royal Caribbean linger longer.

Repositioning Cruises

Ships that cruise the Mediterranean are usually based in the Caribbean during the winter, so they need to cross the Atlantic Ocean each spring and fall. This journey, called a "repositioning cruise," includes a lengthy (5-7 days) stretch where the ship is entirely at sea. Also called a "crossing" or a "transatlantic crossing," these are most common early April (to Europe), or late October and November (from Europe).

If you really want to escape from it all, and just can't get enough of all the shipboard activities, these long trips can be a dream come true; if you're a fidgety manic sightseer, they're a nightmare. Before committing to a repositioning cruise, consider taking a cruise with a day or two at sea just to be sure you really, really enjoy being on a ship that much. Several notes of warning: The seas can be rougher on transatlantic crossings than in the relatively protected Mediterranean; the weather will probably be cooler; and there are a couple of days in the middle of the voyage where most ships lose all satellite communication—no shipboard phones, Wi-Fi, or cable channels. While the officers are in touch with land in the event of emergencies, your own day-to-day contact with the outside world will disappear.

If you're considering a repositioning cruise, don't be misled by the sometimes astonishingly low sticker price (as these typically don't sell as well as the more destination-oriented cruises). Yes, you'll only need a one-way plane ticket between the US and Europe—but that may exceed the cost of a round-trip ticket (don't expect to simply pay half the round-trip price), plus you'll also need to get home from your US destination port—so be sure to figure those costs into your total budget.

Cruise Lines

I don't pretend to be an expert on all the different cruise lines—the focus of this book is on the destinations rather than the ships. But this section is designed to give you an overview of options to get you started. (To dig deeper, consider some of the sources listed under "Gathering Information," at the beginning of this chapter.)

While nobody in the cruise industry formally recognizes different "classes" of companies, just about everybody acknowledges that cruise lines fall into four basic categories: **Mass-Market, Premium, Luxury,** and **Ultra-Luxury.** Of course, a few exceptions straddle these classifications and buck the trends, and some cruise lines are highly specialized—such as Disney Cruise Line (very kid-friendly and experience-focused) and Star Clippers (an authentic tall-ship experience with a mainsail that passengers can help hoist).

Most cruise lines are owned by the same handful of companies. For example, Carnival Corporation owns Carnival, Costa, Cunard, Holland America, Princess, Seabourn, and five other lines (representing about half of the worldwide cruise market).

Royal Caribbean owns Celebrity and Azamara Club Cruises.

The Fine Print: In assembling the following information, I've focused exclusively on Mediterranean cruises. The average cost per day is for two people in the lowest-price, double-occupancy cabin (outside cabins have windows, inside cabins don't). Prices are based on Web-advertised rates offered at the beginning of 2011; you may find even lower rates, if your timing is right. Taxes, port fees, and additional expenses aren't included. The average hours in port are based on a selection of each line's Mediterranean cruises sailing in late spring 2011; your cruise could be different, so check carefully. Within each category, the lines are arranged in alphabetical order.

Mass-Market Lines

The cheapest cruise lines, these huge ships have a "resort-hotel-at-sea" ambience. Prices are enticingly low, but these lines try to make up the difference with a lot of upselling on board (specialty restaurants, photographers, shopping, and so on). The clientele is wildly diverse (including lots of families and young people) and, generally speaking, not particularly well-traveled; they tend to be more interested in being on vacation and enjoying the ship than in sightseeing. Mass-Market lines provide an affordable way to sample cruising.

Carnival

Contact Information: www.carnival.com, tel. 888-CARNIVAL

Number and Capacity of Ships: *Carnival Magic* (their only ship currently sailing in Europe) carries 3,690 passengers

Daily Cost of Cheapest Cabin: Approximately $200 for inside cabin/$230 outside cabin

Average Hours in Port: 11-12 hours

Description: After two years away from Europe, Carnival—the world's largest cruise line—re-entered the Mediterranean market in 2011 with its brand-new, 3,690-passenger megaship, the *Carnival Magic*. Carnival has long had a reputation for their floating-frat-party "Fun Ship" ambience; the company is trying to tone down this image, though it's kept its discos and flashy decor. The line's Mediterranean offerings are limited; it makes most of its money on short vacations to Alaska and the Caribbean. It tries to entice Mediterranean travelers with low prices and the huge new ship—a great value, but for some, it's a "lowest common denominator" cruise experience.

Overall, expect a younger demographic with mostly Americans on board. There are plenty of youth programs, and lots of activities aimed at singles and young couples, such as a Caribbean-themed pub, an outdoor fitness area, and mini-golf. The main dining room tends to serve American cuisine, but there are also plenty of specialty restaurants. Because the *Magic* is so big, it is an attractive low-cost option, but that also means huge crowds—especially when tendering. However, the long times in port help make up for any time lost waiting in line.

Costa
Contact Information: www.costacruise.com, tel. 800-GO-COSTA

Number and Capacity of Ships: 15 ships, ranging from 800 to 3,780 passengers

Daily Cost of Cheapest Cabin: About $230 for inside cabin/$300 outside cabin

Average Hours in Port: 6-7 hours

Description: With frequent sales that can drive prices much lower than what's listed here, Costa is one of the cheapest cruise lines in the Mediterranean, and also has the largest fleet and the most seven-day cruises in the region. Originally an Italian company, it's now owned by Carnival but retains its Italian identity. Most of your fellow passengers will be Europeans (only about 20 percent of passengers are from the US or Canada). While some North Americans relish Costa's truly European ambience, others have reported language-barrier issues or "rude" behavior from some passengers (some Europeans are not always polite about waiting in line). The ships' over-the-top, wildly colorful decor can be either appealing or appalling, depending on your perspective. Onboard activities also have an Italian pizzazz—such as singing waiters or heated international bocce-ball tournaments (though these flourishes are toned down a bit for their Mediterranean cruises). Outrageous ambience aside, the cruising experience itself is quite traditional (there's no open seating in the dining room, and the two formal nights per week are taken seriously).

Costa attracts a wide demographic—from twentysomethings to retirees—and you can expect families during the summer and

school breaks. While Costa boasts about its Italian cuisine, some American cruisers have found the food disappointing. In addition to visiting the predictable big ports, Costa is more likely to venture to some lesser-known stops, such as Malta, Tunisia, and secondary ports on Sicily. The short hours in port draw criticism—and Costa's shore excursion packages are relatively expensive.

MSC Cruises

Contact Information: www.msccruises.com, tel. 877-655-4655

Number and Capacity of Ships: 11 ships, each carrying 1,000–3,275 passengers

Daily Cost of Cheapest Cabin: Roughly $230 for inside cabin/$285 outside cabin

Average Hours in Port: 6 hours

Description: "Beautiful. Passionate. Italian." MSC's slogan sums it up. This low-priced, Italian-owned company caters mostly to Europeans—only about 5 percent of the passengers on their Mediterranean cruises are from the US or Canada. This is a plus if you want to escape America entirely on your vacation, but can come with some language-barrier and culture-shock issues. Since children ride free, summer and school breaks tend to be dominated by families, while at other times passengers are mostly retirees.

The basic price is often a bargain (deep discounts are common), but MSC charges for amenities that are free on many other cruise lines—such as basic drinks, room service, and snacks. In the dining room, you even have to pay for tap water. MSC also has shorter hours in port than most cruise lines, and their shore excursions have a heightened emphasis on shopping. The food and entertainment are average; your choices at the breakfast and lunch buffets are the same for the entire cruise. Keep your expectations low— as one passenger noted, "It's  not really a cruise—just a bus tour that happens on a nice boat."

Norwegian Cruise Line (NCL)

Contact Information: www.ncl.com, tel. 866-234-7350

Number and Capacity of Ships: 11 ships, ranging from 2,000 to 4,100 passengers

Daily Cost of Cheapest Cabin: Approximately $240 for inside cabin/$280 outside cabin

Average Hours in Port: 8-9 hours

Description: Norwegian was an industry leader in the now-widespread trend toward flexibility, and is known for its "Freestyle Cruising" approach. "Whatever" is the big word here (as in, "You're free to do...whatever"). For example, their ships typically have no assigned seatings for meals (though reservations are encouraged), and offer the widest range of specialty restaurants, which can include French, Italian, Mexican, sushi, steakhouse, Japanese teppanyaki, and more. Norwegian also has a particularly wide range of cabin categories, from very basic inside cabins to top-of-the-line, sprawling suites that rival the Luxury lines' offerings.

Norwegian has a Las Vegas-style glitz. On the newer ships, such as the gigantic, 4,100-passenger, much-publicized *Norwegian Epic,* the entertainment is ramped up, with world-class shows—such as Blue Man Group and Cirque de Soleil—requiring advance ticket purchase. Their vessels tend to be brightly decorated—bold murals curl across the prows of their ships, and the public areas are colorful (some might say garish or even tacky). This approach, coupled with relatively low prices, draws a wide range of passengers: singles and families, young and old, American and European, middle-class and wealthy.

Onboard amenities cater to this passenger diversity; along with all of the usual services, some ships have climbing walls and bowling alleys. The crew is also demographically diverse, and the service is acceptable, but not as doting as on some cruise lines, making some passengers feel anonymous. Education and enrichment activities are a low priority—most lectures are designed to sell you something (port excursions, artwork, and so on), rather than prepare you for the port.

Royal Caribbean International

Contact Information: www.royalcaribbean.com, tel. 866-562-7625

Number and Capacity of Ships: 22 ships, ranging from 1,800 to 5,400 passengers

Daily Cost of Cheapest Cabin: Around $215 for inside cabin/$265 outside cabin

Average Hours in Port: 10 hours

Description: Royal Caribbean is the world's second-largest cruise line (after Carnival). Similar to Carnival and Norwegian, but a step up in both cost and (in their mind, at least) amenities, Royal Caribbean edges toward the Premium category.

Offering an all-around, quintessential cruising experience, Royal Caribbean attracts first-time cruisers. The majority are from the US and Canada. The line likes to think of itself as catering to a more youthful demographic: couples and singles in their 30s to 50s on shorter cruises; 50 and up on cruises longer than seven nights. With longer hours in port and onboard fitness facilities (every ship has a rock-climbing wall, some have water parks and mini-golf), they try to serve more active travelers.

The food on board is American cuisine, and its entertainment style matches other cruise lines in this category—expect Vegas-style shows and passenger-participation games. Even though some of its ships are positively gigantic, Royal Caribbean, which prides itself on service, delivers; most of its passengers feel well-treated.

Premium Lines

A step up from the Mass-Market lines (described earlier), both in price and in elegance, most Premium lines evoke the "luxury cruises" of yore. The ships can be nearly as big as the Mass-Market options, but are designed to feel more intimate. The upselling is still there, but it's more restrained, and the clientele tends to be generally older, better-traveled, and more interested in sightseeing. While the Mass-Market lines can sometimes feel like a cattle call, Premium lines ratchet up the focus on service, going out of their way to pamper their guests.

Celebrity

Contact Information: www.celebritycruises.com, tel. 800-647-2251

Number and Capacity of Ships: 10 ships, ranging from 1,800 to 2,850 passengers

Daily Cost of Cheapest Cabin: About $370 for inside cabin/$425 outside cabin

Average Hours in Port: 10-11 hours

Description: Originally a Greek company, Celebrity was bought by Royal Caribbean in 1997 and operates as its upscale sister cruise line. (The "X" on the smokestack is the Greek letter "chi," which stands for Chandris—the founder's family name.) Celebrity distinguishes itself from the other Premium category lines with bigger ships and a slightly younger demographic. Celebrity likes to point out that its larger ships have more activities and restaurants than the smaller Premium (or even Luxury category) ships. Most of its passengers are from the US or Canada, and it's reportedly popular with baby boomers, seniors, gay cruisers, and honeymooners. Among the Premium lines, Celebrity offers some of the best amenities for kids (aside from Disney, of course).

Celebrity's smallest stateroom is quite spacious compared to those on other lines in this category. On its European cruises, the main dining room cuisine seems more European than American (with some high-end options—a plus for many travelers), but there are plenty of specialty restaurants, ranging from Asian-fusion to a steakhouse. Most ships are decorated with a mod touch—with all the bright lights and offbeat art, you might feel like you're in Miami Beach. Adding to the whimsy, some ships even come with a real grass lawn on the top deck. Its service consistently gets high marks, and the onboard diversions include the usual spas, enrichment lectures, Broadway revues, cabarets, discos, theme parties, and a casino.

Cunard Line
Contact Information: www.cunard.com, tel. 800-728-6273
Number and Capacity of Ships: *Queen Elizabeth* carries 2,092 passengers; *Queen Victoria* carries 2,014.
Daily Cost of Cheapest Cabin: Roughly $325 for inside cabin/ $400 outside cabin
Average Hours in Port: 10 hours
Description: Cunard Line plays to its long historic tradition and caters to an old-fashioned, well-traveled, and well-to-do clientele in their 50s and older. Passengers on their Mediterranean cruises tend to be mostly British, along with some Americans and other Europeans. Although the line is suitable for families (kids' programs are staffed by trained British nannies), it's not seriously family-friendly. This line features large ships and offers a pleasantly elegant experience with a British bent—you can even have afternoon tea or enjoy bangers and mash in a pub.

About a sixth of the passengers book suites and have access to specialty restaurants—a remnant of the traditional class distinctions in jolly olde England. The entertainment and lecture programs tend to be more "distinguished"; there's a good library; and activities include ballroom dancing, croquet, tennis, fencing, and lawn bowling. Each ship has a viewable collection of historic Cunard artifacts. The famously refined Cunard dress code seems to be more of a suggestion these days, as many show up in relatively casual dress at formal dining events. Passengers report mixed reviews—some feel that the experience doesn't quite live up to the line's legacy.

Disney Cruise Line
Contact Information: www.disneycruise.disney.go.com, tel. 800-951-3532
Number and Capacity of Ships: 3 ships, ranging from 2,700 to 4,000 passengers
Daily Cost of Cheapest Cabin: Approximately $385 for inside cabin/$465 outside cabin
Average Hours in Port: 10-11 hours
Description: Disney is the gold standard for family cruise vacations. The majority of the passengers are families and multigenerational—expect at least one-third of the passengers to be kids. There'll be plenty of Disney flicks, G-rated floor shows, and mouse ears wherever you turn. Like its amusement parks, Disney's ships have high standards for service and cleanliness. The food is kid-friendly, but the ships also have a high-end Italian restaurant

for a break for parents. While your kids will never be bored, there are a few adult diversions as well (including an adults-only swimming pool)—but no casino. Disney doesn't do a lot of cruising in this region (and itineraries are limited to the western part of the Mediterranean), but it may be the best option if you're taking along your kids or grandkids. Be warned: Parents who think a little Disney goes a long way might overdose on this line.

Holland America Line (HAL)

Contact Information: www.hollandamerica.com, tel. 877-932-4259

Number and Capacity of Ships: 15 ships, ranging from 835 to 2,100 passengers

Daily Cost of Cheapest Cabin: Around $290 for inside cabin/$325 outside cabin

Average Hours in Port: 9-10 hours

Description: Holland America, with a history dating back to 1873 (it once carried immigrants to the New World), prides itself on tradition. Generally, this line has one of the most elderly clienteles in the business, though they're trying to promote their cruises to a wider demographic (with some success). Cruisers appreciate the line's delicate balance between a luxury and a casual vacation—it's formal, but not *too* formal.

Ship decor emphasizes a connection to the line's nautical past, with lots of wood trim and white railings; you might feel like you're on an oversized yacht at times. That's intentional: When building their biggest ships, Holland America designers planned public spaces to create the illusion that passengers are on a smaller vessel (for example, hallways bend every so often so you can't see all the way to the far end). This line also has high service standards; they operate training academies in Indonesia and the Philippines, where virtually all of their crew hails from. These stewards are trained to be good-natured and to make their guests feel special. Dining options  on board tend to be limited; there isn't a wide range of specialty restaurants.

Holland America takes seriously the task of educating their passengers about the ports; most ships have a "Travel Guide" who lectures on each destination and is available for questions, and some excursions—designated "Cruise with Purpose"—are designed to promote a more meaningful, participatory connection with the destinations (though these are relatively rare in Europe).

Princess

Contact Information: www.princess.com, tel. 800-774-6237

Number and Capacity of Ships: 17 ships, ranging from 680 to 3,080 passengers

Daily Cost of Cheapest Cabin: About $300 for inside cabin/$330 outside cabin

Average Hours in Port: 9-10 hours

Description: Princess appeals to everyone from solo travelers to families, with most passengers over 50. Because their market reach is so huge, expect many repeat cruisers enjoying their mainstream cruise experience. While Princess has long been considered a Premium-category line, cruise insiders agree that the line has been lowering its prices—and, many say, its standards—so these days it effectively straddles the Premium and Mass-Market categories. Still, Princess passengers tend to be very loyal.

Princess got a big boost when the 1970s *Love Boat* TV series featured two Princess ships. Those "love boats" have now been  retired, and the Princess fleet is one of the most modern in the industry—half have been launched in the last 10 years. It's known for introducing innovative features such as a giant video screen above the main swimming pool showing movies and sports all day...and into the night. Still, while the ships are new, the overall experience is traditional— some cruisers might even say "stuck in the past," compared to some of the bold and brash Mass-Market lines. The line has the usual activities, such as trivia contests, galley tours, art auctions, and middle-of-the-road musical revues—though some passengers report that they found fewer activities and diversions on Princess ships than they expected for vessels of this size. While its service gets raves and the food is fine, there is some repetition in the main dining room—expect the same dessert choices each night.

Luxury Lines

These lines typically use smaller ships, offer better food and service, command high prices, and have a more exclusive clientele. You get what you pay for—this is a more dignified experience, with longer days in port and less emphasis on selling you extras. In general, while Luxury ships are very comfortable, the cruise is more focused on the destinations than the ship.

Once you're in this price range, you'll find that the various lines are variations on a theme (though there are a few notable exceptions, such as the unique casual-sailboat ambience of

Windstar, or the opportunity to actually rig the sails on Star Clippers). It can be hard to distinguish among the lines; within the Luxury category, passengers tend to go with a cruise line recommended to them by a friend.

Note: The Luxury and Ultra-Luxury lines (described later) generally run smaller ships, which can visit out-of-the-way ports that larger cruise ships can't. However, remember the drawbacks of smaller ships: fewer onboard activities, a narrower range of restaurants, and—for some travelers prone to seasickness—a slightly rougher ride.

Azamara Club Cruises

Contact Information: www.azamaraclubcruises.com, tel. 877-999-9553

Number and Capacity of Ships: *Journey* and *Quest* each carry 694 passengers.

Daily Cost of Cheapest Cabin: Approximately $510 for inside cabin/$585 outside cabin

Average Hours in Port: 11-12 hours

Description: Azamara Club Cruises attracts a moderately affluent, educated, and active middle-aged to retired traveler. This relatively new line (they were revamped and rebranded in early 2010) is still finding its way in the Luxury cruise market. Some passengers call Azamara a "work in progress," but it seems to be developing a successful formula. Their stated aim is to allow their customers to immerse themselves in each destination. Azamara passengers want value and are interested in more unusual destinations and longer port stays—their itineraries include more frequent overnight stops. The clientele is mainly American and British, along with a few Germans and other nationalities. There are no programs or facilities for children.

The atmosphere is casual, with open seating at meals and a focus on good food and wine; the cuisine is Mediterranean-influenced with other international dishes and healthy options. With a high crew-to-passenger ratio, the service is attentive. Live entertainment is more limited than on larger ships; the types of programs encourage meeting other guests,  which contributes to a cozier, more social experience. Cabins and bathrooms can be small, but are well laid-out. The company's good-value all-inclusive pricing covers many amenities you'd pay extra for on other lines, such as good house wine, specialty coffees, bottled water and sodas, basic gratuities (for cabin stewards, bar, and dining), self-service laundry, and shuttle buses in some ports.

Oceania Cruises

Contact Information: www.oceaniacruises.com, tel. 800-531-5658

Number and Capacity of Ships: *Marina* carries 1,250 passengers (its sister ship, *Riviera*, debuts in 2012); *Insignia, Nautica,* and *Regatta* each carry 684.

Daily Cost of Cheapest Cabin: Roughly $665 for inside cabin/ $870 outside cabin

Average Hours in Port: 9-10 hours

Description: Oceania Cruises appeals to well-traveled baby boomers and older retirees who want fine cuisine, excellent service, and a destination-oriented experience. Passengers are mostly North American, along with Brits and other travelers from English-speaking nations. The atmosphere is casually sophisticated. Although the line does not discourage children, there are no children's programs, and there are typically few kids on board. Their itineraries tend to be on the longer side; sailings under 10 days are rare in the Mediterranean.

This line's smaller ships feel like stylish boutique hotels, and have a cozy and intimate atmosphere. The cuisine has French and Italian influences, with a good proportion of healthy fare, and their dining program includes alternative restaurants at no additional charge. They are noted for courting experienced crew members and for low crew turnover. Oceania offers few organized activities, some entertainment, and extensive onboard libraries—their cruises are best for those who can entertain themselves. The larger ships do have a culinary arts center with hands-on workshops. On the smaller ships, the staterooms and bathrooms are smaller than on most Luxury ships—but with reportedly great beds and fine linens. The pricing is not all-inclusive—you'll pay separately for drinks, gratuities, and other extras (considered pricier than average by some of their customers).

Star Clippers

Contact Information: www.starclippers.com, tel. 800-442-0551

Number and Capacity of Ships: *Royal Clipper* carries 227 passengers; *Star Clipper* and *Star Flyer* each carry 170.

Daily Cost of Cheapest Cabin: Around $600 for inside cabin/$715 outside cabin

Average Hours in Port: 8-9 hours

Description: Star Clippers takes its sailing heritage very seriously, and its three ships are among the world's largest and tallest sailing vessels (actual "tall ships," with diesel engines for backup power).

While the Windstar ships (described next) also have sails, those are mostly for show—Star Clippers' square-riggers are real sail-boats. Passengers with nautical know-how are invited to pitch in when sails are hoisted or lowered. If the weather is right during the trip, you can even climb the main mast up to the crow's nest (wearing a safety harness, of course). There's a goose-bump-inducing ceremony every time you leave port: The crew raises the sails while the haunting music plays over the loudspeakers.

With its sailing focus, Star Clippers draws more active, adventurous customers, ranging in age from 30s to 70s, who don't need to be pampered. Passengers are primarily Europeans (one recent sailing had passengers from 38 countries), and almost 60 percent are repeat customers. People who choose Star Clippers love the simple life on board a sailboat; enjoy a casual, easygoing cruise experience; and don't want the nightclubs and casinos offered by mainstream cruise lines. Kids are welcome, but there are no children's programs, counselors, or video-game parlors. Given the constraints of a small vessel, the cabins are not as big or luxurious as you might expect at this price range (for example, none have verandas).

The food, while adequate, comes in modest (European-size) portions. There's open seating in the dining room, the dress code is casual, and there are no rigid schedules. Activities include beach barbecues, crab races, scavenger hunts, talent nights, fashion shows, and performances by local musicians. You'll also have access to complimentary water activities, including snorkeling, kayaking, and sailing.

Windstar Cruises

Contact Information: www.windstarcruises.com, tel. 800-258-7245

Number and Capacity of Ships: *Wind Surf* carries 312 passengers; *Wind Star* and *Wind Spirit* each carry 148.

Daily Cost of Cheapest Cabin: About $885 (all are outside cabins)

Average Hours in Port: 10 hours

Description: Windstar's gimmick is its sails—each of its ships has four big, functional sails that unfurl dramatically each time the ship leaves port. (While the sails are capable of powering the ship in strong winds, they're more decorative than practical—although they do reduce the amount of fuel used by the engines.) This line provides an enticing bridge between the more rough-around-the-edges sailboat experience of Star Clippers (described above) and the comforts of mainstream lines. For many, it's an ideal combination—the romance of sails plus the pampering of a Luxury cruise. For this price range, it has a relatively casual atmosphere, with no formal nights.

Windstar passengers are professionals and experienced independent-minded travelers who range in age from 40s to 70s. First-time cruisers, honeymooners, and anniversary celebrants are enticed by Windstar's unique approach. The smaller ships favor more focused itineraries and smaller ports, with generous time ashore. Passengers are more "travelers" than "cruisers"—they're here to spend as much time as possible exploring the port towns.

The small vessels also mean fewer on-ship activities. The casino and swimming pool are miniscule, the smaller ships have only one specialty restaurant, and nightlife is virtually nonexistent. However, the lounge hosts talented musicians, and each stateroom has a DVD player (there's a free DVD library). On some days when the ship is tendered, they lower a platform from the stern, allowing passengers to swim and enjoy other water-sports activities right off the back of the vessel. The food is high-quality, and there's a barbecue night on the open deck. Windstar also touts its green-ness (thanks to those sails) and its rare open-bridge policy, whereby passengers can visit the bridge during certain times to see the instruments and chat with the captain and officers.

Ultra-Luxury

You'll pay top dollar for these cruises, but get an elite experience in return. The basic features of the previously described Luxury cruises apply to this category as well: small ships (with the exception of Crystal), upscale clientele, a classier atmosphere, less emphasis on onboard activities, and a more destination-focused experience. There's less focus on selling you extras—at these prices, you can expect more and more extras to be included (ranging from alcoholic drinks to shore excursions).

Crystal Cruises

Contact Information: www.crystalcruises.com, tel. 866-446-6625 or 1-888-722-0021

Number and Capacity of Ships: *Serenity* carries 1,070 passengers; *Symphony* carries 922 passengers.

Daily Cost of Cheapest Cabin: Approximately $1,175 (suites only)

Average Hours in Port: 10 hours

Description: While most Luxury and Ultra-Luxury lines have smaller ships, Crystal Cruises distinguishes itself by operating larger ships, closer in size to the less expensive categories. This allows it to offer more big-ship activities and amenities, while still fostering a genteel, upper-crust ambience (which some may consider "stuffy"). Crystal attracts a retired, well-traveled, well-heeled crowd (although there are also a fair number of people under 50). Approximately 75 percent of the travelers are from the US and Canada, and the rest are mainly British. There are basic programs for children (most kids seem to come with multi-generational family groups) that are better than most Ultra-Luxury lines.

The food and the service are both well-regarded (and their seafood comes from sustainable and fair-trade sources). Their acclaimed enrichment programs are noted for having a wide range of mini-courses in everything from foreign languages to computer skills, and excursions include opportunities where passengers can participate in a local volunteering effort.

Note: Crystal Cruises are sold exclusively through travel agents.

Regent Seven Seas Cruises (RSSC)

Contact Information: www.rssc.com, tel. 877-505-5370

Number and Capacity of Ships: *Voyager* and *Mariner* each carry 700 passengers.

Daily Cost of Cheapest Cabin: Roughly $1,125 (suites only)

Average Hours in Port: 10-11 hours

Description: Regent Seven Seas Cruises appeal to well-educated, sophisticated, and affluent travelers—generally from mid-40s to retirees—looking for a destination-oriented experience. Their exclusive, clubby, understatedly elegant atmosphere attracts many repeat cruisers (the *Voyager* seems especially popular). Most passengers are from North America, with the rest from Great Britain, New Zealand, and Australia. The line welcomes families during summer and school breaks, when it offers a children's program; the rest of the year, there's little to occupy kids.

Their "ultra-inclusive" prices are, indeed, among the most inclusive in the industry, covering premium soft drinks, house wines, tips, ground transfers, round-trip airfare from the US, one night's pre-cruise hotel stay, and unlimited excursions. The ships are known for their spacious, elegantly appointed suites (all with verandas). This line has some of the industry's highest space-per-guest and crew member-per-guest ratios, and customers report outstanding service. The French-based cuisine has an international flair, and also attempts to mix in local fare from the ships' ports of call. Passengers tend to be independent-minded and enjoy making their own plans, rather than wanting to be entertained by the cruise line (the entertainment is low-key, and notably, there is no onboard photography service). The crew tries to incorporate the ship's destinations into the entertainment, events, and lectures.

Excursions include private tours, strenuous walking tours, and some soft-adventure offerings such as kayaking.

Seabourn Cruise Line

Contact Information: www.seabourn.com, tel. 800-929-9391
Number and Capacity of Ships: *Odyssey, Sojourn,* and *Quest* each carry 450 passengers; *Pride, Spirit,* and *Legend* each carry 208.
Daily Cost of Cheapest Cabin: About $810 (suites only)
Average Hours in Port: 10 hours
Description: Seabourn Cruise Line attracts affluent, well-traveled couples in their late 40s to late 60s and older, who are not necessarily cruise aficionados but are accustomed to the "best of the best." Deep down, Seabourn passengers want to be on a yacht, but don't mind sharing it with other upper-class travelers—who, as the line brags, are "both interesting and interested." The focus is on exploring more exotic destinations rather than just relaxing on the ship. Most passengers are American, and the onboard atmosphere is classically elegant. Kids are present in summer and during school vacations, usually with multi-generational groups.

These ships feel like private clubs, with pampering as a priority. The extremely high crew member-to-guest ratio is about 1:1, and the crew addresses guests by name. Activities are designed for

socializing with other passengers. Most of the ships offer a stern platform for snorkeling and kayaking right off the back of the ship. The line's all-inclusive pricing includes freebies like a welcome bottle of champagne, an in-suite bar (with full bottles of your pre-selected booze), and nearly all drinks, including decent wines at mealtime (you pay extra only for premium brands). Also included are tips, some excursions, poolside mini-massages, and activities such as exercise classes and wine-tasting seminars.

SeaDream Yacht Club

Contact Information: www.seadreamyachtclub.com, tel. 800-707-4911
Number and Capacity of Ships: *SeaDream I* and *SeaDream II* each carry 110 passengers.
Daily Cost of Cheapest Cabin: Around $1,210
Average Hours in Port: 12+ hours
Description: SeaDream's tiny, intimate ships—the smallest of all those described here—are essentially chic, Ultra-Luxury megayachts. This line appeals to active travelers who are well-heeled and

well-traveled, ranging in age from 40s to 70s (the shorter itineraries appeal to those still working). Passengers are primarily from North America and Europe, the atmosphere is laid-back, and the dress code is country-club casual (with no formal nights). There are no kids' facilities or services on board.

The attentive crew anticipates guests' needs without being fawning. The unstructured environment is best for independent-minded passengers, as you're pretty much on your own for entertainment. The line is perfect for those who want to relax on deck and be outdoors as much as possible. In fact, a unique—and extremely popular—activity is sleeping out under the stars on double loungers. Itineraries include overnight stays in port (allowing guests the option to experience local nightlife) and are somewhat flexible, allowing the captain to linger longer in a port or depart early. Rather than hiring local guides for all their shore excursions, some trips are led by the ship's officers or other crew members. (Note that organized excursions may be canceled if the quota isn't reached, which can happen, given the small number of passengers.) The ships have a sports platform off the stern with water-sports toys such as kayaks and water skis, and there's a fleet of mountain bikes for exploring the destinations. Prices include decent house wines, cocktails, tips, water-sports equipment, DVDs, and shore excursions.

Silversea Cruises

Contact Information: www.silversea.com, tel. 877-760-9052

Number and Capacity of Ships: *Silver Spirit* carries 540 passengers; *Silver Whisper* carries 382; *Silver Wind* and *Silver Cloud* each carry 296.

Daily Cost of Cheapest Cabin: Approximately $1,320 (suites only)

Average Hours in Port: 11 hours

Description: The Italian-owned, Monaco-based Silversea Cruises is popular with well-educated, well-traveled, upper-crust cruisers, generally ranging in age from late 40s to 80s (with many in their 70s). Most passengers are accustomed to the finest and are very discriminating. The ships' Art Deco design lends an elegant 1930s ambience, and the atmosphere on board is clubby. Half of their clientele is from North America, with the other half predominantly from the UK, Europe, and Australia. There are no organized children's programs, and you'll see few children on board.

The cuisine is considered very good, and the spacious suites even have an assigned butler. The service is reported excellent. Partly as a function of the ships' small size and fewer passengers, the events and entertainment are low-key.

BOOKING A CRUISE

Once you've narrowed down your cruise-line options, it's time to get serious about booking. This chapter covers where, when, and how to book your cruise, including pointers on cruise pricing, cabin assignments, trip insurance, pre- and post-cruise plans, and other considerations.

Where to Book a Cruise

While plane tickets, rental cars, hotels, and most other aspects of travel have gradually migrated to do-it-yourself, cruises are the one form of travel that is still booked predominantly through a travel agent. In fact, 90 percent of cruises are booked through travel agencies.

While it's possible to book a cruise directly with the cruise line, most lines actually prefer that you go through an intermediary. That's because their customers are rarely just booking a cruise—while they're at it, they want to look into airfares, trip insurance, maybe some hotels at either end of the cruise, and so on. Because that's beyond the scope of what cruise lines want to sell—their booking offices mainly take orders, not advise—they reduce their overhead by letting travel agents do all that hard work.

It can also be cheaper to book through a travel agent. Some cruise lines discount fares that are sold through their preferred agents; because they've built up relationships with these agents over the years, they don't want to undersell them. In other cases, the travel agency reserves a block of cabins to secure the lowest possible price, and then passes the savings on to their customers.

There are, generally speaking, two different types of cruise-sales agencies: Your neighborhood travel agent, where you can get in-person advice; or a giant company that sells most of its inventory online or by phone. Because cruise prices vary based on volume, a big agency can usually undersell a small one. Big agencies are also more likely to offer incentives (such as onboard credit or cabin upgrades) to sweeten the pot. However, some small agencies belong to a consortium that gives them as much collective clout as a big agency. And some travelers figure the intangible value of personal service they get at a small agency is worth the possibility of paying a little extra. (Although most travel agents don't charge a fee, their commission is built into the cruise price.)

The big cruise agencies often have websites where you can easily shop around for the best price. These include www.vacations togo.com, www.cruisecompete.com, and www.crucon.com. One site, www.cayole.com, tries to predict when prices for a particular departure may be lowest—giving you advice about how soon you should book.

I use the big websites to do my comparison-shopping. But— call me old-fashioned—when it comes time to book, I prefer to sit down with a travel agent to make my plans in person. Ideally, find a well-regarded travel agent in your community who knows cruising and will give you the personal attention you need to sort through your options. Tell them the deals you've seen online, and ask if they can match or beat them. A good travel agent knows how to look at the whole picture of your trip (airfare, hotels, and so on), not just the cruise component. And they can advise you about "insider" information, such as how to select the right cabin. Keep in mind that if you do solicit the advice of a travel agent, you should book the cruise through them—that's the only way they'll get their hard-earned commission.

When to Book a Cruise

Most cruise lines post their Mediterranean cruise schedules a year or more in advance. A specific departure is called a "sailing." If you want to cruise in the summertime, and your plans are very specific (for example, you have your heart set on a certain sailing, or a particular cabin setup, such as adjoining staterooms), it's best to begin looking around the previous November. (For cruises in shoulder season—spring and fall—you may have a little more time to shop around.) Because the cruise lines want to fill up their ships as fast as possible, they typically offer early-booking discounts if you buy your cruise well in advance (at least 6-12 months, depending on the company).

Meanwhile, the most popular time of year to book a cruise is during the first few weeks of January. Dubbed "wave season" by industry insiders, this is when a third of all cruises are booked. If you wait until this time, you'll be competing with other travelers

Sample Pre-Trip Timeline

While this can vary, here's a general timeline for what to do and when—but be sure to carefully confirm with your specific cruise line.

What to Do	Time Before Departure
Book cruise and pay initial deposit	8-10 months (for best selection)
Buy trip insurance, if desired	At time of booking (if through cruise line); within about 2 weeks of booking (if through a third party)
Full payment due	45-60 days
Online check-in	Between booking and full payment (check with cruise line)
Fly to meet your cruise	1-2 days ahead (remember you lose one day when flying from the US to Europe)

for the deals. The sooner you book, the more likely you are to have your choice of sailing and cabin type—and potentially an even better price.

If a cruise still has several cabins available 90 days before departure, they're likely to put them on sale—but don't count on it. People tend to think the longer they wait, the more likely they'll find a sale. But this isn't always the case. Last-minute sales aren't as likely in the Mediterranean as they are for some other destinations, such as the Caribbean. Unlike the Caribbean market, the Mediterranean market has a much shorter season and fewer ships, which means fewer beds to fill...and fewer deals to fill them. And even if you do find a last-minute deal, keep in mind that last-minute airfares to Europe can be that much more expensive.

If you're unsure of when to book, consult your travel agent.

How to Book a Cruise

Once you find the cruise you want, your travel agent may be able to hold it for you for a day or two to think it over. When you've decided, you'll secure your passage on the cruise by paying a deposit. While this varies by cruise line, it averages about $500 per person (this becomes nonrefundable after a specified date, sometimes immediately—ask when you book). No matter how far ahead you book, you generally won't have to pay the balance of your cruise until 45-60 days before departure. After this point, cancellation comes at a heftier price; as the departure date approaches, your cruise becomes effectively nonrefundable.

Cruise Pricing

Like cars or plane tickets, cruises are priced very flexibly. In fact, some cruise lines don't even bother listing prices in their brochures—they just send customers to the Web. In general, for a mass-market cruise, you'll rarely pay the list price. Higher-end cruises are less likely to be discounted (although some of the Luxury lines had to offer sales during the recent financial downturn).

The main factor that determines the actual cost of a cruise is demand (that is, the popularity of the date, destination, and specific ship). Other factors play a role:

Cruise lines and travel agencies use **sales and incentives** to entice new customers. With the recent proliferation of megaships, there are plenty of cabins to fill, and cruise industry insiders rigidly follow the mantra, "Empty beds are not tolerated!" The obvious approach to fill up a slow-selling cruise is to reduce prices. But they may also offer "onboard credit," which can be applied to your expenses on the ship (such as tips, alcoholic drinks, or excursions). In other cases, they may automatically upgrade your stateroom ("Pay for Category C, and get a Category B cabin for no extra charge!"). To sweeten the pot, they might even throw in a special cocktail reception with the captain, or a night or two at a hotel at either end of your cruise. Your travel agent should be aware of these sales; you can also look online, or—if you're a fan of a particular cruise line—sign up to get their email offers.

Some cruise lines offer **discounts** for seniors (including AARP members), AAA members, firefighters, military, union workers, teachers, those in the travel industry, employees of certain corporations, and so on. It never hurts to ask.

Keep in mind that you'll pay a premium for **novelty.** It usually costs more to go on the cruise line's newest, most loudly advertised vessel. If you go on a ship that's just a few years older—with most of the same amenities—you'll likely pay less.

If you are a **repeat cruiser**—or think you may become one—sign up for the cruise line's "frequent cruiser" program. Like the airlines' mileage-rewards programs, these offer incentives, upgrades, and access to special deals.

No matter who you book your cruise through, use a **credit card** to give yourself a measure of consumer protection. A credit-card company can be a strong ally in resolving disputes.

Taxes, Port Fees, and Other Hidden Charges

The advertised price for your cruise isn't all you'll pay. All of the miscellaneous taxes, fees, and other expenses that the ship incurs in port are divvied up and passed on to passengers, under the category "**taxes and port fees.**" While this can vary dramatically from port to port, it'll run you a few hundred dollars per person (for example, around $200 for a 7-day cruise, or around $300 for a 12-day cruise). These amounts are not locked in at the time you book; if the port increases their fees, you'll pay the difference.

Like airlines, cruise lines reserve the right to tack on a **"fuel surcharge"** in the event that the price of oil goes over a certain amount per barrel. Unlike airlines, this can be added onto your bill even after you book the cruise.

Once you're on the cruise, most lines automatically levy an **"auto-tip"** of around $10-12/day per person (which you can adjust upward or downward once on board). While this won't be included in your up-front cruise cost, you should budget for it. For more details on tipping, see page 74.

Special Considerations

Families, singles, groups, people celebrating milestones, and those with limited mobility are all special in my book.

If you're traveling with a family, note that fares for **kids** tend to be more expensive during spring break and summertime, when they're out of school and demand is high; it can be cheaper to bring them off-season. Adjoining staterooms (also called "connecting" rooms) that share an inside door tend to book up early, particularly in the summertime. If those are sold out, consider an inside cabin across from an outside cabin. Some rooms have fold-down bunk beds (or "upper berths"), so a family of three or four can cram into one room (each passenger after the second pays a reduced fare)—but the tight quarters, already cramped for two people, can be challenging for the whole clan.

Single cabins are rare on cruise ships; almost all staterooms are designed with couples in mind. Therefore, cruise rates are quoted per person, based on double occupancy. If you're traveling solo, you'll usually have to pay a "single supplement." This can range from reasonable (an additional 10 percent of the per-person double rate) to exorbitant ("100 percent" of the double rate—in other words, paying as much as two people would). On average, figure paying about 50 percent above the per-person double rate for your own single cabin. Sometimes it's possible to avoid the single supplement by volunteering to be assigned a random roommate by the cruise line, but this option is increasingly rare.

Groups of eight people or more may be eligible for discounts if they book together—ask.

If you'll be celebrating a **special occasion**—such as a birthday or anniversary—on board, mention it when you book. You may get a special bonus, such as a fancy dessert or cocktails with the captain.

If you have **limited mobility**, cruising can be a good way to go—but not all cruise lines are created equal. Some ships are wheelchair-accessible, including fully adapted cabins; others (especially small vessels) may not even have an elevator. When shopping for your cruise, ask the cruise line about the features you'll need, and be very specific. Unfortunately, once you reach port, all bets are off. While some cities are impressively accessible, others (especially smaller towns) may have fewer elevators than the ship you arrived on. The creaky and cobbled Old World doesn't accommodate wheelchairs or walkers very well. Taking a shore excursion can be a good way to see a place with minimum effort; cruise lines can typically inform you of the specific amount of walking and stairs you'll need to tackle for each excursion.

Cabin Classes

Each cruise ship has a variety of staterooms. In some cases, it can be a pretty narrow distinction ("Category A" and the marginally smaller "Category B"). On other ships, it can be the difference between a "Class 1" suite with a private balcony and a "Class 10" windowless bunk-bed closet below the waterline. On its website, each cruise line explains the specific breakdown of its various categories, along with the amenities in each one.

You'll see these terms:

Inside/Interior: An inside cabin has no external windows (though there's often a faux-porthole to at least create the illusion of outside light). While these terrify claustrophobes, inside cabins offer a great value that tempts budget travelers. And many cruisers figure that with a giant ship to explore—not to mention Europe at your doorstep each morning—there's not much point hanging out

in your room anyway.

Outside: With a window to the sea, an outside cabin costs more—but for some travelers, it's worth the splurge to be able to see the world go by. But be aware that you're rarely able to open those windows (for that, you need a veranda—see next). If your view is blocked (by a lifeboat, for example), it should be classified as "obstructed."

Veranda: Going one better than an outside cabin, a "veranda" is cruise jargon for a small outdoor balcony attached to your room. Because windows can't be opened, one big advantage of a veranda is that you can slide open the door to get some fresh air. The size and openness of verandas can vary wildly; for wind-shear reasons, some verandas can be almost entirely enclosed, with only a big picture window-sized opening to the sea. Sitting on the veranda while you cruise the Med sounds appealing, but keep in mind that most of the time you're sailing, it'll be dark outside.

Suite: A multi-room suite represents the top end of cruise accommodations. These are particularly handy for families, but if you can't spring for a suite, ask about adjoining staterooms (see earlier).

Location Within Ship: In general, the upper decks (with higher vantage-point views, and typically bigger windows and more light) are more desirable—and more expensive—than the lower decks. Cabins in the middle of the ship (where the "motion of the ocean" is less noticeable) are considered better than those at either end. And cabins close to the engines (low and to the rear of the ship) can come with extra noise and vibrations.

Look for the **deck plan** on your cruise line's website. If you have a chance to select your own cabin (see next section), study the deck plan carefully to choose a good location. You'd want to avoid a cabin directly below a deck that has a lot of noisy foot traffic (such as the late-night disco or stewards dragging pool chairs across the deck).

Cabin Assignments and Upgrades

Cruise lines handle specific cabin assignments in different ways. While some cruise lines let you request a specific stateroom when you book, others don't offer that option; they'll assign your stateroom number at a future date. In other cases, you can request a "guarantee"—you pay for a particular class and are guaranteed of getting that class of cabin (or better), but are not yet assigned a specific stateroom. As time passes and the cruise line gets a better sense of occupancy on your sailing, there's a possibility that they will upgrade you to a better cabin for no extra charge. There's no way of predicting when you'll find out your specific cabin assignment—it can be months before departure, or days before. (Cabin assignments seem to favor repeat cruisers to reward customers for their loyalty.)

If you need a specific type of stateroom—for instance, you have limited mobility and need to be close to the elevator, or you're traveling with a large family and want to be as close together as possible—opt for a specific cabin assignment as early as you can.

If you don't have special needs, you might as well take your chances with a "guarantee"; you're assured of getting the class of cabin that you paid for...and you could wind up with a bonus veranda.

Assigned Dining: Traditionally, cruisers pre-reserved not only their stateroom, but also which table and at what time they'd like to have dinner each night. Called a "seating," this tradition is fading. It's still mandatory on a few lines, but most lines either make it optional or have done away with it entirely. If your cruise line requires (or you prefer) a specific seating, reserve it when you book your cruise or cabin. (For more on assigned dining, see page 91.)

Travel Insurance

Travel insurance is a way to minimize the considerable financial risks of traveling. These risks include accidents, illness, cruise cancellations due to bad weather, missed flights, lost baggage, medical expenses, and emergency evacuation. If you anticipate any hiccups that may prevent you from taking your trip, travel insurance can protect your investment.

Trip-cancellation insurance lets you bail out without losing all of the money you paid for the cruise, provided you cancel for an acceptable reason, such as illness or a death in the family. This insurance also covers trip interruptions—if you begin a journey but have to cut it short for a covered reason, you'll be reimbursed for the portion of the trip that you didn't complete.

Travel insurance is also handy in the unlikely event that your ship breaks down mid-trip. Though the cruise line should reimburse you for the cruise itself, travel insurance provides more surefire protection and can cover unexpected expenses, such as hotels or additional transportation you might need once you've gotten off the ship.

Travel insurance also includes basic medical coverage—up to a certain amount. If you have an accident or come down with a case of the "cruise-ship virus," your policy will cover doctor visits, treatment, and medication (though you'll generally have to pay a deductible). This usually includes medical evacuation—in the event that you become seriously ill and need to be taken to the nearest adequate medical care (that is, a big, modern hospital).

Baggage insurance, included in most comprehensive policies (and in some homeowner or renter insurance policies—sometimes with a "floater" supplement), reimburses you for luggage that's lost or stolen. However, some items aren't covered (ask for details when you buy). When you check a bag on a plane, it's covered by the airline (though, again, there are limits—ask).

Insurance prices vary dramatically, but most packages cost between 5 and 12 percent of the price of your trip. Two factors affect the price: the trip cost and your age at the time of purchase (rates go up dramatically for every decade over 50). For instance, to insure a 70-year-old traveler for a $3,000 cruise, the prices can range from about $150 to $350, depending on the level of coverage. To insure a 40-year-old for that same cruise, the cost can be about $90-215. Coverage is generally inexpensive or even free for children 17 and under. To ensure maximum coverage, purchase insurance within a couple of weeks of the date you pay your initial trip deposit. Research policies carefully; if you wait too long to purchase insurance, you may be denied certain coverage, such as for pre-existing medical conditions.

Cruise lines offer their own travel insurance, but these generally aren't as comprehensive as policies from third-party insurance companies. For example, a cruise-line policy only covers the cruise itself; if you book your airfare and pre- and post-cruise hotels separately, they will not be covered.

Reputable independent providers include K & K Consulting Services (www.betins.com, tel. 866-552-8834 or 253/238-6374), Access America (www.accessamerica.com, tel. 800-284-8300), Travelex (www.travelex-insurance.com, tel. 800-228-9792), Travel Guard (www.travelguard.com, tel. 800-826-4919), and Travel Insured International (www.travelinsured.com, tel. 800-243-3174). Insuremytrip.com allows you to compare insurance policies and costs among various providers (they also sell insurance; www .insuremytrip.com, tel. 800-487-4722).

Some credit-card companies may offer limited trip-cancellation or interruption coverage for cruises purchased with the card—it's worth checking before you buy a policy.

Airfare and Pre- and Post-Cruise Travel

When booking your airfare, think carefully about how much time you want before and after your cruise. Remember that most Europe-bound flights from the US travel overnight and arrive the following day. The airport will rarely be anywhere near the cruise port; allow plenty of time to get to your ship. You'll need to check in at least two hours before your cruise departs (confirm with your cruise line; most passengers show up several hours earlier). If you miss the ship, you're on your own to catch up with it at its next port. Cutting it close is risky—even a short flight delay can cause huge headaches.

If your travel plans are flexible, consider arriving a few days before your cruise and/or departing a few days after it ends—particularly if the embarkation and disembarkation points are places you'd like to explore. Remember, if you arrive just hours before (or depart just hours after) your cruise, you won't actually have any time to see the beginning and ending ports at all. Common starting and ending points include Barcelona, Rome, Venice, Athens, and Istanbul—all of which merit plenty of time.

Arriving at least a day early also makes it less likely that you'll miss the start of your cruise in case your flight is delayed. In talking with fellow cruisers, while I've rarely heard of people missing the boat at a port of call, I've heard many horror stories about flight delays causing passengers to miss the first day of the cruise—and often incurring a time-consuming, stressful, and costly overland trip to meet their ship at the next stop.

In the past, most cruises included what they called "free air" (or "air/sea"), but these days your airfare to and from Europe costs extra—and you're usually best off booking it yourself. (Relatively few cruise passengers book airfare through their cruise line.) If you book your airfare through the cruise line, you'll typically pay more, but in case of a flight delay, the cruise line will help you meet the cruise at a later point. However, booking your airfare this way has its disadvantages—the cruise line chooses which airline and routing to send you on. They'll select an airline they have a contract with, regardless of whether it's one you want to fly (though it's sometimes possible to pay a "deviation fee" to switch to an airline and routing of your choice).

If you decide to add some days on either end of your trip, it's also best to make your own arrangements for hotels and transfers. While most cruise lines offer pre- and post-tour packages (that include the hotel, plus transfers to and from the airport and the cruise port), they tend to be overpriced. For each of the arrival and departure cities in this book, I've recommended a few hotels for you to consider.

In some rare circumstances, it's convenient for a cruise passenger to leave the ship before the cruise is completed—for example, you want to get off to have some extra time in Barcelona, rather than ride another day down to Cádiz. Cruise lines usually permit this, but you'll pay for the full cost of the cruise (including the portion you're not using), and you'll need to get permission in advance.

Online Check-in

At some point between when you book and when your final payment is due, you'll be invited to check in online for your cruise. This takes only a few minutes. You'll register your basic information and sometimes a credit-card number (for onboard purchases—or you can do this in person when you arrive at the ship). Once registered, you'll be able to print out e-documents (such as your receipt and boarding pass), access information about shipboard life, and learn about and pre-book shore excursions.

PART II: TRAVEL SKILLS FOR CRUISING

BEFORE YOUR CRUISE

As any sailor knows, prepare well and you'll enjoy a smoother voyage. This chapter covers what you should know before you go (including red tape, money matters, and other practicalities), as well as pointers for packing.

Know Before You Go

Red Tape

You need a **passport** to travel to the countries covered in this book. You may be denied entry into certain European countries if your passport is due to expire within three to six months of your ticketed date of return. Get it renewed if you'll be cutting it close. Either getting or renewing a passport can take up to six weeks (for more on passports, see www.travel.state.gov).

For entrance into Turkey, you may also need a **visa** (a sticker that's affixed to a page of your passport); this is most likely if your journey originates or ends in Turkey, or if you are making multiple stops there. If your cruise begins in Turkey, you must buy a visa when you arrive at the airport (windows are located before the passport-control checkpoint). You can make day trips into Turkish ports without a visa, but you can't spend the night on shore without one. If you do need a visa, your cruise crew will notify you. They'll probably collect your passport the evening before arrival and process the paperwork for you (and add the fee to your shipboard bill); your passport will be returned with the needed visa attached.

If you're traveling with **kids,** each minor must possess a passport. Grandparents or guardians can bring kids on board sans parents only if they have a written, notarized letter of consent from the parents. Even a single parent traveling with children has to prove the other parent has given approval. Specifically, the

Specific Concerns

Here are a few things to consider as you prepare for your cruise:

- Contact your **credit- and debit-card companies** to tell them you're going abroad and to ask about fees, limits, and more; see the next page.
- Ask your **health insurance** provider about overseas medical coverage, both on the ship and on shore. For more on health care, see page 76.
- Consider buying **trip insurance** for your cruise. For details, see page 40.
- For cruises with **assigned dining,** request your preference for seating time and table size when you reserve. See page 91.
- Vegetarians, those with food allergies, or anyone with a **special diet** should notify their cruise line at least 30 days before departure. See page 90.
- Your US **mobile phone** may work in Europe; if you want the option to use it while traveling, contact your mobile phone service provider for details. See page 82.
- Some major sights in Italy accept **reservations,** which can help you avoid long lines. For a list of sights to book in advance, see page 48.
- **Smokers,** or those determined to avoid smoke, can ask about their ship's smoking policy. See page 80.
- If you're prone to **seasickness,** ask your doctor for advice; certain medication requires a prescription. For a rundown of seasickness treatments, see page 76.
- If you're taking a **child** on a cruise without both parents, you'll need a notarized letter of permission. See below.

letter should grant permission for the accompanying adult to travel internationally with the child, including dates, destination countries, and address and phone number where the parent(s) at home can be reached. Family Travel Forum provides a sample form that you can print or use as a guideline (www.myfamilytravels.com; click on the "Tips & Gear" tab, select "Tips & Documents," and go to "Required Documents for Travel with Minors"). If you have a different last name from your child, it's smart to bring a copy of the birth certificate (with your name on it). For parents of adopted children, it's a good idea to bring the birth certificate and adoption decree.

Before you leave on your trip, make two sets of **photocopies** of your passport, tickets, and other valuable documents. Pack one set of copies and leave the other set at home (for someone to fax or scan and email to you if necessary). It's easier to replace a lost or stolen passport if you have a photocopy proving that you really had what you lost. A couple of passport-type pictures brought from home can expedite the replacement process.

Money

At the start of your cruise, you must register your credit card (either at check-in or on board the ship). All purchases are made using your room number, and you'll be billed for onboard purchases when you disembark. Be aware that the cruise line may put a hold on your credit card during your trip to cover anticipated shipboard expenses; if you have a relatively low limit, you might come uncomfortably close to it. If you're concerned, ask the cruise line what the amount of the hold will be.

For your time on **land,** bring both a credit card and a debit card. You'll use the debit card at cash machines (ATMs) to withdraw local cash for most purchases, and the credit card to pay for larger items. Some travelers carry a third card as a backup, in case one gets demagnetized or eaten by a temperamental machine. As an emergency backup, I also carry a few hundred dollars in hard cash (in easy-to-exchange $20 bills).

Cash

Most cruise ships are essentially cashless (though you may want to bring some US cash for tipping at casinos). But on land, cash is just as desirable as it is at home. Don't bother changing money before you leave home—ATMs in Europe are easy to find and use (for details, see page 122). And skip traveler's checks—they're a waste of time (long waits at slow banks) and a waste of money in fees.

Credit and Debit Cards

For maximum usability, bring cards with a Visa or MasterCard logo. You'll also need to know your PIN code in numbers, as there are no letters on European keypads. Before your trip, contact the company that issued your debit or credit cards and ask them a few questions.

• Confirm your card will work overseas, and alert them that you'll be using it in Europe; otherwise, they may deny transactions if they perceive unusual spending patterns.

• Ask for the specifics on transaction **fees.** When you use your credit or debit card—either for purchases or ATM withdrawals—you'll often be charged additional "international transaction" fees of up to 3 percent of the amount plus $5 per transaction. Some banks have agreements with European partners that reduce or eliminate the $5 transaction fee. If your fees are too high, consider getting a card just for your trip: Capital One (www.capitalone .com) and most credit unions have cards with low or no international fees.

• If you plan to withdraw cash from ATMs, confirm your daily **withdrawal limit.** Some travelers prefer a high limit that allows them to take out more cash at each ATM stop, while others choose to set a lower limit in case their card is stolen. Note that if you use a credit card for ATM transactions, it's technically a "cash advance" rather than a "withdrawal"—and subject to an additional cash-advance fee.

• Find out your card's **credit limit.** Some cruise lines put a hold on your credit card to cover anticipated onboard expenses; if this or your on-shore spending is likely to crowd your limit, ask for a higher amount or bring a second credit card.

• Ask for your credit card's **PIN** in case you encounter Europe's chip-and-PIN system (most likely in France; for details, see page 123). For security reasons, most banks will only mail a PIN, so give yourself plenty of time to get the code if you don't already know it.

Practicalities

Time: Spain, France, Italy, Croatia, and most of the rest of continental Europe are generally six/nine hours ahead of the East/West Coasts of the US. Greece and Turkey are one hour ahead of most of Europe, and seven/ten hours ahead of the East/West Coasts of the US. (If you cross a time zone on your ship, your cabin steward will leave a reminder on your bed the evening before to set your watch.)

Europe "springs forward" for Daylight Savings Time on the last Sunday in March (two weeks after most of North America) and "falls back" the last Sunday in October (one week before North America). For a handy online time converter, try www.timeand date.com/worldclock.

Watt's Up? Virtually all cruise ships have American-style outlets, so you don't need an adapter or converter to charge your phone or blow-dry your hair. (If you're cruising with a European line, you may want to confirm the outlet type.) But if you're staying at a hotel before or after the cruise, you'll need to adapt to Europe's electrical system, which differs from North America's in two ways: the shape of the plug (round instead of flat prongs) and the voltage of the current (220 instead of 110 volts). For your North American plug to work in Europe, you'll need an adapter, sold inexpensively at travel stores in the US. Most newer electronics or travel appliances (such as hair dryers, laptops, and battery chargers) automatically convert the voltage—if you see a range of voltages printed on the item or its plug (such as "110-220"), it'll work in Europe. It's not worth trying to make older appliances work overseas—while you can buy a voltage converter in the US ($20), they're heavy and unreliable. Either go without or buy a cheap replacement appliance in Europe.

Driving in Europe: If you're planning on renting a car, you'll need to bring your driver's license. An International Driving Permit—a translation of your driver's license—is recommended in France and technically required in some countries, such as Greece, Spain, Turkey, and Italy (though I've often rented cars in these countries without having—or being asked to show—this permit). International Driving Permits are sold at your hometown AAA office for $15 plus the cost of two passport-type photos.

Reservations at Major Museums in Italy: Several popular sights take reservations, allowing you to skip their long, boring, ticket-buying lines. Making reservations to visit the following sights is not mandatory, but it's smart:

For **Florence's** Uffizi Gallery (Renaissance paintings), book at least a month ahead (see page 406). For the Accademia (Michelangelo's *David*), a minimum of a few days is enough (see page 408).

If you want to climb **Pisa's** Leaning Tower, you can book online (see page 488).

In **Rome,** the Vatican Museum (Sistine Chapel) takes online reservations (see page 565).

Free Audio Tours: If you're bringing an MP3 player or smartphone, download free information from **Rick Steves Audio Europe,** featuring audio tours of major sights in Athens, Florence, Rome, and Venice; hours of travel interviews; and more (at www .ricksteves.com/audioeurope, from iTunes, or through the Rick Steves Audio Europe smartphone app).

Discounts: While this book does not list discounts for sights and museums, seniors (age 60 and over), students with International Student Identification Cards, teachers with proper identification, and youths under 18 often get discounts—but you have to ask. To get a teacher or student ID card, visit www.statravel.com or www .isic.org.

Packing

One of the advantages of cruising is unpacking just once—in your stateroom. But don't underestimate the importance of packing light. Cruise-ship cabins are cramped, and large suitcases can consume precious living space. Plus, you'll still need to get to the airport, on and off the plane, and between the airport and the cruise port. The lighter your luggage is, the easier your transitions will be. And when you carry your own luggage, it's less likely to get lost, broken, or stolen.

Consider packing just one carry-on-size bag (9" by 22" by 14"). I know—realistically, you'll be tempted to bring more. But cruising with one bag can be done without adversely impacting your trip (I've done it, and was happy I did). No matter how much you'd like to bring along that warm jacket or extra pair of shoes, be strong and do your best to pack just what you need.

Here's another reason to favor carry-on bags: If your checked luggage gets lost and doesn't find its way to your embarkation port by the time your ship sets sail, it's unlikely to catch up to you. If you booked air travel through the cruise line, the company will do what it can to reunite you with your lost bags. But if you arranged your own flights, the airline decides whether and how to help you—and rarely will it fly your bags to your next port of call. (If you purchase travel insurance, it may cover lost luggage—ask when you buy; for details on insurance, see page 40.) For this reason, even if you check a bag, be sure you pack essentials (medications, change of clothes, travel documents) in your carry-on.

If you're traveling as part of a couple, and the one-piece-per-person idea seems impossible, consider this compromise: Pack one bag each, as if traveling alone, then share a third bag for bulky cruise extras (such as formal wear). If traveling before or after the cruise, you can leave that third, nonessential bag at a friendly hotel or in a train-station luggage locker, then be footloose and fancy-free for your independent travel time.

Remember, packing light isn't just about the trip over and back—it's about your traveling lifestyle. Too much luggage marks you as a typical tourist. With only one bag, you're mobile and in control. You'll never meet a traveler who, after five trips, brags: "Every year I pack heavier."

Baggage Restrictions

Baggage restrictions provide a built-in incentive for packing light. Some cruise lines limit you to two bags up to 50 pounds apiece; others don't enforce limits (or request only that you bring "a reasonable amount" of luggage). But all airlines have restrictions on the number, size, and weight of both checked and carry-on bags. These days, you'll most likely pay for each piece of luggage you check—and if your bag is overweight, you'll pay even more. Check the specifics on your airline's website (or read the fine print on your airline e-ticket).

Knives, lighters, and other potentially dangerous items are not allowed in airplane carry-on or on board your cruise. Large quantities of liquids or gels must be packed away in checked baggage. Because restrictions are always changing, visit the Transportation Security Administration's website (www.tsa.gov/travelers) for an up-to-date list of what's allowed on the plane.

If you plan to check your bag for your flight, mark it inside and out with your name, address, and emergency phone number. If you have a lock on your bag, you may be asked to remove it due to increased security checks, or it may be cut off so the bag can be

Cruise Ship Dress Code

First-time cruisers sometimes worry about the need to dress up on their vacation. Relax. Cruise ships aren't as dressy as they used to be. And, while on certain nights you may see your fellow cruisers in tuxes and formal gowns, there's usually a place to go casual as well. (In general, the more upscale a cruise is, the more formal the overall vibe—though some luxury lines, such as Windstar, have a reputation for relaxed dress codes.)

During the day, the dress code is casual. People wear shorts, T-shirts, swimsuits with cover-ups, flip-flops, or whatever they're most comfortable in. (On pricier cruises, you may see more passengers in khakis or dressy shorts and polo shirts.)

But in the evenings, a stricter dress code emerges. On most nights, dinner is usually **"smart casual"** in the main dining room and at some (or all) specialty restaurants. People are on vacation, so they generally aren't too dressed up—though jeans, shorts, and T-shirts are no-nos. For men, slacks and a button-down or polo shirt is the norm; most women wear dresses, or pants or skirts with a nice top. Plan to wear something a little nicer on the first evening; after you get the lay of the land, you can adjust your wardrobe for the rest of the meals.

Most cruises host one or two **"formal"** nights per week. On these evenings, men are expected to put on jackets (and sometimes ties), while women generally wear cocktail dresses—or pair a dressy skirt or pants with something silky or sparkly on top. Basically, dress as you would for a nice church wedding or a night at the theater. A few overachievers show up wearing tuxedos or floor-length dresses. Note that formal nights will sometimes extend beyond the dining room into the ship's main theater venue.

Some cruises also have **"semiformal"** nights, which fall

inspected (to avoid this, consider a TSA-approved lock). I've never locked my bag, and I haven't had a problem. Still, just in case, I wouldn't pack anything valuable (such as cash or a camera) in my checked luggage.

As baggage fees increase, more people are carrying on their luggage. Arrive early for aircraft boarding—and increase the odds that you'll snare coveted storage space in the passenger cabin.

What to Bring

How do you fit a whole trip's worth of luggage into one bag? The answer is simple: Don't bring much. You don't need to pack for the worst-case scenario. Pack for the best-case scenario and simply buy yourself out of any jams. Risk shivering for a day rather than taking a heavy coat. Think in terms of what you can do without—not what will be handy on your trip. When in doubt, leave it out.

between the standard "smart casual" dress code and the formal nights—for example, men might wear slacks and a tie, but no jacket.

Cruise passengers are evenly split on the "formal night" phenomenon: Some look forward to dressing up and do so with gusto; others just want to be as casual as possible while on vacation. For those who don't want to dress up at all, most cruise ships have dining venues that are completely casual—the buffet, the poolside grill, and so on. Here you'll see people wearing shorts, swimsuits, cover-ups, and flip-flops. If you never want to put on a collared shirt, you can simply eat at these restaurants for the entire cruise. But be aware that you'll be passing gussied-up passengers in the hallways on formal nights—so you might feel a bit out of place if you go totally casual. Bring along a presentable top and pair of pants or skirt for the nights you want to spiff up a bit.

To pack light for your cruise, bring along multifunctional clothing that allows you to go minimally formal. Men can get by with slacks and a sports coat—which, because they can be worn in port as well, are more versatile than a suit. Women can wear a sundress and jazz it up with accessories, such as nice jewelry or a wrap. A scarf, wrap, or jacket makes a regular outfit (such as black pants and a tank top) more formal.

If you want to get decked out without lugging excess clothing on board, ask if your cruise line has a tuxedo-rental program (some cruise lines also offer a rental program for women's formal wear). You may be able to borrow a loaner jacket or rent a tux on the spot, but selection can be limited—so it's better to order in advance. Simply provide your measurements beforehand, and a tux will be waiting in your cabin when you board.

The shops on your cruise ship (or on shore) are sure to have any personal items you forgot or have run out of.

Use the "Packing Checklist" on page 56 to organize and make your packing decisions.

Clothing

Most cruisers will want two to three changes of clothes each day: comfortable, casual clothes for sightseeing in port; more formal evening wear for dinners on the ship; and sportswear, whether it's a swimsuit for basking by the pool or athletic gear for hitting the gym or running track. But that doesn't mean you have to bring along 21 separate outfits for a seven-day cruise. Think versatile. Some port wear can double as evening wear. Two pairs of slacks can be worn on alternating nights, indefinitely. As you choose clothes for your trip, a good rule of thumb is: If you're not going to wear an item more than three times, don't pack it. Every piece of clothing you bring should complement every other item or have at least two uses (for example, a scarf doubles as a shoulder wrap; a sweater provides warmth and dresses up a short-sleeve shirt). Accessories, such as a tie or scarf, can break the monotony and make you look snazzy.

First-time cruisers may worry about "formal nights." While most cruises do have a few formal nights with a dress code, they're not as stuffy as you might think. And those formal nights are optional—you can always eat somewhere other than the formal dining room. So dress up only as much as you want to (but keep in mind that if you plan to eat every meal in the dining room, you must adhere to its dress code—most cruise lines forbid shorts or jeans there at dinnertime). For a general idea of what people typically wear on board, read the sidebar on the previous page, then find out what your ship's dress code is.

When choosing clothes for days in port, keep a couple of factors in mind: First, the Mediterranean can be very hot in the summer, so it's smart to bring breathable, light-colored clothes and a hat. Also, some European churches (particularly in Italy) enforce a strict "no shorts or bare shoulders" dress code. Pants with zip-off/zip-on legs can be handy in these situations.

Laundry options vary from ship to ship, but in general, don't count on an affordable shipboard laundry service. Ask your cruise line in advance about available laundry options. And remember that you can still bring fewer clothes and wash as needed in your stateroom sink. It helps to pack items that don't wrinkle, or look good wrinkled. You should have no trouble drying clothing overnight in your cabin (though it might take longer in humid climates).

Some travelers worry about sticking out and "looking American." But no matter how carefully you dress, your clothes probably will mark you as an American. Frankly, so what? I fit in and am culturally sensitive by watching my manners, not the cut of my clothes. Ultimately—as long as you don't wear something that's outrageous or offensive—it's important to dress in a way that makes you comfortable.

Here are a few specific considerations:

Shirts/blouses. Bring short-sleeved or long-sleeved shirts or blouses in a cotton/polyester blend. A sweater or lightweight fleece is good for layering (handy in the spring and fall, when evenings can be chilly). Dark colors don't show wrinkles or stains, though light colors can be more comfortable on sunny days in port. Indoor areas on the cruise ship can be heavily air-conditioned, so you may need a sweater or a wrap even in the height of summer.

Pants/skirts and shorts. Bring lightweight pants or skirts for hot and muggy big cities and churches with modest dress codes. Jeans can be too hot for summer travel. Button-down wallet pockets are safest (though still not as thief-proof as a money belt, described later). Shorts are perfectly acceptable aboard your ship, but on land in Europe they're considered beachwear, exclusively worn in coastal or lakeside resort towns. While most Europeans won't be offended if you wear shorts, you may be on the receiving end of some second glances or puzzled stares.

Shoes. Take a broken-in, light, and cool pair of casual shoes, with Vibram-type soles and good traction. Comfort is essential even on board, where you'll sometimes be walking considerable distances just to get to dinner. And getting on and off tenders can involve a short hop to a pier—practical shoes are a must for port days. Sandals or flip-flops are good for poolside use or in case your shoes get wet. And don't forget appropriate footwear to go with your dinner clothes (though again, think versatile—for women, a nice, stylish pair of sandals is nearly as good as heels).

Jacket. Bring a light and water-resistant windbreaker that has a hood. Gore-Tex is good if you expect rain. For summer travel, I wing it without rain gear.

Swimsuit and cover-up. If you plan on doing a lot of swimming, consider bringing a second swimsuit so that you always have a dry one to put on. Most cruise lines forbid swimsuits anywhere beyond the pool area, so cover-ups are a necessity.

Packing Essentials

Money belt. This hidden pouch—strapped around your waist and tucked under your clothes—is crucial for the peace of mind it brings. If you were to lose everything except your money belt, your trip could still go on. Lightweight and low-profile beige is best. Pack your **passport, driver's license, credit card, debit card,** and an emergency stash of **hard cash** in your money belt, and wear it whenever you're in port. (Fanny packs are magnets for pickpockets and should never be used as money belts.)

Toiletries kit. Sinks in staterooms come with meager countertop space. You'll have an easier time if you bring a nylon toi-

letries kit that can hang on a hook or a towel bar. Cruise ships provide small bottles of shampoo and itsy-bitsy bars of soap, so you may prefer to bring along your own supplies. Put all squeeze bottles in sealable plastic baggies, since pressure changes in flight can cause even good bottles to leak. (If you plan to carry on your bag, all liquids and gels must be in 3.4-ounce or smaller containers, and all of these items must fit within a single, quart-size sealable plastic bag.)

Bring any **medication** and vitamins you need (keep medicine in original containers, if possible, with legible prescriptions), along with a basic **first-aid kit.** If you're prone to motion sickness, consider some sort of **seasickness remedy.** For various options, see page 76. There are different schools of thought on **hand sanitizers** in preventing the spread of germs. Some cruise lines embrace them, others shun them (see page 78)—but they can come in handy when soap and water aren't readily available.

If you wear **eyeglasses** or **contact lenses,** bring a photocopy of your prescription—just in case. Contact solutions are widely available in Europe, but because of dust and smog, many travelers find their contacts aren't as comfortable over there. A strap for your glasses/sunglasses is handy for water activities or for peering over the edge of the ship in a strong breeze.

Sunscreen and sunglasses. Bring protection for your skin and your eyes. Many passengers underestimate the power of the Mediterranean sun, get a massive sunburn the first day, and spend the rest of the cruise recovering.

Laundry supplies (soap and clothesline). If you plan to wash any of your clothes, bring a small squeeze bottle of detergent. Some cruise-ship bathrooms have built-in clotheslines, but you can bring your own just in case (the handy twisted-rubber type needs no clothespins).

Packing aides. Packing cubes, clothes-compressor bags, and shirt-folding boards can help keep your clothes tightly packed and looking good.

Sealable plastic baggies. Bring a variety of sizes. In addition to holding your carry-on liquids, they're ideal for packing a picnic lunch, storing damp items, and bagging potential leaks before they start. Some cruisers use baggies to organize their materials (cruise-line handouts, maps, ripped-out guidebook chapters, receipts) for each port of call. If you bring them, you'll use them—and they can be hard to find in Europe.

Small daypack. This is ideal for carrying your sweater, camera, literature, and picnic goodies when you visit sights on shore.

Small extra bag. A collapsible tote bag can come in handy for bringing purchases home from your trip. It's also useful for the first and last days of your cruise, when you'll be without your luggage for several hours (after you check in your bag on the first day and before you claim it upon disembarking on the last morning). During these times, you'll want to pack a change of clothes, any medications, and valuables you want to keep with you.

Water bottle. If you bring one from home, make sure it's empty before you go through airport security (fill it at a fountain once you're through). The plastic half-liter mineral water bottles sold throughout Europe are reusable and work great.

Travel information. This book will likely be all you need. But if you want more in-depth coverage of the destinations or information on a place not covered in this book, consider collecting some other sources. (For suggestions, see page 1234.) I like to rip out appropriate chapters from guidebooks and staple them together. When I'm done, I give them away.

Address list. If you plan to send postcards, consider printing your mailing list onto a sheet of adhesive address labels before you leave.

Postcards from home and photos of your family. A small collection of show-and-tell pictures (either printed or digital) is a fun, colorful conversation piece with fellow cruisers, your crew, and Europeans you meet.

Small notepad and pen. A tiny notepad in your back pocket is a great organizer, reminder, and communication aid.

Journal. An empty book to be filled with the experiences of your trip will be your most treasured souvenir. Attach a photocopied calendar page of your itinerary. Use a hardbound type designed to last a lifetime, rather than a spiral notebook.

Electronics and Entertainment

From preserving memories of your trip to keeping in touch with people at home, electronics can enhance your vacation. Consider packing along the following gadgets: **camera** (and associated gear); **mobile phone or smartphone** (for details on using a US phone in Europe—or on a cruise ship—see page 82); **iPod** or other MP3 player; and a **laptop, netbook,** or **tablet computer** (though Wi-Fi aboard a cruise ship is slow and expensive—see page 81). For each item, remember to bring the **charger** and/or extra **batteries** (you can buy batteries on cruise ships and in Europe, but at a higher price).

Some travelers use **digital recorders** to capture pipe organs, tours, or journal entries. Having a portable **radio** can be fun if you want to tune in to European stations as you travel. If renting a car, a **GPS** loaded with European maps can help you navigate to your destination.

Most cruises have limited TV offerings and charge a premium for pay-per-view movies (though you'll find DVD players in some staterooms). If you crave digital distraction, pack your iPod/iPad, laptop/netbook, or portable DVD player with a selection of downloaded videos and/or DVDs. (Travel partners can bring a Y-jack for two sets of earphones.)

For long days at sea, bring some leisure reading, whether on an **ebook reader** (such as a Kindle or iPad) or just a good old

Packing Checklist

*Indicates items you can purchase online at www.ricksteves.com.

- ❏ Shirts/blouses: long- and short-sleeve
- ❏ Sweater or lightweight fleece
- ❏ Pants/skirts
- ❏ Formal night clothes: Dress pants/skirt with nice shirt/top or cocktail dress
- ❏ Formal wear (optional): Sports coat or tux for men, evening gown for women
- ❏ Shorts
- ❏ Swimsuit and cover-up
- ❏ Underwear and socks
- ❏ Shoes: walking/sandals/dress-up
- ❏ Rainproof jacket with hood
- ❏ Tie or scarf
- ❏ Pajamas/nightgown
- ❏ *Money belt
- ❏ Money—your mix of:
  - ❏ Debit card (for ATM withdrawals)
  - ❏ Credit card
  - ❏ Hard cash (in easy-to-exchange $20 bills)
- ❏ Documents plus photocopies:
  - ❏ Passport
  - ❏ Printout of airline and cruise e-tickets
  - ❏ Driver's license
  - ❏ Student or teacher ID card
  - ❏ Insurance details
- ❏ *Daypack
- ❏ *Extra, collapsible tote bag
- ❏ Sealable plastic baggies

paperback. Most ships also have free lending libraries and sell US paperbacks at reasonable prices.

Note: Most ships use North American electrical outlets, but if you're staying at a European hotel, you'll need an **adapter** to plug in electronics (for details, see "Watt's Up?," page 47). Many stale-rooms have a limited number of outlets, so a lightweight **power strip** can be helpful if you have a lot of gadgets to charge at one time.

Miscellaneous Supplies

The following items are not necessities, but they generally take up little room and can come in handy in a pinch.

Basic **picnic supplies,** such as a Swiss Army-type knife and plastic cutlery, enable you to shop for a very European lunch at a market or neighborhood grocery store (but remember not to pack a

❑ Electronics—your choice of:
  ❑ Camera (and related gear)
  ❑ Mobile phone or smartphone
  ❑ iPod/MP3 player/portable DVD player
  ❑ laptop/netbook
  ❑ ebook reader
  ❑ chargers for each of the above
❑ Leisure reading
❑ Empty water bottle
❑ Wristwatch and *alarm clock
❑ *Toiletries kit
  ❑ Toiletries (soap, shampoo, toothbrush, toothpaste, floss, deodorant)
  ❑ Medicines (including seasickness remedies if needed)
  ❑ First-aid kit
  ❑ Hand sanitizer
  ❑ Glasses/contacts (with prescriptions)
❑ Sunscreen and sunglasses
❑ *Laundry soap and *clothesline
❑ *Earplugs/*neck pillow
❑ *Travel information (guidebooks and maps)
❑ Address list (for sending postcards)
❑ Postcards and photos from home
❑ *Notepad/journal and pen
❑ Miscellaneous supplies (list on previous page and below)

If you plan to carry on your luggage, note that all liquids must be in 3.4-ounce or smaller containers and fit within a single quart-size sealable baggie. For details, see www.tsa.gov/travelers.

knife in your carry-on bag when flying).

Sticky notes (such as Post-Its) are great for keeping your place in your guidebook. **Duct tape** cures a thousand problems. A **tiny lock** will keep the zippers on your checked baggage shut.

A small **flashlight** is handy for reading under the sheets while your partner snoozes, or for finding your way through an unlit passage (tiny-but-powerful LED flashlights—about the size of your little finger—are extremely bright and compact). Not every stateroom comes with an **alarm clock,** so bring a small portable one just in case (or you can use the alarm on your mobile phone).

If night noises bother you, you'll love a good set of expandable foam **earplugs;** if you're sensitive to light, bring an **eye mask.** For snoozing on planes, trains, and automobiles, consider an inflatable **neck pillow.**

Spot remover (such as Shout wipes) or a dab of Goop grease remover in a small plastic container can rescue stained clothes. A small **sewing kit** can help you mend tears and restore lost buttons. Because European restrooms are often not fully equipped, carry some toilet paper or **tissue packets** (sold at all newsstands in Europe).

What Not to Pack

Don't bother packing **beach towels,** as these are provided by the cruise line.

Candles, incense, or anything else that burns is prohibited on a cruise ship—leave them at home. The same goes for clothes irons, coffee makers, and hot plates.

Virtually every cruise-ship bathroom comes equipped with a **hair dryer** (though if you need one for before or after your cruise, you may want to check with your hotels). The use of **flat irons, curlers,** or other hair-care appliances that heat up (and present a potential fire hazard) are discouraged, though most cruise lines tolerate their use.

Walkie-talkies can be handy for families who want to keep in touch when they split up to explore a giant ship, but because they transmit on European emergency channels, US models are illegal in Europe.

ON THE SHIP

Now that you've booked your cruise and packed your bags, it's time to set sail. This chapter focuses on helping you get to know your ship and adjust to the seafaring lifestyle.

Initial Embarkation

You've flown across the Atlantic, made your way to the port, and now finally you see your cruise ship along the pier, looming like a skyscraper turned on its side. The anticipation is palpable. But unfortunately, getting checked in and boarding the ship can be the most taxing and tiring part of the entire cruise experience. Instead of waltzing up a gangway, you'll spend hours waiting around as hundreds or even thousands of your fellow passengers are also processed. Add the fact that ports are generally in ugly and complicated- or expensive-to-reach parts of town (not to mention that you're probably jet-lagged), and your trip can begin on a stressful note. Just go with the flow and be patient; once you're on the ship, you're in the clear.

Arrival at the Airport

Cruise lines offer hassle-free airport transfers directly to the ship. While expensive, these are convenient and much appreciated if you're jet-lagged and packing heavy. Taxis are always an option for easy door-to-door service but can be needlessly expensive (especially since, in many cities, taxis levy additional surcharges for both the airport and the cruise port). Public transportation can be a bit more complicated, and may be a drag with bags, but usually saves you plenty of money. For cities where cruises are likely to begin or end, I've included details on connecting to the airport on your own—either by taxi or by public transit—so you can easily compare the cost and hassle with the transfer options offered by your cruise line. I've also included hotel recommendations.

Remember: Do not schedule your arrival in Europe too close to the departure of your cruise, as flights are prone to delays. Arriving on the same day your cruise departs—even with hours to spare—can be risky. And keep in mind that flights departing from the US to Europe generally get in the next calendar day. For more on these topics, see page 41.

Arriving in Europe a day or more before your cruise gives you the chance to get over jet lag, see your departure city, and avoid the potential stress of missing your cruise.

Checking in at the Port

Before you leave home, be clear on the exact location of the port for your ship (some cities have more than one port, and some ports have multiple terminals), as well as the schedule for checking in and setting sail. On their initial sailing, most ships depart around 17:00, but cruise lines usually request that passengers be checked in and on board by 15:30 or 16:00. (Note that, like Europe, this book uses the 24-hour clock.) Better yet, arrive at the port at least an hour or two before that to allow ample time to find your way to the ship and get settled in. Most cruise lines are open for check-in as early as 13:00, and you might be able to drop off your bags even several hours before that—allowing you to explore your embarkation port baggage-free until final boarding time. Early check-in also helps you avoid the longest check-in lines of the day, which are typically in the midafternoon.

When you arrive at the terminal, cruise-line representatives will direct you to the right place. There are basically three steps to getting on the ship, each of which might involve some waiting: 1) dropping off bags; 2) check-in; and 3) embarkation (security check-point and actually boarding the ship to go to your stateroom).

First, you need to **drop off your bags**—usually at a separate location from check-in. Your cruise materials (mailed to you prior to your trip) likely included luggage tags marked with your cabin number; to save time, affix these to your bags before dropping them off (though if you don't have these tags, baggage stewards can give you some on the spot). From here, the crew will deliver your bags to your stateroom. On a big ship, this can take hours—if you'll need anything from your luggage soon after departure, such as a swimsuit, a jacket for dinner, or medication, take it with you now. Don't leave anything fragile in your bags. And be aware that your bags might be sitting in the hallway for quite some time, where passersby have access to them; while theft is rare, you shouldn't leave irreplaceable documents or other valuables in them. Pack as you would for bags being checked on an airline.

At **check-in,** you'll be photographed (for security purposes) and given a credit-card-like room key that you'll need to show whenever you leave and reboard the ship. Crew members will inspect your passport. They also may ask for your credit-card number to cover any onboard expenses (though some cruise lines have you do this after boarding, at the front desk). Remember that they may place a hold on your credit card to cover anticipated charges. If you're accompanying a child on board, see page 44 for the documentation you may need.

As part of check-in, you'll fill out a form asking whether you've had any flu-like symptoms (gastrointestinal or nose/throat) over the last several days. If you have, the ship's doctor will evaluate you free of charge before you are allowed to board. This is a necessary public-health measure, considering that contagious diseases spread like wildfire on a cruise ship (see page 78).

After check-in, you'll be issued a boarding number and asked to wait in a large holding area until your number is called. It could take minutes...or hours.

When your number comes up, you'll have to clear immigration control/customs (usually just a formality—you may not even have to flash your passport) and go through a **security check** to make sure you have no forbidden items, ranging from firearms to alcohol (many cruise lines won't let you BYOB on board, and others limit how much you can bring; for details, see page 96).

Your First Few Hours on Board

Once you're on the ship, head to your **stateroom** and unpack. (For more on your stateroom, see "Settling In," later.) During this time, your cabin steward will likely stop by to greet you. This person is responsible for cleaning your room (generally twice a day—after breakfast and during dinner) and taking care of any needs you might have.

As soon as you step on board, you'll be very aware that you're on a seaborne vessel. You'll quickly remember the old truism about landlubbers having to find their **"sea legs."** At first, you may stagger around like you've had one too many. Hang onto handrails (on stairways and, if it's really rough, in the hallways) and step carefully. You'll eventually get used to it, and you might even discover when you return to shore that you'll need to find your "land legs" all over again. While you may worry that the motion of the ocean will interfere with sleep, many cruisers report exactly the opposite. There's just something soothing about being rocked gently to sleep at night, along with the white noise of the engines.

It's traditional—and fun—for passengers to assemble on the deck while the ship **sets sail,** waving to people on shore and on other ships. On some lines, the ship's loudspeakers play

Cruising Terms Glossary

To avoid sounding like a naive landlubber, learn a few nautical terms: It's a "line," not a "rope." It's a "ship," not a "boat."

aft/stern	back of ship
all aboard	time that all passengers must be on board the ship (typically 30 minutes before departure)
astern	ahead of the stern (that is, in front of the ship)
beam	width of the ship at its widest point
bearing/course	direction the ship is heading (on a compass, usually presented as a degree)
berth	bed (in a cabin) or dock (at a port)
bridge	command center, where the ship is steered from
bulkhead	wall between cabins or compartments
colors	ship's flag (usually the country of registration)
deck	level or "floor" of the ship
deck plan	map of the ship
disembark	leave the ship
draft	distance from the waterline to the deepest point of the ship's keel
embark	board the ship
even keel	the ship is level (keel/mast at 90 degrees)
fathom	unit of nautical depth; 1 fathom = 6 feet
flag	ensign of the country in which a ship is officially registered (and whose laws apply on board)
fore/bow	front of the ship
funnel/stack	ship's smokestack
galley	kitchen
gangway	stairway between the ship and shore
gross registered tonnage	unit of a ship's volume; 1 gross registered ton = 100 cubic feet of enclosed space
hatch	covering for a hold
helm	steering device for the ship; place where steering device is located
HMS	His/Her Majesty's Ship (before the vessel name); British-flagged ships only
hold	storage area below decks
hotel manager	officer in charge of accommodations and food operations
hull	the body of the ship
keel	the "fin" of the ship that extends below the hull
knot	unit of nautical speed; 1 knot = 1 nautical mile/hour = 1.15 land miles/hour
league	unit of nautical distance; 1 league = 3 nautical miles, or 3.45 land miles
leeward	direction against the wind (that is, into the wind); downwind
lido (lido deck)	deck with outdoor swimming pools, athletic area, and other amenities

ON THE SHIP

line	rope
list/listing	tilt to one side
maître d'	host who seats diners and manages dining room
manifest	list of the ship's passengers, crew, and cargo
midship/ amidships	a spot halfway between the bow and the stern
MS/MSY	motor ship/motorized sailing yacht (used before the vessel name)
muster station	where you go if there's an emergency and you have to board the lifeboats
nautical mile	unit of nautical distance; 1 nautical mile = 1.15 land miles
pilot	local captain who advises the ship's captain, or even steers the ship, on approach to a port
pitch/pitching	rise and fall of the ship's bow as it maneuvers through waves
port	left side of the ship (here's a mnemonic device: both "left" and "port" have four letters)
prow	angled front part of the ship
purser/bursar	officer in charge of finances, sometimes also with managerial responsibilities
quay	dock or pier (pron. "key")
rigging	cables, chains, and lines
roll/rolling	side-to-side movement of a ship
seating	assigned seat and time for dinner in the dining room (often optional)
stabilizer	fin that extends at an angle from the hull of the ship into the water to create a smoother ride
starboard	right side of the ship
stateroom/cabin	"hotel room" on the ship
stem	very front of the prow
steward	serving staff, including the cabin steward (housekeeping), dining steward (waiter), or wine steward (sommelier)
superstructure	parts of the ship above the main deck
swell	wave in the open sea
tender	small boat that carries passengers between an anchored ship and the shore
tendered	when a ship is anchored (in the open water) rather than docked (at a pier); passengers reach land by riding tender boats
upper berth	fold-down bed located above another bed
veranda	private balcony off a stateroom
wake	trail of disturbed water that a ship leaves behind it
weigh	raise (for example, "weigh anchor")
windward	in the direction the wind is blowing (with the wind); upwind

melodramatic, corny, but infectious music as the ship glides away from land. Sometimes the initial departure comes with live musicians, costumed crew members, and a festive cocktail-party atmosphere.

Just before or after departure, the crew holds an **emergency drill** to brief you on the location of lifejackets in your cabin, how to put them on, and where to assemble in the event that the ship is evacuated (called a "muster station"). After being given a lifeboat number, you must gather at your muster station, along with others assigned to the same lifeboat.

You'll also get acquainted with the ship's **dining room** or other restaurants. If your ship has traditional "seatings"—an assigned time and seat for dinner each night—this first evening is an important opportunity to get to know the people you'll be dining with. If you have any special requests, you can drop by the dining room a bit before dinnertime to chat with the maître d'.

Memorize your **stateroom number** immediately—you'll be asked for it constantly (when arriving at meals, disembarking, making any onboard purchases, and so on). And be aware of not only your cruise line, but the name of your specific ship (e.g., Norwegian *Gem*, Royal Caribbean *Splendour of the Seas*, Celebrity *Constellation*, Holland America *Noordam*)—people in the cruise industry (including those in port) refer to the ship, not the company.

Various **orientation activities** are scheduled for your first evening; these may include a ship tour or a presentation about the various shore excursions that will be offered during the cruise. While this presentation is obviously promotional, it can be a good use of time to find out your options.

Life on Board

Your cruise ship is your home away from home for the duration of your trip. This section provides an overview of your ship and covers many of the services and amenities that are offered on board.

Settling In

From tiny staterooms to confusing corridors, it might take a couple of days to adjust to life on board a ship. But before long, you will be an expert at everything from getting to the dining room in the shortest amount of time to showering in tight spaces.

Your Stateroom

While smaller than most hotel rooms, your cabin is plenty big enough if you use it primarily as a place to sleep, spending the majority of your time in port and in the ship's public areas. As you unpack, you'll discover that storage space can be minimal. But—as sailors have done for centuries—cruise-ship designers are experts at cramming little pockets of storage into every nook and cranny. Remember where you tuck things so you can find them when it's time to pack up at the end of your trip.

Staterooms usually have a safe, coffee maker, mini-fridge, phone for calling the front desk or other cabins, and television. Channels include information about the ship, sales pitches for shore excursions and other cruises, various American programming (such as ESPN or CNN), and pay-per-view movies. The beds are usually convertible—if you've got a double bed but prefer twins, your cabin steward can pull them apart and remake them for you (or vice versa). Inside the cabin is a lifejacket for each passenger. Make note of where these are stored, as you would the locations of emergency exits on an airplane.

Cabin **bathrooms** are generally tight but big enough to take care of business. Bathrooms come equipped with hair dryers.

First-time cruisers are sometimes surprised at the high water pressure and the dramatic suction that powers each flush. Read and heed the warnings not to put any foreign objects down the toilet: Clogged toilets are not uncommon, and on a cruise ship, this can jam up the system for your whole hallway...not a good way to make friends.

Getting to Know Your Ship

After you're settled in your stateroom, start exploring. As you wander, begin to fill in your mental map of the ship with the things you want to find later: front desk, restaurants, theater, and so on. Many cruises offer a tour of the ship early on, which can help you get your bearings on a huge, mazelike vessel. Deck plans (maps of the ship) are posted throughout the hallways, and you can often pick up a pocket-size plan to carry with you.

As you walk down long hallways,

ON THE SHIP

it's easy to get turned around and lose track of whether you're headed for the front (fore) or the back (aft) of the ship. For the first couple of days, I carry around my ship deck plan and try to learn landmarks: For example, the restaurants (and my cabin) are near the back of the ship, while entertainment venues (casino, big theater) are at the front. Several banks of elevators are usually spread evenly throughout the ship. Before long you'll figure out the most direct way between your stateroom and the places you want to go. It can also be tricky to find your room in a very long, anonymous hall

with identical doors. Consider marking yours in a low-profile way (for example, tape a small picture below your room number) to help you find it in a hurry.

The double-decker main artery running through the middle of the ship, usually called the **promenade deck,** connects several key amenities: theater, main dining room and other eateries, shopping area, library, Internet café, art gallery, photography sales point, and so on. Wrapping around the outside of the promenade deck

is the namesake outdoor (but covered) deck, where you can go for a stroll.

At the center of the promenade deck is the main **lobby** (often called the atrium). This area, usually done up with over-the-top decor, has bars, a big screen for occasional presentations, tables of stuff to buy, and not enough seating. If you get lost exploring the ship, just find your way to the lobby and reorient yourself.

The lobby is also where the **guest services desk** is located. Like the reception desk of a hotel, this is your point of contact if you have concerns about your stateroom or other questions. Nearby you'll usually find the excursions desk (where you can get information about and book seats on shore excursions), a "cruise consultant" (selling seats on the line's future sailings), and the financial services desk (which handles any monetary issues that the guest services desk can't).

If the lobby is the hub of information, then the **lido deck** is

the hub of recreation. Generally the ship's sunny top deck, the lido has swimming areas, other outdoor activities, and usually the buffet restaurant. With a variety of swimming pools (some adults-only, others for kids) and hot tubs; a casual poolside "grill" serving up burgers and hot dogs; long rows of sunbathing chairs; and "Margaritaville"-type live music at all hours, the lido deck screams, "Be on vacation!"

Information

Each evening, the **daily program** for the next day is placed inside your cabin or tucked under your door. These information-packed leaflets offer an hour-by-hour schedule for the day's events, from arrival and all-aboard times to dinner seatings, bingo games, and AA meetings. (It's also peppered with ads touting various duty-free sales and drink specials.) With a staggering number of options each day, this list is crucial for keeping track of where you want to be and when. I tuck this in my back pocket and refer to it constantly. Bring it with you in port to avoid that moment of terror when you suddenly realize you don't remember what time you have to be back on the ship.

Most cruise lines also give you an **information sheet** about each port of call. These usually include a map and some basic historical and sightseeing information. But the dominant feature is a list of the cruise line's "recommended" shops in that port and discounts offered at each one. Essentially, these are the shops that pay the cruise line a commission. These stores can be good places to shop, but they aren't necessarily the best options. For more details on shopping in port, see page 125.

Most cruise lines also offer **"port talks"**—lectures about upcoming destinations. The quality of these can vary dramatically, from educational seminars that will immeasurably deepen your appreciation for the destination to thinly veiled sales pitches for shore excursions.

Better cruises have a **destination expert** standing by when you get off the ship to answer your questions about that port (usually near the gangway or in the lobby). Again, beware: While some are legitimate experts, most are employees of local shops. They can give you some good sightseeing advice, but any shopping tips they offer should be taken with a grain of salt.

English is generally the first **language** on the ship, though—especially on bigger ships—announcements are repeated in other languages as well (often French, German, Italian, and/or Spanish, depending on the clientele). Most crew members who interact with passengers speak good English—though usually it's their second language.

When passing important landmarks, especially on days at sea, the **captain** may periodically come over the loudspeaker to offer commentary. Or, if the seas are rough, the captain may try to soothe rattled nerves (and stomachs) with an explanation of the weather that's causing the turbulence.

Speaking of **announcements,** cruise lines have varying philosophies about these: Some lines barrage you with announcements every hour or so. On other lines, they're rare. If you can't make out the announcement inside your cabin, crack the door to hear the hallway loudspeakers, or tune your TV to the ship-information channel, which also broadcasts announcements.

Your Crew

Your hardworking crew toils for long hours and low pay to make sure you have a great vacation. Whether it's the head waiter who remembers how you like your coffee; the cabin steward who cleans your room with a smile and shows you pictures of his kids back in Indonesia; or the unseen but equally conscientious workers who prepare your meals, wash your laundry, scrub the deck, or drive the tender boats, the crew is an essential and often unheralded part of your cruise experience.

The all-purpose term for crew members is "steward"—cabin steward (housekeeping), wine steward (sommelier), dining steward (waiter), and so on. Your cabin steward can be very helpful if you have a basic question or request; for something more complicated, ask the front-desk staff or the concierge. In the dining room, the maître d' assigns tables and man-

ages the dining room, the head waiter takes your order, and the assistant waiters bring your food and bus your dishes.

The ship's cruise director (sometimes called a host or hostess) is a tireless cheerleader, keeping you informed about the various activities and other happenings on board, usually via perky announcements over the ship's loudspeaker several times a day. The cruise director manages a (mostly American) "cruise staff" that leads activities throughout the ship. I have a lot of sympathy for these folks, partly because of my own background as a tour guide—I can't imagine the responsibility of keeping thousands of people informed and entertained 24/7. Experienced cruisers report that the more enthusiastic and energetic the cruise director and

Running a Cruise Ship

The business of running a ship is divided into three branches, which work together to create a smooth experience: the engine room; the hotel (rooms and food service); and the deck. This last branch includes the physical decks and railings as well as the bridge (the area from which the ship is navigated) and tendering (shore transport). Each department has its leader (chief engineer, hotel manager, and chief officer, respectively), with the captain overseeing the entire operation.

Of course, these days the captain doesn't actually steer the ship while standing at a big wooden wheel. Modern cruise ships are mostly computerized. The "watch"—responsibility

for guiding the ship and dealing with any emergencies—rotates among the officers, who usually work four hours on, then eight hours off. The watch continues when the ship is at anchor or docked, when officers must keep an eye on moorings, make sure the ship is in the correct position, and so on.

The ship is dry-docked (taken out of the water) every two years or so to clean algae, barnacles, and other buildup from the hull and to polish the propeller. A very smooth propeller is crucial for a fluid ride—a dented or porous one can lead to lots of noise and bubbles. Sometimes a crew engineer will put on a wetsuit and dive down to polish the rudder underwater.

As you approach a port (or a challenging-to-navigate passage), a little boat zips out to your cruise ship, and a

"pilot"—a local captain who's knowledgeable about that port—hops off. The pilot advises your ship's captain about the best approach to the dock and sometimes even takes the helm. Once the job is done, another boat might zip out to pick up the pilot.

If you're intrigued by the inner workings of your ship, ask about a behind-the-scenes tour. Many ships offer the opportunity to see the galley (kitchen), food stores, crew areas, and other normally off-limits parts of the ship (usually for a fee).

staff are, the more likely you are to enjoy your cruise. Gradually you'll come to feel respect, appreciation, and even affection for these people who really, really want you to have a great time on your vacation.

Crew Wages

Other than the officers and cruise staff, a ship's crew is primarily composed of people, mostly men, from the developing world. With rare exception, these crew members are efficient, patient, and friendly (or, at least, always smiling). For many cruisers, getting to know the crew is a highlight of their trip.

It's clear that crew members work hard. But most passengers would be surprised to learn just how long they work—and for how little. Because US labor laws don't apply to sailing vessels, cruise lines can pay astonishingly low wages for very long hours of work. Crew members who receive tips are paid an average base salary (before tips) of about $1 each day. This makes tips an essential part of the crew's income (see "Tipping" on page 74). After tips, the English-speaking service crew who interact with passengers make about $2,000-3,000 per month, while the anonymous workers toiling at entry-level jobs below decks can make less than $1,000 per month. While clear industry-wide numbers are hard to come by, the following monthly wages (after tips) are typical:

Cabin steward	$2,000
Waiter	$3,000
Bartender	$1,800
Cook	$1,500-2,100
Dishwasher	$600
Seaman (maintenance)	$1,500
Cruise staff	$2,000
Cruise director	$5,800
Captain	$10,000

These earnings don't seem unreasonable...until you factor in the long hours. Most crew sign a nine- to ten-month contract, then get two or three months off. While they are under contract, they work seven days a week, at least 10 hours a day; the international legal maximum is 14 hours a day, but according to insiders, some crew members put in up to 16 hours. The hours worked are rarely consecutive—for example, a crew member might work six hours, have two or three hours off, then work seven more hours. They rarely if ever get a full day off during their entire months-long contract, though they get enough sporadic time off during the day to be able to rest and occasionally enjoy the ports of call. Do the math: If most crew members work an average of 12 hours a day, 30 days a month, that's 360 hours a month—more than double the 160 hours of a 9-to-5 worker.

Cruise lines do cover their crew's accommodations, food, medical care, and transportation (including a flight home once their contract is completed). This means the crew can pocket or send home most of their earnings. While income-tax laws do not apply on the ship, crew members are required to pay taxes in their home country.

The Secret Lives of Crew Members

Most cruise lines have somewhere between 1 and 1.5 passengers per crew member. So a 3,000-passenger ship has more than 2,000 crew members who need to be housed and fed—in some ways, a vast second set of passengers. The crew's staterooms—the lowest (below the waterline, close to the rumbling engine noise) and smallest on the ship—are far more humble than your own, and usually shared by two to six people. Some cruise staff may have nicer cabins in the passenger areas, but only officers get outside cabins.

While you may see officers eating in the passenger dining room or buffet, most of the crew dines in mess halls with menus that reflect the cuisine of their native countries. Working long

hours and far from home, the crew expects to eat comfort food from their home countries—Southeast Asians want fish and rice; Italians get pasta; and so on. A well-fed crew is a happy crew, which leads to happy passengers—so substantial effort and resources go toward feeding the crew.

The more diverse the crew, the more complicated and expensive it can be to keep everyone satisfied. On some ships, each nationality has its own mess hall and menu that changes day to day. Some cruise lines have found it more efficient to hire employees predominantly from one or two countries. For example, on Holland America, the cabin crew is entirely Indonesian, while the kitchen and dining room crew is Filipino (to recruit employees, the cruise line operates training academies in those two countries).

Many crew members have wives back home who are raising their children; in port, they buy cheap phone cards or use Skype to keep in touch. In fact, most Internet cafés and calling shops target the crew rather than the passengers ("Cheap rates to the Philippines!"). If a café near the port offers free Wi-Fi for customers, you'll invariably see a dozen of your crew huddled over their laptops, deep in conversation.

While many crew members have wives and kids to feed,

others are living the single life. The crew tends to party together (the crew bar is even more rollicking than the passenger bars), and inter-crew romances are commonplace—though fraternization between crew members and passengers is strictly forbidden.

Is It Exploitation?

The national and racial stratification of the entire crew evokes the exploitation and indentured servitude of colonial times: The officers and cruise staff are often Americans, Brits, or Europeans, while those in menial roles (kitchen, waitstaff, cleaning crew, engineers) are Indonesian, Filipino, or another developing-world nationality. It's a mark of a socially conscious company when Southeast Asian employees are given opportunities to rise through the ranks and take on office roles with greater responsibility.

The cruise lines argue that these people are making far more money at sea in glamorous locations—where they get occasional time off to leave the ship and explore the ports—than they would at menial jobs back home. What some see as exploitation, others see as empowerment. (Think of it as "insourcing"—importing cheap labor from the lowest bidder.) For better or for worse, the natural gregariousness of the crew gives cruisers the impression that they can't be so terribly unhappy with their lives. And the remarkable loyalty of many crew members (working many, many years for the same cruise line)—especially on certain lines—is a testament to the success of the arrangement.

Is it wrong to employ Third World people at low wages to wait on First World, mostly white, generally wealthy vacationers? I don't know. But I do know that your crew members are some of the friendliest people on board. Get to know them. Ask about their families back home. And make sure they know how much you appreciate everything they're doing to make your trip more meaningful.

Money Matters

Most cruise ships are essentially cashless. Your stateroom key card doubles as a credit card. When buying anything on board, simply provide your cabin number, then sign a receipt for the expense. You'll likely need cash on board only for tipping (explained later), paying a crew member to babysit, or playing the casino (most slot machines and table games take cash; you can use your onboard account to finance your gambling, but you'll pay a fee for the privilege). To avoid exorbitant cash-advance fees at the front desk, bring along some US cash for these purposes.

Most cruise lines price everything on board (from drinks to tips to souvenirs) in US dollars, regardless of the countries visited during the trip.

Onboard Expenses

First-time cruisers thinking they've paid up front for an "all-inclusive" trip are sometimes surprised by how many add-ons they are offered on board. Your cruise ticket covers accommodations, all the meals you can eat in the ship's main dining room and buffet, and transportation from port to port. You can have an enjoyable voyage and not spend a penny more (except for expenses in port). But the cruise industry is adept at enticing you with extras that add up quickly. These include shore excursions, casino games, premium drinks (alcohol, name-brand soft drinks, and lattes), specialty restaurant surcharges (explained later, under "Eating"), duty-free shopping, fitness classes, spa treatments, photos, and many other goods and services.

It's very easy to get carried away—a round of drinks here, a night of blackjack there, a scuba dive, an ancient-ruins tour, and more. First-timers—even those who think they're keeping a close eye on their bottom line—can be astonished when they get their final onboard bill, which can easily exceed the original cost of the trip (or so hope the cruise lines).

With a little self-control, you can easily limit your extra expenditures, making your seemingly "cheap" cruise actually cheap. It's a good idea to check your current balance (and look for mistaken charges) at the front desk—just drop by at any time. You don't have to avoid extras entirely. After all, you're on vacation—go ahead and have that "daily special" cocktail to unwind after a busy day of sightseeing, or stick a $20 bill into a slot machine. But you always have the right to say, "No, thanks." As long as you're aware of these additional expenses and keep your spending under control, a cruise can still be a great value.

Getting Local Cash on Board

While you don't need much cash on board the ship, you will need local money for your time in port, as many European vendors will not accept credit cards or dollars. It's possible to get local cash on board the ship—but it's expensive. At the front desk, you can exchange cash or traveler's checks to the local currency (at bad rates and often with high commissions), or you can get a cash advance on your credit card (at a decent exchange rate but typically with exorbitant fees). You'll save money if you plan ahead and make use of ATMs near the cruise port (for more on withdrawing money in port, see page 122).

One exception: For places that don't use the euro—such as Croatia, Turkey, or North Africa—it can be worth the added expense to change a small amount of cash on board the ship to finance your trip into town.

Money-Saving Tips

Many people choose cruising because it's extremely affordable. When you consider that you're getting accommodations, food, and transportation for one low price, it's simply a steal. But reckless spending on a cruise can rip through a tight budget like a grenade in a dollhouse. If you're really watching your money, consider these strategies:

Buy as little on board as possible. Everything—drinks, Internet access, knickknacks—is priced at a premium for a captive audience. For most items, you're paying far more than you would off the ship. To check your email, visit an Internet café in port rather than on board. To satisfy a soda craving, buy a bottle of Coke at a convenience store in port rather than ordering one at dinner.

Skip the excursions. While cruise-line excursions are easy and efficient, it's worth a little extra time and hassle to get into town on your own, then use this book's sightseeing information or join a local walking tour. For example, the cruise line may charge $80-100/person for a transfer into town and a walking tour of the old center. But for the cost of a $2 bus ticket, you can get downtown yourself and join a $15 walking tour that covers most of the same sights. This book's destination chapters are designed to help you understand your options.

Stick with the main dining room. If your ship has specialty restaurants that levy a surcharge, skip them in favor of the "free" (included) meals in the main dining room—which are typically good quality.

Save some breakfast for lunch. If you're heading out for a long day in port, help yourself to a big breakfast and bag up the

Tipping

Tipping procedures aboard cruise ships have changed dramatically over the last two decades. Through the late 1980s, cruising was a pastime of the wealthy, and passengers enjoyed tipping the crew royally as part of the experience. Each crew member—cabin steward, maître d', head waiter, assistant waiter, and so on—expected to be tipped a specific amount per day. After the final passenger disembarked, the crew would meet and dump all their tip money into a communal pot, to be divided equally among themselves. But as cruising went mass-market, more frugal middle-class passengers began signing up. Having already paid for their trip, many resented the expectation to tip...so they simply didn't. The crew's take-home pay plummeted, and many workers quit, leaving the cruise lines in dire straits (from which they're still recovering).

These days, cruise lines use a standard "auto-tip" system, in which a set gratuity (generally about $10-12/person per day) is automatically billed to each passenger's account and then divided

leftovers to keep you going until dinnertime.

Minimize premium beverage purchases. Because alcohol, soda, and specialty coffee drinks all cost extra, drink tabs can add up fast. Since many cruise lines prohibit or limit bringing your own alcohol on board, you'll pay dearly for whetting your whistle. Instead of getting a Diet Coke at every meal, develop a taste for iced tea or fruit juice, which is usually included.

Stay out of the casino. With a casino and slots on board, it's easy to fall into a gambling habit. Most cruise lines allow you to use your key card to get cash from your room account for gambling. But read the fine print carefully—you're paying a percentage for this convenience. There's nothing wrong with rolling a few dice or playing a hand or two of blackjack. Just be smart: Keep gambling in line with your overall budget, establish a daily limit, and stick with it.

Don't buy onboard photos. Come to think of it, don't even let them take your photo—so you won't be tempted to buy it later.

Take advantage of free services on board. Rather than buy a book, check one out from the ship's library. Instead of ordering a pricey pay-per-view movie in your cabin, enjoy the cruise's free musical performances, classes, and activities. Read your daily program: There's something free going on, somewhere on the ship, virtually every minute of every day.

Don't cheap out at the expense of fun. If you're having a nice dinner, spring for a glass of wine—but keep a mental tally of all these little charges so you're not shocked by the bill.

among the crew (this system, started around 2000, effectively formalizes the process that was going on for decades). About a third of this tip goes to your cabin steward, a third to the restaurant stewards, and a third to others, including people who worked for you behind the scenes (such as the laundry crew). While overall tips are still not what they were 20 years ago, auto-tipping has proven to be a suitable compromise for both passengers and crew.

Cruise lines explain that, with auto-tipping, additional tipping is "not expected." But it is still most certainly appreciated by the crew. This can cause stress for passengers who are unsure whom, how much, and when to tip; conscientious tippers miss the "good old days" when there was a clearly prescribed amount earmarked for each crew member. Even more confusing, with all the new alternative dining options, you likely won't be served by the same waiter every night—in fact, you might never eat at the same restaurant twice. In general, the rule of thumb is to give a cash tip at the end of the cruise to those crew members who have provided exceptional service (for specific guidelines, see page 97).

At any point, you can increase or decrease your auto-tip amount to reflect your satisfaction with the service you've received. So, if you don't have cash for your final tip, you can simply go to the front desk and increase the auto-tip amount instead (but try to do so before the final night, when accounts are being finalized).

Some passengers prefer to zero out their auto-tip, then pay their favorite crew members in cash to make sure the money winds up with the "right" person. But this can backfire in two ways: First, many crew members adhere to the old system of pooling and dividing tips, including those received in cash—so your cash tip might be split after all. Second, your preferred crew member may choose not to split the cash tip at all—so somebody who worked hard for you, unseen, misses out on much-needed income. The fairest option is to let the auto-tip do what it's designed to do, and then add a cash bonus for the people you wish to reward.

In addition to a monetary tip, crew members appreciate it when you pass along positive feedback. Most cruise lines provide guests with comment cards for this purpose, and they can be taken very seriously when determining promotions. If someone has really gone above and beyond for you, fill out a comment card on their behalf.

Health

Health problems can strike anywhere—even when you're relaxing on a cruise ship in the middle of the Mediterranean. Every ship has an onboard doctor (though he or she may not be licensed in the US). If you have to visit the shipboard physician, you will be charged. Before you leave home, ask your health insurance company if the cost is covered or reimbursable; if you buy travel insurance, investigate how it covers onboard medical care.

Fortunately, some of the most common health concerns on cruise ships, while miserable, are temporary and relatively easy to treat.

Seasickness

Naturally, one concern novice cruisers have is whether the motion of the ship will cause them to spend their time at sea with their head in the toilet. And, in fact, a small percentage of people discover (quickly and violently) that they have zero tolerance for life at sea. But the vast majority of cruisers do just fine.

Fortunately, the Mediterranean is an almost entirely enclosed sea with very little tide or turbulence, compared to the open ocean. And remember that you're on a gigantic floating city—it takes a lot of agitation to really get the ship moving. Cruise ships are also equipped with stabilizers—wing-like panels that extend below the water's surface and automatically tilt to counteract rolling (side-to-side movement) caused by big swells.

But rough seas can occur, and when they do, waves and winds may toss your ship around like it's a toy boat. (As one captain told me, "If you're in a storm in the middle of the Atlantic, no ship is big enough.") When this happens, chandeliers and other fixtures begin to jiggle and clink, motion sickness bags discreetly appear in the hallways, and the captain comes over the loudspeaker to comfortingly explain what's being done to smooth out the ride. Lying in bed, being rocked to sleep like a baby, you hear the hangers banging the sides of your closet. Some cruisers actually enjoy this experience; for others, it's pure misery.

If you're prone to motion sickness, visit your doctor before your cruise, and be prepared with a remedy in case you're laid low. Below are several options that veteran cruisers swear by.

Dramamine (generic name: Dimenhydrinate) is easy to get over the counter but is highly sedating—not ideal unless you are desperate. Some cruisers prefer the less-drowsy formula, which is actually a different drug (called Meclozine, sometimes marketed as **Bonine**). **Marezine** (generic name: Cyclizine) has similar properties and side effects as Dramamine.

Scopolamine patches (sometimes called by the brand name Transderm) are small (dime-sized) and self-adhesive; just stick it on a hairless area behind your ear. They work well for many travelers (the only major side effect is dry mouth), but require a prescription and are expensive (figure $15 for a three-day dose). Some cruisers apply them prophylactically just before first boarding the ship (especially if rough weather is forecast). After removing one of these patches, wash your hands carefully—getting the residue in your eyes can cause dilated pupils and blurry vision.

Elasticized **Sea-Bands** have little buds that press on the pressure points on your wrist associated with nausea. You can buy them in any drugstore. They are easy to wear (if a bit goofy-looking—they look like exercise wristbands), and many people prefer them as a cheap and nonmedicinal remedy.

The similar but more sophisticated **Reletex** resembles (and is worn like) a wristwatch. It operates on the same principle as Sea-Bands but is designed to be less constricting (direct pressure delivered to exactly the right spot). But it's quite expensive ($100–200) and best for those who have a big problem with seasickness.

Every cruise aficionado has a favorite homegrown seasickness remedy. Some say that eating green apples or candied ginger can help settle a queasy stomach. Others suggest holding a peeled orange under the nose. Old sea dogs say that if you stay above deck, as close to the middle of the ship as possible, and keep your eyes on the horizon, it will reduce the effects of the motion.

Illness

Like a college dorm or a day-care center, a cruise ship is a veritable incubator for communicable disease. Think about everything that you (and several thousand other passengers) are touching: elevator buttons, railings, serving spoons in the buffet, and on and on. If one person gets sick, it's just a matter of time before everyone else does.

The common cold is a risk. But perhaps even more likely are basic gastrointestinal upsets, most often caused by the norovirus (a.k.a. the Norwalk virus)—tellingly nicknamed the "cruise-ship virus." Most often spread through fecally contaminated food or person-to-person contact, the norovirus is your basic nasty stomach bug, resulting in nausea, diarrhea, vomiting, and sometimes fever or cramps. It usually goes away on its own after a day or two.

Because contagious maladies are a huge concern aboard a ship, the cruise industry is compulsive about keeping things clean. Between cruises, ships are thoroughly disinfected with a powerful cleaning agent. When you check in, you'll be quizzed about recent symptoms to be sure you aren't bringing any nasty bugs on board. Some cruise lines won't allow passengers to handle the serving spoons at the buffet for the first two days—the crew serves instead. And, if you develop certain symptoms, the cruise line reserves the right to expel you from the ship at the next port of call (though, in practice, this is rare—more likely, they'll ask you to stay in your stateroom until you're no longer contagious).

Many cruise lines douse their passengers with waterless hand sanitizers at every opportunity. Dispensers are stationed around the ship, and smiling stewards might squirt your hands from a spray bottle at the entrance to restaurants or as you reboard the ship after a day in port. Whether this works is up for debate. Several studies have demonstrated that using these sanitizers can be counterproductive. The United States Centers for Disease Control (CDC) recommend them only as an adjunct to, rather than a replacement  for, hand washing with soap and warm water. The gels work great against bacteria but not viruses (such as the norovirus). Following the CDC's lead, some cruise lines have discontinued the use of waterless sanitizers—and have seen an immediate drop in their rate of outbreaks. The logic is that hand sanitizers actually discourage proper hand-washing behavior. When people apply sanitizers, they assume their hands are clean—and don't bother to wash with soap and water. All the while, that spunky norovirus survives on their hands, gets transferred to the serving spoon at the buffet, and winds up all over everyone else's hands while they're eating dinner.

On your stateroom TV set, you might find a channel with instructions on how to wash your hands. Patronizing, yes. But not undeservedly. In a recent international study, Americans were found to be less diligent than other nationalities when it comes to washing their hands after using the bathroom. They then go straight to the buffet, and...you know the rest. It's disgusting but true. If you're a total germophobe, you have two options: Avoid the buffet entirely—or just get over it.

Staying Fit on Board

While it's tempting to head back to the buffet for a second dessert (or even a second dinner) at 11:00 p.m., file away this factoid: A typical cruise passenger gains about a pound a day. After two weeks at sea, you've put on the "Seafaring Fifteen."

Whether you're a fitness buff or simply want to stave off weight gain, cruise ships offer plenty of opportunities to get your body moving. Most ships have fit-

ness centers with exercise equipment, such as bikes, treadmills, elliptical trainers, and weight machines. Some offer the services of personal trainers, plus classes like boot camp, spinning, Pilates, and yoga (newbies and yoga-heads alike will find it an interesting challenge to hold tree pose on a moving ship). These services usually cost extra, though some classes can be free (usually things like stretching or ab work).

If you're not the gym type, there are other ways to burn calories. Besides swimming pools, many ships have outdoor running tracks that wrap around the deck, complete with fresh air and sometimes views. And some ships have

more extreme-type sports, such as rock-climbing walls and surfing simulators.

Even if you don't take advantage of sports-related amenities, simply staying active throughout your cruise will help keep those multicourse dinners from going straight to your hips. With multiple levels, your cruise ship is one giant StairMaster. Take the stairs instead of the elevator, or run down to the bottom floor and hike back up to the top a couple of times a day. Opt for a walking

Water, Trash, and Poo: The Inside Scoop

Wondering how cruise ships deal with passengers' basic functions? Here are the answers to some often-asked questions:

Is the water clean and drinkable? Drinking water is usually pumped into the ship at the point of embarkation. Throughout the duration of the cruise, this supply is what comes out of your bathroom tap and is used in restaurant drinks.

Larger ships also have the capacity to desalinize (remove salt from) seawater for use aboard. While perfectly safe to drink, this water doesn't taste good, so it's reserved primarily for cleaning. The water in your stateroom's toilet or shower might be desalinated.

Waste water from the ship is purified on board. While theoretically safe to drink, it's usually deposited into the sea.

Where does the trash go? Trash from shipboard restaurants is carefully sorted into garbage, recyclables, and food waste. Garbage is removed along with other solid waste in port. Cruise lines pay recycling companies to take the recyclables (interestingly, in the US it's the other way around: the companies pay the ship for their recyclables). Food waste is put through a powerful grinder that turns it into a biodegradable puree. This "fish food" is quietly piped out the end of the ship as it sails through the night.

What happens to poo? You may wonder whether shipboard waste is deposited into the sea as you cruise. These things are dictated by local and international law as well as by the policies of individual cruise lines. Most mainstream cruise lines do not dump solid waste into the sea. Instead it is collected, stored, and removed from the ship for proper disposal in port.

ON THE SHIP

tour instead of a bus tour when you're in port. Hit the dance floor at night. And just in case, bring along your roomy "Thanksgiving pants."

Smoking

Smoking presents both a public health issue and a fire hazard for cruise lines. While policies are evolving, these days most cruise lines prohibit smoking in nearly all enclosed public spaces as well as in many outdoor areas. You may be able to smoke in certain bars or lounges and in dedicated outdoor spots. Most cruise lines allow passengers to light up in their staterooms or on their verandas but do not have designated "smoking" cabins—they simply clean the cabin thoroughly after a smoker has stayed there (generally with impressive success). If you're a dedicated smoker or an adamant nonsmoker, research the various cruise lines' policies when choosing your vacation.

Communicating

Because phoning and Internet access are prohibitively expensive on board—and because the times you'll be in port are likely to coincide with late-night or early-morning hours back home (8:00-17:00 in most of Europe is 2:00-11:00 a.m. on the East Coast and 23:00-8:00 a.m. on the West Coast)—keeping in touch affordably can be tricky. Let the folks back home know not to expect too many calls, or figure out if there are any late evenings in ports when it might be convenient to call home.

Consider asking any crew members you befriend about the cheapest, easiest places in each port to get online or to make cheap phone calls. They spend many months away from home and are experts at staying in touch. (But keep in mind some of the options at the ports are "seamen's clubs"—open only to crew members, not the general public.)

Getting Online

It's useful to get online periodically as you travel—to confirm trip plans, get weather forecasts, catch up on email, or blog or post pho-

tos from your trip. But with high prices and slow speeds, shipboard Internet is not the best option.

Most cruise ships have an Internet café with computer terminals, and many also have Wi-Fi (some offer it in select areas of the ship, others provide it in staterooms). Either way, onboard Internet access is very expensive—figure $0.50-1/minute (the more minutes you buy, the cheaper they are, and special deals can lower the cost substantially).

Before you pay for access, be warned that—since it's satellite-based rather than hard-wired—onboard Internet is tortoise-slow compared to high-speed broadband (remember dial-up?). And while using VoIP (Skype or Google Talk) to make voice or video calls over a Wi-Fi connection is an excellent budget option on land, it's impractical on the ship. Onboard Internet access has such limited bandwidth that these services often don't work well, or at all.

If you can, wait until you're in port to get online. If you have an iPhone, iPad, or other wireless-capable device, find a café where you can sit and download your email over Wi-Fi while enjoying a cup of coffee—at a fraction of the shipboard cost. Or hop on a computer at an Internet café to quickly check your email. For more pointers on getting online in port, see page 120.

Phoning

If you want to make calls during your trip, you can do it either from land or at sea. It's much cheaper to call home from a pay phone on shore (explained on page 120) or from a mobile phone on a land-based network (explained later). Calling from the middle of the Mediterranean is pricey, but if you're in a pinch, you can dial direct from your stateroom telephone or use a mobile phone while roaming on the costly onboard network. For details on how to dial European phone numbers, see page 1228.

Stateroom Telephones: Calling within the ship (such as to the front desk or another cabin) is free on your stateroom telephone. Calling to shore (over a satellite connection) is usually possible, but expensive—anywhere from $6 to $15 a minute (ask for specifics at the front desk). Similar charges apply if someone calls your stateroom from shore.

Mobile Phones: To use a mobile phone on a cruise ship, you can either bring your own (if it's compatible with European networks) or buy a cheap phone once you're in Europe.

Your **US mobile phone** works in Europe if it's GSM-enabled, tri-band or quad-band, and on a calling plan that allows international calls. Phones from T-Mobile and AT&T, which use the same GSM technology that Europe does, are more likely to work overseas than Verizon or Sprint phones (if you're not sure, ask your service provider).

Many mobile-phone companies offer international roaming access; there's generally no monthly fee for this, but the actual calling and messaging rates can add up (usually $1.29/minute for calls and 20-50 cents for text messages). Contact your service provider to authorize international roaming for calls on your account. When you do, tell them which countries you're visiting, and mention that you're taking a cruise. (Cell-phone companies have received furious complaints from customers who've rung up huge bills because they didn't realize they were incurring roaming charges, so they can be a little over-the-top in making sure you understand all the potential costs. But it's better to be informed.)

Many **smartphones,** such as the iPhone, Android, or BlackBerry, work in Europe. For voice calls and text messaging, they work more or less the way standard US mobile phones do (described above). But if you're sending or downloading data (checking email, browsing the Internet, streaming videos, and so on), beware of sky-high fees. Ask your provider in advance how to avoid unwittingly roaming your way to a huge bill. It's safest to

ON THE SHIP

simply turn off international data roaming on your phone (if it has this feature).

You'll pay cheaper rates for calls if your phone is electronically "unlocked" (ask your provider about this). Once in Europe, simply  buy a tiny **SIM card,** which gives you a European phone number—and the ability to make calls at cheaper European rates using prepaid calling credit (around 5-50 cents/minute for domestic calls). SIM cards are sold at mobile-phone stores and some newsstand kiosks for about $5-10, and generally include several minutes' worth of prepaid calling credit. It's easy to insert the SIM card in your phone (usually in a slot behind the battery or on the side). When buying a SIM card, you may need to show ID, such as your passport. Be sure to ask about the SIM card's coverage area, fees for domestic and international calls, roaming charges, and how to check your credit balance and buy more time.

You can also **buy a cheap mobile phone in Europe.** Phones that are "locked" to work with a single provider start around $20; "unlocked" phones—which allow you to switch out SIM cards to use your choice of provider—start at around $60.

Once you have a mobile phone that works in Europe, it can access both land and sea networks. Because many Mediterranean cruise itineraries stay fairly close to land, you can often roam on the cheaper **land-based networks,** even when you're at sea. Your phone will automatically find land-based networks if you're within several miles of shore. The **onboard network,** which doesn't even turn on until the ship is about 10 miles out, is insanely expensive—about $2.50-6/minute, compared to land rates of about $1.29/minute (and even lower if using a European SIM card). Ask your mobile service provider for details about your ship.

Before placing a call from your ship, carefully note which network you're on (this is displayed on your phone's readout, generally next to the signal bars). You might not recognize the various land-based network names; to be safe, learn the name of the cruise-line network (usually something obvious, such as "Phone at Sea")—then avoid making any calls if that name pops up. To prevent accidentally roaming on the sea-based network, simply turn off your phone (or disable roaming, if your phone has that feature) as soon as you board the ship. And be warned that receiving a call—even if you don't answer it—costs the same as making a call.

Satellite Phones: If you want the freedom to make calls anywhere, anytime, at a fixed rate, consider renting a satellite phone.

For example, www.bluecosmo.com rents phones for $40/week, with calling rates of $1.35-1.89/minute (depending on how many minutes you pre-purchase), plus $10-55 for shipping. Once you add up all those costs, this option isn't cheap—but it's versatile.

Onboard Activities

Large cruise ships are like resorts at sea. In the hours spent cruising between ports, there's no shortage of diversions: swimming pools,

hot tubs, and water slides; sports courts, exercise rooms, shuffle-board courts, giant chessboards, and rock-climbing walls; casinos with slots and table games; mini-shopping malls; art galleries with works for sale; children's areas with playground equipment and babysitting services; and spas

where you can get a facial, massage, or other treatments. Many activities have an extra charge associated—always ask before you participate.

To avoid crowds, take advantage of shipboard activities and amenities at off times. The gym is quieter late in the evenings, when many cruisers are already in bed. Onboard restaurants are typically less crowded for the later seatings. If you're dying to try out that rock-climbing wall, drop by as soon as you get back on the ship in the afternoon; if you wait an hour or two, the line could get longer.

Days at sea are a good time to try all the things you haven't gotten around to on busy port days, but be warned that everyone else on the ship has the same idea. Services such as massages are particularly popular on sea days—book ahead and be prepared to pay full price (if you get a massage on a port day, you might get a discount). Premium restaurants and other activities tend to fill up far earlier for days at sea, so don't wait around too long to book anything you have your heart set on.

Remember, the schedule and locations for all of these options—classes, social activities, entertainment, and more—are listed in your daily program.

Social Activities

Many ships offer a wide array of activities, ranging from seminars on art history to wine- and beer-tastings to classes on how to fold towels in the shape of animals (a skill, you'll soon learn, that your cabin steward has perfected). Quite a few of these are sales pitches in disguise, but others are just for fun and a great way to make friends. Bingo, trivia contests, dancing lessons, cooking classes, goofy poolside games, newlywed games, talent shows, nightly mixers for singles, scrapbooking sessions, high tea—there's something for everyone. Note that a few offerings might use code words or abbreviations: "Friends of Bill W" refers to a meeting of Alcoholics Anonymous; "Friends of Dorothy" or "LGBT" refers to a meeting of gay people.

Entertainment and Nightlife

Most cruise ships have big (up to 1,000-seat) theaters with nightly shows. An in-house troupe of singers and dancers generally puts

on two or three schmaltzy revue-type shows a week (belting out crowd-pleasing hits). On other nights, the stage is taken up by guest performers (comedy acts, Beatles tribute bands, jugglers, hypnotists, and so on). While not necessarily Broadway quality, these performances are a fun diversion; since they're typically free and have open seating, it's easy to drop by for just a few minutes (or even stand in the back) to see if you like the show before you commit. Note that on some of the biggest new megaships, the cruise lines are experimenting with charging a fee and assigning seats for more elaborate shows.

Smaller lounges scattered around the ship offer more intimate entertainment with just-as-talented performers—pianists, singers, duos, or groups who attract a faithful following night after night. Some cruisers enjoy relaxing in their favorite lounge to cap their day.

Cruises often screen second-run or classic movies for passengers to watch. Sometimes there's a dedicated cinema room; otherwise, films play in the main theater at off times.

Eating, always a popular pastime, is encouraged all hours of the day and night. While the main shipboard eateries tend to close by about midnight, large ships have one or two places that remain open 24 hours a day.

ON THE SHIP

And if you enjoy dancing, you have plenty of options ranging from classy ballroom-dance venues to hopping nightclubs that pump dance music until the wee hours.

Shopping

In addition to touting shopping opportunities in port, cruise ships have their own shops on board, selling T-shirts, jewelry, trinkets, and all manner of gear emblazoned with their logo. At busy times,

they might even set up tables in the lobby to lure in even more shoppers. In accordance with international maritime law, the ship's casino and duty-free shops can open only once the ship is seven miles offshore.

While shopping on board is convenient and saves on taxes, most of the items sold on the ship can be found at home or on the Internet—for less. If you like to shop, have fun doing it in port, seeking out locally made mementos in European shops. (If you enjoy both sightseeing and shopping, choosing how to balance your port time can be a challenge; I'd suggest doing a quick surgical shopping strike in destinations where you have something in particular you'd like to buy.) You'll find more information on shopping in port on page 125, and in the destination chapters, I've given some suggestions about specific local goods to shop for.

Casino

Cruise ships offer Vegas-style casinos with all the classic games, including slots, blackjack, poker, roulette, and craps. But unlike

Vegas—where casinos clamor for your business with promises of the "loosest slots in town"— cruise ships know they have a captive audience. And that means the odds are even more against you than they are in Vegas. Onboard casinos also offer various trumped-up activities to

drum up excitement. Sure, a poker tournament can be exciting and competitive—but I can't for the life of me figure out the appeal of a slot tournament (no joking). If you want to test your luck—but you're not clear on the rules of blackjack, craps, or other casino games—take advantage of the free gambling classes that many cruise lines offer early in the trip.

Art Gallery

Many ships have an art gallery, and some even display a few genuinely impressive pieces from their own collection (minor works by major artists). But more often the focus is on selling new works by lesser-known artists. Your ship might offer lectures about the art, but beware: These often turn out to be sales pitches for "up-and-coming" artists whose works are being auctioned on board. While the artists may be talented, the "valuation" prices are dramatically inflated. Art auctions ply bidders with free champagne to drive up the prices...but no serious art collector buys paintings on a cruise ship.

Photography

A big feature of many cruise ships is the photo center. Once upon a time, photographers snapped a free commemorative portrait of you and your travel partner as you boarded the ship. But when the cruise lines figured out that people were willing to shell out $8-15 for one of these pictures, they turned it into big business. Roving photographers snap photos of you at dinner, and makeshift studios with gauzy backgrounds suddenly appear in the lobby on formal night. As you disembark at each port, photographers ask you to pose with models in tacky costumes (flamenco danc-

ers in Spain, toga-clad "ancients" in Greece, and—inexplicably—parrots in Croatia). Later that day, all

those photos appear along one of the ship's hallways for all to see (perusing my fellow passengers' deer-in-the-headlights mug shots is one of my favorite onboard activities). While it's hard to justify spending 10 bucks on a cheesy snapshot, you might be able to bargain the price down toward the end of the trip. Repeat cruisers have reported that if you swing by the photography area on the last evening, the salespeople—eager to unload their inventory—may cut a deal if you pay cash.

Spa/Beauty Salon

Most cruise ships have spa facilities, where you can get a massage, facial, manicure, pedicure, and so on. There may also be a beauty salon where you can get your hair done. While convenient, obviously these services are priced at a premium—though specials are often available. When you receive any of these treatments, tip as you would back home (either in cash or by adding a tip when you sign the receipt).

Library

The onboard library has an assortment of free loaner books, ranging from nautical topics to travel guidebooks to beach reading.

Usually outfitted with comfortable chairs and tables, this can also be a good place to stretch out and relax while you read. If the ship's staterooms are equipped with DVD players, the library may have DVDs for loan or rent.

Chapel

Many ships have a nondenominational chapel for prayer or silent reflection. If you're cruising during a religious holiday, the cruise line may invite a clergy member on board to lead a service.

Cruising with Kids

Cruises can be a great way to vacation with a family. But do your homework: Cruise lines cater to kids to varying degrees. Disney, Celebrity, and Royal Caribbean, for example, are extremely kid-friendly, while other lines (especially the higher-end luxury ones) offer virtually nothing extra for children—a hint that they prefer you to leave the kiddos at home.

Kids' Programs and Activities

Family-friendly cruise lines have "kids clubs" that are open for most of the day. It's a win-win situation for both parents and children. Kids get to hang out with their peers and fill their time with games, story time, arts and crafts, and other fun stuff, while parents get to relax and enjoy the amenities of the ship.

Most kids clubs are for children ages three and older, and require your tots to be potty-trained (Norwegian's program is for two and up). Kids are separated by age so that tweens don't have to be subjected to younger children. For older kids, there are teen-only hangouts. If you have kids under three, options are limited: You might find parent/baby classes (no drop-and-go) and, in rare cases, onboard day care (Disney offers this on some ships).

Rules for kids clubs differ across cruise lines. Some charge for it, others include it. While kids clubs are generally open throughout the day (about 9:00-22:00), some close at mealtimes, so you'll have to collect your kids for lunch and dinner. Port-day policies vary—some kids clubs require a parent or guardian to stay on board (in case they need to reach you); others are fine with letting you off your parental leash.

There are also plenty of activities outside the kids club. All ships have pools, and some take it to the next level with rock-

climbing walls, bowling alleys, and inline skating. Arcades and movies provide hours of entertainment, and shows are almost always appropriate for all ages. Many scheduled activities are fun for the whole family, such as art classes, ice-carving contests, or afternoon tea.

Babysitting

Because cruise lines want you to explore the ship and have fun (and, of course, spend money at bars and the casino), many have babysitting services. On some ships, you can arrange for a babysitter to come to your stateroom, while others offer late-night group babysitting for a small fee.

To line up babysitting, ask at the front desk or the kids club. Or, if your child takes a shine to one of the youth counselors at the kids club, hit him or her up for some private babysitting. Often times, crew members have flexible hours and are looking to earn extra money. Some have been separated from their families and even relish the opportunity to play with your kids—let them!

When hiring a babysitter, ask up front about rates; otherwise, offer the standard amount you pay at home. And remember to have cash on hand so you can compensate the babysitter at the end of the evening.

Food

Pizza parlors, hamburger grills, ice cream stands...Thanks to the diverse dining options on ships, even the pickiest of eaters should be satisfied. Here are some tips for dining with children:

If you prefer to eat with your kids each night, choose the first dinner seating, which has more families and suits kids' earlier eating schedules. If your kids are too squirmy to sit through a five-course formal dinner every night, choose the buffet or a casual poolside restaurant (described later, under "Eating").

Don't forget about room service. This can be a nice option for breakfast, so you don't have to rush around in the morning. It's also an easy solution if you're cabin-bound with a napping child in the afternoon.

If your kids have convinced you to let them drink soda (which costs extra on a cruise), buy a soft drink card for the week to save over-ordering à la carte.

In Port

If you plan to take your kids off the ship and into town, remember that a lot of Europe's streets and sidewalks are old, cobbled, and uneven—not ideal for a stroller. If your kids can't walk the whole way themselves, consider bringing a backpack carrier rather than a stroller for more mobility.

While excursions are often not worth the expense, they make sense for some ports and activities, especially when you have kids in tow. You don't have to deal with transportation, nor do you have to worry about missing the boat. (For more on excursions, see page 99).

If you do take your kids into port, consider draping a lanyard around their necks with emergency contact information in case you get separated. Include your name and mobile phone number, your itinerary, a copy of the child's passport, and some emergency cash. Hopefully your kids won't blow it on junk food or some tacky souvenir—though perhaps that's the price you'll have to pay for peace of mind.

Eating

While shipboard dining used to be open-and-shut (one restaurant, same table, same companions, same waitstaff, same time every night), these days you have choices ranging from self-service buffets to truly inspired specialty restaurants. On some ships, you could spend a week on board and never eat at the same place twice.

Note that if you have food allergies or a special diet—such as vegetarian, vegan, or kosher—most cruise lines will do their best to accommodate you. Notify them as far ahead as possible (when you book your cruise or 30 days before you depart).

Types of Dining

Most cruise ships have a main dining room, a more casual buffet, a variety of specialty restaurants, and room service.

Main Dining Room

The main restaurant venue on your ship is the old-fashioned dining room. With genteel decor, formal waiters, and a rotating menu of upscale cuisine, dining here is an integral part of the classic cruise experience.

Traditionally, each passenger was assigned a particular seating time and table for all dinners in the dining room. But over the last decade or so, this **"assigned dining"** policy has been in flux, with various cruise lines taking different approaches. Some lines (including Royal Caribbean, Costa, MSC, Celebrity, and Disney) still have assigned dining. Others (such as Holland America, Princess, and Cunard) make it optional: You can choose whether you want an assigned seating (if you don't, just show up, and you'll be seated at whichever table is available next). Norwegian Cruise Line, along with several of the smaller luxury lines (Oceania, Silversea, Azamara, Windstar, Star Clippers, Seabourn, Regent Seven Seas), have no assigned dining—it's first-come, first-served, in any dining venue.

If you choose assigned dining, you'll eat with the same people every night (unless you opt to dine elsewhere on some evenings). Tables for two are rare, so couples will likely wind up seated with others. You'll really get to know your tablemates...whether you like it or not. Some cruisers prefer to be at a table that's as large as possible—if you are seated with just one other couple, you risk running out of conversation topics sooner than at a table with 10 or 12 people.

Diners are assigned either to an early seating (typically around 18:30) or a late seating (around 20:45). Avid sightseers might prefer the second seating, so they can fully enjoy the port without rushing back to the ship in time to change for dinner (on the other hand, the first seating lets you turn in early to rest up for the next day's port). In general, families and older passengers seem to opt for the first seating, while younger passengers tend to prefer the later one.

If your cruise line has assigned dining (whether mandatory or optional), you can request your seating preferences (time and table size) when you book your cruise. These assignments are first-come, first-served, so the earlier you book and make your request, the

Formal Nights

Many cruises have one or two designated formal nights each week in the main dining room, when passengers get decked out for dinner in suits and cocktail dresses—or even tuxes and floor-length gowns (for tips on how to pack for formal night, see the sidebar on page 50). In general, on formal nights the whole ambience of the ship is upscale, with people hanging out in the bars, casinos, and other public areas dressed to the nines. And cruises like formal nights because passengers behave better and spend more money (for example, order a nicer bottle of wine or buy the posed photos).

Some ships also have semiformal nights (also one or two per week), which are scaled-down versions of the formal nights—for example, men wear slacks and a tie, but no jacket.

Some passengers relish the opportunity to dress up on formal nights. But if you don't feel like it, it's fine to dress however you like—as long as you stay out of the dining room. Skip the formal dinners and eat at another restaurant or the buffet, or order room service.

better. If you don't get your choice, you can ask to be put on a waiting list.

If you're not happy with your assignment, try dropping by the dining room early on the first night to see if the maître d', who's in charge of assigning tables, can help you. He'll do his best to accommodate you (you won't be the only person requesting a change—so there's always some shuffling around). If the maître d' is able to make a switch, it's appropriate to thank him with a tip.

Some people really enjoy assigned dining. It encourages you to socialize with fellow passengers and make friends. Tablemates sometimes team up and hang out in port together as well. And some cruisers form lasting friendships with people they were, once upon a time, randomly assigned to dine with. If, on the other hand, you're miserable with your dinner companions, ask the maître d' to re-seat you. But the longer you wait to request a change, the more difficult (and potentially awkward) it becomes.

If you get tired of assigned dining, you can always find variation by eating at the buffet or a specialty restaurant, or by ordering room service. And if you have an early seating but decide to skip dinner one night to stay late in port, you can still dine at the other onboard restaurants. Since the various onboard eateries are all included (except for specialty-restaurant surcharges), money is no object.

Note that the main dining room is typically also open for breakfast and lunch. At these times, it's generally open seating (no pre-assigned tables), but you'll likely be seated with others. The majority of travelers prefer to have a quick breakfast and lunch at the buffet (or in port). But some cruisers enjoy eating these meals in the dining room (especially on leisurely sea days) as a more civilized alternative to the mob scene at the buffet; it's also an opportunity to meet fellow passengers who normally sit elsewhere at dinner.

Dress Code: In the main dining room, most cruise lines institute a "smart casual" dress code on most nights. This means no jeans, shorts, or t-shirts. Men wear slacks and button-down or polo shirts; women wear dresses or nice separates. "Formal night" dress codes apply in the dining room (see sidebar, opposite page).

Casual Dining: Buffet and Poolside Restaurants

Besides the main dining room, most ships have at least one additional restaurant, generally a casual buffet. This has much longer hours than the dining room, and the food can be quite good. In

fact, the buffet often has some of the same options as in the dining room, and it may even have some more unusual items, often themed (Greek, Indian, sushi, and so on). Most ships also have an even more casual "grill" restaurant, usually near the pool, where you can grab a quick burger or hot dog and other snacks. These options are handy if you're in a hurry, or just want a break from the dining room.

When eating at the buffet, keep in mind that this situation—with hundreds of people handling the same serving spoons and tongs, licking their fingers, then handling more spoons and tongs—is nirvana for communicable diseases. Compound that with the fact that some diners don't wash their hands (incorrectly believing that hand sanitizer is protecting them from all illness), and you've got a perfect storm. At the risk of sounding like a germophobe, wash your hands before, during, and after your meal. For more on this cheerful topic, see page 78.

Dress Code: The buffet and "grill" restaurants have a casual dress code all the time. You'll see plenty of swimsuits and flip-flops, though most cruise lines require a shirt or cover-up in the buffet.

Specialty Restaurants

A relatively recent cruising trend is the proliferation of specialty restaurants on board. Most ships (even small ones) have at least one specialty eatery, but some have a dozen or more. If there's just one specialty restaurant on board, it serves food (such as steak or seafood) that's a notch above what's available in the dining room. If there are several, they specialize in different foods or cuisines: steakhouse, French, sushi, Italian, Mexican, and so on.

Because specialty restaurants are more in-demand than the traditional dining room, it's smart to make reservations if you have your heart set on a particular one. At the beginning of your cruise, scope out the dining room's menu for the week; if one night seems less enticing to you, consider booking a specialty restaurant for that evening. Days at sea are also popular nights in specialty restaurants.

Occasionally these restaurants are included in your cruise price, but more often they require a special "cover charge" (typically $10-30). In addition to the cover charge, certain entrées incur a "supplement" ($10-20). A couple ordering specialty items and a bottle of wine can quickly ring up a $100 dinner bill. If you're on a tight budget, remember: Specialty restaurants are optional. You can eat every meal at the included dining room and buffet if you'd rather not spend the extra money.

Some routine cruisers allege that the cruise lines are making the food in their dining room intentionally worse in order to steer passengers to the specialty restaurants that charge a cover. But from a dollars-and-cents perspective, this simply doesn't add up. The generally higher-quality ingredients used in specialty restaurants typically cost far more than the cover charge; for example, you might pay $20 to eat a steak that's worth $30. The cover charge was designed not to be a moneymaker, but to limit the number of people who try to dine at the specialty restaurants. It's just expensive enough to keep the place busy every night, but not cheap enough that it's swamped. So if cruise food is getting worse, it's not on purpose.

Dress Code: Specialty restaurants usually follow the same dress code as the main dining room (including on formal nights), though it depends on how upscale the menu is. The steakhouse might be more formal than the main dining room; the sushi bar could be less formal. If you're unsure, ask.

Room Service

Room service is temptingly easy and is generally included in the cruise price (no extra charge). Its menu is usually much more limited than what you'd get in any of the restaurants, but it can be convenient, especially on mornings when the ship arrives in port early. By eating breakfast in your room (place your order the night before), you can get ready at a more leisurely pace and avoid the mob at the buffet. You can also arrange for room service to be waiting when you get back on the ship from exploring a port.

Dress Code: From tuxes and gowns to your birthday suit, it's up to you.

Cruise Cuisine

Reviews of the food on cruise ships range wildly, from raves to pans. It's all relative: While food snobs who love locally sourced

bistros may turn up their noses at cruise cuisine, fans of chain restaurants are perfectly satisfied on board. True foodies should lower their expectations. High-seas cuisine is not exactly high cuisine.

Cruise food is as good as it can be, considering that thousands of people are fed at each

meal. Most cruise lines replenish their food stores about every two weeks, so everything you eat—including meat, seafood, and produce—may be less than fresh. Except on some of the top-end lines, the shipboard chefs are afforded virtually no room for creativity: The head office creates the recipes, then trains all kitchen crews to prepare each dish. To ensure cooks get it just right, cruise lines hang a photo in the galley (kitchen) of what each dish should look like—important since most of the cooks and servers come from countries where the cuisine is quite different.

Cruise-ship food is not local cuisine. Today's menu, dreamed up months ago by some executive chef in New York City, bears

no resemblance to the food you saw this afternoon in port. It can be frustrating to wander through a Greek village, passing tavernas with luscious tomato salads and succulent seafood, then go back to your ship and be served Caesar salad and prime rib.

On the other hand, cruise menus often feature famous but

unusual dishes that would cost a pretty penny in a top-end restaurant back home. It can be fun to sample a variety of oddball items (such as frog legs, escargot, or foie gras) and higher-end meats (filet mignon, fowl, lobster, crab)...with no expense and no commitment. (If you don't like it, don't finish it.)

Whether cruise food is good or bad, one thing's for sure: There's plenty of it. A ship with 2,500 passengers and 1,500 crew members might brag that they prepare "17,000 meals a day." Do the math: Someone's going back for seconds. A lot of someones, in fact. (If you're one of them, see "Staying Fit on Board" on page 79.)

All things considered, cruise lines do an impressive job of providing variety and quality. But it still pales in comparison to the food you can get in port, lovingly prepared with fresh ingredients and local recipes. Some travelers figure there's no point paying for a meal in port when you can just eat for free on the ship. But after a few days of cruise cuisine, I can't wait to sit down at a real European restaurant or grab some authentic street food...and I can really taste the difference.

Drinks

In general, tap water, milk, iced tea, coffee and tea, and fruit juices are included. Other drinks cost extra: alcohol of any kind, name-brand soft drinks, fresh-squeezed fruit juices, and premium espresso drinks (lattes and cappuccinos). You'll also pay for any drinks you take from your stateroom's minibar (generally the same price as the restaurants). Beverages are priced approximately the same as in a restaurant on land.

Early in your cruise, ask about special offers for reduced drink prices, such as discount cards or six-for-the-price-of-five beer offers. This also goes for soft drinks—if you guzzle Diet Coke, you can buy an "unlimited drink card" at the start of the cruise and order as many soft drinks as you want without paying more.

Cruise lines want to encourage alcohol sales on board, but without alienating customers. Before you set sail, find out your cruise line's policy on taking alcohol aboard so you can BYOB to save money. Some cruise lines ban it outright; others prohibit only hard liquor but allow wine and sometimes beer. On some ships, you may be able to bring one or two bottles of wine when you first board the ship. Keep in mind that if you bring aboard your own bottle of wine to enjoy with dinner on the ship, you'll most likely face a corkage fee (around $10-20).

To monitor the alcohol situation, cruise lines require you to go through a security checkpoint every time you board the ship. It's OK to purchase a souvenir bottle of booze in port, but you may have to check it for the duration of the cruise. Your purchases will be returned to you on the final night or the morning of your last disembarkation.

If you're a scofflaw who enjoys a nip every now and again, note that various cruising websites abound with strategies for getting around the "no alcohol" rules.

Eating on Port Days

For some travelers, port days present a tasty opportunity to sample the local cuisine. Others prioritize their port time for sightseeing or shopping rather than sitting at a restaurant waiting for their food to arrive. And still others economize by returning to the ship for lunch (which, to me, seems like a waste of valuable port time). For more tips on eating while in port, see page 128.

Some cruise passengers suggest tucking a few items from the

breakfast buffet into a day bag for a light lunch on the go. While this is, to varying degrees, frowned upon by cruise lines, they recognize that many people do it—and, after all, you are paying for the food. If you do this, do so discreetly. Some experienced cruisers suggest ordering room service for breakfast, with enough extra for lunch. Or you can get a room-service sandwich the evening before and tuck it into your minifridge until morning. To make it easier to pack your lunch, bring along sealable plastic baggies from home.

Final Disembarkation

When your cruise comes to an end, there are a few steps before you actually get off the ship. The crew will give you written instructions, and you'll often be able to watch a presentation about the process on your stateroom TV. Many ships even have a "disembarkation talk" on the final day to explain the procedure. While the specifics vary from cruise to cruise, most include the following considerations.

On your last full day on the ship, you'll receive an itemized copy of your **bill.** This includes the auto-tip for the crew (explained earlier, on page 74), drinks, excursions, shopping, restaurant surcharges, and any other expenses you've incurred. This amount will automatically be charged to the credit card you registered with the cruise line. If there are any mistaken charges, contest them as soon as you discover them (to avoid long lines just as everyone is disembarking).

If you'd like to give an additional cash **tip** to any crew members (especially those with whom you've personally interacted or who have given you exceptional service), it's best to do so on the final night in case you can't find the tippee in the morning. It's most common to tip cabin stewards and maybe a favorite waiter or two, particularly if you dined with them several times over the course of your cruise. There is no conventional amount or way to calculate tips; simply give what you like, but keep in mind that the crew has extremely low base wages (about $1/day). Traditionally, the cruise lines provide envelopes (either at the front desk or sometimes left in your stateroom on the final evening) for you to tuck a cash tip inside and hand it to the crew member.

The night before disembarking, leave any **bags** you don't want to carry off the ship (with luggage tags attached) in the hall outside your room. The stewards will collect these bags during the night, and they'll be waiting for you when you step off the ship. Be sure *not* to pack any items you may need before disembarking the next morning (such as medications, a jacket, or a change of clothes).

Before leaving your cabin, check all the drawers, other hidden stowage areas, and the safe—after a week or more at sea, it's easy to forget where you tucked away items when you first unpacked.

In the morning, you'll be assigned a **disembarkation time.** At that time, you'll need to vacate your cabin (so the crew can clean it for the passengers arriving in a few hours) and gather in a designated public area for further instructions on where to leave the ship and claim your luggage.

It's possible to get an **early disembarkation**—particularly if you're in a hurry to catch a plane or train, or if you just want to get started on your sightseeing. Request early disembarkation near the start of your cruise, as there is a set number of slots, and they can fill up. Another option is to walk off with all your luggage (rather than leaving it in the hall overnight and reclaiming it once off the ship). Again, as this opportunity may be limited to a designated number of passengers, ask about it near the start of your cruise.

If you're hungry, you can have breakfast—your last "free" meal before re-entering the real world. Once you do leave the ship, the bags you left outside your room the night before will be waiting for you in the terminal building (though if you're earlier than your appointed time, they may not be ready).

If you're sightseeing around town and need to **store your bags,** there is often a bag-storage service at or near the cruise terminal (I've listed specifics for certain ports in this book). If you're staying at a hotel after the cruise, you can take your bags straight there when you leave the ship; even if your room is not ready, the hotelier is usually happy to hold your bags until check-in time.

Most cruise lines offer a **transfer** service to take you to your hotel or the airport. Typically you'll do better arranging this on your own (taxis wait at the cruise terminal, and this book's destination chapters include detailed instructions for getting into town). Some cruise lines also offer excursions at the end of the journey that swing by the city's top sights before ending at your hotel or the airport. This can be a good way to combine a sightseeing excursion with a transfer.

For **customs** regulations on returning to the US, see page 128.

IN PORT

While some people care more about shipboard amenities than the destinations, most travelers who take a European cruise see it mainly as a fun way to get to the ports. This is your chance to explore some of Europe's most fascinating cities, characteristic seaside villages, and engaging regions.

Prior to reaching each destination, you'll need to decide whether you want to go on an excursion (booked on board through your cruise line) or see it on your own. This chapter explains the pros and cons of excursions and provides a rundown of which destinations are best by excursion—and which are easy to do independently (see the sidebar on page 104). It also fills you in on the procedure for getting off and back on the ship, and provides tips on how to make the most of your time on land.

Excursions

In each port, your cruise line offers a variety of shore excursions. In Europe, these are mostly sightseeing tours on a bus, with some walking tours, led by a freelance local guide who is hired for the day by the cruise line. While the majority of excursions involve bus tours, town walks, and guided visits to museums and archaeological sites, others are more active (snorkeling, riding ATVs, horseback-riding), and some are more passive (a trip to a beach, spa, or even a luxury-hotel swimming pool for the day). Most also include a shopping component (such as a visit to a glassmaker's studio in Venice, a jewelry shop in Santorini, or a carpet-weaving demonstration in Turkey). When shopping is involved, kickbacks are common. Local merchants may pay the cruise line or guide to bring the group to their shops, give them a cut of whatever's bought, or both. The prices you're charged are likely inflated to cover these payouts.

Excursions aren't cheap. On Mediterranean cruises, a basic two- to three-hour town walking tour runs about $40-60/person; a half-day bus tour to a nearby sight can be $70-100; and a full-day bus-plus-walking-tour itinerary can be $100-150 or more. Extras (such as a boat ride or a lunch) add to the cost. There seems to be little difference in excursion costs between a Mass-Market and a Luxury line (in fact, excursions can be more expensive on a cheap cruise than on a pricey one).

On the day of your excursion, you'll gather in a large space (often the ship's theater, sometimes with hundreds of others), wait-ing for your excursion group to be called. You're given a sticker to wear with a number that corresponds to your specific group/bus number. Popular excursion itineraries can have several different busloads. Once called, head down the gangway—or to the tender boats—to meet your awaiting tour bus and local guide.

Excursion Options

The types of excursions you can book vary greatly, depending on the port. In a typical mid-sized port city, there might be two different themed walking tours of the city itself (one focusing on the Old Town and art museum, and another on the New Town and architecture); a panoramic drive into the countryside for scenery, sometimes with stops (such as a wine-tasting, a restaurant lunch, or a folk-dancing show); and trips to outlying destinations, such as a neighboring village or an archaeological site.

Some ports have an even wider range of options. For example, if you dock at either Marseille or Toulon in southern France, you'll be offered various Provençal itineraries that combine appealing towns and sights, such as Avignon, Arles, Aix-en-Provence, the ruined castle at Les Baux, the Roman aqueduct of Pont du Gard, and countryside wineries. In these regions, excursions feature destinations bundled in different ways—look for an itinerary that covers just what you're interested in (see the "Excursions" sidebars in each destination chapter to help you sort through your options).

In some cases, there's only one worthy destination, but it takes some effort to reach it. For example, from the port of Civitavecchia, it's nearly 50 miles into Rome, with little else to see or do nearby. It's possible—using this book—to get to these places by public transportation. But the cruise line hopes you'll pay them to take you instead.

Most excursions include a guided tour of town, but for those who want more freedom, cruise lines also offer "transfer-only" or "transportation-only" excursions: A bus will meet you as you disembark, and you might have a guide who narrates your ride into town. But once you reach the main destination, you're set free and given a time to report back to the bus. While much more expensive than public transportation, these transfers cost less than fully guided excursions and are generally cheaper than hiring a taxi to take you into town (although you can split the cost of a taxi with other travelers).

Most cruise lines can also arrange a private driver or guide for you. While this is billed as an "excursion," you're simply paying the cruise line to act as a middleman. It's much more cost-effective to make these arrangements yourself (you can use one of the guides or drivers I recommend in this book).

Booking an Excursion

The cruise lines make it easy to sign up for excursions. There's generally an excursions presentation sometime during the first few days of your cruise (or during a day at sea), and a commercial for the different itineraries runs 24/7 on your stateroom TV. You can sign up at the excursions desk, through the concierge, or (on some ships) through the interactive menu on your TV. You can generally cancel 24 to 48 hours before the excursion leaves (ask when you book); if you cancel with less notice—for any reason—you will probably have to pay for it.

You can also book shore excursions on the cruise line's website prior to your trip. But be warned: It's common for someone to sign up in advance, then realize once on board that their interests have changed. The cancellation deadline may sneak up on you—and you could be stuck on an excursion you no longer want.

Cruise lines use the words "limited space" to prod passengers to hurry up and book various extra services—especially excursions. Sometimes excursions truly do fill up quickly; other times, you can sign up moments before departure. This creates a Chicken Little situation: Since they *always* claim "limited space," it's hard to know whether a particular excursion truly is filling up fast. If you have your heart set on a particular excursion, book it as far ahead as you can. But if you're on the fence, ask at the excursions desk how many seats are left and how soon they anticipate filling up. If your choice is already booked when you ask, request to be added to the wait list—it's not unusual for the cruise line to have last-minute cancellations or to add more departures for popular excursions.

Take an Excursion, or Do It on My Own?

Excursions are (along with alcohol sales and gambling) the cruise lines' bread and butter. To sell you on them, they like to convey the "insurance" aspect of joining their excursion. They'll tell you that you can rest easy, knowing that you're getting a vetted local tour guide on a tried-and-true itinerary that will pack the best experience into your limited time.

Some excursions are a great value, whisking you to top-tier and otherwise-hard-to-reach sights with an eloquent guide on a well-planned itinerary. But others can be disappointing time- and money-wasters, carting passengers to meager "sights" that are actually shopping experiences in disguise.

This book is designed not necessarily to discourage you from taking the cruise lines' excursions, but to help you make an informed decision, on a case-by-case basis, whether a particular excursion is a good value for your interests and budget. In some situations (such as the Ephesus excursion from Kuşadası), I would happily pay a premium for a no-sweat transfer with a hand-picked, top-notch local guide who can teach me about one of the world's great ancient sites. In other cases (such as a trip from Barcelona's port to its bustling, sights-packed city center—an easy bus ride on your own), the information in this book will allow you to have at least as good an experience, with more flexibility and freedom for a fraction of the price.

Pros and Cons of Excursions

Here are some of the benefits of taking an excursion, as touted by the cruise lines. Evaluate how these selling points fit the way you travel—and whether they are actually perks, or might cramp your style.

Returning to the Ship on Time: Cruise lines try to intimidate you into signing up for excursions by gravely reminding you that if you're on your own and fail to make it back to the ship on time, it could leave without you. If, however, a cruise-line excursion runs late for some reason, the ship will wait. In most places, provided that you budget your time conservatively (and barring an unforeseen strike or other crisis), there's no reason you can't have a great day in port and easily make it back on board in time. But if you don't feel confident about your ability to navigate back to the ship on time, or you have a chronic issue with lateness, an excursion may be a good option.

Getting Off First: Those going on excursions have priority for getting off the ship. This is especially useful when tendering, as tender lines can be long soon after arrival. But if you're organized and get a tender ticket as early as possible, you can make it off the ship almost as fast as the excursion passengers. (For more on tendering, see page 110.)

Optimizing Time in Port: Most excursions are well-planned by the cruise line to be an efficient use of your limited time in port.

Rather than waiting around for a bus or train to your destination, you're whisked dockside-to-destination by the excursion bus. However, when weighing the "time savings" of an excursion, remember to account for how long it takes 50 people (compared to two people) to do everyday tasks: boarding a bus, walking through an ancient site, even making bathroom stops. If you're on your own and want to check out a carpet shop, you can stay as long as you like—or just dip in and out; with a cruise excursion, you're committed to a half-hour, an hour, or however long the shopkeeper is paying your guide to keep you there. Every time your group moves somewhere, you're moving with dozens of other people, which always takes time. In many ports, you may actually reach the city center faster than you can with an excursion, provided you are ready to hop off the ship as soon as you can, you don't waste time getting to the terminal building, and you know how, when, and where to grab public transport.

Accessing Out-of-the Way Sights: In most destinations, there's a relatively straightforward, affordable public-transportation option for getting from the cruise port to the major city or sight. But in a few cases, minor sights (or even the occasional major sight) are challenging, if not impossible, to reach without paying for a pricey taxi. For example, if your cruise is coming in to Toulon, and you've always wanted to see the Pont du Gard aqueduct, you'll find it next to impossible to get there on your own—you'll need an excursion. This book is designed to help you determine how easy—or difficult—it is to reach the places you're interested in seeing.

Touring with Quality Guides: Most excursions are led by local guides contracted through the cruise line. While all guides have been vetted by the cruise line and are generally high-quality, a few oddball exceptions sneak through occasionally. The guide is the biggest wildcard in the success of your tour, but it's also one thing you have very little control over. You won't know which guide is

Excursion Cheat Sheet

This (admittedly oversimplified) roundup shows which major ports are best by excursion and which are doable on your own

Destination (Port)	Excursion?
BARCELONA	No

Details: Ride the shuttle bus right into the heart of town, within easy walking distance (or Metro ride) of most sights.

Destination (Port)	Excursion?
PROVENCE (Marseille/Toulon)	Yes

Details: Various great destinations within reach of the underwhelming port towns; an excursion can efficiently combine several.
From Toulon port: 30-minute walk (or short bus ride) to train station, then 1-hour train to Marseille for onward connections.
From Marseille port: Shuttle bus to Old Port, walk or ride Métro to train station, then take a train to Aix-en-Provence (45 minutes), Arles (1.5 hours), or Avignon (1 hour).

Destination (Port)	Excursion?
FRENCH RIVIERA (Nice/Villefranche/ Monaco)	No

Details: All three ports—and more—are connected by frequent, fast, and easy trains and buses (10-20 minutes between each one by train, longer but more scenic by bus). Train stations are an easy walk, public-transit ride, or taxi trip from each port.

Destination (Port)	Excursion?
FLORENCE, PISA, LUCCA (Livorno)	Maybe

Details: Shuttle bus into downtown Livorno; then public bus to train station; then train to Pisa (20 minutes), Lucca (1 hour), or Florence (1.5 hours). Excursions offer a no-hassle connection that also includes tours of the major sights.

Destination (Port)	Excursion?
ROMA (Civitavecchia)	Maybe

Details: Short walk to train station, then 45-80-minute train into Rome. Doable on your own, but an excursion helps you sightsee efficiently in this big city.

Destination (Port)	Excursion?
NAPLES, POMPEII (Naples/Sorrento)	No

Details From Naples port: Walk or take local buses or taxis to most sights in the city; Pompeii is an easy 35-minute train ride away.
Details From Sorrento port: Easy train ride to Pompeii (35 minutes) or Naples (70 minutes).

Destination (Port)	Excursion?
AMALFI COAST, CAPRI (Naples/Sorrento)	Yes

Details: Both are doable on your own from either port (especially Capri by boat—45 minutes from Naples, 20-25 minutes from Sorrento), but crowded and unreliable public transit risks not making it back in time. An excursion buys you peace of mind.

IN PORT

(with this book in hand). For the full story, read the arrival information in each chapter.

Destination (Port)	Excursion?
VENICE	No

Details: It's an easy 5-minute monorail ride to Grand Canal for a slow vaporetto cruise through town; or a speedy 20-minute express boat directly to St. Mark's Square. Even walking (about 45 minutes to St. Mark's Square) is delightful in this unique city.

SPLIT	No

Details: The port is just a few steps from the easy-to-tour Old Town.

DUBROVNIK	No

Details: Cruisers are either tendered directly to the heart of the Old Town, or docked at the port (15-minute bus or taxi ride from Old Town). Once in the Old Town, everything worth seeing is walkable.

ATHENS (Piraeus)	Maybe

Details: It takes 20-60 minutes by public bus, Metro, or taxi into downtown (depending on traffic). But the important ancient sites benefit from a good guide, and an excursion offers easy connections.

MOST GREEK ISLANDS (Mykonos, Santorini, Corfu, Rhodes, Heraklion) and other ports **(Katakolo/Olympia, Nafplio)**	No

Details: Usually easy and fast to get into town or beaches. Just relax and be on vacation. Exceptions: Katakolo port (an excursion makes seeing Olympia easier) and Heraklion (an excursion allows you to connect both in-town sights and out-of-town palace).

ISTANBUL	No

Details: Cruise ship drops you off near the Golden Horn, an easy walk or tram or taxi ride from virtually every major sight in town.

EPHESUS (Kuşadası)	Yes

Details: Reaching Ephesus requires a complicated ride in shared minibus taxis (30-40 minutes) plus a 15-minute walk; or a pricey taxi. An excursion makes transport easy, and the magnificent site warrants a good guide.

leading your tour until he or she shows up to collect you. Instead, you can hire a good local guide to show you around on a private tour. For two people, this can cost about as much as buying the excursion, but you get a much more personalized experience, tailored to your interests. And if you can enlist other passengers to join you to split the cost, it's even more of a bargain. I've recommended my favorite guides for most destinations; many of them are the same ones who are hired by the cruise lines to lead their excursions. Because guides tend to book up when a big cruise ship is in town, it's smart to plan ahead and email these guides well ahead of your trip.

Cruise lines keep track of which guides get good reviews, and do their best to use those guides in the future. If you do go on an excursion, take the time to give the cruise line feedback, good or bad, about the quality of your guide. They really want to know.

Beware of Crew Members' Advice

While most cruise lines understand that their passengers won't book an excursion at every port, there is some pressure to get you to take them. And if you ask crew members for advice on sightseeing (independent of an excursion), they may be less than forthcoming, so take crew members' destination advice with a grain of salt.

Philosophically, most cruise lines don't consider it their responsibility to help you enjoy your port experience—unless you pay them for an excursion. The longer you spend on the ship, the more likely you are to spend more money on board, so there's actually a financial disincentive for crew members to help you get off the ship and find your own way in the port. You're lucky if the best they offer is, "Take a taxi. I have no idea what it costs."

I have actually overheard excursion staff dispense misinformation about the time, expense, and difficulty involved in reaching downtown from a port ("The taxi takes 25-30 minutes, and I've never seen a bus at the terminal"—when in fact, the taxi takes 10 minutes and there's an easy bus connection from the terminal). Was the crew being deceptive, or just ignorant? Either way, it was still misinformation.

Friendly as they are, the crew members on your cruise don't work for a tourist information office. You're on your own for information. That's why detailed instructions for getting into town from the port are a major feature of this book. Once in town, make your first stop at the local tourist information office (abbreviated **TI** in this book).

The Bottom Line on Excursions

Some passengers are on a cruise because they simply don't want to invest the time and energy needed to be independent...they want to be on vacation. Time is money, and you spend 50 weeks a year figuring things out back home; on vacation, you want someone else to do the thinking for you. If that's you, excursions can be a good way to see a place.

But in many destinations, it honestly doesn't take that much additional effort or preparation to have a good experience without paying a premium for an excursion. And cost savings aside, if you have even a middling spirit of adventure, doing it on your own can actually be a fun experience in itself.

Planning Your Time

Whether you're taking an excursion, sightseeing on your own, or doing a combination of the two, it's important to plan your day on land carefully. Be sure to read this book's sightseeing information and walking tours the night before to make the most of your time in a destination, even if you're taking an excursion—many include free time at a sight or neighborhood, or leave you with extra time in port.

First, keep in mind that the advertised amount of time in port can be deceptive. If the itinerary says that the ship is in town from 8:00 to 17:00, mentally subtract an hour or two from that time. It can take a good half-hour to get off a big ship and to the terminal building (or even longer, if you're tendering), and from the terminal, you still have to reach the town center. At the end of the day, the "all aboard" time is generally a half-hour before the ship departs. Not only do you have to be back on board by 16:30, but you must also build in the time it takes to get from downtown to the ship. Your nine-hour visit in port just shrank to seven hours... still plenty of time to really enjoy a place, but not quite as much as you expected.

It's essential to realize that if you are late returning to the ship, you cannot expect them to wait for you (unless you're on one of the cruise line's excursions, and it's running late). The cruise line has the right to depart without you...and trust me, they will. While this seems harsh, cruise lines must pay port fees for every *minute* they are docked, so your half-hour delay could cost them more than your cruise ticket. Also, they have a tight schedule to keep and can't be waiting around for stragglers (for tips on what to do if this happens to you, see the end of this chapter).

To avoid missing the boat, work backwards from the time you have to be back on board. Be very conservative, especially if you're going far—for example, riding a train or bus to a neighboring town. Public transportation can be delayed, and traffic can be snarled at rush hour—just when you're heading back to the ship. One strategy is to do the farthest-flung sights first, then gradually work your way back to the ship. Once you know you're within walking distance of the ship, you can dawdle to your heart's content, confident you can make it back on time.

If you're extremely concerned about missing the ship, just pretend it departs an hour earlier than it actually does. You'll still have several hours to enjoy that destination and be left with an hour to kill back at the cruise port.

Note that transportation strikes can be a problem in Europe (particularly in France, Italy, and Greece). These can hit at any time, although they are usually publicized in advance. If you're going beyond the immediate area of the port, ask the local tourist information office, "Are there any strikes planned for today that could make it difficult for me to return to my ship?" Even when there is a planned strike, a few trains and buses will still run—ask for the schedule.

If you're an early riser, you'll notice that your ship typically arrives at the port some time before the official disembarkation time. That's because local officials need an hour or more to "clear" the ship (process paperwork, passports, and so on) before passengers are allowed off. Even if you wake up and find the ship docked, you'll most likely have to wait for the official disembarkation time to get off.

While you have to plan your time smartly, don't let anxiety paralyze you: Some travelers—even adventurous ones—get so nervous about missing the boat that they spend all day within view of the cruise port, just in case. Anyone who does that is missing out: In very few cities is the best sightseeing actually concentrated near the port.

Managing Crowds

Unless you're on a luxury line, you can't go on a cruise and expect to avoid crowds. It's simply a fact of life. So be prepared to visit

sights at the busiest possible time—just as your cruise ship funnels a few thousand time-pressed tourists into town (or, worse, when three or four ships simultaneously disgorge).

Keep in mind that my instructions for getting into town might sound easy—but when you're jostling with several hundred others to cram onto a public bus that comes once every 20 minutes, the reality check can be brutal. Be patient...and most importantly, be prepared. You'll be amazed at how many

What Should I Bring to Shore?

- Your room **key card.** No matter how you leave the ship—tendering or docking, with an excursion or on your own—the crew must account for your absence. Any time you come or go, a security guard will swipe your room key. Your photo will flash onscreen to ensure it's really you.
- **Local cash.** After living on a cashless cruise ship, this is easy to forget. If you plan to take out local currency at an ATM, be sure to bring your **debit card** (and a **credit card** if you plan to make purchases).
- **Passport.** It's smart to carry your passport at all times (safely tucked away in a money belt—explained on page 53). While you typically won't have to show a passport when embarking or disembarking at each port (except the first and possibly the last), you may need it as a deposit for renting something (such as an audioguide or a scooter), or as ID when making a credit-card purchase or requesting a VAT refund. And you'll certainly want it in case you miss the boat and have to make your way to the next port.
- **Hot-weather gear,** including sunscreen, a hat for shade, sunglasses, lightweight and light-colored clothing, and a water bottle (or buy one in port). Mediterranean climates can be scorchingly hot in the summertime.
- **Long pants,** if you plan to visit any major churches in Italy. These enforce a strict "no shorts, no bare shoulders" dress code for everyone (even kids).
- Your cruise's **destination information sheet** (or daily program). At a minimum, jot down the "all aboard" time and (if applicable) the time of the last tender or shuttle bus to the ship.
- This **guidebook,** or—better yet—tear out just the pages you need for today's port.

of your fellow cruisers will step off the ship knowing nothing about what their options are for seeing the place. By buying and reading this book, and doing just a bit of homework before each destination, you're already way ahead of the game.

Make it a point to be the first person down the gangway (or in line for tender tickets) each day, and make a beeline for what you most want to see. While your fellow passengers are lingering over that second cup of coffee or puzzling over the bus schedules, you can be the first person on top of the city wall or on the early train to your destination. Yes, you're on vacation, so if you want to take it easy, that's your prerogative. But you can't be lazy and avoid the crowds. Choose one.

Getting Off the Ship

Your ship has arrived at its destination, and it's time to disembark and enjoy Europe. This section explains the procedure for getting off the ship and also provides a rundown of the services you'll find at the port.

Docking Versus Tendering

There are two basic ways to disembark from the ship: docking or tendering.

Docking

When your ship docks, it means that the vessel actually ties up to a pier, and you can simply walk off onto dry land. However, cruise piers (like cruise ships) can be massive, so you may have to walk 10-15 minutes from the ship to the terminal building. Sometimes the port area is so vast, the cruise line will offer a shuttle bus between the ship and the terminal building.

Tendering

If your ship is too big or there's not enough room at the pier, the ship will anchor offshore and send passengers ashore using small boats called tenders. Passengers who have paid for excursions usually go first; then they go in order of tender ticket (or tender number).

Tender tickets are generally distributed the night before or on the morning of arrival. Show up as early as you can to get your tender ticket (you may have to wait in line even before the official start time); the sooner you get your ticket, the earlier you can board your tender. Even then, you'll likely have to wait. (Sometimes passengers in more expensive staterooms are given a "VIP tender ticket," allowing them to skip the line whenever they want.)

The tenders themselves are usually the ship's lifeboats, but

in some destinations, the port authority requires the cruise line to hire local tenders. Because tenders are small vessels prone to turbulence, transferring from the ship to the tender and from the tender to shore can be treacherous. Take your time, be sure of your footing, and let the tender attendants give you a hand—it's their job to prevent you from going for an unplanned swim.

Tendering is, to many passengers, the scourge of cruising, as it can waste a lot of time. Obviously, not everyone on your big ship can fit on those little tender boats all at once. Do the math: Your ship carries some 2,000 passengers. There are three or four tenders, which can carry anywhere from 30 to 150 people apiece, and it takes at least 20 minutes round-trip. This can all translate into a lot of waiting around.

There are various strategies for navigating the tender line: Some cruisers report that if you show up at the gangway, ready to go, before your tender ticket number is called, you might be able to slip on early. A crush of people will often jam the main stairwells and elevators to the gangway. Some of these folks might block your passage despite having later tender tickets than yours. If you use a different set of stairs or elevators, then walk through an alternate hallway, you might be able to pop out near the gangway rather than get stuck in the logjam on the main stairwell. If you anticipate crowd issues while tendering, scope out the ship's layout in advance, when it's not busy.

Another strategy to avoid the crush of people trying to get off the ship upon arrival is to simply wait an hour or two, when you can waltz onto a tender at will. While you'll miss out on some valuable sightseeing time on shore, some cruisers figure that's a fair trade-off for avoiding the stress of tendering at a prime time.

If there's an advantage to tendering, it's that you're more likely to be taken to an arrival point that's close to the town's main  points of interest (for example, in Dubrovnik, tenders bring cruise passengers right to the super-central Old Port, while anchored ships put in at a dock a long bus ride away from the Old Town). When you figure in the time it would take to get from the main cruise port to the city center, tendering might actually save you some time—provided you get an early tender ticket. In fact, on smaller ships, it can actually be an advantage to tender—little to no waiting, and you're deposited in the heart of town.

Strangely, crowds are rare on tenders returning to the ship; apparently passengers trickle back all through the day, so even the last tenders of the day are rarely jam-packed. (And if they are, the ship won't leave without you, provided you're waiting in the tender line.)

The Port Area

In most cases, the port is not in the city center; in some cases (such as Livorno for Florence, Civitavecchia for Rome, or Piraeus for Athens), the port is actually in a separate town or city a lengthy train or bus ride away. In this book's destination chapters, I describe how near (or far) the port is from the town center. Be warned that the port area is, almost as a rule, the ugliest part of town—but once you're in the heart of town, none of that will matter.

Many ports have a terminal building, where you'll find passport check/customs control, and usually also ATMs, some duty-free shops, sometimes a travel agency and/or car-rental office, and (out front) a taxi stand and bus stop into town. Better terminals also have a TI that's staffed at times when cruise ships arrive.

Note: Your passport will rarely be checked on a Mediterranean cruise. Spain, France, Italy, and Greece are all part of the open-borders Schengen Agreement, so you don't need to show a passport when crossing the border. Even in other countries, it likely won't be checked—they know you're on a cruise ship, that you'll be returning to the ship that evening, and that you're likely to drop a lot of moola in port, so they want to make things easy for you. Of the destination countries in this book, only Turkey requires a visa, although it's often not necessary for cruise-ship passengers (explained on page 44). So, while it's wise to carry your passport for identification purposes, don't be surprised if you never actually need it.

Port Agents

In every port, your cruise line has an official port agent—a local representative who's designated to watch out for their passengers while they're in port. This person's name and contact information is listed on the destination information sheet distributed by your cruise line; if you have an emergency and can't contact anyone from your ship, call this person for help. Likewise, if you're running late and realize that you won't make it back to the ship by departure time, get in touch with your port agent, who will relay the information to the ship so they know you aren't coming. If you do miss the ship, sometimes the port agent can point you in the right direction for making your way to the next port of call on your own (for details, see "What If I Miss My Boat?" at the end of this chapter).

Sightseeing On Your Own

If you're planning to strike out on your own, you need to figure out where you're going, how to get there, and what you want to do once you're there.

Getting into Town

When it's a long distance from the ship to the cruise terminal, cruise lines usually offer a free shuttle bus to the terminal; if it's a short distance, you can walk. Either way, once you're at the terminal, you'll need to find your own way into town.

By Taxi

Exiting the terminal, you'll usually run into a busy taxi stand, with gregarious, English-speaking cabbies offering to take you for a tour around the area's main sights. While taxis are efficient, be aware that most cabbies' rates are ridiculously inflated to take advantage of cruisers. You may be able to persuade them to just take you into town (generally at a hiked-up rate), though they usually prefer to find passengers willing to hire them for several hours. Sometimes just walking a block or two and hailing a cab on the street can save you half the rate.

To keep the fare reasonable, consider taking the taxi only as far as you need to (for example, to the nearest subway station to hop a speedy train into the city, rather than pay to drive all the way across town in congested traffic). Also keep in mind that there must be somebody on your ship who's going to the same place you are—strike up a conversation at breakfast or on the gangway to find someone you can team up with to split the fare.

Remember: Taxis aren't just for getting from the port to town; they can also be wonderful time-savers for connecting sights within a big city. For more taxi tips, see the sidebar on page 114.

By Bus

Near the terminal, often just beyond the taxi stand, you'll almost always find a **public bus** stop for getting into town. This is significantly cheaper than a taxi, and often not much slower. But with an entire cruise ship emptying all at once, there can be a line for the bus. These buses usually take local cash only and sometimes require exact change. If you see a kiosk near the bus stop, try to purchase a bus ticket there, or at least buy something small to break big bills and get the correct change.

Occasionally, the cruise line offers a **shuttle bus** into town; while handy, this is rare and reserved mostly for ports that lack a good public-transit connection (such as Barcelona, Marseille, and Mykonos). If the cruise line does offer a shuttle bus into town,

Taxi Tips

There's no denying that taxis are the fastest way to get from your ship to what you want to see. But you'll pay for that convenience. Regular fares tend to be high, and many cabbies are adept at overcharging tourists—especially cruise passengers—in shameless and creative ways. Here are some tips to avoid getting ripped off by a cabbie.

Finding a Cab: In most cruise-port towns, it's generally easy to flag down a cab. A taxi stand is usually right at the cruise terminal. If not (or if you're already in town), ask a local to direct you to the nearest taxi stand. Taxi stands are often listed prominently on city maps; look for the little *T*s.

Whether you're at a taxi stand or flagging down a cab, get into the car only if it's marked with a prominent taxi-company logo and telephone number. Fly-by-night cabbies with a makeshift "Taxi" sign on top of the car are less likely to be honest. Be aware that if a taxi is called for you (for example, by a restaurant), the meter often starts running when the phone call is received.

Establishing a Price: To figure the fare, you can either use the taxi meter or agree on a set price up front. In either case, it's important to know the going rate (the destination chapters include the prevailing rates for the most likely journeys from each port). Even if I'm using the taxi meter, I still ask for a rough estimate up front, so I know generally what to expect.

In most cities, it's best to use the **taxi meter**—and cabbies are legally required to do so if the passenger requests it. So insist. The cabbie may get feisty and refuse. (When this happens, it's almost invariably because the meter fare will turn out lower than the fixed rate.) Do your best, and consider getting out and hailing another taxi.

Even with the meter, cabbies can still find ways to scam

that's usually your best option. The bus typically costs about $4-10 round-trip (buses run frequently when the ship arrives, then about every 15-20 minutes; pay attention to where the bus leaves you downtown, as you'll need to find that stop later to take the bus back to the ship).

The shuttle bus can get very crowded when the ship first unloads—do your best to get off the ship and onto the bus quickly. If you see a long line, consider hiring a taxi—team up with other travelers eager to avoid the crowds and split the tab. At slower times, you might have to wait a little while for the bus to fill up

you. For instance, they may try to set it to the pricier weekend tariff, even if it's a weekday (since trips on nights and weekends generally cost more). Check the list of different meter rates (posted somewhere in the cab, often in English) to make sure your driver has set the meter to the correct tariff. If you're confused about the tariff your cabbie has selected, ask for an explanation.

It's also possible (though obviously illegal) for cabbies to tinker with a taxi meter to make it spin like a pinwheel. If you glance away from the meter, then look back and see that it's mysteriously doubled, you've likely been duped. However, some extra fees are on the level (for instance, in most cities, there's a legitimate surcharge for picking you up at the cruise port). Again, these should be listed clearly on the tariff sheet. If you suspect foul play, following the route on your map or conspicuously writing down the cabbie's license information can shame him into being honest.

Agreeing to a **set price** for the ride is another option. While this is usually higher than the fair metered rate would be, sometimes it's the easiest way to go. Just be sure that the rate you agree to is more or less in the ballpark of the rate I've listed in this book. Consider asking a couple of cabbies within a block or two of each other for estimates. You may be surprised at the variation.

Many cabbies hire out for an hourly rate; if you want the taxi to take you to a variety of outlying sights and wait for you, this can be a good value. You can also arrange in advance to hire a driver for a few hours or the whole day (for some destinations, I've listed my favorite local drivers).

Settling Up: It's best to pay in small bills. If you use a large bill, state the denomination out loud as you hand it to the cabbie. They can be experts at dropping a €50 note and picking up a €20. Count your change. To tip a good cabbie, round up about 5-10 percent (to pay a €4.50 fare, give €5; for a €28 fare, give €30). But if you feel like you're being driven in circles or otherwise ripped off, skip the tip.

before it departs. Note that the port bus sometimes doesn't start running until some time after your ship actually docks (for example, you disembark at 7:00, but the bus doesn't start running until 8:30). This is another case when it can be worth springing for a taxi to avoid waiting around.

By Excursion

Cruise lines sometimes offer transfer-only excursions that include transportation into town, then free time on your own. This may be worthwhile in places where the port is far from the main point of interest (such as the port of Livorno for Florence or the port of Civitavecchia for Rome). While far more expensive than public transportation, this is a low-stress option that still allows you some freedom. For details, see page 100.

Seeing the Town

If you're touring a port on your own, you have several options for getting around town and visiting the sights (see the destination chapters for specifics).

On a Tour

It's easy to get a guided tour without having to pay excessively for an excursion. And there are plenty of choices, from walking to bus tours.

At or near the terminal, you'll generally find travel agencies offering **package tours.** These tours are similar to the cruise-ship excursions but usually cost far less (half or even a third as much). However, what's offered can change from day to day, so they're not as reliable as the cruise line's offerings. It's possible to reserve these in advance, typically through a third party (like a travel agency).

A great budget alternative is to join a regularly scheduled

local walking tour (in English, departing at a specified time every day). Again, these are very similar to the cruise lines' walking tours and often use the same guides. Look for my walking tour listings in the destination chapters or ask at the local TI.

In a large city where sights are spread out, it can be convenient to join a **hop-on, hop-off bus tour.** These buses make a circle through town every 30 minutes or so, stopping at key points where passengers can hop on or off at will. While relatively expensive (figure around €25-30 for an all-day ticket), these tours are easier than figuring out public

transportation, come with commentary (either recorded or from a live guide), and generally have a stop at or near the cruise port.

Some cruisers hire a **private guide** to meet them at the ship and take them around town (see page 103). Book them direct, using the contact information in this book; if you arrange the guide through a

"Cruise" in Six Languages

Need to find your way back to port? Ask a local or look for these words on signs.

Spanish	*crucero*	kruh-THEH-roh
French	*croisière*	kwah-shee-yay
Italian	*crociere*	kroh-cheeAY-reh
Croatian	*krstarenje*	kur-STAH-rehn-yeh
Greek	κρουαζιέρα	krow-SHEH-rah
Turkish	*seyir*	seh-YEER

third party—such as a local travel agent or the cruise line—you'll pay a premium.

On Your Own

If you prefer to sightsee independently, check out my free **audio tours** to some of the top destinations in this book, including the most interesting neighborhoods and most famous sights in Rome, Florence, Venice, and Athens. Audio tours allow your eyes to enjoy the wonders of the place while your ears learn its story. If you have an MP3 player (such as an iPod) or a smartphone, download the tours before your trip at www.ricksteves.com/audioeurope, on iTunes, or via my Rick Steves' Audio Europe smartphone app.

You can also **rent a car** to see the sights. While this makes sense for covering a wide rural area (such as the far-flung beaches on a Greek isle or charming villages in Provence), I would never rent a car to tour a big city—public transportation is not only vastly cheaper, but it avoids the headaches of parking, unfamiliar traffic patterns, and other problems. In general, given the relatively short time you'll have in port and the high expense of renting a car for the day (figure €40-100/day, depending on the port), this option

doesn't make much sense. However, if you're interested, you'll often find car-rental offices or travel agencies at or near the terminal that are accustomed to renting cars for short time periods to cruisers. You can also look for deals online (on rental companies' websites or travel-booking sites) in advance.

On some Greek islands (especially Mykonos), it can be fun to rent an **ATV** (four-wheeled all-terrain vehicle) or a **scooter**—much cheaper and easier, but potentially more dangerous than renting a car. For details, see page 986. In some places, renting a **bicycle** can

IN PORT

be a good option (though the typically hilly terrain and potentially sweltering heat in Mediterranean port areas can make it tough). A bike enables you to get out into the countryside or to zip around a city at your own pace without relying on public transit. Along the French Riviera, various shops rent bikes with supplemental electric power to help you over the hills—a nice boost when you need it.

With Fellow Passengers

The upside of traveling with so many other people is that you have ample opportunities to make friends. On a ship with thousands of people, I guarantee you'll find someone who shares your style of travel. If you and your traveling companion hit it off with others, consider teaming up for your shore time. This "double-dating" can save both money (splitting the cost of an expensive taxi ride) and stress (working together to figure out the best way into town). But be sure you're all interested in the same things before you head ashore—you don't want to end up on the corner in front of the Colosseum, bickering about whether to go to the Forum or the Vatican.

In-Port Travel Skills

Whether you're taking an excursion or tackling a port on your own, this practical advice will come in handy. This section includes tips on useful services, avoiding theft, using money, sightseeing, shopping, eating, and in general, making the most of your time in port.

Travel Smart

Europe is like a complex play—easier to follow and really appreciate on a second viewing. While no one does the same trip twice to gain that advantage, reading about the places you'll visit before you reach each destination accomplishes much the same thing.

Though you're bound to your ship's schedule, note the best times to visit various sights, and try to hit them as best as you can. Pay attention to holidays, festivals, and days when sights are closed. For example, many museums are closed on Mondays. Big sights and museums often stop admitting people 30-60 minutes before closing time.

Sundays have the same pros and cons as they do for travelers in the US (special events, limited hours, banks and many shops closed, limited public transportation, no rush hour). Saturdays are virtually weekdays with earlier closing times and no rush hour (though transportation connections can be less frequent than on weekdays).

When in port, visit the tourist information office. Get online to research sights, make reservations (maybe book a guide or tour for your next destination), keep in touch with home, and so on. And head for the sights you came so far to see.

Most importantly, connect with the culture. Set up your own quest to find the tastiest gelato in Italy or the best baklava in Greece. Be open to unexpected experiences. Slow down and enjoy the hospitality of the European people. Ask questions—most locals are eager to point you in their idea of the right direction. Wear your money belt, get used to the local currency, and learn how to estimate prices in dollars. Those who expect to travel smart, do.

Services

Tourist Information: No matter how well I know a town, my first stop is always the TI. TIs are usually located on the main square, in the city hall, or at the train station (just look for signs). Many cruise ports also have a temporary TI office, which hands out maps and answers questions for arriving cruisers. Their job is to make sure your few hours in town are enjoyable, so you'll come back on your own later. At TIs, you can get information on sights and public transit, and pick up a city map and a local entertainment guide. Ask if guided walks, self-guided walking-tour brochures, or audioguides are available. If you need a quick place to eat, ask where the TI staff goes for lunch.

Medical Help: If you get sick or injured while in port—assuming you're not in need of urgent care—do as the Europeans

do and go to a pharmacist for advice. European pharmacists diagnose and prescribe remedies for most simple problems. They are usually friendly and speak English, and some medications that are only available by prescription in the US are available over the counter (surprisingly cheaply) in Europe. If necessary, the pharmacist will send you to a doctor or the health clinic. For most destinations, I've listed pharmacies close to the cruise port.

Lost or Stolen Passport: To avoid the time-consuming hassle of replacing a passport, do your best to hang on to it; keep it in your money belt. To replace a passport, you must go in person to a US embassy or consulate (neither of which is usually located in a port town) during their business hours, which are generally limited and restricted to weekdays. This can take a day or two. Contact the port agent or the ship's guest services desk immediately—and be aware that you may not be able to continue your cruise if a replacement passport is not available before the ship sails. Having a backup form of ID—ideally a photocopy of your passport and driver's license, as well as an extra passport photo—speeds up a replacement. You may want to clarify this situation with your cruise company before traveling. For more info, see www.ricksteves.com/help.

Internet Cafés: Finding an Internet café in Europe is a breeze. While these places don't always serve food or drinks—

sometimes they're just one big, functional, sweaty room filled with computers—they are an easy and affordable way to get online. It's even easier if you have a Wi-Fi-enabled smartphone or netbook. There are hotspots at Internet cafés and at other businesses. Sometimes Wi-Fi is free; other times you may have to pay by the minute or buy something in exchange for the network password.

Public Phones: Because calling from the ship or a mobile phone can be costly (see page 82), you may want to seek out a pay phone in port to make calls. Coin-op phones are rare in Europe, so you'll need to purchase one of two types of prepaid phone cards. An **insertable phone card,** which you physically slide into the telephone, can be used only at pay phones. It offers reasonable rates for domestic calls, and steeper but still acceptable rates for international calls (rarely exceeding $1/minute). You use an **international phone card** by dialing a toll-free number, then punching in a scratch-to-reveal PIN. Though designed for international calls, which cost as little as 5 cents/minute, they also work for domestic calls. Both types of cards are sold in various denominations at tobacco shops, newsstands, and hole-in-the-wall long-distance shops. Generally these work only in the country where you buy them.

Outsmarting Thieves

In Europe, it's rare to encounter violent crime, but petty purse-snatching and pickpocketing are quite common. Thieves target Americans, especially cruise passengers—not because the thieves are mean, but because they're smart. Loaded down with valuables in a strange new environment, we stick out like jeweled thumbs. But being savvy and knowing what to look out for can dramatically reduce your risk of being targeted.

Pickpockets are your primary concern. To avoid them, be aware of your surroundings, don't keep anything valuable in your pockets, and wear a money belt (explained on page 53). In your money belt, carry your passport, credit and debit cards, and large

cash bills. Keep just a day's spending money in your pocket—if you lose that, it's no big deal.

Thieves thrive on tourist-packed public-transportation routes—especially buses that cover major sights (such as Rome's notorious #64). When riding the subway or bus, be alert at stops, when thieves can dash on and off with your day bag. Criminals—often dressed as successful professionals or even as tourists—will often block a bus or subway entry, causing the person behind you to "bump" into you.

Be wary of any unusual contact or commotion in crowded public places (especially touristy spots). For example, while being jostled at a crowded market, you might end up with ketchup or fake pigeon poop on your shirt. The perpetrator offers profuse apologies while dabbing it up—and pawing your pockets. Treat any disturbance (a scuffle breaking out, a beggar in your face) as a smokescreen for theft—designed to distract unknowing victims.

Europe also has its share of scam artists, from scruffy old women offering you sprigs of rosemary (and expecting money in return) to con artists running street scams, such as the shell game, in which players pay to guess which of the moving shells hides the ball (don't try it—you'll lose every time).

The most rampant scams are more subtle, such as being overcharged by a taxi driver (see the "Taxi Tips" sidebar, earlier). Another common scam is the "slow count": A cashier counts change back with odd pauses, in hopes the rushed tourist will gather up the money quickly without checking that it's all there. Waiters often pad the bill with mysterious charges—carefully scan the itemized bill and account for each item. If paying a small total with a large bill, clearly state the amount you're handing over, and be sure you get the correct change back.

Nearly all crimes suffered by tourists are nonviolent and avoidable. Be aware of the pitfalls of traveling, but relax and have fun.

Money

Whenever you leave the ship, you must use local currency. Most countries in this book (Spain, France, Italy, and Greece) use the euro; stock up on euros early in your trip, and use them throughout the region.

Some popular cruise-ship destinations, including Croatia and Turkey, as well as Israel and North African countries, don't officially use the euro. I've heard cruise-line employees tell their passengers, "We're only in the country for a day, and everyone takes euros, so you don't need to change money." It's true: Many merchants in these countries do accept euros. But exchange rates are bad, and some vendors might flat-out refuse euros. Plus, euros often aren't accepted on public transportation. That's why it's better to get local cash, even if in town just for a few hours. In most port cities, ATMs are easy to find (I've listed the nearest locations for each destination). But in some of the more out-of-way ports, exchanging a small amount of money for local currency at the cruise ship's front desk can save you time looking for an ATM.

Withdrawing Cash

Throughout Europe, cash machines (ATMs) are the standard way for travelers to get cash. When using an ATM, taking out large sums of money can reduce the number of per-transaction bank fees you'll pay. If the machine refuses your request, try again and select a smaller amount (some cash machines limit the amount you can withdraw—don't take it personally). If that doesn't work, try a different machine. For security, it's best to shield the keypad when entering your PIN at the ATM.

Most ATMs in Europe are located outside of a bank. Try to use the ATM when the branch is open; if your card is eaten by the machine, you can immediately go inside for help. If the ATM dispenses big bills, try to break them at a bank or larger store, since it's easier to pay for purchases at small businesses using smaller bills.

Avoid using currency exchange booths (lousy rates and/or outrageous fees); if you have foreign currency to exchange, take it to a bank.

To keep your cash safe, use a money belt (described on page 53). Don't waste time in every port tracking down a cash machine—withdraw several days' worth of money, stuff it in your money belt, and see the sights!

Using Credit and Debit Cards

Just like at home, credit or debit cards are generally accepted by larger restaurants and shops (smaller, family-run places usually

Damage Control for Lost or Stolen Cards

If you lose your credit, debit, or ATM card, you can stop people from using it by reporting the loss immediately to the respective global customer-assistance centers. Call these 24-hour US numbers collect: Visa (410/581-9994), MasterCard (636/722-7111), and American Express (623/492-8427).

At a minimum, you'll need to know the name of the financial institution that issued you the card, along with the type of card (classic, platinum, or whatever). Providing the following information will allow for a quicker cancellation of your missing card: full card number, whether you are the primary or secondary cardholder, the cardholder's name exactly as printed on the card, billing address, home phone number, circumstances of the loss or theft, and identification verification (your birth date, your mother's maiden name, or your Social Security number—memorize this, don't carry a copy). If you are the secondary cardholder, you'll also need to provide the primary cardholder's identification-verification details.

If you promptly report your card lost or stolen, you typically won't be responsible for any unauthorized transactions on your account, although many banks charge a liability fee of $50.

require cash). Some vendors will charge you extra for using a credit card. I typically use my credit card only in a few specific situations: to book hotel reservations by phone (for example, if staying in Europe before or after a cruise), to make major purchases, and to pay for things near the end of my trip (to avoid another visit to the ATM).

While you can use either a credit or a debit card for most purchases, using a credit card offers a greater degree of fraud protection (since debit cards draw funds directly from your bank account).

Chip and PIN: If your card is declined for a purchase in Europe, it may be because of chip and PIN, which requires cardholders to punch in a PIN instead of signing a receipt. Much of Europe—especially the north—is adopting this system (though, of the countries covered in this book, it's widely used only in France). Chip and PIN is used by some merchants and also at automated payment machines—such as those at train stations, parking garages, luggage lockers, and self-serve pumps at gas stations. If you're prompted to enter your PIN (but don't know it), ask if the cashier can print a receipt for you to sign instead, or just pay cash. If you're dealing with an automated machine that won't take your card, look for a cashier nearby who can make your card work. The easiest solution is to carry sufficient cash.

Dynamic Currency Conversion: If merchants offer to convert your purchase price into dollars (called dynamic currency conversion, or DCC), refuse this "service." You'll pay even more in fees for the expensive convenience of seeing your charge in dollars.

At Sights

Most cruise passengers are faced with far more to see and do than they have time for. That's why it's helpful to know what you can typically expect when visiting sights:

A modest **dress code** (no bare shoulders, shorts, or above-the-knee skirts) is enforced at some larger churches in Italy, such as St. Mark's in Venice and St. Peter's in Rome, but is often overlooked elsewhere. This applies to everyone, including kids. If you are caught by surprise, you can improvise, using maps to cover your shoulders and a jacket tied around your waist to hide your legs. (I wear a super-lightweight pair  of long pants rather than shorts for my hot and muggy, big-city Italian sightseeing.)

Some important sights have **metal detectors** or conduct **bag searches** that will slow your entry, while others may require you to check daypacks and coats. They'll be kept safely. If you have something you can't bear to part with, stash it in a pocket or purse. To avoid checking a small backpack, carry it under your arm like a purse as you enter. From a guard's point of view, a backpack is generally a problem, while a purse is not.

Flash **photography** is sometimes banned, but taking photos without a flash is usually OK. Look for signs or ask. Flashes damage oil paintings and distract others in the room. Even without a flash, a handheld camera will take a decent picture (or buy postcards or posters at the museum bookstore). If photos are permitted, video cameras are generally OK, too.

 Museums may have **special exhibits** in addition to their permanent collection. Some temporary exhibits are included in the entry price; others come at an extra cost (which you may have to pay even if you don't want to see that exhibit).

Many sights rent **audio-guides,** which generally

IN PORT

offer excellent recorded descriptions of the artwork. If you bring along your own pair of headphones and a Y-jack, two people can sometimes share one audioguide and save. Guided tours in English (widely ranging in quality) are most likely to occur during peak season. For information on my free audio tours, see page 1232.

Some sights run **short films** featuring their highlights and history. These are generally well worth your time—I make it standard operating procedure to ask when I arrive at a sight if there is a film.

Expect changes—artwork can be on tour, on loan, out sick, or shifted at the whim of the curator. To adapt, pick up any available free floor plans as you enter. Ask museum staff if you can't find a particular piece.

Most important sights have an **on-site café or cafeteria** (usually a good place to rest and have a snack or light meal). Museum WCs are free and generally clean.

Many places sell **postcards** that highlight their attractions. Before you leave, scan the postcards and thumb through the biggest guidebook (or skim its index) to be sure you haven't overlooked something at that sight that you'd like to see.

Most sights **stop admitting people** 30-60 minutes before closing time, and some rooms shut down early (often 45 minutes before the actual closing time). Guards will usher people out, so don't save the best for last.

For details on making **reservations** at major sights, see page 48.

Every sight or museum offers more than what's covered in this book. Use the information in this book as an introduction—not the final word.

Shopping

Shopping can be a fun part of any traveler's European trip. To have a good experience when you go ashore, be aware of the ins and outs of shopping in port.

At every stop, your cruise line will give you an information sheet that highlights local shopping specialties and where to buy them. Remember that these shops commonly give kickbacks to cruise lines and guides. This doesn't mean that the shop (or what it sells) isn't good quality; it just means you're probably paying top dollar.

Regardless of whether a store is working with the cruise line or not, many places jack up their rates when ships arrive, knowing they're about to get hit with a tidal wave of rushed and desperate

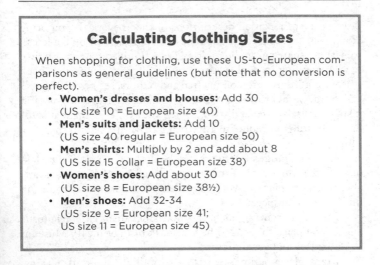

Calculating Clothing Sizes

When shopping for clothing, use these US-to-European comparisons as general guidelines (but note that no conversion is perfect).

- **Women's dresses and blouses:** Add 30
  (US size 10 = European size 40)
- **Men's suits and jackets:** Add 10
  (US size 40 regular = European size 50)
- **Men's shirts:** Multiply by 2 and add about 8
  (US size 15 collar = European size 38)
- **Women's shoes:** Add about 30
  (US size 8 = European size 38½)
- **Men's shoes:** Add 32-34
  (US size 9 = European size 41;
  US size 11 = European size 45)

shoppers. Remember: Europe's cruise season lasts approximately six months, and many people who live and work in that town must extract a year's worth of earnings from visitors during that period.

Finding Deals

So how can you avoid paying over-the-top, inflated prices for your treasured souvenirs? Go ahead and patronize the obvious tourist shops, but be sure to check out local shopping venues, too. Large department stores often have a souvenir section with standard knickknacks and postcards at prices way below those at cruise-recommended shops. These large stores generally work just like ours, and in big cities, most department-store staff are accustomed to wide-eyed foreign shoppers and can speak some English.

If you're adept at bargaining, head over to some of Europe's vibrant outdoor flea markets, where you can find local specialties and soft prices. In much of the Mediterranean world, haggling is the accepted (and expected) method of finding a compromise between the wishful thinking of both the merchant and the tourist.

Bargaining Tips: To be a successful haggler-shopper, first determine the item's value to you. Many tourists think that if they can cut the price by 50 percent they are doing great. So merchants quadruple their prices and the tourist happily pays double the fair value. The best way to deal with crazy prices is to ignore them. Show some interest in an item but say, "It's just too much money." You've put the merchant in a position to make the first offer.

Many merchants will settle for a nickel profit rather than lose a sale entirely. Work the cost down to rock bottom. When it seems to have fallen to a record low, walk away. That last price hollered out as you turn the corner is often the best price you'll get. If the price is right, go back and buy. And don't forget that prices often drop at the end of the day, when flea-market merchants have to think about packing up. For more specifics on haggling in Turkey—where bargaining is practically obligatory—see page 1176.

Getting a VAT Refund

Every year, tourists visiting Europe leave behind millions of dollars of refundable sales taxes. While for some, the headache of collecting the refund is not worth the few dollars at stake, if you do any serious shopping, it's hard cash—free and easy.

Wrapped into the purchase price of your souvenirs is a Value-Added Tax (VAT) of between 18 and 25 percent, depending on the country. Almost all European countries require a minimum purchase for a refund, ranging from about $30 to several hundred dollars. If you spend that minimum at a store that participates in the VAT-refund scheme, you're entitled to get most of that tax back. Getting your refund is usually straightforward and, if you buy a substantial amount of souvenirs, well worth the hassle. If you're lucky, the merchant will subtract the tax when you make your purchase. (This is more likely to occur if the store ships the goods to your home.) Otherwise, you'll need to:

Get the paperwork. Have the merchant completely fill out the necessary refund document, called a "Tax-Free Shopping Cheque." You'll have to present your passport at the store.

Get your stamp at the border or airport. Process your cheque(s) at your last stop in the EU (for example, at the airport) with the customs agent who deals with VAT refunds. It's best to keep your purchases in your carry-on for viewing, but if they're too large or dangerous (such as knives) to carry on, track down the proper customs agent to inspect them before you check your bag. You're not supposed to use your purchased goods before you leave. If you show up at customs wearing your chic Greek shirt, officials might look the other way—or deny you a refund.

Collect your refund. You'll need to return your stamped document to the retailer or its representative. Many merchants work with a service, such as Global Blue (www.global-blue.com) or Premier Tax Free (www.premiertaxfree.com), which have offices at major airports, ports, or border crossings. These services, which extract a 4 percent fee, can refund your money immediately in your currency of choice or credit your card (within two billing cycles). If the retailer handles VAT refunds directly, it's up to you to contact the merchant for your refund. You can also mail the documents from your point of departure (using a stamped, addressed envelope you've prepared or one that's been provided by the merchant). You'll then have to wait—it can take months.

Customs for American Shoppers

You are allowed to take home $800 worth of items per person duty-free, once every 30 days. The next $1,000 is taxed at a flat 3 percent. After that, you pay the individual item's duty rate. You can also bring in duty-free a liter of alcohol (slightly more than a standard-size bottle of wine; you must be at least 21), 200 cigarettes, and up to 100 non-Cuban cigars.

As for food, you can take home vacuum-packed cheeses; dried herbs, spices, or mushrooms; and canned fruits or vegetables, including jams and vegetable spreads. Baked goods, candy, chocolate, oil, vinegar, mustard, and honey are OK. Fresh fruits or vegetables (even that banana from your airplane breakfast) are not permitted. Meats are generally not allowed. Just because a duty-free shop in an airport sells a food product doesn't mean it will automatically pass US customs. Be prepared to lose your investment.

Note that you'll need to carefully pack any bottles of wine, jam, honey, oil, and other liquid-containing items in your checked luggage, due to the 3.2-ounce limit on liquids in carry-on baggage. To check customs rules and duty rates, visit www.cbp.gov, and click on "Travel," then "Know Before You Go."

Eating in Port

Eating in Europe is sightseeing for your taste buds. The memories of good meals can satisfy you for years. Even though most of your meals will be on the ship, you can still experience Europe's amazing cuisine when you're in port. Your options range from grabbing a lunch on the run to lingering over a leisurely meal at a sit-down restaurant. When deciding where to eat, be aware that table service in Europe is slow—sometimes painfully so—by American standards. Don't expect to dine and dash, but you can try explaining to the waitstaff that you're in a hurry.

Lunch on the Go

You can eat quickly and still have a local experience. Every country has its own equivalent of the hot-dog stand, where you can grab a filling bite on the go: French *crêperies,* Greek souvlaki stands, Italian pizza rustica take-out shops, and Turkish-style *döner kebab* and falafel kiosks. Or stop into a heavenly-smelling bakery and buy a pastry or sandwich.

Ethnic eateries are usually cheap; eat in, or get your meal to go. Cafeterias, delis, and fast-food chains with salad bars are tourist-friendly and good for a quick meal.

Picnicking takes a little more time and planning but can be an even more exciting cultural experience: It's fun to dive into a marketplace and actually get a chance to do business there. Europe's colorful markets overflow with varied cheeses, meats, fresh fruits, vegetables, and still-warm-out-of-the-oven bread. Most markets are not self-service: You point to what you want and let the merchant weigh and bag it for you. The unit of measure throughout the Continent is a kilo, or 2.2 pounds. A kilo has 1,000 grams. One hundred grams is a common unit of sale for cheese or meat—and just the right amount to tuck into a chunk of French bread for a satisfying sandwich.

Sit-Down Restaurants

For some cruisers, it's unimaginable to waste valuable port time lingering at a sit-down restaurant when they could be cramming their day with sightseeing. For others, a good European restaurant experience beats a cathedral or a museum by a mile.

To find a good restaurant, head away from the tourist center and stroll around until you find a place with a happy crowd of locals. Look for menus handwritten in the native language (usually posted outside) and offering a small selection. This means they're cooking what was fresh in the market that morning for loyal return customers.

Restaurants in Europe usually do not serve meals throughout the day, so don't wait too long to find a place for lunch. Typically restaurants close from the late afternoon (about 14:00) until the dinner hour.

When entering a restaurant, feel free to seat yourself at any table that isn't marked "reserved." Catch a server's eye and signal to be sure it's OK to sit there. If the place is full, you're likely to simply be turned away: There's no "hostess" standing by to add your name to a carefully managed waiting list.

If no English **menu** is posted, ask to see one. And be aware that the word "menu" can mean a fixed-price meal, particularly in France and Italy. What we call the menu in the US usually goes by some variation on the word "card" in Europe—for instance, *la carte* in French.

Many small eateries offer an economical "*menu* of the day" (*menú del día* in Spain, *plat du jour* in France, and *menù del giorno* in Italy)—a daily special with a fixed price. The "tourist *menu*" (*menù turistico* in Italy, *menu touristique* in France, *menú de turista* in Spanish), popular in restaurants throughout Europe's tourist zones, offers confused visitors a no-stress, three-course meal for a painless price that usually includes service, bread, and a drink. You normally get a choice of several options for each course. Locals rarely order this, but if the options intrigue you, the tourist *menu* can be a convenient way to sample some regional flavors for a reasonable, predictable price.

In restaurants, Europeans generally drink bottled **water** (for taste, not health), served with or without carbonation. You can normally get free tap water, but you may need to be polite, patient, inventive, and know the correct phrase. There's nothing wrong with ordering tap water, and it is safe to drink in all the countries in this book, except for Turkey.

One of the biggest surprises for Americans at Europe's restaurants is the service, which can seem excruciatingly slow when you're eager to get out and sightsee (or in a hurry to get back to your cruise ship). Europeans will spend at least two hours enjoying a good meal, and fast service is considered rude service. If you need to eat and run, make it very clear when you order.

To get the **bill,** you'll have to ask for it. Don't wait until you are in a hurry to leave. Catch the waiter's eye and, with raised hands, scribble with an imaginary pencil on your palm. Before it comes, make a mental tally of roughly how much your meal should cost. If the total is a surprise, ask to have it itemized and explained.

Tipping: Virtually anywhere in Europe, if you're pleased with the service, round up a euro or more. In most restaurants, 5 percent is adequate and 10 percent is considered a big tip. Please believe me—tipping 15-20 percent in Europe is unnecessary, if not culturally insensitive. Tip only at restaurants with waitstaff; skip the tip if you order food at a counter. Servers prefer to be tipped in cash even if you pay with your credit card; otherwise the tip may never reach them (specifics on tipping are also provided in each country's introduction chapter).

Cafés

Europeans are into café-sitting, coffee-sipping, and people-watching. If you simply want to slam down a cup of coffee, order and drink it at the bar. If you want to sit a while and check out the scene, grab a table with a view, and a waiter will take your order. This will cost you about double what it would at the bar (and sometimes an outdoor table is more expensive than an indoor one). If you're on a budget, always confirm the price for a sit-down drink. If you pay for a seat in a café with an expensive drink, that seat's yours for the entire afternoon if you like.

Returning to the Ship

When it's time to head back to your ship, remember that the posted departure time is a bit misleading: The "all aboard" time (when you

absolutely, positively must be on your ship) is usually a half-hour before departure. And the last shuttle bus or tender back to the ship might leave an hour before departure...trimming your port time even more. If you want to max out on time ashore, research alternative options—such as a taxi or a public bus—that get you back to the ship even closer to the "all aboard" time (but, of course, always be cautious not to cut it *too* close). Before leaving the ship, make sure you understand when you need to be back on board, and (if applicable) when the last shuttle bus or tender departs.

All of that said, feel free to take every minute of the time you've got. If the last tender leaves at 16:30, don't feel you need to get back to the dock at 16:00. I make it a point to be the last person back on the ship at every port...usually five minutes or so before "all aboard" time. I sometimes get dirty looks from early birds who've been waiting for a few minutes on that last tender, but I didn't waste their time...they did.

What If I Miss My Boat?

You can't count on the ship to wait for you if you get back late. If you're cutting it close, call ahead to the port agent and let them know you're coming. They will notify the ship's crew, so at least they know they didn't miscount the returning passengers. And there's a possibility (though a very slim one) that the ship could wait for you. But if it sets sail, and you're not on it, you're on your own to reach the next port. The cruise line will not cover any of your transportation or accommodations expenses, and you will not be reimbursed for any unused portion of your cruise.

You have approximately 24 hours to reach the ship before it departs from its next destination. Be clear on where the next stop is. If you're lucky, it's an easy two-hour train ride away, giving you bonus time in both destinations. If you're unlucky, it's a 20-hour overland odyssey or an expensive last-minute flight—or worse, the ship is spending the day at sea, meaning you'll miss out on two full cruising days.

First, ask the **port agent** for advice. The agent can typically give you a little help or at least point you in the right direction. Be aware that you'll be steered to the easiest, but not necessarily the most affordable, solution. For example, the agent might suggest hiring a private driver for hundreds of dollars, rather than taking a $50 bus ride.

You can also ask for help from the **TI,** if it's still open. Local **travel agencies** should know most or all of your connection options and can book tickets for you (they'll charge you a small commission). Or—to do it yourself—find an **Internet café** and get online to research your train, flight, and bus options. German Rail's handy, all-Europe train timetables are a good place to start: http://bahn.hafas.de/bin/query.exe/en. Check the website of the nearest airport; these usually show the schedule of upcoming flights in the next day or two. You can also search for cheap flights on www.skyscanner.net, www.wegolo.com, and www.whichbudget.com.

Don't delay in making your plans. The sooner you begin investigating your options, the more choices you may have. If you realize you've missed your ship at 20:00, there may be an affordable night train to the next stop departing from the train station across town at 21:00...and if you're not on it, you could pay through the nose for a last-minute flight instead.

The prospect of missing your ship is daunting, but don't let it scare you into not enjoying your shore time. As long as you keep a close eye on the time and are conservative in estimating how long it'll take you to get back to the ship, it's easy to enjoy a very full day in port and be the last tired but happy tourist sauntering back onto the ship.

Overnighting in Port

At some major destinations (most often in Barcelona, Rome, Venice, and Istanbul), the cruise ship might spend two full days and an overnight in port. This allows you to linger in the evening and really feel like you've been to a place—treating your cruise ship like a hotel.

With two-day port stops—or with two ports in a row that are close to each other (such as the French Riviera and Toulon, or Naples and Civitavecchia)—some adventurous travelers might opt to spend a night off the ship in order to get a break from the cruising lifestyle or overnight in a town away from the seafaring crowds. This is extra credit for very eager travelers—not recommended in most situations, but possible. If you do this, be sure to notify the officials aboard your ship that you won't be back that night. Any expenses you incur on land (hotels, train tickets, and so on) will be out of your own pocket, and you won't get any money back from the cruise line for days not spent on board.

PART III: MEDITERRANEAN CRUISE PORTS

MEDITERRANEAN CRUISE PORTS

The rest of this book focuses on specific cruise ports where you'll be spending your days. For each one, I've provided specific instructions for getting from the port into town, and included my suggested self-guided tours and walks for the best one-day plan in that town.

Rick Steves' Mediterranean Cruise Ports is a personal tour guide in your pocket, organized by destination. Each major destination is a mini-vacation on its own, filled with exciting sights, strollable neighborhoods, and memorable places to eat. You'll find the following sections in most of the destination chapters (although, because cruise port details can vary from place to place, not every destination will include all of these elements):

Planning Your Time suggests a schedule, with thoughts on how best to use your limited time in port. These plans are what I'd do with my time if I had only a few hours to spend in a particular destination, and assume that you're ambitious about spending the maximum amount of time in port sightseeing, rather than relaxing, shopping, or dining. For each option, I've suggested the amount of time you can reasonably expect to spend to get a good look at the highlights. If you find that my plan packs too much in, or shortchanges something you'd like to focus on, modify the plan by skipping one or two time-consuming options (read the descriptions in the chapters to decide which items interest you).

The **Excursions** sidebars help you make informed, strategic decisions about which cruise-line excursions to outlying destinations best match your interests.

Arrival at the Port sections provide detailed, step-by-step instructions for getting from your cruise ship to wherever you're going (whether it's to the city center, or, in some cases, to a nearby town). Each one begins with a brief "Arrival at a Glance" section to help you get oriented to your options. I've also tracked down helpful services (such as ATMs and Internet cafés) at or near each port.

Orientation includes specifics on public transportation, helpful hints, local tour options, easy-to-read maps, and tourist information.

Self-Guided Walk and Tours take you through interesting neighborhoods and world-class museums.

Sights describes the top attractions and includes their cost and hours. In these sections, the "At a Glance" sections offer a quick overview of the sightseeing options in town (though I've provided additional coverage only of the sights you're most likely to see during your limited time).

Eating serves up a range of options, from inexpensive fast food to fancy restaurants.

Shopping offers advice on the most authentic local souvenirs, and where to buy them.

The **What If I Miss My Boat?** sections give you a quick list of your options for reaching your next port, in case you get stranded.

The **Starting or Ending Your Cruise** sections in the most common embarkation/disembarkation ports (Barcelona, Rome/Civitavecchia, Venice, Athens/Piraeus, and Istanbul) give advice about how to connect from the airport to the cruise port, and list a few of my favorite hotels.

I've also included **country introductions** for each of the six countries with ports in this book (Spain, France, Italy, Croatia, Greece, and Turkey), including a quick description of the country and its main ports, and helpful logistical tips unique to that place (such as phoning, taking the train, and restaurant protocol).

Key to This Book
Updates
This book is updated regularly, but things change. For the latest, visit www.ricksteves.com/update, and for a valuable list of reports and experiences—good and bad—from fellow travelers, check www.ricksteves.com/feedback.

Abbreviations and Times
I use the following symbols and abbreviations in this book:

Sights are rated:

▲▲▲	Don't miss
▲▲	Try hard to see
▲	Worthwhile if you can make it
No rating	Worth knowing about

Tourist information offices are abbreviated as **TI,** and bathrooms are **WCs.**

CRUISE PORTS

Like Europe, this book uses the **24-hour clock** for schedules. It's the same through 12:00 noon, then keep going: 13:00, 14:00, and so on. For anything over 12, subtract 12 and add p.m. (14:00 is 2:00 p.m.).

When giving **opening times,** I include both peak season and off-season hours if they differ. So, if a museum is listed as "May-Oct daily 9:00-16:00," it should be open from 9 a.m. until 4 p.m. from the first day of May until the last day of October (but expect exceptions).

For **transit** or **tour departures,** I first list the frequency, then the duration. So, a train connection listed as "2/hour, 1.5 hours" departs twice each hour, and the journey lasts an hour and a half.

Sleep Code

In the cities where you're likely to begin or end your trip, I list a few of my favorite accommodations. To help you easily sort through these listings, I've divided the rooms into three categories, based on the price for a double room with bath:

$$$ Higher Priced
$$ Moderately Priced
$ Lower Priced

To give maximum information in a minimum of space, I use the following code to describe accommodations. Prices in this book are listed per room, not per person.

S = Single room, or price for one person in a double.
D = Double or twin room.
T = Three-person room.
Q = Four-person room.
b = Private bathroom with toilet and shower or tub.
s = Private shower or tub only. (The toilet is down the hall.)

SPAIN
España

SPAIN

España

Spain is in Europe, but not *of* Europe—it has a unique identity and history, thanks largely to the Pyrenees Mountains that physically isolate it from the rest of the Continent. Spain's seclusion contributed to the creation of unusual customs—bullfights, flamenco dancing, and a national obsession with ham.

Tourism is huge in Spain. With 45 million inhabitants, the country entertains 50 million visitors annually. The country's special charm lies in its people. From the stirring sardana dance to the sizzling rat-a-tat-tat of flamenco, Spain creates its own beat amid the heat.

The country's top cruise destination is Barcelona—a vibrant city that's a mix of old (the Barri Gòtic) and new (the Eixample), sprawling through a sun-baked basin, and hemmed in by dramatic mountains. This city of Romans, Visigoths, sailors, explorers, Pablo Picasso, and Modernista architect Antoni Gaudí offers a wide range of attractions within easy striking distance of its centrally located cruise port.

Practicalities

This section covers just the basics on traveling in Spain.

Tourist Information: www.spain.info

Money: Spain uses the euro currency: 1 euro (€) = about $1.40.

Theft Alert: Thieves target tourists throughout Spain, especially in Barcelona. They pick pockets and snatch purses. Thieves zipping by on motorbikes even grab handbags from pedestrians. Be on guard, use a money belt, and treat any disturbance around you as a smokescreen for theft. Don't believe any "police officers" looking for counterfeit bills.

Business Hours: Many shops are generally open Monday-Friday 9:00-13:00 and 16:00-20:00, open Saturday morning, and closed on Sunday.

Internet Access: It's easily available in Internet cafés; in Barcelona, try Navega Web on the Ramblas (see page 150).

Dress Code: At many churches, a modest dress code is encouraged and sometimes required (no bare shoulders, miniskirts, or shorts).

Trains: You can buy tickets at any train station, but many travelers prefer to buy tickets at travel agencies in Spain because there's less of a language barrier than at the station. El Corte Inglés department stores, located in bigger cities, often have handy travel agencies inside; in Barcelona, one is centrally located on Plaça de Catalunya.

Eating

By our standards, Spaniards eat late, having lunch—their biggest meal of the day—around 13:00-16:00, and dinner starting about 21:00.

For a quick and inexpensive meal, stop at a bar any time of day. Besides *bocadillos* (sandwiches), bars often have slices of *tortilla española* (potato omelet) and fresh-squeezed orange juice. For a fun early dinner at a bar, build a light meal out of tapas—small appetizer-sized portions of seafood, salads, meat-filled pastries, deep-fried tasties, and so on. While the smaller "tapa" size is handiest for maximum tasting opportunities, many bars sell only larger sizes: the *ración* (full portion) and *media-ración* (half-portion).

Jamón, an air-dried ham similar to prosciutto, is a Spanish

staple. Other key terms include *queso* (cheese), *tortilla* (omelet), *frito* (fried), *a la plancha* (grilled), and *surtido* (assortment).

Many bars have three price tiers. It's cheapest to eat or drink while standing at the bar (*barra*), slightly more to sit at a table inside (*mesa* or *salón*), and most expensive to sit outside *(terraza)*. Wherever you are, be assertive or you'll never be served. Saying *"Por favor"* (please) grabs the attention of the server or bartender.

If you're having tapas, don't worry about paying as you go (the bartender keeps track). When you're ready to leave, ask for the bill: "*¿La cuenta?*"

For a budget meal in a restaurant, try a *plato combinado* (combination plate), which usually includes portions of one or two main dishes, a vegetable, and bread for a reasonable price. The *menú del día* (menu of the day, also known as *menú turístico*) is a substantial three- to four-course meal that usually comes with a carafe of house wine.

Tipping: Most restaurants include a service charge in the bill *(servicio incluido)*, though it's customary to tip 5 percent extra for good service. If service is not included *(servicio no incluido)*, tip up to 10 percent.

Phoning

To make calls in Spain from any type of phone, get an international phone card *(tarjeta telefónica con código)*, sold locally at newsstands. The insertable cards *(tarjetas telefónicas)* work only at pay phones. For tips on using either kind of card, see page 120.

Dialing: All phone numbers in Spain are nine digits (no area codes) that can be dialed direct throughout the country. To **call within Spain,** just dial the nine-digit number. To **call to Spain,** start with the international access code (00 if calling from Europe, or 011 from North America), then dial 34 (Spain's country code), then the phone number. To **call home from Spain,** dial 00, 1, then your area code and phone number.

Directory Assistance: Tel. 11811 (€0.40/minute) or 11818 (€0.55/call from private numbers, free from phone booths)

Emergency Telephone Numbers:

Police Help: Tel. 091

Ambulance: Tel. 112 or 061

Passport Problems: Consulate General in Barcelona (tel. 932-802-227, after-hours emergency tel. 915-872-200) or US Embassy in Madrid (tel. 915-872-240, after-hours emergency tel. 915-872-200); Canadian Consulate in Barcelona (tel. 934-127-236) or Embassy in Madrid (tel. 913-828-400).

BARCELONA

Barcelona is Spain's second city, and the capital of the proud and distinct region of Catalunya. With Franco's fascism now ancient history, Catalan flags wave once again. And the local language and culture are on a roll in Spain's most cosmopolitan and European corner.

Barcelona bubbles with life in its narrow Barri Gòtic alleys, along the grand boulevards, and throughout the chic, grid-planned, new part of town, called Eixample. While Barcelona had an illustrious past as a Roman colony, Visigothic capital, 14th-century maritime power, and—in more modern times—a top Mediterranean textile and manufacturing center, you'll have more fun if you throw out the history books and just drift through the city. If you're in the mood to surrender to a city's charms, let it be in Barcelona.

Many cruises start or end in Barcelona. If that's the case for you, check the end of this chapter for airport information and recommended hotels.

Planning Your Time

You have several good options:

• Follow my self-guided walk down **the Ramblas,** the city's colorful pedestrian drag. Allow one hour.

• Visit the **Sagrada Família** church-in-progress started by Modernista architect Antoni Gaudí. Figure on two hours.

• Tour the **Picasso Museum.** Allow 1.5 hours (but note that it's closed Mon).

• Take my self-guided walk of the **Barri Gòtic** (historical center), including the cathedral. Allow two hours total.

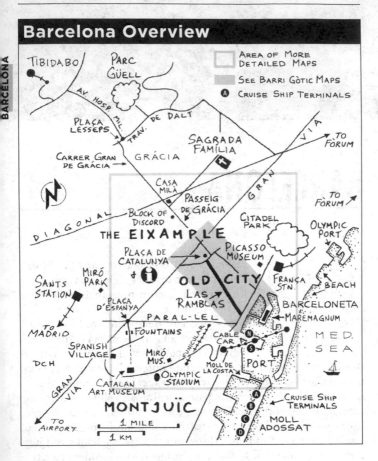

Barcelona Overview

BARCELONA

- TIBIDABO
- PARC GÜELL
- ☐ AREA OF MORE DETAILED MAPS
- ▨ SEE BARRI GÒTIC MAPS
- Ⓐ CRUISE SHIP TERMINALS

AV. HOSP. MIL.

PLAÇA LESSEPS

TRAV. DE DALT

SAGRADA FAMÍLIA

GRAN VIA

TO FORUM

CARRER GRAN DE GRÀCIA →

GRÀCIA

N

CASA MILÀ

PASSEIG DE GRÀCIA

GRAN VIA

TO FORUM

DIAGONAL

BLOCK OF DISCORD

THE EIXAMPLE

CITADEL PARK

OLYMPIC PORT

PLAÇA DE CATALUNYA

PICASSO MUSEUM

OLD CITY

FRANÇA STN.

BEACH

SANTS STATION

MIRÓ PARK

PLAÇA D'ESPANYA

LAS RAMBLAS

BARCELONETA

PARAL-LEL

MAREMAGNUM

TO MADRID

FOUNTAINS

FUNICULAR

CABLE CAR

MED. SEA

PORT

DCH

SPANISH VILLAGE

MIRÓ MUS.

MOLL DE LA COSTA

GRAN VIA

CATALAN ART MUSEUM

OLYMPIC STADIUM

MONTJUÏC

Ⓐ Ⓑ Ⓒ Ⓓ

CRUISE SHIP TERMINALS

MOLL ADOSSAT

TO AIRPORT

1 MILE

1 KM

Crowd Warning: Expect lines at the Sagrada Família and Picasso Museum, particularly in the morning.

Possible Itineraries

Gaudí Fans: Go to the Sagrada Família first (by bus, Metro, or taxi), then head to Plaça de Catalunya (by taxi or on foot), and take the self-guided walk down the Ramblas. (It's three miles from the Sagrada Família to the bottom of the Ramblas.) With any additional time, explore the Barri Gòtic. Allow at least five hours total.

If you want to see other Gaudí sights (such as Casa Milà and Casa Batlló on the Block of Discord), start with the Sagrada Família, taxi to the Block of Discord to visit the sights, then taxi to Plaça de Catalunya and walk down the Ramblas. Allow an additional hour to tour either Casa Milà (better choice) or Casa Batlló.

BARCELONA

Picasso Fans: Go to the Picasso Museum (by foot or taxi), then walk through the Barri Gòtic to Plaça de Catalunya, and take the self-guided walk down the Ramblas. Figure on a minimum of five hours.

Combining Picasso and Gaudí: Walk (or taxi) to the Picasso Museum, taxi to the Sagrada Família, taxi to Plaça de Catalunya, and walk down the Ramblas. Allow six hours.

Arrival at the Port of Barcelona

Arrival at a Glance: A shuttle bus zips you right to the center of town, within walking distance (or an easy Metro ride) of most sights. Or pay €10 for a taxi downtown.

Port Overview

Cruise ships arrive in Barcelona at one of seven different terminals, spread among three different ports (all of them just southwest of the Old Town, beneath the hill called Montjuïc). Most of the cruise terminals have a small TI desk, which is typically staffed when a big ship arrives.

Moll Adossat/Muelle Adosado: Most American cruise lines put in here, a long two miles from the bottom of the Ramblas. This port has four different modern, airport-like terminals (lettered A through D); each one has slightly different amenities (most have a café and shops; some have Internet access, a tour excursions counter, and other services).

Moll de la Costa: Tucked just beneath the hill called Montjuïc, this port has one cruise terminal.

World Trade Center: Just off the southern end of the Ramblas pedestrian street, this pier has two terminals: Terminal N (north) and Terminal S (south). Overhead is the Eiffel-like Torre Jaume I observation tower.

Getting into Town

Barcelona's port is relatively close to its main sights—from any of the cruise terminals, it's easy to reach the Ramblas, either by foot or by shuttle bus. Or you can splurge on a taxi.

By Taxi

Taxis meet each arriving ship and are waiting as you exit any of the terminal buildings. The short trip into town (to the bottom of the Ramblas) runs about €10—a good deal if you split the fare with

Excursions from Barcelona

Barcelona itself can easily occupy a visitor for a full day (and beyond). But you may also see excursions to the following out-of-town sights advertised. While each of these may appeal to someone with a special interest in the topic, for most visitors, they pale in comparison to the sights in Barcelona.

The town of **Figueres,** two hours north of Barcelona, is of sightseeing interest only for its Salvador Dalí Theater-Museum. But if you like Dalí, this is one of Europe's most enjoyable museums. Painted pink, studded with golden loaves of bread, and topped with monumental eggs and a geodesic dome, the building exudes Dalí's outrageous public persona. Because it's so far from town, it's worth considering only if you're a die-hard Dalí devotee.

The resort town of **Sitges,** 45 minutes south of Barcelona, has two attractions: Its tight-and-tiny Old Town, crammed with cafés and boutiques; and its nine long, luxurious beaches, extending about a mile south from town. If beach time is more appealing to you than big-city sights, this is a good option.

The dramatic mountaintop **Montserrat** monastery (about 1.5 hours northwest of Barcelona) has been Catalunya's most important pilgrimage site for a thousand years. A scenic cable-car ride takes you to the monastery, nestled in the jagged peaks at 2,400 feet. In a quick day trip, you can tour the basilica and museum, view a statue of the Black Virgin, hike to a sacred cave, and listen to Gregorian chants by the world's oldest boys' choir. Interesting as this site is, its substantial distance from Barcelona makes it worth a pilgrimage only for the faithful.

other travelers. During high season (May-Sept), when as many as six ships dock on the same day, a ride into town can take twice as long and cost €10 more. Legal supplements are posted on the taxi window: €2.10 port fee and €1 per bag.

For a one-way journey to other parts of town, expect to pay these fares:

- To the Picasso Museum or Plaça de Catalunya: €15
- To the Sagrada Família: €20
- To the airport: €35-40
- To Montserrat: €65

As always, it can cost more in busy times (for details, see page 154). The hourly touring rate is about €40. A round-trip to Montserrat (including waiting time at the site) costs about €150-160.

By Public Transportation

Getting to the sights requires two steps: First, you'll head to the Christopher Columbus Monument (Monument a Colóm), in the middle of the roundabout at the bottom of the Ramblas (at the square called Plaça de Colón). Then you'll connect—by foot, Metro, or bus—to wherever you're going in town.

Step 1: From Your Ship to the Columbus Monument

The procedure varies based on where you arrive: Remember that most cruise ships arrive at the Moll Adossat/Muelle Adosado terminals.

From the Moll Adossat/Muelle Adosado (Terminals A, B, C, and D): The walk into town, mostly through dreary docklands, is long (figure about 20 minutes from terminal A, and double that from terminal D). Instead, take the **shuttle bus** (*lanzadera*, #T3, a.k.a. Portbús, departs from parking lot in front of terminal—follow *Public Bus* signs, €3 round-trip, €2 one-way, buses leave every 20-30 minutes, timed to cruise ship arrival, tel. 932-986-000). This drops you right at the Columbus Monument; pay careful attention to where they drop you off, since you'll catch the return bus here later. Note: If your cruise arrives very early (before 8:30 or so), the shuttle bus may not be operating yet—you can either wait for the bus to start running, or pay for a taxi into town (about €10) to buy yourself a little more port time.

From the Moll de la Costa: Because you're not allowed to walk through this port area, you'll ride a free, private shuttle bus to near the World Trade Center, described next.

From the World Trade Center (Terminals N and S): From either terminal (or the bus stop from Moll de la Costa), you can easily walk into town: Head straight up the wide pier for about five minutes, bear right along the waterfront (walking alongside the long sandstone building), and you'll pop out at the Columbus Monument.

Step 2: From the Columbus Monument to Barcelona's Top Sights

From the Columbus Monument, you can already see (across the roundabout) Barcelona's main attraction: the delightful, tree-lined main people drag, the Ramblas. At the base of the Columbus Monument are a handy TI kiosk (pick up a free town map and get your questions answered here) and stops for both of the city's hop-on, hop-off tour buses (a handy way to get a quick look at this sprawling city—see page 153).

For most destinations in town (including the Barri Gòtic, cathedral, and Picasso Museum), the best plan is to walk to the Ramblas, then walk or take the Metro from there. For the Sagrada Família church, you can either take the Metro or ride a bus.

To the Ramblas and Points Beyond: From the Columbus Monument, it takes two minutes to walk to the Ramblas. From

Services near the Columbus Monument

Some of the cruise terminals offer an impressive array of services. But if you can't find what you want there, head for the Columbus Monument, which is the entry point into the city for cruise passengers.

ATMs: From the Columbus Monument, cross the two streets to the Ramblas. The first ATM you reach (at Santander Bank) is a block up from the bottom of the Ramblas, on the right-hand side. You'll find more ATMs farther up the Ramblas, and elsewhere in town.

Internet Access: If your cruise terminal doesn't have access, try one of the Internet cafés lining the Ramblas; the one closest to the Columbus Monument is inside the Subway/Sports Bar, two blocks up the Ramblas on the left-hand side (terminals and Wi-Fi inside the sports bar area, does not open until 12:00). A bigger place, Navega Web, is farther up the Ramblas; see page 150.

Pharmacy: From the Columbus Monument (with your back to the sea), cross the street on your right, then turn right down the street called Carrer de Josep Anselm Clavé (at the red corner house); a pharmacy is a block down on your right-hand side.

the shuttle-bus stop, stand with the sea to your back and cross the two streets ahead and to your right; you'll circle the roundabout and end up right at the bottom of the tree-lined Ramblas.

A few steps up the Ramblas, you'll come to the red "M" sign

marking the Drassanes **Metro** stop. This is on the handy L3 (green) line, with connections to the stops at Plaça de Catalunya (city center, explained below), Passeig de Gràcia (at the Block of Discord, and a connection to the L2/purple line to the Sagrada Família), and more. For a list of stops on this line—and how to buy and use tickets for the Metro—see page 151.

Before hopping on the Metro, consider your options: Both of this chapter's self-guided walks—of the Ramblas itself, and of the Barri Gòtic neighborhood—begin at the square called **Plaça de Catalunya,** which is at the top of the Ramblas, straight ahead. You can either walk, or—to save time—zip there on the Metro (take it two stops, to Plaça de Catalunya). If you choose to walk, you'll find it's an easy, fascinating, gently uphill, 30-minute stroll; however, if you're planning on taking my self-guided downhill walk of the Ramblas, you'll see all the same scenery on the way back down. While the Ramblas can get crowded, it's typically not too congested in the morning (when most cruise ships arrive).

To the Sagrada Família Church: You have two public-transit options for reaching Gaudí's fanciful cathedral. To take the **Metro,** follow the directions above, and change to the L2/purple line at Passeig de Gràcia, then ride to the Sagrada Família stop. If you want to avoid the transfer—and see some of the city as you travel—consider the **bus,** which you can catch less than a 10-minute walk from the Columbus Monument: With your back to the Ramblas, head out the long, skinny walkway across the harbor called Rambla del Mar. After crossing this bridge, turn left, go around the side of the big Maremagnum building, and find the Port Vell stop for bus #19 next to the building. This bus runs every 8-12 minutes to within a block of the church (València-Av Diagonal stop; ask the driver to tell you where to get off—sah-GRAH-dah fah-MEE-lee-yah?). From the bus stop, turn left around the corner (onto Carrer de Sicilia), then walk a block and you'll pop out at a park near the church. The Sagrada Família is also a stop on the **hop-on, hop-off bus tours** of the city.

By Tour

For information on local tour options in Barcelona—including local guides for hire, walking tours, and bus tours—see "Tours in Barcelona" on page 154.

Returning to Your Ship

If you're heading to the **World Trade Center** terminals—or the shuttle bus back to the **Moll de la Costa**—you can just walk there from the Ramblas.

If you're riding the shuttle bus back to the **Moll Adossat/Muelle Adosado,** you'll catch your bus at the Columbus Monument, but headed in the opposite direction from the bus you rode in on (as you face the water, buses going to the right head toward the port). If you miss the bus, you can hire a taxi to zip you to your ship. If you miss your boat, see the sidebar at the end of this chapter.

If you have some time to kill before heading back, linger along the Ramblas. Or dip into the Maritime Museum (partly closed through 2013), which is just across the roundabout from the Columbus Monument.

Orientation to Barcelona

Like Los Angeles, Barcelona is a basically flat city that sprawls out under the sun between the sea and the mountains. It's huge (1.6 million people, with about 4 million people in greater Barcelona), but cruise-ship travelers need only focus on three areas: the Old City, the harbor/Barceloneta, and the Eixample.

A large square, Plaça de Catalunya, sits at the center of Barcelona, dividing the older and newer parts of town. Sloping downhill from the Plaça de Catalunya is the Old City, with the boulevard called the Ramblas running down to the harbor. Above Plaça de Catalunya is the modern residential area called the Eixample. The Montjuïc hill overlooks the harbor. Outside the Old City, Barcelona's sights are widely scattered, but with a map and a willingness to figure out the sleek Metro system (or a few euros for taxis), all is manageable.

Here are more details per neighborhood:

The **Old City** is where you'll probably spend most of your time. This is the compact soul of Barcelona—your strolling, shopping, and people-watching nucleus. It's a labyrinth of narrow streets that once were confined by the medieval walls. The lively pedestrian drag called the **Ramblas**—one of Europe's great people-watching streets—runs through the heart of the Old City from Plaça de Catalunya down to the harbor. The Old City is divided into thirds by the Ramblas and another major thoroughfare, Via Laietana. To the west of the Ramblas is the **Raval,** enlivened by its university and modern-art museum. The Raval is of least interest to tourists (and, in fact, some parts of it are quite seedy and should be avoided). Far better is the **Barri Gòtic** (Gothic Quarter), between the Ramblas and Via Laietana, with the cathedral as its navel. To the east of Via Laietana is the trendy **Ribera** district (a.k.a. "El Born"), centered on the Picasso Museum and the Church of Santa Maria del Mar.

The **harborfront** has been energized since the 1992 Olympics. A pedestrian bridge links the Ramblas with the modern Maremagnum shopping/aquarium complex. On the peninsula across the harbor is **Barceloneta,** a traditional fishing neighborhood that's home to some good seafood restaurants and a string of sandy beaches. Beyond Barceloneta, a man-made beach, several miles long, leads east to the commercial and convention district called the **Fòrum.**

North of the Old City, beyond the bustling hub of Plaça de Catalunya, is the elegant **Eixample** district—its grid plan is softened by cut-off corners. Much of Barcelona's Modernista architecture is found here. To the north is the **Gràcia** district and, beyond that, Antoni Gaudí's **Parc Güell.**

The large hill overlooking the city to the southwest is **Montjuïc,** home to a variety of attractions, including some museums (Catalan Art, Joan Miró) and the Olympic Stadium. On a short visit, most cruisers skip this area in favor of other sights in town.

Apart from your geographical orientation, you'll need to orient yourself linguistically to a language distinct from Spanish. Although Spanish ("Castilian"/*castellano*) is widely spoken, the native tongue in this region is Catalan—nearly as different from Spanish as Italian (see the sidebar on pages 164-165).

Tourist Information

Barcelona's TI has numerous branches. Cruise passengers may find TI outposts in their cruise terminal, or visit the one at the Columbus Monument. The main branch is at **Plaça de Catalunya** (daily 9:00-21:00, under the main square—look for red sign, tel. 932-853-832). Other convenient branches include at the top of the **Ramblas** (daily 9:00-21:00, at #115); **Plaça de Sant Jaume,** just south of the cathedral (Mon-Fri 8:30-20:00, Sat 9:00-19:00, Sun 10:00-14:00); **Plaça d'Espanya** (daily July-Sept 10:00-20:00, Oct-June 10:00-16:00); **Plaça de Joan Carlos I** (Mon-Sat 10:00-19:00, Sun 10:00-14:00, at the intersection of Diagonal and Passeig de Gràcia at #107, tel. 932-388-091); the **airport** (daily 9:00-21:00, offices in both sections A and B of terminal 2); **Sants train station** (Mon-Fri 8:00-20:00, Sat-Sun 8:00-14:00, near track 6); **Nord bus station** (daily July-Sept 9:00-21:00, Oct-June 9:00-15:00); and more. Throughout the summer, young red-jacketed tourist-info helpers appear in the most touristy parts of town. The central information number for all TIs is 932-853-834 (www.barcelona turisme.cat).

At any TI, pick up the free city map, the small Metro map, and the free quarterly *See Barcelona* guide (practical information on museum hours, restaurants, transportation, history, festivals, and so on). The monthly *Barcelona Metropolitan* magazine and quarterly *What's On Barcelona* (both free and in English) have timely and substantial coverage of topics and events. The *Metro Walks* booklet (€2) details seven city walks combined with Metro rides. The TI is a handy place to buy tickets for the Tourist Bus (described later, under "Getting Around Barcelona").

The main TI, at Plaça de Catalunya, offers guided walks (described later, under "Tours in Barcelona"). Its Modernisme desk gives out a handy route map showing all the Modernista buildings and offers a sightseeing discount package (€12 for a great guidebook and 20 percent discounts to many Modernisme sites—worthwhile if going beyond my big three; for €18 you'll also get a guidebook to Modernista bars and restaurants).

Articket Card: This card is worth it only if you're planning to blitz through at least three art museums. It includes admission to seven art museums and their temporary exhibits, including the Picasso Museum, Casa Milà, Catalan Art Museum, and Fundació Joan Miró (€22, sold at TIs and participating museums, www .articketbcn.org). To skip the ticket-buying line at a museum, show your Articket Card (to the ticket-taker, at the info desk, or at the group entrance), and you'll get your entrance ticket pronto.

Helpful Hints

Theft Alert: You're more likely to be pickpocketed here—especially on the Ramblas—than about anywhere else in Europe. Most of the crime is nonviolent, but muggings do occur. Leave your valuables back on the ship and wear a money belt.

Street scams are easy to avoid if you recognize them. Most common is the too-friendly local who tries to engage you in conversation by asking for the time, talking sports, asking whether you speak English, and so on. Beware of thieves posing as lost tourists who ask for your help. A typical street gambling scam is the pea-and-carrot game, a variation on the shell game. The people winning are all ringers, and you can be sure that you'll lose if you play. Also beware of groups of women aggressively selling carnations, people offering to clean off a stain from your shirt, and people picking things up in front of you on escalators. If you stop for any commotion or show on the Ramblas, put your hands in your pockets before someone else does. Assume any scuffle is simply a distraction by a team of thieves. Crooks are inventive, so keep your guard up. Don't be intimidated...just be smart.

Some areas feel seedy and can be unsafe, especially after dark; I'd avoid the southern part of the Barri Gòtic (basically the two or three blocks directly south and east of Plaça Reial), and I wouldn't venture too deep into the Raval (just west of the Ramblas). One block can separate a comfy tourist zone from the junkies and prostitutes.

Internet Access: Navega Web has hundreds of computers for accessing the Internet and burning pictures onto a disk. It's conveniently located across from La Boquería market, downstairs in the bright Centre Comercial New Park (daily 10:00-24:00, Ramblas 88-94, tel. 933-179-193).

Pharmacy: A 24-hour pharmacy is near La Boquería market at #98 on the Ramblas.

Getting Around Barcelona

By Metro: Barcelona's Metro, among Europe's best, connects just about every place you'll visit. Rides cost €1.40. If you're traveling with a group, the shareable T10 Card is a great deal—€7.85 gives

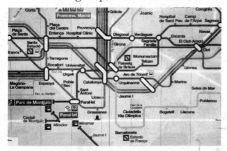

you 10 rides (cutting the per-ride cost nearly in half). It's good on all Metro and local bus lines as well as the RENFE train lines (including rides to the airport and train station). A day pass is also available (€5.90, www.tmb.cat). Automated machines at the Metro entrance have English instructions and sell all types of tickets (these can be temperamental about accepting bills, so try to have change on hand).

Pick up the free Metro map (at any TI) and study it to get familiar with the system. There are several color-coded lines, but most useful for tourists is the **L3 (green) line;** if you're sticking to my recommended sights and neighborhoods, you'll barely have use for any other line. Handy city-center stops on this line include (in order):

Sants Estació—Main train station

Espanya—Plaça d'Espanya

Paral-lel—Funicular to top of Montjuïc

Drassanes—Bottom of the Ramblas, near Columbus Monument, Maremagnum mall, and the cable car up to Montjuïc

Liceu—Middle of the Ramblas, near the heart of the Barri Gòtic and cathedral

Plaça de Catalunya—Top of the Ramblas and main square with TI, airport bus, and lots of transportation connections

Passeig de Gràcia—Classy Eixample street at the Block of Discord; also connection to L2 (purple) line to Sagrada Família and L4 (yellow) line (described below)

Diagonal—Gaudí's Casa Milà

Lesseps—Walk or catch bus #24 to Gaudí's Parc Güell

The **L4 (yellow) line,** which crosses the L3 (green) line at Passeig de Gràcia, is also useful. Helpful stops include **Jaume I** (between the Barri Gòtic/cathedral and La Ribera/Picasso Museum) and **Barceloneta** (at the south end of the Ribera, near the harbor action).

When you enter the Metro, first look for your line number

Barcelona at a Glance

In the sight listings below, a page number directs you to a fuller description in this chapter; sights without page numbers are not described further and generally don't make the cut for a one-day visit.

▲▲▲**Ramblas** Barcelona's colorful, gritty, tourist-filled pedestrian thoroughfare. **Hours:** Always open. See page 155.

▲▲▲**Picasso Museum** Extensive collection offering insight into the brilliant Spanish artist's early years. **Hours:** Tue-Sun 10:00-20:00, closed Mon. See page 173.

▲▲▲**Sagrada Família** Gaudí's remarkable, unfinished cathedral. **Hours:** Daily April-Sept 9:00-20:00, Oct-March 9:00-18:00. See page 184.

▲▲**City History Museum** One-stop trip through town history, from Roman times to today. **Hours:** Tue-Sat April-Oct 10:00-19:00, Nov-March 10:00-17:00, Sun 10:00-20:00, closed Mon. See page 172.

▲▲**Catalan Concert Hall** Best Modernista interior in Barcelona. **Hours:** 50-minute English tours daily every hour 10:00-15:00, plus frequent concerts. See page 177.

▲▲**Casa Milà** Barcelona's quintessential Modernista building, the famous melting-ice-cream Gaudí creation. **Hours:** Daily March-Oct 9:00-20:00, Nov-Feb 9:00-18:30. See page 180.

▲▲**Catalan Art Museum** World-class collection of this region's art, including a substantial Romanesque collection. **Hours:** Tue-Sat 10:00-19:00, Sun 10:00-14:30, closed Mon.

▲**Maritime Museum** Housed in an impressive medieval shipyard, it's a sailor's delight. **Hours:** Some exhibits closed for renovation, others daily 10:00-20:00. See page 167.

---

and color, then follow signs to take that line in the direction you're going. Insert your ticket into the turnstile (with the arrow pointing in), then reclaim it. On board, most trains have Metro-line diagrams with dots that light up next to upcoming destinations. Because the lines cross one another multiple times, there can be several ways to make any one journey. (It's a good idea to keep a general map with you—especially if you're transferring.) Watch your valuables. If I were a pickpocket, I'd set up shop along the

▲**Columbus Monument** Elevator ride to the best easy view in town. **Hours:** Daily May-Oct 9:00-20:30, Nov-April 10:00-18:30. See page 168.

▲**Cathedral of Barcelona** Colossal Gothic cathedral ringed by distinctive chapels. **Hours:** Daily 8:00-12:45 (until 13:45 on Sun) and 17:15-19:30. See page 168.

▲*Sardana* **Dances** Patriotic dance in which proud Catalans join hands in a circle. **Hours:** Every Sun at 12:00, usually also Sat at 18:00, no dances in Aug. See page 170.

▲**Church of Santa Maria del Mar** Catalan Gothic church in La Ribera, built by wealthy medieval shippers. **Hours:** Daily 9:00-13:30 & 16:30-20:00. See page 178.

▲**Barcelona's Beach** Fun-filled, man-made stretch of sand reaching from the harbor to the Fòrum. **Hours:** Always open.

▲**Block of Discord** Noisy block of competing Modernista facades by Gaudí and his rivals. **Hours:** Always viewable. See page 183.

▲**Palau Güell** Exquisitely curvy Gaudí interior. **Hours:** Tue-Sat 10:00-14:30, closed Sun-Mon. See page 184.

▲**Parc Güell** Colorful park at the center of an unfinished Gaudí-designed housing project. **Hours:** Daily 10:00-20:00. See page 189.

▲**Fundació Joan Miró** World's best collection of works by Catalan modern artist Joan Miró. **Hours:** Tue-Sat July-Sept 10:00-20:00, Oct-June 10:00-19:00, Thu until 21:30, Sun 10:00-14:30, closed Mon.

▲**Magic Fountains** Lively fountains near Plaça d'Espanya. **Hours:** Almost always May-Sept Thu-Sun 21:00-23:30, no shows Mon-Wed; Oct-April Fri-Sat 19:00-21:00, no shows Sun-Thu.

made-for-tourists L3/green line.

By Public Bus: Given the excellent Metro service, it's less likely you'll take a local bus (also €1.40 or covered by T10 Card, insert ticket in machine behind driver), although I've noted places where the bus makes sense—for example, bus #19 from near the Columbus Monument to the Sagrada Família.

By Tourist Bus: The handy hop-on, hop-off **Tourist Bus** (Bus Turístic) offers three multi-stop circuits in colorful double-decker buses that go topless in sunny weather. The two-hour blue route covers north Barcelona (most Gaudí sights); the two-hour red route covers south Barcelona (Barri Gòtic, Montjuïc); and the shorter, 40-minute green route covers the beaches and Fòrum. All have headphone commentary (44 stops, daily 9:00-22:00 in summer, 9:00-21:00 in winter, buses run every 5-25 minutes, most frequent in summer, no green route Oct-March). Ask for a brochure (includes city map) at

the TI or at a pickup point. One-day (€22) and two-day (€29) tickets, which you can buy on the bus or at the TI, offer 10-20 percent discounts on the city's major sights and walking tours, which will likely save you about the equivalent of half the cost of the Tourist Bus (www.barcelonabusturistic.cat). **Barcelona City Tour** has a similar operation and the same prices, but offers a €4 discount if you're over 65 (www.barcelonacitytour.com).

By Taxi: Barcelona is one of Europe's best taxi towns. Taxis are plentiful (there are more than 10,000) and honest (whether they like it or not—the light on top shows which tariff they're charging). They're also reasonable (€2 drop charge, €1/kilometer, these "*Tarif 2*" rates are in effect 7:00-21:00, pay higher "*Tarif 1*" rates off-hours, luggage-€1/piece, other fees posted in window). Save time by hopping a cab.

Tours in Barcelona

Walking Tours—The TI at Plaça de Sant Jaume offers great guided walks through the **Barri Gòtic** in English only (€12.50, daily at 10:00, 2 hours, groups limited to 35, buy your ticket 15 minutes early at the TI desk—not from the guide, in summer call ahead to reserve, tel. 932-853-832, www.barcelonaturisme.cat). A local guide explains the medieval story of the city as you walk from Plaça de Sant Jaume through the cathedral neighborhood, finishing back at City Hall on Plaça de Sant Jaume. The TI on Plaça de Catalunya offers a **Picasso** walk, taking you through the streets of his youth and early career and finishing in the Picasso Museum (€18, includes museum admission; Tue, Thu, and Sat at 16:00; 2 hours plus museum visit). The same TI also offers **gourmet** walks (€19, Fri and Sat at 10:00, 2 hours) and **Modernisme** walks (€12.50, Fri and Sat June-Sept at 18:00, Oct-May at 16:00, 2 hours).

Guided Bus Tours—The Barcelona Guide Bureau offers several sightseeing tours leaving from Plaça de Catalunya. Departure times can vary—confirm locally. The **Gaudí** tour visits the facades of Casa Batlló and Casa Milà, as well as Parc Güell and the Sagrada Família (€45, includes Sagrada Família admission, daily at 9:00, also at 15:15 mid-April-Oct, 3 hours). Other tours offered year-round include the **Montjuïc** tour (€33, includes Spanish Village admission, daily at 12:00, 3 hours); the **All Barcelona Highlights** tour (€60, includes Sagrada Família and Spanish Village admissions, daily at 9:00, 6 hours); and the **Montserrat** tour (€40, daily at 15:00, 4 hours), which offers a convenient way to get to this mountaintop monastery. From April through October, there's also the **Gaudí Plus** tour of "off-the-beaten-path masterpieces" (€30, daily at 12:30, 3 hours); and—for soccer fans—the **Barça** tour, which takes you to the Camp Nou stadium (€35, daily at 15:15, 3 hours). You can get detailed information and book tickets at a TI, on their website, or simply by showing up at their departure point on Plaça de Catalunya in front of the Hard Rock Café—look for the guides holding orange umbrellas. Buying tickets online can save you a few euros—usually about 10 percent (tel. 933-152-261, www.barcelonaguidebureau.com).

Local Guides—The Barcelona Guide Bureau is a co-op with about 20 local guides who give personalized four-hour tours (weekdays-€216, per-person price drops as group gets bigger; weekends and holidays-€256, no price break with size of group); **Joana Wilhelm** and **Carles Picazo** are excellent (Via Laietana 54, tel. 932-682-422 or 933-107-778, www.bgb.es). **Jose Soler** is a great and fun-to-be-with local guide who enjoys tailoring a walk through his hometown to your interests (€195/half-day per group, mobile 615-059-326, www.pepitotours.com, info@pepitotours .com).

Self-Guided Walks in Barcelona

Most visitors to Barcelona spend much of their time in the twisty, atmospheric Old City. These two walks will give meaning to your wandering. The first begins at Barcelona's main square and leads you down the city's main drag through one of Europe's best public spaces: the Ramblas. The second walk starts at the same square but guides you into the heart of the Barri Gòtic, to the neighborhood around Barcelona's impressive cathedral.

▲▲▲The Ramblas Ramble:
From Plaça de Catalunya down the Ramblas

Barcelona's central square and main boulevard exert a powerful pull. Many visitors spend the majority of their time doing laps on the Ramblas. While the allure of the Ramblas is fading (as tacky tourist shops and fast-food joints replace its former elegance), this

The Ramblas Ramble

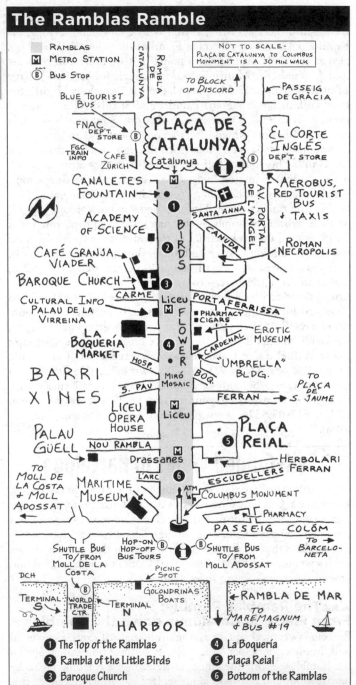

Ramblas
Ⓜ Metro Station
Ⓑ Bus Stop

NOT TO SCALE -
PLAÇA DE CATALUNYA TO COLUMBUS
MONUMENT IS A 30 MIN. WALK

RAMBLA DE CATALUNYA

TO BLOCK OF DISCORD

PASSEIG DE GRÀCIA

BLUE TOURIST BUS

FNAC DEP'T. STORE
Ⓑ

FGC TRAIN INFO

CAFÉ ZÜRICH

PLAÇA DE CATALUNYA
Catalunya ℹ

EL CORTE INGLÉS DEP'T. STORE

Ⓑ

CANALETES FOUNTAIN
Ⓜ Catalunya
❶

AV. PORTAL DE L'ANGEL

AEROBUS, RED TOURIST BUS + TAXIS

ACADEMY OF SCIENCE

BIRDS

SANTA ANNA

CAFÉ GRANJA VIADER
❷

CANUDA

ROMAN NECROPOLIS

BAROQUE CHURCH ✝ ❸

CARME

PORTAFERRISSA

CULTURAL INFO PALAU DE LA VIRREINA

Liceu Ⓜ

PHARMACY
CIGARS

EROTIC MUSEUM

LA BOQUERÍA MARKET

FLOWER

CARDENAL

"UMBRELLA" BLDG.

BARRI XINES

HOSP.

❹

R

TO PLAÇA DE S. JAUME

S. PAV

MIRÓ MOSAIC

BOQ.

FERRAN

LICEU OPERA HOUSE

Ⓜ Liceu

PLAÇA REIAL
❺

PALAU GÜELL

NOU RAMBLA

Ⓜ Drassanes

HERBOLARI FERRAN

TO MOLL DE LA COSTA + MOLL ADOSSAT

L'ARC

MARITIME MUSEUM

❻

ATM

ESCUDELLERS

COLUMBUS MONUMENT

PHARMACY

PASSEIG COLÓM

TO BARCELO- NETA

SHUTTLE BUS TO/FROM MOLL DE LA COSTA

HOP-ON HOP-OFF BUS TOURS Ⓑ

ℹ Ⓑ SHUTTLE BUS TO/FROM MOLL ADOSSAT

DCH

PICNIC SPOT

Ⓑ

TERMINAL S

WORLD TRADE CTR.

TERMINAL N

GOLONDRINAS BOATS

RAMBLA DE MAR

TO MAREMAGNUM + BUS #19

HARBOR

❶ The Top of the Ramblas
❷ Rambla of the Little Birds
❸ Baroque Church
❹ La Boquería
❺ Plaça Reial
❻ Bottom of the Ramblas

is still a fun people zone that offers a good introduction to the city. See it, but be sure to venture farther afield. Here's a top-to-bottom orientation walk.

Plaça de Catalunya: This vast central square divides old and new Barcelona. It's also the hub for the Metro, bus, airport

shuttle, and Tourist Bus (red northern route leaves from El Corte Inglés; blue southern route leaves from the west, or Ramblas, side of the square). Overlooking the square, the huge **El Corte Inglés** department store offers everything from bonsai trees to a travel

agency, plus one-hour photo developing, haircuts, and cheap souvenirs (Mon-Sat 10:00-22:00, closed Sun, pick up English directory flier, supermarket in basement, ninth-floor terrace cafeteria/restaurant has great city view—take elevator from entrance nearest the TI, tel. 933-063-800). Across the square from El Corte Inglés is **FNAC,** a French department store popular for electronics, music, and books (on west side of square—behind blue Tourist Bus stop; Mon-Sat 10:00-22:00, closed Sun).

Four great boulevards radiate from Plaça de Catalunya: the Ramblas; the fashionable Passeig de Gràcia (top shops, noisy with traffic); the cozier, but still fashionable, Rambla de Catalunya (most pedestrian-friendly); and the stubby, shop-filled and delightfully traffic-free Avinguda Portal de l'Angel. Homesick Americans can even find a Hard Rock Café. Locals traditionally start or end a downtown rendezvous at the venerable Café Zürich (at the corner near the Ramblas).

• *Cross the street from the café to...*

❶ **The Top of the Ramblas:** Begin your ramble 20 yards down at the ornate fountain (near #129). More than a Champs-Elysées, this grand boulevard takes you from rich (at the top) to rough (at the port) in a one-mile, 30-minute stroll. You'll raft the river of Barcelonan life past a grand opera house, elegant cafés, retread prostitutes, brazen pickpockets, power-dressing con men, artists, street mimes, an outdoor bird market, great shopping, and people looking to charge more for a shoeshine than what you paid for the shoes.

Grab a bench and watch the scene. Open up your map and read some history into it: You're about to walk right across medieval

Barcelona, from Plaça de Catalunya to the harbor. Notice how the higgledy-piggledy street plan of the medieval town was contained within the old town walls—now gone, but traced by a series of roads named Ronda (meaning "to go around"). Find the Roman town, occupying about 10 percent of what became the medieval town—with tighter roads yet around the cathedral. The sprawling modern grid plan beyond the Ronda roads is from the 19th century. Breaks in this urban waffle show where a little town was consumed by the growing city. The popular Passeig de Gràcia was literally the "Road to Gràcia" (once a separate town, now a characteristic Barcelona neighborhood).

Rambla means "stream" in Arabic. The Ramblas used to be a drainage ditch along the medieval wall that once defined what's now called the Barri Gòtic (Gothic Quarter). "Ramblas" is plural, a succession of five separately named segments, but address numbers treat it as a single long street. (In fact, street signs label it as "La Rambla," singular.) Because no streets cross the Ramblas, it has a great pedestrian feel.

You're at Rambla Canaletes, named for the fountain. The black-and-gold **Fountain of Canaletes** is the starting point for celebrations and demonstrations. Legend says that a drink from the fountain ensures that you'll return to Barcelona one day. All along the Ramblas, you'll see newspaper stands (open 24 hours, selling phone cards) and ONCE booths (selling lottery tickets that support Spain's organization of the blind, a powerful advocate for the needs of people with disabilities).

Got some change? As you wander downhill, drop coins into the cans of the human statues (the money often kicks them into entertaining gear). If you take a photo, it's considered good etiquette to drop in a coin. Warning: Wherever people stop to gawk, pickpockets are at work.

• *Walk 100 yards downhill to #115 and the...*

❷ **Rambla of the Little Birds:** Traditionally, kids bring their parents here to buy pets, especially on Sundays. Apartment-dwellers find birds, turtles, and fish easier to handle than dogs and cats. If you're walking by after-hours, you'll hear the sad sounds of little

tweety birds locked up in their collapsed kiosks.

Along the Ramblas, buildings with balconies that have flowers are generally living spaces; balconies with air-conditioners generally indicate offices. The Academy of Science's clock (at #115) marks official Barcelona time—synchronize. The Carrefour Express supermarket has cheap groceries (at #113, Mon-Sat 10:00-22:00, closed Sun, shorter checkout lines in back of store).

A recently discovered **Roman necropolis** is in a park across the street from the bird market, 50 yards behind the big, modern Citadines Hotel (go through the passageway at #122). Local apartment-dwellers blew the whistle on contractors, who hoped they could finish their building before anyone noticed the antiquities they had unearthed. Imagine the tomb-lined road leading into the Roman city of Barcino 2,000 years ago.

• *Another 50 yards takes you to Carrer del Carme (at #105), and a...*

❸ **Baroque Church:** The big Betlem church fronting the boulevard is Baroque, unusual in Barcelona. Note the Baroque-style sloping roofline, ball-topped pinnacles, and the scrolls above the entrance. And though Barcelona's Gothic age was rich (with buildings to prove it), the Baroque age hardly left a mark. (The city's importance dropped when New World discoveries shifted lucrative trade to ports on the Atlantic.)

For a sweet treat, head down the narrow lane behind the church (going uphill parallel to the Ramblas about 30 yards) to the recommended **Café Granja Viader,** which has specialized in baked and dairy delights since 1870. (For more sugary treats, follow "A Short, Sweet Walk" on page 195, which begins at the intersection in front of the church.)

• *Continue down the boulevard and stroll through the Ramblas of Flowers to the Metro stop marked by the red M (near #96), where you'll find...*

❹ **La Boquería:** This lively produce market is an explosion of chicken legs, bags of live snails, stiff fish, delicious oranges, and sleeping dogs (Mon-Sat 8:00-20:00, best mornings after 9:00, closed Sun, at #91). Originally outside the walls (as many medieval markets were), it expanded into the colonnaded courtyard of a now-gone monastery. Wander around—as local architect Antoni Gaudí used to—and gain inspiration. The Francesc Conserves shop sells 25 kinds of olives (straight in, near back on right, 100-gram minimum). Full legs of ham *(jamón serrano)* abound; *Paleta Ibérica de Bellota* hams are the best, and cost about €120 each. Beware:

Huevos del toro are bull testicles—surprisingly inexpensive...and oh so good. Drop by a café for an *espresso con leche* or breakfast *tortilla española* (potato omelet).

For a quick bite, visit the recommended **Pinotxo Bar** (just to the right as you enter the market), where animated Juan and his family are busy feeding shoppers. (Getting Juan to crack a huge smile and a thumbs-up for your camera makes a great shot...and he loves it.) The stools nearby are a fine perch for enjoying both your coffee and the people-watching. The market and lanes nearby are busy with tempting little eateries (see page 191).

• *Now turn your attention across the boulevard.*

The **Museum of Erotica** is your standard European sex museum (€9, daily 10:00-20:00, across from market at #96).

To the left, at #100, **Gimeno** sells cigars (appreciate the dying art of cigar boxes). Go ahead, do something forbidden in America but perfectly legal here...buy a Cuban (little singles for less than €1). Tobacco shops sell stamps and phone cards—and plenty of bongs and marijuana gear (the Spanish approach to pot is very casual).

Fifty yards farther, underfoot in the center of the Ramblas, find the much-trod-upon **anchor mosaic**—a reminder of the city's attachment to the sea. Created by noted abstract artist Joan Miró, it marks the midpoint of the Ramblas. (The towering Columbus Monument in the distance—hidden by trees—is at the end of this walk.)

Continue a few more steps down to the **Liceu Opera House.** From the Opera House, cross the Ramblas to Café de l'Opera for a beverage (#74). This bustling café, with Modernista decor and a historic atmosphere, boasts that it's been open since 1929, even during the Spanish Civil War.

• *Continue down the Ramblas to #46; turn left down an arcaded lane (Correr de Colom) to a square filled with palm trees.*

❺ **Plaça Reial:** This elegant Neo-classical square has a colonial (or maybe post-colonial) ambience. It comes complete with old-fashioned taverns, modern bars with patio seating, a Sunday coin-and-stamp market (10:00-14:00), Gaudí's first public works (the two colorful helmeted lampposts), and characters who don't need the palm trees to be shady. **Herbolari Ferran** is a fine and aromatic shop of herbs, with fun souvenirs such as top-quality saffron, or *safra* (Mon-Fri 9:30-14:00 & 16:30-20:00, closed Sat-Sun, downstairs at Plaça Reial 18—to the right as you enter the square). The small streets stretching toward the water from the square are intriguing, but less safe.

Back on the other side of the Ramblas, **Palau Güell** offers an enjoyable look at a Gaudí interior (Carrer Nou de la Rambla 3, partly closed for renovation in 2011, see page 184). This apartment was the first of Gaudí's innovative buildings, with a parabolic front doorway that signaled his emerging nonrectangular style.

• *Continue farther downhill on the Ramblas.*

❻ **Bottom of the Ramblas:** The neighborhood on the right-hand side, Barri Xines, is the world's only Chinatown with nothing even remotely Chinese in or near it. Named for the prejudiced notion that Chinese immigrants go hand-in-hand with poverty, prostitution, and drug dealing, the neighborhood's actual inhabitants are poor Spanish, North African, and Roma (Gypsy) people. At night, the Barri Xines is frequented by prostitutes, many of them transvestites, who cater to sailors wandering up from the port. Prostitution is nothing new here. Check out the thresholds at #22 and #24 (along the left side of the Ramblas)—with holes worn in long ago by the heels of anxious ladies.

The bottom of the Ramblas is marked by the city's giant medieval shipyards (on the right, now the Maritime Museum—partly closed for restoration through 2013) and the Columbus Monu-

ment (they are described on pages 167 and 168). Just beyond the Columbus Monument, **La Rambla del Mar** ("Rambla of the Sea") is a modern extension of the boulevard into the harbor. A popular wooden pedestrian bridge—with waves like the sea—leads to Maremagnum, a soulless Spanish mall with a cinema, a huge aquarium, restaurants, and piles of people.

▲▲The Barri Gòtic:
From Plaça de Catalunya to the Cathedral

Barcelona's Barri Gòtic, or Gothic Quarter, is a bustling world of shops and bars packed between otherwise uninteresting 14th- and 15th-century buildings. The section near the port is generally dull and seedy. But the area around the cathedral is a tangled-yet-inviting grab bag of undiscovered courtyards, grand squares, schoolyards, Art Nouveau storefronts, baby flea markets (on Thursdays), musty junk shops, classy antiques shops (on Carrer de

BARCELONA

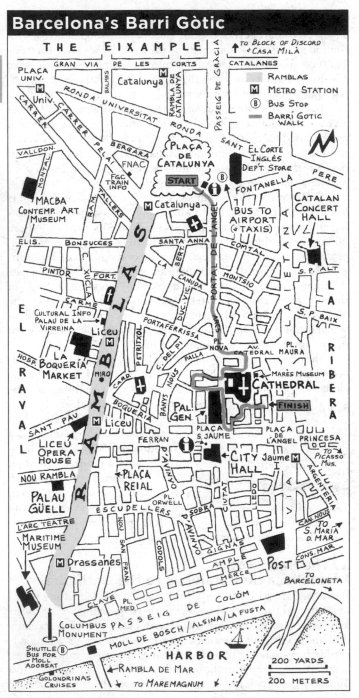

Barcelona's Barri Gòtic

THE EIXAMPLE

TO BLOCK OF DISCORD + CASA MILÀ

CATALANES

GRAN VIA DE LES CORTS

PLAÇA UNIV.

M Univ.

RONDA UNIVERSITAT

Catalunya

RAMBLA DE CATALUNYA

BALMES

CARRER PELAI

BERGARA

VALLDON.

TALLERS

FNAC

FGC TRAIN INFO

PLAÇA DE CATALUNYA

START

RONDA

SANT

El Corte Inglés Dep't. Store

PERE

| Ramblas |
| M Metro Station |
| B Bus Stop |
| Barri Gòtic Walk |

MACBA CONTEMP. ART MUSEUM

ELIS. BONSUCCES

PINTOR

XUCLA FORT.

CARME

CULTURAL INFO PALAU DE LA VIRREINA

M Catalunya

SANTA ANNA

LA BERT.

CANUDA

DUC. VIC.

PORTAFERRISSA

FONTANELLA

BUS TO AIRPORT (+ TAXIS)

COMTAL

MONTSIO

CATALAN CONCERT HALL

S. P. ALT

S. P. BAIX

LA

E L   R A V A L

Liceu M

LA BOQUERIA MARKET

HOSP.

SANT PAU

PINTOR XUCLA

C.

PETRITXOL

DEL PI

CARD.

PALLA

PL. NOVA

AV. CATEDRAL MAURA

MARÈS MUSEUM

CATHEDRAL

FINISH

R I B E R A

Liceu M

BOQUERIA

BANYS NOUS

PAL GEN.

PLAÇA S. JAUME

PLAÇA DE L'ANGEL

PRINCESA

LICEU OPERA HOUSE

FERRAN

D'AVINYO

i

CITY HALL

Jaume I M

TO PICASSO MUS.

NOU RAMBLA

PLAÇA REIAL

PL. ORWELL

CIUTAT

LEDO

ARGENTERIA

PALAU GÜELL

ESCUDELLERS

D'AVINYO

SOBRA

CAN. NOUS

TO S. MARÍA D. MAR

L'ARC TEATRE

NOU

CODOLS

GIGNAS

CONS. MAR

MARITIME MUSEUM

M Drassanes

SAN FRAN.

AMPLE

MERCE

POST

TO BARCELONETA

CLAVE

PL. MED.

AMPLE

COLUMBUS MONUMENT

PASSEIG   DE   COLÓM

MOLL DE BOSCH / ALSINA / LA FUSTA

SHUTTLE B BUS FOR MOLL ADOSSAT

GOLONDRINAS CRUISES

HARBOR

RAMBLA DE MAR

TO MAREMAGNUM

200 YARDS

200 METERS

la Palla), street musicians strumming Catalan folk songs, and balconies with domestic jungles behind wrought-iron bars. Go on a cultural scavenger hunt. Write a poem. This self-guided walk gives you a structure, covering the main sights and offering a historical overview before you get lost.

• *Start on Barcelona's bustling main square.*

Plaça de Catalunya: This square is the center of the world for seven million Catalan people. The square (described on page 157) is decorated with the likenesses of important Catalans. From here, walls that contained the city until the 19th century arc around in each direction to the sea. Looking at your map of Barcelona, you'll see a regimented waffle design—except for the higgledy-piggledy old town corralled by these walls.

The city grew with its history. Originally a Roman town, Barcelona was ruled by the Visigoths from the fall of Rome until 714, when the Moors arrived (they were, in turn, sent packing by the French in 801—because their stay was cut so short, there are few Moorish-style buildings here). Finally, in the 10th century, the Count of Barcelona unified the region, and the idea of Catalunya came to be. The area between Plaça de Catalunya and the old Roman walls (circling the smaller ancient town, down by the cathedral) was settled by churches, each a magnet gathering a small community outside the walls (or "extra muro"). Around 1250, when these "extra muro" communities became numerous and strong enough, the king agreed to invest in a larger wall, and Barcelona expanded. This outer wall was torn down in the 1850s and replaced by a series of circular boulevards (named Rondas).

• *From Plaça de Catalunya's TI, head downhill, crossing the busy street (Calle Fontanella) into a broad pedestrian boulevard called...*

Avinguda Portal de l'Angel: This boulevard is named "Gate of the Angel" for the gate in the medieval wall—crowned by an angel—that once stood here. The angel kept the city safe from plagues and bid voyagers safe journey as they left the security of the city. Imagine the fascinating scene here at the Gate of the Angel, where Barcelona stopped and the wilds began.

While walking down the Avinguda Portal de l'Angel, consider an optional detour a half-block right on **Carrer de Santa Ana,** where a lane on the right leads into a courtyard facing one of those "extra muro" churches, with a fine cloister and simple, typically Romanesque facade.

Continuing down the main boulevard (Avinguda Portal de l'Angel), you reach a fork in the road with a blue-and-yellow-tiled **fountain.** This was once a freestanding well—in the 17th century, it was the last watering stop for horses before leaving town. Take the left fork to the cathedral (past the Architects' House, with its Picasso-inspired frieze).

"You're not in Spain, You're in Catalunya!"

This is a popular nationalistic refrain you might see on T-shirts or stickers around town. Catalunya is *not* the land of bullfighting and flamenco that many visitors envision when they think of Spain (best to wait until you're in Madrid or Sevilla for those).

The region of Catalunya—with Barcelona as its capital—has its own language, history, and culture, and the people have a proud, independent spirit. Historically, Catalunya ("Cataluña" in Spanish, sometimes spelled "Catalonia" in English) has often been at odds with the central Spanish government in Madrid. The Catalan language and culture were discouraged or even outlawed at various times in Spanish history, as Catalunya often chose the wrong side in wars and rebellions against the kings in Madrid. In the Spanish Civil War (1936-1939), Catalunya was one of the last pockets of democratic resistance against the military coup of the fascist dictator Francisco Franco, who punished the region with four decades of repression. During that time, the Catalan flag was banned—but locals vented their national spirit by flying their football team's flag instead.

Three of Barcelona's monuments are reminders of Franco-era suppression. Citadel Park (Parc de la Ciutadella) was originally a much-despised military citadel, constructed in the 18th century to keep locals in line. The Castle of Montjuïc, built for similar reasons, has been the site of numerous political executions, including hundreds during the Franco era. The Sacred Heart Church atop Tibidabo, completed under Franco, was meant to atone for the sins of Barcelonans during the Spanish Civil War—the main sin being opposition to Franco. Although rivalry between Barcelona and Madrid has calmed down in recent times, it rages any time

Enter the square, where you'll stand before two bold **towers**— the remains of the old Roman wall that protected a smaller Barcino, as the city was called in ancient times. The big stones that make up the base of the towers are actually Roman. The wall stretches left of the towers, incorporated into the Deacon's House, which you'll enter from the other side later.

• *The sights from here on are located on the map on page 162. Walk around—past the modern bronze letters* BARCINO *and the mighty façade of the cathedral (which we'll enter momentarily)—and go inside the...*

the two cities' football clubs meet.

To see real Catalan culture, look for the *sardana* dance (described on page 170) or an exhibition of *castellers*. These teams of human-castle builders come together for festivals throughout the year to build towers of flesh that can reach more than 50 feet high, topped off by the bravest member of the team—a child! The Gràcia festival in August and the Mercè festival in September are good times to catch the *castellers*.

The Catalan language is irrevocably tied to the history and spirit of the people here. Since the end of the Franco era in the mid-1970s, the language has made a huge resurgence. Now most school-age children learn Catalan first and Spanish second. Although Spanish is understood here (and the basic survival words are the same), Barcelona speaks Catalan.

Here are the essential Catalan phrases:

English	Catalan	Pronounced
Hello	*Hola*	OH-lah
Please	*Si us plau*	see oos plow
Thank you	*Gracies*	GRAH-see-es
Goodbye	*Adéu*	ah-DAY-oo
Exit	*Sortida*	sor-TEE-dah
Long live Catalunya!	*¡Visca Catalunya!*	BEE-skah kah-tah-LOON-yah

Most place names in this chapter are listed in Catalan. Here's a pronunciation guide:

Plaça de Catalunya	PLAS-sah duh cat-ah-LOON-yah
Eixample	eye-SHAM-plah
Passeig de Gràcia	PAH-sage duh grass-EE-ah
Catedral	KAH-tah-dral
Barri Gòtic	BAH-ree GOH-teek
Montjuïc	MOHN-jew-eek

Deacon's House (Casa de l'Ardiaca): Visitors are welcome inside this mansion, which today functions as the city archives (its front door faces the wall of the church). It's free to enter and a good example of a Renaissance nobleman's palace. Notice how the century-old palm tree seems to be held captive by urban man. Inside you can see the Roman stones up close. Upstairs affords a good view of the cathedral's exterior—textbook Catalan Gothic (plain and practical, like this merchant community) next to textbook Romanesque (the smaller, once freestanding, more humble church adjacent on the right, which you'll visit entering from its cloister later).

• *Exit the house to the left and follow the lane. You'll emerge at the entrance to the...*

Cathedral of Barcelona (Catedral de Barcelona): This huge house of worship is worth a look. Its vast size, peaceful cloister, and many ornate chapels—each one sponsored by a local guild—are impressive. For a self-guided tour, see the "Cathedral of Barcelona" listing on page 168.

• *After visiting the cathedral's cloister, exit and walk to the tiny lane ahead on the right (far side of the statue, Carrer de Montjuïc del Bisbe). This leads to the cute...*

Plaça Sant Felip Neri: This square serves as the playground of an elementary school bursting with youthful energy. The Church of Sant Felip Neri, which Gaudí attended, is still pocked with bomb damage from the Civil War. As a stronghold of democratic, anti-Franco forces, Barcelona saw a lot of fighting. The shrapnel that damaged this church was meant for the nearby Catalan government building (Palau de la Generalitat, described below).

Study the medallions on the wall. Guilds powered the local economy, and the carved reliefs here show that this building must have housed the shoemakers. In fact, on this square you'll find a fun little Shoe Museum (described on page 172).

• *Circle the block back to the cathedral's cloister and take a right, walking along Carrer del Bisbe next to the huge building (on the right), which stretches all the way to the next square.*

Palau de la Generalitat: For more than 600 years, this place has been the home of the Catalan government. Through good times and bad, the Catalan spirit has survived, and this building has housed its capital.

• *Continue along Carrer del Bisbe to...*

Plaça de Sant Jaume (jow-mah): This stately central square of the Barri Gòtic, once the Roman forum, has been the seat of city government for 2,000 years. Today the two top governmental buildings in Catalunya face each other: the Barcelona City Hall (Ajuntament; free but only open to the public Sun 10:00-13:30) and the seat of the autonomous government of Catalunya (Palau de la Generalitat, described above). It always flies the Catalan flag (red and yellow stripes) next to the obligatory Spanish one. From these balconies, the nation's leaders (and soccer heroes) greet the people on momentous days.

• *Take two quick left turns from the corner of Carrer Bisbe (just 10 yards away), and climb Carrer del Paridís. Follow this street as it turns right, but pause when it swings left, at the summit of...*

"Mont" Tàber: A millstone in the corner marks ancient Barcino's highest elevation, a high spot in the road called Mount Tàber. A plaque on the wall says it all: "Mont Tàber, 16.9 meters." Step into the courtyard for a peek at a surviving corner of the imposing **Roman temple** (Temple Roma d'August) that once stood here on Mont Tàber, keeping a protective watch over Barcino (free, well-explained on wall in English, daily 10:00-14:00 & 16:00-20:00).

• *Continue down Carrer del Paridís back to the cathedral, take a right, and go downhill about 100 yards to...*

Plaça del Rei: The Royal Palace sat on this "King's Square" (a block from the cathedral) until Catalunya became part of Spain in the 15th century. Then it was the headquarters of the local Inquisition. In 1493, a triumphant Christopher Columbus, accompanied by six New World natives (whom he called "Indians") and several pure-gold statues, entered the Royal Palace. King Ferdinand and Queen Isabel rose to welcome him home, and they honored him with the title "Admiral of the Oceans."

• *Your tour is over. Nearby, just off Plaça del Rei, is the City History Museum. The Frederic Marès Museum is just up the street (toward the cathedral entrance; both described later). Or simply wander and enjoy Barcelona at its Gothic best.*

Sights in Barcelona

While Barcelona's attractions could easily fill a longer visit (see the "Barcelona at a Glance" sidebar, earlier), for a one-day cruiser visit, I've listed just the sights that are most important and centrally located.

Barcelona's Old City

I've divided Barcelona's Old City sights into three neighborhoods: near the harbor, at the bottom of the Ramblas; the cathedral and nearby (Barri Gòtic); and the Picasso Museum and nearby (La Ribera).

On the Harborfront, at the Bottom of the Ramblas

▲**Maritime Museum (Museu Marítim)**—Barcelona's medieval shipyard, the best preserved in the entire Mediterranean, has an impressive collection covering the salty history of ships and navigation from the 13th to the 20th centuries. Riveting for nautical types, and interesting for anyone, its modern and beautifully presented exhibits will put you in a seafaring mood. The museum is undergoing a major renovation, closing off large sections one at a time through 2013, so what you see will depend on when you visit. The museum's cavernous halls evoke the 14th-century days when Catalunya was a naval and shipbuilding power, crank-

ing out 30 huge galleys a winter. As in the US today, military and commercial ventures mixed and mingled as Catalunya built its trading empire. The excellent included audioguide tells the story and explains the various seafaring vessels displayed—including an impressively huge and richly decorated royal galley (€2.50, prices may change as more exhibits reopen, daily 10:00-20:00, last entry at 19:30, breezy courtyard café, Avinguda de la Drassanes, tel. 933-429-920, www.mmb.cat).

▲**Columbus Monument (Monument a Colóm)**—Marking the point where the Ramblas hits the harbor, this 200-foot-tall monument built for an 1888 exposition offers an elevator-assisted view from its top. The tight four-person elevator takes you to the glassed-in observation area at the top for congested but sweeping views (€3, daily May-Oct 9:00-20:30, Nov-April 10:00-18:30). It was here in Barcelona that Ferdinand and Isabel welcomed Columbus home after his first trip to America. It's ironic that Barcelona would so honor the man whose discoveries ultimately led to its downfall as a great trading power.

***Golondrinas* Cruises**—At the harbor near the foot of the Columbus Monument, tourist boats called *golondrinas* offer two different unguided trips. The shorter version goes around the harbor in 35 minutes (€6.50, daily on the hour 11:30-19:00, every 30 minutes mid-June-mid-Sept, may not run Nov-April—call ahead, tel. 934-423-106). The longer 1.5-hour trip goes up the coast to the Fòrum complex and back (€13.50, can disembark at Fòrum in summer only, about 7/day, daily 11:30-19:30, shorter hours in winter).

▲Cathedral of Barcelona

Most of the construction on Barcelona's vast cathedral (Catedral de Barcelona) took place in the 14th century, during the glory days of

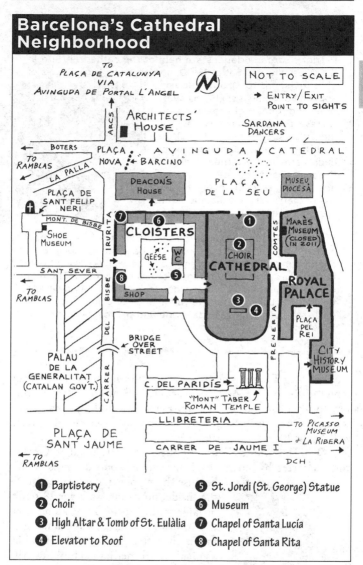

Barcelona's Cathedral Neighborhood

TO PLAÇA DE CATALUNYA VIA AVINGUDA DE PORTAL L'ANGEL

NOT TO SCALE

→ ENTRY / EXIT POINT TO SIGHTS

ARCHITECTS' HOUSE

SARDANA DANCERS

ARCS

BOTERS

TO RAMBLAS

LA PALLA

PLAÇA NOVA

BARCINO

AVINGUDA CATEDRAL

DEACON'S HOUSE

PLAÇA DE LA SEU

MUSEU DIOCESÀ

PLAÇA DE SANT FELIP NERI

MONT. DE BISBE

SHOE MUSEUM

SANT SEVER

IRURITA

❼ ❻ CLOISTERS

GEESE WC

❺

❶

❷ CHOIR CATHEDRAL

COMTES

MARÈS MUSEUM (CLOSED IN 2011)

ROYAL PALACE

BISBE

❽

SHOP

❸

❹

DEL

BRIDGE OVER STREET

FRENERIA

PLAÇA DEL REI

CITY HISTORY MUSEUM

PALAU DE LA GENERALITAT (CATALAN GOV'T.)

CARRER

C. DEL PARIDÍS

"MONT" TÀBER ROMAN TEMPLE

LLIBRETERIA

TO PICASSO MUSEUM & LA RIBERA

PLAÇA DE SANT JAUME

TO RAMBLAS

CARRER DE JAUME I

DCH

❶ Baptistery
❷ Choir
❸ High Altar & Tomb of St. Eulàlia
❹ Elevator to Roof
❺ St. Jordi (St. George) Statue
❻ Museum
❼ Chapel of Santa Lucía
❽ Chapel of Santa Rita

the Catalan nation. The facade was humble, so in the 19th century the proud local bourgeoisie redid it in a more ornate Neo-Gothic style.

Cost and Hours: Strangely, even though the cathedral is free to enter daily 8:00-12:45 (until 13:45 on Sun) and 17:15-19:30, you must pay €5 to enter between 12:45 and 17:15 (tel. 933-151-554). The dress code is strictly enforced; don't wear tank tops, short shorts, or short skirts.

Sardana Dances

Patriotic *sardana* dances are held at the cathedral (Sun at 12:00, usually also Sat at 18:00, no dances in Aug). Locals of all ages seem to spontaneously appear. For some it's a highly sym-  bolic, politically charged action representing Catalan unity—but for most it's just a fun chance to kick up their heels. Participants gather in circles after putting their things in the center—symbolic of community and sharing (and the ever-present risk of theft). All are welcome, even tourists cursed with two left feet.

Holding hands, dancers raise their arms—slow-motion, *Zorba the Greek*-style—as they hop and sway gracefully to the music. The band *(cobla)* consists of a long flute, tenor and soprano oboes, strange-looking brass instruments, and a tiny bongo-like drum *(tambori)*. The rest of Spain mocks this lazy circle dance, but considering what it takes for a culture to survive within another culture's country, it is a stirring display of local pride and patriotism. The event lasts between one and two hours.

Getting There: The huge, can't-miss-it cathedral is in the center of the Barri Gòtic, on Plaça de la Seu. For an interesting way to reach the cathedral from Plaça de Catalunya, and some commentary on the surrounding neighborhood, see my self-guided walk of the Barri Gòtic (page 161).

◉ **Self-Guided Tour:** Though the cathedral is Gothic and supported by buttresses, it has smooth outside walls. That's

because the supporting buttresses are on the inside, providing walls for 28 richly ornamented chapels. This, along with the interior's open and spacious feeling, is characteristic of Catalan Gothic. Typical of all medieval churches, the cathedral has an "ambulatory" plan, allowing worshippers to amble around to the chapel of their choice.

Although the main part of the church is fairly plain, the **chapels,** sponsored by local guilds, show great wealth. Located in the community's most high-profile space, they provided a kind of advertising to illiterate worshippers. The Native Americans that Columbus brought to town were supposedly **baptized** in the first chapel on the left.

The chapels ring a finely carved 15th-century **choir** *(coro)*. For €2.20 (no charge if you paid church entry fee), you can enter and get a close-up look (with the lights on) of the ornately carved stalls and the emblems representing the various Knights of the Golden Fleece who once sat here. The chairs were folded up, giving VIPs stools to lean on during the standing parts of the Mass. Each was creatively carved, and—since you couldn't sit on sacred things—the artists were free to enjoy some secular and naughty fun here. Study the upper tier of carvings.

The **high altar** sits upon the **tomb** of Barcelona's patron saint, Eulàlia. She was a 13-year-old local girl tortured 13 times by Romans for her faith before finally being crucified on an X-shaped cross. Her X symbol is carved on the pews. Climb down the stairs for a close look at her exquisite marble sarcophagus. Many of the sarcophagi in this church predate the present building.

You can ride the **elevator** to the roof for a view (€2.50, no charge if you paid church entry fee, Mon-Fri 10:30-18:00, Sat 10:00-12:00, closed Sun, start from chapel left of high altar).

Enter the **cloisters** (through arch, right of high altar). Once inside, look back at the arch, an impressive mix of Romanesque

and Gothic. Nearby, a tiny **statue** of St. George slaying the dragon stands in the garden. Jordi (George) is one of the patron saints of Catalunya and by far the most popular boy's name here. Cloisters are generally found in monasteries, but this church has one because it needed to accommodate more chapels—to make more money. With so many wealthy merchants in town who believed that their financial generosity would impress God and win them favor, the church needed more private chapel space. Merchants wanted to be buried close to the altar, and their tombs also spill over into the cloister. Notice on the pavement stones, as in the chapels, the symbols of the trades or guilds: scissors, shoes, bakers, and so on.

Long ago the resident **geese**—there are always 13, in memory of Eulàlia—functioned as an alarm system. Any commotion would get them honking, alerting the monk in charge. They honk to this very day.

From the statue of St. Jordi, circle to the right (past a WC hidden on the left). The skippable little €2 **museum** (far corner; no charge if you paid church entry fee) is one plush room with a dozen old religious paintings. Just beyond the museum, in the corner, built into the outside wall of the cloister, is the dark, barrel-vaulted

Romanesque **Chapel of Santa Lucía,** a small church that predates the cathedral. People hoping for good eyesight (Santa Lucía's specialty) leave candles outside. Farther along the cloister, the **Chapel of Santa Rita** (her forte: impossible causes) usually has the most candles.

In the Barri Gòtic, near the Cathedral

For an interesting route from Plaça de Catalunya to the cathedral neighborhood, see my self-guided walk of the Barri Gòtic (page 161). And if you're in town on a weekend, don't miss the *sardana* dances (see sidebar).

Shoe Museum (Museu del Calçat)—Shoe-lovers enjoy this two-room shoe museum, watched over by an earnest attendant. The huge shoes at the entry are designed to fit the foot of the Columbus Monument at the bottom of the Ramblas (€2.50, Tue-Sun 11:00-14:00, closed Mon, one block beyond outside door of cathedral cloister, behind Plaça de G. Bachs on Plaça Sant Felip Neri, tel. 933-014-533).

▲▲**City History Museum (Museu d'Història de la Ciutat)**— Walk through the history of the city with the help of an included audioguide. First watch the nine-minute introductory video in the small theater (playing alternately in Catalan, Spanish, and English)—it's worth viewing in any language. Then take an elevator down 65 feet (and 2,000 years—see the date spin back while you descend) to stroll the streets of Roman Barcelona. You'll see sewers, models of domestic life, and bits of an early-Christian church. Finally, an exhibit in the 11th-century count's palace shows you Barcelona through the Middle Ages (€7, free all day first Sun of month and other Sun from 15:00 in summer; Tue-Sat April-Oct 10:00-19:00, Nov-March 10:00-17:00, Sun 10:00-20:00, last entry 30 minutes before closing, closed Mon; Plaça del Rei, enter on Vageur street, tel. 932-562-122).

Frederic Marès Museum (Museu Frederic Marès)—This museum, which has been closed for renovation, may reopen by the summer of 2011. When open, its eclectic collection of local artist (and packrat) Frederic Marès sprawls around a peaceful courtyard through several old Barri Gòtic buildings. The biggest part of the collection is sculpture, hailing from ancient times to the early 20th century. But even more interesting is Marès' vast collection of items he found representative of everyday life in the 19th century—rooms upon rooms of fans, stamps, pipes, and other bric-a-brac, all lovingly displayed. There are also several sculptures by Frederic Marès himself, and temporary exhibits (closed for part of 2011; when it reopens, €4.20 admission may change, but hours and free days will stay the same: free Wed and Sun from 15:00; open Tue-Sat 10:00-19:00, Sun 10:00-20:00, closed Mon; Plaça de Sant Iu 5-6, tel. 932-563-500, www.museumares.bcn.cat). The delightfully tranquil courtyard café offers a nice break, even when the museum is closed.

▲▲▲Picasso Museum (Museu Picasso)

This is the best collection in the country of the work of Spaniard Pablo Picasso (1881-1973), and—since he spent his formative years

(age 14-21) in Barcelona— it's the best collection of his early works anywhere. By seeing his youthful, realistic art, you can more fully appreciate the artist's genius and better understand his later, more challenging art. The collection is scattered through several connected Gothic palaces, six blocks from the cathedral in the Ribera district (for more on this area, see page 177).

Cost and Hours: €9, free all day first Sun of month and other Sun from 15:00, open Tue-Sun 10:00-20:00, closed Mon, Montcada 15-23, ticket office at #21, Metro: Jaume I, tel. 932-563-000, www.museupicasso.bcn.cat. The ground floor has a required bag check, as well as a handy array of other services (bookshop, WC, and cafeteria).

Crowd-Beating Tips: There's almost always a line, sometimes with waits of more than an hour (about 25 people are admitted every 10 minutes). Mornings until 13:00 and all day Tuesday are busiest. If you have an Articket Card (see page 149), skip the line by going to the "Meeting Point" entrance. You can also skip the line by buying your ticket online at www.museupicasso.bcn.cat (no additional fee).

Eating: The museum itself has a good **café**. Nearby, the **Textil Café,** hiding in a beautiful and inviting museum courtyard across the street, is a decent place to sip a *café con leche* or eat a light meal (Tue-Sun 12:00-24:00, closed Mon, 30 yards from Picasso Museum at Montcada 12-14, tel. 932-954-657; also hosts jazz concerts Sunday nights 20:30-23:00, weather permitting—usually not in winter, no cover, but you have to order something). And just down the street is a neighborhood favorite for tapas, the recommended **El Xampanyet** (closed Mon).

Background: Picasso's personal secretary amassed a huge collection of his work and bequeathed it to the city. Picasso, happy to have a museum showing off his work in the city of his youth, added to the collection throughout his life. (Sadly, since Picasso vowed never to set foot in a fascist, Franco-ruled Spain, and died two years before Franco, the artist never saw the museum.)

❍ **Self-Guided Tour:** Though the rooms are sometimes rear-ranged, the collection (291 paintings) is always presented chronologically. With the help of thoughtful English descriptions for each stage (and blue-shirted guards who don't let you stray), it's easy to follow the evolution of Picasso's work. The room numbers—though not exact—can help you get oriented in the museum. You'll see his art evolve in these stages:

Room 1—Boy Wonder, Age 12-14: Pablo's earliest art is realistic and serious. A budding genius emerges at age 12, as Pablo moves to Barcelona and gets serious about art. Even this young, his portraits of grizzled peasants show great psychological insight and flawless technique. You'll see portraits of Pablo's first teacher, his father *(El Padre del Artista)*. Displays show his art-school work. Every time Pablo starts breaking rules, he's sent back to the standard classic style. The assignment: Sketch nude models to capture human anatomy accurately. Early self-portraits (1896, 1897) show the self-awareness of a blossoming intellect (and a kid who must have been a handful in junior high school). When Pablo was 13, his father quit painting to nurture his young prodigy. Look closely at the portrait of his mother *(Retrato de la Madre del Artista)*. Pablo, then age 15, is working on the fine details and gradients of white in her blouse and the expression in her cameo-like face. Notice the signature. Spaniards keep both parents' surnames, with the father's first, followed by the mother's: Pablo Ruiz Picasso. Pablo was closer to his mom than his dad, and eventually he kept just her name.

Room 2—Adolescence, Developing Talent: During a short trip to Málaga, Picasso dabbles in Impressionism (otherwise unknown in Spain at the time). As a 15-year-old, Pablo dutifully enters art-school competitions. His first big work—while forced to show a religious subject *(Primera Comunión, or First Communion)*—is more an excuse to paint his family. Notice his sister Lola's exquisitely painted veil. This piece was heavily influenced by local painters.

Room 3—Early Success: *Ciencia y Caridad (Science and Charity)*, which won second prize at a fine-arts exhibition, got Picasso the chance to study in Madrid. Now Picasso conveys real feeling. The doctor (Pablo's father) represents science. The nun represents charity and religion. From her hopeless face and lifeless hand, it seems that Picasso believes nothing will save this woman from death. Pablo painted a little perspective trick: Walk back and forth across the room to see the bed stretch and shrink. Three small studies for this painting, hanging in the back of the room, show how this was an exploratory work. The frontier: light.

Picasso travels to Madrid for further study. Finding the stuffy fine-arts school in Madrid stifling, Pablo hangs out in the Prado Museum and learns by copying the masters. Notice his nearly perfect copy of Philip IV by Diego Velázquez. Having absorbed the wisdom of the ages, in 1898 Pablo visits Horta de San Juan, a rural Catalan village, and finds his artistic independence. Poor and without a love in his life, he returns to Barcelona.

Room 4—Barcelona Freedom, 1900: Art Nouveau is all the rage. Upsetting his dad, Pablo quits art school and falls in with the avant-garde crowd. These bohemians congregate daily at Els Quatre Gats ("The Four Cats," slang for "a few crazy people"—a popular restaurant to this day). Further establishing his artistic freedom, he paints portraits—no longer of his family...but of his new friends. Still a teenager, Pablo puts on his first one-man show.

Rooms 5-7—Paris, 1900-1901: Nineteen-year-old Picasso arrives in Paris, a city bursting with life, light, and love. Dropping the paternal surname Ruiz, Pablo establishes his commercial brand name: "Picasso." Here the explorer Picasso goes bohemian and befriends poets, prostitutes, and artists. He paints Impressionist landscapes like Claude Monet, cancan dancers like Toulouse-Lautrec, still lifes like Paul Cézanne, and bright-colored Fauvist works like Henri Matisse. (*La Espera*—with her bold outline and strong gaze—pops out from the Impressionistic background.) It was Cézanne's technique of "building" a figure with "cubes" of paint that inspired Picasso to invent Cubism soon.

Temporary Exhibits: As if to cleanse the museumgoer's palate before plunging into the major works, you'll now walk through some temporary exhibits.

Room 8—Blue Period, 1901-1904: The bleak Paris weather, the suicide of his best friend, and his own poverty lead Picasso to his "Blue Period." He cranks out piles of blue art just to stay housed and fed. With blue backgrounds (the coldest color) and depressing subjects, this period was revolutionary in art history. Now the artist is painting not what he sees but what he feels. The touching portrait of a mother and child, *Desamparados* (*Despair*, 1903), captures the period well. Painting misfits and street people, Picasso, like Velázquez and Toulouse-Lautrec, sees "the beauty in ugliness." Back home in Barcelona, Picasso paints his hometown at night from rooftops *(Azoteas de Barcelona)*. The paintings still blue, here we see proto-Cubism...five years before the first real Cubist painting.

Room 9—Rose Period, 1904-1907: The woman in pink *(Retrato de la Señora Canals),* painted with classic "Spanish melancholy," finally lifts Picasso out of his funk, moving him out of the blue and into a happier "Rose Period" (of which this museum has only the one painting).

Room 11—Cubism, 1907-1920: Pablo's invention in Paris of the shocking Cubist style is well-known—at least I hope so, since this museum has no true Cubist paintings. In the age of the camera, the Cubist gives just the basics (a man with a bowl of fruit) and lets you finish it. (In the museum you'll see some so-called "Synthetic Cubist" paintings—a later variation that flattens the various angles, as opposed to the purer, original "Analytical Cubist" paintings, in which you can simultaneously see several 3-D facets of the subject.)

Also in Rooms 9 and 10—Eclectic, 1920-1950: Picasso is a painter of many styles. In *Mujer con Mantilla* (Room 9), we see a little Post-Impressionistic Pointillism in a portrait that looks like a classical statue. After a trip to Rome, he paints beefy women, inspired by the three-dimensional sturdiness of ancient statues. To Spaniards, the expressionist horse symbolizes the innocent victim (Room 10). In bullfights, the horse—clad with blinders and pummeled by the bull—has nothing to do with the fight. To Picasso, the horse symbolizes the feminine, and the bull, the masculine. Picasso mixes all these styles and symbols—including this image of the horse—in his masterpiece *Guernica* (in Madrid's Centro de Arte Reina Sofía) to show the horror and chaos of modern war.

• *From here, backtrack through Rooms 8-11, and follow signs for* Ending/Collection *to Rooms 12-14.*

Rooms 12-14—Picasso and Velázquez, 1957: Notice the small print of Velázquez's *Las Meninas* (the original is displayed in Madrid's Prado). Picasso, who had great respect for Velázquez, painted more than 50 interpretations of this piece that many consider the greatest painting by anyone, ever. These two Spanish geniuses were artistic equals. Picasso seems to enjoy a relationship with Velázquez. Like artistic soul mates, they spar and tease. He dissects Velázquez, and then injects playful uses of light, color, and perspective to horse around with the earlier masterpiece. In the big black-and-white canvas, the king and queen (reflected in the mirror in the back of the room) are hardly seen, while the self-portrait of the painter towers above everyone. The two women of the court on the right look like they're in a tomb—but they're wearing party shoes. In these rooms, see the fun Picasso had playing paddleball with Velázquez's masterpiece—filtering Velázquez's realism through the kaleidoscope of Cubism.

Picasso said many times that "Paintings are like windows open to the world." In Room 14, we see the French Riviera—with simple black outlines and Crayola colors, Picasso paints sun-splashed nature and the joys of the beach. He died with brush in hand, still growing. To the end, Picasso continued exploring and loving life through his art. As a child, he was taught to paint as an adult. Now, as an old man (with little kids of his own and also-childlike artist Marc Chagall for a friend), he paints like a child.

Rooms 15-16—Ceramics, 1947: As a wrap-up, walk through this room with 41 ceramic works Picasso made during his later years.

In La Ribera, near the Picasso Museum

There's more to the Ribera neighborhood than just the Picasso Museum. While the nearby waterfront Barceloneta district was for the working-class sailors, La Ribera housed the wealthier shippers and merchants. Its streets are lined with their grand mansions—which, like the much-appreciated Church of Santa Maria del Mar, were built with shipping wealth.

La Ribera (also known as "El Born") is separated from the Barri Gòtic by Via Laietana, a four-lane highway built through the Old City in the early 1900s to alleviate growing traffic problems. From the Plaça de l'Angel (nearest Metro stop: Jaume I), cross this busy street to enter an up-and-coming zone of lively and creative restaurants and nightlife. The Carrer de l'Argenteria ("Goldsmiths Street"—streets in La Ribera are named after the workshops that used to occupy them) runs diagonally from the Plaça de l'Angel straight down to the Church of Santa Maria del Mar. The Catalan Concert Hall is to the north.

▲▲Catalan Concert Hall (Palau de la Música Catalana)— This concert hall, finished in 1908, features my favorite Modernista interior in town (by Lluís Domènech i Muntaner). Inviting arches lead you into the 2,138-seat hall. A kaleidoscopic skylight features a choir singing around the sun, while playful carvings and mosaics celebrate music and Catalan culture. You can only get in by tour, which starts with a relaxing 12-minute video (€12, 50-minute tours in English run daily every hour 10:00-15:00, may have longer hours on weekends and holidays, tour times may change based on performance schedule, about 6 blocks northeast of cathedral, tel. 932-957-200, www.palaumusica.org).

The Catch: You must buy your ticket in advance to get a spot on an English guided tour (tickets available up to 7 days in advance—ideally buy yours at least 2 days before, though they're sometimes available the same day or day before). You can buy the ticket in person at the concert hall box office (open daily 9:30-15:30); by phone with your credit card (toll tel. 902-485-475); or online at the concert hall website (€1 fee, www.palaumusica.org).

It might be easier to get tickets for a **concert** (300 per year, tickets for some performances as cheap as €7, see website for details).

Barcelona's La Ribera

TO CATALAN
CONCERT HALL

M METRO STATION

TO
CATHEDRAL
+ RAMBLAS

CHOCOLATE
MUSEUM

PL. PONS
I CLERCH

CARDERS

C. DE LA BORIA

BOUGER

ASSAONADORS

PLAÇA
DE
L'ANGEL

CARRER   DE   LA   PRINCESA

M Jaume I

COTONERS

BARRA DE FERRO

CARRER   DE

COMERÇ

PICASSO
MUSEUM

VIGATANS

FUSINA

CARRER DE L'ARGENTERIA

GRUNYÍ

5

FLASSADERS

C. DEL REC

DE BAYS VELLS

3   BROSOL

D'EN ROSIC

MIRALLERS

DEL

BORN
MARKET

MANRESA

2

4   MONTCADA

MOSQUES

DE LA NAU

ABAIX

SOMBRERERS

PASSEIG DEL BORN

ANT

LAIETANA

SANTA
MARIA
DEL MAR

VIDRIERA

RIBERA

VIA

CANVIS NOUS

PL. STA.
MARIA

STA. MARIA

ESPARTERIA

1

PESCATERIA

REC

SANT JOAN

CARRER

AGULLERS

CANVIS VELLS

ASES

PL.
OLLES

RERA PAL.

POST

CONSOLAT DE MAR

LA
LLOTJA

PLAÇA
DEL
PALAU

MARQUÈS   DE   L'ARGENTERIA

FRANÇA
TRAIN
STN.

PLAÇA
ANTONI
LOPEZ

AVINGUDA   DEL

TO
MAREMAGNUM
+ BARCELONETA

TO
M Barceloneta

❶ 1714 Massacre
   Monument

❷ Sagardi Euskal Taberna
   Rest. & Bar

❸ Taller de Tapas

❹ El Xampanyet Bar

❺ Textil Café

▲**Church of Santa Maria del Mar**—This church is the proud centerpiece of La Ribera. "Del Mar" means "of the sea," and that's where the money came from. The proud shippers built this church in only 55 years, so it has a harmonious style that is considered pure Catalan Gothic. As you step in, notice the figures of workers carved into the big front doors. During the Spanish Civil War (1936-1939), the Church sided with the conservative forces of Franco against the people. In retaliation, the working class took their anger out on this church, burning all of its wood furnishings

and decor (carbon still blackens the ceiling). Today it's stripped down—naked in all its Gothic glory. The tree-like columns inspired Gaudí (their influence on the columns inside his Sagrada Família church is obvious). Sixteenth-century sailors left models of their ships at the foot of the altar for Mary's protection. Even today there remains a classic old Catalan ship at Mary's feet. As within Barcelona's cathedral, here you can see the characteristic Catalan Gothic buttresses flying inward, defining the chapels that ring the nave (free entry, daily 9:00-13:30 & 16:30-20:00).

Exit the church from the side, and you arrive at a square with a modern **monument** to a 300-year-old massacre that's still part of the Catalan consciousness. On September 11, 1714, the Bourbon king ruling from Madrid massacred Catalan patriots, who were buried in a mass grave on this square. From that day on, the king outlawed Catalan culture and its institutions (no speaking the language, no folk dances, no university, and so on). The eternal flame burns atop this monument, and 9/11 is still a sobering anniversary for the Catalans.

From behind the church, the **Carrer de Montcada** leads two blocks to the Picasso Museum (described earlier). The street's mansions—built by rich shippers centuries ago—now house galleries, shops, and even museums. The Picasso Museum itself consists of five such mansions laced together.

Passeig del Born—Just behind the church, this long square was formerly a jousting square (as its shape indicates). This is the neighborhood center and a popular springboard for exploring tapas bars and fun restaurants in the narrow streets all around. Wandering around here, you'll find piles of inviting and intriguing little restaurants (I've listed my favorites on page 194). Enjoy a glass of wine on the square facing the church.

Chocolate Museum (Museu de la Xocolata)—This museum, only a couple of blocks from the Picasso Museum, is a delight for chocolate-lovers. Operated by the local confectioners' guild, it tells the story of chocolate from Aztecs to Europeans via the port of Barcelona, where it was first unloaded and processed. But the history lesson is just an excuse to show off a series of remarkably ornate candy sculptures. These works of edible art—which change every year but often include such Spanish themes as Don Quixote or bullfighting—begin as store-window displays for Easter or Christmas. Once the holiday passes, the confectioners bring the sculptures here to be enjoyed (€4.30, Mon and Wed-Sat

10:00-19:00, Sun 10:00-15:00, closed Tue, Carrer Comerç 36, tel. 932-687-878, www.museuxocolata.com).

The Eixample: Modernisme and Antoni Gaudí

Wide sidewalks, hardy shade trees, chic shops, and plenty of Art Nouveau fun make the Eixample a refreshing break from the Old City. For the best Eixample example, ramble Rambla de Catalunya (unrelated to the more famous Ramblas) and pass through Passeig de Gràcia (Metro for Block of Discord: Passeig de Gràcia, or Metro for Casa Milà: Diagonal).

The 19th century was a boom time for Barcelona. By 1850 the city was busting out of its medieval walls. A new town was planned to follow a grid-like layout. The intersection of three major thoroughfares—Gran Via, Diagonal, and Meridiana—would shift the city's focus uptown. But uptown Barcelona is a unique variation on the common grid-plan city: Barcelona snipped off the building corners to create light and spacious eight-sided squares at every intersection.

The Eixample, or "Expansion," was a progressive plan in which everything was made accessible to everyone. Each 20-block-square district would have its own hospital and large park, each 10-block-square area would have its own market and general services, and each five-block-square grid would house its own schools and day-care centers. The hollow space found inside each "block" of apartments would form a neighborhood park.

Although much of that vision never quite panned out, the Eixample was an urban success. Rich and artsy big shots bought plots along the grid. The richest landowners built as close to the center as possible. For this reason, the best buildings are near the Passeig de Gràcia. While adhering to the height, width, and depth limitations, they built as they pleased—often in the trendy new Modernista style.

For many visitors, Modernista architecture is Barcelona's main draw. (The TI even has a special desk set aside just for Modernisme-seekers.) And one name tops them all: **Antoni Gaudí** (1852-1926). Barcelona is an architectural scrapbook of Gaudí's galloping gables and organic curves. A devoted Catalan and Catholic, he immersed himself in each project, often living on-site. At various times, he called Parc Güell, Casa Milà, and the Sagrada Família home.

Gaudí Sights near the Old City

▲▲**Casa Milà (La Pedrera)**—This Gaudí exterior laughs down on the crowds filling Passeig de Gràcia. Casa Milà, also called La Pedrera ("The Quarry"), has a much-photographed roller coaster of melting-ice-cream eaves. This is Barcelona's quintessential Modernista building and was Gaudí's last major work (1906-1910)

Modernisme

The Renaixensa (Catalan cultural revival) gave birth to Modernisme (Catalan Art Nouveau) at the end of the 19th century. Barcelona is its capital. Its Eixample neighborhood shimmers with the colorful, leafy, flowing, blooming shapes of Modernisme in doorways, entrances, facades, and ceilings.

Meaning "a taste for what is modern"—things like streetcars, electric lights, and big-wheeled bicycles—this free-flowing organic style lasted from 1888 to 1906. Breaking with tradition, artists experimented with glass, tile, iron, and brick. The structure was fully modern, using rebar and concrete, but the decoration was a clip-art collage of nature images, exotic Moorish or Chinese themes, and fanciful Gothic crosses and knights to celebrate Catalunya's medieval glory days. It's Barcelona's unique contribution to the Europe-wide Art Nouveau movement. Modernisme was a way of life as Barcelona burst into the 20th century.

Antoni Gaudí (1852-1926), Barcelona's most famous Modernista artist, was descended from four generations of metalworkers, a lineage of which he was quite proud. He incorporated ironwork into his architecture and came up with novel approaches to architectural structure and space.

Two more Modernista architects famous for their unique style are Lluís Domènech i Muntaner and Josep Puig i Cadafalch. You'll see their work on the Block of Discord.

before dedicating his final years to the Sagrada Família.

You can visit three sections of Casa Milà: the apartment, the attic, and the rooftop (€14, good audioguide-€4, daily March-Oct 9:00-20:00, Nov-Feb 9:00-18:30, last entry 30 minutes before closing, Passeig de Gràcia 92, Metro: Diagonal, toll tel. 902-400-973). It's best to reserve ahead—sometimes there's a 1.5-hour wait to get in (advanced tickets toll tell. 902-101-212, www.lapedreraeducacio.org).

After entering, head upstairs. Two elevators take you up to either the apartment or the attic. Normally you're directed to the

BARCELONA

Modernista Sights

Ⓑ Bus Stop Ⓜ Metro Station

- RONDA DE DALT
- TORRE DE BELLESGUARD
- GAUDÍ HOUSE & MUSEUM
- PARC GÜELL
- #24, #92 & TOURIST BUS Ⓑ
- FINCA GÜELL
- COL·LEGI DE LAS TERESIANES
- FINCA MIRALLES
- GIRONA
- LESSEPS
- TERRACE & FRONT ENTRANCE
- TRAV. DALT
- CASA VICENS
- Ⓑ #24
- GRACIA
- HOSPITAL DE LA SANTA CREU I SANT PAU (BY MUNTANER)
- SANTS TRAIN STN.
- DIAGONAL
- TRAV. GRACIA
- FONTANA Ⓜ
- CASA MILA
- Ⓑ #92
- AV. GAUDÍ
- **BLOCK OF DISCORD**
  - •CASA BATLLÓ - BY GAUDÍ
  - •CASA AMATLLER BY CADAFALCH
  - •CASA LLEÓ MORERA BY MUNTANER
- DIAGONAL Ⓜ
- PROVENÇA
- PASSEIG DE GRACIA
- ⓉⒷ #19 • #50
- SAGRADA FAMÍLIA
- GRAN VIA
- CASA CALVET
- PLAÇA D'ESPANYA
- PLAÇA DE CATALUNYA & Ⓑ #24
- RAMBLAS
- CATALAN CONCERT HALL (BY MUNTANER)
- PARAL·LEL
- MONTJUÏC
- LICEU Ⓜ
- BARRI GÒTIC
- PALAU GÜELL
- DRASS. Ⓜ
- FRANÇA TRAIN STN.
- OLYMPIC PORT & "FISH" (BY GEHRY)
- NOT TO SCALE
- HARBOR
- DCH

apartment, but if you arrive late in the day, go to the attic elevator first, then climb right up to the rooftop to make sure you have enough time to enjoy Gaudí's works and the views.

The typical fourth-floor **apartment** is decorated as it might have been when the building was first occupied by middle-class urbanites (a seven-minute video explains Barcelona society at the time). Notice Gaudí's clever use of the atrium to maximize daylight in all of the apartments.

The **attic** houses a sprawling multimedia "Gaudí Space," tracing the history of the architect's career with models, photos, and videos of his work. It's all displayed

Visit Casa Milà or Casa Batlló?

These two Antoni Gaudí houses offer similar, up-close looks at Modernista architecture. Casa Batlló's rooftop (above right) is smaller, all on one level, and less impressive than the expansive rooftop at Casa Milà (above left). But the unfurnished Casa Batlló is less of a museum and better allows the architecture to speak for itself. If you're choosing one, Casa Milà is cheaper and has the superior rooftop, but Gaudí fans will find both worthwhile.

under distinctive parabola-shaped arches. While evocative of Gaudí's style in themselves, the arches are formed this way partly to support the multilevel roof above. This area was also used for ventilation, helping to keep things cool in summer and warm in winter. Tenants had storage spaces and did their laundry up here.

From the attic, a stairway leads to the fanciful, undulating, jaw-dropping **rooftop,** where 30 chimneys play volleyball with the clouds.

Back at the **ground level** of Casa Milà, poke into the dreamily painted original entrance courtyard. The first floor hosts free art exhibits.

Eating: Stop by the recommended **La Bodegueta,** a long block away (daily lunch special).

▲**Block of Discord**—Four blocks from Casa Milà, you can survey a noisy block of competing late-19th-century facades. Several of Barcelona's top Modernista mansions line Passeig de Gràcia (Metro: Passeig de Gràcia). Because the structures look as though they are trying to outdo each other in creative twists, locals nicknamed the block between Consell de Cent and Arago the "Block of Discord."

First (at #43) and most famous is Gaudí's **Casa Batlló,** with skull-like balconies and a tile roof that suggests a cresting dragon's back; Gaudí based the work on the popular legend of St. Jordi (George) slaying the dragon. You can tour the house—a rival of Casa Milà (described earlier) (€17.80, includes

audioguide, daily 9:00-20:00, may close early
for special events—closings posted in advance
at entrance, tel. 932-160-306, www.casabatllo
.cat). You'll see the main floor (with a funky
mushroom-shaped fireplace nook), the blue-
and-white-ceramic-slathered atrium, the attic
(more parabolic arches), and the rooftop, all
with the help of the good audioguide. Because
preservation of the place is privately funded,
the entrance fee is steep—but the interior
is even more fanciful and over-the-top than
Casa Milà's. There's barely a straight line in
the house. By the way, if you're tempted to
snap photos from the middle of the street, be careful—Gaudí died
under a streetcar.

Next door, at **Casa Amatller** (#41), check out architect Josep
Puig i Cadafalch's creative mix of Moorish- and Gothic-inspired
architecture and iron grillwork, which decorates a step-gable like
those in the Netherlands. Pop inside for a peek at the elaborate
entrance hall.

On the corner (at #35), **Casa Lleó Morera** has a wonderful
interior highlighted by the dining room's fabulous stained glass.
The architect, Lluís Domènech i Muntaner, also designed the
Catalan Concert Hall (you'll notice similarities).

The recommended **La Rita** restaurant, just around the corner
on Carrer Arago, serves a fine three-course lunch for a great price
(Mon-Fri from 13:00).

▲**Palau Güell**—Just as the Picasso Museum reveals a young
genius on the verge of a breakthrough, this early Gaudí building
(completed in 1890) shows the architect taking his first tenta-
tive steps toward what would become his trademark curvy style.
The parabolic-arch doorways, viewable from the outside, are the
first clue that this is not a typical townhouse. In the midst of an
extensive renovation, only part of the house is open to the public:
the main floor and the Neo-Gothic cellar (which was used as a
stable—notice the big carriage doors in the back and the rings on
some of the posts used to tie up the horses). By 2011, they hope to
have more of the house open...and start charging admission (free,
Tue-Sat 10:00-14:30, closed Sun-Mon, a half-block off the Ramblas
at Carrer Nou de la Rambla 3-5, tel. 933-173-974, www.palauguell
.cat). Even if the rooftop—with its fanciful mosaic chimneys (visible from the street if you crane your neck)—is open, I'd skip it if
you plan to see the more interesting one at Casa Milà.

▲▲▲Sagrada Família (Holy Family Church)

Gaudí's most famous and persistent work is this unfinished land-

mark church. He worked on the Sagrada Família from 1883 until his death in 1926. Since then, construction has moved forward in fits and starts. Even today, the half-finished church is not expected to be completed for another quarter-century. (But over 30 years of visits, I've seen considerable progress.) The temple is funded exclusively by private donations and entry fees, which is another reason its completion has taken so long. Your admission helps pay for the ongoing construction.

Cost and Hours: €12, daily April-Sept 9:00-20:00, Oct-March 9:00-18:00, Metro: Sagrada Família puts you right on the doorstep—exit toward *Pl de la Sagrada Família*, tel. 932-073-031, www.sagradafamilia.cat.

Crowd-Beating Tips: The ticket line can be very long (up to about 30-45 minutes at peak times). In summer, it's generally least crowded during lunch and after 18:30, and most crowded right when the church opens. To skip the ticket-buying line, purchase tickets in advance online (www.servicaixa.com, pick up at ServiCaixa terminal outside the Passion Facade) or at any ServiCaixa machine (located throughout the city).

Tours: The 45-minute English tours cost €4 (May-Oct daily at 11:00 and 13:00, Nov-April usually Fri-Mon only, same times). Or rent the good 70-minute audioguide (also €4).

Elevators: Two different elevators take you partway up the towers for a great view of the city and a gargoyle's-eye perspective of the loopy church. Each one costs €2.50 (pay as you board elevator). The **Passion facade elevator** takes you 215 feet up, where you can climb higher if you want; then an elevator takes you back down. The **Nativity facade elevator** is similar, but you can also cross the dizzying bridge between the towers—and you must walk all the way down. (Some people prefer the Nativity elevator despite the additional steps because it offers close views of the facade that Gaudí actually worked on.) For the climbing sections, expect the spiral stairs to be tight, hot, and congested. Lines for both elevators can be very long (up to a 2-hour wait at the busiest times); signs along the stanchions give you an estimated wait time. To avoid long lines, follow the "Crowd-Beating Tips" (above) and go directly to the elevators when you arrive. The Nativity facade elevator generally has a shorter line.

The Construction Project: There's something powerful about an opportunity to feel a community of committed people with a vision, working on a church that will not be finished in their lifetime (as was standard in the Gothic age). Local craftsmen often cap off their careers by spending a couple of years on this exciting construction site. The church will trumpet its completion with 18 spires: A dozen "smaller" 330-foot spires (representing the apostles) will stand in groups of four and mark the three entry facades of the building. Four taller towers (dedicated to the four Evangelists) will surround the two tallest, central towers: a 400-foot-tall tower of Mary and the grand 550-foot Jesus tower, which will shine like a spiritual lighthouse—visible even from out at sea. A unique exterior ambulatory will circle the building, like a cloister turned inside out. If there's any building on earth I'd like to see, it's the Sagrada Família...finished.

◐ Self-Guided Tour: To get a good rundown, follow this commentary.

• *Begin by facing the western side of the church (where you'll enter).*

Passion Facade: It seems strange to begin with something that Gaudí had nothing to do with...but that's where they put the

entrance. When Gaudí died in 1926, only the stubs of four spires stood above the building site. The rest of the church has been inspired by Gaudí's vision but designed and executed by others. Gaudí knew he wouldn't live to complete the church and recognized that later architects and artists would rely on their own muses for inspiration. This artistic freedom was amplified in 1936, when Civil War shelling burned many of Gaudí's blueprints. Judge for yourself how the recently completed and controversial Passion facade by Josep María Subirachs (b. 1927) fits with Gaudí's original formulation (which you'll see downstairs in the museum).

Subirachs' facade is full of symbolism from the Bible. The story of Christ's Passion unfolds in the shape of a Z, from bottom to top. Find the stylized Alpha and Omega over the door; Jesus—hanging on the cross—with an open book (the word of God) for hair; and the grid of numbers adding up to 33 (Jesus' age at the time of his death). The distinct face of the man below and just left of Christ is a memorial to Gaudí.

Now look high above: The figure perched on the bridge between the towers is the soul of Jesus, ascending to heaven. The colorful ceramic caps of the towers symbolize the miters (formal hats) of bishops.

Grand and impressive as this seems, keep in mind it's only the *side* entry to the church. The nine-story apartment building to the right will be torn down to accommodate the grand front entry. The three facades—Passion, Nativity, and Glory—will chronicle Christ's life from birth to death to resurrection.

• *We'll enter the church later. For now, look right to find the...*

School: Gaudí erected this school for the children of the workers building the church. Now it houses an exhibit focusing on the architect's use of geometric forms. You'll also see a classroom and a replica of Gaudí's desk as it was the day he died, and a model for the proposed Glory facade...the next big step.

• *Leaving the school, turn right and go down the ramp under the church, into the...*

Museum: Housed in what is someday intended to be the church's crypt, the museum runs underground from the Passion facade to the Nativity facade. The first section tells the chronological story of the Sagrada Família. Look for the replicas of the pulpit and confessional that Gaudí, the micro-manager, designed for his church. As you wander through the plaster models used for the church's construction, you'll notice that they don't always match the finished product—these are ideas, not blueprints set in stone. Photos show the construction work as it was when Gaudí died in 1926 and how it's progressed over the years. See how the church's design is a fusion of nature, architecture, and religion. The columns seem light, with branches springing forth and capitals that look like palm trees.

Walking down the long passage to the other side of the church, you'll pass under a giant plaster model of the nave (you'll see the real thing soon). Find the hanging model showing how Gaudí used gravity to calculate the perfect parabolas incorporated into the church design (the mirror above this model shows how the right-side-up church is derived from this). Nearby, you'll find some original Gaudí architectural sketches in a dimly lit room and a worthwhile 20-minute movie (generally shown in English at :50 past each hour).

Then you'll peek into a busy workshop for making plaster models of the planned construction, just like what Gaudí used—he found these helpful for envisioning the final product in 3-D. The museum wraps up with an exhibit on the design and implementation of the Passion facade.

• *Climb up the ramp and hook left to see the...*

Nativity Facade (east side): This, the only part of the church essentially finished in his lifetime, shows Gaudí's original vision. (Cleverly, this facade was built and finished first to inspire financial support, which Gaudí knew would be a challenge.) Mixing Gothic-style symbolism, images from nature, and Modernista asymmetry, it is the best example of Gaudí's unmistakable cake-in-the-rain style. The sculpture shows a unique twist on the Nativity, with Jesus as a young carpenter and angels playing musical instruments.

• *From here you have two options:*

To take the elevator up the Nativity facade, go through the small door to the right of the main door. The line stretches through an area called the Rosary Cloister.

*To enter the church (where you'll also find the Passion facade elevator entrance), go in the door to the left of the main entry. First you'll pass the Montserrat Cloister, with the **Gaudí and Nature** exhibition that compares nature, waves, shells, mushrooms, the ripple of a leaf, and so on, to Gaudí's work. Then you'll enter the...*

Construction Zone (the Nave): The cranking cranes, rusty forests of rebar, and scaffolding require a powerful faith, but the Sagrada Família offers a fun look at a living, growing bigger-than-life building. Part of Gaudí's religious vision was a love for nature. He said, "Nothing is invented; it's written in nature." His columns blossom with life, and little windows let light filter in like the canopy of a rain forest, giving both privacy and an intimate connection with God. The U-shaped choir hovers above the nave, tethered halfway up the columns. A relatively recent addition—hanging out in the middle of the back wall—is a statue of Barcelona's patron saint, St. Jordi (George of dragon-slaying fame). The nave's roof was just completed in 2010. At the far end of the nave, you'll see the line to take the elevator up the Passion facade.

Finishing the floors in the nave was a priority before Pope Benedict XVI's visit on November 7, 2010, to consecrate the church. Currently, the construction is focused on a few major tasks: stabilizing the existing nave (which has been rattled by vibrations from the Metro and AVE train lines underground) and eventually adding the third, biggest entry—the Glory facade. They're also in the process of replacing the temporary clear windows with stained-glass ones. The final phase is the central tower (550 feet tall), which, it's estimated, will require four underground support pylons, each consisting of 8,000 tons of cement.

Gaudí lived on the site for more than a decade, and is buried in a Neo-Gothic 19th-century crypt (which is where the church began). His tomb is viewable for free from the small church around the corner from the main ticket entrance (during Mass—Mon-Sat 8:30-10:00 & 18:30-21:00, longer hours on Sun). There's a move afoot to make Gaudí a saint. Perhaps someday his tomb will be a place of pilgrimage. Gaudí—a faithful Catholic whose medieval-style mysticism belied his Modernista architecture career—was certainly driven to greatness by his passion for God. When undertaking a lengthy project, he said, "My client"—meaning God—"is in no hurry."

Bus Connections: From the Sagrada Família, bus #19 makes an easy 15-minute journey to the Old City (stops near the cathedral and La Ribera district), including the Columbus Monument near the shuttle-bus stop back to the cruise port; bus #50 goes from the Sagrada Família, to the corner of Gran Via de les Corts Catalanes and Passeig de Gràcia. If your next stop is Parc Güell (described next), and you don't want to spring for a taxi, try this route: Walk up the pleasant, pedestrianized Avinguda Gaudí four blocks gradually uphill (about 10 minutes). When you reach the striking Modernista-style Hospital de la Santa Creu i Sant Pau, cross the street and go up one block (left) on St. Antonio Maria Claret street to catch bus #92, which will take you to the side entrance of Parc Güell.

▲Parc Güell

Gaudí fans enjoy the artist's magic in this colorful park. Gaudí intended this 30-acre garden to be a 60-residence housing project—a kind of gated community. As a high-income housing development, it flopped; but as a park, it's a delight, offering another peek into Gaudí's eccentric genius. Notice the mosaic medallions that say "park" in English, reminding folks that this is modeled on an English garden.

Cost and Hours: Free, daily 10:00-20:00, tel. 932-130-488.

Getting There: From Plaça de Catalunya, the red Tourist Bus or bus #24 will leave you at the park's side entrance, or a €8 taxi will drop you off at the main entrance. From elsewhere in the city, do a Metro-plus-bus combination: Go by Metro to the Lesseps stop. To avoid the tiring uphill 20-minute walk to the park, don't follow the *Parc Güell 1300 metros* sign; instead, exit the Metro station, cross the streets Princep d'Astúries and Gran de Gràcia, and catch bus #24 (on Gran de Gràcia), which takes you to the park's side entrance in less than 10 minutes. For a more scenic approach (on bus #92) from the Sagrada Família, see the previous listing.

Eating in Barcelona

Along the Ramblas

Within a few steps of the Ramblas you'll find handy lunch places, an inviting market hall, and a slew of vegetarian options.

Lunching Simply yet Memorably near the Ramblas

Although these places are enjoyable for a lunch break during your Ramblas sightseeing, many are also open for dinner. For locations, see the map on page 192.

Taverna Basca Irati serves 40 kinds of hot and cold Basque *pintxos* for €1.80 each. These are open-faced sandwiches—like sushi on bread. Muscle in through the hungry local crowd, get an empty plate from the waiter, and then help yourself. Every few minutes, waiters prance proudly by with a platter of new, still-warm munchies. Grab one as they pass by...it's addictive. You pay on the honor system: You're charged by the number of toothpicks left on your plate when you're done. Wash it down with €2-3 glasses of Rioja (full-bodied red wine), Txakolí (sprightly Basque white wine), or *sidra* (apple wine) poured from on high to add oxygen and bring out the flavor (daily 11:00-24:00, a block off the Ramblas, behind arcade at Carrer Cardenal Casanyes 15, Metro: Liceu, tel. 933-023-084).

Restaurant Elisabets is a happy little neighborhood eatery packed with antique radios, and is popular with locals for its €11 "home-cooked" three-course lunch special. Stop by for lunch, survey what those around you are enjoying, and order what looks best (Mon-Sat 7:30-23:00, closed Sun and Aug, lunch special served 13:00-16:00, otherwise only €3 tapas—not full meals, 2 blocks west of Ramblas on far corner of Plaça Bonsucces at Carrer Elisabets 2, tel. 933-175-826, run by Pilar).

Café Granja Viader is a quaint time capsule, family-run since 1870. They boast about being the first dairy business to bottle and distribute milk in Spain. This feminine-feeling place—specializing in baked and dairy delights, toasted sandwiches, and light meals—is ideal for a traditional breakfast. Or indulge your sweet tooth: Try a glass of *orxata* (or *horchata*—*chufa*-nut milk, summer only), *llet mallorquina* (Majorca-style milk with cinnamon, lemon, and sugar), *crema catalana* (crème brûlée, their specialty), or *suis* ("Swiss"—hot chocolate with a snowcap of whipped cream). *Mel y mato* is fresh cheese with honey...very Catalan (Tue-Sat 9:00-13:45 & 17:00-20:45, Mon 17:00-20:45 only, closed Sun, a block off the Ramblas behind El Carme church at Xucla 4, tel. 933-183-486).

Picnics: Shoestring tourists buy groceries at **El Corte Inglés** (Mon-Sat 10:00-22:00, closed Sun, supermarket in basement, Plaça de Catalunya) and **Carrefour Express supermarket** (Mon-Sat 10:00-22:00, closed Sun, Ramblas 113).

In and near La Boquería Market

Try eating at La Boquería market at least once (#91 on the

Ramblas). Like all farmers markets in Europe, this place is ringed by colorful, good-value eateries. Lots of stalls sell fun take-away food—especially fruit salads and fresh-squeezed fruit juices. There are several good bars around the market busy with shoppers munching at the counter (breakfast, tapas all day, coffee). The market, and most of the eateries listed here (unless noted), are open Monday through Saturday from 8:00 until 20:00 (though things get very quiet after about 16:00) and are closed on Sunday.

Pinotxo Bar is just to the right as you enter the market. It's a great spot for coffee, breakfast (spinach tortillas, or whatever's cooking with toast), or tapas. Fun-loving Juan and his family are La Boquería fixtures. Grab a stool across the way to sip your drink with people-watching views. Have a Chucho?

Kiosko Universal is popular for its great prices on wonderful fish dishes. As you enter the market from the Ramblas, it's all the way to the left in the first alley. If you see people waiting, ask who's last in line *("¿El último?").* You'll eat immersed in the spirit of the market (€14 fixed-price lunches with different fresh-fish options 12:00-16:00, always packed but better before 12:30, tel. 933-178-286).

Restaurant la Gardunya, at the back of the market, offers tasty meat and seafood meals made with fresh ingredients bought directly from the market (€13 fixed-price lunch includes wine and bread, €16 three-course dinner specials don't include wine, €10-20 à la carte dishes, Mon-Sat 13:00-16:00 & 20:00-24:00, closed Sun, mod seating indoors or outside watching the market action, Carrer Jerusalem 18, tel. 933-024-323).

Bar Terrace Restaurant Ra is a lively terrace immediately behind the market (at the right end of the big parking lot) with outdoor tables filled by young, trendy, happy eaters. At lunch they serve one great salad/pasta/wine meal for €11. If you feel like eating a big salad under an umbrella...this is the place (€9-15 à la carte dishes, daily 10:00-12:30 & 13:30-16:00 & 21:00-24:00, fancier menu at night, mobile 615-959-872).

Vegetarian Eateries near
Plaça de Catalunya and the Ramblas

Biocenter, a Catalan soup-and-salad restaurant popular with local vegetarians, takes its cooking very seriously and feels a bit more

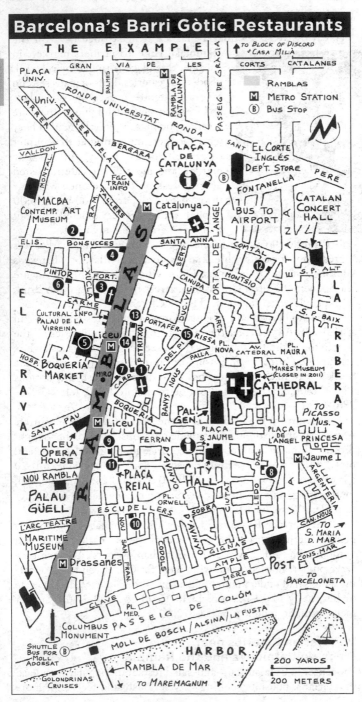

Barcelona's Barri Gòtic Restaurants

Restaurants Key

1. Taverna Basca Irati
2. Restaurant Elisabets
3. Café Granja Viader
4. Supermarket
5. La Boquería Market Eateries
6. Biocenter Veggie Rest.
7. Juicy Jones
8. Café de l'Academia
9. La Crema Canela
10. La Fonda
11. Les Quinze Nits
12. La Dolça Herminia
13. Casa Colomina
14. Granja La Pallaresa
15. Fargas Chocolate Shop

like a real restaurant than most (€6-9.75 weekday lunch specials include soup or salad and plate of the day, €15 dinner specials, Mon-Sat 13:00-23:00, Sun 13:00-16:00, 2 blocks off the Ramblas at Pintor Fortuny 25, Metro: Catalunya, tel. 933-014-583).

Juicy Jones is a tutti-frutti vegan/vegetarian eatery with colorful graffiti decor, a hip veggie menu (served downstairs), groovy laid-back staff, and a stunning array of fresh-squeezed juices served at the bar. Pop in for a quick €3 "juice of the day." For lunch you can get the Indian-inspired €6 *thali* plate, the €6.25 plate of the day, or an €8.50 meal including one of the two plates plus soup or salad and dessert (daily 12:30-23:30, also tapas and salads, Carrer Cardenal Casanyes 7, tel. 933-024-330). There's another location on the other side of the Ramblas (Carrer Hospital 74).

In the Barri Gòtic

These eateries populate Barcelona's atmospheric Gothic Quarter, near the cathedral. Choose between a sit-down meal at a restaurant or a string of very old-fashioned tapas bars.

Restaurants in the Barri Gòtic

Café de l'Academia is a delightful place on a pretty square tucked away in the heart of the Barri Gòtic—but patronized mainly by the neighbors. They serve "honest cuisine" from the market with Catalan roots. The candlelit, air-conditioned interior is rustic yet elegant, with soft jazz, flowers, and modern art. And if you want to eat outdoors on a convivial, mellow square...this is the place (€10-12 first courses, €12-15 second courses, fixed-price lunch for €10 at the bar or €14 at a table, Mon-Fri 13:30-16:00 & 20:30-23:30, closed Sat-Sun, near the City Hall square, off Carrer de Jaume I up Carrer Dagueria at Carrer Lledo 1, tel. 933-198-253).

Popular Chain Restaurants: Barcelona enjoys a chain of several bright, modern restaurants. These are a hit for their modern, artfully presented Spanish and Mediterranean cuisine, crisp ambience, and unbeatable prices. Because of their three-course

€9 lunches and €16-20 dinners (both with wine), all are crowded with locals and in-the-know tourists (all open daily 13:00-15:45 & 20:30-23:30, unless otherwise noted). My favorite of the bunch is **La Crema Canela,** which feels cozier than the others and is the only one that takes reservations (opens at 20:00 for dinner, 30 yards north of Plaça Reial at Passatge de Madoz 6, tel. 933-182-744). The rest are notorious for long lines at the door—arrive 30 minutes before opening, or be prepared to wait. Like La Crema Canela, the next two are also within a block of the Plaça Reial: **La Fonda** (opens at 19:00 for dinner, Carrer dels Escudellers 10, very close to a seedy stretch of street—approach it from the Ramblas rather than from Plaça Reial, tel. 933-017-515) and **Les Quinze Nits** (on Plaça Reial at #6—you'll see the line, tel. 933-173-075). The fourth place, **La Dolça Herminia,** is near the Catalan Concert Hall (2 blocks toward Ramblas from Catalan Concert Hall at Carrer de les Magdalenes 27, tel. 933-170-676).

In the Ribera District, near the Picasso Museum

La Ribera, the hottest neighborhood in town, sparkles with eclectic and trendy as well as subdued and classy little restaurants hidden in the small lanes surrounding the Church of Santa Maria del Mar. While I've listed a few well-established tapas bars that are great for light meals, to really dine, simply wander around for 15 minutes and pick the place that tickles your gastronomic fancy. I think those who say they know what's best in this area are kidding themselves—it's changing too fast and the choices are too personal. One thing's for sure: There are a lot of talented and hardworking restaurateurs with plenty to offer. Consider starting your evening off with a glass of fine wine at one of the *enotecas* on the square facing the Church of Santa Maria del Mar. Sit back and admire the pure Catalan Gothic architecture. My first three listings are all on the main drag, Carrer de l'Argenteria. For locations, see the map on page 178.

Sagardi offers a wonderful array of Basque goodies—tempting *pinchos* and *montaditos* at €1.80 each—along its huge bar. Ask for a plate and graze (just take whatever looks good). You can sit on the square with your plunder for 20 percent extra. Wash it down with Txakolí, a Basque white wine poured from the spout of a huge wooden barrel into a glass as you watch. When you're done, they'll count your toothpicks to tally your bill (daily 12:00-24:00, Carrer de l'Argenteria 62-64, tel. 933-199-993).

Sagardi Euskal Taberna, hiding behind the thriving Sagardi tapas bar (described above), is a mod, rustic, and minimalist woody restaurant committed to serving Basque T-bone steaks and grilled specialties with only the best ingredients. Crisp, friendly service and a big open kitchen with sizzling grills contribute to the ambience. Reservations are smart (€10-20 first courses, €20-30 second courses, plan on €45 for dinner, daily 13:00-16:00 & 20:00-24:00, Carrer de l'Argenteria 62, tel. 933-199-993).

Taller de Tapas ("Tapas Workshop") is an upscale, trendier tapas bar and restaurant that dishes up well-presented, sophisticated morsels and light meals in a medieval-stone-yet-mod setting. Pay 10 percent more to sit on the square. Elegant, but a bit stuffy, it's favored by local office workers who aren't into the Old World Gothic stuff. Four plates will fill a hungry diner for about €20 (daily 8:30-24:00, Carrer de l'Argenteria 51, tel. 932-688-559).

El Xampanyet, a colorful family-run bar with a fun-loving staff (Juan Carlos, his mom, and the man who may be his father), specializes in tapas and anchovies. Don't be put off by the seafood from a tin: Catalans like it this way. A *sortido* (assorted plate) of *carne* (meat) or *pescado* (fish) with *pa amb tomaquet* (bread with crushed-tomato spread) makes for a fun meal. It's filled with tourists during the sightseeing day, but this is a local favorite after dark. The scene is great but—especially during busy times—it's tough without Spanish skills. When I asked about the price, Juan Carlos said, "Who cares? The ATM is just across the street." Plan on spending €20 for a meal with wine (same price at bar or table, Tue-Sat 12:00-16:00 & 19:00-23:30, Sun 12:00-16:00 only, closed Mon, a half-block beyond the Picasso Museum at Montcada 22, tel. 933-197-003).

A Short, Sweet Walk

Let me propose this three-stop dessert (or, since these places close well before the traditional Barcelona dinnertime, a late-afternoon snack). You'll try a refreshing glass of *orxata,* munch some *churros con chocolate,* and visit a fine *xocolateria,* all within a three-minute walk of one another in the Barri Gòtic just off the Ramblas. Start at the corner of Carrer Portaferrissa midway down the Ramblas. For the best atmosphere, if possible, begin your walk at about 18:00 (note that the last place is closed on Sun). For locations, see the map on page 192.

Turrón at **Casa Colomina:** Walk down Carrer Portaferrissa to #8 (on the right). Casa Colomina, founded in 1908, specializes in homemade *turróns*—a variation of nougat made with almond, honey, and sugar, brought to Spain by the Moors 1,200 years ago. Three different kinds are sold in big €12 slabs: *blando, duro,* and *yema*—soft, hard, and yolk (€2 smaller chunks also available). In the summer, the shop also sells ice cream and the refreshing *orxata* (or *horchata*—a drink made from the *chufa* nut). Order a glass and ask to see and eat a *chufa* nut (a.k.a. earth almond or tiger nut; Mon-Sat 10:00-20:30, Sun 12:30-20:30, tel. 933-122-511).

Churros con Chocolate at **Granja La Pallaresa:** Continue down Carrer Portaferrissa, taking a right at Carrer Petritxol to this fun-loving *xocolateria*. Older, elegant ladies gather here for the Spanish equivalent of tea time—dipping their greasy *churros* into pudding-thick cups of hot chocolate (€4.10 for five *churros con chocolate*, Mon-Fri 9:00-13:00 & 16:00-21:00, Sat-Sun 9:00-13:00 & 17:00-21:00, Carrer Petritxol 11, tel. 933-022-036).

Homemade Chocolate at Fargas: For your last stop, head for the ornate Fargas chocolate shop. Continue down Carrer Petritxol to the square, hook left through the two-part square, and then left up Carrer del Pi—it's on the corner of Portaferrissa and Carrer del Pi. Since the 19th century, gentlemen with walking canes have dropped by here for their chocolate fix. Founded in 1827, this is one of the oldest and most traditional chocolate shops in Barcelona. If they're not too busy, ask to see the old chocolate mill *("¿Puedo ver el molino?")* to the right of the counter. They sell even tiny quantities (one little morsel) by the weight, so don't be shy. A delicious chunk of the crumbly semisweet house specialty costs €0.45 (tray by the mill). The tempting bonbons in the window cost about €1 each (Mon-Fri 9:30-13:30 & 16:00-20:00, Sat 10:00-14:00 & 16:00-20:00, closed Sun, tel. 933-020-342).

Starting or Ending Your Cruise in Barcelona

If your cruise begins and/or ends in Barcelona, you'll want some extra time here; for most travelers, two days is a minimum to see the highlights of this grand, sprawling city. For a longer visit here, pick up my *Rick Steves' Snapshot Barcelona* guidebook—or, if your trip extends to other points in the country, consider my *Rick Steves' Spain* guidebook.

Airport Connections

Barcelona's **El Prat de Llobregat Airport,** eight miles southwest of town, has two large terminals: 1 and 2. Terminal 2 is divided into sections A, B, and C. Terminal 1 and the bigger sections of terminal 2 (A and B) each have a post office, a pharmacy, a left-luggage office, plenty of good cafeterias in the gate areas, and ATMs (avoid the gimmicky machines before the baggage carousels; instead, use the bank-affiliated ATMs at the far-left end of the arrivals hall as you face the street). Airport info tel. 913-211-000.

There is no direct public-transportation connection between the cruise ports and this airport. The easiest option is to arrange a transfer through your cruise line, or just hire a **taxi** (€35-40, depending on number of bags and traffic, includes legitimate sur-

What If I Miss My Boat?

Remember that you can get help from the cruise line's port agent (listed on the destination information sheet distributed on the ship) and the local TI (see page 149). If the port agent suggests a costly solution (such as a private car with a driver), you may instead want to consider public transit.

Frequent **trains** leave from Barcelona's Sants Station to points all over Spain and France: **Valencia** (every 1-2 hours, 3-3.5 hours), **Málaga** (every 1-2 hours, 5.75-6.5 hours), **Nice** (1/day via Montpelier; cheaper connections with multiple changes including Cerbère), **Cartagena** (3/day, 7.75-9.5 hours), **Marseille** (3/day, 6.25-8 hours), **Toulon** (3/day 7.25-9 hours), and more. For other connections, ask at the train station or check www.renfe.com or http://bahn.hafas.de/bin /query.exe/en (Germany's excellent all-Europe website). Spain has a train-info toll number (tel. 902-320-320). Some trains also stop at other Barcelona stations closer to the downtown tourist zone: França Station, Passeig de Gràcia, or Plaça de Catalunya.

You can take a **ferry** to **Ibiza** (8.5-9.5 hours) or **Palma de Mallorca** (7-8 hours). For more information, see www.direct ferries.es.

If you need to catch a **plane** to your next destination, see the opposite page for information on Barcelona's airport.

For more advice on what to do if you miss the boat, see page 131.

charges for the cruise terminal and the airport).

The much more affordable (€5-7 total per person) but time-consuming **public-transportation connection** involves three steps: A bus from the airport to Barcelona's Plaça de Catalunya; from there, walk or ride the Metro two stops to the Columbus Monument (near Drassanes Metro stop); and from there, connect to your cruise terminal: to reach the Moll Adossat/Muelle Adosado terminals (A, B, C, or D), ride the shuttle bus (€2 one-way); to reach the World Trade Center terminals (N or S), you can walk; or to reach the Moll de la Costa terminal, you can walk to the World Trade Center, then take a free shuttle bus.

The Details: The **Aerobus** (#A1 and #A2, corresponding with airport terminals 1 and 2) stops immediately outside the arrivals lobby of both terminals (and in each section of terminal 2). It takes about 30 minutes to go downtown, where it makes several stops, including Plaça de Catalunya (departs every 6 minutes, from airport 6:00-1:00 in the morning, from downtown 5:30-24:15, €5 one-way, €8.65 round-trip, buy ticket from machine or from driver, tel. 934-156-020). The line to board the bus can be very long, but—since buses run every six minutes—it moves fast.

From Plaça de Catalunya, you'll need to head down to the waterfront to connect to the cruise terminals. If you're in the mood for a stroll, you can walk down the bustling Ramblas pedestrian boulevard through the heart of town. It's a short walk downhill (about 20 minutes, if you don't dawdle), but it can be very congested and is packed with pickpockets—perhaps not ideal if you're jetlagged and carrying bags. Therefore, it might be easier to find the Metro station on Plaça de Catalunya (look for red *M* sign), and ride the L3 (green) line two stops to Drassanes. From the bottom of the Ramblas, cross to the far side of the roundabout, and catch the port shuttle bus (#T3) from the stop near the TI kiosk at the bottom of the Columbus Monument (€2 one-way, runs every 20-30 minutes).

If you're going from the cruise terminal *to* the airport, simply reverse these directions: Take the port shuttle bus to the Columbus Monument, cross over to the bottom of the Ramblas, walk or take the Metro up to Plaça de Catalunya, and catch the Aerobus to the airport.

Alternative Airport: Some budget airlines, including Ryanair, use **Girona-Costa Brava Airport,** located 60 miles north of Barcelona near Girona. Sagalés buses link this airport to Barcelona (departures timed to meet flights, 1.25 hours, €12, tel. 935-931-300 or 902-361-550, www.sagales.com). You can also go to Girona on a Sagalés bus (hourly, 25 minutes, €3) or in a taxi (€25), then catch a train to Barcelona (at least hourly, 1.25 hours, €15-20). A taxi between the Girona airport and Barcelona costs at least €120. Airport info tel. 972-186-600.

Hotels

If you need a hotel in Barcelona before or after your cruise, here are a few to consider.

$$$ Hotel Catalonia Duques de Bergara, with a garden courtyard and pool, has 150 comfortable but simple rooms (Db-€200 but can drop to as low as €100, non-smoking rooms available, air-con, free Internet access and Wi-Fi, a half-block off Plaça de Catalunya at Carrer de Bergara 11, tel. 933-015-151, fax 933-173-442, www.hoteles-catalonia.com, duques@hoteles-catalonia.es).

$$$ Hotel Neri is chic, posh, and sophisticated, with 22 rooms in the Barri Gòtic, overlooking an overlooked square (Plaça Sant Felip Neri) a block from the cathedral (Db-€265, air-con, free Wi-Fi, rooftop tanning deck, St. Sever 5, tel. 933-040-655, fax 933-040-337, www.hotelneri.com, info@hotelneri.com).

$$ Hotel Reding, on a quiet street a five-minute walk west of the Ramblas and Plaça de Catalunya action, is a slick and sleek place renting 44 mod rooms at a good price (Db-€120, non-smoking rooms, air-con, free Internet access and Wi-Fi, near Metro: Universitat, Gravina 5-7, tel. 934-121-097, fax 932-683-482, www.hotelreding.com, recepcion@hotelreding.com).

$$ Hotel Duc de la Victoria, with 156 rooms, is professional yet friendly, buried in the Barri Gòtic just three blocks off the Ramblas (Db-€140, non-smoking, air-con, Internet access, pay Wi-Fi, Duc 15, tel. 932-703-410, fax 934-127-747, www.nh-hotels .com, nhducdelavictoria@nh-hotels.com).

$ Hotel Continental Barcelona, overlooking the top of the Ramblas, offers an inviting lounge and comfortable rooms with wildly clashing decor (Sb-€90, Db-€100, twin Db-€110, Db with Ramblas balcony-€120, free breakfast, all-day snack bar, non-smoking, air-con, free Internet access and Wi-Fi, Ramblas 138, tel. 933-012-570, fax 933-027-360, www.hotelcontinental.com, barcelona@hotelcontinental.com).

FRANCE

FRANCE

 *Bienvenue!* France is Europe's most diverse, tasty, and, in many ways, most exciting country to explore. Nearly as big as Texas, with 62 million people and striking natural beauty, France dazzles the senses and nourishes the soul. For the palate, velvety wines and exceptional foods are *magnifique*. Come with a willingness to experience subtle pleasures such as people-watching from a sun-dappled café. Accept France on its own terms, and above all, slo-o-o-ow down.

The French value politeness. If you learn only five phrases, learn and use these: *bonjour* (good day), *pardon* (pardon me), *s'il vous plaît* (please), *merci* (thank you), and *au revoir* (goodbye). Begin every encounter with: *Bonjour* (or *S'il vous plaît*), *madame* or *monsieur*. End every encounter with: *Au revoir, madame* or *monsieur*.

Cruisers are most likely to visit the world-renowned South of France. Stretching along the country's southeast Mediterranean coast, the regions of Provence and the French Riviera are an intoxicating bouillabaisse of enjoyable cities, warm stone villages, archaeological marvels, contemporary art, and breathtaking vistas. Sun-baked and windswept Provence offers Roman ruins and rustic charm, while the trendy and upscale Riviera has sunny beaches and top-notch modern art.

The two regions are accessible from a variety of ports. Provence is accessed through the ports of Marseille (a big, gritty city with its own share of good sights) or Toulon. Consider the range of enticing Provençal destinations: genteel Aix-en-Provence, the beach resort of Cassis, Roman-flavored Arles with its Van Gogh connections, the former papal capital of Avignon with its famous broken bridge, and a variety of Roman ruins (such as the Pont du Gard aqueduct), deserted castles (including Les Baux), hill towns, and wineries.

The Riviera's three main ports also double as fine destinations: The vibrant city of Nice, with great museums, a beachfront promenade, and a charming old quarter; the sleepy port town of Villefranche-sur-Mer, with a fine beach of its own and good hiking nearby; and the tiny principality of Monaco, with its casino and ritzy skyscrapers. (Some cruises tender to glamorous Cannes, just west of Nice.) Fortunately, all of these ports are connected to each other by frequent and fast train and bus connections, making it easy to get a good taste of the region even on a short visit.

Practicalities

This section covers just the basics on traveling in France.

Tourist Information: www.franceguide.com

Money: France uses the euro currency: 1 euro (€) = about $1.40.

Theft Alert: Troublesome thieves thrive near high-profile tourist sights. Beware of pickpockets working busy lines (e.g., at sights and ticket windows). Watch out for strangers who attempt to distract you with a petition to sign or who pretend to be deaf and need help—these ruses can be smokescreens for theft.

Business Hours: Many businesses in small-town France close from noon to 14:00 for lunch, and all day on Sunday.

Internet Access: If you can't find an Internet café, look for a post office that offers Internet access *(cyberposte)*. Little hole-in-the-wall Internet-access shops, while common in the rest of Europe, are not prevalent in France.

Trains: At any train station, you can get schedule information, make reservations, and buy tickets for any destination. You can also buy tickets on the train for a small surcharge. At bigger stations, you'll see helpful information agents—wearing red or blue vests—at *Accueil* (information) booths or roaming the station.

Eating

The French eat long and well—nowhere more so than in the south. Relaxed and tree-shaded lunches with a chilled rosé and endless afternoons at outdoor cafés are the norm.

But busy sightseers can easily get food on the go. You'll find bakeries and small stands selling baguette sandwiches, quiche, and pizza-like items for about €4. Sandwich varieties include *fromage* (cheese), *jambon beurre* (ham and butter), *jambon* or *poulet crudités* (ham or chicken with tomatoes, lettuce, cucumbers, and mayonnaise), *saucisson beurre* (sausage and butter), and *thon crudités* (tuna with tomatoes, lettuce, and mayonnaise). Typical quiches at shops and bakeries are *fromage*, *lorraine* (ham and cheese), *aux oignons* (onion), *aux poireaux* (leek), *aux champignons* (mushroom), *au saumon* (salmon), or *au thon* (tuna).

If you're planning to gather supplies for a picnic lunch, start early: Many small stores close at noon. Be daring. Try the smelly cheeses, ugly pâtés, and minuscule yogurts. Shopkeepers are accustomed to selling small quantities. Get a tasty salad to go, and ask for a plastic fork *(une fourchette en plastique)*. A small container is *une barquette*. A slice is *une tranche*.

Cafés and brasseries provide user-friendly meals. At either, feel free to order only a bowl of soup or a salad or *plat* (main course) at any time of day. The daily special—*plat du jour*—is a fast, hearty, and garnished hot plate for €10-15. Unlike restaurants, which open only for lunch and dinner and close in between, some cafés and all brasseries serve food throughout the day, making them the best option if you want  a late lunch or an early dinner. There are two sets of prices: You'll pay more for the same drink if you're seated at a table *(salle)* than if you're at the bar or counter *(comptoir)*.

Restaurants are generally more formal and pricier; you're expected to order more of a meal. If a restaurant serves lunch, it generally begins at 11:30 and goes until 14:00, with last orders taken about 13:30. Dinner service usually begins at 19:00.

To get a waiter's attention, say, "*s'il vous plait.*" A *menu* is a fixed-price meal which usually includes two or three courses; these are a good value, particularly at lunch (the same menu costs more at dinner). Ask for *la carte* if you'd rather see a menu and order à la carte.

Service seems slow to Americans, but the French consider it polite not to rush you. When you're ready for the bill, ask for it: "*L'addition, s'il vous plait.*"

Tipping: At cafés and restaurants, a 12-15 percent service charge is always included in the bill *(service compris)*, and most French never tip. However, if you feel the service was exceptional, it's fine to tip up to 5 percent.

Phoning

To make calls in France from any type of phone, use an international phone card *(carte à code)*, available at newsstand kiosks and tobacco shops. An insertable phone card *(télécarte)* can be used only at pay phones. For more information on these cards, see page 120.

Dialing: France has a direct-dial 10-digit phone system (no area codes). To **call within France,** just dial the 10-digit number. To **call to France,** dial the international access code (00 if calling from Europe, or 011 from North America), then 33 (France's country code, then the phone number (but drop the initial zero). To **call home from France,** dial 00, 1, then your area code and phone number.

Directory Assistance: Tel. 12 (some English spoken); collect calls to the US: 00 00 11

Emergency Telephone Numbers:
Police: Tel. 17
Emergency Medical Assistance: Tel. 15
Riviera Medical Services: Tel. 04 93 26 12 70

Passport Problems: US Consulate in Marseille (tel. 04 91 54 92 00, after-hours emergency tel. 01 43 12 22 22) or US Consulate and Embassy in Paris (24-hour tel. 01 43 12 22 22); Canadian Consulate in Nice (tel. 04 93 92 93 22) or Canadian Consulate and Embassy in Paris (tel. 01 44 43 29 00).

FRANCE

PROVENCE

"There are treasures to carry away in this land, which has not found a spokesman worthy of the riches it offers."

—Paul Cézanne

This magnificent region is shaped like a giant wedge of quiche. From its sunburned crust, fanning out along the Mediterranean coast from the Camargue to Marseille, it stretches north along the Rhône Valley to Orange. The Romans were here in force and left many ruins—some of the best anywhere. Seven popes, artists such as Vincent van Gogh and Paul Cézanne, and author Peter Mayle all enjoyed their years in Provence. This destination features a splendid recipe of arid climate, oceans of vineyards, dramatic scenery, captivating cities, and adorable hill-capping villages.

On a cruise, you'll enter this region through one of two gloomy port cities that (let's be frank) are not representative of the world-renowned romanticism of Provence: Marseille or Toulon. While some travelers enjoy exploring Marseille's swiftly rejuvenating cityscape, most prefer to get out of town—on the train, with a shore excursion, or with a rental car—to experience some of Provence's more famous stops. For a Provençal beach fix, find Cassis, between Marseille and Toulon. Stylish and self-confident Aix-en-Provence lies 45 minutes from the sea (an easy train ride from Marseille). Or delve deeper into the Provençal interior: Spend a few Van Gogh–inspired starry, starry hours in Arles. Stroll the streets of youthful but classy Avignon, which bustles in the shadow of its brooding Palace of the Popes. Explore the ghost town that is ancient Les Baux, and see one of France's greatest Roman ruins, the Pont du Gard aqueduct. Or hop into the splendid scenery and villages of

Provence

the Côtes du Rhône and Luberon regions. Admire the skill of ball-tossing *boules* players in small squares in every Provençal village and city.

Planning Your Time

Provence's ports are Marseille and Toulon, about 40 miles apart. Marseille is within striking distance of several great destinations, but your choices from Toulon are more limited.

Docking at **Marseille,** you can head to the train station and

Provençal Sights near the Ports

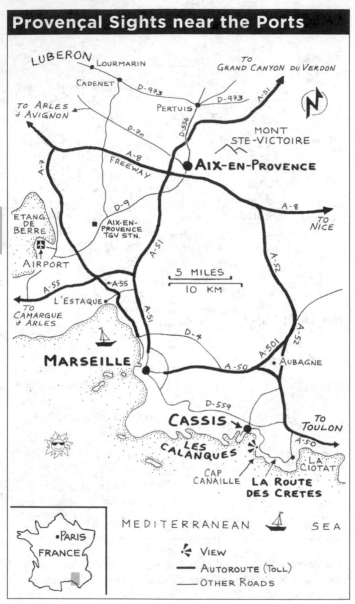

PROVENCE

LUBERON
Lourmarin
Cadenet
D-973
TO
GRAND CANYON du VERDON
PERTUIS
D-973
D-556
A-51
TO ARLES
& AVIGNON
D-7n
MONT
STE-VICTOIRE
A-8
FREEWAY
A-7
AIX-EN-PROVENCE
D-9
A-8
TO
NICE
ETANG
DE
BERRE
AIX-EN-
PROVENCE
TGV STN.
A-51
5 MILES
10 KM
A-52
AIRPORT
A-55
A-55
A-51
L'ESTAQUE
TO
CAMARGUE
& ARLES
D-4
A-52
MARSEILLE
A-50
A-501
AUBAGNE
D-559
CASSIS
TO
TOULON
LES
CALANQUES
A-50
CAP
CANAILLE
LA ROUTE
DES CRETES
LA
CIOTAT

MEDITERRANEAN   SEA

FRANCE
PARIS

⬕ VIEW
━━ AUTOROUTE (TOLL)
── OTHER ROADS

Excursions from Marseille or Toulon

Fascinating and varied excursions abound in this region. Depending on your port of call, you can easily visit **Cassis, Aix-en-Provence, Arles,** or **Avignon** on your own (all described in this chapter). The following are best done by excursion:

Pont du Gard, a well-preserved ancient aqueduct, is one of the most remarkable surviving Roman ruins anywhere (see page 278).

Les Baux is a medieval castle and hill town packed with boutiques and cafés (see page 279).

The **Hill Towns of Provence** are villages that are pretty to look at and fun to explore, including Roussillon, Gordes, Lourmarin, and Isle-sur-la-Sorgue (see page 280).

St-Tropez is a fine seaside experience (see page 378 in the French Riviera chapter), but it's far from the Provençal ports, especially Marseille—Cassis is much closer.

PROVENCE

---

make a quick visit to any one of the following: Aix-en-Provence, Cassis, Arles, or Avignon.

Docking at **Toulon,** take the train either to Cassis or Marseille. To go farther, take a cruise-line excursion or rent a car.

Your Top Options

Here are descriptions, with time estimates, of your choices; you'll probably have to choose just one:

• **Cassis** is a seaside, Riviera-like resort town that's an easy 25-minute train ride from Marseille's station, or a 35-minute ride from Toulon's. It's pleasant to stroll, but with more time, hike or take a boat to the beaches tucked between the cliffs called *calanques* (access can be limited during busy times). Allow five hours for a quick visit from either port, and add up to two hours for the *calanques.*

• **Aix-en-Provence** is a manicured city just a 45-minute train ride away from Marseille's station. With no major sights, Aix is purely Provençal life on display. Follow my self-guided walk through town. Allow a total of six hours from Marseille's cruise port; make sure your train stops at Aix's Centre-Ville station.

• **Arles,** a workaday city, has an impressive Roman Arena; allow two hours to explore, including the nearby Classical Theater and Forum Square. Van Gogh fans can follow a trail of the artist's sites through town; figure on two hours. The Ancient History Museum occupies armchair historians for an hour or two. To get to Arles, catch a train from Marseille (about 1.5 hours each way); allow at least seven hours for your visit, including transportation.

PROVENCE

Services near the Port of Marseille

The main terminal at Porte 4 has Wi-Fi and an **ATM** outside the front door. The smaller terminals have fewer services. Instead, head into town on the cruise line's shuttle bus, and find the nearest services from the Old Port (ask at the TI near the Old Port).

There is no TI at the cruise port, but there is one where the shuttle drops you off at the Old Port (see next page).

Renting a car for the day can be an efficient use of your time in this region. There are car-rental offices at Marseille's train station, including Europcar (tel. 08 25 82 56 80), Avis (tel. 08 20 61 16 36), and Hertz (tel. 04 91 14 04 24).

• **Avignon,** a fashionable walled city, is famous for its medieval bridge and Palace of the Popes. From Marseille, take a high-speed TGV train (35 minutes), then a shuttle bus or taxi from Avignon's TGV train station into town. (Skip the slower trains that go to a more central station, Gare Avignon Centre-Ville; these take 1.5 hours from Marseille). On a quick visit, follow my self-guided walk through downtown Avignon and tour the Palace of the Popes. Allow at least seven hours, starting from the dock in Marseille.

• **Marseille,** a seedy port city with some interesting sights, can fill four hours: explore the street called La Canebière, wander the Old Port, visit La Charité Museum (lunch café) and the cathedral, then head to Notre-Dame de la Garde. (If coming from Toulon, skip Notre-Dame, and allow up to six hours, including transportation.)

Arrival at the Port of Marseille

Arrival at a Glance: A shuttle bus takes you to the Old Port, where you can either start sightseeing Marseille, or continue to the train station (a 20-minute walk or quick Métro ride). From the station, trains head for Cassis (25 minutes), Aix-en-Provence (45 minutes), Arles (1.5 hours), and Avignon (35 minutes plus a 15-minute shuttle bus). Taxis are available for outlying towns, but they're pricey.

Port Overview

Marseille's enormous port sprawls for miles beneath a bluff west of downtown. In this gritty industrial zone, most cruise ships tuck themselves in between cargo vessels at **Porte 4.** This cruise pier has several terminals (called *poste,* or "dock"): Poste 163, Poste 181, and

Poste 186 feed into a new, modern terminal complex near the tip of the pier. A bit closer to the base of the pier, Poste 162 and Postes 2/3 each have their own, much smaller terminal buildings.

Alternative Port: On busy days, a few cruises may anchor offshore and tender passengers to a pier much closer to the town center (just below the cathedral), called **La Joliette.** Smaller ships may even dock here. La Joliette has two docks (Poste 94 and Poste 95). From here, you can walk to the Old Port in just 10 minutes (simply stroll with the port area on your right).

Getting to the Sights

Choose between seeing Marseille or heading to a nearby town via train or bus. The best plan may be to begin the day out of town, then work your way back to Marseille and spend any remaining time sightseeing here before returning to your ship.

By Taxi

Taxis meet arriving ships and take passengers all over Marseille and Provence. Here are the official maximum rates:

- To the Old Port, train station, or Notre-Dame de la Garde church (20 minutes): €15-20
- To Aix-en-Provence (45 minutes): €55
- To Cassis (45 minutes): €63
- Round-trip to Arles (5.5 hours): €205
- Round-trip to Les Baux (5 hours): €175
- Round-trip to both Arles and Les Baux (6.5 hours): €200
- Round-trip to Avignon (5 hours): €220
- Round-trip to Isle-sur-la-Sorgue (5.5 hours): €200

If possible, agree on the above fixed rates up front. If they use the meter, make sure they have it set to the correct tariff: You'll most likely be charged "one-way" fares: tariff C on weekdays (Mon-Sat), or tariff D on Sundays, holidays, or at night. Round-trip fares are cheaper: tariff A on weekdays; tariff B on Sundays, holidays and at night. For any trip, you will pay about 20 percent more on Sundays and holidays. For rides in town, there's a legitimate €1.10 port supplement. The official hourly rate is €22.20.

By Public Transportation

First you'll go to the Old Port, and from there you'll either begin exploring town, or head to the train station to get to another Provençal destination.

Step 1: To Marseille's Old Port

The easiest solution by far is to take the cruise line's **shuttle bus** into downtown Marseille (price varies by cruise line, generally around €7-14 round-trip, departs every 20 minutes, 15-20-minute trip). The bus deposits you at the Old Port in the heart of town, within walking distance of most of Marseille's sights, and a quick Métro ride from the train station (see "Step 2," next). The TI is a block up the main street (La Canebière) on the right.

It's possible but obnoxiously time-consuming to try to get into town on your own (involving a 30-minute walk plus a bus-and-Métro ride). Doing it yourself could easily eat up an hour or more—spring for the shuttle bus instead.

Step 2: From the Old Port to Marseille's Train Station

To reach the train station from the Old Port, **walk** straight uphill on the main drag called La Canebière, then turn left up boulevard Dugommier, which becomes boulevard d'Athènes—take this up to the station (about a 20-minute walk).

To save time and sweat, zip to the station on the **Métro**: Find an entrance to the Vieux-Port Métro stop (there are several; a handy one is right in front of the TI). Go down into the Métro, buy a €2 ticket at the automated machine, and get on a train going toward La Rose. Ride it two stops, to the St. Charles stop, and escalate up into the train station.

Step 3: From Marseille's Train Station to Provençal Sights

The main train station is called Marseille St. Charles. It has both automated ticket machines and staffed ticket windows; its electronic boards show all of the upcoming departures. Before taking off, be sure to plan your return journey. Trains go to **Cassis** (20/day, 25 minutes), **Aix-en-Provence Centre-Ville** station (2/hour, 45 minutes), **Arles** (20/day, 1.5 hours), **Avignon TGV** station (10/day, 35 minutes), and **Isle-sur-la-Sorgue** (8/day, 1-2 hours).

From the train station, you can also take a bus to **Cassis** (8/day, 50 minutes) or **Aix-en-Provence** (4/hour, 50 minutes).

By Tour

For information on hiring a local guide or joining a tour of the region, see the "Tours" section for each destination. Most guides and tour companies are based in Aix, Arles, or Avignon, but Mike Rijken's Wine Safari can pick you up in Marseille (see page 220).

Returning to Your Ship

If you stay in Marseille for the day, catch a shuttle bus at the Old Port back to your terminal. If you left Marseille and are returning by train, get off at Marseille's St. Charles Station and take the

Métro directly back to the Old Port to catch your shuttle bus: Buy a €2 ticket at the machine, descend the long escalator, and take the blue line #1 (direction: La Fourragère) two stops to Vieux-Port. Exiting the Métro train, follow *Sortie la Canebière* signs to emerge at the TI. If you have time to spare, consider walking 20 minutes downhill from the train station instead of taking the Métro (described on page 217).

See page 281 for help if you miss your boat.

Arrival at the Port of Toulon

Arrival at a Glance: Walk (25-30 minutes) or ride a local bus to Toulon's train station for connections to Cassis (35 minutes), Marseille (45-60 minutes), and beyond.

Port Overview

The pleasant if unspectacular city of Toulon (pop. 170,000), situated between mountains and a large bay, is used by some cruise lines to access the sights of Provence. Historically the city served as a fortified royal port (expanded by Louis XIV), and later as a modern military one—leading to its destruction by Allied bombs in World War II. The city was rebuilt more modern than quaint, leaving little for tourists to see. Today, the harborfront is lined not by a salty old fishermen's quarter, but by a stern row of modern apartment blocks. The best plan is to join a cruise-line excursion, rent a car, or head immediately to the train station to visit nearby towns on your own (Cassis and Marseille are easiest). If you wind up with extra time in Toulon, you can visit the city's smattering of museums, including art, natural history, folklore, Asian art, naval history, photography, and more. A cable car leads up to the mountain above town. Ask at the TI for details on any of these options.

Tourist Information: The TI is a five-minute walk from the port, on place Louis Blanc (see walking directions below). Pick up their free brochure/map for cruise passengers (mid-June-Sept Mon-Sat 9:00-19:00, Tue until 22:00, Sun 9:00-13:00; Oct-mid-June Mon-Sat 9:00-18:00, Tue until 22:00, Sun 9:00-13:00; 12 place Louis Blanc, tel. 04 94 18 53 00, www.toulontourisme.com).

Getting to the Sights

The main part of Toulon's old town (and the TI) is just a 5- to 10-minute walk from the cruise ships; to reach the train station, it's a 25- to 30-minute walk or a ride on a local bus. If there are no

Services near the Port of Toulon

Most services cluster near place Louis Blanc, the old town market square (see directions under "Getting to the Sights," below). Here you'll find the **TI** (on the right side of the square), **Pharmacie de la place Louis Blanc** (just beyond the TI), and an **ATM** (on the left, behind the flower stand). The nearest **Internet café** is three blocks away on place Gambetta (just follow the busy avenue de la République).

A **rental car** can be handy to reach Provence's more far-flung destinations. Agencies are at the Toulon train station, including Europcar (tel. 04 94 92 52 92), Avis (toll tel. 08 20 61 16 45), and Hertz (tel. 04 94 22 02 88).

taxis waiting, you can call one at tel. 04 94 93 51 51; figure about €7-10 one-way to the train station.

Step 1: To Toulon's Old Town Market Square (Place Louis Blanc)

It's an easy walk from your cruise ship to the small old town market square called place Louis Blanc, where you'll find the TI, ATMs, and the stop for buses headed to the train station. (If you get turned around, just look for signs to *Office du Tourisme*.) From your ship, walk toward the row of apartment blocks that line the top of the harbor. When you reach this embankment, swing left and walk alongside the apartments until you reach the big gap in the buildings. Hook right between the buildings; place Louis Blanc is straight ahead. The TI is on the right side of the square, and other services are nearby (see "Services near the Port of Toulon").

The mostly traffic-free old town sprawls beyond this square; it's pleasant to explore, but nothing special. The most direct route to the train station (described below) skirts the old town entirely, but if you want to linger, you can cut through the middle of the old town and feel your way to the train station (ideally, after picking up a free town map at the TI).

Step 2: From the Old Town Market Square (Place Louis Blanc) to Toulon's Train Station

From place Louis Blanc, the walk to the train station takes about 20 minutes through not-very-interesting neighborhoods. Buses also run to the station from the square.

By Foot: With your back to place Louis Blanc, turn right onto busy avenue de la République and follow it for a few blocks until it runs into a major intersection. At this point, swing right with the road up rue Henri Pastoureau—passing the square called place d'Armes on your left-hand side—and continue straight up to the big square called place de la Liberté. Cross diagonally through this square and out the top-left corner, on rue Dumont d'Urville. You'll pop out on boulevard de Tessé; the train station is just to your left.

By Bus: Bus #7 runs frequently from place Louis Blanc up to the train station (€1.40, buy ticket from driver, 4/hour Mon-Fri, 3-4/hour Sat, 1-2/hour Sun, 10-15-minute trip depending on traffic). You can catch it just a few steps off of place Louis Blanc (look for the bus stop alongside the church, on avenue de la République). Take this bus to the Gare stop at the end of the line, two blocks below the train station; from there, walk up avenue Vauban to the station.

Step 3: From Toulon's Train Station to Marseille or Cassis

The only destinations close enough for an easy side-trip by train are **Marseille** (hourly, 45-60 minutes) and **Cassis** (about hourly, 35 minutes). For connections beyond Marseille (most of them too far to be advisable on a short port visit), see page 212. While St-Tropez is sometimes offered as an excursion from Toulon, there's no convenient public-transportation connection.

By Tour

For information on hiring a local guide or joining a tour of the region, see the "Tours" section for each destination.

Returning to Your Ship

From Toulon's train station, it's a 25- to 30-minute downhill walk through town back to the cruise port, or you can catch bus #7 from two blocks in front of the station (down avenue Vauban) and take it to the Louis Blanc stop, near the TI and a 5- to 10-minute stroll from the port. If you return to Toulon with time to spare, you could poke around its old town (see ideas under "Port Overview," earlier). See page 281 for help if you miss your boat.

Marseille

Those who think of Marseille as the "Naples of France"—a big, gritty, dangerous port—are missing the boat. Today's Marseille (mar-say), though hardly pristine, is closer to the "Barcelona of France." It's a big, gritty port, *sans* question, but it has a distinct culture, a proud spirit, and a populace determined to clean up its act. That's a tall order, but they're off to a fair start. Thousands of Marseille's historic buildings are undergoing a massive renovation

program, and a new tramway system is up and running. In 2013 Marseille takes over as European Capital of Culture, allowing it to show off its cultural highlights.

France's oldest (600 B.C.) and second-biggest city (and Europe's third-largest port) owns a history that goes back to ancient Greek times—and challenges you to find its charm. Marseille is a world apart from France's other leading cities and has only one essential sight to visit—Notre-Dame de la Garde. Here the city is the museum, the streets are its paintings, and the happy-go-lucky residents provide its ambience.

The influence of immigrants matters: More than 25 percent of the city's population came from countries in North Africa. You're likely to hear as much Arabic as French. These migrants have created residential ghettos where nary a word of French is uttered—infuriating anti-immigrant French people certain that this will be the destiny for the rest of "their" country.

Most tourists leave Marseille off their itinerary—it doesn't fit their idea of the French Riviera or of Provence (and they're right). But it would be a shame to come to the south of France and not experience—however briefly—the region's leading city and namesake of the French national anthem. This much-maligned city seems eager to put on a welcoming face.

Orientation to Marseille

Marseille is big, with 820,000 people, so keep it simple and focus on the area immediately around the Old Port (Vieux Port). A main boulevard (La Canebière) meets the colorful Old Port at a cluster of small (and skippable) museums and the TI. The Panier district is the old town, blanketing a hill that tumbles down to the port. The harborside is a lively, broad promenade lined with inviting eateries, amusements, and a morning fish market. Everything described here (except Notre-Dame de la Garde) is within a 30-minute walk of the Old Port.

Tourist Information

The main TI is right at the Old Port (Mon-Sat 9:00-19:00, Sun 10:00-17:00, 4 La Canebière, toll tel. 08 26 50 05 00, www.marseille-tourisme.com). Pick up the good city map, the flier with a self-guided walk through the old town, and information on museums and the weekly walking tours.

Arrival in Marseille

By Train: If you're coming from Toulon, get off at St. Charles Station (Gare St. Charles). To get from the train station to the

Old Port, you can walk, take the Métro, or catch a taxi.

On **foot** it's an exhilarating 20-minute downhill gauntlet along grimy streets from the station to the Old Port. Leave the station through the exit at track A (by the big departure board), veer right, and walk down the stairs and straight on boulevard d'Athènes, which becomes boulevard Dugommier. Turn right at McDonald's onto the grand boulevard, La Canebière, which leads directly to the Old Port and the main TI.

By **Métro** it's an easy subterranean trip from the train station to the Old Port: Go down the escalator opposite track E and buy a ticket (from the machines or inside the *Accueil* office, €2 ticket is good for one hour of travel on Métro and buses, all-day pass costs about €5). Descend the long escalator, and take the blue line #1 (direction: La Fourragère) two stops to Vieux Port. Following *Sortie la Canebière* exit signs, you'll pop out at the TI (and smell the fish market). To return to the station from here, take the blue line #1 (direction: La Rose) two stops and get off at the stop called St. Charles.

If you take a **taxi**, allow €10 to the Old Port and €15 to Notre-Dame de la Garde—though train station cabbies may refuse these short trips if business is hopping (tel. 04 91 02 20 20). Taxis along the port will take you on shorter rides.

Helpful Hints

Pickpockets: As in any big city, thieves thrive in crowds and target tourists. Wear your money belt, and assume any commotion is a smokescreen for theft.

PROVENCE

Marseille

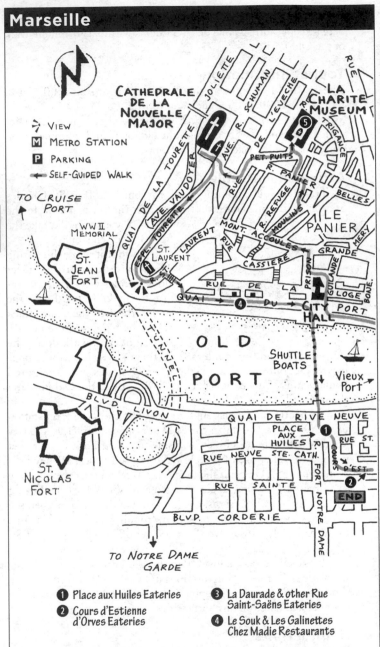

PROVENCE

Map labels:

N

VIEW
M METRO STATION
P PARKING
← SELF-GUIDED WALK

TO CRUISE PORT

CATHEDRALE DE LA NOUVELLE MAJOR

LA CHARITE MUSEUM

WW II MEMORIAL

ST. JEAN FORT

QUAI DE LA TOURETTE

AVE. VAUDOYER

ESPL. ST.-TOURETTE

ST. LAURENT

JOLIETTE

R. SCHUMAN

AVE. DE L'EVECHE

R. TRIGANCE

PET. PUITS

R. PANIER

R. REFUGE

MONT. ACCOULES

RUE CASSIERE

MOULINS

LE PANIER

BELLES

GRANDE

MERY

GUILANDE

LOGE

BONE

QUAI DU

RUE DE LA

PRISON

CITY HALL

PORT

OLD PORT

TUNNEL

SHUTTLE BOATS

VIEUX PORT

BLVD. LIVON

ST. NICOLAS FORT

QUAI DE RIVE NEUVE

PLACE AUX HUILES

RUE NEUVE STE. CATH.

RUE SAINTE

R. FORT NOTRE DAME

COURS D'EST

RUE ST.

END

BLVD. CORDERIE

TO NOTRE DAME GARDE

1 Place aux Huiles Eateries
2 Cours d'Estienne d'Orves Eateries
3 La Daurade & other Rue Saint-Saëns Eateries
4 Le Souk & Les Galinettes Chez Madie Restaurants

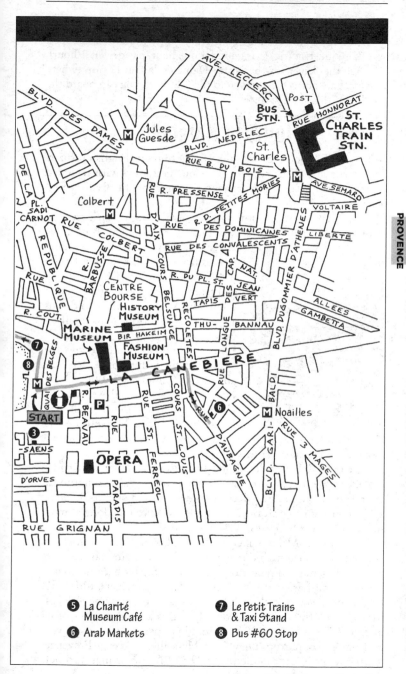

5 La Charité
Museum Café

6 Arab Markets

7 Le Petit Trains
& Taxi Stand

8 Bus #60 Stop

PROVENCE

Bus #60 to the Basilica: This handy bus scoots you from the Old Port up to Notre-Dame de la Garde in 10 minutes for about a €2 round-trip (ticket is good for one hour, pay driver, 3/hour). Ask the driver for the Notre-Dame de la Garde stop (where most are going). To return to the Old Port, you can board the bus at this same stop.

Tours in Marseille

Ask at the TI about occasional **walking tours** in English (usually Sat afternoons, about €7) and two-hour **taxi tours** with recorded information in English (arranged through the TI, €90/up to 4 people).

Le Petit Train's helpful little tourist trains with skimpy recorded information make two routes through town. Both leave

at least hourly from the Old Port (across from TI). The more interesting Notre-Dame de la Garde route (#1) saves you the 30-minute climb to the basilica's fantastic view, and runs along a nice section of Marseille's waterfront (€7, allow one hour round-trip, including 20 minutes to visit the church, runs daily, April-Oct usually every 20 minutes 10:00-13:00 & 14:00-18:30, March and Nov hourly, Dec-Feb 5/day, tel. 04 91 25 24 69). I'd skip the Vieux Marseille route (#2), which toots you through the Panier district—better done on foot (€6, 40 minutes, April-Oct only).

Le Grand Tour's double-decker buses with open seating up top offer a 16-stop, hop-on, hop-off route that is very similar to Le Petit Train's routes. The pricey buses depart from next to the Petit Train stop and run only once an hour, leaving you too long at most stops. Skip these buses (€18 for one-day pass).

Dutchman Mike Rijken's **Wine Safari** is a one-man show, taking travelers through the region he adopted more than 20 years ago. Mike came to France to train as a chef, later became a wine steward, and has now found his calling as a driver/guide. His English is fluent, and though his focus is wine and wine villages, Mike knows the region thoroughly and is a good teacher of its history (€55/half-day, €100/day, priced per person, group size varies from 2 to 6; pickups possible in Marseille or Aix-en-Provence; tel. 04 90 35 59 21, mobile 06 19 29 50 81, www.winesafari.net, mikeswinesafari@wanadoo.fr).

Sights in Marseille

I've listed these sights starting at the Old Port, jogging up and back on La Canebière, and then wandering in the Panier district. I've also included some commentary to help you connect the dots (see the map on page 218).

• *Start where the cruise ship's shuttle bus (or the Métro from the train station) deposits you in the heart of town, the...*

Old Port (Vieux Port)

Protected by two impressive fortresses at its mouth, Marseille's Vieux Port has long been the economic heart of town. These citadels were built in the 17th century under Louis XIV, suppos-edly to protect the city. But locals figured the forts were actually designed to keep an eye on Marseille—a city that was essentially autonomous until 1660, and a challenge to thoroughly incorporate into the growing kingdom of France.

Today, the serious shipping is away from the center, and the Old Port is the happy domain of pleasure craft. The fish market

along quai des Belges (where you're standing) thrives each morning (unless the wind kept the boats home the day before). The stalls are gone by 13:00, but the smells linger. Looking out to sea from here, Le Panier (the old town) rises to your right. The harborfront below Le Panier was destroyed in 1943 by the Nazis, who didn't want a tangled refuge for resistance fighters so close to the harbor. Today, it's been rebuilt with modern condos and trendy restaurants.

• *Walk uphill on the busy retail street called...*

La Canebière

The boulevard La Canebière (pronounced "can o' bee-air") with its new facelift—and classy tramway—is the celebrated main drag of Marseille. Strolling this stubby thoroughfare, you feel surrounded by a teeming, diverse city. Along this street, you'll find a thriving international market scene, three museums, and a stylish shopping district.

• *For a taste of Africa, head five blocks up La Canebière and turn right at rue Longue des Capucins. Walk down this street a few blocks (to rue d'Aubagne).*

Arab Markets—Marseille's huge Moroccan, Algerian, and Tunisian populations give the city a special spice. Strolling this area, you're immersed in an exotic and fragrant little medina filled with commotion—and no one's speaking French. Stop by **Soleil d'Egypte** and try a *bourek* wrap (apple and ground round) or, better, try the *pastilla* wrap (chicken, almonds, onions, and egg). Double back to La Canebière on rue d'Aubagne, stopping to pick up dessert (Tunisian pastries) at **La Carthage** bakery.

• *Return to La Canebière and walk back toward the Old Port. The grand triumphal arch you see far to the right at cours Belsunce marks the historic gateway to the city of Aix-en-Provence. Next, the big building that seals the street to the left at rue Ferréol is Marseille's préfecture, or regional administration. Now, cross back to the north side of La Canebière and you'll come to the...*

Fashion Museum (Musée de la Mode)—The exhibits here are as skimpy as most of its dresses, with two rooms full of creative and colorful outfits from the 1950s to today. The museum may close for renovation in 2012-2013 (if open: €3, Tue-Sun June-Sept 11:00-18:00, Oct-May 10:00-17:00, closed Mon year-round, 11 La Canebière, in Espace Mode Mediterranée).

For more fashion, cross back over La Canebière, continue across place du Général de Gaulle (passing the merry-go-round), and find the tiny rue de la Tour, Marseille's self-proclaimed "rue de la Mode." It's lined with shops proudly displaying the latest fashions, mostly from local designers. Just beyond that is the 1920s Art Deco facade of Marseille's opera house.

• *Near the end of La Canebière, on the right side, find the tall, grandiose chamber of commerce building that houses the...*

▲Marine Museum—Step inside (free entry) and take in the grand 1860s interior. A relief on the ceiling shows great moments in Marseille's history and a large court with a United Nations of plaques, reminding locals how their commerce comes from trade around the world.

The small ground-floor exhibit on the city's maritime history starts (to the right as you enter) with an impressive portrait of Emperor Napoleon III (who called for the building's construction) and his wife. Sketches show the pomp surrounding its grand opening. The next room traces the growth of the city through charts of its harbor, and the following rooms display models of big ships over the centuries (€2, daily 10:00-18:00, tel. 04 91 39 33 33).

• *In La Centre Bourse, the modern shopping center behind the chamber of commerce, you'll find the...*

Marseille History Museum (Musée d'Histoire de Marseille)— Come here for a French-only introduction to Marseille's remarkable history, including the remains of an old Roman ship and bits of a Greek vessel—both found here (closed until early 2012, €2, no English, Mon-Sat 12:00-19:00, closed Sun, tel. 04 91 90 42 22).

• *When La Canebière ends, walk around the right side of the Old Port and find the small ferry dock (La Ligne du Ferry Boat) that crosses the port. You'll be back here soon. But for now, turn around and find the City Hall.*

Le Panier District (Old Town)

Until the mid-19th century, Marseille was just the hill-capping old town and its fortified port. Today, it's the best place to find the town's soul. The ornate **City Hall** (Hôtel de Ville) stands across from the three-masted sailboat and the little shuttle ferry. Its bust of Louis XIV overlooks the harbor. Rue de la Prison leads behind the City Hall and up the hill (where we're headed shortly). At the crest of the hill—the highest point in the old town—is the peaceful place des Moulins, named for the 15 windmills that used to spin and grind from this windy summit. (Today, only the towers of three windmills remain.)

• *Walk up the broad stairway, passing the City Hall, turn left at the top, then track the brown signs up—and up some more—to la Vieille Charité. As you walk, read the thoughtful English-information plaques (posted on iron stands at points of historic interest) and listen for the sounds of local life being played out, on the streets and in the rooms just above.*

▲**La Charité Museum (Centre de la Vieille Charité)**—Now a museum, this was once a poorhouse. In 1674 the French king

decided that all the poor people on the streets were bad news. He built a huge triple-arcaded home to house a thousand needy subjects. In 1940 the famous architect Le Corbusier declared it a shame that such a fine building was so underappreciated. Today, the striking building—wonderfully renovated and beautiful in its arcaded simplicity—is used as a collection of art galleries surrounding a Pantheonesque church. You can stroll around the courtyard for free. (Good WCs are in the far-left corner.)

The pediment of the church features the figure of Charity taking care of orphans (as the state did with this building). She's flanked by pelicans (symbolic of charity, for the way they were said to pick flesh from their own bosom to feed their hungry chicks, according to medieval legend). The ground floor outside the church houses temporary exhibits. Upstairs you'll find rooms with interesting collections of Celtic (c. 300 B.C.), Greek, and Roman artifacts from this region. There's also a surprisingly good Egyptian collection, and masks from Africa and the South Pacific (€3-6 depending on exhibits, no English information, Tue-Sun June-Sept 11:00-18:00, Oct-May 10:00-17:00, closed Mon year-round, idyllic restaurant/bar, tel. 04 91 14 58 80).

• *From La Charité, cross the small cobbled triangular square, turn right on rue du Petit Puits, and follow the street down, curving left, then right, to find...*

Cathédrale de la Nouvelle Major—Bam. This huge, striped

cathedral seems lost out here, away from the action and above the nondescript port. The cathedral was built in the late 1800s to replace the old cathedral that the city had outgrown. It's more impressive from the outside, but worth a quick peek inside for its floor and wall mosaics over the nave (Tue-Sun 10:00-19:00, closed Mon).

• *Return to the Old Port by walking up the tree-lined esplanade de la Tourette. Marseille's sprawling modern port is behind you and becomes visible as you climb.*

The Great Maritime Port of Marseille (GPMM)—The economy of Marseille is driven by its modern commercial ports, which extend 30 miles west from here (a nearby canal links Marseille inland via the Rhône River, adding to the port's importance). Over 100 million tons of freight pass through this port each year (60 percent of which is petroleum), making this one of Europe's top three ports. Container traffic is significant but is hampered by crippling strikes for which the left-leaning city is famous. By contrast, cruise-ship tourism has taken off in a big way, bringing more than 550,000 passengers to Marseille each year.

• *Keep walking. A fabulous view awaits you at the bend.*

View Terrace—Voilà! This is one of the best views of Marseille, with Notre-Dame de la Garde presiding above, and twin forts below protecting the entrance to the Old Port. The ugly, boxy building marked "Memorial" at the base of the fort (below and to your right) is a memorial to those lost during the Nazi occupation of the city in World War II. The small church to your left is the Church of St. Laurent, which once served as a parish church for

sailors and fishermen—notice the lighthouse-like tower.
• *Continue down the steps back to the Old Port.*

From the Old Port to the New Town

Halfway along the promenade (quai du Port), at the City Hall, you'll see the fun little **shuttle boat** that ferries locals across the harbor to the new town (free, every 10 minutes 8:00-17:00, lunch break from about 12:30-13:15). Note the unusual two-way steering wheel as you sail. You'll dock in the new town—which, because of the 1943 bombings, is actually older than the "old" town along the harborfront.

Directly in front of the ferry landing, you'll find popular bars and brasseries, good for a quick meal or memorable drink. Wander in along place aux Huiles, make your way left, and find a smart pedestrian zone crammed with cafés and restaurants (see "Eating in Marseille," later).
• *Our walk is over. Don't miss a trip up to Notre-Dame de la Garde, described next.*

Overlooking the Old Port

▲▲**Notre-Dame de la Garde**—Crowning Marseille's highest point, 500 feet above the harbor, is the city's landmark sight. This massive Neo-Romanesque-Byzantine basilica, built in the 1850s during the reign of Napoleon III, is a radiant collection of domes, gold, and mosaics. The monumental statue of Mary and the Baby Jesus towers above everything (Jesus' wrist alone is 42 inches around, and the statue weighs nine tons). And though people come here mostly for the commanding city view, the interior will bowl you over (open daily in summer 7:00-20:00, until 19:00 in winter, cafeteria and WCs just below the view terrace). This hilltop has served as a lookout, as well as a place of worship, since ancient times. Climb to the highest lookout for an orientation table and the best views. Those islands straight ahead are the Iles du Frioul, including the island of If—where the Count of Monte Cristo spent time.

Getting There: To reach the church, you can hike 30 minutes straight up from the harbor. To save some sweat, catch a taxi (about €10), hop on bus #60, or ride the tourist train—all stop on the harborfront near the fish market (see map on page 218 and "Helpful Hints" on page 217).

PROVENCE

Eating in Marseille

In the New Town: For the best combination of trendiness, variety, and a fun people scene, eat in the new town, on or near quai de Rive-Neuve (on the left side of the Old Port as you look out to sea). Look for **place aux Huiles, cours d'Estienne d'Orves,** and **rue Saint-Saëns** for a melting pot of international eateries ranging from giant salads and fresh seafood to crêpes, Vietnamese dishes, Belgian waffles, and Buffalo wings. Come here for ambience, not for top cuisine. **La Daurade** is worth considering, with fresh seafood at fair prices served in a classy setting (€18 *menus,* €20 bouillabaisse, closed Wed, 36 rue Saint-Saëns, tel. 04 91 33 82 42).

Near the Old Port: For good views *en terrasse,* go to the other side of the port. Have a real Moroccan meal at **Le Souk** (€16 couscous and *tajine* dishes, €20 three-course *menu,* intimate and authentic interior, closed Mon, 100 quai du Port, tel. 04 91 91 29 29). If you must have bouillabaisse, try **Les Galinettes Chez Madie** (€26 *menu,* €35/person for bouillabaisse, closed Sun, 138 quai du Port, tel. 04 91 90 40 87).

Near La Charité: **La Charité Museum** has a lovely, quiet courtyard café (lunch only).

Cassis

Hunkered below impossibly high cliffs, Cassis (kah-see) is an unpretentious port town that gives travelers a sunny time-out from their busy vacation. Two hours away from the fray of the Côte d'Azur, Cassis is a poor man's St-Tropez. Outdoor cafés line the small port on three sides, where boaters clean their crafts as they chat up café clients. Cassis is popular with the French and close enough to  Marseille to be busy on weekends and all summer. Come to Cassis to dine portside, swim in the glimmering-clear water, and explore its rocky *calanques* (inlets).

Orientation to Cassis

The Massif du Puget mountain hovers over little Cassis, with hills spilling down to the port. Cap Canaille cliff rises from the southeast, and the famous *calanques* inlets hide along the coast northwest of town. Hotels, restaurants, and boats line the attractive little port.

Tourist Information

The TI is in the modern building in the middle of the port among the boats (Mon-Sat 9:00-12:30 & 14:00-18:00, Sun 10:00-12:30 except July-Aug 9:00-19:00, quai des Moulins, toll tel. 08 92 25 98 92—€0.34/minutes, www.ot-cassis.fr, info@ot-cassis.com).

Arrival in Cassis

By Train: Cassis' hills forced the train station to be built two miles away, and those last two miles can be a challenge. It's a small station with limited hours (no baggage storage, ticket windows open Mon-Fri 6:15-13:15 & 13:45-20:45, Sat-Sun 9:30-13:15 & 13:45-18:10). If you need to buy tickets when the station is closed, use the machines (coins only).

A **taxi** into town costs up to €10 and is well worth the expense unless a bus is soon to arrive (see below). If there's no taxi waiting, call 04 42 01 78 96 (a pay phone is outside the train station). Otherwise, it's a 50-minute walk into town (turn left out of the station and follow signs).

Marcouline **buses** link the station with the town center, but service is spotty (about hourly with longer intervals in the afternoon, schedule posted at all stops). Call the TI in advance to get the schedule and plan your arrival accordingly—but be ready to take a taxi. The bus drops you at the Casino stop in Cassis: From here, turn right on rue de l'Arène and walk downhill five minutes to reach the port.

By Bus: Regional buses (including those from Marseille) stop a five-minute walk from the port on avenue du 11 Novembre (stop is labeled Gendarmerie).

Helpful Hints

Market Days: The market hops on Wednesdays and Fridays until 12:30 (on the streets around the Hôtel de Ville).

Beaches: Cassis' beaches are pebbly. The big beach behind the TI is sandier than others, though water shoes still help. You can rent a mattress with a towel (about €15/day) and pedal boats (about €10/hour). Underwater springs just off the Cassis shore make the water clean, clear, and a bit cooler than at other beaches.

Internet Access: Avelit Télécom is a few blocks from the port, across from Parking la Viguerie, on avenue de la Viguerie (at #23, tel. 04 42 98 81 94).

Grocery Store: The **Casino** market is next door to Hôtel le Liautaud (daily 8:30-12:30 & 15:30-20:00, Sun until 18:00).

PROVENCE

Cassis

1. El Sol, L'Oustau de la Mar, Bar Canaille & Chez César Rests.
2. Le 8 et Demi Café & Grand Marnier Crêpes
3. Restaurant le Clos des Arômes
4. Le Grand Large Restaurant
5. La Girondole Restaurant
6. Le Bonaparte Restaurant
7. Le Chai Cassidain Wine Bar
8. Avelit Télécom (Internet Access)
9. Casino Grocery
10. Tourist Train (Afternoon Only)
11. Motorboat Rental & WC
12. Pedal Boat Rental
13. Kayak Rental
14. To "Gendarmerie" Bus Stop (Regional Buses to/from Marseille)

B. BUS STOP TO/FROM TRAIN STATION
T. TAXI STAND
P. PARKING

Wine-Tasting: Le Chai Cassidain is a wine bar that welcomes visitors, with red-leather stools and a good selection of regional wines offered by the bottle or by the glass (daily 10:00-13:00 & 15:00-22:00 and often later, 4 blocks from port at 6 rue Séverin Icard, tel. 04 42 01 99 80).

Taxi: Call 04 42 01 78 96 or find the main taxi stand across from Hôtel Cassitel by the *boules* court.

Tourist Train: The little white *train touristique*, with commentary in French and English, will take you on a worthwhile 45-minute circuit out to the peninsula on the Port-Miou *calanque* and back (€6, March-Oct, afternoons only, catch it next to the TI, tel. 04 42 01 09 98).

PROVENCE

Self-Guided Tour of Cassis

Visual Tour from the Port

Find a friendly bench in front of Hôtel le Golfe—or, better, enjoy a drink at their café—and read this quick town intro.

Cassis was born more than 2,500 years ago (on the hill with the castle ruins, across the harbor). Ligurians, Phoenicians, maybe Greeks, certainly Romans, and plenty of barbarians all found this spot to their liking. Parts of the castle date from the eighth century, and the **fortress walls** were constructed in the 13th century to defend against seaborne barbarian raids. The Michelin family recently sold the fortress to investors who wanted to turn it into a luxury hotel. Cassis' planning commission had other ideas.

In the 18th century, when things got safer, people moved their homes back to the waterfront. Since then, Cassis has made its living through fishing, quarrying its famous white stone, and producing well-respected white wines—which, conveniently, pair well with the local seafood dishes, and *bien sûr*, with tourists like us.

With improvements in transportation following the end of World War II, tourism rose gradually in Cassis, though crowds are still sparse by Riviera standards. While foreigners overwhelm nearby resorts, Cassis is popular mostly with the French and still feels unspoiled. The town's protected status limits the height of the buildings along the waterfront. Cassis' port is home to some nice boats...but they're chump change compared to the glitzier harbors farther east.

The big cliff towering above the castle hill is **Cap Canaille.** Europe's highest maritime cliff, it was sculpted by receding glaciers (wrap your brain around that concept), and today drops 1,200 feet straight down. You can—and should—take a taxi along the top for staggering views.

If you can overcome your inertia, walk to your right, then veer left on top of the short wall in front of the public WCs. The rocky shore over your right shoulder looks cut away just for sunbathers. But Cassis was once an important **quarry,** and stones were sliced right out of this beach for easy transport to ships. The Statue of Liberty's base sits on this rock, and even today, Cassis stone remains highly valued throughout the world...but yesterday's quarrymen have been replaced by today's sunbathers.

Sights in Cassis

▲▲▲The Calanques

Until you see these exotic Mediterranean fjords—with their translucent blue water, tiny intimate beaches, and stark cliffs plunging into the sea or forming rocky promontories—it's hard to understand what all the excitement is about.

Calanques (kah-lahnk) are narrow, steep-sided valleys partially flooded by the sea, surrounded by rugged white cliffs usually made of limestone (quarries along the *calanques* have provided building stone for centuries). The word comes from the Corsican word *calanca,* meaning "inlet"—the island of Corsica also has *calanques.* These inlets began as underwater valleys carved by the seaward flow of water at river mouths, and were later gouged out deeper by glaciers. About 12,000 years

(In the margin: PROVENCE)

ago, when the climate warmed and glaciers retreated at the end of the last Ice Age, the sea level rose partway up the steep rocky sides of the *calanques*. Today the cliffs harbor a unique habitat that includes rare plants and nesting sites for unusual raptors.

The most famous inlets are in the Massif des Calanques, which runs along a 13-mile stretch of the coast from Marseille to Cassis. This area and part of the surrounding region became a national park in 2011.

You can hike, or cruise by boat or kayak, to many *calanques*. Bring plenty of water, sunscreen, and anything else you need for the day, as there's nary a baguette for sale. Don't dawdle—to limit crowds and because of fire hazards, the most popular *calanques* can be closed to visitors between 11:00 and 16:00 in high season (late June-mid-Sept) and on weekends. When they are "closed," the only way to see the *calanques* is by boat or kayak. The TI can give you plenty of advice.

Cruising the *Calanques*: Several boats offer trips of various lengths (3 *calanques*-€13, 2/hour, 45 minutes; 5 *calanques*-€15, 3/day, one hour; 8-10 *calanques*-€19, 1-3/day, 2 hours; tel. 04 42 01 90 83, www.calanques-cassis.com). The three-*calanque* tour is most popular. Tickets are sold (and boats depart) from a small booth on the port opposite the Hôtel Lieutaud. *Prochain départ* means "next departure." Boats vary in size (some seat up to 100). Closer to the TI, Didier Crespi offers more personal cruises on his smaller boat *Le Calendal* (seats 12 max). His commentary is in French only, but he can give you the basics in English (3 *calanques*-€13, one hour, drop by or call for the day's schedule, mobile 06 63 35 66 51).

Hiking to the *Calanques*: The trail lacing together *calanques* Port-Miou, Port-Pin, and d'En-Vau will warm a hiker's heart. Views are glorious and the trail is manageable if you have decent shoes (though shade is minimal).

For most, the best *calanque* by foot is Calanque Port-Pin, about an hour from Cassis (30 minutes after the linear, boat-lined Calanque Port-Miou, which also works as a destination if time is short). Calanque Port-Pin is intimate and well-forested, with a small beach.

The TI's map of Cassis gives a general idea of the *calanques* trail, though you don't really need a map. Start along the road behind Hôtel le Golfe and walk past Plage du Bestouan, then look for green hiker signs to *Calanque Miou* (pay attention to your route for an easier return). You'll climb up, then drop down residential streets, eventually landing at the foot of Calanque Port-Miou, where the dirt trail begins. Follow signs to *Calanques Port-Pin* and *d'En Vau*, walking 500 yards along a wide trail and passing through an old quarry.

You're now on the *GR (Grande Randonnée)* trail, indicated by red, white, and green markers painted on rocks, trees, and other landmarks. Follow those markers as they lead uphill (great views at the top), then connect to a rough stone trail leading down to Calanque Port-Pin (nice beach, good scampering). *Bonne route!*

Other Ways to Reach the *Calanques*: From about mid-April to mid-October, you can rent a **kayak** in Cassis—or in nearby Port Miou, which is closer to the *calanques* (one-seater-€25/4 hours, two-seater-€40/4 hours, tel. 04 42 01 80 01 in Cassis, mobile 06 75 70 00 73 in Port Miou). The TI has brochures for more kayak companies. You can also take a **kayak tour** (€35/half-day, €55/day, depart from nearby town of La Ciotat, advance reservations smart, mobile 06 12 95 20 12, www.provencekayakmer.fr). If the hiking trails are closed, this is the only way you'll be able to get to those *calanques* beaches.

You can rent a small motorboat without a special boating license (€100/half-day, €140/day, €700 cash or credit-card imprint as deposit; at Loca'Bato office, a few steps away from Hôtel le Golfe; mobile 06 73 11 63 65). Another option is a **skippered boat rental** (up to 8 people, about €350/half-day, €410/day, ask at TI).

Eating in Cassis

Peruse the lineup of tempting restaurants along the port, window-shop the recommended places below, and then decide for yourself (all have good interior and exterior seating). You can have a ham-and-cheese crêpe or go all out for bouillabaisse with the same great view. Picnickers can enjoy a beggars' banquet on the benches at Hôtel le Golfe or on the beach, or discover your own quiet places along the lanes away from the port (small grocery stores open until 19:30). Local wines are terrific: red from Bandol and whites/rosés from Cassis.

Dining Portside

The first four places offer €23-28 *menus* and are ideally situated side by side, allowing diners to comparison shop. I've enjoyed good meals at each of them.

El Sol is sharp and popular with discerning diners (closed Sun eve and all day Mon, 20 quai des Baux, tel. 04 42 01 76 10).

L'Oustau de la Mar is a good choice, with a loyal following, fair prices, and welcoming owner Dominique. Try the *dos de loup de mer à la crème d'olives*—a whitefish smothered in a delectable sauce (closed Thu, 20 quai des Baux, tel. 04 42 01 78 22).

Bar Canaille specializes in fresh seafood platters, oysters, and other shellfish (closed Tue, 22 quai des Baux, tel. 04 42 01 72 36).

Chez César was most popular with locals on my last visit, with good prices and selection (€25 *marmite de pêcheur*—a poor man's bouillabaisse, €12.50 *plats, menus* from €22, closed Sun-

Mon, 21 quay des Baux, tel. 04 42 01 75 47).

Le 8 et Demi serves crêpes, pizza, salads, and good Italian gelato on plastic tables with front-and-center portside views (closed Thu, 8 quai des Baux, tel. 04 42 01 94 63).

The **Grand Marnier crêpe stand** cooks delicious dessert crêpes to go for €3—the Grand Marnier crêpe rules. This is ideal for strollers (next to Le 8 et Demi).

Dining Away from the Port

Restaurant le Clos des Arômes is the place to come for a refined, candlelit meal. Dine on a lovely enclosed terrace (€26 *menu*, closed all day Mon and Tue-Wed for lunch, near Parking la Viguerie at 10 rue Abbé Paul Mouton, tel. 04 42 01 71 84).

Le Grand Large is indeed large and owns the scenic beach-front next to the TI. Come here for a quiet drink, or to dine sea-side rather than portside (€27 *menu* with good choices, open daily, Plage de Cassis, tel. 04 42 01 81 00).

La Girondole is an easy place for families, with cheap pizza, pasta, and salads. It's a block off the port (open daily in summer, take-away also possible, closed Tue off-season, 1 rue Thérèse Rastit, tel. 04 42 01 13 39).

Le Bonaparte attracts budget travelers with good prices, sufficient quality, and a big selection (€12 two-course *menu*, €16 three-course *menu*, closed Sun-Mon, 14 rue Général Bonaparte, tel. 04 42 01 80 84).

PROVENCE

Aix-en-Provence

Aix-en-Provence is famous for its outdoor markets, beautiful people, and ability to embrace the good life. It was that way when the French king made the town his administrative capital of Provence, and it's that way today. For a tourist, Aix-en-Provence (the "Aix" is pronounced "X") is happily free of any obligatory turn-stiles. And there's not a single ancient sight to see. It's just a wealthy town filled with 140,000 people—most of whom, it seems, know how to live well and look good. Aix-en-Provence's 40,000 stu-dents (many from other countries) give the city a youthful energy and its well-deserved nickname, "Sex-en-Provence."

Aix-en-Provence

1 Thé à Thème
2 Chez Feraud
3 Pasta Cosy
4 Les Agapes
5 Charlotte
6 Hôtel Cézanne Restaurant
7 Le Papagayo Café, Paniers des Salades & Juste en Face
8 Café l'Archevêché
9 La Médina de Fez
10 Aux Deux Garçons & Le Grillon
11 La Brocherie
12 Maison Béchard Patisserie
13 Café de l'Unic & Brûlerie Richelme
14 Paradox Bookshop
15 Monoprix (Groceries)
16 Electric Minibus Stop

PROVENCE

Orientation to Aix-en-Provence

With no "must-see" sights (unless you're a student), Aix works well as a day trip, and is best on days when the most markets thrive (Tue, Thu, and Sat). The city can be seen in a 1.5-hour stroll from the TI or train station, though connoisseurs of southern French culture will want more time to savor this lovely place.

Cours Mirabeau (the grand central boulevard) divides the stately, quiet Mazarin Quarter from the lively old town. In the old sections, picturesque squares are connected by fine pedestrian shopping lanes, many of which lead to the cathedral.

Tourist Information

The TI anchors the west end of cours Mirabeau at La Rotonde traffic circle (although be aware that it will probably move to 300 avenue Giuseppe Verdi sometime in 2011). Get the walking-tour brochure *In the Footsteps of Cézanne*, with the best city-center map and a good overview of excursions in the area. The TI has other maps that cover areas beyond old Aix (Mon-Sat 8:30-19:00, Sun 10:00-13:00 & 14:00-18:00, longer hours in the summer, shorter hours in the winter, 2 place du Général de Gaulle, tel. 04 42 16 11 61, www.aixenprovencetourism.com). English-language **walking tours** of the old town are offered at 10:00 on Tuesdays, Thursdays, and Saturdays (€8, depart from the TI).

Arrival in Aix-en-Provence

By Train: Aix-en-Provence has two train stations: Centre-Ville, near the city center; and the faraway TGV station, which cruisers should avoid. From the Centre-Ville station, it's a breezy 10-minute stroll to the TI and pedestrian area (cross the boulevard and walk straight up avenue Victor Hugo, turn left at first intersection, still on Victor Hugo; TI is on the left when you reach La Rotonde, the big traffic circle).

By Bus: From the sidewalk bus station *(gare routière)*, it's a 10-minute walk to the TI: Head uphill to the flowery roundabout and turn left toward the splashing fountain (La Rotonde, the big traffic circle by the TI). There is talk of relocating the *gare routière*, but most residents don't take it seriously—still, beware of possible changes.

By Car: Day-trippers should look for the La Rotonde parking area (near the TI) or park in any pay lot near the old city. Allow €14 for 24 hours of parking.

Helpful Hints

Markets: Aix-en-Provence bubbles over with photogenic open-air morning markets in several of its squares: **Richelme** (produce daily, my favorite), **Palace of Justice** (flea market Tue, Thu, and Sat), and **L'Hôtel de Ville** (flower market Tue, Thu, and Sat; book market first Sun of each month). Most pack up at 13:00, except the book market, which runs all day. It's well worth planning your visit for a market day, as these markets are the sightseeing highlights of the town. WineInProvence leads market tours (described below).

Internet Access: There are many options; ask the TI for suggestions.

English Bookstore: Located on the quiet side of Aix-en-Provence, the low-key **Paradox Bookshop** has a modest collection of adult and children's books, a good selection of tourist guides (Cassis, Arles, Avignon, and so on), and a small supply of American grocery staples such as peanut butter. The owner, Ms. Graillon, carries my guidebooks, speaks fluent English, and is a good source for information (Mon-Sat 10:00-12:30 & 14:00-18:30, closed Sun, 15 rue du 4 Septembre, tel. 04 42 26 47 99).

Supermarket: Monoprix, on cours Mirabeau two long blocks up from La Rotonde, has a grocery store in the basement (Mon-Sat 8:30-21:00, closed Sun).

Taxi: Call 04 42 27 71 11 or mobile 06 16 23 82 39.

Famous Local Product: Signs at fancy bakeries advertise *calissons d'Aix,* the city's homemade pastries (which don't do much for me). They're made with almond paste—kind of like a marzipan cake—and make good souvenirs. I prefer the *macarons.*

Dark Sunglasses: You may want to pick up a pair of especially dark glasses (to be more discreet when appreciating the beautiful people of Aix-en-Provence).

Tours in Aix-en-Provence

Local Guides—**Caroline Bernard** speaks great English and enjoys teaching visitors the wonders of her city (bernardcaro@aol.com, or contact her through the TI). **Catherine d'Antuono** is a smart, capable guide for Aix-en-Provence and the region (mobile 06 17 94 69 61, tour.designer@provence-travel.com).

WineInProvence—Smart, young, and enthusiastic Americans Hilary and Brian are eager to help you discover French wine and food in a fun loft apartment just off a market square. Their dream is to show you a side of Provence that you wouldn't otherwise see—through the lens of French food and wines (2-hour tasting of 5 French wines-€50, 5-hour cooking and wine-tasting class-€150). Hilary and Brian also lead tours of Aix's open markets and specialty food shops, allowing you to experience shopping for food in Provence like a local. You'll meet their favorite cheese-makers, bakers, and produce vendors (€75, 2 hours). They also run half-day and full-day wine tours, covering the lesser-known areas of Cassis, Bandol, and Aix-en-Provence (€155/person for half-day, €225/person for all day, mobile 06 33 69 42 95, www.tastesofprovence.com).

Wine Safari—Dutchman Mike Rijken can pick you up at the Aix train station for a wine tour (see page 220).

Electric Minibus Joyride—For a mere €0.50, take an orientation ride on a *Diabline*—a six-seater electric-powered minibus. It leaves every 10 minutes from the La Rotonde fountain, opposite the TI (Mon-Sat 8:30-13:00 & 15:00-19:30, none on Sun, 40 minutes round-trip). You can also wave down the young drivers anywhere and hop on. There are two routes (A and B); ask the driver for a map when you board. Line A gives you a better overview of the city and runs a route similar to the self-guided walk described below. It also gets you near Cézanne's Studio. Designed with local seniors in mind, the minibus provides a fun (and less glamorous) slice-of-life experience in Aix-en-Provence.

Petit Train—Rest your feet and discover Aix-en-Provence's historic center on a 50-minute tour on the little train, while listening to English commentary (€6, departs from La Rotonde fountain). Ask about the longer tours that cover Cézanne's steps.

Self-Guided Walk in Aix-en-Provence

I've listed these streets, squares, and sights in the order of a handy, lazy orientation stroll. This walk is highlighted on the map on page 234.

• *Start across from the TI, on cours Mirabeau near the small fountain.*

La Rotonde: In the 1600s, the roads from Paris and Marseille met just outside the Aix-en-Provence town wall at a huge roundabout called La Rotonde. From here locals enjoyed a sweeping view of open countryside before entering the town. As time passed, Aix-en-Provence needed space more than fortifications. The wall was destroyed and replaced by a grand boulevard (cours Mirabeau). A modern grid-plan town, the Mazarin Quarter, arose across the boulevard from the medieval town (to the right as you look up cours Mirabeau). In 1860, to give residents water and shade, the town graced La Rotonde with a fountain and the boulevard with trees. Voilà: The modern core of Aix-en-Provence was created.

• *Saunter up cours Mirabeau.*

Cours Mirabeau: This "Champs-Elysées of Provence" divides the higgledy-piggledy old town and the stately Mazarin Quarter. Designed for the rich and famous to strut their fancy stuff, cours Mirabeau survives much as it was: a single lane for traffic and an extravagant pedestrian promenade, shaded by plane trees and lined by 17th- and 18th-century mansions for the nobility. Rich

folks lived on the right side (in the Mazarin Quarter); common folk lived on the left side (in the old town). Cross-streets were gated to keep everyone in their place.

The street follows a plan based on fours: 440 meters long, 44 meters wide, plane trees (originally elms) 4 meters apart, and decorated by 4 fountains. The "mossy fountains," covered by 200 years of neglect, trickle with water from the thermal spa that gave Aix its first name (in France, "Aix" refers to a city built over a hot spring). At the end of the boulevard, a statue celebrates the last count of Provence, under whose rule this region joined France.

Cours Mirabeau was designed for showing off. Today, it remains a place for *tendance* (trendiness)—or even *hyper-tendance*. Show your stuff and strut the broad sidewalk. As you stroll up the boulevard, stop in front of Aix's oldest and most venerated *patisserie*, **Maison Béchard** (12 cours Mirabeau), and get a whiff coming from the vent under the entry. Grab a seat in an upscale café and observe.

• *From the mossy fountain at rue du 4 Septembre, turn right onto Aix-en-Provence's quiet side, the pleasing little place des Quatre Dauphins. This marks the center of the...*

Mazarin Quarter (Quartier Mazarin): Built in a grid plan during the reign of King Louis XIV, the Mazarin Quarter remains a peaceful, elegant residential neighborhood—although each of its mansions now houses several families rather than just one. Study the quarter's Baroque and Neoclassical architecture (from the 17th and 18th centuries). The square's Fountain of the Four Dolphins, inspired by Bernini's fountains in Rome, dates from an age when Italian culture set the Baroque standard across Europe.

Wander up rue Cardinale to the **Musée Granet,** which faces a handsome square and features Aix's home-grown artists (including a few paintings by Cézanne—see sidebar on page 241). The vertical St. Jean de Malte church sits across from the museum.

• *Return to the cours Mirabeau and pop into #53, the venerable...*

Aux Deux Garçons: This café, once frequented by Paul Cézanne, is now popular with—and controlled by—the local mafia. Don't take photos here (and don't open a competing café—the mafia is a serious problem for many independent restaurateurs in Aix). Still, it's worth a peek for its beautiful circa-1790 interior and, for many, worth the higher (mafia-inflated) prices for the sidewalk setting. The Cézanne family hat shop was next door (#55). Cézanne's dad must have been some hatter. He parlayed that successful business into a bank, then into greater wealth, setting up his son to be free to enjoy his artistic pursuits.

• *From here we'll enter the lively Old Town, where pedestrian streets are filled with strolling beauties and romantic street musicians. This is the place in Aix-en-Provence for shopping. Leave cours Mirabeau down the tiny passage Agard, 10 steps past Aux Deux Garçons. It leads to the* **Palace of Justice Square,** *which hosts a bustling flea market (Tue, Thu, and Sat mornings). If the market is on, dally awhile. Leave this square heading left along the first street you crossed to enter it. The street you're on, rue Marius Reinaud, hosts the top designer shops in town. Pause several blocks down at the peaceful courtyard square called...*

Place d'Albertas: This sweet little square was created by the guy who lived across the street. He hated the medieval mess of buildings facing his mansion, so he drew up a harmonious facade with a fountain, and hired an architect to build his ideal vision and mask the ugly neighborhood. The neighbors got a nice new facade, and the rich guy got the view of his dreams. The long-overdue restoration of this once run-down square is making a remarkable difference. But since only two-thirds of the property owners agreed to help fund the work, one third remains undone.

• *From here turn right on rue Aude, the main street of medieval Aix-en-Provence (which turns into rue du Maréchal Foch and eventually leads to the cathedral). Notice how effectively the green bollards keep cars from parking in this virtually car-free zone. Notice also the side streets, with their traffic-barrier stumps that lower during delivery hours. Stop where rue du Maréchal Foch crosses rue de la Fauchier for a decadent* macaron *sensation at* **Brunet Chocolatier** *(ooh la la). Make your way to...*

Richelme Square (Place Richelme): This wonderful square hosts a lively market, as it has since the 1300s (daily 7:00-13:00). It's the perfect Provençal scene—lovely buildings, plane trees, farmers selling local produce, and a guy in the goat-cheese stall near the Bar de l'Horloge who looks just like Paul Cézanne—or Jerry Garcia, if that's more your style. (He works Tue, Thu, and Sat and is fully aware of his special good looks; drop by for a sample and a photo if you like.) The cafés at the end of the square are ideal for market observation. To savor the market scene, pause for a drink at **Café de l'Unic** (also draws a lively and young pre-dinner crowd). To experience the best coffee and hot chocolate in Aix,

Paul Cézanne in Aix-en-Provence

Post-Impressionist artist Paul Cézanne (1839-1906) loved Aix-en-Provence. He studied law at the university (opposite the cathedral), and produced most of his paintings in and around Aix-en-Provence—even though this conservative town didn't understand him or his art. Today the city fathers milk anything remotely related to his years here. But because the conservative curator of the town's leading art gallery, the Granet Museum, decreed "no Cézannes," you can see only a few of Cézanne's lesser original paintings in Aix-en-Provence. Bad curator.

Instead, fans of the artist will want to pick up the *In the Footsteps of Cézanne* self-guided-tour flier at the TI, and follow the bronze pavement markers around town.

Cézanne's **last studio** (Atelier Cézanne)—preserved as it was when he died—is open to the public. It's a 30-minute walk from the TI, or you can get there on electric minibus A (see "Tours in Aix-en-Provence," earlier). Although there is no art here, his tools and personal belongings make it almost interesting for enthusiasts—I'd skip it. If you must go, it's best (and essential in high season) to reserve a visit time in advance at the TI or at www.aixenprovencetourism.com (€6, daily July-Aug 10:00-18:00, April-June and Sept 10:00-12:00 & 14:00-18:00, Oct-March until 17:00, English-language tours usually at 16:00 or 17:00, 2 miles from TI at 9 avenue Cézanne, tel. 04 42 16 10 91, www.atelier-cezanne.com).

grab an outdoor stool and go local at **Brûlerie Richelme** (Tue-Sat 8:30-18:15, closed Sun-Mon).

• *One block uphill is the stately...*

L'Hôtel de Ville Square (Place de l'Hôtel de Ville): This square, also known as place de la Mairie, is anchored by a Roman column. Stand with your back to the column and face the Hôtel de Ville. The center niche of this 17th-century City Hall once featured a bust of Louis XIV. But since the Revolution, Marianne (the Lady of the Republic) has taken his place. As throughout Europe, the

three flags represent the region (Provence), country (France), and the European Union. Provence's flag carries the red and yellow of Catalunya (the region in Spain centered on Barcelona) because the counts of Provence originated there. The coat of arms over the doorway combines the Catalan flag and the French fleur-de-lis.

The 18th-century building on your left was once the town's corn exchange (today it's a letter exchange). Its exuberant pediment features figures representing the two rivers of Provence: old man Rhône and madame Durance. While the Durance River floods frequently (here depicted overflowing its frame), it also brings fertility to the fields (hence the cornucopia).

Back toward the Hôtel de Ville (where you're heading), the 16th-century bell tower was built in part with stones scavenged from ancient Roman buildings—notice the white stones at the tower's base. The niche above the arch once displayed the bust of the king. Since the Revolution, it has housed a funerary urn that symbolically honors all who gave their lives for French liberty. Under the arch, a small plaque honors the American 3rd Division that liberated the town in 1944 (with the participation of French troops; Aix-en-Provence got through World War II relatively unscathed).

History aside, the square is a delight for its colorful morning markets: flowers (Tue, Thu, and Sat) and old books (first Sun of month). On non-market days and each afternoon, café tables replace the market stalls.

• *Stroll under the bell tower and up rue Gaston de Saporta, to the yellow-bannered...*

Musée Etienne de St. Jean: This museum—which may close in 2011—fills a 17th-century mansion with a scant collection of artifacts. The building interior itself is of most interest. The exhibits include lots of *santons*—painted clay figurines popular in old-time manger scenes (if open: €4, pick up the English handout, April-Sept Tue-Sun 10:00-13:00 & 14:00-18:00, Oct-March until 17:00, closed Mon, 17 rue Gaston de Saporta).

• *A block farther uphill, facing the historic university building (where Cézanne studied), is the...*

Cathedral of the Holy Savior (Saint-Sauveur): This church was built atop the Roman forum—likely on the site of a pagan temple. As the cathedral grew with the city, its interior became a parade of architectural styles. The many-faceted interior is at once confusing and fascinating, with three distinct sections: Standing at the entrance, you face the Romanesque section; to the left are the Gothic and then the Baroque sections. We'll visit each in turn.

In the **Romanesque section,** branching off to the right is the baptistery, with its early Christian (fourth-century) Roman font. It's big enough for immersion, which was the baptismal style in Roman times. Also notice that it's eight-sided, symbolizing eternity: one side more than the seven days it took God to create everything. The font is surrounded by ancient columns with original fourth-century capitals below a Renaissance cupola. Farther down is the door to the 12th-century cloister (visits on the half-hour except 12:00-14:00, or just open the outer door and peer through the iron gate). Beyond that, find the closet-sized architectural footprint of the original Christian chapel from the Roman era.

In the **Gothic section,** two organs flank the nave: One works, but the other is a prop, added for looks...an appropriately symmetrical Neoclassical touch, as was the style in the 18th century. The precious door (facing the street from this section) is carved of chestnut with a Gothic top (showing sibyls, or ancient female prophets) and Renaissance lower half (depicting prophets). Because it faces the street, it's covered by a second, protective door (viewable on request).

In the **Baroque section,** don't miss the finely detailed three-paneled altar painting of the burning bush (15th century, by Nicolas Froment).

• *Your tour is over. Walking back through town, drop by a designer bakery to try a* calisson, *Aix-en-Provence's local candy (see "Helpful Hints," earlier). Or, for fewer calories and just as much fun, marvel at a town filled with people who seem to be living life very, very well.*

Eating in Aix-en-Provence

In Aix-en-Provence, you can dine on bustling squares, along a grand boulevard, or in little restaurants on side streets (where you'll find the best values). Cours Mirabeau is good for desserts and drinks, as are many of the outdoor places lining leafy squares. Aix is filled with tempting but mediocre restaurants. To eat higher on the food chain, try one of the following places.

In the Old Town
Thé à Thème delivers wonderful lunches at colorful tables, with cheery ambience inside and on the charming back terrace. The portions are big and the prices are small, making this a popular place with locals. Call ahead for an outside table (€10 *plats,* wonderful desserts, Tue-Sat 9:30-18:00, closed Sun-Mon, 7 rue Mignet, tel. 04 42 63 04 05).

Chez Feraud, in a lovely vine-covered building, is a good choice for a refined meal of authentic Provençal dishes. Here, clients speak in hushed voices, the table settings are carefully arranged, and Mama serves with formal grace while son handles the grill (€30 *menu,* 8 rue du Puits Juif, tel. 04 42 63 07 27).

Pasta Cosy is unique, serving a Franco-Italian fusion of original dishes in a small, cozy setting (inside and out). Welcoming owner Fabien greets every client with the same enthusiasm and ensures good service and top quality (his wife is le chef). Be tempted by their rich Pastacosy dish (pasta cooked inside a wheel of parmesan cheese). Try the *fiocchetti* (pasta cooked with pears and gorgonzola) or the gourmet white truffle pasta. Desserts are homemade and delicious. The reasonably priced wine list features wines from Burgundy and Provence (closed Sun, across from Hôtel le Manoir at 5 rue d'Entecasteaux, tel. 04 42 38 02 28).

Les Agapes is a top choice for Provençal cuisine, offering generous portions, good prices, and attentive service (€20-25 *menus*, 11 rue des Bernardines, tel. 04 92 70 45 45).

Charlotte is Aix's low-key, down-and-dirty diner, where locals come for a good meal at a good price in simple surroundings. The entrance is the epitome of low-profile (€19 three-course *menu* only, no à la carte, 32 rue des Bernardines, tel. 04 42 26 77 56).

Hôtel Cézanne serves up a gourmet champagne brunch *à la francaise*. For €20 you can feast on a great selection of omelets (made with caramelized goat cheese or truffles) and sample real French toast (brunch served daily 7:00-12:00, 40 avenue Victor Hugo, tel. 04 42 91 11 11).

On Forum des Cardeurs: Just off L'Hôtel de Ville Square, the forum des Cardeurs is café-crammed. Browse the selection from top to bottom, then decide. **Le Papagayo** has a good selection of salads and a quiche of the day (big €14 salads, open daily for lunch and dinner, 22 forum des Cardeurs, tel. 04 42 23 98 35). **Paniers des Salades** is *the* place for salads (€10 buys a salad big enough for two; the goat-cheese salad is particularly good, 34 forum des Cardeurs, tel. 04 42 21 35 80). **Juste en Face,** facing Papagayo, features excellent grilled meats (the duck and rabbit are tasty) and Mediterranean cuisine, specializing in North African *tajine*—a vegetable-based stew usually served with meat (€16 *plats*, open daily, 6 rue Verrerie, tel. 04 42 96 47 70).

On and near place des Martyrs de la Resistance: A short block below the cathedral, this quiet square is good for a light meal. **Café l'Archevêché** is a fine bet for café fare and is understandably proud of its pizzas (lunch only except June-mid-Sept, tel. 04 42 21 43 57). For a change of pace, find **La Médina de Fez** a few blocks away, offering authentic Moroccan cuisine at fair prices (*menus* from €19, closed Mon, 35 rue Campra, tel. 04 42 21 68 58).

Along Cours Mirabeau

If you're interested in a delicious view more than delicious food, eat with style on cours Mirabeau.

Aux Deux Garçons has always been the place to see and be seen: a vintage brasserie with door-to-door waiters in aprons, a lovely interior, and well-positioned outdoor tables with properly placed silverware on white tablecloths. It's busy at lunchtime (€20 *plats*, two-course *menus* from €28, great steak *tartare*, open daily, 53 cours Mirabeau, tel. 04 42 26 00 51). Even if you're not eating here, pop in to see the decor.

Le Grillon is a younger, more boisterous, and less pricey choice for dining on cours Mirabeau (white tablecloths, €15 *plats*, €24 *menu*). Its bar is a hit with locals for the prime seating: front and center on the boulevard's strolling fashion show (open daily for lunch and dinner, corner of rue Clémenceau and cours Mirabeau, tel. 04 42 27 58 81).

In the Mazarin Quarter

La Brocherie dishes up French rather than Provençal cuisine. Its stone-rustic, indoors-only ambience is best for cooler days. This family-owned bistro—run by Messieurs Soudain and Tourville—is deep in the Mazarin Quarter and highlights food from the farm (it's about beef). Dig into the hearty self-service salad buffet (all you can eat, €12) and meats grilled over a wood fire (skip the fish options). The €20 *menu* includes the salad bar (closed Sun, indoor seating only, 5 rue Fernand Dol, tel. 04 42 38 33 21).

Arles

By helping Julius Caesar defeat Marseille, Arles (pronounced "arl") earned the imperial nod and was made an important port city. With the first bridge over the Rhône River, Arles was a key stop on the Roman road from Italy to Spain, the Via Domitia. After reigning as the seat of an important archbishop and a trading center for centuries, the city became a sleepy backwater of little importance in the 1700s. Vincent van Gogh settled here in the late 1800s, but left only a chunk of his ear (now long gone). American bombers destroyed much of Arles in World War II as the townsfolk hid out in its underground Roman galleries. But today Arles thrives again, with its evocative Roman ruins, an eclectic assortment of museums, made-for-ice-cream pedestrian zones, and squares that play hide-and-seek with visitors.

The city's unpolished streets and squares are not to everyone's taste. This workaday city has not sold out to tourism, so you won't see dolled-up lanes and perfectly preserved buildings. But to me, that's part of its charm.

Arles

← Van Gogh Walking Tour

P Parking

B Bus Stop

↙ View

🖼 Easel

100 YARDS
100 METERS

1 The Yellow House (Easel)
2 Starry Night Over the Rhône (Easel)
3 Rue de la Cavalerie
4 Arena (Easel)
5 Fondation Van Gogh
6 Alpilles Mountains View
7 Jardin d'Eté (Easel)
8 To Les Alyscamps Cemetery
9 Place du Forum & Café la Nuit (Easel)
10 Espace Van Gogh (Easel)
11 Trinquetaille Bridge (Easel)
12 Le Petit Train Departure Point
13 Bus #1 (to Ancient History Museum)

PROVENCE

TRINQUETAILLE BRIDGE

QUAI   MARX   TRUCHET

DR. FANTON

RUE A. FRANCE

TO ANCIENT HISTORY MUSEUM

R. JOUVE   R. LIBERTE

ARLATEN FOLK MUSEUM (CLOSED UNTIL 2013)

RUE GAMBETTA

RUE REPUB.

ESPACE VAN GOGH

MOLIERE   R.

RUE

END

TO ANCIENT HISTORY MUSEUM ←   BLVD.   BUS STN.

DCH

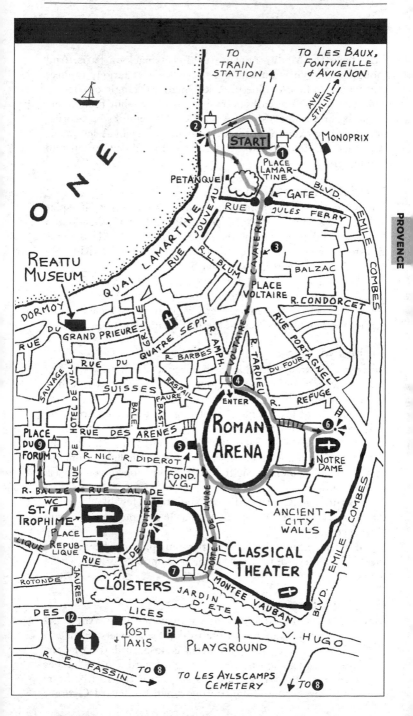

TO TRAIN STATION

TO LES BAUX, FONTVIEILLE & AVIGNON

AVE. STALIN

MONOPRIX

R Ô N E

START ❶

❷

PLACE LAMARTINE

PETANQUE

GATE

BLVD.

RUE   JULES FERRY

CAVALERIE

❸

BALZAC

EMILE COMBES

QUAI LAMARTINE

RUE JOUVEAU

R. L. BLUM

PLACE VOLTAIRE

R. CONDORCET

REATTU MUSEUM

DORMOY

RUE DU GRAND PRIEURE

QUATRE SEPT.

R. BARBES

R. AMPH.

VOLTAIRE

RUE TARDIEU

DU FOUR

RUE PORTAGNEL

RUE

SAUVAGE

RUE DU

SUISSES

RASPAIL

FAURE

BAIE

R. BAST.

REFUGE

R.

DE HOTEL DE VILLE

RUE DES ARENES

❹
ENTER

ROMAN ARENA

❻

NOTRE DAME

PLACE DU FORUM

❾

R. NIC.   R. DIDEROT

❺

FOND. V.G.

DE LAURE

ANCIENT CITY WALLS

R. BALZE ← RUE CALADE

WC

ST. TROPHIME

PLACE REPUB-LIQUE

LIQUE

RUE

DE CLOITRE

PORTE

CLASSICAL THEATER

ROTONDE

CLOISTERS

❼

JARDIN D'ETE

MONTEE VAUBAN

EMILE COMBES

BLVD.

V. HUGO

JAURES

DES

❶❷

POST & TAXIS

P

LICES

PLAYGROUND

R. E. FASSIN

TO ❽

TO LES AYLSCAMPS CEMETERY

TO ❽

Orientation to Arles

Arles faces the Mediterranean, turning its back on Paris. And though the town is built along the Rhône, it largely ignores the river. Landmarks hide in Arles' medieval tangle of narrow, winding streets. Virtually everything is close—but first-timers can walk forever to get there. Arles provides helpful street-corner signs that point you toward sights. Racing cars enjoy Arles' medieval lanes, turning sidewalks into tightropes and pedestrians into leaping targets.

Tourist Information

The **main TI** is on the ring road boulevard des Lices, at esplanade Charles de Gaulle (April-Sept daily 9:00-18:45; Oct-March Mon-Sat 9:00-16:45, Sun 10:00-13:00; tel. 04 90 18 41 20, www.arlestourisme.com). There's also a **train station TI** (Mon-Fri 9:00-13:30 & 14:30-16:45, closed Sat-Sun).

At either TI, pick up the city map, note the bus schedules (displayed in binders), and ask about walking tours of Arles. Skip the useless €1 brochure describing several walks in Arles, including one that locates Van Gogh's "easels" (better explained on page 256).

Arrival in Arles

By Train: The train station is on the river, a 10-minute walk from the town center. Before heading into town, get what you need at the train station TI.

To reach the town center, turn left out of the train station and walk 15 minutes; or wait for the free Navia bus at the shelter across the street (3/hour, Mon-Sat only). Taxis usually wait in front of the station, but if you don't see any, call the posted telephone numbers, or dial 04 89 73 36 00. If the train station TI is open, you can ask them to call.

By Bus: The Centre-Ville bus station is a few blocks below the main TI, located on the ring road at 16-24 boulevard Georges Clemenceau.

By Car: Parking des Lices (Arles' only parking garage), near the TI on boulevard des Lices, is the best option (€3/hour, €8/24 hours).

Helpful Hints

Market Days: On Wednesday and Saturday mornings, Arles' ring road erupts into an open-air festival of fish, flowers, produce... and you name it. The main event is on Saturday, with vendors jamming the ring road from boulevard Emile Combes to the east, along boulevard des Lices near the TI (the heart of the market), and continuing down boulevard Georges

Clemenceau to the west. Wednesday's market runs only along boulevard Emile Combes.

Internet Access: Internet cafés in Arles change with the wind. Ask at the TI.

English Book Exchange: A small exchange is available at the recommended **Soleileis** ice-cream shop.

Getting Around Arles

In this flat city, everything's within **walking** distance. Only the Ancient History Museum requires a healthy walk (or you can take a taxi or bus). The elevated riverside promenade provides Rhône views and a direct route to the Ancient History Museum (to the southwest) and the train station (to the northeast). Keep your head up for *Starry Night* memories, but eyes down for decorations by dogs with poorly trained owners.

Arles' **taxis** charge a set fee of about €10, but nothing except the Ancient History Museum is worth a taxi ride. To call a cab, dial 04 89 73 36 00 or 04 90 96 90 03.

The free **Navia bus** circles the town (3/hour, Mon-Sat only), but is only useful for access to the train station.

Tours in Arles

Tourist Train—Le Petit Train d'Arles provides a helpful orientation to the lay of the land—if you prefer sitting to walking (€7, 35 minutes, stops in front of the main TI and at the Arena).

Local Guides—Charming **Jacqueline Neujean,** an excellent guide, knows Arles and nearby sights intimately and loves her work (€90/2 hours, tel. & fax 04 90 98 47 51). Gregarious **Daniela Wedel** happily organizes personalized excursions (about €160/half day, €270 full day—price varies according to itinerary and number of people, mobile 06 43 86 30 83, daniela@treasure-europe.com).

Sights in Arles

Most sights cost €3.50-7, and though any sight warrants a few minutes, many aren't worth their individual admission price. The TI sells three different monument passes (called Passeports). **Le Passeport Avantage** covers almost all of Arles' sights (€13.50, under 18 for €12; Fondation Van Gogh discounted); and the €9 **Le Passeport Liberté** lets you choose any five monuments (one must be a museum). Depending on your interests, one of the €9 Passeports is probably best.

Start at the Ancient History Museum for a helpful overview (drivers should try to do this museum on their way into Arles), then dive into the city-center sights. Remember, many sights stop selling tickets 30-60 minutes before closing (both before lunch and at the end of the day).

▲▲Ancient History Museum (Musée de l'Arles et de la Provence Antiques)

Begin your town visit here, for Roman Arles 101. Located on the site of the Roman chariot racecourse (the arc of which is built into the parking lot), this air-conditioned, all-on-one-floor museum is just west of central Arles along the river. Models and original sculptures (with almost no posted English translations but a decent hand-out) re-create the Roman city, making workaday life and culture easier to imagine.

Cost and Hours: €6, Wed-Mon April-Oct 9:00-19:00, Nov-March 10:00-18:00, closed Tue year-round, presqu'île du Cirque Romain.

Information: Ask for the English booklet, which provides a helpful if not in-depth background on the collection, and inquire whether there are any free English tours (usually daily July-Sept at 17:00, 1.5 hours). Tel. 04 90 18 88 88, www.arles-antique.cg13.fr.

Getting There: To reach the museum on foot from the city center (a 20-minute **walk**), turn left at the river and take the riverside path to the big, blue, modern building. As you approach the museum, you'll pass the verdant Hortus Garden—designed to recall the Roman circus and chariot racecourse that were located here, and to give residents a place to gather and celebrate civic events. A **taxi** ride costs €10 (museum can call a taxi for your return). **Bus #1** gets you within a few minutes' walk (€0.80, 3/hour Mon-Sat, none Sun). Catch the bus in Arles (clockwise direction on boulevard des Lices), then get off at the Musée de l'Arles Antique stop (before the stop, you'll see the bright-blue museum ahead on the right). Turn left as you step off the bus, and follow the sidewalk. (To return to the center, the bus stop is across the street from where you got off.)

◉ Self-Guided Tour: A huge map of the Roman Arles region greets visitors and shows the key Roman routes accessible to Arles. Find the impressive row of pagan and early-Christian **sarcophagi** (from the second to fifth centuries). These would have lined the Via Aurelia outside the town wall. In the early days of the Church, Jesus was often portrayed beardless and as the good shepherd, with a lamb over his shoulder.

Next you'll see **models** of every Roman structure in (and near)

Arles. These are the highlight for me, as they breathe life into the buildings as they looked 2,000 years ago. Start with the model of Roman Arles, and imagine the city's splendor. Find the Forum—still the center of town today, though only two columns survive. Look at the space Romans devoted to their Arena and huge racecourse—a reminder that an emphasis on sports is not unique to modern civilizations. The model also illustrates how little Arles seems to have changed over two millennia, with its houses still clustered around the city center, and warehouses still located on the opposite side of the river.

Look for individual models of the major buildings shown in the city model: the elaborately elegant forum; the floating bridge that gave Arles a strategic advantage (over the widest, and therefore slowest, part of the river); the theater (with its magnificent stage wall); the Arena (with its movable stadium cover to shelter spectators from sun or rain); and the circus, or chariot racecourse. Part of the original racecourse was just outside the windows, and, though long gone, it must have resembled Rome's Circus Maximus in its day—its obelisk is now the centerpiece of Arles' place de la République.

Finally, check out the **3-D model** of the hydraulic mill of Barbegal, with its 16 waterwheels and eight grain mills cascading down a nearby hillside.

Other rooms in the museum display pottery, jewelry, metal and glass artifacts, and well-crafted mosaic floors that illustrate how Roman Arles was a city of art and culture. The many **statues** that you see are all original, except for the greatest—the *Venus of Arles*, which Louis XIV took a liking to and had moved to Versailles. It's now in the Louvre—and, as locals say, "When it's in Paris...bye-bye."

In Central Arles

Ideally, visit these sights in the order listed below. I've included some walking directions to connect the dots.

▲▲**Forum Square (Place du Forum)**—Named for the Roman forum that once stood here, place du Forum was the political and religious center of Roman Arles. Still lively, this café-crammed square is a local watering hole and popular for a *pastis* (anise-based apéritif). The bistros on the square, though no place for a fine meal, can put together a good-enough salad or *plat du jour*—and when you sprinkle on the ambience, that's €10 well spent.

At the corner of Grand Hôtel Nord-Pinus (a favorite of Pablo

Picasso), a plaque shows how the Romans built a foundation of galleries to make the main square level in order to compensate for Arles' slope down to the river. The two columns are all that survive from the upper story of the entry to the Forum. Steps leading to the entrance are buried—the Roman street level was about 20 feet below you (you can get a glimpse of it by peeking through the street-level openings under the Hôtel d'Arlatan, two blocks below place du Forum on rue Sauvage).

The statue on the square is of **Frédéric Mistral** (1830-1914). This popular poet, who wrote in the local dialect rather than in French, was a champion of Provençal culture. After receiving the Nobel Prize in Literature in 1904, Mistral used his prize money to preserve and display the folk identity of Provence. He founded the regional folk museum (the Arlaten Folk Museum, closed for renovation until 2013) at a time when France was rapidly centralizing. (The local mistral wind—literally "master"—has nothing to do with his name.)

The **bright-yellow café**—called Café la Nuit—was the subject of one of Vincent van Gogh's most famous works in Arles. Although his painting showed the café in a brilliant yellow from the glow of gas lamps, the facade was bare limestone, just like the other cafés on this square. The café's current owners have painted it to match Van Gogh's version...and to cash in on the Vincent-crazed hordes who pay too much to eat or drink here.

• *Walk a block uphill (past Grand Hôtel Nord Pinus) and turn left. Walk through the Hôtel de Ville's vaulted entry (or take the next right if it's closed), and pop out onto the big...*

Republic Square (Place de la République)—This square used to be called "place Royale"...until the French Revolution. The obelisk was the former centerpiece of Arles' Roman Circus. The lions at its base are the symbol of the city, whose slogan is (roughly) "the gentle lion." Find a seat and watch the peasants—pilgrims, locals, and street musicians. There's nothing new about this scene.

• *Near the corner of the square where you entered, look for...*

▲▲**St. Trophime Church**—Named after a third-century bishop of Arles, this church sports the finest Romanesque main entrance (west portal) I've seen anywhere.

Like a Roman triumphal arch, the church facade trumpets the promise of Judgment Day. The tympanum (the semicircular area above the door) is filled with Christian symbolism. Christ sits in majesty, surrounded by symbols of the four evangelists: Matthew (the winged man), Mark (the winged lion), Luke (the ox), and John (the eagle). The 12 apostles are lined up below Jesus. It's Judgment Day...some are saved and others aren't. Notice the condemned (on the right)—a chain gang doing a sad bunny-hop over the fires of hell. For them, the tune trumpeted by the three angels above Christ is not a happy one. Below the chain gang, St. Stephen is being stoned to death, with his soul leaving through his mouth and instantly being welcomed by angels. Ride the exquisite detail back to a simpler age. In an illiterate medieval world, long before the vivid images of our Technicolor time, this was a neon billboard over the town square.

Enter the church (free, daily April-Sept 9:00-12:00 & 14:00-18:30, Oct-March 9:00-12:00 & 14:00-17:00). Just inside the door on the right, a chart locates the interior highlights and helps explain the carvings you just saw on the tympanum.

Tour the church counterclockwise. The tall 12th-century Romanesque nave is decorated by a set of tapestries showing scenes from the life of Mary (17th century, from the French town of Aubusson). Amble around the Gothic apse. Just to the left of the high altar, check out the relic chapel—with its fine golden boxes that hold long-venerated bones of obscure saints. Farther down is a chapel built on an early-Christian sarcophagus from Roman Arles (dated about A.D. 300). The heads were lopped off during the French Revolution.

This church is a stop on the ancient pilgrimage route to Santiago de Compostela in northwest Spain. For 800 years pilgrims on their way to Santiago have paused here...and they still do today. As you leave, notice the modern-day pilgrimages advertised on the far right near the church's entry.

• *Leaving the church, turn left, then left again through a courtyard to enter the cloisters.*

The adjacent **cloisters** are worth a look only if you have a pass (big cleaning under way, enter at the far end of the courtyard). The many small columns were scavenged from the ancient Roman theater. Enjoy the sculpted capitals, the rounded 12th-century Romanesque arches, and the pointed 14th-century Gothic ones. The pretty vaulted hall exhibits 17th-century tapestries showing scenes from the First Crusade to the Holy Land. On the second floor, you'll walk along an angled rooftop designed to catch rainwater—notice the slanted gutter that channeled the water into a cistern and the heavy roof slabs covering the tapestry hall below (€3.50, daily March-Oct 9:00-18:00, Nov-Feb 10:00-17:00).

• *Turn right out of the cloisters, then take the first right on rue de la Calade to reach the...*

Classical Theater (Théâtre Antique)—This first-century B.C. Roman theater once seated 10,000. It was an elegant, three-level structure with 27 arches radiating out to the street level. From the outside, it looked much like a halved version of Arles' Roman Arena. For more on Roman theaters, spring for the helpful €3 brochure.

Start with the video outside, which provides helpful background information and images that make it easier to put the scattered stones back in place (crouch in front to make out the small English subtitles). Next, walk to a center aisle and pull up a stone seat. To appreciate the theater's original size, look to the upper-left side of the tower and find the protrusion that supported the highest seating level. The structure required 33 rows of seats covering three levels to accommodate demand. During the Middle Ages, the old theater became a convenient town quarry—St. Trophime Church was built from theater rubble. Precious little of the original theater survives—though it still is used for events, with seating for 3,000 spectators.

Two lonely Corinthian columns are all that remain of a three-story stage wall that once featured more than 100 columns and statues painted in vibrant colors. The orchestra section is defined by a semicircular pattern in the stone in front of you. Stepping up onto the left side of the stage, look down to the slender channel that allowed the brilliant-red curtain to disappear below, like magic. The stage, which was built of wood, was about 160 feet across and 20 feet deep. Go backstage and browse through the actors' changing rooms, then loop back to the entry behind the grass (€6, daily May-Sept 9:00-19:00, March-April and Oct 9:00-18:00, Nov-Feb 10:00-17:00). Budget travelers can peek over the fence from rue du Cloître, and see just about everything for free.

• *A block uphill is the...*

▲▲▲**Roman Arena (Amphithéâtre)**—Nearly 2,000 years ago, gladiators fought wild animals here to the delight of 20,000 screaming fans. Today local daredevils still fight wild animals here—"bullgame" posters around the Arena advertise upcoming

spectacles. A lengthy restoration process is well under way, giving the amphitheater an almost bleached-teeth whiteness.

In Roman times, games were free (sponsored by city bigwigs), and fans were seated by social class. The many exits allowed for rapid

Le Mistral

Provence lives with its vicious mistral winds, which blow 30-60 miles per hour, about 100 days out of the year. Locals say it blows in multiples of threes: three, six, or nine days in a row. The mistral clears people off the streets and turns lively cities into ghost towns. You'll likely spend a few hours or days taking refuge—or searching for cover. The winds are strongest between noon and 15:00.

When the mistral blows, it's everywhere, and you can't escape. Author Peter Mayle said it could blow the ears off a donkey (I'd include the tail). According to the natives, it ruins crops, shutters, and roofs (look for stones holding tiles in place on many homes). They'll also tell you that this pernicious wind has driven many people crazy (including young Vincent van Gogh). A weak version of the wind is called a *mistralet*.

The mistral starts above the Alps and Massif Central mountains and gathers steam as it heads south, gaining momentum as it screams over the Rhône Valley (which acts like a funnel between the Alps and the Cévennes mountains) before exhausting itself when it hits the Mediterranean. And though this wind rattles shutters throughout the Riviera and Provence, it's strongest over the Rhône Valley...so Avignon, Arles, and the Côtes du Rhône villages bear its brunt. While wiping the dust from your eyes, remember the good news: The mistral brings clear skies.

PROVENCE

dispersal after the games—fights would break out among frenzied fans if they couldn't leave quickly. Through medieval times and until the early 1800s, the arches were bricked up and the stadium became a fortified town—with 200 humble homes crammed within its circular defenses. Three of the medieval towers survive (the one above the ticket booth is open and rewards those who climb it with terrific views). To see two still-sealed arches—complete with cute medieval window frames—turn right as you leave, walk to the Andaluz restaurant, and look back to the second floor (€6, daily May-Sept 9:00-19:00, March-April and Oct 9:00-18:00, Nov-Feb 10:00-17:00).

• *Our last stop is a museum that's been on the move a lot recently. If you're here in early 2011, turn left out of the Arena and walk uphill to find the...*

▲**Fondation Van Gogh**—A refreshing stop for modern-art-lovers and Van Gogh fans, this two-level gallery shows works by contemporary artists (including **Roy Lichtenstein** and **Robert Rauschenberg**), who pay homage to Vincent through thought-provoking interpretations of his works. The black-and-white photographs (both art and shots of places that Vincent painted) complement the paintings. (But be warned that the collection contains no Van

Gogh originals.) Unfortunately, this collection is often on the road July through September, when non-Van Gogh material is displayed (€6, €4 with Le Passeport Avantage; good collection of Van Gogh souvenirs, prints, and postcards for sale in gift shop; Tue-Sat 10:00-12:30 & 14:00-17:00, closed Sun-Mon, tel. 04 90 49 94 04, www.fondationvangogh-arles.org). In late 2011, you'll find the museum at 17 rue des Suisses, three blocks west of the Arena. In Spring 2012, it moves across town to 35 rue du Dr. Fanton, near the Trinquetailla Bridge. For more on Vincent, see "Van Gogh Sights in and near Arles," next.

Van Gogh Sights in and near Arles

In the dead of winter in 1888, 35-year-old Dutch artist Vincent van Gogh left big-city Paris for Provence, hoping to jump-start his floundering career and personal life. He was inspired, and he was lonely. Coming from the gray skies and flat lands of the north, Vincent was bowled over by everything Provençal—the sun, bright colors, rugged landscape, and unspoiled people. For the next two years he painted furiously, cranking out a masterpiece every few days.

None of the 200-plus paintings that Van Gogh did in the south can be found today in the city that so moved him. But you can walk the same streets he knew and see places he painted, marked by about a dozen steel-and-concrete "**easels**," with photos of the final paintings for then-and-now comparisons. The TI has a €1 brochure that locates all the easels (those described in this walk are easily found without the brochure—see the map on page 246). Small stone markers with yellow accents embedded in the pavement lead to the easels.

• *Take a walk in Vincent's footsteps (roughly north to south through Arles' center) and watch his paintings come to life by putting yourself in his shoes. Start at* **place Lamartine** *and find the stone easel across the grass from the Crêperie-Brasserie.*

Vincent arrived in Arles on February 20, 1888, to a foot of snow. He rented a small house on the north side of place Lamartine. The house was destroyed in 1944 by an errant bridge-seeking bomb, but the four-story building behind it—where you see the Civette Arlesienne—still stands (find it in the painting). The house had four rooms, including a small studio and the cramped trapezoid-shaped bedroom made famous  in paintings. It was painted yellow inside and out, and Vincent named it..."**The Yellow House.**"

• *Walk to the river, passing a monument in honor of two American pilots killed in action during the liberation of Arles. The monument was erected in 2002 as a post-9/11 sign of solidarity with Americans. Find the easel in the wall where ramps lead down to the river.*

One night, Vincent set up along this river west of place Lamartine and painted the stars boiling above the city skyline—*Starry Night over the Rhône.* Vincent looked to the night sky for the divine and was the first to paint outside after dark, adapting his straw hat to hold candles (which must have blown the minds of locals back then). As his paintings progressed, the stars became larger and more animated (like Vincent himself). Note: This painting is not the *Starry Night* you're thinking of.

PROVENCE

• *Turn around and walk through the small park, then go into town between the stone towers along **rue de la Cavalerie.***

Van Gogh walked into town the same way, underneath the arch and along this street. Arles' 19th-century red light district was just east of rue de la Cavalerie, and the far-from-home Dutchman spent many lonely nights in its bars and brothels.

• *Pass through place Voltaire, continue walking up rue Voltaire to the **Arena**, and then find the easel at the top of the Arena steps, to the right.*

All summer long, fueled by sun and alcohol, Vincent painted the town. He loved the bullfights in the Arena (note the bull in the easel), and sketched the colorful surge of the crowds, spending more time studying the people than watching the bullfights. Vincent had little interest in Arles' antiquity—it was people and nature that fascinated him. (Near the Arena, the Fondation Van Gogh—described on page 255—exhibits paintings by artists inspired by Van Gogh.)

• *Walk clockwise around the Arena, then up the cobbled lane next to Andaluz restaurant. Keep left in the parking lot to find a viewpoint.*

This view to the **Alpilles Mountains** (no easel) pretty much matches what Vincent would have seen (be here late in the day for the best light). Vincent was an avid walker. Imagine him hauling his easel into those fields under intense sun, leaning against a ferocious wind, struggling to keep his hat on. He did this about 50 times during his stay in Arles, just to paint the farm workers.

• *Continue past the upper end of the Arena, turn left before the Classical Theater, and walk out rue de Porte de Laure. At the end of the street, step down into the park and find the easel on the last path before the end of the park to the right.*

Vincent spent many a sunny day painting the leafy **Jardin**

d'Eté. In a letter to his sister, Vincent wrote, "I don't know whether you can understand that one may make a poem by arranging colors.... In a similar manner, the bizarre lines, purposely selected and multiplied, meandering all through the picture may not present a literal image of the garden, but they may present it to our minds as if in a dream."

Packing his paints and a picnic in a rucksack, he day-tripped to the old Roman cemetery of **Les Alyscamps** (a 10-minute detour from this route, across the busy street and to the left).

• *Continue through the gardens and exit at the far-right corner. Work your way past the Classical Theater on rue du Cloître, and take the first left on rue de la Calade. Continue to* **place du Forum** *and locate an easel one café down from the yellow Café la Nuit.*

In October, lonely Vincent—who dreamed of making Arles a magnet for fellow artists—persuaded his friend Paul Gauguin to come. Their plan was for Gauguin to be the "dean" of a new art school in Arles, and Vincent its instructor-in-chief. At first, the two got along well. They spent days side by side, rendering the same subject in their two distinct styles. At night they hit the bars and brothels. Van Gogh's well-known *Café at Night* captures the glow of an absinthe buzz at Café la Nuit on place du Forum.

After two months together, the two artists clashed over art and personality differences (Vincent was a slob around the house, whereas Gauguin was meticulous). The night of December 23, they were drinking absinthe at the café when Vincent suddenly went ballistic. He threw his glass at Gauguin. Gauguin left. Walking through place Victor Hugo, Gauguin heard footsteps behind him and turned to see Vincent coming at him, brandishing a razor. Gauguin quickly fled town. The local paper reported what happened next: "At 11:30 p.m., Vincent Vaugogh [*sic*], painter from Holland, appeared at the brothel at no. 1, asked for Rachel, and gave her his cut-off earlobe, saying, 'Treasure this precious object.' Then he vanished." He woke up the next morning at home with his head wrapped in a bloody towel and his earlobe missing. Was Vincent emulating a successful matador, whose prize is cutting off the bull's ear?

• *From here retrace your steps a bit, then walk through the place de la République, turn right in the far corner, and find the Arlaten Folk Museum. Turn left on rue Président Wilson, and find Espace Van Gogh (on the right). There's an easel in the center of the courtyard.*

Vincent was checked into the local hospital—today's **Espace Van Gogh** cultural center (the Espace is free, but only the courtyard is open to the public). It surrounds a flowery courtyard that the artist loved and painted when he was being treated for blood loss as well as for hallucinations and severe depression that left him bed-ridden for a month.

In the spring of 1890, Vincent left Provence to be cared for by a doctor in Auvers-sur-Oise, north of Paris. On July 27, he wandered into a field and shot himself. He died two days later.

The next easels are less central, but easily located and worth the effort for Van Gogh fans: the **Trinquetaille Bridge,** on the river walkway toward the Ancient History Museum (the current bridge is a 1951 replacement); and the most famous, the **Langlois Drawbridge** (1.5 miles south of town along a Rhône canal—today's bridge is a 1926 duplicate of the original).

Eating in Arles

You can dine well in Arles on a modest budget—in fact, it's hard to blow a lot on a meal here (most of my listings have *menus* for €22 or less). The bad news is that restaurants here change regularly, so double-check my suggestions. Before you eat, go local on place du Forum and enjoy a *pastis.* This anise-based apéritif is served straight in a glass with ice, plus a carafe of water—dilute to taste. Sundays are dead, though most eateries on place du Forum are open.

For **picnics,** a big, handy Monoprix supermarket/department store is on place Lamartine (Mon-Sat 8:30-19:25, closed Sun).

On or near Place du Forum

Great atmosphere and mediocre food at fair prices await on place du Forum. By all accounts, the garish yellow Café la Nuit is worth avoiding. Most other cafés on the square deliver acceptable quality and terrific ambience. A half-block below the Forum, on rue du Dr. Fanton, you'll find a lineup of more tempting restaurants. The first three are popular, and all have good indoor and outdoor seating.

Le 16 is a warm, affordable place to enjoy a fresh salad (€10)—though it's almost too popular for its own good (€13 *plats,* €21 three-course *menu,* closed Sat-Sun, 16 rue du Dr. Fanton, tel. 04 90 93 77 36).

Le Gaboulet has created a buzz in Arles by blending a cozy interior, classic French cuisine, and service with a smile (thanks to owner Frank). It's the most expensive of the places I list on this street, but it's still jammed—book ahead or come early (€27 *menu,* great fries, closed Sun-Mon, 18 rue du Dr. Fanton, tel. 04 90 93 18 11).

Au Brin de Thym, next door, has long been reliable and specializes in traditional Provençal cuisine at fair prices—the bull steak

PROVENCE

Arles Restaurants

← Van Gogh Walking Tour
🅿 Parking
Ⓑ Bus Stop
View

100 YARDS
100 METERS

❶ Le 16, Le Gaboulet & Au Brin de Thym
❷ La Gueule du Loup
❸ La Cuisine de Comptoir
❹ Café de la Major
❺ Le Grillon
❻ Le Criquet
❼ Hôtel le Calendal Café/Rest.
❽ Hôtel Voltaire Restaurant
❾ Soleileis Ice Cream

R   H

TRINQUETAILLE BRIDGE

MARX

QUAI   TRUCHET

DR. FANTON

❸

R. JOUVE.   R. LIBERTE

RUE A. FRANCE

TO ANCIENT HISTORY MUSEUM

ARLATEN FOLK MUSEUM
(CLOSED UNTIL 2013)

RUE GAMBETTA

REPUB-

ESPACE VAN GOGH

RUE   MOLIÈRE   R.

TO ANCIENT HISTORY MUSEUM ←   BLVD.   Ⓑ   BUS STN.

DCH

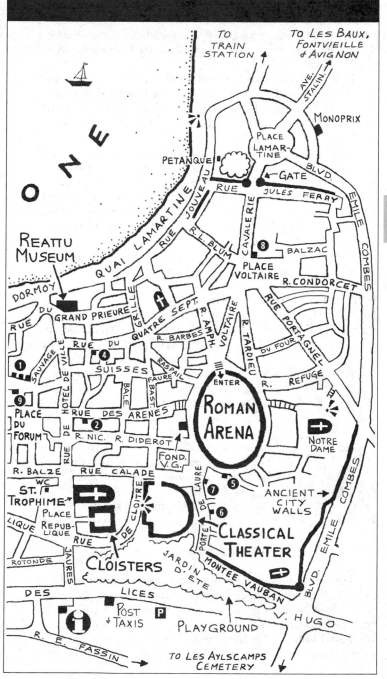

PROVENCE

is delicious. Arrive early for an outdoor table or call ahead, and let hardworking and sincere Monsieur and Madame Colombaud take care of you. Monsieur does *le cooking* while Madame does *le serving* (€19 three-course *menu*, closed Tue, 22 rue du Dr. Fanton, tel. 04 90 49 95 96).

La Gueule du Loup is a small, traditional place with a loyal following (reserve ahead). Its fine blend of Provençal and classic French cuisine is served in an intimate setting under wood beams in an upstairs room (€31 three-course *menu*, closed Wed, 39 rue des Arènes, tel. 04 90 96 96 69).

At **La Cuisine de Comptoir,** a cool little bistro, locals of all ages abandon Provençal decor. Welcoming owners Alexandre and Vincent offer light *tartines*—a delicious cross between pizza and bruschetta, served with soup or salad for just €10 (a swinging deal). Sit at the counter and watch *le chef* at work (closed Sun, indoor dining only, just off place du Forum's lower end at 10 rue de la Liberté, tel. 04 90 96 86 28).

Café de la Major is *the* place to go to recharge with some serious coffee or tea (closed Sun, 7 bis rue Réattu, tel. 04 90 96 14 15).

Near the Roman Arena

For about the same price as on place du Forum, you can enjoy regional cuisine with a point-blank view of the Arena. Because

they change regularly, the handful of (mostly) outdoor eateries that overlook the Arena are pretty indistinguishable.

Le Grillon owns the best view above the Arena and serves good-enough salads, crêpes, and *plats du jour* for €9-12 (closed all day Wed and Sun nights, at the top of the Arena on rond-point des Arènes, tel. 04 90 96 70 97).

Le Criquet is a sweet little place serving Provençal classics at good prices two blocks above the Arena (€18 three-course *menu,* closed Mon, indoor dining only, 21 rue Porte de Laure, tel. 04 90 96 80 51).

Hôtel le Calendal serves lunch in its lovely courtyard (€12-18, daily 12:00-15:00) or delicious little sandwiches for €2 each (three make a good meal) at its small café (just above the Arena at 5 rue Porte de Laure, tel. 04 90 96 11 89).

Hôtel Voltaire, well-situated on a pleasing square, serves simple three-course lunches at honest prices to a loyal clientele

(€13 *menus*; hearty *plats* and filling salads for €10—try the *salade fermière, salade Latine*, or the filling *assiette Provençale;* closed Sun evening, a few blocks below the Arena at 1 place Voltaire, tel. 04 90 96 49 18).

And for Dessert...

Soleileis has Arles' best ice cream, with all-natural ingredients and unusual flavors such as *fadoli*—olive oil mixed with nougatine. There's also a shelf of English books for exchange (open daily 14:00-18:30, across from recommended Le 16 restaurant at 9 rue du Dr. Fanton).

Avignon

Famous for its nursery rhyme, medieval bridge, and brooding Palace of the Popes, contemporary Avignon (ah-veen-yohn) bustles and prospers behind its mighty walls. During the 68 years (1309-1377) that Avignon starred as the *Franco Vaticano*, it grew from a quiet village into a thriving city. With its large student population and fashionable shops, today's Avignon is an intriguing blend of medieval history, youthful energy, and urban sophistication. Street performers entertain the international throngs who fill Avignon's ubiquitous cafés and trendy boutiques. If you're here in July, be prepared for big crowds

and higher prices, thanks to the rollicking theater festival. Clean, sharp, and popular with tourists, Avignon is more impressive for its outdoor ambience than for its museums and monuments.

Orientation to Avignon

The cours Jean Jaurès, which turns into rue de la République, runs straight from the Centre-Ville train station to place de l'Horloge and the Palace of the Popes, splitting Avignon in two. The larger eastern half is where the action is. Climb to Le Jardin du Rochers des Doms for the town's best view, tour the pope's immense palace, lose yourself in Avignon's back streets, and find a shady square to call home. Avignon's shopping district fills the traffic-free streets near where rue de la République meets place de l'Horloge.

Tourist Information

The main TI is between the Centre-Ville train station and the old town, at 41 cours Jean Jaurès (April-Oct Mon-Sat 9:00-18:00—until 19:00 in July, Sun 9:45-17:00; Nov-March Mon-Fri 9:00-18:00, Sat 9:00-17:00, Sun 10:00-12:00; tel. 04 32 74 32 74, www.avignon-tourisme.com). From April through mid-October, branch TI offices are open inside the St. Bénezet Bridge entrance (daily 10:00-13:00 & 14:00-18:00) and inside Les Halles market (Fri-Sun 10:00-13:00, closed Mon-Thu). At any TI, get the helpful map.

Everyone should pick up the free **Avignon Passion Pass** (valid 15 days, for up to five family members). Get the pass stamped when you pay full price at your first sight, and then receive reductions at the others (for example, €2 less at the Palace of the Popes and €3 less at the Petit Palais). The discounts add up—always show your Passion Pass when buying a ticket. The pass comes with the Avignon "Passion" map and guide, which includes several good (but tricky-to-follow) walking tours.

Arrival in Avignon

By Train

Avignon has two train stations: TGV (linked to downtown by frequent shuttle buses) and Centre-Ville. Trains from Marseille serve only the TGV station, a 15-minute shuttle bus ride from downtown Avignon.

TGV Station (Gare TGV): This shiny new station is on the outskirts of town. To get to the city center, take the *navette/*

shuttle bus (marked *Navette/ Avignon Centre;* €1.20, buy ticket from driver, 3/hour, 15 minutes). To find the bus stop, leave the station by the north exit *(sortie nord),* walk down the stairs, and find the long bus shelter to the left. In downtown Avignon you'll arrive at a stop just inside the city walls, in front of the post office on cours Président Kennedy (see the map on page 266). From here, you're three blocks from the city's main TI, and two blocks from Centre-Ville Station. A **taxi** ride between the TGV station and downtown Avignon costs about €16-20 (to find taxis, exit the TGV station via *sortie nord*).

Centre-Ville Station (Gare Avignon Centre-Ville): All non-TGV trains (and a few TGV trains) serve the central station. To reach the town center, cross the busy street in front of the station and walk through the city walls onto cours Jean Jaurès. The TI is three blocks down, at #41.

By Bus

The dingy bus station *(gare routière)* is 100 yards to the right as you leave the Centre-Ville train station (beyond and below Ibis Hôtel).

By Car

Drivers entering Avignon follow *Centre-Ville* and *Gare SNCF* (train station) signs. You'll find central pay lots (about €10/half-day, €14/day) in the garage next to Centre-Ville Station, at the Parking Jean Jaurès under the ramparts across from the train station; or at the Parking Palais des Papes (follow signs on the riverside road, boulevard St. Lazare, just past St. Bénezet Bridge). There are two free lots nearby with free shuttle buses to the center (follow *P Gratuit* signs): One is just across Daladier Bridge (pont Daladier); the other is along the river past the Palace of the Popes, just northeast of the walls. Leave nothing in your car.

Helpful Hints

Local Help: David at **Imagine Tours** (see "Tours in Avignon," later) can help with emergencies or tickets to special events (mobile 06 89 22 19 87, www.imagine-tours.net, imagine.tours @gmail.com).

Internet Access: The TI has a current list of Internet cafés.

English Bookstore: Try **Shakespeare Bookshop** (Tue-Sat 9:30-12:00 & 14:00-18:30, closed Sun-Mon, 155 rue Carreterie, in Avignon's northeast corner, tel. 04 90 27 38 50).

Grocery Store: Carrefour City is central and has long hours (Mon-Sat 7:00-21:00, Sun 9:00-12:00, next to McDonald's, 2 blocks from the TI, toward place de l'Horloge on rue de la République).

Shuttle Boat: A free shuttle boat, the *Navette Fluviale,* plies back and forth across the river (as it did in the days when the town had no functioning bridge) from near St. Bénezet Bridge (daily July-Aug 11:00-21:00, Sept-June roughly 10:00-12:30 & 14:00-18:00, 3/hour). It drops you on the peaceful Ile de la Barthélasse, with its riverside restaurant, grassy walks, and bike rides with terrific city views.

Commanding City Views: For great views of Avignon and the river, walk or drive across Daladier Bridge, or ferry across the Rhône on the *Navette Fluviale* (described above). I'd take the boat across the river, walk the view path to Daladier Bridge, and then cross back over the bridge (45-minute walk over mostly level ground). You can enjoy other impressive vistas from the top of Le Jardin du Rochers des Doms, from the tower in the Palace of the Popes, and from the end of the famous, broken St. Bénezet Bridge.

PROVENCE

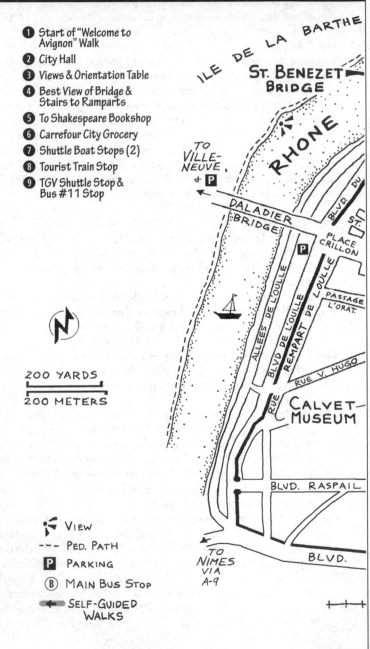

Avignon

1. Start of "Welcome to Avignon" Walk
2. City Hall
3. Views & Orientation Table
4. Best View of Bridge & Stairs to Ramparts
5. To Shakespeare Bookshop
6. Carrefour City Grocery
7. Shuttle Boat Stops (2)
8. Tourist Train Stop
9. TGV Shuttle Stop & Bus #11 Stop

ILE DE LA BARTHE

ST. BENEZET BRIDGE

RHONE

TO VILLE-NEUVE

DALADIER BRIDGE

BLVD. DU ST.

PLACE CRILLON

PASSAGE L'ORAT.

ALLEES DE L'OULLE

BLVD DE L'OULLE

REMPART DE L'OULLE

RUE V. HUGO

RUE

CALVET MUSEUM

BLVD. RASPAIL

TO NIMES VIA A-9

BLVD.

200 YARDS
200 METERS

View
Ped. Path
P Parking
B Main Bus Stop
Self-Guided Walks

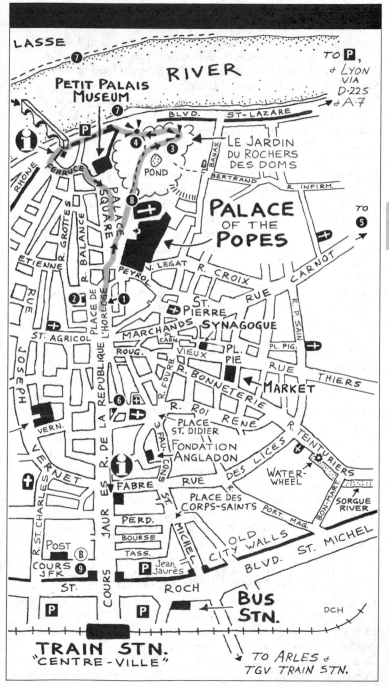

LASSE

7

RIVER

Petit Palais Museum

TO **P**, & LYON VIA D-225 & A-7

7

BLVD. ST-LAZARE

RHONE

FERRUCE

P

4

3

POND

Le JARDIN du ROCHERS DES DOMS

BANAS.

BERTRAND

R. INFIRM.

PALACE SQUARE

R. BALANCE

R. GROTTES

ETIENNE

RUE

JOSEPH

ST. AGRICOL

VERN.

8

PLACE DE L'HORLOGE

PEYROL.

V. LEGAT

R. CROIX

PALACE OF THE **POPES**

CARNOT

TO **5**

PROVENCE

2

1

ST. PIERRE

SYNAGOGUE

MARCHANDS

PL. CARN.

VIEUX

ROUG.

R. FOURB

R. BONNETERIE

PL. PIE

RUE

R. SAIN

PL. PIG.

RUE THIERS

MARKET

VERNET

R. ROI RENE

6

R. TEINTURIERS

PLACE ST. DIDIER

FONDATION ANGLADON

3 FAUCONS

RUE

DES LICES

WATER-WHEEL

SORGUE RIVER

BON-MART.

FABRE

ST.

PLACE DES CORPS-SAINTS

RUE

R

PORT. MAG.

R. ST. CHARLES

PERD.

BOURSE

TASS.

MICHEL

OLD CITY WALLS

ST. MICHEL

Post

B

9

COURS JFK

COURS

Jean Jaures

P

ROCH

BLVD. ST. MICHEL

BUS STN.

DCH

ST.

P

P

TRAIN STN. "CENTRE-VILLE"

TO ARLES & TGV TRAIN STN.

Tours in Avignon

Walking Tours—The TI offers informative two-hour English walking tours of Avignon (€11, discounted with Avignon Passion Pass, April-Oct Wed and Fri-Sat at 10:00, depart from main TI; Nov-March on Sat only, depart from Palace of the Popes).

Tourist Trains—The little train leaves regularly from in front of the Palace of the Popes and offers a decent overview of the city, including Le Jardin du Rochers des Doms and St. Bénezet Bridge (€7, 2/hour, 40 minutes, mid-March-mid-Oct daily 10:00-19:00, English commentary).

Avignon Wine Tour—For a playful, informative, and distinctly French perspective on wines of the Côtes du Rhône region, contact François Marcou, who runs his tours with passion and energy, offering travelers different itineraries every day. Based in Avignon, François can pick you up at either of the city's train stations (€75/person for all-day wine tours that include 4-5 tastings, €350 for private groups, mobile 06 28 05 33 84, www.avignon-wine-tour .com, avignon.wine.tour@modulonet.fr).

Imagine Tours—Unlike most tour operators, this organization runs on a not-for-profit basis, with a focus on cultural excursions. It offers low-key, personalized tours that allow visitors to discover the "true heart of Provence." The itineraries adapt to your interests, and the volunteer guides will meet you at the departure point of your choice (€150/half-day, €275/day, prices are for up to 4 people, mobile 06 89 22 19 87, fax 04 90 24 84 26, www.imagine-tours .net, imagine.tours@gmail.com). They also offer free assistance to travelers, should you want advice planning your itinerary or run into problems during your trip.

Visit Provence—This company runs trips from Avignon (and a few from Arles) to many Provençal destinations, and provides introductory commentary to what you'll see (but no guiding at the actual sights). They have eight-seat minivans (about €60/half-day, €100/day). Ask about their cheaper big-bus excursions, or consider hiring a van and driver for your private use (plan on €210/half-day, €400/day, tel. 04 90 14 70 00, check website for current destinations, www.provence-reservation.com).

Self-Guided Walk in Avignon

Before starting this walk—which connects the city's top sights—be sure to pick up the Avignon Passion Pass at the TI, then show it when entering each attraction to receive discounted admission (explained earlier, under "Tourist Information").

• *Start your tour where the Romans did, on place de l'Horloge, in front of City Hall (Hôtel de Ville).*

Place de l'Horloge

This café square was the town forum during Roman times and the market square through the Middle Ages. (Restaurants here offer good people-watching, but they also have less ambience and low-quality meals—you'll find better squares elsewhere to hang your beret in.) Named for a medieval clock tower that the City Hall now hides (find plaque in English), this square's present popularity arrived with the trains in 1854. Walk a few steps to the center of the square, and look down the main drag, rue de la République. When the trains came to Avignon, proud city fathers wanted a direct, impressive way to link the new station to the heart of the city (just like in Paris)—so they plowed over homes to create rue de la République and widened place de l'Horloge. This main drag's Parisian feel is intentional—it was built not in the Provençal manner, but in the Haussmann style that is so dominant in Paris (characterized by broad, straight boulevards lined with stately buildings).

• *Walk uphill past the carousel (public WCs behind). You'll see a golden statue of Mary, floating high above the buildings. Veer right at the street's end, and continue into...*

Palace Square (Place du Palais)

This grand square is lined with the Palace of the Popes, the Petit Palais, and the cathedral. In the 1300s the entire headquarters of the Catholic Church was moved to Avignon. The Church bought Avignon and gave it a complete makeover. Along with clearing out vast spaces like this square and building this three-acre palace, the Church erected more than three miles of protective wall (with 39 towers), "appropriate" housing for cardinals (read: mansions), and residences for its entire bureaucracy. The city was Europe's largest construction zone. Avignon's population grew from 6,000 to 25,000 in short order. (Today, 13,000 people live within the walls.) The limits of pre-papal Avignon are outlined on city maps: Rues Joseph Vernet, Henri Fabre, des Lices, and Philonarde all follow the route of the city's earlier defensive wall.

The Petit Palais (Little Palace) seals the uphill end of the square and was built for a cardinal; today it houses medieval paintings (museum described later). The church just to the left of the Palace of the Popes is Avignon's cathedral. It predates the Church's purchase of Avignon by 200 years. Its small size reflects Avignon's modest, pre-papal population. The gilded Mary was added in 1854, when the Vatican established the doctrine of her Immaculate Conception. Mary is taller than the Palace of the Popes by design: The Vatican never accepted what it called the "Babylonian Captivity" and had a bad attitude about Avignon long after the pope was definitively back in Rome. There hasn't been a French pope since the Holy See returned to Rome—over 600 years. That's what I call a grudge.

Directly across the square from the palace's main entry stands a cardinal's residence, built in 1619 (now the Conservatoire National de Musique). Its fancy Baroque facade was a visual counterpoint to the stripped-down Huguenot aesthetic of the age. During this time, Provence was a hotbed of Protestantism—but, buried within this region, Avignon was a Catholic stronghold. Notice the stumps in front and nearby. Nicknamed *bites* (slang for the male anatomy), they effectively keep cars from double-parking in areas designed for people. Many of the metal ones slide up and down by remote control to let privileged cars come and go.

• *You can visit the massive **Palace of the Popes** (described on page 272) now, but it works better to visit that palace at the end of this walk. Now is a good time to take in the...*

Petit Palace Museum (Musée du Petit Palais)

This former cardinal's palace now displays the Church's collection of mostly medieval Italian painting (including one delightful Botticelli) and sculpture. All 350 paintings deal with Christian themes. A visit here before going to the Palace of the Popes helps furnish and populate that otherwise barren building, and a quick peek into its courtyard shows the importance of cardinal housing (€6, €2 English brochure, some English explanations posted; June-Sept Wed-Mon 10:00-13:00 & 14:00-18:00, closed Tue; Oct-May Wed-Mon 9:30-13:00 & 14:00-17:30, closed Tue; at north end of Palace Square, tel. 04 90 86 44 58).

From Palace Square we'll head up to the rocky hilltop where Avignon was first settled, then drop down to the river. With this short loop, you can enjoy a park, hike to a grand river view, and visit Avignon's beloved broken bridge—an experience worth ▲▲.

• *Start by climbing to the church level, then take the switchback ramps up to...*

▲▲Le Jardin du Rochers des Doms

Though the park itself is a delight—with a sweet little café (good prices for food and drinks) and public WCs—don't miss the climax: a panoramic view of the Rhône River Valley and the broken bridge (park gates open daily April-Sept 7:30-20:00, Oct-March 7:30-18:00). For the best views (and the favorite make-out spot for local teenagers later in the evening), find the terrace behind the odd zodiac display (across the grass from the

pond-side park café, facing the statue of Jean Althen). On a clear day, the tallest peak you see, with its white limestone cap, is Mont Ventoux ("Windy Mountain"). Below and just to the right, you'll spot free passenger ferries shuttling across the river (great views from path on other side of the river), and—tucked amidst the trees on the far side of the river—a highly recommended restaurant, Le Bercail. The island in the river is the Ile de la Barthélasse, a nature preserve where Avignon can breathe.

St. André Fortress (across the river on the hill; see the info plaque to the left) was built by the French in 1360, shortly after the pope moved to Avignon, to counter the papal incursion into this part of Europe. The castle was across the border, in the kingdom of France. Avignon's famous bridge was a key border crossing, with towers on either end—one was French, and the other was the pope's. The French one, across the river, is the Tower of Philip the Fair.

• *From this viewpoint, take the stairs to the left down to the tower. As the stairs spiral down, just before St. Bénezet Bridge, catch a glimpse of the...*

Ramparts

The only bit of the rampart you can walk on is accessed from St. Bénezet Bridge (pay to enter—see next). When the pope arrived in the 1360s, small Avignon had no town wall...so he built one. What you see today was restored in the 19th century.

• *When you come out of the tower on street level, take the right-side exit and walk left along the river. Pass under the old bridge to find its entrance shortly after.*

▲▲St. Bénezet Bridge (Pont St. Bénezet)

This bridge, whose construction and location were inspired by a shepherd's religious vision, is the "pont d'Avignon" of nursery-rhyme fame. The ditty (which you've probably been humming all day) dates back to the 15th century: *Sur le pont d'Avignon, on y danse, on y danse, sur le pont d'Avignon, on y danse tous en rond* ("On the bridge of Avignon, we will dance, we will dance, on the bridge of Avignon, we will dance all in a circle").

But the bridge was a big deal even outside of its kiddie-tune fame. Built between 1171 and 1185, it was the only bridge crossing the mighty Rhône in the Middle Ages. It was damaged several times by floods and subsequently rebuilt, until 1668, when most of it was knocked down by a disastrous icy flood. Lacking a government stimulus package, the townsfolk decided not to rebuild this time, and for more than a century, Avignon had no bridge across the Rhône. While only four arches survive today, the original bridge was huge: Imagine a 22-arch, 3,000-foot-long bridge extending from Vatican territory to the lonely Tower of Philip the Fair, which marked the beginning of France (see displays of the bridge's original length). A Romanesque chapel on the bridge is dedicated to St. Bénezet. Though there's not much to see on the bridge, the audioguide included with your ticket tells a good enough story. It's also fun to be in the breezy middle of the river with a sweeping city view.

Cost and Hours: €4.50, €13 combo-ticket includes Palace of the Popes, same hours as the Palace of the Popes (next), tel. 04 90 27 51 16. The ticket booth is housed in what was a medieval hospital for the poor (funded by bridge tolls). Admission includes a small room dedicated to the song of Avignon's bridge and your only chance to walk a bit of the ramparts (enter both from the tower).

• *To get to the Palace of the Popes from here, exit left, then turn left again back into the walls. Walk to the end of the short street, then turn right following signs to* Palais des Papes. *Look for the brown signs leading left under the passageway. After a block of uphill walking, find the stairs to the palace.*

▲Palace of the Popes (Palais des Papes)

In 1309 a French pope was elected (Pope Clément V). At the urging of the French king, His Holiness decided that dangerous Italy was no place for a pope, so he moved the whole operation to Avignon for a secure rule under a supportive king. The Catholic Church literally bought Avignon (then a two-bit town), and popes resided here until 1403. Meanwhile, Italians demanded a Roman pope, so from 1378 on, there were twin popes—one in Rome and one in Avignon—causing a schism in the Catholic Church that wasn't fully resolved until 1417.

A visit to the mighty yet barren papal palace comes with an audioguide that leads you along a one-way route and does a credible job of overcoming the complete lack of furnishings. It teaches the basic history while allowing you to tour at your own pace.

As you wander, ponder that this palace—the largest surviving Gothic palace in Europe—was built to accommodate 500 people as the

administrative center of the Holy See and home of the pope. This was the most fortified palace of the age (remember, the pope left Rome to be more secure). Nine popes ruled from here, making this the center of Christianity for 100 years. You'll walk through the pope's personal quarters (frescoed with happy hunting scenes), see many models of how the various popes added to the building, and learn about its state-of-the-art plumbing. The rooms are huge. The "pope's chapel" is twice the size of the adjacent Avignon cathedral.

The last pope checked out in 1403 (escaping a siege), but the Church owned Avignon until the French Revolution in 1789. During this interim period, the pope's "legate" (official representative, normally a nephew) ruled Avignon from this palace. Avignon residents, many of whom had come from Rome, spoke Italian for a century after the pope left, making it a linguistic ghetto within France. In the Napoleonic age, the palace was a barracks, housing 1,800 soldiers. You can see cuts in the wall where high ceilings gave way to floor beams. Climb the tower (Tour de la Gâche) for grand views and a rooftop café with surprisingly good food at very fair prices.

A room at the end of the tour (called *la boutellerie*) is dedicated to the region's wines, of which they claim the pope was a fan. Sniff "Le Nez du Vin"—a black box with 54 tiny bottles designed to develop your "nose." (Blind-test your travel partner.) The nearby village of Châteauneuf-du-Pape is where the pope summered in the 1320s. Its famous wine is a direct descendant of his wine. You're welcome to taste here (€6 for three to five fine wines and souvenir tasting cup).

Cost and Hours: €10.50 (more for special exhibits), €13 combo-ticket includes St. Bénezet Bridge, daily mid-March-Oct 9:00-19:00, until 20:00 July and Sept, until 21:00 in Aug, Nov-mid-March 9:30-17:45, last entry one hour before closing, tel. 04 90 27 50 74, www.palais-des-papes.com.

• *You'll exit at the rear of the palace. To return to Palace Square, make two rights after exiting.*

Eating in Avignon

Skip the overpriced places on place de l'Horloge and find a more intimate location for your meal. Avignon has many delightful squares filled with tables ready to seat you.

Near the Church of St. Pierre

The church divides two enchanting squares. One is quiet and intimate, the other is lively.

L'Epicerie, sitting alone on an intimate square, serves the

Avignon Restaurants

1. Church of St. Pierre Eateries
2. Place Crillon Eateries
3. Place des Corps-Saints Eateries
4. Restaurant Françoise
5. L'Isle Sonnante Restaurant
6. La Cantina Restaurant
7. Le Caveau du Théâtre Rest.
8. Hôtel la Mirande Restaurant
9. La Vache à Carreaux Rest.
10. L'Epice and Love Rest.
11. Le Bercail Rest.
12. Carrefour City Grocery

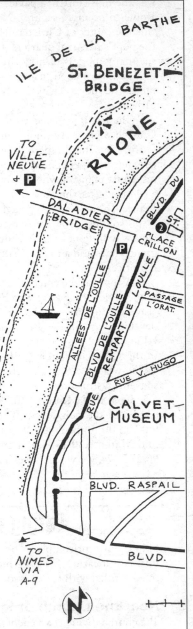

200 YARDS

200 METERS

🏴 VIEW

--- PED. PATH

🅿 PARKING

Ⓑ MAIN BUS STOP

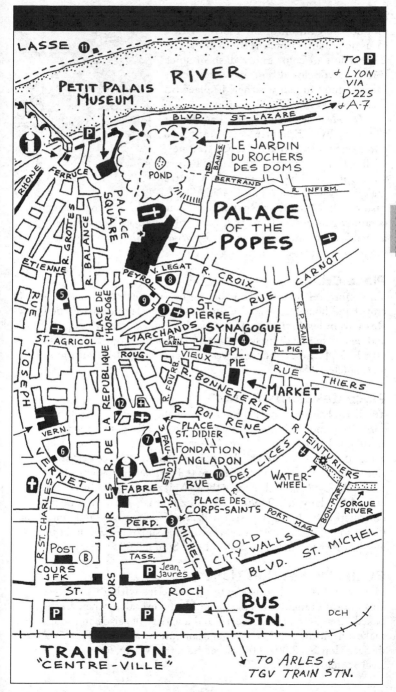

PROVENCE

highest-quality and highest-priced cuisine around the Church of St. Pierre, with a focus on products from the south of France. Expect lots of color and a dash of spice (€18-24 *plats,* closed Sun off-season, cozy interior good in bad weather, 10 place St. Pierre, tel. 04 90 82 74 22).

On place des Châtaignes: Pass under the arch by L'Epicerie restaurant and enter enchanting place des Châtaignes, with a fun commotion of tables. Peruse your options. The **Crêperie du Cloître** makes mediocre crêpes and salads (daily, cash only). Vietnamese **Restaurant Nem,** tucked in the corner, is family-run (*menus* from €12, cash only). **Pause Gourmande** is a small, lunch-only eatery with €9 *plats du jour,* and always has a veggie option (closed Sun).

Place Crillon

This more refined square just off the river attracts a stylish crowd and houses a variety of dining choices. Traditional French **Restaurant les Artistes** and *italiano* **La Piazza** are both popular and owned by the same folks (good €11 lunch deals, daily, tel. 04 90 82 23 54). **La Comédie** serves €9 crêpes and salads with mod seating (closed Sun).

Place des Corps-Saints

You'll find several youthful and reasonable eateries with tables sprawling under big plane trees on this locally popular square. **Bistrot à Tartines** specializes in—you guessed it—*tartines* (big slices of toast smothered with toppings), and has the coziest interior and best desserts on the square (€8 *tartines* and salads, daily, tel. 04 90 85 58 70). I also enjoy the €10 pizzas and friendly service at **Le Pili** (daily, tel. 04 90 27 39 53). **Zeste** is a friendly, modern deli offering fresh soups, pasta salads, wraps, smoothies, and more. Get it to go, or eat inside or on the scenic square—all at unbeatable prices (Mon-Sat 7:30-19:00, closed Sun, tel. 09 51 49 05 62).

By the Market (Les Halles)

Here you'll find a good selection of eateries with good prices. **Restaurant Françoise** is a pleasant café and tea salon, where fresh-baked tarts—savory and sweet—and a variety of salads and soups make a healthful meal, and vegetarian options are plentiful (€7-12 dishes, Mon-Sat 8:00-19:00, closed Sun, free Wi-Fi, 6 rue Général Leclerc, tel. 04 32 76 24 77).

Elsewhere in Avignon

At **L'Isle Sonnante,** join chef Boris and wife Anne to dine intimately in their formal and charming one-room *bistrot*. You'll choose from a small menu offering only fresh products and will be served by owners who care (*menus* from €30, closed Sun-Mon, 100 yards from the carousel on place de l'Horloge at 7 rue Racine, tel. 04 90 82 56 01, best to book ahead).

La Cantina delivers fine Italian cuisine in a beautiful courtyard (€15 pizzas, €20-30 *plats*, closed Sun evening, 83 rue Joseph Vernet, tel. 04 90 85 99 04).

Le Caveau du Théâtre is a welcoming place where Richard invites diners to have a glass of wine or meal at a sidewalk table, or inside in one of two carefree rooms (€13 *plats*, €18 *menus*, fun ambience for free, closed for lunch Sat and all day Sun, 16 rue des Trois Faucons, tel. 04 90 82 60 91).

Hôtel la Mirande is the ultimate Avignon splurge. Reserve ahead here for understated elegance and Avignon's top cuisine (€35 lunch *menu*; closed Tue-Wed—but for a price break, dine in the kitchen with the chef on these "closed" days for €85-140 including wine; behind Palace of the Popes, 4 place de la Mirande, tel. 04 90 86 93 93).

La Vache à Carreaux is a unique place with a passion for cheese in all its forms (non-cheese dishes are also available). The decor is as warm as the welcome, the wine list is extensive and reasonable, and it's a hit with the locals—so reserve ahead (€12-20 *plats*, daily, just behind Palace of the Popes at 14 rue Peyrolerie, tel. 04 90 80 09 05).

At **L'Epice and Love** (the name is a fun French-English play on words, pronounced "lay peace and love"), English-speaking owner Marie creates a playful atmosphere in her cozy, friendly restaurant. A few colorfully decorated tables and tasty meat, fish, and vegetarian dishes at good prices greet the hungry traveler (*menus* from €16, daily, 30 rue des Lices, tel. 04 90 82 45 96).

Across the River

Le Bercail offers a fun opportunity to get out of town (barely) and take in *le fresh air* with a terrific riverfront view of Avignon, all the while enjoying inexpensive Provençal cooking served in big portions. Book ahead, as this restaurant is popular (*menus* from €17, serves late, daily April-Oct, tel. 04 90 82 20 22). To get there, take the free shuttle boat (located near St. Bénezet Bridge; stops running at about 18:00) to the Ile de la Barthélasse, turn right, and walk five minutes.

More Sights in Provence

The cities listed above are all worthwhile destinations. But some of Provence's best bits are buried in its countryside—best reached by shore excursion or rental car.

▲▲▲Pont du Gard

This perfectly preserved Roman aqueduct was built in about 19 B.C. as the critical link of a 30-mile canal that, by dropping one inch for every 350 feet, supplied nine million gallons of water per day (about 100 gallons per second) to Nîmes—one of ancient Europe's largest cities. Though most of the aqueduct is on or below the ground, at Pont du Gard it spans a canyon on a massive bridge—one of the most remarkable surviving Roman ruins anywhere. Wear sturdy shoes if you plan to climb around the aqueduct (footing is tricky), and bring swimwear and flip-flops if you plan to backstroke beneath the monument.

This was the biggest bridge in the whole 30-mile-long aqueduct. It seems exceptional because it is: The arches are twice the width of standard aqueducts, and the main arch is the largest the Romans ever built—80 feet (so it wouldn't get its feet wet). The bridge is about 160 feet high and was originally about 1,100 feet long. Today, 12 arches are missing, reducing the length to 790 feet.

The bridge and the river below provide great fun for holiday-goers. While parents suntan on rocks, kids splash into the gorge from under the aqueduct. Some daredevils actually jump from the aqueduct's lower bridge—not knowing that crazy winds scrambled by the structure cause painful belly flops (and sometimes even accidental deaths). For the most refreshing view, float flat on your back underneath the structure.

The stones that jut out—giving the aqueduct a rough, unfinished appearance—supported the original scaffolding. The protuberances were left, rather than cut off, in anticipation of future repair needs. The lips under the arches supported wooden templates that allowed the stones in the round arches to rest on something until the all-important keystone was dropped into place. Each stone weighs four to six tons. The structure stands with no mortar—taking full advantage of the innovative Roman arch, made strong by gravity.

Hike over the bridge for a closer look and the best views. Steps lead up a high trail (marked *panorama*) to a superb viewpoint (go right at the top; best views are soon after the trail starts descending). You'll also see where the aqueduct meets a rock tunnel. Walk through the tunnel and continue for a bit, following a trail that meanders along the canal's path.

Other Sights: Near the aqueduct, a state-of-the-art museum (well-presented in English) explains the critical role fresh water played in the Roman "art of living." A corny, romancing-the-aqueduct 25-minute film plays in the same building as the museum. There is also a cafeteria, a kids' museum (called *Ludo*), and an extensive outdoor *garrigue* nature area.

Cost and Hours: The aqueduct, museum, film, and *garrigue* nature area are all free, but parking is €15 per car. The museum is open daily May-Sept 9:00-19:00, Oct-April 9:00-17:00, closed two weeks in Jan. The aqueduct itself is open until 1:00 in the morning, as is the parking lot. The *garrigue* is always open. The aqueduct is between Remoulins and Vers-Pont du Gard, 13 miles from Avignon. Toll tel. 08 20 90 33 30, www.pontdugard.fr.

▲▲Les Baux

The hilltop town of Les Baux crowns the rugged Alpilles (ahl-pee) Mountains, evoking a tumultuous medieval history. Here, you can imagine the struggles of a strong community that lived a rough-and-tumble life—thankful more for their top-notch fortifications than for their dramatic views.

Les Baux is actually two visits in one: castle ruins perched on an almost lunar landscape, and a medieval town below. Savor the castle, then tour—or blitz—the lower streets on your way out. Whereas the town, which lives entirely off tourism, is packed with shops, cafés, and tourist knickknacks, the castle above stays manageable because crowds are dispersed over a big area. The lower town's polished-stone gauntlet of boutiques is a Provençal dream come true for shoppers.

The Castle Ruins (The "Dead City"): The sun-bleached ruins of the "dead city" of Les Baux are carved into, out of, and on top

of a rock 650 feet above the valley floor. Many of the ancient walls of this striking castle still stand as a testament to the proud past of this once-feisty village.

As you walk on the wind-blown spur (*baux* in French), you'll pass kid-thrilling medieval siege weaponry (go ahead, try the battering ram). Good displays in English and images help reconstruct the place. Try to imagine 4,000 people living up here. Notice the water-catchment system (a slanted field that caught rainwater and drained it into cisterns—necessary during a siege) and find the reservoir cut into the rock below the castle's highest point. Look for post holes throughout the stone walls that reveal where beams once supported floors.

For the most sensational views, climb to the blustery top of the citadel. Hang on. The mistral wind just might blow you away.

Cost and Hours: €8 (ask about family rates), includes excellent audioguide, daily July-Aug 9:00-20:00, Easter-June and Sept-Oct 9:00-19:00, Nov-Easter 9:30-17:00. From April to October, medieval pageantry, tournaments, or fun-for-kids demonstrations enliven the mountaintop. If you bring your lunch, enjoy the picnic tables.

Lower Town: After your castle visit, you can shop and eat your way back through the new town. Or you can escape some of the crowds by visiting these minor but worthwhile sights: The 15th-century **Manville Mansion City Hall** flies the red-and-white flag of Monaco, a reminder that the Grimaldi family (which has long ruled the tiny principality of Monaco) owned Les Baux until the French Revolution (1789). The enjoyable **Yves Brayer Museum** (Musée Yves Brayer) lets you peruse three floors of paintings (Van Gogh-like Expressionism, without the tumult) by Yves Brayer (1907-1990), who spent his final years here in Les Baux. The free **Museum of *Santons*** displays a collection of *santons* ("little saints"), popular folk figurines that decorate local Christmas mangers and make festive souvenirs.

For lunch, the **Hostellerie de la Reine Jeanne** offers friendly service and good-value meals indoors or out (€12 salads, €16 *menus*, try the *salade Estivale*, open daily, 150 feet to your right after entry to the village of Les Baux, tel. 04 90 54 32 06).

▲▲Hill Towns and Villages

If your cruise line offers excursions to the faraway towns of the Côtes du Rhône and Luberon regions, or if you plan to rent a car, here's a rundown on some of my favorites. Minivan tours and basic bus excursions are also available—ask at a TI, or see "Tours in Marseille" on page 220 and "Tours in Avignon" on page 268.

Lourmarin—the closest to Marseille—is a lovely, busy, upscale village.

Isle-sur-la-Sorgue, sitting within a split in its crisp, happy little river, hosts a bustling market on Sundays and Thursdays. It's a sturdy, workaday town, with a gritty charm that feels refreshingly real amid so many adorable villages.

Roussillon is a beautiful hill town sitting atop a huge ochre

What If I Miss My Boat?

Remember that you can get help from the cruise line's port agent (listed on the destination information sheet distributed on the ship) and the local TI (see page 217 for Marseille or page 213 for Toulon). If the port agent suggests a costly solution (such as a private car with a driver), you may want to consider public transit.

Frequent **trains** leave from Marseille's St. Charles Station to points all over France and beyond: **Barcelona** (2/day, 6.5 hours, change in Montpellier and Figueras), **Nice** (almost hourly, 2.5 hours), **Livorno** (4/day, 9.5-10.5 hours, change in Nice, Ventimiglia, and Genoa), **Civitavecchia** (3/day, 12-13.5 hours, change in Nice, Ventimiglia, and Genoa), **Naples** (1/day, 13.25 hours, change in Nice, Ventimiglia, and Milan).

There are also trains from Toulon to other Mediterranean ports: **Barcelona** (3/day, 7.5-8 hours, change in Marseille, Montpellier, and Figueras), **Nice** (hourly, 2 hours), **Livorno** (3/day, 9.5-10 hours, change in Nice, Ventimiglia, and Genoa), **Civitavecchia** (4/day, 11.5 hours, change in Nice, Ventimiglia, and Genoa), and **Naples** (1/day, 12.5 hours, change in Nice, Ventimiglia, and Milan).

If you need to catch a **plane** to your next destination, Marseille's airport (Aéroport Marseille-Provence), about 16 miles north of the city center, is small and easy to navigate (tel. 04 42 14 14 14, www.marseille.aeroport.fr).

Local **travel agents** in Marseille and Toulon can help you.

For more advice on what to do if you miss the boat, see page 131.

PROVENCE

deposit, giving it a red-rock appeal. It's popular with American tourists.

Uzès, a chic town with manicured pedestrian streets, is more popular with European tourists.

Joucas, popular with artists, is an adorable little village where flowers and stones are lovingly maintained.

Brantes is a spectacularly situated cliff village with little tourism.

Le Crestet, often overlooked, enjoys a sensational hilltop location and has only one commercial enterprise.

Séguret, busy with day-trippers, is a linear hillside village with memorable views.

Gigondas, a world-famous wine village, offers a nice balance of commercial activity and quiet.

Vaison la Romaine is a popular midsize town with Roman ruins and lots of activity, spanning both sides of a river.

THE FRENCH RIVIERA

La Côte d'Azur

A hundred years ago, celebrities from London to Moscow flocked to the French Riviera to socialize, gamble, and escape the dreary weather at home. Today, cruise passengers, budget vacationers, and heat-seeking Europeans fill belle époque resorts at France's most sought-after fun-in-the-sun destination.

The region got its nickname from turn-of-the-20th-century vacationing Brits, who simply extended the Italian Riviera west to France. Their original definition of the French Riviera only went as far as Nice, though the Riviera label has been stretched even farther westward since these Victorian Brits strolled their promenade. Today, this summer fun zone is *La Côte d'Azur* to the French.

Three main cruise ports (which line up along a 12-mile seafront stretch) serve this region: Nice, Villefranche-sur-Mer, and Monaco. Once ashore at any of them, the region's biggest draw is Nice—with world-class museums, a splendid beachfront promenade, a seductive old town, and all the headaches of a major city (traffic, crime, pollution, and so on). Monaco welcomes everyone and will happily take your cash. Between Nice and Monaco lies the Riviera's richest stretch of real estate, paved with famously scenic roads (called the Three Corniches) and peppered with cliff-hanging villages, million-dollar vistas, and sea-view walking trails connecting beach towns. Fifteen minutes from Nice (on the way to Monaco), little Villefranche-sur-Mer stares across the bay to woodsy and exclusive Cap Ferrat. The eagle's-nest Eze-le-Village surveys the same scene from high above. West of Nice (and practical to visit only if your ship arrives in Nice) are more options: Antibes has a thriving port and silky sand beaches; image-conscious Cannes (also a port for some smaller cruise ships) is the Riviera's self-appointed queen, with an elegant veneer hiding... very little; and yacht-happy St-Tropez swims alone at the western fringe of the region.

Planning Your Time

Three main ports serve this area: Nice, Villefranche-sur-Mer, and Monaco. A few cruises tender to Cannes, farther to the west. Once you reach your destination, turn to the "Arrival" information in that section of this chapter.

If Arriving at Nice, Villfranche-sur-Mer, or Monaco: Conveniently, all three of these ports are easily connected to each other by frequent trains and buses—so your sightseeing options are effectively the same from any of them. It can be hard to choose among the many good destinations described in this chapter. If it's a toss-up, an easy plan is to visit **your port city plus Nice**. (If your ship docks at Nice, you could consider a speedy side-trip to Monaco or Antibes; either is within 15-30 minutes one-way by train.)

If Arriving at Cannes: Your best, nearest option is to visit Antibes (with its Picasso Museum), just 15 minutes by train. Nice is about 40 minutes away. Or just enjoy relaxing in Cannes.

Your Top Options

Here are quick descriptions, with time estimates, of your choices:

• The big city of **Nice** has a beachfront promenade, an atmospheric old town, and two excellent art museums (Chagall and Matisse). With a day here, start with my two self-guided walks: "Welcome to the Riviera" and "Old Nice" (allow an hour each). Art-lovers can spend an hour apiece in the Chagall and Matisse museums (plus 15-20 minutes each way by taxi or bus—but note that both museums are closed Tue amd the Matisse Museum may close for renovation in 2012), while others can just relax at the beach. Allow six to seven hours for everything. With less time, choose between the walks or museums.

• **Villefranche-sur-Mer** is simply an easygoing harbor town of steep narrow streets on a lovely bay filled with yachts. You can spend anywhere from a few minutes to a few hours here, enjoying the ambience or the beach. It's just 10 minutes by train from Nice.

• The glamorous principality of **Monaco** has two main sightseeing zones: Monaco-Ville, a cliff-capping old town with great views (follow my self-guided walk and allow up to two hours); and the glitzy district of Monte Carlo, with little to see except its famous casino (which doesn't open until 14:00; allow one hour or less). All said, figure on a total of three hours in Monaco for a satisfying experience (and it's 20 minutes from Nice by train).

Excursions from French Riviera Ports

The best destinations are all doable by public transportation. **Nice** is better than nice—it's tops. Other winners are peaceful **Villefranche-sur-Mer,** elegant **Cap Ferrat,** hilltop **Eze-le-Village,** and glitzy **Monaco.** (All destinations mentioned in this sidebar are described at greater length in this chapter.)

Other than Antibes, the following destinations west of Nice are not as appealing. They're farther afield and more suited for excursions, but why bother when Nice is near?

Antibes is a ramparted medieval town of narrow streets and red-tiled roofs, with a big yacht harbor, sandy beaches, and the prized Picasso Museum. It's the best stop west of Nice.

Cannes is a wealthy seafront town, catering to the rich and famous, and made for window-shopping. Go here only if your ship docks here.

St-Tropez is a trendy, busy, traffic-free port town smothered with fashion boutiques, fancy restaurants, and luxury boats. Other seafront resorts are at least as good, and closer, to the main Riviera ports.

St-Paul-de-Vence is a cobblestoned hill town jammed with shops and waves of tourists, and near the Fondation Maeght's modern-art collection. Difficult to reach on your own, this worthwhile town is usually bundled into an excursion with other sights.

Grasse is the historic and contemporary capital of perfume-making, with a museum and aggressive perfume merchants. A popular excursion destination (for its kickbacks as much as for its perfume), Grasse doesn't merit as much time as most excursions give it.

• **Cap Ferrat,** a 30-minute bus ride from Nice (and next door to Villefranche), is an exclusive, beautiful peninsula where groomed trails pass by villas, beaches, and a village port. I've outlined hikes lasting from 30 minutes to three hours.

• **Eze-le-Village** is a hilltop village with upscale boutiques, steep cobbled lanes, and magnificent views. Allow at least one hour to enjoy its back lanes and views, plus another 30 minutes or so each way to get there by bus.

• **Antibes,** with its Picasso Museum, is a fine side-trip, particularly if you're arriving in Nice or Cannes. Figure on four or five hours round-trip from either destination, including train time (15-30 minutes from Nice, 15 minutes from Cannes).

Tips: If your destination is accessible by either train or bus, it's substantially faster to take the train. And no matter where you go, bring along a swimsuit if the weather's sunny—good beaches are plentiful.

Public Transportation in the French Riviera

Many key Riviera destinations are connected by bus or train service, and some are served by both. See the chart on the following pages for a summary of available services. While bus fare for any trip is only €1, the pricier train can be a better choice because it saves you time. The bus frequencies are for Monday-Saturday (Sunday often has limited or no bus service)—confirm all connections and last train/bus times locally. I've listed some connections as "not recommended" due to the amount of time spent in transit; for example, while it is possible to connect Cannes and Monaco by train, at over two hours round-trip, you'd spend a good portion of your day on the train instead of enjoying the sights. Stick closer to your port.

THE FRENCH RIVIERA

Public Transportation in the French Riviera

From	To Cannes	To Antibes	To Nice	
Cannes by Train	N/A	2/hour, 15 minutes	2/hour, 30-40 minutes	
Cannes by Bus	N/A	#200, 35 minutes or more with traffic	#200, 2-4/hour, 1.5-1.75 hours or more with traffic	
Antibes by Train	2/hour, 15 minutes	N/A	2/hour, 15-30 minutes	
Antibes by Bus	#200, 35 minutes or more with traffic	N/A	#200, 2-4/hour, 1-1.5 hours or more with traffic	
Nice by Train	2/hour, 30-40 minutes	2/hour, 15-30 minutes	N/A	
Nice by Bus	#200, 2-4/hour, 1.5-1.75 hours or more with traffic	#200, 2-4/hour, 1-1.5 hours or more with traffic	N/A	
Villefranche-sur-Mer by Train	2/hour, 50 minutes	2/hour, 40 minutes	2/hour, 10 minutes	
Villefranche-sur-Mer by Bus	Not recommended	Not recommended	#100, 3-4/hour, 15 minutes; also #81, 2/hour, 15 minutes	
Cap Ferrat by Train	Not recommended	Not recommended	N/A	
Cap Ferrat by Bus	Not recommended	Not recommended	#81, 2/hour, 30 minutes; also #100, 3-4/hour, 30 minutes plus 20-minute walk	
Eze-le-Village by Train	Not recommended	Not recommended	Bus #83 to Eze-Bord-de-Mer (8/day), then train to Nice (2/hour, 15 minutes)	
Eze-le-Village by Bus	Not recommended	Not recommended	#82/#112, 8-16/day, 25 minutes	
Monaco by Train	Not recommended	Not recommended	2/hour, 20 minutes	
Monaco by Bus	Not recommended	Not recommended	#100, 3-4/hour, 45 minutes	

To Villefranche-sur-Mer	To Cap Ferrat	To Eze-le-Village	To Monaco
2/hour, 50 minutes	Not recommended	Not recommended	Not recommended
Not recommended	Not recommended	Not recommended	Not recommended
2/hour, 40 minutes	Not recommended	Not recommended	Not recommended
Not recommended	Not recommended	Not recommended	Not recommended
2/hour, 10 minutes	N/A	2/hour, 15 minutes, to Eze-Bord-de-Mer, then bus #83 to Eze, 8/day	2/hour, 20 minutes
#100, 3-4/hour, 15 minutes; also #81, 2/hour, 15 minutes	#81, 2/hour, 30 minutes; also #100, 3-4/hour, 30 minutes plus 20-minute walk	#82/#112, 16/day, 25 minutes	#100, 3-4/hour, 45 minutes
N/A	N/A	N/A	2/hour, 10 minutes
N/A	#81, 2/hour, 15 minutes; also #100, 3-4/hour, 15 minutes plus 20-minute walk	#80 to upper Villefranche, then bus #82/#112, 8-16/day, 25 minutes	#100, 3-4/hour, 25 minutes
N/A	N/A	N/A	N/A
#81, 2/hour, 15 minutes; also #100, 3-4/hour, 15 minutes plus 20-minute walk	N/A	#100 direction: Monaco to Gare d'Eze stop, then bus #83 to village	#100, 3-4/hour, 15 minutes
N/A	N/A	N/A	N/A
#82/#112 to upper Villefranche (16/day, 25 minutes), then bus #80 to Villefranche's center	#83 to Gare d'Eze stop, then bus #100 direction Nice	N/A	#112, 7/day Mon-Sat, none on Sun, 25 minutes
2/hour, 10 minutes	N/A	N/A	N/A
#100, 3-4/hour, 25 minutes	#100, 3-4/hour, 20 minutes	#112, 7/day Mon-Sat, none on Sun, 25 minutes	N/A

Getting Around the Riviera

By Train: There is no faster way to move about the Riviera than by train (especially useful if you're rushing to get back to your ship). Speedy trains link the Riviera's beachfront destinations—Nice, Villefranche-sur-Mer, Monaco, Cannes, and Antibes (see previous pages for approximate travel times; see www.sncf.com for details).

Train fares are cheap, but you need plenty of change to buy train tickets from machines at smaller, unstaffed stations. Never board a train without a ticket or valid pass—fare inspectors don't accept any excuses, and the minimum fine is €70.

By Bus: To reach sights between the main towns (such as Cap Ferrat and Eze-le-Village), buses do better than the train. For other destinations, the bus may be cheaper than the train and allows you to enjoy the winding scenery, but can be agonizingly slow in heavy traffic.

Buses are an amazing deal. Any one-way ride costs €1—whether you're riding 15 minutes from Nice to Villefranche-sur-Mer, 45 minutes to Monaco, or an hour to Antibes. Two private bus companies provide service to Riviera destinations: the more important Ligne d'Azur (www.lignedazur.com, in English) and the smaller TAM. The same tickets work on buses for both companies (and for local buses and trams within Nice)—you can even transfer between the buses of the two different companies. The €1 single ticket (called **"Ticket Azur"**), available on all Ligne d'Azur buses, lets you take a one-way ride anywhere within the bus system (if you board a TAM bus and want to transfer, ask for a transfer: *un ticket correspondance*). Bring change to buy bus tickets from drivers (who can't make change for large bills).

By Boat: Trans Côte d'Azur offers boat service from Nice to Monaco (tel. 04 92 98 71 30, www.trans-cote-azur.com).

By Car: While public transportation is easy in this region, some cruisers enjoy renting a car to joyride between towns—especially along the three dramatically scenic roads, called the Corniches, that connect Nice and Monaco. For this reason, I've included a few car-rental offices (listed in each destination chapter) and driving pointers.

Tours of the French Riviera

To efficiently see several Riviera destinations in one short day, consider hiring a guide or joining a tour.

Local Guides: Sylvie Di Cristo offers terrific full-day tours throughout the French Riviera in a car or minivan. She adores educating people about this area's culture and history, and loves adapting her tour to your interests, from overlooked hill towns to wine, cuisine, art, or perfume (€170/person for 2-3 people, €120/person for 4-6 people, €100/person for 7-8 people, 2-person mini-

mum, mobile 06 09 88 83 83, www.frenchrivieraguides.net, sylvie
.di.cristo@wanadoo.fr).

Sofia Villavicencio can expertly guide you in Nice and around
the Riviera. Her English is flawless, and art is her passion (€135/
half-day, €200/full-day, tel. 04 93 32 45 92, mobile 06 68 51 55 52,
sofia.villavicencio@laposte.net).

Minivan Tours: The Nice TI has information on minivan
excursions from Nice (roughly €50-60/half-day, €80-110/day).
Med-Tour is one of many (tel. 04 93 82 92 58, mobile 06 73 82 04
10, www.med-tour.com); **Tour Azur** is another (tel. 04 93 44 88
77, www.tourazur.com). **Revelation Tours** specializes in English-
language excursions (tel. 04 93 53 69 85, www.revelation-tours
.com). All also offer private tours by the day or half-day (check
with them for their outrageous prices, about €90/hour).

Helpful Hints

Closed Days: The following sights are closed on Mondays: Nice's
  Modern and Contemporary Art Museum, the Fine Arts
  Museum, and cours Saleya market, along with Antibes'
  Marché Provençal market from September through May.
  On Tuesdays the Chagall and Matisse museums in Nice are
  closed.

Events: The Riviera is famous for staging major events. Unless
  you're actually taking part in the festivities, these events give
  you only traffic jams. The three biggies are the **Nice Carnival**
  (late Feb, www.nicecarnaval.com), **Grand Prix of Monaco**
  (late May, www.grand-prix-monaco.com), and Festival de
  Cannes, better known as the **Cannes Film Festival** (mid-
  May, www.festival-cannes.com).

Nice

Nice (sounds like "niece"), with its spectacular Alps-to-Mediterranean surroundings, is an enjoyable big-city highlight of the Riviera. Its traffic-free old city mixes Italian and French flavors to create a spicy Mediterranean dressing, while its broad seaside walkways invite lounging and people-watching. Nice may be nice, but it's hot and jammed in July and August. Everything you'll want to see in Nice is either within walking distance, or a short bus or tram ride away.

Nice is perfectly situated for exploring the Riviera by public transport. Monaco, Villefranche-sur-Mer, Eze-le-Village, Antibes, and Cannes are all within about a one-hour bus or train ride. See "Getting Around the Riviera" on page 288 for more specifics.

Arrival at the Port of Nice

Arrival at a Glance: You can easily walk or take public transit (bus or tram) to most sights in Nice. To reach nearby towns, the train is faster than the bus. Go to Nice's train station (walk 10 minutes, then take the tram; or pay €15-20 for a taxi), where you can catch a train to Villefranche-sur-Mer (10 minutes), Monaco (20 minutes), or Antibes (15-30 minutes). Or, at the top of the port, you can catch bus #100 to Villefranche-sur-Mer (15 minutes) or Monaco (45 minutes); additional buses depart from the main bus station (a 20-25-minute walk away). Taxis are available for any of these (€35-40 one-way to Villefranche, €80 one-way to Monaco).

Port Overview

Nice's port is at the eastern edge of the town center, below Castle Hill. Cruise ships dock at either end of the mouth of this port: **Terminal 1** to the east (along the embankment called quai du Commerce), or **Terminal 2** to the west (along quai Infernet). From either terminal, it's a free shuttle bus ride or about a 10-minute walk to the top of the port. The picturesque port is filled with yachts, sailboats, and fishing boats, and surrounded by seafood restaurants and brasseries. There's a tiny, rocky, partially nude beach at the mouth of the port, just beyond Terminal 1.

A free **shuttle bus** *(navette)* circles the port, connecting the two terminals and place Ile de Beauté, the street that runs along

Services at the Port of Nice

As the port is close to Nice's city center, you'll easily find ample ATMs, Internet cafés, and other services, either at or near the port. For some of the options in town, see "Helpful Hints" on page 298.

Internet Access: You may be able to pick up a free Wi-Fi signal around the port (though this is sporadic). Several places around the port have Internet terminals.

Pharmacy: There are several within a block or two of the port, including Pharmacie Port Lympia (a block from Terminal 2, at 50 boulevard Stalingrad); Pharmacie du Port (at the top-left corner of the port, on the street leading to place Garibaldi at rue Cassini 17); and another one at 3 Boulevard Carnot (at the top-right corner of the port).

the top of the port (where you'll find bus stops—including for the bus to Villefranche and Monaco—and easy access to place Garibaldi, Nice's entry square). If a shuttle bus is departing soon, it can save you a few minutes' walk. But the port area is charming enough that walking is an enjoyable alternative to the bus.

Tourist Information: TI kiosks at both terminals are timed to be open when cruises arrive—just look for the TI attendants under the pointy white tents.

Getting into Town

The atmospheric streets of Old Nice—and the beaches and grand promenade that stretch between the city and the sea—are just on the other side of Castle Hill from the port. The tram and all city and regional buses cost only €1 per trip, making this one of the cheapest and easiest cities in France to get around in. Note that the **Le Grand Tour Bus** hop-on, hop-off bus circuit, which conveniently connects many of Nice's major sights, has a stop at the top of the port (for details, see "Tours in Nice," later).

By Taxi

Taxis meet arriving cruise ships; if you can't find one, ask the TI at the terminal to call one for you. Rates can be slippery, but expect to pay about €15-20 to points within Nice (such as to the train station or to the Matisse or Chagall museums), €35-40 one-way to Villefranche-sur-Mer, or €80 one-way to Monaco.

By Foot and Public Transportation

If your ship docks at **Terminal 2,** and you're heading for the old town, just walk around the base of the castle-topped hill (with the

Nice

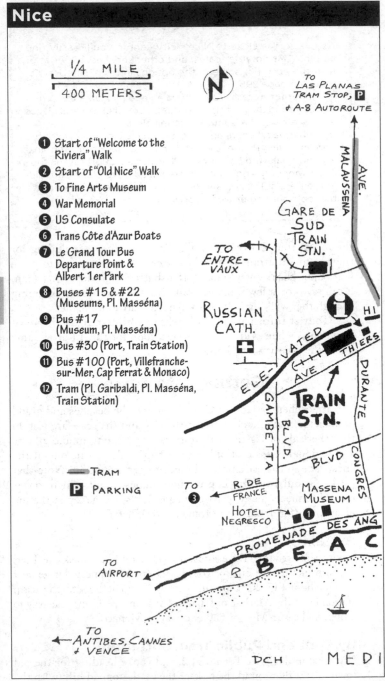

THE FRENCH RIVIERA

1/4 MILE
400 METERS

N

TO LAS PLANAS TRAM STOP, **P** & A-8 AUTOROUTE

1 Start of "Welcome to the Riviera" Walk
2 Start of "Old Nice" Walk
3 To Fine Arts Museum
4 War Memorial
5 US Consulate
6 Trans Côte d'Azur Boats
7 Le Grand Tour Bus Departure Point & Albert 1er Park
8 Buses #15 & #22 (Museums, Pl. Masséna)
9 Bus #17 (Museum, Pl. Masséna)
10 Bus #30 (Port, Train Station)
11 Bus #100 (Port, Villefranche-sur-Mer, Cap Ferrat & Monaco)
12 Tram (Pl. Garibaldi, Pl. Masséna, Train Station)

AVE. MALAUSSENA

GARE DE SUD TRAIN STN.

TO ENTRE-VAUX

RUSSIAN CATH.

ELE-VATED
AVE. THIERS

TRAIN STN.

GAMBETTA BLVD.

DURANTE

CONGRES

BLVD

R. DE FRANCE

TO 3

MASSENA MUSEUM

TRAM
P PARKING

HOTEL NEGRESCO

1

PROMENADE DES ANG

B E A C

TO AIRPORT

R

TO ANTIBES, CANNES & VENCE

DCH   M E D I

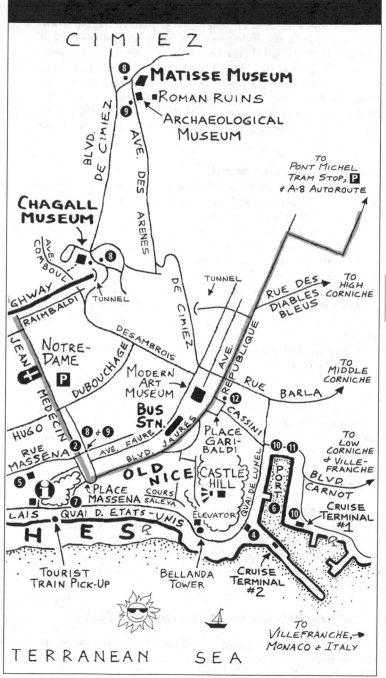

THE FRENCH RIVIERA

sea on your left), and you'll be there in about 10-15 minutes.

Terminal 1 is at the far end of the port from the old town. If you arrive here, it's slightly faster to circle around the back of Castle Hill: Walk or ride the shuttle bus to the top of the port, take the angled rue Cassini to place Garibaldi (described next), then walk into the old town from there. The total walk takes about 20-25 minutes. (From this end of the port, it's more scenic—but takes a few minutes more—to walk all the way around the port to Terminal 2, then along the promenade between Castle Hill and the sea.)

Walking to Place Garibaldi

The square called place Garibaldi serves as a sort of gateway between the port of Nice and the rest of the city. It's about a 15- to 20-minute walk from either cruise terminal. First, walk (or ride the shuttle bus) to the top-left corner of the port area (i.e., with the port to your back, go all the way to the left), and head up the angled street called rue Cassini toward the square with the palm trees. After three short blocks, you'll pop out at place Garibaldi.

Once in place Garibaldi, to reach **Old Nice,** walk straight through the middle of the square and out the other side, then turn left and walk down the broad boulevard Jean Jaurès; the old town sprawls to your left.

To reach the **tram stop** from place Garibaldi, walk along the right side of the square, then turn right on avenue de la République and walk a half-block. From here, you can ride the tram to various points of interest in town. For example, the tram connects the train station (see below). Or, to reach the Chagall or Matisse museums, you can ride the tram to the place Masséna stop, then transfer to bus #15 or #22 (bus #17 also goes to the Matisse Museum, but not the Chagall Museum); for details, see "Getting There" on pages 322 (for the Matisse Museum) or 312 (for the Chagall Museum)—or, for a more direct bus to Matisse, see below.

By Direct Bus to the Matisse Museum

The most direct way to the Matisse Museum—which may close for renovation in 2012—is to walk to the top of the port, then go a block to the right to boulevard de Stalingrad. From here, you can catch bus #20 to the Arènes-Matisse stop (3/hour Mon-Fri, 1-2/hour Sat-Sun, 30 minutes).

Getting to Sights Beyond Nice

To go from Nice to Villefranche-sur-Mer, Monaco, or other destinations, you can take either a train or a bus. The train is faster, but the bus stop is closer to Nice's port.

By Train

Trains go from Nice eastward to **Villefranche-sur-Mer** (2/hour, 10 minutes, €1.90) and **Monaco** (2/hour, 20 minutes, €3.60); and westward to **Antibes** (2/hour, 15-30 minutes, €4) and **Cannes** (2/hour, 30-40 minutes, €6.20).

From the cruise port, you can get to the train station by bus or by tram. The bus stop is closer to the port, but the bus departs less frequently.

Bus #30 goes from the top of the port to the train station (2/hour, 15 minutes). If you arrive at Terminal 2, you'll catch the bus at the top-left corner of the port, along place Ile de Beauté (the bus stop is to your left, with the port to your back). If you arrive at Terminal 1, you can catch bus #30 closer to the terminal: As you walk along the port, look for the steps on your right leading up to boulevard de Stalingrad; once on that street, find the bus stop. From either stop, take bus #30 in the direction of Gare SNCF to the end of the line (Gare SNCF stop), right at the train station.

Rather than wait for the bus, it can be faster to walk three blocks from the top of the port to catch the more frequent **tram** (see directions to place Garibaldi, earlier): Hop on a tram (going back the direction you just came from) and ride to the Gare Thiers stop. From that stop, cross the tracks and walk straight one long block on avenue Thiers; you'll see the train station on the right.

By Bus

To Villefranche-sur-Mer, Cap Ferrat, and Monaco (from Nice's Port)

Exiting either terminal, walk up to the top of the port (place Ile de Beauté). Near the right end of this strip (with your back to the port) is the stop for bus #100, which runs about every 15 minutes to **Villefranche-sur-Mer** (15 minutes), **Cap Ferrat** (20 minutes), or **Monaco** (45 minutes).

To Cap Ferrat, Eze-le-Village, and Cannes (from Nice's Bus Station/*Gare Routière*)

From Nice's bus station, you can reach **Cap Ferrat** (bus #81, offers more stops on the Cap than bus #100 noted above; 2/hour, 30 minutes), **Eze-le-Village** (buses #82/#112, 16/day, 8 on Sun, 25 minutes), and **Cannes** (and other points west; bus #200, 4/hour, Sun 2-3/hour, 1.5-1.75 hours).

Nice's **bus station** is about a 20- to 25-minute walk from either cruise terminal: First, walk to place Garibaldi (described earlier). From here, either catch the tram and ride it one stop to Gare Routière; or simply walk an additional 5-10 minutes to the bus station: Head straight through place Garibaldi, turn left onto busy boulevard Jean Jaurès, and walk until you see the bus station *(gare routière)* on your right. At Nice's ramshackle bus station, you'll find several bus companies and WCs (but no baggage storage). You can get timetables and prices from the English-speaking clerk at the information desk (Mon-Sat 8:00-12:00 & 13:00-17:00, closed Sun, tel. 04 93 85 61 81). Buy tickets from the driver. Television monitors by the central bus bays list platforms, destinations, and departure times.

By Boat to Monaco

From June to mid-September, Trans Côte d'Azur offers scenic boat trips from Nice to Monaco (Tue, Thu, and Sat only, 45 minutes each way). The boat departs at 9:30; you can either come straight back (€27, arriving back in Nice at 11:00), or you can return to Nice in the afternoon (€32, arriving at 18:00—do this only if your ship is departing late and you'll have plenty of time to absorb any potential delays). Reservations are required, so try to book a few days ahead (tel. 04 92 98 71 30 or 04 92 00 42 30, www.trans-cote-azur .com, croisieres@trans-cote-azur.com). The boat leaves from the port, near Terminal 2—look for the blue ticket booth *(billeterie)* on quai de Lunel. The same company also runs one-hour round-trip cruises along the coast to Cap Ferrat (see "Tours in Nice," later), as well as boats to St-Tropez (but the return boat from St-Tropez likely won't get you back in time to catch your ship—I'd skip this option).

By Tour

For information on local tour options around the French Riviera, see page 288; for options within Nice—including bus tours, guided boat cruises, walking tours, and more—see "Tours in Nice" on page 300.

Returning to Your Ship

From Old Nice, walk around Castle Hill to find the port. If you're coming on bus #100 from Villefranche-sur-Mer or Monaco, get off at the "Le Port" stop, right at the top of the port. If arriving by train, either take a taxi to the port, or ride the tramway to place Garibaldi and walk 15-20 minutes from there (down rue Cassini straight to the port).

Orientation to Nice

Everything of interest lies between the beach and the train tracks (about 15 blocks apart—see map on page 292). The city revolves around its grand place Masséna, where pedestrian-friendly avenue Jean Médecin meets Old Nice and the Albert 1er parkway (with

quick access to the beaches). It's a 20-minute walk (or a €10 taxi ride) from the train station to the beach, and a 20-minute walk along the promenade from the fancy Hôtel Negresco to the heart of Old Nice.

A 10-minute ride on the smooth-as-silk tramway takes you through the center of the city, connecting the train station, place Masséna, Old Nice, the bus station, and place Garibaldi (near the cruise port).

Tourist Information

Nice's helpful TI has two locations: next to the **train station** (usually busy; summer Mon-Sat 8:00-20:00, Sun 9:00-18:00; rest of year Mon-Sat 9:00-19:00, Sun 10:00-17:00) and facing the **beach** at 5 promenade des Anglais (usually quiet, daily 9:00-18:00, until 20:00 July-Aug, closed Sun off-season, toll tel. 08 92 70 74 07—€0.34/minute, www.nicetourisme.com). Pick up the thorough *Practical Guide to Nice* and a free Nice map. You can also get information here on day trips (including maps of Monaco or Antibes; details on boat excursions; and bus schedules to Eze-le-Village).

Arrival in Nice

By Train: All trains stop at Nice's main station, Nice-Ville. The station area is gritty and busy: Never leave your bags unattended and don't linger here longer than necessary.

Turn left out of the station to find a **TI** next door. Continue a few more blocks down for the Gare Thiers **tram stop** (this will take you to place Masséna, the old city, bus station, and port). Board the tram heading toward the right, direction Pont Michel (see "Getting Around Nice," later).

To walk from the station to the beach, cross avenue Thiers in front of the station, go down the steps by Hôtel Interlaken, and continue walking down avenue Durante, which turns into rue des Congrés. You'll soon reach the heart of Nice's beachfront promenade.

Taxis wait in front of the train station. **Car rental** offices are to the right as you exit the station.

By Bus: Nice's bus station *(gare routière)* is sandwiched between boulevard Jean Jaurès and avenue Félix Faure, next to the old city. Cross boulevard Jean Jaurès to enter Old Nice. Trams run along boulevard Jean Jaurès; take the tram in the direction of Las Planas to reach place Masséna and the train station.

Helpful Hints

Theft Alert: Nice has its share of pickpockets. Thieves target fanny packs: Have nothing important on or around your waist, unless it's in a money belt tucked out of sight. Be wary of scooters when standing at intersections, don't leave things unattended on the beach while swimming, and if you're in Old Nice after dark, stick to main streets.

US Consulate: You'll find it at 7 avenue Gustave V (tel. 04 93 88 89 55, fax 04 93 87 07 38, http://france.usembassy.gov/nice .html, usca.nice@orange.fr).

Museums: Some Nice museums (Chagall, Matisse) are closed on Tuesdays, while others (Modern and Contemporary Art, Fine Arts) close on Mondays. City museums are free of charge—so all of the sights in town (except the Chagall Museum and the Russian Cathedral) cost zilch to enter, making rainy-day options a swinging deal here.

Internet Access: There's no shortage of places to get online in Nice—they're everywhere. Just look up as you walk (keep your eye out for the @ symbol).

English Bookstore: The Cat's Whiskers has an eclectic selection of novels and regional travel books, including mine (Tue-Sat 10:00-12:00 & 14:00-19:00, closed Sun-Mon, 26-30 rue Lamartine, tel. 04 93 80 02 66).

Grocery Store: The big **Monoprix** on avenue Jean Médecin and rue Biscarra has it all, including deli counter, bakery, and cold drinks (Mon-Sat 8:30-21:00, closed Sun, see map on page 332).

Renting a Bike (and Other Wheels): Roller Station rents bikes (*vélos*, €5/hour, €10/half-day, €15/day), rollerblades (*rollers*, €6/day), Razor-type scooters (*trotinettes*, €6/half-day, €9/day), and skateboards (€6/half-day, €9/day). You'll need to leave your ID as a deposit (daily 9:30-19:00, July-Aug until 20:00, next to yellow awnings of Pailin's Asian restaurant at 49 quai des Etats-Unis—see map on page 328, another location at 10 rue Cassini near place Garibaldi, tel. 04 93 62 99 05, owner Eric). If you need more power, try the electric-assisted bikes or scooters at **Energy Scoot** (2 rue St. Philippe, near the promenade des Anglais and avenue Gambetta, tel. 04 97 07 12 64).

Car Rental: You'll find most companies represented at Nice's train station and near Albert 1er Park.

Views: For panoramic views, climb Castle Hill (see page 305), or take a one-hour boat trip (described later, under "Tours in Nice").

Beach Gear: To make life tolerable on the rocks, swimmers should buy a pair of the cheap plastic beach shoes sold at many shops

THE FRENCH RIVIERA

(flip-flops fall off in the water). **Go Sport** at #13 on place Masséna sells beach shoes, flip-flops, and cheap sunglasses (daily 10:00-19:00—see map on page 328).

Getting Around Nice

Although you can walk to most attractions in Nice, smart travelers make good use of the buses and tram. Both are covered by the same single-ride €1 ticket (good for 74 minutes in one direction, including transfers between bus and tram; can't be used for a round-trip). The €4 all-day ticket **(Carte Journée)** is good on Nice's city buses and tramway, as well as on buses throughout the region. This all-day ticket makes sense if you plan to take the bus to museums or use the tramway several times. Either ticket is valid on local buses and trams, as well as buses to nearby destinations (see "Getting Around the Riviera," on page 288).

The **bus** is handy for reaching the Chagall and Matisse museums and the Russian Cathedral. Make sure to validate your ticket in the machine just behind the driver—watch locals do it and imitate.

Nice's **tramway** makes an "L" along avenue Jean Médecin and boulevard Jean Jaurès, and connects the main train station (Gare

Thiers stop), place Masséna (Masséna stop, a few blocks' walk from the sea), Old Nice (Opéra-Vieille Ville), the bus station (Cathédrale-Vieille Ville), and the Modern and Contemporary Art Museum (place Garibaldi, near the port).

Taking the tram in the direction of Pont Michel takes you from the train station toward the beach and bus station (direction Las Planas goes the other way). Buy tickets at the machines on the platforms (coins only, no credit cards). Choose the English flag to change the display language, turn the round knob and push the green button to select your ticket, press it twice at the end to get your ticket, or press the red button to cancel. Once you're on the tram, validate your ticket by inserting it into the top of the white box, then reclaiming it.

Taxis are useful for getting to Nice's outlying sights, and worth it if you're nowhere near a bus or tram stop (figure €15 from promenade des Anglais). They normally only pick up at taxi stands *(tête de station),* or you can call 04 93 13 78 78.

The hokey **tourist train** gets you up Castle Hill (see "Tours in Nice," next).

THE FRENCH RIVIERA

Tours in Nice

Bus Tour—Le Grand Tour Bus provides a 12-stop, hop-on, hop-off service on an open-deck bus with headphone commentary (2/hour, 1.5-hour loop) that includes the promenade des Anglais, the old port, Cap de Nice, and the Chagall and Matisse museums on Cimiez Hill (€20/1-day pass, cheaper for seniors and students, €10 for last tour of the day at about 18:00, buy tickets on bus, main stop is near where promenade des Anglais and quai des Etats-Unis meet, across from plage Beau Rivage, tel. 04 92 29 17 00). This tour is a pricey way to get to the Chagall and Matisse museums, but it's an acceptable option if you also want a city overview. Check the schedule if you plan to use this bus to visit the Russian Cathedral, as it may be faster to walk there.

Tourist Train—For €7 (or €4 for children under 9) you can spend 40 embarrassing minutes on the tourist train tooting along the promenade, through the old city, and up to Castle Hill. This is a sweat-free way to get to Castle Hill...but so is the elevator, which is much cheaper (every 30 minutes, daily 10:00-18:00, June-Aug until 19:00, recorded English commentary, meet train near Le Grand Tour Bus stop on quai des Etats-Unis, tel. 04 93 62 85 48).

▲Boat Cruise—Here's your chance to join the boat parade and see Nice from the water. On this one-hour star-studded tour, you'll cruise in a comfortable yacht-size vessel to Cap Ferrat and past Villefranche-sur-Mer, then return to Nice with a final lap along promenade des Anglais. It's a scenic trip (the best views are from the seats on top), and worthwhile if you won't be hiking along the Cap Ferrat trails that provide similar views.

French (and sometimes English-speaking) guides play Robin Leach, pointing out mansions owned by some pretty famous people, including Elton John (just as you leave Nice, it's the soft-yellow square-shaped place right on the water), Sean Connery (on the hill above Elton, with rounded arches and tower), and Microsoft co-founder Paul Allen (in saddle of Cap Ferrat hill, above yellow-umbrella beach with sloping red-tile roof). Guides also like to point out the mansion where the Rolling Stones recorded *Exile on Main Street* (between Villefranche-sur-Mer and Cap Ferrat). I wonder if this gang ever hangs out together? The boats leave from the port, near Terminal 2 (€15; May-Oct Tue-Sun 2/day, usually at 11:00 and 15:00, no boats Mon; March-April Tue-Wed, Fri, and Sun at 15:00; no boats Nov-Feb; call ahead to verify schedule, arrive 30 minutes early to get best seats, drinks and WCs available).

Walking Tours—The TI on promenade des Anglais organizes weekly walking tours of Old Nice in French and English (€12, May-Oct only, usually Sat morning at 9:30, 2.5 hours, reservations

Nice at a Glance

▲▲▲**Chagall Museum** The world's largest collection of Chagall's work, popular even with people who don't like modern art. **Hours:** Wed-Mon 10:00-17:00, May-Oct until 18:00, closed Tue. See page 321.

▲▲▲**Promenade des Anglais** Nice's four-mile sun-struck seafront promenade. **Hours:** Always open. See page 320.

▲▲**Old Nice** Charming old city offering enjoyable atmosphere and a look at Nice's French-Italian cultural blend. **Hours:** Always open. See page 306.

▲**Matisse Museum** A worthwhile collection of Henri Matisse's paintings. May close for renovation sometime in 2012. **Hours:** Wed-Mon 10:00-18:00, closed Tue. See page 322.

▲**Modern and Contemporary Art Museum** Ultramodern museum with enjoyable collection from the 1960s-1970s, including Warhol and Lichtenstein. **Hours:** Tue-Sun 10:00-18:00, closed Mon. See page 324.

▲**Russian Cathedral** Finest Orthodox church outside of Russia. **Hours:** Mon-Sat 9:00-12:00 & 14:30-18:00, Sun 14:30-18:00, until 17:00 off-season. See page 326.

▲**Castle Hill** Site of an ancient fort boasting great views—especially in early mornings and evenings. **Hours:** Park closes at 20:00 in summer, earlier off-season. Elevator runs daily 10:00-19:00, until 20:00 in summer. See page 327.

Fine Arts Museum Lush villa shows off impressive paintings by Monet, Sisley, Bonnard, and Raoul Dufy. **Hours:** Tue-Sun 10:00-18:00, closed Mon. See page 326.

Molinard Perfume Museum Small museum tracing the history of perfume. **Hours:** Daily July-Aug 10:00-19:00, Sept-June 10:00-13:00 & 14:00-18:30, sometimes closed Mon off-season. See page 326.

THE FRENCH RIVIERA

necessary, depart from TI, tel. 08 92 70 74 07). They also have evening art walks on Fridays at 19:00.

Nice's cultural association (Centre du Patrimoine) offers incredibly cheap €5 walks on varying themes (in English, minimum 5 people). Call 04 92 00 41 90 a few days ahead to make a reservation. Most tours start at their office at 75 quai des Etats-Unis; look for the red plaque next to Musée des Ponchettes.

Local Guides—**Sofia Villavicencio** and **Sylvie Di Cristo** each give expert tours of Nice (for contact info, see page 288). Lovely **Pascale Rucker** tailors her tours in Nice to your interests. Book in advance, though it's also worth a try on short notice (€179/half-day, €274/day, tel. & fax 04 93 87 77 89, mobile 06 16 24 29 52).

Les Petits Farcis Cooking Tour and Classes—Charming Canadian Francophile Rosa Jackson, a food journalist and Cordon Bleu-trained cook, offers popular cooking classes in Old Nice. Her single-day classes include a morning trip to the open-air market on cours Saleya to pick up ingredients, and an afternoon session spent creating an authentic *niçois* meal from your purchases (€195/person, mobile 06 81 67 41 22, www.petitsfarcis.com).

Self-Guided Walks & Tours in Nice

My self-guided "Welcome to the Riviera Walk" and "Old Nice Walk" introduce you to Nice's waterfront promenade and its historic center, while my "Chagall Museum Tour" walks you through that museum's collection. Allow an hour apiece.

Welcome to the Riviera Walk

This leisurely, level walk begins on the promenade des Anglais (near the landmark Hôtel Negresco) and ends on Castle Hill above Old Nice. Allow one hour at a promenade pace to reach the elevator up to Castle Hill. A quick visit to the Masséna Museum (free, daily 10:00-18:00), next to the starting point of this walk, sets the Riviera stage for this stroll.

• *Begin at the walkway running along Nice's beach. This is the...*

Promenade des Anglais

Welcome to the Riviera. There's something for everyone along this four-mile-long seafront circus. Watch the Europeans at play, admire the azure Mediterranean, anchor yourself on a blue seat, and prop your feet up on the made-to-order guardrail. Come back to join the late-afternoon parade of tans along the promenade.

For now, stroll like the belle époque English aristocrats for whom the promenade was paved (see map on page 292). The broad sidewalks of the promenade des Anglais ("walkway of the English") were financed by upper-crust English tourists who wanted a safe place to stroll and admire the view. The walk was done in marble in 1822 for aristocrats who didn't want to dirty their shoes or smell the fishy gravel. This grand promenade leads to the old city and Castle Hill.

• *Check out the pink-domed...*

Hôtel Negresco

Nice's finest hotel is also a historic monument, offering up the city's most expensive beds and a free "museum" interior (always open—

provided you're dressed decently, absolutely no beach attire). The hotel recently underwent a massive renovation, so expect some changes to the following description.

March straight through the lobby (as if you're staying here) into the exquisite **Salon Royal,** a cozy place for a drink and a frequent host to art exhibits (opens at 11:00). The chandelier hanging from the Eiffel-built dome is made of 16,000 pieces of crystal. It was built in France for the Russian czar's Moscow palace...but because of the Bolshevik Revolution in 1917, he couldn't take delivery. Read the explanation of the bucolic dome scene, painted in 1913 for the hotel, then saunter around the perimeter counterclockwise. If the bar door is open (after about 15:00), wander up the marble steps for a look. Farther along, nip into the toilets for either an early 20th-century powder room or a Battle of Waterloo experience. The chairs nearby were typical of the age (cones of silence for an afternoon nap sitting up).

The hotel's Chantecler **restaurant** is one of the Riviera's best (allow €90 per person before drinks; described on page 334). A few years ago, it lost one of its Michelin stars, so you'll understand if the staff doesn't smile. In France, big-time chefs are like famous athletes: People know about them and talk about who's hot and who's not. Cooking is serious business—a few years ago, a famous Burgundian chef lost a star and committed suicide. On your way out, pop into the **Salon Louis XIV** (right of entry lobby as you leave), where the embarrassingly short Sun King models his red platform boots (English descriptions explain the room).

Once outside, turn left and walk past the bar to the back to see the hotel's original **entrance** (grander than today's)—in the 19th century, classy people stayed out of the sun, and any posh hotel that cared about its clientele would design its entry on the shady north side.

• *Cross the promenade des Anglais, and—before you begin your seaside promenade—grab a blue seat and gaze out to the...*

Bay of Angels (Baie des Anges)

Face the water. The body of Nice's patron saint, Réparate, was supposedly escorted into this bay by angels in the fourth century. To your right is where you might have been escorted into France—Nice's airport, built on a massive landfill. On that tip of land way

THE FRENCH RIVIERA

beyond the runway is Cap d'Antibes. Until 1860, Antibes and Nice were in different countries—Antibes was French, but Nice was a protectorate of the Italian kingdom of Savoy-Piedmont, a.k.a. the Kingdom of Sardinia. (During that period, the Var River—just west of Nice—was the geographic border between these two peoples.) In 1850 the people here spoke Italian and ate pasta. As Italy was uniting, the region was given a choice: Join the new country of Italy or join good old France (which was enjoying good times under the rule of Napoleon III). The vast majority voted in 1860 to go French...and voilà!

The first green hill to your left (Castle Hill) marks the end of this walk. Farther left lies Villefranche-sur-Mer (marked by the tower at land's end, and home to lots of millionaires), then Monaco (which you can't see, with more millionaires), then Italy (with lots of, uh, Italians). Behind you are the foothills of the Alps (Alpes Maritimes), which trap threatening clouds, ensuring that the Côte d'Azur enjoys sunshine more than 300 days each year. While half a million people live here, pollution is carefully treated—the water is routinely tested and very clean.

• With the sea on your right, begin...

Strolling the Promenade

The block next to Hôtel Negresco houses a lush park and the Masséna Museum of city history. Nearby sit two other belle époque establishments: the West End and Westminster **hotels,** both boasting English names to help those original guests feel at home (the West End is now part of the Best Western group...to help American guests feel at home). These hotels symbolize Nice's arrival as a tourist mecca a century ago, when the combination of leisure time and a stable economy allowed visitors to find the sun even in winter.

As you walk, be careful to avoid the green bike lane. You'll pass a number of separate **beaches**—some private, others public. In spite of the rocks, they're still a popular draw. You can rent gear—about €12-18 for a *chaise longue* (long chair) and a *transat* (mattress), €3-5 for an umbrella, and €4 for a towel—and kick

back. You'll also pass several beach restaurants (a highly recommended experience). Some of these eateries serve breakfast, all serve lunch, some do dinner, and a few have beachy bars...tailor-made for a break from this walk. A few promote package deals, including a lounge chair, an umbrella, a locker, and a meal, all for about €26. Why all this gear rental?

In Europe, most beach-going families take planes or trains, since parking and gas are pricey (even worse than in the US) and traffic is ugly. So, unlike my family's beach trips, they can't stuff chairs, coolers, and the like in the trunk of their car and park right near the beach.

Even a hundred years ago, there was sufficient tourism in Nice to justify building its first **casino** (a leisure activity imported from Venice). Part of an elegant casino, La Jetée Promenade stood on those white-covered pilings just offshore, until the Germans destroyed it during World War II.

Although La Jetée Promenade is gone, you can still see the striking 1927 Art Nouveau facade of the Palais de la Méditerranée, a grand casino, hotel, and theater. This intimidating edifice was built during the great Depression by American financier Frank Jay Gould, who was looking for a better return on his investments when America's economy was tanking. It soon became the grandest casino in Europe, and today is one of France's most exclusive hotels.

The unappealing Casino Ruhl stands nearby. Anyone can drop in for some one-armed-bandit fun, but if you're in town in the evening and want to play the tables, you'll need to dress up and bring your passport. **Albert 1er Park** is named for the Belgian king who enjoyed wintering here. While the English came first, the Belgians and Russians were also big fans of 19th-century Nice. That tall statue at the edge of the park commemorates the 100-year anniversary of Nice's union with France.

Continue along the promenade, past the park. You're now on **quai des Etats-Unis** ("quay of the United States"). This name was given as a tip-of-the-cap to the Americans for finally entering World War I in 1917. Five minutes past the Hôtel Suisse (brilliant views as you walk), there's a monumental **war memorial** sculpted out of the rock in honor of the thousands of local boys who died serving their country in World Wars I and II.

• Take the elevator next to the Hôtel Suisse up to Castle Hill (elevator runs daily 10:00-19:00, until 20:00 in summer, €0.70 one-way, €1.10 round-trip).

Castle Hill (Colline du Château)

This hill—in an otherwise flat city center—offers sensational views over Nice, the port (to the east), the foothills of the Alps, and the Mediterranean. The views are best early or at sunset, or whenever the weather's clear (park closes at 20:00 in summer, earlier off-season). Nice was founded on this hill. Its residents were crammed onto the hilltop until the 12th century, as it was too risky to live in the flatlands below. Today you'll find a waterfall, a playground, two cafés (with fair prices), and a cemetery—but no castle—on Castle Hill.

• *Your tour is finished. Enjoy the vistas. To walk down to Old Nice, follow signs from just below the upper café to* Vieille Ville *(not Le Port), turn right at the cemetery, and then look for the walkway down on your left. If you're planning a boat tour (one hour, see page 300 for details), follow the* Le Port *signs to the bassin des Amiraux.*

Old Nice Walk

This self-guided walking tour gives you a helpful introduction to Nice's bicultural heritage and its most interesting neighborhoods. Allow about an hour at a leisurely pace for this level walk, including a stop for coffee and *socca* (chickpea crêpe). It's best done in the morning (while the outdoor market thrives and the *socca*'s hot), and preferably not on a Sunday, when many shops are closed. This walk ends near the bus station—handy for returning to your ship in Villefranche-sur-Mer or Monaco (but remember that the train is faster).

• *Start on avenue Jean Médecin, near the Café Ritz, a block north of the Galleries Lafayette department store (see map on page 308).*

Avenue Jean Médecin

Nice's newly renovated "main street," once a nightmare of cars and delivery vehicles tangling with pedestrians, has been turned into a pedestrian and cyclist nirvana. As you walk along this major street, notice how quiet it is. Now think of a major street like this in your city, teeming with vehicles; then imagine it without the cars and trucks. Bravo, Nice. I used to avoid this street at all costs. Now I can't get enough of it. Places like the Café Ritz flourish in an environment of generous sidewalks and no traffic.

• *Stroll toward place Masséna and drink in the Italianesque colors and street theater that surround you. Find a bench on place Masséna.*

Place Masséna

This vast square pays tribute to Jean-André Masséna, a French military leader during the Revolutionary and Napoleonic Wars.

He's not just another pretty face in a long lineup of French military heroes, but is considered among the greatest commanders in history—anywhere, anytime. Napoleon thought of him as "the greatest name of my military Empire." No wonder this city is proud of him.

This grand *place* is Nice's drawing room, where old meets

new, and where the tramway bends between the bus and train stations. The square's black-and-white pavement feels like an elegant
outdoor ballroom, with the sleek tram waltzing across its dance
floor. The men you see on pedestals high above are modern-art
additions that arrived with the new tram.

There's also no better place than place Masséna to appreciate
the city's Italian heritage (standing here makes me feel as if I'm in
Venice's St. Mark's Square). The rich colors of the buildings reflect
the taste of previous Italian rulers, back when Nice's residents
rooted for Italian soccer teams. The fountains are the product of
more recent tastes—to save money, they only have high pressure
after 17:00. The distant hills behind the fountains separate Nice
from Villefranche-sur-Mer, and that Italianesque clock tower is
barely beyond Nice's bus station.

Look west across place Masséna and down a grassy parkway.
You're standing on Nice's historic river, the Paillon. It's been covered since the late 1800s and runs under place Masséna, then under
the parkway to the sea. For centuries this river was Nice's natural
defense to the north and west (the sea protected the south, and
Castle Hill defended the east). Imagine the fortified wall that once
ran along its length from the hills behind you to the sea.

With the arrival of tourism in the 1800s, Nice spread north,
beyond the river to your right. The modern can't-miss-it sculpture in the parkway is meant to represent the "curve of the French
Riviera"—whatever that means—but looks more like an answer to
local skateboarders' prayers. The tram is the first of three planned
routes, and is Nice's first serious stab at managing its debilitating
traffic problems.

• *Cross the square toward the Caisse d'Epargne Côte d'Azur bank, and
walk between the curved buildings along rue de l'Opéra, turning left
on...*

Rue St. François de Paule

You've entered Old Nice. Peer into the **Alziari** olive-oil shop at
#14 (on the right, Mon-Sat 8:30-12:00 & 14:00-1900, closed Sun).
Dating from 1868, the shop produces top-quality stone-ground
olive oil. The proud and charming owner, Gilles Piot, claims
that stone wheels create less acidity (since metal grinding builds
up heat). Locals fill their own containers from the huge vats (the
cheapest one is peanut oil, not olive oil). Consider a gift for the
olive oil-lover on your list. (Some may want to backpedal one block
to the **Molinard** perfume shop and museum before continuing—
see page 326.)

A block down on the left (at #7), **Pâtisserie Auer's** grand
old storefront has changed little since the pastry shop opened in
1820 (closed Sun). The writing on the window says, "Since 1820

Old Nice Walk

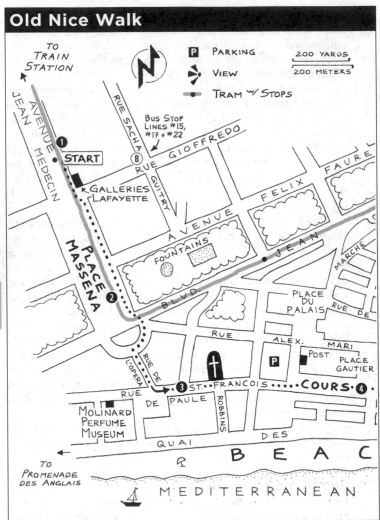

from father to son." The gold royal shields on the back wall remind shoppers that Queen Victoria indulged her sweet tooth here.

Across the street is Nice's grand **opera house,** dating from the same era. Imagine this opulent jewel back in the 19th century, buried deep in the old town of Nice. With all the fancy big-city folks wintering here, this rough-edged town needed some high-class entertainment. The four statues on top represent theater, dance, music, and song.

• *Continue on, sifting your way through souvenirs to the cours Saleya (koor sah-lay-yuh).*

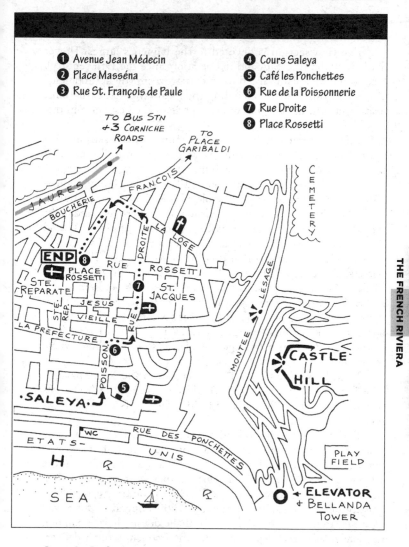

1. Avenue Jean Médecin
2. Place Masséna
3. Rue St. François de Paule
4. Cours Saleya
5. Café les Ponchettes
6. Rue de la Poissonnerie
7. Rue Droite
8. Place Rossetti

TO BUS STN + 3 CORNICHE ROADS

TO PLACE GARIBALDI

JAURES

BOUCHERIE

FRANCOIS

RUE DROITE

LA LOGE

CEMETERY

END 8

PLACE ROSSETTI

STE. REPARATE

RUE ROSSETTI

ST. JACQUES

7

LESAGE

STE. REP.

JESUS

VIEILLE

RUE

LA PREFECTURE

6

POISSON.

MONTEE

CASTLE HILL

SALEYA

5

WC

RUE DES PONCHETTES

ETATS-UNIS

PLAY FIELD

H   R

SEA   R

ELEVATOR + BELLANDA TOWER

Cours Saleya

Named for its broad exposure to the sun *(soleil)*, this commotion of color, sights, smells, and people has been **Nice's main market square** since the Middle Ages (produce market held Tue-Sun until 13:00—on Mon, an antiques market takes center stage). Amazingly, part

of this square was a parking lot until 1980, when the mayor of Nice had an underground garage built.

The first section is devoted to the Riviera's largest flower market (all day Tue-Sun and in operation since the 19th century). Here you'll find plants and flowers that grow effortlessly and ubiquitously in this climate, including the local favorites: carnations, roses, and jasmine. Fresh flowers are perhaps the best value in this otherwise pricey city.

The boisterous produce section trumpets the season with mushrooms, strawberries, white asparagus, zucchini flowers, and more—whatever's fresh gets top billing.

Place Pierre Gautier (also called Plassa dou Gouvernou—bilingual street signs include the old Niçoise language, an Italian dialect) is where farmers set up stalls to sell their produce and herbs directly. For a great market overview, climb the steps by Le Grand Bleu restaurant; you may have to step over the trash sacks.

Look up to the **hill** that dominates to the east. The city of Nice was first settled up there by Greeks (circa 400 B.C.). In the Middle Ages, a massive castle stood there with soldiers at the ready. Over time, the city grew down to where you are now. With the river guarding one side and the sea the other, this mountain fortress seemed strong—until Louis XIV leveled it in 1706. Nice's medieval seawall ran along the line of two-story buildings where you're standing.

Now, look across place Pierre Gautier to the large "palace." The **Ducal Palace** was where the kings of Sardinia (the city's Italian rulers until 1860) would reside when in Nice. Today, it's police headquarters.

Resume your stroll down the center of cours Saleya, stopping when you see La Cambuse restaurant on your left. In front, hovering over the black-barrel fire with the paella-like pan on top, is the self-proclaimed **Queen of the Market,** Thérèse (tehr-ehz). When she's not looking for a husband, Thérèse is cooking *socca,* Nice's chickpea crêpe specialty (until about 13:00). Spend €3 for a wad of *socca* (careful—it's hot, but good). If she doesn't have a pan out, that means it's on its way (watch for the frequent scooter deliveries). Wait in line...or else it'll be all gone when you return.

• *Continue down cours Saleya. The fine golden building that seals the end of the square is where Henri Matisse spent 17 years with a brilliant view onto Nice's world. If you're in the mood, the* **Café les Ponchettes** *is perfectly positioned for a people-watching break. If not, turn left a block before the end of the square and head down...*

Rue de la Poissonnerie

Look up at the first floor of the first building on your right. **Adam and Eve** are squaring off, each holding a zucchini-like gourd. This scene (post-apple) represents the annual rapprochement in Nice to make up for the sins of a too-much-fun Carnival (Mardi Gras). Residents of Nice have partied hard during Carnival for more than 700 years.

Now, walk a few doors down to #6 (right side). That filthy **iron grille** above the door allows air to enter the building, but keeps out uninvited guests. You'll see lots of these open grilles in Old Nice. They were part of a clever system that sucked in cool air from the sea, circulating it through homes and blowing it out through vents in the roof.

A few steps away, check out the small **Baroque church** (Notre-Dame-de-l'Annonciation) dedicated to St. Rita, the patron saint of desperate causes. She holds a special place in locals' hearts, making this the most popular church in Nice.

• *Turn right on the next street, where you'll pass Old Nice's most happening café/bar (**Distilleries Ideales**), with a Pirates of the Caribbean-style interior. Now turn left on "Right" Street (rue Droite), and enter an area that feels like a Little Naples.*

Rue Droite

In the Middle Ages, this straight, skinny street provided the most direct route from wall to wall, or river to sea. Stop at **Esipuno's bakery** (at place du Jésus, closed Mon-Tue) and say *bonjour* to the friendly folks. Thirty years ago, this baker was voted the best in France—the trophies you see were earned for bread-making, not bowling. His son now runs the place. Notice the firewood stacked by the oven. Try the house specialty, *tourte aux blettes* (pastry stuffed with pine nuts, raisins, and white beets).

Farther along, at #28, Thérèse (whom you met earlier) cooks her *socca* in the wood-fired oven here before she carts it to her barrel on cours Saleya. The balconies of the mansion in the next block mark the **Palais Lascaris** (1647), a rare souvenir from one of Nice's most prestigious families. It's worth popping inside for its Baroque Italian architecture, antique musical instruments, tapestries, and furniture (free, Wed-Mon 10:00-18:00, closed Tue). Look up and make faces back at the guys under the balconies.

• *Turn left on the rue de la Loge, then left again on rue Centrale, to reach...*

Place Rossetti

The most Italian of Nice's piazzas, place Rossetti feels more like Roma than Nice. Fenocchio is popular for its many gelato flavors, ranging from classic to innovative (daily March-Nov 9:00-24:00; mouth-watering preview at www.fenocchio.fr).

Walk to the fountain and stare back at the church. This is the **Cathedral of St. Réparate**—an unassuming building for a major city's cathedral. It was relocated here in the 1500s, when Castle Hill was temporarily converted to military-only. The name comes from Nice's patron saint, a teenage virgin named Réparate whose martyred body floated to Nice in the fourth century accompanied by angels (remember the Bay of Angels?). The interior of the cathedral gushes Baroque, a response to the Protestant Reformation. With the Catholic Church's Counter-Reformation, the theatrical energy of churches was cranked up—with re-energized, high-powered saints and eye-popping decor.

• *Our tour is over. If you're re-energized, take a walk up* **Castle Hill.** *To get there, cross place Rossetti and follow the lane leading uphill (see Castle Hill description at the end of the "Welcome to the Riviera Walk"). To visit the Chagall or Matisse museums, return to place Masséna to catch a bus there (see "Getting There," below, for the Chagall Museum, and page 322 for the Matisse Museum). Or, if you want to head for the bus station, take a left outside the church and you'll eventually get there.*

Chagall Museum Tour

Even if you're suspicious of modern art, the Chagall Museum (Musée Chagall)—with the world's largest collection of Marc Chagall's work in captivity—is a delight. After World War II, Chagall returned from the United States to settle in Vence, not far from Nice. Between 1954 and 1967, he painted a cycle of 17 large murals designed for, and donated to, this museum. These paintings, inspired by the biblical books of Genesis, Exodus, and the Song of Songs, make up the "nave," or core, of what Chagall called the "House of Brotherhood."

Orientation

Cost: €7.50, free first Sun of the month (but crowded).

Hours: Wed-Mon 10:00-17:00, May-Oct until 18:00, closed Tue year-round.

Getting There: You can reach the museum, located on avenue Docteur Ménard, by bus or on foot.

    Buses #15 and #22 serve the Chagall Museum from the Masséna Guitry stop, near place Masséna (5/hour Mon-Sat, 3/hour Sun, €1; stop faces eastbound on rue Sacha Guitry, a block east of Galeries Lafayette department store—see map on page 292). The museum's bus stop (called Musée Chagall, shown on the bus shelter) is on boulevard de Cimiez (walk uphill from the stop to find the museum).

Chagall Museum

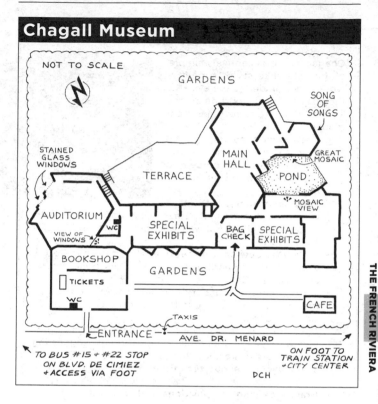

NOT TO SCALE

GARDENS

SONG OF SONGS

STAINED GLASS WINDOWS

MAIN HALL

GREAT MOSAIC

TERRACE

POND

MOSAIC VIEW

AUDITORIUM

VIEW OF WINDOWS

WC

SPECIAL EXHIBITS

BAG CHECK

SPECIAL EXHIBITS

BOOKSHOP

TICKETS

GARDENS

WC

CAFE

TAXIS

ENTRANCE

AVE. DR. MENARD

TO BUS #15 + #22 STOP ON BLVD. DE CIMIEZ + ACCESS VIA FOOT

ON FOOT TO TRAIN STATION + CITY CENTER

DCH

To **walk** from central Nice to the Chagall Museum (30 minutes), go to the train-station end of avenue Jean Médecin and turn right onto boulevard Raimbaldi. Walk four long blocks along the elevated road, then turn left onto avenue Raymond Comboul, and follow *Musée Chagall* signs.

Information: Although Chagall would suggest that you explore his works without help, the free audioguide gives you detailed explanations of his works and covers temporary exhibits. The free *Plan du Musée* helps you locate the rooms, though you can do without, as the museum is pretty simple. Tel. 04 93 53 87 20, www.musee-chagall.fr.

Leaving the Museum: To take **buses** #15 or #22 back to downtown Nice, turn right out of the museum, then make another right down boulevard de Cimiez, and catch the bus heading downhill. To continue on to the Matisse Museum (which may be closed—call first), catch buses #15 or #22 using the uphill stop located across the street. **Taxis** usually wait in front of the museum. It's about €12 for a ride to the city center.

To **walk** to the train station area from the museum (20 minutes), turn left out of the museum grounds, then left again

Chagall's Style

Chagall uses a deceptively simple, almost childlike style to paint a world that's hidden to the eye—the magical, mystical world below the surface. Here are some of his techniques:

- **Deep, radiant colors,** inspired by Expressionism and Fauvism (an art movement pioneered by Matisse and other French painters).
- **Personal imagery,** particularly from his childhood in Russia—smiling barnyard animals, fiddlers on the roof, flower bouquets, huts, and blissful sweethearts.
- **A Hasidic Jewish perspective,** the idea that God is everywhere, appearing in everyday things like nature, animals, and humdrum activities.
- **A fragmented Cubist style,** multifaceted and multidimensional, a perfect style to mirror the complexity of God's creation.
- **Overlapping images,** like double-exposure photography, with faint imagery that bleeds through, suggesting there's more to life under the surface.
- **Stained-glass-esque technique** of dark, deep, earthy, "potent" colors, and simplified, iconic, symbolic figures.
- **Gravity-defying compositions,** with lovers, animals, and angels twirling blissfully in midair.
- **Happy (not tragic) mood** depicting a world of personal joy, despite the violence and turmoil of world wars and revolution.
- **Childlike simplicity,** drawn with simple, heavy outlines, filled in with Crayola colors that often spill over the lines. Major characters in a scene are bigger than the lesser characters. The grinning barnyard animals, the bright colors, the magical events presented as literal truth...Was Chagall a lightweight? Or a lighter-than-air-weight?

on the street behind it (avenue Docteur Ménard). As the street bends right, take the ramps and staircases down on your left, turn left at the bottom, cross under the freeway and the train tracks, then turn right on boulevard Raimbaldi to reach the station.

Length of This Tour: Allow one hour.

Cuisine Art and WCs: An idyllic café (€10 salads and *plats*) awaits in the corner of the garden. A spick-and-span WC is next to the ticket desk (there's one inside, too).

The Tour Begins

This small museum consists of six rooms: two rooms with the 17 large murals, two rooms for special exhibits, an auditorium with stained-glass windows, and a mosaic-lined pond (viewed from inside). In the main hall you'll find the core of the collection (Genesis and Exodus scenes). The adjacent octagonal room houses five paintings—the Song of Songs room.

• *Buy your ticket, pass through the garden, and enter the museum at the baggage-check counter (daypacks must be checked). Find the main hall filled with Chagall's colorful paintings of...*

Old Testament Scenes

Each painting is a lighter-than-air collage of images that draw from Chagall's Russian folk-village youth, his Jewish heritage, biblical themes, and his feeling that he existed somewhere between heaven and earth. He believed that the Bible was a synonym for nature, and that color and biblical themes were key ingredients for understanding God's love for his creation. Chagall's brilliant blues and reds celebrate nature, as do his spiritual and folk themes. Notice the focus on couples. To Chagall, humans loving each other mirrored God's love of creation.

The paintings are described below in the order you should see them, going counterclockwise around the room (some paintings might be on loan to other museums). Look for posted explanations of each work in English.

Abraham and the Three Angels

In the heat of the day, Abraham looked up and saw three men. He said, "Let a little food and water be brought, so you can be refreshed..." (Genesis 18:1-5)

Abraham refreshes God's angels on this red-hot day, and in return, they promise Abraham a son (in the bubble, at right), thus making him the father of the future Israelite nation.

The Sacrifice of Isaac

Abraham bound his son Isaac and laid him on the altar. Then he took the knife to slay his son. But the angel of the Lord called out to him from heaven, "Abraham!" (Genesis 22:9-11)

Tested by God, Abraham prepares to kill his only son, but the angel stops him in time. Notice that Isaac is posed exactly as Adam is in *The Creation* (described below). Abraham's sacrifice echoes three others: the sacrifice all men must make (i.e., Adam, the everyman), the sacrifice of atonement (the goat tied to a tree at left), and even God's sacrifice of his own son (Christ carrying the cross, upper right).

The Creation

God said, "Let us make man in our image, in our likeness..." (Genesis 1:26)

A pure-white angel descends through the blue sky and carries a still-sleeping Adam from radiant red-yellow heaven to earth. Heaven is a whirling dervish of activity, spinning out all the events of future history, from the tablets of the Ten Commandments to the Crucifixion—an overture of many images that we'll see in later paintings. (Though not a Christian, Chagall saw the Crucifixion as a universal symbol of man's suffering.)

Moses Receives the Ten Commandments

The Lord gave him the two tablets of the Law, the tablets of stone inscribed by the finger of God... (Exodus 31:18)

An astonished Moses is tractor-beamed toward heaven, where God reaches out from a cloud to hand him the Ten Commandments. While Moses tilts one way, Mount Sinai slants the other, leading our eye up to the left, where a golden calf is being worshipped by the wayward Children of Israel. But down to the right, Aaron and the menorah assure us that Moses will set things right. In this radiant final panel, the Jewish tradition—after a long struggle—is finally established.

Driven from Paradise

So God banished him from the Garden of Eden...and placed cherubim and a flaming sword to guard the way... (Genesis 3:23-24)

An angel drives them out with a fire hose of blue (there's Adam still cradling his flaming-red coq), while a sparkling yellow sword prevents them from ever returning. Deep in the green colors, the painting offers us glimpses of the future—Eve giving birth (lower-right corner) and the yellow sacrificial goat of atonement (top right).

Paradise

God put him in the Garden of Eden...and said, "You must not eat from the tree of the knowledge of good and evil..." (Genesis 2:15-17)

Paradise is a rich, earth-as-seen-from-space pool of blue, green, and white. Amoebic, still-evolving animals float around Adam (celibately practicing yoga) and Eve (with lusty-red hair). On the right, an angel guards the tempting tree, but Eve offers an apple, and Adam reaches around to sample the forbidden fruit.

The Rainbow

God said, "I have set my rainbow in the clouds as a sign of the covenant between me and the earth." (Genesis 9:13)

A flaming angel sets the rainbow in the sky, while Noah rests beneath it and his family offers a sacrifice of thanks. The

Marc Chagall
(1887-1985)

1887-1910: Russia

Chagall is born in the small town of Vitebsk, Belarus. He's the oldest of nine children in a traditional Russian Hasidic Jewish family. He studies realistic art in his hometown. In St. Petersburg, he is first exposed to the Modernist work of Paul Cézanne and the Fauves.

1910-1914: Paris

A patron finances a four-year stay in Paris. Chagall hobnobs with the avant-garde and learns technique from the Cubists, but he never abandons painting recognizable figures or his own personal fantasies. (Some say his relative poverty forced him to paint over used canvases, which gave him the idea of overlapping images that bleed through. Hmm.)

1914-1922: Russia

Returning to his hometown, Chagall marries Bella Rosenfeld (1915), whose love will inspire him for decades. He paints happy scenes despite the turmoil of wars and the Communist Revolution. Moving to Moscow (1920), he paints his first large-scale works, sets for the New Jewish Theatre. These would inspire many of his later large-scale works.

1923-1941: France and Palestine

Chagall returns to France. In 1931 he travels to Palestine, where the bright sun and his Jewish roots inspire a series of gouaches (opaque watercolor paintings). These gouaches would later inspire 105 etchings to illustrate the Bible (1931-1952), which would eventually influence the 17 large canvases of biblical scenes in the Chagall Museum (1954-1967).

1941-1947: United States/World War II

Fearing persecution for his Jewish faith, Chagall emigrates to New York, where he spends the war years. The Crucifixion starts to appear in his paintings—not as a Christian symbol, but as a representation of the violence mankind perpetrates on itself. In 1947 his beloved Bella dies, and he stops painting for months.

1947-1985: South of France

After the war, Chagall returns to France, eventually settling in St-Paul-de-Vence. In 1952 he remarries. His new love, Valentina Brodsky, plus the southern sunshine, bring Chagall a revived creativity—he is extremely prolific for the rest of his life. He experiments with new techniques and media—ceramics, sculpture, book illustrations, tapestry, and mosaic. In 1956 he's commissioned for his first stained-glass project. Eventually he does windows for cathedrals in Metz and Reims, and a synagogue in Jerusalem (1960). The Chagall Museum opens in 1973.

pure-white rainbow's missing colors are found radiating from the features of the survivors.

Jacob's Ladder

He had a dream in which he saw a ladder resting on the earth with its top reaching to heaven, and the angels of God were ascending and descending on it... (Genesis 28:12)

In the left half, Jacob (Abraham's grandson) slumps asleep and dreams of a ladder between heaven and earth. On the right, a spinning angel with a menorah represents how heaven and earth are bridged by the rituals of the Jewish tradition.

Jacob Wrestles with an Angel

So Jacob wrestled with him till daybreak. Jacob said, "I will not let you go unless you bless me..." (Genesis 32: 24, 26)

Jacob holds on while the angel blesses him with descendants (the Children of Israel) and sends out rays from his hands, creating, among others, Joseph (stripped of his bright-red coat and sold into slavery by his brothers).

Noah's Ark

Then he sent out a dove to see if the water had receded... (Genesis 8:8)

Adam and Eve's descendants have become so wicked that God destroys the earth with a flood, engulfing the sad crowd on the right. Only righteous Noah (center), his family (lower right), and the animals (including our yellow goat) are spared inside an ark. Here Noah opens the ark's window and sends out a dove to test the waters.

Moses Brings Water from the Rock

The Lord said, "Strike the rock, and water will come out of it for the people to drink..." (Exodus 17:5-6)

In the brown desert, Moses nourishes his thirsty people with water miraculously spouting from a rock. From the (red-yellow) divine source, it rains down actual (blue) water, but also a gush of spiritual yellow light.

Moses and the Burning Bush

The angel of the Lord appeared to him in flames of fire from within a bush... (Exodus 3:2)

Horned Moses—Chagall depicts him according to a medieval tradition—kneels awestruck before the burning bush, the event that calls him to God's service. On the left, we see Moses after the call, his face radiant, leading the Israelites out of captivity across the Red Sea, while Pharaoh's men drown (lower half of Moses' robe). The Ten Commandments loom ahead.

Song of Songs

Song of Solomon 7:11
Come, my lover, let us go to the countryside,
let us spend the night in the villages.

Song of Solomon 5:2
I slept but my heart was awake.

Song of Solomon 2:17
Until the day breaks and the shadows flee,
turn, my lover, and be like a gazelle or like
a young stag on the rugged hills.

Song of Solomon 3:4
I held him and would not let him go.

Song of Solomon 7:7
Your stature is like that of the palm,
and your breasts like clusters of fruit.

• *Return to* Moses Receives the Ten Commandments, *then walk past a stained-glass window on your way to the octagonal room.*

Song of Songs

Chagall wrote, "I've been fascinated by the Bible ever since my earliest childhood. I have always thought of it as the most extraordinary source of poetic inspiration imaginable. As far as I am concerned, perfection in art and in life has its source in the Bible, and exercises in the mechanics of the merely rational are fruitless. In art as well as in life, anything is possible, provided there is love."

Chagall enjoyed the love of two women in his long life—his first wife, Bella, then Valentina, who gave him a second wind as he was painting these late works. Chagall was one of the few "serious" 20th-century artists to portray unabashed love. Where the Bible uses the metaphor of earthly, physical, sexual love to describe God's love for humans, Chagall uses unearthly colors and a mystical ambience to celebrate human love. These red-toned canvases are hard to interpret on a literal level, but they capture the rosy spirit of a man in love with life. The sidebar above reflects the order of the verses displayed in the painting.

• *Head back toward the entry and turn left at* The Sacrifice of Isaac *to find...*

The Pond

The great mosaic reflected in the pond evokes the prophet Elijah in his chariot of fire (from the Second Book of Kings)—with Chagall's addition of the 12 signs of the zodiac, which he used to symbolize Time.

• *Return to the main hall, veer left, and exit the hall to the right. Pass through the exhibition room with temporary displays. At the end, you'll find...*

The Auditorium

This room is worth a peaceful moment to enjoy three Chagall stained-glass windows: the creation of light, elements, and planets (a visual big bang that's four "days" wide); the creation of animals, plants, man and woman, and the ordering of the solar system (two "days" wide, complete with fish and birds still figuring out where they belong); and the day of rest, with angels singing to the glory of God (the narrowest—only one "day" wide). If you like these windows, make sure to visit the cathedral in Reims on a future trip.

Sights in Nice

Walks and Beach Time

▲▲▲**Promenade des Anglais and Beach**—Meandering along Nice's four-mile seafront promenade on foot or by bike is a must.

This stretch is *the* place to be in Nice, from the days when wealthy English tourists filled the grand seaside hotels to today's Europeans seeking fun in the sun.

For a self-guided walk of this strip, see the "Welcome to the Riviera Walk," earlier. To rev up the pace of your promenade saunter, rent a bike and glide along the coast in both directions (about 30 minutes each way; for rental info, see "Helpful Hints," earlier). Both of the following paths start along promenade des Anglais.

The path to the **west** stops just before the airport, at perhaps the most scenic *boules* courts in France. Pause here to watch the old-timers while away their afternoon tossing shiny metal balls. If you take the path heading **east,** you'll round the hill—passing a scenic cape and the town's memorial to both world wars—to the harbor of Nice, with a chance to survey some fancy yachts. Pedal around the harbor and follow the coast past the Corsica ferry terminal (you'll need to carry your bike up a flight of steps). From there the path leads to an appealing tree-lined residential district.

And of course, there's the **beach.** Settle in to the smooth pebbles and consider your options: you can play beach volleyball, table tennis, or *boules;* rent paddleboats, personal watercraft, or windsurfing equipment; explore ways to use your zoom lens and pretend you're a paparazzo; or snooze on a comfy beach bed.

THE FRENCH RIVIERA

To rent a spot on the beach, compare rates, as prices vary—

beaches on the east end of the bay are usually cheaper (chair and mattress—*chaise longue* and *transat*-€12-18, umbrella-€3-5, towel-€4). Consider having lunch in your bathing suit (€12 salads and pizzas in bars and restaurants all along the beach). Or, for a peaceful café au lait on the Mediterranean, stop here first thing in the morning before the crowds hit. *Plage Publique* signs explain the 15 beach no-nos (translated into English).

▲▲**Wandering Old Nice (Vieux Nice)**—Offering an intriguing look at Nice's melding of French and Italian cultures, the old city is a fine place to linger. Enjoy its narrow lanes, bustling market squares, and colorful people.

For details on this neighborhood, see the "Old Nice Walk" on page 306.

Museums and Monuments

To bring culture to the masses, the city of Nice has nixed the entry fee to all municipal museums—so it's free to enter any of the following sights except the Chagall Museum and the Russian Cathedral. Cool.

The first two museums (Chagall and Matisse) are a long walk northeast of Nice's city center. Because they're in the same direction and served by the same bus line (buses #15 and #22 stop at both museums), it makes sense to visit them on the same trip. From place Masséna, the Chagall Museum is a 10-minute bus ride or a 30-minute walk, and the Matisse Museum is a 20-minute bus ride or a one-hour walk.

▲▲▲**Chagall Museum (Musée National Marc Chagall)**—Inspired by the Old Testament, modern artist Marc Chagall

custom-painted works for this building, which he considered a "House of Brotherhood." In typical Chagall style, these paintings are lively, colorful, and simple (some might say simplistic). The museum is a can't-miss treat for Chagall fans, and a hit even for people who usually don't like modern art.

For a complete self-guided tour of the museum, and directions on how to get here, see the "Chagall Museum Tour" on page 312.

Cost and Hours: €7.50, free first Sun of the month (but crowded), open Wed-Mon 10:00-17:00, May-Oct until 18:00, closed Tue year-round, avenue Docteur Ménard, tel. 04 93 53 87 20, www.musee-chagall.fr.

▲**Matisse Museum (Musée Matisse)**—This small museum contains a sizeable sampling of Henri Matisse paintings. It offers a painless introduction to the artist, whose style was shaped by Mediterranean light and by fellow Côte d'Azur artists Pablo Picasso and Pierre-Auguste Renoir. The collection is scattered throughout several rooms with a few worthwhile works, though it lacks a certain *je ne sais quoi* when compared to the Chagall Museum. The museum may close for renovation sometime in 2012—confirm it's open before heading out.

Cost and Hours: Free, Wed-Mon 10:00-18:00, closed Tue, 164 avenue des Arènes de Cimiez, tel. 04 93 81 08 08, www.musee-matisse-nice.org. The museum is housed in a beautiful Mediterranean mansion set in an olive grove amid the ruins of the Roman city of Cemenelum. Part of the ancient Roman city of Nice, Cemenelum was a military camp that housed as many as 20,000 people.

Getting to the Matisse Museum: It's a long uphill walk from the city center. Take the bus (details follow) or a cab (about €20 from promenade des Anglais). Once here, walk into the park to find the pink villa. **Bus #20** connects the port to the museum. **Buses #15, #17,** and **#22** offer regular service to the Matisse Museum from just off place Masséna on rue Sacha Guitry (Masséna Guitry stop, a block east of the Galeries Lafayette department store—see map on page 308; 20 minutes; note that bus #17 does not stop at the Chagall Museum). On any bus, get off at the Arènes-Matisse bus stop. (For bus tips on leaving the museum, see the end of this listing.)

Background: Henri Matisse, the master of leaving things out, could suggest a woman's body with a single curvy line—letting the viewer's mind fill in the rest. Ignoring traditional 3-D perspective, he used simple dark outlines saturated with bright blocks of color to create recognizable but simplified scenes composed into a decorative pattern to express nature's serene beauty. You don't look "through" a Matisse canvas, like a window; you look "at" it, like wallpaper.

Matisse understood how colors and shapes affect us emotionally. He could create either shocking, clashing works (Fauvism) or geometrical, balanced, harmonious ones (later pieces). Whereas other modern artists reveled in purely abstract design, Matisse (almost) always kept the subject matter at least vaguely recognizable. He used unreal colors and distorted lines not just to portray what an object looks like, but to express its inner nature (even inanimate objects). Meditating on his paintings helps you connect with nature—or so Matisse hoped.

As you tour the museum, look for Matisse's favorite motifs—including fruit, flowers, wallpaper, and sunny rooms—often with a window opening onto a sunny landscape. Another favorite subject is the *odalisque* (harem concubine), usually shown sprawled in a seductive pose and with a simplified, masklike face. You'll also see a few souvenirs from his travels, which influenced much of his work.

Viewing the Collection: Enter the museum at park level from the door opposite the olive grove (not the basement entry). The museum features temporary exhibits about Matisse that change frequently.

Rooms on the entry level usually house paintings from Matisse's formative years as a student (1890s). Notice how quickly his work evolves: from dark still lifes to colorful Impressionist works to more abstract pieces, all in a matter of a few years. A beige banner describes his "discovery of light," which the Riviera (and his various travels to sun-soaked places like Morocco and Tahiti) brought to his art. You may see photographs of his apartment on cours Saleya, which is described in my "Old Nice Walk," earlier.

Other rooms on this floor may highlight Matisse's fascination with dance and the female body (these subjects sometimes move upstairs). You'll see pencil and charcoal drawings, and a handful of bronze busts; he was fascinated by sculpture. *The Acrobat*—painted only two years before Matisse's death—shows the artist at his minimalist best. Look also for the orange-bearded 1905 portrait of Matisse by André Derain.

The floor above features sketches and models of Matisse's famous Chapel of the Rosary, located in nearby Vence, and related religious works. On the same floor, you may find paper cutouts from his *Jazz* series, more bronze sculptures, various personal objects, and linen embroideries inspired by his travels to Polynesia.

The bookshop, WCs, and additional temporary exhibits are in the basement levels. The fantastic wall-hanging near the bookshop—Matisse's colorful paper cutout *Flowers and Fruits*—shouts, "Riviera!"

Leaving the Museum: When leaving the museum, find the stop for buses #15 and #22 (frequent service downtown and stops en route at the Chagall Museum): Turn left out of the Matisse Museum into the park and keep straight, exiting the park at the Archeological Museum, then turn right. Pass the bus stop across the street (#17 goes to the city center but not the Chagall Museum, and #20 goes to the port), and walk to the small roundabout. Cross the roundabout to find the shelter (facing downhill) for buses #15

Henri Matisse
(1869-1954)

Here's an outline of Henri Matisse's busy life:

1880s and 1890s—At age 20, Matisse, a budding lawyer, is struck down with appendicitis. Bedridden for a year, he turns to painting as a healing escape from pain and boredom. After recovering, he studies art in Paris and produces dark-colored, realistic still lifes and landscapes. His work is exhibited at the Salons of 1896 and 1897.

1897-1905—Influenced by the Impressionists, he experiments with sunnier scenes and brighter colors. He travels to southern France, including Collioure (on the coast near Spain), and seeks still more light-filled scenes to paint. His experiments are influenced by Vincent van Gogh's bright, surrealistic colors and thick outlines, and by Paul Gauguin's primitive visions of a Tahitian paradise. From Paul Cézanne, he learns how to simplify objects into their basic geometric shapes. He also experiments (like Cézanne) with creating the illusion of 3-D not by traditional means, but by using contrasting colors for the foreground and background.

1905—Back in Paris, Matisse and his colleagues (André Derain and Maurice de Vlaminck) shock the art world with an exhibition of their experimental paintings. The thick outlines, simple forms, non-3-D scenes, and—most of all—bright, clashing, unrealistic colors seemed to be the work of "wild animals" (fauves). Fauvism is hot, and Matisse is instantly famous. (Though notorious as a "wild animal," Matisse himself was a gentle, introspective man.)

1906-1910—After just a year, Fauvism is out, and African masks are in. This "primitive" art form inspires Matisse to simplify and distort his figures further, making them less realistic but more expressive.

1910-1917—Matisse creates his masterpiece paintings. Cubism is the rage, pioneered by Matisse's friend and rival for the World's Best Painter award, Pablo Picasso. Matisse dabbles in Cubism,

and #22 by the apartment building with the oval portico (see map on page 292).

▲**Modern and Contemporary Art Museum (Musée d'Art Moderne et d'Art Contemporain)**—This ultramodern museum features an explosively colorful, far-out, yet manageable collection focused on American and European-American artists from the 1960s and 1970s (Pop Art and New Realism styles are highlighted).

simplifying forms, emphasizing outline, and muting his colors. But ultimately it proves to be too austere and analytical for his deeply sensory nature. The Cubist style is most evident in his sculpture.

1920s—Burned out from years of intense experimentation, Matisse moves to Nice (spending winters there from 1917, settling permanently in 1921). Luxuriating under the bright sun, he's reborn, and he paints colorful, sensual, highly decorative works. Harem concubines lounging in their sunny, flowery apartments epitomize the lush life.

1930s—A visit to Tahiti inspires more scenes of life as a sunny paradise. Matisse increases playing around with the lines of the figures he draws to create swirling arabesques and decorative patterns.

1940s—Duodenal cancer (in 1941) requires Matisse to undergo two operations and confines him to a wheelchair for the rest of his life. Working at an easel becomes a struggle for him, and he largely stops painting in 1941. But as World War II ends, Matisse emerges with renewed energy. Now in his 70s, he explores a new medium: paper cutouts pasted onto a watercolored surface (découpages on gouache-prepared surface). The medium plays to his strengths: The cutouts are essentially blocks of bright color (mostly blue) with a strong outline. Scissors in hand, Matisse says, "I draw straight into the color." (His doctor advises him to wear dark glasses to protect his weak eyes against the bright colors he chooses.) In 1947, Matisse's book Jazz is published, featuring the artist's joyful cutouts of simple figures. Like jazz music, the book is a celebration of artistic spontaneity. And like music in general, Matisse's works balance different tones and colors to create a mood.

1947-1951—Matisse's nurse becomes a Dominican nun in Vence. To thank her for her care, he spends his later years designing a chapel there. He oversees every aspect of the Chapel of the Rosary (Chapelle du Rosaire) at Vence, from the stained glass to the altar to the colors of the priest's robe. Though Matisse is not a strong Christian, the church exudes his spirit of celebrating life and sums up his work.

1954—Matisse dies.

THE FRENCH RIVIERA

The exhibits cover three floors and include a few works by Andy Warhol, Roy Lichtenstein, and Jean Tinguely, and small models of Christo's famous wrappings. You'll find rooms dedicated to Robert Indiana, Yves Klein, and Niki de Saint Phalle (my favorite). The temporary exhibits can be as appealing to modern-art-lovers as the permanent collection: Check the museum website for what's playing. Don't leave without exploring the rooftop terrace.

Cost and Hours: Free, Tue-Sun 10:00-18:00, closed Mon, about a 15-minute walk from place Masséna, near bus station on promenade des Arts, tel. 04 93 62 61 62, www.mamac-nice.org.

Fine Arts Museum (Musée des Beaux-Arts)—Housed in a sumptuous Riviera villa with lovely gardens, this museum holds 6,000 works from the 17th to 20th centuries. Start on the first floor and work your way up to experience an appealing array of paintings by Monet, Sisley, Bonnard, and Raoul Dufy, as well as a few sculptures by Rodin and Carpeaux (free, Tue-Sun 10:00-18:00, closed Mon, 3 avenue des Baumettes, inconveniently located at the western end of Nice, take buses #12 or #23 from the train station or bus #38 from the bus station to the Rosa Bonheur stop, tel. 04 92 15 28 28, www.musee-beaux-arts-nice.org).

Molinard Perfume Museum—The Molinard family has been making perfume in Grasse (about an hour's drive from Nice) since 1849. Their Nice store has a small museum in the rear that illustrates the story of their industry. Back when people believed water spread the plague (Louis XIV supposedly bathed less than once a year), doctors advised people to rub fragrances into their skin and then powder their body. At that time, perfume was a necessity of everyday life.

Tiny Room 1 shows photos of the local flowers, roots, and other parts of plants used in perfume production. Room 2 explains the earliest (18th-century) production method. Petals would be laid out in the sun on a bed of animal fat, which would absorb the essence of the flowers as they baked. Petals were replaced daily for two months until the fat was saturated. Models and old photos show the later distillation process (660 pounds of lavender produced only a quarter-gallon of essence). Perfume is "distilled like cognac and then aged like wine." The small bottles on the table in the corner demonstrate the role of the "blender" and the perfume mastermind called the "nose" (who knows best). Notice the photos of these lab-coat-wearing perfectionists. Of the 150 real "noses" in the world, more than 100 are French. You are welcome to enjoy the testing bottles.

Cost and Hours: Free, daily July-Aug 10:00-19:00, Sept-June 10:00-13:00 & 14:00-18:30, sometimes closed Mon off-season, just between beach and place Masséna at 20 rue St. François de Paule, see map on page 308, tel. 04 93 62 90 50, www.molinard.com.

▲Russian Cathedral (Cathédrale Russe)—Nice's Russian Orthodox church—claimed by some to be the finest outside Russia—is worth a visit. Five hundred rich Russian families wintered in Nice in the late 19th century. Since they couldn't pray in a Catholic church, the community needed a worthy Orthodox house of worship. Czar Nicholas I's widow provided the land (which required tearing down her house), and Czar Nicholas II gave this

church to the Russian community in 1912. (A few years later, Russian comrades who *didn't* winter on the Riviera assassinated him.) Here in the land of olives and anchovies, these proud onion domes seem odd. But, I imagine, so did those old Russians.

Step inside (pick up English info sheet). The one-room interior is filled with icons and candles, and the old Russian music adds to the ambience. The wall of icons (iconostasis) divides things between the spiritual world and the temporal world of the worshippers. Only the priest can walk between the two worlds, by using the "Royal Door." Take a close look at items lining the front (starting in the left corner). The angel with red boots and wings—the protector of the Romanov family—stands over a symbolic tomb of Christ. The tall black hammered-copper cross commemorates the massacre of Nicholas II and his family in 1918. Notice the Jesus icon to the right of the Royal Door. According to a priest here, as worshippers meditate, staring deep into the eyes of Jesus, they enter a lake where they find their soul. Surrounded by incense, chanting, and your entire community...it could happen. Farther to the right, the icon of the unhappy-looking Virgin and Child is decorated with semiprecious stones from the Ural Mountains. Artists worked a triangle into each iconic face—symbolic of the Trinity.

Cost and Hours: €3, Mon-Sat 9:00-12:00 & 14:30-18:00, Sun 14:30-18:00, until 17:00 off-season, chanted services Sat at 17:30 or 18:00, Sun at 10:00, no tourist visits during services, no short shorts, 17 boulevard du Tzarewitch, tel. 04 93 96 88 02, www.acor-nice.com. The park around the church stays open at lunch and makes a fine setting for picnics.

Getting to the Russian Cathedral: It's a 10-minute walk from the train station. Exit the station to the right onto avenue Thiers, turn right on avenue Gambetta, go under the freeway, and turn left following *Eglise Russe* signs. Or, from the station, take any bus heading west on avenue Thiers and get off at avenue Gambetta (then follow the previous directions).

▲**Castle Hill (Colline du Château)**—Nice was first settled on this hill, which offers sweeping views over the city—best by far in the early morning or late in the day (park closes at 20:00 in summer, earlier off-season). You can get to the top by foot, by elevator (€0.70 one-way, €1.10 round-trip, runs daily 10:00-19:00, until 20:00 in summer, next to beachfront Hôtel Suisse), or by pricey tourist train (described under "Tours in Nice," earlier). Up top

THE FRENCH RIVIERA

Old Nice Restaurants

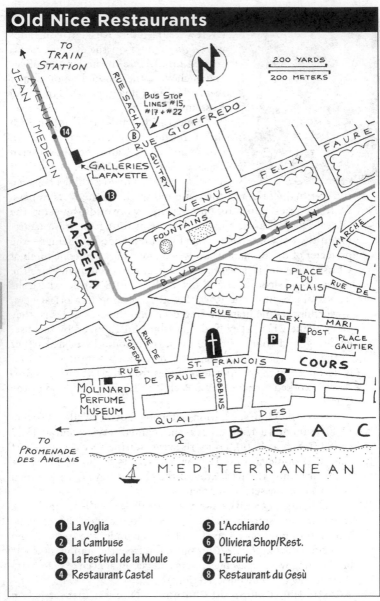

THE FRENCH RIVIERA

❶ La Voglia   **❺** L'Acchiardo

❷ La Cambuse   **❻** Oliviera Shop/Rest.

❸ La Festival de la Moule   **❼** L'Ecurie

❹ Restaurant Castel   **❽** Restaurant du Gesù

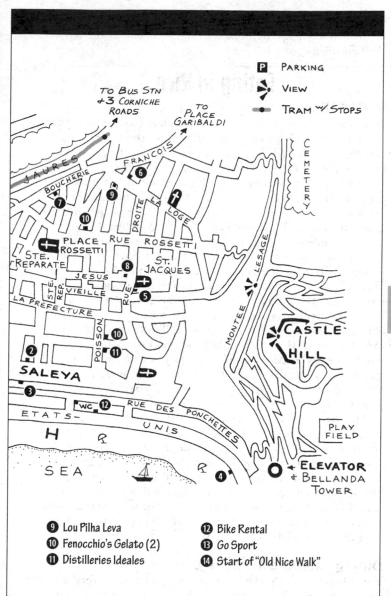

TO BUS STN
+ 3 CORNICHE
ROADS

TO
PLACE
GARIBALDI

P PARKING

▶ VIEW

━●━ TRAM ᵂ/ STOPS

JAURES

BOUCHERIE

FRANCOIS

CEMETERY

LA LOGE

RUE DROITE

RUE ROSSETTI

PLACE ROSSETTI

STE. REPARATE

STE. REP.

JESUS

VIEILLE

ST. JACQUES

RUE

LA PREFECTURE

POISSON.

LESAGE

MONTEE

CASTLE HILL

SALEYA

RUE DES PONCHETTES

WC

ETATS-UNIS

PLAY FIELD

H   R

SEA   R

ELEVATOR
+ BELLANDA
TOWER

⑨ Lou Pilha Leva
⑩ Fenocchio's Gelato (2)
⑪ Distilleries Ideales

⑫ Bike Rental
⑬ Go Sport
⑭ Start of "Old Nice Walk"

THE FRENCH RIVIERA

you'll find cafés and an extensive play area for kids.

For more on Castle Hill, see the "Welcome to the Riviera Walk," earlier.

Eating in Nice

In Old Nice

Nice's cuisine scene converges on cours Saleya (koor sah-lay-yuh), which is entertaining enough in itself to make the generally mediocre food a good deal. It's a fun, festive spot to compare tans and mussels. For locations, see the map on previous page.

La Voglia is all about good Italian food at fair prices. It's popular with locals, lively, and offers fun inside and outside seating (€14 pizza and pasta, open daily, at the western edge of cours Saleya at 2 rue St Francois de Paule, tel. 04 93 80 99 16).

La Cambuse is a classy place by cours Saleya standards, and may be the only restaurant along here that doesn't try to reel in passersby. The cuisine is Franco-Italian with an emphasis on Italy. There's attentive service and good seating indoors and out (€14 starters, €18-24 *plats*, 5 cours Saleya, tel. 04 93 80 82 40).

La Festival de la Moule is a simple, touristy place for lovers of mussels (or for just plain hungry folks). For €14 you get all-you-can-eat mussels (11 sauces possible) and fries in a youthful outdoor setting. Let twins Alex and Marc tempt you with their spicy and cream sauces—be daring and try several (other bistro fare available, across the square from la Cambuse, 20 cours Saleya, tel. 04 93 62 02 12).

Restaurant Castel is a fine eat-on-the-beach option, thanks to its location at the very east end of Nice looking over the bay. You almost expect Don Ho to step up and grab a mic. Lose the city hustle and bustle by dropping down the steps below Castle Hill. The views are unforgettable even if the cuisine is not; you can even have lunch at your beach chair if you've rented one here (€10/half-day, €14/day). Linger long enough to merit the few extra euros the place charges (€16 salads and pastas, €20-26 main courses, 8 quai des Etats-Unis, tel. 04 93 85 22 66).

Dining Cheap à la Niçoise

Try at least one of these five places—not just because they're terrific budget options, but primarily because they offer authentic *niçoise* cuisine.

L'Acchiardo, hidden away in the heart of Old Nice, is a dark and homey eatery that does a good job mixing a loyal clientele with hungry tourists. Its simple, hearty *niçoise* cuisine is served at fair prices by gentle Monsieur Acchiardo. The small plaque under the menu outside says it's been run by father and son since 1927 (€7 starters, €14 *plats*, €5 desserts, cash only, closed Sat-Sun, indoor seating only, 38 rue Droite, tel. 04 93 85 51 16).

Oliviera venerates the French olive. This shop/restaurant sells a variety of oils, offers free tastings, and serves a menu of dishes paired with specific oils (think of a wine pairing). Welcoming owner Nadim, who speaks excellent English, knows all of his producers and provides "Olive Oil 101" explanations with his tastings (best if you buy something afterward or have a meal). You'll learn how passionate he is about his products, and once you come to taste, you'll want to stay and eat (€14-22 main dishes, Tue-Sat 10:00-22:00, closed Sun-Mon, indoor seating only, 8 bis rue du Collet, tel. 04 93 13 06 45).

L'Ecurie, a favorite for Nice residents, is off the beaten path in Old Nice. The cuisine is a mix of traditional *niçoise* and Italian specialties, and the ambience is warm inside and out (€23 three-course *menu*, €11 wood-fired pizza, open daily, 4 rue du Marché, tel. 04 93 62 32 62).

Restaurant du Gesù, a happy-go-lucky greasy spoon, squeezes plastic tables into a slanting square deep in the old city (sailors accustomed to dining off-balance will feel right at home). Arrive early or join the mobs waiting for an outside table; better yet, have fun in the soccer-banner-draped interior. The *raviolis sauce daube* is popular (€10 pizzas and pastas, closed Sun, 1 place du Jésus, tel. 04 93 62 26 46).

Lou Pilha Leva delivers fun and cheap lunch or dinner options with *niçoise* specialties and outdoor-only benches that are swimming in pedestrians (open daily, located where rues de la Loge and Centrale meet in Old Nice).

And for Dessert...

Gelato-lovers should save room for the tempting ice-cream stands in Old Nice. **Fenocchio** is the city's favorite, with mouth-watering displays of 86 flavors ranging from tomato to lavender to avocado—all of which are surprisingly good (daily March-Nov until 24:00, two locations: 2 place Rossetti and 6 rue de la Poissonnerie).

Near Promenade des Anglais

Cave de l'Origine is a warm, local spot run by kind Isabelle and Carlo, where you'll find a quality food shop *(épicerie)* and wine bar/*bistrot* serving a small selection. Carlo loves talking about his all-natural wines and other products. Stop by for a glass of wine, to peruse the shop, or better, to reserve a table for a meal (€10 starters, €19 *plats,* open Tue-Sat for lunch, Thu-Sat for dinner, reservations smart, indoor seating only; shop open Tue-Sat 10:00-20:00, closed Sun-Mon; 3 rue Dalpozzo, tel. 04 83 50 09 60).

Place Grimaldi nurtures several appealing restaurants with

Nice Restaurants

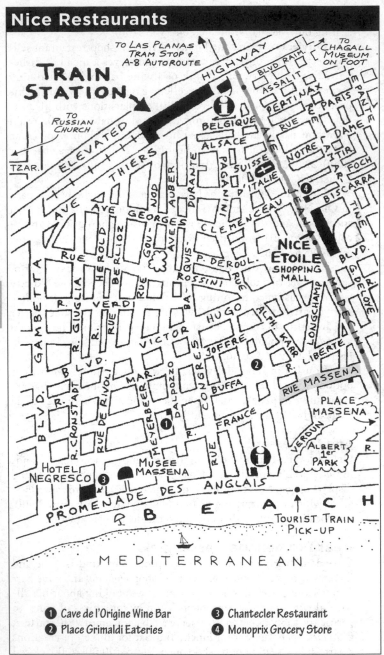

THE FRENCH RIVIERA

1 Cave de l'Origine Wine Bar
2 Place Grimaldi Eateries
3 Chantecler Restaurant
4 Monoprix Grocery Store

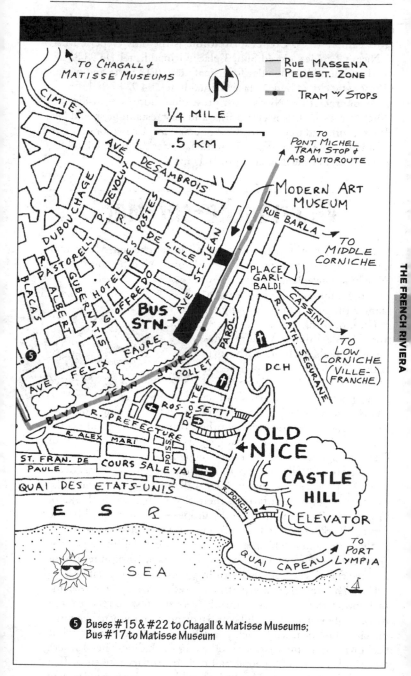

TO CHAGALL &
MATISSE MUSEUMS

RUE MASSENA
PEDEST. ZONE

TRAM w/ STOPS

N

1/4 MILE

.5 KM

CIMIEZ

AVE DESAMBROIS

TO
PONT MICHEL
TRAM STOP &
A-8 AUTOROUTE

MODERN ART
MUSEUM

RUE BARLA

TO
MIDDLE
CORNICHE

DUBOUCHAGE

P. DEVOLUI

R. POSTES

R. DE CILLE

ST-JEAN

PLACE
GARI-
BALDI

R. CASSINI

PASTORELLI

HOTEL DES GIOFFREDO

AVE PAROL.

R. CATH. SEGURANE

TO
LOW
CORNICHE
(VILLE-
FRANCHE)

BLACAS

ALBERT

GUBERNATIS

BUS
STN.

FELIX FAURE

BLVD. JEAN JAURES

COLLET

TE

DCH

AVE

R. PREFECTURE

ROS-SETTI

DR.

POISS.

OLD
NICE

R. ALEX MARI

ST. FRAN. DE
PAULE

COURS SALEYA

CASTLE
HILL

QUAI DES ETATS-UNIS

R. PONCH.

ELEVATOR

E   S   R

SEA

QUAI CAPEAU

TO
PORT
LYMPIA

⑤ Buses #15 & #22 to Chagall & Matisse Museums;
Bus #17 to Matisse Museum

THE FRENCH RIVIERA

good indoor and outdoor seating along a broad sidewalk and under tall sycamore trees. **Crêperie Bretonne** is the only crêperie I list in Nice (€8 crêpes, closed Sun, 3 place Grimaldi, tel. 04 93 82 28 47). **Le Grimaldi** is popular for its café fare (€12 pasta and pizza, €15-19 *plats*, closed Sun, 1 place Grimaldi, tel. 04 93 87 98 13).

Chantecler has Nice's most prestigious address—inside the Hôtel Negresco. This is everything a luxury restaurant should be: elegant, soft, and top-quality. Call or email for reservations (*menus* from €90, closed Mon-Tue, 37 promenade des Anglais, tel. 04 93 16 64 00, chantecler@hotel-negresco.com).

Villefranche-sur-Mer

In the glitzy world of the Riviera, Villefranche-sur-Mer offers travelers an easygoing slice of small-town Mediterranean life.

From here convenient day trips allow you to gamble in style in Monaco, saunter the promenade des Anglais in Nice, or drink in immense views from Eze-le-Village. Villefranche-sur-Mer feels Italian, with soft-orange buildings; steep, narrow streets spilling into the sea; and pasta on most menus. Luxury sailing yachts glisten in the bay—an inspiration to those lazing along the harborfront to start saving when their trips are over. Sand-pebble beaches, a handful of interesting sights, and quick access to Cap Ferrat keep other visitors just busy enough.

Originally a Roman port, Villefranche-sur-Mer was overtaken by fifth-century barbarians. Villagers fled into the hills, where they stayed and farmed their olives. In 1295 the Duke of Provence—like many in coastal Europe—was threatened by the Saracen Turks. He asked the hillside olive farmers to move down to the water and establish a front line against the invaders, thus denying the enemy a base from which to attack Nice. In return for tax-free status, they stopped farming, took up fishing, and established *Ville-* (town) *franche* (without taxes). Since there were many such towns, this one was specifically "Tax-free town on the sea" *(sur Mer)*. In about 1560, the Duke of Savoy built an immense, sprawling citadel in the town (which you can still tour). And today, while the town has an international following (including Tina Turner), two-thirds of its 8,000 people call it their primary residence. That makes Villefranche-sur-Mer feel more like a real community than many neighboring Riviera towns.

Arrival at the Port of Villefranche-sur-Mer

Arrival at a Glance: Villefranche's sights and beach are easily walkable from the cruise terminal. To reach other towns, you can walk 10 minutes to the train station for trains to Nice (10 minutes) or Monaco (10 minutes); or hike 10-15 minutes up to the main road to catch bus #100 to Nice (15 minutes) or Monaco (25 minutes). Cap Ferrat's lush hiking trails are a 50-minute walk or 15-minute bus ride away. Taxis go to Nice (€35-40), Monaco (€50-60), and Cap Ferrat (€20-25)—all one-way rates.

Port Overview

Tenders deposit passengers at a slick terminal building (Gare Maritime) at the Port de la Santé, right in front of Villefranche-sur-Mer's old town. The main road (with the main TI and bus stop) is a steep hike above.

Smaller and less famous than its neighbors Nice and Monaco, Villefranche-sur-Mer hustles to impress its cruise passengers. On days when cruises are in town, local vendors set up kiosks to show off their wares on place Amélie Pollonnais (just to the left as you exit the terminal). Because Villefranche is a small town, it's a low-impact, pleasant place to arrive. And, while it lacks flashy sights and big-name museums, Villefranche is simply a delightful place to kill time. Leave yourself some time at the end of the day to just hang out in Villefranche as you wait for that last tender.

Tourist Information: There's a TI inside the terminal building (opening timed to cruise-ship arrivals). Pick up the free town map that's tailor-made for arriving cruise passengers. The main TI is on the main road up above, near the bus stops (see page 340).

Getting into Town

Your tender leaves you in the heart of town—staring right at the main square. A pleasant maze of tight streets climbs the hill behind Hôtel Welcome. The walls of the imposing citadel squat boldly just down the coast (just walk with the water on your left), with the port de la Darse beyond. For details on all of these sights, see "Sights in Villefranche-sur-Mer," later.

It's easy to **walk** to various points in town. Leaving the terminal, you'll see directional sights pointing left, to *Town center/bus* (a 10- to 15-minute, steeply uphill walk); and right, to *Gare SNCF/ train station* (a 10-minute, mostly level stroll with some stairs up at the end).

THE FRENCH RIVIERA

Services at the Port of Villefranche-sur-Mer

You'll find several helpful services inside the terminal building, including a phone that lets you make a free call to local excursion companies to see if you can join a last-minute tour of the region.

Wi-Fi is planned for the cruise terminal (possibly free) in the near future. Otherwise, two places with both Internet terminals and Wi-Fi sit side by side on place du Marché: **Chez Net,** an "Australian International Sports Bar Internet Café," has American keyboards, whereas **L'Ex Café** has French keyboards (both are open daily).

An **ATM** is on place Wilson, near the cruise terminal.

Right at the terminal building is a fun, characteristic little **"Exposition Marine,"** displaying old nautical paintings and model ships, with a very local-feeling, hole-in-the-wall bar in the back (free entry).

The nearest **pharmacy** is on the main road up above, near the TI.

If you want to go for a bike ride around the area (such as the nearby Cap Ferrat) but don't feel like pedaling too hard, consider renting an **electric bike** from Henri at Eco-Loc. The adventurous can also try this as an alternative to taking the bus to Cap Ferrat, Eze-le-Village, or even Nice (although the road to Nice is awfully busy). You get about 25 miles on a fully charged battery (less on hilly terrain—after that you're pedaling; €5/hour, €20/day, April-Sept daily 9:00-17:30, deposit and ID required, best to call for reservations 24 hours in advance; helmets, locks, baskets, and child seats available; find the small tent on the port next to Café Calypso, mobile 06 66 92 72 41).

You can be your own skipper and **rent a motor boat** at Dark Pelican (€75-90/half-day, €130/day, deposit required, on the harbor at the Gare Maritime, tel. 04 93 01 76 54, www .darkpelican.com).

Little **minibus #80,** which departs from in front of the cruise terminal, saves you the sweat of going from the harbor up the hill to the TI and main road—but it only runs once per hour (daily 7:00-19:00; €1 ticket also covers bus to Nice—but to go to Monaco, you'll need to buy a separate €1 ticket on that bus). The minibus travels from the port to the top of the hill, stopping near Hôtel la Fiancée du Pirate and the stop for buses #82 and #112 to Eze-le-Village.

It's possible to **taxi** to points in town (see "By Taxi," below), but it's overpriced and unnecessary, given the small size of the place.

Skip the useless white **Petit Train,** which goes nowhere interesting (€6, 20-minute ride).

Getting to Sights Beyond Villefranche-sur-Mer

To reach Nice, Monaco, and other Riviera sights, your options include taxi, train, and bus.

By Taxi

Taxis wait in the parking lot in front of the cruise terminal. Their exorbitant rates start with a minimum €10-20 charge for a ride to the train station (an easy 10-minute stroll along the beach), but many drivers will flat-out refuse such a short ride. For farther-flung trips, here are the rates you'll likely pay (one-way):

- To Nice: €35-40
- To Cap Ferrat: €20-25
- To Eze-le-Village: €35-40
- To Monaco: €50-60

Ask your driver to write down the price before you get in, and get a receipt when you pay. For an all-day trip, you can try negotiating a flat fee (e.g., €300 for a 4-hour tour). For a reliable taxi in Villefranche-sur-Mer, call or email **Didier** (mobile 06 15 15 39 15, taxididier.villefranchesurmer@orange.fr). Other numbers to try are mobile 06 09 33 36 12 or mobile 06 39 32 54 09.

By Public Transportation

Villefranche's train station and bus stop are both a short walk from the cruise terminal. There's some uphill climbing to either one; the bus stop is closer but steeper, while the train station has fewer stairs.

By Train

To reach the train station from the terminal, simply stroll with the water on your right for about 10 minutes along the sun-drenched promenade, then look for the stairs on your left leading steeply up to the station. From here, trains go west to **Nice** (2/hour, 10 minutes), **Antibes** (2/hour, 40 minutes), and **Cannes** (2/hour, 50 minutes); and east to **Monaco** (2/hour, 10 minutes).

By Bus

Villefranche's primary bus stop is uphill from the cruise terminal: Follow signs for *Octroi/centre-ville/TI* up the switchback path through the park, pass the soccer field and the TI, and find the Octroi bus stop (just above the TI). From here, buses go to **Monaco** (#100, 4/hour Mon-Sat, 3/hour Sun, 25 minutes) and **Nice** (#100, 4/hour Mon-Sat, 3/hour Sun, 15 minutes; or #81, 2/hour daily, 15 minutes).

To reach **Eze-le-Village,** you have two bus options, either of

Villefranche-sur-Mer

1. Le Cosmo Bistrot/Brasserie
2. La Grignotière
3. La Serre
4. La Mère Germaine
5. Souris Gourmande
6. Casino Grocery
7. Chez Net Bar & L'Ex Café (Internet Access)
8. Boat Rides & Electric Bike Rental
9. Octroi Bus Stop (from Nice; to Monaco & Cap Ferrat)
10. Octroi Bus Stop (to Nice; from Monaco & Cap Ferrat)

P PARKING
T TAXI STAND
⌗ STEPPED STREETS

200 YARDS
200 METERS

THE FRENCH RIVIERA

TO EZE-LE VILLAGE & MONACO VIA MIDDLE CORNICHE ROAD

ALBERT 1er AVE.

POST

AVE. CH. JEUN.

AVE.

AVE. JOF.

AVE. FOCH

JARDIN BINON

PLAY AREA

AVENUE

DE GAULLE

AVE. PRINCESSE GRACE

PLAY AREA

CORDERIE

QUAI

TO MONT-ALBAN FORT & NICE

DCH

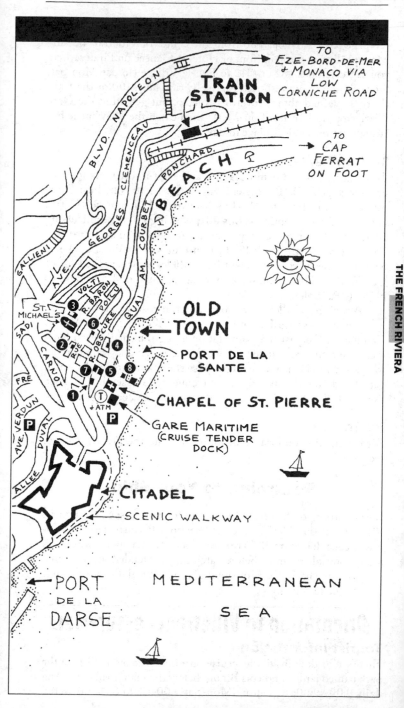

THE FRENCH RIVIERA

which requires a transfer. (For more on this cliff-capping village, see page 351.) Take bus #80 from the center of Villefranche-sur-Mer uphill to the stop in front of Hôtel la Fiancée du Pirate, where you can catch bus #82 or #112 to Eze-le-Village (16/day Mon-Sat, 8/day Sun, 25 minutes). Alternatively, ride bus #100 or the train (both explained above) toward Monaco, but get off at the Gare d'Eze stop (in Eze-Bord-du-Mer). Then catch the #83 shuttle bus straight up to Eze-le-Village (8/day).

To Cap Ferrat

The nearby, forested peninsula of Cap Ferrat is a magnet for hikers (see page 345). The easiest way to get there is by bus: First, follow the directions for "By Bus," above, to Villefranche's Octroi bus stop. The best option is **bus #81,** which goes to Beaulieu-sur-Mer, then all Cap Ferrat stops, ending at the port in St. Jean-Cap-Ferrat (2/hour daily until 19:30, 15 minutes from Villefranche to St. Jean). The twice-as-frequent **bus #100** leaves you at the edge of Cap Ferrat (a 20-minute walk to Villa Ephrussi de Rothschild or plage de Passable).

A **taxi** from Villefranche to Cap Ferrat costs about €20-25.

You can also **walk** 50 minutes from Villefranche-sur-Mer to Cap Ferrat: Go past the train station along the small beach lane, then climb the steps at the far end of the beach and walk parallel to the tracks. Continue straight past the mansions (with ornate gates) and take the first right on avenue de Grasseuil. You'll see signs to *Villa Ephrussi de Rothschild,* then to Cap Ferrat's port.

By Tour

For information on local tour options around the French Riviera, see page 288.

Returning to Your Ship

If returning to Villefranche by bus or train, see "Arrival in Villefranche-sur-Mer" in the next section. If you're early back to town, consider yourself fortunate. There are few ports where it's more enjoyable to linger before catching your tender. Just kill time exploring the back streets or sipping a coffee until it's time to stroll back to the terminal.

Orientation to Villefranche-sur-Mer

Tourist Information

There's a TI desk inside the cruise terminal. The main TI is in the park named jardin François Binon, below the main road (July-Aug daily 9:00-19:00; Sept-June Mon-Sat 9:00-12:00 & 14:00-18:00, closed Sun; 20-minute walk or €10 taxi ride from train station, tel. 04 93 01 73 68, www.villefranche-sur-mer.com). Pick up schedules for buses #81 to Cap Ferrat and #83 to Eze-le-Village (via an easy transfer). Also ask for the brochure detailing a self-guided walking tour of Villefranche-sur-Mer and information on boat rides (usually mid-June-Sept). Either TI also has a simple brochure-map showing the walks around neighboring Cap Ferrat.

Arrival in Villefranche-sur-Mer

By Bus: Bus #100 from either Nice or Monaco stops at Villefranche-sur-Mer's Octroi stop, at the jardin François Binon, just above the TI. To reach the old town and cruise terminal, walk past the TI down avenue Général de Gaulle, take the first stairway on the left, then make a right at the street's end.

By Train: Villefranche-sur-Mer's train station is a 15-minute walk along the water from the old town and cruise terminal. Find your way down toward the water, and turn right to walk into town.

By Car: For a quick visit to the TI, park at the pay lot just below the TI. A bit farther down, you'll find free parking in the small lot off avenue Verdun, and—beyond that—more parking down in the moat areas within the boundaries of the citadel (well-signed from main road—look for *Parking Fossés*).

Helpful Hints

Market Day: A fun bric-a-brac market enlivens Villefranche-sur-Mer on Sundays (on place Amélie Pollonnais by Hôtel Welcome, and in jardin François Binon by the TI). On Saturday mornings, a small food market sets up near the TI (only in jardin François Binon).

Last Call: If your ship is staying late in town, be aware that the last bus back from Nice or Monaco is at about 20:00. After that, take the train or a cab.

Sights in Villefranche-sur-Mer

Conveniently, most of Villefranche-sur-Mer's modest sights cluster near the cruise terminal.

The Harbor—Browse Villefranche-sur-Mer's minuscule harbor. Although the town was once an important fishing community, only eight families still fish here to make money. Find the footpath that leads beneath the citadel to the sea (by the port parking lot). Stop where the path hits the sea and marvel at the scene: a bay filled with beautiful sailing yachts. (You might see well-coiffed captains being ferried in by dutiful mates to pick up their statuesque call girls.) Local guides keep a list of the world's 100 biggest yachts and talk about some of them as if they're part of the neighborhood.

Looking far to the right, that last apartment building on the sea was the headquarters for the US Navy's Sixth Fleet following World War II, and remained so until 1966, when de Gaulle pulled France out of the military wing of NATO. (The Sixth Fleet has been

based in Naples ever since.) A wall plaque at the bottom of rue de l'Eglise commemorates the US Navy's presence in Villefranche. Now look left into the hills and notice the impressive arch-supported Low Corniche road that leads to Monaco. Until that road was built in 1860, those hills were free of any development...all the way to Monaco.

• *You are standing at the base of Villefranche's massive...*

Citadel—The town's mammoth castle was built in the 1500s by the Duke of Savoy to defend against the French. When the region joined France in 1860, it became just a barracks. In the 20th century, the city had no military use for the space and started using the citadel to house its police station, city hall, a summer outdoor theater, and two art galleries. There's still only one fortified entry to this huge complex.

• *To continue along this footpath, see "Seafront Walks," later; otherwise, wander back along the harbor toward the Hôtel Welcome and find the...*

Chapel of St. Pierre (Chapelle Cocteau)—This chapel, decorated by artist Jean Cocteau, is the town's cultural highlight. Cocteau was a Parisian transplant who adored little Villefranche-sur-Mer and whose career was distinguished by his work as an artist, poet, novelist, playwright, and filmmaker. Influenced by his pals Marcel Proust, André Gide, Edith Piaf, and Pablo Picasso, Cocteau was a leader among 20th-century avant-garde intellectuals. At the door, Marie-France—who is passionate about Cocteau's art—collects a €2.50 donation for a fishermen's charity. She then sets you free to enjoy the chapel's small but intriguing interior. She's happy to give some explanations if you ask.

In 1955 Jean Cocteau covered the barrel-vaulted chapel with heavy black lines and pastels. Each of Cocteau's surrealist works—the Roma (Gypsies) of Stes-Maries-de-la-Mer who dance and sing to honor the Virgin, girls wearing traditional outfits, and three scenes from the life of St. Peter—is explained in English. Is that Villefranche-sur-Mer's citadel in the scene above the altar? (Tue-Sun 10:00-12:00 & 15:00-19:00, closed Mon and when Marie-France is tired, below Hôtel Welcome).

A few blocks north along the harbor (past Hôtel Welcome),

rue de May leads to the mysterious **rue Obscura**—a covered lane running 400 feet along the medieval rampart. This street served as an air-raid shelter during World War II. Much of the lane is closed indefinitely for repair.

St. Michael's Church—The town church, a few blocks up rue de l'Eglise from the harbor, features an 18th-century organ and a fine statue of a recumbent Christ—carved, they say, from a fig tree by a galley slave in the 1600s.

Seafront Walks—A seaside walkway originally used by customs agents to patrol the harbor leads under the citadel and connects the old town with the interesting workaday harbor (port de la Darse). At the port you'll find a few cafés, France's Institute of Oceanography (an outpost for the University of Paris oceanographic studies), and an 18th-century dry dock. You can also wander along Villefranche-sur-Mer's waterfront and continue beyond the train station for postcard-perfect views back to Villefranche-sur-Mer. You can even extend your walk to Cap Ferrat (see "To Cap Ferrat" on page 340).

Eating in Villefranche-sur-Mer

Le Cosmo Bistrot/Brasserie takes center stage on place Amélie Pollonnais with a great setting—a few tables have views to the harbor and to Cocteau chapel's facade (after some wine, Cocteau pops). Manager Arnaud runs a tight-but-friendly ship and offers well-presented, tasty meals with good wines (I love their red Bandol). Ask for the daily suggestions and consider the €12 *omelette niçoise* (€13-16 fine salads and pastas, €15-27 *plats*, open daily, place Amélie Pollonnais, tel. 04 93 01 84 05).

Disappear into Villefranche-sur-Mer's walking streets and find cute little **La Grignotière,** serving generous and delicious €18 *plats*, and plenty of other options. The mixed seafood grill is a smart order, as is the spaghetti and *gambas* (shrimp). They also offer a hearty €30 *menu*, but good luck finding room for it. Gregarious Michel speaks English fluently and runs the place with his sidekick Bridget. Dining is primarily inside, making this a good choice for cooler days (daily May-Oct, closed Wed Nov-April, 3 rue Poilu, tel. 04 93 76 79 83).

La Serre, nestled below the church in the old town, is a simple place with a hardworking owner. Sylvie serves well-priced meals to a loyal local clientele, always with a smile. Choose from the many pizzas (all named after US states and €10 or less), salads, and meats; or try the good-value, €17 three-course *menu* (open daily, cheap house wine, 16 rue du May, tel. 04 93 76 79 91).

La Mère Germaine, right on the harbor, is the only place in town classy enough to lure a yachter ashore. It's dressy, with formal service and a price list to match. The name commemorates the

The Three Corniches

Nice, Villefranche-sur-Mer, and Monaco are linked by three coastal routes: the Low, Middle, and High Corniches. The roads are nicknamed after the decorative frieze that runs along the top of a building (cornice). Each Corniche (kor-neesh) offers sensational views and a different perspective.

Low Corniche: The Basse Corniche (also called "Corniche Inférieure") strings ports, beaches, and seaside villages together for a traffic-filled ground-floor view. It was built in the 1860s (along with the train line) to bring people to the casino in Monte Carlo. When this Low Corniche was finished, many hill-town villagers descended to the shore and started the communities that now line the sea. Before 1860, the population of the coast between Villefranche-sur-Mer and Monte Carlo was zero.

Middle Corniche: The Moyenne Corniche is higher, quieter, and far more impressive. It runs through Eze-le-Village and provides breathtaking views over the Mediterranean, with several scenic pullouts.

High Corniche: Napoleon's crowning road-construction achievement, the Grande Corniche caps the cliffs with staggering views from almost 1,600 feet above the sea. It is actually the Via Aurelia, used by the Romans to conquer the West.

Villas: Between Villefranche-sur-Mer and Monaco are many impressive villas. A particularly grand entry leads to the sprawling estate built by King Leopold II of Belgium in the 1920s. Those heading up to the Middle Corniche from Villefranche-sur-Mer can look down on this yellow mansion and its lush garden, which fill an entire hilltop. This estate was later owned by the Agnelli family (of Fiat fame and fortune), and then by the Safra family (American bankers).

current owner's grandmother, who fed hungry GIs during World War II. Try the bouillabaisse, served with panache (€72/person with 2-person minimum, €45 mini-version for one, €41 *menu*, open daily, reserve harborfront table, tel. 04 93 01 71 39).

Souris Gourmande ("Gourmet Mouse") is handy for a made-to-order sandwich, either to take away or to eat there (€5 sandwiches, daily 11:00-22:00, closed Fri in winter, at base of steps behind Hôtel Welcome). Sandwich in hand, you'll find plenty of great places to enjoy a harborside sit.

There's a handy **Casino market/grocery store** a few blocks above Hôtel Welcome at 12 rue Poilu (Thu-Tue 7:30-12:30 & 15:00-19:30, Wed 7:30-13:00 only).

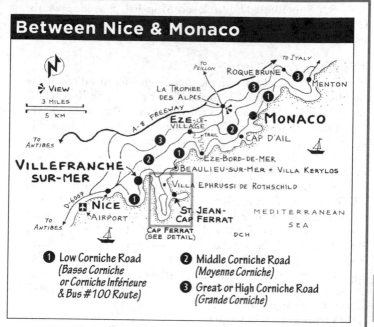

Between Nice & Monaco

❶ Low Corniche Road
(Basse Corniche
or Corniche Inférieure
& Bus #100 Route)

❷ Middle Corniche Road
(Moyenne Corniche)

❸ Great or High Corniche Road
(Grande Corniche)

The Best Route: Buses travel each route; the higher the Corniche, the less frequent the buses (4/hour on Low, 12/day on Middle, and 5/day on High; get details at Nice's bus station). For a ▲▲▲ route, **drivers** should take the Middle Corniche from Nice or Villefranche-sur-Mer to Eze-le-Village; from there, follow signs to the *Grande Corniche* and *La Turbie* (*La Trophée des Alpes*), then finish by dropping down into Monaco.

Cap Ferrat

This exclusive peninsula, rated ▲▲, decorates Villefranche-sur-Mer's bay views. Cap Ferrat is a peaceful eddy off the busy Nice-Monaco route (Low Corniche). You could spend a leisurely day on this peninsula, wandering the sleepy port village of St. Jean-Cap-Ferrat (a.k.a. St. Jean), touring the Villa Ephrussi de Rothschild mansion and gardens and the nearby Villa Kérylos, and walking on sections of the beautiful trails that follow the coast. If you have a house here, former Microsoft mogul Paul Allen is your neighbor.

Tourist Information: The main TI is between the port and Villa Ephrussi (Mon-Fri 9:00-16:00, closed Sat-Sun, 59 avenue Denis Séméria, bus #81 stops here at *Office du Tourisme*). A smaller TI is in the village of St. Jean-Cap-Ferrat (unpredictable hours, likely Sat-Sun 10:00-17:00, closed Mon-Fri, 5 avenue Denis Séméria). The two TIs share a phone number and email address (tel. 04 93 76 08 90, office-tourisme@saintjeancapferrat.fr).

Planning Your Time

Here's how I'd spend a day on the Cap: From Nice or Villefranche-sur-Mer, take the bus (#81) to the Villa Ephrussi de Rothschild stop (called Passable), then visit the villa. Walk 30 minutes, mostly downhill, to St. Jean-Cap-Ferrat for lunch (many options, including grocery shops for picnic supplies) and poke around the village. Consider the 45-minute walk on the plage de Paloma trail (ideal for picnics). After lunch, follow a beautiful 30-minute trail to Villa Kérylos in Beaulieu-sur-Mer and tour that villa. Return to Nice, Villefranche-sur-Mer, or Monaco by train or bus.

You can add Eze-le-Village to this day if you skip the small town of St. Jean-Cap-Ferrat and walk directly from Villa Ephrussi de Rothschild to Villa Kérylos. Take bus #100 (direction: Monaco) from the stop near Villa Kérylos and get off at the Gare d'Eze stop, where you meet bus #83 that shuttles up and up to the village (one €1 ticket covers both buses, get #83 schedule at a TI or check online at www.lignedazur.com).

Warning: Late-afternoon buses back to Villefranche-sur-Mer or Nice along the Low Corniche can be slammed (worse on weekends), potentially leaving passengers stranded at stops for long periods. To avoid this, either take the train or board bus #81 on the Cap itself (before it gets crowded).

Arrival in Cap Ferrat

If arriving on **bus #81** from Nice or Villefranche, you can either get off at the Passable stop (for Villa Ephrussi de Rothschild), or stay on until St. Jean-Cap-Ferrat village. **Bus #100** from Nice, Villefranche, or Monaco drops you at Cap Ferrat's edge (Ange Gardien or Pont St. Jean stops); from there, you can walk 20 minutes to Villa Ephrussi de Rothschild (after crossing over the main road from bus stop, look for the center alleyway—chemin des Moulins—running straight up the Cap, turn left at the end, go down a stone stairway, then turn right on the small road).

Sights on Cap Ferrat

▲**Villa Ephrussi de Rothschild**—In what seems like the ultimate in Riviera extravagance, Venice, Versailles, and the Côte d'Azur come together in the pastel-pink Villa Ephrussi. Rising above Cap Ferrat, this 1905 mansion has views west to Villefranche-sur-Mer and east to Beaulieu-sur-Mer.

Start with the well-furnished belle époque **interior** (helpful

Cap Ferrat

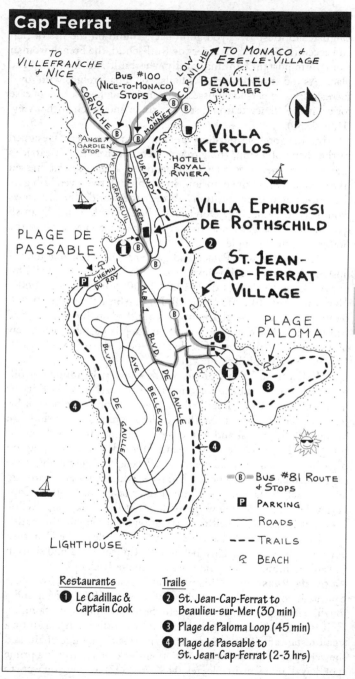

TO VILLEFRANCHE & NICE

TO MONACO & EZE-LE-VILLAGE

LOW CORNICHE

Bus #100 (Nice-to-Monaco) Stops

BEAULIEU-SUR-MER

LOW CORNICHE

"ANGE GARDIEN" STOP

AVE. MONNET

AVE. DE GRASSEUIL

DENIS SEM

DURANDY

VILLA KERYLOS

HOTEL ROYAL RIVIERA

VILLA EPHRUSSI DE ROTHSCHILD

PLAGE DE PASSABLE

CHEMIN DU ROY

ALB. 1

BLVD. DE GAULLE

ST. JEAN-CAP-FERRAT VILLAGE

PLAGE PALOMA

BLVD. DE GAULLE

AVE. DE BELLEVUE

LIGHTHOUSE

THE FRENCH RIVIERA

Bus #81 Route & Stops

P Parking

— Roads

--- Trails

R Beach

Restaurants
1 Le Cadillac & Captain Cook

Trails
2 St. Jean-Cap-Ferrat to Beaulieu-sur-Mer (30 min)
3 Plage de Paloma Loop (45 min)
4 Plage de Passable to St. Jean-Cap-Ferrat (2-3 hrs)

English handout provided). Upstairs, an 18-minute film (with English subtitles) gives you good background on the life of rich and eccentric Beatrice, Baroness de Rothschild, the French woman from an important banking family who built and furnished the place. As you stroll through the halls, you'll pass rooms with royal furnishings and personal possessions, including her bathroom case for cruises. A fancy tearoom serves drinks and lunch with a view (11:00-17:30).

But the gorgeous **gardens** are why most come here. Designed in the shape of a ship, the gardens were motivated by Beatrice's many ocean-liner trips. Her small army of gardeners even dressed like sailors. Behind the mansion, stroll through the seven lush gardens re-created from locations all over the world. The sea views from here are amazing. Don't miss the Alhambra-like Spanish gardens, the rose garden at the far end, and the view back to the house from the "Temple of Love" gazebo.

Cost and Hours: Palace and gardens-€10, skippable tour of upstairs-€3 extra, combo-ticket with Villa Kérylos-€15—valid for one week; mid-Feb-Oct daily 10:00-18:00, July-Aug until 19:00; Nov-mid-Feb Mon-Fri 14:00-18:00, Sat-Sun 10:00-18:00; tel. 04 93 01 33 09, www.villa-ephrussi.com. Kids will enjoy the free treasure-hunt booklet. The nearest bus stop is Passable, just a few minutes after turning onto Cap Ferrat—be ready (only via bus #81, 10-minute walk uphill to the villa).

Walks from Villa Ephrussi: It's a lovely 30-minute stroll, mostly downhill and east, from Villa Ephrussi to Villa Kérylos in Beaulieu-sur-Mer (described on page 350) or to the port of St. Jean-Cap-Ferrat. To get to either, make a hard left at the stop sign below Villa Ephrussi and follow signs along a small road toward the Hôtel Royal Riviera on avenue Henri Honoré (see map on page 347). When the road comes to a T, keep going straight, passing a green gate down a pedestrian path, which ends at a trail—go left to reach Villa Kérylos, or head right to get to St. Jean-Cap-Ferrat (be careful to follow the path left at the Villa Sonja Rello). It's about 15 minutes to either destination once you join this path.

To get to plage de Passable, on the west side of the Cap, turn left along the main road just below Villa Ephrussi and find signs in 50 yards (5 minutes down, at least 10 minutes back up).

Plage de Passable—This pleasant beach, located below Villa Ephrussi, comes with great views of Villefranche-sur-Mer and a rough, pebbly surface. It's a peaceful beach, popular with families. Half is public (free, with shower), and the other half is run by a small restaurant (€20 includes changing locker, lounge chair, and shower; reserve ahead in summer or on weekends as this is a prime spot, kayak rental available, tel. 04 93 76 06 17). If ever you were to do the French Riviera rent-a-beach ritual, this is the place.

St. Jean-Cap-Ferrat—This quiet village port (also called St. Jean) lies in Cap Ferrat's center, yet off most tourist itineraries. St.

Jean houses yachts, boardwalks, views, and boutiques packaged in a "take your time, darling" atmosphere. It's a few miles off the busy Nice-to-Monaco road, yet it feels overlooked. A string of restaurants line the port, with just enough visitors to keep them in business.

There's a small TI in the village center with limited hours (see page 345). The bus stop back to Villefranche-sur-Mer is a block above the port near Hôtel la Frégate (if you need a taxi, call 04 93 76 86 00). The hiking trail to Beaulieu-sur-Mer (with access to Villa Ephrussi) begins past the beach, to the left of the port as you look out to the water (details below).

▲▲Walks Around Cap Ferrat

The Cap is perfect for a walk, as you'll find well-maintained foot trails covering most of its length. Depending on how much time you have, there are three easy, mostly level options (30 minutes, 45 minutes, or 2-3 hours). The TIs in Villefranche-sur-Mer and St. Jean-Cap-Ferrat have maps of Cap Ferrat with walking paths marked, or you can use this book's directions (below) and map

(page 347). During segments of all of the hikes, you can make out the three Corniche roads cut into the side of the massive cliffs.

Between St. Jean-Cap-Ferrat and Beaulieu-sur-Mer (30 minutes): A level walk takes you past sumptuous villas, great views, and fun swimming opportunities. From St. Jean-Cap-Ferrat's port, walk along the harbor with the water on your right, and work your way past the beach. Head up the steps to promenade Maurice Rouvier and continue; before long you'll see smashing views of the whitewashed Villa Kérylos (and you might be able to make out the hill town of Eze-le-Village crowning the last peak on the right across the bay). To get from Beaulieu-sur-Mer to St. Jean-Cap-Ferrat, start walking at Villa Kérylos (with the sea on your left) toward the Hôtel Royal Riviera, and find the trail (be careful to stay left at the Villa Sonja Rello about halfway down).

You can also reach this trail by walking 10 minutes downhill from Villa Ephrussi (described above).

Plage de Paloma Loop Trail (45 minutes): Just east of St. Jean's port, a sea-soaked, view-loaded trail offers you a terrific sampling of Cap Ferrat's beauty for a modest effort. From the port, walk about a quarter-mile east (with the port on your left, passing Hôtel La Voile d'Or); you'll find the trailhead where the road comes to a T—look for a *Plage Paloma* sign. Cross the small dirt park to start the trail, and do this walk counterclockwise. The trail is level and paved, yet uneven enough that good shoes are helpful. Plunk your picnic on one of the benches along the trail, or eat at the café on plage de Paloma at the end of the walk (sandwiches and salads). If time is tight, walk up the road toward *Plage Paloma* signs and find the trail for great views.

Plage de Passable to St. Jean-Cap-Ferrat (2-3 hours): For a longer hike that circles the Cap, follow the signs below Villa Ephrussi marked *Plage Passable* (10 minutes downhill on foot from the villa, parking available near the trailhead). Walk down to the beach (you'll find a good café that's ideal for lunch), turn left, and cross the beach. Go along a paved road behind a big apartment building, and after about 300 feet, take the steps down to the trail *(Sentier Littoral)*. Near the end of the trail, you'll pass by the port of St. Jean-Cap-Ferrat, where you have three options: take bus #81 back to Villefranche-sur-Mer, walk back to Villa Ephrussi and plage de Passable via the shorter inland route (by reversing the directions under "Walks from Villa Ephrussi," earlier), or continue on to Beaulieu-sur-Mer and take a bus to Monaco or Nice.

Near Cap Ferrat: Villa Kérylos

This town, right on the Low Corniche road (just after Cap Ferrat), is busy with traffic. It's a good place to pick up the hiking trail to St. Jean-Cap-Ferrat and to visit the unusual **Villa Kérylos.** In 1902, an eccentric millionaire modeled his new mansion after a Greek villa from the island of Delos from about 200 B.C. No expense was spared in re-creating this Greek fantasy, from the floor mosaics to Carrara marble

columns to exquisite wood furnishings. The rain-powered shower is fun, and the included audioguide will increase your Greek IQ. The ceramics workshop—open only high season and weekend afternoons—offers a chance to test your talents (€9, combo-ticket with Villa Ephrussi de Rothschild-€15—valid for one week; mid-

Feb-Oct daily 10:00-18:00, July-Aug until 19:00; Nov-mid-Feb Mon-Fri 14:00-18:00, Sat-Sun 10:00-18:00; tel. 04 93 01 47 29, www.villa-kerylos.com).

Getting to and from Villa Kérylos: The Monaco-Nice bus #100 (4/hour Mon-Sat, 3/hour Sun, 20 minutes from Nice or Monaco) drops you at the Eglise stop at the Hôtel Metropole in Beaulieu (turn right off the bus and find signs to Villa Kérylos). Trains (2/hour, 10 minutes from Nice or Monaco) leave you a 10-minute walk away: Turn left out of the train station and left again down the main drag. Walk to the end, turn right, then find signs to Villa Kérylos. The walking trail from Villa Kérylos to Cap Ferrat and Villa Ephrussi de Rothschild begins on the other side of the bay, beneath Hôtel Royal Riviera.

Eating on Cap Ferrat

For **picnics,** the short pedestrian street in St. Jean-Cap-Ferrat has all you need (grocery store, bakery, charcuterie, and pizza to go), and you'll have no trouble finding portside or seaside seating. Plage de Paloma is a 10-minute walk away.

Le Cadillac is *the* place for outdoor seating and café fare in St. Jean-Cap-Ferrat. It's at the top of the small pedestrian street (good €13 pizza, €16 *plats,* daily, 1 rue Mermoz, tel. 04 93 76 16 44).

Captain Cook is a sweet little eatery that takes its fish seriously. There's a small patio in front, a bigger one out back (no view), and a cozy interior between (good €26 *menu,* ask about bouillabaisse, closed Wed, a few steps past the port toward plage de Paloma at 11 avenue Jean Mermoz, tel. 04 93 76 02 66).

Eze-le-Village

Floating high above the sea, flowery and flawless Eze-le-Village (don't confuse it with the seafront town of Eze-Bord-de-Mer) is entirely consumed by tourism. This *village d'art et de gastronomie* (as

it calls itself) nurtures perfume outlets, upscale boutiques, steep cobbled lanes, and magnificent views. Touristy as this place certainly Eze, its stony state of preservation and magnificent hilltop setting over the Mediterranean may draw you away from the beaches. Day-tripping by bus to Eze-le-Village from Nice, Monaco, or Villefranche-sur-Mer works well, provided you know the bus schedules (ask at TIs or check www.lignedazur.com; the trip from Villefranche-sur-Mer requires a transfer).

Getting to Eze-le-Village

There are two Ezes: Eze-le-Village (the spectacular hill town) and Eze-Bord-de-Mer (a modern beach resort far below Eze-le-

Village). Eze-le-Village is about 20 minutes east of Villefranche-sur-Mer on the Middle Corniche.

From Nice's bus station and upper Villefranche-sur-Mer, buses #82 and #112 provide 16 buses per day to Eze-le-Village (8/day on Sun, 25 minutes). (For details on where to catch this bus in Villefranche, see page 337.)

From Nice, Villefranche, or Monaco, you can also take the train or bus #100 to Eze-Bord-de-Mer, getting off at the Gare d'Eze stop. From here, take the #83 shuttle bus straight up to Eze-le-Village (8/day, daily 9:45-18:00, schedule is posted at the stop, but it's best to know schedule before you go).

To connect Eze-le-Village directly with Monte Carlo in Monaco, take bus #112 (7/day Mon-Sat, none on Sun, 25 minutes).

You could take a pricey taxi between the two Ezes (allow €25 one-way, mobile 06 09 84 17 84).

Orientation to Eze-le-Village

Bus stops and parking lots weld the town to the highway (Middle Corniche) that passes under its lowest wall. Eze-le-Village's main parking lot is a block below the town's entry. The stop for buses to Nice is across the road by the Avia gas station, and the stops for buses to Eze-Bord-de-Mer and Monaco are on the village side of the main road, near the Casino Market. The helpful **TI**, in the lot's far corner, has bus schedules (April-Oct daily 9:00-18:00, July-Aug until 19:00; Nov-March Mon-Sat 9:00-18:30, closed Sun; place de Gaulle, tel. 04 93 41 26 00, www.eze-riviera.com). English-language tours of the village and gardens are available for €8 (call to arrange in advance). Public WCs are located just behind the TI and in the village behind the church, though the cleanest and best-smelling are at either perfume showroom.

Self-Guided Walk in Eze-le-Village

• *From the TI, wander uphill into the town. You'll come to an exclusive hotel gate and the start of a steep trail down to the beach, marked Eze/Mer. For a panoramic view and an ideal picnic perch, walk 80 steps down this path (for more details, see "Trail to Eze-Bord-de-Mer," later). Continuing up into the village, find the steps just after the ritzy hotel gate and climb to...*

Place du Centenaire: In this square, a stone plaque in the flower bed celebrates the 100th anniversary of the 1860 plebiscite, the time when all 133 Eze residents voted to leave the Italian Duchy of Savoy and join France. *Vive la France!* A town map here helps you get oriented.

• *Now pass through the once-formidable town gate (designed to keep the Ottomans out) and climb into the 14th-century village. You'll find occasional English information plaques on walls in the old city that together give a good history of the village. Wandering the narrow lanes, follow signs to the...*

Château Eza: This was the winter getaway of the Swedish royal family from 1923 until 1953; today it's a hotel. The château's tearoom (Salon de Thé), on a cliff overlooking the jagged Riviera and sea, offers you the most scenic coffee or beer break you'll ever enjoy—for a price. The sensational view terrace is also home to an expensive-but-sensational restaurant (€7 beer, €50 lunch *menus*, open daily, tel. 04 93 41 12 24, www.chateaueza.com, info@chateaueza.com).

• *The uphill lanes end at the hilltop castle ruins—now blanketed by the...*

Jardins d'Eze: Here you'll find a prickly festival of cactus. Since 1949, these ruins have been home to 400 different plants 1,300 feet above the sea (€5, open daily, hours change frequently but usually May-Sept 9:00-19:00, Oct-April until dusk, well-described in English, tel. 04 93 41 10 30). At the top, you'll be treated to a commanding 360-degree view, with a helpful *table d'orientation*. On a crystal-clear day (they say...), you can see Corsica. The castle was demolished by Louis XIV in 1706. Louis destroyed castles like this all over Europe (most notably along the Rhine), because he didn't want to risk having to do battle with rebellious nobles inside them at some future date.

• *As you descend, drop by the...*

Eze Church: Though built during Napoleonic times, it has an uncharacteristic Baroque fanciness—a reminder that 300 years of Savoy rule left the townsfolk with an Italian savoir faire and a sensibility for decor.

Sights in Eze-le-Village

Perfume Factory Fragonard—This factory, with its huge tour-bus parking lot, lies on the Middle Corniche, 350 feet below Eze-le-Village. Designed for tour groups, it cranks them through all day long. If you've never seen mass tourism in action, this place will open your eyes. (The gravel is littered with the color-coded stickers each tourist wears so that the salespeople know which guide gets the kickback.) Drop in for an informative and free tour, which can last anywhere from 20 to 40 minutes depending on the walking ability of the group (daily 9:00-18:00, but best Mon-Fri 9:00-11:00 & 14:00-15:30, when the "factory" actually has people working, tel. 04 93 41 05 05). You'll see how the perfume and scented soaps are made and bottled before you're herded into the gift shop.

For a more personal and intimate (but unguided) look at perfume, cross the main road in Eze-le-Village to visit the **Gallimard** shop. Explore the small museum and let the lovely ladies show you their scents (daily 9:00-18:30, handy and free WCs).

Trail to Eze-Bord-de-Mer—This steep trail leaves Eze-le-Village from the foot of the hill-town entry, near the fancy hotel gate, and descends 1,300 feet to the sea along a no-shade, all-view trail. Allow 45 minutes at a steady but manageable pace (good walking shoes are essential). Once in Eze-Bord-de-Mer, you can catch a bus or train to all destinations between Nice and Monaco. While walking this trail in the late 1800s, Friedrich Nietzsche was moved to write his unconventionally spiritual novel, *Thus Spoke Zarathustra*.

Eating in Eze-le-Village

There's a handy **Casino** market at the foot of the village by the bus stop (daily 8:00-20:00) and a sensational picnic spot at the beginning of the trail to Eze-Bord-de-Mer. **Le Cactus** serves cheap crêpes, salads, and sandwiches at outdoor tables near the entry to the old town (daily, tel. 04 93 41 19 02). For a real splurge, dine at **Château Eza** (described earlier).

Monaco

Despite high prices, wall-to-wall daytime tourists, and a Disney-esque atmosphere, Monaco is a Riviera must. Monaco is on the go.

Since 1929, cars have raced around the port and in front of the casino in one of the world's most famous auto races, the Grand Prix de Monaco (see sidebar on page 367). The modern breakwater—constructed elsewhere and towed in by sea—enables big cruise ships to dock here. The district of Fontvieille, reclaimed from the sea, bristles with luxury high-rise condos. But don't look for anything too deep in this glittering tax haven. Two-thirds of its 30,000 residents live here because there's no income tax—leaving fewer than 10,000 true Monegasques.

This minuscule principality (0.75 square mile) borders only France and the Mediterranean. The country has always been tiny, but it used to be...less tiny. In an 1860 plebiscite, Monaco lost two-thirds of its territory when the region of Menton voted to join France. To compensate, France suggested that Monaco build a fancy casino and promised to connect it to the world with a road (the Low Corniche) and a train line. This started a high-class tourist boom that has yet to let up.

Although "independent," Monaco is run as a piece of France. A French civil servant appointed by the French president—with the blessing of Monaco's prince—serves as state minister and manages the place. Monaco's phone system, electricity, water, and so on, are all French.

The death of Prince Rainier in 2005 ended his 56-year career of enlightened rule. Today Monaco is ruled by Prince Rainier's unassuming son, Prince Albert Alexandre Louis Pierre, Marquis of Baux. At 50-some years old, Prince Albert has long been considered Europe's most eligible bachelor—though he has admitted to fathering two children out of wedlock—but finally plans to marry in 2011. A graduate of Amherst College, Albert is a bobsled enthusiast who raced in several Olympics, and an avid environmentalist who seems determined to clean up Monaco's tarnished tax-haven, money-laundering image. (Monaco is infamously known as a "sunny place for shady people.")

Monaco is big business, and Prince Albert is its CEO. Its famous casino contributes only 5 percent of the state's revenue, whereas its 43 banks—which offer an attractive way to hide your money—are hugely profitable. The prince also makes money with a value-added tax (19.6 percent, the same as in France), plus real estate and corporate taxes.

The glamorous romance and marriage of the American actress Grace Kelly to Prince Rainier added to Monaco's fairy-tale mystique. Grace Kelly (Prince Albert's mother) first came to Monaco to star in the 1955 Hitchcock movie *To Catch a Thief*, in which she was filmed racing along the Corniches. Later, she married the prince and adopted the country. Tragically, in 1982 Monaco's much-loved Princess Grace died in a car wreck on that same Corniche. She was just 52 years old.

Monaco is a special place: There are more people in Monaco's philharmonic orchestra (about 100) than in its army (about 80 guards). The princedom is well-guarded, with police and cameras on every corner. (They say you could win a million dollars at the casino and walk to the train station in the wee hours without a worry...and I believe it.) Stamps are so few that they increase in value almost as soon as they're printed. And collectors snapped up the rare Monaco versions of euro coins (with Prince Rainier's portrait) so quickly that many Monegasques have never even seen one.

Arrival at the Port of Monaco

Arrival at a Glance: It's a long walk or a short bus ride to most sights in town (including the Monaco-Ville old town and the ritzy Monte Carlo casino district). To reach other towns, you can walk 20 minutes to the train station for trains to Villefranche-sur-Mer (10 minutes), then Nice (20 minutes); or walk 10 minutes to place d'Armes to catch bus #100 to Villefranche-sur-Mer (25 minutes), then Nice (45 minutes).

Port Overview

Cruise ships tender passengers to the end of Monaco's yacht harbor, a short walk from downtown. *Très elegant!*

To summon a **taxi** (assuming none are waiting when you disembark), look for the gray taxi-call box near the tender dock—just press the button and wait for your cab to arrive.

Port Services: The seasonal **TI** right next to the tender dock is open on busy days May through September. If it's closed when you visit, try one of the TIs listed on page 362. There's a **pharmacy** at the top-right corner of place d'Armes (described later) and another one just across the street.

Getting into Town

There are two parts of Monaco you may want to visit: the cliff-top old town, **Monaco-Ville;** and the ritzy skyscraper zone of **Monte Carlo,** with its famous casino. Everything in town is accessible by foot and/or local bus.

Getting to Place d'Armes

The first step for reaching the train station, the stop for bus #100 to Nice and Villefranche, or the stop for bus #1 or #2 to Monaco-Ville, is walking 10 minutes to the market square called place d'Armes. (Note: To get to Monte Carlo and the casino, you don't need to go to place d'Armes—for details, see "Getting to Monte Carlo," page 360.)

It's an easy, mostly level walk from the tender dock to place d'Armes. Head straight along the yacht harbor until you reach the busy street, boulevard Albert 1er. Use the white overpass (with an elevator) to cross the street, then follow green *Gare S.N.C.F.* signs through a maze of skyscrapers, across the street, and up a charming lane lined with motorcycle shops. Continue straight into the peach-and-yellow building, and ride the free public elevator up to *Marché Place d'Armes* (level 0). Exiting the elevator, you'll pop out into a little market square. At the far end of this square is a roundabout and the busy rue Grimaldi. From here, you have several options (described in the next few pages).

Getting to Monaco-Ville

To reach the sights of Monaco-Ville, you can either ride a bus, or hike steeply up to the top of the hill next to the harbor.

To ride **bus** #1 or #2 up to Monaco-Ville, first walk to the bus stop near place d'Armes (described earlier). As you exit the elevator into place d'Armes, turn left and cross the street, then continue up to the second, uphill street (which leads up to the hilltop). Cross this second street and bear right to find the bus stop, where you can catch bus #1 or #2 to Monaco-Ville. (Note: Don't take bus #1 and #2 from the stop on the lower street—from here, the bus runs in the opposite direction and will just take you right back to the port.)

There are several routes up to Monaco-Ville **by foot.** The fastest, steepest ascent (with an elevator option partway) is near the tip of the Monaco-Ville peninsula, just above where tenders arrive: From the tender port, head toward downtown, but keep an eye out on your left for the easy-to-miss steps at the corner of the port, next to the Yacht Club de Monaco. These stairs take you steeply up to the base of the hill. Turn left, then curl to the right around the tip of land (with the water on your left-hand side), following signs for *Palais/Musées.* Eventually you'll reach a parking garage; you

Monaco

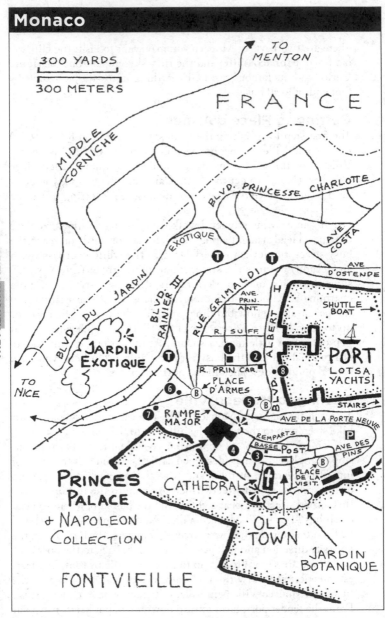

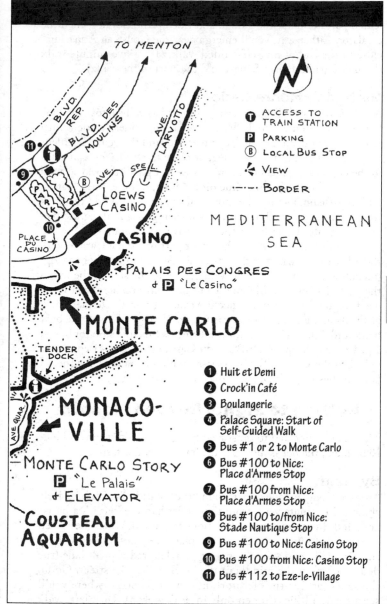

TO MENTON

BLVD. REP.
BLVD. DES MOULINS
AVE. LARVOTTO
AVE.
SPE. L.
PARK

ACCESS TO TRAIN STATION
PARKING
LOCAL BUS STOP
VIEW
BORDER

LOEWS CASINO

MEDITERRANEAN SEA

PLACE DU CASINO

CASINO

PALAIS DES CONGRES
& "Le Casino"

MONTE CARLO

TENDER DOCK

MONACO-VILLE

AVE. QUAR.

MONTE CARLO STORY
"Le Palais"
& ELEVATOR

COUSTEAU AQUARIUM

1 Huit et Demi
2 Crock'in Café
3 Boulangerie
4 Palace Square: Start of Self-Guided Walk
5 Bus #1 or 2 to Monte Carlo
6 Bus #100 to Nice: Place d'Armes Stop
7 Bus #100 from Nice: Place d'Armes Stop
8 Bus #100 to/from Nice: Stade Nautique Stop
9 Bus #100 to Nice: Casino Stop
10 Bus #100 from Nice: Casino Stop
11 Bus #112 to Eze-le-Village

THE FRENCH RIVIERA

can either bypass the garage and keep hiking up through the manicured park, or enter the garage and ride up the elevator, then the escalator. Either way, you'll emerge near the Cousteau Aquarium, close to the end of my self-guided walk. (It's a five-minute walk through town to Palace Square and the start of the walk.)

Getting to Monte Carlo

Monte Carlo (and its landmark casino) is basically across the harbor from the tender dock. While the casino doesn't open until 14:00, its architecture is easy to appreciate, and the genteel gardens that sprawl behind it are an elegant place to stroll. You can **walk** to the casino area in about 25 minutes—just go all the way around the harbor. To shave some time off the hike, ride the little "bateau bus" **shuttle boat** across the mouth of the harbor (to find the dock from your tender, walk toward town, then go right along the pier extending into the harbor; €1, €3/all-day pass, 3/hour).

To ride **bus** #1 or #2 to the upper part of Monte Carlo—with the TI, views down over the casino gardens, and handy bus stops (including the one for Eze-le-Village)—find the stop at the top of the yacht harbor. (Unlike many options outlined here, you won't need to go all the way to place d'Armes.) From the tender dock, just walk along the harbor toward town. When you reach the busy boulevard Albert 1er, look for the Princess Stefanie stop for bus #1 and #2. Ride it up to the Place du Casino stop; bus #1 continues uphill to the Casino Tourisme stop, which is handier for the TI (and the bus stop for Eze-le-Village).

Getting to Sights Beyond Monaco

Monaco is connected to most nearby sights by both train and bus. Remember, the bus is more scenic, but the train is faster.

By Train

Monaco's long, mostly underground train station sits unobtrusively about a 20-minute walk from the tender harbor—but it's a pleasant stroll. First, follow the directions to place d'Armes (described earlier). Head up to the far end of place d'Armes, cross the busy rue Grimaldi, and take the narrow, angled, red-asphalt lane (rue de la Turbie) in the middle of the block across the street. Go up the stairs (or ride the elevator) into the little plaza, where you'll see a small TI kiosk (open only in peak season). Turn left, walk up more stairs, and enter the train station (the big, pink building on your right; the easy-to-miss entrance is at the far end—look for *Acces Gare* signs). You'll go down a long marble hallway with moving walkways to the tracks, then hike to the right along the tracks to reach the ticket offices. From here, the train goes twice hourly to **Villefranche-sur-Mer** (10 minutes), then on to **Nice** (20 minutes).

By Bus

The stop for bus #100—which conveniently connects Monaco along the Lower Corniche to most other sights in this chapter—is near place d'Armes. First, follow the instructions to that square (described earlier). Once in place d'Armes, head up to the far end of the square, along rue Grimaldi. Across the roundabout on the left, on the right-hand side of the street, is the stop for bus #100 to Nice, Villefranche-sur-Mer, and Cap Ferrat; cross the street two times in either direction (circling halfway around the roundabout) to get there. While the stop may not be marked for bus #100, it's the right one. If you're concerned, verify with a local by asking, *"Direction Nice?"* From here, the bus runs every 15 minutes (less on Sun) to **Cap Ferrat** (20 minutes), **Villefranche-sur-Mer** (25 minutes), and **Nice** (45 minutes). A ticket for any ride costs €1.

If you're going first to the TI and Monte Carlo area, and want to catch bus #100 to Nice from there, you don't need to go all the way down to place d'Armes: There's a stop a few blocks above the casino on avenue de la Costa (under the arcade to the left of Barclays Bank).

To Eze-le-Village: To ride the bus along the scenic Upper Corniche to the charming, cliffhanging village of Eze-le-Village (bus #112, 7/day Mon-Sat, none on Sun, 25 minutes), you'll catch the bus from place de la Crémaillère, one block above the main TI and casino park. First, ride bus #1 or #2 to the TI and casino, following the directions for "Getting to Monte Carlo," earlier. Then, from the TI, walk up rue Iris with Barclays Bank to your left, curve right, and find the bus shelter across the street by the green Costa à la Crémaillère café. Bus numbers for these routes are not posted, but this is the stop.

By Tour

For information on local tour options around the French Riviera, see page 288.

Returning to Your Ship

The tender dock is easy to find: Just head down to the water, and out along the right side of the yacht harbor. If you have some time to kill before the last tender, notice that Monaco-Ville is directly above the tender dock. You could linger up there, then head toward the Cousteau Aquarium, ride down the escalator, then transfer to the elevator (inside the parking garage), and finally walk around the

THE FRENCH RIVIERA

point to the stairs leading down to the tender area. To stick closer, you can luxuriate along the harbor in front of the Yacht Club.

Orientation to Monaco

The principality of Monaco consists of three distinct tourist areas: Monaco-Ville, Monte Carlo, and La Condamine. Monaco-Ville fills the rock high above every- thing else and is referred to by locals as Le Rocher ("The Rock"). This is the oldest sec- tion, home to the Prince's Palace and all the sights except the casino. Monte Carlo is the area around the casino. La Condamine is the port (which divides Monaco-Ville and Monte Carlo).

From here it's a 25-minute walk up to the Prince's Palace or to the casino, or three minutes by local bus (see "Getting Around Monaco," later). A fourth, less-interesting area, Fontvieille, forms the west end of Monaco and was reclaimed from the sea by Prince Rainier in the 1970s.

The surgical-strike plan for most travelers is to start at Monaco-Ville (where you'll spend the most time), wander down along the port area, and finish by gambling away whatever you have left in Monte Carlo (the casino doesn't open until 14:00). You can walk the entire route in about 1.5 hours, or take three bus trips and do it in 15 minutes.

Tourist Information

The main TI is at the top of the park above the casino (Mon-Sat 9:00-19:00, Sun 10:00-12:00, 2 boulevard des Moulins, tel. 00-377/92 16 61 16 or 00-377/92 16 61 66, www.visitmonaco.com). A branch TI is in the train station (Tue-Sat 9:00-17:00, closed Sun-Mon except July-Aug).

Arrival in Monaco

By Bus from Nice and Villefranche-sur-Mer: Bus riders need to pay attention, since stops are not announced. Cap d'Ail is the town before Monaco, so be on the lookout after that (the last stop before Monaco is called Cimitière). You'll enter Monaco through the modern cityscape of high-rises of the Fontvieille district. When you see the rocky outcrop of old Monaco, be ready to get off.

There are three stops in Monaco. Listed in order from Nice, they are Place d'Armes (in front of a tunnel at the base of Monaco-Ville's rock), Stade Nautique (center on the port—handiest for the cruise tender dock), and Casino (near the casino on avenue d'Ostende). The Place d'Armes stop is the best starting point. From there you can walk up to Monaco-Ville and the palace (10 minutes straight up), or catch a quick local bus (#1 or #2, details under "Getting Around Monaco," below). To reach the bus stop and steps up to Monaco-Ville, cross the street right in front of the tunnel and walk with the rock on your right for about 200 feet (good WCs at the local-bus stop). To begin at the Casino stop, walk uphill to the Häagen-Dazs and turn right to find the casino.

For directions on returning to Nice by bus, see "By Bus," earlier.

By Train from Nice and Villefranche-sur-Mer: This loooooong underground train station is in central Monaco, about a 15-minute walk to the casino or to the port, and about 25 minutes to the palace. The station has no baggage storage.

The TI and ticket windows are up the escalator at the Italy end of the station. There are three exits from the train platform level (one at each end and one in the middle).

To reach Monaco-Ville and the palace from the station, take the platform-level exit at the Nice end of the tracks (signed *Sortie Fontvieille/Monaco Ville*), which leads through a long tunnel (TI annex at end) to the foot of Monaco-Ville; turn left at the end of the walkway and hike 15 minutes up to the palace, or take the bus (#1 or #2).

To reach Monaco's port and the casino, take the mid-platform exit, closer to the Italy end of the tracks. Follow *Sortie la Condamine* signs down the steps and escalators, then follow *Accès Port* signs until you pop out at the port, where you'll see the stop for buses #1 and #2. It's a 25-minute walk from the port to the palace (to your right) or 20 minutes to the casino (up avenue d'Ostende to your left), or a short trip via buses #1 or #2 to either.

If you plan to return to Nice by train after 20:30, when ticket windows close, buy your return tickets now or be sure to have about €4 in coins (the ticket machines only take coins).

Helpful Hints

Telephone Tip: To call Monaco from France, dial 00, then 377 (Monaco's country code) and the eight-digit number. Within Monaco, simply dial the eight-digit number.

Loop Trip by Bus: From Nice, consider visiting Monaco by bus, taking a bus from Monaco directly to Eze-le-Village (#112, no Sun bus), then returning to Nice by bus from Eze.

Getting Around Monaco

By Local Bus: Buses #1 and #2 link all areas with fast and frequent service (single ticket-€1, 10 tickets-€6, day pass-€3, pay driver,

10/hour, fewer on Sun, buses run until 21:00). You can split a 10-ride ticket with your travel partners, since you're unlikely to take more than two or three rides in Monaco.

By Open Bus Tour: You could pay €17 for a hop-on, hop-off open-deck bus tour that makes 12 stops in Monaco, but I wouldn't. You must begin at the top of the Monaco-Ville hill—inconvenient for those arriving by cruise—and, besides, most of Monaco is walkable. If you want a scenic tour of the principality that includes its best views, pay €1 to take local bus #2, and stay on board for a full loop (or hop on and off as you please).

By Tourist Train: "Monaco Tour" tourist trains begin at the aquarium and pass by the port, casino, and palace (€7, 2/ hour, 10:30-18:00 in summer, 11:00-17:00 in winter depending on weather, 30 minutes, recorded English commentary).

By Taxi: If you've lost track of time at the casino, you can call the 24-hour taxi service (tel. 08 20 20 98 98)...provided you still have enough money to pay the fare.

Self-Guided Walk of Monaco-Ville

All of Monaco's sights (except the casino) are in Monaco-Ville, packed within a few cheerfully tidy blocks. This walk makes a tidy loop around Monaco-Ville.

• *To get from anywhere in Monaco to the palace square (Monaco-Ville's sightseeing center, home of the palace and the Napoleon Collection), take bus #1 or #2 to place de la Visitation (end of the line). Turn right as you step off the bus and walk five minutes straight down the*

street leading from the left corner of the little square. You'll pass the post office, a worthwhile stop for its collection of valuable Monegasque stamps (we'll go there later—to visit it now, see next page).

Palace Square (Place du Palais): This square is the best place to get oriented to Monaco. Facing the palace, go to the right and look out over the city (er...principality). This rock gave birth to the little pastel Hong Kong look-alike in 1215, and it's managed to remain an independent country for most of its nearly 800 years. Looking beyond the glitzy port, notice the faded green roof above and to the right: It belongs to the casino that put Monaco on the map. The famous Grand Prix runs along the port, and then up the ramp to the casino. And Italy is so close, you can almost smell the pesto. Just beyond the casino is France again (which flanks Monaco on both sides)—you could walk one-way from France to France, passing through Monaco in about 60 minutes.

The odd statue of a woman with a fishing net is dedicated to **Prince Albert I's** glorious reign (1889-1922). Albert was a Renaissance man with varied skills and interests. He had a Jacques Cousteau-like fascination with the sea (and built Monaco's famous aquarium), and was a determined pacifist who made many attempts to dissuade Germany's Kaiser Wilhelm II from becoming involved in World War I. It was Albert I's dad, Charles III, who built the casino.

• *Now walk toward the palace and find the statue of the monk grasping a sword.*

Meet **François Grimaldi,** a renegade Italian dressed as a monk, who captured Monaco in 1297 and began the dynasty that still rules the principality. Prince Albert is his great-great-great... grandson, which gives Monaco's royal family the distinction of being the longest-lasting dynasty in Europe.

• *Walk to the opposite side of the square.*

At the Louis XIV cannonballs, look down at Monaco's newest area, the reclaimed-from-the-sea **Fontvieille** district, which has seen much of Monaco's post-World War II growth (residential and commercial—notice the lushly planted building tops). Prince Rainier continued—some say, was obsessed with—Monaco's economic growth, creating landfills (topped with apartments, such as Fontvieille), flashy ports, more beaches, and a new rail station. Today, thanks to Prince Rainier's efforts, tiny Monaco is a member of the United Nations. (If you have kids with you, check out the nifty play area just below.)

• *If you're into stamps, detour down rue Comte Félix Gastaldi, then follow the jog to the right onto rue Emile de Loth to find the...*

Post Office: Philatelists and postcard-writers with panache can buy—or just gaze in awe at—this post office's impressive collection of Monegasque stamps (Mon-Sat 9:00-12:00 & 13:00-17:00, closed Sun, tel. 00-377/93 15 28 63).

•*Backpedal a few steps to the...*

Prince's Palace (Palais Princier): A medieval castle sat where Monaco's palace is today. Its strategic setting has had a lot to do with Monaco's ability to resist attackers. Today, Prince Albert lives in the palace, whereas Princesses Stephanie and Caroline live down the street a few blocks. The palace guards protect the prince 24/7 and still stage a **Changing of the Guard** ceremony with all the pageantry of an important nation (daily at 11:55, fun to watch but jam-packed). Audioguide tours take you through part of the prince's lavish palace in 30 minutes. The rooms are well-furnished and impressive, but interesting only if you haven't seen a château lately (€8 combo-ticket includes audioguide and the Napoleon Collection, April-Oct daily 10:00-18:00, last entry 30 minutes

before closing, closed Nov-March, tel. 00-377/93 25 18 31).
• *Next to the palace entry is the...*

Napoleon Collection: Napoleon occupied Monaco after the French Revolution. This is the prince's private collection of items Napoleon left behind: military medals, swords, guns, letters, and—best—his hat. I found this collection more interesting than the palace (€4 includes audioguide, €8 combo-ticket includes Prince's Palace, same hours as palace).

• *With your back to the palace, leave the square through the arch to the right (under the most beautiful police station I've ever seen) and find the...*

Cathedral of Monaco (Cathédrale de Monaco): The somber but beautifully lit cathedral, rebuilt in 1878, shows that Monaco cared for more than just its new casino. It's where centuries of Grimaldis are buried, and where Princess Grace and Prince Rainier were married. Circle slowly behind the altar (counterclockwise). The second tomb is that of Albert I, who did much to put Monaco on the world stage. The second-to-last tomb—inscribed *"Gratia Patricia, MCMLXXXII"*—is where Princess Grace was buried in 1982. Prince Rainier's tomb lies next to Princess Grace's (daily 8:30-18:45, until 18:00 in winter).

• *As you leave the cathedral, find the 1956 wedding photo of Princess Grace and Prince Rainier (keep an eye out for other photos of the couple as you walk), then walk left through the immaculately maintained Jardin Botanique, with more fine views. Find the...*

Cousteau Aquarium (Musée Océanographique): Prince Albert I built this impressive, cliff-hanging aquarium in 1910 as a monument to his enthusiasm for things from the sea. The aquarium, which Captain Jacques Cousteau directed for 32 years, has 2,000 different specimens, representing 250 species. The bottom floor features Mediterranean fish and colorful tropical species (all nicely described in English). My favorite is the zebra lionfish, though I'm keen on eels too. Rotating exhibits occupy the entry floor. Upstairs, the fancy Albert I Hall houses a museum (included in entry fee, very little English information) and features ship models, whale skeletons, oceanographic instruments and tools, and scenes of Albert and his beachcombers hard at work. Find the display on Christopher Columbus with English explanations. Don't miss the elevator to the rooftop terrace view, where you'll also find convenient WCs and a reasonable café (€13, kids-€7, daily July-Aug 9:30-19:30, April-June and Sept 9:30-19:00, Oct-March

Le Grand Prix Automobile de Monaco

Each May, the Grand Prix de Monaco focuses the world's attention on this little country. The race started as an enthusiasts' car rally by the Automobile Club of Monaco (and is still run by the same group, more than 80 years later). The first race, held in 1929, was won by a Bugatti at a screaming average speed of...48 mph (today's cars double that speed). To this day, drivers consider this one of the most important races on their circuits.

By Grand Prix standards, it's an unusual course, running through the streets of this tiny principality, sardined between mountains and sea. The hilly landscape means that the streets are narrow, with tight curves, steep climbs, and extremely short straightaways. Each lap is about two miles, beginning and ending at the port. Cars climb along the sea from the port, pass in front of the casino, race through the commercial district, and do a few dandy turns back to the port. The race lasts 78 laps, and whoever is still rolling at the end wins (most don't finish).

The Formula 1 cars look like overgrown toys that kids might pedal up and down their neighborhood street (if you're here a week or so before the race, feel free to browse the parking structure below Monaco-Ville, where many race cars are kept). Time trials to establish pole position begin three days before the race, which is always on a Sunday (for dates, see www.yourmonaco.com/grand_prix). More than 150,000 people attend the gala event; like the nearby film festival in Cannes, it's an excuse for yacht parties, restaurant splurges, and four-digit bar tabs at luxury hotels.

THE FRENCH RIVIERA

10:00-18:00; down the steps from Monaco-Ville bus stop, at the opposite end of Monaco-Ville from the palace; tel. 00-377/93 15 36 00, www.oceano.mc).

• *The red–brick steps, across from the aquarium to the right, lead up to buses #1 and #2, both of which run to the port, the casino, and the train station. To walk back to the palace and through the old city, turn left at the top of the brick steps. For a brief movie break, take the escalator to the right of the aquarium as you leave it and drop into the parking garage, then take the elevator down and find the...*

Monte Carlo Story: This informative 35-minute film gives an entertaining and informative account of Monaco's fairy-tale history, from fishing village to jet-set principality, and offers a comfortable, soft-chair break from all that walking. The last part of the film was added to the original version after the death of Prince Rainier, which is why your sound stops early (€7, headphone commentary in English; daily showings usually on the hour at 14:00, 15:00, 16:00, and 17:00; there may be a morning showing for groups that you can join—ask, tel. 00-377/93 25 32 33).

Sights in Monaco

Above Monaco-Ville

Jardin Exotique—This cliffside municipal garden, located above Monaco-Ville, has eye-popping views from France to Italy. It's a fascinating home to more than a thousand species of cacti (some giant) and other succulent plants, but probably worth the entry only for view-loving botanists (some posted English explanations provided). Your ticket includes entry to a skippable natural cave and an anthropological museum, as well as a not-to-be-missed view snack bar/café (€7, daily mid-May-mid-Sept 9:00-19:00, mid-Sept-mid-May 9:00-18:00 or until dusk, tel. 00-377/93 15 29 80). Bus #2 runs here from any stop in Monaco, and makes for a worthwhile mini tour of the country, even if you don't visit the gardens. You can get similar views over Monaco for free from behind the souvenir stand at the Jardin's bus stop; or, for even grander vistas, cross the street and hike toward La Turbie.

In Monte Carlo

▲**Casino**—Monte Carlo, which means "Charles' Hill" in Spanish, is named for the prince who presided over Monaco's 19th-century makeover. Begin your visit opposite Europe's most famous casino, in the park above the pedestrian-unfriendly traffic circle. In the mid-1800s, olive groves stood here. Then, with the construction of the casino and spas, and easy road and train access, one of Europe's poorest countries was on the Grand Tour map—*the* place for the vacationing aristocracy to play. Today, Monaco has the world's highest per-capita income.

The casino is intended to make us feel comfortable while losing money. Charles Garnier designed the place (with an opera house inside) in 1878, in part to thank the prince for his financial help in completing Paris' Opéra Garnier (which the architect also designed). The central doors provide access to slot machines, private gaming rooms, and the opera house. The private gaming rooms occupy the left wing of the building.

Count the counts and Rolls-Royces in front of Hôtel de Paris (built at the same time, visitors allowed in the hotel, no shorts, www.montecarloresort.com), then strut inside past the slots to the sumptuous atrium. This is the lobby for the opera house (open only for performances). There's a model of the opera at the end of the room, and marble WCs on the right. If you're over 21, you can try your luck at the one-armed bandits (push button on slot machines to claim your winnings). If it's before 20:00, shorts are allowed at the slots, though you'll need decent attire to go any farther. After 20:00, shorts are off-limits everywhere.

The scene, flooded with camera-toting tourists during the day, is downright James Bond-like after dark in the private rooms. The park behind the casino offers a peaceful café and a good view of the building's rear facade and of Monaco-Ville.

If paying an entrance fee to lose money is not your idea of fun, you can access all games for free in the plebeian, American-style Loews Casino, adjacent to the old casino.

Cost and Hours: The slot machines and the first gaming rooms *(salons européens)* open daily at 14:00. Slots are free, but you'll pay €10 to enter *les salons européens*. Most of the glamorous private game rooms open Mon-Fri at 16:00 and Sat-Sun at 15:00, though some don't open until 21:00 or 22:00. Here you can rub elbows with high rollers—provided you're 18 or older (bring your passport for proof) and properly attired (tie and jacket for men, dress standards for women are far more relaxed—only tennis shoes are a definite no-no). Men might be able to rent a tie and jacket at a nearby store (ask at the TI or casino before you go, casino tel. 00-377/92 16 20 00, www.montecarlocasinos.com).

Take the Money and Run: The stop for buses returning to Nice and Villefranche-sur-Mer, and for local buses #1 and #2, is at the top of the park, above the casino on avenue de la Costa (under the arcade on the left). To get back to the train station from the casino, take bus #1 or #2 from this stop, or walk about 15 minutes down avenue d'Ostende (just outside the casino) toward the port, and follow signs to *Gare SNCF* (see map).

Eating in Monaco

Several cafés serve basic, inexpensive fare on the port. I prefer the eateries that line the flowery and traffic-free rue de la Princesse Caroline, which runs between rue Grimaldi and the port. The best this street has to offer is **Huit et Demi.** It has a white-tablecloth-meets-director's-chair ambience, mostly outdoor tables, and cuisine worth returning for (€13 salads, €14 pizzas, €18-24 *plats*, closed Sat for lunch and all day Sun, 7 rue de la Princesse Caroline, tel. 00-377/93 50 97 02). For a simple and cheap salad or sandwich, find the **Crock'in** café farther down at 2 rue de la Princesse (closed

Sun, tel. 04 93 15 02 78).

In Monaco-Ville you'll find incredible *pan bagnat* (*salade niçoise* sandwich), quiche, and sandwiches at the yellow-bannered **Boulangerie,** a block off Palace Square (open daily until 19:00, 8 rue Basse). Try a *barbajuan* (a spring roll-size beignet with wheat, rice, and parmesan), the *tourta de bléa* (pastry stuffed with pine nuts, raisins, and white beets), or the focaccia sandwich (salted bread with herbs, mozzarella, basil, and tomatoes, all drenched in olive oil). For dessert, order the *fougasse monégasque* (a soft-bread pastry topped with sliced almonds and anise candies). Monaco-Ville has many pizzerias, *crêperies,* and sandwich stands.

West of Nice

Cannes

Cannes (pronounced "can"), famous for its annual film festival, is the sister city of Beverly Hills. That says it all. When I asked the

TI for a list of museums and sights, they just smiled. Cannes—with big, exclusive hotels lining mostly private stretches of perfect, sandy beach—is for strolling, shopping, dreaming of meeting a movie star, and lounging on the seafront. Cannes has little that's unique to offer the traveler...except a mostly off-limits film festival and quick access to two undeveloped islands. You can buy an ice-cream cone at the train station and see everything before you've had your last lick. Money is what Cannes has always been about—wealthy people come here to make the scene, so there's always enough *scandale* to go around. The king of Saudi Arabia purchased a serious slice of waterfront just east of town and built his compound with no regard to local zoning regulations. Money talks on the Riviera...and always has.

Arrival at the Port of Cannes

Cruise ships tender passengers to the west side of Cannes' port. From here, it's an easy walk into town: Just head inland, with the port on your right-hand side. As you walk, you'll pass ticket windows selling seats for various offshore excursions, and across the port you'll see the famous Film Festival Hall. (The tender dock is near the end of my self-guided walk; you can either do the walk from here in reverse; or you can walk about 10 minutes around the port to the walk's starting point—in the park just beyond the Film Festival Hall—and do it in order.)

It's about a 15-minute walk from the tender dock to the **train station:** Go up to the square at the top of the port. Walk to the far end of the square, and exit the square at its top-right corner, onto rue Maréchal. Bear right up rue Vénizélos, and you'll pop out at the train station. From here, trains run twice hourly to **Antibes** (15 minutes), **Nice** (30-40 minutes), **Villefranche-sur-Mer** (40-50 minutes), and points beyond.

Orientation to Cannes

It's a breeze to visit Cannes (the train is faster, but the bus is cheaper). Buses arrive next to the train station. From the train station (baggage storage available 8:30-20:30), turn left to find the busy **TI,** and pick up the nifty little city map (Mon-Sat 9:00-13:00 & 14:00-18:00, closed Sun, tel. 04 93 99 19 77, www.cannes.fr). On Sundays, when the train station TI is closed, drop by the glamorously quiet main TI, in the film festival building at 1 boulevard de la Croisette (daily 9:00-19:00).

Self-Guided Walk of Cannes

This self-guided walking tour will take you to Cannes' sights in a level, one-hour walk at a movie-star pace. Well-kept WCs are available in the lobbies of any large hotel you pass.

• *From the train station TI, cross the street and walk for five unimpressive minutes down rue des Serbes to the beachfront. Cross the busy boulevard de la Croisette and make your way past snack stands to the sea. Find the round lookout and get familiar with...*

The Lay of the Land: Cannes feels different from its neighbors to the east. You won't find the distinctive pastel oranges and pinks of Old Nice and Villefranche-sur-Mer. Cannes was never part of Italy—and through its architecture and cuisine, it shows.

Face the water. The land jutting into the sea on your left is actually two islands, St. Honorat and Ste. Marguerite. **St. Honorat**

has been the property of monks for over 500 years; today its abbey, vineyards, trails, and gardens can be visited by peace-seeking travelers. **Ste. Marguerite,** which you also can visit, is famous for the stone prison that housed the 17th-century Man in the Iron

Handy Cannes Phrases

Where is a movie star?	*Où est une vedette?*
I am a movie star.	*Je suis une vedette.*
I am rich and single.	*Je suis riche et célibataire.*
Are you rich and single?	*Etes-vous riche et célibataire?*
Are those real?	*Ils sont des vrais?*
How long is your yacht?	*Quelle est la longeur de votre yacht?*
How much did that cost?	*Combien coûtait-il?*
You can always dream...	*On peut toujours rêver...*

Mask (whose true identity remains unknown).

Now look to your right. Those striking mountains sweeping down to the sea are the Massif de l'Esterel. Their red-rock outcrops oversee spectacular car and train routes. Closer in, the hill with the medieval tower caps Cannes' old town (Le Suquet). This hilltop offers grand views and pretty lanes, but little else. Below the old town, the port welcomes yachts of all sizes...provided they're big.

Face inland. On the left, find the modern, rust-colored building that's home to the famous film festival (we'll visit there soon). Back the other way, gaze up the boulevard. That classy building with twin black-domed roofs is Hôtel Carlton, our eventual target and as far as we'll go together in that direction.

• *Continue with the sea on your right and stroll the...*

Promenade (La Croisette): You're walking along boulevard de la Croisette—Cannes' famed two-mile-long promenade. First

popular with kings who wintered here after Napoleon fell, the elite parade was later joined by British aristocracy. Today, boulevard de la Croisette is fronted by some of the most expensive apartments and hotels in Europe. If it's lunchtime, you might try one of the beach cafés—Brad Pitt did. **Plage le Goéland's** café has fair-enough prices and appealing decor (€13 mussels, €15 roasted chicken, daily, closest private beach to the Film Festival Hall, tel. 04 93 38 22 05).

• *Stop when you get to...*

Hôtel Carlton: This is the most famous address on boulevard de la Croisette (allow €1,200-5,800 per night). Face the beach. The iconic Cannes experience is to slip out of your luxury hotel (prefer-

ably this one), into a robe (ideally, monogrammed with your initials), and onto the beach—or, better yet, onto the pier (this avoids getting irritating sand on your carefully oiled skin). While you may not be doing the "fancy hotel and monogrammed robe" ritual on this Cannes excursion, you can—for about €18—rent a chair and umbrella and pretend you're tanning for a red-carpet premiere. Cannes does have a few token public beaches, but most beaches are private and run by hotels like the Carlton. You could save money by sunning among the common folk, but the real Cannes way to flee the rabble and paparazzi is to rent a spot on a private beach (best to reserve ahead in July-Aug).

Cross over and wander into the hotel—you're welcome to browse (except during the festival). Ask for a hotel brochure, verify room rates, check for availability. Can all these people really afford this? Imagine the scene here during the film festival (see anyone famous?). A surprisingly affordable café (considering the cost of a room) lies just beyond.

• *You can continue your stroll down La Croisette, but I'm doubling back to the dull orange building that is Cannes'...*

Film Festival Hall: Cannes' film festival (Festival de Cannes), staged since 1939, completes the "Big Three" of Riviera events (with Monaco's Grand Prix and Nice's Carnival). The hall where the festival takes place—a busy-but-nondescript convention center—sits like a plump movie star on the beach. You'll recognize the formal grand entryway—but the red carpet won't be draped for your visit.

Find the famous (Hollywood-style) handprints in the sidewalk all around. To get inside during the festival, you have to be a star (or a photographer—some 3,000 paparazzi attend the gala event, and most bring their own ladders to get above the crowds). Though off-limits to us, the festival is all that matters around here—and worth a day trip if you're here while it's on. The town buzzes with megastar energy, press passes, and revealing dresses. Locals claim that it's the world's third-biggest media event, after the Olympics and the World Cup (soccer). The festival prize is the Palme d'Or (like the Oscar for Best Picture). The French press can't cover the event enough, and the average Jean in France follows it as Joe would the

World Series in the States. In 2008, the French surprised everyone by winning the prize for the first time in 21 years, for the unhyped, realistic drama *Entre les Murs (The Class,* about a teacher's struggles in a Paris middle school). The Thai film *Uncle Boonmee Who Can Recall His Past Lives* took the prize in 2010.

• *Around the other side of the festival hall is the port (Gare Maritime).*

The Port and Old Town (Le Suquet): The big-boy yachts line up closest to the Film Festival Hall. After seeing this yacht frenzy, everything else looks like a dinghy. Boats to St-Tropez and the nearby islands of St. Honorat and Ste. Marguerite depart from the far side of the port (at quai Laubeuf; see "Sights in Cannes," below, for boat info).

Cannes' oldest neighborhood, Le Suquet, crowns the hill past the port. Locals refer to it as their Montmartre. It's artsy and charming, but it's a steep 15-minute walk above the port, with little of interest except the panoramic views from its ancient church, Notre-Dame-de-l'Espérance (Our Lady of Hope).

• *To find the views from Le Suquet, walk past the bus station at the northwest corner of the port and find your way up cobbled rue Saint-Antoine (next to the Café St. Antoine). Turn left on place du Suquet, and then follow signs to* Traverse de la Tour *for the final leg.*

Cue music. Roll end credits. Our film is over. For further exploration, look for Cannes' "underbelly" between Le Suquet and the train station—narrow lanes with inexpensive cafés and shops that regular folks can afford.

Sights in Cannes

Shopping—Cannes is made for window-shopping (the best streets are between the station and the waterfront). For the trendiest boutiques, stroll down handsome rue d'Antibes (it parallels the sea about three blocks inland). Rue Meynadier anchors a pedestrian zone with more affordable shops closer to the port. To bring home a real surprise, consider cosmetic surgery. Cannes is well-known as *the* place on the Riviera to have your face (or other parts) realigned.

Excursions to St. Honorat and Ste. Marguerite Islands—Boats ferry tourists 15 minutes to these twin islands just off Cannes' shore (€12 round-trip, daily 9:00-18:00, 1-2/hour, www.trans-cote-azur .com, no ferry runs between two islands). The islands offer a refreshing change from the frenetic mainland, with almost no

development, good swimming, and peaceful walking paths. On Ste. Marguerite you can visit the castle and cell where the mysterious Man in the Iron Mask was imprisoned (good little museum with decent English explanations featuring cargo from a sunken Roman vessel). On St. Honorat you can hike seafront trails and visit the abbey where monks still live and pray.

Excursions to St-Tropez—Trans Côte d'Azur runs boat excursions from Cannes to St-Tropez. This boat trip is popular—book a few days ahead from June to September (€42 round-trip, 75 minutes each way; July-mid-Sept daily 2/day; June and late Sept 1/day Tue, Thu, and Sat-Sun only; no service Oct-May; tel. 04 92 98 71 30, fax 04 92 00 42 31, www.trans-cote-azur.com).

Eating in Cannes

For a tasty, easy lunch in Cannes, consider **Fournil St. Nicholas.** You'll get mouthwatering quiche and sandwiches and exquisite salads at affordable prices (leaving the train station, turn right and walk a few blocks to 5 rue Venizelos, tel. 04 93 38 81 12).

Antibes

Antibes has a down-to-earth, easygoing ambience that's rare in this area. Its old town is a maze of narrow streets and red-tile roofs rising above the blue Med, protected by twin medieval towers and wrapped in extensive ramparts. Visitors can browse Europe's biggest yacht harbor, snooze on a sandy beach, loiter through an enjoyable old town, and hike along a sea-swept trail. The town's cultural claim to fame, the Picasso Museum, shows off its great collection in a fine old building.

Antibes' old town lies between the port and boulevard Albert 1er and avenue Robert Soleau. Place Nationale is the old town's hub of activity. The restaurant-lined rue Aubernon connects the port and the old town. Stroll along the sea between the old port and place Albert 1er (where boulevard Albert 1er meets the water). The best beaches lie just beyond place Albert 1er, and the walk is beautiful. Good play areas for children are along this path and on place des Martyrs de la Résistance.

Orientation to Antibes

Tourist Information

Antibes has three TIs: one in a kiosk at the **train station** (April-Sept only, Mon-Sat 9:00-18:00, closed Sun), one near the **port** at 32 boulevard d'Aguillon (Mon-Sat 10:00-12:00 & 13:30-18:00, closed Sun), and the main TI on **place Général de Gaulle** where the fountains squirt (July-Aug daily 9:00-19:00; Sept-June Mon-Sat 9:00-12:30 & 13:30-18:00, Sun 9:00-12:00; tel. 04 97 23 11 11, www.antibesjuanlespins.com). At any TI, pick up the excellent city map and the self-guided walking tour of old Antibes.

Arrival in Antibes

By Train: Bus #14 runs every 20 minutes from the train station (the bus stop is 50 yards to right as you exit station) to the *gare routière* (bus station; near the main TI and old town), and continues to the fine plage de la Salis which has quick access to the Phare de la Garoupe trail. **Taxis** are usually waiting in front of the train station.

To **walk** to the port, the old town, and the Picasso Museum (15-20-minute walk), cross the street in front of the station, skirting left of the Piranha Café, and follow avenue de la Libération downhill as it bends left. At the end of the street, head right along the port, and continue until you reach the end of the parking lots; turn right into the old town.

By Bus: Slow bus #200 stops a few blocks from the TI (turn right as you leave the TI to find the stops just off boulevard Dugommier: buses from Nice and to Cannes stop on avenue Aristide Briand—second shelter down; buses to Nice and from Cannes stop on boulevard Gustave Chancel).

Helpful Hints

Monday, Monday: Avoid Antibes on Mondays, when all sights are closed.

Internet Access: Centrally located **l'Outil du Web** is two blocks from place Général de Gaulle TI—walk toward the train station (Mon and Thu 9:30-18:00, Tue-Wed and Fri 9:30-13:00, closed Sat-Sun, 11 avenue Robert Soleau, tel. 04 93 74 11 86).

English Bookstore: Heidi's English Bookshop has a welcoming vibe and a great selection of new and used books, with many guidebooks—including mine (Mon-Fri 10:00-19:00, Sat-Sun 11:00-18:00, 24 rue Aubernon).

Grocery Store: Picnickers will appreciate Casino's **Epicerie de la Place market** (daily until 22:00 in summer, until 21:00 off-season, where rue Sade meets place Nationale).

Bike Rental: Ask at the TI for bike-rental options.

Taxi: For a taxi, call 08 25 56 07 07 or 04 93 67 67 67.

Boat Rental: You can motor your own seven-person yacht thanks to **Antibes Bateaux Services** (€300/half-day, at the small fish market on the port, mobile 06 15 75 44 36, www.antibes -bateaux.com).

Getting Around Antibes

Though most sights and activities are within easy walking distance, buses are a great value in Antibes, allowing three hours of travel for €1 (one-way or round-trip). **Bus #2** provides access to the best beaches and hikes. It runs from the bus station down boulevard Albert 1er, with stops every few blocks (daily 7:00-19:00, every 40 minutes). **Bus #14** links the train station, bus station, old town, and plage de la Salis.

A **tourist train** offers circuits around old Antibes, the port, and the ramparts (€7, departs from place de la Poste, mobile 06 03 35 61 35).

Sights in Antibes

Antibes' **port** was enlarged in the 1970s to accommodate ever-expanding yacht dimensions. The work was financed by wealthy yacht owners (mostly Saudi Arabian) eager for a place to park their aircraft carriers. That old four-pointed structure crowning the opposite end of the port is Fort Carré, which protected Antibes from foreigners for more than 500 years. The pathetic remains of a once-hearty fishing fleet are moored in the port. The Mediterranean is pretty much fished out. Most of the seafood you'll eat here comes from fish farms or the Atlantic.

Antibes' **old town** is the haunt of a large community of English, Irish, and Aussie boaters who help crew those giant yachts in Antibes' port. (That helps explain the Irish pubs and English bookstores.) Antibes' market hall (daily until 13:00, except closed Mon Sept-May) does double duty—market by day, restaurants by night. Near the market is the pretty, pastel **Church of the Immaculate Conception,** built on the site of a Greek temple (worth a peek inside). A church has stood here since the 12th century; this version served as the area's cathedral until the mid-1200s. The stone bell tower stands apart from the church and predates it by 600 years, when it was part of the city's defenses.

Looming above the church on prime real estate is the white-stone **Château Grimaldi.** This site has been home to the acropolis of the Greek city of Antipolis, a Roman fort, and a medieval bishop's palace (once connected to the cathedral below). Today this is where you'll find the compact, three-floor **Picasso Museum,** which offers a manageable collection of Picasso's paintings, sketches, and ceramics. Picasso lived in this castle for four months in 1946, when he cranked out an amazing amount of art. He was elated by the end of World War II, and his works show a celebration of color and a rediscovery of light after France's long nightmare of war (€6; mid-June-mid-Sept Tue-Sun 10:00-18:00, July-Aug Wed and Fri until 20:00; mid-Sept-mid-June Tue-Sun 10:00-12:00 &

14:00-18:00; closed Mon year-round, last entry 30 minutes before closing, tel. 04 92 90 54 20, www.antibes-juanlespins.com/eng /culture/musees).

The best **beaches** stretch between Antibes' port and Cap d'Antibes. The first you'll cross is the plage Publique (no rentals required). Next are the groomed plages de la Salis and du Ponteil, with mattress, umbrella, and towel rental. All are busy but manageable in summer and on weekends, with cheap snack stands and exceptional views of the old town. The closest beach to the old town is at the port (plage de la Gravette), which seems calm in any season.

More Sights on the French Riviera

St-Tropez

St-Tropez is a busy, charming, and traffic-free port town smothered with fashion boutiques, elegant restaurants, and luxury boats. The village itself is the attraction, as the nearest big beach is miles away. Wander the harborfront, where fancy yachts moor stern-in, their carefully coiffed captains and first mates enjoying *pu-pus* for happy hour—they're seeing and being seen. Take time to stroll the back streets while nibbling a chocolate-and-Grand Marnier crêpe.

In St-Tropez, window-shopping, people-watching, tan maintenance, and savoring slow meals fill people's days, weeks, and, in some cases, lives. Here, one dresses up, sizes up one another's yachts, and trolls for a partner. While the only models you'll see are in the shop windows, Brigitte Bardot—who turns 78 in 2012—sometimes hangs out on a bench in front of the TI signing autographs.

St-Paul-de-Vence

The most famous of Riviera hill towns is also the most-visited village in France. And it feels that way—like an overrun and over-restored artist-shopping-mall. Its attraction is understandable, as every cobble and flower seems *just-so,* and the setting is memorable. The inviting, pricey, and far-out Fondation Maeght, a private museum, is situated a steep 20-minute walk or short taxi ride above St-Paul-de-Vence.

Fondation Maeght (fohn-dah-shown mahg) offers an excellent introduction to modern Mediterranean art by gathering many of the Riviera's most famous artists under one roof. The unusual museum building is purposefully low-profile, to let its world-

What If I Miss My Boat?

Remember that you can get help from the cruise line's port agent (listed on the destination information sheet distributed on the ship) and the local TI. If the port agent suggests a costly solution (such as a private car with a driver), you may want to consider public transit.

Frequent **trains** connect **Nice, Villefranche-sur-Mer, Monaco,** and **Cannes** (2/hour; 10 minutes from Nice to Villefranche, 20 minutes to Monaco, 30-40 minutes to Cannes). The train is also a good option for **Marseille** (18/day from Nice, 2.5 hours) and **Toulon** (1-2/hour from Nice, 1.75 hours). Trains are less frequent to **Barcelona** (1 direct/day from Nice, 10.5 hours, more with changes), **Livorno** (3/day from Nice, 7.5 hours with 1 change), **Civitavecchia** (7/day from Nice, 9.5 hours with 2 changes), and **Naples** (8/day from Nice, 10-14 hours with 2-4 changes).

For other connections, ask at the train station or check http://bahn.hafas.de/bin/query.exe/en (Germany's excellent all-Europe website).

Nice's easy-to-navigate **airport** (Aéroport de Nice Côte d'Azur) is a 20- to 30-minute taxi or bus ride west of the city center. Figure €35 for a taxi to the airport from Nice or €55 from Villefrance-sur-Mer. Express buses #99 and #98 connect the airport with Nice (€4). Airport info: toll tel. 08 20 42 33 33 (€0.12/minute), www.nice.aeroport.fr.

Any local **travel agent** also should be able to help.

For more advice on what to do if you miss the boat, see page 131.

THE FRENCH RIVIERA

class modern-art collection take center stage. Works by Fernand Léger, Joan Miró, Alexander Calder, Georges Braque, and Marc Chagall are thoughtfully arranged in well-lit rooms. The backyard of the museum has views, a Gaudí-esque sculpture labyrinth by Miró, and a courtyard filled with the wispy works of Alberto Giacometti.

Grasse

The only good reason to visit Grasse is if you care about perfume. Grasse has been at the center of the fragrance industry since the 1500s, when it was known for its scented leather gloves. The cultivation of aromatic plants around Grasse slowly evolved to produce ingredients for soaps and perfumes, and by the 1800s, Grasse was recognized as the center for perfume (thanks largely to its flower-friendly climate), making it a wealthy city.

Grasse's **International Museum of Perfume** is a magnificent tribute to perfume, providing a thorough examination of its history and production from ancient Greece to today. The museum is well-designed, with excellent English explanations, a good audioguide, and impressive multimedia exhibits that could keep a perfume fan busy for days. The museum also offers a self-guided visit to their gardens near Grasse, featuring five acres of important plants and flowers used in perfume production. The well-run, functioning **Fragonard Perfume** Factory, located dead-center in Grasse, provides frequent, fragrant, informative 20-minute tours and an interesting "museum" to explore while you wait.

ITALY
Italia

ITALY

Italia

Bella Italia! Italy has Europe's richest, craziest culture. If you take Italy on its own terms, you'll experience a cultural keelhauling that actually feels good. Savor your cappuccino, dangle your feet over a Venetian canal, and imagine what it was like centuries ago. Look into the famous sculpted eyes of Michelangelo's *David* and understand Renaissance Man's assertion of himself. Ramble through the rabble and rubble of Rome and mentally resurrect those ancient stones. Italy is for romantics.

Almost completely surrounded by water, Italy has no shortage of ports. This book focuses on the most popular cruise stops.

The port of Livorno is the gateway to an impressive range of Tuscan destinations, including Florence, the birthplace of the Renaissance; Pisa and its famed Leaning Tower; and the delightful walled town of Lucca.

The port of Civitavecchia serves Rome, the Eternal City.

The ports of Naples and nearby Sorrento are worthwhile destinations on their own, and are near Pompeii's ancient ruins, smoldering Mount Vesuvius, the trendy isle of Capri, and the scenic Amalfi Coast.

And always, there's Venice, the one-of-a-kind medieval city of islands, canals, and *bellissimo* romance.

Practicalities

This section covers just the basics on traveling in Italy.

Tourist Information: www.italiantourism.com

Money: Italy uses the euro currency: 1 euro (€) = about $1.40.

Theft Alert: Italy has particularly hardworking pickpockets. Assume that beggars (such as women with babies, or gangs of scruffy children pushing pieces of cardboard at you) are pickpockets and any scuffle is simply a distraction by a team of thieves. Some thieves are well-dressed and even carry guidebooks to fool you.

Business Hours: Many businesses are open throughout the day Monday through Saturday, but some businesses close for lunch (roughly 13:00-15:30).

Internet Access: You may be asked to show your passport before using terminals at Internet cafés.

Sights: Opening and closing hours of sights can change unexpectedly; confirm the latest times with the local tourist information office or the sights' websites.

Dress Code: Some major churches enforce a modest dress code (no bare shoulders or shorts) for everyone, even children.

Trains: You can buy tickets at Italian train stations (at the ticket window or at automated machines with English instructions) or from travel agencies. Before boarding the train, you must validate your train documents by stamping them in the yellow box near the platform.

Eating

Italians eat lunch from about 12:00 to 14:00. They eat dinner a bit later than we do; better restaurants start serving around 19:00.

For a quick bite any time of day, stop by an Italian "bar." These  aren't taverns, but small cafés selling sandwiches, coffee, and other drinks. At bars, it's cheaper to eat and drink while standing at the counter (*banco*) rather than sitting at a table (*tavolo*) or outside (*terrazza*). This tiered pricing system is clearly posted on the wall. Sometimes you'll pay for your meal at a cash register, then take the receipt to another counter to claim your drink. Watch the locals and imitate.

Take-away food from pizza shops and delis (such as a *rosticcería* or *tavola calda*) makes an easy picnic. You can stop by a gelato shop for dessert. An *enoteca* is a wine bar with snacks and light meals.

If you have time to dine, look for a *ristorante*, *trattoria*, or *osteria*. A full meal consists of an appetizer (antipasto), a first course (*primo piatto*, pasta or soup), and a second course (*secondo piatto*, expensive meat and fish dishes). Steak and seafood are sometimes sold

by weight, priced by the kilogram (just over 2 pounds) or *etto* (100 grams, one-tenth of a kilogram); the letters "s.q." means according to quantity. Make sure you're really clear on the price before ordering. Vegetables *(verdure)* may come with the *secondo* or cost extra, as a side dish *(contorni)*. The euros can add up in a hurry, but you don't have to order each course. My approach is to mix antipasti and *primi piatti* family-style with my dinner partners (skipping *secondi*).

For an unexciting but hearty meal, look for a *menù turistico* (or *menù del giorno*), a three- or four-course, fixed-price deal.

When you want the bill, ask for *"Il conto."*

Tipping: At restaurants, the service charge is usually built into your bill's grand total in one of two ways: either the menu prices include the fee *(servizio incluso)* or a percentage is added to the bottom of your bill *(servizio non incluso;* usually 10-15 percent). In either case, the total you pay already includes a tip. If you're pleased with the service, you can round up the bill by a euro or two (though most Italians rarely do). If you order your food at a counter, there's no need to tip.

Phoning

To make cheap calls from any type of phone, buy an international phone card from a newsstand, tobacco shop, or Internet café (I've had good luck with the Europa brand card). Insertable cards, which work only at payphones, are sold at tobacco shops, post offices, and machines near public phones (rip off a corner to activate the card, then insert it into a payphone). For tips on using either type of card, see page 120.

Dialing: Italian phone numbers begin with 0. To **call within Italy**, just dial the number as it appears in this book—whether you're calling across the street or across the country. To make an international **call to Italy**, start with the international access code (00 if calling from Europe, or 011 from North America), then dial 39 (Italy's country code), then the local number. To **call home from Italy** (or from anywhere in Europe), dial 00, 1, then your area code and phone number.

Directory Assistance: Telephone help: tel. 170 (in English; free directory assistance); directory assistance: tel. 12 (for €0.50, an Italian-speaking robot gives the number twice, very clearly)

Emergency Telephone Numbers:

English-Speaking Police Help: Tel. 113

Ambulance: Tel. 118

Passport Problems: US Embassy in Rome (24-hour line, tel. 06-46741), US Consulates in Florence (tel. 055-266-951) and Naples (tel. 081-583-8111); Canadian Embassy in Rome (tel. 06-854-441), Canadian Consulate in Naples (tel. 081-401-338).

FLORENCE, PISA, LUCCA
& the PORT of LIVORNO

The port of Livorno gives cruisers access to Italy's justifiably famous region of Tuscany. While there are many Tuscan treats to consider, for most the top attraction is Florence.

Florence is Europe's cultural capital. As the home of the Renaissance and the birthplace of the modern world, Florence practiced the art of civilized living back when the rest of Europe was rural and crude. Democracy, science, and literature, as well as painting, sculpture, and architecture, were all championed by the proud and energetic Florentines of the 1400s.

Today, Florence is geographically small but culturally rich, with more artistic masterpieces per square mile than anyplace else. In a single day, you could look Michelangelo's *David* in the eyes, fall under the seductive sway of Botticelli's *Birth of Venus,* and climb the modern world's first dome, which still dominates the skyline.

The port of Livorno is also within easy striking distance of two other great cities. Pisa's famous Field of Miracles (Leaning Tower, Duomo, and Baptistery) is touristy but worth a visit. Lucca, contained within its fine Renaissance wall, has a charm that causes many connoisseurs of Italy to claim it as a favorite stop.

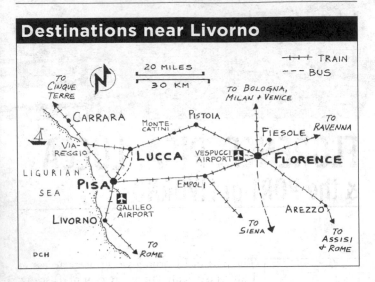

Planning Your Time

For most travelers, the best choice is to make a beeline to Florence. Another good option is going to Pisa and, if you're interested, the neighboring town of Lucca as well. Read the descriptions in this book to decide which destination(s) most appeals to you.

If you choose Florence, don't try to combine it with any other destination; it'll take you two hours just to get from the port of Livorno to Florence. I'd suggest taking the train, though a "transportation-only" excursion can be convenient (see page 100).

No matter where you go, if you're taking the train, keep in mind that it takes 30 minutes just to get from Livorno's cruise port to the train station across town (details covered later). Also, be sure to plan your day conservatively, as trains can be delayed.

Florence

Florence's sights are concentrated in its compact core. The city's two top sights—the Accademia and Uffizi Gallery—are plagued with long ticket-buying lines; it's smart to book entry times in advance (see page 406 for instructions). If you don't reserve ahead and plan to wait in line, visit your preferred sight first, then see if you have time for the other. Note that both sights are closed on Monday. Allow nine hours for visiting Florence, including transportation from your cruise ship and back.

I'd suggest seeing the sights in this order, following my self-guided tours:

• Tour the Accademia, starring Michelangelo's *David*. Allow 30 minutes inside. Then head down Via Ricasoli to the Duomo (10-minute walk).

Excursions from Livorno

The top choices, of course, are **Florence, Pisa,** and **Lucca.**

The following destinations are farther afield, with less-straightforward public-transportation connections—they're best done by shore excursion or with a hired driver.

Siena is a red-brick hilltop city known for its pageantry, Palio horse race, and a stunning traffic-free main square. See page 506.

The Cinque Terre consists of five idyllic Riviera hamlets along a rugged coastline, connected by scenic hiking trails and dotted with beaches. See page 507.

San Gimignano is a small, picturesque hill town, spiked with medieval towers and swarming with tourists. See page 509.

Volterra, a more remote hill town, has wine bars, alabaster workshops, Etruscan sights, and few crowds. See page 509.

• Take my self-guided Renaissance Walk, starting at the Duomo. If you're in a hurry, you can walk to the Uffizi Gallery in 10 minutes, but I'd allow up to two hours.

• Tour the Uffizi Gallery, famous for its Renaissance art. Allow up to two hours inside.

• Any additional time is well spent at Ponte Vecchio (shop-lined bridge over the Arno), the Bargello (sculpture museum near the Uffizi), or shopping at the San Lorenzo Market (a short walk north of the Duomo). If you're more interested in shopping than sightseeing, see page 469.

Pisa and Lucca

You can visit either or both towns easily from Livorno using public transportation. Both Pisa and Lucca deserve at least a two-hour stop (plus transportation time from your ship).

For **Pisa,** allow a minimum of four hours, including transportation from your cruise ship and back. Add two hours if you want to climb the Leaning Tower and didn't reserve ahead (at www .opapisa.it; see page 488).

Lucca alone deserves at least five hours (including transportation—which gives you enough time to stroll the town and rent a bike for a spin around the wall.

To do **both Pisa and Lucca,** allow yourself six hours minimum (including transportation), and skip climbing Pisa's Leaning Tower; it's more satisfying with more time. It's logistically wise to begin in Lucca (the farthest point), then work your way back toward Livorno. Starting in Livorno, catch the train to the Pisa Centrale station, where you'll change to the Lucca-bound train.

LIVORNO

After you visit Lucca, take the hourly, 30-minute, direct bus from Lucca's Piazzale Verdi to Pisa's Field of Miracles and Leaning Tower. When you're done, ride the city bus across town to the Pisa Centrale train station for the 20-minute ride back to Livorno's station (remember, it's another 30 minutes from Livorno's station back to your ship).

If you have your heart set on Pisa, but are only so-so on Lucca, head straight to Pisa, then decide if you have enough time to squeeze in a side-trip to Lucca—you'll be halfway there already.

Pisa Only

If you're going only to Pisa, you'll have time to see the city beyond its famous tower. After arriving at the train station, follow this plan:

• Take the self-guided walk (allow up to an hour) from the train station to the Field of Miracles to see the Leaning Tower. To get there quicker, take the city bus from the station (15 minutes).

• If you want to climb the Leaning Tower and don't have a reservation, go straight to the Tower's ticket office to snag an appointment—usually for a couple of hours later. Allow an hour if you ascend the Tower.

• Visit the sights on Field of Miracles, specifically the Baptistery (eerie acoustics) and Duomo (distinctive architecture). Allow one hour.

Lucca Only

Lucca is a pleasant town with a walkable wall. Note that many of the town's stores and museums are closed on Sundays and Mondays.

When in Lucca:

• Walk part or all of the 2.5-mile wall that encircles the city. Or do it by rental bike.

• Stroll the town, dipping into a few churches or museums if you like.

Arrival at the Port of Livorno

Arrival at a Glance: From the port, ride the shuttle bus or walk into Livorno's town center. From here, you can catch a local public bus to the train station (10 minutes). From Livorno, trains go to Florence (1 hour 22 minutes), Pisa (20 minutes), and Lucca (1-1.25 hours, change in Pisa). There's also a direct bus from downtown Livorno to Pisa (55 minutes). Taxis cost €60 to Pisa, €80 to Lucca, and €250 to Florence (all one-way rates).

Livorno

To More Cruise Docks

Bucino Firenze

Piazza del Portuale

VIA DELLA CINTA ESTERNA

Bacino Cappellini

QUARTIERE DELLA VENEZIA

Fosso Reale

FORTEZZA NUOVA

Piazza Garibaldi

To Central Train Station

FORTEZZA VECCHIA

Piazza della Fort. Vecchia

Piazza dei Marmi

V. BORRA

VIA MADONNA

CITY HALL

Piazza del Municipio

VIA AVVALORATI

VIA D. POSTA

VIA D. GALERE

Piazza della Repubblica

WC

❶

Piazza Grande

ATM

VIA GRANDE

Darsena Vecchia

MOLO CAPITINERA

Piazza Unità d'Italia

VIA FIUME

PHARMACY

Piazza del Pamiglione

VIA GRANDE

COGORANO

❷

DUOMO

Piazza Cavallotti

❸

VIA BUONTALENTI

COVERED MARKET

❹

VIA DEL CARDINALE

MOLO 75

Piazza Micheli

VIA S. FRANCESCO

V. TEMPIO

POST

PRODUCE MARKET

Porto Mediceo

Piazza Arsenale

VIA CRISPI

SCALI D'AZEGLIO

Darsena Nuova

To Molo Mediceo Cruise Terminal

200 Meters

200 Yards

❶ Shuttle to/from Port   ❸ Bus #101 to Pisa
❷ Bus #1 to Train Stn.   ❹ Pizzeria da Gagari

Port Overview

The city of Livorno (sometimes called "Leghorn" in English), with 160,000 inhabitants, is located on Italy's west coast, about 60 miles west of Florence. As a city devastated during World War II and then rebuilt with the help of the American army, Livorno's unkempt postwar architecture still shows scars of its rough past. While this Tuscan city does have an interesting history—particularly in the time of the Renaissance—it pales in comparison to the tidier and more compelling nearby cities. Around 900,000 cruise passengers pass through Livorno each year. Most of them are side-tripping into Florence, Pisa, and Lucca, but it's also possible to reach farther destinations, including Siena, Tuscan hill towns (such as San Gimignano and Volterra), and the Cinque Terre.

Livorno's port (at the western edge of town) is vast and sprawling, but most arriving cruise ships dock in one of two places: Molo

LIVORNO

75, at the **Porto Mediceo;** or the adjacent **Molo Capitaniera.** From either port, unless you're taking a taxi or shore excursion, you'll head to the city's main square, where you'll find the TI and connections to other points.

Tourist Information: There is no TI at the port. For details about Livorno's TI, see "Services in Downtown Livorno," later.

Getting to Florence, Pisa, and Lucca

Taxis to Florence, Pisa, and Lucca are very expensive; any budget-minded traveler with patience can use public transportation to go from Livorno to any of these places, and back again before your ship departs. If it's the one time in your life that you're this close to Michelangelo's *David* or Pisa's famous Leaning Tower, it's worth the effort.

By Taxi

Taxis meet arriving cruises and offer various day trips around the area (the cabbie drops you off for a designated amount of time in one or two cities). In general, drivers prefer to take passengers who will pay them for the whole day, so it can be difficult to get one to take you just one-way (especially the long haul into Florence). Here are some ballpark fares:

- One-way to Pisa: €60
- Round-trip to Pisa: €120
- One-way to Lucca: €80
- One-way between Pisa and Lucca: €50
- Round-trip from Livorno to both Pisa and Lucca: €220
- One-way to Florence: €250
- Round-trip to Florence: €320

Taxis both at the port and in the city offer the same rates. Clarify the fare beforehand, even though by law the driver must have the meter on (the quoted price will usually be less than the meter). The fare can vary, depending on the number of people and the season. Some cabs fit up to eight people, bringing the per-person cost down substantially. The TI (in downtown Livorno) might be willing to help you arrange taxi-sharing with other cruisers to split the cost. Better yet, buddy up with your fellow passengers at breakfast or on the gangway.

By Excursion

Many cruise lines offer a "transportation-only" excursion from the ship to Florence. This includes a bus ride from the ship directly to a point in downtown Florence, ample free time to explore the city, then a bus ride back to your ship. While expensive (around $100-125—which is about €70-90), for two people this is still cheaper than a taxi and almost as easy—worth considering if the directions explained next seem just too complicated.

By Public Transportation

The basic plan is this: Walk or ride the cruise line's shuttle bus from the port to downtown Livorno; then ride a public bus to Livorno's train station; then take the train to wherever you're going. (Unfortunately, most taxi drivers at the port will not consider the brief ride to the Livorno Centrale train station; if they do, they'll charge you a premium at about €10-20, and may try to extract an even higher fare.)

When planning your day, factor in the time it takes to get from Livorno's dock to its train station (estimate at least half an hour each way: 15-minute walk to the town center, then another 10 minutes by bus to the station).

Step 1: From the Ship to Downtown Livorno

From the port, you can either ride the cruise line's shuttle bus or walk to downtown.

Most cruise lines offer a **shuttle bus** to the center of Livorno, dropping you off at a bus stop near the TI kiosk in Piazza del Municipio (sometimes free, possibly about €5 round-trip). Particularly if your boat is docked at the far end of the port, this is a handy option.

If the line for the shuttle bus is too long—or if you're in the mood for a stroll—you can **walk** from most areas of the port to downtown Livorno in about 10 to 20 minutes. If you're arriving at Molo 75/Porto Mediceo, walk around the little sailboat harbor, then bear right over the wide bridge and up Via Grande. From Molo Capitaniera, walk through the port area, cross the wide bridge, and continue straight up Via Grande. Via Grande—an elegant-feeling, arcaded street lined with local shops and fashion boutiques—takes you straight to Piazza Grande in the heart of town (where you can catch bus #1 to the train station).

Note: Particularly when there are multiple cruise ships in town, it can be unpredictable exactly where your ship will dock. On very busy days, you might even put in at the cargo docks, much farther out from the two piers described above. If this is the case, the shuttle bus is the better option.

Step 2: From Downtown Livorno to the Train Station

Livorno's city center clusters around two nearby squares: **Piazza Grande** (stop for bus #1 to train station) and **Piazza del Municipio** (TI, public WCs, stop for shuttle bus to the port). The squares are connected by the two-block-long Via Cogorano (ATM).

Livorno's public **bus** #1 departs from the middle of Piazza

---

Services in Downtown Livorno

The **TI** kiosk is on Piazza del Municipio, right next to the stop for the shuttle bus to the port (May-Oct daily 8:00-18:00; Nov-April Mon-Sat 9:00-17:00, closed Sun; tel. 0586-204-611). The TI arranges taxi-sharing and local guides, and has a free brochure with self-guided walks. They can also inform you about local tours, such as a boat trip around the canals of Livorno plus a visit to Pisa (€20), or a visit to Pisa including a brief opera performance and a wine-tasting (€16)—though it's more satisfying to explore these towns on your own. If you'd like to linger in Livorno, see "**Sights in Livorno**," later.

ATMs: A handy ATM is at UniCreditBanca, next to the port shuttle bus stop on Via Cogorano (between Piazza Grande and Piazza del Municipio).

Pharmacy: You'll find the **Farmacia Internazionale** on Via Grande, between the port area and downtown (Mon-Fri 8:30-13:00 & 15:00-20;00, Sat 8:30-12:30, closed Sun, one block before Piazza Grande, on the left with your back to the port, Via Grande 140, tel. 0586-890-346). Another pharmacy is on Via Cogorano between Piazza Grande and Piazza del Municipio (open 24 hours daily).

WCs: Public bathrooms are in the stark city hall, across the street from the TI on Piazza del Municipio.

Grande, and heads to Livorno Centrale train station (€1, 8/hour Mon-Sat, 4-6/hour Sun, 10 minutes). If you're arriving on the shuttle bus from the port, remember that you'll get off that bus on the nearby Piazza del Municipio—just turn right out of the bus and walk two short blocks on Via Cogorano to Piazza Grande. At Piazza Grande, buy tickets at any *tabacchi* (tobacco shop) or newsstand, or at the ATL bus office on the street to the left of the church (buy a second ticket now for your return trip, to save time later). The bus stop is on the island in front of the church. When the bus drives around a tree-filled piazza, you've arrived at the station.

The **walk** from Piazza Grande to the train station (continue straight up Via Grande with the port at your back) takes about 35 minutes, and is not particularly pretty.

Pisa Bus Alternative: If you want to go straight to Pisa, consider taking bus #101, which leaves from downtown Livorno and heads to Pisa (1/hour, no buses Sat-Sun, 55 minutes, €2.30, schedule posted at stop or at www.atl.livorno.it—click on "Pisa Aeroporto Galilei/Pisa Stazione FS"). In Livorno, catch bus #101 at the Largo Duomo stop behind the cathedral (which faces Piazza Grande). The bus first goes to Pisa's airport and then leaves you about a block from Pisa's train station, across town from the Field of Miracles and Leaning Tower (see "Arrival in Pisa," page 480).

Notice that the bus runs less frequently than the train, and not at all on weekends. It also takes more than twice as long as the train (which takes only 20 minutes)—but it saves you the trip from downtown Livorno to the train station.

Step 3: From Livorno Centrale Train Station to Florence, Pisa, and Lucca

From Livorno Centrale Station, trains zip to Florence, Pisa, Lucca, and other points in Italy. Check the *partenze* (departures) board for the next departure to your destination. In Italian, Florence is "Firenze." If you're going to Pisa, note that it's usually listed as an intermediate station (for example, on the way to Firenze, Milano, or Torino) rather than the final destination.

While the lines can be long at the ticket windows, the self-service machines are fast and generally less crowded. There are two types of machines: The machines marked *Rete Regionale* accept cash only and sell tickets for regional trains (not the faster IC or ES trains to Pisa—explained next). The TrenItalia machines accept credit cards and sell all tickets. Before boarding the train, be sure to validate your ticket by sticking it in the *convalida* slot.

Note that all train lines go first to Pisa, then split: north to Lucca or east to Florence. Most trains are regional and cheap, but a few Pisa-bound trains are high-speed InterCity (IC) or Eurostar (ES) trains; if you take these to Pisa—even if it's just to transfer to a Lucca- or Florence-bound train—you'll pay a premium (about €4 extra on IC, or €6 extra on ES), and it will only save you a few minutes.

To Florence: Hourly, usually departs at :10 after the hour, arrives in Florence at :32 past the following hour—1 hour and 22 minutes total, €6.70 on a regional train. (There are also occasional departures that are a few minutes shorter, but require you to change trains at Pisa Centrale.) For details on what to do when you get to Florence, see "Arrival in Florence," page 397.

To Pisa: 2-3/hour, 20 minutes, €1.90 on a regional train. Once in Pisa, turn to "Arrival in Pisa," page 480.

To Lucca: About hourly, around 1 hour (or up to 1.25 hours), transfer at Pisa Centrale, €3.70 on a regional train. See "Arrival in Lucca," page 496.

To Other Destinations: From Livorno Centrale station, you can ride to **Monterosso** on the **Cinque Terre** (nearly hourly, 1.5-1.75 hours, some direct, others transfer at La Spezia Centrale) or **Siena** (hourly, 2-2.5 hours, transfer in Empoli)—though both of these are too far to be particularly convenient as a side-trip from Livorno. For more about these destinations, see "More Sights near Livorno" at the end of this chapter.

By Tour

Karin Kibby, an Oregonian living in Livorno who leads Rick Steves tours, also offers day tours from the cruise port throughout Tuscany and the Cinque Terre. She'll work with you to find the best solution for your budget and interests (2-10 people, mobile 333-108-6348, karinkintuscany@yahoo.it). For information on local tour options in Florence—see "Tours in Florence" on page 404. There are also tour options in Pisa (page 482) and Lucca (page 497).

Sights in Livorno

If you find yourself with extra time to spend in Livorno itself, you have a few options.

The TI's brochure of **self-guided walks** is worthwhile, including one that ends at the waterfront a 15-minute walk from the cruise docks. You'll meander through the "Quartiere della Venezia," a historic district

with canals (though that's about all it has in common with Venice). Starting at the TI kiosk, and ending at the harbor's fortress, the walk takes you by 18th-century palaces and churches, including buildings still displaying damage from World War II (allow 45 minutes).

A cluster of **markets** are a 10-minute walk southeast of Piazza Grande. Find produce on Piazza Cavallotti (Mon-Sat 8:00-13:30, closed Sun), artisanal food products in the covered market (*mercato coperto*, Mon-Sat 8:00-13:30, closed Sun), and home goods and clothes on Via Buontalenti (Mon-Sat 8:00-20:00, closed Sun).

You can grab a taste of *torta di ceci*. This local culinary specialty is a savory chickpea-flour crêpe with oil and pepper. Get a piece "to go" at Pizzeria da Gagari (10-minute walk from Piazza Grande at Via del Cardinale 24, Mon-Sat 8:30-14:00 & 16:00-21:00, closed Sun).

Seafood-lovers will want to seek out *cacciucco*, a flavorful stew made from seasonal fish swimming in a zesty garlic tomato broth.

Returning to Your Ship

Remember, trains can be delayed, and it's a several-step process to get back to your ship (train to Livorno, then bus to downtown Livorno, then shuttle bus or walk to the port). Schedule your day conservatively, and if you wind up with extra time in Livorno, see "Sights in Livorno," above.

If returning by train from Florence, Pisa, or Lucca, get off at Livorno Centrale and head straight out the front door to the awaiting bus #1, which brings you back to Piazza Grande. From there, walk straight up Via Grande to the port, or walk two short blocks (down Via Cogorano) to Piazza del Municipio to catch the shuttle bus back to your ship.

See page 510 for help if you miss your boat.

Florence

Florence (Firenze), the home of the Renaissance and birthplace of our modern world, has the best Renaissance art in Europe.

Get your bearings with a Renaissance walk. Florentine art goes beyond paintings and statues—there's food, fashion, and handicrafts. You can lick Italy's best gelato while enjoying some of Europe's best people-watching.

Orientation to Florence

The best of Florence lies on the north bank of the Arno River. The

main historical sights cluster around the red-brick dome of the cathedral (Duomo). Everything is within a 20-minute walk of the train station, cathedral, or Ponte Vecchio (Old Bridge). The less-impressive but more characteristic Oltrarno area (south bank) is just over the bridge. Though small, Florence is intense. Prepare for scorching summer heat, kamikaze motor scooters, slick pickpockets, few WCs, steep prices, and long lines.

Tourist Information

There are three TIs in Florence: across from the train station, near Santa Croce Church, and on Via Cavour.

The TI across the square from the train station is most crowded—expect long lines (Mon-Sat 8:30-19:00, Sun 8:30-14:00; with your back to tracks, exit the station—it's 100 yards away, across the square in wall near corner of church at Piazza Stazione 4; tel. 055-212-245, www.firenzeturismo.it). In the train station, avoid the Hotel Reservations "Tourist Information" window (marked *Informazioni Turistiche Alberghiere*) near the McDonald's; it's not a real TI but a hotel-reservation business instead.

The TI near Santa Croce Church is pleasant, helpful, and uncrowded (Mon-Sat 9:00-19:00, Sun 9:00-14:00, shorter hours off-season, Borgo Santa Croce 29 red, tel. 055-234-0444, turismo2 @comune.fi.it).

FLORENCE

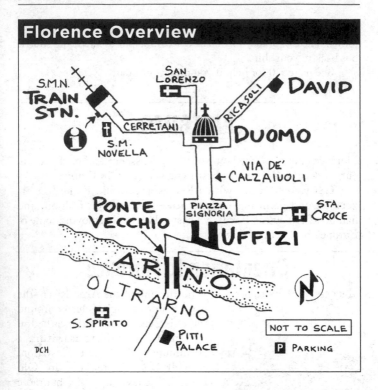

Florence Overview

Another winner is the TI three blocks north of the Duomo (Mon-Sat 8:30-18:30, Sun 8:30-13:30, Via Cavour 1 red, tel. 055-290-832, international bookstore across street).

At any TI, pick up these free, handy resources:

- a city map (ask for the "APT" map, which has bus routes of interest to tourists on the back)

- a current museum-hours listing (extremely important, since no guidebook—including this one—has ever been able to accurately predict the hours of Florence's sights for the coming year). Also check www.comune.fi.it (select "Museums," then "Museums' Opening Hours").

- information on entertainment, including the TI's monthly *Florence and Tuscany News* (good for events and entertainment listings)

- the ad-driven monthly *Florence Concierge Information* magazine (which lists museums, plus concerts, markets, sporting events, church services, shopping ideas, some bus and train connections, and an entire similar section on Siena)

- *The Florentine* newspaper (published every other Thu in English, for expats and tourists, with great articles giving cultural insights; download latest issue at www.theflorentine.net).

These English freebies are available at TIs and hotels all over town.

Arrival in Florence

By Train: Florence's main train station is called **Santa Maria Novella** (*Firenze S.M.N.* on schedules and signs). Built in Mussolini's "Rationalism" style back between the wars, in some ways the station seems to have changed little—notice the 1930s-era lettering and architecture.

Florence also has two suburban train stations: **Firenze Rifredi** and **Firenze Campo di Marte.** Note that some trains don't stop at the main station—before boarding, confirm that you're heading for S.M.N., or you may overshoot the city. (If this happens, don't panic; the other stations are a short taxi ride from the center.)

Minimize time in the main station—doing business here is generally intense, crowded, and overpriced. It's also rife with pickpockets. The banks of user-friendly automated ticket machines are handy. They take euros and credit cards, display schedules, issue tickets, and even make reservations for railpass-holders. Still, it can be quicker to get tickets and train info from travel agencies in town.

With your back to the tracks, look left to see a 24-hour pharmacy (*Farmacia,* near McDonald's), the fake "Tourist Information" office (funded by hotels), city buses, bus ticket booth, the taxi stand (fast-moving line, except on holidays), and the entrance to the Galleria S.M. Novella underground mall/passage that leads from the station under the square to the Church of Santa Maria Novella. (Warning: Pickpockets—often dressed as tourists—frequent this tunnel, especially the surface point near the church.)

To get to the TI, walk away from the tracks and exit the train station to the left (going straight out of the station leads you to an uninviting wasteland of construction). The real TI is across the square by the stone church, 100 yards in front of the station (see "Tourist Information"). Pick up picnic supplies at the Conad supermarket, located along the west side of the station on Via Luigi Alamanni (Mon-Sat 8:00-20:00, closed Sun).

The Duomo, though not visible from here, is located to the left (east) down busy Via dei Panzani, a 10-minute walk away. The Uffizi Gallery is about a 10-minute walk south of the Duomo on the car-free Via de' Calzaiuoli. The Accademia (home of *David*) is a 15-minute walk east of the station. To save time getting to the Accademia, take bus #1, #6, #14, or #23 to Piazza San Marco. Taxis are a reasonable alternative; see "Getting Around Florence," page 401.

Daily Reminder

Sunday: The Duomo's dome, Museum of Precious Stones, and Mercato Centrale are closed. At the Church of Santa Maria Novella, the Museum and Cloisters are closed, but the church itself is open (11:00-17:00). These sights close early: Duomo Museum (at 13:40) and the Baptistery's interior (at 14:00). A few sights are open only in the afternoon: Duomo (13:30-16:45), Santa Croce Church (13:00-17:30), Church of San Lorenzo (13:30-17:00), Brancacci Chapel and Church of Santa Maria Novella (both 13:00-17:00), and Santo Spirito Church (15:00-17:30). The Museum of San Marco and the Bargello are closed on the first, third, and fifth Sundays of the month. Palazzo Davanzati and the Medici Chapels close on the second and fourth Sundays.

It's not possible to reserve tickets by phone on Sunday for the major sights (Accademia and Uffizi Gallery) because the telephone-reservation office for both is closed; try other options instead (see page 406 for details).

Monday: The biggies are closed, including the Accademia *(David)* and the Uffizi Gallery, as well as the Orsanmichele Church, and the Pitti Palace's Palatine Gallery, Royal Apartments, and Modern Art Gallery.

The Museum of San Marco and the Bargello close on the second and fourth Mondays. At the Pitti Palace, the Argenti Museum and the Boboli and Bardini Gardens close on the first and last Mondays. Palazzo Davanzati is closed on the first, third, and fifth Mondays. The San Lorenzo Market is closed Monday in winter.

Helpful Hints

Theft Alert: Florence has particularly hardworking thief gangs who hang out where you do: near the train station, the station's underpass (especially where the tunnel surfaces), and major sights. American tourists—especially older ones—are considered easy targets. Some thieves even dress like tourists to fool you. Also be on guard at two squares frequented by drug pushers (Santa Maria Novella and Santo Spirito). Bus #7 (to the nearby town of Fiesole, with great Florence views) is a favorite with tourists and, therefore, with thieves.

Pharmacies: There are 24-hour pharmacies at the train station and on Borgo San Lorenzo (near the Baptistery).

Reservations: To avoid standing in long lines, book ahead to visit the Accademia and Uffizi Gallery (see page 406 for details); you'll pay about a €4 booking fee, but it's worth it for the efficiency and peace of mind of having an assured entry time.

Price Hike Alert: Some of Florence's museums have found a clever way to squeeze more money out of visitors. They host a

Target these sights on Mondays: Duomo and its dome, Duomo Museum, Campanile, Baptistery, Medici-Riccardi Palace, Brancacci Chapel, Mercato Nuovo, Mercato Centrale, Casa Buonarroti, Galileo Science Museum, Palazzo Vecchio, and churches (including Santa Croce and Santa Maria Novella). Or take a walking tour.

Tuesday: All sights are open except Casa Buonarroti and the Brancacci Chapel. The Galileo Science Museum closes early (13:00).

Wednesday: All sights are open, except the Medici-Riccardi Palace and Santo Spirito Church.

Thursday: All sights are open. These sights close early: Duomo (15:30 in May and Oct, 16:30 in winter, 17:00 in summer) and Palazzo Vecchio (14:00).

Friday: All sights are open except the Museum and Cloisters at the Church of Santa Maria Novella (church open 11:00-17:30).

Saturday: All sights are open, but the Duomo's dome closes earlier than usual, at 17:40.

Early-Closing Warning: Some of Florence's sights close surprisingly early every day (or most days). Palazzo Davanzati closes daily at 13:50, the Museum of San Marco closes at 13:50 on weekdays (open later Sat and some Sun), and the Medici Chapels close at 13:50 in winter. The Museum of Precious Stones and Casa Buonarroti close at 14:00, as does the Mercato Centrale (except in winter, when it stays open until 17:00 on Sat).

special exhibit that few tourists really care to see and require you to pay extra for your ticket, even if all you want to see is the permanent collection.

Churches: Many churches now operate like museums, charging an admission fee to see their art treasures. Modest dress for men, women, and even children is required in some churches, and recommended for all of them—no bare shoulders, short shorts, or short skirts. Be respectful of worshippers and the paintings; don't use a flash. Churches usually close from 12:00 or 12:30 to 15:00 or 16:00.

Addresses: Street addresses list businesses in red and residences in black (color-coded on the actual street number and indicated by a letter following the number in printed addresses: "r" = red; no indication or "n" = black, for *nero*). The red and black numbers each appear in roughly consecutive order on streets but bear no apparent connection with each other. I'm lazy and don't concern myself with the distinction (if one number's wrong, I look for the other) and can easily find my way around.

Internet Access: In bustling, tourist-filled Florence, you'll see small Internet cafés on virtually every street (remember to bring your passport). **V.I.P. Internet** has cheap rates, numerous terminals, and long hours (€1.50/hour, daily 9:00-24:00, Via Faenza 49 red, tel. 055-264-5552). **Internet Train,** the dominant chain, is pricier, with bright and cheery rooms, speedy computers, and decent hours (€4.30/hour, cheaper for students, reusable card good for any other Internet Train location, open daily roughly 9:00-20:00, www.internettrain.it).

Find branches near Piazza della Repubblica (Via Porta Rossa 38 red), behind the Duomo (Via dell'Oriolo 40), on Piazza Santa Croce (Via de Benci 36 red), near *David* (Via Guelfa 54 red), and near Ponte Vecchio (Borgo San Jacopo 30 red). Internet Train also offers Wi-Fi, phone cards, CD-burning, and other related services.

Bookstores: Local guidebooks (sold at kiosks) are cheap and give you a map and a decent commentary on the sights. For brand-name guidebooks in English, try **Feltrinelli International** (Mon-Sat 9:00-19:30, closed Sun, a few blocks north of the Duomo and across the street from TI and Medici-Riccardi Palace at Via Cavour 12 red, tel. 055-219-524); **Edison Bookstore** (also has CDs, plus novels on the Renaissance and much more on its four floors; Mon-Sat 9:00-24:00, Sun 10:00-24:00, facing Piazza della Repubblica, tel. 055-213-110); **Paperback Exchange** (cheaper, all books in English, bring in your used book for a discount on a new one, Mon-Fri 9:00-19:30, Sat 10:30-19:30, closed Sun, just south of the Duomo on Via delle Oche 4 red, tel. 055-293-460); or **BM Bookshop** (with perhaps the city's largest collection of English books and guidebooks—including mine; Mon-Sat 9:30-19:30, closed Sun, near Ponte alla Carraia at Borgognissanti 4 red, tel. 055-294-575).

Maps: While the city is awash in free tourist maps, which work fine for most visits, if you want to invest in a durable, detailed, and smartly designed map, consider Rough Guide's *Map of Florence & Siena* (€9).

Travel Agency: Get train tickets, reservations, and supplements at travel agencies rather than at the congested train station. The cost is either the same or the charge is minimal.

Water: Carry a water bottle to refill at Florence's twist-the-handle public fountains.

Chill Out: Schedule several cool breaks into your sightseeing where you can sit, pause, and refresh yourself with a sandwich, gelato, or coffee.

Getting Around Florence

I organize my sightseeing geographically and do it all on foot. I think of Florence as a Renaissance treadmill—it requires a lot of walking.

Buses: The city's full-size buses don't cover the old center well, especially now that the whole area around the Duomo has been declared off-limits to motorized traffic. Of the many bus lines, I found these of most value for seeing outlying sights: Lines #12 and #13 go from the train station to Porta Romana, up to San Miniato Church and Piazzale Michelangelo, and on to Santa Croce.

Florence at a Glance

▲▲▲**Accademia** Michelangelo's *David* and powerful (unfinished) *Prisoners*. Reserve ahead. **Hours:** Tue-Sun 8:15-18:50, closed Mon. See page 453.

▲▲▲**Uffizi Gallery** Greatest collection of Italian paintings anywhere. Reserve at least one month in advance. **Hours:** Tue-Sun 8:15-18:50, closed Mon. See page 463.

▲▲▲**Duomo Museum** Underrated cathedral museum with sculptures. **Hours:** Mon-Sat 9:00-19:30, Sun 9:00-13:40. See page 459.

▲▲▲**Bargello** Underappreciated sculpture museum (Michelangelo, Donatello, Medici treasures). **Hours:** Tue-Sat April-Oct 8:15-16:50, Nov-March 8:15-13:50; also open first, third, and fifth Mon of each month and second and fourth Sun of each month. See page 460.

▲▲**Museum of San Marco** Best collection anywhere of artwork by the early Renaissance master Fra Angelico. **Hours:** Tue-Fri 8:15-13:50, Sat 8:15-16:50; also open 8:15-16:50 on second and fourth Sun and 8:15-13:50 on first, third, and fifth Mon of each month. See page 455.

▲▲**Medici Chapels** Tombs of Florence's great ruling family, designed and carved by Michelangelo. **Hours:** Tue-Sat April-Oct 8:15-16:50, Nov-March 8:15-13:50; also open first, third, and fifth Sun and second and fourth Mon of each month. See page 456.

▲▲**Duomo (Santa Maria del Fiore)** Gothic cathedral with colorful facade and the first dome built since ancient Roman times. **Hours:** Mon-Fri 10:00-17:00, Thu until 15:30 in May and Oct and until 16:30 in winter, Sat 10:00-16:45, Sun 13:30-16:45. See page 458.

▲▲**Galileo Science Museum** Fascinating old clocks, telescopes, maps, and Galileo's fingers. **Hours:** Wed-Mon 9:30-18:00, Tue 9:30-13:00. See page 463.

▲▲**Santa Croce Church** Precious art, tombs of famous Florentines, and Brunelleschi's Pazzi Chapel in 14th-century church. **Hours:** Mon-Sat 9:30-17:30, Sun 13:00-17:30. See page 464.

▲▲**Church of Santa Maria Novella** Thirteenth-century Dominican church with Masaccio's famous 3-D painting. **Hours:** Mon-Thu 9:00-17:30, Fri 11:00-17:30, Sat 9:00-17:00, Sun 13:00-17:00. See page 465.

▲▲**Pitti Palace** Several museums in lavish palace plus sprawling Boboli and Bardini Gardens. **Hours:** Palatine Gallery, Royal Apartments, and Modern Art Gallery: Tue-Sun 8:15-18:50, closed Mon; Argenti Museum, Costume Gallery, Porcelain Museum, and Boboli and Bardini Gardens: Daily 8:15-18:30, until 19:30 June-Aug, closed first and last Mon of the month, shorter hours in winter. See page 466.

▲▲**Brancacci Chapel** Works of Masaccio, early Renaissance master who reinvented perspective. **Hours:** Mon and Wed-Sat 10:00-17:00, Sun 13:00-17:00, closed Tue. Reservations required. See page 467.

▲▲**San Miniato Church** Sumptuous Renaissance chapel and sacristy showing scenes of St. Benedict. **Hours:** Daily April-Oct 8:00-19:30, Nov-March 8:00-13:00 & 14:30-18:00. See page 469.

▲**Medici-Riccardi Palace** Lorenzo the Magnificent's home, with fine art, frescoed ceilings, and Gozzoli's lovely Chapel of the Magi. **Hours:** Thu-Tue 9:00-19:00, closed Wed. See page 457.

▲**Climbing the Duomo's Dome** Grand view into the cathedral, close-up of dome architecture, and, after 463 steps, a glorious Florence vista. **Hours:** Mon-Fri 8:30-19:00, Sat 8:30-17:40, closed Sun. Long and slow lines, go early, no reservations accepted. See page 458.

▲**Campanile** Views similar to Duomo's, 50 fewer steps, and fewer lines. **Hours:** Daily 8:30-19:30. See page 459.

▲**Baptistery** Bronze doors fit to be the gates of paradise. **Hours:** Doors always viewable; interior open Mon-Sat 12:15-19:00 except first Sat of month 8:30-14:00, Sun 8:30-14:00. See page 459.

▲**Palazzo Vecchio** Fortified palace, once the home of the Medici family, wallpapered with history and Renaissance themes. **Hours:** Fri-Wed 9:00-19:00, Thu 9:00-14:00. See page 463.

▲**Ponte Vecchio** Famous bridge lined with shops selling gold and silver. **Hours:** Bridge always open (shops closed at night). See page 464.

▲**Casa Buonarroti** Early, lesser-known works by Michelangelo. **Hours:** Wed-Mon 9:30-14:00, closed Tue. See page 465.

▲**Piazzale Michelangelo** Hilltop square with stunning view of Duomo and Florence. **Hours:** Always open. See page 468.

Fun little *elettrico* **minibuses** wind through the tangled old center of town and up and down the river—just €1.20 gets you a 90-minute joyride. These buses, which run every 10 minutes, are popular with sore-footed sightseers and eccentric local seniors. *Elettrico* #C2 twists through the congested old center from the train station to Piazza Beccaria. *Elettrico* #C3 goes up and down the Arno River from Ognissanti to Santa Croce Church and beyond; #C1 winds around Piazza Repubblica, then heads north up to Piazza Libertà. *Elettrico* #D goes from the train station to Ponte Vecchio, cruising through Oltrarno, and finishing at Ponte San Niccolò. Routes are shown on the free TI map (see the handy inset) and the "La Rete dei Bussini Potenziata" leaflet, free at the ATAF bus office, located just east of the train station, on Piazza della Stazione.

Buy bus tickets at *tabacchi* (tobacco) shops, newsstands, or the ATAF bus office (€1.20/90 minutes, €4.50/4 tickets, validate in machine on the bus, tel. 800-424-500, www.ataf.net). You can buy tickets on board, but you'll pay more (€2) and you'll need exact change. Follow general bus etiquette: Board at front or rear doors, exit out the center.

Hop-on, hop-off bus tours stop at the major sights (see "Hop-on, Hop-off Bus Tours" on the next page).

Taxi: The minimum cost for a taxi ride is €5, or €6 after 22:00 and on Sundays (rides in the center of town should be charged as tariff #1). A taxi ride from the train station to Ponte Vecchio costs about €9. Taxi fares and supplements (e.g., €2 extra if you call a cab rather than hail one) are clearly explained on signs in each taxi.

Tours in Florence

For extra insight with a personal touch, consider the tour companies and individual Florentine guides listed here. They are hardworking, creative, and offer a worthwhile array of organized sightseeing activities. Study their websites for details. If you're taking a city tour, remember that individuals save money with a scheduled public tour (such as those offered daily by Artviva Tours of Florence, listed next). If you're traveling as a family or with a small group, however, you're likely to save money by booking a private guide (since rates are based on roughly €55/hour for any size of group).

Artviva Walking Tours—This company offers a variety of tours (up to 12/day year-round) featuring downtown Florence, museum highlights, and Tuscany day trips. Their guides are native English-speakers. The three-hour "Original Florence" walk hits the main sights but gets offbeat to weave a picture of Florentine life in medieval and Renaissance times. Tours go rain or shine with as few as four participants (€25, daily at 9:15). Museum tours include the Uffizi (€39, includes admission, 2 hours), Accademia (called "Original *David*" tour, €35, includes admission, 1 hour), and "Original Florence in One Day" (€94, includes admission to Uffizi and Accademia, 6 hours).

Reservations are necessary for all tours and talks. For specifics and schedules, pick up their extensive brochure in a hotel lobby or their office (Mon-Sat 8:00-18:00, Sun 8:30-13:30 but off-season closed Sun and for lunch, near Piazza della Repubblica at Via dei Sassetti 1, second floor, above Odeon Cinema, tel. 055-264-5033 during day or mobile 329-613-2730 18:00-20:00, www.italy .artviva.com, staff@artviva.com).

Florentia—Top-notch private walking tours—geared for thoughtful, well-heeled travelers with longer-than-average attention spans—are led by Florentine scholars. The tours range from introductory city walks and museum visits to in-depth thematic walks, such as the Oltrarno neighborhood, "Unusual Florence," and side-trips into Tuscany (tours-€175/half-day, €350/day, reserve in advance, tel. 338-890-8625, www.florentia.org, info@florentia .org).

Context Florence—This scholarly group of graduate students and professors leads "walking seminars," such as a three-hour study of Michelangelo's work and influence (€85/person, includes Accademia admission). I enjoyed the fascinating three-hour fresco workshop (€75/person, you take home a fresco you make yourself). See their website for other innovative offerings: Medici walk, lecture series, food walks, kids' tours, and programs in Venice, Rome, Naples, London, and Paris (tel. 069-762-5204, US tel. 888-467-1986, www.contexttravel.com, info@contexttravel.com).

Local Guides—Good guides include **Paola Barubiani** and her art historian partners at Walks Inside Florence (€55/hour for up to 4 people, €50/person for small-group 3-hour tour, €165/group of 2-6 people for private 3-hour tour, special rates for family tours, ask about Rick Steves discount, mobile 335-526-6496, www.walksinsideflorence.com, paola@walksinsideflorence .it). **Alessandra Marchetti,** a Florentine who has lived in the US, gives private walking tours of Florence and driving tours of Tuscany (€60-75/hour, mobile 347-386-9839, aleoberm@tin .it). **Paola Migliorini** and her partners at Tuscany Tours offer museum tours, city walking tours, private cooking classes, wine tours, and Tuscan excursions by van—you can tailor tours as you like (€55/hour without car, €65/hour in an 8-seat van, tel. 055-472-448, mobile 347-657-2611, www.florencetour.com, info @florencetour.com).

Hop-on, Hop-off Bus Tours—Around town, you'll see big double-decker sightseeing buses double-parking near major

FLORENCE

Make Reservations to Avoid Lines

Florence has an optional reservation system for its state-run sights, which include the Accademia, Uffizi Gallery, Bargello, Medici Chapels, and Pitti Palace. I highly recommend getting reservations for the Accademia (Michelangelo's *David*) and the Uffizi (Renaissance paintings), but not the others.

The Brancacci Chapel is the only sight in Florence that requires reservations. These are free and simple to make. If possible, call at least a day in advance and sign up for the film, too. Sometimes same-day reservations are available (tel. 055-276-8224 or 055-276-8558, English spoken, call center open daily 9:00-17:00). For more information, see page 467.

The Uffizi and Accademia

Your best strategy is to get reservations for these two top sights as soon as you know when you'll be in town. Although you can generally get an entry time for the Accademia within a few days, the Uffizi can be booked more than a month in advance.

There are several ways to make a reservation: Call the reservation number directly, book online, take a tour, or go in person in advance to the museums or the Orsanmichele Church ticket window. Here are details on the options:

• Reserve by **phone** before you leave the States (from the US, dial 011-39-055-294-883, or within Italy call 055-294-883; €4/ticket reservation fee; booking office open Mon-Fri 8:30-18:30, Sat 8:30-12:30, closed Sun). The reservation line

sights. Tourists on the top deck can listen to brief recorded descriptions of the sights, snap photos, and enjoy an effortless drive-by look at the major landmarks. Tickets cost €22, are valid for two days, and include two bus lines. Line A takes one hour with a trip up to Piazzale Michelangelo; Line B takes two hours with a side-trip to Fiesole (first bus at 9:30, last bus at 18:00, pay as you board, www.firenze.city-sightseeing.it). As the name implies, you can hop off when you want and catch the next bus (usually every 30 minutes, depending on the season). Hop-on stops include the train station and Pitti Palace. As most sights are buried in the old center where big buses can't go, Florence doesn't really lend itself to this kind of tour bus. Look at the route map before committing.

is often busy, and even if you get through, you may be dis-connected while on hold. Be persistent and try again. When you do get through, an English-speaking operator walks you through the process, and a few minutes later you say *grazie*, with an appointment and a six-digit confirmation number. Bring the confirmation(s) with you and pay cash at the sight(s). The advantage to phoning versus booking online is that you pay nothing upfront when you phone.

- Using a credit card, you can reserve your visit **online.** Pricey middleman sites—such as www.uffizi.com and www.tickitaly .com—are reliable, but their booking fees are exorbitant, run-ning about €10 per ticket. Or you could take your chances with the city's troublesome official site (www.firenzemusei .it) in the hopes that its glitches have been fixed. It's the cheapest place to make reservations online (€4/ticket reser-vation fee), but even when it's working, the site often reverts to Italian-only (*"Annulia Operazione"* means "cancel"), you can't book a time before noon, and some readers report not receiving vouchers they've paid for.

- Take a **tour** that includes your museum admission. Artviva Walking Tours offers tours of the Uffizi (€39/person, 2 hours), Accademia (€35/person, 1 hour), and both museums (€94/person, 6 hours; see listing on page 404, or visit www .italy.artviva.com).

- To **reserve in Florence:** call the reservation number (see above) or head to the booking window at Orsanmichele Church (€4 reservation fee, daily 10:00-17:00, along Via Calzaiuoli—see location on map on page 421). For another Uffizi option, go to its ticket office and pay cash (Tue-Sun 8:15-18:50, use the *Main Entrance*—door #2, enter to the left of the line).

Self-Guided Walks & Tours in Florence

Florence is a walker's paradise—and it's even better now that traffic has been banned from the area near the Duomo. What follows are guided tours of two of my favorite museums: the Accademia (Michelangelo's *David*) and the Uffizi (world's best Italian paintings), linked by a two-hour stroll through the heart of Florence.

Free Audio Tours: You can download free audio versions of these tours at www.ricksteves.com/audioeurope, from iTunes, or through the Rick Steves Audio Europe smartphone app.

Accademia Tour:
Michelangelo's *David*

One of Europe's great thrills is actually seeing Michelangelo's *David* in the flesh. Seventeen feet high, gleaming white, and exalted by a halo-like dome over his head, *David* rarely disappoints, even for those with high expectations. And the Galleria dell'Accademia doesn't stop there. With a handful of other Michelangelo statues and a few other interesting sights, it makes for an uplifting visit that isn't overwhelming. *David* is a must-see on any visit to Florence, so plan for it (and consider reserving an entry time—see page 406 for info).

Orientation

Cost: €6.50 (plus €4 fee for recommended reservation).

Hours: Tue-Sun 8:15-18:50, closed Mon, last entry 45 minutes before closing.

Reservations: It's smart to reserve ahead. For details on all of your reservation options, see page 406. Reservation-holders should line up at the entrance labeled *With Reservations*. On off-season weekdays (Oct-March) before 8:30 or after 16:00, you can sometimes get in with no reservation and no lines.

When to Go: In peak season, the museum is most crowded on Sun, Tue, and right when it opens.

Getting There: It's at Via Ricasoli 60, a 15-minute walk from the train station or a 10-minute walk northeast of the Duomo. Taxis are reasonable.

Information: Exhibits are explained in English, and a small bookstore sells guidebooks near the ticket booths at the entrance. Several shops outside the museum sell postcards, books, and posters. Museum tel. 055-238-8609 or 055-294-883, www .polomuseale.firenze.it.

Audioguides: The museum rents a €5.50 audioguide (€8/2 people). Remember that you can download a free audio tour of this sight (see page 48).

Length of This Tour: While *David* and the *Prisoners* can be seen in 30 minutes, allow an hour if you wish to linger and explore other parts of the museum.

Services: The WCs are downstairs near the entrance/exit.

Photography: Photos and videos are prohibited.

Cuisine Art: Gelateria Carabè, popular for its sumptuous *granita* (Italian ice) is a block toward the Duomo, at Via Ricasoli

FLORENCE

Accademia Overview

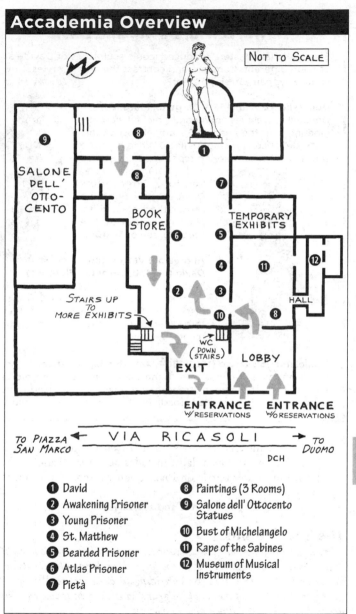

NOT TO SCALE

SALONE DELL' OTTO-CENTO

BOOK STORE

TEMPORARY EXHIBITS

STAIRS UP TO MORE EXHIBITS →

WC (DOWN STAIRS)

HALL

LOBBY

EXIT

ENTRANCE w/ RESERVATIONS

ENTRANCE w/o RESERVATIONS

TO PIAZZA SAN MARCO ← **VIA RICASOLI** → TO DUOMO

DCH

FLORENCE

❶ David
❷ Awakening Prisoner
❸ Young Prisoner
❹ St. Matthew
❺ Bearded Prisoner
❻ Atlas Prisoner
❼ Pietà

❽ Paintings (3 Rooms)
❾ Salone dell' Ottocento Statues
❿ Bust of Michelangelo
⓫ Rape of the Sabines
⓬ Museum of Musical Instruments

David, David, David, and *David*

Several Italian masters produced iconic sculptures of David—all of them different. Compare and contrast the artists' styles. How many ways can you slay a giant?

Donatello's *David* (1430, Bargello, Florence)
Donatello's *David* is young and graceful, casually gloating over the head of Goliath, almost Gothic in its elegance and smooth lines. While he has a similar weight-on-one-leg *(contrapposto)* stance

as Michelangelo's later version, Donatello's *David* seems feminine rather than masculine. (For more about the Bargello, see page 406.)

Andrea del Verrocchio's *David* (c. 1470, Bargello, Florence)
Wearing a military skirt and armed with a small sword, Verrocchio's *David* is just a boy. The statue is only four feet tall—dwarfed by Michelangelo's monumental version.

Michelangelo's *David* (1501–1504, Accademia, Florence)
Michelangelo's *David* is pure Renaissance: massive, heroic in size, and superhuman in strength and power. The tensed right hand, which grips a stone in readiness to hurl at Goliath, is more

60 red. Picnickers can stock up at Il Centro Supermercati, a half-block north (open daily, includes deli, Via Ricasoli 109). I refill my water bottle on Piazza San Marco, in the traffic circle park.

Starring: Michelangelo's *David* and *Prisoners.*

The Tour Begins

• *From the entrance lobby, show your ticket, turn left, and look right down the long hall with* David *at the far end, under a halo-like dome. Yes, you're really here. With* David *presiding at the "altar," the* Prisoners *lining the "nave," and hordes of "pilgrims" crowding in to look, you've arrived at Florence's "cathedral of humanism."*

Start with the ultimate...

David (1501-1504)

When you look into the eyes of Michelangelo's *David,* you're looking into the eyes of Renaissance man. This 17-foot-tall

powerful than any human hand. It's symbolic of divine strength. A model of perfection, Michelangelo's *David* is far larger and grander than we mere mortals. We know he'll win. Renaissance man has arrived.

Gian Lorenzo Bernini's *David* (1623, Borghese Museum, Rome)

Flash forward more than a century. In this self-portrait, 25-year-old Bernini is ready to take on the world, slay the pretty-boy *David*s of the Renaissance, and invent Baroque. Unlike Michelangelo's rational, cool, restrained *David*, Bernini's is a doer: passionate, engaged, dramatic. While Renaissance *David* is simple and unadorned—carrying only a sling— Baroque Dave is "cluttered" with a braided sling, a hairy pouch, flowing cloth, and discarded armor. Bernini's *David*, with his tousled hair and set mouth, is one of us; the contest is less certain than with the other three *David*s.

To sum up: Donatello's *David* represents the first inkling of the Renaissance; Verrocchio's is early Renaissance in miniature; Michelangelo's is textbook Renaissance; and Bernini's is the epitome of Baroque.

symbol of divine victory over evil represents a new century and a whole new Renaissance outlook. This is the age of Columbus and classicism, Galileo and Gutenberg, Luther and Leonardo—of Florence and the Renaissance.

In 1501, Michelangelo Buonarroti, a 26-year-old Florentine, was commissioned to carve a large-scale work for the Duomo. He was given a block of marble that other sculptors had rejected as too tall, shallow, and flawed to be of any value. But Michelangelo picked up his hammer and chisel, knocked a knot off what became *David*'s heart, and started to work.

The figure comes from a Bible story. The Israelites, God's chosen people, are surrounded by barbarian warriors led by a brutish giant named Goliath. The giant challenges the Israelites to

FLORENCE

send out someone to fight him. Everyone is afraid except for one young shepherd boy—David. Armed only with a sling, which he's thrown over his shoulder, David gathers five smooth stones from the stream and faces Goliath.

The statue captures David as he's sizing up his enemy. He stands relaxed but alert, leaning on one leg in a classical pose known as *contrapposto*. In his powerful right hand, he fondles the handle of the sling, ready to fling a stone at the giant. His gaze is steady—searching with intense concentration, but also with extreme confidence. Michelangelo has caught the precise moment when David is saying to himself, "I can take this guy."

Note that while the label on *David* indicates that he's already slain the giant, the current director of the Accademia believes, as I do, that Michelangelo has portrayed David facing the giant. Unlike most depictions of David after the kill, this sculpture does not show the giant's severed head. There's also a question of exactly how David's sling would work. Is he holding the stone in his right or left hand? Does the right hand hold the sling's pouch or the retention handle of a sling? Scholars debate Sling Theory endlessly.

David is a symbol of Renaissance optimism. He's no brute. He's a civilized, thinking individual who can grapple with and overcome problems. He needs no armor, only his God-given body and wits. Look at his right hand, with the raised veins and strong, relaxed fingers—many complained that it was too big and overdeveloped. But this is the hand of a man with the strength of God. No mere boy could slay the giant. But David, powered by God, could...and did.

Originally, the statue was commissioned to stand along the southern roofline of the Duomo. But during the three years it took to sculpt, they decided instead to place it guarding the entrance of

the Town Hall, or Palazzo Vecchio. (If the relationship between *David*'s head and body seems a bit out of proportion, it's because Michelangelo designed it to be seen "correctly" from far below the rooftop of the church.)

The colossus was placed standing up in a cart and dragged across rollers from Michelangelo's workshop (behind the Duomo) to the Palazzo Vecchio, where the statue replaced a work by Donatello. There *David* stood—naked and outdoors—for 350 years. In the right light, you can see signs of weathering on his shoulders. Also, note the crack in *David*'s left arm where it was broken off during a 1527 riot near the Palazzo Vecchio. In 1873, to conserve the masterpiece, the statue was finally replaced with a copy and moved here. The real *David* now stands under a wonderful Renaissance-style dome designed just for him.

Circle *David* and view him from various angles. From the front, he's confident, but a little less so when you gaze directly into his eyes. Around back, see his sling strap, buns of steel, and Renaissance mullet. Up close, you can see the blue-veined Carrara marble and a few cracks and stains. From the sides, Michelangelo's challenge becomes clear: to sculpt a figure from a block of marble other sculptors said was too tall and narrow to accommodate a human figure.

Renaissance Florentines could identify with *David*. Like him, they considered themselves God-blessed underdogs fighting their city-state rivals. In a deeper sense, they were civilized Renaissance people slaying the ugly giant of medieval superstition, pessimism, and oppression.

• *Hang around a while. Eavesdrop on tour guides. The Plexiglas shields at the base of the statue went up after an attack by a frustrated artist, who smashed the statue's feet in 1991.*

Lining the hall leading up to David *are other statues by Michelangelo—his* Prisoners, St. Matthew, *and* Pietà. *Start with the* Awakening Prisoner, *the statue at the far end of the nave (farthest from* David*). He's on your left as you face* David.

The *Prisoners* (*Prigioni,* c. 1516-1534)

These unfinished figures seem to be fighting to free themselves from the stone. Michelangelo believed the sculptor was a tool of God, not creating but simply revealing the powerful and beautiful figures that God had encased in the marble. Michelangelo's job was to chip away the excess, to reveal. He needed to be in tune with God's will, and whenever the spirit came upon him, Michelangelo worked in a frenzy, without sleep, often for days on end.

The *Prisoners* give us a glimpse of this fitful process, showing the restless energy of someone possessed, struggling against the rock that binds him. Michelangelo himself fought to create the image he saw in his mind's eye. You can still see the grooves from the chisel, and you can picture Michelangelo hacking away in a cloud of dust. Unlike most sculptors, who built a model and then marked up their block of marble to know

FLORENCE

where to chip, Michelangelo always worked freehand, starting from the front and working back. These figures emerge from the stone (as his colleague Vasari put it) "as though surfacing from a pool of water."

The so-called *Awakening Prisoner* (the names are given by scholars, not Michelangelo) seems to be stretching after a long nap, still tangled in the "bedsheets" of uncarved rock. He's more block than statue.

On the right, the *Young Prisoner* is more finished. He buries his face in his forearm, while his other arm is chained behind him.

The *Prisoners* were designed for the never-completed tomb of Pope Julius II (who also commissioned the Sistine Chapel ceiling). Michelangelo may have abandoned them simply because the project itself petered out, but he may have deliberately left them unfinished. Having satisfied himself that he'd accomplished what he set out to do, and seeing no point in polishing them into their shiny, finished state, he went on to a new project.

Walking up the nave toward *David*, you'll pass by Michelangelo's **St. Matthew** (1503). Though not one of the *Prisoners* series, he is also unfinished, perfectly illustrating Vasari's "surfacing" description.

The next statue, the *Bearded Prisoner,* is the most finished of the four, with all four limbs, a bushy face, and even a hint of daylight between his arm and body.

Across the nave on the left, the *Atlas Prisoner* carries the unfinished marble on his stooped shoulders, his head still encased in the block.

As you study the *Prisoners,* notice Michelangelo's love and understanding of the human body. His greatest days were spent sketching the muscular, tanned, and sweating bodies of the workers in the Carrara marble quarries. The prisoners' heads and faces are the least-developed part—they "speak" with their poses. Comparing the restless, claustrophobic *Prisoners* with the serene and confident *David* gives an idea of the sheer emotional range in Michelangelo's work.

Pietà

In the unfinished *Pietà* (the threesome closest to *David*), the figures struggle to hold up the sagging body of Christ. Michelangelo (or, more likely, one of his followers) emphasizes the heaviness of Jesus' dead body, driving home the point that this divine being suffered a very human death. Christ's massive arm is almost the size of his bent and broken legs. By stretching his body—if he stood up, he'd be more than seven feet tall—the weight is exaggerated.

• *After getting your fill of Michelangelo, consider taking a spin around the rest of the Accademia. Michelangelo's statues are far and away the highlight here, but the rest of this small museum—housed in a former convent/hospice—has a few bonuses.*

Paintings

Browse the pleasant-but-underwhelming collection of paintings in the hall near *David* and the adjoining corridor; you'll be hard-pressed to find even one by a painter whose name you recognize. (You'll find better art in the Giambologna Room near the exit; described below.) Upstairs (climb the stairs near the exit), there's a collection of icons.

Salone dell'Ottocento Statues

At the end of the hall to the left of *David* is a long room crammed with plaster statues and busts. These were the Academy art students' "final exams"—preparatory models for statues, many of which were later executed in marble. The black dots on the statues are sculptors' "points," guiding them on how deep to chisel. The Academy art school has been attached to the museum for centuries, and you may see the next Michelangelo wandering the streets nearby.

Bust of Michelangelo by Da Volterra

At the end of the nave (farthest from *David*), a bronze bust depicts a craggy, wrinkled Michelangelo, age 89, by Daniele da Volterra. (Da Volterra, one of Michelangelo's colleagues and friends, is best known as the one who painted loincloths on the private parts of Michelangelo's nudes in the Sistine Chapel.) As a teenager, Michelangelo got his nose broken in a fight with a rival artist. Though Michelangelo went on to create great beauty, he was never classically handsome.

• *Enter the room near the museum entrance dominated by a large, squirming statue.*

Giambologna Room—*Rape of the Sabines* (1582)

This full-size plaster model guided the Giambologna's assistants in completing the marble version in the Loggia (next to the Palazzo Vecchio, described on page 429). A Roman warrior tramples a fighter from the Sabine tribe and carries off the man's wife. Husband and wife exchange one final, anguished glance. Circle the statue and watch it spiral around its axis. Giambologna was clearly influenced (as a plaque with photo points out) by

Michelangelo's groundbreaking *Victory* in the Palazzo Vecchio (1533-1534, described on page 463). Michelangelo's statue of a man triumphing over a fallen enemy introduced both the theme and the spiral-shaped pose that many artists imitated.

The room also contains minor paintings by artists you'll encounter elsewhere in Florence: Botticelli (whose *Birth of Venus* hangs in the Uffizi), Filippino Lippi (whose work appears in the Brancacci Chapel and Church of Santa Maria Novella), Domenico Ghirlandaio (Church of Santa Maria Novella), Fra Bartolomeo (Museum of San Marco), and Benozzo Gozzoli (Medici-Riccardi Palace).

• *From the Giambologna Room, head down a short hallway leading to a few rooms containing...*

The Museum of Musical Instruments

Between 1400 and 1700, Florence was one of Europe's most sophisticated cities, and the Medici rulers were trendsetters. Musicians like Scarlatti and Handel flocked to the court of Prince Ferdinando (1663-1713). You'll see late-Renaissance cellos, dulcimers, violins, woodwinds, and harpsichords. (Listen to some on the computer terminals.)

As you enter, look for the two paintings of the prince (he's second from the right in both paintings, with the yellow bowtie) hanging out with his musician friends. The gay prince played a mean harpsichord, and he helped pioneer new variations. In the adjoining room, you'll see several experimental keyboards, including some by Florence's keyboard pioneer, Bartolomeo Cristofori. The tall piano on display (from 1739) is considered by some to be the world's first upright piano.

• *The tour is finished. From here, it's a 10-minute walk to the Duomo— the starting point of my Florence Renaissance Walk (next).*

Florence Renaissance Walk

From the Duomo to the Arno River

After centuries of labor, Florence gave birth to the Renaissance. We'll start with the soaring church dome that stands as the proud symbol of the Renaissance spirit. Next door, you'll find the Baptistery doors that opened the Renaissance. Finally, we'll reach Florence's political center, dotted with monuments of that proud time. Great and rich as this city is, it's easily covered on foot. This walk through the top sights is less than a mile long, running from the Duomo to the Arno River.

Renaissance Walk

TO S. MARCO

TO ACCADEMIA (DAVID)

V. ALFANI

MEDICI CHAPELS

STREET MKT.

MEDICI-RICCARDI PALACE

TO TRAIN STN.

SERVI

V. PUCCI

LEONARDO MUSEUM

GIGLIO

PANZ.

SAN LORENZO

B.S. LOR.

MARTELLI

RICASOLI

DUOMO

DUOMO MUSEUM

CERRETANI

BAPT.

START

CAMPANILE

ORIUOLO

AGLI

PEC.

TOSINGHI

S. MARIA RICCI

CASA DI DANTE

STROZZI

PZZA. REP.

SPEZ.

CORSO

TAVO. DANTE

BARGELLO

ORSAN-MICHELE

CALZAIUOLI

PROCO.

VIA

V. G. VECCHIA

PORTA ROSSA

CONDOTTA

V. PAL. DAVAN-ZATI

TERME

COV. MKT.

MARIA

VACC.

PIAZZA SIGNORIA

ANG.

B.S. APOST.

BORGO GRECI

PALAZZO VECCHIO

TO SANTA CROCE

FINISH

ACCIAIUOLI

EXIT

GALILEO SCIENCE MUSEUM

D. NERI

V. BENCI

BORGO S. CROCE

TINT.

S. JAC.

GUICC.

PONTE VECCHIO

UFFIZI GALLERY

LUNG. DIAZ

ARNO

DCH

TO PITTI PALACE

ENTRY POINT TO SIGHTS

VIEW

200 YARDS

200 METERS

FLORENCE

Orientation

Duomo (Cathedral): Free, Mon-Fri 10:00-17:00, Thu until 15:30 in May and Oct and until 16:30 in winter, Sat 10:00-16:45, Sun 13:30-16:45. A modest dress code is enforced. Tel. 055-230-2885, www.operaduomo.firenze.it.

Climbing the Dome: €8, Mon-Fri 8:30-19:00, Sat 8:30-17:40, closed Sun, last entry 40 minutes before closing. Enter from outside the church on the north side.

Tip for Cathedral and Dome Visit: Whenever you decide to visit the cathedral and dome, you can avoid a long wait in line by taking the €15 "Terraces of the Cathedral and Dome" tour; see page 458.

Campanile (Giotto's Tower): €6, daily 8:30-19:30, last entry 40 minutes before closing.

Baptistery: €4, interior open Mon-Sat 12:15-19:00 except first Sat of month 8:30-14:00, Sun 8:30-14:00, last entry 30 minutes before closing, audioguide-€2, tel. 055-230-2885. The famous bronze doors are on the outside so they're always "open" (viewable) and free. The original panels are in the Duomo Museum.

Medici-Riccardi Palace: €5, €7 with mandatory special exhibits, Thu-Tue 9:00-19:00, last entry 30 minutes before closing, closed Wed, Via Cavour 3, tel. 055-276-0340.

Orsanmichele Church: Free, Tue-Sun 10:00-17:00, closed Mon. The niche sculptures are always viewable from the outside. At the ticket window, you can book tickets for the Uffizi and Accademia.

Information: The nearest TI is on Via Cavour, two blocks north of the Duomo (ask for updates of museum hours).

Length of This Tour: Allow two hours for the walk, including interior visits of the Baptistery and Orsanmichele Church (but not the other sights mentioned).

Services: Many cafés along the walk have WCs. You can refill your water bottle at public twist-the-handle fountains at the Duomo (left side, by the dome entrance) and the Palazzo Vecchio (behind the Neptune fountain).

Photography: In churches and other sights along this walk, photos without a flash are generally OK.

Cuisine Art: You'll find plenty of cafés, self-service cafeterias, bars, and gelato shops along the route. Some good eateries along this walk are described later in "Eating in Florence," including Self-Service Ristorante Leonardo (closed Sat, a block from the Duomo, southwest of the Baptistery, Via Pecori 11) and the famous L'Antico Trippaio tripe-selling sandwich cart a block east of Orsanmichele. For an inexpensive drink and sandwich a half-block north of the Duomo, sneak up to the quiet upstairs café at the Libreria Martelli bookstore (26 Via de' Martelli).

Starring: Brunelleschi's dome, Ghiberti's doors, the Medicis' palaces, and the city of Florence—old and new.

The Tour Begins
Overview

The Duomo, the cathedral with the distinctive red dome, is the center of Florence and the orientation point for this walk. If you ever get lost, home's the dome. We'll start here, see several sights in the area, and then stroll down the city's pedestrian-only main street to the Palazzo Vecchio and the Arno River. Consider prefacing this walk with a visit to the ultimate Renaissance man: Michelangelo's *David* (see "Accademia Tour," page 408).

The Florentine Renaissance (1400-1550)

In the 13th and 14th centuries, Florence was a powerful center of banking, trading, and textile manufacturing. The resulting wealth fertilized the cultural soil. Then came the Black Death in 1348. Nearly half of the population died, but the infrastructure remained strong, and the city rebuilt better than ever. Led by Florence's chief family—the art-crazy Medicis—and propelled by the naturally aggressive and creative spirit of the Florentines, it's no wonder that the long-awaited Renaissance finally took root here.

The Renaissance—the "rebirth" of Greek and Roman culture that swept across Europe—started around 1400 and lasted about 150 years. In politics, the Renaissance meant democracy; in science, a renewed interest in exploring nature. The general mood was optimistic and "humanistic," with a confidence in the power of the individual.

In medieval times, poverty and ignorance had made life "nasty, brutish, and short" (for lack of a better cliché). The church was the people's opiate, and their lives were only a preparation for a happier time in heaven after leaving this miserable vale of tears.

Medieval art was the church's servant. The noblest art form was architecture—churches themselves—and other arts were considered most worthwhile if they embellished the house of God. Painting and sculpture were narrative and symbolic, designed to tell Bible stories to the devout and illiterate masses.

As prosperity rose in Florence, so did people's confidence in life and themselves. Middle-class craftsmen, merchants, and bankers felt they could control their own destinies, rather than be at the whim of nature. They found much in common with the ancient Greeks and Romans, who valued logic and reason above superstition and blind faith.

Renaissance art was a return to the realism and balance of Greek and Roman sculpture and architecture. Domes and

round arches replaced Gothic spires and pointed arches. In painting and sculpture, Renaissance artists strove for realism. Merging art and science, they used mathematics, the laws of perspective, and direct observation of nature to paint the world on a flat surface.

This was not an anti-Christian movement, though it was a logical and scientific age. Artists saw themselves as an extension of God's creative powers. At times, the church even supported the Renaissance and commissioned many of its greatest works—for instance, Raphael frescoed images of Plato and Aristotle on the walls of the Vatican. But for the first time in Europe since Roman times, there were rich laymen who wanted art simply for art's sake.

After 1,000 years of waiting, the smoldering fires of Europe's classical heritage burst into flames in Florence.

• *The dome of the Duomo is best viewed just to the right of the facade, from the corner of the pedestrian-only street.*

FLORENCE

The Duomo—Florence's Cathedral

The dome of Florence's cathedral—visible from all over the city—inspired Florentines to do great things. (Most recently, it inspired

the city to make the area around the cathedral delightfully traffic-free.) The big church itself (called the Duomo) is Gothic, built in the Middle Ages by architects who left it unfinished.

Think of the confidence of the age: The Duomo was built with a big hole in its roof, just waiting for a grand dome to cover it...but the technology needed to create such a dome had yet to be invented. *No problema.* They knew that someone would soon be able to handle the challenge. In the 1400s, the architect Filippo Brunelleschi was called on to finish

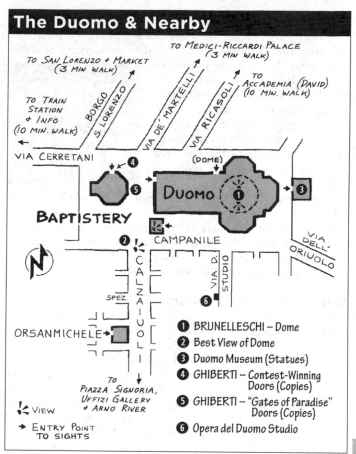

The Duomo & Nearby

TO MEDICI-RICCARDI PALACE (3 MIN. WALK)

TO SAN LORENZO & MARKET (3 MIN. WALK)

TO TRAIN STATION & INFO (10 MIN. WALK)

TO ACCADEMIA (DAVID) (10 MIN. WALK)

BORGO S. LORENZO

VIA DE' MARTELLI

VIA RICASOLI

VIA CERRETANI

(DOME)

DUOMO

BAPTISTERY

CAMPANILE

VIA DELL' ORIUOLO

N

CALZAIUOLI

VIA D. STUDIO

SPEZ.

ORSANMICHELE→

TO PIAZZA SIGNORIA, UFFIZI GALLERY & ARNO RIVER

VIEW

ENTRY POINT TO SIGHTS

① BRUNELLESCHI – Dome
② Best View of Dome
③ Duomo Museum (Statues)
④ GHIBERTI – Contest-Winning Doors (Copies)
⑤ GHIBERTI – "Gates of Paradise" Doors (Copies)
⑥ Opera del Duomo Studio

FLORENCE

the job. Brunelleschi capped the church Roman-style—with a tall, self-supporting dome as grand as the ancient Pantheon's (which he had studied).

He used a dome within a dome. First, he built the grand white skeletal ribs, which you can see, then filled them in with interlocking bricks in a herringbone pattern. The dome grew upward like an igloo, supporting itself as it proceeded from the base. When they reached the top, Brunelleschi arched the ribs in and fixed them in place with the lantern. His dome, built in only 14 years, was the largest since Rome's Pantheon.

Brunelleschi's dome was the wonder of the age, the model for many domes to follow, from St. Peter's to the US Capitol. People gave it the ultimate compliment, saying, "Not even the ancients could have done it." Michelangelo, setting out to construct the dome of St. Peter's, drew inspiration from the dome of Florence.

He said, "I'll make its sister...bigger, but not more beautiful."

The church's facade looks old, but is actually Neo-Gothic—only from 1870. The facade was rushed to completion (about 600 years after the building began) to celebrate Italian unity, here in the city that for a few years served as the young country's capital. Its "retro" look captures the feel of the original medieval facade, with green, white, and pink marble sheets that cover the brick construction; Gothic (pointed) arches; and three horizontal stories decorated with mosaics and statues. Still, the facade is generally ridiculed.

The interior feels bare after being cleaned out during the Neoclassical age and by the terrible flood of 1966 (free entry, but not worth a long wait). To climb the dome (€8), enter from outside the church on the north side (see page 458).

Campanile (Giotto's Tower)

The bell tower (to the right of the facade) offers an easier, less crowded, and faster climb than the Duomo's dome (€6), though the unobstructed views from the Duomo are better. Giotto, like any good Renaissance genius, wore several artistic hats. Considered the father of modern painting, he designed this 270-foot-tall bell tower for the Duomo two centuries before the age of Michelangelo. In his day, Giotto was called the ugliest man to ever walk the streets of Florence, but he designed for the city what many in our day call the most beautiful bell tower in all of Europe.

The bell tower served as a sculpture gallery for Renaissance artists—notice Donatello's four prophets on the side that faces out (west). These are copies—the originals are at the wonderful Duomo Museum, just behind the church (see page 459). In the museum, you'll also get a close-up look at Brunelleschi's wooden model of his dome, Ghiberti's doors (described next), and a late *Pietà* by Michelangelo. A couple of blocks away, at the Opera del Duomo Studio, workers sculpt and restore statues for the cathedral (Via dello Studio 23a—you can peek through the doorway).

• *The Baptistery is the small octagonal building in front of the church.*

Ghiberti's Bronze Doors

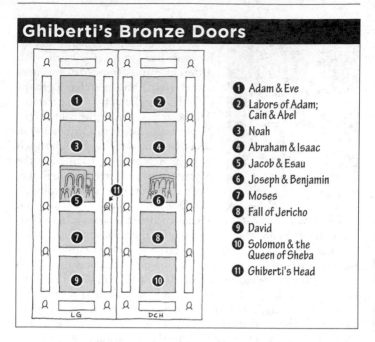

1. Adam & Eve
2. Labors of Adam; Cain & Abel
3. Noah
4. Abraham & Isaac
5. Jacob & Esau
6. Joseph & Benjamin
7. Moses
8. Fall of Jericho
9. David
10. Solomon & the Queen of Sheba
11. Ghiberti's Head

Baptistery and Ghiberti's Bronze Doors

Florence's Baptistery is dear to the soul of the city. In medieval and Renaissance times, the locals—eager to link themselves to the classical past—believed (wrongly) that this was a Roman building. It is, however, Florence's oldest building (11th century). Most festivals and parades either started or ended here.

Interior: For a modest €4 fee, you'll see a fine example of pre-Renaissance mosaic art (1200s-1300s) in the Byzantine style. Workers from St. Mark's in Venice came here to make the remarkable ceiling mosaics (of Venetian glass) in the late 1200s.

The Last Judgment on the ceiling gives us a glimpse of the medieval worldview. Life was a preparation for the afterlife, when you would be judged and saved, or damned, with no in-between. Christ, peaceful and reassuring, would bless you with heaven (on his right hand, thumbs up) or send you to hell (below Christ's ultimate thumbs down) to be tortured by demons and gnashed between the teeth of monsters. This hellish scene looks like something right out of the *Inferno* by Dante...who was dipped into the baptismal waters right here.

Doors: The Baptistery's bronze doors bring us out of the Middle Ages and into the Renaissance. Some say the Renaissance began precisely in the year 1401, when Florence staged a competition to find the best artist to create the Baptistery's north doors (on

the right side as you face the Baptistery with the Duomo at your back). Florence had strong civic spirit, with different guilds (powerful business associations) and merchant groups embellishing their city with great art. All the greats entered the contest, but 25-year-old Lorenzo Ghiberti won easily, beating out heavyweights such as Brunelleschi (who, having lost the Baptistery gig, was free to go to Rome, study the Pantheon, and later design the Duomo's dome). The original entries of Brunelleschi and Ghiberti are in the Bargello, where you can judge them for yourself.

Later, in 1425, Ghiberti was given another commission, for the east doors (facing the church). This time there was literally no contest. The bronze panels of these doors (the ones with the crowd of tourists looking on) added a whole new dimension to art—depth. Michelangelo said these doors were fit to be the "Gates of Paradise." (These panels are copies; the originals are in the nearby Duomo Museum.) Here we see how the Renaissance was a merging of art and science. Realism was in, and Renaissance artists used math, illusion, and dissection to get it.

In the "Jacob and Esau" panel (just above eye level on the left), receding arches, floor tiles, and banisters create a background for a realistic scene. The figures in the foreground stand and move like real people, telling the Bible story with human details. Amazingly, this spacious, 3-D scene is made from bronze only a few inches deep.

Ghiberti spent 27 years (1425-1452) working on these panels. That's him in the center of the door frame, atop the second row of panels—the head on the left with the shiny, male-pattern baldness.

• *Before we head south to the river, detour a block north up Via de' Martelli (which becomes Via Cavour). At the intersection with Via dei Pucci is the imposing Medici-Riccardi Palace.*

Medici-Riccardi Palace

Renaissance Florence was ruled by the Medicis, the rich banking family who lived here. Studying this grand Florentine palace, you'll notice fortified lower walls and elegance limited to the fancy upper stories. The Medici family may have been the local Rockefellers, but having self-made wealth rather than actual noble blood, they were always a bit defensive. The Greek motifs along the eaves highlight the palace's Renaissance roots. Back then, rather than having parking spots, grand buildings came with iron rings to which you'd tether your horse.

You can step into the doorway at Via Cavour 1 and view the courtyard through an iron gate (though the entrance is farther up the street). If you pay admission, you get access to a quintessential Florentine palazzo with a courtyard and a couple of impressive rooms, most notably the sumptuous little Chapel of the Magi.

• *Though we won't visit them on this walk, one block west of here are the Church of San Lorenzo (page 455), San Lorenzo street market (page 457), and Medici Chapels (page 456). For now, return to the Duomo and continue south, entering the pedestrian-only street that runs from here toward the Arno River.*

Via de' Calzaiuoli

The pedestrian-only Via de' Calzaiuoli (kahlts-ay-WOH-lee) is lined with high-fashion shops, as Florence is a trendsetting city in trendsetting Italy. This street has always been the main axis of the city, and it was part of the ancient Roman grid plan that became Florence. In medieval times, this street connected the religious center (where we are now) with the political center (where we're heading), a five-minute walk away. In the 20th century, this historic core was a noisy snarl of car traffic. However, traffic jams have been replaced by potted plants, and now this is a pleasant place to stroll, people-watch, window-shop, lick the drips on your gelato cone, and wonder why American cities can't become more pedestrian-friendly.

And speaking of gelato...the recommended **Grom,** which keeps its *gelati* in covered metal bins, the old-fashioned way, is just a half-block detour away (daily 10:30-24:00, take your first left, to Via delle Oche 24 red). Or you could drop by any of the several nearby gelato shops. *Perché no?* (Why not?)

Continue down Via de' Calzaiuoli. Two blocks down from the Baptistery, look right on Via degli Speziali to see a triumphal arch that marks Piazza della Repubblica. The arch celebrates the unification of Italy in 1870 and stands as a reminder that, in ancient Roman times, this piazza was the city center.

• *A block farther, at the intersection with Via Orsanmichele, is the...*

Orsanmichele Church—Florence's Medieval Roots

The Orsanmichele Church provides an interesting look at Florentine values. It's a combo church/granary. Originally, this was an open loggia (covered porch) with a huge grain warehouse

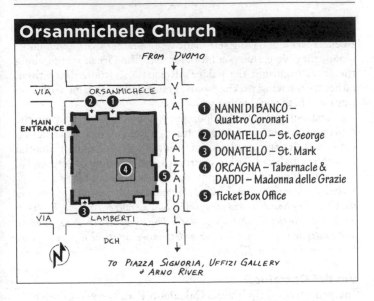

Orsanmichele Church

FROM DUOMO

VIA ORSANMICHELE

MAIN ENTRANCE

VIA CALZAIUOLI

VIA LAMBERTI

DCH

TO PIAZZA SIGNORIA, UFFIZI GALLERY & ARNO RIVER

1 NANNI DI BANCO – Quattro Coronati

2 DONATELLO – St. George

3 DONATELLO – St. Mark

4 ORCAGNA – Tabernacle & DADDI – Madonna delle Grazie

5 Ticket Box Office

upstairs. The arches of the loggia were artfully filled in (14th century), and the building gained a new purpose—as a church. This was prime real estate on what had become the main drag between the church and palace.

The niches in the walls stood empty for decades while they waited for sponsors to fill them with statues. That job fell to the rising middle class of merchants and their guilds.

Florence in 1400 was a republic, a government working for the interests not of a king, but of these guilds (much as modern America caters to corporate interests). Over time, various guilds commissioned statues as PR gestures, hiring the finest artists of the generation. As a result, the statues that ring the church (generally copies of originals stored safely in nearby museums) function as a textbook of the evolution of Florentine art.

Orsanmichele Exterior

In earlier Gothic times, statues were set deep into church niches, simply embellishing the house of God. Here at the Orsanmichele Church, we see statues—as restless as man on the verge of the Renaissance—stepping out from the protection of the Church.

• *Circle the church exterior counterclockwise, looking out for these statues.*

Nanni di Banco's *Quattro Coronati* (c. 1400)

These four early Christians were sculptors martyred by the Roman emperor Diocletian because they refused to sculpt pagan gods. They seem to be contemplating the consequences of the fatal decision they're about to make. Beneath some of the niches, you'll find the symbol of the guilds that paid for the art. Art historians differ here. Some think the work was commissioned by the carpenters' and masons' guild. Others contend it was by the guys who did discount circumcisions.

Donatello's *St. George* (c. 1417)

George is alert, perched on the edge of his niche, scanning the horizon for dragons and announcing the new age with its new outlook. His knitted brow shows there's a drama unfolding. Sure, he's anxious, but he's also self-assured. Comparing this Renaissance-style *St. George* to *Quattro Coronati,* you can psychoanalyze the heady changes under way. This is humanism.

This *St. George* is a bronze copy of the marble original (located in the Bargello).
• *Continue around the corner of the church, bypassing the entrance for now.*

Donatello's *St. Mark* (1411-1413)

The evangelist cradles his gospel in his strong, veined hand and gazes out, resting his weight on the right leg while bending the

left. Though subtle, St. Mark's *contrapposto* pose (weight on one foot) was the first seen since antiquity. Commissioned by the linen-sellers' guild, the statue has elaborately detailed robes that drape around the natural contours of his weighty body. When the guild first saw the statue, they thought the oversized head and torso made it top-heavy. Only after it was lifted into its raised niche did Donatello's cleverly designed proportions look right—and the guild accepted it. Eighty years after young Donatello carved this statue, a teenage Michelangelo Buonarroti stood here and marveled at it.
• *Backtrack to the entrance and go inside.*

Orsanmichele Interior

Here's a chance to step into Florence, circa 1350. The church has a double nave because it was adapted from a granary. Look for the pillars (on the left) with rectangular holes in them about three feet off the ground. These were once used as chutes for delivering grain from the storage rooms upstairs. Look up to see the rings hanging from the ceiling, which were likely used to make pulleys for lifting grain, and the iron bars spanning the vaults for support.

The fine **tabernacle** is by Andrea Orcagna. Notice how it was designed exactly for this space: Like the biggest Christmas tree possible, it's capped by an angel whose head touches the ceiling. Take in the Gothic tabernacle's medieval elegance. What it lacks in depth and realism it makes up for in color, with an intricate assemblage of marble, glass, gold, and expensive lapis lazuli. Florence had just survived the terrible bubonic plague of 1348, which killed half the population. The elaborate tabernacle was built to display Bernardo Daddi's *Madonna delle Grazie*, which received plague survivors' grateful prayers. While it's great to see art in museums, it's even better to enjoy it in its original setting—or "in situ"— where the artist intended it to be seen. When you view similar altarpieces out of context in the Uffizi, think back on the candlelit medieval atmosphere that surrounds this altarpiece.

• *The Bargello, with Florence's best collection of sculpture, is a few blocks east, down Via dei Tavolini (see page 460). But let's continue down the mall 50 more yards, to the huge and historic square.*

Palazzo Vecchio—Florence's Political Center

The main civic center of Florence is dominated by the Palazzo Vecchio, the Uffizi Gallery, and the marble greatness of old Florence littering the cobbles. This square still vibrates with the echoes of Florence's past—executions, riots, and great celebrations. There's even Roman history: Look for the **chart** showing the ancient city (on a waist-high, freestanding display to your right as you enter the square). Today, it's a tourist's world with pigeons, postcards, horse buggies, and tired hubbies. And, if it would make your tired companion happy, stop in at the expensive **Rivoire** café to enjoy its fine desserts, pudding-thick hot chocolate, and the best view seats in town.

Before you towers the Palazzo Vecchio, the Medicis' palatial City Hall—a fortress designed to contain riches and survive the

many riots that went with local politics. The windows are just beyond the reach of angry stones, the tower was a handy lookout post, and justice was doled out sternly on this square. Until 1873, Michelangelo's *David* stood where you see the replica today. The original was damaged in a 1527 riot (when a bench thrown out of a palace window knocked its left arm off), but remained here for several centuries, vulnerable to erosion and pollution until it was

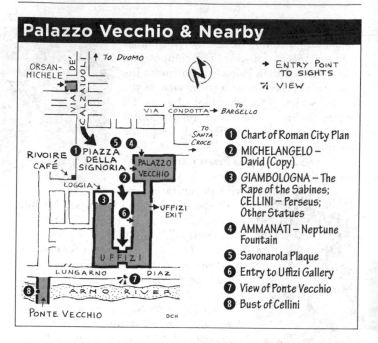

Palazzo Vecchio & Nearby

ORSAN-MICHELE

VIA DE' CALZAIUOLI

↑ To DUOMO

→ ENTRY POINT TO SIGHTS

↗ VIEW

VIA CONDOTTA → TO BARGELLO

TO SANTA CROCE

RIVOIRE CAFÉ

PIAZZA DELLA SIGNORIA

LOGGIA

PALAZZO VECCHIO

UFFIZI EXIT

UFFIZI

LUNGARNO DIAZ

ARNO RIVER

PONTE VECCHIO

DCH

1. Chart of Roman City Plan
2. MICHELANGELO – David (Copy)
3. GIAMBOLOGNA – The Rape of the Sabines; CELLINI – Perseus; Other Statues
4. AMMANATI – Neptune Fountain
5. Savonarola Plaque
6. Entry to Uffizi Gallery
7. View of Ponte Vecchio
8. Bust of Cellini

moved indoors for its own protection.

While the palace interior is not worth touring on a short visit, be sure to step past the replica *David* through the front door into the Palazzo Vecchio's courtyard (free). This palace was Florence's civic center. You're surrounded by art for art's sake—a statue frivolously marking the courtyard's center, and ornate walls and columns. Such luxury represented a big change 500 years ago. The squiggly wall painting is called *grotteschi*, inspired by the art that decorated the walls of ancient Roman villas being excavated at the time (c. 1500, named for "grotto" because the ancient villas were actually well below 15th-century Roman street level).

• *Back outside, check out the statue-filled Loggia.*

The Loggia, once a forum for public debate, was perfect for a city that prided itself on its democratic traditions. But later, when the Medicis figured that good art was more desirable than free speech, it was turned into an outdoor sculpture gallery. Notice the squirming Florentine themes—conquest, domination, rape, and decapitation. The statues lining the back are Roman originals brought back to Florence by a Medici when he moved home after living in Rome. Two statues in the front deserve a closer look.

The Rape of the Sabines, with its pulse-quickening rhythm of muscles, is from the restless Mannerist period, which followed the stately and confident Renaissance (c. 1560). The sculptor,

FLORENCE

Giambologna, proved his mastery of the medium by sculpting three entangled bodies from one piece of marble. The composition is best viewed from below and in front. The relief panel below shows a wider view of the terrible scene. Note what looks like an IV tube on the arm of the horrified husband. It's an electrified wire that effectively keeps the pigeons away.

Benvenuto **Cellini's** *Perseus,* the Loggia's most noteworthy piece, shows the Greek hero

who decapitated the snake-headed Medusa. They say Medusa was so ugly she turned humans who looked at her to stone.

• *Cross the square to the big* **fountain of Neptune** *by Bartolomeo Ammanati that Florentines (including Michelangelo) consider a huge waste of marble.*

The guy on the horse, to the left, is Cosimo I, one of the post-Renaissance Medicis. Find the round bronze plaque on the ground 10 steps in front of the fountain.

Savonarola Plaque

The Medici family was briefly thrown from power by an austere monk named Savonarola, who made Florence a constitutional republic. He organized huge rallies lit by roaring bonfires here on the square where he preached. While children sang hymns, the devout brought their rich "vanities" (such as paintings, musical instruments, and playing cards) and threw them into the flames.

But not everyone wanted a return to the medieval past. Encouraged by the pope, the Florentines fought back and arrested Savonarola. For two days, they tortured him, trying unsuccessfully to persuade him to see their side of things. Finally, on the very spot where Savonarola's followers had built bonfires of vanities, the monk was burned. The bronze plaque, engraved in Italian *("Qui dove...")*, reads, "Here, Girolamo Savonarola and his Dominican brothers were hanged and burned" in the year "MCCCCXCVIII" (1498).

• *Stay cool, we have 200 yards to go. Follow the gaze of the fake David into the courtyard of the two-tone horseshoe-shaped building...*

Uffizi Courtyard—The Renaissance Hall of Fame

The top floor of this building, known as the *uffizi* (offices) during Medici days, is filled with the greatest collection of Florentine painting anywhere. It's one of Europe's top four or five art galleries (see "Uffizi Gallery Tour," next page).

The Uffizi courtyard, filled with merchants and hustling young artists, is watched over by 19th-century statues of the great figures of the Renaissance. Tourists zero in on the visual accomplishments of the era—not realizing that it was many-faceted. Let's pay tribute to the nonvisual Renaissance as well, as we wander through Florence's Hall of Fame.

• *Stroll down the left side of the courtyard from the Palazzo Vecchio to the river, noticing the following greats.*

1. Lorenzo the Magnificent—whose statue is tucked under the arcade, by an Uffizi doorway—was a great art patron and cunning power broker. Excelling in everything except modesty, he set the tone for the Renaissance.

2. Giotto, an architect (holding the plan to the city's great bell tower—named for him), was the first great modern painter.

3. Donatello, the sculptor who served as a role model for Michelangelo, holds a hammer and chisel.

4. Alberti wrote a famous book, *On Painting*, which taught early Renaissance artists the mathematics of perspective.

5. Leonardo da Vinci was a scientist, sculptor, musician, engineer...and not a bad painter either.

6. Michelangelo ponders the universe and/or stifles a belch.

7. Dante, with the laurel-leaf crown and lyre of a poet, says, "I am the father of the Italian language." He was the first Italian to write a popular work *(The Divine Comedy)* in non-Latin, using the Florentine dialect, which soon became "Italian" throughout the country.

8. The poet **Petrarch** wears laurel leaves from Greece, a robe from Rome, and a belt from Wal-Mart.

9. Boccaccio wrote *The Decameron,* stories told to pass the time during the 1348 Black Death.

10. The devious-looking **Machiavelli** is hatching a plot—his book *The Prince* taught that the end justifies the means, paving the way for the slick-and-cunning "Machiavellian" politics of today.

11. Vespucci (in the corner) was an explorer who gave his first name, Amerigo, to a fledgling New World.

12. Galileo (in the other corner) holds the humble telescope he used to spot the moons of Jupiter.

• *Pause at the Arno River, overlooking Ponte Vecchio.*

FLORENCE

Ponte Vecchio

Before you is Ponte Vecchio (Old Bridge). A bridge has spanned this narrowest part of the Arno since Roman times. While Rome "fell," Florence really didn't, remaining a bustling trade center along the river. To get into the exclusive little park below (on the north bank), you'll need to join the Florence rowing club.

• *Finish your walk by hiking to the center of the bridge.*

A fine bust of the great gold-smith, Cellini, graces the central point of the bridge. This statue is a reminder that, in the 1500s, the Medicis booted out the bridge's butchers and tanners and installed the gold- and silversmiths who still tempt visitors to this day. This is a very romantic spot late at night (when lovers gather, and a top-notch street musician performs).

Look up to notice the Medicis' protected and elevated passageway that led from the Palazzo Vecchio through the Uffizi, across Ponte Vecchio, and up to the immense Pitti Palace, four blocks beyond the bridge. During World War II, the Nazi occupiers were ordered to blow up Ponte Vecchio. An art-loving German consul intervened and saved the bridge. The buildings at either end were destroyed, leaving the bridge impassable but intact. *Grazie.*

• *From here it is an easy stroll back to the Uffizi, described next.*

Uffizi Gallery Tour

In the Renaissance, Florentine artists rediscovered the beauty of the natural world. Medieval art had been symbolic, telling Bible stories. Realism didn't matter. But Renaissance people saw the beauty of God in nature and the human body. They used math and science to capture the natural world on canvas as realistically as possible.

The Galleria degli Uffizi (Uffizi Gallery, oo-FEED-zee) has the greatest overall collection anywhere of Italian painting. We'll trace the rise of realism and savor the optimistic spirit that marked the Renaissance.

My eyes love things that are fair,
and my soul for salvation cries.
But neither will to Heaven rise
unless the sight of Beauty lifts them there.
— Michelangelo Buonarroti, sculptor, painter, poet

Orientation

Cost: €6.50, but mandatory special exhibitions generally bump the price to €10; plus there's a €4 fee for optional but highly recommended reservations. If you've reserved tickets, you'll need to bring cash to pick them up.

Hours: Tue-Sun 8:15-18:50, closed Mon, last entry 45 minutes before closing.

Reservations: It's smart to book ahead to avoid the notoriously long ticket-buying lines. During summer and on weekends, the Uffizi can be booked up a month or more in advance. Sometimes, by the end of the day (an hour before closing), there are no lines and you can just walk right in, but generally you'll encounter lines even off-season. The busiest days are Tuesday, Saturday, and Sunday. Avoid the three-hour peak-season wait by reserving ahead. For details, see the "Make Reservations to Avoid Lines" sidebar on page 406.

Getting There: It's on the Arno River between the Palazzo Vecchio and Ponte Vecchio, a 15-minute walk from the train station.

Getting In: Once you have your reservation (or voucher), go to the Uffizi 10 minutes before your appointed time. You'll notice that there are several entrances. Walk briskly across the courtyard from the 200-yard-long ticket-buying line—pondering the IQ of this gang—to the reserved-ticket pickup desk at door #3 (labeled *Reservation Ticket Office,* see map on page 435). Give your reservation number or voucher, pay in cash (if you didn't already pay when you made the reservation), and get your ticket. Then take it back across the courtyard again to door #1 (labeled  *Reservation Entrance*), close to the Palazzo Vecchio. There are two lines at this entrance: Get in the line for individuals, not groups. Show your ticket and walk in.

Renovation: The Uffizi is undergoing a massive, years-long renovation that may affect your visit. In particular, the Tribune room (with *Venus de' Medici*, page 445) may be closed. On the plus side, new exhibition space on the first floor (the area you pass through on your way to the exit) is likely to open up in time for your visit.

Information: There's no English (or Italian) information in the museum's rooms. You can buy cheap Uffizi guidebooks at the ground-floor bookstore immediately upon entering, or from street vendors. Also see "Audioguide Tours," below. Museum info tel. 055-238-8651, reservation tel. 055-294-883, www.polomuseale.firenze.it.

Audioguide Tours: The museum rents an audioguide (€5.50, €8/2 people, 1.5 hours, must leave ID). Remember you can download free audio tours of this sight (see page 1232).

Length of This Tour: Allow two hours.

Cloakroom: Baggage check is available. No bottled liquids are allowed inside the museum.

Services: The Uffizi has a post office and book/gift shop in the entrance/exit hall on the ground floor; there's also a public entrance for these. You'll find WCs before and after your museum tour, but facilities are scarce in between. The main WC is in the entrance/exit hall on the ground floor near the post office. There are no WCs on the top floor (the focus of this tour), and only two often-crowded WCs on the way to the exit.

Photography: No photos are allowed.

Cuisine Art: The simple café at the end of the gallery has an outdoor terrace with stunning views of the Palazzo Vecchio and the Duomo's dome. They serve reasonably priced sandwiches, salads, desserts, and fruit cups (you'll pay more to sit on the view terrace). A €5 cappuccino outside, with that view, is one of Europe's great treats.

A block away, a quiet wine-and-olive-oil shop called 'Ino Bottega di Alimentari e Vini has good sandwiches (daily 11:00-17:00, walking from the Uffizi along the Arno to Ponte Vecchio, take the first right to Via dei Georgofili 3 red).

Starring: Botticelli, Venus, Raphael, Giotto, Titian, Leonardo, and Michelangelo.

The Tour Begins
The Ascent
• *Buy your ticket, then walk up the four long flights of the monumental staircase to the top floor (or take the elevator). Your brain should be fully aerated from the hike up. Past the ticket-taker, look out the window.*

The Uffizi is U-shaped, running around the courtyard. Except for a little Baroque spillover, the entire collection is on this one floor, displayed chronologically. This left wing contains Florentine

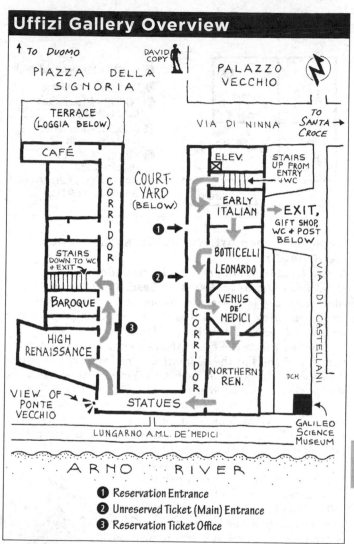

Uffizi Gallery Overview

↑ To DUOMO

DAVID COPY

PIAZZA DELLA SIGNORIA

PALAZZO VECCHIO

TERRACE (LOGGIA BELOW)

VIA DI NINNA

TO SANTA CROCE →

CAFÉ

CORRIDOR

COURT-YARD (BELOW)

ELEV.

STAIRS UP FROM ENTRY + WC

EARLY ITALIAN

1 →

→ EXIT, GIFT SHOP, WC & POST BELOW

STAIRS DOWN TO WC + EXIT

BOTTICELLI LEONARDO

2 →

BAROQUE

VENUS DE' MEDICI

CORRIDOR

VIA DI CASTELLANI

HIGH RENAISSANCE

3

NORTHERN REN.

DCH

VIEW OF PONTE VECCHIO →

STATUES

GALILEO SCIENCE MUSEUM

LUNGARNO A.M.L. DE'MEDICI

ARNO RIVER

1 Reservation Entrance
2 Unreserved Ticket (Main) Entrance
3 Reservation Ticket Office

paintings from medieval to Renaissance times. The right wing (which you can see across the courtyard) has art from the Roman and Venetian High Renaissance, works from the Baroque period that followed, and a café terrace facing the Duomo. A short hallway with sculpture connects the two wings. We'll concentrate on the Uffizi's forte, the Florentine section, then get a taste of the art it inspired.

• *Down the hall, enter the first door on the left and face Giotto's giant* Madonna and Child.

Medieval Art

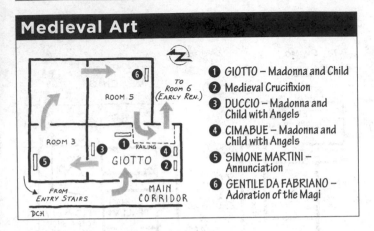

1. GIOTTO – Madonna and Child
2. Medieval Crucifixion
3. DUCCIO – Madonna and Child with Angels
4. CIMABUE – Madonna and Child with Angels
5. SIMONE MARTINI – Annunciation
6. GENTILE DA FABRIANO – Adoration of the Magi

Medieval—When Art Was as Flat as the World (1200-1400)

Giotto (c. 1266-1337)—Madonna and Child
(Madonna in trono col Bambino Gesù, Santi e Angeli)

Mary and baby Jesus sit on a throne in a golden never-never land symbolizing heaven. It's as if medieval Christians couldn't imagine holy people inhabiting our dreary material world. It took Renaissance painters to bring Mary down to earth and give her human realism. For the Florentines, "realism" meant "three-dimensional." In this room, pre-Renaissance paintings show the slow process of learning to paint a 3-D world on a 2-D surface.

Before concentrating on the Giotto, look at some others in the room. The **crucifixion** (on your right as you face the Giotto) was medieval 3-D—paint a crude two-dimensional work...then physically tilt the head forward. Nice try.

The three similar-looking Madonna-and-Bambinos in this room—all painted within a few decades of each other in about the year 1300—show baby steps in the march to realism. **Duccio**'s piece (on the left as you face Giotto) is the most medieval and two-dimensional. There's no background. The angels are just stacked one on top of the other, floating in the golden atmosphere. Mary's throne is crudely drawn—the left side is at a three-quarters angle while the right is practically straight on. Mary herself is a wispy cardboard-cutout figure seemingly floating just above the throne.

On the opposite wall, the work of **Cimabue**—mixing the iconic Byzantine style with budding Italian realism—is an improvement. The large throne creates an illusion of depth. Mary's

foot actually sticks out over the lip of the throne. Still, the angels are stacked totem-pole-style, serving as heavenly bookends.

Giotto (JOT-oh) employs realism to make his theological points. He creates a space and fills it. Like a set designer, he builds a three-dimensional "stage"—the canopied throne—then peoples it with real beings. The throne has angels in front, prophets behind, and a canopy over the top, clearly defining its three dimensions. The steps up to the throne lead

from our space to Mary's, making the scene an extension of our world. But the real triumph here is Mary herself—big and monumental, like a Roman statue. Beneath her robe, she has a real live body, with knees and breasts that stick out at us. This three-dimensionality was revolutionary in its day, a taste of the Renaissance a century before it began.

Giotto was one of the first "famous" artists. In the Middle Ages, artists were mostly unglamorous craftsmen, like carpenters or cable-TV repairmen. They cranked out generic art and could have signed their work with a bar code. But Giotto was recognized as a genius, a unique individual. He died in a plague that devastated Florence. If there had been no plague, would the Renaissance have started 100 years earlier?

• Enter Room 3, to the left of Giotto.

Simone Martini (c. 1285-1344)—*Annunciation* (*Annunciazione con i Santi Ansano e Massima*)

Simone Martini boils things down to the basic figures needed to get the message across: (1) The angel appears to sternly tell (2)

Mary that she'll be the mother of Jesus. In the center is (3) a vase of lilies, a symbol of purity. Above is (4) the Holy Spirit as a dove about to descend on her. If the symbols aren't enough to get the message across, Simone Martini has spelled it right out for us in Latin: *"Ave Gratia Plena..."* or, "Hail, favored one, the Lord is with you." Mary doesn't exactly look pleased as punch.

FLORENCE

This is not a three-dimensional work. The point was not to re-create reality but to teach religion, especially to the illiterate masses. This isn't a beautiful Mary or even a real Mary. She's a generic woman without distinctive features. We know she's pure—not from her face, but only because of the halo and symbolic flowers. Before the Renaissance, artists didn't care about the beauty of individual people.

Simone Martini's *Annunciation* has medieval features you'll see in many of the paintings in the next few rooms: (1) religious subject, (2) gold background, (3) two-dimensionality, and (4) meticulous detail.

• *Pass through Room 4, full of golden altarpieces, stopping at the far end of Room 5.*

Gentile da Fabriano (c. 1370-1427)—*Adoration of the Magi (Adorazione dei Magi)*

Look at the incredible detail of the Three Kings' costumes, the fine horses, and the cow in the cave. The canvas is filled from top
to bottom with realistic details—but it's far from realistic. While the Magi worship Jesus in the foreground, their return trip home dangles over their heads in the "background."

This is a textbook example of the International Gothic style popular with Europe's aristocrats in the early 1400s: well-dressed, elegant people in a colorful, design-oriented setting. The religious subject is just an excuse to paint secular luxuries such as jewelry and clothes made of silk brocade. And the scene's background and foreground are compressed together to create an overall design that's pleasing to the eye.

Such exquisite detail work raises the question: Was Renaissance three-dimensionality truly an improvement over Gothic, or simply a different style?

• *Exit to your right and hang a U-turn left into Room 7.*

Early Renaissance (mid-1400s)
Paolo Uccello (1397-1475)—*The Battle of San Romano (La Battaglia di San Romano)*

(Consider yourself lucky if this painting, long under restoration, has returned for your visit.) In the 1400s, painters worked out the problems of painting realistically, using mathematics to create the illusion of three-dimensionality. This colorful battle scene, which may be out for restoration in 2011, is not so much a piece of art as an exercise in perspective. Paolo Uccello (oo-CHEL-loh) has

Early Renaissance

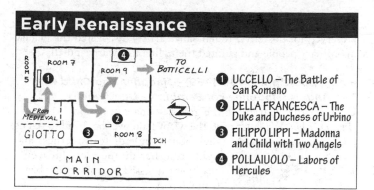

❶ UCCELLO – The Battle of San Romano

❷ DELLA FRANCESCA – The Duke and Duchess of Urbino

❸ FILIPPO LIPPI – Madonna and Child with Two Angels

❹ POLLAIUOLO – Labors of Hercules

challenged himself with every possible problem.

The broken lances at left set up a 3-D "grid" in which to place this crowded scene. The fallen horses and soldiers are experiments

in "foreshortening"—shortening the things that are farther away from us (which appear smaller) to create the illusion of distance. Some of the figures are definitely A-plus material, like the fallen gray horse in the center and the white horse at the far right walk-

ing away. But some are more like B-minus work—the kicking red horse's legs look like ham hocks at this angle, and the fallen soldier at far right would be child-size if he stood up.

And then there's the D-minus "Are you on drugs?" work. The converging hedges in the background create a nice illusion of a distant hillside maybe 250 feet away. So what are those soldiers the size of the foreground figures doing there? And jumping the hedge, is that rabbit 40 feet tall?

Paolo Uccello almost literally went crazy trying to master the three dimensions (thank God he was born before Einstein discovered one more). Uccello got so wrapped up in it he kind of lost...perspec-tive.

• *Enter Room 8. In the center of the room stands a double portrait.*

Piero della Francesca (c. 1412-1492)—*The Duke and Duchess of Urbino (Ritratti dei Duchi di Urbino)* In medieval times, only saints and angels were worthy of being painted. In the humanistic Renaissance, however, even

FLORENCE

non-religious folk like this husband and wife had their features preserved for posterity. Renaissance artists discovered the beauty in ordinary people and painted them, literally, warts and all.

Fra Filippo Lippi (1406-1469)—*Madonna and Child with Two Angels (Madonna col Bambino e Due Angeli)*

Compare this Mary with the generic female in Simone Martini's *Annunciation*. We don't need the wispy halo over her head to tell us

she's holy—she radiates sweetness and light from her divine face. Heavenly beauty is expressed by a physically beautiful woman.

Fra (Brother) Lippi, an orphan raised as a monk, lived a less-than-monkish life. He lived with a nun who bore him two children. He spent his entire life searching for the perfect Virgin. Through his studio passed Florence's prettiest girls, many of whom decorate the walls here in this room.

Lippi painted idealized beauty, but his models were real flesh-and-blood human beings. You could look through all the thousands of paintings from the Middle Ages and not find anything so human as the mischievous face of one of Lippi's little angel boys.

• *Enter Room 9, with two small works by Pollaiuolo in the glass case between the windows.*

Antonio Pollaiuolo (c. 1431-1498)—*Labors of Hercules (Fatiche di Ercole)*

Hercules gets a workout in these two small panels showing the human form at odd angles. The poses are the wildest imaginable, to show how each muscle twists and tightens. While Uccello

worked on perspective, Pollaiuolo studied anatomy. In medieval times, dissection of corpses was a sin and a crime (the two were the same then). Dissecting was a desecration of the human body, the temple of God. But Pollaiuolo was willing to sell his soul to the devil for artistic knowledge. He dissected.

There's something funny about this room that I can't put my finger on...I've got it—no Madonnas. Not one. (No, that's not a Madonna; she's a Virtue.)

We've seen how Early Renaissance artists worked to conquer reality. Now let's see

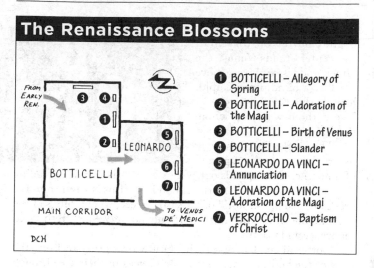

The Renaissance Blossoms

FROM EARLY REN.

LEONARDO

BOTTICELLI

MAIN CORRIDOR

To VENUS DE' MEDICI

DCH

❶ BOTTICELLI – Allegory of Spring

❷ BOTTICELLI – Adoration of the Magi

❸ BOTTICELLI – Birth of Venus

❹ BOTTICELLI – Slander

❺ LEONARDO DA VINCI – Annunciation

❻ LEONARDO DA VINCI – Adoration of the Magi

❼ VERROCCHIO – Baptism of Christ

the fruits of their work, the flowering of Florence's Renaissance.

• *Enter the large Botticelli room and take a seat.*

Florence—The Renaissance Blossoms (1450-1500)

Florence in 1450 was in a Firenz-y of activity. There was a can-do spirit of optimism in the air, led by prosperous merchants and bankers and a strong middle class. The government was reasonably democratic, and Florentines saw themselves as citizens of a strong republic—like ancient Rome. Their civic pride showed in the public monuments and artworks they built. Man was leaving the protection of the church to stand on his own two feet.

Lorenzo de' Medici, head of the powerful Medici family, epitomized this new humanistic spirit. Strong, decisive, handsome, poetic, athletic, sensitive, charismatic, intelligent, brave, clean, and reverent, Lorenzo was a true Renaissance man, deserving of the nickname he went by—the Magnificent. He gathered Florence's best and brightest around him for evening wine and discussions of great ideas. One of this circle was the painter Botticelli (bot-i-CHEL-ee).

Sandro Botticelli (1445-1510)—*Allegory of Spring (Allegoria della Primavera)*

It's springtime in a citrus grove. The winds of spring blow in (Mr. Blue, at right), causing the woman on the right to sprout flowers from her lips as she morphs into Flora, or Spring—who walks by, spreading flowers from her dress. At the left are Mercury and the Three Graces, dancing a delicate maypole dance. The Graces may be symbolic of the three forms of love—love of beauty, love of people, and sexual love, suggested by the raised intertwined

fingers. (They forgot love of peanut butter on toast.) In the center stands Venus, the Greek goddess of love. Above her flies a blindfolded Cupid, happily shooting his arrows of love without worrying whom they'll hit.

Here is the Renaissance in its first bloom, its "springtime" of innocence. Madonna is out, Venus is in. Adam and Eve hiding their nakedness are out, glorious flesh is in. This is a return to the pre-Christian pagan world of classical Greece, where things of the flesh are not sinful. But this is certainly no orgy—just fresh-faced innocence and playfulness.

Botticelli emphasizes pristine beauty over gritty realism. The lines of the bodies, especially of the Graces in their see-through nighties, have pleasing, S-like curves. The faces are idealized but have real human features. There's a look of thoughtfulness and even melancholy in the faces—as though everyone knows that the innocence of spring will not last forever.

• Look at the next painting to the right.

Botticelli—*Adoration of the Magi (Adorazione dei Magi)*

Here's the rat pack of confident young Florentines who reveled in the optimistic pagan spirit—even in a religious scene. Botticelli included himself among the adorers, looking vain in the yellow robe at far right. Lorenzo's the Magnificent-looking guy at the far left.

Botticelli—*Birth of Venus (Nascita di Venere)*

According to myth, Venus was born from the foam of a wave. Still only half awake, this fragile, newborn beauty floats ashore on a clam shell, blown by the winds, where her maid waits to dress her. The pose is the same S-curve of classical statues (as we'll soon see). Botticelli's pastel colors make the world itself seem fresh and newly born.

This is the purest expression of Renaissance beauty. Venus' naked body is not sensual, but innocent. Botticelli thought that physical beauty was a way of appreciating God. Remember Michelangelo's poem: Souls will never ascend to heaven "...until

the sight of Beauty lifts them there."

Botticelli finds God in the details—Venus' wind-blown hair, the translucent skin, the maid's braided hair, the slight ripple of the wind god's abs, and the flowers tumbling in the slowest of slow motions, suspended like musical notes, caught at the peak of their brief life.

Mr. and Mrs. Wind intertwine—notice her hands clasped around his body. Their hair, wings, and robes mingle like the wind. But what happened to those splayed toes?

• *"Venus on the Half-Shell" (as many tourists call this) is one of the masterpieces of Western art. Take some time with it. Then find the small canvas on the wall to the right, near the* Allegory of Spring.

Botticelli—*Slander (La Calunnia)*

The spring of Florence's Renaissance had to end. Lorenzo died young. The economy faltered. Into town rode the monk Savonarola, preaching medieval hellfire and damnation for those who embraced the "pagan" Renaissance spirit. "Down, down with all gold and decoration," he roared. "Down where the body is food for the worms." He presided over huge bonfires, where the people threw in their fine clothes, jewelry, pagan books...and paintings.

Slander spells the end of the Florentine Renaissance. The setting is classic Brunelleschian architecture, but look at what's

taking place beneath those stately arches. These aren't proud Renaissance men and women but a ragtag, medieval-looking bunch, a Court of Thieves in an abandoned hall of justice. The accusations fly, and everyone is condemned. The naked man pleads for mercy, but the hooded black figure, a symbol of his execution, turns away. The figure of Truth (naked Truth)—straight out of *The Birth of Venus*—looks up to heaven as if to ask, "What has happened to us?" The classical statues in their niches look on in disbelief.

Botticelli listened to Savonarola. He burned some of his own paintings and changed his tune. The last works of his life were darker, more somber, and pessimistic about humanity.

The German poet Heinrich Heine said, "When they start by

burning books, they'll end by burning people." After four short years of power, Savonarola was burned on his own bonfire in Piazza della Signoria, but by then the city was in shambles. The first flowering of the Renaissance was over.

• *Enter the next room.*

Leonardo da Vinci (1452-1519)—*Annunciation*

A scientist, architect, engineer, musician, and painter, Leonardo was a true Renaissance man. He worked at his own pace rather than to please an employer, so he often left works unfinished. The

two paintings in this room aren't his best, but even a lesser Leonardo is enough to put a museum on the map, and they're definitely worth a look.

Gabriel has walked up to Mary, and now kneels on one knee like an ambassador, saluting her. See how relaxed his other hand is, draped over his knee. Mary, who's been reading, looks up with a gesture of surprise and curiosity.

Leonardo constructs a beautifully landscaped "stage" and puts his characters in it. Look at the bricks on the right wall. If you extended lines from them, the lines would all converge at the center of the painting, the distant blue mountain. Same with the edge of the sarcophagus and the railing. This subtle touch creates a subconscious feeling of balance, order, and spaciousness in the viewer.

Think back to Simone Martini's *Annunciation* to realize how much more natural, relaxed, and realistic Leonardo's version is. He's taken a miraculous event—an angel appearing out of the blue—and presented it in a very human way.

Leonardo da Vinci—*Adoration of the Magi*

Leonardo's human insight is even more apparent here, in this

unfinished work. The poor kings are amazed at the Christ child—even afraid of him. They scurry around like chimps around a fire. This work is as agitated as the *Annunciation* is calm, giving us an idea of Leonardo's range. Leonardo was pioneering a new era of painting, showing not just the outer features but the inner personality.

The next painting to the right, ***Baptism of Christ,*** is by Andrea del

Verrocchio, Leonardo's teacher. Leonardo painted the angel on the far left when he was only 14 years old. Legend has it that when Verrocchio saw that some kid had painted an angel better than he ever would...he hung up his brush for good.

Florence saw the first blossoming of the Renaissance. But when the cultural climate turned chilly, artists flew south to warmer climes. The Renaissance shifted to Rome.

• *Exit into the main hallway. Breathe. Sit. Admire the ceiling. Look out the window. See you in five.*

Back already? Now continue down the hallway. On your left is the doorway to the Tribune room (may be closed when you visit). If it's open, you'll see the famous Venus de' Medici *statue behind glass.*

Classical Sculpture

If the Renaissance was the foundation of the modern world, the foundation of the Renaissance was classical sculpture. Sculptors, painters, and poets alike turned for inspiration to these ancient Greek and Roman works as the epitome of balance, 3-D perspective, human anatomy, and beauty.

Venus de' Medici, or Medici Venus
(Venere de' Medici, Ancient Greece)

Is this pose familiar? Botticelli's *Birth of Venus* has the same position of the arms, the same S-curved body, and the same lifting of the right leg. A copy of this statue stood in Lorenzo the Magnificent's garden, where Botticelli used to hang out. This one is a Roman copy of the lost original by the great Greek sculptor Praxiteles. The *Venus de' Medici* is a balanced, harmonious, serene statue from Greece's "Golden Age," when balance was admired in every aspect of life.

Perhaps more than any other work of art, this statue has been the epitome of both ideal beauty and sexuality. In the 18th and 19th centuries, sex was "dirty," so the sex drive of cultured aristocrats was channeled into a love of pure beauty. Wealthy sons and daughters of Europe's aristocrats made the pilgrimage to the Uffizi to complete their classical education... where they swooned in ecstasy before the cold beauty of this goddess of love.

Louis XIV had a bronze copy made. Napoleon stole her away to Paris for himself. And in Philadelphia in the 1800s, a copy had to be kept under lock and key to prevent the innocent from catching the Venere-al disease. At first, it may be difficult for us to appreciate such passionate love of art, but if any generation

Classical Sculpture & Northern Renaissance

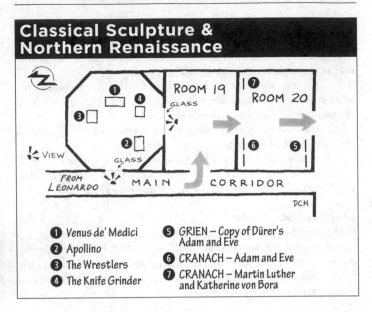

1. Venus de' Medici
2. Apollino
3. The Wrestlers
4. The Knife Grinder
5. GRIEN – Copy of Dürer's Adam and Eve
6. CRANACH – Adam and Eve
7. CRANACH – Martin Luther and Katherine von Bora

knows the power of sex to sell something—be it art or underarm deodorant—it's ours.

The Other Statues

Venus de' Medici's male counterpart is on the right, facing Venus. *Apollino* (a.k.a. "Venus with a Penis") is also by the master of smooth, cool lines: Praxiteles.

The other works are later Greek (Hellenistic), when quiet balance was replaced by violent motion and emotion. *The Wrestlers*, to the left of Venus, is a study in anatomy and twisted limbs—like Pollaiuolo's paintings a thousand years later.

The drama of *The Knife Grinder* to the right of Venus stems from the off-stage action—he's sharpening the knife to flay a man alive.

This fine room was a showroom, or a "cabinet of wonders," back when this building still functioned as the Medici offices. Filled with family portraits, it's a holistic statement that symbolically links the Medici family with the four basic elements: air (weathervane in the lantern), water (inlaid mother of pearl in the dome), fire (red wall), and earth (inlaid stone floor).

• *Enter the next room past the Tribune room and find Room 20.*

Northern Renaissance

Hans Baldung Grien (c. 1484-1545)—
Copy of Dürer's *Adam and Eve*

The warm spirit of the Renaissance blew north into Germany.

Albrecht Dürer (1471-1528), the famous German painter and engraver, traveled to Venice, where he fell in love with all things

Italian. Returning home, he painted the First Couple in the Italian style—full-bodied, muscular (check out Adam's abs and Eve's knees), "carved" with strong shading, fresh-faced, and innocent in their earthly Paradise.

This copy of Dürer's original (now in the Prado) by Hans Baldung Grien was a training exercise. Like many of Europe's artists—including Michelangelo and Raphael—Baldung Grien learned technique by studying Dürer's meticulous engrav-

ings, spread by the newly invented printing press.

Lucas Cranach (1472-1553)—*Adam and Eve*

Eve sashays forward, with heavy-lidded eyes, to offer the forbidden fruit. Adam stretches to display himself and his foliage to Eve. The

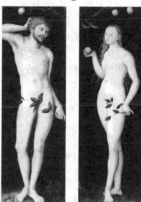

two panels are linked by smoldering eye contact, as Man and Woman awaken to their own nakedness. The Garden of Eden is about to be rocked by new ideas that are both liberating and troubling.

Though the German Lucas Cranach occasionally dabbled in the "Italian style," he chose to portray his Adam and Eve in the now-retro look of International Gothic.

They are slimmer than Dürer's, as well as smoother, more S-shaped, elegant, graceful, shapely, and erotic, with the dainty pinkies of the refined aristocrats who were signing Cranach's paycheck.

Though life-size, Adam and Eve are not lifelike, not monumental, not full-bodied or muscular, and are not placed in a real-world landscape with distant perspectives. Even so, Cranach was very much a man of the Renaissance, a friend of Martin Luther, and a champion of humanism.

• *Find a small, two-panel portrait featuring Martin Luther with his wife (or possibly a panel featuring Luther's colleague, Melanchthon; the museum rotates these two).*

FLORENCE

Cranach—*Martin Luther*

Martin Luther—German monk, fiery orator, and religious whistle-blower—sparked a century of European wars by speaking out against the Catholic Church.

Luther (1483-1546) lived a turbulent life. In early adulthood, the newly ordained priest suffered a severe personal crisis of faith, before finally emerging "born again." In 1517, he openly protested against Church corruption and was excommunicated. Defying

both the pope and the emperor, he lived on the run as an outlaw, watching as his ideas sparked peasant riots. He still found time to translate the New Testament from Latin to modern German, write hymns such as "A Mighty Fortress," and spar with the humanist Erasmus and fellow-Reformer Zwingli.

Now 46 years old, Martin Luther is easing out of the fast lane. Recently married to an ex-nun, he has traded his monk's habit for street clothes, bought a house, had several kids...and has clearly been enjoying his wife's home cooking and home-brewed beer.

Cranach—*Katherine von Bora* (Luther's wife)

When "Katie" decided to leave her convent, the famous Martin Luther agreed to help find her a husband. She rejected his nominees, saying she'd marry no one...except Luther himself. In 1525, the 42-year-old ex-priest married the 26-year-old ex-nun "to please my father and annoy the pope." Martin turned his checkbook over to "my lord Katie," who also ran the family farm, raised their six children and 11 adopted orphans, and hosted Martin's circle of friends (including Cranach) at loud, chatty dinner parties.

• *Pass through the next couple of rooms, exiting to a great view of the Arno and Ponte Vecchio. Stroll through the...*

Sculpture Hall

A hundred years ago, no one even looked at Botticelli—they came to the Uffizi to see the sculpture collection. And today, these 2,000-year-old Roman copies of 2,500-year-old Greek originals are hardly noticed...but they should be. Only a few are displayed here now.

The purple statue in the center of the hall—headless and

limbless—is a female wolf (or "Lupa") done in porphyry stone. This was the animal that raised Rome's legendary founders and became the city's symbol. Renaissance Florentines marveled at the ancient Romans' ability to create such lifelike, three-dimensional works. They learned to reproduce them in stone...and then learned to paint them on a two-dimensional surface.

• *Grab a seat at one of the benches scattered throughout the hall for a...*

View of the Arno

Enjoy Florence's best view of the Arno and Ponte Vecchio. You can also see the red-tiled roof of the Vasari Corridor, the "secret" passage connecting the Palazzo Vecchio, Uffizi, Ponte Vecchio, and Pitti Palace on the other side of the river—a half-mile in all. This was a private walkway, wallpapered in great art, for the Medici family's commute from home to work.

As you appreciate the view (best at sunset), remember that it's this sort of pleasure that Renaissance painters wanted you to get from their paintings. For them, a canvas was a window you looked through to see the wide world. Their paintings re-create natural perspective: Distant objects (such as bridges) are smaller, dimmer, and higher up the "canvas," while closer objects are bigger, clearer, and lower.

We're headed down the home stretch now. If your little U-feetsies are killing you, and it feels like torture, remind yourself that it's a pleasant torture and smile...like the statue next to you.

• *In the far hallway, turn left into the first room (#25) and grab a blast of cold from the air-conditioning vent on the floor to the left.*

High Renaissance (1500-1550)— Michelangelo, Raphael, Titian
Michelangelo Buonarroti (1475-1564)—
Holy Family (Sacra Famiglia)

This is the only completed easel painting by the greatest sculptor in history. Florentine painters were sculptors with brushes; this shows it. Instead of a painting, it's more like three clusters of statues with some clothes painted on.

The main subject is the holy family—Mary, Joseph, and baby Jesus—and in the background are two groups of nudes looking like classical statues. The background represents the old pagan world, while Jesus in the foreground is the new age of Christianity. The figure of young John the Baptist at right is the link between the two.

This is a "peasant" Mary, with a plain face

High Renaissance

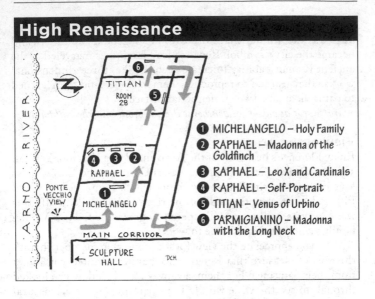

1 MICHELANGELO – Holy Family

2 RAPHAEL – Madonna of the Goldfinch

3 RAPHAEL – Leo X and Cardinals

4 RAPHAEL – Self-Portrait

5 TITIAN – Venus of Urbino

6 PARMIGIANINO – Madonna with the Long Neck

(map labels: ARNO RIVER, TITIAN ROOM 28, RAPHAEL, PONTE VECCHIO VIEW, MICHELANGELO, MAIN CORRIDOR, SCULPTURE HALL, DCH)

and sunburned arms. Michelangelo shows her from a very unflattering angle—we're looking up her nostrils. But Michelangelo himself was an ugly man, and he was among the first artists to recognize the beauty in everyday people.

Michelangelo was a Florentine—in fact, he was like an adopted son of the Medicis, who recognized his talent—but much of his greatest work was done in Rome as part of the Pope's face-lift of the city. We can see here some of the techniques he used on the Sistine Chapel ceiling that revolutionized painting—monumental figures; dramatic angles (looking up Mary's nose); accentuated, rippling muscles; and bright, clashing colors (all the more apparent since both this work and the Sistine Chapel ceiling have recently been cleaned). These elements added a dramatic tension that was lacking in the graceful work of Leonardo and Botticelli.

Michelangelo painted this for Angelo Doni for 70 ducats. (Michelangelo designed, but didn't carve, the elaborate frame.) When the painting was delivered, Doni tried to talk Michelangelo down to 40. Proud Michelangelo took the painting away and would not sell it until the man finally agreed to pay double...140 ducats.

• *Enter Room 26 and welcome back Raphael's* Madonna of the Goldfinch *after a laborious 10-year restoration.*

Raphael (Raffaello Sanzio, 1483-1520)—*Madonna of the Goldfinch (La Madonna del Cardellino)*

Raphael (roff-eye-ELL) brings Mary and Bambino down from heaven and into the real world of trees, water, and sky. He gives

FLORENCE

baby Jesus (right) and John the Baptist a realistic, human playfulness. It's a tender scene painted with warm colors and a hazy background that matches the golden skin of the children.

Raphael perfected his craft in Florence, following the graceful style of Leonardo. In typical Leonardo fashion, this group of Mary, John the Baptist, and Jesus is arranged in the shape of a pyramid, with Mary's head at the peak.

The two halves of the painting balance perfectly. Draw a line down the middle, through Mary's nose and down through her knee. John the Baptist on the left is balanced by Jesus on the right. Even the trees in the background balance each other, left and right. These things aren't immediately noticeable, but they help create the subconscious feelings of balance and order that reinforce the atmosphere of maternal security in this domestic scene—pure Renaissance.

Raphael—*Leo X and Cardinals* (*Ritratta di Papa Leone X con i Cardinali*)

Raphael was called to Rome at the same time as Michelangelo, working next door while Michelangelo painted the Sistine Chapel ceiling. Raphael peeked in from time to time, learning from Michelangelo's monumental, dramatic figures, and his later work is grittier and more realistic than the idealized, graceful, and "Leonardoesque" Madonna.

Pope Leo X is big, like a Michelangelo statue. And Raphael captures some of the seamier side of Vatican life in the cardinals' eyes— shrewd, suspicious, and somewhat cynical. With Raphael, the photographic realism pursued by painters since Giotto was finally achieved.

The Florentine Renaissance ended in 1520 with the death of Raphael. Raphael (see his **self-portrait** to the left of Leo X) is considered both the culmination and conclusion of the Renaissance. The realism, balance, and humanism we associate with the Renaissance are all found in Raphael's work. He combined the grace of Leonardo with the power of Michelangelo. With his death, the Renaissance shifted again—to Venice.

• *Pass through the next room and enter Room 28.*

Titian (Tiziano Vecellio, c. 1490-1576)—*Venus of Urbino* (*La Venere di Urbino*)

Compare this *Venus* with Botticelli's newly hatched *Venus,* and you get a good idea of the difference between the Florentine and Venetian Renaissance. Botticelli's was pure, innocent, and oth-

erworldly. Titian's should have a staple in her belly button. This isn't a Venus, it's a centerfold— with no purpose but to please the eye and other organs. While Botticelli's allegorical *Venus* is a message, this is a massage. The bed is used.

Titian and his fellow Vene-tians took the pagan spirit pioneered in Florence and carried it to its logical hedonistic conclusion. Using bright, rich colors, they captured the luxurious life of happy-go-lucky Venice.

While Raphael's *Madonna of the Goldfinch* was balanced with a figure on the left and one on the right, Titian balances his painting in a different way—with color. The canvas is split down the middle by the curtain. The left half is dark, the right half lighter. The two halves are connected by a diagonal slash of luminous gold—the nude woman. The girl in the background is trying to find her some clothes.

By the way, visitors from centuries past also panted in front of this Venus. The poet Byron called it "*the* Venus." With her sensual skin, hey-sailor look, and suggestively placed hand, she must have left them blithering idiots.

• *Find the n–n–n–next painting...in Room 29.*

Parmigianino (1503-1540)—*Madonna with the Long Neck* (*Madonna della Collo Lungo*)

Raphael, Michelangelo, Leonardo, and Titian mastered reality.

They could place any scene onto a canvas with photographic accuracy. How could future artists top that?

Mannerists such as Parmigianino tried, by going beyond realism, exaggerating it for effect. Using brighter colors and twisting poses (two techniques explored by Michelangelo), they created scenes more elegant and more exciting than real life.

By stretching the neck of his Madonna, Parmigianino (like the cheese) gives her an unnatural, swanlike beauty.

FLORENCE

She has the same pose and position of hands as Botticelli's *Venus* and the *Venus de' Medici*. Her body forms an arcing S-curve—down her neck as far as her elbow, then back the other way along Jesus' body to her knee, then down to her foot. The baby Jesus seems to be blissfully gliding down this slippery slide of sheer beauty.

In the Uffizi, we've seen many images of female beauty: from ancient goddesses to medieval Madonnas to wicked Eves, from Botticelli's pristine nymphs to Michelangelo's peasant Mary, from Raphael's Madonna-and-baby to Titian's babe. Their physical beauty expresses different aspects of the human spirit.

• *Pass through several rooms, returning to the main hallway. Head to the end of the hallway to the café for a true aesthetic experience.*

The Little Cappuccin Monk (Cappuccino)

This drinkable art form, born in Italy, is now enjoyed all over the world. It's called "The Little Cappuccin Monk" because the coffee's frothy light- and dark-brown foam looks like the two-toned cowls of the Cappuccin order. Sip it on the terrace in the shadow of the towering Palazzo Vecchio, and be glad we live in an age where you don't need to be a Medici to enjoy all this fine art. *Salute.*

Sights in Florence

While Florence has a wealth of interesting museums well-worth knowing about on a longer visit (see the "Florence at a Glance sidebar, earlier), for a one-day cruiser visit, I've listed just the main sights within walking distance of each other in the center. Don't let the length of my descriptions determine your sightseeing priorities. In this section, Florence's most important sights may have the shortest listings. These sights are covered in the much more detail in one of the earlier walks or tours.

North of the Duomo (Cathedral)

▲▲▲**Accademia (Galleria dell'Accademia)**—This museum houses Michelangelo's *David*, the consummate Renaissance statue of the buff, biblical shepherd boy ready to take on the giant. Nearby are some of the master's other works, including his powerful (unfinished) *Prisoners*, *St. Matthew*, and a *Pietà* (possibly by one of his disciples). For a self-guided tour, see page 408.

Cost and Hours: €6.50, plus €4 fee for recommended reservation (see page 406 for details), Tue-Sun 8:15-18:50, closed Mon, last entry 45 minutes before closing (Via Ricasoli 60, tel.

Heart of Florence

055-238-8609 or 055-294-883, www.polomuseale.firenze.it).

▲▲**Museum of San Marco (Museo di San Marco)**—Located one block north of the Accademia, this 15th-century monastery

houses the greatest collection anywhere of frescoes and paintings by the early Renaissance master Fra Angelico. The ground floor features the monk's paintings, along with some works by Fra Bartolomeo. Upstairs are 43 cells decorated by Fra Angelico and his assistants. While the monk-painter was trained in the medieval religious style, he also learned and adopted Renaissance techniques and sensibilities, producing works that blended Christian symbols and Renaissance realism. Don't miss the cell of Savonarola, the charismatic monk who rode in from the Christian right, threw out the Medicis, turned Florence into a theocracy, sponsored "bonfires of the vanities" (burning books, paintings, and so on), and was finally burned himself when Florence decided to change channels.

Cost and Hours: €4, Tue-Fri 8:15-13:50, Sat 8:15-16:50; also open 8:15-16:50 on second and fourth Sun and 8:15-13:50 on first, third, and fifth Mon of each month; last entry 30 minutes before closing, reservations possible but unnecessary, on Piazza San Marco, tel. 055-238-8608, www.polomuseale.firenze.it.

Museum of Precious Stones (Museo dell'Opificio delle Pietre Dure)—This unusual gem of a museum features room after room of exquisite mosaics of inlaid marble and stones. Upstairs, you'll see remnants of the Medici workshop from 1588, including 500 different precious stones and the tools used to cut and inlay them. The helpful loaner booklet available next to the ticket window describes it all in English.

Cost and Hours: €4, Mon-Sat 8:15-14:00, closed Sun, around corner from Accademia at Via degli Alfani 78, tel. 055-265-1357.

Church of San Lorenzo—This red-brick dome—which looks

like the Duomo's little sister—is the Medici church and the burial place of the family's founder, Giovanni di Bicci de' Medici (1360-1429). The facade is big, ugly, and unfinished, because Pope Leo X (also a Medici) pulled the plug on the project due to dwindling funds—after Michelangelo had labored on it for four years (1516-1520). Inside,

FLORENCE

though, is the spirit of Florence in the 1420s, with gray-and-white columns and arches in perfect Renaissance symmetry and simplicity. The Brunelleschi-designed church is lit by an even, diffused light. The Medici coat of arms (with the round pills of these "medics") decorates the ceiling, and everywhere are images of St. Lawrence, the Medici patron saint who was martyred on a grill.

Highlights of the church include two finely sculpted Donatello pulpits (in the nave). In the Martelli Chapel (left wall of the left transept), Filippo Lippi's *Annunciation* features a smiling angel greeting Mary in a sharply 3-D courtyard. Light shines through the vase in the foreground, like the Holy Spirit entering Mary's womb. The Old Sacristy (far left corner), designed by Brunelleschi, was the burial chapel for the Medicis. Bronze doors by Donatello flank the sacristy's small altar. Overhead, the dome above the altar shows the exact arrangement of the heavens on July 4, 1442, leaving scholars to hypothesize about why that particular date was used. Back in the nave, the round inlaid marble in the floor before the main altar marks where Cosimo the Elder—Lorenzo the Magnificent's grandfather—is buried. Assistants in the church provide information on request, and the information brochure is free and in English.

Cost and Hours: €3.50, Feb-Oct Mon-Sat 10:00-17:00, Sun 13:30-17:00, closed Nov-Jan, www.basilicasanlorenzo.it.

Nearby: A street market bustles outside the church (listed after the Medici Chapels, below).

Around the back end of the church is the entrance to the Medici Chapels and the New Sacristy, designed by Michelangelo for a later generation of dead Medicis.

▲▲**Medici Chapels (Cappelle Medicee)**—The burial site of the ruling Medici family in the Church of San Lorenzo includes

the dusky Crypt; the big, domed Chapel of Princes; and the magnificent all-Michelangelo New Sacristy, featuring the master's architecture, tombs, and statues. The Medicis made their money in textiles and banking and patronized a dream team of Renaissance artists that put Florence on the cultural map. Michelangelo, who spent his teen years living with the Medicis, was commissioned for the family's final tribute.

Cost and Hours: €6, Tue-Sat April-Oct 8:15-16:50, Nov-March 8:15-13:50; also open first, third, and fifth Sun and second and fourth Mon of each month; last entry 30 minutes before closing, confirm latest hours at TI or chapel, tel. 055-238-8602, www.polomuseale.firenze.it. Don't waste money on a reservation to visit this sight.

▲**San Lorenzo Market**—Florence's vast open-air market sprawls around the Church of San Lorenzo. Most of the leather stalls are run by Iranians selling South American leather that was tailored in Italy. Prices are soft (daily 9:00-19:00, closed Mon in winter, between the Duomo and train station).

▲**Mercato Centrale (Central Market)**—Florence's giant iron-and-glass-covered central market, a wonderland of picturesque produce, is fun to explore. While the nearby San Lorenzo Market—with its garment stalls in the streets—feels like a step up from a haphazard flea market, the Mercato Centrale retains a Florentine elegance. Wander around. You'll see parts of the cow you'd never dream of eating (no, that's not a turkey neck), enjoy generous free samples, watch pasta-making, and have your pick of plenty of fun eateries sloshing out cheap and tasty pasta to locals (Mon-Sat 7:00-14:00, in winter open Sat until 17:00, closed Sun). For eating ideas in and around the market, see "Eating in Florence," page 471.

▲**Medici-Riccardi Palace (Palazzo Medici-Riccardi)**— Lorenzo the Magnificent's home is worth a look for its art. The

tiny Chapel of the Magi contains colorful Renaissance gems like the *Procession of the Magi* frescoes by Benozzo Gozzoli. The former library has a Baroque ceiling fresco by Luca Giordano, a prolific artist from Naples known as "Fast Luke" *(Luca fa presto)* for his ambidextrous painting abilities. While the Medicis originally occupied this 1444 house, in the 1700s it became home to the Riccardi family, who added the Baroque flourishes.

Cost and Hours: €5, €7 with mandatory special exhibits, Thu-Tue 9:00-19:00, closed Wed, last entry 30 minutes before closing; kitty-corner from Church of San Lorenzo, one long block north of Duomo, ticket entrance is north of the main gated entrance, Via Cavour 3, tel. 055-276-0340.

Leonardo Museum—This small entrepreneurial venture is fun for anyone who wants to crank the shaft and spin the ball bearings of Leonardo's genius inventions. While there are no actual historic artifacts, it shows about 30 of Leonardo's

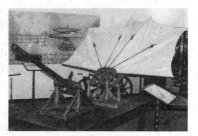

FLORENCE

inventions and experiments made into models. You'll see a full-size armored tank, walk into a chamber of mirrors, operate a rotating crane, and watch experiments in flying. Each is described in English. What makes this exhibit special is that you're encouraged to touch and play with the models—it's great for kids.

Cost and Hours: €6, daily 10:00-19:00, closes at 18:00 in winter, Via dei Servi 66 red, tel. 055-282-966, www.mostredileonardo.com.

Duomo and Nearby

For more information on the Duomo and associated sights, see page 420.

▲▲**Duomo (Cattedrale di Santa Maria del Fiore)**—Florence's Gothic cathedral has the third-longest nave in Christendom. The church's noisy Neo-Gothic facade from the 1870s is covered with pink, green, and white Tuscan marble. In the interior, you'll see a huge *Last Judgment* by Giorgio Vasari and Federico Zuccari (inside the dome). Much of the church's great art is stored in the Duomo Museum behind the church.

The cathedral's claim to artistic fame is Brunelleschi's magnificent dome—the first Renaissance dome and the model for domes to follow.

Massive crowds line up to see the huge church. The church is a major sight, but not worth a long wait. Either go late (the crowds subside by late afternoon), or take the Terraces tour mentioned below.

Cost and Hours: Free entry, Mon-Fri 10:00-17:00, Thu until 15:30 in May and Oct and until 16:30 in winter, Sat 10:00-16:45, Sun 13:30-16:45, modest dress code enforced, tel. 055-230-2885, www.operaduomo.firenze.it.

Crowd-Beating Tip: Taking the "**Terraces of the Cathedral and Dome**" tour allows you to skip the long lines to enter the cathedral and to climb the dome. After a short guided tour of the interior, you'll climb up onto the exterior terrace, where great views reward the stair hike (see "Climbing the Duomo's Dome," next). When the tour is finished on the terrace, you can continue on your own up to the top of the dome (€15, 45 minutes; offered Mon-Fri at 10:30, 12:00, and 15:00; at 10:30 and 12:00 on Sat, no tours on Sun, buy tickets at nearby Duomo Museum and they'll tell you where to meet your guide). If you're planning to climb the dome anyway (€8), the tour is a fine value.

▲**Climbing the Duomo's Dome**—For a grand view into the cathedral from the base of the dome, a peek at some of the tools used in the dome's construction, a chance to see Brunelleschi's "dome-within-a-dome" construction, a glorious Florence view from the top, and the equivalent of 463 plunges on a Renaissance StairMaster, climb the dome. To avoid the long, dreadfully slow-moving line, arrive by 8:30 or drop by very late. Those taking the "Terraces" tour of the Duomo (see above) can skip the line.

Cost and Hours: €8, Mon-Fri 8:30-19:00, Sat 8:30-17:40, closed Sun, last entry 40 minutes before closing, enter from outside church on north side, tel. 055-230-2885.

▲**Campanile (Giotto's Tower)**—The 270-foot bell tower has 50 fewer steps than the Duomo's dome (but that's still 414 steps—no elevator); offers a faster, less-crowded climb; and has a view of the Duomo to boot, but the cage-like top makes taking good photographs difficult.

Cost and Hours: €6, daily 8:30-19:30, last entry 40 minutes before closing.

▲**Baptistery**—Michelangelo said its bronze doors were fit to be the gates of paradise. Check out the gleaming copies of Lorenzo Ghiberti's bronze doors facing the Duomo. Making a breakthrough in perspective, Ghiberti used mathematical laws to create the illusion of receding distance on a basically flat surface.

The doors on the north side of the building were designed by Ghiberti when he was young; he'd won the honor and opportunity by beating Brunelleschi in a competition (the rivals' original entries are in the Bargello).

Inside, sit and savor the medieval mosaic ceiling, where it's always Judgment Day and Jesus is giving the ultimate thumbs-up and thumbs-down. The rest of the ceiling mosaics tell the history of the world, from Adam and Eve (over the north/entrance doors, top row) to Noah and the Flood (over south doors, top row), to the life of Christ (second row) to the beheading of John the Baptist (bottom row), all bathed in the golden glow of pre-Renaissance heaven.

Cost and Hours: €4, interior open Mon-Sat 12:15-19:00 except first Sat of month 8:30-14:00, Sun 8:30-14:00, last entry 30 minutes before closing, audioguide-€2, photos allowed inside, tel. 055-230-2885; bronze doors are on the outside, so always "open"; original panels are in the Duomo Museum.

▲▲▲**Duomo Museum (Museo dell'Opera del Duomo)**—The underrated cathedral museum, behind the church (at Via del Proconsolo 9), is great if you like sculpture. On the ground floor,

look for a late Michelangelo *Pietà,* the eight
restored panels of Ghiberti's north doors for
the Baptistery, and statues from the original Baptistery facade. Upstairs, you'll find
Brunelleschi's models for his dome, as well
as Donatello's anorexic *Mary Magdalene* and
playful choir loft. The museum features most
of Ghiberti's original "Gates of Paradise"
panels; the panels on the Baptistery's doors
today are copies.

Cost and Hours: €6, Mon-Sat 9:00-
19:30, Sun 9:00-13:40, last entry 40 minutes
before closing, one of the few museums in
Florence always open on Mon, Via del Proconsolo 9, tel. 055-
230-2885. At this museum, you can purchase €15 tickets for the
"Terraces of the Cathedral and Dome" tour mentioned earlier
(page 458), which allows you to bypass the long cathedral-entry
and dome-climbing lines.

Between the Duomo
and Piazza della Signoria

▲▲▲**Bargello (Museo Nazionale)**—This underappreciated
sculpture museum is in a former police station-turned-prison that
looks like a mini-Palazzo Vecchio. It has Donatello's painfully
beautiful *David* (the very influential first male nude to be sculpted

in a thousand years), works
by Michelangelo, and rooms
of Medici treasures explained
only in Italian (politely suggest to the staff that English
descriptions would be wonderful). Moody Donatello,
who embraced realism with
his lifelike statues, set the per-
sonal and artistic style for many Renaissance artists to follow. The
best works are in the ground-floor room at the foot of the outdoor
staircase and in the room directly above.

Cost and Hours: €4, but mandatory special exhibitions often
increase the price to €7, Tue-Sat April-Oct 8:15-16:50, Nov-March
8:15-13:50; also open first, third, and fifth Mon and the second
and fourth Sun of each month; last entry 40 minutes before closing, reservations possible but unnecessary, Via del Proconsolo 4,
reservation tel. 055-238-8606, www.polomuseale.firenze.it.

Casa di Dante (Dante's House)—Dante Alighieri (1265-1321),
the poet who gave us *The Divine Comedy,* is the Shakespeare of
Italy, the father of the modern Italian language, and the face on

the country's €2 coin. However, most Americans know little of him, and this museum is not the ideal place to start. Even though it has English information, this small museum (in a building near where he likely lived) assumes visitors have prior knowledge of the poet. Dante-lovers can trace his interesting life and works through pictures, models, and artifacts. And because the exhibits are as much about medieval Florence as they are about the man, novices can learn a little about Dante and the city he lived in.

Cost and Hours: €4, summer daily 10:00-18:00; winter Tue-Sun 10:00-17:00, closed Mon; last entry 30 minutes before closing, near the Bargello at Via Santa Margherita 1, tel. 055-219-416, www.museocasadidante.it.

▲**Orsanmichele Church**—In the ninth century, this loggia (covered courtyard) was a market used for selling grain (stored upstairs). Later, it was enclosed to make a church.

Outside are dynamic statue-filled niches, some with accompanying symbols from the guilds that sponsored the art. Donatello's *St. Mark* and *St. George* (on the northeast and northwest corners) step out boldly in the new Renaissance style.

The interior has a glorious Gothic tabernacle (1359) housing the painted wooden panel that depicts *Madonna delle Grazie* (1346). The iron bars spanning the vaults were the Italian Gothic answer to the French Gothic external buttresses. Look for the rectangular holes in the piers—these were once wheat chutes that connected to the upper floors.

For more information on the church, see page 425.

Cost and Hours: Free entry, Tue-Sun 10:00-17:00, closed Mon, niche sculptures always viewable from the outside.

Ticket Office: You can give the *Madonna della Grazie* a special thanks if you need Uffizi or Accademia tickets (sold from door facing Via de' Calzaiuoli; ticket window open daily 10:00-17:00).

A block away, you'll find the...

▲**Mercato Nuovo (a.k.a. the Straw Market)**—This market loggia is how Orsanmichele looked before it became a church. Originally a silk and straw market, Mercato Nuovo still functions as a rustic yet touristy market (at the intersection of Via Calimala and Via Porta Rossa). Prices are soft, but the San Lorenzo Market (listed earlier) is much better for haggling. Notice the circled X in the center, marking the spot where people hit the ground after being hoisted up to the top and dropped as punishment for bankruptcy. You'll also find *Porcellino* (a statue of a wild boar nicknamed "little pig"), which people rub and give coins to in order to ensure their return to Florence. This new copy, while only a few years old, already has a polished snout. At the back corner, a wagon sells tripe (cow innards) sandwiches—a local favorite (daily 9:00-20:00).

▲**Piazza della Repubblica and Nearby**—This large square sits on the site of Florence's original Roman Forum. The lone column—nicknamed "the belly button of Florence"—once marked the intersection of the two main Roman roads. All that survives of Roman Florence is its grid street plan and this column. Look at any map of Florence today (there's one by the benches—where the old boys hang out to talk sports and politics), and you'll see the ghost

of Rome in its streets: a grid-plan city center surrounded by what was the Roman wall. Roman Florence was a garrison town, a rectangular fort with this square marking the intersection of the two main roads (Via Corso and Via Roma).

Today's piazza, framed by a triumphal arch, is a nationalistic statement celebrating the unification of Italy. Florence, the capital of the country (1865-1870) until Rome was "liberated" (from the Vatican), lacked a square worthy of this grand new country. So the neighborhood here—once the Jewish quarter—was razed to open up an imposing, modern forum surrounded by stately circa-1890 buildings.

Venerable cafés and stores line the square. The La Rinascente department store, facing Piazza della Repubblica, is one of the city's mainstays (WC on fourth floor, continue up the stairs from there to the bar with a view terrace).

▲**Palazzo Davanzati**—This five-story late-medieval tower house offers a rare look at a noble dwelling built in the 14th century. Currently only the ground and first floors are open to visitors, though the remaining floors can be visited by appointment. Like other buildings of the age, the exterior is festooned with 14th-century horse-tethering rings made out of iron, torch holders, and poles upon which to hang laundry and fly flags. Inside, though the furnishings are pretty sparse, you'll see richly painted walls, a long chute that functioned as a well, plenty of fireplaces, a lace display, and even a modern toilet.

Cost and Hours: €2, Tue-Sat 8:15-13:50; also open second and fourth Mon and first, third, and fifth Sun; Via Porta Rossa 13, tel. 055-238-8610.

On and near Piazza della Signoria

Piazza della Signoria, the main civic center of Florence, is dominated by Palazzo Vecchio, the Uffizi Gallery, and the marble greatness of old Florence littering the cobbles. For more information on this area, see page 428.

▲▲▲**Uffizi Gallery**—This greatest collection of Italian paintings anywhere features works by Giotto, Leonardo, Raphael, Caravaggio, Rubens, Titian, and Michelangelo, and a roomful of Botticellis, including his *Birth of Venus.* For a self-guided tour, see page 432.

Cost and Hours: €6.50 but mandatory special exhibits generally bump the price to €10, extra €4 for recommended reservation, cash required to pick up reserved tickets, Tue-Sun 8:15-18:50, closed Mon, last entry 45 minutes before closing, museum info tel. 055-238-8651, www.polomuseale.firenze.it. To avoid the long ticket lines, get reservations at least a month ahead in high season. For details on making reservations, check the sidebar on page 406.

▲**Palazzo Vecchio**—With its distinctive castle turret, this fortified palace—the Town Hall, officially called the Palazzo della Signoria—is a Florentine landmark. But if you're visiting only one palace interior in town, the Pitti Palace is better. The interior of Palazzo Vecchio is best for fans of coffered and gilded ceilings, of Florentine history, or of the artist Giorgio Vasari, who wallpapered the place with mediocre magnificence.

The museum's most famous statues are Michelangelo's *Victory* and Donatello's bronze statue of *Judith and Holofernes.*

Cost and Hours: €6, €8 combo-ticket with Brancacci Chapel, skippable audioguide, tours are free and in English but require reservation, Fri-Wed 9:00-19:00, Thu 9:00-14:00, ticket office closes one hour earlier, tel. 055-276-8224.

▲▲**Galileo Science Museum (Museo Galilei e Istituto di Storia della Scienza)**—When we think of the Florentine Renaissance, we think of visual arts: painting, mosaics, architec-

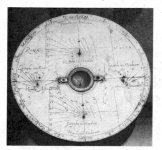

ture, and sculpture. But when the visual arts declined in the 1600s (abused and co-opted by political powers), music and science flourished in Florence. The first opera was written here. And Florence hosted many scientific breakthroughs, as you'll see in this fascinating collection of Renaissance and later clocks, telescopes, maps, and ingenious gadgets. Trace the technical innovations as modern science emerges from 1000 to 1900. One of the most talked-about bottles in Florence is the one here that contains Galileo's finger. Exhibits include various tools for gauging the world, from a compass and thermometer to Galileo's telescopes. Other displays delve into clocks, pumps, medicine, and chemistry. Some English information is available, and the docents are helpful. It's friendly, comfortably cool, never crowded, and just a block east of the Uffizi on the Arno River.

FLORENCE

Cost and Hours: €8, €20 family ticket, Wed-Mon 9:30-18:00, Tue 9:30-13:00, Piazza dei Giudici 1, tel. 055-265-311, recorded info tel. 055-293-493, www.museogalileo.it.

▲**Ponte Vecchio**—Florence's most famous bridge is lined with shops that have traditionally sold gold and silver. A statue of Benvenuto Cellini, the master goldsmith of the Renaissance, stands in the center, ignored by the flood of tacky tourism.

Notice the "prince's passageway" above the bridge, called the **Vasari Corridor.** In less-secure times, the city leaders had a fortified passageway connecting Palazzo Vecchio and the Uffizi with the mighty Pitti Palace, to which they could flee in times of attack. This passageway is sometimes open to the public, but a visit is almost impossible to arrange, and if you do manage it, it's usually a disappointment (you could check at the Uffizi to see if it's open or try a private tour company such as Artviva Walking Tours; see page 404).

East of Piazza della Signoria

▲▲**Santa Croce Church**—This 14th-century Franciscan church, decorated with centuries of precious art, holds the tombs of great Florentines.

The loud 19th-century Victorian Gothic facade faces a huge square ringed with tempting shops and littered with tired tour-

ists. Escape into the church and admire its sheer height and spaciousness. Start at the back of the nave (farthest from the altar). On the left wall (as you face the altar) is the **tomb of Galileo Galilei** (1564-1642), the Pisan who lived his last years under house arrest near Florence. Having defied the Church by saying that the earth revolved around the sun, his heretical remains were not allowed in the church until long after his death. Directly opposite (on the right wall) is the **tomb of Michelangelo Buonarroti** (1475-1564).

The first chapel to the right of the main altar features the famous fresco by Giotto of the *Death of St. Francis.* With simple but eloquent gestures, Francis' brothers bid him a sad farewell. One folds his hands and stares longingly at Francis' serene face. Another bends to kiss Francis' hand, while others raise their

arms in grief. It's one of the first expressions of human emotion in modern painting. It's also one of the first to create a real three-dimensional grouping of figures.

At the end of the right transept, a left turn at the first door leads into the sacristy, where you'll find a rumpled bit of **St. Francis' tunic** (*Parte della Tonaca,* scrunched up in a small gold frame). In the hallway near the bookstore, notice the photos of the devastating flood of 1966. Beyond that is the leather school, the first shop of what is now a popular leather district. Wander through the former dorms for monks, watch the leatherworking in action, and browse the finished products—for sale, of course.

Exit between the Rossini and Machiavelli tombs into the cloister (open-air courtyard). On the left, enter Brunelleschi's Pazzi Chapel, which captures the Renaissance in miniature.

Cost and Hours: €5 includes the church, Pazzi Chapel, and museum; Mon-Sat 9:30-17:30, Sun 13:00-17:30, last entry 30 minutes before closing, modest dress code enforced, 10-minute walk east of Palazzo Vecchio along Borgo de' Greci, tel. 055-246-6105. The leather school is free and sells tickets to the church. If the church has a long line, come here to avoid the line (daily 10:00-18:00, has own entry behind church plus an entry within the church, www.leatherschool.com).

▲**Casa Buonarroti (Michelangelo's House)**—Fans enjoy a house standing on property once owned by Michelangelo. The house was built after Michelangelo's death by the artist's grand-nephew, who turned it into a little museum honoring his famous relative. You'll see some of Michelangelo's early, less-than-monumental statues and a few sketches. Be warned: Michelangelo's descendants attributed everything they could to their famous relative, but very little here (beyond two marble relief panels and a couple of sketches) is actually by Michelangelo.

Cost and Hours: €6.50, Wed-Mon 9:30-14:00, closed Tue, English descriptions, Via Ghibellina 70, tel. 055-241-752.

Near the Train Station

▲▲**Church of Santa Maria Novella**—This 13th-century Dominican church is rich in art. Along with crucifixes by Giotto

and Brunelleschi, there's every textbook's example of the early Renaissance mastery of perspective: *The Holy Trinity* by Masaccio. The exquisite chapels trace art in Florence from medieval times to early Baroque. The outside of the church features a dash of Romanesque (horizontal stripes),

Gothic (pointed arches), Renaissance (geometric shapes), and Baroque (scrolls). Step in and look down the 330-foot nave for a 14th-century optical illusion.

Cost and Hours: €3.50, Mon-Thu 9:00-17:30, Fri 11:00-17:30, Sat 9:00-17:00, Sun 13:00-17:00, last entry 30 minutes before closing, tel. 055-219-257.

Nearby: A palatial **perfumery** (Farmacia di Santa Maria Novella) is a block from Piazza Santa Maria Novella, 100 yards down Via della Scala at #16 (free but shopping encouraged, inconsistent hours but likely daily 9:30-19:30, see map on page 400, tel. 055-216-276, www.smnovella.com). Thick with the lingering aroma of centuries of spritzes, it started as the herb garden of the Santa Maria Novella monks. Well-known even today for its top-quality products, it is extremely Florentine. Pick up the history sheet at the desk, and wander deep into the shop. From the back room, you can peek at one of Santa Maria Novella's cloisters with its dreamy frescoes and imagine a time before Vespas and tourists.

You can get a closer look inside the **Museum and Cloisters,** adjacent to the church, but they're definitely lesser sights (€2.70, entry to the left of the church's facade; Mon-Thu and Sat 9:00-17:00, closed Fri and Sun).

South of the Arno River

▲▲**Pitti Palace**—The imposing Pitti Palace, several blocks southwest of Ponte Vecchio, is not only home to the second-best collection of paintings in town, the **Palatine Gallery,** but also happens

to be the most sumptuous palace you can tour in Florence. The building itself is mammoth, holding several different museums and anchoring two gardens. Stick primarily to the gallery, forget about everything else, and the palace becomes a little less exhausting.

You'll walk through one palatial room after another, walls sagging with masterpieces by 16th- and 17th-century masters, including Rubens, Titian, and Rembrandt. Its Raphael collection is the second-biggest anywhere—the Vatican beats it by one. Each room has some descriptions in English, though the paintings themselves have limited English labels.

The collection is all on one floor. To see the highlights, walk straight down the spine through a dozen or so rooms. Before you exit, consider a visit to the Royal Apartments. These 14 rooms (of which only a few are open at any one time) are where the Pitti's rulers lived in the 18th and 19th centuries. Each room features a

different color and time period. Here, you get a real feel for the splendor of the dukes' world.

The Rest of the Pitti Palace: If you've got the energy and interest, it'd be a Pitti to miss the palace's other offerings.

The **Modern Art Gallery,** on the second floor, features Romantic, Neoclassical, and Impressionist works by 19th- and 20th-century Tuscan painters.

The **Argenti Museum** (on the ground and mezzanine floors) is the Medici treasure chest, with jeweled crucifixes, exotic porcelain, and gilded ostrich eggs, made to entertain fans of the applied arts.

The **Boboli and Bardini Gardens,** located behind the palace, offer a pleasant and shady refuge from the city heat. Enter the Boboli Gardens from the Pitti Palace courtyard. The less-visited Bardini Gardens are behind the Boboli, rising in terraces toward Piazzale Michelangelo.

Cost and Hours: The main reason to visit is to see the Palatine Gallery, but you can't buy a ticket for the gallery alone; to see it you'll need to buy ticket #1, which includes the Palatine Gallery, Royal Apartments, and Modern Art Gallery (€8.50 but often €12 with mandatory special exhibits, Tue-Sun 8:15-18:50, closed Mon, tel. 055-238-8614, www.polomuseale.firenze.it). Ticket #2 covers the Boboli and Bardini Gardens, Argenti Museum (the Duke's treasures), Costume Gallery, and Porcelain Museum (€6, more with special exhibits, daily 8:15-18:30, until 19:30 June-Aug, same phone and website as above). An €11.50 combo-ticket covers the whole palace complex (valid 3 days). If there's a long line, you can bypass it by buying a reservation for immediate entry at the ticket window (€3 reservation fee).

▲▲**Brancacci Chapel**—For the best look at works by Masaccio (the early Renaissance master who reinvented perspective), see his restored frescoes here. Instead of medieval religious symbols, Masaccio's paintings feature simple, strong human figures with facial expressions that reflect their emotions. The accompanying works of Masolino and Filippino Lippi provide illuminating contrasts.

Reservations are free and required (see below). Your ticket includes a 40-minute film in English on the church, the frescoes, and Renaissance Florence (reserve a viewing time when you book your entry). The film starts promptly at the top of the hour. Computer animation brings the paintings to life—making them appear to move and giving them

FLORENCE

3-D depth—while narration describes the events depicted in the panels. Yes, it's a long time commitment, and the film takes liberties with the art. But it's visually interesting and your best way to see the frescoes close up. The film works great either before or after you visit the frescoes.

Cost and Hours: €4, free reservations required—it's very easy...just call at least a day in advance, €8 combo-ticket with Palazzo Vecchio, both tickets include worthwhile 40-minute film in English—reserve film when you book entry, limit of 30 visitors every 15 minutes, Mon and Wed-Sat 10:00-17:00, Sun 13:00-17:00, closed Tue, ticket office closes at 16:30; in Church of Santa Maria del Carmine—cross Ponte Vecchio and turn right on Borgo San Jacopo, walk 10 minutes, then turn left into Piazza del Carmine; tel. 055-276-8224 or 055-276-8558.

Reservations: Call the chapel at least a day ahead for free, mandatory reservations; tickets are sometimes available for the same day (tel. 055-276-8224 or 055-276-8558, English spoken, call center open daily 9:00-17:00). If the line is busy, keep trying—it's best to call around 14:00-15:00 or just before the ticket office closes at 16:30. Reservation times begin every 15 minutes, with a maximum of 30 visitors per time slot (you have 15 minutes inside the chapel). When you call to reserve, you can also book a time to see the film.

Santo Spirito Church—This church has a classic Brunelleschi interior and a painted, carved wooden crucifix attributed to 17-year-old Michelangelo. The sculptor donated this early work to the monastery in appreciation for allowing him to dissect and learn about bodies. The Michelangelo *Crocifisso* is displayed in the sacristy, through a door midway down the left side of the nave (if it's closed, ask someone to let you in). Copies of Michelangelo's *Pietà* and *Risen Christ* flank the nave. Beer-drinking, guitar-playing rowdies decorate the church steps.

Cost and Hours: Free entry, Mon-Tue and Thu-Sat 9:30-12:30 & 16:00-17:30, Sun 15:00-17:30 only, closed Wed, Piazza Santo Spirito, tel. 055-211-716.

▲**Piazzale Michelangelo**—Overlooking the city from across the river (look for the huge statue of *David*), this square has a superb view of Florence and the stunning dome of the Duomo.

It's worth the 30-minute hike or bus ride (either #12 or #13 from the train station—takes a long time). It makes sense to take a taxi or ride the bus up, and then enjoy the easy downhill walk back into town. An inviting café with great views is just below the overlook. The best photos are taken from the street immediately below the overlook (go around to the right and down a few steps). Off the west side of the piazza is a somewhat hidden terrace, an excellent place to retreat from the mobs. After dark, the square is

FLORENCE

packed with school kids licking ice cream and each other. About 200 yards beyond all the tour groups and teenagers is the stark, beautiful, crowd-free Romanesque San Miniato Church (next listing).

The hike down is quick and enjoyable. Take the steps between the two bars on the San Miniato Church side of the parking lot (Via San Salvatore al Monte), and in a couple of minutes you walk through the old wall (Porta San Miniato) and emerge in the delightful little Oltrarno neighborhood of San Niccolò.

▲▲**San Miniato Church**—According to legend, the martyred St. Minias—this church's namesake—was beheaded on the banks of

the Arno in A.D. 250. He picked up his head and walked here (this was before the #12 bus), where he died and was buried in what became the first Christian cemetery in Florence. In the 11th century, this church was built to house Minias' remains. Imagine this fine church all alone— without any nearby buildings or fancy stairs—a peaceful refuge

where white-robed Benedictine monks could pray and work (their motto: *ora et labora*). The church's green-and-white marble facade (12th century) is classic Florentine Romanesque. The church has wonderful 3-D paintings, a plush ceiling of glazed terra-cotta panels by Luca della Robbia, and a sumptuous Renaissance chapel (located front and center). The highlight for me is the brilliantly preserved art in the sacristy (behind altar in the room on right) showing scenes from the life of St. Benedict (circa 1350, by a follower of Giotto). Drop a euro into the box to light the room for five minutes.

Cost and Hours: Free entry, daily April-Oct 8:00-19:30, Nov-March 8:00-13:00 & 14:30-18:00, Gregorian chants April-Sept daily at the 17:30 Mass—17:00 in winter, 200 yards above Piazzale Michelangelo, bus #12 or #13 from train station, tel. 055-234-2731.

Shopping in Florence

Florence is a great shopping town—known for its sense of style since the Medici days. Many people spend entire days shopping. Smaller stores are generally open 9:00-13:00 and 15:30-19:30, usually closed on Sunday, often closed on Monday, and sometimes closed for a couple of weeks around August 15. Many stores have promotional stalls in the market squares.

For shopping ideas, ads, and a list of markets, see *The Florentine* newspaper or *Florence Concierge Information* magazine (free from TI and many hotels). For a list of bookstores, see page 401.

If you end up going overboard on Florentine finds, you can buy a cheap extra suitcase at the stalls outside the Church of Santa Maria Novella, opposite the train station. A big suitcase with wheels costs about €25, and should last long enough to haul your purchases home.

Markets

Busy street scenes and markets abound. Prices are soft in the markets—go ahead and bargain. Perhaps the biggest market is the one that fills the streets around the Church of San Lorenzo (see page 455), with countless stalls selling lower-end leather, clothing, T-shirts, handbags, and souvenirs (daily 9:00-19:00, closed Mon in winter, between the Duomo and train station). Beware of fake "genuine" leather and "Venetian"

glass. The neighboring Mercato Centrale (Central Market) is a giant covered food market (see "Edible Goodies," later).

Other popular shopping centers are the Santa Croce area (known for leather; check out the leather school, which is actually inside the Santa Croce Church—enter to the right of the altar or use the outside entrance); Ponte Vecchio (traditional spot for gold and silver); and the old, covered Mercato Nuovo (three blocks north of Ponte Vecchio, described on page 461).

For antiques, artisan shops, and fashionable clothing boutiques, wander the city's "Left Bank," the Oltrarno (south side of river).

A **flea market** litters Piazza dei Ciompi with antiques and odds and ends daily, but is only really big on the last Sunday of each month (9:00-20:00, near Piazza Santa Croce).

Boutiques and High Fashion

The entire area between the river and the cathedral is busy with inviting boutiques that show off ritzy Italian fashions. The street Via de' Tornabuoni is best for boutique browsing.

The main **Ferragamo** store fills a classy 800-year-old building with a fine selection of shoes and bags (daily 10:00-19:30, Via de' Tornabuoni 2). They have an interesting, four-room shoe museum (€5, Wed-Mon 10:00-18:00, closed Tue, near the Santa Trinità bridge at Piazza Santa Trinità 5, tel. 055-336-0846). For more boutiques, meander the following streets: Via della Vigna Nuova (runs west from Via de' Tornabuoni), Via del Parione, and Via Strozzi (runs east from Via de' Tornabuoni to Piazza della Repubblica).

Department Stores

Typical chain department stores are **Coin,** the Italian equivalent of Macy's (Mon-Sat 10:00-19:30, Sun 10:30-19:30, on Via de' Calzaiuoli, near Orsanmichele Church); the similar, upscale **La Rinascente** (Mon-Sat 9:00-21:00, Sun 10:30-20:00, on Piazza della Repubblica); and **Oviesse,** a discount clothing chain, the local JCPenney (Mon-Sat 9:00-19:30, Sun 9:00-13:00 & 15:00-17:30, near train station at intersection of Via Panzani and Via del Giglio).

Souvenir Ideas

Shoppers in Florence can easily buy art reproductions (posters, calendars, books, prints, and so on—a breeze to find in and near the Uffizi and Accademia museums). With its history as a literary center, Florence offers traditional marbled stationery and leather-bound journals (try the Il Papiro chain stores), plus reproductions of old documents, maps, and manuscripts. Find silk ties, scarves, and Tuscan ceramics at the San Lorenzo street market, where haggling is expected. Goofy knickknacks featuring Renaissance masterpieces are fun gifts: Botticelli mouse pads, Raphael lipstick-holders, and plaster *David*s. For soaps, skin creams, herbal remedies, and perfumes, sniff out the antique and palatial perfumery, **Farmacia di Santa Maria Novella** (Via della Scala 16, see page 466).

Edible Goodies

The **Mercato Centrale** is a prime spot for stocking up on culinary souvenirs (Mon-Sat 7:00-14:00, Sat in winter until 17:00, closed Sun, a block north of the Church of San Lorenzo). Classic purchases include olives, Parmigiano-Reggiano cheese (must be vacuumed-packed to pass US customs), unusually shaped and colored pasta, and jars of pestos and sauces (such as pesto *genovese* or *tartufo*—truffle).

Upstairs, where produce and bulk products are sold, the price of dried porcini mushrooms is less than a quarter of what it is at the airport Duty Free. While many bring home a special bottle of Chianti Classico or Brunello di Montalcino, I take home only the names of my favorite wines—and buy them later at my hometown wine shop (rather than flying with hard-to-pack bottles).

Eating in Florence

To save money and time for sights, keep lunches fast and simple, eating in one of the countless pizzerias and self-service cafeterias (or picnicking your way through the Mercato Centrale).

Italian restaurateurs like to serve what's fresh. If you're into flavor, go for the seasonal best bets—featured in the *piatti del giorno* ("special of the day") sections of menus.

For dessert, it's gelato (see the sidebar on page 476).

Near the Mercato Centrale

Notice that all of these eateries are open only for lunch.

Mercato Centrale (Central Market) is great for an ad-lib lunch. It offers colorful piles of picnic produce, people-watching, and rustic sandwiches (Mon-Sat 7:00-14:00, Sat in winter until 17:00, closed Sun, a block north of San Lorenzo street market). Meat, fish, and cheese are sold on the ground level, with fruit and veggies mostly upstairs. The thriving ground-level eateries within the market (such as Nerbone, described next) serve some of the cheapest hot meals in town. The fancy deli, Perini, is famous for its quality products and generous free samples. Buy a picnic of fresh mozzarella cheese, olives, fruit, and crunchy bread to munch on the steps of the nearby Church of San Lorenzo, overlooking the bustling street market.

Nerbone in the Market is a venerable café and the best place for a sit-down meal within Mercato Centrale. Join the shoppers and workers who crowd up to the bar to grab their €5 plates—tripe is very big here—and then find an informal table to eat at nearby. Of the several cheap market diners, this feels the most authentic (lunch only, cash only, inside Mercato Centrale on the side closest to the Church of San Lorenzo, mobile 339-648-0251).

Trattoria Mario has been serving hearty lunches to market-goers since 1953 (Fabio and Romeo are the latest generation). Their simple formula: bustling service, old-fashioned good value, a lunch-only fixed-price meal, and shared tables. It's *cucina casalinga*—home cooking *con brio*. This place is extremely popular, and their best dishes often sell out first, so go early. If there's a line, put your name on the list (€5 pastas, €8 *secondi*, cash only, Mon-Sat 12:00-15:30, closed Sun and Aug, no reservations, Via Rosina 2, tel. 055-218-550).

Casa del Vino, Florence's oldest operating wine shop, offers glasses of wine from among 25 open bottles. Owner Gianni, whose family has owned the Casa for more than 70 years, is a class act. Gianni's *carta dei panini* lists many delightful €3.50 sandwiches (the crostini are notable). Some opened bottles behind the counter are marked with prices for wine by the glass; otherwise, see the list tacked to the bar. During busy times, it's a mob scene. You'll eat standing outside, with workers on a quick lunch break (Mon-Sat 9:30-17:00, closed Sat in summer and Sun year-round, hidden behind stalls of San Lorenzo Market at Via dell'Ariento 16 red, tel. 055-215-609).

Döner Kebab—Cheap, Fast, and Not a Hint of Pasta

Because of the influx of Middle Eastern immigrants into Italy, "ethnic cuisine" has become more prevalent in recent years. Today, shops selling döner kebab (roasted meat wrapped in thin bread) are sprouting everywhere.

Döner kebab shops offer cheap, filling, healthy alternatives to your average slice of pizza or ham-and-cheese *panino*. The kebab itself consists of chicken or veal and turkey, which has been cut into thick slabs, piled high onto a skewer, and slow-roasted on a vertical spit. Once it's cooked, the rich, savory meat is sliced ultra-thin with a razor and stuffed into your choice of pita bread (*panino*) or a wrap (*piadina*), along with tomatoes, onions, lettuce, tangy yogurt sauce, and (optional) hot chili sauce. A vegetarian alternative is falafel (a fried garbanzo-bean patty) served with the same works. Either dish costs about €3-4, and shops are generally open from 11:00 in the morning until midnight.

Budget Lunches Between the Duomo and the Accademia

Pasticceria Robiglio, a smart little café, opens up its stately dining area and sets out a few tables on the sidewalk for lunch on workdays. They have a small menu of daily pasta and *secondi* specials, and seem determined to do things like they did in the elegant pre-tourism days (generous €8 plates, a great €7.50 *niçoise*-like "fantasy salad," pretty pastries, good wines by the glass, smiling service, daily 12:00-15:00, longer hours as a café, a block toward the Duomo off Piazza S.S. Annunziata at Via dei Servi 112 red, tel. 055-212-784). Before you leave, be tempted by their pastries—famous among Florentines.

La Mescita Fiaschetteria is a characteristic hole-in-the-wall just around the corner from *David*—but a world away from all the tourism. It's where locals and students enjoy daily pasta specials and hearty sandwiches with good €1 house wine. You can trust Mirco—just point to what looks good (such as their €5 pasta plate), and you'll soon be eating well and inexpensively. The place can either be mobbed by students or in a peaceful time warp, depending on when you stop by (Mon-Sat 12:00-16:00, closed Sun, Via degli Alfani 70 red, mobile 347-795-1604).

Picnic on the Ultimate Renaissance Square: Il Centro Supermercati, a handy supermarket across from the Accademia *(David)*, happily makes sandwiches to your specs (Mon-Sat 8:00-20:00, Sun 10:00-19:00, Via Ricasoli 109). Choose your fresh bread and tasty meat and cheese (assembled and sold by the weight);

FLORENCE

Florence Restaurants

1. Mercato Centrale & Nerbone in the Market
2. Trattoria Mario
3. Casa del Vino
4. Pasticceria Robiglio
5. La Mescita Fiaschetteria
6. Il Centro Supermercati
7. Self-Service Rist. Leonardo
8. The Oil Shoppe
9. Cantinetta dei Verrazzano
10. Osteria Vini e Vecchi Sapori
11. I Fratellini
12. L'Antico Trippaio
13. 'Ino Bottega di Alimentari e Vini
14. Gelateria Grom
15. Gelateria Carrozze
16. Gelateria Carabè
17. Festival del Gelato
18. Perchè No! Gelateria
19. Vivoli's Gelateria
20. Gelateria de' Neri

FLORENCE

Gelato

Gelato is an edible art form. Italy's best ice cream is in Florence—one souvenir that can't break and won't clutter your luggage.

But beware of scams at touristy joints on busy streets that turn a simple request for a cone into a €10 "tourist special" rip-off. To avoid this, survey the size options and be very clear in your order (for example, "a €3 cone").

A key to gelato appreciation is sampling liberally and choosing flavors that go well together. Ask, as Italians do, for *"Un assaggio, per favore?"* (A taste, please?; oon ah-SAH-joh pehr fah-VOH-ray) and *"Che si sposano bene?"* (What marries well?; kay see spoh-ZAH-noh BEN-ay).

Artiginale, nostra produzione, and *produzione propia* mean gelato is made on the premises; also, gelato displayed in covered metal tins (rather than white plastic) is more likely to be homemade. Gelato aficionados avoid colors that don't appear in nature—for fewer chemicals and real flavor, go for mellow hues (bright colors attract children). These places are open daily for long hours.

Near the Duomo: The recent favorite in town, **Grom** uses organic ingredients and seasonal fresh fruit, along with biodegradable spoons and tubs. Their traditional approach and quality give locals déjà vu, reminding them of the good old days and the ice cream of their childhood. Mario, who really cares, sees "gelato as cuisine," and adjusts the menu monthly to fit what's in season (daily 10:30-24:00, Via delle Oche 24 red). Their *liquirizia*

embellish with some veggies, milk, yogurt, or juice; and hike around the block to Piazza S.S. Annunziata, the first Renaissance square in Florence. There's a fountain for washing fruit on the square. Grab a stony seat anywhere you like, and savor one of my favorite cheap Florence eating experiences. (Or, drop by either of the two places listed earlier for a sandwich and juice to go.)

Fast and Cheap near the Duomo

Self-Service Ristorante Leonardo is inexpensive, air-conditioned, quick, and handy. Eating here, you'll get the sense that they're passionate about the quality of their food. Stefano and Luciano (like Pavarotti) run the place with enthusiasm, and put out free pitchers of tap water. It's just a block from the Duomo, southwest of the Baptistery (tasty €4 pastas, €5 main courses, Sun-Fri 11:45-14:45 & 18:45-21:45, closed Sat, upstairs at Via Pecori 11, tel. 055-284-446).

(licorice) flavor is worth a sample.

Near Ponte Vecchio: **Gelateria Carrozze** is a longtime favorite (daily 11:00-20:00, until 1:00 in the morning in summer, on riverfront 30 yards from Ponte Vecchio toward the Uffizi at Piazza del Pesce 3).

Near the Accademia: A Sicilian choice on a tourist thoroughfare, **Gelateria Carabè** is particularly famous for its luscious *granite*—Italian ices made with fresh fruit. Antonio, whose family has made ice cream the Sicilian way for more than 100 years, can tell you why that's important (daily 11:00-20:00; from the Accademia, it's a block toward the Duomo at Via Ricasoli 60 red).

Near Orsanmichele Church: For gelato served in a brash, neon environment, it's **Festival del Gelato** or **Perchè No!,** both located just off the busy main pedestrian drag (Via de' Calzaiuoli). They serve a stunning array of brightly colored kid-pleasing flavors (Festival del Gelato is at Via del Corso 75; Perchè No! is at Via dei Tavolini 19).

Near the Church of Santa Croce: The venerable favorite, **Vivoli's** still serves great gelato—but it's more expensive and stingy in its servings. Before ordering, try a free sample of their rice flavor—*riso* (closed Mon, Aug, and Jan; opposite the Church of Santa Croce, go down Via Torta a block and turn right on Via Stinche). Locals flock to **Gelateria de' Neri** (Via de' Neri 26 red), also owned by Vivoli's.

Across the River: If you want an excuse to check out the little village-like neighborhood across the river from Santa Croce, enjoy a gelato at the tiny **Il Gelato di Filo** (named for Filippo and Lorenzo) at Via San Miniato 5 red, a few steps toward the river from Porta San Miniato. Gelato chef Edmir is proud of his fruity sorbet as well.

FLORENCE

The Oil Shoppe cobbles together huge gourmet hot and cold sub sandwiches *all'Italiana* from creative ingredients (€3.50). You can get a sandwich plus fries and water (€5), or build your own salad and pair it with a homemade soup of the day for a fast, cheap, and hearty lunch. Eat at the skinny counter or take your food to go (generally Mon-Fri 10:30-18:00 or until the bread runs out, closed Sat-Sun, 2 long blocks east of the Duomo at Via S. Egidio 22 red, cheery Alberto runs the show).

Near Piazza della Signoria and Ponte Vecchio

Cantinetta dei Verrazzano, a long-established bakery-café-wine bar, serves delightful sandwich plates in an old-time setting. Their *specialità Verrazzano* is a fine plate of four little crostini (like mini-bruschetta) proudly featuring different breads, cheeses, and meats from the Chianti region (€7.50). The *tagliere di focacce*, a sampler plate of mini-focaccia sandwiches, is also fun (price depends on quantity). Add a glass of Chianti to either of these dishes to make a fine light meal. Office workers pop in for a quick lunch, and it's traditional to share tables (Mon-Sat 8:00-21:00, closed Sun, just off Via de' Calzaiuoli on a side street across from Orsanmichele Church at Via dei Tavolini 18, tel. 055-268-590). They also have benches and tiny tables for eating at "take-out" prices. Simply step to the back and point to the hot *focacce* sandwich (€3) you'd like, order a drink at the bar, and take away your food or sit with locals and watch the action while you munch.

Osteria Vini e Vecchi Sapori, half a block north of Palazzo Vecchio, is a colorful 16-seat hole-in-the-wall serving Tuscan food, including plates of mixed crostini (€1 each—step right up and choose at the bar) and €10 daily specials. Be sure to try their raspberry *(lampone)* tiramisu. In the evening, it becomes a little restaurant with a fun, accessible menu of delicious €8 pastas and €10 *secondi* (Tue-Sat 12:30-15:00 & 19:30-22:00, Sun 12:30-15:00, closed Mon, reserve for dinner; facing the bronze equestrian statue in Piazza della Signoria, go behind its tail into the corner and to your left; Via dei Magazzini 3 red, tel. 055-293-045, run by Mario while wife Rosanna cooks and son Thomas serves).

I Fratellini is an informal little eatery where the "little brothers" have served peasants 29 different kinds of sandwiches and cheap glasses of Chianti wine (see list on wall) since 1875. Join the local crowd to order, then sit on a nearby curb or windowsill to munch, placing your glass on the wall rack before you leave (€4 for sandwich and wine, daily 9:00-20:00 or until the bread runs out, closed Sun in winter, 20 yards in front of Orsanmichele Church on Via dei Cimatori, tel. 055-239-6096). Be adventurous with the menu (easy-order by number). Consider *finocchiona* (a special Tuscan salami), *lardo di Colonnata* (lard aged in Carrara marble), and *cinghiale piccante* (spicy wild boar) sandwiches. Order the most expensive wine they're selling by the glass (Brunello for €4; bottles are labeled).

L'Antico Trippaio, an antique tripe stand, is a fixture in the town center (daily 9:00-20:00, on Via Dante Alighieri, mobile 339-742-5692). Cheap and authentic as can be, this is where Florentines come daily for €3.50 sandwiches *(panini)* featuring specialties like *trippa alla fiorentina* (tripe), *lampredotto* (cow's stomach), and a list of more appetizing sandwiches. The best people-watching place to munch your sandwich is three blocks away, on Piazza della Signoria.

'Ino Bottega di Alimentari e Vini is a mod little shop filled with gifty edibles. Serena and Alessandro serve sandwiches and wine—you'll get your €5-7 sandwich on a napkin with an included glass of their wine of the day as you perch on a tiny stool. They can also make a fine *piatto misto* of cheeses and meats; just say how much you'd like to spend (daily 11:00-17:00, immediately behind Uffizi Gallery on Ponte Vecchio side, Via dei Georgofili 3 red, tel. 055-219-208).

Pisa

In A.D. 1200, Pisa's power peaked. For nearly three centuries (1000-1300), Pisa rivaled Venice and Genoa as a sea-trading power, exchanging European goods for luxury items in Muslim lands. As a port near the mouth of the Arno River (six miles from the coast), the city enjoyed easy access to the Mediterranean, plus the protection of sitting a bit upstream. The Romans had made it a navy base, and by medieval times it was a major player.

Pisa's 150-foot galleys cruised the Mediterranean, gaining control of the islands of Corsica, Sardinia, and Sicily, and trading with other Europeans, Muslims, and Byzantine Christians as far south as North Africa and as far east as Syria. European Crusaders hired Pisan boats to carry them and their supplies as they headed off to conquer the Muslim-held Holy Land. The Pisan "Republic" prided itself on its independence from both popes and emperors. The city used its sea-trading wealth to build the grand monuments of the Field of Miracles, including the now-famous Leaning Tower.

But the Pisan fleet was routed in battle by Genoa (1284, at Meloria, off Livorno), their overseas outposts were taken away, the port silted up, and Pisa was left high and dry, with only its Field of Miracles and its university keeping it on the map.

Pisa's three important sights—the Duomo, Baptistery, and the Tower—float regally on the best lawn in Italy. The style throughout is Pisa's very own "Pisan Romanesque." Even as the church was being built, Piazza del Duomo was nicknamed the "Campo dei Miracoli," or Field of Miracles, for the grandness of the undertaking.

The Tower has reopened after a decade of restoration and topple-prevention. To ascend, you'll have to make a reservation when you buy your €15 ticket (for details, see page 488).

Orientation to Pisa

The city of Pisa is framed on the north by the Field of Miracles (Leaning Tower) and on the south by Pisa Centrale train station.

The Arno River flows east to west, bisecting the city. Walking from Pisa Centrale train station directly to the Tower takes about 30 minutes (but allow up to an hour if you take my self-guided walk). The two main streets for tourists and shoppers are Via Santa Maria (running south from the Tower) and Corso Italia/Borgo Stretto (running north from the station).

Tourist Information

One TI is about 200 yards from Pisa Centrale train station—exit and walk straight up the left side of the street to the big circular Piazza Vittorio Emanuele II. The TI is on the left, around the corner from #16 (Mon-Sat 9:00-19:00, Sun 9:00-16:00, tel. 050-42291, www.pisaturismo.it). Another, less-enthusiastic TI is east of the Tower, in the Duomo Museum (daily April-Sept 9:30-19:30, Oct-March 10:00-17:00).

Arrival in Pisa

By Train: Most trains (and visitors) arrive at **Pisa Centrale** station, about a mile south of the Tower and Field of Miracles. A few trains also stop at the smaller Pisa S. Rossore station, which is just four blocks from the Tower (not all trains stop here, but if yours does, hop off).

To get from this station to the Field of Miracles, you can **walk** (get free map from TI, 30 minutes direct, 60 minutes if you follow my self-guided walk), take a **taxi** (€7-10, tel. 050-541-600, taxi stand at station), or go by **bus.** Take bus LAM Rossa (4-6/hour, after 20:00 3/hour, 15 minutes), which stops across the street from the train station, in front of the NH Cavalieri Hoteles. Buy a €1 bus ticket from the *tabacchi*/magazine kiosk in the train station's main hall or at any *tabacchi* shop (€1.50 if you buy it on board, smart to have exact change, good for 1 hour, round-trip permitted). Before getting on the bus, confirm that it is indeed going to "Campo dei Miracoli" (ask driver, a local, or TI) or risk taking a long tour of Pisa's suburbs. The correct buses let you off at Piazza Manin, in front of the gate to the Field of Miracles; drivers make sure tourists don't miss the stop.

PISA

Pisa

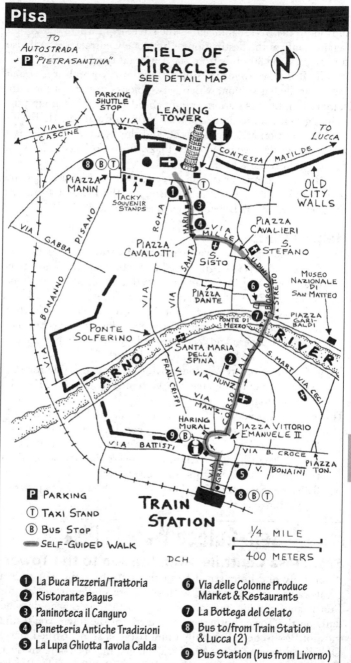

TO
AUTOSTRADA
& **P** "PIETRASANTINA"

FIELD OF
MIRACLES
SEE DETAIL MAP

PARKING
SHUTTLE
STOP

VIA

VIALE
CASCINE

LEANING
TOWER

TO
LUCCA

CONTESSA MATILDE

PIAZZA
MANIN

TACKY
SOUVENIR
STANDS

OLD
CITY
WALLS

VIA GABBA

BONANNO PISANO

PISANO

PIAZZA
CAVALOTTI

ROMA

SANTA MARIA

VIA MILLE

PIAZZA
CAVALIERI

S.
STEFANO

S.
SISTO

U. DINI

BORGO STRETTO

MUSEO
NAZIONALE
DI
SAN MATTEO

PIAZZA
DANTE

VIA

VIA

PONTE
SOLFERINO

PONTE DI
MEZZO

PIAZZA
GARI-
BALDI

ARNO

SANTA MARIA
DELLA
SPINA

RIVER

FRAT. CRISPI

VIA NUNZ.

CORSO ITALIA

VIA MANZ.

S. MART

VIA CECI

HARING
MURAL

PIAZZA VITTORIO
EMANUELE II

VIA BATTISTI

VIA B. CROCE

V. BONAINI

PIAZZA
TON.

VIA GRATI

TRAIN
STATION

P PARKING

T TAXI STAND

B BUS STOP

SELF-GUIDED WALK

¼ MILE

400 METERS

DCH

PISA

❶ La Buca Pizzeria/Trattoria

❷ Ristorante Bagus

❸ Paninoteca il Canguro

❹ Panetteria Antiche Tradizioni

❺ La Lupa Ghiotta Tavola Calda

❻ Via delle Colonne Produce Market & Restaurants

❼ La Bottega del Gelato

❽ Bus to/from Train Station & Lucca (2)

❾ Bus Station (bus from Livorno)

To return to the train station from the Tower, catch the bus in front of the BNL bank, across the street from where you got off (again, confirm the destination—"Stazione Centrale"). You'll also find a taxi stand 30 yards from the Tower (at Bar Duomo).

By Bus from Livorno: Bus #101 from Livorno leaves you at Gate 2 at the bus station, which is two blocks in front of the train station. Exit the bus station straight ahead and bear left around the building to reach the circular Piazza Vittorio Emanuele II. The TI and train station are to your right, and the Field of Miracles is a 25-minute walk to your left (see "Piazza Vittorio Emanuele II" in my self-guided walk, later).

By Bus from Lucca: The direct bus from Lucca drops you outside the walls behind the Baptistery at the Field of Miracles; the stop is called Via Bonanno (see map on page 487).

Helpful Hints

Markets: An open-air **produce market** attracts picnickers to Piazza della Vettovaglie, one block north of the Arno River near Ponte di Mezzo, and nearby Piazza Sant'Uomobuono (Mon-Sat 7:00-18:00, main section closes at 13:00, closed Sun). A **street market**—with more practical goods than food—bustles on Wednesday and Saturday mornings between Via del Brennero and Via Paparrelle (8:00-13:00, just outside of wall, about 6 blocks east of the Tower).

Local Guide: Dottore Vincenzo Riolo is a great guide for Pisa and the surrounding area (€130/3 hours, mobile 338-211-2939, www.pisatour.it, info@pisatour.it).

Tours: To get beyond the tourist mobs and understand the cultural powerhouse that was Pisa, consider the "Self-Guided Walk" next. Local guides lead a two- to three-hour walking tour in English (and Italian) that covers the city rather than the famous Tower sights (€12, check website for times, tel. 050-830-253, mobile 328-144-6855 after hours, www.pisatour .it, Vincenzo).

PISA

Self-Guided Walk in Pisa

From Pisa Centrale Train Station to the Tower

A leisurely one-hour stroll from the station to the Tower is a great way to get acquainted with the more subtle virtues of this Renaissance city. Because almost none of the hordes who descend daily on the Tower bothers with the rest of the town, you'll find most of Pisa to be delightfully untouristy—a student-filled classy Old World town with an Arno-scape much like its upstream rival, Florence. Pisa is pretty small, with just 100,000 people. But its 45,000 students keep it lively, especially at night.

• *From Pisa Centrale train station, walk north up Viale Gramsci to the circular square called...*

Piazza Vittorio Emanuele II

As Pisa was considered strategic in World War II, both the train station and its main bridge were targeted. For that reason, 40 per-

cent of this district was destroyed. Looking at the makeshift walls that surround the square, you may think it's still a bombed-out zone. The piazza is being rebuilt to include an underground parking lot, but the project was delayed after workers accidentally damaged an ancient structure while digging. The entire wall of a building just to the left of the piazza was painted by American artist Keith Haring in 1989 to create *Tuttomondo (Whole Wide World)*. Haring (who died of AIDS in 1990) brought New York City graffiti into the mainstream. This painting is a celebration of diversity, chaos, and the liveliness of our world, vibrating with energy. On the piazza, you'll also find a TI.

• *Walk up Corso Italia to the river.*

Corso Italia

Cutting through the center of town, this is Pisa's main drag. As it leaves Piazza Vittorio Emanuele II, look to the right to see the circa-1960 wall map of Pisa with a steam train (on the wall of the bar on the corner). You'll also see plenty of youthful fashions, as kids are out making the scene here. Be on guard for pickpockets—too young to arrest, they can only be kicked out of town. Pushed out of their former happy hunting grounds, the Field of Miracles, they now work the crowds here, often dressed as tourists.

• *Follow the pedestrianized Corso Italia straight north to the Arno River and Ponte di Mezzo. Stop in the center of the bridge.*

Ponte di Mezzo

This modern bridge, constructed on the same site where the Romans built one, marks the center of Pisa. In the Middle Ages, this bridge (like Florence's Ponte Vecchio) was lined with shops. It's been destroyed several times by floods and in 1943 by British and American bombers. Enjoy the view from the center of the bridge, with its long lines of elegant mansions recalling days of trading glory—the cityscape feels a bit like Venice's Grand Canal. Pisa sits on shifting delta sand, making construction tricky. The entire town leans. With innovative arches above ground and below, architects didn't stop the leaning—but they have made buildings that wobble without falling down.

• *Cross the bridge to...*

Piazza Garibaldi

This square is named for the charismatic leader of the Risorgimento, the unification movement that led to Italian independence in 1870. Knowing Pisa was strongly nationalist, Garibaldi came here when wounded to be nursed back to health. Many Pisans died in the national struggle. **La Bottega del Gelato,** Pisa's favorite gelato place, is on Piazza Garibaldi (daily 11:30-24:00). You can side-trip about 100 yards downstream to **Caffè dell'Ussero** (famous for its fine 14th-century red terra-cotta original facade, at #28, Sun-Fri 7:00-21:00, closed Sat) and browse its time-warp interior, lined with portraits and documents from the struggle for Italian independence.

• *Continue north up the elegantly arcaded...*

Borgo Stretto

Welcome to Pisa's main shopping street. On the right, the Church of St. Michael, with its fine Pisan Romanesque facade, still sports some 16th-century graffiti. I'll bet you can see some modern graffiti across the street. Students have been pushing their causes here—or simply defacing things—for five centuries.

From here, look farther up the street and notice how it undulates like a flowing river. In the sixth century B.C., Pisa was born when two parallel rivers were connected by canals. This street echoes the flow of one of those canals. An 11th-century landslide rerouted the second river, destroying ancient Pisa, and the entire city regenerated.

• *After a few steps, detour left onto Via delle Colonne, and walk one block down to...*

Piazza delle Vettovaglie

Pisa's historic market square, Piazza delle Vettovaglie, is lively day and night. Its Renaissance loggia has hosted the fish and vegetable market for generations. The stalls are set up in this piazza during the morning (Mon-Sat 7:00-13:00, closed Sun), and stay open later in the neighboring piazza to the west (Piazza Sant'Uomobuono, Mon-Sat 7:00-18:00, closed Sun). You could cobble together a picnic from the sandwich shops and fruit-and-veggie stalls ringing these squares.

• *Continue north on Borgo Stretto another 100 yards, passing an ugly bomb site on the right, with its horrible 1960s reconstruction. Take the second left on nondescript Via Ulisse Dini (it's not obvious—turn left*

*immediately at the arcade's end, just before the pharmacy). This leads to
Pisa's historic core, Piazza dei Cavalieri.*

Piazza dei Cavalieri

With its old clock and colorfully decorated palace, this piazza was
once the seat of the independent Republic of Pisa's government.

Around 1500, Florence decapitated Pisa and made
this square the training place for the knights of its
navy. The statue of Cosimo I de' Medici shows the
Florentine who ruled Pisa in the 16th century. With
a foot on a dolphin, he reminded all who passed
that the Florentine navy controlled the sea—at
least a little of it. The frescoes on the exterior of
the square's buildings, though damaged by salty sea
air and years of neglect, reflect Pisa's fading glory
under the Medicis.

With Napoleon, this complex of grand buildings became part of the University of Pisa. The university is one of Europe's oldest, with roots in a law
school that dates back as far as the 11th century. In the mid-16th
century, the city was a hotbed of controversy, as spacey professors like Galileo Galilei studied the solar system—with results
that challenged the Church's powerful doctrine. More recently,
the blind tenor Andrea Bocelli attended law school in Pisa before
embarking on his well-known musical career.

From here, take Via Corsica (to the left of the clock). The
humble **Church of San Sisto,** ahead on the left (side entrance on
Via Corsica), is worth a quick look. With simple bricks, assorted
reused columns, heavy walls, and few windows, this was the typical Romanesque style before the more lavish Pisan Romanesque of
the Field of Miracles structures.

Follow Via Corsica as it turns into Via dei Mille (and grab a
quick bite at the recommended **Panetteria Antiche Tradizioni**),
and then turn right on Via Santa Maria, which leads north,
through increasingly touristy claptrap, directly to the Field of
Miracles and the Tower.

Sights in Pisa

▲▲▲Leaning Tower

A 15-foot lean from the vertical makes the Tower one of Europe's
most recognizable images. You can see it for free; it's always viewable. And, after years of stabilization efforts, it's open again if you
want to climb it for a fee.

Rising up alongside the cathedral, the Tower is nearly 200

feet tall and 55 feet wide, weighing 14,000 tons and currently leaning at a five-degree angle (15 feet off the vertical axis). It started to lean almost immediately after construction began. There are eight stories— a simple base, six stories of columns (forming arcades), and a belfry on top. The inner structural core is a hollow cylinder built of limestone bricks, faced with white marble barged here from San Giuliano, northeast of the city. The thin columns of the open-air arcades make the heavy Tower seem light and graceful.

The Tower was built over two centuries by at least three different architects. You can see how each successive architect tried to correct the leaning problem—once halfway up (after the fourth story), once at the belfry on the top.

The first stones were laid in 1173, probably under the direction of the architect Bonanno Pisano (who also designed the Duomo's bronze back door). Five years later, just as they'd finished the base and the first arcade, someone said, "Is it just me, or does that look crooked?" The heavy Tower—resting on a very shallow 13-foot foundation—was obviously sinking on the south side into the marshy, multilayered, unstable soil. (Actually, all the Campo's buildings tilt somewhat.) They carried on anyway, until they'd finished four stories (the base, plus three arcade floors). Then, construction suddenly halted—no one knows why—and for a century the Tower sat half-finished and visibly leaning.

Around 1272, the next architect continued, trying to correct the problem by angling the next three stories backward, in the opposite direction of the lean. The project then again sat mysteriously idle for nearly another century. Finally, Tommaso Pisano put the belfry on the top (c. 1350-1372), also kinking it backward.

After the Tower's completion, several attempts were made to stop its slow-motion fall. The architect-artist-writer Giorgio Vasari reinforced the base (1550), and it actually worked. But in 1838, well-intentioned engineers pumped out groundwater, destabilizing the Tower and causing it to increase its lean at a rate of a millimeter per year.

It got so bad that in 1990 the Tower was closed for repairs, and $30 million was spent trying to stabilize it. Engineers dried the soil with steam pipes, anchored the Tower to the ground with steel cables, and buried 600 tons of lead on the north side as a counterweight (not visible)—all with little success. The breakthrough came when they drilled 15-foot holes in the ground on the north side and sucked out 60 tons of soil, allowing the Tower to sink on

Pisa's Field of Miracles

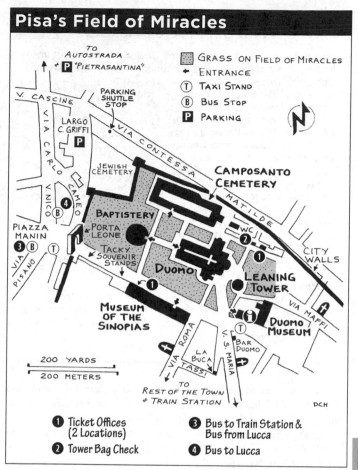

TO AUTOSTRADA & "PIETRASANTINA"

GRASS ON FIELD OF MIRACLES
ENTRANCE
(T) TAXI STAND
(B) BUS STOP
(P) PARKING

V. CASCINE
VIA CARLO CAMEO
VIA CONTESSA
PARKING SHUTTLE STOP
LARGO C. GRIFFI
P
JEWISH CEMETERY
CAMPOSANTO CEMETERY
MATILDE
(4)
(B)
BAPTISTERY
PORTA LEONE
TACKY SOUVENIR STANDS
DUOMO
WC
(2)
(1)
CITY WALLS
PIAZZA MANIN
(3)
(B)
(T)
VIA PISANO
LEANING TOWER
MUSEUM OF THE SINOPIAS
VIA ROMA
V. S. MARIA
LA BUCA TASSI
BAR DUOMO
(T)
VIA MAFFI
DUOMO MUSEUM

200 YARDS
200 METERS

TO REST OF THE TOWN & TRAIN STATION

DCH

① Ticket Offices (2 Locations)
② Tower Bag Check
③ Bus to Train Station & Bus from Lucca
④ Bus to Lucca

PISA

the north side and straighten out its lean by about six inches.

In addition to gravity, erosion threatens the Tower. Since its construction, 135 of the Tower's 180 marble columns have had to be replaced. Stone decay, deposits of lime and calcium phosphate, accumulations of dirt and moss, cracking from the stress of the lean—all of these are factors in its decline.

Thanks to the Tower's lean, there are special trouble spots. The lower south side (which is protected from cleansing rain and wind) is black from dirty airborne particles, while the stone on the upper areas, though clean, has more decay (from eroding rain and wind).

The Tower, now stabilized, has also been thoroughly cleaned. Cracks have been filled, and accumulations removed, using atomized water sprays and poultices of various solvents.

Field of Miracles Tickets

Pisa has a combo-ticket scheme designed to get you into its neglected secondary sights: the Baptistery, Camposanto Cemetery, Duomo Museum, and Museum of the Sinopias (fresco pattern museum).

For €5, you get your choice of one of the following: the Baptistery, Camposanto Cemetery, Museum of the Sinopias, or Duomo Museum; for two of these sights or one plus the Duomo, the cost is €6; for three of the above you pay €8; and for the works, you'll pay €10 (credit cards accepted). By comparison, the Duomo alone is a bargain (€2).

You can buy any of these tickets either behind the Leaning Tower or at the Museum of the Sinopias (near Baptistery, almost suffocated by souvenir stands). Both ticket offices have big yellow triangle-shaped signs.

No matter what ticket you get, you'll have to pay an additional €15 if you want to climb the Tower. Tickets for the Tower are sold at the ticket offices or online at least 15 days in advance at www.opapisa.it (€2 fee).

All the work to shore up, straighten, and clean the Tower has turned the clock back a few centuries. In fact, art historians figure it leans today as much as it did for Galileo.

Cost and Hours: €15, kids under six not allowed, daily March 9:00-18:00, April-May and Sept 8:30-20:30, June-Aug 8:00-23:30, Oct 9:00-19:30, Nov-Feb 10:00-16:30, ticket office opens 30 minutes early, last entry 30 minutes before closing.

Reservations: Reservations are required to climb the Tower. You can reserve in person or, for an extra €2, book a time at www.opapisa.it.

Online bookings are accepted no more than 45 days—and no fewer than 15 days—in advance. You must pick up your ticket(s) at least 30 minutes before your time slot. Show up 10 minutes before your appointment at the meeting point outside the ticket office.

To reserve in person, go to the ticket office behind the Tower, on the left in the yellow building, or to the Museum of the Sinopias ticket office hidden behind the souvenir stalls. You choose a 30-minute time slot for your visit. If you visit in summer, it will likely be a couple of hours before you're able to go up (see the rest of the monuments and grab lunch while waiting). The wait is usually much shorter at the beginning or end of the day.

PISA

Climbing the Tower: Every 30 minutes, 40 people can clamber up the 294 tilting stairs to the top. Note that children under age eight are not allowed to go up. Children ages 6-12 must be accompanied by—and hold hands at all times with—an adult. Teenagers between 12 and 18 are allowed with an adult.

You can't take any bags up the Tower, but day bag-size lockers are available at the ticket office—show your Tower ticket to check your bag. You may check your bag 10 minutes before your reservation time and must pick it up immediately after your Tower visit.

You wind your way up the outside of the Tower along a spiraling ramp. For your 30-minute time slot, figure about 10 minutes to climb and 10 to descend, leaving about 10 minutes for vertigo at the top. Even though it's technically a "guided" visit, that only means you're accompanied by a museum guard who makes sure you don't stay up past your scheduled appointment time.

Caution: There are skinny railings, the steps are slanted, and rain makes the marble slippery. Anyone with balance issues of any sort should think twice before ascending.

▲▲Duomo (Cathedral)

The gargantuan Pisan Romanesque cathedral, with its carved pulpit by Giovanni Pisano, is artistically more important than its

more famous bell tower.

Begun in 1063, the Duomo is the centerpiece of the Field of Miracles' complex of religious buildings. The architect Buschetto created the style of Pisan Romanesque that set the tone for the Baptistery and Tower.

PISA

The **bronze back doors** (Porta San Ranieri) at the Tower end were designed by Bonnano Pisano (c. 1186). The doors have

24 different panels that show Christ's story using the same simple, skinny figures found in Byzantine icons. (The doors are actually copies; the originals are housed—but not always on display—in the Duomo Museum.) Cast using the lost-wax technique, these doors were an inspiration for Lorenzo Ghiberti's bronze doors in Florence.

The 320-foot nave was the longest in Christendom when

it was built. The striped marble and arches-on-columns give it an exotic, almost mosque-like feel. Dim light filters in from the small upper windows of the galleries, where the women worshipped. The gilded coffered ceiling has shields of Florence's Medicis, including the round symbols (pills). This powerful family—who began as doctors, later became cloth merchants, and finally bankers—took over Pisa after its glory days.

In the apse (behind the altar) is a **mosaic** (c. 1300, partly done by Cimabue) showing Christ as the Ruler of All (Pantocrator) between Mary and John the Evangelist. Looking up into the **dome,** the heavens open, and rings of saints and angels spiral up to a hazy God. Beneath the dome is an inlaid-marble Cosmati-style mosaic floor.

The 15-foot-tall octagonal **pulpit** by Giovanni Pisano (c. 1250-1319) is the last, biggest, and most complex of the four pulpits by the Pisano father-and-son team. Christ's

life unfolds in a series of panels crammed with figures. Giovanni left no stone uncarved in his pursuit of beauty. Originally, this and the other pulpits were frosted with paint, gilding, and colored pastes.

The bronze **incense burner** that hangs from the ceiling (near the pulpit) is a replica of the one that supposedly caught teenage Galileo's attention when a gust of wind set the lamp swinging. He timed the swings, and realized that the burner swung back and forth in the same amount of time regardless of how wide the arc. (This pendulum motion was a constant that allowed Galileo to measure this ever-changing universe.) Legend says the Pisa-born Galileo also threw objects off the Tower to time their falls, fascinated by gravity.

Pause at the **tomb of Holy Roman Emperor Henry VII,** the German king (c. 1275-1313) who invaded Italy and was welcomed by Pisans as a leader of unity and peace. Unfortunately, Henry took ill and died young, leaving Ghibelline Pisa at the mercy of its Guelph rivals, such as rising Florence. Pisa never recovered.

In a glass-lined casket on the altar, Pisa's patron saint—**St. Ranieri**—lies mummified, encased in silver at his head and feet, with his hair shirt covering his body. The son of a rich sea-trader, Ranieri (1117-1161) was a hard-partying touring musician who was later inspired to give away his money, join a monastery, and give spirited sermons from the Duomo pulpit.

Cost and Hours: €2; Mon-Sat March 10:00-18:00, April-Sept 10:00-20:00, Oct 10:00-19:00, Nov-Feb 10:00-17:00; Sun 13:00-17:30 all year; last entry 30 minutes before closing. Shorts are OK as long as they're not too short, and shoulders should be covered (although it's not really enforced). Big backpacks are not allowed, nor is storage provided. If you have a day bag, carry it.

▲▲▲Field of Miracles (Campo dei Miracoli)

Scattered across a golf course-green lawn are five grand buildings: the cathedral (or Duomo), its bell tower (the Leaning Tower), the

Baptistery, the hospital (today's Museum of the Sinopias), and the Camposanto Cemetery (see map on page 487). The buildings are constructed from similar materials—bright white marble—and have comparable decoration. Each has a simple ground floor and rows of delicate columns and arches that form open-air arcades, giving the Campo a pleasant visual unity.

The style is dubbed Pisan Romanesque. Where traditional Romanesque has a heavy fortress-like feel—thick walls, barrel arches, few windows—Pisan Romanesque is light and elegant. At ground level, most of the structures have simple half-columns and arches. On the upper levels, you'll see a little of everything—tight rows of thin columns; pointed Gothic gables and prickly spires; Byzantine mosaics and horseshoe arches; and geometric designs (such as diamonds) and striped colored marbles inspired by mosques in Muslim lands.

Architecturally, the Campo is unique and exotic. Theologically, the Campo's buildings mark the main events of every Pisan's life: christened in the Baptistery, married in the Duomo, honored in ceremonies at the Tower, healed in the hospital, and buried in the Camposanto Cemetery.

Lining this field of artistic pearls is a gauntlet of Europe's tackiest souvenir stands, as well as dozens of amateur mimes "propping up" the Leaning Tower while tourists take photos.

▲Baptistery

Located in front of the Duomo, the round Baptistery is the biggest in Italy. It's interesting for its pulpit and interior ambience, and especially great for its acoustics.

The building is 180 feet tall—John the Baptist on top looks

eye-to-eye with the tourists atop the nearly 200-foot Leaning Tower. Notice that the Baptistery leans nearly six feet to the north (the Tower leans 15 feet to the south). The building (begun 1153) is modeled on the circular domed Church of the Holy Sepulchre in Jerusalem, seen by Pisan Crusaders who occupied Jerusalem in 1099.

Inside, it's simple, spacious, and baptized with light. Tall arches encircle just a few pieces of religious furniture. In the center sits the **octagonal font** (1246, topped with a statue of the first baptist, John), which contains plenty of space for baptizing adults by immersion (the medieval custom), plus four wells for dunking babies.

Nicola Pisano's **pulpit** is arguably the world's first Renaissance sculpture. It's the first authenticated (signed) work by the "Giotto of sculpture," working in what came to be called the Renaissance style. The pulpit is a freestanding sculpture that has classical columns, realistic people and animals, and 3-D effects in the carved panels.

The speaker's platform stands on columns that rest on the backs of animals, representing Christianity's triumph over paganism. The relief panels, with scenes from the life of Christ, are more readable than the Duomo pulpit. Read left to right, starting from the back: Nativity, Adoration of the Magi, Presentation in the Temple, Crucifixion, Last Judgment.

Make a sound in here and it echoes for a good 10 seconds. A priest standing at the baptismal font (or a security guard today) can sing three tones within the 10 seconds—"Ave Maria"—and make a chord, singing haunting harmonies with himself. This medieval form of digital delay is due to the 250-foot-wide dome. Recent computer analysis suggests that the 15th-century architects who built the dome intended this building to function not just as a Baptistery, but also as a musical instrument. A security guard sings every half-hour, starting when the doors open in the morning. Climb 75 steps to the interior gallery (midway up) for an impressive view back down on the baptismal font.

Cost and Hours: €5, for combo-ticket see "Field of Miracles Tickets" sidebar, daily March 9:00-17:30, April-Sept 8:00-19:30, Oct 8:30-19:00, Nov-Feb 10:00-17:00, last entry 30 minutes before closing.

More Sights in Pisa

Camposanto Cemetery—This site, bordering the Field of Miracles on the north, has been a cemetery since ancient times.

Lined with faint frescoes, the ancient cemetery is famous for its "Holy Land" dirt, said to reduce a body into a skeleton within a day. Highlights are the building's cloistered open-air courtyard (with intricately carved arches); some ancient Roman and Greek sarcophagi; and the 1,000-square-foot 14th-century fresco, *The Triumph of Death*. The fresco captures Pisa's mood in the wake of the bubonic plague (1348), which killed one in three Pisans. Grim stuff, but appropriate for the Camposanto's permanent residents.

Cost and Hours: €5, for combo-ticket see "Field of Miracles Tickets" sidebar, same hours as Baptistery.

Museum of the Sinopias (Museo delle Sinopie)—Across from the Baptistery, housed in a 13th-century hospital (with its entrance nearly obscured by souvenir stands), this museum displays some of the original sketches (made on walls) that were used to make the frescoes in the Camposanto Cemetery.

This museum comes with two free short introductory videos that you can watch even without a ticket. Good students might want to start here first for this orientation to the square: a 10-minute 3-D computer tour of the complex, and a 15-minute story of the Tower, its tilt, and its fix.

"Sinopias" are sketches in red paint made directly on the wall, designed to guide the making of the final colored fresco. The master always did the sinopia himself; if he liked the results, his assistants made a "cartoon" by tracing the sinopia onto large sheets of paper *(cartone)*. Then the sinopia was plastered over and the assistants redrew the outlines, using the cartoon as a guide. While the plaster was still wet, the master and his team quickly filled in the color and details, producing the final frescoes (now on display at the Camposanto). These sinopias—never meant to be seen—were uncovered by the bombing and restoration of the Camposanto and brought here.

Cost and Hours: €5, for combo-ticket see "Field of Miracles Tickets" sidebar, same hours as Baptistery.

Duomo Museum (Museo dell'Opera del Duomo)—This museum behind the Leaning Tower is big on Pisan art, displaying treasures of the cathedral, paintings, silverware, and sculptures (from the 12th to 14th centuries, particularly by the Pisano dynasty), as well as ancient Egyptian, Etruscan, and Roman artifacts. It houses many of the original statues and much of the artwork that once adorned the Campo's buildings (where copies stand today), notably the statues by Nicola and Giovanni Pisano. You can stand face-to-face with the Pisanos' very human busts that once ringed the outside of the Baptistery. You'll see a mythical sculpted hippogriff (a medieval jackalope) and other oddities brought back from the Holy Land by Pisan Crusaders. The museum also has several large-scale wooden models of the Duomo, Baptistery, and Tower.

Cost and Hours: €5, for combo-ticket see "Field of Miracles Tickets" sidebar, same hours as Baptistery, Piazza Arcivescovado 18.

Museo Nazionale di San Matteo—On the river and in a former convent, this art museum displays 12th- to 15th-century sculptures, illuminated manuscripts, and paintings on wood by Martini, Masaccio, and others. This fine collection—especially its painted wood crucifixes—gives you a chance to see Pisan innovation in 11th- to 13th-century art, before Florence took the lead.

Cost and Hours: €4, Tue-Sat 8:30-19:00, Sun 8:30-13:00, closed Mon, near Piazza San Paolo at Lungarno Mediceo, a 5-minute walk upriver from the main bridge, tel. 050-541-865.

Eating in Pisa

La Buca, a pizzeria-trattoria just a block from the Tower, is adequate and convenient for a quick lunch or dinner (Sat-Thu 12:00-15:00 & 18:00-22:30, closed Fri, at Via Santa Maria 171 and Via A. G. Tassi 6b, tel. 050-560-660).

Ristorante Bagus boasts trendy twists on Tuscan fare—their specialty is an extra-rare burger made with the famous Chianina beef. For a change from the basic Italian trattoria or tourist traps, this place promises an upscale lunch or dinner (€25 fixed-price meal, Mon-Fri 12:30-14:30 & 19:30-22:00, Sat 19:30-22:00 only, closed Sun, heading south on Corso Italia turn right on Via Nunziata and take your first right, Piazza dei Facchini 13, tel. 050-26196).

At **Paninoteca il Canguro,** friendly Fabio makes warm, hearty sandwiches to order. Try the popular primavera sandwich (Mon-Sat 10:00-24:00, closed Sun, Via Santa Maria 151, tel. 050-561-942).

Panetteria Antiche Tradizioni—not to be confused with another *panetteria* across the street—is a sandwich/bread shop with complete fixings for a picnic on the lawn at the Field of Miracles or a sit-down lunch ordered from their menu (limited pastas, soups, and salads). Build your own sandwich with homemade bread or focaccia, then choose fruit from the counter, fresh pastries from the window, and cold drinks or wine to round out your meal (daily 8:00-20:00, Via Santa Maria 66, mobile 347-675-2940).

Drop by cheery **La Lupa Ghiotta Tavola Calda** for a cheap, fast, and tasty meal a few steps from Pisa Centrale train station. It's got everything you'd want from a *ristorante* at half the price and with faster service (build your own salad—five ingredients for €4.50; Mon and Wed-Sat 12:15-15:00 & 19:15-23:30, Tue 12:15-15:00 only, closed Sun, Viale F. Bonaini 113, tel. 050-21018).

The street that houses the daily market, **Via delle Colonne** (a block north of the Arno, west of Borgo Stretto), has a few atmospheric mid-priced restaurants and several fun greasy take-out options.

Lucca

Surrounded by well-preserved ramparts, layered with history, alternately quaint and urbane, Lucca charms its visitors. The city

is a paradox. Though it hasn't been involved in a war since 1430, it is Italy's most impressive fortress city, encircled by a perfectly intact wall. Most cities tear down their wall to make way for modern traffic. But Lucca's wall effectively keeps out both traffic and, it seems, the stress of the modern world. Locals are very protective of their wall, which they

enjoy like a community roof garden.

Lucca, known for being Europe's leading producer of toilet paper and Kleenex (with a monopoly on the special machinery that makes it), is nothing to sneeze at. However, the town has no single monumental sight to attract tourists—it's simply a uniquely human and undamaged never-bombed city. Romanesque churches seem to be around every corner, as do fun-loving and shady piazzas filled with soccer-playing children. Still, it's hard to focus on anything in particular within the walls.

Locals say Lucca is like a cake with a cherry filling in the middle...every slice is equally good. Despite Lucca's charm, few tourists seem to put it on their maps, and it remains a city for the Lucchesi (loo-KAY-zee).

Orientation to Lucca

Tourist Information

The main TI is just inside the Porta Santa Maria gate, on Piazza Santa Maria (daily May-Oct 9:00-20:00, Nov-April 9:00-12:30 & 15:00-18:30, pricey Internet access, WCs, no-fee room booking, Piazza Santa Maria 35, tel. 0583-919-931, www.luccatourist.it, info@luccaturismo.it).

Another TI, on Piazzale Verdi, offers information, a no-fee room-booking service, and baggage check (daily 9:00-18:30, futuristic WC, bike rental, 80-minute city-walk audioguide-€9, additional audioguide-€3 more; bag storage-€1.50/hour per bag, they need to photocopy your passport; tel. 0583-583-150).

A third TI, at Piazza Curtatone, has the handiest baggage check near the train station (daily 9:00-17:30, bag storage-€1.50/day per bag; exit the station, cross the square, and it's just ahead on the right; tel. 0583-583-150).

Arrival in Lucca

To reach the city center from the **train** station, walk toward the walls and head left, to the entry at Porta San Pietro. Taxis are sparse, but try calling 0583-333-434 (ignore any recorded message—just wait for a live operator); a ride from the station to Piazza Anfiteatro costs about €6.

Connecting Lucca and Pisa

If you want to visit Lucca and Pisa in one day, direct buses #R008 or #P731 from Lucca's Piazzale Verdi drop you near the Leaning Tower, making Pisa an easy connection. These buses are usually marked by their final destination, *Pisa Aeroporto* (hourly, 30 minutes, buy €3 ticket on bus, toll-free tel. 800-602-947).

Helpful Hints

Shops and Museums Alert: Shops close most of Sunday and Monday mornings. Many museums are closed on Monday as well.

Markets: Lucca's atmospheric markets are worth visiting. Every third Sunday and the preceding Saturday of the month, one of the largest **antiques markets** in Italy unfurls in the blocks from Piazza Antelminelli to Piazza San Giovanni (8:00-19:00). The last weekend of the month, local artisans sell **arts and crafts** around town, mainly near the cathedral (also 8:00-19:00). At the **general market,** held Wednesdays and Saturdays, you'll find produce and household goods (8:30-13:00, from Porta Elisa to Porta San Jacopo on Via dei Bacchettoni).

Internet Access: You can get online at the main **TI** (see "Tourist Information," earlier) or at **Betty Blue,** a wine bar (€4.50/hour, two terminals and cables to plug in your laptop, Thu-Tue 11:00-24:00, closed Wed, Via del Gonfalone 16, tel. 0583-492-166).

Bike Rental: Several places with identical prices cluster around Piazza Santa Maria (€2.50/hour, €12.50/day, tandem bikes available, free helmets, daily about 9:00-19:30 or sunset). These easygoing shops rent good bikes: **Antonio Poli** (Piazza Santa Maria 42, tel. 0583-493-787, enthusiastic Cristiana) and **Cicli Bizzarri** (Piazza Santa Maria 32, tel. 0583-496-682, Australian Dely). At the west end of town, the **TI** on Piazzale Verdi rents bikes. At the south end, you'll find **Promo Turist** at Porta San Pietro (same rates and hours as the competition,

Via Francesco Carrara, mobile 348-380-0126, Marco). A one-hour rental gives you two leisurely loops around the ramparts.

Magazine: For insights into American and British expat life and listings of concerts, markets, festivals, and other special events, pick up a copy of *The Grapevine* (€2), available at newsstands.

Local Guide: Gabriele Calabrese knows and shares his home-town well (€120/3 hours, by foot or bike, mobile 347-788-0667, www.turislucca.com, turislucca@turislucca.com).

Sights in Lucca

▲▲**Bike the Ramparts**—Lucca's most remarkable feature, its Renaissance wall, is also its most enjoyable attraction—especially when circled on a rental bike. Stretching for 2.5 miles, this is an ideal place to come for an over-view of the city by foot or bike.

Lucca has had a protective wall for 2,000 years. You can read three walls into today's map: the first rectangular Roman wall, the later medieval wall (nearly the size of today's), and the 16th-century Renaissance wall that survives today.

With the advent of cannons, thin medieval walls were suddenly vulnerable. A new design—the same one that stands today—was state-of-the-art when it was built (1550-1650). Much of the old medieval wall (look for the old stones) was incorporated into the Renaissance wall (with uniform bricks). The new wall was squat: a 100-foot-wide mound of dirt faced with bricks, engineered to absorb a cannonball pummel-ing. The townspeople cleared a wide no-man's-land around the town, exposing any attackers from a distance. Eleven heart-shaped bastions (inviting picnic areas today) were designed to minimize exposure to cannonballs and to maximize defense capabilities. The ramparts were armed with 130 cannons.

The town invested a third of its income for more than a cen-tury to construct the wall, and—since it kept away the Florentines and nasty Pisans—it was considered a fine investment. In fact, nobody ever bothered to try to attack the wall. Locals say that the only time it actually defended the city was during an 1812 flood of the Serchio River, when the gates were sandbagged and its ram-parts kept out the high water.

Today, the ramparts seem made-to-order for a leisurely bike ride (20-minute pedal, wonderfully smooth). You can rent bikes cheaply and easily from one of several bike-rental places in town

Lucca

RAMPARTS

••• PATHWAY ATOP RAMPARTS

--- OTHER PATHS

P PARKING

1 Ristorante Canuleia

2 Vineria I Santi & Osteria Baralla

3 Osteria Via San Giorgio

4 Vecchia Trattoria Buralli

5 Trattoria da Leo

6 Bella 'Mbriana Pizzeria

LUCCA

(listed earlier, under "Helpful Hints").

Piazza Anfiteatro—Just off the main shopping street, the architectural ghost of a Roman amphitheater can be felt in the delightful Piazza Anfiteatro. With the fall of Rome, the theater (which seated 10,000) was gradually cannibalized for its stones and inhabited by a mishmash of huts. The huts were cleared away at the end of the 19th century to better appreciate the town's illustrious

7 Il Cuore Enogastronomia & Ristorante

8 Pizzeria da Felice

9 Betty Blue Wine Bar & Internet Access

10 Bike Rentals (3)

11 Bus to Pisa's Leaning Tower

past. Today, the square is a circle of touristy shops and mediocre restaurants that becomes a lively bar-and-café scene after dark. Today's street level is nine feet above the original arena floor. The only bits of surviving Roman stonework are a few arches on the northern exterior (at Via Fillungo 42 and on Via Anfiteatro).

Via Fillungo—This main pedestrian drag stretches southwest from Piazza Anfiteatro. *The* street to stroll, Via Fillungo takes you from the amphitheater almost all the way to the cathedral. Along the way, you'll get a taste of Lucca's rich past, including several elegant century-old storefronts. Many of the original storefront paintings, reliefs, and mosaics survive—even if today's shopkeeper sells something entirely different.

At #97 is a classic old **jewelry store** with a rare storefront that has kept its T-shaped arrangement (when closed, you see a wooden T, and during open hours it unfolds with a fine old-time display). This design dates from a time when the merchant sold his goods in front, did his work in the back, and lived upstairs.

Di Simo Caffè, at #58, has long been the hangout of Lucca's artistic and intellectual elite. Composer and hometown boy Giacomo Puccini tapped his foot while sipping coffee here. Pop in to check out the 1880s ambience (handy €10 buffet lunch served daily 12:30-14:30, café open 9:00-24:00).

A surviving five-story **tower house** is at #67. There was a time when nearly every corner sported its own tower. The stubby stones that still stick out once supported wooden staircases (there were no interior connections between floors). So many towers cast shadows over this part of town that the street just before it is called Via Buia (Dark Street). Look away from the tower down Via San Andrea for a peek at the town's tallest tower, Guinigi, in the distance—with its characteristic oak trees sprouting from the top.

At #45 and #43, you'll see two more good examples of tower houses. Across the street, the **Clock Tower** (Torre delle Ore) has a hand-wound Swiss clock that has clanged four times an hour since 1754 (€3.50 to climb up and see the mechanism flip into action on the quarter-hour—if it's actually working, €5 combo-ticket includes Guinigi Tower, daily April-Oct 9:30-18:30, Nov-March 9:30-16:30, corner of Via Fillungo and Via del'Arancio).

The intersection of Via Fillungo and Via Roma/Via Santa Croce marks the center of town (where the two original Roman roads crossed). As you go right down Via Roma, you'll pass the fine Edison Bookstore on your left before reaching Piazza San Michele.

Piazza San Michele—This square has been the center of town since Roman times, when it was the forum. It's dominated by the Church of San Michele. Towering above the church's fancy Pisan Romanesque facade, the archangel Michael stands ready to flap his wings—which he actually did on special occasions.

The square is surrounded by an architectural hodgepodge. The loggia, which dates from 1495, is the first Renaissance building in town. There's a late-19th-century interior in Buccellato Taddeucci, a 130-year-old pastry shop (#34). The left section of the BNL bank (#5; in front of the church) sports an Art Nouveau facade that celebrates both Amerigo Vespucci and Cristoforo Colombo.

You'll notice that no statues of big shots decorate Lucca squares. That's because unlike Venice, Florence, and Milan—which were dominated by a few powerful dynasties—Lucca was traditionally run by an oligarchy of a hundred leading families. But after Italian unification, when leaders were fond of saying, "We have created Italy...now we need to create Italians," stirring statues of national heroes popped up everywhere—even in Lucca. The statue on Piazza San Michele is of a two-bit local guy, dredged up centuries after his death because he favored strong central government.

Look back at the church facade, which also has an element of patriotism—designed to give roots and legitimacy to Italian statehood. Perched above many of the columns are the faces of heroes in the Italian independence and unification movement: Victor Emmanuel II (above the short red column on the right), the Count of Cavour (next to Victor, above the column with black zigzags), and Giuseppe Mazzini.

▲**San Martino Cathedral**—This cathedral, begun in the 11th century, is an entertaining mix of architectural and artistic styles. Its elaborate Pisan Romanesque **facade**—featuring Christian teaching scenes, animals, and candy-cane-striped columns—dominates the piazza. The facade's central figure is St. Martin, a Roman military officer from Hungary who, by offering his cloak to a beggar, more fully understood the beauty of Christian compassion. (The impressive original, a fine example of Romanesque sculpture, hides from pollution just inside, to the right of the main entrance.) Each of the columns on the facade is unique. Notice how the facade is asymmetrical: The 11th-century bell tower was already in place when the rest of the cathedral was built, so the builders cheated on the right side to make it fit the space. Over the right portal (as if

leaning against the older tower), the architect Guideo from Como holds a document declaring that he finished the facade in 1204. On the right (at eye level on the pilaster), a labyrinth is set into the wall. The maze relates the struggle and challenge our souls face in finding salvation. (French pilgrims on their way to Rome could relate to this, as it's the same pattern they knew from the floor of the church at Chartres.) The Latin plaque just left of the main door is where moneychangers and spice traders met to seal deals (on the doorstep of the church—to underscore the reliability of their promises). Notice the date: *An Dni MCXI* (A.D. 1111).

The **interior** features Gothic arches, Renaissance paintings, and stained glass from the 19th century. On the left side of the nave, a small, elaborate birdcage-like temple contains the wooden crucifix—beloved by locals—called Volto Santo. It's said to have been sculpted by Nicodemus in Jerusalem and set afloat in an unmanned boat that landed on the coast of Tuscany, from where wild oxen miraculously carried it to Lucca in 782. The sculpture (which is actually 12th-century Byzantine-style) has quite a jewelry collection, which you can see in the Cathedral Museum (described next).

On the right side of the nave, the sacristy houses the enchantingly beautiful **memorial tomb of Ilaria del Carretto** by Jacopo della Quercia (1407). Pick up a handy English description to the right of the door as you enter the sacristy. This young bride of silk baron Paolo Guinigi is decked out in the latest, most expensive fashions, with the requisite little dog curled up at her feet in eternal sleep. She's so realistic that the statue was nicknamed "Sleeping Beauty." Her nose is partially worn off because of a long-standing tradition of lonely young ladies rubbing it for luck in finding a boyfriend.

Cost and Hours: Cathedral—free, Ilaria tomb—€2, €6 combo-ticket includes Cathedral Museum and San Giovanni Church; Mon-Fri 9:30-17:45, Sat 9:30-18:45; Sun open sporadically between Masses: 9:30-10:45 & 12:00-17:45; Piazza San Martino.

Cathedral Museum (Museo della Cattedrale)—This beautifully presented museum houses original paintings, sculptures, and vestments from the cathedral and other Lucca churches. The first room displays jewelry made to dress up the Volto Santo crucifix, including gigantic gilded silver shoes. Upstairs, notice the fine red brocaded silk—a reminder that this precious fabric is what brought riches and power to the city. The exhibits in this museum have very brief descriptions and are meaningful only with the slow-talking €1 audioguide—if you're not in the mood to listen, skip the place altogether.

Cost and Hours: €4, €6 combo-ticket includes Ilaria tomb and San Giovanni Church; April-Oct daily 10:00-18:00; Nov-March Mon-Fri 10:00-14:00, Sat-Sun 10:00-17:00; to the left of the cathedral as you're facing it, Piazza Antelminelli, tel. 0583-490-530, www.museocattedralelucca.it.

San Giovanni Church—This first cathedral of Lucca is interesting only for its archaeological finds. The entire floor of the 12th-century church has been excavated in recent decades, revealing layers of Roman houses, ancient hot tubs that date back to the time of Christ, early churches, and theological graffiti. Eager students can request an English translation of the floor plans from the ticket office to learn what's what. As you climb under the church's present-day floor and wander the lanes of Roman Lucca, remember that the entire city sits on similar ruins.

Cost and Hours: €2.50, €6 combo-ticket includes Ilaria tomb and Cathedral Museum, audioguide-€1; mid-March-Oct daily 10:00-18:00; Nov-mid-March Sat-Sun 10:00-17:00, closed Mon-Fri; kitty-corner from cathedral at Piazza San Giovanni.

Church of San Frediano—This impressive church was built in 1112 by the pope to counter Lucca's bishop and his spiffy cathedral. Lucca was the first Mediterranean stop on the pilgrim route from northern Europe, and the pope wanted to remind pilgrims that the action, the glory, and the papacy awaited them in Rome. Therefore, he had the church made "Roman-esque." The pure marble facade frames an early Christian Roman-style mosaic of Christ with his 12 apostles. Step inside and you're struck by the sight of 40 powerful (if recycled) ancient Roman columns. The message: Lucca may be impressive, but the finale of your pilgrimage—in Rome—is worth the hike.

Inside, there's a notable piece of art in each corner: At rear left is the 12th-century baptistery, with some interesting Church propaganda showing the story of Moses (the evil Egyptians are played by Holy Roman Empire troops). At rear right is St. Zita's actual body, put there in 1278. At front left is a particularly elegant Virgin Mary, depicted at the moment she gets the news that she'll bring the Messiah into the world (carved and painted by Lucchesi artist Matteo Civitali, c. 1460). And at front right is a painting on wood of the *Assumption of the Virgin* (c. 1510), with Doubting Thomas receiving Mary's red belt as she ascends so he'll doubt no more. The pinball-machine composition serves as a virtual catalog of the fine silk material produced in Lucca—a major industry in the 16th century.

Cost and Hours: Free, Mon-Sat 8:30-12:00 & 15:00-17:30, Sun 9:00-11:30 & 15:00-17:30, Piazza San Frediano, tel. 0583-493-627.

Palazzo Mansi—Minor paintings by Tintoretto, Pontormo, Veronese, and others vie for attention, but the palace itself—a sumptuously furnished and decorated 17th-century confection—steals the show. This is your chance to appreciate the wealth of Lucca's silk merchants.

LUCCA

Cost and Hours: €4, Tue-Sat 8:30-19:30, Sun 8:30-13:30, closed Mon, no photos, request English booklet at ticket desk, Via Galli Tassi 43, tel. 0583-55-570, www.luccamuseinazionali.it. All visitors must be accompanied by a museum employee, so there

may be a bit of a wait during high season.

Guinigi Tower (Torre Guinigi)— Many Tuscan towns have towers, but none is quite like the Guinigi family's. Up 227 steps is a small garden with fragrant trees surrounded by fantastic views.

Cost and Hours: €3.50, €5 combo-ticket includes Clock Tower, likely open daily April-Sept 9:00-19:30, Oct 10:00-18:00, Nov-March 9:30-16:30, Via Sant'Andrea 41.

Eating in Lucca

Ristorante Canuleia makes everything fresh in their small kitchen. While the portions aren't huge, the food is tasty. You can eat in their dressy little dining room or outside on the garden courtyard (€9 pastas, €15 *secondi*, Mon-Sat 12:30-14:00 & 19:30-21:30, closed Sun, Via Canuleia 14, tel. 0583-467-470, reserve for dinner).

Vineria I Santi is pricey but good if you appreciate quality food and fine wine, and just want to lie back and be pampered. Leonardo serves food with a sexy jazz ambience that would work well in a bordello. Relax in the peaceful indoors among wine bottles, or on a quiet square outside (€11 pastas, €18 *secondi*, Thu-Tue 12:30-14:30 & 19:30-22:00, closed Wed, Via Anfiteatro 29, tel. 0583-496-124).

Osteria Via San Giorgio, owned by Daniela and her brother Piero, is a cheery family eatery that satisfies both fish-lovers and meat-lovers. Sample the splittable *antipasto fantasia*—five small courses such as *ceviche* (seafood salad), scallops au gratin, squid sautéed with potatoes, or whatever else was caught that day in Viareggio. Dinner-size salads are bright and fresh, pasta is home-made, and Daniela's desserts tempt (daily 12:00-16:00 & 19:00-23:00, Via San Giorgio 26, tel. 0583-953-233).

Vecchia Trattoria Buralli, on quiet Piazza Sant'Agostino, is a good bet for traditional cooking and juicy steaks, with fine indoor and piazza seating (€7 pastas, €10 *secondi*, €12-30 fixed-price meals, Thu-Tue 12:00-14:45 & 19:00-22:30, closed Wed, Piazza Sant'Agostino 10, tel. 0583-950-611).

Osteria Baralla, on the street that circles Piazza Anfiteatro, is popular with locals for its quality mid-priced meals. They have a breezy, spacious dining room under medieval vaults, and a few quiet tables on the pedestrian street (Mon-Sat 12:30-14:15 & 19:30-22:15, closed Sun, reservations smart for dinner, Via Anfiteatro 7/9, tel. 0583-440-240).

Trattoria da Leo, a brother of Vecchia Trattoria Buralli, packs in chatty locals for typical, cheap home-cooking in a hash-slingin' Mel's Diner atmosphere. This place is a high-energy winner...you know it's going to be good as soon as you step in. Arrive early or reserve in advance (€6 pastas, €10 *secondi*, Mon-Sat 12:00-14:30 & 19:30-22:30, sometimes open Sun, cash only, leave Piazza San Salvatore on Via Asili and take the first left to Via Tegrimi 1, tel. 0583-492-236).

Bella 'Mbriana Pizzeria focuses on doing one thing very well: turning out piping-hot wood-fired pizzas to happy locals in a welcoming wood-paneled dining room. Order and pay at the counter, take a number, and they'll call you when your pizza's ready. Consider take-out to munch atop the nearby walls. Prices range from €5 for your basic *Napolitano* to €8 for their specialty, with buffalo mozzarella and other gourmet ingredients (Wed-Mon 12:30-14:30 & 18:30-23:00, closed Tue, to the right as you face the Church of San Frediano, Via della Cavalerizza 29, tel. 0583-495-565).

Il Cuore Enogastronomia includes a delicatessen and restaurant. For a fancy picnic, drop in the deli for ready-to-eat lasagna, saucy meatballs, grilled and roasted vegetables, vegetable soufflés, Tuscan bean soup, fruit salads, and more, sold by weight and dished up in disposable trays to go. Ask them to heat your order *(riscaldare)*, then picnic on nearby Piazza Napoleone. For curious traveling foodies on a budget who want to eat right there, they can assemble a €10 "degustation plate"—point to direct the construction from among the array of tasty treats under the glass (Tue-Sun 9:30-19:30, closed Mon, Via del Battistero 2, tel. 0583-493-196, Marianna).

Il Cuore Ristorante, located across the way, is a trendy find for wine-tasting or a meal on a piazza. Feast on fresh pastas and other high-quality dishes from their lunch and dinner menus (Wed-Sun 12:00-22:00 with limited menu 15:00-19:30, Tue 12:00-15:00, closed Mon, Via del Battistero, tel. 0583-493-196).

Pizzeria da Felice is a little mom-and-pop hole-in-the-wall serving *cecina* (chickpea crêpes) and slices of freshly baked pizza to throngs of snackers. Grab a *cecina* and a short glass of wine for €2.50 (Mon-Sat 10:00-20:30, closed Sun and 3 weeks in Aug, Via Buia 12, tel. 0583-494-986).

LUCCA

More Sights near Livorno

If your cruise line offers shore excursions to other Tuscan destinations, or if you plan to hire a private driver, here's a brief description of what to expect. For more information, consider two of my guidebooks, *Rick Steves' Snapshot Hill Towns of Central Italy* or *Rick Steves' Snapshot Cinque Terre*.

Siena

Siena's thriving historic center, with red-brick lanes cascading every which way, offers Italy's best medieval city experience. While Florence has the blockbuster museums, Siena has an easy-to-enjoy soul: Courtyards sport flower-decked wells, alleys dead-end at rooftop views, and the sky is a rich blue dome.

For those who dream of a Fiat-free Italy, Siena is a haven. Pedestrians rule in the old center of Siena. Sit at a café on the main square. Wander narrow streets lined with colorful flags and iron rings to tether horses. Take time to savor the first European city to eliminate automobile traffic from its main square (1966) and then, just to be silly, wonder what would happen if they did it in your hometown.

Il Campo, Siena's main square, is the heart—geographically and metaphorically—of Siena. The square fans out from the City Hall (Palazzo Pubblico) to create an amphitheater, where the citizens are the stars. The square and its buildings are the color of the soil upon which they stand...a color known to Crayola-users and other artists as "Burnt Sienna."

Picture Il Campo during the famous **Palio** horse races (every year on July 2 and Aug 16). Ten snorting horses and their nervous riders (selected from 17 *contrade,* or neighborhoods) line up near the Antica Siena shop (right side of square) to await the starting signal. Then they race like crazy three times around the perimeter (the gray pavement), which is covered with dirt. The winner crosses the line, and 1/17th of Siena goes berserk for the next 365 days. For easy-to-pack souvenirs, get some of the colorful scarves/flags that depict the symbols of Siena's 17 neighborhoods (such as the wolf, the turtle, and the snail).

If the Campo is the heart of Siena, the **Duomo** (or cathedral) is its soul. The white-and-dark-green-striped church, sitting on an artificial platform atop Siena's highest point, is visible for miles around. This ornate but surprisingly secular shrine to the Virgin Mary is stacked with colorful art inside and out, from the inlaid-marble floors to the stained-glass windows. The interior is a Renaissance riot of striped columns, intricate marble inlays, Michelangelo statues, and Bernini sculptures.

Located at the back of the Duomo on the right, the **Duomo Museum** (Siena's most enjoyable) was built to house the cathedral's art. The ground floor is filled with the cathedral's original Gothic sculptures by Giovanni Pisano (who spent 10 years in the late 1200s carving and orchestrating the decoration of the cathedral) and a fine Donatello *Madonna and Child*. Be sure to climb onto the Panorama del Facciatone for a surprise view of Siena.

While you're here, look for Siena's claim to caloric fame—*panforte*, a rich, chewy concoction of nuts, honey, and candied fruits that impresses even fruitcake-haters.

With extra time, you could climb the City Hall Tower, visit the Church of San Domenico (with relics of St. Catherine), or see Sienese art in the Pinacoteca. But I like to just hang out on Il Campo.

Cinque Terre

The Cinque Terre (CHINK-weh TAY-reh), a remote chunk of the Italian Riviera, is the traffic-free, lowbrow, underappreciated alternative to the French Riviera.
There's not a museum in sight. Just sun, sea, sand (pebbles), wine, and pure, unadulterated Italy. Enjoy the villages, swimming, hiking, and romance of one of God's great gifts to tourism. Each of the five *(cinque)* villages fills a ravine with a lazy hive of human activity—callused locals, sunburned travelers, and no Vespas. While the Cinque Terre is now discovered (and can be quite crowded midday, when tourist boats drop by), I've never seen happier, more relaxed tourists.

The five towns from east to west are: **Riomaggiore** (a workaday town), **Manarola** (picturesque), **Corniglia** (on a hilltop), **Vernazza** (the region's cover girl, the most touristy and dramatic), and **Monterosso al Mare** (the closest thing to a beach resort of the five towns). If you take the train here, note that some trains stop only in Monterosso and Riomaggiore.

With its harbor overseen by a ruined castle and a stout stone church, Vernazza is the jewel of the Cinque Terre. But you get fewer crowds and better value for your money in other towns. Monterosso is a good choice for sun-worshipping softies and the younger crowd. Hermits, anarchists, wine-lovers, and mountain goats like Corniglia. Sophisticated Italians and Germans choose Manarola.

With limited time, choose just one town to wander. With more time, consider a hike. All five towns are connected by trail #2, marked with red-and-white paint, white arrows, and some signs. If you hike, you'll need to get a Cinque Terre Card (€5, sold at trailheads, good for one day, includes map). The entire seven-mile hike can be done in about four hours, but allow five for dawdling. If you have time for only one segment, consider the wide, easy Riomaggiore-Manarola path. In comparison, the rest of the trail is narrow, rocky, and comes with lots of steps.

Every town in the Cinque Terre has a beach or a rocky place to swim. Monterosso has the biggest and sandiest, with beach umbrellas and beach-use fees (but it's free where there are no umbrellas). Vernazza's is tiny—better for sunning than swimming. Manarola and Riomaggiore have the worst beaches (no sand), but Manarola offers the best deep-water swimming.

This region is the birthplace of pesto. Basil, which loves the temperate Ligurian climate, is ground with cheese (half parmigiano cow cheese and half pecorino sheep cheese), garlic, olive oil, and pine nuts, and then poured over pasta. Try it on spaghetti, *trenette*, or *trofie* (made of flour with a bit of potato, designed specifically for pesto to cling to). If you become addicted, small jars of pesto are sold in the local grocery stores and gift shops—they make tasty souvenirs.

The Cinque Terre is where you can melt into small-town Italy. Sit on the breakwater to enjoy the views, and munch a picnic to the soundtrack of the surf.

Hill Towns near Livorno: San Gimignano and Volterra

The sun-soaked hill towns of central Italy offer what to many is the quintessential Italian experience: sun-dried tomatoes, homemade pasta, wispy cypress-lined driveways following desolate ridges to fortified 16th-century farmhouses, atmospheric *enoteche* serving Tuscany's famously tasty wines, and dusty old-timers warming the same bench day after day while soccer balls buzz around them like innocuous flies.

Multi-towered San Gimignano is a classic, but because it's such an easy hill town to visit from Florence, peak-season crowds can overwhelm the town's charms. For rustic vitality not completely trampled by tourist crowds, out-of-the-way Volterra is the clear winner.

San Gimignano

The epitome of a Tuscan hill town, with 14 medieval towers still standing (out of an original 72), San Gimignano (sahn jee-meen-

YAH-noh) is a perfectly pre-served tourist trap. There are no important interiors to sight-see, and the town is packed with crass commercialism. But San Gimignano is visually so beautiful that it remains a good destination.

While the basic sight here is the town of San Gimignano itself, there are a few worth-while stops. From the town gate, head straight up the traffic-free town's cobbled main drag to Piazza della Cisterna (with its 13th-century well). The town sights cluster around the adjoining Piazza del Duomo. The **Duomo** (or Collegiata) is San Gimignano's Romanesque cathedral. Inside, Sienese Gothic art (14th century) lines the nave with parallel themes, Old Testament on the left and New Testament on the right. The **Civic Museum and Tower** is a small, fun museum, consisting of just three unfurnished rooms and a tower, inside City Hall. The highlight for most visitors is a chance to climb the Tower (Torre Grossa), the city's tallest at 200 feet and 218 steps.

San Gimignano's cuisine is typical Tuscan home cooking. *Cinghiale* (cheeng-GAH-lay, wild boar) is served in almost every way: stews, soups, cutlets, and, my favorite, salami. Most shops will give you a sample before you commit to buying.

Volterra

Encircled by impressive walls and topped with a grand fortress, Volterra sits high above the rich farmland. More than 2,000 years ago, Volterra was one of the most important Etruscan cities, a city much larger than the one we see today. Greek-trained Etruscan artists worked here, leaving a sig-nificant stash of art, particularly funerary urns.

Compact and walkable, the city stretches out from the pleasant

What If I Miss My Boat?

Remember that you can get help from the cruise line's port agent (listed on the destination information sheet distributed on the ship) and the local TI (for Florence, see page 395; for Pisa, see page 480; for Lucca, see page 495). If the port agent suggests a costly solution (such as a private car with a driver), you may want to consider public transit.

Florence is Tuscany's transportation hub, with fine train, bus, and plane connections to virtually anywhere in Italy. The city has several train stations, a bus station (next to the main train station), and Amerigo Vespucci Airport. Pisa is on a main train line and has a major airport (Galileo Galilei Airport); Lucca is on a minor train line. It's easy to reach Florence by train from Pisa (2-3/hour, 1.25 hours) or from Lucca (2/hour, 1.5 hours).

Frequent trains leave from Florence's Santa Maria Novella Station (the same one with train connections to Livorno) to: **Venice** (hourly, 2-3 hours), **Civitavecchia** (at least hourly, transfer in Rome, 3.5 hours), **Naples** (hourly, 3-5 hours, some change in Rome), **Sorrento** (hourly, 5-6 hours, transfer to Circumvesuviana commuter train in Naples), **Nice** (6/day, 7-8 hours, transfer in Milan and Ventimiglia), **Marseille** (3/day, 10-11 hours, transfer in Milan, Ventimiglia, and Nice), and more. For other connections, ask at the train station or check http://bahn.hafas.de/bin/query.exe/en (Germany's excellent all-Europe website). Italy has a train-info toll number 892-021 (answered 24 hours daily in Italian only; have a local person call for you).

Any local **travel agent** should be able to help. For more advice on what to do if you miss the boat, see page 131.

Piazza dei Priori to the old city gates. While the town itself is a pleasing postcard, it has some top-notch sights.

The **Etruscan Arch** (Porta all'Arco), built of massive volcanic tuff stones in the fourth century B.C., is Volterra's most dramatic ruin. The three seriously eroded heads, dating from the first century B.C., show what happens when you leave something outside for 2,000 years. The **Etruscan Museum** (Museo Etrusco Guarnacci) is filled top to bottom with rare Etruscan artifacts, making it easy to appreciate how advanced this pre-Roman culture was. The 12th-century **Duomo** is not as elaborate as its cousin in Pisa, but the simple facade and central nave are beautiful examples of the Pisan Romanesque style. Built in about 10 B.C., the town's well-preserved **Roman Theater** is considered to have some of the best acoustics of its kind.

As you stroll up Via Matteotti, the town's main shopping street, stop in an alabaster workshop or showroom. Alabaster, mined nearby, has long been a big industry here. Or visit a bakery to munch the local *cantuccini* (almond biscotti).

Unlike other famous towns in Tuscany, Volterra feels not cutesy or touristy...but real, vibrant, and almost oblivious to the allure of the tourist dollar. A refreshing break from its more commercial neighbors, it's my favorite small town in Tuscany.

ROME
& the PORT of CIVITAVECCHIA

Roma

Rome is magnificent and brutal at the same time. It's a showcase of Western civilization, with astonishingly ancient sights and a modern vibrancy. But if you're careless, you'll be run down or pickpocketed. And with the wrong attitude, you'll be frustrated by the kind of chaos that only an Italian can understand. On my last visit, a cabbie struggling with the traffic said, *"Roma chaos."* I responded, *"Bella chaos."* He agreed.

While Paris is an urban garden, Rome is a magnificent tangled forest. If you pace yourself; if you're well-organized for sightseeing; and if you protect yourself and your valuables with extra caution and discretion, you'll love it. (And Rome is much easier to live with if you can avoid the midsummer heat.)

For me, Rome is in a three-way tie with Paris and London as Europe's greatest city. Two thousand years ago, the word "Rome" meant civilization itself. Everything was either civilized (part of the Roman Empire, Latin- or Greek-speaking) or barbarian. Today, Rome is Italy's political capital, the capital of Catholicism, and the center of the ancient world, littered with evocative remains. As you peel through its fascinating and jumbled layers, you'll find Rome's buildings, cats, laundry, traffic, and 2.6 million people endlessly entertaining. And then, of course, there are its stupendous sights.

Visit St. Peter's, the greatest church on earth, and scale Michelangelo's 448-foot-tall dome, the world's tallest. Learn something about eternity by touring the huge Vatican Museum. You'll find the story of creation—bright as the day it was painted—in the restored Sistine Chapel. Do the "Caesar Shuffle" through ancient Rome's Forum and Colosseum, or enjoy a walk from Campo de' Fiori to the Spanish Steps.

Excursions from Civitavecchia

The top options are **Rome, Rome,** and **Rome.** You could easily fill a week without ever leaving the city limits.

Here are other typical excursions that cruise lines offer:

The excavated ancient city **Ostia Antica** (one hour south of Civitavecchia) was a working port town, and its ruins show a more complete and grittier view of Roman life than wealthier Pompeii (near Naples). Wandering around today, you'll see ruins of warehouses, apartments, shopping arcades, and baths that once served 60,000 inhabitants.

The Etruscan necropolis of **Tarquinia,** about a half-hour north of Civitavecchia, contains 6,000 graves cut in the rock; the earliest date from the seventh century B.C. (that's pre-"ancient Rome"). Aristocratic tombs contain large-scale wall paintings rich in details. Excavated treasures are displayed in the Tarquinian National Museum.

Lake Bracciano, an hour's ride east of Civitavecchia, is part of the Parco Bracciano Nature Reserve. As pretty as it must be, it's hard to imagine missing Rome for this excursion.

The grand, classic hill town of **Orvieto** (1.75 hours north of Civitavecchia), perched high above a vineyard-filled valley, is famous for its white wine, colorful ceramics, and resplendent Gothic cathedral. Take this side-trip only if you'd rather see a charming hill town than the enormous city of Rome.

Many cruises start or end in Rome. If yours does, check the end of this chapter for airport information and recommended hotels.

Planning Your Time

Rome is wonderful, but it's huge and exhausting. With just a few hours, you'll have to be very selective—getting just a first nibble of this grand city. Keep in mind that it takes approximately 1.5 hours each way to get between your ship and downtown Rome—so you'll need to mentally subtract at least three hours from the time you have in port.

If all you have left is a few hours, they'll be full and memorable. On a brief first-time visit to Rome, there are two main choices, each taking several hours. For a short stop, you'll need to choose between the two. (Note that the Vatican sights are prone to long lines.) I've also included a third option, a mile-long Walk Across Rome, which could be the focus of your visit, or could be added to the end of one of the other plans. If shopping is your main interest, see page 618.

• **Ancient Roman Sites** (in this order): Colosseum, Forum, and Pantheon. Allow three hours. (If you have extra time, it's easy to add on much of the Walk Across Rome: Piazza Navona, Trevi Fountain, and Spanish Steps.)

• **Vatican City:** Vatican Museum (with the Sistine Chapel) and St. Peter's Basilica. Tour the Vatican Museum first; ideally, reserve the Vatican Museum online before your trip (see page 565). Then exit from the Sistine Chapel directly into St. Peter's. Allow four hours, and up to five hours if you haven't reserved ahead for the Vatican Museum and have to wait in line.

• **Walk Across Rome:** Take my self-guided walk from Campo de' Fiori to the Spanish Steps, exploring the characteristic squares, Pantheon, and Trevi Fountain en route. Allow two hours or more, especially if you tour the Pantheon.

Arrival at the Port of Civitavecchia

Arrival at a Glance: Ride a shuttle bus to the port entrance, then walk 10-15 minutes to the train station and catch a train into Rome (45-80 minutes, depending on type of train and destination in Rome). A taxi straight into Rome takes 1.5 hours and costs around €110-150.

Port Overview

Cruise ships dock at Civitavecchia (chee-vee-tah-VEH-kyah), a small, manageable port city about 45 miles northwest of Rome. Civitavecchia is historic: With foundations dating back to Etruscan times, this "Ancient Town" (as its name means) was built up by the Emperor Trajan, then favored by the popes with "free port" status. By the 20th century, it had become Rome's main port before being leveled by

Allied bombs in World War II, and later rebuilt. Today, this town of 50,000 has little for visitors to see. Virtually every cruise passenger disembarking at Civitavecchia is headed for Rome, which is a train ride away (45-80 minutes, depending on which train and which Rome station you use).

Civitavecchia's large port area stretches west from its main crossroads, Largo Plebiscito. Several cruise terminals line up along a long pier. The stout 16th-century Michelangelo Fortress (Forte Michelangelo) stands where the port area meets the town, next to the port gate. Tourist services cluster just outside the port gate, on Largo Plebiscito; others line the main road (Viale Garibaldi) between the gate and the train station (a 10- to 15-minute walk away).

Civitavecchia

To Tarquinia

VIA SANGALLO

VIA XX SETTEMBRE

100 Meters
100 Yards

BOATS TO SARDINIA & CORSICA

Piazzetta S. Maria

Piazza Regina Magherita

MKT.

Piazza del Conservatorio

CENTOCELLE

CRUISE TERMINAL

Piazza V. Emanuele

CORSO

PORT GATE

Largo Plebiscito

Piazza Fratti

FORTE MICHELANGELO

Piazza d. Eroi

V. TOTI

V. BRUNO

DIRECT ROUTE TO/FROM TRAIN STATION

Piazza degli Eventi

ATM

VIA CRISPI

VIA DELLA REPUBBLICA

TRAIN STATION

Mediterranean Sea

PEDESTRIAN PROMENADE

GARIBALDI

VIA VITTORIA

To Rome

VIA DUCA D'AOSTA

1 Hotel San Giorgio & Hotel Mediterraneo
2 Hotel de La Ville
3 Cruises Services Center (Internet Access, Etc.)
4 Mr. G Caffè (Wi-Fi)
5 Casa del Gelato (Wi-Fi)

Tourist Information: A small Civitavecchia TI is at the shuttle bus stop, next to the Michelangelo Fortress (daily 9:00-13:00, opens earlier on days with early cruise arrivals, tel. 0766-1892-667). Just outside the port gate, in a green kiosk on the small leafy square, is an often-unstaffed Rome provincial TI.

Getting into Rome

Road traffic between Civitavecchia and Rome is terrible, making the train faster and more economical than a taxi.

From Your Ship to the Port Gate

To reach either Civitavecchia's train station or taxi stand, you'll need to get from your cruise ship to the port entrance. Each cruise ship is met by a free shuttle bus, which brings you to the port gate, in front of the fortress (buses run at least every 20 minutes, likely more often with demand). Some shuttle buses may take you all the way to the train station—ask when you board.

If there's a long line to board the shuttle bus, consider walking from your ship to the port gate. It's a 10- to 20-minute walk, depending on how far your terminal is from the port entrance

ROME

Services in Civitavecchia

Here are the nearest services to the port, though if you can wait, Rome has everything you need (see "Helpful Hints" on page 523).

ATM: An ATM is at **Banca delle Marche,** between the port gate and the train station on Viale Garibaldi.

Internet Access: As you exit the port gate, the first shop on your right, **Cruises Services Center,** has Internet terminals (€3/hour), cheap telephone cards and calling cabins, and other basic services (daily 9:00-19:00). Two other nearby places offer free Wi-Fi with a purchase: **Mr. G Caffè** (near Cruises Services Center) and **Casa del Gelato** (across the small square).

Pharmacy: A pharmacy is on Viale Garibaldi.

Baggage Storage: If Civitavecchia is your first or last stop, and you need a place to store bags, you can stow them at the Cruises Services Center described above (€5/day per bag).

(though be aware that from some areas of the port, you may not be allowed to walk—ask as you leave the ship).

From the Port Gate to Rome by Taxi

Taxis wait at the port gate, attempting to extort €15 for the very short ride to the train station (at least triple the fair metered rate), or significantly more for the ride into Rome (figure about 1.5 hours each way, depending on traffic; the going rate should be €110-150 one-way, or €300-400 for an all-day Rome city tour, but many cabbies inflate their prices dramatically). Taxis generally meet arriving ships, or you can call 076-626-121.

From the Port Gate to Rome by Train

Here's the basic plan: From the port gate, walk about 10-15 minutes to Civitavecchia's train station; ride the train into Rome; then connect by taxi or public transportation to what you'd like to see in Rome. For a preview before your trip, check out the Rome Walks website (www.romewalks.com), which has a useful step-by-step video on this approach.

Step 1: Walk from the Port Gate to the Train Station

From the shuttle-bus stop, **walk** through the security checkpoint at the port gate to reach Largo Plebiscito, Civitavecchia's hub of activity. On your right is a row of hole-in-the-wall shops and businesses catering to cruise passengers, and dead ahead is the main road, Viale Garibaldi. From here, it's about a half-mile,

gently uphill, 10- to 15-minute walk to Civitavecchia's train station: Just walk straight ahead up Viale Garibaldi, with the sea on your right-hand side. After about three blocks, at Hotel de La Ville, bear left and uphill through a long parking lot to the pale-orange train station (marked *Civitavecchia*—see photo). If you get turned around, look for signs to *Stazione FF. SS.*

Local **buses #B, #C,** and **#D** also go from just above the port gate on Largo Plebiscito (Viale Garibaldi stop) one stop to the train station (Stazione FF. SS. stop; €0.80, 3-4/hour, 5 minutes, buy ticket at *tabacchi*—tobacco shop—before you board). The bus only saves you a few minutes of walking: Unless it happens to be departing just as you arrive, you'll likely wind up spending more time waiting for the next bus than you would simply walking to the station. Take the bus only if you're carrying heavy bags or have limited mobility.

Step 2: Take the Train from Civitavecchia to Rome

Frequent trains connect Civitavecchia and two different stations in Rome. First decide whether you want to go to Rome's main **Termini Station** (where all trains stop, closer to the ancient sites) or Rome's secondary **San Pietro Station** (served only by regional trains, closer to the Vatican). All together, there are approximately three trains per hour in each direction. In case your timing works out, consider the once-daily "Special Express Train" mentioned below. All train tickets must be validated in the yellow box before getting on train.

Civitavecchia Station: Inside the station, you'll find the "food village" café and cafeteria, a *tabacchi* shop, and a newsstand, but no lockers or baggage storage (the nearest baggage storage is at the port gate—described earlier). Look for the *partenze* screens, which show upcoming departures. The columns show each train's destination *(destinazione)*; category *(cat)*; time of departure *(ore)*; delay, if any *(rit)*; and which track the train leaves from *(bin)*.

Fast Trains (no Vatican stop): In the category *(cat)* column, trains marked IC (InterCity) and ES (Eurostar) are faster and more expensive (45-60 minutes to Termini Station; ES trains—€12.50 each way second-class including required seat reservation; IC—€9 each way second-class); however, these trains do not stop at the San Pietro Station closer to the Vatican.

Regional Trains (with stop near Vatican): Trains designated as REG (regional) are slower, but they're also cheaper and give you the option of getting off at the San Pietro Station near the Vatican (to Termini: 60-80 minutes, €4.50 each way; to San Pietro: 40-55 minutes, €4.10 each way). Another advantage of a regional train is that it's covered by the €9 BIRG ticket, which includes all-day, unlimited travel on regional trains in second class and on the Metro and bus system in Rome. You cannot buy a BIRG ticket from a machine—you must buy one at the ticket counter, from a customer-service agent, or at the newsstand inside the station (sells only BIRG tickets, no other kind). Be sure to write your name on the back of your BIRG ticket.

Special Express Train (with stop near Vatican): A once-daily, special express train departure, which runs only during the cruising season, is designed specifically for cruise passengers; it goes from Civitavecchia directly to Rome's San Pietro Station (near the Vatican), then on to Termini Station (times in 2010: depart Civitavecchia 9:24, arrive San Pietro 10:00, arrive Termini 10:15; depart Termini 16:45, arrive San Pietro 17:02, arrive Civitavecchia 17:37). This journey is not covered by the BIRG ticket, and tickets must be bought at a ticket window or from a customer-service agent. If this train's departure is timed to your cruise, it's the fastest way into town.

Self-Service Ticket Machines: There's often a long line for the ticket windows, but you can use the self-service machines. There are two types of machines: Those labeled *Biglietto Veloce/Fast Ticket* accept only credit cards, are much easier to use, and sell tickets for all types of trains (except the special express train—see above); on these machines, when prompted, select "base" fare. Machines labeled *Biglietti Self-Service/Rete Regionale* have instructions only in Italian, accept only cash, and sell tickets only for regional trains.

Platforms: The Civitavecchia train station has five main platforms (*binario*, or *bin*; numbered 1 through 5), connected by an underground tunnel. There are also two "short" *(tronco)* platforms, 1T and 2T, at the far-right end of the station as you face the tracks; these are *not* the same as tracks 1 and 2. Be sure you're waiting at the correct platform.

Step 3: From Rome's Train Stations to the Sights

Once you arrive in Rome, your plan depends on which station you ride to: San Pietro (best if you plan to start at the Vatican) or Termini (easy Metro connection to the Colosseum or a taxi to Campo de' Fiori).

San Pietro Station

This small station has basic services (ticket window, ticket machines, WC, and café). If you're going to the Vatican Museum, it's smart to take a taxi if you'd like to avoid the 30-minute walk. From the station, St. Peter's Basilica is about a 10- to 15-minute **walk** to your left—just look for its giant dome. From the station, follow Via della Stazione San Pietro to Via Porta Cavalleggeri, where you'll see the wall of Vatican City across the street. Cross the street and follow the wall to the right (east). Soon you'll see St. Peter's Basilica on your left. To reach the Vatican Museum, cross the square, pass through the colonnades, then the arches of the brick wall, and continue straight, following the wall north another 10-15 minutes along Via di Porta Angelica until it turns left at Viale Vaticano, where you'll find the main museum entrance. **Bus #64** goes from San Pietro Station to the Cavalleggeri stop near St. Peter's Square, but it may be faster to walk than to wait for the bus.

Termini Station

Termini, Rome's main train station, is a buffet of tourist services. While information desks are jammed with travelers, the staff at very handy red info kiosks at the head of the tracks can answer your simple questions. Along track 24, about 100 yards down, you'll find the **TI** (daily 8:00-20:30), a **post office** (Mon-Fri 8:30-14:00, Sat 8:30-13:00, closed Sun), and **car rental** desks. A good self-service **cafeteria,** Ciao, is near the head of track 24, upstairs, with fine views (daily 11:00-22:30). Near track 1, you'll find a **pharmacy** (daily 7:30-22:00); along the same track is a **waiting room** and **train information** office (daily 6:00-24:00). The handy **Drugstore Conad,** selling everything from groceries to electronics, is just downstairs (daily 6:00-24:00). Elsewhere in the station are **ATMs,** late-hours banks, and 24-hour thievery. In the station's main entrance lobby, **Borri Books** sells books in English, including popular fiction, Italian history and culture, and kids' books, plus maps upstairs (daily 7:00-23:00). The station has some sleazy sharks with official-looking business cards; avoid anybody selling anything unless they're in a legitimate shop at the station.

Termini is a local transportation hub, ideal for using Rome's excellent public transportation network—which includes the Metro (subway) and buses—to reach whatever you'd like to see in Rome. For all the details on this system and its tickets, see page 527. Note that the Metro and bus areas are under construction until sometime in 2011—look for signs directing you to the nearest Metro platform or bus stop.

The city's two **Metro** lines (A and B) intersect at Termini Metro station downstairs. If you're heading for the Colosseum and ancient sites, ride line B (direction Laurentina) two stops, to Colosseo. For the Vatican, ride line A (direction Battisini) seven stops, to Cipro (still a 10-minute walk from the Vatican)—or take a bus, described next.

ROME

Buses (including Rome's hop-on, hop-off bus tours—see "Tours in Rome" on page 531) leave across the square directly in front of the main station hall. To reach the Pantheon or the Vatican, hop on bus #64 or #40 (requires an additional 10- to 15-minute walk to the Vatican Museum, or a 5-minute walk to the Pantheon).

Consider hiring a **taxi** to save time getting around Rome. Taxis queue in front of the station; avoid con men hawking "express taxi" services in unmarked cars (only use cars marked with the word *taxi* and a phone number). To avoid the long taxi line, simply hike out past the buses to the main street and hail one. For details on taking taxis in Rome, see page 530.

By Tour

For information on local tour options in Rome—including local guides for hire, walking tours, and hop-on, hop-off bus tours—see "Tours in Rome" on page 531.

Returning to Your Ship

If you return to the port from Rome's Termini Station, note that trains to Civitavecchia generally leave from tracks 27-30, a 10- to 15-minute walk from the main station entrance...seriously. Allow plenty of time to make this hike.

Once back at Civitavecchia's train station, exit to the right and head straight back down to the port. When boarding the free shuttle bus inside the port gate, check to make sure it's the right one (marked with the name of your cruise ship).

If you have extra time in Civitavecchia before heading back to your ship, consider checking out the National Archaeological Museum's collection of Roman and Etruscan artifacts (free, open until 18:00, a block uphill from the port gate at Largo Camillo Benso Conte di Cavour 1). To squeeze in some beach time before getting back on board, the handy beach at Pirgo—directly in front of the train station—is as good as it gets around here (which isn't saying much).

Note: Not all taxis have permission to enter the port area (they can only go as far as the port gate, a long walk or shuttle-bus ride from your ship). If you're taking a taxi *to* the port, ensure that they have authorization to the pier *(molo)* to bring you all the way to your ship; otherwise, you'll have to ride the shuttle bus.

See page 630 for help if you miss your boat.

ROME

Rome's Neighborhoods

VATICAN MUSEUM
VATICAN CITY
ST. PETER'S
SAN PIETRO TRAIN STN.

PIAZZA DEL POPOLO
NORTH ROME
"SHOPPING TRIANGLE"
SPANISH STEPS

VILLA BORGHESE
BORGHESE GALLERY

PANTHEON NEIGHBORHOOD

TIBER RIVER

PIAZZA VENEZIA

TERMINI
NAT'L. MUSEUM
TRAIN STATION

CAPITOL HILL
FORUM
ANCIENT ROME
COLOSSEUM

PILGRIM'S ROME
SAN GIOVANNI IN LATERANO

STA. MARIA
TRASTEVERE

TESTACCIO
SOUTH OF TESTACCIO
SOUTH ROME
APPIAN WAY
E.U.R.

NOT TO SCALE

DCH

Orientation to Rome

Sprawling Rome actually feels manageable once you get to know it. The old core, with most of the tourist sights, sits in a diamond formed by Termini train station (in the east), the Vatican (west), Villa Borghese Gardens (north), and the Colosseum (south). The Tiber River runs through the diamond from north to south. In the center of the diamond sits Piazza Venezia, a busy square and traffic hub. It takes about an hour to walk from Termini train station to the Vatican.

Think of Rome as a series of neighborhoods, huddling around major landmarks.

Ancient Rome: In ancient times, this was home for the grandest buildings of a city of a million people. Today, the best of the classical sights stand in a line from the Colosseum to the Forum to the Pantheon.

Pantheon Neighborhood: The Pantheon anchors the neighborhood I like to call the heart of Rome. It stretches eastward from the Tiber River through Campo de' Fiori and Piazza Navona, past the Pantheon to the Trevi Fountain.

Daily Reminder

Sunday: These sights are closed—the Vatican Museum (except for the last Sunday of the month, when it's free and even more crowded), Villa Farnesina, Santa Susanna Church, and the Catacombs of San Sebastiano. In the morning, the Porta Portese flea market hops, and the old center is delightfully quiet.

Monday: Many sights are closed, including the National Museum of Rome, Borghese Gallery, Capitoline Museums, Catacombs of Priscilla, Museum of the Bath (at the Baths of Diocletian), Museum of the Imperial Forums (includes Trajan's Market and Trajan's Forum), Castel Sant'Angelo, Ara Pacis, Montemartini Museum, E.U.R.'s Museum of Roman Civilization, Etruscan Museum, Museum of the Liberation of Rome, some Appian Way sights (Tomb of Cecilia Metella, Circus and Villa of Maxentius, and the San Sebastiano Gate and Museum of the Walls), and Ostia Antica. Many of the ancient sights (e.g., Colosseum and Forum) and the Vatican Museum, among others, are open. Churches are open as usual. The Baths of Caracalla closes early in the afternoon.

Tuesday: All sights are open.

Wednesday: All sights are open, except for the Catacombs of San Callisto. St. Peter's Basilica may be closed in the morning for a papal audience.

Thursday: All sights are open (though the Cappuccin Crypt occasionally closes).

Friday: All sights are open.

Saturday: Most sights are open in Rome, except for the Synagogue, Jewish Museum, and Santa Susanna Church.

North Rome: With the Spanish Steps, Villa Borghese Gardens, and trendy shopping streets (Via Veneto and the "shopping triangle"), this is a more modern, classy area.

Vatican City: Located west of the Tiber, it's a compact world of its own, with two great, huge sights: St. Peter's Basilica and the Vatican Museum.

Trastevere: This seedy, colorful wrong-side-of-the-river neighborhood is the city at its crustiest.

Termini: Though light on sightseeing highlights, the train-station neighborhood has many public-transportation connections.

Pilgrim's Rome: Several prominent churches dot the area south of Termini train station.

South Rome: South of the city center are the gritty/colorful Testaccio neighborhood, the 1930s suburb of E.U.R., and the Appian Way.

Within each of these neighborhoods, you'll find elements from the many layers of Rome's 2,000-year history: the marble ruins of ancient times; tangled streets of the medieval world; early Christian churches; grand Renaissance buildings and statues; Baroque fountains and church facades; 19th-century apartments; and 20th-century boulevards choked with traffic.

Since no one is allowed to build taller than St. Peter's dome, and virtually no buildings have been constructed in the city center since Mussolini got distracted in 1938, Rome has no modern skyline. The Tiber River is basically ignored—after the last floods (1870), the banks were built up very high, and Rome turned its back on its naughty river.

Tourist Information

Rome has two tourist information offices and numerous kiosks (generally open daily 9:30-19:00). The TI offices are at the airport (terminal 3) and Termini train station (open until 20:30, way down track 24, look for signs). Little kiosks are near the Forum (on Piazza del Tempio della Pace), on Via Nazionale (at Palazzo delle Esposizioni), near Castel Sant'Angelo (at Piazza Pia), at the Church of Santa Maria Maggiore (on Via dell'Olmata), near Piazza Navona (at Piazza delle Cinque Lune), and near the Trevi Fountain (at Via del Corso and Via Minghetti). The TI's website is http://en.turismoroma.it.

At any TI, ask for a city map, a listing of sights and hours (in the free *Museums of Rome* booklet), and the free *Evento* booklet, with English-language pages listing the month's cultural events.

The best map I found is published by Rough Guide (€8 in bookstores).

Rome's single best source of up-to-date tourist information is its **call center,** with English-speakers on staff. Dial 06-0608 (answered daily 9:00-21:00, press 2 for English).

Several English-oriented **websites** provide insight into events and daily life in the city: www.inromenow.com (light tourist info on lots of topics), www.wantedinrome.com (events and accommodations), and http://rome.angloinfo.com (on living in and moving to Rome).

Helpful Hints

Internet Access: Rome has plenty of Internet cafés. Bring your passport, which you may be asked to show before going online.

Bookstores: These stores (all open daily except Anglo American and Open Door) sell travel guidebooks, including mine. The first two are chains, while the others have a more personal touch. **Borri Books** is at Termini train station, and **Feltrinelli**

ROME

International has two branches (at Largo Argentina, and just off Piazza della Repubblica at Via Vittorio Emanuele Orlando 84, tel. 06-482-7878). **Anglo American Bookshop** has great art and history sections (closed Sun and Mon morning, a few blocks south of Spanish Steps at Via della Vite 102, tel. 06-679-5222). **Libreria Fanucci** is centrally located (a block toward the Pantheon from Piazza Navona at Piazza Madama 8, tel. 06-686-1141). In Trastevere, Irishman Dermot at the **Almost Corner Bookshop** stocks an Italian-interest section (Via del Moro 45, tel. 06-583-6942), and the **Open Door Bookshop** carries the only used books in English in town (closed Sun, Via della Lungaretta 23, tel. 06-589-6478).

Travel Agencies: You can get train tickets and railpass-related reservations and supplements at travel agencies (at little or no additional cost), avoiding a trip to a train station. The **American Express** office near the Spanish Steps sells train tickets and makes reservations for no extra fee (may close in 2011—be sure to call ahead, Piazza di Spagna 38, tel. 06-67641).

Theft Alert: While violent crime is rare in the city center, petty theft is rampant. With sweet-talking con artists meeting you at the station, well-dressed pickpockets on buses, and thieving gangs of children at the ancient sites, Rome is a gauntlet of rip-offs. While it's not as bad as it was a few years ago, and pickpockets don't want to hurt you—they usually just want your money—green or sloppy tourists will be scammed. Thieves strike when you're distracted. Don't trust kind strangers. Keep nothing important in your pockets. Be most on guard while boarding and leaving buses and subways. Thieves crowd the door, then stop and turn while others crowd and push from behind. You'll find less crowding and commotion—and less risk—waiting for the end cars of a sub-way rather than the middle cars. The sneakiest thieves pretend to be well-dressed businessmen (generally with something in their hands), or tourists wearing fanny packs and toting cameras and even Rick Steves guidebooks.

Scams abound: Don't give your wallet to self-proclaimed "police" who stop you on the street, warn you about counterfeit (or drug) money, and ask to see your cash. If a bank machine eats your ATM card, see if there's a thin plastic insert with a tongue hanging out that thieves use to extract it.

If you know what to look out for, fast-fingered moms with babies and gangs of children picking the pockets and hand-bags of naive tourists are not a threat, but an interesting, albeit sad, spectacle. Pickpockets troll through the tourist crowds around the Colosseum, Forum, Piazza della Repubblica, and train and Metro stations. Watch them target tourists who are overloaded with bags or distracted with a video camera. The kids look like beggars and hold up newspapers or cardboard signs to confuse their victims. They scram like stray cats if you're on to them.

Reporting Losses: To report lost or stolen passports and documents, or to make an insurance claim, you must file a police report (at Termini train station, with *polizia* at track 11 or with carabinieri at track 20; offices are also at Piazza Venezia). To replace a passport, file the police report, then call your embassy to make an appointment (see page 384). To report lost or stolen credit cards, see page 123.

Pedestrian Safety: Your main safety concern in Rome is crossing streets safely, using extreme caution. Scooters don't need to stop at red lights, and even cars exercise what drivers call the "logical option" of not stopping if they see no oncoming traffic. As noisy gasoline-powered scooters are replaced by electric ones, they are quieter (hooray) but more dangerous for pedestrians. Follow locals like a shadow when you cross a street (or spend a good part of your visit stranded on curbs). When you do cross alone, don't be a deer in the headlights. Find a gap in the traffic and walk with confidence while making eye contact with approaching drivers—they won't hit you if they can tell where you intend to go.

Staying/Getting Healthy: In the heat of summer, take frequent rest breaks. I drink lots of cold, refreshing water from Rome's many drinking fountains (the Forum has three).

Pharmacies: There's a pharmacy (marked by a green cross) in every neighborhood. Several pharmacies stay open late in Termini train station (daily 7:30-22:00) and at Piazza dei Cinquecento 51 (open 24 hours daily, next to Termini train station on the corner of Via Cavour, tel. 06-488-0019).

Getting Around Rome

Sightsee on foot, by city bus, by Metro, or by taxi. I've grouped your sightseeing into walkable neighborhoods. Make it a point to visit sights in a logical order. Needless backtracking wastes precious time.

The public-transportation system, which is cheap and efficient, consists primarily of buses, a few trams, and the two underground subway (Metro) lines. Consider it part of your Roman experience.

Buying Tickets

All public transportation uses the same ticket (€1, valid for one Metro ride—including transfers underground—plus unlimited city buses and *elettrico* buses during a 75-minute period). A

Tips on Sightseeing in Rome

These tips will help you use your time and money efficiently, making the Eternal City seem less eternal and more entertaining.

Combo-Ticket for Colosseum, Forum, and Palatine Hill: A €12 combo-ticket covers these three adjacent sights (no individual tickets are sold per sight). The combo-ticket allows one entry per sight, and is valid for two days. To avoid ticket-buying lines at the Colosseum and Forum, purchase your combo-ticket at the lesser-visited Palatine Hill.

Roma Pass: The Roma Pass (€25, valid three days, www.romapass.it) isn't worthwhile for a short, one-day visit to Rome.

Museum Reservations: You can reserve online to avoid long lines at the Vatican Museum (http://mv.vatican.va; see page 565 for more details).

Opening Hours: Rome's sights have notoriously variable hours from season to season. Get a current listing of opening times from one of Rome's TIs—ask for the free booklet *Museums of Rome*. Or check online at www.060608.it (click on "Culture and Leisure"; although the pages are in English, search by using the Italian names of sights). On holidays, expect shorter hours or closures.

Churches: Many churches, which have divine art and free entry, open early (around 7:00-7:30), close for lunch (roughly 12:00-15:00), and close late (about 19:00). When possible, kamikaze tourists maximize their sightseeing hours by visiting churches before 9:00 or late in the day, and during the siesta, seeing major sights that stay open all day (St. Peter's, Colosseum, Forum, Capitoline Museums, and National Museum of Rome). Many churches have "modest dress" requirements, which means no bare shoulders, miniskirts, or shorts—for men, women, or children. However, this dress code is strictly enforced throughout Vatican City and St. Paul's Outside the Walls. Elsewhere, you'll see many tourists in shorts (but not skimpy shorts) touring churches.

Picnic Discreetly: Public drinking and eating is not allowed at major sights, though the ban is difficult to enforce. To avoid the risk of being fined, choose an empty piazza for your picnic, or keep a low profile.

WCs: Because public restrooms are scarce, use toilets at museums, restaurants, and bars.

one-day pass good on buses and the Metro is €4 (good until midnight). Remember, if you bought a €9 BIRG ticket to cover your regional train ride from Civitavecchia, it's good for your Metro and bus travel in Rome.

You can purchase transit tickets and passes at some newsstands, tobacco shops (*tabacchi*, marked by a black-and-white *T* sign), and major Metro stations and bus stops, but not onboard. It's smart to stock up on tickets, so you don't have to run around searching for an open *tabacchi* when you spot your bus approaching. Metro stations rarely have human ticket-sellers, and the machines are often either broken or require exact change (it helps to insert your smallest coin first).

Validate your ticket by sticking it in the Metro turnstile (magnetic strip-side up, arrow-side first) or in the machine when you board the bus (magnetic strip-side down, arrow-side first)—watch others and imitate. To get through a Metro turnstile with a transit pass, use it just like a ticket (on buses, however, you only need to validate your pass if that's your first time using it). If the validation machine won't work, you can ride with your ticket unstamped, but you must write the date, time, and bus number on it, or risk getting fined. For more information, visit www.atac.roma.it (which has a useful route planner in English), or call 800-431-784 or 06-57003.

By Metro

The Roman subway system (Metropolitana, or "Metro") is simple,

with two clean, cheap, fast lines—A and B—that intersect at Termini train station. The Metro runs from 5:30 to 23:30 (Fri-Sat until 1:30 in the morning). The subway's first and last compartments are generally the least crowded (and the least likely to harbor pickpockets).

You'll notice lots of big holes in the city as a new line is built. Line C, from the Colosseum to Largo Argentina, will likely be done in 2020.

While much of Rome is not served by its skimpy subway, the following stops are helpful:

Termini (intersection of lines A and B): Termini train station (including trains to Civitavecchia), shuttle train to airport, and National Museum of Rome

Repubblica (line A): Baths of Diocletian/Octagonal Hall, Via Nazionale

Barberini (line A): Cappuccin Crypt, Trevi Fountain, and Villa Borghese

ROME

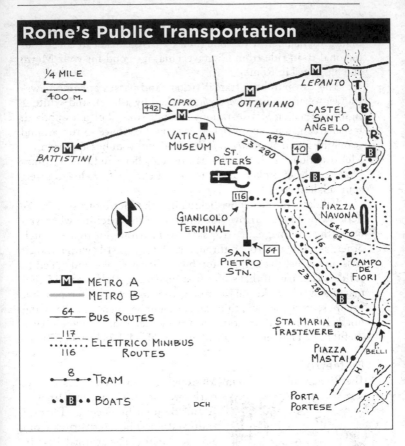

Rome's Public Transportation

Spagna (line A): Spanish Steps, and classy shopping area
Flaminio (line A): Piazza del Popolo
Ottaviano (line A): St. Peter's and Vatican City
Cipro (line A): Vatican Museum
Tiburtina (line B): Tiburtina train and bus station
Colosseo (line B): Colosseum, Roman Forum, bike rental
Piramide (line B): Protestant Cemetery and trains to Ostia
Antica
E.U.R. (line B): Mussolini's futuristic suburb

By Bus

The Metro is handy, but it won't get you everywhere—take the bus. Bus routes are clearly listed at the stops. TIs usually don't have bus maps, but with some knowledge of major stops, you won't necessarily need one (though if you do want a route map, buy it from *tabacchi* shops; bus info: www.atac.roma.it with good route planner in English, or tel. 06-57003, usually not in English).

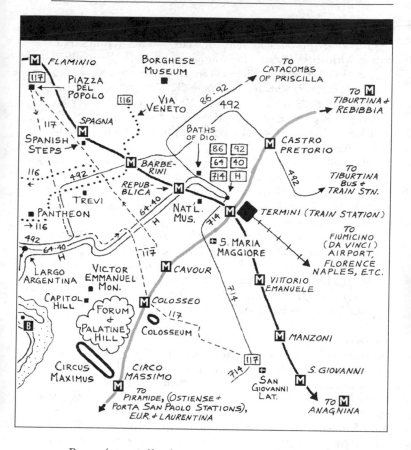

Buses (especially the touristy #40 and #64) are havens for thieves and pickpockets. Assume any commotion is a thief-created distraction. If one bus is packed, there's likely a second one on its tail with far fewer crowds and thieves. Once you know the bus system, you'll find it's easier than searching for a cab.

Tickets have a barcode and must be stamped on the bus in the yellow box with the digital readout (be sure to retrieve your ticket). Validate your ticket as you board (magnetic strip-side down, arrow-side first), or you are cheating. While relatively safe, riding without a stamped ticket on the bus is stressful. Inspectors fine even innocent-looking tourists €50. There's no need to validate a transit pass on the bus, unless your pass is new and hasn't yet been stamped elsewhere in the transit system. Bus etiquette (not always followed) is to board at the front or rear doors and exit out the middle.

Regular bus lines start running at about 5:30, and during the day they run every 5-10 minutes. After 23:30, and sometimes earlier (such as on Sundays), buses are less frequent but dependable.

Bus #64: This bus cuts across the city, linking Termini train station with the Vatican, stopping at Piazza della Repubblica (sights), Via Nazionale, Piazza Venezia (near Forum), Largo Argentina (near Pantheon), St. Peter's Basilica (get off just past the tunnel), and San Pietro Station. Ride it for a city overview and to watch pickpockets in action. The #64 can get horribly crowded, awkward for female travelers uncomfortably close to male strangers.

Bus #40: This express bus following the #64 route is especially helpful—fewer stops and crowds.

Elettrico **Minibuses:** Two cute *elettrico* minibuses wind through the narrow streets of old and interesting neighborhoods, and are great for transport or simple joyriding:

Elettrico **#116:** Through the medieval core of Rome: Ponte Vittorio Emanuele II (near Castel Sant'Angelo) to Campo de' Fiori, Pantheon, Piazza Barberini, and the southern edge of the scenic Villa Borghese Gardens.

Elettrico **#117:** San Giovanni in Laterano, Colosseo, Via dei Serpenti, Trevi Fountain, Piazza di Spagna, and Piazza del Popolo.

By Taxi

I use taxis in Rome more often than in other cities. They're reasonable and useful for efficient sightseeing in this big, hot metropolis. Taxis start at €2.80, then charge about €1.30 per kilometer (surcharges: €1 on Sun, €3 for nighttime hours of 22:00-7:00, one regular suitcase or bag rides free, tip by rounding up to the nearest euro). Sample fares: Termini train station to Vatican-€10; Termini train station to Colosseum-€6 (or look up your route at www.worldtaximeter.com). Three or four companions with more money than time should taxi almost everywhere.

It's tough to wave down a taxi in Rome. Find the nearest taxi stand by asking a passerby or a clerk in a shop, *"Dov'è una fermata dei taxi?"* (doh-VEH OO-nah fehr-MAH-tah DEHee TAHK-see). Some taxi stands are listed on my maps. To call a cab on your own, dial 06-4994 or 06-6645. To save time and energy, have your restaurant call a taxi for you; the meter starts when the call is received (generally adding a euro or two to the bill). It's routine for Romans to ask the waiter in a restaurant to call a taxi when they ask for the bill. The waiter will tell you how many minutes you have to enjoy your coffee.

Beware of corrupt taxis. A common cabbie scam is to take your €20 note, drop it, and pick up a €5 note (similar color), claiming that's what you gave him. To avoid this scam, pay in small bills; if you only have a large bill, show it to the cabbie as you state its face value.

If hailing a cab on the street, be sure the meter is restarted when you get in (should be around €2.80, or around €5 if you or your restaurant phoned for the taxi). Many meters show both the fare and the time elapsed during the ride—and some tourists pay €10 for an eight-and-a-half-minute trip (more than the fair meter rate).

When you arrive at the train station, beware of hustlers conning naive visitors into unmarked rip-off "express taxis." Only use official taxis, with a *taxi* sign and phone number marked on the door. By law, they must display a multilingual official price chart. If you have any problems with a taxi, point to the chart and ask the cabbie to explain it to you. Making a show of writing down the taxi number (to file a complaint) can motivate a driver to quickly settle the matter.

By Car with Driver

You can hire your own private car with driver through Autoservizi Monti Concezio, run by gentle, capable, and English-speaking Ezio (car-€35/hour, minibus-€40/hour, 3-hour minimum for city sightseeing, long rides outside Rome are more expensive, mobile 335-636-5907 or 349-674-5643, www.montitours.com, concezio monti@gmail.com).

Tours in Rome

Walking Tours

Finding the best guided tours in Rome is challenging. Local guides are good but pricey. Tour companies are cheaper, but quality and organization are unreliable. To help, I've produced a series of **free audio tours** that illuminate Rome's major sights (Colosseum, Roman Forum, St. Peter's Basilica, the Sistine Chapel, and more), covered the way my readers appreciate. You can download my free audio tours at www.ricksteves.com/audioeurope, from iTunes, or through the Rick Steves Audio Europe smartphone app.

Other options include hiring a private Italian guide (around €150-180 for a half-day tour—those listed here are excellent and worth every euro, if you can afford it); organizing a group of 4-6 people from your cruise to split the cost of hiring a private guide (this ends up costing about the same as joining a tour from one of the companies listed here); or going on a scheduled walking tour with one of the companies listed below (about €25, generally expat guides).

Local Guides—Consider hiring your own personal tour guide. I've worked with each of these licensed independent local guides. They speak excellent English and enjoy tailoring tours to your interests. Their prices (roughly €50/hour, €180/half-day) flex with the day, season, and demand. Arrange your date and price by email.

Rome at a Glance

In the sight listings below, a page number directs you to a fuller description in this chapter; sights without page numbers are not described further and generally don't make the cut for a one-day visit.

▲▲▲**Colosseum** Huge stadium where gladiators fought. **Hours:** Daily 8:30 until one hour before sunset: April-Sept until 19:15, Oct until 18:30, off-season closes as early as 16:30. See page 603.

▲▲▲**Roman Forum** Ancient Rome's main square, with ruins and grand arches. **Hours:** Same hours as Colosseum. See page 606.

▲▲▲**Pantheon** The defining domed temple. **Hours:** Mon-Sat 8:30-19:30, Sun 9:00-18:00, holidays 9:00-13:00, closed for Mass Sat at 17:00 and Sun at 10:30. See page 615.

▲▲▲**National Museum of Rome** Greatest collection of Roman sculpture anywhere. **Hours:** Tue-Sun 9:00-19:45, closed Mon.

▲▲▲**Borghese Gallery** Bernini sculptures and paintings by Caravaggio, Raphael, and Titian. Reservations mandatory. **Hours:** Tue-Sun 9:00-19:00, closed Mon.

▲▲▲**Vatican Museum** Four miles of the finest art of Western civilization, culminating in Michelangelo's glorious Sistine Chapel. **Hours:** Mon-Sat 9:00-18:00, last entry at 16:00, they start ushering you out at 17:30. Closed religious holidays and Sun, except last Sun of the month (when it's open 9:00-14:00, last entry at 12:30). May be open some Fri nights April-Oct 19:00-23:00 (last entry at 21:30) by reservation only. Hours are notoriously subject to constant change. See page 617.

▲▲▲**St. Peter's Basilica** Most impressive church on earth, with Michelangelo's *Pietà* and dome. **Hours:** Church—daily April-Sept 7:00-19:00, Oct-March 7:00-18:00, often closed Wed mornings; dome—daily April-Sept 8:00-18:00, Oct-March 8:00-17:00. See page 618.

▲▲**Palatine Hill** Ruins of emperors' palaces, Circus Maximus view, and museum. **Hours:** Same as Colosseum. See page 607.

▲▲**Capitoline Museums** Ancient statues, mosaics, and view of Forum. **Hours:** Tue-Sun 9:00-20:00, closed Mon. See page 611.

▲▲**Ara Pacis** Shrine marking the beginning of Rome's Golden Age. **Hours:** Tue-Sun 9:00-19:00, closed Mon. See page 616.

▲▲**Catacombs** Underground tombs, mainly Christian, outside the city. **Hours:** Generally open 9:00-12:00 & 14:00-17:00.

▲**Arch of Constantine** Honors the emperor who legalized Christianity. **Hours:** Always viewable. See page 603.

▲**St. Peter-in-Chains** Church with Michelangelo's *Moses*. **Hours:** Daily 8:00-12:30 & 15:00-19:00, until 18:00 in winter. See page 604.

▲**Trajan's Column** Tall column with narrative relief, on Piazza Venezia. **Hours:** Always viewable. See page 608.

▲**Museum of the Imperial Forums** Includes entry to Trajan's Market. **Hours:** Tue-Sun 9:00-19:00, closed Mon. See page 608.

▲**Capitol Hill Square** Hilltop piazza designed by Michelangelo, with a museum, grand stairway, and Forum overlooks. **Hours:** Always open. See page 611.

▲**Trevi Fountain** Baroque hot spot into which tourists throw coins to ensure a return trip to Rome. **Hours:** Always flowing. See page 616.

▲**Baths of Diocletian** Once ancient Rome's immense public baths, now a Michelangelo church. **Hours:** Mon-Sat 7:00-18:30, Sun 7:00-19:30.

▲**Santa Maria della Vittoria** Church with Bernini's swooning *St. Teresa in Ecstasy*. **Hours:** Mon-Sat 8:30-12:00 & 15:30-18:00, Sun 15:30-18:00.

▲**Rome from the Sky** Elevator to the top of the Victor Emmanuel Monument for a 360-degree city view. **Hours:** Mon-Thu 9:30-18:30, Fri-Sun 9:30-19:30. See page 614.

▲**Cappuccin Crypt** Decorated with the bones of 4,000 Franciscan friars. **Hours:** Daily 9:00-12:00 & 15:00-18:00, may be closed Thu.

▲**Castel Sant'Angelo** Hadrian's Tomb turned castle, prison, papal refuge, now museum. **Hours:** Tue-Sun 9:00-19:30, closed Mon.

▲**Galleria Doria Pamphilj** Aristocrat's ornate palace shows off paintings by Caravaggio, Titian, and Raphael. **Hours:** Daily 10:00-17:00.

ROME

Francesca Caruso loves to teach and share her appreciation of her city, and has contributed generously to this chapter (francesca inroma@gmail.com). Popular with my readers, Francesca understandably books up quickly; if she's busy, she'll recommend one of her colleagues. **Carla Zaia** is an engaging expert on all things Roman (mobile 349-759-0723, carlaromeguide@gmail.com). **Cristina Giannicchi** has an archaeology background (mobile 338-111-4573, www.crisacross.com, crisgiannicchi@gmail.com). **Sara Magister** is a Roman with a doctorate in art history, who wrote a book on Renaissance Rome (tel. 06-583-6783, mobile 339-379-3813, a.magister@iol.it). **Giovanna Terzulli** is a personable, knowledgeable art historian (terzulli@tiscali.it).

Walking-Tour Companies—Rome has many highly competitive tour companies, each offering a series of themed walks through various slices of Rome. Three-hour guided walks generally cost €25-30 per person. Guides are usually native English-speakers, often American expats. Tours are limited to small groups, geared to American tourists, and given in English only. I've listed some here, but without a lot of details on their offerings. Before your trip, spend some time on these companies' websites to get to know your options, as each company has a particular teaching and guiding personality. Some are highbrow, and others are less scholarly. It's sometimes required, and always smart, to book a spot in advance (easy online). I must add that we get a lot of negative feedback on some of these tour companies. Readers report that their advertising can be misleading, and that scheduling mishaps are not uncommon.

Context Rome's walking tours are more intellectual than most, designed for travelers with longer-than-average attention spans. They are more expensive than others, and are led by "docents" rather than guides (tel. 06-9762-5204, US tel. 800-691-6036, www.contextrome.com). **Enjoy Rome** offers five different walks and a website filled with helpful information (Via Marghera 8a, tel. 06-445-1843, www.enjoyrome.com, info@enjoyrome.com). **Rome Walks** has put together several particularly creative itineraries (mobile 347-795-5175, www.romewalks.com, info@romewalks.com, Annie). **Roman Odyssey** gives readers of this book a 10 percent discount on their walks and private tours (tel. 06-580-9902, mobile 328-912-3720, www.romanodyssey.com, Rahul). **Through Eternity** offers travelers with this book a 10 percent discount on most tours and a 20 percent discount on its Underground Rome and Secret Rome tours; book through their website for the best discount (tel. 06-700-9336, mobile 347-336-5298, www.througheternity.com, info@througheternity.com, Rob).

Hop-on, Hop-off Bus Tours

Several different agencies, including the ATAC public bus company, run hop-on, hop-off tours around Rome. These tours are constantly evolving and offer varying combinations of sights. You can grab one (and pay as you board) at any stop; Termini train station and Piazza Venezia are handy hubs. Although the city is perfectly walkable and traffic jams can make the bus dreadfully slow, these open-top bus tours remain popular.

Trambus #110 seems to be the best. Operated by the ATAC city-bus lines, it offers an orientation tour on big red double-decker buses with an open-air upper deck. In less than two hours, you'll have 80 sights pointed out to you (with a next-to-worthless recorded narration). While you can hop on and off, the service can be erratic (mobbed midday, not ideal in bad weather) and it can be very slow in heavy traffic. It's best to think of this as a two-hour quickie orientation with scant information and lots of images. The 11 stops include Via Veneto, Via Tritone, Ara Pacis, Piazza Cavour, St. Peter's Square, Corso Vittorio Emanuele (for Piazza Navona), Piazza Venezia, Colosseum, and Via Nazionale. Bus #110 departs every 20 minutes. You can catch it at any stop, including Termini Station (runs daily 8:30-20:30, tel. 06-684-0901, www.trambus open.com). Buy the €20 ticket as you board.

Archeobus is an open-top bus, also operated by ATAC, that runs twice hourly from Termini Station out to the Appian Way (with stops at the Colosseum, Baths of Caracalla, San Callisto, San Sebastiano, and the Tomb of Cecilia Metella). This is a handy way to see the sights down this ancient Roman road, but it can be frustrating for various reasons—sparse narration, sporadic service, and not ideal for hopping on and off (€15, €30 combo-ticket with Trambus 110, ticket valid 24 hours, 1.5-hour loop, daily 8:30-16:30, from Termini train station and Piazza Venezia, tel. 06-684-0901, www.trambusopen.com). A similar bus laces together all the Christian sights.

Self-Guided Walks & Tours in Rome

ROME

With one day in Rome, most travelers will focus on either Ancient Rome—the Colosseum, Forum, and Pantheon—or the Vatican, with the Vatican Museum (Sistine Chapel) and St. Peter's Basilica. What follows are self-guided tours through each of these sights. For those with more time, or who prefer a less-intense approach to the city, I've also included a picturesque walk through the heart of Rome.

Free Audio Tours: Remember that you can download free audio versions of these tours at www.ricksteves.com/audioeurope, from iTunes, or through the Rick Steves Audio Europe smartphone app.

Colosseum Tour

Rome has many layers—modern, Baroque, Renaissance, Christian. But let's face it: "Rome" is Caesars, gladiators, chariots, centurions, *Et tu, Brute*," trumpet fanfares, and thumbs-up or thumbs-down. That's the Rome we'll look at. Our "Caesar Shuffle" begins with the downtown core of ancient Rome, the Colosseum (Colosseo). A logical next stop is the Roman Forum, just next door.

Orientation

Cost: €12 combo-ticket also includes Roman Forum and Palatine Hill.

Hours: The Colosseum, Roman Forum, and Palatine Hill are all open daily 8:30 until one hour before sunset: April-Sept until 19:15, Oct until 18:30, off-season closes as early as 16:30; last entry one hour before closing.

Getting There: The Colosseo Metro stop on line B is just across the street from the monument.

Avoiding Lines: The lines in front of the Colosseum are for buying tickets and for security checks, not for actually entering the sight. Everyone has to wait in the security line to go through the metal detectors first, but once you're through that—if you have your ticket already—stay to the left and muscle your way past the ticket-buying crowd to go directly to the turnstile, which never has a line. Enter

by inserting your ticket in the turnstile or flashing your pass.

If you're buying a combo-ticket, you'll likely save lots of time if you get your ticket at the less-crowded Palatine Hill entrance. Or buy and print it online in advance at www.ticket clic.it (€1.50 booking fee, good for two consecutive days, not changeable). Note that the "free tickets" you'll see listed are valid only for EU citizens with ID.

Another way to avoid the line is to pay to join an official

guided tour (€4 plus €12 combo-ticket, see "Tours," later). Once past the security check, tell one of the guards that you want to purchase a guided tour and he will usher you toward the ticket booth marked *Visite Guidate* (you'll also pay for your ticket here).

Private walking-tour guides (or their American assistants) linger outside the Colosseum, offering tours that include the admission fee and allow you to skip the line. This will cost you a few extra euros (€22 for two-hour tours of the Colosseum, Palatine Hill, and Forum, including the €12 ticket), but can save time; however, see the warning below.

Warnings: It can be hard to judge the length of the ticket line because it's tucked into the Colosseum arcade. Unscrupulous private guides tell tourists that there's a long line, when there really might be no line at all. If you do sign up with a private guide, confirm that your tour will start right away, and look at your ticket to make sure that it includes admission to Palatine Hill and Forum (some guides, claiming to cover all three sights, will purchase a group Colosseum-only ticket, then say "ciao" after the Colosseum tour).

Also beware of the **greedy gladiators.** For a fee, the incredibly crude modern-day gladi-  ators snuff out their cigarettes and pose for photos. They take easy-to-swindle tourists for too much money. Watch out if you tangle with these guys (they're accustomed to getting as much as €100 from naive tourists). If you go for it, €4-5 for one photo usually keeps them appeased.

And finally, look out for **pick-pockets.** The Colosseum's exterior is traditionally a happy hunting ground for pickpockets and con artists.

Information: Tel. 06-3996-7700.

Tours: A dry but fact-filled **audioguide** is available just past the turnstiles (€4.50/2 hours). A handheld **video-guide** senses where you are in the site and plays related video clips (€5.50, pick up after turnstiles). Guided **tours** in English (which let you skip the ticket line) depart nearly hourly between 10:00 and 17:00, and last 45 minutes to one hour (€4 plus your €12 ticket, purchase inside the Colosseum near the ticket booth marked *Visite Guidate*).

Length of This Tour: Allow an hour.

Services: For tips on where to eat, drink, and find a WC in the area, see the sidebar on page 542.

ROME

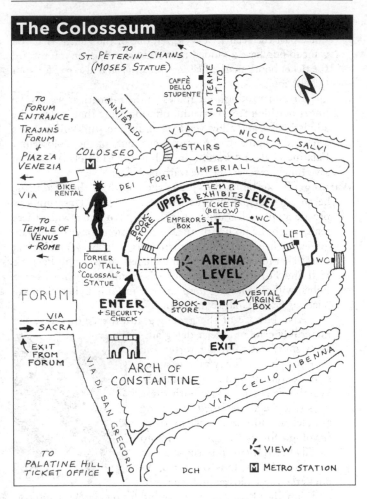

The Tour Begins

Exterior

• *View the Colosseum from the Forum fence, across the street from the Colosseo Metro station.*

Built when the Roman Empire was at its peak in A.D. 80, the Colosseum represents Rome at its grandest. The Flavian Amphitheater (the Colosseum's real name) was an arena for gladiator contests and public spectacles. When killing became a spectator sport, the Romans wanted to share the fun with as many people as possible, so they stuck two semicircular theaters together to create a freestanding amphitheater. The outside (where slender cypress trees stand today) was decorated with a 100-foot-tall bronze statue of Nero that gleamed in the sunlight. In a later age, the colossal structure was nicknamed a "coloss-eum," the wonder of its age. It could accommodate 50,000 roaring fans (100,000 thumbs).

The Romans pioneered the use of concrete and the rounded arch, which enabled them to build on this tremendous scale. The exterior is a skeleton of 3.5 million cubic feet of travertine stone. (Each of the pillars flanking the ground-level arches weighs five tons.) It took 200 ox-drawn wagons shuttling back and forth every day for four years just to bring the stone here from Tivoli. They stacked stone blocks (without mortar) into the shape of an arch, supported temporarily by wooden scaffolding. Finally, they wedged a keystone into the top of the arch—it not only kept the arch from falling, it could bear even more weight above. Iron pegs held the larger stones together—notice the small holes that pockmark the sides.

The exterior says a lot about the Romans. They were great engineers, not artists, and the building is more functional than beautiful. (If ancient Romans visited the US today as tourists, they might send home postcards of our greatest works of "art"—freeways.) While the essential structure of the Colosseum is Roman, the four-story facade is decorated with mostly Greek columns—Doric-like Tuscan columns on the ground level, Ionic on the second story, Corinthian on the next level, and at the top, half-columns with a mix of all three. Originally, copies of Greek statues stood in the arches of the middle two stories, giving a veneer of sophistication to this arena of death.

Only a third of the original Colosseum remains. Earthquakes destroyed some of it, but most was carted off as easy pre-cut stones for other buildings during the Middle Ages and Renaissance.

• *To enter, first go through the security line. Once past security, queue up. If you need to buy a ticket, line up along the right. If you already have a ticket, get in the fast lane to the left of the ticket line and go directly to the turnstile. To pay for an official tour, bypass the ticket line and head directly to the ticket booth marked* Visite Guidate. *Once past the turnstiles, there may be signs directing you on a specific visitors' route.*

Interior

Entrances and Exits: As you walk through passageways and up staircases, admire the ergonomics. Fans could pour in through ground-floor entrances; there were eight total, including the emperor's private entrance on the north side. Your ticket was a piece of broken pottery marked with entrance, section, row, and seat number. You'd pass by concession stands selling fast food and souvenirs, such as wine glasses with the names of famous gladiators. The hallways leading to the seats were called by the Latin word *vomitorium*. At exit time, the Colosseum would "vomit" out its contents, giving us the English word. It's estimated that all

50,000 fans could enter and exit in 15 minutes.

• *Soon you'll spill out into the arena. Wherever you end up—upstairs or downstairs, at one side of the arena or the other—just take it all in and get oriented. The tallest side of the Colosseum (with the large Christian cross) is the north side. You might notice that the arena is currently undergoing renovation. It's being cleaned from top to bottom and given permanent lighting. This ambitious project has opened up new areas previously closed to visitors, including some underground corridors.*

Arena: The games took place in this oval-shaped arena, 280 feet long by 165 feet wide. The ratio of length to width is 5:3, often called the golden ratio. Since the days of the Greek mathematician Pythagoras, artists considered that proportion to be ideal, with almost mystical properties. The Colosseum's architects apparently wanted their structure to embody the perfect 3-by-5 mathematical order they thought existed in nature.

When you look down into the arena, you're seeing the underground passages beneath the playing surface (there are plans to open these up for tours). The arena was originally covered with a wooden floor, then sprinkled with sand (*arena* in Latin). The new bit of reconstructed floor gives you an accurate sense of the original arena level, and the subterranean warren where animals and prisoners were held. As in modern stadiums, the spectators ringed the playing area in bleacher seats that slanted up from the arena floor. Around you are the big brick masses that supported the tiers of seats.

A variety of materials were used to build the stadium. Look around. Big white travertine blocks stacked on top of each other formed the skeleton. The brick pillars for the bleachers were made with a shell of brick, filled in with concrete. Originally the bare brick was covered with marble columns or ornamental facing, so the interior was a brilliant white (they used white plaster for the upper-floor cheap seats).

The Colosseum's seating was strictly segregated. At ringside,

the emperor, senators, Vestal Virgins, and VIPs occupied marble seats with their names carved on them (a few marble seats have been restored, at the east end). The next level up held those of noble birth. The level tourists now occupy was for ordinary free Roman citizens, called plebeians. Up at the very top (a hundred yards from the action), there were once wooden bleachers for the poorest people—foreigners, slaves, and women.

The top story of the Colosseum is mostly ruined—only the north side still retains its high wall. This was not part of the

original three-story structure, but was added around A.D. 230 after a fire necessitated repairs. Picture the awning that could be stretched across the top of the stadium by armies of sailors. Strung along horizontal beams that pointed inward to the center, the awning only covered about a third of the arena—so those at the top always enjoyed shade, while many nobles down below roasted in the sun.

Looking into the complex web of passageways beneath the arena, you can imagine how busy the backstage action was. Gladiators strolled down the central passageway, from their warm-up yard on the east end to the arena entrance on the west. Some workers tended wild animals. Others prepared stage sets of trees or fake buildings, allowing the arena to be quickly transformed from an African jungle to a Greek temple. Props and sets were hauled up to arena level on 80 different elevator shafts via a system of ropes and pulleys. (You might be able to make out some small rectangular shafts, especially near the center of the arena.) That means there were 80 different spots from which animals, warriors, and stage sets could pop up and magically appear.

The games began with a few warm-up acts—dogs bloodying themselves attacking porcupines, female gladiators fighting each other, or a dwarf battling a one-legged man. Then came the main event—the gladiators.

"Hail, Caesar! *(Ave, Cesare!)* We who are about to die salute you!" The gladiators would enter the arena from the west end,

parade around to the sound of trumpets, acknowledge the Vestal Virgins (on the south side), then stop at the emperor's box (supposedly marked today by the cross that stands at the "50-yard line" on the north side—although no one knows for sure where it was). They would then raise their weapons, shout, and salute—and begin fighting. The fights pitted men against men, men against beasts, and beasts against beasts. Picture 50,000

Modern Amenities in the Ancient World

The area around the Colosseum, Forum, and Palatine Hill is rich in history, but pretty barren when it comes to food, shelter, and WCs. Here are a few options:

The Colosseum has a few crowded **WCs** inside, but don't count on them being available. A nice big WC is behind (east of) the structure (facing ticket entrance, go counterclockwise; WC is under stairway). If you can wait, the best WCs in the area are at Palatine Hill—at the Via di San Gregorio entrance, in the museum, or in the Farnese Gardens. The Forum also has one WC at the entrance and another near the Temple of Vesta (#8 on map on page 549).

Because there are limited **eateries** in the area, consider assembling a small picnic. The Colosseo Metro stop has €5 hot sandwiches. Snack stands on street corners sell drinks, sandwiches, fruit, and candy. If you prefer to dine in, you'll find a few restaurants behind the Colosseum (with expansive views of the structure), a few recommended places a block away (no views but better value—see page 626), and a cluster of places near the Forum's main entrance (where Via Cavour spills into Via dei Fori Imperiali).

To refill your **water** bottle, stop at one of the water fountains in the area. You'll find them along a few city streets, as well as inside the Forum and Palatine Hill.

A nice oasis is the free tourist center, **I Fori di Roma,** located near the Forum entrance. It's across Via dei Fori Imperiali and a bit east, toward the Colosseum. It has a small café, a WC, and a few exhibits.

If your sightseeing takes you as far as **Capitol Hill,** you'll find services at the Capitoline Museums, including a nice view café.

---

screaming people around you (did gladiators get stage fright?), and imagine that they want to see you die.

Some gladiators wielded swords, protected only with a shield and a heavy helmet. Others represented fighting fishermen, with a net to snare opponents and a trident to spear them. The gladiators were usually slaves, criminals, or poor people who got their chance for freedom, wealth, and fame in the ring. They learned to fight in training schools, then battled their way up the ranks. The best were rewarded like our modern sports stars, with fan clubs, great wealth, and, yes, product endorsements.

The animals came from all over the world: lions, tigers, and bears (oh my!), crocodiles, elephants, and hippos (not to mention exotic human "animals" from the "barbarian" lands). They were

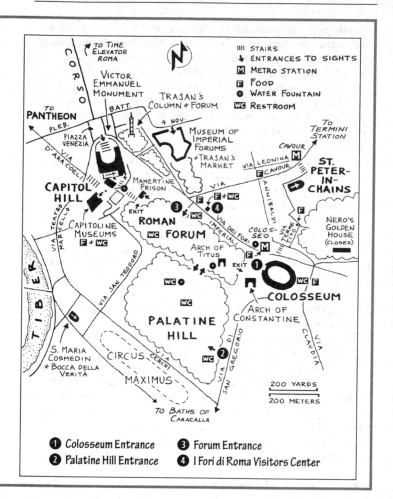

1 Colosseum Entrance   **3** Forum Entrance
2 Palatine Hill Entrance   **4** I Fori di Roma Visitors Center

kept in cages beneath the arena floor, then lifted up in the elevators. Released at floor level, animals would pop out from behind
blinds into the arena—the gladiator didn't know where, when, or
by what he'd be attacked. Many a hapless warrior met his death
here, and never knew what hit him. (This brought howls of laughter from the hardened fans in the cheap upper seats who had a
better view of the action.)

Nets ringed the arena to protect the crowd. The stadium was
inaugurated with a 100-day festival in which 2,000 men and 9,000
animals were killed. Colosseum employees squirted perfumes
around the stadium to mask the stench of blood.

If a gladiator fell helpless to the ground, his opponent would
approach the emperor's box and ask: Should he live or die?

ROME

Sometimes the emperor left the decision to the crowd, who would judge based on how valiantly the man had fought. They would make their decision—thumbs-up or thumbs-down. Consider the value of these games in placating and controlling the huge Roman populace. Seeing the king of beasts—a lion—slain by a gladiator reminded the masses of man's triumph over nature. Seeing exotic animals from Africa heralded their conquest of distant lands. And having the thumbs-up or thumbs-down authority over another person's life gave them a real sense of power. Imagine the psychological boost the otherwise downtrodden masses felt when the emperor granted them this thrilling decision.

Did they throw Christians to the lions like in the movies? Christians were definitely thrown to the lions, made to fight gladiators, crucified, and burned alive...but probably not here in this particular stadium. Maybe, but probably not.

Rome was a nation of warriors that built an empire by conquest. The battles fought against Germans and other barbarians, Egyptians, and strange animals were played out daily here in the Colosseum for the benefit of city-slicker bureaucrats, who got vicarious thrills by watching brutes battle to the death. The contests were always free, sponsored by the government to bribe the people's favor or to keep Rome's growing masses of unemployed rabble off the streets.

• *With these scenes in mind, wander around, then check out the upper level. There are stairs on both the east and the west sides, as well as an elevator at the east end. The upper deck offers more colossal views of the arena, plus a bookstore and temporary exhibits. Wherever you may Rome, find a spot at the west end of the upper deck, where you can look out over some of the sights nearby. Start with the big, white, triumphal Arch of Constantine.*

Views from the Upper Level

Arch of Constantine: If you are a Christian, were raised a Christian, or simply belong to a so-called "Christian nation,"

ponder this arch. It marks one of the great turning points in history—the military coup that made Christianity mainstream. In A.D. 312, Emperor Constantine defeated his rival Maxentius in the crucial Battle of the Milvian Bridge. The night before, he had seen a vision of a cross in the sky.
Constantine—whose mother and sister were Christians—became sole emperor and legalized Christianity. With this one battle, a once-obscure Jewish sect with a handful of followers was now the

state religion of the entire Western world. In A.D. 300, you could be killed for being a Christian; a century later, you could be killed for not being one. Church enrollment boomed.

The restored arch is like an ancient museum. It's decorated entirely with recycled carvings originally made for other buildings. By covering it with exquisite carvings of high Roman art—works that glorified previous emperors—Constantine put himself in their league. Hadrian is featured in the round reliefs, with Marcus Aurelius in the square reliefs higher up. The big statues on top are of Trajan and Augustus. Originally, Augustus drove a chariot similar to the one topping the modern Victor Emmanuel II Monument. Fourth-century Rome may have been in decline, but Constantine clung to its glorious past.

Surrounding Hills: Looking southwest, beyond the Arch of Constantine, you see Palatine Hill, dotted with umbrella pines. Next to the Arch of Constantine is the road called the Via Sacra, or Sacred Way, once Rome's main street. It heads west up an incline toward the Arch of Titus (you can just make out its white top from here). That marks the head of the Forum, the religious, political, and commercial heart of ancient Rome.

The Colosseum was built between three of Rome's legendary seven hills—the Palatine (to the southwest), the Esquiline (to the north), and the Caelian (to the south). The Colosseum stands on land where the notorious Emperor Nero once had his sumptuous Golden House, which stretched from the Arch of Titus, across the valley, and up onto Esquiline Hill. After the house was replaced by the Colosseum, Nero's statue (or colossus) became the Colosseum's 100-foot-tall doorman.

• *Looking west, in the direction of the Forum, you'll see some ruins sitting atop a raised, rectangular-shaped hill. (You can recognize the hill by some door-like openings cut into the hill's support wall.) The ruins—consisting of an arched alcove made of brick and backed by a church bell tower—are all that remain of the once great Temple of Venus and Rome.*

The Temple of Venus and Rome: At 100 feet tall, this temple atop a pedestal was one of the most prominent temples in Rome—and also its biggest. The size of a football field, it once covered the entire hill. The style of the temple was Greek—surrounded by white columns and topped with a triangular pediment above the entrance. Today, the perimeter of the complex is still visible, marked by a few massive white columns, six feet thick.

The main ruin in the center—the tall brick arch with a cross-hatched ceiling—

was once the *cella*, or sacred chamber of the temple. Here sat two monumental statues, back to back. Venus, the goddess of love, faced the Colosseum. The goddess called Roma Aeterna faced the Forum. Paired together, they symbolized the birth and eternal destiny of the race of people meant to endure forever. The goddesses' Latin names were written in the twin *cella*s. On one side it read "Roma," and on the other "Amor." Roma and Amor—a perfectly symmetrical palindrome, showing how Rome and Love were meant to go together. In ancient times, newlyweds ascended the staircase from the Colosseum (some parts are still visible) to the temple, to ask Venus and Roma Aeterna to bring them good luck. These days, Roman couples get married at the church with the bell tower to ensure themselves love and happiness for eternity.

The temple was designed by Hadrian, the second-century emperor and amateur architect who also designed the Pantheon. Hadrian's design was critiqued by Rome's best-known architect, who complained that the huge statues would be so cramped they'd bump their heads if they stood up. Hadrian listened patiently to the criticism...then had the architect killed.

The Colosseum's Legacy: A.D. 500 to the Present

With the coming of Christianity to Rome, the Colosseum and its deadly games slowly became politically incorrect. However, some gladiator contests continued here sporadically until they were completely banned in A.D. 435. Animal hunts continued a few decades longer. As the Roman Empire dwindled and the infrastructure crumbled, the stadium itself was neglected. Finally, around A.D. 523—after nearly 500 years of games—the last animal was slaughtered, and the Colosseum shut its doors.

For the next thousand years, the structure was inhabited by various squatters. It was used for makeshift apartments or shops, as a church, a cemetery, and as a refuge during invasions and riots. Over time, the Colosseum was eroded by wind, rain, and the strain of gravity. Earthquakes weakened it, and a powerful quake in 1349 toppled the south side.

More than anything, the Colosseum was dismantled by the Roman citizens themselves, who carted off pre-cut stones to be re-used for palaces and churches, including St. Peter's. The marble facing was pulverized into mortar, and 300 tons of iron brackets were pried out and melted down, resulting in the pock-marking you see today.

After centuries of neglect, a series of 16th-century popes took pity on the pagan structure. In memory of the Christians who may (or may not) have been martyred here, they shored up the south and west sides with bricks and placed the big cross on the north side of the arena.

Today, the Colosseum links Rome's glorious past with its vital present. Major political demonstrations begin or end here, providing protesters with an iconic backdrop for the TV cameras. On Good Friday, the pope comes here to lead pilgrims as they follow the Stations of the Cross.

The legend goes that so long as the Colosseum shall stand, the city of Rome shall also stand. For nearly 2,000 years, the Colosseum has been the enduring symbol of Rome, the Eternal City.

• *The Roman Forum is 100 yards to the right of the arch. You can enter it through the Forum entrance on Via dei Fori Imperiali or from the Palatine Hill entrance along Via di San Gregorio—see the map on page 543. (Note that what looks like an entrance gate up Via Sacra is currently exit-only.) If you're ready for a visit, read on.*

Roman Forum Walk

The Forum (Foro Romano) was the political, religious, and commercial center of the city. Rome's most important temples and halls of justice were here. This was the place for religious processions, political demonstrations, elections, important speeches, and parades by conquering generals. As Rome's empire expanded, these few acres of land became the center of the civilized world.

Orientation

Cost: €12 combo-ticket also includes Colosseum and Palatine Hill. To avoid standing in a long ticket-buying line, see tips on "Avoiding Lines" on page 536 of the Colosseum Tour.

Hours: The Roman Forum, Colosseum, and Palatine Hill are all open daily 8:30 until one hour before sunset: April-Sept until 19:15, Oct until 18:30, off-season closes as early as 16:30; last entry one hour before closing.

Tips: The ancient paving at the Forum is uneven; wear sturdy shoes. I carry a water bottle and refill it at the Forum's public drinking fountains.

Getting There: The closest Metro stop is Colosseo. The Forum has two entrances. The main entrance is on Via dei Fori Imperiali ("Road of the Imperial Forums"). From the Colosseum Metro stop, walk away from the Colosseum on Via dei Fori Imperiali to find the low-profile Forum ticket office, located where Via Cavour spills into Via dei Fori Imperiali.

The other entrance is at the Palatine Hill ticket office on Via di San Gregorio—after buying your ticket, take the path to the right (not up the hill), and wind around to enter the Forum at the Arch of Titus.

Information: A free visitors center (called I Fori di Roma), located across Via dei Fori Imperiali from the Forum's main entrance, has a TI, bookshop, small café, WCs, and a film (daily 9:30-18:30). A bookstore is at the Forum entrance. Vendors at the Forum sell small *Rome: Past and Present* books with plastic overlays that restore the ruins (includes DVD, smaller book marked €15, prices soft, so offer €10). Info office tel. 06-3996-7700.

Tours: An unexciting yet informative **audioguide** helps decipher the rubble (€4, €6 version includes Palatine Hill, must leave ID), but you'll have to return it to one of the Forum entrances instead of being able to exit directly to Capitol Hill or the Colosseum. Official **guided tours** in English run Monday through Friday at around 13:00 (€4, 45 minutes, confirm time at ticket office).

Length of This Tour: Allow 1.5 hours.

Services: There's a WC at the main entrance and another in the middle of the Forum, near #8 on the map. For information on food and other WCs in the area, see the sidebar on page 542.

The Tour Begins

• *Start at the Arch of Titus (Arco di Tito). It's the white triumphal arch that rises above the rubble on the east end of the Forum (closest to the Colosseum). Stand at the viewpoint alongside the arch and gaze over the valley known as the Forum.*

Overview

The Forum is a rectangular valley running roughly east (the Colosseum end) to west (Capitol Hill, with its bell tower). The rocky path at your feet is the Via Sacra. It leads from the Arch of Titus, through the trees, past the large brick Senate building, through the triumphal arch at the far end, and up Capitol Hill. The hill to your left (with all the trees) is Palatine Hill.

Picture being here when a conquering general returned to Rome with crates of booty. The valley was full of gleaming white buildings topped with bronze roofs. The Via Sacra—Main Street of the Forum—would be lined with citizens waving branches and carrying torches. The trumpets would

ROME

Roman Forum

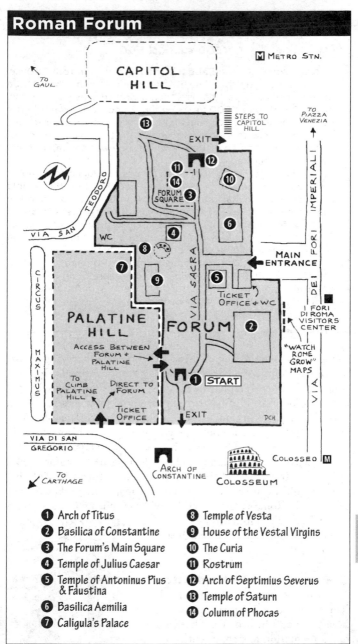

1. Arch of Titus
2. Basilica of Constantine
3. The Forum's Main Square
4. Temple of Julius Caesar
5. Temple of Antoninus Pius & Faustina
6. Basilica Aemilia
7. Caligula's Palace
8. Temple of Vesta
9. House of the Vestal Virgins
10. The Curia
11. Rostrum
12. Arch of Septimius Severus
13. Temple of Saturn
14. Column of Phocas

ROME

Rome: Republic and Empire
(500 B.C.-A.D. 500)

Ancient Rome spanned about a thousand years, from 500 B.C. to A.D. 500. During that time, Rome expanded from a small tribe of barbarians to a vast empire, then dwindled slowly to city size again. For the first 500 years, when Rome's armies made her ruler of the Italian peninsula and beyond, Rome was a republic governed by elected senators. Over the next 500 years, a time of world conquest and eventual decline, Rome was an empire ruled by a military-backed dictator.

Julius Caesar bridged the gap between republic and empire. This ambitious general and politician, popular with the people because of his military victories and charisma, suspended the Roman constitution and assumed dictatorial powers in about 50 B.C. A few years later, he was assassinated by a conspiracy of senators. His adopted son, Augustus, succeeded him, and soon "Caesar" was not just a name but a title.

Emperor Augustus ushered in the Pax Romana, or Roman peace (A.D. 1-200), a time when Rome reached her peak and controlled an empire that stretched even beyond Eurail—from England to Egypt, Turkey to Morocco.

sound as the parade began. First came porters, carrying chests full of gold and jewels. Then a parade of exotic animals from the conquered lands—elephants, giraffes, hippopotamuses—for the crowd to "ooh" and "ahh" at. Next came the prisoners in chains, with the captive king on a wheeled platform so the people could jeer and spit at him. Finally, the conquering hero himself would drive down in his four-horse chariot, with rose petals strewn in his path. The whole procession would run the length of the Forum and up the face of Capitol Hill to the Temple of Saturn (the eight big columns midway up the hill—#13 on the map), where they'd place the booty in Rome's coffers. Then they'd continue up to the summit to the Temple of Jupiter (only ruins of its foundation remain today) to dedicate the victory to the King of the Gods.

❶ Arch of Titus (Arco di Tito)

The Arch of Titus commemorated the Roman victory over the province of Judaea (Israel) in A.D. 70. The Romans had a reputation as benevolent conquerors who tolerated the local customs and rulers. All they required was allegiance to the empire, shown by worshipping the

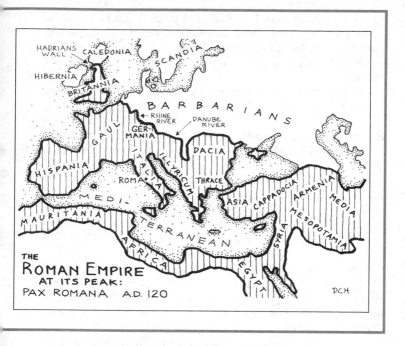

THE
ROMAN EMPIRE
AT ITS PEAK:
PAX ROMANA A.D. 120

emperor as a god. No problem for most conquered people, who already had half a dozen gods on their prayer lists anyway. But Israelites believed in only one god, and it wasn't the emperor. Israel revolted. After a short but bitter war, the Romans defeated the rebels, took Jerusalem, destroyed their temple (leaving only the foundation wall—today's revered "Wailing Wall"), and brought home 50,000 Jewish slaves...who were forced to build this arch (and the Colosseum).

Roman propaganda decorates the inside of the arch, where a relief shows the emperor Titus in a chariot being crowned by

the goddess Victory. (Thanks to modern pollution, they both look like they've been through the wars.) The other side shows booty from the sacking of the temple in Jerusalem—soldiers carrying a Jewish menorah and other plunder. The two (unfin-

ished) plaques on poles were to have listed the conquered cities. Look at the top of the ceiling. Constructed after Titus' death, the relief shows him riding an eagle to heaven, where he'll become one of the gods.

The brutal crushing of the A.D. 70 rebellion (and another one

60 years later) devastated the nation of Israel. With no temple as a center for their faith, the Jews scattered throughout the world (the Diaspora). There would be no Jewish political entity again for almost 2,000 years, until modern Israel was created after World War II.

• *Walk down the Via Sacra into the Forum. After about 50 yards, turn right and follow a path uphill to the three huge arches of the...*

❷ Basilica of Constantine (a.k.a. Basilica Maxentius)

Yes, these are big arches. But they represent only one-third of the original Basilica of Constantine, a mammoth hall of justice. The arches were matched by a similar set along the Via Sacra side (only a few squat brick piers remain). Between them ran the central hall, which was spanned by a roof 130 feet high—about 55 feet higher than the side arches you see. (The stub of brick you see sticking up began an arch that once spanned the central hall.) The hall itself was as long as a football field, lavishly furnished with color-ful inlaid marble, a gilded bronze ceiling, and statues, and filled with strolling Romans. At the far (west) end was an enormous marble statue of Emperor Constantine on a throne. (Pieces of this statue, including a hand the size of a man, are on display in Rome's Capitoline Museums.)

The basilica was begun by the emperor Maxentius, but after he was trounced in battle, the victor Constantine completed the massive building. No doubt about it, the Romans built monuments on a more epic scale than any previous Europeans, wowing their "barbarian" neighbors.

• *Now stroll deeper into the Forum, downhill along Via Sacra, through the trees. Many of the large basalt stones under your feet were walked on by Caesar Augustus 2,000 years ago. Pass by the only original bronze door still swinging on its ancient hinges (the green door at the Tempio di Romolo, on the right) and continue between ruined buildings until the Via Sacra opens up to a flat, grassy area.*

ROME

❸ The Forum's Main Square

The original Forum, or main square, was this flat patch about the size of a football field, stretching to the foot of Capitol Hill. Surrounding it were temples, law courts, government buildings, and triumphal arches.

Rome was born right here. According to legend, twin brothers Romulus (Rome) and Remus were orphaned in infancy and raised by a she-wolf on top of Palatine Hill. Growing up, they found it hard to get dates. So they and their cohorts attacked the nearby Sabine tribe and kidnapped their women. After they made peace, this marshy valley became the meeting place and then the trading center for the scattered tribes on the surrounding hillsides.

The square was the busiest and most crowded—and often the seediest—section of town. Besides the senators, politicians, and currency exchangers, there were even sleazier types—souvenir hawkers, pickpockets, fortune-tellers, gamblers, slave marketers, drunks, hookers, lawyers, and tour guides.

The Forum is now rubble, but imagine it in its prime: blinding white marble buildings with 40-foot-high columns and shining bronze roofs; rows of statues painted in realistic colors; processional chariots rattling down Via Sacra. Mentally replace tourists in T-shirts with tribunes in togas. Imagine the buildings towering and the people buzzing around you while an orator gives a rabble-rousing speech from the Rostrum. If things still look like just a pile of rocks, at least tell yourself, "But Julius Caesar once leaned against these rocks."

• *At the near (east) end of the main square (the Colosseum is to the east) are the foundations of a temple now capped with a peaked wood-and-metal roof.*

❹ Temple of Julius Caesar (Tempio del Divo Giulio, or Ara di Cesare)

Julius Caesar's body was burned on this spot (under the metal roof) after his assassination. Peek behind the wall into the small apse area, where a mound of dirt usually has fresh flowers—given to remember the man who, more than any other, personified the greatness of Rome.

Caesar (100-44 B.C.) changed Rome—and the Forum—dramatically. He cleared out many of the wooden market stalls and began to ring the square with even grander buildings. Caesar's house was located behind the temple, near that clump of trees. He walked right by here on the day he was assassinated ("Beware the Ides of March!" warned a street-corner Etruscan preacher).

Though he was popular with the masses, not everyone liked Caesar's urban design or his politics. When he assumed dictatorial powers, he was ambushed and stabbed to death by a conspiracy of senators, including his adopted son, Brutus *("Et tu, Brute?")*.

The funeral was held here, facing the main square. The citizens gathered, and speeches were made. Mark Antony stood up to say (in Shakespeare's words), "Friends, Romans, countrymen, lend me your ears. I come to bury Caesar, not to praise him." When Caesar's body was burned, the citizens who still loved him threw anything at hand on the fire, requiring the fire department to come put it out. Later, Emperor Augustus dedicated this temple in his name, making Caesar the first Roman to become a god.

• *Behind and to the left of the Temple of Julius Caesar are the 10 tall columns of the...*

❺ Temple of Antoninus Pius and Faustina

The Senate built this temple to honor Emperor Antoninus Pius (A.D. 138-161) and his deified wife, Faustina. The 50-foot-tall Corinthian

(leafy) columns must have been awe-inspiring to out-of-towners who grew up in thatched huts. Although the temple has been inhabited by a church, you can still see the basic layout—a staircase led to a shaded porch (the columns), which admitted you to the main building (now a church), where the statue of the god sat. Originally, these columns supported a triangular pediment decorated with sculptures.

Picture these columns, with gilded capitals, supporting brightly painted statues in the pediment, and the whole building capped with a gleaming bronze roof. The stately gray rubble of today's Forum is a faded black-and-white photograph of a 3-D Technicolor era.

The building is a microcosm of many of the changes that

occurred after Rome fell. In medieval times, the temple was pillaged. Note the diagonal cuts high on the marble columns—a failed attempt by scavengers to cut through the pillars to pull them down for their precious stone. (They used vinegar and rope to cut the marble...but because vinegar also eats through rope, they abandoned the attempt.) In 1550, a church was housed inside the ancient temple. The door shows the street level at the time of Michelangelo. The long staircase was underground until excavated in the 1800s.

• *There's a ramp next to the Temple of A. and F. Walk halfway up it and look to the left to view the...*

❻ Basilica Aemilia

A basilica was a covered public forum, often serving as a Roman hall of justice. In a society that was as legal-minded as America is today, you needed a lot of lawyers—and a big place to put them. Citizens came here to work out matters such as inheritances and building permits, or to sue somebody.

Notice the layout. It was a long, rectangular building. The stubby columns all in a row form one long, central hall flanked by two side aisles. Medieval Christians required a larger meeting hall for their worship services than Roman temples provided, so they used the spacious Roman basilica as the model for their churches. Cathedrals from France to Spain to England, from Romanesque to Gothic to Renaissance, all have the same basic floor plan as a Roman basilica.

• *Return again to the Temple of Julius Caesar. To the right of the temple are the three tall Corinthian columns of the Temple of Castor and Pollux. Beyond that is Palatine Hill—the corner of which may have been...*

❼ Caligula's Palace (a.k.a. the Palace of Tiberius)

Emperor Caligula (ruled A.D. 37-41) had a huge palace on Palatine Hill overlooking the Forum. It actually sprawled down the hill into the Forum (some supporting arches remain in the hillside).

Caligula was not a nice person. He tortured enemies, stole senators' wives, and parked his chariot in handicap spaces. But Rome's luxury-loving emperors only added to the glory of the Forum, with each one trying to make his mark on history.

• *To the left of the Temple of Castor and Pollux, find the remains of a small white circular temple.*

❽ Temple of Vesta

This is perhaps Rome's most sacred spot. Rome considered itself one big family, and this temple represented a circular hut, like the kind that Rome's first families lived in. Inside, a fire burned, just as in a Roman home. And back in the days before lighters and butane, you never wanted your fire to go out. As long as the sacred flame burned, Rome would stand. The flame was tended by priestesses known as Vestal Virgins.

• *Around the back of the Temple of Vesta, you'll find two rectangular brick pools. These stood in the courtyard of the...*

❾ House of the Vestal Virgins

The Vestal Virgins lived in a two-story building surrounding a long central courtyard with these two pools at one end. Rows of

statues depicting leading Vestal Virgins flanked the courtyard. This place was the model—both architecturally and sexually—for medieval convents and monasteries.

Chosen from noble families before they reached the age of 10, the six Vestal Virgins served a 30-year term. Honored and revered by the Romans, the Vestals even had their own box opposite the emperor in the Colosseum.

As the name implies, a Vestal took a vow of chastity. If she served her term faithfully—abstaining for 30 years—she was given a huge dowry, and allowed to marry. But if they found any Virgin who wasn't, she

was strapped to a funeral car, paraded through the streets of the Forum, taken to a crypt, given a loaf of bread and a lamp...and

ROME

Rome Falls

Remember that Rome lasted 1,000 years—500 years of growth, 200 years of peak power, and 300 years of gradual

decay. The fall had many causes, among them the barbarians who pecked away at Rome's borders. Christians blamed the fall on moral decay. Pagans blamed it on Christians. Socialists blamed it on a shallow economy based on the spoils of war. (Republicans blamed it on Democrats.) Whatever the reasons, the far-flung empire could no longer keep its grip on conquered lands, and it pulled back. Barbarian tribes from Germany and Asia attacked the Italian peninsula and even looted Rome itself in A.D. 410, leveling many of the buildings in the Forum. In 476, when the last emperor checked out and switched off the lights, Europe plunged into centuries of ignorance, poverty, and weak government—the Dark Ages.

But Rome lived on in the Catholic Church. Christianity was the state religion of Rome's last generations. Emperors became popes (both called themselves "Pontifex Maximus"), senators became bishops, orators became priests, and basilicas became churches. The glory of Rome remains eternal.

buried alive. Many women suffered the latter fate.

• *Return to the Temple of Julius Caesar and head to the Forum's west end (opposite from the Colosseum). As you pass alongside the big open space of the Forum's main square, consider how the piazza is still a standard part of any Italian town. It has reflected and accommodated the gregarious and outgoing nature of the Italian people since Roman times.*

Stop at the big, well-preserved brick building (on right) with the triangular roof. Look in at...

⑩ The Curia (Senate House)

The Curia was the most important political building in the Forum. While the present building dates from A.D. 283, this was the site of Rome's official center of government since the birth of the republic. (Note that ongoing archaeological work may restrict access to the Curia, as well as the Arch of Septimius

ROME

Severus—described later—and the exit to Capitol Hill.) Three hundred senators, elected by the citizens of Rome, met here to debate and create the laws of the land. Their wooden seats once circled the building in three tiers; the Senate president's podium sat at the far end. The marble floor is from ancient times. Listen to the echoes in this vast room—the acoustics are great.

Rome prided itself on being a republic. Early in the city's history, its people threw out the king and established rule by elected representatives. Each Roman citizen was free to speak his mind and have a say in public policy. Even when emperors became the supreme authority, the Senate was a power to be reckoned with. The Curia building is well-preserved, having been used as a church since early Christian times. In the 1930s, it was restored and opened to the public as a historic site. (Note: Although Julius Caesar was assassinated in "the Senate," it wasn't here—the Senate was temporarily meeting across town.)

A statue and two reliefs inside the Curia help build our mental image of the Forum. The statue, made of porphyry marble in about A.D. 100 (with its head, arms, and feet now missing), was a tribute to an emperor, probably Hadrian or Trajan. The two relief panels may have decorated the Rostrum. Those on the left show people (with big stone tablets) standing in line to burn their debt records following a government amnesty. The other shows the distribution of grain (Rome's welfare system), some buildings in the background, and the latest fashion in togas.

• *Go back down the Senate steps and find the 10-foot-high wall just to the left of the big arch, marked...*

⓫ Rostrum (Rostri)

Nowhere was Roman freedom more apparent than at this "Speaker's Corner." The Rostrum was a raised platform, 10 feet high and 80 feet long, decorated with statues, columns, and the prows of ships (rostra).

On a stage like this, Rome's orators, great and small, tried to draw a crowd and sway public opinion. Mark Antony rose to offer Caesar the laurel-leaf crown of kingship, which Caesar publicly (and hypocritically) refused while privately becoming a dictator. Men such as Cicero railed against the corruption and decadence that came with the city's newfound wealth. In later years, daring citizens even spoke out against the emperors, reminding them that Rome was once free. Picture the backdrop these speakers would have had—a mountain of marble buildings piling up on Capitol Hill.

In front of the Rostrum are trees bearing fruits that were sacred to the ancient Romans: olives (provided food, light, and preservatives), figs (tasty), and wine grapes (made a popular export product).

ROME

• *The big arch to the right of the Rostrum is the...*

⓬ Arch of Septimius Severus

In imperial times, the Rostrum's voices of democracy would have

been dwarfed by images of the empire, such as the huge six-story-high Arch of Septimius Severus (A.D. 203). The reliefs commemorate the African-born emperor's battles in Mesopotamia. Near ground level, see soldiers marching captured barbarians back to Rome for the victory parade. Despite Severus' efficient rule, Rome's empire was crumbling under the weight of its own corruption, disease, decaying infrastructure, and the constant attacks by foreign "barbarians."

• *Pass underneath the Arch of Septimius Severus and turn left. On the slope of Capitol Hill are the eight remaining columns of the...*

⓭ Temple of Saturn

These columns framed the entrance to the Forum's oldest temple (497 B.C.). Inside was a humble, very old wooden statue of the god Saturn. But the statue's pedestal held the gold bars, coins, and jewels of Rome's state treasury, the booty collected by conquering generals.

• *Standing here, at one of the Forum's first buildings, look east at the lone, tall...*

⓮ Column of Phocas—Rome's Fall

This is the Forum's last monument (A.D. 608), a gift from the

powerful Byzantine Empire to a fallen empire—Rome. Given to commemorate the pagan Pantheon's becoming a Christian church, it's like a symbolic last nail in ancient Rome's coffin. After Rome's 1,000-year reign, the city was looted by Vandals, the population of a million-plus shrank to about 10,000, and the once-grand city center—the Forum—was abandoned, slowly covered up by centuries of silt and dirt. In the 1700s, an English historian named Edward Gibbon overlooked this spot from Capitol Hill. Hearing Christian monks

ROME

singing at these pagan ruins, he looked out at the few columns poking up from the ground, pondered the "Decline and Fall of the Roman Empire," and thought, "Hmm, that's a catchy title...."

• *There are several ways to exit the Forum:*

1. *Exiting past the Arch of Titus lands you at the Colosseum.*
2. *Exiting near the Arch of Septimius Severus leads you to the stairs up to Capitol Hill.*
3. *The Forum's main entrance spills you back out onto Via dei Fori Imperiali.*
4. *From the Arch of Titus, you can climb Palatine Hill.*

Pantheon Tour

If your imagination is fried from trying to reconstruct ancient buildings out of today's rubble, visit the Pantheon, Rome's best-preserved monument. Engineers still admire how the Romans built such a mathematically precise structure without computers, fossil fuel-run machinery, or electricity. (Having unlimited slave power didn't hurt.) Stand under the Pantheon's solemn dome to gain a new appreciation for the sophistication of these ancient people.

Orientation

Pantheon: Free, Mon-Sat 8:30-19:30, Sun 9:00-18:00, holidays 9:00-13:00, closed for Mass Sat at 17:00 and Sun at 10:30. Audioguide-€5, €8.50/2 people, 25 minutes. Tel. 06-6830-0230.

Getting There: To reach the Pantheon neighborhood, you can walk (it's a 20-minute walk from Capitol Hill), take a taxi, or catch a bus. Buses #64 and #40 carry tourists and pickpockets frequently between Termini train station and Vatican City, stopping at a chaotic square called Largo Argentina, located a few blocks south of the Pantheon. (Take either Via dei Cestari or Via di Torre Argentina north to the Pantheon.) The *elettrico* minibus #116 runs between Campo de' Fiori and Piazza Barberini via the Pantheon. The most dramatic approach is on foot coming from Piazza Navona along Via Giustiniani, which spills directly into Piazza della Rotunda, offering the classic Pantheon view. See my "Walk Across Rome" on page 595.

Length of This Tour: Allow a half-hour to see the Pantheon, and at least another hour to visit all the churches.

Photography: It's allowed—even with flash—in the Pantheon. No flash in churches.

WCs: The nearest WCs are at bars and downstairs in the McDonald's on the Pantheon's square.

Cuisine Art: Restaurants abound. Several reasonable eateries are a

ROME

block or two north up Via del Pantheon. Some of Rome's best gelato is nearby. For recommendations, see page 624.

Drinks: A drinking fountain spurts near the obelisk in Piazza della Rotonda. For those who prefer their liquids caffeinated, two of Rome's most venerable (and busiest) coffee shops are just steps away: **Tazza d'Oro Casa del Caffè** (their icy *granita di caffè* is heaven on a hot day, Via degli Orfani 84) and **Bar Sant'Eustachio** (they add sugar to their coffee drinks unless you request otherwise, Piazza di Sant'Eustachio 82).

The Tour Begins

• *Start the tour at the top of the square called Piazza della Rotunda, with cafés and restaurants around the edges and an obelisk-topped fountain in the center. You're looking at...*

The Pantheon
Exterior

The Pantheon was a Roman temple dedicated to all *(pan)* of the gods *(theos)*. The original temple was built in 27 B.C. by Augustus'

son-in-law, Marcus Agrippa. In fact, the inscription below the triangular **pediment** proclaims in Latin, "Marcus Agrippa, son of Lucio, three times consul made this." But after a couple of fires, the structure we see today was completely rebuilt by the emperor Hadrian around A.D. 120. Some say that Hadrian, an amateur architect (and voracious traveler), helped design it.

The Pantheon looks like a pretty typical temple from the outside, but this is perhaps the most influential building in art history. Its dome was the model for the Florence cathedral dome, which launched the Renaissance, and for Michelangelo's dome of St. Peter's, which capped it all off. Even Washington, D.C.'s capitol building was inspired by this dome.

The 40-foot-high columns of the **portico** (entrance porch) are made from single pieces of red-gray granite (not the standard stacks of cylindrical pieces). They were taken from an Egyptian temple. The holes in the triangular pediment once held a huge bronze Roman eagle. Back up or step to one side to look above the pediment to the building itself. You'll see a roofline that was abandoned mid-construction. The pediment was originally intended to be higher, but when the support columns arrived, they were shorter than expected. Even the most enlightened can forget to "measure twice, cut once."

Pantheon Cross-Section

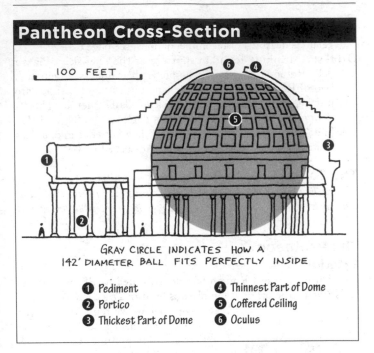

100 FEET

GRAY CIRCLE INDICATES HOW A
142' DIAMETER BALL FITS PERFECTLY INSIDE

❶ Pediment
❷ Portico
❸ Thickest Part of Dome
❹ Thinnest Part of Dome
❺ Coffered Ceiling
❻ Oculus

• *Pass through the portico, with its forest of enormous columns. Look up at the porch roof, and imagine the ceiling covered in its original bronze plating. It was removed in the 17th century by a scavenging pope from the Barberini family, inspiring the well-known quip, "What the barbarians didn't do, the Barberini did." Melted down, some of the bronze was used to build the huge bronze canopy over the altar at St. Peter's. Now pass through the giant* **bronze door**—*a copy of the original. Take a seat and take it all in.*

Interior

The dome, which was the largest made until the Renaissance, is set on a circular base. The mathematical perfection of this dome-on-a-base design is a testament to Roman engineering. The dome is as high as it is wide—142 feet from floor to rooftop and from side to side. To picture it, imagine a basketball set inside a wastebasket so that it just touches bottom.

The dome—recently cleaned and feeling loftier than ever—is made from concrete (a Roman invention) that gets lighter and thinner as it reaches the top. The

Pantheon

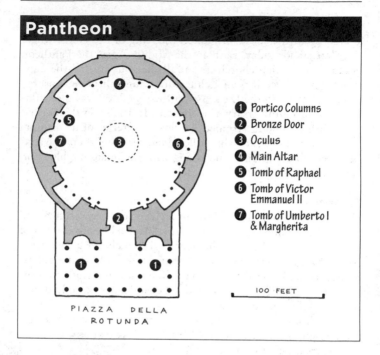

1. Portico Columns
2. Bronze Door
3. Oculus
4. Main Altar
5. Tomb of Raphael
6. Tomb of Victor Emmanuel II
7. Tomb of Umberto I & Margherita

100 FEET

PIAZZA DELLA ROTUNDA

base of the dome is 23 feet thick and made from heavy concrete mixed with travertine, while near the top, it's less than 5 feet thick and made with a lighter volcanic rock (pumice) mixed in. Note the square indentations in the surface of the dome. This **coffered ceiling** reduces the weight of the dome without compromising strength. The walls are strengthened by blind arches built into the wall (visible outside).

Both Brunelleschi and Michelangelo studied this dome before building their own (in Florence and the Vatican, respectively). Remember, St. Peter's Basilica is really only the dome of the Pantheon atop the Forum's Basilica of Constantine.

At the top, the **oculus**, or eye-in-the-sky, is the building's only light source and is almost 30 feet across. The 1,800-year-old floor

has holes in it and slants toward the edges to let the rainwater drain. Though some of the floor's marble has been replaced over the years, the design—alternating circles and squares—is original.

In ancient times, this was a one-stop-shopping temple where you could worship any of the gods whose statues decorated the niches. Entering the temple, Romans came face-to-face with a larger-than-life statue of Jupiter, the King of the Gods, where the **altar** stands today. Early in the Middle Ages, the Pantheon became a Christian church (from "all the gods" to "all the martyrs"), which saved it from architectural cannibalism and ensured its upkeep through the Dark Ages. (The year 2009 was the building's 1,400th anniversary as a church.) In the seventh century, a Byzantine emperor stripped the dome's interior of its original golden-tile ceiling. The twin, grilled windows just right of the altar (at 2 o'clock) are original and, along with the inlaid marble floor, give you a sense of the ancient decor.

Tombs

The only new things in the interior are the decorative statues and the tombs of famous people. The artist Raphael lies to the left of the main altar, which is in the lighted glass niche (pictured here). Above him is a statue of the Madonna and Child that Raphael himself commissioned for his tomb. The Latin inscription on his tomb reads, "In life, Nature feared to be outdone by him. In death, she feared she too would die."

You'll also see the tombs of modern Italy's first two kings. To the right is Victor Emmanuel II (*"Padre della Patria,"* father of his country). To the left is Umberto I (son of the father). These tombs are a hit with royalists. In fact, there is often a guard standing by a guestbook, where visitors can register their support for these two kings' now-controversial family, the Savoys. And finally, under Umberto lies his queen, Margherita...for whom the classic pizza Margherita (mozzarella, tomato sauce, and basil) was named in 1889.

The Pantheon is the only ancient building in Rome continuously used since its construction. When you leave, notice that the building is sunken below current street level, showing how the rest of the city has risen on 20 centuries of rubble.

The Pantheon also contains the world's greatest Roman column. There it is, spanning the entire 142 feet from heaven to earth—the pillar of light from the oculus.

Vatican Museum Tour

The four miles of displays in the Vatican Museum (Musei Vaticani)—from ancient statues to Christian frescoes to modern paintings—culminate in the Raphael Rooms and Michelangelo's glorious Sistine Chapel. (If you have binoculars, bring them.) This is one of Europe's top three or four houses of art. It can be exhausting, so plan your visit carefully. Allow two hours for a quick visit, three or four hours for enough time to enjoy it.

Overview

Cost and Hours: €15 plus optional €4 reservation fee, Mon-Sat 9:00-18:00, last entry at 16:00 (though the official closing time is 18:00, the staff starts ushering you out at 17:30), closed on religious holidays and Sun except last Sun of the month (when it's free, more crowded, and open 9:00-14:00, last entry at 12:30). Hours are subject to constant change and museum closes for frequent holidays; check http://mv.vatican.va for current times. Lines are extremely long in the morning—skip the ticket-buying line altogether by reserving an entry time on their website for €19 (€15 ticket plus €4 booking fee, pay with credit card). Guided tours and audioguides are available.

The Sistine Chapel closes before the museum. Individual rooms may close at odd hours, especially in the afternoon. The rooms described here are usually open.

Getting There: If you're taking a regional train from Civitavecchia, get off at San Pietro Station (see page 518). If you're coming from Termini or elsewhere in town, you can catch the Metro to the Cipro stop, a 10-minute walk from the entrance, including a climb up a big flight of stairs. The Ottaviano Metro stop is slightly farther from the entrance, but may be closer to the end of the ticket-buying line. Bus #64 stops on the other side of St. Peter's Square, a 10- to 15-minute walk (facing the church from the obelisk, take a right through the colonnade and follow the Vatican wall). Taxis are reasonable (hop in and say, "moo-ZAY-ee vah-tee-KAH-nee").

Dress Code: Modest dress (no short shorts or bare shoulders) is required. This dress code is strictly enforced here and throughout Vatican City especially at St. Peter's Basilica (which you can visit after leaving the Sistine Chapel).

Avoiding Lines: You can buy a ticket and **reserve an entry time online** at http://mv.vatican.va for €19 (€15 ticket plus €4 booking fee, pay with credit card). You choose your day and time, they email you a confirmation immediately, and you print out the voucher with its reservation bar code. At the Vatican Museum, bypass the ticket-buying line and queue up at the "Entrance with Reservations" line (to the right). Show your voucher to the guard, who will scan it and let you in. Once inside the museum, go to a ticket window (either in the lobby or upstairs), present your voucher and ID, and they'll issue your ticket.

ROME

If you book a **guided tour through the Vatican Museum** (see below), you can also skip the ticket-buying line and approach the guard with your voucher. If you book with a private tour company, you may still have a short wait at crowded times.

If you don't have a reservation, **try arriving after 14:00,** when crowds subside somewhat. Another good time is during the papal audience on Wednesday after 10:30, when many tourists are at St. Peter's Basilica.

Make sure you get in the right line. Generally, individuals without tickets line up against the Vatican City wall (to the left of the entrance as you face it), and individuals with reservations enter on the right.

Tours: The Vatican offers English tours that are easy to book online (€31, includes admission, http://mv.vatican.va). As with individual ticket reservations, present your confirmation voucher to a guard to the right of the entrance, then, once inside, go to the Guided Tours desk (in the lobby, up a few stairs).

Both private tour companies and private guides offer guided English tours of the museum, usually allowing you to skip the long ticket-buying line. For a listing of several companies, see page 531.

Audioguide Tours: If you rent an **audioguide** (€7 plus ID, available at the top of the ramp/escalator), you lose the option of taking the shortcut from the Sistine Chapel to St. Peter's (since audioguides must be returned to the museum entrance/exit).

Length of This Tour: Until you expire, the museum closes, or 2.5 hours, whichever comes first.

Services: The post office, with stamps that make collectors drool, is upstairs. WCs are mainly at the entrance/exit, plus a few scattered within the collection.

Museum Strategies: There are two exits from the museum, and you'll want to decide which you'll take before you enter. The main exit is right near the entrance. Use this one if you plan on renting an audioguide (which you must return at the entrance).

The other exit is a shortcut that leads from the Sistine Chapel directly to St. Peter's Basilica (spilling out alongside the church; see map on page 581). This route saves you a 30-minute walk (15 minutes back to the Vatican Museum entry/exit, then 15 minutes to St. Peter's) and lets you avoid the often-long security line at the basilica's main entrance. If you take this route, you'll have to do the following: adhere to St. Peter's stricter dress code (no shorts, miniskirts, or bare shoulders), forgo an audioguide, skip the Pinacoteca or tour it

Vatican Museum Overview

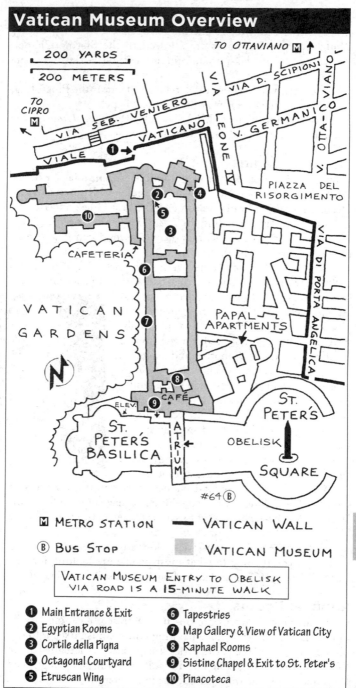

TO OTTAVIANO M ↑

200 YARDS
200 METERS

TO CIPRO M

VIA SEB. VENIERO
VIALE VATICANO
VIA LEONE IV
VIA D. SCIPIONI
V. GERMANICO
OTTAVIANO

PIAZZA DEL RISORGIMENTO

VIA DI PORTA ANGELICA

CAFETERIA

VATICAN GARDENS

N

PAPAL APARTMENTS

ELEV.

CAFÉ

ST. PETER'S BASILICA

ATRIUM

OBELISK

ST. PETER'S SQUARE

#64 B

M METRO STATION — VATICAN WALL

B BUS STOP ▨ VATICAN MUSEUM

VATICAN MUSEUM ENTRY TO OBELISK
VIA ROAD IS A **15**-MINUTE WALK

1 Main Entrance & Exit
2 Egyptian Rooms
3 Cortile della Pigna
4 Octagonal Courtyard
5 Etruscan Wing

6 Tapestries
7 Map Gallery & View of Vatican City
8 Raphael Rooms
9 Sistine Chapel & Exit to St. Peter's
10 Pinacoteca

ROME

earlier, and be prepared for the odd chance that the shortcut is simply closed (which sometimes happens).

Photography: No photos are allowed in the Sistine Chapel. Elsewhere in the museum, photos without a flash are permitted.

Cuisine Art: A self-service cafeteria is inside, near the Pinacoteca, and a smaller café is near the Sistine Chapel.

Starring: World history, Michelangelo, Raphael, *Laocoön*, the Greek masters, and their Roman copyists.

The Tour Begins

Start, as civilization did, in **Egypt and Mesopotamia.** Next, the Pio Clementino collection features **Greek and Roman statues.** Decorating its courtyard are some of the best Greek and Roman statues in captivity, including the *Laocoön* group (first century B.C., Hellenistic) and the *Apollo Belvedere* (a second-century Roman copy of a Greek original).

The centerpiece of the next hall is the *Belvedere Torso* (just a 2,000-year-old torso, but one that had a great impact on the art of Michelangelo). Finishing off the classical statuary are two fine fourth-century porphyry sarcophagi. These royal purple tombs were made (though not used) for the Roman emperor Constantine's mother and daughter. They were Christians—and therefore outlaws—until Constantine made Christianity legal in A.D. 312. Both sarcophagi were quarried and worked in Egypt. The technique for working this extremely hard stone (a special tempering of metal was required) was lost after this, and porphyry was not chiseled again until Renaissance times in Florence.

Overachievers may first choose to pop into the **Etruscan wing**—labeled Museo Etrusco—located a few steps up from this level. Others have permission to save their aesthetic energy for the Sistine.

After long halls of tapestries, old maps, broken penises, and fig leaves, you'll come to what most people are looking for: the Raphael Rooms (or *stanza*) and Michelangelo's Sistine Chapel.

Raphael Rooms

These outstanding works are frescoes. A fresco (meaning "fresh" in Italian) is technically not a painting. The color is mixed into wet plaster, and, when the plaster dries, the painting is actually part of the wall. This is a durable but difficult medium, requiring speed and accuracy, as the work is built one patch at a time.

After fancy rooms illustrating the "Immaculate Conception of Mary" (in the 19th century, the Vatican codified this hard-to-sell

doctrine, making it a formal part of the Catholic faith) and the triumph of Constantine (with divine guidance, which led to his conversion to Christianity), you enter rooms frescoed by Raphael and his assistants. The highlight is the restored *School of Athens*. This is remarkable for its blatant pre-Christian classical orientation, especially since it originally wallpapered the apartments of Pope Julius II. Raphael honors the great pre-Christian thinkers—Aristotle, Plato, and company—who are portrayed as the leading artists of Raphael's day. The bearded figure of Plato is Leonardo da Vinci. Diogenes, history's first hippie, sprawls alone in bright blue on the stairs, while Michelangelo broods in the foreground—supposedly added later. Apparently, Raphael snuck a peek at the Sistine Chapel and decided that his arch-competitor was so good that he had to put their personal differences aside and include him in this tribute to the artists of his generation. Today's St. Peter's was under construction as Raphael was working. In the *School of Athens*, he gives us a sneak preview of the unfinished church.

• *Leaving this final Raphael Room, you'll see two arrows. Follow the one to the left—the route that goes directly to the Sistine Chapel.*

The Sistine Chapel

The brilliantly restored Sistine Chapel contains Michelangelo's ceiling and his huge *The Last Judgment*. The Sistine is the personal chapel of the pope and the place where new popes are elected. (The small, old-fashioned stove that burns pope-vote ballots—which sends out puffs of telltale smoke—is placed near today's shortcut exit.)

When Pope Julius II asked Michelangelo to take on this important project, he said, "No, *grazie*." Michelangelo insisted he was a sculptor, not a painter. The Sistine ceiling was a vast undertaking, and he didn't want to do a half-vast job. But the pope pleaded, bribed, and threatened until Michelangelo finally consented, on the condition that he be able to do it all his own way.

ROME

Julius had asked for only 12 apostles along the sides of the ceiling, but Michelangelo had a grander vision—the entire history of the world until Jesus. He spent the next four years (1508-1512) craning his neck on scaffolding six stories up, covering the ceiling with frescoes of biblical scenes.

In sheer physical terms, it's an astonishing achievement: 5,900 square feet, with the vast majority done by his own hand. (Raphael only designed most of his rooms, letting assistants do the grunt work.)

First, he had to design and erect the scaffolding. Any materials had to be hauled up on pulleys. Then, a section of ceiling would be plastered. With fresco—painting on wet plaster—if you don't get it right the first time, you have to scrape the whole thing off and start over. And if you've ever struggled with a ceiling light fixture or worked underneath a car for even five minutes, you know how heavy your arms get. The physical effort, the paint dripping in his eyes, the creative drain, and the mental stress from a pushy pope combined to almost kill Michelangelo.

But when the ceiling was finished and revealed to the public, it simply blew 'em away. Like the *Laocoön* statue discovered six years earlier, it was unlike anything seen before. It both caps the Renaissance and turns it in a new direction. In perfect Renaissance spirit, it mixes Old Testament prophets with classical figures. But the style is more dramatic, shocking, and emotional than the balanced Renaissance works before it. This is a very personal work—the Gospel according to Michelangelo—but its themes and subject matter are universal. Many art scholars contend that the Sistine ceiling is the single greatest work of art by any one human being.

The Sistine Ceiling: Understanding What You're Standing Under

The ceiling shows the history of the world before the birth of Jesus. We see God creating the world, creating man and woman, destroying the earth by flood, and so on. God himself, in his purple robe, actually appears in the first five scenes. Along the sides (where the ceiling starts to curve), we see the Old Testament prophets and pagan Greek prophetesses who foretold the coming of Christ. Dividing these scenes and figures are fake niches (a painted 3-D illusion) decorated with nude statue-like figures with symbolic meaning.

The key is to see three simple divisions in the tangle of bodies:
1. The central spine of nine rectangular biblical scenes;
2. The line of prophets on either side; and
3. The triangles between the prophets showing the ancestors of Christ.

• *Ready? Within the chapel, grab a seat along the side (if there's room).*

The Sistene Schematic

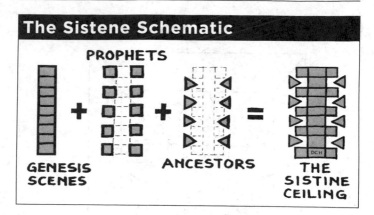

PROPHETS

GENESIS SCENES **+** **+** ANCESTORS **=** THE SISTINE CEILING

Face the altar with the big The Last Judgment *on the wall (more on that later). Now look up to the ceiling and find the central panel of...*

The Creation of Adam

God and man take center stage in this Renaissance version of creation. Adam, newly formed in the image of God, lounges dreamily in perfect naked innocence. God, with his entourage, swoops in with a swirl of activity (which—with a little imagination—looks like a cross-section of a human brain...quite a strong humanist statement). Their reaching hands are the center of this work. Adam's is limp and passive; God's is strong and forceful, his finger twitching upward with energy. Here is the very moment of creation, as God passes the spark of life to man, the crowning work of his creation.

This is the spirit of the Renaissance. God is not a terrifying giant reaching down to puny and helpless man from way on high. Here they are on an equal plane, divided only by the diagonal patch of sky. God's billowing robe and the patch of green upon which Adam is lying balance each other. They are like two pieces of a jigsaw puzzle, or two long-separated continents, or like the yin and yang symbols finally coming together—uniting, complementing each other, creating wholeness. God and man work together in the divine process of creation.

• *This celebration of man permeates the ceiling. Notice the Adonises-come-to-life on the pedestals that divide the central panels. And then came woman.*

The Garden of Eden: Temptation and Expulsion

In one panel, we see two scenes from the Garden of Eden. On the left is the leafy garden of paradise where Adam and Eve lie around blissfully. But the devil comes along—a serpent with a woman's torso—and winds around the forbidden Tree of Knowledge. The

ROME

The Sistine Ceiling

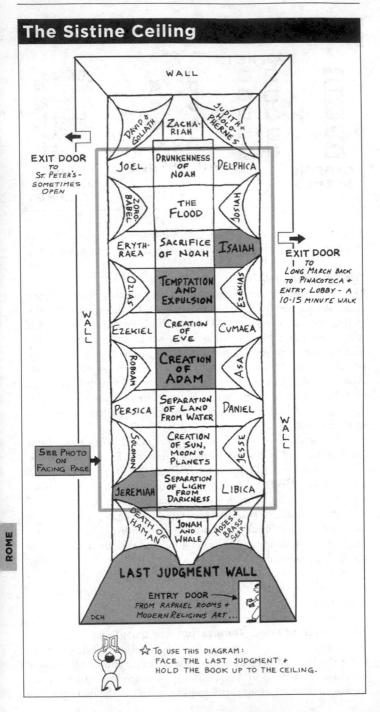

WALL

DAVID & GOLIATH
ZACHARIAH
JUPITH + HOLOFERNES

EXIT DOOR
TO ST. PETER'S – SOMETIMES OPEN

JOEL
DRUNKENNESS OF NOAH
DELPHICA

ZORO-BABEL
THE FLOOD
JOSIAH

ERYTH-RAEA
SACRIFICE OF NOAH
ISAIAH

EXIT DOOR
↑ TO LONG MARCH BACK TO PINACOTECA + ENTRY LOBBY – A 10·15 MINUTE WALK

OZIAS
TEMPTATION AND EXPULSION
EZEKIAS

WALL

EZEKIEL
CREATION OF EVE
CUMAEA

ROBOAM
CREATION OF ADAM
ASA

PERSICA
SEPARATION OF LAND FROM WATER
DANIEL

WALL

SOLOMON
CREATION OF SUN, MOON & PLANETS
JESSE

SEE PHOTO ON FACING PAGE →

JEREMIAH
SEPARATION OF LIGHT FROM DARKNESS
LIBICA

DEATH OF HAMAN
JONAH AND WHALE
MOSES + BRASS SERP.

LAST JUDGMENT WALL

ENTRY DOOR →
FROM RAPHAEL ROOMS + MODERN RELIGIOUS ART...

DCH

ROME

☆ TO USE THIS DIAGRAM:
FACE THE LAST JUDGMENT +
HOLD THE BOOK UP TO THE CEILING.

temptation to gain new knowledge is too great for these Renaissance people. They eat the forbidden fruit.

At right, the sword-wielding angel drives them from Paradise into the barren plains. They're grieving, but they're far from helpless. Adam's body is thick and sturdy, and we know they'll survive in the cruel world. Adam firmly gestures to the angel, like he's saying, "All right, already! We're going!"

The Nine Scenes from Genesis

Take some time with these central scenes to understand the story that the ceiling tells. They run in sequence, starting at the front:

1. God, in purple, divides the light from darkness.
2. God creates the sun (burning orange) and the moon (pale white, to the right). Oops, I guess there's another moon.
3. God bursts toward us to separate the land and water.
4. *The Creation of Adam.*
5. God creates Eve, who dives into existence out of Adam's side.
6. *The Garden of Eden: Temptation and Expulsion.*
7. Noah kills a ram and stokes the altar fires to make a sacrifice to God.
8. The great flood, sent by God, destroys the wicked, who desperately head for higher ground. In the distance, the Ark carries Noah's family to safety. (The blank spot dates to 1793, when a nearby gunpowder depot exploded, shaking the building.)
9. Noah's sons see their drunken father. (Perhaps Michelangelo chose to end it with this scene as a reminder that even the best of men are fallible.)

Prophets

You'll notice that the figures at the far end of the chapel are a bit smaller than those over *The Last Judgment*.

Michelangelo started at the far end, with the Noah scenes. By 1510, he'd finished the first half of the ceiling. When they took the scaffolding down and could finally see what he'd been working on for two years, everyone was awestruck—except Michelangelo. As powerful as his figures are, from the floor they didn't look dramatic enough for Michelangelo. For the other half, he pulled out all the stops.

Compare the Noah scenes (far end) with their many small figures to the huge images of God at the other end. Similarly, Isaiah (near the lattice screen, marked "Esaias") is stately and balanced, while Jeremiah ("Hieremias," in the corner by *The Last Judgment*) is a dark, brooding figure. This prophet who witnessed the destruction of Israel slumps his chin in his hand and ponders the fate of his people. Like the difference between the stately *Apollo Belvedere* and the excited *Laocoön*, Michelangelo added a new emotional dimension to Renaissance painting.

The Last Judgment

When Michelangelo returned to paint the altar wall 23 years later (1535), the mood of Europe—and of Michelangelo—was completely different. The Protestant Reformation had forced the Catholic Church to clamp down on free thought, and religious wars raged. Rome had recently been pillaged by roving bands of mercenaries. The Renaissance spirit of optimism was fading. Michelangelo himself had begun to question the innate goodness of mankind.

It's Judgment Day, and Christ—the powerful figure in the center, raising his arm to spank the wicked—has come to find out

who's naughty and who's nice. Beneath him, a band of angels blows its trumpets Dizzy Gillespie-style, giving a wake-up call to the sleeping dead. The dead at lower left leave their graves and prepare to be judged. The righteous, on Christ's right hand (the left side of the picture), are carried up to the glories of heaven. The wicked on the other side are hurled down to hell, where demons wait to torture them. Charon, from the underworld of Greek mythology, waits below to ferry the souls of the damned to hell.

It's a grim picture. No one, but no one, is smiling. Even many of the righteous being resurrected (lower left) are either skeletons or cadavers with ghastly skin. The angels have to play tug-of-war with subterranean monsters to drag them from their graves.

Over in hell, the wicked are tortured by gleeful demons. One of the damned (to the right of the trumpeting angels) has an utterly lost expression, as if saying, "Why did I cheat on my wife?!" Two demons grab him around the ankles to pull him down to the bowels of hell, condemned to an eternity of constipation.

But it's the terrifying figure of Christ that dominates this scene. He raises his arm to smite the wicked, sending a ripple of fear through everyone. Even the saints around him—even Mary beneath his arm (whose interceding days are clearly over)—shrink back in terror at loving Jesus' uncharacteristic outburst. His expression is completely closed, and he turns his head, refusing even to

The Last Judgment

1	Christ with Mary	**5**	Charon the Ferryman
2	Trumpeting Angels	**6**	Demon/Critic Wrapped in Snake
3	Righteous Dead Ascending	**7**	St. Bartholomew Holding Flayed Skin (Michelangelo's Face)
4	Damned Man		

listen to the whining alibis of the damned. Look at Christ's bicep. If this muscular figure looks familiar to you, it's because you've seen it before—the Belvedere Torso.

When *The Last Judgment* was unveiled to the public in 1541, it caused a sensation. The pope is said to have dropped to his knees and cried, "Lord, charge me not with my sins when thou shalt come on the Day of Judgment."

And it changed the course of art. The complex composition, with more than 300 figures swirling around the figure of Christ, was far beyond traditional Renaissance balance. The twisted figures shown from every imaginable angle challenged other painters to try and top this master of 3-D illusion. And the sheer terror and drama of the scene was a striking contrast to the placid optimism of, say, Raphael's *School of Athens*. Michelangelo had Baroque-en all the rules of the Renaissance, signaling a new era of art.

With the Renaissance fading, the fleshy figures in *The Last Judgment* aroused murmurs of discontent from Church authorities. Michelangelo rebelled by painting his chief critic into the scene—in hell. He's the jackassed demon in the bottom right corner, wrapped in a snake. Look at how Michelangelo covered his privates. Sweet revenge.

(After Michelangelo's death, prudish Church authorities painted the wisps of clothing that we see today.)

Now move up close. Study the details of the lower part of the painting from right to left. Charon, with Dr. Spock ears and a Dalí moustache, paddles the damned in a boat full of human turbulence. Look more closely at the J-Day band. Are they reading music, or is it the Judgment Day tally? Before the cleaning, these details were lost in murk.

The Last Judgment marks the end of Renaissance optimism epitomized in *The Creation of Adam*, with its innocence and exaltation of man. There, he was the wakening man-child of a fatherly

God. Here, man cowers in fear and unworthiness before a terrifying, wrathful deity.

Michelangelo himself must have wondered how he would be judged—had he used his God-given talents wisely? Look at St. Bartholomew, the bald, bearded guy at Christ's left foot (our right). In the flayed skin he's holding is a barely recognizable face—the twisted self-portrait of a self-questioning Michelangelo.

• *There are two exits from the Sistine Chapel. To return to the main entrance/exit, leave the Sistine through the side door next to the screen. You'll soon find yourself facing The Long March back to the museum's entrance (about 15 minutes away) and the Pinacoteca.*

Or, if you're planning to take the shortcut directly to St. Peter's Basilica (see "Museum Strategies," page 566), exit out the far-right corner of the Sistine Chapel (with your back to the altar). This route saves you a 30-minute walk and the wait in the St. Peter's security line, but you can't get back to the main entrance/exit or the Pinacoteca. Though this corner door is likely labeled "Exit for private tour groups only," you can usually just slide through with the crowds (or protest that your group has left you behind). If for some reason this exit is closed, hang out in the Sistine Chapel for a few more minutes—it'll likely reopen shortly.

The Long March Back

Along this corridor (located one floor below the long corridor that you walked to get here), you'll find the Pinacoteca (the Vatican's small but fine collection of paintings, with Raphael's *Transfiguration*, Leonardo's unfinished *St. Jerome*, and Caravaggio's *Deposition*), a cafeteria (long lines, uninspired food), and the underrated early Christian art section, before you exit via the souvenir shop.

St. Peter's Basilica Tour

St. Peter's Basilica (Basilica San Pietro) is the greatest church in Christendom. It represents the power and splendor of Rome's 2,000-year domination of the Western world. Built on the memory and grave of the first pope, St. Peter, this is where the grandeur of ancient Rome became the grandeur of Christianity.

Orientation

Cost: Free entry to basilica and Crypt. Dome climb—€5 to climb stairs all the way up, or €7 to take an elevator partway up to the roof, then climb 323 steps to the top of the dome (for details, see "Dome Climb," later). Museum-Treasury—€6.

Dress Code: No shorts or bare shoulders (applies to men, women, and children), and no miniskirts. This dress code is strictly enforced.

Hours of Church: Daily April-Sept 7:00-19:00, Oct-March 7:00-18:00. The church closes on Wednesday mornings during papal audiences. The best time to visit the church is early or late; at 17:00, when the church is fairly empty, sunbeams can work their magic, and the late-afternoon Mass fills the place with spiritual music.

Mass is held daily—Mon-Sat at 8:30, 9:00, 10:00, 11:00, 12:00, and 17:00; Sun and holidays at 9:00, 10:30 (in Latin), 11:30, 12:15, 13:00, 16:00, and 17:45. Confirm the schedule (on-site or at www.saintpetersbasilica.org) and location; it's generally in the south (left) transept.

The **Museum-Treasury** is open daily (April-Sept 9:00-18:15, Oct-March 9:00-17:15), and the **Crypt** closes one hour earlier than the church does.

Dome Climb (Cupola): Daily April-Sept 8:00-18:00, Oct-March 8:00-17:00. Allow one hour for the round-trip to the top of the dome (or a half-hour to the roof). You can take the elevator or stairs to the roof (231 steps up), then climb another 323 steps to the top of the dome. The entry to the elevator is just outside the basilica on the north side of St. Peter's (near the secret exit from the Sistine Chapel—described on page 577). Look for signs to the cupola. For more on the dome, see page 594.

Getting There: If you're taking a regional train from Civitavecchia, it's easiest to get off at San Pietro Station (see page 518). Coming from Termini or elsewhere in town, take the Metro to Ottaviano, then walk 10 minutes south on Via Ottaviano. There are two good bus options: The #40 express bus drops off at Piazza Pio, next to Castel Sant'Angelo—a 10-minute walk to St. Peter's. The more crowded bus #64 is convenient for pickpockets and stops just outside St. Peter's Square to the south (after crossing the Tiber, take the first stop past the tunnel; backtrack toward the tunnel and turn left when you see the rows of columns). A taxi from Termini train station to St. Peter's costs about €10.

Avoiding the Line: To bypass the long security-checkpoint line, visit the Vatican Museum first (though it has its own long lines and checkpoint), then take the shortcut from the Sistine Chapel directly to St. Peter's. (Note, though, that this shortcut isn't always open; you may need to wait a bit.) If you visit the museum first, remember that St. Peter's dress code is stricter than the Vatican Museum's.

Information: The TI on the left (south) side of the square is excellent (Mon-Sat 8:30-18:30, closed Sun, free Vatican and church map, tel. 06-6988-1662, www.saintpetersbasilica.org—has detailed map).

Services: WCs are to the right and left on St. Peter's Square, near baggage storage past the security checkpoint, and on the roof. **Drinking fountains** are at the obelisk and near WCs. The **post office** is next to the TI (you can buy stamps and postcards and drop them into a postbox).

Tours: The Vatican TI conducts free 1.5-hour tours of **St. Peter's** (depart Mon-Fri from TI, generally at 9:45 and 14:15, confirm schedule at TI, tel. 06-6988-1662). Audioguides can be rented near the checkroom (€5 plus ID, daily 9:00-17:00).

Length of This Tour: Allow one hour, plus another hour if you climb the dome.

Checkroom: The free bag check (mandatory for bags larger than a purse or daypack) is outside the basilica (to the right as you face the entrance), and just inside the security checkpoint.

Starring: Michelangelo, Bernini, St. Peter, a heavenly host...and, occasionally, the pope.

ROME

Vatican City

This tiny independent country of little more than 100 acres, contained entirely within Rome, has its own postal system, dress code (dress modestly—even if you're just wandering through the square), armed guards, helipad, mini-train station, and radio station (KPOP). Politically powerful, the Vatican is the religious capital of 1.1 billion Roman Catholics. If you're not a Catholic, become one for your visit.

The pope is both the religious and secular leader of Vatican City. For centuries, locals referred to him as "King Pope." Italy and the Vatican didn't always have good relations. In fact, after unification (in 1870), when Rome's modern grid plan was built around the miniscule Vatican, it seemed as if the new buildings were designed to be just high enough so no one could see the dome of St. Peter's from street level. Modern Italy was created in 1870, but the Holy See didn't recognize it as a country until 1929, when the pope and Mussolini signed the Lateran Pact, giving sovereignty to the Vatican and a few nearby churches.

Like every European country, Vatican City has its own versions of the euro coin (with a portrait of the pope). You're unlikely to find one in your pocket, though, as they are snatched up by collectors before falling into actual circulation.

Small as it is, Vatican City has two huge sights: St. Peter's Basilica (with Michelangelo's *Pietà*) and the Vatican Museum (with the Sistine Chapel). The Vatican post office, with offices on St. Peter's Square (next to TI) and in the Vatican Museum, is famous for its stamps (Mon-Sat 8:30-18:30, closed Sun). Vatican stamps are good throughout Rome, but to use the Vatican's mail service, you need to mail your cards from the Vatican; write your postcards ahead of time. (Note that the Vatican won't mail cards with Italian stamps.)

The Tour Begins

• *Find a shady spot where you like the view under the columns around St. Peter's oval-shaped "square." If the pigeons left a clean spot, sit on it.*

Background

Nearly 2,000 years ago, this area was the site of Nero's Circus—a huge cigar-shaped Roman chariot racecourse. The tall obelisk you see in the middle of the square once stood about 100 yards from its current location, in the center of the circus course (to the left of where St. Peter's is today). The Romans had no marching bands, so for halftime entertainment they killed Christians. This persecuted minority was forced to fight wild animals and gladiators, or they were simply crucified. Some were tarred up, tied to posts, and burned—human torches to light up the evening races.

One of those killed here, in about A.D. 65, was Peter, Jesus'

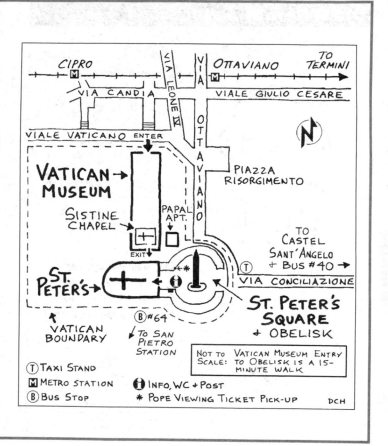

right-hand man, who had come to Rome to spread the message of love. At his own request, Peter was crucified upside-down, because he felt unworthy to die as his master had. His remains were buried in a nearby cemetery located where the main altar in St. Peter's is today. For 250 years, these relics were quietly and secretly revered.

Peter had been recognized as the first "pope," or bishop of Rome, from whom all later popes claimed their authority as head of the Church. When Christianity was finally legalized in 313, the Christian emperor Constantine built a church on the site of Peter's martyrdom. "Old St. Peter's" lasted 1,200 years (A.D. 329-1500).

By the time of the Renaissance, Old St. Peter's was falling apart and was considered unfit to be the center of the Western Church. The new, larger church we see today was begun in 1506 by the architect Bramante. He was succeeded by Michelangelo and a number of other architects, each with his own designs. Carlo

Old & New St. Peter's

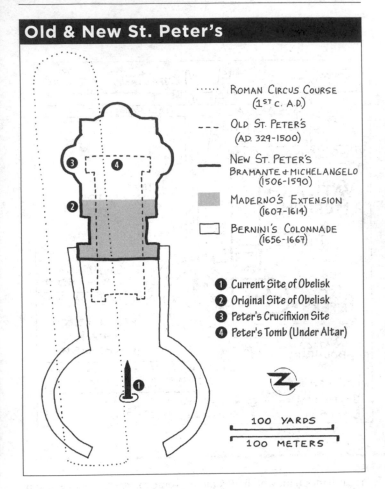

...... ROMAN CIRCUS COURSE
(1ST C. A.D.)

--- OLD ST. PETER'S
(A.D. 329-1500)

— NEW ST. PETER'S
BRAMANTE & MICHELANGELO
(1506-1590)

MADERNO'S EXTENSION
(1607-1614)

BERNINI'S COLONNADE
(1656-1667)

❶ Current Site of Obelisk
❷ Original Site of Obelisk
❸ Peter's Crucifixion Site
❹ Peter's Tomb (Under Altar)

100 YARDS

100 METERS

Maderno took Michelangelo's Greek cross-shaped church and lengthened it, adding a long nave. As the construction proceeded, they actually built the new church around the old one (see diagram above). The project was finally finished 120 years later, and Old St. Peter's was dismantled and carried out of the new church. (A few bits survive from the first church: the central door, some columns in the atrium, eight spiral columns around the tomb from the Jerusalem Temple, the venerated statue of Peter, and Michelangelo's *Pietà*.)

Michelangelo designed the magnificent dome. Unfortunately, although it soars above

ROME

St. Peter's, it's barely visible from the center of the square due to Maderno's extended nave. To see the entire dome, you'll need to step outside the open end of the square, where in the 1930s Benito Mussolini opened up the broad boulevard, finally letting people see the dome that had been hidden for centuries by the facade. Though I don't make a habit of thanking fascist dictators, in this case I'll make an exception: *"Grazie, Benito."*

• *More on the church later—for now, let's talk about the square. Ideally, you should head out to the obelisk to view the square and read this. But let me guess—it's 95 degrees outside, right? OK, read on in the shade of these stone sequoias.*

St. Peter's Square

St. Peter's Square, with its ring of columns, symbolizes the arms of the church welcoming everyone—believers and non-believers—with its motherly embrace. It was designed a century after Michelangelo by the Baroque architect Gian Lorenzo Bernini, who did much of the work that we'll see inside. Numbers first: 284 columns, 56 feet high, in stern Doric style. Topping them are Bernini's 140 favorite saints, each 10 feet tall. The "square" itself is actually elliptical, 660 by 500 feet. Though large, it's designed like a saucer, a little higher around the edges, so that even when full of crowds (as it often is), it allows those on the periphery to see above the throngs.

The obelisk in the center is 90 feet of solid granite weighing more than 300 tons. Think for a second about how much his-

tory this monument has seen. Originally erected in Egypt more than 2,000 years ago, it witnessed the fall of the pharaohs to the Greeks and then to the Romans. Then the emperor Caligula moved it to imperial Rome, where it stood impassively watching the slaughter of Christians at the racecourse and the torture of Protestants by the Inquisition (in the yellow-and-rust building just outside the square, to the left of the church). Today, it watches over the church, a reminder that each civilization builds on the previous ones. The puny cross on top reminds us that Christian culture has cast but a thin veneer over our pagan origins.

• *Now venture out across the burning desert to the obelisk, which provides a narrow sliver of shade.*

As you face the church, the gray building to the right at two o'clock, rising up behind Bernini's colonnade, is where the pope

ROME

St. Peter's Square

ST. PETER'S
BASILICA

(DOME)

B
BUS
#64

WALL

SISTINE
CHAPEL

BERNINI'S
COLONNADE

ST. PETER'S
SQUARE

VATICAN
WALL

VIA DI PTA.
ANGELICA

VIA DELLA
CONCILIAZIONE

N

❶ Obelisk

❷ Papal Apartments
(Top Story, Right)

❸ Sistine Chapel
(in Vatican Museum)

❹ "Centro del Colonnato"
Plaque

❺ Swiss Guard at Vatican
City Entrance

❻ Papal Ticket Pick-up
at Bronze Doors

❼ Tourist Info, Vatican Post
Office, Bookstore & WC

❽ Baggage Checkroom,
Audioguides & WC

❾ Exit from Sistine Chapel

❿ Elevator to Dome &
Crypt Entrance

⓫ To Ottaviano Metro (10 min),
Cipro Metro (20 min) &
Vatican Museum (15 min)

lives. The last window on the right
of the top floor is his bedroom.
To the left of that window is his
study window, where he appears
occasionally to greet the masses. If
you come to the square at night as
a Poping Tom, you might see the
light on—the pope burns much
midnight oil.

ROME

On more formal occasions (which you may have seen on TV),
the pope appears from the church itself, on the small balcony above
the central door.

The Sistine Chapel is just to the right of the facade—the
small gray-brown building with the triangular roof, topped by an
antenna. The tiny chimney (the pimple along the roofline midway up the left side) is where the famous smoke signals announce
the election of each new pope. If the smoke is black, a two-thirds
majority hasn't been reached. White smoke means a new pope has
been selected.

Walk to the right, five pavement plaques from the obelisk,

to one marked *Centro del Colonnato.* From here, all of Bernini's columns on the right side line up. The curved Baroque square still pays its respects to Renaissance mathematical symmetry.

• *Climb the gradually sloping pavement past crowd barriers, the security checkpoint, and the huge statues of St. Paul (with his two-edged sword) and St. Peter (with his bushy hair and keys). Along the way, you'll pass by the dress-code enforcers and a gaggle of ticked-off guys in shorts.*

On the square are two entrances to Vatican City: one to the left of the facade, and one to the right in the crook of Bernini's "arm" (the same entrance that hands out pope-viewing tickets). Guarding this small but powerful country's border crossing are the mercenary guards from Switzerland. You have to wonder if they really know how to use those pikes. Their colorful uniforms are said to have been designed by Michelangelo, though he was not known for his sense of humor.

• *Enter the atrium (entrance hall) of the church.*

The Basilica

The atrium is itself bigger than most churches. The huge white columns on the portico date from the first church (fourth century). Five famous bronze doors lead into the church.

Made from the melted-down bronze of the original door of Old St. Peter's, the central door was the first Renaissance work in Rome (c. 1450). It's only opened on special occasions. The panels (from the top down) feature Jesus and Mary, Paul and Peter, and (at the bottom) how each was martyred: Paul decapitated, Peter crucified upside-down.

The far-right entrance is the **Holy Door,** opened only during Holy Years. On Christmas Eve every 25 years, the pope knocks three times with a silver hammer and the door opens, welcoming pilgrims to pass through. After Pope John Paul II opened the door on Christmas Eve, 1999, he bricked it up again with a ceremonial trowel a year later to wait another 24 years. (A plaque above the door fudges a bit for effect: it says that Pope "IOANNES PAULUS II" opened the door in the year "MM"—2000—and closed it in "MMI.") On the door itself, note crucified Jesus' shiny knees, polished by pious pilgrims who touch them for a blessing.

• *Now for one of Europe's great "wow" experiences. Enter the church. Gape for a while. But don't gape at Michelangelo's famous* Pietà *(on the right). That's this tour's finale. I'll wait for you at the round maroon pavement stone on the floor near the central doorway.*

The Church

This church is appropriately huge. Size before beauty: The golden window at the far end is two football fields away. The dove in the window has the wingspan of a 747 (OK, maybe not quite, but it *is* big). The church covers six acres. The babies at the base of the pillars along the main hall (the nave) are adult-size. The lettering in the gold band along the top of the pillars is seven feet high. Really. The church has a capacity of 60,000 standing worshippers (or 1,200 tour groups).

The church is huge and it feels huge, but everything is designed to make it seem smaller and more intimate than it really is. For example, the statue of St. Teresa near the bottom of the first pillar on the right is 15 feet tall. The statue above her near the top looks the same size, but is actually six feet taller, giving the impression that it's not so far away. Similarly, the fancy bronze canopy over the altar at the far end is as tall as a seven-story building. That makes the great height of the dome seem smaller.

Looking down the nave, we get a sense of the splendor of ancient Rome that was carried on by the Catholic Church. The floor plan is based on the ancient Roman basilica, or law-court building, with a central aisle (nave) flanked by two side aisles. In fact, many of the stones used to build St. Peter's were scavenged from the ruined law courts of ancient Rome.

On the floor near the central doorway is a round slab of porphyry stone in the maroon color of ancient Roman officials. This is the spot where, on Christmas night in A.D. 800, the French king Charlemagne was crowned Holy Roman Emperor. Even in the Dark Ages, when Rome was virtually abandoned and visitors reported that the city had more thieves and wolves than decent people, its imperial legacy made it a fitting place to symbolically establish a briefly united Europe.

St. Peter's was very expensive to build and decorate. The popes financed it by selling "indulgences," allowing the rich to buy forgiveness for their sins from the Church. This kind of corruption inspired an obscure German monk named Martin Luther to rebel and start the Protestant Reformation.

The ornate, Baroque-style interior decoration—a riot of

St. Peter's Basilica

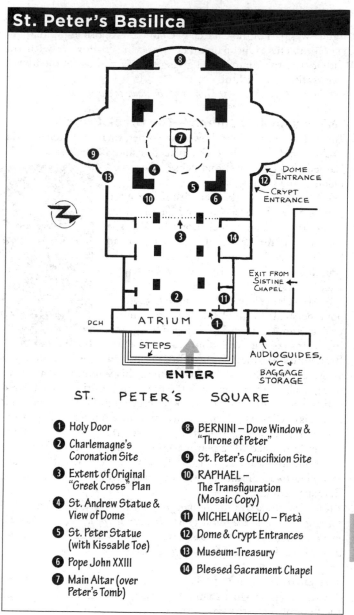

ST. PETER'S SQUARE

1. Holy Door
2. Charlemagne's Coronation Site
3. Extent of Original "Greek Cross" Plan
4. St. Andrew Statue & View of Dome
5. St. Peter Statue (with Kissable Toe)
6. Pope John XXIII
7. Main Altar (over Peter's Tomb)

8. BERNINI – Dove Window & "Throne of Peter"
9. St. Peter's Crucifixion Site
10. RAPHAEL – The Transfiguration (Mosaic Copy)
11. MICHELANGELO – Pietà
12. Dome & Crypt Entrances
13. Museum-Treasury
14. Blessed Sacrament Chapel

ROME

marble, gold, stucco, mosaics, columns of stone, and pillars of light—was part of the Church's "Counter-" Reformation. Baroque served as cheery propaganda, impressing followers with the authority of the Church, and giving them a glimpse of the heaven that awaited the faithful.

• *Now, walk straight up the center of the nave toward the altar.*

"Michelangelo's Church"—The Greek Cross

The plaques on the floor show where other, smaller churches of the world would end if they were placed inside St. Peter's: St. Paul's Cathedral in London (Londinense), Florence's Duomo, and so on.

You'll also walk over circular golden grates. Stop at the second one (at the third pillar from the entrance). Look back at the entrance and realize that if Michelangelo had had his way, this whole long section of the church wouldn't exist. The nave was extended after his death.

Michelangelo was 71 years old when the pope persuaded him to take over the church project and cap it with a dome. He agreed, intending to put the dome over Donato Bramante's original "Greek Cross" floor plan, with four equal arms. In optimistic Renaissance times, this symmetrical arrangement symbolized perfection—the orderliness of the created world and the goodness of man (who was created in God's image). But Michelangelo was a Renaissance man in Counter-Reformation times. The Church, struggling against Protestants and its own corruption, opted for a plan designed to impress the world with its grandeur—the Latin cross of the Crucifixion, with its nave extended to accommodate the grand religious spectacles of the Baroque period.

• *Continue toward the altar, entering "Michelangelo's Church." Park yourself in front of the statue of St. Andrew to the left of the altar, the guy holding an X-shaped cross. Like Andrew, gaze up into the dome, and also like him, gasp. (Never stifle a gasp.)*

The Dome

The dome soars higher than a football field on end, 448 feet from the floor of the cathedral to the top of the lantern. It glows with light from its windows, the blue and gold mosaics creating a cool, solemn atmosphere. In this majestic vision of heaven (not painted by Michelangelo), we see (above the windows) Jesus, Mary, and a ring of saints, more rings of angels above them, and, way up in the ozone, God the Father (a blur of blue and red without binoculars).

When Michelangelo died (1564), he'd completed only the drum of the dome—the circular base up as far as the windows—but the next architects were guided by his designs.

Listen to the hum of visitors echoing through St. Peter's and reflect on our place in the cosmos: half animal, half angel, stretched between heaven and earth, born to live only a short while, a bubble of foam on a great cresting wave of humanity.

• *But I digress.*

Peter

The base of the dome is ringed with a gold banner telling us in massive blue letters why this church is so important. According

to Catholics, Peter was selected by Jesus to head the church. The banner in Latin quotes from the Bible where Jesus says to him, "You are Peter *(Tu es Petrus)* and upon this rock I will build my church, and to you I will give the keys of the kingdom of heaven" (Matthew 16:18). (Every quote from Jesus to Peter found in the Bible is written out in seven-foot-tall letters that continue around the entire church.)

Peter was the first bishop of Rome. His prestige and that of the city itself made this bishopric more illustrious than all others, and Peter's authority has supposedly passed in an unbroken chain to each succeeding bishop of Rome—that is, the 250-odd popes that followed.

Under the dome, under the bronze canopy, under the altar, some 23 feet under the marble floor, rest the bones of St. Peter, the "rock" upon which this particular church was built. You can't see the tomb, but go to the railing and look down into the small, lighted niche below the altar with a box containing bishops' shawls—a symbol of how Peter's authority spread to the other churches. Peter's tomb (not visible) is just below this box.

Are they really the bones of Jesus' apostle? According to a papal pronouncement: definitely maybe. The traditional site of his tomb was sealed up when Old St. Peter's was built on it in A.D. 326, and it remained sealed until 1940, when it was opened for archaeological study. Bones were found, dated from the first century, of a robust man who died in old age. His body was wrapped

ROME

in expensive cloth. Various inscriptions and graffiti in the tomb indicate that second- and third-century visitors thought this was Peter's tomb. Does that mean it's really Peter? Who am I to disagree with the pope? Definitely maybe.

If you line up the cross on the altar with the dove in the window, you'll notice that the niche below the cross is just off-center compared with the rest of the church. Why? Because Michelangelo built the church around the traditional location of the tomb, not the actual location—about two feet away—discovered by modern archaeology.

Back in the nave sits a bronze statue of Peter under a canopy. This is one of a handful of pieces of art that were in the earlier church. In one hand he holds the keys, the symbol of the authority given him by Christ, while with the other hand he blesses us. He's wearing the toga of a Roman senator. It may be that the original statue was of a senator and that the bushy head and keys were added later to make it Peter. His big right toe has been worn smooth by the lips of pilgrims and foot-fetishists. Stand in line and kiss it, or, to avoid foot-and-mouth disease, touch your hand to your lips, then rub the toe. This is simply an act of reverence with no legend attached, though you can make one up if you like.

• *Circle to the right around the statue of Peter to find another popular stop among pilgrims: the lighted glass niche with the red-robed body of...*

Pope John XXIII

Pope John XXIII, who reigned 1958-1963, is nicknamed "the good pope." He is best known for initiating the landmark Vatican II Council (1962-1965) that instituted major reforms, bringing the Church into the modern age. The Council allowed Mass to be conducted in the vernacular rather than in Latin. Lay people were invited to participate more in services, Church leadership underwent some healthy self-criticism, and a spirit of ecumenism flourished. Pope John was a populist, referring to people as "brothers and sisters"...a phrase popular today among popes. In 2000, during the beatification process (a stop on the way to sainthood), Church authorities checked his body, and it was surprisingly fresh. So they moved it upstairs, put it behind glass, and now old Catholics who remember him fondly enjoy another stop on their St. Peter's visit.

The Main Altar

The main altar beneath the dome and canopy (the white marble slab with cross and candlesticks) is used only when the pope him-

self says Mass. He sometimes conducts the Sunday morning service when he's in town, a sight worth seeing. I must admit, though, it's a little strange being frisked at the door for weapons at the holiest place in Christendom.

The tiny altar would be lost in this enormous church if it weren't for Gian Lorenzo Bernini's seven-story bronze canopy (God's "four-poster bed"), which "extends" the altar upward and reduces the perceived distance between floor and ceiling. The corkscrew columns echo the marble ones that surrounded the altar/tomb in Old St. Peter's. Some of the bronze used here was taken and melted down from the ancient Pantheon. On the marble base of the columns are three bees on a shield, the symbol of the Barberini family, who commissioned the work and ordered the raid on the Pantheon. As the saying went, "What the barbarians didn't do, the Barberini did."

Starting from the column to the left of the altar, walk clockwise around the canopy. Notice the female faces on the marble bases, about eye level above the bees. Someone in the Barberini family was pregnant during the making of the canopy, so Bernini put the various stages of childbirth on the bases. Continue clockwise to the last base to see how it came out.

Bernini (1598-1680), the Michelangelo of the Baroque era, is the man most responsible for the interior decoration of the church. The altar area was his masterpiece, a "theater" for holy spectacles. Bernini did: 1) the bronze canopy; 2) the dove window in the apse, surrounded by bronze work and statues; 3) the statue of lance-bearing St. Longinus ("The hills are alive..."), which became the model for the other three statues; 4) much of the marble floor decoration; and 5) the balconies above the four statues, incorporating some of the actual corkscrew columns from Old St. Peter's, said to have been looted by the Romans from the Temple of Herod (called "Solomon's Temple") in Jerusalem. Bernini, the father of Baroque, gave an impressive unity to an amazing variety of pillars, windows, statues, chapels, and aisles.

• *Approach the apse, the front area with the golden dove window.*

The Apse

Bernini's dove window shines above the smaller front altar used for everyday services. The Holy Spirit, in the form of a six-foot-high dove, pours sunlight onto the faithful through the alabaster windows, turning into artificial rays of gold and reflecting off swirling gold clouds, angels, and winged babies. During a service, real sunlight passes through real clouds of incense, mingling with

ROME

Bernini Blitz

Nowhere is there such a conglomeration of works by the flamboyant genius who remade the church—and the city—in the Baroque style. Here's your scavenger-hunt list. You have 20 minutes. Go!

1. St. Peter's Square: design and statues
2. Constantine equestrian relief (right end of atrium)
3. Decoration (stucco, gold leaf, marble, etc.) of side aisles (flanking the nave)
4. Tabernacle (the temple-like altarpiece) inside Blessed Sacrament Chapel
5. Much of the marble floor throughout church
6. Bronze canopy over the altar
7. St. Longinus statue (holding a lance) near altar
8. Balconies (above each of the four statues) with corkscrew, Solomonic columns
9. Dove window, bronze sunburst, angels, "Throne," and Church Fathers (in the apse)
10. Tomb of Pope Urban VIII (far end of the apse, right side)
11. Tomb of Pope Alexander VII (between the apse and the left transept, over a doorway, with the gold skeleton smothered in jasper poured like maple syrup)

Bizarre...Baroque...Bernini.

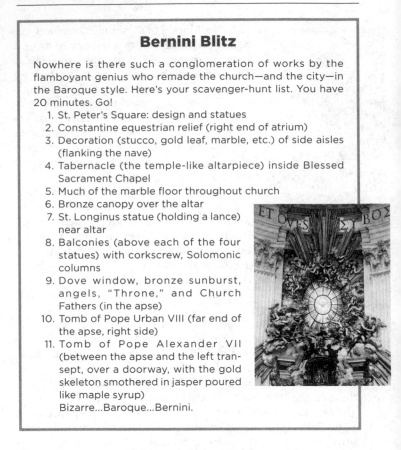

Bernini's sculpture. This is the epitome of Baroque—an ornate, mixed-media work designed to overwhelm the viewer.

Beneath the dove is the centerpiece of this structure, the so-called "Throne of Peter," an oak chair built in medieval times for a king. Subsequently, it was encrusted with tradition and encased in bronze by Bernini as a symbol of papal authority. Statues of four early Church Fathers support the chair, a symbol of how bishops should support the pope in troubled times—times like the Counter-Reformation.

Remember that St. Peter's is a church, not a museum. In the apse, Mass is said daily (Mon-Sat at 17:00, Sun at 17:45—after vespers at 17:00) for pilgrims, tourists, and Roman citizens alike. Wooden confessional booths are available in the north transept (to the right of the main altar) for Catholics to tell their sins to a listening ear and receive forgiveness and peace of mind (daily, usually mornings and late afternoons—see website). The faithful renew their faith, and the faithless gain inspiration. Look at the

ROME

light streaming through the windows, turn and gaze up into the dome, and quietly contemplate your deity (or lack thereof).

• *To the left of the main altar is the south transept. At the far end, left side, find the dark "painting" of St. Peter crucified upside-down.*

South Transept—Peter's Crucifixion Site

This marks the exact spot (according to tradition) where Peter was killed 1,900 years ago. Peter had come to the world's greatest city

to preach Jesus' message of love to the pagan, often hostile Romans. During the reign of Nero, he was arrested and brought to Nero's Circus so all Rome could witness his execution. When the authorities told Peter he was to be crucified just like his Lord, Peter said "I'm not worthy" and insisted they nail him on the cross upside-down.

The Romans were actually quite tolerant of other religions, but they required their conquered peoples to worship the Roman emperor as a god. For most religions, this was no problem, but monotheistic Christians refused to worship the emperor even when burned alive, crucified, or thrown to the lions. Their bravery, optimism in suffering, and message of love struck a chord among slaves and members of the lower classes. The religion started by a poor carpenter grew, despite occasional pogroms (persecution of minorities) by fanatical emperors. In three short centuries, Christianity went from a small Jewish sect in Jerusalem to the official religion of the world's greatest empire.

This and all the other "paintings" in the church are actually mosaic copies made from thousands of colored chips the size of your little fingernail. Smoke and humidity would damage real paintings. Around the corner on the right (heading back toward the central nave), pause at the copy of Raphael's huge "painting" (mosaic) of *The Transfiguration*, especially if you won't be seeing the original in the Vatican Museum.

• *Back near the entrance to the church, in the far corner, behind bullet-proof glass, is the...*

Pietà

Michelangelo was 24 years old when he completed this *Pietà* (pee-ay-TAH) of Mary with the dead body of Christ taken from the cross. It was Michelangelo's first major commission (by the French ambassador to the Vatican), done for Holy Year 1500.

Pietà means "pity." Michelangelo, with his total mastery of the real world, captures the sadness of the moment. Mary cradles her crucified son in her lap. Christ's lifeless right arm drooping down lets us know how heavy this corpse is. His smooth skin is accented by the rough folds of Mary's robe. Mary tilts her head down, looking at her dead son with sad tenderness. Her left hand turns upward, asking, "How could they do this to you?"

Michelangelo didn't think of sculpting as creating a figure, but as simply freeing the God-made figure from the prison of marble around it. He'd attack a project like this with an inspired passion, chipping away to find what God put inside.

The bunched-up shoulder and rigor-mortis legs show that Michelangelo learned well from his studies of cadavers. But realistic as this work is, its true power lies in the subtle "unreal" features. Life-size Christ looks childlike compared with larger-than-life Mary. Unnoticed at first, this accentuates the subconscious impression of Mary enfolding Jesus in her maternal love. Mary—the mother of a 33-year-old man—looks like a teenager, emphasizing how Mary was the eternally youthful "handmaiden" of the Lord, always serving him, even at this moment of supreme sacrifice. She accepts God's will, even if it means giving up her son.

The statue is a solid pyramid of maternal tenderness. Yet within this, Christ's body tilts diagonally down to the right and Mary's hem flows with it. Subconsciously, we feel the weight of this dead God sliding from her lap to the ground.

At 11:30 on May 23, 1972, a madman with a hammer entered St. Peter's and began hacking away at the *Pietà*. The damage was repaired, but that's why there's now a shield of bulletproof glass.

This is Michelangelo's only signed work. The story goes that he overheard some pilgrims praising his finished *Pietà*, but attributing it to a second-rate sculptor from a lesser city. He was so enraged that he grabbed his chisel and chipped "Michelangelo Buonarroti of Florence did this" in the ribbon running down Mary's chest.

On your right (covered in gray concrete with a gold cross) is the inside of the Holy Door. It won't be opened until Christmas Eve, 2024, the dawn of the next Jubilee Year. If there's a prayer inside you, ask that St. Peter's will no longer need security checks or bulletproof glass when this door is next opened.

Up to the Dome (Cupola)

A good way to finish a visit to St. Peter's is to go up to the dome for the best view of Rome anywhere (daily April-Sept 8:00-18:00, Oct-March 8:00-17:00). The entrance to the dome is along the

right side of the church, but the line begins to form out front, at the church's right door (as you face the church).

There are two levels: the rooftop of the church and the very top of the dome. Climb (for €5) or take an elevator (€7) to the first level, on the church roof just above the facade. From the roof, you have a commanding view of St. Peter's Square, the statues on the colonnade, Rome across the Tiber in front of you, and the dome itself—almost terrifying in its nearness—looming behind you.

From here, you can also go inside to the gallery ringing the interior of the dome, where you can look down inside the church. Notice the dusty top of Bernini's seven-story-tall canopy far below. Study the mosaics up close—and those huge letters! It's worth the elevator ride for this view alone.

From this level, if you're energetic, continue all the way up to the top of the dome. The staircase actually winds between the outer shell and the inner one. It's a sweaty, crowded, claustrophobic 15-minute, 323-step climb, but worth it. The view from the summit is great, the fresh air even better. Admire the arms of Bernini's colonnade encircling St. Peter's Square. Find the big, white Victor Emmanuel Monument, with the two statues on top; and the Pantheon, with its large, light, shallow dome. The large rectangular building to the left of the obelisk is the Vatican Museum, stuffed with art. Survey the Vatican

grounds, with its mini-train system and lush gardens. Look down into the square on the tiny pilgrims buzzing like electrons around the nucleus of Catholicism.

ROME

Walk Across Rome

From Campo de' Fiori to the Spanish Steps

Rome can be grueling. But taking a walk is a fine way to mix romance into all the history, and enliven everything with some of Europe's best people-watching. This walk shows Rome at its most colorful, as it meanders through narrow streets and past important monuments. Allow anywhere from one to three hours for this walk, depending on whether you linger (yes, do) and tour the Pantheon (another good idea).

Walk Across Rome

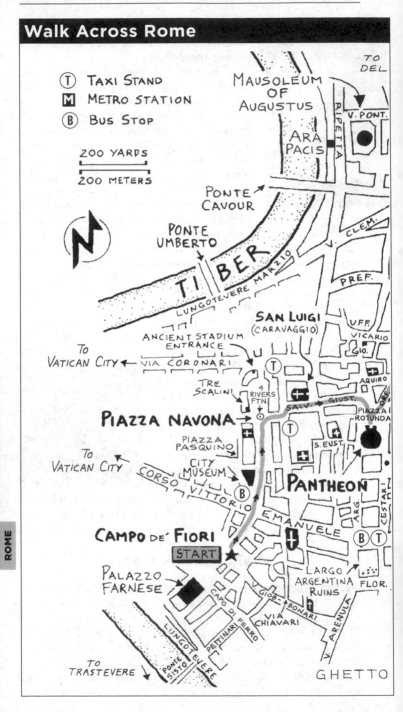

(T) Taxi Stand
(M) Metro Station
(B) Bus Stop

200 YARDS
200 METERS

MAUSOLEUM OF AUGUSTUS

TO DEL

V. PONT.

RIPETTA

ARA PACIS

PONTE CAVOUR

V. CLEM.

PONTE UMBERTO

TIBER

LUNGOTEVERE MARZIO

PREF.

SAN LUIGI (CARAVAGGIO)

V. UFF.

VICARIO GIO.

To Vatican City ←

ANCIENT STADIUM ENTRANCE

VIA CORONARI

(T)

AQUIRO

TRE SCALINI

4 RIVERS FTN.

SALV. → GIUST.

PIAZZA ROTUNDA

PIAZZA NAVONA

(T)

PIAZZA PASQUINO

S. EUST.

To Vatican City ←

CORSO VITTORIO

CITY MUSEUM

(B)

PANTHEON

ARG.

CESTARI

EMANUELE

CAMPO DE' FIORI

(B)(T)

START

PALAZZO FARNESE

LARGO ARGENTINA RUINS

FLOR.

CAPO DI FERRO

V. GIOB-BONARI

VIA CHIAVARI

V. ARENULA

PETTINARI

LUNGOTEVERE

PONTE SISTO

To TRASTEVERE ↓

GHETTO

ROME

PIAZZA POPOLO

M SPAGNA

VILLA BORGHESE

S. TRINITÀ MONTI

SPANISH STEPS

END

BABUINA

VITTORIO

CROCE

CAROZZE

CONDOTTI

V. BORGOGNONA

V. FRATTINA

V. VITE

POST

PIAZZA MIGNANELLI

McD

DUE MACELLI

To BARBERINI

M

S. AND

NAZ

DEL TRITONE

PIAZZA COLONNA

PARL.

P. MONTE.

P. COLONNA

Galleria DEL SORDI

VIA

STAMP.

SABINI

MURATTE

CORSO

DATARIA

Trevi Fountain

GUGLIA

PZZA PIETRA

PASTINI

SEMINARIO

San Ignazio

STA. MARIA SOPRA MINERVA

Galleria DORA PAMPHILJ

V. IV

B

NOV.

To TERMINI

V. PLEBISCITO

Gesù

BOTT. OSC.

ARACOELI

PIAZZA VENEZIA

T

FORI IMPERIALI

CAPITOL HILL

V.E. MON.

To COLOSSEUM & M

F O R U M

DCH

ROME

Sitting so close to a Bernini fountain that traffic noises evaporate; jostling with local teenagers to see all the gelato flavors; observing lovers straddling more than the bench; jaywalking past *polizia* in flak-proof vests; and marveling at the ramshackle elegance that softens this brutal city for those who were born here and can imagine living nowhere else—these are the flavors of Rome.

The Walk Begins

• *Start this mile-long walk at Campo de' Fiori, my favorite outdoor dining room. This walk is equally pleasant in reverse order: You could ride the Metro to the Spanish Steps and finish at Campo de' Fiori.*

Campo de' Fiori

The center of the great, colorful square is marked with the statue of Giordano Bruno, an intellectual heretic who was burned on this spot in 1600. Bruno overlooks this  "Field of Flowers," the site of a busy produce market in the morning and a favorite of strollers after sundown. This neighborhood is still known for its free spirit and occasional demonstrations. When the statue of Bruno was erected in 1889, local riots overcame Vatican protests against honoring a heretic. Bruno faces his nemesis, the Vatican Chancellory (the big white building just outside the far-right corner of the square), while his pedestal reads, "And the flames rose up." Check out the reliefs on the pedestal for scenes from Bruno's trial and execution.

At the east end of the square (behind Bruno), the ramshackle apartments are built right into the old outer wall of ancient Rome's mammoth Theater of Pompey. This entertainment complex covered several city blocks, stretching from here to Largo Argentina. Julius Caesar was assassinated in the Theater of Pompey, where the Senate was renting space.

The square is lined with and surrounded by fun eateries. Bruno faces the **Forno** (in the left corner of the square, closed Sun), a popular place for hot and tasty take-out *pizza bianco*. Step in, at least to observe the frenzy as pizza is sold hot out of the oven. You can order *un etto* (100 grams, an average serving) by pointing, then take your snack to the counter to pay. The many bars lining the square are fine for drinks and people-watching. Late at night on weekends, the place is packed with beer-drinking kids, turning what was once a charming medieval square into one vast Roman street party.

• *If Bruno did a hop, step, and jump forward, then turned right on Via dei Baullari and marched 200 yards, he'd cross the busy Corso Vittorio Emanuele; then, continuing another 150 yards on Via Cuccagna, he'd find...*

Piazza Navona

Rome's most interesting scene features street music, artists, fire-eaters, local Casanovas, ice cream, fountains by Bernini, and outdoor cafés that are worthy of a splurge if you've got time to sit and enjoy Italy's human river.

This oblong square retains the shape of the original race-track that was built around A.D. 80 by the emperor Domitian. (To see the ruins of the original entrance, exit the square at the far—or north—end, then take an immediate left, and look down to the left 25 feet below the current street level.) Since ancient times, the square has been a center of Roman life. In the 1800s, the city would flood the square to cool off the neighborhood.

The **Four Rivers Fountain** in the center is the most famous fountain by the man who remade Rome in Baroque style, Gian Lorenzo Bernini. Four burly river gods (representing the four continents that were known in 1650) support an Egyptian obelisk. The water of the world gushes everywhere. The Nile has his head covered, since the headwaters were unknown then. The Ganges holds an oar. The Danube turns to admire the obelisk, which Bernini had moved here from a stadium on the Appian Way. And Uruguay's Río de la Plata tumbles backward in shock, wondering how he ever made the top four. Bernini enlivens the fountain with horses plunging through the rocks and exotic flora and fauna from these newly discovered lands. Homesick Texans may want to find the armadillo. (It's the big, weird armor-plated creature behind the Plata river statue.)

The Plata river god is gazing upward at the church of St. Agnes, worked on by Bernini's former student-turned-rival, Francesco Borromini. Borromini's concave facade helps reveal the dome and epitomizes the curved symmetry of Baroque. Tour guides say that Bernini designed his river god to look horrified at Borromini's work. Or maybe he's shielding his eyes from St. Agnes' nakedness, as she was stripped before being martyred. But either explanation is unlikely, since the fountain was completed two years before Borromini even started work on the church.

• *Leave Piazza Navona directly across from Tre Scalini (famous for its rich chocolate ice cream), and go east down Corsia Agonale, past rose peddlers and palm readers. Jog left around the guarded building (where Italy's senate meets), and follow the brown sign to the Pantheon, which is straight down Via del Salvatore.*

The Pantheon

Sit for a while under the floodlit and moonlit portico of the Pantheon.

The 40-foot single-piece granite columns of the Pantheon's entrance show the scale the ancient Romans built on. The columns

support a triangular Greek-style roof with an inscription that says "M. Agrippa" built it. In fact, it was built *(fecit)* by Emperor Hadrian (A.D. 120), who gave credit to the builder of an earlier structure. This impressive entranceway gives no clue that the greatest wonder of the building is inside—a domed room that inspired later domes, including Michelangelo's St. Peter's and Brunelleschi's Duomo (in Florence).

For more information, see "Pantheon Tour" on page 560.

• *With your back to the Pantheon, veer to the right, uphill toward the yellow sign that reads* Casa del Caffè *at the Tazza d'Oro coffee shop on Via Orfani.*

From the Pantheon to Piazza Colonna

Tazza d'Oro Casa del Caffè, one of Rome's top coffee shops, dates back to the days when this area was licensed to roast coffee beans. Locals come here for its fine *granita di caffè con panna* (coffee slush with cream).

• *Continue up Via Orfani to...*

Piazza Capranica is home to the big, plain Florentine Renaissance-style Palazzo Capranica (directly opposite as you enter the square). Big shots, like the Capranica family, built towers on their palaces—not for any military use, but just to show off.

• *Leave the piazza to the right of the palace, heading down Via in Aquiro.*

The street Via in Aquiro leads to a sixth-century B.C. **Egyptian obelisk** taken as a trophy by Augustus after his victory in Egypt over Mark Antony and Cleopatra.

The obelisk was set up as a sundial. Walk the zodiac markings to the well-guarded front door. This is Italy's **parliament building,** where the lower house meets, and you may see politicians, political demonstrations, and TV cameras.

• *To your right is Piazza Colonna, where we're heading next—unless you like gelato...*

A two-block detour to the left (past Albergo Nazionale) brings you to Rome's most famous *gelateria.* **Giolitti's** is cheap for take-out or elegant and splurge-worthy for a sit among classy locals (open daily until past midnight, Via Uffici del Vicario 40); get your gelato in a cone *(cono)* or cup *(coppetta).*

Piazza Colonna features a huge second-century column. Its reliefs depict the victories of Emperor Marcus Aurelius over the barbarians. When Marcus died in A.D. 180, the barbarians began to get the upper hand, beginning Rome's long three-century fall. The big, important-looking palace houses the headquarters for the deputies (or cabinet) of the prime minister.

Noisy **Via del Corso** is Rome's main north-south boulevard. It's named for the Berber horse races—without riders—that took place here during Carnevale. This wild tradition continued until the late 1800s, when a series of fatal accidents (including, reportedly, one in front of Queen Margherita) led to its cancellation. Historically the street was filled with meat shops. When it became one of Rome's first gas-lit streets in 1854, these butcher shops were banned and replaced by classier boutiques, jewelers, and antiques dealers. Nowadays most of Via del Corso is closed to traffic for a few hours every evening and becomes a wonderful parade of Romans out for a stroll.

• *Cross Via del Corso to enter a big palatial building with columns, which houses the Galleria del Sordi shopping mall. Inside, take the fork to the right and exit out the back. (If you're here after 22:00, when the mall is closed, circle around the right side of the Galleria on Via dei Sabini.) Once out the back, head up Via de Crociferi, to the roar of the water, lights, and people of...*

ROME

The Trevi Fountain

The Trevi Fountain shows how Rome took full advantage of the abundance of water brought into the city by its great aqueducts. This watery Baroque avalanche by Nicola Salvi was completed in 1762. Salvi used the palace behind the fountain as a theatrical backdrop for the figure of "Ocean," who represents water in every form. The statue surfs through his wet kingdom—with water

gushing from 24 spouts and tumbling over 30 different kinds of plants—while Triton blows his conch shell.

The magic of the square is enhanced by the fact that no streets directly approach it. You can hear the excitement as you approach, and then—*bam!*—you're there. The scene is always lively, with lucky Romeos clutching dates while unlucky ones clutch beers. Romantics toss a coin over their shoulder, thinking it will give them a wish and assure their return to Rome. That may sound silly, but every year I go through this tourist ritual...and it actually seems to work.

Take some time to people-watch (whisper a few breathy *bellos* or *bellas*) before leaving. There's a peaceful zone at water level on the far right.

• *From the Trevi Fountain, we're 10 minutes from our next stop, the Spanish Steps. Just use a map to get there, or follow these directions: Facing the Trevi Fountain, go forward, walking along the right side of the fountain on Via della Stamperia. Cross the busy Via del Tritone. Continue 100 yards and veer right at Via delle Fratte, a street that changes its name to Via Propaganda before ending at...*

The Spanish Steps

Piazza di Spagna, with the very popular Spanish Steps, is named

for the Spanish Embassy to the Vatican, which has been here for 300 years. It's been the hangout of many Romantics over the years (Keats, Wagner, Openshaw, Goethe, and others). In the 1700s, British aristocrats on the "Grand Tour" of Europe came here to ponder Rome's decay. The British poet John Keats pondered his mortality, then died of tuberculosis at age 25 in the pink building on the right side of the steps. Fellow Romantic Lord Byron lived across the square at #66.

The Sinking Boat Fountain at the foot of the steps, built by Bernini or his father, Pietro, is powered by an aqueduct. Actually, all of Rome's fountains are aqueduct-powered; their spurts are determined by the water pressure provided by the various aqueducts. This one, for instance, is much weaker than Trevi's gush.

The piazza thrives day and night. It's clear that the main

sight here is not the famous steps, but the people who sit on them. Window-shop along Via Condotti, which stretches away from the steps. This is where Gucci and other big names cater to the trendsetting jet set. Facing the Spanish Steps, you can walk right, about a block, to tour one of the world's biggest and most lavish McDonald's (salad bar, WC).

• *Our walk is finished. If you'd like to reach the top of the steps sweat-free, there's a free elevator just outside the Spagna Metro stop (elevator closes at 21:00; Metro stop is to the left of the Spanish Steps). Afterward, you can zip elsewhere on the Metro (usually open until 22:00) or grab a taxi at either the north or south side of the piazza.*

Sights in Rome

I've clustered Rome's sights into walkable neighborhoods, some quite close together (see the "Rome's Neighborhoods" map on page 521). For example, the Colosseum and the Forum are a few minutes' walk from Capitol Hill; a 10-minute walk beyond that is the Pantheon.

While Rome has other sights worth knowing about on a longer visit (see the "Rome at a Glance" sidebar, earlier), for a one-day cruiser visit, I've listed just the main sights within the city center.

Don't let the length of my descriptions determine your sightseeing priorities. In this section, Rome's most important sights have the shortest listings. These sights are covered in much more detail in one of the earlier walks or tours.

Ancient Rome

The core of the ancient city, where the grandest monuments were built, is between the Colosseum and Capitol Hill. To the north, this ancient area flows into the Renaissance at Capitol Hill, then into the modern era at Piazza Venezia.

The Colosseum and Nearby

▲▲▲**Colosseum (Colosseo)**—This 2,000-year-old building is the classic example of Roman engineering. Used as a venue for entertaining the masses, this colossal, functional stadium is one of Europe's most recognizable landmarks. For a self-guided tour, see page 536.

Cost and Hours: €12 combo-ticket includes Roman Forum and Palatine Hill, audioguide and tours available; open daily 8:30 until one hour before sunset: April-Sept until 19:15, Oct until 18:30, off-season closes as early as 16:30; last entry one hour before closing, Metro: Colosseo.

▲**Arch of Constantine**—This well-preserved arch, which stands between the Colosseum and the Forum, commemorates a military

ROME

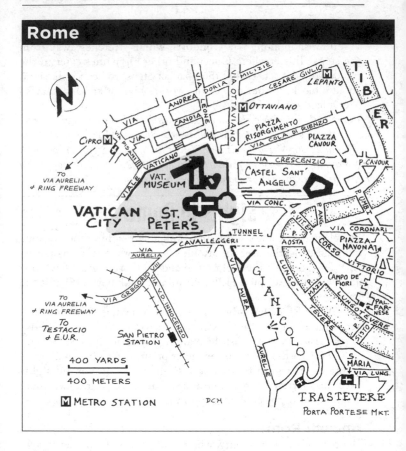

Rome

coup and, more importantly, the acceptance of Christianity by the Roman Empire. The arch is free to see—always open and viewable. For more information, see page 544.

▲**St. Peter-in-Chains Church (San Pietro in Vincoli)**—Built in the fifth century to house the chains that held St. Peter, this church is most famous for its Michelangelo statue. Check out the much-venerated chains under the high altar, then focus on mighty *Moses*. (Note that this isn't the famous St. Peter's Basilica, which is at Vatican City.)

Pope Julius II commissioned Michelangelo to build a massive tomb, with 48 huge statues, crowned by a grand statue of this egomaniacal pope. The pope had planned to have his tomb placed in the center of St. Peter's Basilica. When Julius died, the work had barely been started, and no one had the money or necessary commitment to Julius to finish the project.

In 1542, some of the remnants of the tomb project were brought

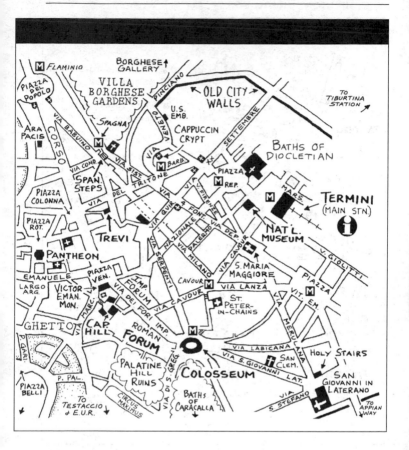

to St. Peter-in-Chains and pieced together by Michelangelo's assistants. Some of the best statues ended up elsewhere, like the *Prisoners* in Florence, and the *Slaves* in the Louvre. *Moses* and the Louvre's *Slaves* are the only statues Michelangelo personally completed for the project. Flanking *Moses* are the Old Testament sister-wives of Jacob, Leah (to our right) and Rachel, both begun by Michelangelo but probably finished by pupils.

This powerful statue of Moses—mature Michelangelo—is worth studying. The artist worked on it in fits and starts for 30 years. Moses has received the Ten Commandments. As he holds the stone tablets, his eyes show a man determined to stop his tribe from worshipping the golden calf and idols...a man determined to win salvation for the people of Israel. Why the horns? Centuries ago, the Hebrew word for "rays" was mistranslated as "horns."

Cost and Hours: Free, April-Sept 8:00-12:30 & 15:30-19:00, Oct-March 8:00-12:30 & 15:00-18:00, modest dress required; the

ROME

Ancient Rome

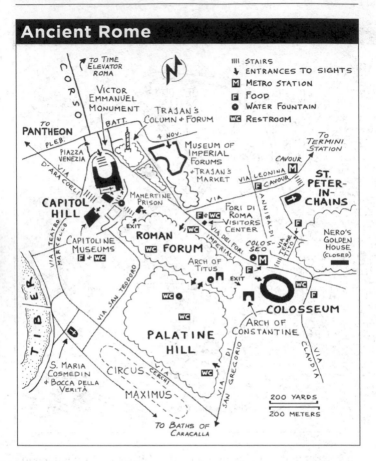

church is a 15-minute uphill, zigzag walk from the Colosseum, or a shorter, simpler walk from the Cavour Metro stop—from that station, go downhill on Via Cavour a half-block, then climb the pedestrian staircase called Via di San Francesco di Paola, which leads right to the church.

Nero's Golden House (Domus Aurea)—The sparse underground remains of Emperor Nero's "Golden House" are a faint shadow of their ancient grandeur. While it's exciting to think that Nero's house survives, it's in a sad state of ruin, and has been closed to the public indefinitely.

The Roman Forum and Nearby

▲▲▲**Roman Forum (Foro Romano)**—This is ancient Rome's birthplace and civic center, and the common ground between Rome's famous seven hills. As just about anything important that happened in ancient Rome happened here, it's arguably the most important piece of real estate in Western civilization. For a self-guided tour, see page 547.

Cost and Hours: €12 combo-ticket includes Colosseum and Palatine Hill, audio-guide available; open daily 8:30 until one hour before sunset: April-Sept until 19:15, Oct until 18:30, off-season closes as early as 16:30; last entry one hour before closing, Metro: Colosseo, tel. 06-3996-7700.

▲▲**Palatine Hill (Monte Palatino)**—The hill overlooking the Forum is jam-packed with history—"the huts of Romulus," the

huge Imperial Palace, a view of the Circus Maximus—but there's only the barest skeleton of rubble left to tell the story.

We get our word "palace" from this hill, where the emperors chose to live. The Palatine Hill was once so filled with palaces that later emperors had to build out. (Looking up at it from the Forum, you see the substructure that supported these long-gone palaces.)

The Palatine museum contains statues and frescoes that help you imagine the luxury of the imperial Palatine. From the pleasant garden, you'll get an overview of the Forum. On the far side, look down into an emperor's private stadium and then beyond at the dusty Circus Maximus, once a chariot course. Imagine the cheers, jeers, and furious betting.

While many tourists consider the Palatine Hill just extra credit after the Forum, it offers an insight into the greatness of Rome that's well worth the effort. (And, if you're visiting the Colosseum or Forum, you've got a ticket whether you like it or not.)

Cost and Hours: €12 combo-ticket also includes Roman Forum and Colosseum; open same hours as Roman Forum and Colosseum, Metro: Colosseo. Audioguides cost €4 (€6 version includes Roman Forum, must leave ID). Guided tours in English are offered once daily at 11:30 (€4, 45 minutes, not always available off-season); ask for information at the ticket booth. The entrance is on Via di San Gregorio (facing the Forum with the Colosseum at your back, it's down the street to your left). You can also enter the Palatine from within the Roman Forum—just climb the hill from the Arch of Titus.

▲**Mamertine Prison**—This 2,500-year-old cistern-like prison, which once held the bodies of Saints Peter and Paul, is worth a

ROME

look—unless it's still closed for renovation when you visit. When you step into the room, ignore the modern floor and look up at the hole in the ceiling, through which prisoners were lowered. Then take the stairs down to the level of the actual prison floor. Downstairs, you'll see the column to which Peter was chained. It's said that a miraculous fountain sprang up in this room so that Peter could convert and baptize his jailers, who were also subsequently martyred. The upside-down cross commemorates Peter's upside-down crucifixion.

Imagine humans, amid fat rats and rotting corpses, awaiting slow deaths. On the walls near the entry are lists of notable prisoners (Christian and non-Christian) and the ways they were executed: *strangolati, decapitato, morto per fame* (died of hunger). The sign by the Christian names reads, "Here suffered, victorious for the triumph of Christ, these martyr saints."

Cost and Hours: Ovepriced at €10, daily 9:00-19:00 if renovation completed, at the foot of Capitol Hill, near Forum's Arch of Septimius Severus.

▲**Trajan's Column, Market, and Imperial Forums**—This grand column is the best example of "continuous narration" that we have from antiquity. More than 2,500 figures scroll around the 140-foot-high column, telling of Trajan's victorious Dacian campaign (circa A.D. 103, in present-day Romania), from the assembling of the army at the bottom to the victory sacrifice at the top. The ashes of Trajan and his wife were once held in the base, and the sun once glinted off a polished bronze statue of Trajan at the top. (Today, St. Peter is on top.) Study the propaganda that winds up the column like a scroll, trumpeting Trajan's wonderful military exploits. Viewing balconies once stood on either side, but it seems likely that Trajan fans came away only with a feeling that the greatness of their emperor and empire was beyond comprehension (for a rolled-out version of the column's story, visit the E.U.R.'s Museum of Roman Civilization). This column marked "Trajan's Forum," which was built to handle the shopping needs of a wealthy city of more than a million people. Commercial, political, religious, and social activities all mixed in the forum.

Nestled into the cutaway curve of Quirinal Hill is the semi-circular brick complex of **Trajan's Market.** It was likely part shopping mall, part warehouse, and part administration building. Or, as some archaeologists have recently suggested, it may have contained mostly government offices.

Paying the admission fee gets you inside Trajan's Market, Trajan's Forum, and the **Museum of the Imperial Forums.** The museum takes you through discoveries from the forums of emperors Julius Caesar, Augustus, Nerva, and Trajan, with fragments of statues and a slideshow that reconstructs how the forum looked in each emperor's time.

Trajan's Column is just a few steps off Piazza Venezia (a hub for major bus routes #40 and #64), on Via dei Fori Imperiali, across the street from the Victor Emmanuel Monument. Trajan's Market can be entered only through the Museum of the Imperial Forums at Via IV Novembre 94. Trajan's Forum stretches southeast of the column toward the Colosseo Metro stop and the Colosseum itself.

Cost and Hours: €7, includes entry to the market ruins, Tue-Sun 9:00-19:00, closed Mon, last entry 30 minutes before closing, Via IV Novembre 94, up the staircase from Trajan's Column; tel. 06-0608, ww.mercatiditraiano.it.

Bocca della Verità—The legendary "Mouth of Truth" at the Church of Santa Maria in Cosmedin draws a playful crowd. Stick your hand in the mouth of the gaping stone face in the porch wall. As the legend goes (and was popularized by the 1953 film *Roman Holiday*, starring Gregory Peck and Audrey Hepburn), if you're a liar, your hand will be gobbled up. The mouth is only accessible when the church gate is open.

Cost and Hours: €0.50, daily 9:30-17:50, closes earlier off-season, Piazza Bocca della Verità, near the north end of Circus Maximus.

Capitol Hill and Nearby

Of Rome's famous seven hills, this is the smallest, tallest, and most famous—home of the ancient Temple of Jupiter and the center of

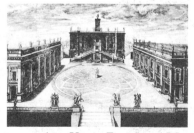

city government for 2,500 years. There are several ways to get to the top of Capitol Hill. (While I call it "Capitol Hill" for simplicity, it's correctly called "Capitoline Hill.") If you're coming from the north (from Piazza Venezia), take Michelangelo's impressive stairway to the right of the big, white Victor Emmanuel Monument. Coming from the southeast (the Forum), take the steep staircase near the Arch of Septimius Severus. From near Trajan's Forum along Via dei Fori Imperiali, take the winding road. All three converge at the top, in the square called Campidoglio (kahm-pee-DOHL-yoh).

Shortcut: A clever little "back door" gives you access from the top of Capitol Hill directly to the top of the Victor Emmanuel Monument and the Santa Maria in Aracoeli church, saving lots of uphill stair-climbing. To find the back door, locate the She-Wolf statue (to the left of the mayoral palace). Climb the wide set of stairs near the statue (the highest set of stairs you see). To reach the church, turn left at the column in the middle of the staircase,

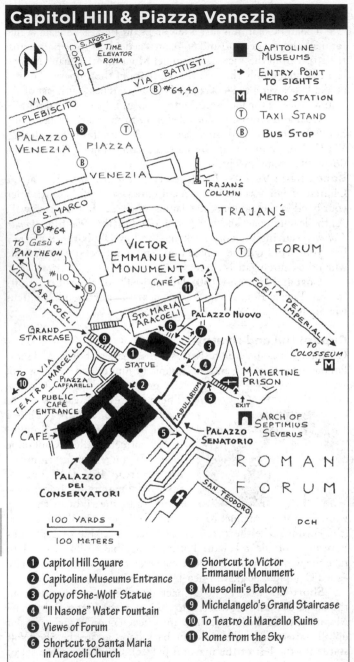

Capitol Hill & Piazza Venezia

CAPITOLINE MUSEUMS

→ ENTRY POINT TO SIGHTS

M METRO STATION

T TAXI STAND

B BUS STOP

1 Capitol Hill Square

2 Capitoline Museums Entrance

3 Copy of She-Wolf Statue

4 "Il Nasone" Water Fountain

5 Views of Forum

6 Shortcut to Santa Maria in Aracoeli Church

7 Shortcut to Victor Emmanuel Monument

8 Mussolini's Balcony

9 Michelangelo's Grand Staircase

10 To Teatro di Marcello Ruins

11 Rome from the Sky

following signs to *Aracoeli*. To reach the Victor Emmanuel Monument, continue up to the top of the steps, pass through the iron gate, and enter the small unmarked door at #13 on the right. You'll soon emerge on a café terrace midway up the monument with vast views. The Rome from the Sky elevator to the top is just around the corner.

▲**Capitol Hill Square (Campidoglio)**—This square atop the hill, once the religious and political center of ancient Rome, is still the home of the city's government. In the 1530s, the pope called on Michelangelo to re-establish this square as a grand center. Michelangelo placed the ancient equestrian statue of Marcus Aurelius as the square's focal point. Effective. (The original statue is now in the adjacent museum.) The twin buildings on either side are the Capitoline Museums. Behind the replica of the statue is the mayoral palace (Palazzo Senatorio).

Michelangelo intended that people approach the square from his grand stairway off Piazza Venezia. From the top of the stairway, you see the new Renaissance face of Rome, with its back to the Forum. Michelangelo gave the buildings the "giant order"—huge pilasters make the existing two-story buildings feel one-storied and more harmonious with the new square. Notice how the statues atop these buildings welcome you and then draw you in.

The terraces just downhill (past either side of the mayor's palace) offer grand views of the Forum. To the left of the mayor's palace is a copy of the famous She-Wolf statue on a column. Farther down is *il nasone* ("the big nose"), a refreshing water fountain. Block the spout with your fingers, and water spurts up for drinking. Romans joke that a cheap Roman boy takes his date out for a drink at *il nasone*. Near the She-Wolf statue is the staircase leading to a shortcut to the Victor Emmanuel Monument (for details, see "Shortcut," page 609).

▲▲**Capitoline Museums (Musei Capitolini)**—This museum encompasses two buildings (Palazzo dei Conservatori and Palazzo Nuovo), connected by an underground passage that leads to the vacant Tabularium and panoramic views of the Roman Forum.

Cost and Hours: €8-11 depending on cost of temporary exhibit, €8.50-13 combo-ticket with Montemartini Museum, Tue-Sun 9:00-20:00, closed Mon, last entry one hour before closing, tel. 06-8205-9127, www.museicapitolini.org.

Overview: The museum's layout—with two different buildings connected by an underground passage—can be confusing. To identify the museum's two buildings, face the equestrian statue (with your back to the grand stairway). You'll enter at the Palazzo dei Conservatori (on your right), cross underneath the square (beneath the Palazzo Senatorio, or mayoral palace, not open to public), and exit from the Palazzo Nuovo (on your left).

ROME

At the Palazzo dei Conservatori entrance, buy your ticket and consider renting the good €5 audioguide (€6.20/2 people).

The **Palazzo dei Conservatori** claims to be one of the world's oldest museums, founded in 1471 when a pope gave ancient statues to the citizens of Rome. In the courtyard, enjoy the massive chunks of Constantine: his head, hand, and foot. When intact, this giant held the place of honor in the Basilica of Constantine in the Forum. The museum is worthwhile, with lavish rooms and several great statues. You'll see the 13th-century *Capitoline She-Wolf* (the little statues of Romulus and Remus were added in the Renaissance). Don't miss the *Boy Extracting a Thorn* and the enchanting *Commodus as Hercules*. Behind Commodus is a statue of his dad, Marcus Aurelius, on a horse. The greatest surviving equestrian statue of antiquity, this was the original centerpiece of the square (where a copy stands today). Christians in the Dark Ages thought that the statue's hand was raised in blessing, which probably led to their misidentifying him as Constantine, the first Christian emperor. While most pagan statues were destroyed by Christians, "Constantine" was spared.

The second-floor café, Caffè Capitolino, has a splendid patio offering city views. It's lovely at sunset (public entrance for non-museum-goers off Piazza Caffarelli and through door #4).

Go downstairs to the **Tabularium.** Built in the first century B.C., these sturdy vacant rooms once held the archives of ancient Rome. The word Tabularium comes from "tablet," on which Romans wrote their laws. You won't see any tablets, but you will see a superb head-on view of the Forum from the windows.

Leave the Tabularium and enter the **Palazzo Nuovo,** which houses mostly portrait busts of forgotten emperors. But it also has two must-see statues: the *Dying Gaul* and the *Capitoline Venus* (both on the first floor up).

Santa Maria in Aracoeli—This church is built on the site where Emperor Augustus (supposedly) had a premonition of the com-

ing of Mary and Christ standing on an "altar in the sky" *(ara coeli)*. The church is Rome in a nutshell, where you can time-travel across 2,000 years by standing in one spot.

Cost and Hours: Daily 9:00-12:30 & 15:00-18:30. It's atop Capitol Hill, squeezed between the Victor Emmanuel Monument and the square called Campidoglio. While dedicated pilgrims climb up the long, steep staircase from street level (the right side of Victor Emmanuel Monument, as you face it), savvy sightseers prefer to enter through the "back door" atop Capitol Hill (see "Shortcut," page 609).

Piazza Venezia

This vast square, dominated by the big, white Victor Emmanuel Monument, is a major transportation hub and the focal point of modern Rome. (The square will be dug up for years—Metro line C is under construction, and when anything of archaeological importance is uncovered, progress is interrupted.) Stand with your back to the monument and look down Via del Corso, the city's axis, surrounded by Rome's classiest shopping district. In the 1930s, Benito Mussolini whipped up Italy's nationalistic fervor from a balcony above the square (with your back to Victor Emmanuel Monument, it's the less-grand balcony on the left). Fascist masses filled the square screaming, "Four more years!"—or something like that. Mussolini created boulevard Via dei Fori Imperiali (to your right) to open up views of the Colosseum in the distance to impress his visiting friend Adolf Hitler. Mussolini lied to his people, mixing fear and patriotism to push his country to the right and embroil the Italians in expensive and regrettable wars. In 1945, they shot and hung Mussolini from a meat hook in Milan.

Circling around the right side of the Victor Emmanuel Monument, look down into the ditch on your left to see the ruins of an ancient apartment building from the first century A.D.; part of it was transformed into a tiny church (faded frescoes and bell tower). Rome was built in layers—almost everywhere you go, there's an earlier version beneath your feet. (The hop-on, hop-off Trambus 110 stops just across the busy intersection from here.)

Continuing on, you reach two staircases leading up Capitol Hill. One is Michelangelo's grand staircase up to the Campidoglio. The longer of the two leads to the Santa Maria in Aracoeli church, a good example of the earliest style of Christian churches (described earlier). The contrast between this climb-on-your-knees ramp to God's house and Michelangelo's elegant stairs illustrates the changes Renaissance humanism brought civilization.

From the bottom of Michelangelo's stairs, look right several blocks down the street to see a condominium actually built upon the surviving ancient pillars and arches of Teatro di Marcello.

Victor Emmanuel Monument—This oversize monument to Italy's first king, built to celebrate the 50th anniversary of the country's unification in 1870, was part of Italy's push to overcome the new country's strong regionalism and create a national identity. The scale of the monument is over-the-top. The 43-foot-long statue of the king on the horse is the biggest equestrian statue in the world. The king's moustache is over five feet wide, and a person could fit into the horse's hoof. Open to the public, the structure

offers a grand view of the Eternal
City (free, 242 punishing steps
to the highest viewpoint accessible on foot—unless you take
the shortcut from Capitol Hill
described on page 609).

Locals love to hate the
"Altar of the Nation." Romans
think of the 200-foot-high,
500-foot-wide monument not as an altar of the fatherland, but as
"the wedding cake," "the typewriter," or "the dentures." (For short,
they call it "the Vittoriano.") It wouldn't be so bad if it weren't sitting on a priceless acre of ancient Rome and if they had chosen
better marble (the in-your-face white picks up the pollution horribly, requiring frequent cleaning). Soldiers guard Italy's Tomb of
the Unknown Soldier as the eternal flame flickers.

The Victor Emmanuel Monument also houses a little-visited
Museum of the Risorgimento, which explains the movement and
war that led to the unification of Italy in 1870 (free, daily 9:30-
18:30, tel. 06-679-3598, café).

▲**Rome from the Sky**—This elevator, located near the top of the
Victor Emmanuel Monument next to the outdoor café, zips you to

the rooftop for the grandest 360-degree view of the
center of Rome (even better
than from the top of St.
Peter's dome). Helpful panoramic diagrams describe
the skyline, with powerful
binoculars available for
zooming in on particular
sights. Go in late afternoon, when it's beginning to cool off and
Rome glows.

Cost and Hours: €7, Mon-Thu 9:30-18:30, Fri-Sun 9:30-
19:30, ticket office closes 45 minutes earlier, tel. 06-6920-2049,
follow signs inside the Victor Emmanuel Monument to *ascensori
panoramici* or take the shortcut from Capitol Hill.

Pantheon Neighborhood

The area around the Pantheon is the heart of Rome. This neighborhood stretches eastward from the Tiber River through Campo de'
Fiori and Piazza Navona, past the Pantheon to the Trevi Fountain.
Besides being home to ancient sights and historic churches, it's
also the place that gives Rome its urban-village feel. Wander narrow streets, sample the many shops and eateries, and gather with
the locals in squares marked by a bubbling fountain.

Pantheon Neighborhood

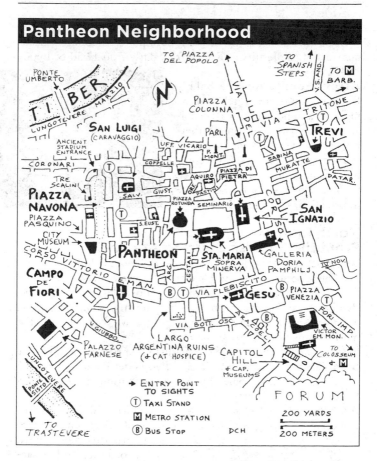

▲▲▲**Pantheon**—For the greatest look at the splendor of Rome, antiquity's best-preserved interior is a must. Built two millennia ago, this influential domed temple served as the model for Michelangelo's dome of St. Peter's and many others. For a self-guided tour, see page 560.

Cost and Hours: Free, Mon-Sat 8:30-19:30, Sun 9:00-18:00, holidays 9:00-13:00, closed for Mass Sat at 17:00 and Sun at 10:30, tel. 06-6830-0230.

▲▲**Churches near the Pantheon**—The Church of San Luigi dei Francesi has a magnificent chapel painted by Caravaggio (free, daily 10:00-12:30 & 16:00-19:00). The only Gothic church in Rome is Santa Maria sopra Minerva, with a little-known Michelangelo statue, *Christ Bearing the Cross* (free, Mon-Fri 7:00-19:00, Sat-Sun 8:00-13:00 & 15:30-19:00, on a little square behind Pantheon, to the east). The Church of San Ignazio, several blocks east of the Pantheon, is a riot of Baroque illusions with a false dome (free,

ROME

daily 7:30-12:30 & 15:00-19:15). A few blocks away, across Corso Vittorio Emanuele, is the rich and Baroque Gesù Church, head-quarters of the Jesuits in Rome (free, daily 7:00-12:30 & 16:00-19:45).

▲**Trevi Fountain**—The bubbly Baroque fountain, worth ▲▲ by night, is a minor sight to art schol-ars...but a major nighttime gather-ing spot for teens on the make and tourists tossing coins. The coins tourists deposit daily are collected to feed Rome's poor. (For more information, see page 601.)

North Rome:
From the Spanish Steps to Ara Pacis

▲**Spanish Steps**—The wide, curving staircase, culminating with an obelisk between two Baroque church towers, makes for one of Rome's iconic sights. Beyond that, it's a people-gathering place. By day, the area hosts shoppers looking for high-end fashions; on warm evenings, it attracts young people in love with the city. (For more information, see page 602.)

"Shopping Triangle"—The triangular-shaped area between the Spanish Steps, Piazza Venezia, and Piazza del Popolo (along Via del Corso) contains Rome's highest concentration of upscale bou-tiques and fashion stores.

▲▲**Ara Pacis (Altar of Peace)**—On January 30, 9 B.C., soon-to-be-emperor Augustus led a procession of priests up the steps

and into this newly built "Altar of Peace." They sac-rificed an animal on the altar and poured an offering of wine, thanking the gods for helping Augustus pacify barbarians abroad and rivals at home. This marked the dawn of the Pax Romana (c. A.D. 1-200), a Golden Age of good living, stability, dominance, and peace (pax). The Ara Pacis (AH-rah PAH-chees) hosted annual sacrifices by the emperor until the area was flooded by the Tiber River. Buried under silt, it was abandoned and forgotten until the 16th century, when various parts were discovered and excavated. Mussolini gathered the altar's scattered parts and reconstructed them here in 1938. In 2006, the Altar of Peace reopened to the public in a striking modern building. As the first new building allowed to be built in the old center since 1938, it's been controver-

ROME

sial, but its quiet, air-conditioned interior may signal the dawn of another new age in Rome.

The Altar of Peace was originally located east of here, along today's Via del Corso. The model shows where it stood in relation to the Mausoleum of Augustus (now next door) and the Pantheon. Approach the Ara Pacis and look through the doorway to see the raised altar. This simple structure has just the basics of a Roman temple: an altar for sacrifices surrounded by cubicle-like walls that enclose a consecrated space.

The reliefs on the north and south sides probably depict the parade of dignitaries who consecrated the altar, while reliefs on the west side (near the altar's back door) celebrate the two things Augustus brought to Rome: peace (goddess Roma as a conquering Amazon, right side) and prosperity (fertility goddess). Imagine the altar as it once was, standing in an open field, painted in bright colors—a mingling of myth, man, and nature.

Cost and Hours: €9, tightwads can look in through huge windows for free; Tue-Sun 9:00-19:00, closed Mon, last entry one hour before closing; €3.50 audioguide also available as free podcast at www.arapacis.it, good WC downstairs. The Ara Pacis is a long block west of Via del Corso on Via di Ara Pacis, on the east bank of the Tiber near Ponte Cavour, Metro: Spagna; a 10-minute walk down Via dei Condotti. Tel. 06-0608.

Vatican City

Vatican City, a tiny independent country, contains the Vatican Museum (with Michelangelo's Sistine Chapel) and St. Peter's

Basilica (with Michelangelo's exquisite *Pietà*). A helpful **TI** is just to the left of St. Peter's Basilica as you're facing it (Mon-Sat 8:30-19:00, closed Sun, tel. 06-6988-1662, Vatican switchboard tel. 06-6982, www.vatican.va). The entrances to St. Peter's and to the Vatican Museum are a 15-minute walk apart (follow the outside of the Vatican wall, which links the two sights). The

nearest Metro stops involve a 10-minute walk to either sight: For St. Peter's, the closest stop is Ottaviano; for the Vatican Museum, it's Cipro.

ROME

▲▲▲**Vatican Museum (Musei Vaticani)**—The four miles of displays in this immense museum—from ancient statues to Christian frescoes to modern paintings—culminate in the Raphael Rooms and Michelangelo's glorious Sistine Chapel. Modest dress is required. For a self-guided tour, see page 564.

Cost and Hours: €15 plus optional €4 reservation fee,

Mon-Sat 9:00-18:00, last entry at 16:00 (though the official closing time is 18:00, the staff starts ushering you out at 17:30), closed on religious holidays and Sun except last Sun of the month (when it's free, more crowded, and open 9:00-14:00, last entry at 12:30). The always-crowded museum now has an online reservation system and a website (http://mv.vatican.va) with up-to-date hours and information. Plan ahead for your visit.

▲▲▲**St. Peter's Basilica (Basilica San Pietro)**—There is no doubt: This is the richest and grandest church on earth. To call it vast is like calling Einstein smart. The church strictly enforces its dress code. Dress modestly—a not-too-short dress or long pants, with shoulders covered (men, women, and children). For a self-guided tour, see page 578.

Cost and Hours: Free, daily April-Sept 7:00-19:00, Oct-March 7:00-18:00. The church often closes on Wednesday mornings during papal audiences. Free guided tours (Mon-Fri) and €5 audioguides are available. Masses occur daily throughout the day. The view from the dome is worth the climb (€7 for elevator to roof, then take stairs; €5 to climb stairs all the way; allow an hour to go up and down, daily April-Sept 8:00-18:00, Oct-March 8:00-17:00, www.saintpetersbasilica.org).

Shopping in Rome

Traditionally, shops are open from 9:00 to 13:00 and from 16:00 to 19:00. They're often closed on Sundays, summer Saturday afternoons, and winter Monday mornings. But in the city center, you'll find that many are now staying open through lunch (generally 10:00-19:00).

For information on VAT refunds and customs regulations, see page 127.

If all you need are souvenirs, a surgical strike at any souvenir shop will do. Otherwise, try...

Department Stores

To conveniently peruse clothes, bags, shoes, and perfume at several major Italian chain stores, wander the shopping complex under Termini Station (most stores open daily 8:00-22:00).

Large department stores offer relatively painless one-stop shopping. A good upscale department store is **La Rinascente** (like Nordstrom or Macy's). Its main branch is on Piazza Fiume, and there's a smaller store on Via del Corso in the **Galleria Alberto Sordi,** an elegant 19th-century "mall" (across from Piazza Colonna). **UPIM** is the Roman JCPenney (many branches, including inside Termini Station, Via Nazionale 111, Piazza Santa Maria Maggiore, and Via del Tritone 172). **Oviesse,** a cheap clothing outlet, is near the Vatican Museum (on the corner of Via Candia and Via Mocenigo, Metro: Cipro).

Shopping Neighborhoods

A good, midrange shopping area is all along **Via del Corso,** with prices increasing as you head toward Piazza di Spagna. **Via Nazionale** also features a range of affordable shops, especially for clothes and shoes. Cheapskates scrounge through the junky but dirt-cheap shops in the gritty area around **Piazza Vittorio.**

Boutiques

For top fashion, stroll the streets around the Spanish Steps, including **Via Condotti, Via Borgognona** (for the big-name shops), and **Via del Babuino** (trendy design shops and galleries). For antiques, stroll **Via de Coronari** (between Piazza Navona and the bend in the river), **Via Giulia** (between Campo de' Fiori and the river), and **Via Margutta** (classier, with art galleries too, from Spanish Steps to Piazza del Popolo). For funkier, unique items, try **Via Giubbonari**—it's packed with artsy little boutiques—and other streets near Campo de' Fiori.

Flea Markets

For antiques and fleas, the granddaddy of markets is the **Porta Portese** *mercato delle pulci* (flea market). This Sunday-morning

market is long and spindly, running between the actual Porta Portese (a gate in the old town wall) and the Trastevere train station. Starting at Porta Portese, walk through the long, tacky parade of stalls selling cheap bras and shoes. Along the way, check out the con artists with the shell games. Each has shills in the crowd "winning big money" to get suckers involved. Hang on to your wallet—literally, in your front pocket (and make sure your money belt is tucked in). This is a den of thieves. The heart of the market for real flea-market junk (hiding a few little antique treasures) is the square in the center near Via Cesare Pascarella. I find that a slow stroll through the entire market and back to the Porta Portese takes about an hour and a half. While the shopping gets old (and the vendor food will make you sick), the people-watching is endlessly entertaining (6:30-13:00 Sun only, on Via Portuense and Via Ippolito Nievo; to get to the market, catch bus #75 from Termini station or tram #8 from Largo Argentina, get off the bus or tram on Viale Trastevere, and walk toward the river—and the noise).

At the **Via Sannio** market, you'll find new and used clothing and leather goods, some handicrafts, and random items that were probably stolen. You won't find antiques (Mon-Sat 9:00-13:30, closed Sun, behind Coin department store, a couple of blocks south of San Giovanni in Laterano, Metro: San Giovanni).

Open-Air Produce Markets

Rome's outdoor markets provide a fun and colorful dimension of the city that even the most avid museumgoer should not miss. Wander through the easygoing neighborhood produce markets, which clog certain streets and squares every morning (7:00-13:00) except Sunday. Consider the huge **Mercato Trionfale** (three blocks in front of Vatican Museum at Via Andrea Doria). Another great food market is the **Mercato Esquilino** (Via Turati near Piazza Vittorio). Smaller but equally charming slices of everyday Roman life are at markets on these streets and squares: **Piazza delle Coppelle** (near the Pantheon), **Via Balbo** (near Termini Station), and **Via della Pace** (near Piazza Navona). The covered **Mercato di Testaccio** sells mostly produce and is a hit with photographers and people-watchers (Piazza Testaccio, near Metro: Piramide). And **Campo de' Fiori,** despite having become quite touristy, is still a fun scene.

Eating in Rome

In the Pantheon Neighborhood

For the restaurants in this central area, I've listed them based on which landmark they're closest to: Campo de' Fiori, Piazza Navona, or the Pantheon.

On and near Campo de' Fiori

While it is touristy, Campo de' Fiori offers a sublimely romantic setting. And, since it's so close to the collective heart of Rome, it remains popular with locals, even though its restaurants offer greater atmosphere than food value. The square is lined with popular and interesting bars, pizzerias, and small restaurants—all great for people-watching over a glass of wine.

Osteria da Giovanni ar Galletto is nearby, on the more elegant and peaceful Piazza Farnese. Angelo entertains an upscale Roman crowd and has magical outdoor seating. Regrettably, service can be horrible, you need to double-check the bill, and single diners aren't treated very well. Still, if you're in no hurry and ready to savor my favorite al fresco setting in Rome (while humoring the waiters), this is a good bet (€10 pastas, €15 *secondi,* Mon-Sat 12:15-15:00 & 19:30-23:00, closed Sun, reservations smart for outdoor seating, tucked in corner of Piazza Farnese at #102, tel. 06-686-1714).

Filetti di Baccalà is a cheap and basic Roman classic, where nostalgic regulars cram into wooden tables savoring their old-school favorites—fried cod finger-food fillets (€5 each) and raw *puntarelle* greens (slathered with anchovy sauce in spring and winter). Study what others are eating, and order from your grease-stained server by pointing at what you want. Sit in the fluorescently lit interior or try to grab a seat out on the little square, a quiet haven a block east of Campo de' Fiori (Mon-Sat 17:30-23:00, closed Sun, cash only, Largo dei Librari 88, tel. 06-686-4018).

Trattoria der Pallaro, an eccentric and well-worn eatery that has no menu, has a slogan: "Here, you'll eat what we want to feed you." Paola Fazi—with a towel wrapped around her head turban-style—and her gang dish up a rustic five-course meal of typically Roman food for €25, including wine and coffee, and capped with a thimble of mandarin juice. While the service is odd and the food is forgettable, the experience can be fun (Tue-Sun 12:00-15:30 & 19:00-24:00, closed Mon, cash only, indoor/outdoor seating on quiet square, a block south of Corso Vittorio Emanuele, down Largo del Chiavari to Largo del Pallaro 15, tel. 06-6880-1488).

Pizzeria da Baffetto 2 makes pizza Roman-style: thin crust, crispy, and wood-fired. Eat in the cramped informal interior, or outside on the busy square (€7-9 pizzas, Wed-Mon 12:00-15:30 & 18:30-24:00, closed Tue, a block north of Campo de' Fiori at Piazza del Teatro di Pompeo 18, tel. 06-6821-0807).

Near Piazza Navona

Piazza Navona is the most quintessential setting for dining on a Roman square. Whether you eat here or not, you'll want to stroll the piazza before or after your evening meal. This is where many people fall in love with Rome. The tangled streets just to the west are lined with popular eateries of many stripes.

Ciccia Bomba is a traditional trattoria where Gianpaolo and crew serve up well-priced homemade pasta, wood-fired pizza, and other Roman specialties. With a name like "Fatso," this place had better have good food...and it does (€7 pastas, €9 *secondi,* Mon-Sat 12:00-15:00 & 19:00-24:00, closed Sun, off-season open Sun and closed Wed, Via del Governo Vecchio 76, a block west of Piazza Navona, just north from Piazza Pasquino, tel. 06-6880-2108).

Cul de Sac is a corridor-wide trattoria lined with wine bottles and packed with enthusiastic locals. Come early for an excellent tasting plate of salami and one of their many bottles of wine (they've got more than 1,000), or come later for a full meal of

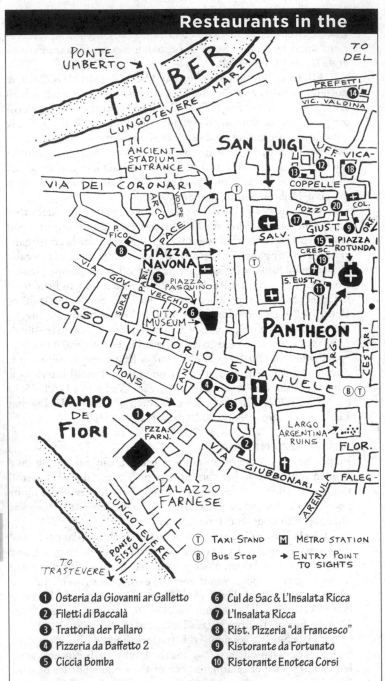

Restaurants in the

- **1** Osteria da Giovanni ar Galletto
- **2** Filetti di Baccalà
- **3** Trattoria der Pallaro
- **4** Pizzeria da Baffetto 2
- **5** Ciccia Bomba
- **6** Cul de Sac & L'Insalata Ricca
- **7** L'Insalata Ricca
- **8** Rist. Pizzeria "da Francesco"
- **9** Ristorante da Fortunato
- **10** Ristorante Enoteca Corsi

T TAXI STAND   **M** METRO STATION
B BUS STOP   → ENTRY POINT TO SIGHTS

Pantheon Neighborhood

PIAZZA POPOLO

IN LUCINA

TO SPANISH STEPS

TO BARB. M

PIAZZA PARL.

PARLIA-MENT

TRI TONE

VIA

RIO

P. MONTE.

P. COLONNA

SABINI

MURATTE

TREVI

LAV.

DATARIA

AQUIRO

P. PIETRA

SEMINARIO

UMILITA

SAN IGNAZIO

N

MARMO

CORSO

GALLERIA DORA PAMPHILJ

STA. MARIA SOPRA MINERVA

16

10

PLEBISCITO

BATT.

VIA IV NOV.

VIA

GESÙ

PIAZZA VENEZIA

200 YARDS
200 METERS

BOTT. OSC.

ARACOELI

V. E. MON.

FORI IMP

NAMI

CAPITOL HILL

TO COLOSSEUM & M

DCH

FORUM

ROME

⑪ Miscellanea
⑫ Osteria da Mario
⑬ Le Coppelle Taverna
⑭ Trattoria dal Cav. Gino
⑮ Antica Salumeria

⑯ Super Market Di per Di
⑰ Supermercato Despar
⑱ Gelateria Caffè Pasticceria Giolitti
⑲ Crèmeria Monteforte
⑳ Gelateria San Crispino

nicely cooked Roman dishes (daily 12:00-16:00 & 18:00-24:00, tel. 06-6880-1094, a block off Piazza Navona on Piazza Pasquino).

L'Insalata Ricca is a popular chain that specializes in hearty and healthy €8 salads and less-healthy pastas (daily 12:00-15:45 & 18:45-24:00). They have a handy branch on Piazza Pasquino (next to Cul de Sac, tel. 06-6830-7881), and a more spacious and enjoyable location a few blocks away, on a bigger square next to busy Corso Vittorio Emanuele (near Campo de' Fiori at Largo dei Chiavari 85, tel. 06-6880-3656).

Ristorante Pizzeria "da Francesco" is a bustling, unpretentious place with hardworking young waitstaff, great indoor seating, and classic outdoor seating on a cluttered little square that makes you want to break out a sketch pad. Their blackboard explains the daily specials (€7 pizzas, €8 pastas, €10 *secondi*, open daily, 3 blocks west of Piazza Navona at Piazza del Fico 29, tel. 06-686-4009).

Close to the Pantheon

Eating on the square facing the Pantheon is a temptation (there's even a McDonald's that offers some of the best outdoor seating in town), and I'd consider it just to relax and enjoy the Roman scene. But if you walk a block or two away, you'll get less view and better value. Here are some suggestions.

Ristorante da Fortunato is an Italian classic, with fresh flowers on the tables and waiters in white coats and black ties politely serving good meat and fish to politicians, foreign dignitaries, and tourists with good taste. Don't leave without perusing the photos of their famous visitors—everyone from former Iraqi Foreign Minister Tariq Aziz to Bill Clinton seems to have eaten here. All are pictured with the boss, Fortunato, who, since 1975, has been a master of simple edible elegance. The outdoor seating is fine for watching the river of Roman street life flow by, but the atmosphere is inside. For a dressy night out, this is a reliable and surprisingly reasonable choice—but be sure to reserve ahead (plan to spend €45 per person, Mon-Sat 12:30-15:00 & 19:30-23:30, closed Sun, a block in front of the Pantheon at Via del Pantheon 55, tel. 06-679-2788).

Ristorante Enoteca Corsi is a wine shop that grew into a thriving lunch-only restaurant. The Paiella family serves straightforward, traditional cuisine at great prices to an appreciative crowd of office workers. Check the blackboard for daily specials (gnocchi on Thursday, fish on Friday, and so on). Friendly Giuliana and Manuela welcome eaters to step into their wine shop and pick out a bottle. For the cheap take-away price, plus €2-4 (depending on the wine), they'll uncork it at your table. With €8 pastas, €11 main dishes, and fine wine at a third of the price you'd pay in normal restaurants, this can be a superb value. Consider finishing with a glass of the family's homemade *limoncello* (Mon-Sat 12:00-15:00, closed Sun, a block toward the Pantheon from the Gesù Church at Via del Gesù 87, no reservations possible, tel. 06-679-0821).

Miscellanea is run by much-loved Mikki, who's on a mission to keep foreign students well-fed. You'll find hearty and fresh €4 sandwiches and a long list of €6 salads, along with pasta and other staples. Mikki (and his son, Romero) often tosses in a fun little extra, including—if you have this book on the table—a free glass of Mikki's "sexy wine" (homemade from *fragoline*—strawberry-flavored grapes). This place is popular with American students on foreign-study programs (daily 8:00-24:00, indoor/outdoor seating, facing the rear of the Pantheon at Via della Palombella 34, tel. 06-6813-5318).

Osteria da Mario, a homey little mom-and-pop joint with a no-stress menu, serves traditional favorites in a fun dining room or on tables spilling out onto a picturesque old Roman square (€8 pastas, €10 *secondi*, Mon-Sat 13:00-15:30 & 19:00-23:00, closed Sun, from the Pantheon walk 2 blocks up Via Pantheon, go left on Via delle Coppelle, take first right to Piazza delle Coppelle 51, tel. 06-6880-6349, Marco).

Le Coppelle Taverna is simple, basic, family-friendly, and inexpensive—especially for pizza—with a checkered-tablecloth ambience (€9 pizzas, daily 12:30-15:00 & 19:30-23:30, Via delle Coppelle 39, tel. 06-6880-6557, Alfonso).

Trattoria dal Cav. Gino, tucked away on a tiny street behind the Parliament, has been a favorite since 1963. Photos on the wall recall the days when it was the haunt of big-time politicians. Grandpa Gino shuffles around grating the parmesan cheese while his sister and son serve up traditional Roman favorites and make sure things run smoothly. Reserve ahead, even for lunch (€8 pastas, €11 *secondi*, cash only, Mon-Sat 13:00-14:45 & 20:00-22:30, closed Sun, fish on Friday, behind Piazza del Parlamento and just off Via di Campo Marzio at Vicolo Rosini 4, tel. 06-687-3434, Fabrizio and Carla—Gino's son and daughter—both speak English).

Picnicking Close to the Pantheon

It's fun to munch a picnic with a view of the Pantheon. (Remember to be discreet.) Here are some options.

Antica Salumeria is an old-time *alimentari* (grocery store) on the Pantheon square. Eduardo speaks English and will help you assemble your picnic: artichokes, mixed olives, bread, cheese, meat (they're proud of their Norcia prosciutto), and wine (with plastic glasses). Just set a price (figure €10 per person), and Eduardo will assemble it. Their pastries are fresh from their own bakery. While you can create your own sandwiches (sold by the weight, more fun, and cheaper), they also sell quality ready-made sandwiches for around €5 (daily 8:00-21:00, mobile 334-340-9014).

ROME

Supermarkets near the Pantheon: Food is relatively cheap at Italian supermarkets. **Super Market Di per Di** is a convenient place for groceries a block from Gesù Church (Mon-Sat 8:00-21:00, Sun 9:00-19:30, 50 yards off Via del Plebiscito at Via del Gesù 59). Another place, **Supermercato Despar,** is a half a block from the Pantheon toward Piazza Navona (daily 9:00-22:00, Via Giustiniani 18).

Gelato Close to the Pantheon

Three fine *gelaterie* are within a two-minute walk of the Pantheon.

Gelateria Caffè Pasticceria Giolitti, Rome's most famous and venerable ice-cream joint, has reasonable take-away prices and elegant Old World seating (daily 7:00-24:00, just off Piazza Colonna and Piazza Monte Citorio at Via Uffici del Vicario 40, tel. 06-699-1243).

Crèmeria Monteforte is known for its traditional, quality gelato and super-creamy sorbets *(cremolati).* The fruit flavors are especially refreshing—think gourmet slushies (Tue-Sun 10:00-24:00, off-season closes earlier, closed Mon and Dec, faces the west side of the Pantheon at Via della Rotonda 22, tel. 06-686-7720).

Gelateria San Crispino, well-respected by Romans, serves small portions of particularly tasty gourmet gelato using creative ingredients. Because of their commitment to natural ingredients, the colors are muted; gelato purists consider bright colors a sign of unnatural chemicals used to attract children. They serve cups, but no cones (daily 12:00-24:00, a block in front of the Pantheon on Piazza della Maddalena, tel. 06-6889-1310).

In Ancient Rome:
Eating Cheaply near the Colosseum

You'll find good views but poor value at the restaurants directly behind the Colosseum. To get your money's worth, eat at least a block away. Here are three handy eateries: one at the foot of Via Cavour, and two at the top of Terme di Tito (a long block uphill from the Colosseum, near St. Peter-in-Chains church—of Michelangelo's *Moses* fame; for directions, see page 605). For a map of the area, see page 538.

Enoteca Cavour 313 is a wine bar with a mission: to offer good wine and quality food with an old-fashioned commitment to value and friendly service. It's also a convenient place for a good lunch near the Forum and Colosseum. Angelo and his three partners enjoy creating a mellow ambience under lofts of wine bottles (daily specials and fine wines by the glass, daily 12:30-14:45 & 19:30-24:00, 100 yards off Via dei Fori Imperiali at Via Cavour 313, tel. 06-6785-496).

Caffè dello Studente is popular with engineering students

ROME

attending the nearby University of Rome. Pina, Mauro, and their perky daughter Simona (speaks English) give my readers a royal welcome and serve typical *bar gastronomia* fare—toasted sandwiches, salads, and pizzas (stick to any of the aforementioned fare to avoid frozen dishes). If they have a "Rick Steves menu," give it a miss. You can get your food to go *(da portar via)*, eat standing at the crowded bar, or wait for table service outside. If it's not busy, show this book when you order at the bar and sit without paying extra at a table (Mon-Sat 7:30-22:30, April-Oct Sun 9:00-22:30, Nov-March closed Sun, Via delle Terme di Tito, tel. 06-488-3240).

Hostaria da Nerone, next door, is a more formal restaurant with much better food and homemade pasta dishes. Their €9 *antipasti* plate—with a variety of veggies, fish, and meat—is a good value for a quick lunch. While the *antipasti* menu indicates specifics, you can have a plate of whatever's out—just direct the waiter to assemble the €9 *antipasti* plate of your lunchtime dreams (Mon-Sat 12:00-15:00 & 19:00-23:00, closed Sun, indoor/outdoor seating, Via delle Terme di Tito 96, tel. 06-481-7952, run by Teo and Eugenio).

Starting or Ending Your Cruise in Rome

If your cruise begins or ends in Rome, you'll want some extra time here; for most travelers, two days is a minimum to see the highlights of the Eternal City. If you're planning a longer visit, pick up my *Rick Steves' Rome* guidebook—or, if your trip extends beyond Rome, consider my *Rick Steves' Italy* guidebook.

Airport Connections

You'll need to take two trains to link Civitavecchia and Fiumicino Airport: one between the airport and Rome's Termini Station, and another between Termini and Civitavecchia. Rome's two airports—**Fiumicino** (a.k.a. Leonardo da Vinci) and the small **Ciampino**—share the same website (www.adr.it).

Fiumicino Airport

Rome's major airport has a TI (in terminal 3, daily 8:00-19:00), ATMs, banks, luggage storage, shops, and bars. The Rome Walks website (www.romewalks.com) has a useful video on options for getting into the city from the airport. A slick, direct **"Leonardo Express" train** connects the airport and Rome's central Termini train station in 30 minutes for €15. Trains run twice hourly in both directions from roughly 6:00 to 23:00 (leaving the airport at :06 and :36). From the airport's arrival gate, follow signs to *Stazione/Railway Station*. Buy your ticket from a machine, the Biglietteria office, or a newsstand at the platform, then validate it in a yellow

ROME

machine near the track. Make sure the train you board is going to the central "Roma Termini" station, not "Roma Orte" or others.

Going from Termini train station to the airport, trains depart at about :22 and :52 past the hour, from track 25 (located way down at the far end of track 24; allow 10 minutes for the hike, moving walkways downstairs). Check the departure boards for "Fiumicino Aeroporto"—the local name for the airport—and confirm with an official or a local on the platform that the train is indeed going to the airport (€15, buy ticket from any *tabacchi* or newsstand in the station, or at the self-service machines, Termini-Fiumicino trains run 5:52-22:52). Read your ticket: If it requires validation, stamp it in the yellow machine near the platform before boarding. From the train station at the airport, you can access all of the terminals—1, 2, 3, or 5.

Allow lots of time going in either direction; there's a fair amount of transportation involved, including moving walkways, escalators, and walking (e.g., getting to Termini, from Termini to the train platform, the ride to the airport, getting from the airport train station to check-in, etc.). Flying to the US involves an extra level of security—plan on getting to the airport even earlier (I like to arrive 2.5 hours ahead of my flight).

A Rome city **taxi** from the airport to central Rome should cost €45 (for four people and their bags). Cabbies not based in Rome can charge €60. Look for a Rome city cab, with the "SPQR" shield on the door. If you're staying the night in Rome, check with your hotel about an airport **shuttle van.**

Ciampino Airport

Rome's smaller airport (tel. 06-6595-9515) handles charter flights and some budget airlines (including all Ryanair and some easyJet flights). The Terravision Express Shuttle connects Ciampino and Rome's Termini train station, leaving every 20 minutes (€4 one-way, €8 round-trip, www.terravision.eu). The SIT Bus Shuttle also connects Termini train station to Ciampino (€6, about 2/hour, 30-60 minutes, runs 7:45-23:15 Ciampino to Termini, 4:30-21:30 Termini to Ciampino, pickup on Via Marsala just outside the train exit closest to track 1, tel. 06-591-7844, www.sitbusshuttle.it).

From Rome's Termini Train Station to Civitavecchia

Once your airport train leaves you at Rome's Termini Station, you're only halfway there. From here, you'll head to Civitavecchia; trains depart about three times per hour (€4.50-12.50, taking 45-80 minutes, depending on the train). Be warned that Civitavecchia trains generally leave from tracks 27-30, a long 10- to 15-minute walk from the station entrance. If you're catching the Civitavecchia-bound train at Termini Station, you'll likely be approached on the platform by bogus "porters" who offer to help you get your bags into the train and find your seat, then demand an exorbitant tip. These are not railway employees; there are no official porters. Don't use them unless you really need to; then, if you do, tip them only what you think is fair.

Once in Civitavecchia, exit the train station to the right and walk about 10 minutes to the port gate, on the square called Largo Plebescito. Go through the port gate and find the cruise line's shuttle-bus stop across the street from the big fortress, next to the TI kiosk. Wait for a bus marked with your cruise ship's name.

From the Airport(s) Directly to Civitavecchia

Shuttle van services run between the port and Rome's airports, such as **Rome Airport Shuttle** (€90/1-2 people, €15 each additional person up to 8, share with others and save, much more for pickup between 21:00 and 7:00, tel. 06-4201-4507 or 06-4201-3469, www.airportshuttle.it). A **taxi** costs about €60 one-way between Civitavecchia and Fiumicino.

Hotels

If you need a hotel in Rome for before or after your cruise, here are a few suggestions near the Termini train station. While the neighborhood is not atmospheric as other areas of Rome, the hotels near Termini are less expensive, restaurants are plentiful, and the good public-transit connections can help you get anywhere in the city.

$$$ Hotel Modigliani, a delightful 23-room place, is energetically run in a clean, bright, minimalist yet in-love-with-life style (Db-€195, check website for deals and ask for a 10 percent Rick Steves discount; air-con, Wi-Fi; northwest of Via Firenze—from Tritone Fountain on Piazza Barberini, go 2 blocks up Via della Purificazione to #42; tel. 06-4281-5226, www.hotel modigliani.com, info@hotelmodigliani.com, Giulia and Marco).

$$ Hotel Aberdeen is warmly run by Annamaria, with support from cousins Sabrina and Cinzia and sister Laura. The 37 rooms are comfy, modern, and air-conditioned (Sb-€102, Db-€160, Tb-€170, Qb-€200, for these rates—or better—book direct via email or use the "Rick Steves reader reservations" link on their website, Internet access and Wi-Fi, Via Firenze 48, tel. 06-482-3920, fax 06-482-1092, www.hotelaberdeen.it, info@hotel aberdeen.it).

$$ Hotel Sonya offers 28 well-equipped, high-tech rooms, a central location, and decent prices (Sb-€90, Db-€150, Tb-€165, Qb-€185, Quint/b-€200, 5 percent discount with this book and cash, air-con, elevator, loaner laptops in room and Wi-Fi, faces the Opera House at Via Viminale 58, Metro: Repubblica or Termini,

ROME

What If I Miss My Boat?

Remember that you can get help from the cruise line's port agent (listed on the destination information sheet distributed on the ship) and the local TI (see page 523). If the port agent suggests a costly solution (such as a private car with a driver), you may want to consider public transit.

Frequent **trains** leave from Rome's very central Termini Station (the same one with train connections to Civitavecchia) to points all over Italy and beyond: to **Venice** (roughly hourly, 3.5 hours, overnight possible), **Livorno** (3/hour, 0.75-1 hour), **Naples** (at least hourly, 1.25 hours on Frecciarossa trains, otherwise 2-2.5 hours), **Sorrento** (go by train to Naples, then transfer to Circumvesuviana train—every 30 minutes, 70 minutes), **Nice** (6/day, 10 hours), and more. For other connections, ask at the train station or check http://bahn.hafas.de /bin/query.exe/en (Germany's excellent all-Europe website). Italy has a train-info toll number 892-021 (answered 24 hours daily in Italian only; have a local person call for you). A few trains depart from Rome's Tiburtina station, four Metro stops from Termini.

If you need to catch a **plane** to your next destination, see page 627 for information on Rome's two airports.

For a recommended local **travel agent,** see page 524. For more advice on what to do if you miss the boat, see page 131.

tel. 06-481-9911, fax 06-488-5678, www.hotelsonya.it, info@hotel sonya.it, Francesca and Ivan).

$$ Hotel Selene spreads its rooms out on a few floors of a big palazzo. With elegant furnishings and room to breathe, its 40 rooms are a good value (Db-€145, Tb-€165, €10 less with cash, air-con, elevator, Via del Viminale 8, tel. 06-482-4460, www.hotel seleneroma.it, reception@hotelseleneroma.it).

$ Hotel Nardizzi Americana has 33 pleasant, air-conditioned rooms and a delightful rooftop terrace (Sb-€95, Db-€125, Tb-€155, Qb-€175, email them or use "Rick Steves readers reservations" link on their website to get these special rates in 2011, normal website sometimes has even lower rates, additional 10 percent off any time with cash, air-con, elevator, Internet access and Wi-Fi, Via Firenze 38, fourth floor, tel. 06-488-0035, fax 06-488-0368, www .hotelnardizzi.it, info@hotelnardizzi.it, Stefano, Fabrizio, Mario, and Samy).

$ Hotel Montreal, run with care, is a bright, solid business-class place with 27 rooms on a big street a block southeast of Santa Maria Maggiore (Sb-€95, Db-€120, Tb-€150, may be less if you email direct and ask for a Rick Steves discount, air-con, eleva-tor, Internet access, communal garden terrace, good security, Via

Carlo Alberto 4, 1 block from Metro: Vittorio Emanuele, 3 blocks west of Termini train station, tel. 06-445-7797, fax 06-446-5522, www.hotelmontrealroma.com, info@hotelmontrealroma.com, Pasquale).

In Civitavecchia: With the glories of one of Europe's best after-dark cities just a short train-ride away, I'd never sleep in ho-hum Civitavecchia. But if you must, several overpriced hotels cater to upscale cruise passengers' tastes along the road between Civitavecchia's train station and cruise port: **Hotel San Giorgio,** with classy public spaces and 41 slightly worn rooms (Db-€200 in cruise season, soft rates, deals online, Viale Garibaldi 34, tel. 0766-5991, www.sangiorgiohotel.biz) and **Hotel de La Ville,** with faded elegance outside and 45 nice rooms inside (standard Db-€180 in cruise season, €45 more for superior room, Viale della Repubblica 4, tel. 0766-580-507, www.roseshotels.it; same website has info on their nearby, cheaper **Hotel Mediterraneo**).

NAPLES, SORRENTO & CAPRI

Naples is southern Italy's leading city, offering a fascinating, gritty mix of museums, churches, and lively street scenes. Just beyond Naples you'll find the impressive ruins of Pompeii and Herculaneum...and see the brooding volcano that did them both in, Mount Vesuvius. Farther away are the resort town of Sorrento, the holiday isle of Capri, and the scenic Amalfi Coast—each of these is, up to a point, reachable from Naples on a day in port.

These destinations are well-connected by Circumvesuviana train, taxi, or boat. Long-distance buses are also possible, but less reliable if you're on a tight cruising timetable. If time permits, consider taking a boat—it's faster, cooler, and more scenic, and you can take coastline photos you can't get from land.

Planning Your Time

Ships call at either Naples or Sorrento. While you have essentially the same options from either port, some destinations are easier to reach from one than from the other.

Docking at Naples, an easy choice is to stay in the city, visiting the Archaeological Museum and following my self-guided walk through the downtown. The ruins at Pompeii and Herculaneum are each a short train ride away. Or you can take a boat across the bay to the island of Capri. But Sorrento and the Amalfi Coast are a bit farther away, and harder to squeeze into a single day.

From Sorrento, you're a short boat ride away from the island of Capri, and a train ride from Pompeii and Herculaneum. You're also near the dramatic Amalfi Coast (which is possible to see by bus, but easier with a hired driver or cruise-line excursion). Note

Excursions from Naples or Sorrento

In this region, the best excursions are those to **Naples,** the ancient Roman archaeological sites of **Pompeii** or smaller **Herculaneum,** the romantic island of **Capri,** or the strikingly vertical **Amalfi Coast.** The following two options—a bit farther afield—round out the possibilities.

To escape the heat and the crowds, visit the desolate, lunar-like 4,000-foot-high **Vesuvius** (an hour southeast of Naples), mainland Europe's only active volcano (it last erupted in 1944). A steep 30-minute climb takes you from the parking lot to the often cold and windy top for a sweeping view of the Bay of Naples. Walk the entire crater lip for the most interesting views; the far end overlooks Pompeii.

Paestum (2 hours southeast of Naples) has one of the best collections of Greek temples anywhere, and its archaeological museum offers the rare opportunity to see beautifully crafted artifacts—dating from prehistoric to Greek to Roman times—at the site where they were discovered.

that some cruise lines advertise a stop in **"Capri,"** but actually dock across the bay, in Naples.

Your Top Options

Here are quick descriptions, with time estimates, of your top choices:

• **Naples** has an excellent Archaeological Museum with Pompeii's best art; it's worth two hours. Note that the museum is closed on Tuesday.

To enjoy Naples' vibrant street life, take my self-guided walk from the museum to Piazza del Plebiscito, near the port (Part 1; allow 1 hour), and with extra time, on to the train station (Part 2; allow 2 more hours, with stops in churches).

Fans of Roman antiquity can spend a marvelous day from Naples by heading to Pompeii, then finishing at Naples' Archaeological Museum (allow up to 9 hours total, including Circumvesuviana train).

• Touring **Pompeii**'s ruins takes three hours (allow up to 5 hours total, including the train from either Naples or Sorrento).

• If time is tight, **Herculaneum**—which is like a small Pompeii—takes only an hour to tour (allow a total of 3 hours for your visit if you're traveling from Naples, or 3.5 hours from Sorrento).

• The resort town of **Sorrento** is pleasant, but has virtually no sightseeing (my self-guided walk takes about an hour). If you're docking in Naples, it's not worth coming to Sorrento just to see

Services at the Port of Naples

You'll find most of what you need right at the cruise terminal. Inside the twin buildings are pay phones, gift shops, and an **ATM** (hiding upstairs, in the middle of the grand, marbled check-in area that bridges the two buildings).

In the covered area between the terminal buildings, you'll find various shops and services, including some cafés and a *tabacchi* shop (where you can buy bus tickets). Caffè Moreno, in the middle of this area, offers free **Wi-Fi** if you sit at a table and order something (not if you buy something to go). Caffè Tovaldo, on the right side of this area as you face the city, has **Internet terminals** upstairs (€3/hour) and cheap calling cards.

the town (about 2 hours round-trip by boat, or 3 hours round-trip by train). If your ship docks in Sorrento, and you want to visit Pompeii and Naples' Archaeological Museum by Circumvesuviana train, allow up to nine hours.

• The island of **Capri** will fill an entire day. Be careful to factor in transportation time for the boat trip from either Sorrento (about 20-25 minutes) or Naples (about 45 minutes); only a few cruises tender passengers directly to Capri. If you're heading to Capri to see the Blue Grotto, be sure to check that the tide isn't too high or the water too rough—ask the TI in Naples or Sorrento before heading over. For specific advice on how to make the most of your time on Capri, see page 687.

• The scenic **Amalfi Coast** takes a full day to see from Sorrento, and is most easily done with a hired driver. If your ship docks in Naples rather than Sorrento, it's best to join a shore excursion if you want to see the Amalfi Coast.

Naples

Neapolis ("new city") was a thriving Greek commercial center 2,500 years ago. Today it's Italy's third-largest city, with more than one million people. Walking through its colorful Old Town is one of my favorite sightseeing experiences anywhere in Italy.

The pulse of Italy throbs in Naples. Like Cairo or Mumbai,

it's appalling and captivating at the same time, the closest thing to "reality travel" that you'll find in Western Europe. But this tangled mess still somehow manages to breathe, laugh, and sing—with a captivating Italian accent.

Arrival at the Port of Naples

Arrival at a Glance: You can either stay in Naples (ride a €12-15 taxi or cheap bus to the Archaeological Museum, which is also the start of my self-guided walk), or head to nearby sights: Take a taxi or bus to the Circumvesuviana train station, then take a train to Herculaneum (25 minutes), Pompeii (35 minutes), or Sorrento (70 minutes). You can also take a boat to Capri (45 minutes) or Sorrento (35 minutes; boats depart from next to the cruise terminal). A round-trip taxi to Pompeii (including waiting time) costs €90; one-way to Sorrento costs €100.

Port Overview

Naples' cruise terminal (Stazione Marittima) is conveniently located at the southeast edge of downtown Naples, near the Castel Nuovo and the grand square called Piazza del Plebiscito. The terminal complex is a stern, blocky, fascist-style bunker with two separate buildings connected by a second-story concourse that forms a covered, garage-like area that contains some helpful services (see sidebar).

Walking straight out from the cruise terminal, you're facing the old center of Naples. A busy street runs in front of the terminal area (called Via Ammiraglio Ferdinando Acton to the left, and Via Cristoforo Colombo to the right). Along this road, to the left are the Molo Beverello dock—with boats to Sorrento and Capri—and, beyond that, Piazza del Plebiscito. To the right is the bus stop to the train station. Straight ahead across the road is a drab square called Piazza Municipio, with the bus stop to Naples' world-class Archaeological Museum nearby. All of these options are explained in detail below.

Tourist Information: As you exit the port terminal complex, you'll head through a little checkpoint (marked *Molo Angiomo*) that has a sporadically staffed TI desk. If that's closed, the nearest TI is at the Galleria Umberto I shopping mall (about a 10-minute walk away, near Piazza del Plebiscito).

Getting to the Sights

Whether you're staying in Naples or heading to nearby sights, you can either pay for a taxi or use public transport.

By Taxi

As you leave the cruise terminal, you'll find a taxi stand ahead and to the left. Here are the standard rates to points both in Naples and throughout the region:

- To the Archaeological Museum or the train station: €12-15
- Two-hour tour around Naples: €70
- Round-trip to Pompeii including a two-hour wait: €90
- Round-trip to Herculaneum including a two-hour wait: €70
- Round-trip to Pompeii and Herculaneum including waiting time: €130
- One-way to Sorrento: €100

Agree on a set price without the meter, and pay upon arrival. You'll pay a legitimate supplement on Sundays and holidays.

Several reputable drivers in this region are available to hire for a full-day tour to whichever sights most appeal to you. But, as they are primarily based in Sorrento, you'll pay a hefty surcharge to have them pick you up in Naples. Check out your options on page 675, and if this option interests you, try to book in advance.

By Public Transportation

If you'll be taking a public bus in Naples, get your **bus tickets** at the *tabacchi* (tobacco shop) inside the terminal complex, under the covered area between the two buildings. You'll find the *tabacchi* inside the coffee shop in the middle of this area. Local transit tickets cost €1.10 apiece; validate the ticket in the yellow box on the bus as you board.

However, if you'd like to stretch your legs, you can **walk**— both the Archaeological Museum and the train station are about 45 gently uphill minutes away (in different directions).

To Sights in Naples

The **Archaeological Museum** stands at the top of town. Head here either to tour its impressive collection, or to begin my self-guided walk downhill through old Naples. You can ride a taxi to the museum, or take public bus #R4 (the bus stop is a few blocks away from the port—about a 10-minute walk). To reach the stop for bus #R4, walk straight out of the cruise terminal and to the busy road. Bear right to the traffic-light crosswalk and cross this road, then continue straight up Piazza Municipio for three short blocks. Cross the busy street called Via Agostino Depretis, then turn right and walk down that same street about a half-block to the Depretis stop for bus #R4 (departs every 10-15 minutes). Ride this bus six stops to Piazza Museo ("p. Museo").

Note: "Part 1" of my self-guided walk ends at Piazza del Plebiscito, an easy 10-minute walk from the cruise terminal. However, "Part 2"—which immerses you even more deeply (and

Getting Around the Region

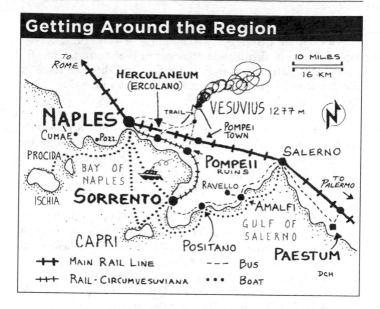

TO ROME

HERCULANEUM (ERCOLANO)

VESUVIUS 1277 M

TRAIL

POMPEI TOWN

NAPLES

CUMAE · POZZ.

PROCIDA

BAY OF NAPLES

ISCHIA

SORRENTO

CAPRI

POSITANO

POMPEII RUINS

RAVELLO

AMALFI

GULF OF SALERNO

SALERNO

TO PALERMO

PAESTUM

10 MILES

16 KM

┼┼ MAIN RAIL LINE

┼┼┼ RAIL · CIRCUMVESUVIANA

- - - BUS

••• BOAT

DCH

enjoyably) in the quirky urban world of Naples—takes you across town, to the train-station area. From Piazza Garibaldi (the giant square in front of the train station), you can catch bus #601 or #152 back to the port.

If you'd like to head straight from the cruise terminal to the nearby **Piazza del Plebiscito,** it's about a 10-minute walk: Cross the busy road in front of the cruise terminal area and turn left along this same road, walking in front of the big castle, then the sailboat harbor. At the big traffic tunnel, look for the elevator just to the right (marked *ascensore Acton,* free, Mon-Sat 7:00-21:30, Sun 8:00-14:30), which will zip you up to the square. (While you could start my self-guided walk in reverse from here, it's uphill in this direction; it's better to ride the bus up to the museum and begin there.)

To Herculaneum, Pompeii, or Sorrento by Circumvesuviana Train

Trains to Herculaneum, Pompeii, Sorrento, and other points near Naples run on the Circumvesuviana line, which has its own designated station in Naples. (Trains to other points in Italy—such as Rome—leave from Centrale Station, very close by.) Be warned that the Circumvesuviana is popular among thieves—keep a close eye on your belongings.

To reach the Circumvesuviana station from the cruise terminal, you can either take a taxi (€12-15, see above) or ride public bus #601 or #152. To reach the bus stop from the cruise terminal, walk

NAPLES

straight out to the main road and bear right to the crosswalk. The stop for bus #601 (runs every 10 minutes) or #152 (runs every 45 minutes) is at the first island in the middle of the street: Cross the street halfway, then turn right and walk along the tram tracks to the stop marked *Colombo Beverello*; you'll board a bus that's going toward your right.

Ride the bus about 10 minutes, then get off at the "c. Garibaldi" stop (that's "c." for Corso Garibaldi—not "p. Garibaldi" for Piazza Garibaldi). Near the bus stop is the terminus for the Circumvesuviana train. When you buy your train ticket, ask which track your train will depart from (*"Quale binario?"*; KWAH-lay bee-NAH-ree-oh). Just beyond, you'll find the gate where you insert your ticket.

If you miss the "c. Garibaldi" bus stop, don't panic. You can ride one more stop to Piazza Garibaldi ("p. Garibaldi")—the vast, grimy square in front of Centrale train station. From here, make the long hike to the far end of Piazza Garibaldi and go inside Centrale Station, then follow the signs to *Circumvesuviana* (across from track 14, downstairs), where you'll find the ticket office and info booth. The train platforms are downstairs.

Look for trains marked *Sorrento* (the end point), which depart twice hourly. These take you to Herculaneum/Ercolano (about 25 minutes, €1.80 one-way), Pompeii (about 35 minutes, €2.40 one-way), and Sorrento, the end of the line (70 minutes, €3.40 one-way, www.vesuviana.it). Not all of the trains go as far as Sorrento; check the schedule or confirm with a local before boarding to make sure the train goes where you want. Express trains marked *DD* (6/day) get you to Sorrento 20 minutes sooner. Once you reach your destination, turn to the "Arrival" information in each section of this chapter.

Note that if you're going to the ancient site of **Pompeii,** be sure to use the Circumvesuviana train's *Pompei Scavi* stop. Don't use national train connections from Centrale Station to the modern-day city of Pompei (which might seem convenient, but it's far from the ruins).

To Capri or Sorrento by Boat

Naples is well-connected by boat to Capri (roughly 2/hour, 45 minutes, €16) and Sorrento (5 hydrofoils/day, departs roughly every 2 hours starting at 9:00, 35 minutes, €10). Taking the hydrofoil to Sorrento is faster—and safer from pickpockets—than taking the Circumvesuviana train, though it doesn't run as frequently.

Conveniently, Naples' local boat dock (called Molo Beverello) is right next to the cruise terminal: As you exit the cruise terminal, bear left, following the well-marked crosswalks to *Molo Beverello*. Pass the row of cafés to reach the blue-and-white Molo Beverello building. Check upcoming departures on the computer screens. Ticket windows clearly display the next available departure. (Local TIs also have schedules.)

Before taking the boat anywhere, first be absolutely certain that you can make it back to your cruise ship with plenty of time to spare. Ask and double-check with the ticket-sellers. Buy a ticket for whichever is leaving soonest to your destination, and also buy your return ticket, reserving a seat in advance if possible. If crowds are expected on the return boat, arrive at the dock early.

The four primary ferry companies that service Naples, Sorrento, and Amalfi Coast are Caremar, SNAV, Metro del Mare, and Alilauro (a.k.a. LMP or Gescab). Many of the schedules can be found together on www.capritourism.com; click "Shipping Timetable." Each company has different destinations and prices; some compete for the same trips. The quicker the trip, the higher the price. The number of boats that run per day depends on the season. Trips are canceled in bad weather.

By Tour

For information on hiring a local guide in Naples, see page 642; for Pompeii, see page 661.

Returning to Your Ship

If you end up on **Piazza del Plebiscito,** you're about a 10-minute walk from your ship: Simply go to the bottom corner of the palace, ride the free elevator or walk down the stairs to the embankment, then head straight to the cruise terminal—you can see your ship from here.

If you're returning to Naples on the **Circumvesuviana,** stay on until the last stop and head out the front door to the street called Corso Garibaldi. Take a taxi, or find bus #601 or #152, and ride it (going toward your left, with your back to the Circumvesuviana station) to the Acton stop, which is in front of the cruise terminal.

If you're returning by **boat,** it couldn't be easier: You'll see your cruise ship from where you disembark.

For information on what to do if you've missed your boat, see the sidebar on page 704.

Orientation to Naples
Tourist Information

The most convenient of Naples' three TIs is in **Centrale train station** (daily 9:00-19:00, near track 23, tel. 081-268-779, www.eptnapoli.info or www.inaples.it). Pick up a map and the *Qui Napoli* booklet, which lists the latest museum hours, events, and transportation info. If they say they're "finished," ask for an old one. In town, you'll find TIs at the **Galleria Umberto I shopping mall** (across from the entrance to the Teatro di San Carlo; Mon-Sat 9:00-19:00, Sun 9:00-14:00, tel. 081-402-394) and across from the **Church of Gesù Nuovo** (same hours as Galleria Umberto I, tel. 081-551-2701). Skip the region's Campania ArteCard, which isn't a good value for a short cruise visit.

Arrival in Naples

By Boat: If you're arriving by cruise ship or by boat from Sorrento or Capri, see "Arrival at the Port of Naples," earlier.

By Circumvesuviana Train: If your cruise ship docks in Sorrento, and you're taking the Circumvesuviana train to Naples, get off at the Garibaldi stop (one stop before the end of the line). I'd recommend making a beeline to the Archaeological Museum, where you can either tour the collection or begin my self-guided walk.

If you'll be taking a taxi to the museum, ride the escalator from the Garibaldi stop up into the vast Napoli Centrale train station. Inside the station, you'll find a TI and an ATM (at Banco di Napoli near track 24). Taxis wait outside; figure on €10 for a ride to the museum (insist on the meter—*tassametro)*.

If you want to take Naples' Metro (Metropolitana) to the Archaeological Museum, follow Metro signs after you get off the Circumvesuviana train. Your train ticket includes a ride anywhere on the Metro system within three hours of validation. At the Metro stop (near track 14, downstairs in Centrale Station), ask which track—*"Quale binario?"* (KWAH-lay bee-NAH-ree-oh)— to Piazza Cavour (direction: Pozzuoli, usually track 4). Validate your ticket in the small yellow boxes near the escalator going down to the tracks. Ride the subway one stop. As you leave the Metro, you can exit and hike uphill, or follow *Linea 1 Museo* signs through a long series of underground moving sidewalks to the Museo stop (on a different line), where you'll exit a bit closer to the museum. No matter where you emerge, look for a grand old red building up a flight of stairs at the top of the block.

Helpful Hints

Theft Alert: Err on the side of caution. Don't venture into neighborhoods that make you uncomfortable. Walk with confidence, as if you know where you're going and what you're doing. Assume able-bodied beggars are thieves.

Stick to busy streets and beware of gangs of hoodlums. A third of the city is unemployed, and past local governments have set an example that the Mafia would be proud of. Assume con artists are more clever than you. Any jostle or commotion

Naples

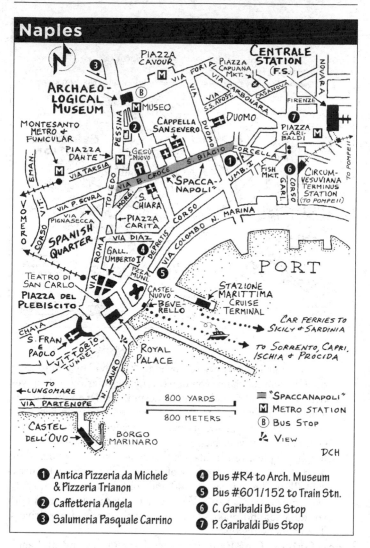

1 Antica Pizzeria da Michele & Pizzeria Trianon

2 Caffetteria Angela

3 Salumeria Pasquale Carrino

4 Bus #R4 to Arch. Museum

5 Bus #601/152 to Train Stn.

6 C. Garibaldi Bus Stop

7 P. Garibaldi Bus Stop

is probably a thief-team smokescreen. Motor-scooter crime (where a thief grabs a bag or a necklace, then races off) is not uncommon. To keep bags safe, it's probably best to store them at Centrale Station.

Perhaps your biggest risk of theft is while catching or riding the Circumvesuviana commuter train. While I ride the Circumvesuviana comfortably and safely, each year I hear of many who get ripped off on this ride. You won't be mugged—just conned or pickpocketed. For maximum safety and peace of mind, sit in the front car, where the driver will double as

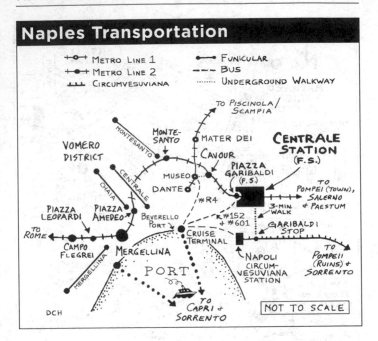

Naples Transportation

┼━o━┼ Metro Line 1
┼━●━┼ Metro Line 2
⊥⊥⊥ Circumvesuviana
●━━● Funicular
━ ━ ━ Bus
·········· Underground Walkway

TO PISCINOLA/ SCAMPIA

VOMERO DISTRICT

MONTESANTO

MONTE-SANTO

MATER DEI

CAVOUR

CENTRALE STATION (F.S.)

CENTRALE

MUSEO

DANTE

PIAZZA GARIBALDI (F.S.)

TO POMPEI (TOWN), SALERNO & PAESTUM

3-MIN. WALK

#R4

PIAZZA LEOPARDI

PIAZZA AMEDEO

CHIAIA

BEVERELLO PORT

#152 & #601

GARIBALDI STOP

TO ROME

CAMPO FLEGREI

MERGELLINA

CRUISE TERMINAL

NAPOLI CIRCUM-VESUVIANA STATION

TO POMPEII (RUINS) & SORRENTO

MERGELLINA

PORT

TO CAPRI & SORRENTO

DCH

NOT TO SCALE

your protector.

Con artists may say you need to "transfer" by taxi to catch the Circumvesuviana; you don't. Anyone offering to help you with your bags is likely a thief, despite displayed credentials. There are no porters at Centrale Station or in the basement where the Circumvesuviana station is located. Wear your money belt, hang on to your bag, and don't display any valuables.

Traffic: In Naples, red lights are discretionary, and pedestrians need to be wary, particularly of motor scooters. Smart tourists jaywalk in the shadow of bold and confident locals, who generally ignore crosswalks. Wait for a break in traffic, cross with confidence, and make eye contact with approaching drivers. The traffic will stop.

Local Guides: Pina Esposito specializes in art and archaeology, and does fine tours of Naples' excellent but somewhat hard-to-appreciate Archaeological Museum (€120/2 hours, 10 percent off with this book, confirm one week in advance, sometimes available on shorter notice, mobile 349-596-8251, annamariaesposito1 @virgilio.it). She also leads tours of Capri, Pompeii, and the surrounding area. For private tours of Capri (if Pina is booked), try the folks at **Mondo Guide** (tel. 081-751-3290, info@mondoguide.it).

NAPLES

Getting Around Naples

Naples' subway, the Metropolitana, has two lines. Line 2, the main line, runs from Centrale Station (catch it downstairs at the Garibaldi stop) through the center of town (direction: Pozzuoli), stopping at Piazza Cavour (a 5-minute walk from the Archaeological Museum) and Montesanto (top of Spanish Quarter and Spaccanapoli street). Line 1 runs from Piscinola/Scampia (suburbs) into the city center, stopping at the Museo station, near the Archaeological Museum (connects to Line 2's Piazza Cavour subway stop). Tickets cost €1.10 and are good for 1.5 hours. All-day tickets cost €3.10. Validate tickets either at the turnstile (if there is one), or in the small yellow boxes you'll see before you reach the track.

Sights in Naples

▲▲▲Archaeological Museum (Museo Archeologico)

For lovers of antiquity, this museum alone makes Naples a worthwhile stop. Considering its popularity and the importance of the collection, it's remarkable how ramshackle, unkempt, and dumpy its displays are. Still, if you can overlook the dust bunnies, this museum offers the best possible peek into the artistic jewelry boxes of Pompeii and Herculaneum. When Pompeii was excavated in the early 1800s, Naples' Bourbon king bellowed, "Bring me the best of what you find!" The actual sites are impressive but barren; the finest art and artifacts ended up here.

Cost and Hours: €6.50, but often €10 with mandatory charge for special exhibits, cash only, Wed-Mon 9:00-19:30, closed Tue.

Getting There: For directions on how to get here from the cruise port, see page 636, and from the Circumvesuviana station, see page 640.

Secret Room Appointment: Depending on how packed the museum is, you may need to make an appointment on arrival to visit the Secret Room (Gabinetto Segreto), which contains erotic art from Pompeii (included in admission, you get a 15-minute window; to schedule a time, go to the information counter—on your immediate left as you enter). When it's not crowded, an appointment is unnecessary.

Information: Tel. 081-442-2149. For the basics, you can follow my self-guided tour (below). If you want a **guided tour,** look for Pina Esposito at the museum (see "Helpful Hints," earlier; €120/2-hour tour, 10 percent less with this book; help her assemble a group of up to 10 to split the fee). **Audioguides,** which haven't been updated for years, cost €4 (at ticket desk). The shop sells a worthwhile *National Archaeological Museum of Naples* guidebook—at €12, it's still a better value than the audioguide. Bag check is obligatory and free. Photos are allowed without a flash.

The museum seems to be in constant chaos due to ongoing renovations. If you can't find a particular work, ask a museum custodian, *"Dov'è?"* (DOH-vay, meaning "Where is?"), followed by the item's name.

Self-Guided Tour

Entering the museum, stand at the base of the grand staircase. To your right, on the ground floor, are larger-than-life statues

from the Farnese Collection, starring the *Toro Farnese*. Up the stairs on the mezzanine level (turn left at the lion) are mosaics and frescoes from Pompeii, including the *Battle of Alexander* and the Secret Room of erotic art. On the top floor is a scale model of Pompeii and bronze statues from Herculaneum (a nearby town destroyed in the same eruption that devastated Pompeii). You'll find WCs by circling behind the staircase.

• *From the base of the grand staircase, turn right and head to the far end.*

Ground Floor: The Farnese Collection

The museum's ground floor alone has enough Greek and Roman art to put any museum on the map. Its highlight is the Farnese Collection, a grand hall of huge, bright, and wonderfully restored statues excavated from Rome's Baths of Caracalla.

The tangled **Toro Farnese** depicts a woman being tied to a bull. At 13 feet, it's the tallest ancient marble group ever found, and the largest intact statue from antiquity. A third-century A.D. copy

of a lost bronze Hellenistic original, it was carved out of one piece of marble. Michelangelo and others "restored" it at the pope's request—meaning that they integrated surviving bits into a new work. Panels on the wall show which pieces were actually carved by Michelangelo (in blue on the chart): the head of the woman in back, the torso of the aunt under the bull, and the dog. (Imagine how the statue would stand out if it was thoughtfully lit and not surrounded by white walls.)

Here's the story behind the statue: Once upon an ancient Greek time, King Lycus was bewitched by Dirce. He abandoned his pregnant wife, Antiope (standing regally in the background). The single mom gave birth to twin boys (shown here). When they grew up, they killed their deadbeat dad and tied Dirce to the horns of a bull to be bashed against a mountain. Captured in marble, the action is thrilling: cape flailing, dog snarling, hooves in the air. You can almost hear the bull snorting. And in the back, Antiope oversees this harsh ancient justice with satisfaction.

At the far end of the hall stands **Hercules.** In a small room behind him is a glass case with the sumptuous **Farnese Cup** *(Tazza Farnese,* second century B.C., from Egypt). This large, ancient cameo made of agates looks less like a cup than a cereal bowl. Its decorations are both Egyptian (the Nile toting a lush cornucopia) and, on the flip side, Greek (Medusa's head).

• *Backtrack a bit, then head up to the mezzanine level.*

Mezzanine: Pompeiian Mosaics and the Secret Room

Most of these mosaics—of animals, musicians, and geometric designs—were taken from Pompeii's House of the Faun (see page 669). The house's delightful centerpiece is a 20-inch-high statue of the *Dancing Faun.* This rare surviving Greek bronze statue (from the fourth century B.C.) is surrounded by some of the best mosaics of that age.

A highlight is the grand *Battle of Alexander,* a second-century B.C. copy of the original Greek fresco, done a century earlier. It decorated a floor in the House of the Faun and was found intact; the damage you see occurred as this treasure was moved from Pompeii to the king's collection here.

The painting (on left, made before it was moved) shows how it once looked. Alexander (left side of the scene, with curly hair and sideburns) is about to defeat the Persians under Darius (central figure, in chariot with turban and beard). This pivotal victory allowed Alexander to quickly overrun much of Asia (331 B.C.). Alexander is the only one without a helmet...a confident master of the battlefield while everyone else is fighting for their lives, eyes bulging with fear. Notice how the horses, already in retreat, add to the scene's propaganda value. Notice also the shading and perspective, which Renaissance artists would later work so hard to accomplish. (A modern reproduction of the mosaic is now in the House of the Faun.)

The **Secret Room** *(Gabinetto Segreto)* contains a sizable assortment of erotic frescoes, well-hung pottery, and perky statues that once decorated bedrooms, meeting rooms, brothels, and even shops at Pompeii and Herculaneum. (On crowded days, you may have to make an appointment on arrival to view the room, though this is rare—see "Secret Room Appointment," page 643.) These bawdy statues and frescoes—many of them once displayed in Pompeii's grandest houses—were entertainment for guests. (By the time they made it to this museum, in 1819, the frescoes could be viewed only with permission from the king—see the letters in the glass case just outside the door.) The Roman nobles commissioned the wildest scenes imaginable. Think of them as ancient dirty jokes.

Circulating counterclockwise through this section, look for: 1) a faun playfully pulling the sheet off a beautiful woman, only to be grossed out by the plumbing of a hermaphrodite (perhaps the original *"Mamma mia!"*); 2) horny pygmies from Africa in action; 3) Venus, the patron goddess of Pompeii, a favorite pin-up girl; 4) a particularly high-quality statue of a goat and a satyr illustrating the act of sodomy; and 5) a toga with an embarrassing bulge.

The next room is furnished and decorated the way an ancient brothel might have been. The 10 frescoes on the wall functioned as both a menu of services offered and as a kind of *Kama Sutra* of sex positions. The walls feature big stone penises that once projected over Pompeii's doorways. A massive phallus was not necessarily a sexual symbol, but a magical amulet used against the "evil eye." It symbolized fertility, happiness, good luck, riches, straight A's, and general well-being. The glass cases contain more phallic art.

• *So, now that your travel buddy is finally showing a little interest in art...finish up your visit by climbing the stairs to the top floor.*

Top Floor: Statues, Artifacts, and a Model of Pompeii

At the top of the stairs, you'll enter a grand, empty hall. This was the great hall of the university (17th and 18th centuries) until the building became the royal museum in 1777. The sundial (from 1791) still works. At noon, a sunray strikes the spot, indicating today's date...if you know your zodiac.

To your right are rooms containing **bronze statues** from Herculaneum—of racers, dancers, and fauns (first-century B.C. copies of fourth-century B.C. originals). They once decorated the

holiday home (Villa dei Papyri in Herculaneum) of Julius Caesar's father-in-law. Look into the lifelike blue eyes of the intense *atleta* (athletes), bent on doing their best. The *Five Dancers*, with their inlaid-ivory eyes and graceful poses, decorated a portico. *Resting Hermes* (with his tired little heel wings) is taking a break. The *Drunken Faun* (singing and snapping his fingers to the beat, a wineskin at his side) is clearly living for today—true to the *carpe diem* preaching of the Epicurean philosophy. Caesar's father-in-law was an Epicurean philosopher, and his library—containing 2,000 papyrus scrolls—supported his outlook.

Return to the grand hall and continue to the other side, passing through several rooms of vases, statuettes, spoons, glassware, and other objects found at Pompeii. Keep going to the far end, where you'll find a **scale model** of the archaeological site of Pompeii, circa 1879 *(plastico di Pompeii)*. Belly up to the railing and find the Porta Marina entrance and the large rectangle of the town's Forum. Another model on the wall shows the site in 2004, after more excavations.

The Rest of the Museum

After years in restoration, the museum's large collection of **frescoes** taken from the walls of Pompeii villas is back (in Rooms LXVI to LXXVIII). Pompeiians loved to decorate their homes with scenes from mythology (Hercules' Labors, Venus and Mars in love), landscapes, everyday market scenes, and faux architecture. The display is roughly chronological.

For extra credit, visit **Doriforo**. (Ask a guard, *"Dov'è il Doriforo?"* He was last spotted on the ground floor, in the hall to the left, as you face the staircase.) This seven-foot-tall "spear-carrier" (the literal translation of *doriforo*) just stands there, as if holding a spear. What's the big deal about this statue, which looks like so many others? It's a marble replica made by the Romans of one of the most-copied statues of antiquity, a fifth-century B.C. bronze Greek original by Polyclitus. This copy once stood in a Pompeii gym, where it inspired ancient athletes with the ideal proportions of Greek beauty. So full of motion, and so realistic in its *contrapposto* pose (weight on one foot), the *Doriforo* would later inspire Donatello and

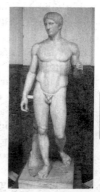

Michelangelo, triggering the Renaissance. And so the glories of ancient Pompeii, once buried and forgotten, live on today.

Self-Guided Walk in Naples

A Slice of Neapolitan Life

Walk from the Archaeological Museum through the heart of town and back to Centrale Station. Allow at least three hours, plus pizza and sightseeing stops. If you have less time, do just Part 1, ending near the port.

Naples, a living medieval city, is its own best sight. Couples artfully make love on Vespas surrounded by more fights and smiles per cobblestone than anywhere else in Italy. Rather than seeing Naples as a list of sights, visit its one great museum and then capture its essence by taking this walk through the core of the city. Should you become overwhelmed or lost, step into a store and ask for directions: "Where is the central station?" in Italian is *"Dov'è la stazione centrale?"* (DOH-vay lah staht-zee-OH-nay chen-TRAH-lay). Or point to the next sight in this book.

Part 1: Via Pessina, Via Toledo, and the Spanish Quarter

The first part of this walk is a straight one-mile ramble down a boulevard to Galleria Umberto I, near the Royal Palace. Ideally, begin by touring the Archaeological Museum (at the top of Piazza Cavour, Metro: Cavour or Museo).

• *Leaving the Archaeological Museum, turn right and go one block, to the head of Via Pessina. Follow this busy street downhill to Piazza Dante—see his statue in the distance.*

Piazza Dante: This square is marked by a statue of Dante, the medieval poet. Here you can feel Italy...but many Neapolitans merely feel the repression of the central state. When Napoleon was defeated, Naples became its own independent kingdom. But with Italian unification in 1861, Naples went from being a thriving cultural and political capital to a provincial town, its money used to help establish the industrial strength of the north. Originally, a statue of a Spanish Bourbon king stood here. The grand red-and-gray building is typical of Bourbon structures from that period. With the unification of Italy, the king, symbolic of Italy's colonial subjugation, was replaced by Dante—considered the father of the Italian language and a strong symbol of nationalism.

Old Dante looks out over an urban area that was once grand, then chaotic, and is now slowly becoming grand again. Behind Dante's right shoulder is the Port'Alba, part of Naples' old wall and the entrance to a small street lined with book vendors. Via Pessina, the long, straight street that you're walking, originated

"A Slice of Neapolitan Life" Walk

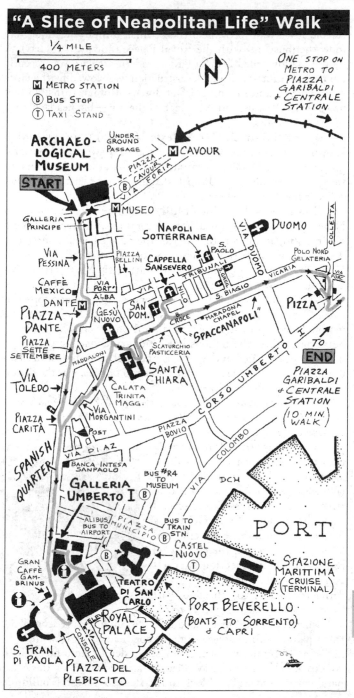

¼ MILE

400 METERS

Ⓜ METRO STATION
Ⓑ BUS STOP
Ⓣ TAXI STAND

N

ONE STOP ON METRO TO PIAZZA GARIBALDI & CENTRALE STATION

ARCHAEO-LOGICAL MUSEUM

START

UNDER-GROUND PASSAGE

Ⓜ CAVOUR

PIAZZA CAVOUR

VIA FORIA

Ⓑ

Ⓜ MUSEO

GALLERIA PRINCIPE

VIA PESSINA

PIAZZA BELLINI

NAPOLI SOTTERRANEA

CAPPELLA SANSEVERO

S. PAOLO

DUOMO

VIA DUOMO

COLLETTA

POLO NORD GELATERIA

VIA FORC.

CAFFÈ MEXICO

VIA PORT' ALBA

SAN DOM.

TRIBUNALI

S. BIAGIO

VICARIA

DANTE Ⓜ

PIAZZA DANTE

GESÙ NUOVO

VIA CROCE

B. CROCE

S. BIAGIO

MARADONA CHAPEL

"SPACCANAPOLI"

PIZZA

PIAZZA SETTE SETTEMBRE

MADDALONI

SCATURCHIO PASTICCERIA

END

VIA TOLEDO

SANTA CHIARA

CORSO UMBERTO I

PIAZZA GARIBALDI & CENTRALE STATION (10 MIN. WALK)

CALATA TRINITA MAGG.

PIAZZA CARITÀ

VIA MORGANTINI

POST

PIAZZA BOVIO

COLOMBO

SPANISH QUARTER

VIA DIAZ

BANCA INTESA SANPAOLO

BUS #R4 TO MUSEUM

VIA DCH

GALLERIA UMBERTO I

Ⓑ

PIAZZA MUNICIPIO

BUS TO TRAIN STN.

PORT

ALIBUS BUS TO AIRPORT

Ⓑ

CASTEL NUOVO

Ⓣ

STAZIONE MARITTIMA (CRUISE TERMINAL)

GRAN CAFFÈ GAMBRINUS

ⓘ

TEATRO DI SAN CARLO

ⓘ

ROYAL PALACE

PORT BEVERELLO (BOATS TO SORRENTO) & CAPRI

S. FRAN. DI PAOLA

PIAZZA DEL PLEBISCITO

CONSOLE

NAPLES

as a military road built by Spain in the 16th century. It skirted the old town wall to connect the Spanish military headquarters (now the museum) with the Royal Palace (down by the bay). A subway station called Dante (with a modern-art flair) was recently built here on Piazza Dante. Construction was slowed by the city's rich underground history: 13 feet down—Roman ruins; 23 feet down—Greek ruins; and every inch of the way—big headaches for construction workers.

Across the street, **Caffè Mexico** (at #86) is an institution known for its espresso, which is served already sweetened—ask for *senza zucchero* if you don't want sugar (pay first, then take receipt to the counter; locals tip €0.10). Most Italians agree that Neapolitan coffee is the best anywhere.

Continue walking downhill, remembering that here in Naples, red lights are considered "decorations." When crossing a street, try to tag along with a native. The people here are survivors: A long history of corrupt and greedy colonial overlords has taught Neapolitans to deal creatively with authority. Many credit this aspect of Naples' past for the advent of organized crime here.

Via Pessina becomes Via Toledo (another reminder of Spanish rule), Naples' principal shopping street. In 1860, from the white marble balcony of the Neoclassical building overlooking Piazza Sette Settembre, the famous revolutionary Giuseppe Garibaldi declared Italy united and Victor Emmanuel II its first king. Not until 1870, when Rome fell to the unification forces, was the dream of Italian unity fully realized.

• *Continue straight on Via Toledo. At the next left (Via Maddaloni), about three blocks below Piazza Dante and a block past Piazza Sette Settembre, you'll come to the long, straight street called...*

Spaccanapoli: Before crossing the street—whose name translates as "split Naples"—look left. Look right. Since ancient times, this thin street (which changes names several times: Maddaloni, Via B. Croce, Via S. Biagio dei Librai, Forecella, and Vicaria) has bisected the city. We'll return to this intersection later. (If you want to abbreviate this walk, turn left here and skip ahead to "Part 2.")

• *Stay on Via Toledo, which runs through...*

Piazza Carità: Surrounded by fascist architecture from 1938, this square is full of stern, straight, obedient lines. (For the best fascist architecture in town, take a slight detour from here—with your back to Via Toledo, leave Piazza Carità downhill on the right-hand corner and walk a block to the Poste e Telegrafi building.

There you'll see several government buildings with stirring reliefs singing the praises of a totalitarian society.)

• *From Piazza Carità, wander south down Via Toledo for a few blocks, looking to your left for more examples of...*

Fascist Architecture (Banks): Notice the two banks. Try robbing the Banco di Napoli (Via Toledo 178). Step across the street and check out its architecture: typical fascist arches and reliefs, built to celebrate the bank's 400th anniversary (est. 1539—how old is *your* bank?).

On the next corner, **Banca Intesa Sanpaolo** fills an older palace—take a free peek at the opulent interior. On the second floor is a great late Caravaggio painting. *The Martyrdom of Saint Ursula* shows a terrible scene: His marriage proposal rejected, the king of the Huns flings an arrow into Ursula's chest. Blood spurts, Ursula is stunned but accepts her destiny sweetly, and Caravaggio himself (far right, his last self-portrait) screams to symbolize the rejection of evil (€3, Mon-Sat 10:00-18:00, closed Sun; includes 40-minute audioguide, a look at old Naples paintings, and a fine WC).

• *From here, side-trip uphill three blocks into the...*

Spanish Quarter: This is a classic world of *basso* (low) living. In such tight quarters, families generally do it in the road.

This is *the* cliché of life in Naples, as shown in so many movies. The Spanish Quarter is Naples at its rawest, poorest, and most characteristic. The only predictable things about this Neapolitan tide pool are the ancient grid plan of its streets (which survives from Greek times), the friendliness of its shopkeepers, and the boldness of its mopeds. Concerned locals will tug on their lower eyelids, warning you to be wary. Hungry? Pop into a grocery shop and ask the man to make you his best prosciutto and mozzarella sandwich (the price should be about €4).

• *Return to Via Toledo (clogged with more people than cars) and work your way down to the immense...*

Piazza del Plebiscito: This square celebrates the 1861 vote (*plebiscito*, plebiscite), when Naples chose to join Italy. Walk to the middle of the square. From here, you'll see the Church of San Francesco di Paola, with its Pantheon-inspired dome and broad, arcing colonnades.

• *Opposite is the...*

Royal Palace (Palazzo Reale): Having housed Spanish, French, and even Italian royalty, this building displays statues of all those who stayed here. Look for eight kings in the niches, each from a different dynasty (left to right): Norman, German, French, Spanish, Spanish, Spanish, French (Napoleon's brother-in-law), and, finally, Italian—Victor Emmanuel II, King of Savoy. The statues were done at the request of V. E. II's son, so his dad is the most dashing of the group. This huge, lavish palace welcomes the public (€4, more with special exhibits, Thu-Tue 9:00-20:00, closed Wed, last entry one hour before closing, audioguide-€4, or €5/2 people, tel. 848-800-288).

The palace's grand Neoclassical staircase leads up to a floor with 30 plush rooms. You'll follow a one-way route (with some English descriptions) featuring paintings by "the Caravaggio Imitators," Neapolitan tapestries, fine inlaid-stone tabletops, and more. Don't miss the huge Hercules room and the chapel with a fantastic nativity scene (a commotion of 18th-century ceramic figurines).

The **Gran Caffè Gambrinus,** facing the piazza, takes you back to the elegance of 1860. It's a classic place to sample a unique Neapolitan treat called *sfogliatella* (crispy scallop shell-shaped pastry filled with sweet ricotta cheese). Or you might prefer the mushroom-shaped, rum-soaked bread-like cakes called *babà*, which come in a huge variety. Stand at the bar *(banco),* pay double to sit *(tavola),* or just wander around as you imagine the café buzzing with the ritzy intellectuals, journalists, and artsy bohemian types who munched on *babà* here during Naples' 19th-century heyday (daily 7:00-24:00, Piazza del Plebiscito 1, tel. 081-417-582).

• *Continue 50 yards past the Royal Palace to enjoy a...*

Fine Harbor View: While boats busily serve Capri and Sorrento, Mount Vesuvius smolders ominously in the distance. (Hey, look—there's your cruise ship in the foreground!) Look back to see the vast "Bourbon red" palace—its color inspired by Pompeii. On the hilltop above Piazza del Plebiscito is Naples' Carthusian Monastery and the Castle of St. Elmo. This street continues to Naples' romantic harborfront—the fishermen's quarters or Borgo Marinaro—a fortified island connected to the mainland by a stout causeway, with its fanciful Castel dell'Ovo (castle of the egg) and trendy harborside restaurants. Farther along the harborfront stretches the Lungomare promenade and Santa Lucia district. (The long harborfront promenade, Via Francesco Caracciolo, is a delightful people-watching scene on balmy nights.)

• *Nearby, notice the free **elevator** (acensore) that can whisk you down to the embankment below, from which it's just a seven-minute walk to your ship.*

But if you have more time to spare, head back to the piazza and go behind the palace, where you can peek inside the Neoclassical...

Teatro di San Carlo: Built in 1737, 41 years before Milan's La Scala, this is Europe's oldest opera house and Italy's second-most-respected (after La Scala). The theater burned down in 1816 and was rebuilt within the year. Guided 40-minute visits basically just show you the fine auditorium with its 184 boxes—each with a big mirror to reflect the candlelight (€5, Mon-Sat 10:00-17:30, tours every 40 minutes, closed Sun, tel. 081-553-4565, www.teatro sancarlo.it).

Beyond Teatro di San Carlo and the Royal Palace is the huge, harborfront Castel Nuovo, which houses government bureaucrats and the **Civic Museum,** featuring 14th- to 16th-century art (€5, Mon-Sat 9:00-19:00, closed Sun, last entry one hour before closing, tel. 081-795-5877).

Across the street from Teatro di San Carlo, go through the tall yellow arch into the Victorian iron and glass of the 100-year-old shopping mall, **Galleria Umberto I.** Gawk up.

• *For Part 2 of this walk, double back up Via Toledo to Piazza Carità, veering right on Via Morgantini to Via Maddaloni (to avoid the backtracking and uphill walk, catch an €8 taxi to the Church of Gesù Nuovo—JAY-zoo noo-OH-voh).*

Part 2: Spaccanapoli to the Station

You're back at the straight-as-a-Greek-arrow Spaccanapoli, formerly the main thoroughfare of the Greek city of Neapolis.
• *Stop at...*

Piazza Gesù Nuovo: This square is marked by a towering 18th-century Baroque monument to the Counter-Reformation. Although the Jesuit order was powerful in Naples because of its Spanish heritage, locals never attacked Protestants here with the full fury of the Spanish Inquisition. The square also has a handy little TI and is the starting point for electric bus #E1, which makes a 40-minute loop through the characteristic old quarter and ends up back here (buy ticket at nearby newsstand before boarding, 2/hour, daily 7:00-24:00).
• *Now visit two bulky old churches, starting with the austere, fortress-like 17th-century...*

Church of Gesù Nuovo: The unique pyramid-grill facade survives from a fortified 15th-century noble palace. Step inside for a brilliant Neapolitan Baroque interior. The second chapel on the right features a much-adored statue of Giuseppe Moscati (1880-1927), a Christian doctor famous for helping the poor. In 1987, Moscati became the first modern doctor to be canonized.

Continue on to the third chapel and enter the **Sale Moscati.** This huge room is filled with "Ex Votos"—tiny red-and-silver plaques of thanksgiving for prayers answered with the help of St. Moscati (each has a symbol of the ailment cured). Naples' practice of using Ex Votos, while incorporated into its Catholic rituals, goes back to its pagan Greek roots. Rooms from Moscati's nearby apartment are on display, and a glass case shows possessions and photos of the great doctor. As you leave the Sale Moscati, notice the big bomb casing that hangs in the left corner. It fell through the church's dome in 1943, but caused almost no damage...yet another miracle (daily 7:00-12:30 & 16:00-19:30).

• *Head across the street, to the simpler...*

Church of Santa Chiara: Dating from the 14th century, this church is from a period of French royal rule under the Angevin dynasty. Consider the stark contrast between this church (Gothic) and the Gesù Nuovo (Baroque). Notice the huge inlaid-marble Angevin coat of arms on the floor. The faded Trinity on the back wall, to the left of the entry, shows a dove representing the Holy Spirit between the heads of God the Father and Christ (c. 1414). This is an example of the fine frescoes that once covered the walls. Most were stuccoed over during Baroque times or destroyed in 1943 by World War II bombs. The altar is adorned with four finely carved Gothic tombs of Angevin kings. A chapel stacked with Bourbon royalty is just to the right (daily 7:00-12:30 & 16:30-20:00).

• *Leaving the church, take a right and head to the back of the building. Continue through the archway straight ahead, and pass all the parked cars to reach the farthest door on the right. Here you'll find the bright, ornate majolica-tiled...*

Cloistered Courtyard of Santa Chiara: Note the sprawling nativity scene immediately on your right as you enter—a cartoon-ish 3-D snapshot of Old World Napoli. Stop in at its museum (€5, Mon-Sat 9:30-17:30, Sun 9:30-14:30, last entry 30 minutes before closing).

• *Now return to the main drag, turn right, and continue straight down traffic-free Via B. Croce. A good little lunch spot, **Trattoria da Titina e Gennaro**, is just down the street across from the church (Via Santa Chiara 6).*

Since this is a university district, you'll see lots of students and bookstores. This neighborhood is also extremely superstitious. Look for incense-burning women with carts full of good-luck charms for sale.

• *Farther down Spaccanapoli, you'll see the next square...*

Piazza San Domenico Maggiore: This square is marked by an ornate 17th-century monument built to thank God for ending the plague. But more important is the well-loved **Scaturchio Pasticceria,** another good place to try *sfogliatella* (€1.50 to go, costs double at a table in the square, daily 7:20-20:40, tel. 081-551-7031).

• *From this square, detour left along the right side of the castle-like church, then follow yellow signs, taking the first right and walking one block to...*

Cappella Sansevero: This small chapel is a Baroque explosion mourning the body of Christ, who lies on a soft pillow under an incredibly realistic veil. It's also the personal chapel of Raimondo de Sangro, an eccentric Freemason. The monuments to his relatives have a second purpose: to share the Freemason philosophy of freedom through enlightenment (€6, Mon and Wed-Sat 10:00-18:00, Sun 10:00-13:30, closed Tue, last entry 20 minutes before closing, no photos, but postcards are sold in gift shop, Via de Sanctis 19, tel. 081-551-8470).

Study the incredible *Veiled Christ* in the center. Carved out of marble, it's like no other statue I've seen (by Giuseppe "Howdee-doodat" Sammartino, 1753). The Christian message (Jesus died for our salvation) is accompanied by a Freemason message (the veil represents how the body and ego are obstacles to real spiritual freedom). As you walk from Christ's feet to his head, notice how the expression on Jesus' face goes from suffering to peace.

Raimondo de Sangro lies buried at the far (altar) end. An inventor, he created the deep-green pigment used on the ceiling fresco. The inlaid M. C. Escher-esque maze on the floor around de Sangro's tomb is another Freemason reminder of how the quest for knowledge gets you out of the maze of life.

To the right of the altar, the statue *Despair* struggles with a marble rope net (carved out of a single piece of stone), symbolic of a troubled mind. The Freemason symbolism shows how knowledge—in the guise of an angel—frees the human mind. On the opposite side of the altar from *Despair,* a veiled woman fingers a broken plaque, symbolizing...something.

Your Sansevero finale is downstairs: two mysterious...skeletons. Perhaps another of the mad inventor's fancies: Inject a corpse with a fluid to fossilize the veins so that they'll survive the body's decomposition. While that's the legend, it was most likely created to illustrate how the circulatory system works.

• *Return to Via B. Croce (a.k.a. Spaccanapoli), turn left, and continue your cultural scavenger hunt. At the intersection of Via Nilo, find the...*

Statue of the Nile (on the left): A reminder of the multi-ethnic makeup of Greek Neapolis, this statue is in what was the Egyptian quarter. Locals like to call this statue *The Body of Naples,* with the overflowing cornucopia symbolizing the abundance of their fine city. (I once asked a Neapolitan man to describe the local women, who are famous for their beauty, in one word. He replied, "Abundant.") This intersection is considered the center of old Naples.

A few blocks farther, at the tiny square, Via San Gregorio

Armeno leads left into a colorful district (and also to the underground Napoli Sotterranea archaeological site). You'll see many shops that sell tiny components of fantastic *presepi* (nativity scenes), including figurines caricaturing local politicians and celebrities. Just as many Americans keep an eye out year-round for Christmas-tree ornaments, Italians regularly add pieces to the family *presepe*, the centerpiece of their holiday celebrations.

• *As Via B. Croce becomes Via S. Biagio dei Librai, notice the...*

Gold and Silver Shops: Some say stolen jewelry ends up here, is melted down immediately, and gets resold in some other form as soon as it cools. The inimitable Sr. Grassi runs the Ospedale delle Bambole (doll hospital) at #81.

• *Cross busy Via Duomo.*

Here, the street and side-street scenes along Via Vicaria intensify. This is known as a center of the Camorra (organized crime).

Paint a picture with these thoughts: Naples has the most intact street plan of any ancient Roman city. Imagine this city during those times (and retain these images as you visit Pompeii), with streetside shop fronts that close up after dark, turning into private homes. Today, it's just one more page in a 2,000-year-old story of a city: all kinds of meetings, beatings, and cheatings; kisses, near misses, and little-boy pisses.

You name it, it occurs right on the streets today, as it has since ancient times. People ooze from crusty corners. Black-and-white death announcements add to the clutter on the walls. Widows sell cigarettes from buckets. For a peek behind the scenes in the shade of wet laundry, venture down a few side streets. Buy two carrots as a gift for the woman on  the fifth floor if she'll lower her bucket to pick them up.

A few blocks on, at the tiny fenced-in triangle of greenery, hang out for a few minutes just to observe the crazy motorbike action and teen scene.

• *From here, veer right onto Via Forcella (which leads to the busy boulevard that takes you to Centrale Station). A tiny, round traffic island protects a chunk of the ancient Greek wall of Neapolis (fourth century* B.C.*). But first, turn right on busy Via Pietro Colletta, walk 50 yards, and step into the North Pole, at the...*

Polo Nord Gelateria: The oldest *gelateria* in Naples has had four generations of family working here since 1931. Before you order, sample a few flavors, including their *bacio*—"kiss"—flavor (chocolate and hazelnut); all are made fresh daily (Mon-Sat

10:00-24:00, Sun 10:00-14:00 & 17:00-24:00, Via Pietro Colletta 41, tel. 081-205-431). Via Pietro Colletta leads past Napoli's two most competitive **pizzerias** (see "Eating in Naples," later) to Corso Umberto I.

• *Turn left on the grand boulevard-like Corso Umberto I. From here to Centrale Station, it's at least a 10-minute walk (if you're tired, hop on a bus; they all go to the station). To finish the walk, continue on Corso Umberto I—past a gauntlet of purse/CD/sunglasses salesmen and shady characters hawking stolen camcorders—to the vast, ugly Piazza Garibaldi. You made it.*

To reach the cruise port, you can either catch bus #601 or #152 from this end of Piazza Garibaldi; or, if you're taking the train back to Sorrento, you can hike to the far end of the giant square to Centrale Station, then head downstairs to the Circumvesuviana train.

More Sights in Naples

Open-Air Fish Market—Naples' fish market squirts and stinks as it has for centuries under the Porta Nolana (gate in the city wall) just four blocks from Centrale train station. Of the town's many boisterous outdoor markets, this will net you the most photos and memories. From Piazza Nolana, wander under the medieval gate and take your first left down Vico Sopramuro, enjoying this  wild and entirely edible cultural scavenger hunt (Tue-Sun 8:00-14:00, closed Mon).

Two other markets with more clothing and less fish are at Piazza Capuana (several blocks northwest of Centrale Station and tumbling down Via Sant'Antonio Abate, Mon-Sat 8:00-18:00, Sun 9:00-13:00) and a similar cobbled shopping zone along Via Pignasecca (just off Via Toledo, west of Piazza Carità).

Grand View from Certosa San Martino—This ultimate view overlooking Naples, its bay, and a volcano comes with a €6 price tag. The monastery, founded in 1325 and dissolved in the early 1800s, is popular today for its dramatic view gardens, church, and museum, which features a history of the kingdoms of southern Italy and the city's best collection of *presepi* manger scenes (Thu-Tue 8:30-19:00, closed Wed, last entry one hour before closing, Metro: Montesanto, well-posted 10-minute walk from top of Montesanto funicular at Largo San Martino 5, tel. 081-558-6408).

Eating in Naples

Cheap and Famous Pizza

Naples—whose pizzerias bake just the right combination of fresh dough, mozzarella, and tomatoes in traditional wood-burning ovens—is the birthplace of pizza. Drop by one of the two most venerable pizzerias in town (both a few long blocks from the station, at the end of my "A Slice of Neapolitan Life" self-guided walk).

Antica Pizzeria da Michele is for pizza purists. Filled with locals (and tourists), it serves just two varieties: *margherita* (tomato sauce and mozzarella) and *marinara* (tomato sauce, oregano, and garlic, no cheese). Come early to sit and watch the pizza artists in action. A pizza with beer costs €6 (Mon-Sat 10:00-24:00, closed Sun; look for the vertical red *Antica Pizzeria* sign at the intersection of Via Pietro Colletta and Via Cesare Sersale at #1; tel. 081-553-9204).

Pizzeria Trianon, across the street, has been da Michele's archrival since 1923. It offers more choices, slightly higher prices (€5-7), air-conditioning, and a cozier atmosphere. For less chaos, head upstairs. While waiting for your meal, you can survey the evolution of a humble wad of dough into a smoldering bubbly feast in their entryway pizza kitchen (daily 11:00-15:30 & 19:00-23:00, Via Pietro Colletta 42, tel. 081-553-9426, Giuseppe).

Near the Archaeological Museum

Caffetteria Angela is a fun little eating complex: coffee bar; *tavola calda* with hot ready-to-eat dishes (€3-4); and a tiny meat, cheese, and bread shop with all you need for a cheap meal to go. It offers honest pricing and simple, peaceful, air-conditioned indoor seating (no cover, open Mon-Sat 7:00-21:00, Sun 9:00-14:00, just off Via Pessina, 3 blocks below museum at Via Conte di Ruvo 21, tel. 081-549-9660).

Salumeria Pasquale Carrino is a tiny salami shop with an exuberant owner—the fun-loving and flamboyant Pasquale—who turns sandwich-making into a show (€6 sandwich good for two people, Mon-Sat 8:00-15:00 & 16:30-20:00, closed Sun, 100 yards from museum—as you leave take two rights and a left to Via Salvator Rosa 10, tel. 081-564-0889).

Pompeii

Stopped in their tracks by the eruption of Mount Vesuvius in A.D. 79, Pompeii and Herculaneum offer the best look anywhere at what life in Rome must have been like 2,000 years ago. These two cities of well-preserved ruins are yours to explore. Of the two sites, Pompeii is grander, while Herculaneum is smaller and more intimate. Vesuvius, still smoldering ominously, rises up on the horizon. It last erupted in 1944 and is still an active volcano.

A once-thriving commercial port of 20,000, Pompeii (worth ▲▲▲) grew from Greek and Etruscan roots to become an important Roman city. Then, at about noon on August 24, A.D. 79, everything changed as the city was buried under 30 feet of hot volcanic ash. For archaeologists, this was a shake-and-bake windfall, teaching them volumes about daily Roman life. Pompeii was rediscovered in the 1600s; excavations began in 1748.

Pompeii is a surprisingly big and impressive site, but its best art is in Naples' Archaeological Museum. If you want to deepen your understanding of Pompeii, try to visit the museum in Naples as well.

Orientation to Pompeii

Cost: €11, €20 combo-ticket includes Herculaneum (called Ercolano) and three lesser sites (valid 3 days).

Hours: Daily April-Oct 8:30-19:30, Nov-March 8:30-17:00 (last entry 1.5 hours before closing).

Getting There: Pompeii is roughly midway between Naples and Sorrento on the Circumvesuviana train line (2/hour, €2.40 and 35 minutes from Naples, €1.90 and 30 minutes from Sorrento, one-way, www.vesuviana.it).

Arrival at Pompeii: Get off the Circumvesuviana train at the *Pompei Scavi, Villa dei Misteri* stop (from Naples, it's the stop after *Torre Annunziata;* from Sorrento, it's the one after *Moregine*). From the Pompei Scavi train station, turn right and walk down the road about a block to the entrance (first left turn). The TI is farther down the street, but it's not a necessary stop for your visit. Parking is available at Camping Zeus near the Circumvesuviana train station (€2.50/hour).

Information: A good map and a helpful information booklet

POMPEII

Pompeii

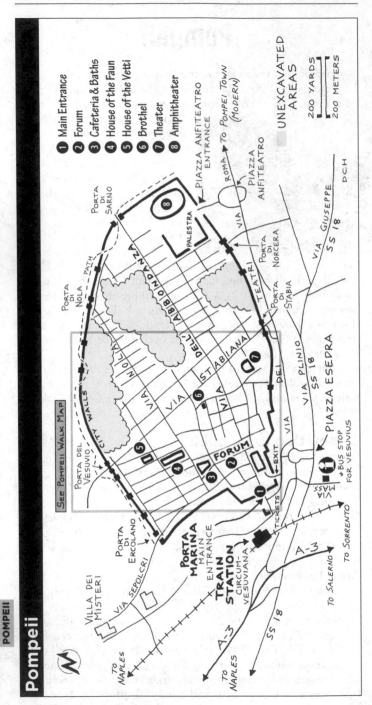

POMPEII

1 Main Entrance
2 Forum
3 Cafeteria & Baths
4 House of the Faun
5 House of the Vetti
6 Brothel
7 Theater
8 Amphitheater

UNEXCAVATED AREAS

200 YARDS
200 METERS

SEE POMPEII WALK MAP

N

TO NAPLES

VILLA DEI MISTERI

VIA SEPOLCRI

PORTA DI ERCOLANO

PORTA DEL VESUVIO

CITY WALLS

VIA NOLANA

PATH

PORTA DI NOLA

VIA DELL'ABBONDANZA

PORTA DI SARNO

PALESTRA

PORTA DI NOCERA

PORTA DI STABIA

VIA STABIANA

VIA DEI TEATRI

PIAZZA ANFITEATRO ENTRANCE

PIAZZA ANFITEATRO

TO POMPEI TOWN (MODERN)

ROMA

VIA GIUSEPPE

SS 18

DCH

PIAZZA ESEDRA

VIA PLINIO

SS 18

BUS STOP FOR VESUVIUS

i

VIA MASS

TICKETS

EXIT

FORUM

PORTA MARINA MAIN ENTRANCE

TRAIN STATION

CIRCUM-VESUVIANA

A-3

TO SORRENTO

TO SALERNO

SS 18

TO NAPLES

A-3

(which describes the most important stops within the site), when available, are included with your admission, but you must pick them up at the information window (to the left of the WCs). Tel. 081-857-5347, www.pompeiisites.org.

The bookshop sells the small Pompeii and Herculaneum *Past and Present* book. Its helpful text and plastic overlays allow you to re-create the ruins (€12 in bookstores, pay no more than that if you buy from a street vendor; look for the current year's edition).

Tours: My self-guided tour covers the basics. **Live guides** (around €115/2 hours) of varying quality can be risky—there really is no guarantee of what you're getting. They cluster near the ticket booth and may try to herd you into a group with other travelers, which makes the price more reasonable for you. For a private tour, hire the knowledgeable **Gaetano Manfredi,** who brings energy, intensity, and theatricality to his tours. He's a joy to follow for two hours as he brings the dusty ruins to life. Avoid impersonators. The real Gaetano takes bookings only in advance, preferably by email (rates vary with season and group size, tel. 338-725-5620, www.pompeiitourguide .com, gaetanoguide@hotmail.it). Parents, note that some sexually explicit frescoes are included on tours.

Audioguide Tours: These are available from a kiosk near the ticket booth at the Porta Marina entrance (€6.50, €10/2 people, ID required), but they offer basically the same info as your free booklet. You can download a free audio version of this tour at www.ricksteves.com/audioeurope, from iTunes, or through the Rick Steves Audio Europe smartphone app.

Length of This Tour: Allow three hours.

Services: The site has two WCs—one near the entrance and another in the cafeteria.

Cuisine Art: Your best bet is to bring your own food. The restaurant within the site serves edible sandwiches, pizza, and pasta at a reasonable price. A few mediocre restaurants cluster between the entrance and the train station.

Starring: Roofless (collapsed) but otherwise intact Roman buildings, plaster casts of hapless victims, a few erotic frescoes, and the dawning realization that these ancient people were no different from us.

Background

Pompeii, founded in 600 B.C., eventually became a booming Roman trading city. Not rich, not poor, it was middle class—a perfect example of typical Roman life. Most streets would have been lined with stalls and jammed with customers from sunup to sundown. Chariots vied with shoppers for street space. Two thousand years

ago, Rome controlled the entire
Mediterranean—making it a kind
of free-trade zone—and Pompeii
was a central and bustling port.

There were no posh neigh-
borhoods in Pompeii. Rich
and poor mixed it up as elegant
houses existed side by side with
simple homes. While nearby
Herculaneum would have been a
classier place to live (traffic-free streets, fancier houses, far better drainage), Pompeii was the place for action and shopping. It
served an estimated 20,000 residents with more than 40 bakeries, 30 brothels, and 130 bars, restaurants, and hotels. With most
of its buildings covered by brilliant white ground-marble stucco,
Pompeii in A.D. 79 was an impressive town.

Self-Guided Tour of Pompeii

• *Just past the ticket-taker, start your approach up to the...*

❶ Porta Marina

The city of Pompeii was born on the hill ahead of you. This was

the original town gate. Before
Vesuvius blew, the sea came
nearly to here. Look to the left
in the distance to see the stone
rings where ships were tied to
the dock. Also notice the two
openings in the gate (ahead,
up the ramp). Both were left
open by day to admit major
traffic. At night, the larger one was closed for better security.

• *Pass through the Porta Marina and continue up the street, pausing at
the three large stepping-stones in the middle.*

❷ Pompeii's Streets

Every day, Pompeiians flooded the streets with gushing water to

clean them. These stepping-
stones let pedestrians cross
without getting their sandals
wet. Chariots traveling in either
direction could straddle the
stones (all had standard-size
axles). A single stepping-stone
in a road means it was a one-way

street, a pair indicates an ordinary two-way, and three (like this) signifies a major thoroughfare. The basalt stones are the original Roman pavement. The sidewalks (elevated to hide the plumbing) were paved with bits of broken pots (an ancient form of recycling) and studded with reflective bits of white marble. These "cats' eyes" helped people get around after dark, either by moonlight or with the help of lamps.

• *Continue straight ahead, don your mental toga, and enter the city as the Romans once did. The road opens up into the spacious main square: the Forum. Stand at the end of this rectangular space and look toward Mount Vesuvius.*

❸ The Forum (Foro)

Pompeii's commercial, religious, and political center stands at the intersection of the city's two main streets. While it's the

most ruined part of Pompeii, it's grand nonetheless. Picture the piazza surrounded by two-story buildings on all sides. The pedestals that line the square once held statues (now safely displayed in the museum in Naples). In its heyday, Pompeii's citizens gathered here in the main square to shop, talk politics, and socialize. Business took place in the important buildings that lined the piazza.

The Forum was dominated by the **Temple of Jupiter,** at the far end (marked by a half-dozen ruined columns atop a stair-step base). Jupiter was the supreme god of the Roman pantheon—you might be able to make out his little white marble head at the center-rear of the temple.

At the near end of the Forum (where you're standing) is the **curia,** or city hall. Like many Roman buildings, it was built with brick and mortar, then covered with marble walls and floors. To your left (as you face Vesuvius and the Temple of Jupiter) is the **basilica,** or courthouse.

Since Pompeii was a typical town, it has the same layout and components that you'll find in any Roman city—main square, curia, basilica, temples, axis of roads, and so on. All power converged at the Forum: religious (the temple), political (the curia), judicial (the basilica), and commercial (this piazza was the main marketplace). Even the power of the people was expressed here, since this is where they gathered to vote. Imagine the hubbub of this town square.

Look beyond the Temple of Jupiter. Five miles to the north looms the ominous backstory to this site: **Mount Vesuvius.**

POMPEII

The Eruption of Vesuvius

At about noon on August 24, A.D. 79, Mount Vesuvius blew, sending a mushroom cloud of ash, dust, cinders, and rocks 12 miles into the air. It spewed for 18 hours straight, as winds blew the cloud southward. The white-gray ash settled like snow on Pompeii, collapsing roofs and floors, but leaving the walls intact. Two thousand of the town's 20,000 residents were entombed under eight feet of fine powder.

The next morning, Vesuvius' upper portion collapsed, picking up speed as it fell to earth, creating a cloud of ash, pumice, and gas. The red-hot avalanche (a "pyroclastic flow") sped down the side of the mountain at nearly 100 miles per hour. Four minutes later, it engulfed the city of Herculaneum (four miles away), burying it in nearly 60 feet of hot mud. The mud cooled into stone, freezing the moment in time.

Mentally draw a triangle up from the two remaining peaks to reconstruct the mountain before the eruption. When it blew, Pompeiians had no idea that they had been living under a volcano, since Vesuvius hadn't erupted for 1,200 years. Imagine the wonder—then the horror—as the column of smoke roared upward, and then began to fall like hail, rain, and snow, collapsing roofs and burying everything in a blanket of ash.

• *As you face Vesuvius, the basilica is to your left, lined with stumps of columns. Step inside and see the layout.*

❹ Basilica

Pompeii's basilica was a first-century palace of justice. This ancient law court has the same floor plan later adopted by many Christian churches (which are also called basilicas). The big central hall (or nave) is flanked by rows of columns marking off narrower side aisles. Along the side walls are traces of the original marble.

The column stumps—all about the same height—were not ruined by the volcano. Rather, they were left unfinished when Vesuvius blew. Pompeii had been devastated by an earthquake in A.D. 62, and was just in the process of rebuilding the basilica when Vesuvius erupted 17 years later. The half-built columns show off the technology of the day. Uniform bricks were stacked around a cylindrical core. Once finished, they would have been coated with marble dust stucco to simulate marble columns—an

POMPEII

Pompeii Walk

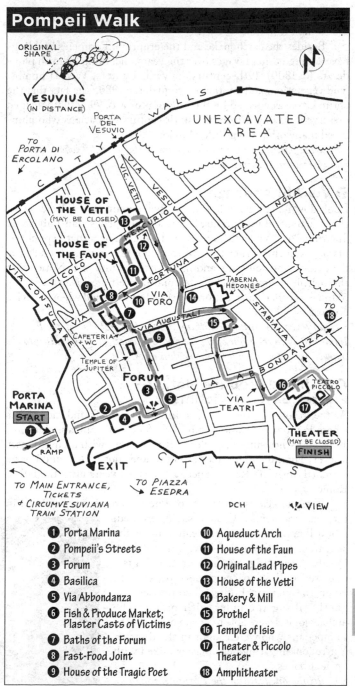

ORIGINAL SHAPE

VESUVIUS (IN DISTANCE)

WALLS

UNEXCAVATED AREA

Porta DEL VESUVIO

TO PORTA DI ERCOLANO

CITY

VIA VETTI

VIA VESUVIO

VIA NOLA

HOUSE OF THE VETTI (MAY BE CLOSED)

MERCURIO

HOUSE OF THE FAUN

VICOLO

VIA FORTUNA

TABERNA HEDONES

VIA CONSULARE

VIA

VIA FORO

STABIANA

TO

CAFETERIA + WC

VIA AUGUSTALI

TEMPLE OF JUPITER

Forum

VIA ABBONDANZA

TEATRO PICCOLO

PORTA MARINA

START

VIA TEATRI

THEATER (MAY BE CLOSED)

FINISH

RAMP

EXIT

CITY WALLS

TO MAIN ENTRANCE, TICKETS & CIRCUMVESUVIANA TRAIN STATION

TO PIAZZA ESEDRA

DCH

VIEW

1. Porta Marina
2. Pompeii's Streets
3. Forum
4. Basilica
5. Via Abbondanza
6. Fish & Produce Market; Plaster Casts of Victims
7. Baths of the Forum
8. Fast-Food Joint
9. House of the Tragic Poet
10. Aqueduct Arch
11. House of the Faun
12. Original Lead Pipes
13. House of the Vetti
14. Bakery & Mill
15. Brothel
16. Temple of Isis
17. Theater & Piccolo Theater
18. Amphitheater

POMPEII

economical construction method found throughout Pompeii (and the Roman Empire).

Besides the earthquake and the eruption, Pompeii's buildings have suffered other ravages over the years, including Spanish plunderers (c. 1800), 19th-century souvenir hunters, WWII bombs, wild vegetation, and another earthquake in 1980. The fact that the entire city was covered by the eruption of A.D. 79 actually helped preserve it, saving it from the sixth-century barbarians who plundered many other towns into oblivion.

• *Exit the basilica and cross the square to the far side, where the city's main street hits the Forum.*

❺ Via Abbondanza

Look down Via Abbondanza, Pompeii's main street. Lined with shops, bars, and restaurants, it was a lively, pedestrian-only zone. The three "beaver-teeth" stones are traffic barriers that kept chariots out. On the corner (just to the left), take a close look at the dark travertine column standing next to a white one. Notice that the marble drums of the white column are not chiseled entirely round—another construction project left unfinished when Vesuvius erupted.

• *Head toward Vesuvius, walking along the right side of the Forum. Immediately to the right of the Temple of Jupiter, a door leads into the market hall, where you'll find two glass cases.*

❻ Fish and Produce Market— Plaster Casts of Victims

As the frescoes on the wall (just inside on the left) indicate, this is where Pompeiians came to buy their food—fish, bread, chickens, and so on. These fine examples of Roman art—with their glimpses of everyday life and mastery of depth and illusion—would not be matched until the Renaissance, a thousand years after the fall of Rome.

The glass cases hold casts of Pompeiians, eerily captured in their last moments. When Vesuvius erupted, 2,000 Pompeii citizens suffocated under the ash, their bodies buried in volcanic debris. While excavating, modern archaeologists detected hollow spaces underfoot, created when the victims' bodies decomposed. By gently filling the holes with plaster, the archaeologists were able to create molds of the Pompeiians who were caught in the disaster. You're looking at modern plaster mixed with ancient bones.

• *Continue on, leaving the Forum through an*

*arch behind the Temple of Jupiter. Here you'll find a pedestrians-only
road sign (ahead on the right corner, above the* REG VII INS IV *sign)
and more "beaver-teeth" traffic blocks. The modern cafeteria is the only
eatery inside the archaeological site (with a coffee bar and WC). Twenty
yards past the cafeteria, on the left-hand side at #24, is the entrance to
the...*

❼ Baths of the Forum (Terme del Foro)

Pompeii had six public baths, each with a men's and a women's section. You're in the men's zone. The leafy courtyard at the entrance
was the gymnasium. After working out, clients could relax with a
hot bath *(caldarium),* warm bath *(tepidarium),* or cold plunge *(frigidarium).*

The first big, plain room you enter served as the **dressing
room.** Holes on the walls were for pegs to hang clothing. The
window (with Neptune underneath) was originally covered with a
less-translucent Roman glass. Walk over the non-slip mosaics into
the next room.

The ***tepidarium*** is ringed by mini-statues or *telamones* (male
caryatids, figures used as supporting pillars), which divided the
lockers. Clients would undress and warm up here, perhaps stretching out on one of the bronze benches near the bronze heater for a
massage. Look at the ceiling—half crushed by the eruption and
half intact, with its fine blue-and-white stucco work.

Next, admire the engineering in the steam-bath room, or
caldarium. The double floor was heated from below—so nice
with bare feet (look into the grate to see the brick support towers). The double walls with brown terra-cotta tiles held the heat.
Romans soaked in the big tub, which was filled with hot water.
Opposite the big tub is a fountain, which spouted water onto the
hot floor, creating steam. The lettering on the fountain reminded
those enjoying the room which two politicians paid for it...and
how much it cost them (5,250 *sestertii*). To keep condensation from
dripping annoyingly from the ceiling, fluting (ribbing) was added
to carry water down the walls.

• *Today's visitors exit the baths through the original entry. If you're a bit
hungry, immediately across the street is an ancient...*

❽ Fast-Food Joint

After a bath, it was only natural to want a little snack. So, just
across the street is a fast-food joint, marked by a series of rectangular marble counters. Most ancient Romans didn't cook for
themselves in their tiny apartments, so to-go places like this were
commonplace. The holes in the counters held the pots for food.
Each container was like a thermos, with a wooden lid to keep
the soup hot, the wine cool, and so on. Notice the groove in the

front doorstep and the holes out on the curb. The holes likely accommodated cords for stretching awnings over the sidewalk to shield the clientele from the hot sun, while the grooves were for the shop's folding accordion doors. Look at the wheel grooves in the pavement, worn down through centuries of use. There are also

more stepping-stones for pedestrians to cross the flooded streets.

• *Just a few steps uphill from the fast-food joint is the...*

❾ House of the Tragic Poet (Casa de Poeta Tragico)

This house is typical Roman style. The entry is flanked by two family-owned shops (each with a track for a collapsing accordion door). The home is like a train running straight away from the street: atrium (with skylight and pool to catch the rain), den (where deals were made by the shopkeeper), and garden (with rooms facing it and a shrine to remember both the gods and family ancestors). In the entryway is the famous "Beware of Dog" *(Cave Canem)* mosaic.

Today's visitors enter the home by the back door (circle around to the left). The modern pipe exposed across the lane is the same as ones used in the ancient plumbing system, hidden beneath the raised sidewalk. Inside the house, the grooves on the marble well head were formed by generations of dragging the bucket up by rope. The richly frescoed dining room is off the garden. Diners lounged on their couches (the Roman custom) and enjoyed frescoes with fake "windows," giving the illusion of a bigger and airier room. Just to the right is a humble BBQ-style kitchen with a little closet for the toilet (the kitchen and bathroom shared the same plumbing).

• *Return to the fast-food place and continue about 10 yards downhill to the big intersection. From the center of the intersection, look left to see a giant arch, framing a nice view of Mount Vesuvius.*

❿ Aqueduct Arch—Running Water

Water was critical for this city of 20,000 people, and this arch was part of Pompeii's water-delivery system. A 100-mile-long aqueduct carried fresh water down from the hillsides to a big reservoir perched at the highest point of the city wall. Since overall water pressure was disappointing, Pompeiians built arches like the brick one you see here (originally covered in marble) with hidden water tanks at the top. Located just below the altitude of the main tank, these smaller tanks were filled by gravity, and provided each neighborhood with reliable pressure.

• *If you're thirsty, fill your water bottle from the modern fountain. Then continue straight downhill one block (50 yards) to #2 on the left.*

⓫ House of the Faun (Casa del Founo)

Stand across the street and marvel at the grand entry with *"HAVE"* (hail to you) as a welcome mat. Go in. Notice the two shrines above the entryway—one dedicated to the gods, the other to this wealthy family's ancestors.

You are standing in Pompeii's largest home, where you're greeted by the delightful small bronze statue of the *Dancing Faun,* famed for its realistic movement and fine proportion. (The original, described on page 645, is in Naples' Archaeological Museum.) With 40 rooms and 27,000 square feet, the House of the Faun covers an entire city block. The next floor mosaic, with an intricate diamond-like design, decorates the homeowner's office. Beyond that is the famous floor mosaic of the *Battle of Alexander.* (The original is also at the museum in Naples.) In 333 B.C., Alexander the Great beat Darius and the Persians. Romans had great respect for Alexander, the first great emperor before Rome. While most of Pompeii's nouveau riche had notoriously bad taste and stuffed their palaces with over-the-top, mismatched decor, this guy had class. Both the faun (an ancient copy of a famous Greek statue) and the Alexander mosaic show an appreciation for history.

The house's back courtyard leads to the exit in the far-right corner. It's lined with pillars rebuilt after the A.D. 62 earthquake. Take a close look at the brick, mortar, and fake marble stucco veneer.

• *Sneak out of the House of the Faun through its back door and turn right. (If this exit is closed, return to the entrance and make a U-turn left, around to the back of the house.) Thirty yards down, along the right-hand side of the street are metal cages protecting...*

⓬ Original Lead Pipes

These 2,000-year-old pipes (made of lead imported from Britannia) were part of the city's elaborate water system. From the aqueduct-fed water tank at the high end of town, three independent pipe systems supplied water to the city: one for baths, one for private homes, and one for public water fountains. If there was a water shortage, democratic priorities prevailed: First the baths were cut off, then the private homes. The last water supply to go was the public fountains, where all citizens could get drinking and cooking water.

• *If the street's not closed off, take your first left (on Vicolo dei Vetti), walk about 20 yards, and find the entrance (on the left) to the...*

⑬ House of the Vetti (Casa dei Vetti)

Pompeii's best-preserved home has been completely blocked off for years; unfortunately it's unlikely to reopen in time for your visit. The House of the Vetti was the bachelor pad of two wealthy merchant brothers. If you can see the entryway, you may spot the huge erection. This is not pornography. There's a meaning here: The penis and the sack of money balance each other on the goldsmith scale above a fine bowl of fruit. Translation: Only with a balance of fertility and money can you have abundance.

If it's open, step into the atrium with its ceiling open to the sky to collect light and rainwater. The pool, while decorative, was a functional water-supply tank. It's flanked by large money boxes anchored to the floor. The brothers were certainly successful merchants, and possibly moneylenders, too.

Exit on the right, passing the tight servant quarters, and go into the kitchen, with its bronze cooking pots (and an exposed lead pipe on the back wall). The passage dead-ends in the little Venus Room, which features erotic frescoes behind glass.

Return to the atrium and pass into the big colonnaded garden. It was replanted according to the plan indicated by traces of roots excavated in the volcanic ash. Richly frescoed entertainment rooms ring this courtyard. Circle counterclockwise. The dining room is finely decorated in black and "Pompeiian red" (from iron rust). Study the detail. Notice the lead humidity seal between the wall and the floor, designed to keep the moisture-sensitive frescoes dry. (Had Leonardo da Vinci taken this clever step, his *Last Supper* in Milan might be in better shape today.) Continuing around, you'll see more of the square white stones inlaid in the floor. Imagine them reflecting like cats' eyes as the brothers and their friends wandered around by oil lamp late at night. Frescoes in the Yellow Room (near the exit) show off the ancient mastery of perspective, which would not be matched elsewhere in Europe for nearly 1,500 years.

• *Facing the entrance to the House of the Vetti, turn left and walk downhill one long block (along Vicolo dei Vetti) to a T-intersection (Via*

*della Fortuna), marked by a stone fountain
with a bull's head for a spout. Intersections
like this were busy neighborhood centers,
where the rent was highest and people gathered. With the fountain at your back, turn
left, then immediately right, walking along
a gently curving road (Vicolo Storto). On the
left side of the street, at #22, find four big
stone cylinders.*

⑭ Bakery and Mill (Forno e Mulini)

The brick oven looks like a modern-day pizza oven. The stubby
stone towers are flour grinders. Grain was poured into the top, and

donkeys or slaves pushed wooden
bars that turned the stones. The
powdered grain dropped out of
the bottom as flour—flavored
with tiny bits of rock. Each neighborhood had a bakery like this.

Continue to the next intersection (Via degli Augustali, where
there's another fast-food joint)
and turn left. As you walk, look at
the destructive power of all the vines, and notice how deeply the
chariot grooves have worn into the pavement. Deep grooves could
break wagon wheels. The suddenly ungroovy stretch indicates that
this road was in the process of being repaved when the big shake
shut everything down.

• *Head about 50 yards down this (obviously one-way) street to #44 (on
the left). Here you'll find the Taberna Hedones (with a small atrium,
den, and garden). This bar still has its original floor and, deeper in, the
mosaic arch of a grotto fountain. Just past the tavern, turn right and
walk downhill to #18, on the right.*

⑮ Brothel (Lupanare)

You'll find the biggest crowds in Pompeii at a place that was likely
popular 2,000 years ago, too—the brothel. Prostitutes were nicknamed *lupe* (she-wolves), alluding to the call they made when trying to attract business. The brothel was a simple place, with beds
and pillows made of stone. The ancient graffiti includes tallies and
exotic names of the women, indicating the prostitutes came from
all corners of the Mediterranean (it also served as feedback from
satisfied customers). The faded frescoes above the cells may have
been a kind of menu for services offered. Note the idealized women
(white, which was considered beautiful; one wears an early bra) and

the rougher men (dark, considered horny). The bed legs came with little disk-like barriers to keep critters from crawling up.

• *Leaving the brothel, go right, then take the first left, and continue going downhill two blocks to the intersection with Pompeii's main drag, Via dell'Abbondanza. The Forum—and exit—are to the right, for those who may wish to opt out from here.*

The huge amphitheater—which is certainly skippable—is 10 minutes to your left. But for now, go left for 60 yards, then turn right just beyond the fountain, and walk down Via dei Teatri. Turn left before the columns (about 50 yards away), and head downhill another 60 yards to #28, which marks the...

⑯ Temple of Isis

This Egyptian temple served Pompeii's Egyptian community. The little white stucco shrine with the plastic roof housed holy water from the Nile. Isis, from Egyptian myth, was one of many foreign gods adopted by the eclectic Romans. Pompeii must have had a synagogue, too, but it has yet to be excavated.

• *Exit the temple where you entered, and go right. At the next intersection, turn right again, and head downhill to the adjacent theaters. Your goal is the large theater, but if it's closed for renovation, look at the smaller but similar theater (Piccolo Theater).*

⑰ Theater

Originally a Greek theater (Greeks built theirs with the help of a hillside), this was the birthplace of the Greek port here in 470 B.C.

During Roman times, the theater sat 5,000 people in three sets of seats, all with different prices: the five marble terraces up close (filled with romantic wooden seats for two), the main section, and the cheap nosebleed section (surviving only on the right). The square stones above the cheap seats once supported a canvas rooftop. Take note of the high-profile boxes, flanking the stage, for guests of honor. From this perch, you can see the gladiator barracks—the colonnaded courtyard beyond the theater. They lived in tiny rooms, trained in the courtyard, and fought in the nearby amphitheater.

• *You've seen Pompeii's highlights. When you're ready to leave, backtrack to the main road and turn left, going uphill to the Forum, where you'll find the main entrance/exit.*

However, there's much more to see—three-quarters of Pompeii's 164 acres have been excavated, but this tour has covered only a third of the site. After the theater—if you still have energy to see more—go back

POMPEII

to the main road, and take a right toward the eastern part of the site, where the crowds thin out. Go straight for about 10 minutes, then turn right down a dirt path (about 75 yards from the wall at the edge of the site), which leads to the...

⑱ Amphitheater

Climb to the upper level of the amphitheater (if the external stairs are blocked, try the entrance to the left). With Vesuvius looming in the background, mentally replace the tourists below with gladiators and wild animals locked in combat. Walk along the top of the amphitheater and look down into the grassy rectangular area surrounded by columns. This is the **Palaestra,** an area once used for athletic training. Facing the other way, look for the bell tower that tops the roofline of the modern city
of Pompei, where locals go about their daily lives in the shadow of the volcano, just as their ancestors did 2,000 years ago. *HAVE!*

Herculaneum (Ercolano)

Though Herculaneum lacks the grandeur of Pompeii, it's smaller, less crowded, and not as ruined as its famous big sister, offering
a closer, more intimate peek into ancient Roman life.

Caked and baked by the same A.D. 79 eruption that pummeled Pompeii, Herculaneum is a small community of intact buildings, surrounded on all sides by the modern town. While Pompeii was initially smothered in ash and pumice, Herculaneum was buried under nearly 60 feet of boiling mud, which hardened into tuff, perfectly preserving the city until excavations began in 1738.

Cost and Hours: €11, open daily April-Oct 8:30-19:30, Nov-March 8:30-17:00, ticket office closes 1.5 hours earlier, tel. 081-732-4311, www.pompeiisites.org.

At the Site: Pick up a free detailed map and excellent booklet (with numbered explanations of each building) at the info desk next to the ticket window. The informative and interesting audioguide sheds light on the ruins and life in Herculaneum in the first century A.D. (€6.50, €10/2 people, ID required, pick up 100 yards after the ticket turnstiles). There is no bookstore or café at the site; WCs are located in the modern building, 200 yards ahead.

Highlights of the excavation site include the **Seat of the Augustali** (Sede degli Augustali), which was a forum for freed slaves climbing their way up the ladder of Roman society, and the *thermopolium*—the Roman equivalent to fast food, with giant tubs for wine, oil, and snacks. The **Bottega ad Cucumas** wine shop still has charred remains of beams, and its drink list remains frescoed on the outside wall. The **House of Neptune and Amphitrite** (Casa di Nettuno e Anfitrite) has colorful mosaics and an intact shell frame.

Don't miss the **gymnasium** *(palestra)* complex and the **House of the Deer** (Casa dei Cervi), with its colorfully frescoed walls. Ancient Herculaneum, like all Roman cities of that age, was filled with color, rather than the stark white we often imagine (even the statues were painted).

The **baths** (Terme Suburbane, sometimes closed) illustrate the city's devastation. Some of Herculaneum's 4,000 citizens had a little more time than the people of Pompeii to flee the eruption. They tried to escape to the sea, but never made it out of Herculaneum.

Sorrento

Arriving in serene Sorrento—a welcoming mid-sized city with plenty of services but little bustle—presents the cruise traveler with an embarrassment of riches. While worth a stroll itself, the city is a jumping-off-place for several exciting destinations.

The jet-setting island of Capri is just a short cruise from Sorrento, offering more charm and fun (outside of the crowded months of July and August) than its glitzy reputation would suggest.

North of Sorrento, and easily accessible on the Circumvesuviana train line, are the ancient sites of Pompeii and Herculaneum, and big-city Naples with its impressive Archaeological Museum.

To the east of Sorrento is the stunning Amalfi Coast, which you can tour with a hired driver or by public bus.

See "Your Top Options" on page 633 for approximate times to allow per destination.

Arrival at the Port of Sorrento

Arrival at a Glance: You can explore the town of Sorrento itself; walk or take a bus to the train station to ride the Circumvesuviana to Pompeii (30 minutes), Herculaneum (45 minutes), or Naples (70 minutes); or catch a boat to Capri (20-25 minutes) or Naples (35 minutes). A taxi or hired driver brings the glorious Amalfi Coast within reach.

Port Overview

Cruise ships tender passengers to Marina Piccola, Sorrento's little harbor. From the boat dock, Sorrento's town center (the main square, Piazza Tasso) and its train station are both steeply uphill. For a description of the town and the services it offers, see page 679.

Getting to the Sights

By Taxi or Hired Car

Taxi: Taxis tend to overcharge—plan on at least €15 for short rides within town (such as from the port to the train station). Because of heavy traffic and the complex one-way road system, you can likely walk faster than you can ride in this city. If you do use a taxi, even if you agree to a set price, be sure it has a meter. All official taxis have one. Better yet, take the bus instead.

For a longer trip, expect to pay €80 for up to four people in a car (or €90 for up to six in a minibus) for a one-way trip from Sorrento to Positano, and 50 percent more to Amalfi. While taxis must use a meter within a city, a fixed rate is OK otherwise. Negotiate—ask about a reduced rate for a round-trip.

Hired Car: If you'd like not just a taxi driver but someone happy to share their knowledge of the area, hire a driver. Several good Sorrento-based drivers can be hired for the day to take you around the region. This splurge is a particularly enticing option on the Amalfi Coast, given the tight turns, impossible parking, congested buses, and potential fun. (It makes much less sense to pay a premium for a driver to take you to Pompeii, Herculaneum, or Naples, as those places are conveniently served by the Circumvesuviana train, and only licensed guides, not drivers, are authorized to take you into the site at Pompeii.)

Here are several services that are worth reserving in advance: The **Monetti** family does Amalfi Coast excursions for roughly €250 for eight hours (and as far as Paestum for €330 for 10 hours). To ensure you get their best price, mention this book. Payment is

SORRENTO

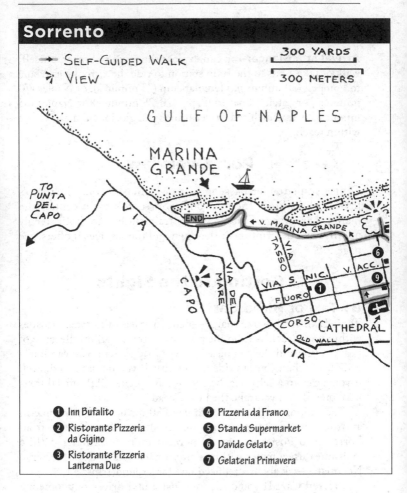

Sorrento

→ SELF-GUIDED WALK

↗ VIEW

300 YARDS

300 METERS

GULF OF NAPLES

MARINA GRANDE

TO PUNTA DEL CAPO

VIA CAPO

VIA DEL MARE

END

V. MARINA GRANDE

VIA TASSO

VIA S. NIC.

V. ACC.

FUORO

CORSO

CATHEDRAL

OLD WALL

VIA

❶ Inn Bufalito

❷ Ristorante Pizzeria da Gigino

❸ Ristorante Pizzeria Lanterna Due

❹ Pizzeria da Franco

❺ Standa Supermarket

❻ Davide Gelato

❼ Gelateria Primavera

by cash only (Raffaele's mobile 335-602-9158 or 338-946-2860, fax 081-807-4531, www.monettitaxi17.it, monettitaxi17@libero.it).

Sorrento Silver Star is recommended by readers for their punctuality, professionalism, and pricing (tel. 081-877-1224, www.sorrentosilverstar.com).

Umberto and Giovanni Benvenuto offer transport and narrated excursions throughout the Amalfi Coast, as well as to Rome, Naples, Pompeii, and more (tel. 089-874-024, mobile 346-684-0226, US tel. 310-424-5640, www.benvenutolimos.com, info@benvenutolimos.com).

Anthony Buonocore is based in Amalfi, but does excursions and transfers throughout the region in his basic but air-conditioned six-person van (rates vary depending on trip, tel. 349-441-0336, www.amalfitransfer.com, buonocoreanthony@yahoo.it).

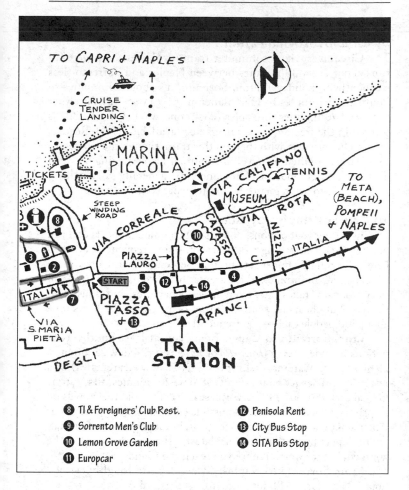

8 TI & Foreigners' Club Rest.
9 Sorrento Men's Club
10 Lemon Grove Garden
11 Europcar
12 Penisola Rent
13 City Bus Stop
14 SITA Bus Stop

By Public Transportation

From Sorrento's harbor, you can head up into the town center; catch a train to nearby destinations; or ride a boat to the isle of Capri or the city of Naples. I've provided arrival information for all the region's outlying destinations I cover (look for it at the top of each section).

To Sorrento's Town Center

To get from the harbor to Piazza Tasso, hike uphill 15 minutes or take a short ride on either a small blue bus (4/hour, €1, buy ticket from driver, day passes not valid) or a red-and-white bus (3/hour, buy €1 tickets at the *tabacchi* or adjacent Metro del Mar kiosk). The train station is a five-minute walk from Piazza Tasso (head down Corso Italia).

To Pompeii, Herculaneum, or Naples by Circumvesuviana Train

The Circumvesuviana commuter train (explained on page 640) runs about every 30 minutes between Naples and Sorrento (less frequently on holidays). From Sorrento, it's about 30 minutes to Pompeii, 45 minutes to Herculaneum (€1.90 one-way for either trip), and 70 minutes to Naples (€3.40 one-way). The schedule is printed in the free *Surrentum* magazine (available at TI). Readers report a big problem with theft on this train, though the risk seems to be largely limited to travel in suburban Naples; going between Sorrento and Pompeii or Herculaneum is generally safer. Still, it makes sense to be on guard, no matter what your destination.

To Capri or Naples by Boat

In considering your options, note that the number of boats that run per day varies according to the season—the frequency indicated here is for roughly mid-May through September, with a few more boats per day in summer. The Caremar line, a subsidized state-run ferry company, takes cars, offers fewer departures, and is just a bit slower—but cheaper—than the other boat. All of the boats take about 500 people each—and frequently fill up.

From Sorrento to Capri: Boats run at least hourly. Your options include a **ferry** (*traghetto* or *nave veloce*, 4/day, 25 minutes, €9.80, run by Caremar, tel. 081-807-3077, www.caremar.it) or a faster but pricier **jet boat** (*aliscafi*, 18/day, 20 minutes, €14, run by Gescab, tel. 081-807-1812, www.gescab.it). To avoid the crowds on Capri, try to depart as early as possible (the best plan is to buy your ticket at 8:00 and take the 8:25 jet boat, but if you arrive after that, try to depart by 9:30 at the very latest). These early boats can be jammed, but it's worth it once you reach the island.

From Sorrento to Naples: 5/day, departs roughly every 2 hours, 35 minutes, €10; for more info, see page 635.

To Positano and Amalfi

Given your time constraints, I'd recommend seeing the Amalfi Coast by shore excursion or by taxi or hired driver. Buses and boats are possible, but subject to crowding (causing people to wait for the next departure), making these a risky choice if you have limited time.

Returning to Sorrento

If returning by train, simply walk or ride a bus back down to the port (see "Arrival in Sorrento," next page).

SORRENTO

Orientation to Sorrento

Wedged on a ledge under the mountains and over the Mediterranean, spritzed by lemon and olive groves, Sorrento is an attractive resort of 20,000 residents and, in summer, just as many tourists. It's as well-located for regional sightseeing as it is a fine place to stay and stroll. The Sorrentines have gone out of their way to create a completely safe and relaxed place for tourists to come and spend money. Everyone seems to speak fluent English and work for the Chamber of Commerce. This gateway to the Amalfi Coast has an unspoiled old quarter, a lively main shopping street,

and a spectacular cliffside setting. Residents are proud of the many world-class romantics who've vacationed here, such as the famed tenor Enrico Caruso, who chose Sorrento as the place to spend his last weeks in 1921.

Sorrento is long and narrow. The main drag, Corso Italia (50 yards in front of the Circumvesuviana train station), runs parallel to the sea from the station through the town center and out to the cape, where the road's name becomes Via Capo. Piazza Tasso marks the town's center. Everything mentioned here is within a 10-minute walk of the train station.

Tourist Information

The TI (labeled *Soggiorno e Turismo*)—located inside the Foreigners' Club—hands out the free monthly *Surrentum* magazine, with a great city map and schedules of boats, buses, concerts, and festivals (Mon-Fri 8:30-16:15, closed Sat-Sun, shorter hours off-season, Via Luigi de Maio 35, tel. 081-807-4033, www.sorrentotourism.com).

To get from Piazza Tasso to the TI, turn right at the end of the square, and go down Via Luigi de Maio through Piazza Sant'Antonino, bearing right downhill about 30 yards to the Foreigners' Club mansion at #35.

If you just need quick advice, the fake tourist office—located in a green caboose just outside the train station—can be of help. While it's a private business run with hopes that you'll purchase an overpriced excursion, the office is willing to give basic information on directions, buses, and ferries.

Arrival in Sorrento

By Boat: Passenger boats from Naples or Capri dock at Sorrento's harbor, Marina Piccola—which is also where cruise ships tender passengers. For details on arriving here, see page 675.

By Train: If you're arriving on the Circumvesuviana from Naples, you're a five-minute walk from the main square, Piazza Tasso: Exit the station straight ahead, then turn left on Corso Italia. From Piazza Tasso, you can walk a few minutes to the TI (see "Tourist Information," earlier for directions), take my self-guided walk, or, if you're taking a boat to Capri or Naples, you can head for the harbor, Marina Piccola. To reach the harbor **on foot,** head down the stairs near the statue's left side (about 10 minutes). Or you can catch a red-and-white **bus** #B or #C (3/hour, €1, buy ticket at *tabacchi*) or the little blue bus (4/hour, €1, buy ticket from driver). Boat tickets are sold only at the port.

Helpful Hints

Bookstore: Libreria Tasso has a decent selection of books in English, including this one (Mon-Sat 10:00-13:20 & 16:30-21:30, Sun 11:30-13:15 & 19:00-22:00, shorter hours off-season, closed Sun Nov-March, Via San Cesareo 96, one block north of cathedral, near Sorrento Men's Club, tel. 081-807-1639).

Local Guides: Giovanna Donadio is a good tour guide for Sorrento, Amalfi, and Capri (€100/half-day, €160/day, same price for any size of group, mobile 338-466-0114, giovanna_dona@hotmail.com). **Giovanni Visetti** is a nature-lover who organizes hikes (www.giovistravels.com).

Where It's At: The **Foreigners' Club** provides reasonably priced snacks and drinks, music, dancing, and magnificent vistas from its cliffside terrace—drop in for the view overlooking the harbor and the Bay of Naples (daily 9:30-24:00, behind TI, public WC, Via Luigi de Maio 35, tel. 081-877-3263).

Getting Around Sorrento

By Bus: City buses (either orange or red-and-white) all stop in the main square, Piazza Tasso. There's only one stop on the square—under the flags closest to the sea. Bus #A runs to Meta beach, buses #B and #C go to the port (Marina Piccola), and bus #D heads to the fishing village (Marina Grande). Tickets for a ride between just the port and Piazza Tasso cost €1 (see "Arrival in Sorrento," earlier); other tickets cost €2.40 and are good for 45 minutes (purchase at *tabacchi* shops and newsstands). Stamp your ticket upon entering the bus. The one-day pass (€7.20) is also valid for the entire Amalfi Coast.

By Rental Wheels: Many places rent motor scooters for about €40 per day, including **Europcar** (Mon-Sat 9:00-13:00 & 16:00-19:30, closed Sun, Corso Italia 210p, tel. 081-878-4956, www.sorrento.it) and **Penisola Rent,** a half-block away (daily 9:00-13:30 & 16:00-20:30, located in Hotel Nice, tel. 081-877-4664, www.penisolarent.com). Don't rent a car in summer unless you enjoy traffic jams.

By Taxi: See page 675.

Self-Guided Walk in Sorrento

Get to know Sorrento with this lazy self-guided town stroll.

• *Begin on the main square. Stand under the flags with your back to the sea, and face...*

Piazza Tasso: As with any southern Italian town, this town's "piazza" is its living room. It may be noisy and congested, but locals want to be where the action is...and be part of the scene. The most expensive apartments and top cafés are on or near this square. Buses stop here on their way to Marina Piccola (where boats depart from the harbor for Naples and Capri, a 10-minute hike below you), to the train station (left), and to Via Capo (right).

This square spans a gorge that divided the town until the 19th century. The old town (on your right) still has some surviving ancient Greek streets. The new town (to your left) was farm country just two centuries ago. A statue of St. Anthony, patron of Sorrento, faces north as if greeting those coming from Naples (often equipped with an armload of fresh lemons and oranges). If you walk a block inland, go right up to the green railing, and look down, you'll see steps carved in the fifth century B.C.

Sorrento's name came from the Greek word for "siren," the legendary half-bird, half-woman who sang an intoxicating lullaby. According to Homer, the sirens lived on an island near here. No one had ever sailed by the sirens without succumbing to their incredible musical charms...and to death. But Homer's hero Ulysses was determined to hear the song. He put wax in his oarsmen's ears and had himself lashed to the mast of his ship. Oh, it was nice. The sirens, thinking they had lost their powers, threw themselves into the sea, and the place became safe to inhabit. Ulysses' odyssey was all about the westward expansion of Greek culture, and to the ancient Greeks, places like Sorrento were the wild, wild west.

• *With your back still to the sea, head to the far-right corner of the square, behind the statue of Torquato Tasso, the square's namesake. (A Sorrento native, he was a lively Renaissance poet.) Peek into the big courtyard of Palazzo Correale (#18, behind the statue in the right corner) to get a feel for an 18th-century aristocratic palace's courtyard, lined with characteristic tiles. Next door, a fun shop sells regional products and offers free biscuits and tastes of liqueurs. As you're leaving the courtyard, on your immediate left you'll see the narrow...*

Via Santa Maria della Pietà: Here, just a few yards off the noisy main drag, is a street that goes back centuries before Christ. About 100 yards down the lane, at #24, find a 13th-century palace (no balconies back then...for security reasons). Continuing on for 10 yards, you'll see a tiny shrine across the street. Typical of southern Italy, it's where the faithful pray to their saint, who contacts Mary, who contacts Jesus, who contacts God. This shrine is a bit more direct—it starts right with Mary.

• *Continue down the lane, which ends at the...*

Cathedral: This is the seat of the local bishop. Pop in for a cool stroll around the ambulatory, checking out the impressive *intarsio* (inlaid-wood) doors. Two sets, inlaid on both sides, show many scenes of the town and its industry. The doors facing the main street include an old town map. These were made to celebrate the pope's visit in 1992. Also notice the intricate inlaid Stations of the Cross, which describe Jesus' last hours.

• *Backtrack 10 yards down Via Santa Maria della Pietà, turn left, cross busy Corso Italia (look back at the bell tower, with its ancient Roman columns at the base), and go straight on Via P. Reginaldo Giuliani, following the...*

Old Greek Street Plan: Notice here how streets are laid out— east-west for the most sunlight and north-south for the prevailing and cooling breeze.

• *One block ahead is a fine old portico, the...*

Sorrento Men's Club: Once the meeting place of the town's nobles, this club has been a retreat for retired working-class men for generations. Strictly no women—and no phones.

Italian men venerate their mothers. (Italians joke that Jesus must have been a southern Italian because his mother believed her son was God, he believed his mom was a virgin, and he lived at home with her until he was 30.) But Italian men have also built into their culture ways to be on their own. Here, men play cards and gossip under a historic emblem of the city and a finely frescoed 16th-century dome, with its marvelous 3-D scenes.

• *At the Men's Club, turn right onto...*

Via San Cesareo: This touristy pedestrian-only shopping street leads four or five blocks back to Piazza Tasso. All along the way, you can peruse (and sample) lemon products in the very competitive shops. Notice the huge ancient doorways with their tiny doors—to carefully let in people during a dangerous age.

• *At the noisy street on the edge of Piazza Tasso, turn left and fight the traffic downhill to the next square, with another...*

Statue of St. Anthony (Antonino): Sorrento's town saint humbly looms among the palms, facing the basilica where his reliquary lies (under the altar in the crypt, surrounded by lots of votives). From here, you can quit the walk and stay in the city center, or continue to the village-like waterfront (if it's before 20:00, you can catch a bus to get back).

• *Exit the square diagonally to the left and gradually wind your way downhill toward Marina Grande (not down the street that leads to the Foreigners' Club and port). After a block or so, on the right you'll see the trees in front of the Imperial Hotel Tramontano and to their right, a path leading to a...*

Cliffside Square: This fine public square, the Villa Communale, overlooks the harbor. Belly up to the banister to enjoy the view of the little harbor and the Bay of Naples. From here, steps zigzag down to Marina Piccola, where lounge chairs, filled by vacationers working on tans, line the sundecks. The Franciscan church fronting this square has a great little cloister (pop in to see Sicilian Gothic—a 13th-century mix of Norman, Gothic, and Arabic styles).

• *Return to the road and continue downhill, walking through the next square (Piazza della Vittoria), which offers another grand view. Stay on the road closest to the water—it eventually leads to stairs that zigzag down to Marina Grande, Sorrento's big harbor. Just before reaching the harbor, you pass under an...*

Ancient Greek Gate: This gate is a reminder that Marina Grande is a separate town from Sorrento, with its own proud residents. It's said that even their cats look different. Because Marina Grande dwellers lived outside the wall and were more susceptible to rape, pillage, and plunder, Sorrentines believe that they come from Saracen (Turkish pirate) stock. Sorrentines still scare their children by saying, "Behave—or the Turks will take you away."

Marina Grande's economy is still based on its fishing fleet. People respect old traditions. Women wear black when a relative dies (one year for an uncle, aunt, or sibling; 2-3 years for a husband or parent). Men get off easy, just wearing a black button if their loved one dies.

From here, buses return to the center at Piazza Tasso every hour (usually at :25 past the hour, note schedule, €2.40 ticket purchased from *tabacchi* shop).

Sights in Sorrento

▲▲**Strolling**—Take time to explore the surprisingly pleasant old city between Corso Italia and the sea. Views from the public park next to Imperial Hotel Tramontano are worth the detour. Each night in summer (May-Oct at 19:30; Nov-April weekends only), the police close off the Corso Italia to traffic, and Sorrento's main drag becomes a thriving people scene. The *passeggiata* peaks at about 22:00. (When Piazza Tasso and the main thoroughfare are closed to traffic, buses for Via Capo leave from up on Via degli Aranci, a short walk from Piazza Tasso along Via Fuorimura.)

▲**Lemon Products Galore**— Via San Cesareo is lined with hardworking rival shops selling a mind-boggling array of lemon products and offering samples of lots of sour goodies. Poke around for a pungent experience.

▲**Lemon Grove Garden (Giardini di Cataldo)**—This small park consists of an inviting organic lemon and orange grove lined with shady, welcoming paths. The owners of the grove are seasoned green thumbs, working the orchard through many generations. You'll see that they've even grafted orange-tree branches onto a lemon tree so that both fruits now grow on the same tree. The garden is dotted with benches, tables, and an inviting little tasting (and buying) stand. You'll get a chance to sniff and taste the varieties of lemons, and enjoy free samples of chilled *limoncello* along with various other homemade liqueurs made from basil, mandarins, or fennel (enthusiastically free, daily April-Sept 10:00-20:00, Oct-March 10:00-16:30, tel. 081-807-4040). The main shop selling their organic homemade products and tasty gelato is across from the Corso Italia entrance at #267; a smaller stand is inside. Enter the garden either on Corso Italia (100 yards north of the train station—where painted tiles show lemon fantasies), or at the intersection of Via Capasso and Via Rota (next to the Hotel La Meridiana Sorrento).

▲**Swimming near Sorrento**—If you require immediate tanning, you can rent a chair on the pier by the port. There are no great beaches in Sorrento—the gravelly, jam-packed private beaches of **Marina Piccola** are more for partying than pampering, and there's just a tiny spot for public use.

A sandy beach is two miles away at **Meta.** While the Meta Circumvesuviana stop is a very long walk from the beach (or a €25 cab ride), the orange or red-and-white bus #A goes directly from Piazza Tasso to the Meta beach (last stop, schedule posted for hourly returns). At Meta, you'll find pizzerias, snack bars, and a little free section of beach, but it's mostly dominated by several sprawling private-beach complexes—if you go, pay for a spot in one of these. Lido Metamare seems best (open May-Sept, €2.50 entry; also available are lockable changing cabins, lounge chairs, etc.). It's a very Italian scene—locals complain that it's "too local" (read: inundated with Naples' riffraff)—with light lunches, a playground, a manicured beach, loud pop music...and no international tourists.

Lemons

Around here, *limoni* are ubiquitous: screaming yellow painted on ceramics, dainty bottles of *limoncello,* and lemons the

size of softballs at the fruit stand. The Amalfi Coast and Sorrento area produces several different kinds of lemons.

The gigantic bumpy lemons are actually citrons, called *cedri,* and are more for show—they're pulpier than they are juicy, and make a good marmalade. The juicy *sfusato sorrentino,* grown only in Sorrento, is shaped like an American football, while the *sfusato amalfitano,* with knobby points on both ends, is less juicy but equally aromatic. These two kinds of luscious lemons are used in sweets such as *granita* (shaved ice doused in lemonade), *limoncello* (a candy-like liqueur with a big kick, called *limoncino* on the Cinque Terre), *delizia* (a dome of fluffy cake filled and slathered with a thick whipped lemon cream), *spremuta di limone* (fresh-squeezed lemon juice), and, of course, gelato or *sorbetto alla limone.*

Tarzan might take Jane to the wild and stony beach at **Punta del Capo,** a 15-minute bus ride from Piazza Tasso (2/hour, get off at stop in front of the American Bar, then walk 10 minutes past ruined Roman Villa di Pollio). From the American Bar bus stop, you can also walk to **Marina di Puolo,** a tiny fishing town popular in the summer for its sandy beach, surfside restaurants, and beach-front disco (15-minute walk, follow signs).

Scuba Diving—To escape the shops, dive deep into the Mediterranean. PADI-certified Futuro Mare offers a one-hour boat ride out to the protected marine zone that lies between Sorrento and Capri, where you can try the beginners' dive (€90, includes instruction and complete supervision, April-Oct usually daily at 9:30). The boat also takes experienced certified divers (1 dive-€60, 2 dives-€95, April-Oct daily at 9:30 and 14:00). The whole experience takes about three hours, and the prices include all equipment, transportation, and the dive itself, which lasts about 40 minutes for both novices and experts (tel. 081-877-1472, mobile 349-653-6323, call a day or two in advance to reserve, www.sorrentodiving.it).

Boat Rental—You can rent motor boats big enough for four people (€150/day, plus gas—figure about €30 for a trip to Capri; "office" is in souvenir store on eastern part of Marina Piccola—with your back to the ferry-ticket offices, it's to the left at Via Marina Piccola 43, tel. 081-807-2283, www.nauticasicsic.com).

Eating in Sorrento

Eating Well and Cheaply Downtown

Inn Bufalito, which focuses on regional specialties, backs up its motto: "Eating well is for everyone." In an informal setting, Franco and his staff serve up a changing menu of pizza, pasta, and all things buffalo, including a delicious selection of *mozzarella di bufala* (€7 salads, €8 pasta, no cover charge, daily 12:00-16:00 & 18:00-24:00, closed Mon off-season and all of Jan-Feb, Vico I Fuoro 21, tel. 081-365-6975).

Ristorante Pizzeria da Gigino, lively and congested, makes huge, tasty Neapolitan-style pizzas in their wood-burning oven (pizza, pasta, and *secondi* all €8-10 each; no cover charge, daily 12:00-24:00, closed Jan-Feb; just off Piazza Sant'Antonino—take first road to the left of Sant'Antonino as you face him, pass under the archway, and take the first left to Via degli Archi 15; tel. 081-878-1927, Antonino).

Ristorante Pizzeria Lanterna Due offers an agreeable family-run atmosphere celebrating the "food, art, and music of Italian cooking," a fun staff, and decent food. Join the other tourists at the long line of tables along the alley, or in the air-conditioned interior (€8 pastas, €9 *secondi*, €2 cover, double-check your bill, daily 12:00-22:00, Via Santa Maria delle Grazie 28, tel. 081-807-4521).

Pizzeria da Franco seems to be Sorrento's favorite place for basic, casual pizza in a fun, untouristy atmosphere. There's nothing fancy about this place—just locals on benches eating hot sandwiches and great pizzas served on waxed paper in a square tin. It's packed to the rafters with a youthful crowd that doesn't mind the plastic cups (€7 pizzas, €5 salads, daily 12:00-2:00 in the morning, just across from Lemon Grove Garden on busy Corso Italia at #265, tel. 081-877-2066).

Picnics: You'll find many markets and take-out pizzerias in the old town. Consider getting a pizza to go at Pizzeria da Franco (listed above) or groceries at the **Standa supermarket** (Mon-Sat 8:30-13:20 & 16:30-20:15, Sun 9:30-13:00 & 17:00-20:30, Corso Italia 223).

Gelato: A few doors downhill from L'Antica Trattoria, **Davide Gelato** has many repeat customers (so many flavors, so little time). In 1957, Augusto Davide opened the shop, and his grandson, Giovanni, proudly carries on the tradition today (look toward the back, where the gelato is made on-site). Walk the most enticing chorus line in Italy before ordering. Sample *Profumi di Sorrento* (an explosive sorbet of mixed fruits) and lemon crème. They also serve simple meals at fair prices (daily 9:30-24:00, shorter hours and closed Wed off-season, 2 blocks off Corso Italia at Via Padre R. Giuliani 39, tel. 081-878-1337).

At **Gelateria Primavera,** another neighborhood favorite, Antonio and Alberta whip up 70 flavors fresh daily—and still have time to make pastries for the pope (and everybody else—check out the photos). Try the *noce* (walnut, pronounced no-CHAY) or pistachio in a homemade waffle cone (€3 for up to three flavors, daily 9:00-2:00 in the morning, tel. 081-807-3252, two-minute walk west of Piazza Tasso at Corso Italia 142).

Capri

Capri was made famous as the vacation hideaway of Roman emperors Augustus and Tiberius. In the 19th century, it was the haunt of Romantic Age aristocrats on their Grand Tour of Europe. But these days, the island is a world-class tourist trap, packed with gawky nametag-wearing visitors searching for the rich and famous, and finding only their prices.

The "Island of Dreams" is a zoo in July and August—overrun with tacky, low-grade group tourism at its worst. Other times of year, while still crowded, it can provide a relaxing and scenic break from the cultural gauntlet of Italy.

Planning Your Time

From Sorrento, you can reach Capri by ferry or jet boat; unfortunately, unless your cruise arrives very early, you'll be making this trip along with every other tourist in town. Do your best to stay ahead of the crowds: Take the soonest, fastest boat possible on arrival. It's wise to get a round-trip boat ticket with a specific return (improving your odds of getting a spot on a boat when they're most crowded); you can use the ticket to return earlier if you like. Once on Capri, go directly to the Blue Grotto, then catch a bus from the grotto to Anacapri and ride the chairlift to Monte Solaro. From the summit, return by chairlift (or hike down). Stroll out from the base of the chairlift to Villa San Michele for the view, then catch a bus to Capri town for the rest of your stay.

At the end of the day, ride the funicular down to Marina Grande (kill time lazing on the free beach or wandering the yacht harbor) to catch the boat back to Sorrento or Naples. Be 20 minutes early for the boat, or risk being bumped. Confirm the schedule carefully—last boats usually leave between 18:00 and 20:10. All departing boats are listed at the port on a handy lighted schedule

Capri

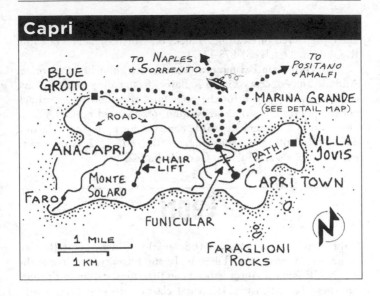

board, which notes exact dock locations for each departure (facing the taxis, the board is just around the corner from the TI).

Orientation to Capri

First thing—pronounce it right: KAH-pree, not kah-PREE like the song or the pants. The island is small—just four miles by two miles—and is separated from the Sorrento Peninsula by a narrow strait. There are only two towns to speak of: Capri and Anacapri. The island also has some scant Roman ruins and a few interesting churches and villas. But its chief attraction is its famous Blue Grotto, and its best activity is a chairlift up the island's Monte Solaro.

Arrival in Capri

For instructions on getting from Sorrento to Capri, see page 678. Get oriented on the boat before you dock. As you near the harbor, Capri spreads out before you: The port is called **Marina Grande** (TI, boats to Blue Grotto, buses to anywhere, funicular to the town of Capri). **Capri town** fills the ridge high above the harbor. The ruins of Emperor Tiberius' palace, **Villa Jovis,** cap the peak on the left. The dramatic *"Mamma mia!"* road arcs around the highest mountain on the island **(Monte Solaro)** on the right, leading up to

Anacapri (the island's second town, just out of sight). Notice the old zigzag steps below that road. Until 1874, this was the only connection between Capri and Anacapri. (Though it's quite old, it's nowhere near as old as its nickname, "The Phoenician Stairway," implies.) The white house on the ridge above the zigzags is **Villa San Michele** (where you can go later for a grand view of boats like the one you're on now).

Upon arrival, get your bearings. Boats dock in two places: on the long pier and directly by the main street. If your boat arrives on the main street, take a right to get to the long pier. Stand with your back to the pier: The **funicular** is across the street. The kiosk that sells **bus and funicular tickets** is to your right in the cluster of buildings at the start of the pier. Behind that are kiosks that sell return **boat tickets** (for the two competing companies). Across the street and uphill from all this are the **public WCs.**

The **TI** is near the ticket kiosk, right by the stubby dock for Blue Grotto boats (April-Oct Mon-Sat 8:30-19:30, Sun 9:00-15:00; Nov-March Mon-Sat 9:00-15:00, closed Sun; pick up free map—or the better €1 map if you'll be venturing to the outskirts of Capri town or Anacapri, tel. 081-837-0634, www.capritourism .com).

From the port, you have three transit options: boat to the Blue Grotto (best early—ideally upon arrival), bus to Anacapri (often with long and frustrating lines), or funicular up to Capri town (4/hour, 5 minutes).

Helpful Hints

Cheap Tricks: A cheap day trip to Capri is tough. From Sorrento to Capri by boat costs from €10 to €14 each way, and Blue Grotto tickets (plus transportation) come to €22.50—that's about €40-55 per person. Taking the bus rather than the boat to the Blue Grotto (see next page) saves about €8 per person.

Best Real Hike: Serious hikers love the peaceful and scenic three-hour Fortress Hike, which takes you entirely away from the tourists. You'll walk under ruined forts along the rugged coast, from the Blue Grotto to the *faro* (lighthouse). From there, three buses per hour return you to Anacapri. The tourist office has a fine map/brochure.

Free Beach: Marina Grande has a free pebbly beach. You can get a shower at the bar for €1.

Local Guide: Roberta Mazzarella is good (about €50/hour, mobile 339-135-7619, robertamazzarella@yahoo.it).

Boat Departure Schedule: A very handy electronic board lists all boats departing in the next hour or so from Capri. It's on the end of the building between the TI and boat-ticket kiosk (on the wall facing the mainland). This is the one way to know all

Capri Harbor

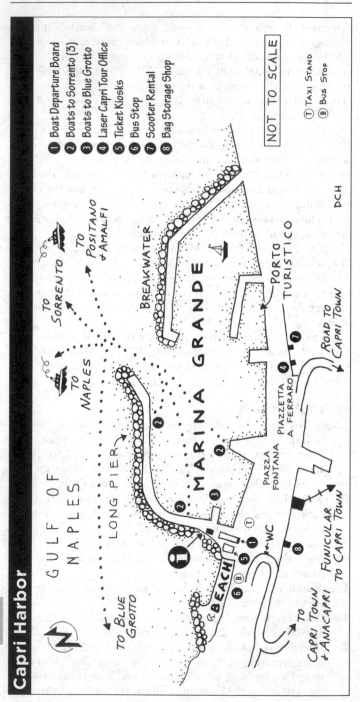

CAPRI

Capri Harbor

1. Boat Departure Board
2. Boats to Sorrento (3)
3. Boats to Blue Grotto
4. Laser Capri Tour Office
5. Ticket Kiosks
6. Bus Stop
7. Scooter Rental
8. Bag Storage Shop

NOT TO SCALE

T Taxi Stand
B Bus Stop

GULF OF NAPLES

TO BLUE GROTTO

TO NAPLES

TO SORRENTO

TO POSITANO & AMALFI

LONG PIER

BREAKWATER

MARINA GRANDE

PORTO TURISTICO

PIAZZETTA A. FERRARO

PIAZZA FONTANA

WC

BEACH

ROAD TO CAPRI TOWN

FUNICULAR TO CAPRI TOWN

TO CAPRI TOWN & ANACAPRI

DCH

the departure options coming up and to confirm your boat's departure time and dock number. The board includes a small chart that locates the many dock numbers in this confusing harbor.

Getting Around Capri

The buses and funicular are covered by the same ticket options: €1.40 per ride (two single tickets are the easiest option if going straight to Blue Grotto by public bus—one to get to Anacapri, then one to get to the Blue Grotto), €2.20 for one hour of unlimited use (even better for the Blue Grotto), or €7.90 for an all-day pass (includes deposit, turn it in at the end of the day to get €1 back). Single-ride tickets are often available at newsstands, *tabacchi* shops, or from the driver. Unlimited use and all-day passes are usually sold only at official ticket offices. Consider an all-day pass if you plan to take more than five rides on the buses and funicular (possible if you go by bus to the Blue Grotto and spend some time in each town). Schedules are clearly posted at all bus stations. Taxis have steep and fixed rates (Marina Grande to Capri-€15; Marina Grande to Anacapri-€20). You can hire a taxi for about €70 per hour—negotiate.

Buses and Funicular from the Port at Marina Grande: Buses pick up just uphill from where you bought your ticket. Get in line under the appropriate sign: either under *San Costanzo* for going up to the town of **Capri** (at least 4/hour), where you could then transfer to Anacapri (4/hour, 10 minutes, there's routinely a long queue for this Capri-Anacapri bus); or direct to **Anacapri** (sporadic schedule, but about every 40 minutes). For most people, the best way from the port to Anacapri is to take the funicular to Capri (4/hour, on the quarter-hour, takes 5 minutes), and then bus from there to Anacapri.

Buses from Anacapri: To use the buses smartly in Anacapri, you need to know that there are two stops: the town center (Piazza Vittoria) and the cemetery stop (Piazza della Pace—pronounced "PAH-chay"—just 200 yards farther down the main road; residents may refer to it by its former name, Piazza del Cimitero). Buses to **Capri town** (at least 4/hour) can be packed. Guarantee a seat by catching the bus from the Piazza della Pace stop, one stop before most people get on. Anacapri-Blue Grotto buses depart only from this stop (not from the town center). If you're coming from the town of Capri and want to transfer to the **Blue Grotto** buses, don't get off when the driver announces "Anacapri." Instead, ride one more stop, then transfer to the Grotta Azzurra (Blue Grotto) buses. If in doubt, ask the driver or a local.

Boat Trips Around the Island: Laser Capri runs quick trips around the island, passing stunning cliffs, caves, and views that most miss when they go only to the Blue Grotto. If you have an hour, it's well worth the extra €3. Their tiny ticket window faces dock #23 at Marina Grande, from where its boats offer three excursions: circle of the island without grotto stop (1 hour, €14), circle the island with a grotto stop (2 hours, €14), and just to the grotto and back (1 hour, €11). The €11.50 grotto admission is always extra (boats leave 9:30-16:30, Via Don Giobbe Ruocco 45, tel. 081-837-5208, www.lasercapri.com). Another company, Motoscafisti Capri, offers the trip for the same price (see listings under the "Blue Grotto," page 694).

Scooter Rental: If you like riding a scooter, this is the perfect way to have the run of the island, although the steep and narrow roads aren't ideal for novice riders. Ciro proudly rents 40 bright-yellow scooters with 50cc engines—strong enough to haul couples. Rental includes a map and instructions with parking tips and other helpful information (€15/hour, €55/day, ask for Rick Steves discount; includes helmet, gas, and insurance; daily 9:00-19:00, Via Don Giobbe Ruocco 55, Marina Grande, tel. 081-837-8018, mobile 338-360-6918, www.capriscooter.com).

Sights in Capri

Capri Town

This is a cute but extremely touristy shopping town. The *funiculare* drops you just around the corner from Piazza Umberto, the town's main square. The **TI** fills a closet under the bell tower on Piazza Umberto (less crowded than its sister on the port and with longer hours: Mon-Sat 8:30-20:30, Sun 9:00-15:00, tel. 081-837-0686, WC downstairs behind TI). With your back to the funicular, the bus stop is 50 yards down Via Roma.

Capri's multi-domed Baroque **cathedral,** which faces the square, is worth a quick look. (Its multicolored marble floor at the altar was scavenged from the Roman Emperor's villa in the 19th century.)

To the left of City Hall (Municipio, lowest corner), a lane leads into the medieval part of town, which has plenty of eateries. The lane to the left of the cathedral (past Bar Tiberio, under the wide arch) has been dubbed "Rodeo Drive" by residents because it's the fashion shopping strip. Walk down Rodeo Drive (past Gelateria Buonocore at #35, famous for its fresh waffle cones) to Quisisana Hotel, the island's top old-time hotel. From there, head left for fancy shops and villas, and right for gardens and views.

Downhill and to the right, a five-minute walk leads to a lovely public garden, Giardini Augusto (free, daily 9:00-18:30).

Villa Jovis and the Emperor's Capri

Even before becoming emperor, Augustus loved Capri so much he traded the family-owned Isle of Ischia to the (then-independent) Neapolitans in exchange for making Capri his personal property. Emperor Tiberius spent a decade here, 26-37 A.D. (Some figure he did so in order to escape being assassinated in Rome.)

Emperor Tiberius' ruined villa, Villa Jovis, is a scenic 45-minute hike from Capri town (€2, daily 9:00-19:00, closes earlier off-season, tel. 081-837-4549). You won't find any statues or mosaics here—just an evocative, ruined complex of terraces fitting a rocky perch over a sheer drop to the sea...and a lovely view. You can make out a large water reservoir for baths, the foundations of servants' quarters, and Tiberius' private apartments (fragments of marble flooring still survive). The ruined lighthouse dates from the Middle Ages.

▲▲Blue Grotto

Three thousand tourists a day spend a couple of hours visiting Capri's Blue Grotto *(Grotta Azzurra)*. I did—early (when the

light is best), without the frustration of crowds and choppy waves nearly making entrance impossible...and it was great.

The actual cave experience isn't much: a five-minute dinghy ride through a three-foot-high entry hole to reach a 60-yard-long cave, where the sun reflects brilliantly blue on its

limestone bottom. But the experience—getting there, getting in, and getting back—is a scenic hoot. You get a fast ride on a 30-foot boat partway around the gorgeous island; along the way you see bird life and dramatic limestone cliffs with scant narration. You'll understand why Roman emperors appreciated the invulnerability of the island—it's surrounded by cliffs, with only one access point, and therefore easy to defend.

At the grotto's "distribution center," you pile into eight-foot dinghies with other tourists; from there, ruffian rowers elbow their way to the tiny hole and pull fast and hard on the cable at the low point of the swells to squeeze you into the grotto. Then your man rows you around, spouting off a few descriptive lines and singing "O Sole Mio." Depending upon the strength of the sunshine that day, the blue light inside is brilliant.

The grotto was actually an ancient Roman *nymphaeum*—

a retreat for romantic hanky-panky. Many believe that, in its day, a tunnel led here directly from a palace, and that the grotto experience was enlivened by statues of Poseidon and company, placed half-underwater as if emerging from the sea. It was ancient Romans who smoothed out the entry hole used to this day.

Typically, your boatman will extort an extra tip out of you before taking you back outside to your big boat (€2 is more than enough, but you don't need to pay a penny...you've already paid plenty).

Cost and Logistics: Two companies make the boat trip from Marina Grande—Motoscafisti Capri and Laser Capri (€11 round-trip, no discount for one-way, daily from 9:00 until an hour before sunset, closes earlier off-season, boats don't run in stormy weather or during high tides—check this out *before* you purchase boat tickets; Motoscafista Capri—tel. 081-837-7714, www.motoscafisticapri.com; Laser Capri—tel. 081-837-5208, www.lasercapri.com).

Once you reach the grotto, you pay €7.50 for a rowboat to take you in for the five-minute row around the inside of the grotto (after your rower jockeys for position for at least 20 minutes), plus €4 to cover the admission to the grotto (€11.50 total for grotto visit, not counting €11 round-trip ride from port; again, tip entirely optional). While it's technically against the rules, some people dive in for free after 18:00, when the boats stop running—a magical experience and a favorite among locals.

When the waves or high tide make entering dangerous, the boats don't go in—the grotto can close with no notice, sending tourists (flush with anticipation) home without a chance to squeeze through the little hole. (If this happens to you, consider a one-hour €14 boat ride around the island—including a look at the Faraglioni Rocks—offered by both companies.)

You can take the boat back, or request to be dropped off on a small dock next to the grotto to return by bus to Anacapri (no discount for one-way boat ticket, stairs lead to bus stop, schedule posted at the stop, roughly 3/hour, buy ticket from driver).

If you're on a budget, you can take the bus from Anacapri directly to the grotto (rather than a boat from Marina Grande). You'll save about €8, and see a beautiful, calmer side of the island (every 20 minutes from Piazza della Pace, a 200-yard walk on the main road beyond the Piazza Vittoria bus stop in Anacapri; €2.20 ticket valid one hour, usually enough time to visit the grotto and take the bus back to town).

If you're coming from Capri's port, allow 1-3 hours for the entire visit, depending on the chaos at the caves (an early trip will get you there at the same time as the boatmen in their dinghies—who hitch a ride behind your boat—resulting in less chaos and a shorter wait at the entry point).

CAPRI

Anacapri

Capri's second town has no sea views but some fun and interesting activities. From the busy Piazza Vittoria, where the bus drops you, head 40 yards down the pedestrian street to reach the tiny **TI** (Mon-Sat 8:30-17:30, Sun 9:00-15:00, often closed Nov-Easter, Via Orlandi 59, tel. 081-837-1524).

For a sweeping island view, go to the top of the stairs in Piazza Vittoria, and take the pedestrian path that heads left, past the deluxe Capri Palace Hotel (venture in if you can get past the treacherously eye-catching swimming pool windows), and below the Villa San Michele. (The view is even better from the villa— listed next.)

Villa San Michele—The 19th-century mansion of Capri's grand personality, Axel Munthe, offers an insight into the scene here when this was the only comfortable refuge for Europe's artsy gay community. Oscar Wilde, D. H. Lawrence, and company hung out here back when being gay could land you in jail...or worse. Munthe, a Swedish doctor who lived here until 1949, left this impressive mansion littered with Roman statues, the Olivetum (museum of native birds and bugs), and a delightful garden. From the sphinx, you'll enjoy one of Capri's best views.

Cost and Hours: €6, daily 9:00-18:00, tel. 081-837-1401.

▲**St. Michael's Church**—This church has a remarkable majolica floor showing paradise on earth in a classic 18th-century Neapolitan style. The entire floor is ornately tiled, featuring an angel (with flaming sword) driving Adam and Eve from paradise. The devil is wrapped around the trunk of a beautiful tree. The animals—happily ignoring this momentous event—all have human expressions. For the best view, climb the spiral stairs from the postcard desk.

Cost and Hours: €2, daily April-Oct 9:00-19:00, Nov-March 10:00-14:00, in town center—after the TI continue walking 5 minutes and take a right to the church, tel. 081-837-2396.

Faro—The lighthouse is a favorite place to enjoy the sunset, with a private beach, pool, small restaurants, and a few fishermen. Reach it by bus from Anacapri (3/hour, departs from Piazza della Pace stop).

▲▲**Chairlift up to Monte Solaro**—From Anacapri, ride the chairlift to the 1,900-foot summit of Monte Solaro for a commanding view of the Bay of Naples. Work on your tan as you float over hazelnut, walnut, chestnut, apricot, peach,

kiwi, and fig trees and past a montage of tourists. As you ascend, consider how real estate has been priced out of the locals' reach. The ride takes 15 minutes each way, and you'll want at least 30 minutes on top.

At the summit, you'll enjoy the best panorama possible: lush cliffs busy with seagulls enjoying the ideal nesting spot. The Faraglioni Rocks—with tour boats squeezing through every few minutes—are an icon of the island. The pink building nearest the rocks was an American R&R base during World War II. Eisenhower and Churchill met here. On the peak closest to Cape Sorrento, you can see the distant ruins of the Emperor Tiberius' palace, Villa Jovis. Pipes from the Sorrento Peninsula bring water to Capri (demand for fresh water here long ago exceeded the supply provided by the island's three natural springs). The Galli Islands mark the Amalfi Coast in the distance. Cross the bar terrace for views of Mount Vesuvius and Naples (€9 round-trip, €7 one-way, daily June-Oct 9:30-17:00, last run down at 17:30, closes earlier Nov-May, confirm schedule with TI, departs from top of the steps in Piazza Vittoria—the first Anacapri bus stop, tel. 081-837-1428).

A highlight for hardy walkers (provided you have strong knees and good shoes) is the 40-minute downhill hike from the top of Monte Solaro, through lush vegetation and ever-changing views, past the 14th-century Chapel of Santa Maria Cetrella (at the trail's only intersection, it's a 10-minute detour to the right), and back into Anacapri. The trail starts downstairs, past the WCs (last chance). Down two more flights of stairs, look for the sign to *Anacapri e Cetrella*—you're on your way. While the trail is well-established, you'll encounter plenty of uneven steps, loose rocks, and few signs.

Amalfi Coast

With its stunning scenery, hill- and harbor-hugging towns, and historic ruins, Amalfi is Italy's coast with the most. The trip from Sorrento to Salerno along the breathtaking Amalfi Coast is one of the world's great scenic drives. It will leave your mouth open and your camera's memory full. You'll gain respect for the Italian engineers who built the roads in the 1800s—and even more respect for anyone who drives it today. Cantilevered garages, hotels, and villas cling to the vertical terrain, and beautiful sandy coves tease from far below and out of reach. As you hyperventilate, notice how the Mediterranean, a sheer 500-foot drop below, really twinkles. All this beautiful scenery apparently inspires local Romeos and Juliets, with the evidence of late-night romantic encounters lit-

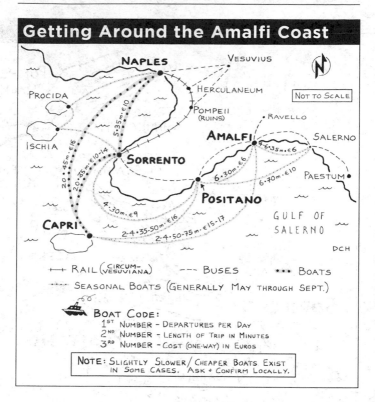

Getting Around the Amalfi Coast

NAPLES · VESUVIUS

PROCIDA · HERCULANEUM

POMPEII (RUINS)

· RAVELLO

AMALFI · SALERNO

ISCHIA · SORRENTO · 4·6·35m·€6

PAESTUM

POSITANO · 6·30m·€6 · 6·70m·€10

20·45m·€16 · 20·35m·€10-14 · 5·35m·€10

4·30m·€9

CAPRI · 2·4·35-50m·€16

2·4·50-75m·€15-17

GULF OF SALERNO

NOT TO SCALE

DCH

⊢—⊣ RAIL (CIRCUM-VESUVIANA)   - - - BUSES   ••• BOATS

···· SEASONAL BOATS (GENERALLY MAY THROUGH SEPT.)

BOAT CODE:
  1ST NUMBER – DEPARTURES PER DAY
  2ND NUMBER – LENGTH OF TRIP IN MINUTES
  3RD NUMBER – COST (ONE-WAY) IN EUROS

NOTE: SLIGHTLY SLOWER / CHEAPER BOATS EXIST IN SOME CASES. ASK & CONFIRM LOCALLY.

tering the roadside turnouts. Over the centuries, the spectacular scenery and climate have been a siren call for the rich and famous, luring Roman emperor Tiberius, Richard Wagner, Sophia Loren, Gore Vidal, and others to the Amalfi Coast's special brand of *la dolce vita*.

Getting to the Amalfi Coast

Amalfi Coast towns are pretty but are generally touristy, congested, overpriced, and a long hike above tiny, pebbly beaches. Most beaches are private, and access is expensive. The real thrill here is the scenic Amalfi drive.

Don't Get Stranded: When deciding how best to see the coast, consider foremost your time restrictions, and the fact that the coastal road is often clogged with gawking drivers, especially in July and August. Taking a **shore excursion** operated by your cruise ship is your safest option, as your

Amalfi Coast

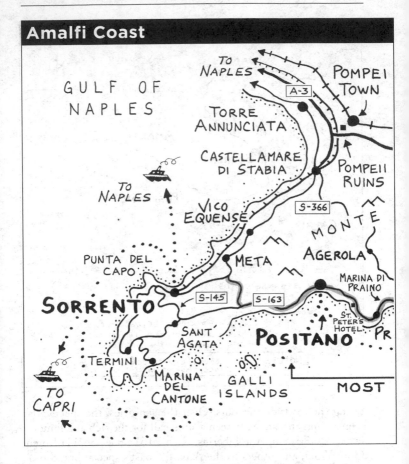

ship will wait if you're caught in traffic. Otherwise, your next best option is either taking a **taxi** or **hiring a driver,** which gives you the most flexibility (see page 675 for recommended services).

The **bus** is by far the cheapest option, and worth considering if you have at least eight hours for the coast. The bus runs fairly frequently (about hourly, daily 7:00-22:00, until 20:00 off-season; 50 minutes to Positano, another 50 minutes to Amalfi; €7.20 all-day ticket or €3.60 90-minute ticket one-way to Positano). It's probably best to go only as far as Positano. Buses carry a risk: Not only can they get stuck in traffic, but they can fill up in the afternoon. If your return bus is full, don't wait for the next one: call a taxi (abut €80-100 from Positano to Sorrento). Even better, don't cut it close; return earlier than you need to.

In Sorrento, look for the *Bus Stop SITA* sign across from the train station (10 steps down) and line up for bus marked *Amalfi via Positano* (buy tickets at the *tabacchi* shop nearest any bus stop

AMALFI COAST DRIVE

OTHER ROADS

AUTOSTRADA

RAIL (CIRCUM-VESUVIANA)

RAIL

TRAIL

BOAT

A-3

LATTARI

RAVELLO

MINORI

VIETRI

A-3

TO PAESTUM

HIKE →
PONTONE

S-163

MAIORI

SALERNO

ATRANI

CETARA

AMALFI

AINO

N

SCENIC SECTION

GULF OF SALERNO

DCH

before boarding, grab a seat on the right for the best views, sitting toward the front minimizes carsickness).

While you can avoid traffic hassles by taking a **boat** to Positano and/or Amalfi, their infrequency makes them even less appealing for the cruise traveler (4/day, run mid-April–mid-Oct only, to Positano: 30 minutes, €9; to Amalfi: 1.25 hours, €11; www .metrodelmare.com).

The Coastal Drive: Sorrento to Positano

The trip from Sorrento along the Amalfi Coast is one of the all-time great white-knuckle rides. Gasp from the right side of the bus or cab as you go out and from the left as you return to Sorrento. (Those on the wrong side really miss out.) Traffic is so heavy that private tour buses are only allowed to go in one direction (south-

bound from Sorrento)—summer traffic is infuriating. Fluorescent-vested policemen are posted at tough bends during peak hours to help fold in side-view mirrors and keep things moving.

Leaving Sorrento, the road winds up into the hills past lemon groves and hidden houses. Traveling the coast, you'll see several watchtowers placed within sight of each other, so that a relay of rooftop bonfires could spread word of a Saracen (Turkish pirate) attack. The gray-green trees are olives. Dark, green-leafed trees planted in dense groves are the source of the region's lemons—many destined to become *limoncello* liqueur. The black nets over the orange and lemon groves create a greenhouse effect, trapping warmth and humidity for maximum tastiness.

As you approach the exotic-looking town of **Positano,** you know you've reached the scenic heart of the Amalfi Coast.

Positano

According to legend, the Greek god Poseidon created Positano for Pasitea, a nymph he lusted after. History says the town was

founded when ancient Greeks at Paestum, nearby, decided to move out of the swamp (to escape malaria). Specializing in scenery and sand, Positano hangs halfway between Sorrento and Amalfi town on the most spectacular stretch of the coast.

The "skyline" looks like it did a century ago. Notice the town's characteristic Saracen-inspired rooftop domes. Filled with sand, these provide low-tech insulation—cool in summer and hot in winter. It's been practically impossible to get a building permit in Positano for 25 years now, and landowners who want to renovate can't make external changes. The steep stairs are a way of life for the 4,000 hardy locals. Only one street in Positano allows motorized traffic; the rest are steep pedestrian lanes. Because hotels don't take large groups (bus access is too difficult), the town—unlike Sorrento—has been spared the ravages of big-bus tourism.

Squished into a ravine, with narrow alleys that cascade down to the harbor, Positano requires you to stroll, whether you're going up or heading down. The center of town has no main square (unless you count the beach). There's little to do here but eat, window-shop, and enjoy the beach and views...hence the town's popularity.

Arrival in Positano: The main coast highway winds above the town. Regional SITA buses (blue or green-and-white) stop at two scheduled bus stops located at either end of town; get off at the second stop, Sponda. Roads lead downhill through the town to the beach. It's a 20-minute stroll/shop/munch from here to the beach (and TI).

Internet Access: Your best bet is at **La Brezza Internet,** on the west side of the beach (to the right as you face the water, €5/30 minutes).

Sights: Positano offers just two main activities: **shopping** (look for locally produced linen and ceramics), and enjoying its **beaches.** Spiaggia Grande, the main beach, is mostly private (€10-15/person, cost includes drink service and use of lounge chair and umbrella, free section near the middle, nearest WC beneath the steps to the right as you face the water), whereas Fornillo Beach, just around the bend (to the west), is less crowded and more affordable.

Eating in Positano

The pizzerias and restaurants facing the beach, while overpriced,

are pleasant and convenient. At the waterfront, I like **La Cambusa** (at the top of the steps), but neighboring places also leave people fat and happy.

Sunny Emilia at **Delikatessen** can supply picnic ingredients (*antipasto misto* to go at €1.40/100 grams, pasta for €1/100 grams, sandwiches made and sold

by weight—about €3.50, she microwaves food and includes all the picnic ware, best selection early; daily March-Oct 7:00-22:00, Nov-Feb 8:00-20:00, just below car park at Via del Mulini 5, tel. 089-875-489). **Vini e Panini,** another small grocery, is a block from the beach a few steps above the TI. Daniela, the fifth-generation owner, speaks English and happily makes sandwiches to order (daily 8:00-22:00, off-season closes 14:00-16:00, tel. 089-875-175, just off church steps).

Getting Back to Sorrento by Bus

Be aware that the SITA bus to Sorrento may leave from the Sponda stop five minutes before the printed departure. There's no room for the bus to wait, so in case the driver is early, you should be, too. Buy tickets from the *tabacchi* shop next to Bar Mulino Verde, at Positour Agency (near Piazza dei Mulini on Via Colombo), or

AMALFI COAST

Positano

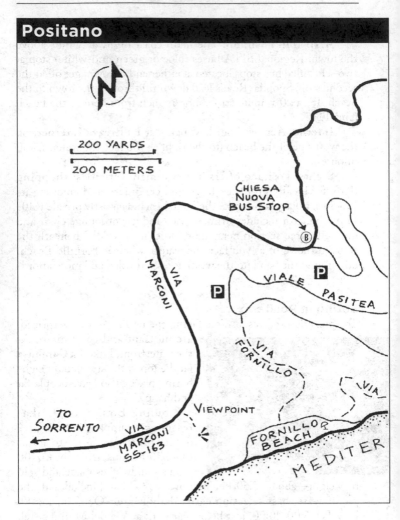

200 YARDS

200 METERS

CHIESA NUOVA BUS STOP

B

VIA MARCONI

P

VIALE PASITEA

P

VIA FORNILLO

VIA

TO SORRENTO

VIA MARCONI SS-163

VIEWPOINT

FORNILLO BEACH

P

MEDITER

just below the bus stop at the Total gas station (across from Hotel Marincanto). If the walk up to the stop is too tough, take the dizzy little local orange bus (marked *Interno Positano*), which constantly loops through Positano, connecting the lower town with the highway's two bus stops (2/hour, €1.10 at *tabacchi* or €1.50 on board, catch it at convenient stop at the corner of Via Colombo and Via dei Mulini, heads up to Sponda).

Amalfi Town

The Amalfi Coast is named for this town. After Rome fell, Amalfi was one of the first cities to trade goods—coffee, carpets, and paper—between Europe and points east. Its heyday was the 10th

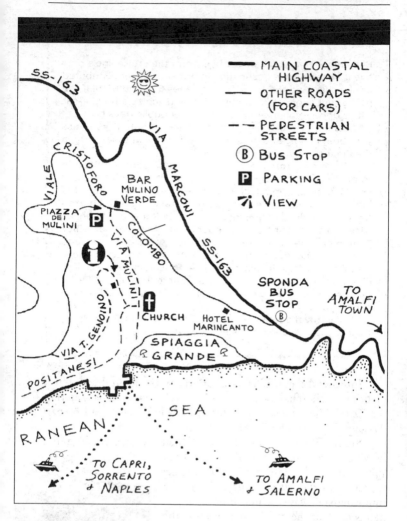

and 11th centuries, when it was a powerful maritime republic—a trading power with a fleet that controlled this region and rivaled Genoa and Venice. Amalfi minted its own coins and established "rules of the sea"—the basics of which survive today.

Venture into the town, and you find its once rich and formidable medieval shell is filled with trendy shops, a main square sporting a springwater-spewing statue of St. Andrew, and a cathedral—the town's most important sight.

AMALFI COAST

What If I Miss My Boat?

Remember that you can get help from the cruise line's port agent (listed on the destination information sheet distributed on the ship) and the local TI (see pages 639 and 679). If the port agent suggests a costly solution (such as a private car with a driver), you may want to consider public transit.

Naples is the region's transportation hub. If you miss your boat in Sorrento, your best bet is to head to Naples via the Circumvesuviana.

Frequent **trains** leave from Naples' Centrale Station to points all over Italy and beyond: **Civitavecchia** (at least hourly, 3 hours, most change in Rome), **Venice** (roughly hourly, 5.5 hours, overnight options take longer), **Livorno** (roughly hourly, 5 hours, most change in Rome or Florence), **Nice** (via overnight trains, 14 hours, 2-4 changes), **Marseille/Toulon** (via overnight trains, 17-20 hours, 3-5 changes), and more. For other connections, ask at the train station or check http://bahn.hafas.de/bin/query.exe/en (Germany's excellent all-Europe website). Italy has a train-info toll number 892-021 (answered 24 hours daily in Italian only; have a local person call for you).

Any **travel agent** can help you. For more advice on what to do if you miss the boat, see page 131.

Internet Access: L'Altra Costiera, on the main drag a block up from the church, looks more like a travel agency but has Internet service (€3/30 minutes, daily 9:00-21:00, 4 terminals, Via Lorenzo d'Amalfi 34, tel. 089-873-6082).

Sights: The town's **cathedral** is "Amalfi Romanesque" (a mix of Moorish and Byzantine flavors, built c. 1000-1300) with a fanciful Neo-Byzantine facade from the 19th century. Climb the imposing stairway—which functions as a handy outdoor theater for town events. The 1,000-year-old bronze door at the top was given to Amalfi by a wealthy local merchant who had it made in Constantinople (€3, daily 7:00-19:00, shorter off-season, closed Jan-Feb, from 10:00-17:00 access church through cloister, pick up English flier, tel. 089-871-324). There's a fine, free WC at the top of the steps (through unmarked green door, just a few steps before ticket booth).

VENICE

Venezia

Soak all day in this puddle of elegant decay. Venice is Europe's best-preserved big city. This car-free urban wonderland of a hundred islands—laced together by 400 bridges and 2,000 alleys—survives on the artificial respirator of tourism.

Born in a lagoon 1,500 years ago as a refuge from barbarians, Venice is overloaded with tourists and is slowly sinking (unrelated facts). In the Middle Ages, the Venetians became Europe's clever middlemen for East-West trade and created a great trading empire. By smuggling in the bones of St. Mark (San Marco) in A.D. 828, Venice gained religious importance as well. With the discovery of America and new trading routes to the Orient, Venetian power ebbed. But as Venice fell, her appetite for decadence grew. Through the 17th and 18th centuries, Venice partied on the wealth accumulated through earlier centuries as a trading power.

Today, Venice is home to just over 60,000 people in its old city, down from a peak population of nearly 200,000. While there are about 500,000 in greater Venice (counting the mainland, not counting tourists), the old town has a small-town feel. Locals seem to know everyone. To see small-town Venice away from the touristic flak, escape the Rialto-San Marco tourist zone and savor the town early and late without the hordes of vacationers day-tripping in from cruise ships and nearby beach resorts. A 10-minute walk from the madness puts you in an idyllic Venice that few tourists see.

Some cruises start or end in Venice. If yours does, see the end of the chapter for airport information and recommended hotels.

VENICE

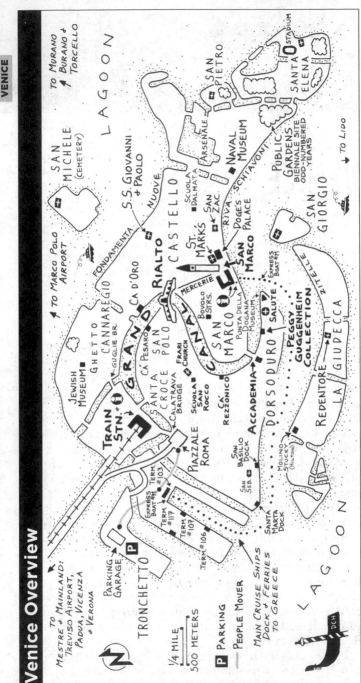

Venice Overview

TO MESTRE + MAINLAND:
TREVISO AIRPORT,
PADUA, VICENZA
+ VERONA

TO MURANO +
BURANO +
TORCELLO

LAGOON

SAN
MICHELE
(CEMETERY)

SAN
PIETRO

STADIUM

SANTA
ELENA

TO MARCO POLO AIRPORT

S.S. GIOVANNI
+ PAOLO

NUOVE

ARSENALE

NAVAL
MUSEUM

PUBLIC
GARDENS
BIENNALE SITE
ODD-NUMBERED
YEARS

TO LIDO

FONDAMENTA

CA D'ORO

GHETTO

CANNAREGIO

RIALTO

CASTELLO

SCUOLA
DALMATA

SAN
ZAC.

ST.
MARKS

DOGE'S
PALACE

RIVA

SCHIAVONI

EXPRESS
BOAT #1

SAN
GIORGIO

JEWISH
MUSEUM

GUGLIE BR.

GRAND

SANTA
CROCE

CA' PESARO

SAN
POLO

MERCERIE

BOVOLO
STRS.

SAN
MARCO

SALUTE

PUNTA DELLA
DOGANA

PEGGY
GUGGENHEIM
COLLECTION

ZITELLE

TRAIN
STN.

CALATRAVA
BRIDGE

FRARI
CHURCH

SCUOLA
SAN
ROCCO

CANAL

CA'
REZZONICO

ACCADEMIA

DORSODURO

REDENTORE

LA GIUDECCA

PIAZZALE
ROMA

TERM.
#103

EXPRESS
BOAT #1

TERM.
#117

TERM.
#107

TERM. #106

SAN
BASILIO
DOCK

SAN
SEB.

MOLINO
STUCKY
(HILTON)

SANTA
MARTA
DOCK

PARKING
GARAGE

TRONCHETTO

N

¼ MILE

500 METERS

P PARKING

PEOPLE MOVER

MAIN CRUISE SHIPS
DOCK + FERRIES
TO GREECE

LAGOON

LAGOON

DCH

Excursions from Venice

Excursion offerings might appeal to cruisers with special interests, but their attractions can't touch the jewel-like confection that is **Venice.**

North of Venice are the islands of **Murano** (40 minutes by boat) and **Burano** (an additional 30 minutes from Murano). Visit the first for its world-class glass artisans and factories, and the second for its fine lace and picturesque pastel houses. Some travelers (especially those who have already spent time in Venice proper) enjoy these islands as a small-town alternative to Venice. As these towns are most famous for their respective products, expect any excursions here to be heavily focused on selling you glass and lace.

Padua is for art-lovers; this elegantly arcaded university town (1.25 hours southwest of Venice) is home to the celebrated Scrovegni Chapel frescoes of the early Renaissance master Giotto.

Serious history buffs might choose to see the impressive Roman ruins in **Verona** (2 hours west of Venice), which is also the pick for star-crossed lovers retracing Romeo and Juliet's steps.

Planning Your Time

Venice is made to order for a wonderful day. I'd suggest tackling the city in this order:

• From the cruise port, head for Piazzale Roma, hop on a vaporetto, and take my self-guided **Grand Canal Cruise,** ending at St. Mark's Square. Allow an hour (15 minutes to Piazzale Roma, 45 minutes on the vaporetto).

• Take these self-guided tours: **St. Mark's Square** (allow 30 minutes) and **St. Mark's Basilica** (1 hour).

• With more time, you could visit the **Doge's Palace** (on St. Mark's Square); take a 15-minute walk from St. Mark's Square to the **Rialto Bridge** and its open-air produce market; ride a gondola (see page 776); or visit the **Accademia** art gallery. If you visit the Accademia, see it on your way in: Take the Grand Canal Cruise tour, get off at the Accademia stop, tour the museum, then continue on the vaporetto to St. Mark's Square (or go by foot—it's a 15-minute walk). If you'd rather shop than sightsee, see page 778.

Allow at least an hour to get back to port. You can catch an express boat from St. Mark's Square directly back to the cruise port, or you can ride a vaporetto from St. Mark's Square or the Rialto to Piazzale Roma, then take the monorail to the port. (It's also fun to walk back from St. Mark's Square—it can be done in an hour, but allowing more time would make it more relaxing.)

Arrival at the Port of Venice

Arrival at a Glance: Hop on express boat #M to St. Mark's Square (20 minutes); or ride the People Mover monorail five minutes to the Grand Canal, where you can ride a slow, scenic vaporetto to St. Mark's—following my self-guided Grand Canal Cruise (25-45 minutes). If all of these options are jammed up (as can happen when multiple cruise ships arrive), you can walk to the Grand Canal in about 15 minutes, or all the way to St. Mark's Square in about 45 minutes. A water taxi downtown costs €80.

Port Overview

Cruise ships dock at Venice's Stazione Marittima, which is at the west end of town, roughly between the Tronchetto parking garage and Santa Lucia train station. The terminal forms the "fish's mouth" of Venice. The cruise port consists of one long, wide, rectangular pier, and a narrower, adjacent pier; together these form a harbor, where most cruise ships dock. There are four different terminal buildings: #117 (along the north side of the main pier), #107 and #108 (along the south/harbor side of the main pier), and #103 (at the top of the harbor, near the base of the main pier). Some ships may dock south of the main port at Santa Marta or San Basilio.

Tourist Information: The local port authority sometimes operates small info kiosks in the terminals that dispense free maps of the city.

Getting into Town

Venice's public transportation is convenient and affordable—there's little reason to pay for a water taxi.

By Taxi

You can hire a **water taxi** to points in central Venice, but it's very expensive (figure €80 minimum for up to six people to anywhere in Venice; book at the kiosks in front of building #103 at the top of the harbor). **Land taxis** wait in front of the cruise terminals, but because virtually nothing of interest in Venice is accessible by car, it's unlikely you'll need them (unless you're going to Marco Polo Airport—about €40).

By Public Transportation

Choose whether you want to make a beeline to St. Mark's Square (by express boat along the Giudecca Canal, around the bottom of Venice); or take the slower, more scenic approach via the more famous Grand Canal.

Services at the Port of Venice

You'll find everything you need in downtown Venice, but here's a rundown on what you'll encounter at the port.

ATMs: These are inside the terminal buildings.

No Internet Access: There is no public Internet access at the port; you'll have to head into Venice, where Internet access is much easier to find; see "Helpful Hints" on page 714. (At the base of the main pier, you may notice the Seamen's Club, with an Internet café—but this is a membership-only organization solely for cruise-line employees.)

Food: The humble self-service cafeteria and coffee bar called La Crociera ("The Cruiser") is easy to find, between terminal building #103 and the People Mover monorail station.

Baggage Storage: If you don't see a kiosk offering this service as you get off your ship, ask around for the office (€5/ day to store bags, €8 to transfer bags to a Venice hotel, €6 to transfer to train station). There's also baggage storage right next to the Piazzale Roma stop for the People Mover monorail (€5/bag, daily 6:00-21:00).

Directly to St. Mark's Square (via the Giudecca Canal)

The handy Alilaguna express boat #M conveniently connects the cruise port directly to St. Mark's Square (San Marco-Giardinetti dock) in just 20 minutes (€6.50 one-way, €12 round-trip, €3 per big bag, 2/hour in each direction, from cruise port 8:10-16:10, from San Marco 9:10-16:10; before boarding, buy ticket at kiosk in front of building #103 at the top of the harbor; www.alilaguna.it). While there's a small round-trip discount, buying a one-way ticket leaves your options open for returning to the cruise port. Because this service is understandably popular, the boats can fill up; if you're arriving on a cruise ship, get to this dock as quickly as possible. If there's already a long line, consider one of the options described next.

If your ship docks outside the main port, Venice's water buses, called *vaporetti*, stop at San Basilio, see page 719.

To St. Mark's Square via the Grand Canal

First, you'll make your way to Piazzale Roma—the bus station/ parking lot on the Grand Canal—by monorail, foot, or bus; from there, you can ride a vaporetto (water bus) to St. Mark's Square.

Step 1—From the Cruise Port to Piazzale Roma: The **People Mover** monorail connects the cruise port to the rest of Venice. To reach it, head away from the water, and you'll see the elevated tracks and station (to the right, beyond terminal building #103). From this Stazione Marittima stop, the monorail goes every few minutes in two different directions: Take it to Piazzale Roma

(€1, buy ticket at automated machine as you enter the terminal, ride takes just 2-3 minutes). You'll exit the station into a busy bus parking lot. Turn left and head for the Grand Canal, where you'll find a vaporetto stop (see "Step 2," below).

Note that, like the Alilaguna boat, the People Mover monorail can be crowded when several cruises arrive; if the line seems too long and you're feeling energetic, it's a drab, urban 15-minute **walk** to the Grand Canal (Piazzale Roma/train station): Continue straight past the People Mover station through the big parking lot, and walk up the red-brick traffic bridge (with a sidewalk for pedestrians). When you reach the busy road at the gas station above, turn right and follow the road straight to Piazzale Roma, and continue straight ahead to the Piazzale Roma vaporetto stop.

Alternatively, a free **shuttle bus** near terminal #103 carries passengers from certain cruise lines back and forth from Piazzale Roma.

Step 2—From Piazzale Roma via the Grand Canal to St. Mark's Square: Walk to Piazzale Roma's waterfront and look for the vaporetto stop. Buy a vaporetto ticket (€6.50 one-way) and hop on the boat: You can choose between the slower boat #1 (about 45 minutes to St. Mark's) or the express boat #2 (25 minutes, skips several stops). My self-guided Grand Canal Cruise is more enjoyable on #1, but workable on #2 if you're in a hurry. You'll hop off at the San Marco stop, right in the heart of historic Venice.

Alternate Plan—Walk All the Way to St. Mark's Square: If the *vaporetti* are too crowded and you'd like to stretch your legs and get a glimpse of untouristy Venice, consider walking all the way to St. Mark's. From Piazzale Roma, it's actually very pleasant to explore Venice as you walk another 30-40 minutes or so (about 1.5 miles) through its back streets and mostly away from the crush of tourists to St. Mark's Square. Follow signs for *San Marco*. Note: It can be even more enjoyable to walk back to the boat at the end of the day.

By Tour

For information on local tour options in Venice—including walking tours and local guides for hire—see "Tours in Venice" on page 723.

Returning to Your Ship

Because every cruise passenger in town will be trying to get back to the port at the same time you are, your return options can be crowded. Plan ahead, keep an eye on lines at the boat docks, and be sure to leave yourself plenty of time. See page 792 for help if you miss your boat.

By Express Boat: The fastest way back to the cruise port is on the Alilaguna express boat #M (catch it at the San Marco-Giardinetti dock: From St. Mark's, head for the waterfront, turn right, and walk into the small park; the boat zips straight to the cruise port in 20 minutes; for specifics, see "Directly to St. Mark's Square," earlier).

By Vaporetto: You can catch a vaporetto to Piazzale Roma (from which it's just a quick People Mover monorail ride to the port). From the San Zaccaria-Jolanda dock, *vaporetti* #42 and #52 both go to Piazzale Roma in about 20 minutes. In a pinch, vaporetto #2 goes from San Zaccaria-M.V.E. to Piazzale Roma, but takes longer (about 40 minutes). Once you make it to Piazzale Roma, you can breathe easy—you're just a quick People Mover ride from the port. If your ship is docked outside the main port, vaporetto #2 stops at San Basilio.

On Foot: One of my favorite activities in Venice is walking through the back streets all the way to Piazzale Roma. Conservatively, allow yourself about an hour (including time for the short People Mover ride from Piazzale Roma back to the cruise port), refer constantly to a map to stay on track, and just keep following signs for *Piazzale Roma*—or, if you don't see that, watch for *Ferrovia* (the train station, across the Grand Canal from Piazzale Roma).

By Water Taxi: In an emergency, you can pay a water taxi to zip you back to the cruise port—but it's extremely expensive.

Orientation to Venice

The island city of Venice is shaped like a fish. Its major thoroughfares are canals. The Grand Canal winds through the middle of the fish, starting at the mouth where all the people and food enter, passing under the Rialto Bridge, and ending at St. Mark's Square (Piazza San Marco). Park your 21st-century perspective at the mouth and let Venice swallow you whole.

Venice is a car-less kaleidoscope of people, bridges, and odorless canals. The city has no major streets, and addresses are hopelessly confusing. There are six districts (shown on map on page 706): San Marco (most touristy), Castello (behind San Marco), Cannaregio (from the train station to the Rialto), San Polo (other side of the Rialto), Santa Croce (the "eye" of the fish, east of the train station), and Dorsoduro (the "belly" of the fish and southernmost district of the city). Each district has about 6,000 address numbers.

To find your way, navigate by landmarks, not streets. Many street corners have a sign pointing you to *(per)* the nearest major landmark, such as San Marco, Accademia, Rialto, and Piazzale Roma, Ferrovia (train station). Obedient visitors stick to the main thoroughfares as directed by these signs...and miss the charm of back-street Venice.

Beyond the city's core lie several other islands, including San Giorgio (with great views of Venice), Giudecca (more views), San Michele (old cemetery), Murano (famous for glass), Burano (lace-making), Torcello (old church), and the skinny Lido beach.

Tourist Information

With this book, a decent city map, and the *Shows and Events* booklet (described below), there's little need to visit a tourist office in Venice. That's fortunate, because the city's TIs are crowded and clunky. If you need to check or confirm something, there are four offices: **train station** (daily 8:00-18:30), **St. Mark's Square** (daily 9:00-15:30, opposite end from church), nearby at the **San Marco-Vallaresso vaporetto stop** (daily 10:00-18:00), and at the **airport** (daily 9:00-21:00). You can save time by phoning 041-529-8711 or visiting www.turismovenezia.it.

At the TI, pick up the free **Shows and Events** pamphlet. Besides upcoming events and nightlife, it also lists museum hours, emergency telephone numbers, and includes a vaporetto route map (www.turismovenezia.it, click on "Venezia")

For a creative travel guide written by young Venetians, consider **My Local Guide Venice,** for its neighborhood histories, self-guided walking tours, and recommendations on sights and activities (sold at TIs for €13).

Maps: In Venice of all places, you need a good map. The TI sells a decent €2.50 map and miniguide—but you can find a wider range at bookshops, newsstands, and postcard stands. The cheap maps are pretty bad, but if you spend €5, you'll get a map that shows you everything. Investing in a good map can be the best €5 you'll spend in Venice. Don't take street names too seriously—spellings change with the dialect. Also, keep in mind that many street names change midway.

Passes for Venice

The sights you probably care the most about (Accademia, Peggy Guggenheim Collection, Scuola San Rocco, Campanile, and the three sights within St. Mark's Basilica that charge admission)

Daily Reminder

Sunday: While anyone is welcome to worship, most churches are closed to sightseers during Mass on Sunday morning. The Church of San Giorgio Maggiore (on an island across from St. Mark's Square) hosts a Mass at 11:00. The Church of San Polo is closed today, and these sights are open only in the afternoon: St. Mark's Basilica (14:00-17:00, until 16:00 Nov-March), Frari Church (13:00-18:00), and the Church of San Zaccaria (16:00-18:00). Today, the Rialto open-air market consists mainly of souvenir stalls (fish and produce sections closed). It's a bad day for a pub crawl, as most pubs are closed.

Monday: All sights are open except the Rialto produce market, Ca' Pesaro, and Torcello Museum (on Torcello Island). The Accademia and Ca' d'Oro close at 14:00.

Tuesday: All sights are open except the Peggy Guggenheim Collection, Ca' Rezzonico (Museum of 18th-Century Venice), and Punta della Dogana.

Wednesday/Thursday/Friday: All sights are open.

Saturday: All sights are open except the Jewish Museum.

Notes: The Accademia is open earlier (daily at 8:15) and closes later (19:15 Tue-Sun) than most sights in Venice. Some sights close earlier off-season (such as the Correr Museum, Campanile bell tower, and St. Mark's Basilica).

Churches: Modest dress is recommended at churches and required at St. Mark's Basilica—no bare shoulders, shorts, or short skirts. Some churches are closed to sightseers on Sunday morning (including St. Mark's Basilica, Frari Church, Church of San Zaccaria, and after 11:00 at San Giorgio Maggiore), and many are closed from roughly 12:00 to 14:30 or 15:30 Monday through Saturday (this includes La Salute and San Giorgio Maggiore).

Crowd Control: The city is inundated with cruise-ship crowds and tours from mainland hotels daily from 10:00 to about 17:00. Crowds can be a serious problem at **St. Mark's Basilica.** If possible, try going early or late.

At the **Doge's Palace,** avoid the long line by purchasing your ticket at the less-crowded Correr Museum. You can also buy your ticket online, book a tour, or—if your schedule allows—visit late in the day.

For the **Campanile,** ascend late (it's open until 21:00 July-Sept), or skip it entirely if you're going to the similar San Giorgio Maggiore bell tower.

For the **Accademia,** go early or late—or you can reserve a ticket in advance by phone or online.

The sights that have crowd problems get even more crowded when it rains.

VENICE

are not covered on any pass. To see the Doge's Palace, you must also pay for the less-visited Correr Museum (both on St. Mark's Square). While this €13 ticket is called a "pass" (described next), think of it as just a combo-ticket.

Doge's Palace/Correr Museum Tickets: The **San Marco Museum Plus Pass** (€13) covers admission to the Doge's Palace and Correr Museum (including two other museums within the Correr—the National Archaeological Museum and the Monumental Rooms of Marciana National Library), plus your choice of **one** of these seven museums: Ca' Rezzonico (Museum of 18th-Century Venice); Palazzo Mocenigo Costume Museum; Casa Goldoni (home of the Italian playwright); Ca' Pesaro (modern art); Museum of Natural History in the Santa Croce district; Murano's Glass Museum; or Burano's Lace Museum. To bypass the long line at the Doge's Palace, purchase this pass at the less-crowded Correr Museum (or any other included museum).

Transportation Passes: Venice also sells a transit-only pass covering *vaporetti* (a good deal only if you plan to take three or more rides in a day), see "Getting Around Venice," later.

Helpful Hints

Get Lost: Accept the fact that Venice was a tourist town 400 years ago. It was, is, and always will be crowded. While 80 percent of Venice is, in fact, not touristy, 80 percent of the tourists never notice. Hit the back streets. Venice is the ideal town to explore on foot. Walk and walk to the far reaches of the town. Don't worry about getting lost. In fact, get as lost as possible. Keep reminding yourself, "I'm on an island, and I can't get off." When it comes time to find your way, just follow the directional arrows on building corners or simply ask a local, *"Dov'è San Marco?"* ("Where is St. Mark's?") People in the tourist business (that's most Venetians) speak some English. If they don't, listen politely, watch where their hands point, say, *"Grazie,"* and head off in that direction. If you're lost, refer to your map, or pop into a hotel and ask for their business card—it comes with a map and a prominent "You are here."

Be Prepared to Splurge: Venice is expensive for residents as well as tourists. Demand is huge, supply is limited, and running a business is costly. Things just cost more here; everything must be shipped in and hand-trucked to its destination. Perhaps the best way to enjoy Venice is just to succumb to its charms and blow a lot of money.

Theft Alert: Pickpockets (often elegantly dressed) work the crowded main streets, docks, and *vaporetti* (wear your money belt, zip up your valuables, and watch your purse or day bag). Your biggest risk of pickpockets is inside St. Mark's Basilica.

A handy Polizia station is on the right side of St. Mark's Square (near Caffè Florian). A service called Counter of Tourist Mediation at the Venice Complaint Office handles complaints about local crooks—including gondolier, restaurant, or hotel rip-offs (tel. 041-529-8710, fax 041-523-0399, complaint.apt@turismovenezia.it).

Immigrants selling items such as knock-off handbags on the streets are doing so illegally—if you buy goods from them, you'll risk getting a big fine.

Take Breaks: Venice's endless pavement, crowds, and tight spaces are hard on the tourist. Schedule breaks in your sightseeing. Grab a cool place to sit down, relax, and recoup—meditate on a pew in an uncrowded church, or stop in a café.

Etiquette: Walk on the right and don't loiter on bridges. On St. Mark's Square, a "decorum patrol" admonishes snackers and sunbathers. Picnicking is forbidden (keep a low profile). The only place for a legal picnic is in Giardinetti Reali, the small park along the waterfront west of the Piazzetta near St. Mark's Square.

Dress Modestly: Men should keep their shirts on. When visiting St. Mark's Basilica or other major churches, men, women, and even children must cover their shoulders and knees (or risk being turned away). Remove hats when entering a church.

Public Toilets: Handy public WCs (€1.50) are near major landmarks, including: St. Mark's Square (one is behind the Correr Museum, to the left of the post office; another is at the waterfront park, Giardinetti Reali), Rialto, and at the Accademia Bridge. Use free toilets whenever you can—in a museum you're visiting or a café you're eating in. Like Mom always said, "Just try."

Best Views: While the best views of Venice may be from water level, there are several upper-altitude viewing spots: On St. Mark's Square, try the soaring Campanile, or St. Mark's Basilica (specifically the balcony of the San Marco Museum, requires admission). The Rialto and Accademia bridges provide free, expansive views of the Grand Canal, along with a cooling breeze. Or get off the main island for a view of the Venetian skyline: Ascend the Church of San Giorgio Maggiore's bell tower, or venture to La Giudecca island to visit the swanky bar of the Molino Stucky Hilton Hotel (free shuttle boat from San Zaccaria-M.V.E. vaporetto stop).

Pigeon Poop: If your head is bombed by a pigeon, resist the initial response to wipe it off immediately—it'll just smear into your hair. Wait until it dries, and it should flake off cleanly. But if the poop splatters on your clothes, wipe it off immediately to avoid a stain.

Venice

TO MAINLAND

CAMPO DI GHETTO NUOVO

JEWISH GHETTO

S. LEO.

MADDA.

PONTE DI GUGLIE

S. MARCUOLA

R. BIASIO

BARI

BEMBO

TINTOR

S. STAE

FERROVIA (TRAIN STN.)

LISTA DI SPAGNA

S. SIMON

LACA

CAMPO S. STIN

CHIESA

CAMPO S. POLO

TO TRONCHETTO & MAINLAND

GARAGE

TO TRONCHETTO & CRUISE PORT

PIAZZALE ROMA

AMAI

S. ROCCO

FRARI CHURCH

TINT

SALON.

S. TOMA

S. POLO

Scuola San Rocco

FOSC.

GRAND

CAMPO SANTA MARG.

CAP.

CA' REZZ.

PAL. GRASSI

S. SAM. BO.

CAMPO S. STEF.

AVOGARIA

CAMPO SAN BARNABA

TOLETTA

CORFU

AGNESE

ACCADEMIA

ZATTERE

PONTE LONGO

RIO TERRA FOSCARINI

ZATTERE SPIRITO E.

200 YARDS

200 METERS

DCH

T TRAGHETTO CROSSING

V VAPORETTO STOP

G GONDOLA STATION

•— PEOPLE MOVER

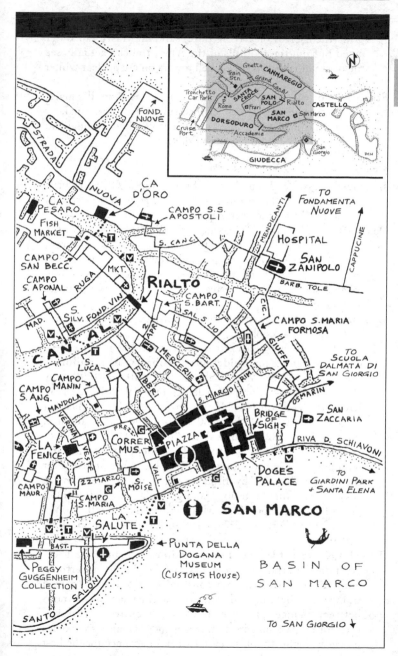

Water: I carry a water bottle to refill at public fountains. Venetians pride themselves on having pure, safe, and tasty tap water piped in from the foothills of the Alps. You can actually see the mountains from Venice's bell towers on crisp, clear winter days.

Street Lingo: *Campo* means square, *campiello* is a small square, *calle* is street, *fondamenta* is the road running along a canal, *rio* is a small canal, *rio terra* is a street that was once a canal and has been filled in, and *ponte* is a bridge.

Services

Internet Access: You'll find handy, if pricey (up to €8/hour), little Internet places all over town. They are usually on back streets: Ask at the TI for the nearest place.

Post Office: The main P.O. is near the Rialto Bridge (on the St. Mark's side, Mon-Sat 8:30-13:00, closed Sun). Use post offices only as a last resort, as simple transactions can take 45 minutes if you get in the wrong line. You can buy stamps from tobacco shops and mail postcards at any of the red postboxes around town.

Bookstores: In keeping with its literary heritage, Venice has classy and inviting bookstores.

The following have great English-language travel sections (and stock my guidebooks): **Libreria Mondadori** is a block behind St. Mark's Square (daily 10:00-20:00, may close in 2011, 1345 Complesso del Ridotto, tel. 041-522-2193); **Libreria Studium** is a block behind St. Mark's Basilica (Mon-Sat 9:00-19:30, Sun 9:30-13:30, Calle de la Canonica, tel. 041-522-2382). **Acqua Alta** ("high water") is a funky secondhand bookstore with bargain books in English and reproduction prints of Venice. Quirky Luigi has prepared for the next "high water" by displaying his wares in a selection of vessels, including bathtubs and a gondola (daily 9:00-21:00, just beyond Campo Santa Maria Formosa at Calle Longa Santa Maria Formosa 5176, tel. 041-296-0841, mobile 340-680-0704).

Travel Agencies: If you need to get train tickets, make seat reservations, or arrange a *cuccetta* (koo-CHET-tah—a berth on a night train) avoid a time-consuming trip to the crowded train station by using a downtown travel agency. Most trains between Venice, Florence, and Rome require reservations, even for railpass-holders. A travel agency can also give advice on cheap flights (book at least a week in advance for the best fares).

Near St. Mark's Square, **Oltrex Change and Travel** sells train and plane tickets and books train reservations for a €3.50 fee (tickets sold daily May-Oct 9:00-18:00, Nov-April 9:00-16:30, one bridge past the Bridge of Sighs, Riva degli Schiavoni 4192, tel. 041-524-2828, Luca and Beatrice).

Near Rialto, **Kele & Teo Travel** sells train tickets for about a €4 fee (Mon-Fri 9:00-18:00, Sat 9:00-12:00, closed Sun; leaving the Rialto Bridge heading for St. Mark's, it's half a block away, tucked down a side street on the right; tel. 041-520-8722).

Getting Around Venice

On Foot: Navigate by major landmarks. There are signs on street corners all over town pointing to *San Marco, Accademia, Ferrovia* (train station), and *Piazzale Roma* (the bus stop behind the train station). Determine whether your destination is in the direction of a major signposted landmark, then follow the signs through the maze of squares, lanes, and bridges.

By Vaporetto: The public-transit system is a fleet of motorized bus-boats called *vaporetti*. They work like city buses except

that they never get a flat, the stops are docks, and if you get off between stops, you might drown.

For most travelers, only two vaporetto lines matter: line #1 and line #2. These lines leave every 10 minutes (less off-season) and go up and down the Grand Canal, between the "mouth" of the fish at one end and San Marco at the other. Line #1 is the slow boat, taking 45 minutes and making every stop along the way. Line #2 is the fast boat that zips down the Grand Canal in 25 minutes, stopping only at Tronchetto (parking lot), Piazzale Roma (bus station), Ferrovia (train station), San Marcuola, Rialto Bridge, San Tomà (Frari Church), Accademia Bridge, San Marco (west end of St. Mark's Square), and San Zaccaria (east end of St. Mark's Square).

Catching a vaporetto is very much like catching a city bus. Helpful charts at the docks show a map of the lines and stops. At one end of the Grand Canal are Tronchetto, Piazzale Roma (Ple. Roma), and Ferrovia. At the other end is San Marco. The sign on the dock lists the line number that stops there and which direction the boat is headed, for example: "#2—Direction San Marco." Nearby is the sign for line #2 going in the other direction, for example: "#2—Direction Tronchetto."

It's simple, but there are a few quirks. Some stops have just one dock for boats going in both directions, so make sure the boat

Handy *Vaporetti* from San Zaccaria, near St. Mark's Square

Several *vaporetti* leave from the San Zaccaria docks, located 150 yards east of St. Mark's Square. There are four separate San Zaccaria docks spaced about 70 yards apart: Danieli, Jolanda, M.V.E., and Pietà. (Note: Although I list which specific dock these lines leave from, they often change from season to season—be prepared.)

- Line #1 goes up the Grand Canal, making all the stops, including San Marco-Vallaresso, Rialto, Ferrovia (train station), and Piazzale Roma (but it does not go as far as Tronchetto). In the other direction, it goes to the Lido. Line #1 departs from the San Zaccaria-Danieli dock.
- Line #2 zips over to San Giorgio Maggiore, the island church across from St. Mark's Square (5 minutes, €2 ride). From there, it continues on to the parking lot at Tronchetto (departs from San Zaccaria-M.V.E.)
- Line #41 goes to San Michele and Murano in 45 minutes (departs from San Zaccaria-Jolanda).
- The "LN" heads to Burano (70 minutes, from San Zaccaria-Pietà dock).
- The Molino Stucky shuttle boat takes even non-guests to the Hilton Hotel, with its popular view bar (free, 20-minute ride, leaves at 0:20 past the hour from near the San Zaccaria-M.V.E. dock).
- Lines #51 and #52 are the *circulare* (cheer-koo-LAH-ray), making a loop around the perimeter of the island, with a stop at the Lido—perfect if you just like riding boats. Line #51 goes counterclockwise (departs from San Zaccaria-Danieli), and #52 goes clockwise (departs from San Zaccaria-Jolanda).
- The Alilaguna airport shuttle to and from the airport stops at the San Zaccaria-Jolanda dock (see page 789).

Note: Alilaguna boat #M—the express boat to the cruise port—goes from the San Marco-Giardinetti stop, a 10-minute walk away (walk with the lagoon on your left).

you get on is pointing in the direction you want to go. Larger stops might have two separate docks side by side (one for each direction), while some smaller stops have docks across the canal from each other (one for each direction). Electronic reader boards on busy docks display which boats are coming next, and when.

To clear up any confusion, ask a ticket-seller or conductor (there's often one stationed on the dock to help confused tourists), or pick up the most current ACTV timetable (free at ticket booths, in English and Italian, tel. 041-2424, www.hellovenezia.com or www.actv.it).

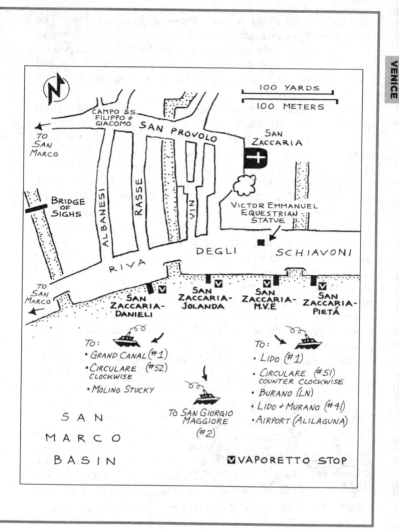

A **single ticket** costs a whopping €6.50. (Don't worry—much cheaper passes are described next.) Tickets are good for 60 minutes in one direction; you can hop on and off at stops during that time. Technically, you're not allowed a round-trip (though in practice, a round-trip is allowed if you can complete it within a 60-minute span). Note that you'll pay only €2 for a few shorter runs, including the route from San Marco to La Salute or from San Zaccaria-Jolanda to San Giorgio Maggiore.

You can also buy a **pass** for unlimited use of *vaporetti* and ACTV buses (€16/12 hours, €18/24 hours). Because single tickets cost a hefty €6.50 a pop, it makes sense to get a pass if you'll be taking three rides or more. Think through your Venice itinerary before you step up to the ticket booth to pay for your first vaporetto trip. And it's fun to be able to hop on and off spontaneously, and avoid long ticket lines. On the other hand, many tourists just walk and rarely use a boat.

Buy vaporetto tickets or passes at ticket booths at main stops (such as Ferrovia, Rialto, Accademia, and San Marco-Vallaresso). You can buy individual tickets on board from a conductor (do it immediately upon boarding, or you risk a €50 fine). Plan your travel so you'll have tickets or a pass handy when you need them—not all stops have ticket booths. Passes are validated and start with your first swipe. The pass system (called iMob) is electronic—just touch your card to the electronic reader on the dock to validate it.

For fun, take my Grand Canal Cruise (see page 724). Boats can be literally packed during the tourist rush hour. Morning rush hour (8:00-10:00) is headed in the direction of St. Mark's Square, as tourists and commuters arrive. Afternoon rush hour (about 17:00) is when they're headed in the other direction for the train station and cruise port. Riding at night—if your schedule allows it—with nearly empty boats and chandelier-lit palace interiors viewable from the Grand Canal, is an entirely different experience.

By *Traghetto:* Only four bridges cross the Grand Canal, but

traghetti (gondolas) shuttle locals and in-the-know tourists across the Grand Canal at eight handy locations (marked on the color map of Venice at the front of this book). Venetians stand while riding, but you shouldn't (€0.50, don't tip—literally). Note that *traghetti* generally don't run in the evening.

By Water Taxi: Venetian taxis, like speedboat limos, hang out at busy points along the Grand Canal. Prices, which average €65, are soft (about €70 to train station or €110 to airport for up to four people, extra fees for very early or late runs). Negotiate and settle on the price before stepping in. For travelers with lots of luggage or small groups who can split the cost, taxi-boat rides can be a worthwhile and time-saving convenience—and skipping across the lagoon in a classic wooden motorboat is a cool indulgence. For €90 an hour, you can have a private unguided taxi-boat tour.

By Gondola: To hire a gondolier for your own private cruise, see page 776.

Tours in Venice

Avventure Bellissime Venice Tours—This company offers a selection of two-hour walks, including a basic St. Mark's Square

introduction called the "Original Venice Walking Tour" (€21, includes church entry, most days at 11:00, Sun at 14:00; 45 minutes on the square, 15 minutes in the church, 60 minutes along back streets). Other walks include Cannaregio/Jewish Ghetto, San Polo/Dorsoduro, and ghost stories and legends (€20, group size 8-22, English-language only, tel. 041-520-8616, see www.tours-italy.com for details, info@tours-italy.com, Monica or Jonathan). Their 70-minute Grand Canal boat tour (€40, daily at 16:30, limited to eight people) is timed for good late-afternoon light. To get a 10 percent discount on any tour, say "Rick sent me."

Classic Venice Bars Tour—Debonair guide Alessandro Schezzini is a connoisseur of Venetian *bacari*—classic old bars serving wine and traditional *cicchetti* snacks. He organizes two-hour Venetian pub tours (€30, any night on request at 18:00, depart from the top of the Rialto Bridge, reserve by phone or email, mobile 335-530-9024, www.schezzini.it, alessandro@schezzini .it). Alessandro's tours include sampling *cicchetti* with wines at three different *bacari*, plus he'll answer all of your questions about Venice. (If you think of this tour as a light dinner with a local friend, you can consider it part of your eating budget.)

Venicescapes—Michael Broderick's private theme tours of Venice are intellectually demanding and beyond the attention span of most mortal tourists. But those with a keen interest in learning and a desire to gain a solid understanding of Venice find him passionate and engaging. Rather than a "sightseeing tour," your time with Michael is more like a rolling graduate-level lecture. For a description of his various itineraries, see his website (book well in advance, tours last 4-6 hours: $275 for 2 people, $50/person after that, pay in dollars or the current euro equivalent, admissions and transportation are extra, tel. 041-520-6361, www.venicescapes.org, info@venicescapes.org).

Artviva: The Original and Best Walking Tours—This company offers a number of tours, including a Venice in One Glorious Day Special and four theme tours (Grand Canal, Venice Walk, Doge's Palace, Gondola Tour). The two-hour "Learn to Be a Gondolier" tour teaches the ancient craft of rowing Venetian-style (€80, 4 people maximum). See the tour details and Rick Steves readers' discounts on their website (book in advance, tours run March-Nov, tel. 055-264-5033, www.italy.artviva.com, staff@art viva.com).

Local Guides—Licensed guides are carefully trained and love explaining Venice to visitors. If you organize a small group to split the cost (figure on roughly €70/hour with a 2-hour minimum), the fee becomes more reasonable. The following companies and guides give excellent tours to individuals, families, and small groups.

Elisabetta Morelli (€65/hour, mention this book, 2-hour minimum, tel. 041-526-7816, mobile 328-753-5220, bettamorelli @inwind.it).

Walks Inside Venice is a group of three women enthusiastic about teaching (€70/hour per group, 3-hour minimum; Roberta: mobile 347-253-0560; Cristina: mobile 348-341-5421; Sara: mobile 335-522-9714; www.walksinsidevenice.com, info@walksinside venice.com).

Venice with a Guide is a co-op of 10 equally good guides (www.venicewithaguide.com).

Alessandro Schezzini, mentioned earlier for his Classic Venice Bars Tour, isn't a licensed Italian guide and therefore can't take you into sights. But his relaxed two-hour back-streets "Rick Steves" tour does a great job of getting you beyond the clichés and into offbeat Venice (€15/person, book by email—alessandro @schezzini.it, mobile 335-530-9024, www.schezzini.it).

Self-Guided Tours in Venice

The following three tours provide a good introduction to this magical city. You can cruise the Grand Canal to St. Mark's Square, then take the self-guided tour of St. Mark's Square, and top it off with a tour of St. Mark's Basilica.

Free Audio Tours: If you'd rather be hearing these tours than reading them, you can download free audio versions at www.rick steves.com/audioeurope, from iTunes, or through the Rick Steves Audio Europe smartphone app. Audio tours free up your eyes to enjoy the sights.

Grand Canal Cruise

Take a joyride and introduce yourself to Venice by boat. Cruise the Grand Canal all the way to San Marco, starting at Ferrovia (the train station). Cruisers can get on at Piazzale Roma.

If it's your first trip down the Grand Canal, you might want to stow this book and just take it all in—Venice is a barrage on the senses that hardly needs narration. But these notes give the cruise a little meaning and help orient you to this great city.

This tour is designed to be done on the slow boat #1 (which takes about 45 minutes). The express boat #2 travels the same route, but it skips many stops and takes only 25 minutes, making it hard to sightsee.

To help you enjoy the visual parade of canal wonders, I've organized this tour by boat stop. I'll point out both what you can see from the current stop and what to look forward to as you cruise to the next stop.

Orientation

Cost: €6.50 for a 60-minute vaporetto ticket (or covered by a pass). For more on riding the vaporetto, see page 719.

When to Go: Boats run every 10 minutes. If you can, enjoy the best light and the fewest crowds by riding late in the day. Avoid the morning rush hour (8:00-10:00), when local workers and tourists commute into town (from Ferrovia to San Marco—in the same direction as this tour). In the evening, the crowds head the opposite way, and boats to San Marco are less crowded. Sunset bathes the buildings in gold. After dark, chandeliers light up building interiors.

Getting There: This tour starts at the Ferrovia vaporetto stop (at Santa Lucia train station). It also works if you board upstream from Ferrovia, either at Tronchetto (where cars arrive) or Piazzale Roma (where airport buses and the People Mover monorail from the cruise port arrive). Just start the tour when your vaporetto reaches Ferrovia.

Tips: You're more likely to find an empty seat if you catch the vaporetto at Piazzale Roma, which is even closer to the cruise port. Wherever you catch your vaporetto, confirm that you're on a boat that goes all the way to San Marco, by way of Rialto (*"San Marco via Rialto"*). If the conductor announces *"Solo Rialto!"*, the boat only goes as far as Rialto.

Stops to Consider: You can break up the tour by hopping on and off at various sights that are described in greater depth elsewhere in this book (but remember, a single-fare vaporetto ticket is good for just 60 minutes). Note that only boat #1 docks at all the stops listed; the faster boat #2 skips some stops.

These are all worth considering as hop-off spots: San Marcuola (near the Jewish Ghetto), Mercato Rialto (fish market and famous bridge), Ca' Rezzonico (Museum of 18th-Century Venice), Accademia (art museum and the nearby Guggenheim Collection), and Salute (huge and interesting church).

Information: Some city maps (on sale at postcard racks) have a handy Grand Canal map on the back.

Sightseeing Tips: As you board the vaporetto, make a beeline for

VENICE

Venice's Grand Canal

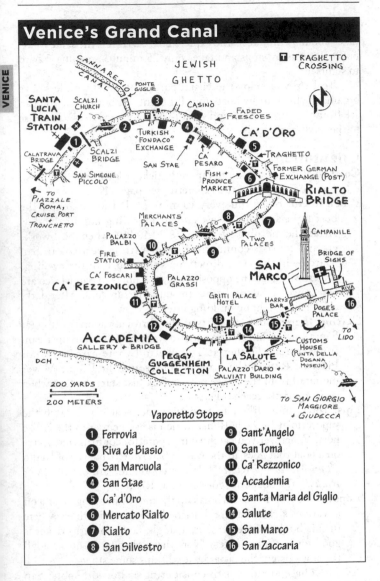

T TRAGHETTO CROSSING

CANNAREGIO CANAL

JEWISH GHETTO

PONTE GUGLIE

SANTA LUCIA TRAIN STATION

SCALZI CHURCH

CASINÒ

FADED FRESCOES

Turkish "Fondaco" Exchange

CA' D'ORO

CALATRAVA BRIDGE

SCALZI BRIDGE

CA' PESARO

SAN STAE

TRAGHETTO

SAN SIMEONE PICCOLO

FISH + PRODUCE MARKET

FORMER GERMAN EXCHANGE (POST)

TO PIAZZALE ROMA, CRUISE PORT + TRONCHETTO

RIALTO BRIDGE

MERCHANTS' PALACES

PALAZZO BALBI

CAMPANILE

FIRE STATION

TWO PALACES

BRIDGE OF SIGHS

CA' FOSCARI

PALAZZO GRASSI

SAN MARCO

CA' REZZONICO

GRITTI PALACE HOTEL

HARRY'S BAR

DOGE'S PALACE

RIVA

ACCADEMIA GALLERY + BRIDGE

PEGGY GUGGENHEIM COLLECTION

LA SALUTE

CUSTOMS HOUSE (PUNTA DELLA DOGANA MUSEUM)

TO LIDO

DCH

PALAZZO DARIO + SALVIATI BUILDING

200 YARDS

200 METERS

TO SAN GIORGIO MAGGIORE + GIUDECCA

Vaporetto Stops

1. Ferrovia
2. Riva de Biasio
3. San Marcuola
4. San Stae
5. Ca' d'Oro
6. Mercato Rialto
7. Rialto
8. San Silvestro
9. Sant'Angelo
10. San Tomà
11. Ca' Rezzonico
12. Accademia
13. Santa Maria del Giglio
14. Salute
15. San Marco
16. San Zaccaria

an open-air seat in the front of the boat, which has the best seats for this tour. From the front, you can easily look left, right, and forward. If you find yourself stuck on the side or in the cabin, do your best. Avoid sitting in the back, only because you'll miss the wonderful forward views.

Some readers do this cruise twice—once in either direction—because it's hard to see it all while trying to read along aboard a moving boat.

Length of This Tour: Allow 45 minutes on vaporetto #1, or 25 minutes on vaporetto #2.

Starring: Palaces, markets, boats, bridges—Venice.

The Tour Begins

While you wait for your boat, here's some background on Venice's "Main Street."

At more than two miles long, nearly 150 feet wide, and nearly 15 feet deep, the Grand Canal is the city's largest, lined with its most impressive palaces. It's the remnant of a river that once spilled from the mainland into the Adriatic. The sediment it carried formed barrier islands that cut Venice off from the sea, forming a lagoon.

Venice was built on the marshy islands of the former delta, sitting on wood pilings driven nearly 15 feet into the clay (alder was the preferred wood). About 25 miles of canals drain the city, dumping like streams into the Grand Canal. Technically, Venice has only three canals: Grand, Giudecca, and Cannaregio. The 45 small waterways that dump into the Grand Canal are referred to as rivers (e.g., Rio Nuovo).

Venice is a city of palaces, dating from the days when the city was the world's richest. The most lavish palaces formed a grand

chorus line along the Grand Canal. Once frescoed in reds and blues, with black-and-white borders and gold-leaf trim, they made Venice a city of dazzling color. This cruise is the only way to truly appreciate the palaces, approaching them at water level, where their main entrances were located. Today, strict laws prohibit any changes in these buildings, so while landowners gnash their teeth, we can enjoy Europe's best-preserved medieval city—slowly rotting. Many of the grand buildings are now vacant. Others harbor chandeliered elegance above mossy, empty (often flooded) ground floors.

❶ Ferrovia

The **Santa Lucia train station,** one of the few modern buildings in town, was built in 1954. It's been the gateway into Venice since 1860, when the first station was built. "F.S." stands for "Ferrovie dello Stato," the Italian state railway system.

More than 20,000 people a day commute in from the mainland, making this the busiest part of Venice during rush hour. The **Calatrava Bridge,** spanning the Grand Canal between the train station and Piazzale Roma upstream, was built in 2008 to alleviate some of the congestion and make the commute easier (for more about the bridge, see page 775).

Opposite the train station, atop the green dome of **San Simeone Piccolo** church, St. Simeon waves *ciao* to whoever enters or leaves the "old" city. The pink church with the white Carrara-marble facade, just beyond the train station, is the **Church of the Scalzi** (Church of the Barefoot, named after the shoeless Carmelite monks), where the last doge (Venetian ruler) rests. It looks relatively new because it was partially rebuilt after being bombed in 1915 by Austrians aiming (poorly) at the train station.

❷ Riva de Biasio

Venice's main thoroughfare is busy with all kinds of **boats:** taxis, police boats, garbage boats, ambulances, construction cranes, and even brown-and-white UPS boats. Somehow they all manage to share the canal in relative peace.

About 25 yards past the Riva de Biasio stop, you'll look left down the broad **Cannaregio Canal** to see what was the **Jewish Ghetto** (see page 774). The twin, pale-pink, six-story "skyscrapers"—the tallest buildings you'll see at this end of the canal—are reminders of how densely populated the world's original ghetto was. Set aside as the local Jewish quarter in 1516, this area became extremely crowded. This urban island developed into one of the most closely knit business and cultural quarters of all the Jewish communities in Italy and gave us our word "ghetto" (from *geto*, the copper foundry located here).

❸ San Marcuola

At this stop, facing a tiny square just ahead, stands the unfinished church of San Marcuola, one of only five churches fronting the Grand Canal. Centuries ago, this canal was a commercial drag of expensive real estate in high demand by wealthy merchants.

About 20 yards ahead on the right stands the stately gray **Turkish "Fondaco" Exchange,** one of the oldest houses in Venice. Its horseshoe arches and roofline of triangles and dingleballs are reminders of its Byzantine heritage. Turkish traders in turbans docked here, unloaded their goods into the warehouse on the bottom story,

then went upstairs for a home-style meal and a place to sleep. Venice in the 1500s was very cosmopolitan, welcoming every religion and ethnicity, so long as they carried cash. (Today the building contains the city's Museum of Natural History—and Venice's only dinosaur skeleton.)

Just 100 yards ahead on the left, Venice's **Casinò** is housed in the palace where German composer Richard *(The Ring)* Wagner died in 1883. See his distinct, strong-jawed profile in the white plaque on the brick wall. In the 1700s, Venice was Europe's Vegas, with casinos and prostitutes everywhere. Casinòs ("little houses") have long provided Italians with a handy escape from daily life. Today they're run by the state to keep Mafia influence at bay. Notice the fancy front porch, rolling out the red carpet for high rollers arriving by taxi or hotel boat.

❹ San Stae

The San Stae Church sports a delightful Baroque facade. Opposite the San Stae stop, look for the peeling plaster that once made up **frescoes** (scant remains on the lower floors). Imagine the facades of the Grand Canal at their finest. As colorful as the city is today, it's still only a faded, sepia-toned remnant of a long-gone era, a time of lavishly decorated, brilliantly colored palaces.

Just ahead, jutting out a bit on the right, is the ornate white facade of **Ca' Pesaro.** *"Ca'"* is short for *casa* (house). Because only

 the house of the doge (Venetian ruler) could be called a palace *(palazzo),* all other Venetian palaces are technically *"Ca'."*

In this city of masks, notice how the rich marble facades along the Grand Canal mask what are generally just simple, no-nonsense brick buildings. Most merchants enjoyed showing off. However, being smart businessmen, they only decorated the side of the buildings that would be seen and appreciated. But look back as you pass Ca' Pesaro (which houses the International Gallery of Modern Art—see page 771). It's the only building you'll see with a fine side facade. Ahead, on the left, with its glorious triple-decker medieval arcade (just before the next stop) is Ca' d'Oro.

❺ Ca' d'Oro

The lacy **Ca' d'Oro** (House of Gold) is the best example of Venetian Gothic architecture on the canal. Its three stories offer different variations on balcony design, topped with a spiny white roofline.

Venetian Gothic mixes traditional Gothic (pointed arches and round medallions stamped with a four-leaf clover) with Byzantine styles (tall, narrow arches atop thin columns), filled in with Islamic frills. Like all the palaces, this was originally painted and gilded to make it even more glorious than it is now. Today the Ca' d'Oro is an art gallery (see page 775).

Look at the Venetian chorus line of palaces in front of the boat doing an architectural cancan. On the right is the arcade of the covered **fish market,** with the open-air **produce market** just beyond. It bustles in the morning but is quiet the rest of the day. This is a great scene to wander through—even though European Union hygiene standards have made it cleaner, but less colorful

than it once was. Find the *traghetto* gondola ferrying shoppers—standing like Washington crossing the Delaware—back and forth. There are eight *traghetto* crossings along the Grand Canal, each one marked by a classy low-key green-and-black sign. Make a point to use them. At €0.50 a ride, they are one of the best deals in Venice.

❻ Mercato Rialto

This stop opened in 2007 to serve the busy market (boats only stop here from 8:00 to 20:00). The long and officious-looking building at this stop is the Venice courthouse. Straight ahead in the distance, rising above the huge post office, is the tip of the Campanile (bell tower) crowned by its golden angel at St. Mark's Square, where this tour will end. The former post office (100 yards directly ahead, on left side, soon to be a shopping center) used to be the German Exchange, the trading center for German metal merchants in the early 1500s.

You'll cruise by some trendy and beautifully situated wine bars on the right, but look ahead as you round the corner and see the impressive Rialto Bridge come into view.

A major landmark of Venice, the **Rialto Bridge** is lined with shops and tourists. Constructed in 1588, it's the third bridge built on this spot. Until the 1850s, this was the only bridge crossing the Grand Canal. With a span of 160 feet and foundations stretch-

ing 650 feet on either side, the Rialto was an impressive engineering feat in its day. Earlier Rialto Bridges could open to let big ships in, but not this one. When this new bridge was completed, much of the Grand Canal was closed to shipping and became a canal of palaces.

When gondoliers pass under the fat arch of the Rialto Bridge, they take full advantage of its acoustics: *"Volare, oh, oh..."*

❼ Rialto

Rialto, a separate town in the early days of Venice, has always been the commercial district, while San Marco was the religious and governmental center. Today, a winding street called the Mercerie connects the two, providing travelers with human traffic jams and a mesmerizing gauntlet of shopping temptations. This is the only stretch of the historic Grand Canal with landings upon which you can walk. They unloaded the city's basic necessities here: oil, wine, charcoal, iron. Today, the quay is lined with tourist-trap restaurants.

Venice's sleek, black, graceful **gondolas** are a symbol of the city (for more on gondolas, see page 776). With about 500 gondoliers joyriding amid the churning *vaporetti*, there's a lot of congestion on the Grand Canal. Pay attention—this is where most of the gondola and vaporetto accidents take place. While the Rialto is the highlight of many gondola rides, gondoliers understandably prefer the quieter small canals. Watch your vaporetto driver curse the better-paid gondoliers.

Ahead 100 yards on the left, two gray-colored **palaces** stand side by side (the City Hall and the mayor's office). Their horseshoe-shaped, arched windows are similar and their stories are the same height, lining up to create the effect of one long balcony.

❽ San Silvestro

We now enter a long stretch of important **merchants' palaces,** each with proud and different facades. Because ships couldn't navigate beyond the Rialto Bridge, the biggest palaces—with the major shipping needs—line this last stretch of the navigable Grand Canal.

Venice at a Glance

In the sight listings below, a page number directs you to a fuller description in this chapter; sights without page numbers are not described further and generally don't make the cut for a one-day visit.

▲▲▲**St. Mark's Square** Venice's grand main square. **Hours:** Always open. See page 764.

▲▲▲**St. Mark's Basilica** Cathedral with mosaics, saint's bones, treasury, museum, and viewpoint of square. **Hours:** Basilica— Mon-Sat 9:45-17:00, Sun 14:00-17:00 (until 16:00 Nov-March); Treasury, Golden Altarpiece, and San Marco Museum close 15 minutes before church (shorter hours in winter). See page 764.

▲▲▲**Doge's Palace** Art-splashed palace of former rulers, with prison accessible through Bridge of Sighs. **Hours:** Daily April-Oct 8:30-18:30, Nov-March 8:00-17:30. See page 765.

▲▲▲**Rialto Bridge** Distinctive bridge spanning the Grand Canal, with a market nearby. **Hours:** Bridge—always open; market— souvenir stalls open daily, produce market closed Sun-Mon, fish market closed Sun. See page 770.

▲▲**Correr Museum** Venetian history and art. **Hours:** Daily April-Oct 10:00-19:00, Nov-March 10:00-17:00. See page 766.

▲▲**Accademia** Venice's top art museum. **Hours:** Mon 8:15-14:00, Tue-Sun 8:15-19:15. See page 769.

▲▲**Peggy Guggenheim Collection** Popular display of 20th-century art. **Hours:** Wed-Mon 10:00-18:00, closed Tue. See page 769.

▲▲**Frari Church** Franciscan church featuring Renaissance masters. **Hours:** Mon-Sat 9:00-18:00, Sun 13:00-18:00. See page 772.

▲▲**Scuola San Rocco** "Tintoretto's Sistine Chapel." **Hours:** Daily 9:30-17:30. See page 774.

▲**Campanile** Dramatic bell tower on St. Mark's Square with elevator to the top. **Hours:** Daily April-June and Oct 9:00-19:00, July-Sept 9:00-21:00, Nov-March 9:30-15:45, closed from Christmas to mid-Jan. See page 766.

▲**Bridge of Sighs** Famous enclosed bridge, part of Doge's Palace, near St. Mark's Square. **Hours:** Generally viewable, but covered with scaffolding during renovation. See page 767.

▲**La Salute Church** Striking church dedicated to the Virgin Mary. **Hours:** Daily 9:00-12:00 & 15:00-17:30. See page 770.

▲**Ca' Rezzonico** Posh Grand Canal palazzo with 18th-century Venetian art. **Hours:** April-Oct Wed-Mon 10:00-18:00, Nov-March Wed-Mon 10:00-17:00, closed Tue. See page 770.

▲**Punta della Dogana** Museum of contemporary art. **Hours:** Wed-Mon 10:00-19:00, closed Tue. See page 770.

▲**Ca' Pesaro** International modern art gallery in a canalside palazzo. **Hours:** Tue-Sun 10:00-17:00, closed Mon. See page 771.

▲**Scuola Dalmata di San Giorgio** Exquisite Renaissance meeting house. **Hours:** Mon 14:45-18:00, Tue-Sat 9:15-13:00 & 14:45-18:00, Sun 9:15-13:00. See page 776.

Church of San Zaccaria Final resting place of St. Zechariah (San Zaccaria), plus a Bellini altarpiece and an eerie crypt. **Hours:** Mon-Sat 10:00-12:00 & 16:00-18:00, Sun 16:00-18:00 only. See page 768.

Church of San Polo Ninth-century church with works by Tintoretto, Veronese, and Tiepolo. **Hours:** Mon-Sat 10:00-17:00, closed Sun. See page 774.

Nearby Islands

▲**San Giorgio Maggiore** Island across the lagoon featuring church with Palladio architecture, Tintoretto paintings, and fine views back on Venice. **Hours:** May-Sept Mon-Sat 9:30-12:30 & 14:30-18:00, Sun 8:30-11:00 & 14:30-18:00; Oct-April until 16:30. See page 768.

San Michele Cemetery island on the lagoon. **Hours:** Always open.

Murano Island famous for glass factories and glassmaking museum. **Hours:** Glass museum open daily April-Oct 10:00-18:00, Nov-March 10:00-17:00.

Burano Sleepy lacemaking island. **Hours:** Always open.

Torcello Near-deserted island with old church, bell tower, and museum. **Hours:** Most sights open daily March-Oct 10:30-18:00, Nov-Feb 10:00-16:30, museum closed Mon.

Palaces like these were multi-functional: ground floor for the warehouse, offices and showrooms upstairs, and the living quarters above the offices on the "noble floors" (with big windows designed to allow maximum light). Servants lived and worked on the top floors (with the smallest windows). For fire safety reasons, the kitchens were also located on the top floors. Peek into the noble floors to catch a glimpse of their still-glorious chandeliers of Murano glass.

❾ Sant'Angelo

Notice how many buildings have a foundation of waterproof white stone *(pietra d'Istria)* upon which the bricks sit high and dry. Many

canal-level floors are abandoned as the rising water level takes its toll.

The **posts**—historically painted gaily with the equivalent of family coats of arms—don't rot under water. But the wood at the waterline, where it's exposed to oxygen, does. On the smallest canals, little blue gondola signs indicate that these docks are for gondolas only (no taxis or motor boats).

❿ San Tomà

Fifty yards ahead, on the right side (with twin obelisks on the rooftop), stands **Palazzo Balbi,** the palace of an early-17th-century captain general of the sea. These Venetian equivalents of five-star admirals were honored with twin obelisks decorating their palaces. This palace, like so many in the city, flies three flags: Italy (green-white-red), the European Union (blue with ring of stars), and Venice (a lion on a field of red and gold). Today it houses the administrative headquarters of the regional government.

Just past the admiral's palace, look immediately to the right, down a side canal. On the right side of that canal, before the bridge, see the traffic light and the **fire station** (with four arches hiding fireboats parked and ready to go).

The impressive **Ca' Foscari,** with a classic Venetian facade (on the corner, across from the fire station), dominates the bend in the canal. This is the main building of the University of Venice, which has about 25,000 students. Notice the

elegant lamp on the corner.

The grand, heavy, white **Ca' Rezzonico,** just before the Ca' Rezzonico stop, houses the Museum of 18th-Century Venice (see page 770). Across the canal is the cleaner and leaner **Palazzo Grassi,** the last major palace built on the canal, erected in the late 1700s. It was recently purchased by a French tycoon and now displays his contemporary art collection.

⓫ Ca' Rezzonico

Up ahead, the Accademia Bridge leads over the Grand Canal to the **Accademia Gallery** (right side), filled with the best Venetian paintings (see page 769). The bridge was put up in 1934 as a temporary structure. Locals liked it, so it stayed.

⓬ Accademia

From here, look through the graceful bridge and way ahead to enjoy a classic view of **La Salute Church,** topped by a crown-

shaped dome supported by scrolls (see page 770). This Church of Saint Mary of Good Health was built to thank God for delivering Venetians from the devastating plague of 1630 (which had killed about a third of the city's population).

The low, white building among greenery (100 yards ahead, on the right, between the Accademia Bridge and the church) is the **Peggy Guggenheim Collection.** The American heiress "retired" here, sprucing up a palace that had been abandoned in mid-construction. Peggy willed the city her fine collection of modern art (see page 769).

As you approach the next stop, notice on the right how the fine line of higgledy-piggledy palaces evokes old-time Venice. Two doors past the Guggenheim, Palazzo Dario has a great set of characteristic **funnel-shaped chimneys.** These forced embers through a loop-the-loop channel until they were dead—required in the days when stone palaces were surrounded by humble, wooden buildings, and a live spark could make a merchant's workforce homeless. Notice this early Renaissance building's flat-feeling facade with "pasted-on" Renaissance motifs. Three doors later is the **Salviati building** (with the fine mosaics), which was once a glassworks.

VENICE

⓭ Santa Maria del Giglio

Back on the left stands the fancy Gritti Palace hotel. Hemingway and Woody Allen both stayed here (but not together).

Take a deep whiff of Venice. What's all this nonsense about stinky canals? All I smell is my shirt. By the way, how's your captain? Smooth dockings? To get to know him, stand up in the bow and block his view.

⓮ Salute

The huge La Salute Church towers overhead as if squirted from a can of Catholic Reddi-wip. Like Venice itself, the church rests upon pilings. To build the foun-dation for the city, more than a million trees were piled together, reaching beneath the mud to the solid clay. Much of the surround-ing countryside was deforested by Venice. Trees were exported and consumed locally to fuel the fur-naces of Venice's booming glass industry, to build Europe's biggest merchant marine, and to prop up this city in the mud.

As the Grand Canal opens up into the lagoon, the last build-ing on the right with the golden ball is the 17th-century **Customs House,** which now houses the Punta della Dogana Museum of Contemporary Art (see page 770). Its two bronze Atlases hold a statue of Fortune riding the ball. Arriving ships stopped here to pay their tolls.

⓯ San Marco

Up ahead on the left, the green pointed tip of the Campanile marks **St. Mark's Square,** the political and religious center of Venice...

and the final destination of this tour. You could get off at the San Marco stop and go straight to St. Mark's Square. But I'm staying on the boat for one more stop, just past St. Mark's Square (it's a quick walk back).

Survey the lagoon. Oppo-site St. Mark's Square, across the water, the ghostly white church with the pointy bell tower is **San Giorgio Maggiore,** with great views of Venice (see page 768). Next to it is the residential island Giudecca, stretching from close to San Giorgio Maggiore past the Venice youth hostel (with a nice view, directly across) to the Hilton Hotel (good nighttime view, far-right end of island).

Still on board? If you are, as we leave the San Marco stop, prepare for a drive-by view of St. Mark's Square. First comes the bold white facade of the old mint (where Venice's golden ducat, the "dollar" of the Venetian Republic, was made) and the library facade. Then the twin columns, topped by St. Theodore and St. Mark, who've welcomed visitors since the 15th century. Between the columns, catch a glimpse of two giant figures atop the **Clock Tower**—they've been whacking their clappers every hour since 1499. The domes of **St. Mark's Basilica** are soon eclipsed by the lacy facade of the **Doge's Palace.** Next you'll see the **Bridge of Sighs** (currently under scaffolding), and then the grand harborside promenade—the **Riva.**

Follow the Riva with your eye, past elegant hotels to the green area in the distance. This is the largest of Venice's few **parks,** which hosts the Biennale art show every odd year. Much farther in the distance is the **Lido,** the island with Venice's beach. Its sand and casinos are tempting, but its car traffic disrupts the medieval charm of Venice.

⑯ San Zaccaria

OK, you're at your last stop. Quick—muscle your way off this boat! (If you don't, you'll eventually end up at the Lido.)

At San Zaccaria, you're right in the thick of the action. A number of other *vaporetti* depart from here (see page 719). Otherwise, it's a short walk back along the Riva to St. Mark's Square. Ahoy!

St. Mark's Square Tour

Venice was once Europe's richest city, and Piazza San Marco was its center. As middleman in the trade between Asia and Europe, wealthy Venice profited from both sides. In 1450, Venice had 180,000 citizens (far more than London) and a gross "national" product that exceeded that of entire countries.

The rich Venetians taught the rest of Europe about the good life—silks, spices, and jewels from the East, crafts from northern Europe, good food and wine, fine architecture, music, theater, and laughter. Venice was a vibrant city full of painted palaces, glittering canals, and impressed visitors. Five centuries after its power began to decline, Venice is all of these still, with the added charm of romantic decay. In this tour, we'll spend an hour in the heart of this Old World superpower.

Orientation

Getting There: Signs all over town point to *San Marco*—meaning both the square and the basilica—located where the Grand Canal spills out into the lagoon. Vaporetto stops: San Marco or San Zaccaria.

Campanile: If you ascend the bell tower, it'll cost you €8 (daily April-June and Oct 9:00-19:00, July-Sept 9:00-21:00, Nov-March 9:30-15:45, closed from Christmas to mid-Jan, tel. 041-522-4064).

Information: There are two TIs. One is in the southwest corner of the square; the other is along the waterfront at the San Marco-Vallaresso vaporetto stop.

Audioguide Tours: You can download a free audio version of this tour at www.ricksteves.com/audioeurope, from iTunes, or through the Rick Steves Audio Europe smartphone app.

WCs: Handy public WCs (€1.50) are behind the Correr Museum and at Giardinetti Reali park.

Cuisine Art: Cafés with live music provide an engaging sound-track for St. Mark's Square (see "Cafés on St. Mark's Square" sidebar, later). The Correr Museum (at the end of the square opposite the basilica) has a quiet coffee shop overlooking the crowded square. For a list of restaurants in the area, see page 786.

Necessary Eyesores: Expect scaffolding and advertising billboards to cover parts of the square and its monuments when you visit. The Campanile's foundation is being fortified, an effort that will take years. The nearby Bridge of Sighs is also covered with scaffolding during restoration.

Cardinal Points: The square is aligned (roughly) east-west. So, facing the basilica, north is to your left.

Starring: Byzantine domes, Gothic arches, Renaissance arches... and the wonderful, musical space they enclose.

The Tour Begins

• *For an overview of this grand square and the buildings that sur-round it, view it from the west end of the square (away from St. Mark's Basilica).*

The Piazza

St. Mark's Basilica dominates the square with its Byzantine-style onion domes and glowing mosaics. Mark Twain said it looked like "a vast warty bug taking a meditative walk." (I say it looks like tiara-wearing ladybugs copulating.) To the right of the basilica is its 300-foot-tall Campanile. Between the basilica and the Campanile, you can catch a glimpse of the pale-pink Doge's Palace. Lining the square are the former government offices *(procuratie)* that administered the Venetian empire's vast net-

work of trading outposts, which stretched all the way to Turkey.

The square is big, but it feels intimate with its cafés and dueling orchestras. By day, it's great for people-watching and pigeon-chasing. By night, under lantern light, it transports you to another century, complete with its own romantic soundtrack. The piazza draws Indians in saris, English nobles in blue blazers, and Nebraskans in shorts. Napoleon called the piazza "the most beautiful drawing room in Europe." Napoleon himself added to the intimacy by building the final wing, opposite the basilica, that encloses the square.

For architecture buffs, here are three centuries of styles, bam, side by side, *uno–due–tre*, for easy comparison:

1. On the left side (as you face the basilica) are the "Old" offices, built in about 1500 in solid, column-and-arch Renaissance style.

2. The "New" offices (on the right), in a High Renaissance style from a century later (c. 1600), are a little heavier and more ornate. This wing mixes arches, the three orders of columns from bottom to top—Doric, Ionic, and Corinthian—and statues in the Baroque style.

3. Napoleon's wing, at the opposite end from the basilica, is Neoclassical (c. 1800)—a return to simpler, more austere classical

columns and arches. Napoleon's architects tried to make his wing bridge the styles of the other two. But it turned out a little too high for one side and not high enough for the other. Nice try.

Imagine this square full of water, with gondolas floating where people now sip cappuccinos.

That happens every so often at very high tides *(acqua alta)*, a reminder that Venice and the sea are intertwined. (Now that one is sinking and the other is rising, they are more intertwined than ever.)

Venice became Europe's richest city from its trade with north-ern Europeans, Ottoman Muslims, and Byzantine Christians.

VENICE

St. Mark's Square

TO RIALTO

SAN ZULIAN

ST. MARK'S BAG CHECK

TO RIALTO

S. MARCO

MERCERIE

FABBRI

C. FIUBERA

4

SPADARIA

PIAZZETTA D. LEONCINI

TRON

OLD OFFICES

CLOCK TOWER

8

ST. MARK'S BASILICA

RAMO SELVA

10

7

CAMPA-NILE

PIAZZA

DOGE'S PALACE

FRENNERIA

CORRER MUSEUM

+ NAPOLEON'S WING

SAN MARCO

6

11

PIAZZETTA

POST

WC

i

NEW OFFICES

9

S. MARCO COLUMN

SAN MOISÈ

CALLE VALLARESSO

SAN MOISÈ

5

GIARDINETTI REALI

G

S. THEODORE COLUMN

SAL.

WC

i

TO ACCADEMIA

V SAN MARCO - GIARDINETTI EXPRESS BOAT #M TO CRUISE PORT

V SAN MARCO - VALLARESSO

SAN MARCO

T

TO SALUTE

TO CRUISE PORT

◄ ENTRANCES TO SIGHTS

V VAPORETTO STOP

T TRAGHETTO CROSSING

G GONDOLA STATION

⚘ VIEW

100 YARDS

100 METERS

DCH

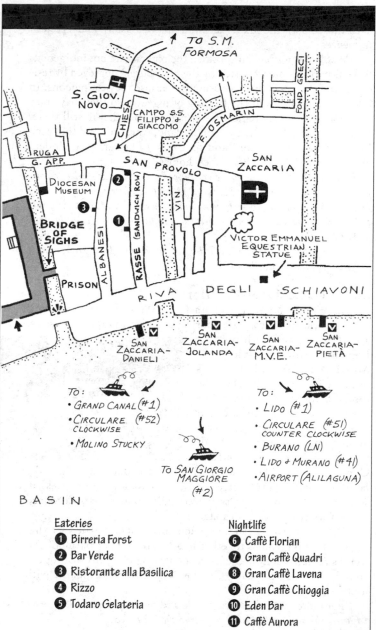

TO S.M. FORMOSA

FOND. GRECI

S. GIOV. NOVO

CHIESA

CAMPO S.S. FILIPPO & GIACOMO

F. OSMARIN

SAN ZACCARIA

RUGA G. APP.

SAN PROVOLO

DIOCESAN MUSEUM

2

VIA

3

1

RASSE (SANDWICH ROW)

BRIDGE OF SIGHS

ALBANESI

VICTOR EMMANUEL EQUESTRIAN STATUE

PRISON

RIVA DEGLI SCHIAVONI

SAN ZACCARIA-DANIELI

SAN ZACCARIA-JOLANDA

SAN ZACCARIA-M.V.E.

SAN ZACCARIA-PIETÀ

TO:
• GRAND CANAL (#1)
• CIRCULARE (#52) CLOCKWISE
• MOLINO STUCKY

TO:
• LIDO (#1)
• CIRCULARE (#51) COUNTER CLOCKWISE
• BURANO (LN)
• LIDO & MURANO (#41)
• AIRPORT (ALILAGUNA)

TO SAN GIORGIO MAGGIORE (#2)

BASIN

Eateries
1 Birreria Forst
2 Bar Verde
3 Ristorante alla Basilica
4 Rizzo
5 Todaro Gelateria

Nightlife
6 Caffè Florian
7 Gran Caffè Quadri
8 Gran Caffè Lavena
9 Gran Caffè Chioggia
10 Eden Bar
11 Caffè Aurora

Here in St. Mark's Square, the exact center of this East-West axis, we see both the luxury and the mix of Eastern and Western influences.

Watch out for pigeon speckle. The pigeons are not indigenous to Venice (they were imported by the Habsburgs) nor loved by residents. In fact, Venetians love seagulls because they eat pigeons. In 2008, Venice outlawed the feeding of pigeons, so their days may be numbered. There are now fewer pigeons, but they're still there. Vermin are a problem on this small island, where it's said that each Venetian has two pigeons and four rats. (The rats stay hidden, except when high tides flood their homes.)

• *The TI is nearby, in the corner of Napoleon's wing. It's wise to confirm your sightseeing plans here and pick up the latest list of opening hours. Behind you (southwest of the piazza), you'll find the public WC (€1.50) and a post office with a helpful stamps-only line (usually closes at 14:00).*

Now approach the basilica. If it's hot and you're tired, grab a shady spot at the foot of the Campanile.

St. Mark's Basilica—Exterior

The facade is a crazy mix of East and West. There are round, Roman-style arches over the doorways, golden Byzantine mosaics, a roofline ringed with pointed French Gothic pinnacles, and Muslim-shaped onion domes (wood, covered with lead) on the roof. The brick-structure building is blanketed in marble that came from everywhere—columns from Alexandria, capitals from Sicily, and carvings from  Constantinople. The columns flanking the doorways show the facade's variety—purple, green, gray, white, yellow, some speckled, some striped horizontally, some vertically, some fluted, all topped with a variety of different capitals.

What's amazing isn't so much the variety as the fact that the whole thing comes together in a bizarre sort of harmony. St. Mark's remains simply the most interesting church in Europe, a church that (paraphrasing Goethe) "can only be compared with itself."

For more on the basilica, inside and out, see page 748.

• *Facing the basilica, turn 90 degrees to the left to see...*

The Clock Tower (Torre dell'Orologio)

Two bronze "Moors" (African Muslims) stand atop the Clock Tower (built originally to be giants, they only gained their ethnic-

Cafés on St. Mark's Square

Cafés line the square. Those with live music feature similar food, prices, and a three- to five-piece combo playing a selection of classical and pop hits, from Brahms to "Bésame Mucho." If you sit outside and get just a drink, expect to pay €12-20, including a €6 cover charge when the orchestra is playing. A coffee—your cheapest option—costs about €6 if you sit at an outside table, plus the €6 cover charge when the music plays, bringing it to €12 total. It's perfectly acceptable to nurse a cappuccino for an hour—you're paying for the music with the cover charge.

Caffè Florian (on the right as you face the church—see map earlier in this chapter) is the most famous Venetian café

and one of the first places in Europe to serve coffee. It's been a popular spot for a discreet rendezvous in Venice since 1720. The orchestra plays a more classical repertoire than at the other cafés. The outside tables are the main action, but do walk inside through the richly decorated, old-time rooms where Casanova, Lord Byron, Charles Dickens, and Woody Allen have all paid too much for a drink (reasonable prices at bar in back).

Gran Caffè Quadri, opposite the Florian, has an equally illustrious history of famous clientele, including the writers Stendhal and Dumas, and composer Richard Wagner. **Gran Caffè Lavena,** near the Clock Tower, is newer and less prestigious.

Gran Caffè Chioggia, on the Piazzetta facing the Doge's Palace, charges slightly less, with one or two musicians, usually a pianist, playing cocktail jazz.

The following less-expensive options don't have live music, but you can enjoy overhearing music from nearby cafés: **Eden Bar,** next to Gran Caffè Quadri, is touristy, but that doesn't matter when you're enjoying your hot dog and Coke while sitting out on the piazza. **Caffè Aurora,** in the shadow of the Campanile, features nearly all the ambience of the orchestra cafés at half the price.

ity when the metal darkened over the centuries). At the top of each hour they swing their giant clappers. The clock dial shows the 24 hours, the signs of the zodiac, and, in the blue center, the phases of the moon. Above the dial is the world's first digital clock, which changes every five minutes. The Clock Tower retains some of its original coloring of blue and gold, a reminder that, in centuries past, this city glowed with bright color.

An alert winged lion, the symbol of St. Mark and the city, looks down on the crowded square. He opens a book that reads *"Pax Tibi Marce,"* or "Peace to you, Mark." As legend goes, these were the comforting words that an angel spoke to the stressed evangelist, assuring him he would find serenity during a stormy night that the saint spent here on the island. Eventually, St. Mark's body found its final resting place inside the basilica, and now his winged-lion symbol is everywhere. (Find four in 20 seconds. Go.)

Venice's many lions express the city's various mood swings through history—triumphant after a naval victory, sad when a favorite son has died, hollow-eyed after a plague, and smiling when the soccer team wins. The pair of lions squatting between the Clock Tower and basilica have probably been photographed being ridden by every Venetian child born since the dawn of cameras.

For a self-guided tour of the basilica, see page 748.

The Campanile

The original Campanile (cam-pah-NEE-lay), or bell tower, was

a lighthouse and a marvel of 10th-century architecture until the 20th century (1902), when it toppled into the center of the piazza. It had groaned ominously the night before, sending people scurrying from the cafés. The next morning...crash! The golden angel on top landed right at the basilica's front door, standing up.

The Campanile was rebuilt 10 years later complete with its golden archangel Gabriel, who always faces the breeze. You can ride a lift to the top for the best view of Venice. It's crowded at peak times, but well worth it.

You may see construction work around the Campanile's base. Hoping to prevent a repeat of the 1902 collapse, they've wrapped the underground foundations with a titanium girdle to shore up a crack that appeared in 1939.

Because St. Mark's Square is the first place in town to start flooding, there are tide gauges at the outside base of the Campanile (near the exit, facing St. Mark's Square) that show the current sea level *(livello marea)*. Find the stone plaque (near the exit door) that commemorates the high-water 77-inch level from the disastrous floods of 1966. In December of 2008, Venice suffered another terrible high tide, cresting at 61 inches.

If the tide is mild (around 20 inches), the water merely seeps up through the drains. But when there's a strong tide (around 40 inches), it looks like someone's turned on a faucet down below. The water bubbles upward and flows like a river to the lowest points in the square, which can be covered with a few inches of water in an hour or so. When the water level rises one meter above mean sea level, a warning siren sounds, and it repeats if a serious flood is imminent.

Many doorways have three-foot-high wooden or metal barriers to block the high water *(acqua alta)*, but the seawater still seeps in through floors and drains, rendering the barriers nearly useless. (To learn the reasons for the flooding, see the sidebar on page 771.)

You might see stacked wooden benches in the square; during floods, the benches are placed end-to-end to create elevated sidewalks. If you think the square is crowded now, when it's flooded it turns into total gridlock, as all the people normally sharing the whole square jostle for space on the narrow wooden walkways.

In 2006, the pavement around St. Mark's Square was taken up, and the entire height of the square was raised by adding a layer of sand, and then replacing the stones. If the columns along the ground floor of the Doge's Palace look stubby, it's because this process has been carried out many times over the centuries.

• *The small square between the basilica and the water is...*

The Piazzetta

This "Little Square" is framed by the Doge's Palace on the left, the library on the right, and the waterfront of the lagoon. In former days, the Piazzetta was closed to the public for a few hours a day so that government officials and bigwigs could gather in the sun to strike shady deals.

The pale-pink Doge's Palace is the epitome of the style known as Venetian Gothic. Columns support traditional, pointed Gothic arches, but with a Venetian flair—they're curved to a point, ornamented with a trefoil (three-leaf clover), and topped with a round medallion of a quatrefoil (four-leaf clover). The pattern is found on buildings

$$\wedge + \cap + \curvearrowright + \clubsuit = $$

all over Venice and on the formerly Venetian-controlled Croatian coast, but nowhere else in the world (except Las Vegas).

The two large 12th-century columns near the water were looted from Constantinople. Mark's winged lion sits on top of one. The lion's body (nearly 15 feet long) predates the wings and is more than 2,000 years old. The other column holds St. Theodore (battling a crocodile), the former patron saint who was replaced by Mark. I guess stabbing crocs in the back isn't classy enough for an upwardly mobile world power. Criminals were executed by being hung from these columns in the hopes that the public could learn its lessons vicariously.

Venice was the "Bride of the Sea" because she depended on sea trading for her livelihood. This "marriage" was celebrated annually by the people. The doge, in full regalia, boarded a ritual boat (his Air Force One equivalent) here at the edge of the Piazzetta and sailed out into the lagoon. There a vow was made, and he dropped a jeweled ring into the water to seal the marriage.

In the distance, on an island across the lagoon, is one of the grandest views in the city, of the Church of San Giorgio Maggiore. With its four tall columns as the entryway, the church, designed by the late-Renaissance architect Andrea Palladio, influenced future government and bank buildings around the world.

Speaking of architects, I will: Sansovino. Around 1530, Jacopo Sansovino designed the library (here in the Piazzetta) and the delicate Loggetta at the base of the Campanile (pictured on page 744; it was destroyed by the collapse of the tower in 1902 and was pieced back together as much as possible).

The Tetrarchs and the Doge's Palace's Seventh Column

Where the basilica meets the Doge's Palace is the traditional entrance to the palace, decorated with four small Roman statues—the Tetrarchs. No one knows for sure who they are, but I like the legend that says they're the scared leaders of a divided Rome during its fall, holding their swords and each other as all hell breaks loose around them. Whatever the legend, these statues—made of precious purple porphyry stone—are symbols of power. They were looted from Constantinople and then placed here proudly as spoils of war. How old are they? They've guarded the palace entrance since the city first rose from the mud.

The Doge's Palace's seventh column (the seventh from the water) tells a story of love, romance, and tragedy in its carved capi-

tal: 1) In the first scene (the carving facing the Piazzetta), a woman on a balcony is wooed by her lover, who says, "Babe, I want *you!*" 2) She responds, "Why, little ol' *me?*" 3) They get married. 4) Kiss. 5) Hit the sack—pretty racy for 14th-century art. 6) Nine months later, guess what? 7) The baby takes its first steps. 8) And as was all too common in the 1300s...the child dies.

The pillars along the Doge's Palace look short—a result of the square being built up over the centuries. It's happening again today. The stones are taken up, sand is added, and the stones are replaced, buying a little more time as the sea slowly swallows the city.

• *At the waterfront in the Piazzetta, turn left and walk (east) along the water. At the top of the first bridge, look inland at...*

The Bridge of Sighs

In the Doge's Palace (on your left), the government doled out justice. On your right are the prisons. (Don't let the palatial facade fool you—see the bars on the

windows?) Prisoners sentenced in the palace crossed to the prisons by way of the covered bridge in front of you. This was called the Prisons' Bridge until the Romantic poet Lord Byron renamed it in the 19th century. From this bridge, the convicted got their final view of sunny, joyous Venice before entering the black and dank prisons. According to the Romantic legend, they sighed. As you will, too, when you see the scaffolding.

Venice has been a major tourist center for four centuries. Anyone who's ever come here has stood on this very spot, looking at the Bridge of Sighs. Lean on the railing leaned on by everyone from Casanova to Byron to Hemingway.

St. Mark's Basilica Tour

Among Europe's churches, St. Mark's is peerless. From the outside, it's a riot of domes, columns, and statues, completely unlike the towering Gothic churches of northern Europe or the heavy Baroque of much of the rest of Italy. Inside, the decor of mosaics, colored marbles, and oriental treasures is rarely seen elsewhere. The Christian symbolism is unfamiliar to Western eyes, done in the style of Byzantine icons and even Islamic designs. Older than most of Europe's churches, it feels like a remnant of a lost world.

This is your best chance in Italy (outside of Ravenna) to glimpse a forgotten and somewhat mysterious part of the human story—Byzantium.

Orientation

Cost: Though entering the church is free, there are three separate, optional sights requiring paid admission inside: the Treasury (€3, includes audioguide—free for the asking), Golden Altarpiece (€2), and San Marco Museum (€4, enter museum from atrium either before or after you tour the church, skip the €3.50 audioguide). The San Marco Museum is the one most worth its entry fee.

Hours: The church is open Mon-Sat 9:45-17:00, Sun 14:00-17:00 (Sun until 16:00 Nov-March). The three sights inside close 15 minutes earlier; in winter, the Treasury and Golden Altarpiece close an hour earlier.

Dress Code: Modest dress (no shorts or bare shoulders) is strictly enforced, even for kids.

Getting There: Signs throughout Venice point to *San Marco,* meaning both the square and the church. Vaporetto stops: San Marco or San Zaccaria.

Lines: There's almost always a long line to get into St. Mark's. Once inside, it's usually crowded, and you just have to shuffle through on a one-way system. It's best to read this section before you go...or while standing in line.

Theft Alert: St. Mark's Basilica is the most dangerous place in Venice for pickpocketing—inside, it's always a crowded jostle.

Information: Guidebooks are sold in the bookstand in the basilica's atrium. Tel. 041-270-8311, www.basilicasanmarco.it.

Tours: Free, hour-long English **tours** (heavy on the mosaics' religious symbolism) are generally offered daily at 11:00; meet in the atrium. But the schedule varies, so see the schedule board in the atrium. Remember that you can download a free **Rick Steves audio tour** at www.ricksteves.com/audioeurope, from iTunes, or through the Rick Steves Audio Europe smartphone app.

WCs: A free WC is inside the San Marco Museum. Public WCs (€1.50) are nearby (one behind the Correr Museum, another at Giardinetti Reali park).

Length of This Tour: Allow one hour.

Cuisine Art: No food is allowed inside the church. For suggestions nearby, see page 786.

Photography: Although forbidden inside the church, it is allowed on the balcony of the San Marco Museum, with great views overlooking the square.

Starring: St. Mark, Byzantium, mosaics, and ancient bronze horses.

The Tour Begins

Start outside in the square, far enough back to take in the whole facade. Then zero in on the details. As you tour the interior, do your best to follow this tour. At busy times, your actual itinerary and pace may be determined by the sheer flow of the masses.

❶ Exterior—Mosaic of Mark's Relics

St. Mark's Basilica is a treasure chest of booty that was looted during Venice's glory days. That's most appropriate for a church built on the stolen bones of a saint.

The **mosaic over the far-left door** shows the theft that put Venice on the pilgrimage map. Two men (in the center, with crooked staffs) enter the church bearing a coffin with the body of St. Mark, who looks somewhat grumpy from the long voyage.

St. Mark was the author of one of the Gospels, the four Bible books telling the story of Jesus' life (Matthew, Mark, Luke, and John). Seven centuries after his death, his holy body was in Muslim-occupied Alexandria, Egypt. In 828, two visiting merchants of Venice "rescued" the body from the "infidels," hid it in a pork barrel (which was unclean to

Muslims), and spirited it away to Venice.

The merchants presented the body—not to a pope or bishop—but to the doge (with white ermine collar, on the right) and his wife, the dogaressa (with entourage, on the left), giving instant status to Venice's budding secular state. They built a church

St. Mark's Basilica

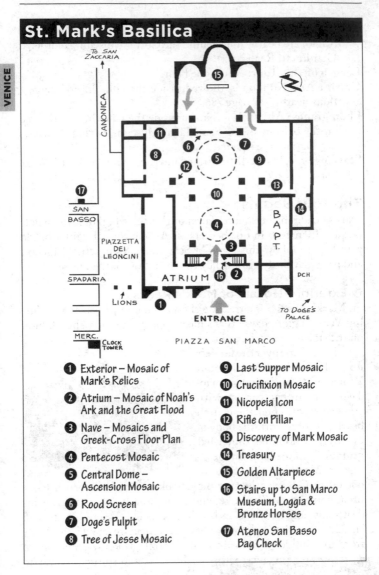

① Exterior – Mosaic of Mark's Relics

② Atrium – Mosaic of Noah's Ark and the Great Flood

③ Nave – Mosaics and Greek-Cross Floor Plan

④ Pentecost Mosaic

⑤ Central Dome – Ascension Mosaic

⑥ Rood Screen

⑦ Doge's Pulpit

⑧ Tree of Jesse Mosaic

⑨ Last Supper Mosaic

⑩ Crucifixion Mosaic

⑪ Nicopeia Icon

⑫ Rifle on Pillar

⑬ Discovery of Mark Mosaic

⑭ Treasury

⑮ Golden Altarpiece

⑯ Stairs up to San Marco Museum, Loggia & Bronze Horses

⑰ Ateneo San Basso Bag Check

here over Mark's bones and made him the patron saint of the city. You'll see his symbol, the winged lion, all over Venice.

The original church burned down in 976. Today's structure was begun in 1063. The mosaic, from 1260, shows that the church hasn't changed much since then—you can see the onion domes and famous bronze horses on the balcony.

The St. Mark's you see today, mostly from the 11th century, was modeled after a sixth-century church in Constantinople.

Venice needed roots. By building a retro church, the city could imply that it had been around for longer than it actually had been. (Throughout European history, upstarts loved to fake deep roots this way. Germany embraced mystic, medieval lore as it emerged as a modern nation in the 19th century, England cooked up the King Arthur legend, and so on.)

In subsequent centuries, the church was encrusted with materials looted from buildings throughout the Venetian empire. Their prize booty was the four bronze horses that adorn the balcony, stolen from Constantinople during the Fourth Crusade (these are copies, as the originals are housed inside the church museum). The architectural style of St. Mark's has been called "Early Ransack."

• *Enter the atrium (entrance hall) of the basilica, through a sixth-century, bronze-paneled Byzantine door.*

Immediately after being admitted by the dress-code guard, look up and to the right into an archway decorated with fine mosaics.

❷ Atrium—Mosaic of Noah's Ark and the Great Flood

St. Mark's famous mosaics, with their picture symbols, were easily understood in medieval times, even by illiterate masses. Today's

literate masses have trouble reading them, so let's practice on these, some of the oldest (13th century), finest, and most accessible mosaics in the church.

Noah and sons are sawing logs to build a boat. Venetians—who were great ship builders—related to the Ark. At its peak, Venice's Arsenale warship-building plant employed several thousand.

Below that are three scenes of Noah putting all species of animals into the Ark, two by two. (Who's at the head of the line? Lions.) Another scene shows the Flood in full force, drowning the wicked. Noah sends out a dove twice to see whether there's any dry land where he can dock. He finds it, leaves the Ark with a gorgeous rainbow overhead, and offers a sacrifice of thanks to God. Easy, huh?

• *Now that our medieval literacy rate has risen, rejoin the slow flow of people. Notice the entrance to the San Marco*

Museum (Loggia dei Cavalli), which you can visit later. Now climb seven steps, pass through the doorway, and enter the nave. Loiter somewhere just inside the door (crowd flow permitting) and let your eyes adjust.

❸ The Nave—Mosaics and Greek-Cross Floor Plan

The initial effect is dark and unimpressive (unless they've got the floodlights on). But as your pupils slowly unclench, you'll notice

that the entire upper part is decorated in mosaic—4,750 square yards (imagine paving a football field with contact lenses). These golden mosaics are in the Byzantine style, though many were designed by artists from the Italian Renaissance and later. The

often-overlooked lower walls are covered with green-, yellow-, purple-, and rose-colored marble slabs, cut to expose the grain, and laid out in geometric patterns. Even the floor is mosaic, mostly geometrical designs. It rolls like the sea. Venice is sinking and shifting, creating these cresting waves of stone.

The church is laid out with four equal arms, topped with domes, radiating out from the center to form a Greek cross (+). Those familiar with Eastern Orthodox churches will find familiar elements in St. Mark's: a central floor plan, domes, mosaics, and iconic images of Mary and Christ as Pantocrator—ruler of all things. As your eyes adjust, the mosaics start to give off a "mystical, golden luminosity," the atmosphere of the Byzantine heaven. The air itself seems almost visible, like a cloud of incense. It's a subtle effect, one that grows on you as the filtered light changes. There are more beautiful, bigger, more overwhelming, and even holier churches, but none is as stately.

• Find the chandelier near the entrance doorway (in the shape of a Greek cross cathedral space station), and run your eyes up the support chain to the dome above.

❹ Pentecost Mosaic

In a golden heaven, the dove of the Holy Spirit shoots out a pinwheel of spiritual lasers, igniting tongues of fire on the heads of the 12 apostles below, giving them the ability to speak other languages without a Rick Steves phrase book. You'd think they'd be amazed, but

Mosaics

St. Mark's mosaics are designs or pictures made with small cubes of colored stone or glass pressed into wet plaster. Ancient Romans paved floors, walls, and ceilings with them. When Rome "fell," the art form died out in the West but was carried on by Byzantine craftsmen. They perfected the gold background effect by baking gold leaf into tiny cubes of glass called *tesserae* (tiles). The surfaces of the tiles are purposely cut unevenly to capture light and give off a shimmering effect. The reflecting gold mosaics helped to light thick-walled, small-windowed, lantern-lit Byzantine churches, creating a golden glow that symbolized the divine light of heaven.

St. Mark's mosaics tell the entire Christian history from end to beginning. Entering the church, you're greeted with

scenes from the end of the world (Apocalypse) and the Pentecost. As you approach the altar, you walk backward in time to the source, experiencing Jesus' Passion and Crucifixion, his miraculous life, and continuing back to his birth and Old Testament predecessors. Over the altar at the far end of the church

(and over the entrance door at the near end) are images of Christ—the beginning and the end, the Alpha and Omega of the Christian universe.

their expressions are as solemn as...icons. One of the oldest mosaics in the church (c. 1125), it has distinct "Byzantine" features: a gold background and apostles with halos, solemn faces, almond eyes, delicate blessing hands, and rumpled robes, all facing forward.

This is art from a society still touchy about the Bible's commandment against making "graven images" of holy things. Byzantium had recently emerged from two centuries of Iconoclasm, in which statues and paintings were broken and burned as sinful "false gods." The Byzantine style emphasizes otherworldliness rather than literal human detail. The poet W. B. Yeats stood here and described what he saw: "O sages standing in God's holy fire as in the gold mosaic of a wall, come from the holy fire...and be the singing-masters of my soul."

• *Shuffle along with the crowds up to the central dome.*

❺ Central Dome—Ascension Mosaic

Gape upward to the very heart of the church. Christ—having lived his miraculous life and having been crucified for man's sins—

Byzantium

The Byzantine Empire was the eastern half of the ancient Roman Empire that *didn't* "fall" in A.D. 476. It remained Christian, Greek-speaking, and enlightened for another thousand years.

In A.D. 330, Constantine, the first Christian emperor, moved the Roman Empire's capital to the newly expanded city of Byzantium, which he humbly renamed Constantinople (modern Istanbul). With him went Rome's best and brightest. When the city of Rome decayed and fell, plunging Western Europe into its "Dark Ages," Constantinople lived on as the greatest city in Europe.

Venice had strong ties with Byzantium from its earliest days. In the sixth century, Byzantine Emperor Justinian invaded northern Italy, briefly reuniting East and West, and making Ravenna his regional capital. In 800, Venetians asked the emperor in Constantinople to protect them from Charlemagne's marauding Franks.

Soon Venetian merchants were granted trading rights to Byzantine ports in the Adriatic and eastern Mediterranean. They traded raw materials from Western Europe for luxury goods from the East.

When Muslim Ottoman Turks threatened the Christian Byzantine Empire, the Venetians joined the Crusades, the series of military expeditions that were designed to "save" Jerusalem and Constantinople. Venetians grew rich renting ships to the Crusaders in exchange for money, favors, and booty.

During the Fourth Crusade (1202-1204), which went horribly awry, the Crusaders—led by the Venetian doge Dandolo—sacked

ascends into the starry sky on a rainbow. He raises his right hand and blesses the universe. This isn't the dead, crucified, mortal Jesus featured in most churches, but a powerful, resurrected god, the ruler of all.

Christ's blessing radiates, rippling down to the ring of white-robed apostles below. They stand amid the trees of the Mount of Olives, waving good-bye as Christ ascends. Mary is with them, wearing blue with golden Greek crosses on each shoulder and looking ready to play patty-cake. From these saints, goodness descends, creating the Virtues that ring the base of the dome between the windows. In Byzantine churches, the window-lit dome represented heaven, while the dark church below represented earth—a microcosm of the hierarchical universe.

Beneath the dome at the four corners, the four Gospel writers ("Matev," "Marc," "Luca," and "Ioh") thoughtfully scribble down the heavenly events. This wisdom flows down like water from the symbolic Four Rivers below them, spreading through the church's four equal arms (the "four corners" of the world), and baptizing

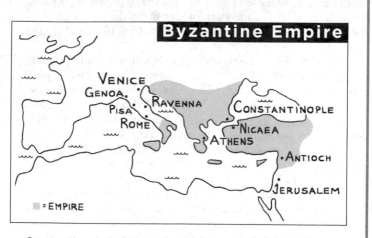

Byzantine Empire

VENICE
GENOA
PISA
ROME
RAVENNA
CONSTANTINOPLE
NICAEA
ATHENS
ANTIOCH
JERUSALEM

■ = EMPIRE

Constantinople, a fellow Christian city. This was, perhaps, the lowest point in Christian history, at least until the advent of TV evangelism. The Venetians carried home the bronze horses, the Pala d'Oro enamels, the Treasury's treasures, the Nicopeia icon, and much of the marble that now covers the (brick) church.

Venice rose while the Byzantine Empire faded. Then both civilizations nose-dived when Constantinople finally fell to the Ottomans in 1453.

Today, we find hints of the Byzantine Empire in the Eastern Orthodox Church, in mosaics and icons, and in the looted treasures shipped back to Venice.

the congregation with God's love. The church building is a series of perfect circles within perfect squares—the cosmic order—with Christ in the center solemnly blessing us. God's in his heaven, saints are on earth, and all's right with the world.

Under the Ascension Dome—The Church as Theater

Look around at the church's furniture and imagine a service here. The **rood screen** ❻, topped with 14 saints, separates the congregation from the high altar, heightening the "mystery" of the Mass.

The **pulpit on the right** was reserved for the doge, who led prayers and made important announcements ❼. Mosaics were visual aids for the priest, telling the whole story of Jesus. It starts with his ancestors perched in the **Tree of Jesse** ❽ (in the north transept, to the left as you face the altar). The story continues through Jesus' life, to the **Last Supper ❾** (in the arch leading to the south transept), and culminates in the **Crucifixion ❿** (in the west arch).

The Crucifixion mosaic features a stick-figure Christ, emphasizing the symbolic solemnity of the moment, not its Mel Gibson-style gruesomeness. In fact, there aren't very many crucifixes at all in the church, giving it an Eastern Orthodox flavor. While Western Christianity focuses on the death of Jesus, to Orthodox believers, Christ's death is just the tragic Act I. Other scenes in the arch show the rest of the story, Christ's triumphant Resurrection and post-death miracles, leading to the climax, his Ascension (in the central dome).

The Venetian church service is a theatrical multimedia spectacle, combining words (prayers, biblical passages, Latin and Greek phrases), music (chants, a choir, organ, horns, strings), costumes and props (priests' robes, golden reliquaries, candles, incense), set design (the mosaics, rood screen, Golden Altarpiece), and even stage direction (processionals through the crowd, priests' motions, standing, sitting, kneeling, crossing yourself). The symmetrical church is itself part of the set design. The Greek-cross floor plan symbolizes perfection, rather than the more common Latin cross of the crucifixion (emphasizing man's sinfulness). Coincidentally or not, the first modern opera—also a multimedia theatrical experience—was written by St. Mark's *maestro di cappella*, Claudio Monteverdi (1567-1643).

North Transept

In the north transept (the arm of the church to the left of the altar), today's Venetians pray to a painted wooden icon of Mary and baby Jesus known as **Nicopeia,** or "Our Lady of Victory" (on the east wall of the north transept, it's a small painting crusted over with a big stone canopy) ⓫. Supposedly painted by the evangelist Luke, it was once enameled with bright paint and precious stones, and Mary was adorned with a crown and necklace of gold and jewels (now on display in the Treasury). This Madonna has helped Venice persevere through plagues, wars, and crucial soccer games. When Mary answers a prayer, grateful Venetians give her offerings, like the old **rifle** that hangs next to a Madonna-and-child on a pillar (as you approach the north transept) ⓬. A wife prayed to the Madonna for her husband's safe return from war with Austria in 1848. When he came home alive, she gave his rifle to the Virgin in thanks.

• *In the south transept (to right of main altar), find the dim mosaic high up on the west wall.*

⓭ Discovery of Mark Mosaic

Not a biblical scene, this mosaic depicts the miraculous event that capped the construction of the present church.

It's 1094, the church is nearly complete (see the domes shown in cutaway fashion), and they're all set to re-inter Mark's bones under the new altar. There's just one problem: During the decades of construction, they forgot where they'd stored his body!

So (in the left half of the mosaic), all of Venice gathers inside the church to bow down and pray for help finding the bones.

The doge (from the Latin *dux*, meaning leader) leads them. Soon after (the right half), the patriarch (far right) is inspired to look inside a hollow column where he finds the relics. Everyone turns and applauds, including the womenfolk (left side of scene), who stream in from the upper-floor galleries. The relics were soon placed under the altar in a ceremony that inaugurated the current structure.

The south transept also features horseshoe arches atop slender columns, giving the transept the exotic flavor of a Muslim mosque. The door under the rose window leads directly from the Doge's Palace. On important occasions, the doge entered the church through here, ascended the steps of his pulpit, and addressed the people.

St. Mark's Three Museums

Inside the church are three sights, each requiring a separate admission. None is a must-see, but they provide the easiest way (outside of Istanbul or Ravenna) to soak up Byzantine ambience—and admission to the San Marco Museum (the best of the bunch) gives you access to great views over the inside of the church, as well as to the square outside.

⓮ Treasury (Tesoro)

• *The tiny Treasury is in the south transept. The admission fee includes an audioguide (when available)—ask for it. The collection is crammed into two small rooms.*

You'll see Byzantine chalices, silver reliquaries, monstrous monstrances (for displaying the Communion wafer), and icons done in gold, silver, enamels, gems, and semiprecious stones. Some pieces represent the fruit of labor by different civilizations over a thousand-year period. For example, an ancient rock-crystal chalice made by the Romans might be decorated centuries later with Byzantine enamels, and then finished still later with gold filigree by Venetian goldsmiths. This is marvelous handiwork, but all the more marvelous for having been done when Western Europe was still mired in mud. Here are some highlights.

• *Enter the main room, to the right. Start with the large glass case in the center of the room.*

Main Room: This display case holds the most precious Byzantine objects (mostly war booty brought here during the Fourth Crusade). The hanging lamp with the protruding fish features fourth-century Roman rock crystal framed in 11th-century Byzantine metalwork. Just behind it, a black bucket, carved with scenes of satyrs chasing nymphs, epitomizes the pagan world that was fading as Christianity triumphed. Also in the case are blue-and-gold lapis lazuli icons of the Crucifixion and of the Archangel Michael, featuring a Byzantine specialty—enamel work (more on that craft at the Golden Altarpiece). See various chalices (cups used for the bread and wine during Mass) made of onyx, agate, and rock crystal, and an incense burner shaped like a domed church.

• *Along the walls, find the following displays (working counterclockwise around the room).*

The first three glass cases have bowls and urns made of glass or rock crystal, gold and silver, and precious stones, and laced with elaborate filigree (twisted wires). The styles blend elements from the three medieval cultures that cross-pollinated in the Eastern Mediterranean: Venetian, Byzantine, and Islamic. Next comes the Urn of Artaxerxes I (middle of the right wall), an Egyptian-made object that once held the ashes of the great Persian king who ruled 2,500 years ago (r. 465-425 B.C.). The next cases hold religious paraphernalia used for High Mass—chalices, reliquaries, candlesticks, bishops' robes, and a 600-year-old crosier (ceremonial shepherd staff) still used today by the chief priest on holy days.

Next is the Ciborio di Anastasia (far-left corner), a small marble canopy that once arched over the blessed communion wafer during Mass. The object may be a gift from "Anastasia," the name carved on it in Greek. She was a lady-in-waiting in the court of the emperor Justinian (483-565). Christian legend has it that she was so beautiful that Justinian (a married man) pursued her amorously, so she had to dress like a monk and flee to a desert monastery.

Moving to the next wall, you'll see two large golden panels that once fronted an altar; flanking the panels are two golden candlesticks. What detail! The smiling angels at the top, the literary lion, the man with the weight on his shoulders, the row of queens... all the way down to the roots. Continuing counterclockwise, see a photo of a Madonna adorned with jewels, gold, and enamel. If you like this, it's just a taste of what the Pala d'Oro offers.

Next to the Madonna, notice the granite column that extends below current floor level—you can see how the floor has risen as things have settled in the last 1,000 years.

Relics/Sanctuary Room: Straight ahead, the glass case over the glowing alabaster altar contains elaborate gold-and-glass reliquaries holding relics of Jesus' Passion—his torture and execution. The reliquary showing Christ being whipped (from 1125) holds a stone from the column he was tied to. You may scoff, but of Europe's many "Pieces of the True Cross" and "Crown of Thorns" relics, these have at least some claim of authenticity. Legend has it that Christ's possessions were gathered up in the fourth century by Constantine's mother and taken to Constantinople. During the Crusade heist of 1204, Venetians brought them here. They've been paraded through the city every Good Friday for 800 years.

Back by the room's entrance is a glass reliquary with the bones of Doge Orseolo (r. 976-978), who built the church that preceded the current structure. Another contains the bones of St. George, legendary dragon slayer.

⓯ Golden Altarpiece (Pala d'Oro)

• *The Golden Altarpiece is located behind the main altar.*

Under the stone canopy sits the high altar. Inside the altar is an urn (not visible) with the mortal remains of Mark, the Gospel writer. (Look through the grate of the altar to read *Corpus Divi Marci Evangelistae*, or "Body of the Evangelist Mark.") He rests in peace, as an angel had promised him. Shh.

As you shuffle along, notice the marble canopy's support columns carved with New Testament scenes in the 13th century. (On the right-hand pillar closest to the altarpiece, fourth row from the bottom: Is that a genie escaping from a bottle while someone tries to stuff him back in?)

The Golden Altarpiece is a stunning golden wall made of 250 blue-backed enamels with religious scenes, all set in a gold frame

and studded with 15 hefty rubies, 300 emeralds, 1,500 pearls, and assorted sapphires, amethysts, and topaz. The Byzantine-made enamels (c. 1100) were part of the Venetians' plunder of 1204, subsequently pieced together by Byzantine craftsmen specifically for St. Mark's high altar. It's a bit much to take in all at once, but get up close and find several details you might recognize:

In the center, Jesus as Ruler of the Cosmos sits on a golden throne, with a halo of pearls and jewels. Like a good Byzantine Pantocrator, he dutifully faces forward and gives his blessing while stealing a glance offstage at Mark ("Marcus") and the other saints.

Along the bottom row, Old Testament prophets show off the books of the Bible they've written. With halos, solemn faces, and elaborately creased robes, they epitomize the Byzantine icon style.

Follow Mark's story in the panels along the sides. In the bottom left panel, Mark meets Peter (seated) at the gates of Rome. It was Peter (legend has it) who gave Mark the eyewitness account of Jesus' life that Mark wrote down in his Gospel. Mark's story ends in the bottom right panel with the two Venetian merchants returning by ship, carrying his coffin here to be laid to rest.

Byzantium excelled in the art of *cloisonné* enameling. A piece of gold leaf is stamped with a design, then filled in with pools of enamel paint, which are baked on. Look at a single saint to see the detail work: The gold background around the saint is the gold-leaf medallion that gets stamped. The golden folds in the robe are the raised edges of the impression. The different colors of the robe are different-colored paints in the recessed areas, each color baked on in a separate firing. Some saints even have pearl crowns or jewel collars pinned on. This kind of craftsmanship—and the social infrastructure that could afford it—made Byzantium seem like an enchanted world during Europe's dim Middle Ages.

After you've looked at some individual scenes, back up as far as this small room will let you and just let yourself be dazzled by the whole picture—this "mosaic" of Byzantine greatness. This magnificent altarpiece sits on a swivel (notice the mechanism at its base) and is swung around on festival Sundays so the entire congregation can enjoy it.

⓰ San Marco Museum (Museo di San Marco)— Mosaics, Bronze Horses, View of the Piazza, and More

• *The staircase up to the museum is in the atrium near the main entrance. The sign says* Loggia dei Cavalli, Museo. *Ascend the steps, buy your ticket, and enter. You'll see several models of the church at various stages of its history. From there, you'll spill out by the museum's three highlights: view of the interior (right), view of the square (out the door to the left), and bronze horses (directly ahead). Belly up to the stone balustrade to survey the interior.*

View of Church Interior

Scan the church, with its 8,000 square meters of mosaics, then take a closer look at the Pentecost Mosaic (first dome above you, described earlier). The unique design at the very top signifies the Trinity: throne (God), Gospels (Christ), and dove (Holy Spirit). The couples below the ring of apostles are the people of the world (I can find Asia, Judaea, and Cappadocia), who, despite their different languages, still understood the Spirit's message.

If you were a woman in medieval Venice, you'd enjoy this same close-up view, because in the Middle Ages, women climbed the same stairs you just did and found a spot along the balconies at your feet. The balcony was for women, the nave for men, and the altar for the priests. Back then the rood screen (the fence with the 15 figures on it) separated the priest from the public, and he officiated with his back to the people.

Appreciate the patterns of the mosaic floor—one of the finest in Italy—that covers the floor like a Persian carpet.

• *From here, the museum loops you to the far (altar) end of the church, then back to the bronze horses. Along the way, you'll see...*

Mosaic Fragments

These mosaics once hung in the church, but when they became damaged or aesthetically old-fashioned, they were replaced by new and more fashionable mosaics. These few fragments avoided the garbage can. You'll see mosaics from the church's earliest days (and most "Byzantine" style, c. 1070) to more recent times (1700s, realistic Renaissance detail). Many are accompanied by small photos that show where the fragment used to fit into a larger scene.

The mosaics—made from small cubes of stone or colored glass pressed into wet clay—were assembled on the ground, then cemented onto the walls. Artists draw the pattern on paper, lay it on the wet clay, and slowly cut the paper away as they replace it with cubes. The first mosaic on your left as you enter shows a reproduction of a paper "cast" of a mosaic.

• *Continuing on, you'll see other artwork and catch glimpses of the interior of the church from the north transept. Here you get a close-up view of the Tree of Jesse mosaic, showing Jesus' distant ancestor at the root and his mom at the top. Continue on to the Sala dei Banchetti (WCs near the room's entrance).*

Sala dei Banchetti

This large, ornate room—once the doge's banquet hall—is filled with religious objects, tapestries and carpets that once adorned the church, Burano lace vestments, illuminated music manuscripts, a doge's throne, and much more.

Try reading some music. The manuscripts date from the 16th century—before the age of treble and bass clefs. You'll see a C clef along the left margin of each staff (which could slide along the staff to locate middle C). From this, you could chant notes in proper relationship to each other, following the rhythm indicated.

In the center of the hall stands the most prestigious artwork here, the Pala Feriale, by Paolo Veneziano (1345). On ordinary workdays, these 14 scenes painted on wood covered the basilica's golden Pala d'Oro. The top row is seven saints (including crucified

Christ). Below are seven episodes in Mark's life. In the first panel, Mark kneels before a red-robed Saint Peter and receives his calling. Next, he arrives in Alexandria and makes his first convert. Then Jesus appears to Mark. Mark is beaten to death and dragged through the streets. The panel of the sailboat tells the story of the Venetian merchants' trip home with Mark's relics. A storm at sea billows their sails, ripples the flag, churns the waves, and scares the crew as the ship heads toward the rocks. But then Mark himself appears miraculously at the stern and calms the storm, bringing the ship (and his own body) safely to Venice. Paolo proudly signed his name (along the bottom) and the names of his two assistants, his sons Luca and Giovanni. In the next panel, Mark's long-lost body is rediscovered hidden in a column. Finally, worshippers gather at Mark's tomb by the altar of the basilica.

• *Now double back toward the museum entrance, through displays of stone fragments from the church, finally arriving at...*

The Bronze Horses (La Quadriga)

Stepping lively in pairs and with smiles on their faces, they exude energy and exuberance. Art historians don't know how old they are—they could be from ancient Greece (fourth century B.C.) or ancient Rome during its Fall (fourth century A.D.). Professor Carbon Fourteen says they're from around 175 B.C. Originally, the horses pulled a chariot *Ben-Hur* style. These bronze statues were not hammered and bent into  shape by metalsmiths, but were cast from clay molds by using the lost-wax technique. The bronze is high quality, with 97 percent copper. Originally gilded, they still have some streaks of gold. Long gone are the ruby pupils that gave the horses the original case of "red eye."

Megalomaniacs through the ages have coveted these horses not only for their artistic value, but because they symbolize Apollo, the Greco-Roman god of the sun...and of secular power. The doge spoke to his people standing between the horses when they graced the balcony atop the church's facade (where the copies—which you'll see next—stand today).

Their expressive faces seem to say, "Oh boy, Wilbur, have we done some travelin'." Legend says they were made in the time of Alexander the Great, then taken by Nero to Rome. Constantine took them to his new capital in Constantinople to adorn the chariot racecourse. The Venetians then stole them from their fellow Christians during the looting of noble Constantinople (in 1204) and brought them to St. Mark's.

What goes around comes around, and Napoleon came around and took the horses when he conquered Venice in 1797. They stood atop a triumphal arch in Paris until Napoleon's empire was "blown-aparte" and they were returned to their "rightful" home.

The horses were again removed from their spot when they were attacked by their most dangerous enemy yet—modern man. The threat of oxidation from pollution sent them galloping for cover inside the church.

• *The visit ends outside on the balcony overlooking St. Mark's Square.*

The Loggia and View of St. Mark's Square

You'll be drawn repeatedly to the viewpoint of the square, but remember to look at the facade to see how cleverly all the looted

architectural elements blend together. Ramble among the statues of water-bearing slaves that serve as drain spouts. The horses are modern copies (note the 1978 date on the hoof of the horse to the right).

Be a doge, and stand between the bronze horses overlooking St. Mark's Square. Under the gilded lion of St. Mark, in front of the four great Evangelists (who once stood atop the columns), and flanked—like Apollo—by the four glorious horses, he inspired the Venetians in the square below to great things.

Admire the mesmerizing, commanding view of the center of this city, which so long ago was Europe's only superpower, and today is just a small town with a big history—one that's filled with tourists.

Sights in Venice

While Venice has many sights worth knowing about on a longer visit (see the "Venice at a Glance" sidebar, earlier), for a one-day cruiser visit, I've listed just the top sights. Don't let the length of my descriptions determine your sightseeing priorities. In this section, Venice's most important sights may have the shortest listings. These sights are covered in much more detail in one of the earlier self-guided tours.

San Marco District

For information on the San Marco Museum Plus Pass, which covers most of the sights on the square, see page 712.

▲▲▲**St. Mark's Square (Piazza San Marco)**—This grand square is surrounded by splashy, historic buildings and sights: St. Mark's Basilica, the Doge's Palace, the Campanile bell tower, and the Correr Museum. The square is filled with music, lovers, pigeons, and tourists by day, and is your private rendezvous with the Venetian past late at night, when Europe's most magnificent dance floor is *the* romantic place to be.

For a slow and pricey thrill, invest about €12-20 (including the cover charge for the music) in a drink at one of the elegant cafés with the dueling orchestras (see "Cafés on St. Mark's Square," page 743). For an unmatched experience that offers the best people-watching, it's worth the small splurge.

The **Clock Tower** (Torre dell'Orologio), built during the Renaissance in 1496, marks the entry to the main shopping drag, called the Mercerie, which connects St. Mark's Square with the Rialto. From the piazza, you can see the bronze men (Moors) swing their huge clappers at the top of each hour.

A good **TI** is on the square (with your back to the basilica, it's in the far-left, southwest corner of the square; daily 9:00-15:30), and a €1.50 WC is 30 yards beyond St. Mark's Square (see *Albergo Diorno* sign marked on pavement, WC open daily 9:00-17:30). Another TI is on the lagoon (daily 10:00-18:00, walk toward the water by the Doge's Palace and go right, €1.50 WCs nearby).

For a self-guided tour of the square, see page 737.

▲▲▲**St. Mark's Basilica (Basilica di San Marco)**—Built in the 11th century to replace an earlier church, this basilica's distinctly Eastern-style architecture underlines Venice's connection with Byzantium (which protected it from the ambition of Charlemagne and his Holy Roman Empire). It's decorated with booty from returning sea captains—a kind of architectural Venetian trophy chest. The interior glows mysteriously with gold mosaics and colored marble. Since about A.D. 830, the saint's bones have been housed on this site.

For a self-guided tour, see page 748.

Cost and Hours: Basilica entry is free, exhibits cost extra, open Mon-Sat 9:45-17:00, Sun 14:00-17:00 (Sun until 16:00 Nov-

March), St. Mark's Square, vaporetto stops: San Marco or San Zaccaria, tel. 041-270-8311, www.basilicasanmarco.it. The dress code is strictly enforced for everyone (no bare shoulders or bare knees). Lines can be long, and bag check is mandatory, free, and can save you time in line; no photos are allowed inside.

▲▲▲**Doge's Palace (Palazzo Ducale)**—The seat of the Venetian government and home of its ruling duke, or doge, this

was the most powerful half-acre in Europe for 400 years. The Doge's Palace was built to show off the power and wealth of the Republic. The doge lived with his family on the first floor near the halls of power. From his once-lavish (now sparse) quarters, you'll follow the one-way tour through the public rooms of the top floor, finishing with the Bridge of Sighs and the prison. The place is wallpapered with masterpieces by Veronese and Tintoretto. Don't worry much about the great art. Enjoy the building.

You'll see the restored facades from the **courtyard.** Notice a grand staircase (with nearly naked Moses and Paul Newman at the top). Even the most powerful visitors climbed this to meet the doge. This was the beginning of an architectural power trip.

In the **Senate Hall,** the 120 senators met, debated, and passed laws. Tintoretto's large *Triumph of Venice* on the ceiling (central painting, best viewed from the top) shows the city in all its glory. Lady Venice is up in heaven with the Greek gods, while barbaric lesser nations swirl up to give her gifts and tribute.

The **Armory**—a dazzling display originally assembled to intimidate potential adversaries—shows remnants of the military might that the empire employed to keep the East-West trade lines open (and the local economy booming).

The giant **Hall of the Grand Council** (175 feet by 80 feet, capacity 2,600) is where the entire nobility met to elect the senate and doge. It took a room this size to contain the grandeur of the Most Serene Republic. Ringing the room are portraits of the first 76 doges (in chronological order). The one at the far end that's blacked out is the notorious Doge Marin Falier, who opposed the will of the Grand Council in 1355. He was tried for treason, beheaded, and airbrushed from history.

On the wall over the doge's throne is Tintoretto's monsterpiece, *Paradise,* the largest oil painting in the world. Christ and Mary are surrounded by a heavenly host of 500 saints. The painting leaves you feeling that you get to heaven not by being a good Christian, but by being a good Venetian.

Cross the covered **Bridge of Sighs** over the canal to the **prisons.** Circle the cells. Notice the carvings made by prisoners—from olden days up until 1930—on some of the stone windowsills of the cells, especially in the far corner of the building.

Cross back over the Bridge of Sighs, pausing to look through the marble-trellised windows at all of the tourists.

Cost and Hours: Covered by €13 San Marco Museum Plus Pass, which also includes admission to the Correr Museum; no individual tickets are sold to this sight. If the line is long at the Doge's Palace, buy your pass at the Correr Museum across the square; then you can go directly through the Doge's turnstile without waiting in line. Open daily April-Oct 8:30-18:30, Nov-March 8:00-17:30, last entry one hour before closing.

Location: Next to St. Mark's Basilica, just off St. Mark's Square. Vaporetto stops: San Marco or San Zaccaria.

Tours: The audioguide costs €5. For a live guided tour, consider the Secret Itineraries Tour, which takes you into palace rooms otherwise not open to the public (€18, or €12 with San Marco Museum Plus Pass; two or three English-language tours each morning). Reserve ahead for this tour in peak season—they can fill up as much as a month in advance. Book online at www .museiciviciveneziani.it, reserve by phone (tel. 848-082-000, or from the US dial 011-39-041-4273-0892), or ask at the info desk.

▲▲Correr Museum (Museo Civico Correr)—This uncrowded museum gives you a good overview of Venetian history and art. In the Napoleon Wing, you'll see fine Neoclassical sculpture by Antonio Canova. Then peruse armor, banners, and paintings that re-create festive days of the Venetian republic. The upper floor lays out a good overview of Venetian art, including several paintings by the Bellini family. There are English descriptions and breathtaking views of St. Mark's Square throughout.

Cost and Hours: Covered by €13 San Marco Museum Plus Pass, which also includes the Doge's Palace, daily April-Oct 10:00-19:00, Nov-March 10:00-17:00, last entry one hour before closing, enter at far end of square directly opposite basilica, tel. 041-240-5211, www.musei civiciveneziani.it.

Avoid long lines at the crowded Doge's Palace by buying the museum pass listed above at the Correr Museum.

▲Campanile (Campanile di San Marco)—This dramatic bell tower replaced a shorter lighthouse, once part of the original fortress that guarded the entry of the Grand Canal. The lighthouse crumbled into a pile of bricks in 1902, a thousand years after it was built. Today, you'll see

construction work being done to strengthen the base of the tower. Ride the elevator 300 feet to the top of the bell tower for the best view in Venice (especially at sunset). For an ear-shattering experience, be on top when the bells ring. The golden archangel Gabriel at the top always faces into the wind.

Cost and Hours: €8, daily April-June and Oct 9:00-19:00, July-Sept 9:00-21:00, Nov-March 9:30-15:45, closed from Christmas to mid-Jan, tel. 041-522-4064. Lines are longest at midday; beat the crowds and enjoy the crisp morning air at 9:00 or the cool evening breeze at 18:00.

La Fenice Opera House (Gran Teatro alla Fenice)—During Venice's glorious decline in the 18th century, this was one of

seven opera houses in the city, and one of the most famous in Europe. For 200 years, great operas and famous divas debuted here, applauded by ladies and gentlemen in their finery. Then in 1996, an arson fire completely gutted the theater. But La Fenice ("The Phoenix") has risen from the ashes, thanks to an eight-year effort to rebuild the historic landmark according to photographic archives of the interior. To see the results at their most glorious, attend an evening performance.

You can also tour the opera house during the day. All you really see is the theater itself; there's no "backstage" tour of dressing rooms, or an opera museum. The auditorium, ringed with box seats, is impressive: pastel blue with sparkling gold filigree, muses depicted on the ceiling, and a starburst chandelier. It's also a bit saccharine and brings sadness to Venetians who remember the place before the fire. Other than a minor exhibit of opera scores and Maria Callas memorabilia, there's little to see from the world of opera. The dry audioguide recounts two centuries of construction.

Cost and Hours: €8, includes 45-minute audioguide, generally open daily 10:00-19:30, but schedule varies greatly depending on rehearsal and performance schedule, concert box office open daily 9:30-18:30, call center open daily 7:30-20:00, on Campo San Fantin between St. Mark's Square and Accademia Bridge, vaporetto stop: Santa Maria del Giglio, tel. 041-2424, www.teatro lafenice.it.

Behind St. Mark's Basilica

▲**Bridge of Sighs**—Connecting two wings of the Doge's Palace high over a canal, this enclosed bridge will be surrounded by scaffolding for the next few years for restoration. Travelers

popularized this bridge in the Romantic 19th century. Supposedly, a condemned man would be led over this bridge on his way to the prison, take one last look at the glory of Venice, and sigh. Though overhyped, when it's uncovered the bridge is undeniably tingle-worthy—especially after dark, when the crowds have dispersed and it's just you and floodlit Venice. A local legend says that lovers will be assured eternal love if they kiss on a gondola at sunset under the bridge.

The bridge is around the corner from the Doge's Palace: Walk toward the waterfront, turn left along the water, and look up the first canal on your left. You can walk across the bridge (from the inside) by visiting the Doge's Palace.

Church of San Zaccaria—This historic church is home to a sometimes-waterlogged crypt, a Bellini altarpiece, a Tintoretto painting, and the final resting place of St. Zechariah, the father of John the Baptist.

Cost and Hours: Free, €1 to enter crypt, €0.50 coin to light up Bellini's altarpiece, Mon-Sat 10:00-12:00 & 16:00-18:00, Sun 16:00-18:00 only, 2 canals behind St. Mark's Basilica.

Across the Lagoon from St. Mark's Square

▲**San Giorgio Maggiore**—This is the dreamy church-topped island you can see from the waterfront by St. Mark's Square. The striking church, designed by Palladio, features art by Tintoretto, a bell tower, and good views of Venice.

Cost and Hours: Free entry to church; May-Sept Mon-Sat 9:30-12:30 & 14:30-18:00, Sun 8:30-11:00 & 14:30-18:00; Oct-April until 16:30.

Mass is held at 11:00 (ring the bell at the door to the right of the main entrance). The bell tower costs €3 and is accessible by elevator (runs from 30 minutes after the church opens until 30 minutes before the church closes).

Getting There: To reach the island from St. Mark's Square, take the five-minute ride on vaporetto #2 (€2, 6/hour, ticket valid for one hour; leaves from San Zaccaria-M.V.E. stop located east of Bridge of Sighs by equestrian statue; catch boat in direction: Tronchetto).

Dorsoduro District

▲▲**Accademia (Gallerie dell'Accademia)**—Venice's top art museum, packed with highlights of the Venetian Renaissance, features paintings by the Bellini family, Titian, Tintoretto, Veronese, Tiepolo, Giorgione, Canaletto, and Testosterone. It's just over the wooden Accademia Bridge from the San Marco action.

The Venetian love of luxury shines through in this collection, which starts in the Middle Ages and runs to the 1700s. Look for grand canvases of colorful, spacious settings, peopled with happy locals in extravagant clothes having a great time. Medieval highlights include elaborate altarpieces and golden-haloed Madonnas. Among early masterpieces of the Renaissance are Mantegna's studly *St. George* and Giorgione's mysterious *The Tempest*. As the Renaissance reaches its heights, so do the paintings, such as Titian's magnificent *Presentation of the Virgin*, a religious scene, yes, but it's really just an excuse to display secular splendor (Titian was the most famous painter of his day—perhaps even more famous than Michelangelo). End your tour with Guardi's and Canaletto's painted "postcards" of the city—landscapes for visitors who lost their hearts to the romance of Venice.

Cost and Hours: €6.50, Mon 8:15-14:00, Tue-Sun 8:15-19:15, last entry 45 minutes before closing, no photos allowed. The dull audioguide costs €5 (€7/2 people). One-hour guided tours in English are €5 (€7/2 people, Sat-Sun at 11:00). At Accademia Bridge, vaporetto stop: Accademia. Tel. 041-522-2247, www.gallerieaccademia.org.

Avoiding Crowds: Expect long lines in the late morning, because they allow only 300 visitors in at a time; visit early or late to miss the crowds, or make a reservation at least a day in advance (€1 fee; calling 041-520-0345 is easier than reserving online at their clunky website).

There's a decent canalside pizzeria (Pizzeria Accademia Foscarini, closed Tue) at the base of the Accademia Bridge.

▲▲**Peggy Guggenheim Collection**—The popular museum of far-out art, housed in the American heiress' former retirement palazzo, offers one of Europe's best reviews of the art of the first half of the 20th century. Stroll through styles represented by artists whom Peggy knew personally—Cubism (Picasso, Braque), Surrealism (Dalí, Ernst), Futurism (Boccioni), American Abstract Expressionism (Pollock), and a sprinkling of Klee, Calder, and Chagall. The place is staffed by international interns working on art-related degrees.

Cost and Hours: €12, generally includes temporary exhibits, Wed-Mon 10:00-18:00, closed Tue, last entry 15 minutes before closing, audioguide-€7, mini-guidebook-€6, free and mandatory baggage check for anything bigger than a small purse, pricey café, photos allowed only in garden and terrace—a fine and relaxing perch overlooking Grand Canal; near Accademia, Dorsoduro 704, a five-minute walk from the Accademia Bridge (vaporetto: Accademia) or from La Salute Church (vaporetto: Salute); tel. 041-240-5411, www.guggenheim-venice.it.

▲La Salute Church (Santa Maria della Salute)—This impressive church with a crown-shaped dome was built and dedicated to the Virgin Mary by grateful survivors of the 1630 plague.

Cost and Hours: Church—free, daily 9:00-12:00 & 15:00-17:30; sacristy—€2, may have shorter hours than church; tel. 041-274-3928. It's a 10-minute walk from the Accademia Bridge; the Salute vaporetto stop is at its doorstep (the hop from San Marco-Vallaresso to Salute on vaporetto #1 is €2).

▲Ca' Rezzonico (Museum of 18th-Century Venice)—This grand Grand Canal palazzo offers the best look in town at the life of Venice's rich and famous in the 1700s. Wander under ceilings by Tiepolo, among furnishings from that most decadent century, enjoying views of the canal and paintings by Guardi, Canaletto, and Longhi.

Cost and Hours: €7, covered by passes, April-Oct Wed-Mon 10:00-18:00, Nov-March Wed-Mon 10:00-17:00, closed Tue, last entry one hour before closing, audioguide-€4 or €6/2 people, free and mandatory baggage check, at Ca' Rezzonico vaporetto stop, tel. 041-241-0100, www.museiciviciveneziani.it.

▲Punta della Dogana—This museum of contemporary art, housed in the former Customs House at the end of the Grand Canal, features cutting-edge 21st-century art in spacious rooms. This isn't Picasso and Matisse, or even Pollock and Warhol—those guys are ancient history. But if you're into the likes of Jeff Koons, Rachel Whiteread, and a host of newer artists, the museum is world-class. The displays change completely about every year, drawn from the museum's large collection. In fact, the art spreads over two locations—the triangular Customs House and Palazzo Grassi.

Cost and Hours: €15 for one locale, €20 for both, Wed-Mon 10:00-19:00, closed Tue, last entry one hour before closing, audioguide-€5 or €8/2 people, small café. The Customs House is near La Salute Church (Dogana *traghetto* or vaporetto: Salute). Palazzo Grassi is a bit upstream, on the east side of the Grand Canal (vaporetto: San Samuele). Tel. 199-139-139, www.palazzograssi.it.

Santa Croce District

▲▲▲Rialto Bridge—One of the world's most famous bridges, this distinctive and dramatic stone structure crosses the Grand Canal with a single confident span. The arcades along the top of

Is Venice Sinking?

Venice has been battling rising water levels since the fifth century. But today, the water is winning. Due to many factors, including global warming, Venice now floods about 100 times a year—usually from October until late winter—a phenomenon called the *acqua alta*.

Simply put, Venice is sinking and the water is rising. Venice sits atop sediments deposited at the ancient mouth of the Po River, which are still compacting and settling. Twentieth-century industry worsened things by pumping out massive amounts of groundwater from the aquifer beneath the lagoon for nearly 50 years before the government stopped it in the 1970s.

So what is Venice doing about the flooding? Since the 1966 flood, officials knew something had to be done, but it took about four decades to come up with a solution that some are still unhappy about. In 2003, a consortium of engineering firms began construction on the MOSE or Moses Project, which is expected to be operational by 2014. Named for the acronym of its Italian name, *Modulo Sperimentale Elettromeccanico*, it's also a nod to Moses and his (albeit temporary) mastery over the sea.

Underwater "mobile" gates are being built on the floor of the sea that will lie flat at the entrances of the three inlets that lead into Venice's lagoon. When the seawater rises above a certain level, air will be pumped into the gates, causing them to rise, and shutting out the Adriatic.

Will it work? Time...and tides...will tell.

the bridge help reinforce the structure...and offer some enjoyable shopping diversions, as does the **market** east of the bridge (souvenir stalls open daily, produce market closed Sun-Mon, fish market closed Sun).

▲**Ca' Pesaro International Gallery of Modern Art**—This museum features 19th- and early-20th-century art in a 17th-century canalside palazzo. The collection is strongest on Italian (especially Venetian) artists, but also presents a broad array of other well-known artists. The highlights are in one large room: Klimt's beautiful/creepy *Judith II*, with eagle-talon fingers; Kandinsky's *White Zig Zags* (plus other recognizable shapes); the colorful *Nude in the Mirror* by Bonnard, which flattens the 3-D scene into a 2-D pattern of rectangles; and Chagall's surprisingly realistic portrait of his hometown rabbi, *The Rabbi of Vitebsk*. The adjoining Room VII features small-scale works by Matisse, Max Ernst, Mark Tobey, and a Calder mobile. Admission also includes an Oriental Art wing.

Cost and Hours: €5.50, covered by passes, Tue-Sun 10:00-17:00, closed Mon, last entry one hour before closing, 2-minute walk from San Stae vaporetto stop, tel. 041-524-0662.

Palazzo Mocenigo Costume Museum—The Museo di Palazzo Mocenigo offers a walk through six rooms of a fine 17th-century mansion with period furnishings, family portraits, ceilings painted (c. 1790) with family triumphs (the Mocenigos produced seven doges), Murano glass chandeliers in situ, and a paltry collection of costumes with sparse descriptions.

Cost and Hours: €6, covered by passes, Tue-Sun 10:00-16:00, closed Mon, a block in from San Stae vaporetto stop, tel. 041-721-798.

San Polo District

▲▲**Frari Church (Chiesa dei Frari)**—My favorite art experience in Venice is seeing art in the setting for which it was designed—
as it is at the Frari Church. The Franciscan "Church of the Brothers" and the art that decorates it is warmed by the spirit of St. Francis. It features the work of three great Renaissance masters: Donatello, Giovanni Bellini, and Titian—each showing worshippers the glory of God in human terms.

In **Donatello's wood carving of St. John the Baptist** (just to the right of the high altar), the prophet of the desert—dressed in animal skins and nearly starving from his diet of bugs 'n' honey—announces the coming of the Messiah. Donatello was a Florentine working at the dawn of the Renaissance.

Bellini's *Madonna and Child with Saints and Angels* painting (in the sacristy farther to the right) came later, done by a Venetian in a more Venetian style—soft focus without Donatello's harsh realism. While Renaissance humanism demanded Madonnas and saints that were accessible and human, Bellini places them in a physical setting so beautiful that it creates its own mood of serene holiness. The genius of Bellini, perhaps the greatest Venetian painter, is obvious in the pristine clarity, rich colors (notice Mary's

Frari Church

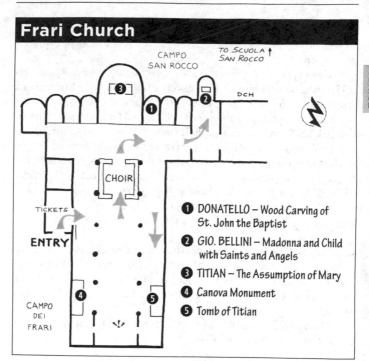

CAMPO SAN ROCCO

TO SCUOLA SAN ROCCO

DCH

VENICE

❸

❶

❷

CHOIR

TICKETS

ENTRY

CAMPO DEI FRARI

❹

❺

❶ DONATELLO – Wood Carving of St. John the Baptist

❷ GIO. BELLINI – Madonna and Child with Saints and Angels

❸ TITIAN – The Assumption of Mary

❹ Canova Monument

❺ Tomb of Titian

clothing), believable depth, and reassuring calm of this three-paneled altarpiece.

Finally, glowing red and gold like a stained-glass window over the high altar, **Titian's *The Assumption of Mary*** sets the tone of exuberant beauty found in the otherwise sparse church. Titian the Venetian—a student of Bellini—painted steadily for 60 years... you'll see a lot of his art. As stunned apostles look up past the swirl of arms and legs, the complex composition of this painting draws you right to the radiant face of the once-dying, now-triumphant Mary as she joins God in heaven.

Feel comfortable to discreetly freeload off passing tours. For many, these three pieces of art make a visit to the Accademia Gallery unnecessary (or they may whet your appetite for more). Before leaving, check out the Neoclassical pyramid-shaped Canova monument and (opposite that) the grandiose tomb of Titian. Compare the carved marble *Assumption* behind Titian's tombstone portrait with the painted original above the high altar.

Cost and Hours: €3, Mon-Sat 9:00-18:00, Sun 13:00-18:00, last entry 15 minutes before closing, no visits during services, modest dress recommended. On Campo dei Frari, near San Tomà vaporetto and *traghetto* stops.

Tours: Audioguides are available (€2, €3/2 people). You can download my free audio tour at www.ricksteves.com/audioeurope, from iTunes, or through the Rick Steves Audio Europe smartphone app.

Concerts: The church occasionally hosts evening concerts (€15, buy ticket at church). For concert details, look for fliers, check www.basilicadeifrari.it, or call the church at 041-272-8611.

▲▲**Scuola San Rocco**—Sometimes called "Tintoretto's Sistine Chapel," this lavish meeting hall (next to the Frari Church) has some 50 large, colorful Tintoretto paintings plastered to the walls and ceilings. The best paintings are upstairs, especially the *Crucifixion* in the smaller room. View the neck-breaking splendor with one of the mirrors available at the entrance.

Cost and Hours: €7, audioguide-€1, daily 9:30-17:30, last entry 30 minutes before closing, tel. 041-523-4864, www.scuola grandesanrocco.it.

Church of San Polo—This nearby church, which pales in comparison to the two sights just listed, is only worth a visit for art-lovers. One of Venice's oldest churches (from the ninth century), San Polo features works by Tintoretto, Veronese, and Tiepolo and son.

Cost and Hours: €3, Mon-Sat 10:00-17:00, closed Sun, last entry 15 minutes before closing.

Cannaregio District

Jewish Ghetto—In medieval times, Jews were grudgingly allowed to do business in Venice, but they weren't permitted to live there until 1385 (subject to strict laws and special taxes). Anti-Semitic forces tried to oust them from the city, but in 1516, the doge compromised by restricting Jews to a special (undesirable) neighborhood. It was located on an easy-to-isolate island near the former foundry *(geto)*, coining the word "ghetto" for a segregated neighborhood.

The population swelled with immigrants from elsewhere in Europe, reaching 5,000 in the 1600s, the Golden Age of Venice's Jews. Restricted within their tiny neighborhood (the Ghetto Nuovo, or "New Ghetto"), they expanded upward, building six-story "skyscrapers" that still stand today. The community's five synagogues were built atop the high-rise tenements. (As space was very tight and you couldn't live above a house of worship, this was the most practical use of precious land.) Only two synagogues are still active. You can spot them (with their five windows) from the square, but to visit them you have to book a tour through the Jewish Museum.

This original Ghetto becomes most interesting after touring the **Jewish Museum** (Museo Ebraico), which consists of two parts: a museum and a synagogue. The humble two-room museum has silver menorahs, cloth covers for the Torah scrolls, various religious objects, artifacts from the old community, and scant English explanations (€3, June-Sept Sun-Fri 10:00-17:00, Oct-May Sun-Fri 10:00-16:30, closed Sat and Jewish holidays, Campo di Ghetto Nuovo, vaporetto stop: San Marcuola, tel. 041-715-359, small café and bookstore). To see the **synagogue,** you must sign up for a half-hour English tour (€8.50, tours run hourly on the half-hour June-Sept Sun-Fri 10:00-19:00, Oct-May Sun-Fri 10:00-17:30, closed Sat and Jewish holidays). Group sizes are limited (the 11:30 tour is often booked full), so show up 20 minutes early to be sure you get in.

Calatrava Bridge (a.k.a. Ponte della Costituzione)—This controversial bridge, officially called "Constitution Bridge," is

just upstream and around the bend from the train station. Only the fourth bridge to cross the Grand Canal, it carries foot traffic between the train station and Piazzale Roma. A modern structure of glass, steel, and stone, the bridge finally opened in 2008 after delays, cost overruns, and questions about its stability.

The bridge was designed by Spanish architect Santiago Calatrava, whose other projects include a museum in his hometown of Valencia, Spain; the twisting torso skyscraper in Malmö, Sweden; and the Olympic Sports complex in Athens, Greece.

The bridge draws snorts from Venetians. With an original price tag of €4 million, the cost rose to around €11 million. The modern design of the bridge is also a sore point for a city with such rich medieval and Renaissance architecture. And, to add practical insult to aesthetic injury, the heavy bridge is crushing the centuries-old foundations at either end, threatening nearby buildings.

Interestingly, Calatrava's modern structure harkens back to the past, employing the same low-arch design of many older Venetian bridges. Pedestrians walk over similar shallow stair steps, and the bridge uses local Istrian stone.

Ca' d'Oro—This "House of Gold" palace, fronting the Grand Canal, is quintessential Venetian Gothic (Gothic seasoned with Byzantine and Islamic accents—see page 729). Inside, the permanent collection includes a few big names in Renaissance painting—Ghirlandaio, Signorelli, and Mantegna; a glimpse at a lush courtyard; and a grand view of the Grand Canal.

Cost and Hours: €5, slow and dry audioguide-€4, Mon 8:15-14:00, Tue-Sun 8:15-19:15, free peek through hole in door of courtyard, vaporetto stop: Ca' d'Oro, Calle Ca' d'Oro 3932.

Castello District

▲Scuola Dalmata di San Giorgio—This little-visited "school" (which means "meeting place") features an exquisite wood-paneled chapel decorated with the world's best collection of paintings by Vittorio Carpaccio (1465-1526).

The Scuola, a reminder that cosmopolitan Venice was once Europe's melting pot, was one of a hundred such community centers for various ethnic, religious, and economic groups, supported by the government partly to keep an eye on foreigners. It was here that the Dalmatians (from the southern coast of present-day Croatia) worshipped in their own way, held neighborhood meetings, and preserved their culture.

Cost and Hours: €4, Mon 14:45-18:00, Tue-Sat 9:15-13:00 & 14:45-18:00, Sun 9:15-13:00, on Calle dei Furlani, tel. 041-522-8828.

Santa Elena—For a pleasant peek into a completely non-touristy, residential side of Venice, walk or catch vaporetto #1 from St. Mark's Square to the neighborhood of Santa Elena (at the fish's "tail"). This 100-year-old suburb lives as if there were no tourism. You'll find a kid-friendly park, a few lazy restaurants, and beautiful sunsets over San Marco.

Experiences in Venice

Gondola Rides

Gondolas cost lots more after 19:00 but are also more romantic and relaxing under the moon. A rip-off for some, this is a tra-ditional must for romantics. Gondoliers charge about €80 for a 40-minute ride during the day; from 19:00 on, figure on €100. To add music (a singer and an accordionist), it'll cost an additional €110 before 19:00, or €130 after 19:00. You can divide the cost—and the romance—among up to six people per boat, but you'll need to save two seats for the musicians if you choose to be serenaded. Only two seats (the ones in back) are next to each other. If you want to haggle, you'll find softer prices during the day. (Note that gondoliers have a trick

where one guy says "No," and another, acting secretive, comes to you a bit later and says, "OK, but don't let my friend know I'm offering you this incredible price.") Establish the price and dura-tion before boarding, enjoy your ride, and pay only when you're finished.

If you've hired musicians and want to hear a Venetian song

(un canto Veneziano), try requesting *"Venezia La Luna e Tu."* Asking to hear *"O Sole Mio"* (which comes from Naples) is like asking a bartender in Cleveland to sing *"The Eyes of Texas."*

Glide through nighttime Venice with your head on someone's shoulder. Follow the moon as it sails past otherwise unseen buildings. Silhouettes gaze down from bridges while window glitter spills onto the black water. You're anonymous in the city of masks, as the rhythmic thrust of your striped-shirted gondolier turns old crows into songbirds. This is extremely relaxing (and, I think, worth the extra cost to experience at night). Because you might get a narration plus conversation with your gondolier, talk with several and choose one you like who speaks English well. Women, beware...while gondoliers can be extremely charming, local women say that anyone who falls for one of these Romeos "has slices of ham over her eyes."

For cheap gondola thrills during the day, stick to the €0.50 one-minute ferry ride on a Grand Canal *traghetto*. At night, *vaporetti* are nearly empty, and it's a great time to cruise the Grand Canal on the slow boat #1. Or hang out on a bridge along the gondola route and wave at romantics.

Festivals

Every odd year, the city hosts the **Venice Biennale International Art Exhibition,** a world-class contemporary art fair spread over the Arsenale and sprawling Castello Gardens. Artists representing 70 nations from around the world offer the latest in contemporary art forms: video, computer art, performance art, and digital photography, along with painting and sculpture (take vaporetto #1 or #2 to Giardini-Biennale; for details and an events calendar, see www.labiennale.org). The actual exhibition usually runs from June through November, but other events—film, dance, theater—loosely connected with the Biennale are held throughout the year (starting as early as Feb) in various venues on the island.

Other typically Venetian festival days filling the city's hotels with visitors and its canals with decked-out boats are **Feast of the Ascension Day** (in May or June), **Feast and Regatta of the Redeemer** (third Sun in July and the preceding evening), and the **Historical Regatta** (old-time boats and pageantry, first Sat and Sun in Sept). Smaller regattas include the **Murano Regatta** (early July) and the **Burano Regatta** (mid-Sept).

Venice's patron saint, **St. Mark,** is commemorated every April 25. Venetian men celebrate the day by presenting roses to the women in their lives (mothers, wives, and lovers).

For more information on festivals, try the TI (www.turismo venezia.it) and the free *Shows and Events* booklet (www .turismovenezia.it).

Shopping in Venice

Long a city of aristocrats, luxury goods, and merchants, Venice was built to entice. While no one claims it's great for bargains, it has a shopping charm that makes paying too much strangely enjoyable. Carnevale masks, lace, glass, antique paper products, designer clothing, fancy accessories, and paintings are all popular with tourists visiting Venice.

Shops are generally open from 9:00 to 13:00 and from 15:00 to 19:30. In touristy Venice, more shops are open on Sunday than in the rest of the country. If you're buying a substantial amount from nearly any shop, bargain—it's accepted and almost expected. Offer less and offer to pay cash; merchants are very conscious of the bite taken by credit-card companies. Anything not made locally is pricey to bring in and therefore generally more expensive than elsewhere in Italy. The shops near St. Mark's Square charge the most.

For ordinary items (not high-priced tourist baubles), the best all-purpose department store is the Coin store on the St. Mark's Square side of the Rialto Bridge. (From the bridge, head north toward Ferrovia, the train station.)

For information on VAT refunds and customs regulations, see page 127.

Shopping Streets

Here's the best route to kick off your Venetian shopping spree:

St. Mark's Square: Walk the entire colonnaded square past pricey jewelry, glass, lace, and clothing stores. A half-block detour out the far end leads to several high-fashion shops along Calle de Vallaresso.

Mercerie: This is the main street between St. Mark's Square (leave the square under the Clock Tower) and the Rialto, noted for its high rent, high prices, fancy windows, and designer labels. Then, go over the...

Rialto Bridge: The streets at either side are a cancan of shopping temptations. Continue down the street to...

Ruga Vecchia San Giovanni (a.k.a. Ruga): Away from the intensity of the tourist center, you'll enter the San Polo neighborhood (west side of Rialto Bridge) with plenty of inviting shops, but fewer crowds and better prices.

Elsewhere in Venice: Art-lovers browse the **art galleries** between the Accademia and the Peggy Guggenheim Collection.

Venetian Glass

Popular Venetian glass is available in many forms: vases, tea sets, decanters, glasses, jewelry, lamps, mod sculptures (such as solid-

Mask Making

In the 1700s, when Venice was Europe's party town, masks were popular—sometimes even mandatory—to preserve the anonymity of visiting nobles doing things forbidden back home. At Carnevale (the weeks-long Mardi Gras leading up to Lent), everyone wore masks. The most popular were based on characters from the lowbrow comedic theater called commedia dell'arte. We all know Harlequin (simple, Lone Ranger-type masks), but there were also long-nosed masks for the hypo-critical plague doctor, pretty Columbina masks, and so on.

Masks are made with the simple technique of papier-mâché. You make a mold of clay, smear it with Vaseline (to make it easy to remove the finished mask), then create the mask by draping layers of paper and glue atop the clay mold.

You'll see mask shops all over town. Just behind St. Mark's Square, on a quiet canal just inland from the Church of San Zaccaria (on Fondamenta dell'Osmarin), is a corner with two fascinating mask and costume shops. The **Ca' del Sol** mask and costume shop (two showrooms connected by a little bridge) and **Atelier Marega** are both worth a look. After you cross the bridge to the second Ca' del Sol shop, head to the next door farther on, the wood-carving shop of **Paolo Brandolisio** (Mon-Fri 9:30-13:00 & 15:30-19:00, tel. 041-522-4155, http://paolobrandolisio.altervista.org). You can pop in to watch Paolo carving traditional oars and *forcola* (the oar-lock of the gondola, a symbol of Venetian life and a popular art piece). To check out Paolo virtually, search for "forcole e remi" on YouTube to watch videos of him working.

Out near the Frari Church, the **"Tragicomica" Mask Shop** is highly respected and likely to have artisans at work (daily 10:00-19:00, 200 yards past Church of San Polo on Calle dei Nomboli, tel. 041-721-102).

glass aquariums), and on and on. Shops will ship it home for you, but you're likely to pay as much or more for the shipping as you are for the item(s). Make sure the shop insures their merchandise *(assicurazione)*, or you're out of luck if it breaks. If your item arrives broken and it has been insured, take a photo of the pieces, send it to the shop, and they'll replace it for free. For a cheap, packable souvenir, consider the glass-bead

necklaces sold at vendors' stalls throughout Venice.

If you're serious about glass, visit the small shops on **Murano Island.** Their glassblowing demonstrations are fun; you'll usually see a vase and a "leetle 'orse" made from molten glass. You'll find greater variety on Murano, but prices are usually the same as in Venice.

Around St. Mark's Square, various companies offer glass-blowing demos for tour groups. **Galleria San Marco,** a tour-group staple just off St. Mark's Square, offers great demos every few minutes. They have agreed to let individual travelers flashing this book sneak in with tour groups to see the show (and sales pitch). And, if you buy anything, show this book and they'll take 20 percent off the listed price. The gallery faces the square behind the orchestra nearest the church; at #139, go through the shop and climb the stairs (daily 9:00-18:00, tel. 041-271-8650, manager Ferdinando).

Souvenir Ideas

The most popular souvenirs and gifts are Murano glass (described above), Burano lace (fun lace umbrellas for little girls), Carnevale masks (fine shops and artisans all over town), art reproductions (posters, postcards, and books), prints of Venetian scenes, traditional stationery (pens and marbled paper products of all kinds), calendars with Venetian scenes, silk ties, scarves, and plenty of goofy knickknacks (Titian

mousepads, gondolier T-shirts, and little plastic gondola condom holders).

Along Venice's many shopping streets, you'll notice fly-by-night street vendors selling knockoffs of famous-maker hand-bags (Louis Vuitton, Gucci, etc.). These vendors are willing to

bargain. But buyer beware: If you're caught purchasing fakes, you could get hit with a fine. Legitimate manufacturers are raising a stink about these street merchants, and the government is trying to rid the city of them. Authorities frustrated in their attempts to actually arrest the merchants have made it illegal to buy counterfeit items. Their hope: The threat of a huge fine will scare potential customers away—so unlicensed merchants will be driven out of business and off the streets.

Nightlife in Venice

Some cruises actually spend an overnight in Venice; many others begin or end here. If your schedule allows, try to experience Venice after dark. **Gondolas** cost more, but are worth the extra expense (see page 776).

Venice has a busy schedule of events, festivals, and entertainment. Check at the TI for listings, and keep an eye out for publications such as the free booklet called *Shows and Events,* available at some hotels and online at www.turismovenezia.it (click on "Venezia").

Baroque Concerts—Venice is a city of the powdered-wig Baroque era. For about €25 (prices vary), you can take your pick of traditional Vivaldi concerts in churches throughout town. Homegrown Vivaldi is as trendy here as Strauss is in Vienna and Mozart is in Salzburg. In fact, you'll find frilly young Vivaldis hawking concert tickets on many corners. The TI has a list of this week's Baroque concerts. Shows start at 21:00 and generally last 1.5 hours. You'll see posters in hotels all over town (hotels sell tickets at face-value). A one-stop shop for concerts is the Vivaldi Store, at the east end of Rialto Bridge (5537 Salizada del Fontego dei Tedeschi). Tickets for Baroque concerts in Venice can usually be bought the same day as the concert, so don't bother with websites that sell tickets with a surcharge.

Consider the venue carefully. The general rule of thumb: Musicians in wigs and tights offer better spectacle; musicians in black-and-white suits are better performers. **San Vitale Church** (at the north end of Accademia Bridge) and the **Interpreti Veneziani orchestra** (which often plays there) are reliably top-notch (tel. 041-277-0561, www.interpretiveneziani.com). For the latest on church concerts, check any TI or visit www.turismovenezia.it.

Other Performances—Venice's most famous theaters are **La Fenice** (grand old opera house, box office tel. 041-2424, see page 767), **Teatro Goldoni** (mostly Italian live theater), and **Teatro della Fondamenta Nuove** (theater, music, and dance).

Musica a Palazzo is a unique evening of opera at the Doge's Palace. You'll spend about 45 minutes in three sumptuous rooms as eight musicians (generally four instruments and four singers) perform. With these kinds of surroundings, under Tiepolo frescoes, you'll be glad you dressed up. As there are only 70 seats, you must book by phone or online in advance. Opera-lovers find this to be a wonderful evening (€50, nightly shows at 20:30, Palazzo Barbarigo-Minotto, Fondamenta Duodo o Barbarigo—on the Grand Canal next to the Santa Maria del Giglio vaporetto stop, mobile 340-971-7272, www.musicapalazzo.com).

St. Mark's Square—For tourists, St. Mark's Square is the highlight, with lantern light and live music echoing from the cafés. Just being here after dark is a thrill, as **dueling café orchestras** entertain (see sidebar on page 743). Every night, enthusiastic musicians play the same songs, creating the same irresistible magic. Hang out for free behind the tables (allowing you to move easily on to the next orchestra when the musicians take a break), or spring for a seat and enjoy a fun and gorgeously set concert. If you sit a while, it can be €12-20 well spent (for a drink and the cover charge for music). Dancing on the square is free (and encouraged). Streetlamp halos, live music, floodlit history, and a ceiling of stars make St. Mark's magic at midnight. You're not a tourist, you're a living part of a soft Venetian night...an alley cat with money. In the misty light, the moon has a golden hue. Shine with the old lanterns on the gondola piers, where the sloppy lagoon splashes at the Doge's Palace...reminiscing.

Eating in Venice

While touristy restaurants are the scourge of Venice, the following places are still popular with Venetians and respect the tourists who happen in. First trick: Walk away from triple-language menus. Second trick: Order the daily special. Third trick: For freshness, eat fish. Most seafood dishes are the catch-of-the-day. Note that seafood can be sold by weight rather than a set price (if you see "100 g" or "*l'etto*" by a too-good-to-be-true price on the menu, that's the cost per 100 grams—about a quarter pound). The abbreviation *s.q.* is similar, meaning according to quantity (you pay for the weight of the particular piece).

Near the Rialto Bridge
East of the Rialto Bridge, near Campo San Bartolomeo
Rosticceria San Bartolomeo is a cheap—if confusing—self-service diner, a throwback budget eatery with a likeably surly staff. Take out, grab a table, munch at the bar, or pay a bit more to eat at the restaurant upstairs (good €6-7 pasta, great fried *mozzarella al prosciutto* for €1.50, delightful fruit salad, €1 glasses of wine, prices listed on wall behind counter, no cover or service charge, daily 9:00-21:30, tel. 041-522-3569). To find it, imagine the statue on Campo San Bartolomeo walking backward 20 yards, turning left, and going under a passageway—now, follow him.

   If you're pub crawling from Rosticceria San Bartolomeo, continue over a bridge to Campo San Lio. Here, turn left, passing Hotel Canada on your right, and follow Calle Carminati straight about 50 yards over another bridge. On the left is the pastry shop (*pasticceria*), and straight ahead is Osteria al Portego (at #6015).

West of the Rialto Bridge

All of these places are informal, serving *cicchetti* and/or light meals. The first group of bars are within 200 yards of each other, a few steps behind the Rialto fish market; the rest are a short walk from this hive of eateries (see map on the next page). This area is very crowded by day.

Cicchetti and Light Meals West of the Rialto

Most bars are closed 15:00-18:00 (though Cantina Do Mori and Ostaria ai Storti stay open all day) and offer glasses of house wine for under a euro, better wine for around €2, and *cicchetti* for €1-2. At each place, look for the list of snacks and wine by the glass at the bar or on the wall. If you're ready for dessert, try dipping a Burano biscuit in a glass of strawberry-flavored *fragolino* or another sweet dessert wine.

Cantina Do Mori has been famous with locals (since 1462) and savvy travelers (since 1982) as a convivial place for fine wine. You'll choose from a forest of little edibles on toothpicks and *francobolli* (a spicy selection of 20 tiny mayo-soaked sandwiches nicknamed "stamps"). Go here to be abused in a fine atmosphere—the frowns are part of the shtick (Mon-Sat 8:00-20:00, closed Sun, stand-up only, arrive early before the *cicchetti* are gone, San Polo 429, tel. 041-522-5401). From the Rialto Bridge, walk 200 yards down Ruga degli Orefici, away from St. Mark's Square—then turn left on Ruga Vecchia S. Giovanni, then right at Sotoportego Do Mori.

Bar all'Arco, a bustling one-room joint across from Cantina Do Mori, is particularly enjoyable for its tiny open-face sandwiches (closed Sun, tel. 041-520-5666).

Ostaria ai Storti serves lots of veggies and a few homemade pastas (check the daily specials) at great prices. With a homey feel, it's a fun place to congregate. Check out the photo of the market in 1909, below the bar. Alessandro speaks English and enjoys helping educate travelers while serving *fragolino* (daily 9:00-22:30, 20 yards from Cantina Do Mori on Calle delle Do Spade 819, tel. 041-523-6861).

Cantina Do Spade is run by Sebastiano, who clearly lists the *cicchetti* and wines of the day (daily 11:00-15:00 & 18:00-21:00, 30 yards down Calle delle Do Spade from Ostaria ai Storti at Calle delle Do Spade 19, tel. 041-521-0583).

At **Pesce Pronto,** you can actually sample fish while watching the market action. Bruno and Umberto serve artful fish hors

VENICE

Restaurants near the Rialto Bridge

TO GHETTO
& TRAIN STN.

TO
TRAIN STN.

STRADA
NOVA

PISTOR

S.S. APOST.

CA'
D'ORO

CAMPO
S.S. APOST.

TO
TRAIN
STN.

FISH
MARKET
BLDG.

BOTERI

Veg.
Mkt.

CANAL

CAMPO
CORN. S.

CAMPO
BECC.

SPEZIALI

C. DO SPADE

DON.

GRIST.

Mercato
Rialto

RIALTO
BRIDGE

SANSONI

S. MATTIA
S. ARCO

S. GIOVANNI

OREFICI

CAMPO
S. GIAC.

SAL.

POST

N

Ruga Vecc.

VIN

STATUE

CAMPO
S. BART.

BISSA

1

TO
CAMPO
SAN POLO
& FRARI
CHURCH

FONDAMENTA

FERRO

RIALTO

2 APRILE

STAGNERI

SAN
SILV.

GRAND

RIVA

CARBON

MAZZINI

BEMBO

MERCERIE

DCH

CAMPO
S. LUCA

FABBRI

BALLOTE

MERC.
REGINA

TO
ACCADEMIA

TO
SAN MARCO

1 Rosticceria San Bartolomeo
2 Cantina Do Mori, Bar all'Arco & Ostaria ai Storti
3 Cantina Do Spade

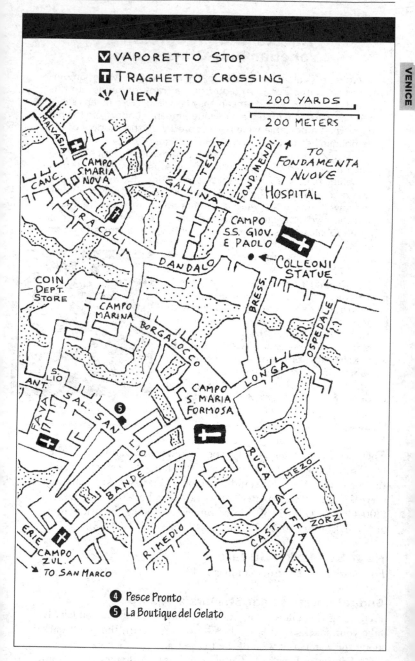

V VAPORETTO STOP
T TRAGHETTO CROSSING
↯ VIEW

200 YARDS
200 METERS

MALVASIA

CAMPO S MARIA NOVA

CANC.

MIRACOLI

TESTA

GALLINA

FOND. MEND.

TO FONDAMENTA NUOVE

HOSPITAL

CAMPO S.S. GIOV. E PAOLO

COLLEONI STATUE

DANDALO

BRESS.

COIN DEPT. STORE

CAMPO MARINA

BORGALOCCO

OSPEDALE

S. LIO

ANT.

FAVA

SAL. SAN

LIO

CAMPO S. MARIA FORMOSA

LONGA

BANDE

RUGA

MEZO

ERIE

CAMPO ZUL.

RIMEDIO

CAST.

CIUFFA

ZORZI

→ TO SAN MARCO

❹ Pesce Pronto
❺ La Boutique del Gelato

The Stand-Up Progressive Venetian Pub-Crawl Dinner

If you're in Venice at dinnertime, try my favorite Venetian dinner. It's a pub crawl (giro d'ombra)—a tradition unique to this island city, where no cars mean easy crawling. (Giro means stroll, and ombra—slang for a glass of wine—means shade, from the old days when a portable wine bar scooted with the shadow of the Campanile bell tower across St. Mark's Square.)

Venice's residential back streets hide plenty of characteristic bars (bacari) with countless trays of interesting toothpick munchies (cicchetti) and blackboards listing the wines that are uncorked and served by the glass. This is a great way to mingle and have fun with the Venetians. Bars don't stay open very late, and the cicchetti selection is best early, so start your evening by 18:00. Most bars are closed on Sunday. For a stress-free pub crawl, consider taking a tour with the charming Alessandro Schezzini (see page 723).

Cicchetti bars have a social stand-up zone and a cozy gaggle of tables where you can generally sit down with your cicchetti or order from a simple menu. In some of the more popular places, the crowds happily spill out into the street. Food generally costs the same price whether you stand or sit.

I've listed plenty of pubs in walking order for a quick or extended crawl. If

d'oeuvres, *sfornato con pesce* (a savory baked pastry), and many other fresh fish tidbits—all at a fair price. This fancy hole-in-the-wall is fun for a quick bite—eat standing up or take it to go. At 12:30, they serve €10-12 "express plates" of pasta and other choices (Tue-Sat 9:00-14:30 & 17:00-19:30, closed Sun-Mon, facing the fish market at Calle de le Beccarie o Panataria 319, tel. 041-822-0298).

Near St. Mark's Square

For locations, see the map on page 740.

Budget Eateries near St. Mark's Square

Picnicking isn't allowed on St. Mark's Square, but you can legally take your snacks to the nearby Giardinetti Reali, the small park along the waterfront west of the Piazzetta.

"Sandwich Row": On Calle delle Rasse, just steps away from the tourist intensity at St. Mark's Square, is a strip I call "Sandwich Row." Lined with sandwich bars, it's the closest place to St. Mark's

you've crawled enough, most of these bars make a fine one-stop, sit-down dinner.

While you can order a plate, Venetians prefer going one-by-one...sipping their wine and trying this...then give me one of those...and so on. Try deep-fried mozzarella cheese, gorgonzola, calamari, artichoke hearts, and anything ugly on a toothpick. *Crostini* (small toasted bread with something on it) are popular, as are marinated seafood, olives, and prosciutto with melon. Meat and fish (*pesce;* PESH-ay) munchies can be expensive; veggies *(verdure)* are cheap, at about €3 for a meal-sized plate. In many places, there's a set price per food item (e.g., €1.50). To get a plate of assorted appetizers for €8 (or more, depending on how hungry you are), ask for *"Un piatto classico di cicchetti misti da €8"* (oon pee-AH-toh KLAH-see-koh dee cheh-KET-tee MEE-stee dah OH-toh ay-OO-roh). Bread sticks *(grissini)* are free for the asking.

Bar-hopping Venetians enjoy an *aperitivo,* a before-dinner drink. Boldly order a Bellini, a *spritz con Aperol,* or a prosecco, and draw approving looks from the natives.

Drink the house wines. A small glass of house red or white wine *(ombra rosso* or *ombra bianco)* or a small beer *(birrino)* costs about €1. The house keg wine is cheap—€1 per glass, about €4 per liter. *Vin bon,* Venetian for fine wine, may run you from €1.50 to €6 per little glass. There are usually several fine wines uncorked and available by the glass. A good last drink is *fragolino,* the local sweet wine—*bianco* or *rosso.* It often comes with a little cookie *(biscotti)* for dipping.

to get a decent sandwich at an affordable price with a place to sit down (most places open daily 7:00-24:00, €1 extra to sit; from the Bridge of Sighs, head down the Riva and take the second lane on the left). I particularly like **Birreria Forst,** which serves a selection of meaty €2.70 sandwiches with tasty sauce on wheat bread, or made-to-order sandwiches for around €3.50 (daily 10:00-20:30, air-con, rustic wood tables, Calle delle Rasse 4540, tel. 041-523-0557) and **Bar Verde,** a more modern sandwich bar with fun people-watching views from its corner tables (big €4 sandwiches, splittable €8 salads, fresh pastries including Sicilian cannoli, at the end of Calle delle Rasse, facing Campo S.S. Filippo e Giacomo).

Ristorante alla Basilica, just one street behind St. Mark's Basilica, is a church-run institutional-feeling place serving a solid €13 three-course lunch daily from 11:45 to 15:00 (modern, air-con, Calle degli Albanesi 4255, tel. 041-522-0524).

Rizzo is a convenient bar/*alimentari* market located north of St. Mark's Square on the main drag of Calle dei Fabbri. Grab

€4.50 homemade lasagna and other reasonably priced snacks, such as yogurt, sautéed spinach, or fried sandwiches. It's stand-and-eat only—there's no seating (Mon-Sat 8:00-20:00, closed Sun, Calle dei Fabbri 933A, tel. 041-522-3388).

In Dorsoduro
Near the Accademia Bridge
Ristorante/Pizzeria Accademia Foscarini, next to the Accademia Bridge and Galleria, offers decent €8-11 pizzas in a great canalside setting. Their toasted *fareiti* sandwich is a local favorite (€6.50 at the table). Though the pizzas may be forgettable, this place is both scenic and practical—on each visit to Venice, I grab a pizza lunch here while I ponder the Grand Canal bustle (May-Oct Wed-Mon 7:00-21:30, Nov-April until 20:00, closed Tue, Dorsoduro 878C, tel. 041-522-7281).

Cheap Meals
The keys to eating affordably in Venice are pizza, bars/cafés, and picnics. *Panini* and *tramezzini* (sandwiches) are sold fast and cheap at bars everywhere and can stave off midmorning hunger. There's a great "Sandwich Row" of cheap cafés near St. Mark's Square (see page 786). For speed, value, and ambience, you can get a filling plate of typically Venetian appetizers at nearly any bar. For budget eating, I like stand-up mini-meals at ***cicchetti*** **bars** best (see sidebar page 786).

Picnics
The **produce market** that sprawls for a few blocks just past the Rialto Bridge is a fun place to assemble a picnic (best Mon-Sat 8:00-13:00, closed Sun). The adjacent fish market is wonderfully slimy (closed Sun-Mon). Side lanes in this area are speckled with fine little hole-in-the-wall munchie bars, bakeries, and cheese shops. Remember that the only legal place to picnic in public in Venice is Giardinetti Reali, the waterfront park near St. Mark's Square.

Gelato
La Boutique del Gelato, as lines attest, is considered the best *gelateria* in Venice. They dish up generous €1.20 scoops (daily 10:00-22:00, closed Dec-Jan, located on map on page 784, leave Campo Santa Maria Formosa from the corner with the bell tower, cross the bridge, turn right on Salizada San Lio, and find it next to Hotel Bruno at #5727).

On St. Mark's Square, there are two venerable *gelaterie:* **Gran Caffè Lavena** (daily until 24:00, first café to left of the Clock Tower, behind the first orchestra) and **Todaro Gelateria** (on the corner of the Piazzetta, near the Grand Canal and just under St. Theodore slaying the dragon, tel. 041-528-5165).

Starting or Ending Your Cruise in Venice

If your cruise begins and/or ends in Venice, you'll want some extra time here; for most travelers, two days is a minimum to see the highlights of this grand city. For a longer visit here, pick up my *Rick Steves' Venice* guidebook—or, if your trip extends to other points in the country, consider my *Rick Steves' Italy* guidebook.

Getting from Marco Polo Airport into Venice

If you want to stay in Venice before your cruise, there are three ways to get between the airport (which is on the mainland) and downtown Venice (on an island):

- Alilaguna water bus—medium in speed and cost
- Water taxis—fastest and most expensive
- Buses to Piazzale Roma—slowest and least expensive

Alilaguna Water Bus

These boats make the scenic (if slow) journey across the lagoon, shuttling passengers between the airport and a number of different stops on the island of Venice (€13, 60-90-minute trip depending on your destination; boats leave every 30-60 minutes). There are several lines (blue, red, orange), but if you know what stop you want, it's easy to find the line that goes there.

From the Airport to Venice: The airport's boat dock is an eight-minute walk from the terminal. Exit the arrivals terminal and turn left, following signs along a paved, level covered sidewalk. You can buy tickets at the airport's TI or the "Public Transport" window, at vending machines inside the airport terminal (cash only), or simply at the ticket booth at the dock. Any ticket-seller can tell you which line to catch; however, none of the lines serving the airport stop at the main cruise port terminal. Boats from the airport run from roughly 7:00 to midnight.

From Venice to the Airport: Give yourself plenty of time to make your flight. Ask your hotelier what dock and what line is best. Boats start leaving Venice as early as 3:40 so that passengers can catch early flights.

Venice Transit Connections

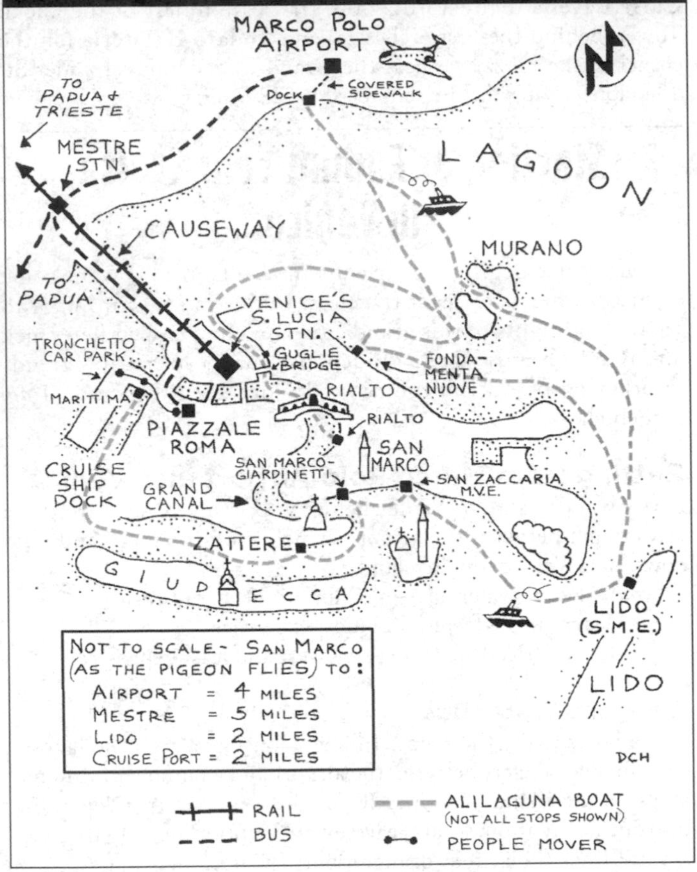
MARCO POLO AIRPORT
COVERED SIDEWALK
DOCK
TO PADUA & TRIESTE
MESTRE STN.
LAGOON
CAUSEWAY
MURANO
TO PADUA
VENICE'S S. LUCIA STN.
TRONCHETTO CAR PARK
GUGLIE BRIDGE
FONDAMENTA NUOVE
RIALTO
MARITTIMA
PIAZZALE ROMA
RIALTO
SAN MARCO
SAN MARCO-GIARDINETTI
SAN ZACCARIA M.V.E.
CRUISE SHIP DOCK
GRAND CANAL
ZATTERE
GIUDECCA
LIDO (S.M.E.)
LIDO
NOT TO SCALE - SAN MARCO (AS THE PIGEON FLIES) TO:
AIRPORT = 4 MILES
MESTRE = 5 MILES
LIDO = 2 MILES
CRUISE PORT = 2 MILES
DCH
RAIL
BUS
ALILAGUNA BOAT (NOT ALL STOPS SHOWN)
PEOPLE MOVER

For a full schedule, see the Alilaguna website (www.alilaguna.it), call 041-523-5775, scan the schedules posted at Alilaguna docks, or ask at the TI. Note that the Alilaguna water bus is not part of the ACTV vaporetto system, so it is not covered by city transit passes.

Water Taxi

Luxury **taxi** speedboats zip directly between the airport and your hotel, getting you within steps of your final destination in about 30 minutes. The official price is €100 for up to four people, though you'll often get a higher quote (around €110)—talk them down. From the airport, arrange your ride at the airport's water-taxi desk or at the dock (next to the Alilaguna dock).

Airport Shuttle Bus

Buses take you across the bridge from the mainland to the island, dropping you at the "mouth" of the fish, on a square called Piazzale Roma. From there, you can catch a vaporetto down the Grand Canal—convenient for hotels near the Rialto Bridge and St. Mark's Square.

Two companies compete for the airport shuttle business. The ATVO "Venezia Express" and the ACTV bus #5 both connect the airport and Piazzale Roma (€2.50-3, 20-40 minutes, 2/hour, 5:00-24:00, www.atvo.it or www.actv.it). The ATVO is slightly faster and pricier.

From the Airport to Venice: Both buses leave from just outside the arrivals terminal and drop you off at Piazzale Roma. Buy tickets at the TI, from ticket machines in the terminal or outside next to the buses, or sometimes directly from the driver. Check which ticket you are buying—ATVO tickets are not valid on ACTV buses and vice versa.

When you arrive at Piazzale Roma, you'll find the vaporetto dock by walking to the six-story white building, then taking a right.

From Venice to the Airport: Buses leave Piazzale Roma between 5:00 and 20:40, departing from the northeast corner of the lot near Hotel Santa Chiara.

Private Shuttle Bus

Treviso Car Service, which offers a private **minivan service** between Marco Polo Airport and Piazzale Roma (€50 per minivan, seats up to 8, tel. 338-204-4390, www.trevisocarservice.com, Andrea).

Getting from Treviso Airport into Venice

Several budget airlines, such as Ryanair, Wizz Air, and Blue, use this small airport, 12 miles northwest of Venice (www.trevisoairport.it). Regular ATVO buses take you to Piazzale Roma (€6, 2-3/hour, 1.25 hours, www.atvo.it, where you can catch the People Mover monorail to the cruise port). Buy your tickets at the ATVO desk in the airport and stamp them on the bus. The buses also stop at Mestre's train station. Treviso Car Service offers minivan service to Piazzale Roma (€55 per minivan, www.trevisocarservice.com).

Getting to the Cruise Port

Whether you're coming from points in Venice (such as the train station or St. Mark's Square), or from the airport, below you'll find instructions for reaching the cruise port.

What If I Miss My Boat?

Remember that you can get help from the cruise line's port agent (listed on the destination information sheet distributed on the ship) and the local TI (see page 712). If the port agent suggests a costly solution (such as a private car with a driver), you may want to consider public transit instead.

Venice has train and plane connections to virtually anywhere in Italy. The city has a train station and two airports—Marco Polo and the small Treviso.

Frequent **trains** leave from Venice's **Santa Lucia train station** (on the Grand Canal) to points all over Italy and beyond: to **Florence** (hourly, 2-3 hours, may transfer in Bologna; often crowded so make reservations), **Rome** (hourly, 3.5 hours, may transfer in Bologna, overnight possible), **Naples** (almost hourly, 5.5-7 hours, with changes in Bologna or Rome). To **Split** or **Dubrovnik,** overland connections are long (16 hours by night train to Split, much longer by train and bus to Dubrovnik); driving all the way is much shorter (consider hiring a driver—figure about 8 hours to Split, 12 hours to Dubrovnik), or look into flights.

For other connections, ask at the train station or check http://bahn.hafas.de/bin/query.exe/en (Germany's excellent all-Europe website).

For recommended local **travel agents,** see page 718. For more advice on what to do if you miss the boat, see page 131.

Getting from Points in Venice to the Cruise Port

If arriving by train and going directly to the port, exit the Venezia Santa Lucia **train station,** turn right, follow the Grand Canal to the modern Calatrava Bridge, cross it, walk through Piazzale Roma (big bus parking lot) to the People Mover station at the far-right corner, then ride the People Mover one stop to Stazione Marittima.

If you're heading to the port from **St. Mark's Square,** you can ride the Alilaguna boat #M (described on page 709). From elsewhere in Venice, it might be easier to take a vaporetto to Piazzale Roma and take the People Mover from there to Stazione Marittima.

Once at the port, you'll need to drop off your bags at the baggage collection area. Follow signs for your cruise line, and ask representatives where you can drop bags (many of them use a huge but easy-to-miss white tented area set back from the piers, between buildings #107/#108 and #117). Once you've deposited your bags, you can head to your terminal building to check in. If your cruise starts in Venice, you may need to check in at the main terminal even if your ship docks outside the main port.

Getting from Marco Polo Airport to the Cruise Port

Venice's modern airport is on the mainland, six miles north of the city. It's a sleek wood beam-and-glass terminal, with a TI (daily 9:00-21:00), ATMs, car-rental agencies, a bank, a post office, and a few shops and eateries. For flight information, call tel. 041-260-9260 or visit www.veniceairport.com.

From the airport, you can take a taxi directly to the port (€40), or you can take an airport shuttle bus to Piazzale Roma (explained earlier), then the People Mover from there (buy €1 People Mover ticket as you enter, take it one stop to Stazione Marittima).

Hotels

If you need a hotel in Venice before or after your cruise, here are a few to consider.

$$$ Hotel Campiello, lacy and bright, was once part of a 19th-century convent. Ideally located 50 yards off the waterfront, on a tiny square, its 16 rooms offer a tranquil, friendly refuge for travelers who appreciate comfort and professional service (Sb-€130, Db-€180, 10 percent discount with cash and this book, air-con, elevator, Wi-Fi; from the waterfront street—Riva degli Schiavoni—take Calle del Vin, between pink Hotel Danieli and Hotel Savoia e Jolanda, to #4647, Castello; tel. 041-520-5764, fax 041-520-5798, www.hcampiello.it, campiello@hcampiello.it; family-run for four generations, currently by Thomas, Monica, Nicoletta, and Marco). They also rent three modern family apartments, under rustic timbers just steps away (up to €380/night).

$$ Locanda al Leon is a basic place renting 14 decent rooms just off Campo S.S. Filippo e Giacomo (Db-€135-150, Tb-€170, Qb-€220, these prices with cash and this book, air-con, Internet access and Wi-Fi, Campo S.S. Filippo e Giacomo 4270, Castello, tel. 041-277-0393, fax 041-521-0348, www.hotelalleon.com, leon @hotelalleon.com, Giuliano and Marcella). From the San Zaccaria-Danieli vaporetto stop, take Calle dei Albanesi (two streets left of pink Hotel Danieli) to its far end.

$$ Hotel Fontana is a two-star, family-run place with 15 rooms near a school, two bridges behind St. Mark's Square. Their annex across the street has much lower ceilings and slightly lower prices (Sb-€110, Db-€140-170, family rooms, 10 percent cash discount, quieter rooms on garden side, 2 rooms have terraces for €10 extra, air-con, elevator, Internet access and Wi-Fi, Campo San Provolo 4701, Castello, tel. 041-522-0579, fax 041-523-1040, www .hotelfontana.it, info@hotelfontana.it, Diego and Gabriele).

$$ Hotel la Residenza is a grand old palace facing a peaceful square. It has 15 great rooms on three levels and a huge, luxurious old lounge. This is a great value for romantics—you'll feel like you're in the Doge's Palace after hours. Hang out in the living room and you become royalty (Sb-€100, Db-€130-165, air-con, Wi-Fi, Campo Bandiera e Moro 3608, Castello, tel. 041-528-5315, fax 041-523-8859, www.venicelaresidenza.com, info@venicela residenza.com, Giovanni).

$$ Locanda Casa Querini rents six bright, high-ceilinged rooms on a quiet square tucked away behind St. Mark's. You can enjoy your breakfast or a sunny picnic/happy hour sitting at their tables right on the sleepy little square (Db-€150, third person-€20-25, one cheaper small double, ask for cash discount, air-con, Wi-Fi, halfway between San Zaccaria vaporetto stop and Campo Santa Maria Formosa at Campo San Giovanni in Oleo 4388, Castello, tel. 041-241-1294, fax 041-523-6188, www.locanda querini.com, casaquerini@hotmail.com, Patrizia and Silvia).

$ Albergo Doni is dark, clean, and quiet—a bit of a time-warp—with 13 dim but once-classy rooms run by a likable smart aleck named Gina, her niece Tessa, and her nephew, an Italian stallion named Nikos (D-€90, Db-€115, T-€120, Tb-€155, reserve with credit card but pay in cash, ceiling fans, three Db rooms have air-con, Fondamenta del Vin 4656, Castello, tel. & fax 041-522-4267, www.albergodoni.it, albergodoni@hotmail.it).

CROATIA
Hrvatska

CROATIA

Hrvatska

Sunny beaches, succulent seafood, and a taste of *la dolce vita*...in Eastern Europe?

Unfamiliar as it might seem, Croatia has some of Europe's most spectacular natural wonders, a fascinating recent history, and a spirit of adventure—much of it still off the beaten path. With thousands of miles of seafront and more than a thousand islands, Croatia's coastline is Eastern Europe's Riviera. Holiday-makers love its sunshine-bathed pebbly beaches, predictably balmy summer weather, and melt-in-your-mouth seafood. Most people flock to the southern Dalmatian Coast, where dramatic limestone cliffs rise from the deep and islands are scattered just offshore.

Aside from its fun-in-the-sun status, Croatia is also historic. From ruined Roman arenas and Byzantine mosaics to Venetian bell towers, Habsburg villas, and even communist concrete, past rulers have left their mark. A trip to Croatia also offers thoughtful travelers the opportunity to understand its complicated role in Europe's most violent war in generations. But most visitors will focus on Croatia's substantial natural wonders: mountains, sun, sand, and sea.

Two major Croatian ports are likely to be on your itinerary. The great medieval walled city of Dubrovnik, poking proudly into the Adriatic, is Croatia's single finest town. Understandably thronged by visitors, its atmospheric Old Town, picturesque beaches, and offbeat museums are a delight. A few years back, Dubrovnik became so popular, so quickly, that they had to turn away cruise ships...

so they began going to Split. But don't think of Split as second fiddle to Dubrovnik. Instead, Split—Croatia's second city, and the unofficial capital of the Dalmatian Coast—is the bustling urban yang to Dubrovnik's trapped-in-the-past yin. In addition to its lively shops, cafés, and promenade, Split has some of Croatia's best

Roman ruins: the remarkable foundations of Diocletian's Palace, which now form the base for Split's Old Town.

Practicalities

This section covers just the basics on traveling in Croatia.

Tourist Information: http://us.croatia.hr

Money: Croatia uses its traditional currency, the kuna: 5 kuna (kn) = about $1 (so a kuna is worth about 20 cents). One kuna is broken down into 100 lipa.

Theft (Minimal): Croatia is relatively free of the petty crime that plagues port cities in other countries, but it's smart to keep alert, especially in crowds and on public transportation.

Business Hours: Particularly in seasonal resort areas along the coast, business hours are unpredictable. Even in touristy Split and Dubrovnik, some shops may be closed on Sunday.

Internet Access: You can generally find a café with Wi-Fi or an Internet hotspot in most towns. T-Mobile operates hotspots in many Croatian towns and big hotels, but it's usually quite pricey.

Sights: Many Croatian museums are closed on Mondays.

Dress Code: A modest dress code (no bare shoulders or shorts) is encouraged, but rarely enforced, at churches.

Buses: Buses in Croatia often take you where trains can't, but confusingly, a single bus route might be operated by several different companies, making it difficult to find comprehensive schedules. Some big cities have handy websites listing all connections (such as www.ak-split.hr for Split), but for smaller towns, the TI is your best source of information.

Eating

Croatia offers good food for reasonable prices. Choosing between strudel and baklava on the same menu, you're constantly reminded

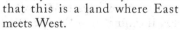

that this is a land where East meets West.

If you're in the mood for a picnic meal, look for bakeries selling *burek* (savory phyllo dough filled with meat, cheese, spinach, or apples), *baklava* (phyllo dough layered with honey and nuts), and other goodies, or try a shop advertising "pizza cut" (pizza by the slice to go). Many grocery stores sell pre-made sandwiches.

There's a cheap pizza or pasta joint on every corner, offering an easy, quick, and inexpensive way to fill the tank. For something heartier, consider the local grilled meats. You'll most often see *čevapčići*, minced meat formed into a sausage shape, and *ražnjići*, steak on a skewer. A Dalmatian specialty is *pašticada*—braised beef in a slightly sweet wine-and-herb sauce. A nice veggie complement is *đuveđ*, a spicy mix of stewed vegetables, flavored with tomatoes and peppers. And you can't eat any of this without the ever-present

condiment *ajvar*, made from red bell pepper and eggplant, like ketchup with a kick.

At fish restaurants, seafood is often priced by weight—either by kilogram or by hectogram (100 grams, or one-tenth of a kilogram). A one-kilogram portion feeds two hungry people or three light eaters.

When restaurant-hunting, venturing even a block or two off the main drag leads to local, higher-quality food for less than half the price of the tourist-oriented places. Only a rude waiter will rush you. Good service is relaxed (slow to an American).

Tipping: At a restaurant with table service, round up the bill 5-10 percent after a good meal. At some tourist restaurants, a 10-15 percent service charge may be added to your bill, in which case an additional tip is not necessary.

Phoning

Pay phones in Croatia take insertable phone cards, sold at newsstands and kiosks. The cheap international telephone cards that are widely available elsewhere in Europe are less common in Croatia.

Dialing: Croatia's phone system uses area codes. If you're dialing within an area code, use just the local number; for long-distance calls, dial the area code (which starts with a 0), then the local number. To **call to Croatia,** dial the international access code (00 if calling from Europe, 011 from North America), then 385 (Croatia's country code), then the area code (without the initial 0) and the local number. To **call home from Croatia,** dial 00, 1, then your area code and phone number.

Directory Assistance: Tel. 988
Emergency Telephone Numbers:
Police: Tel. 92
Medical or Other Emergencies: Tel. 112
Passport Problems: US Embassy in Zagreb (tel. 01/661-2200, after-hours tel. 01/661-2400); Canadian Embassy in Zagreb (tel. 01/488-1200).

SPLIT

Dubrovnik is the darling of the Dalmatian Coast, but Split (pronounced as it's spelled) is Croatia's "second city" (after Zagreb), bustling with 189,000 people. If you've been hopping along the coast, landing in urban Split feels like a return to civilization. While most Dalmatian coastal towns seem made for tourists, Split is real and vibrant—a shipbuilding city with ugly sprawl surrounding an atmospheric Old Town, which teems with Croatians living life to the fullest.

Though today's Split throbs to a modern, young beat, its history goes way back—all the way to the Roman Empire. Along with all the trappings of a modern city, Split has some of the best Roman ruins this side of Italy. In the fourth century A.D., the Roman Emperor Diocletian (245-313) wanted to retire in his native Dalmatia, so he built a huge palace here. Eventually, the palace was abandoned. Then locals, fleeing seventh-century Slavic invaders, moved in and made themselves at home, and a medieval town sprouted from the rubble of the old palace. In the 15th century, the Venetians took over the Dalmatian Coast. They developed and fortified Split, slathering the city with a new layer of Gothic-Renaissance architecture.

But even as Split grew, the nucleus remained the ruins of Diocletian's Palace. To this day, 2,000 people live or work inside the former palace walls. A maze of narrow alleys is home to fashionable boutiques and galleries, wonderfully atmospheric cafés, and Roman artifacts around every corner.

Today's Split is struggling to decide how it fits into Croatia's new tourist-mecca image: Is it a big, drab metropolis; a

Excursions from Split

Split itself offers enough diversions to fill an entire day, all within easy walking distance of the ship. But Split is also a place where cruise lines seem to cobble together excursions based on what's convenient to bus passengers to, rather than on what's really worth seeing.

Of the many options near Split, the small town of **Trogir** is the most appealing (about a 30-minute ride by bus). For more information on Trogir, see page 822.

The Roman ruins at **Solin** (a.k.a. Ancient Salona), located on the outskirts of Split, pale in comparison to ancient ruins elsewhere—including those in the city center of Split. Unless you've never met a Roman ruin you didn't like, I'd skip Solin.

More nature-oriented options are farther afield: the gorgeous waterfalls at **Krka National Park** (1.5 hours northwest of Split); the **Cetina River,** popular for canoe and white-water rafting trips (about 45 minutes southeast of Split); and the rustic island of **Brač,** with its famous sandy beaches (30-minute boat ride south from Split).

And finally, some cruise lines also offer side-trips to nearby towns and cities, including the resort town of **Omiš,** where the Cetina River empties into the Adriatic (about 30 minutes southeast of Split); and the city of **Šibenik,** with its impressive Cathedral of St. James (about 1.25 hours northwest of Split)...though, again, where Dalmatian cities are concerned, both of these decidedly play second fiddle to Split.

Bottom line: Unless you have a special interest in the above sights, save yourself some money and simply enjoy the urban charms, ancient wonders, and artistic gems of Split.

no-nonsense transit point; an impressive destination in its own right, with sights to rival Dubrovnik's...or all three?

Planning Your Time

Compact Split is made to order for a quick visit on a cruise. Here are the top activities, which I'd do in this order:

• **Tour Diocletian's Palace** in the Old Town; allow 1-1.5 hours. It's a short walk from the cruise terminal and tender dock. Stroll the remains of the palace, either using my self-guided walk or joining a walking tour (see page 805).

• Have a **coffee or ice-cream break** along the Riva promenade, or **lunch** in or near the Old Town.

• Browse the **shops** in the Old Town, or visit a couple of Split's **museums** (most can be seen in 30-60 minutes). The **Meštrović Gallery** is tops (allow 1 hour to tour the collection), but it's a 25-minute walk or short bus or taxi ride from the Old Town—leave yourself plenty of time to get back to your ship.

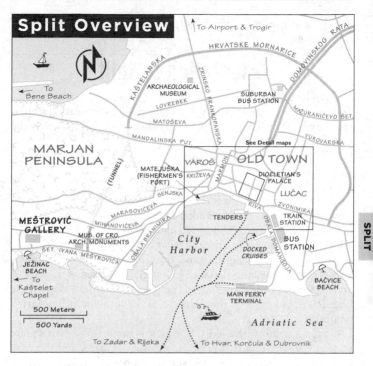

Arrival at the Port of Split

From a cruiser's perspective, Split is one of the easiest cities to arrive in. Cruise ships either dock or tender here; in either case, cruise passengers arrive in downtown Split, just a short walk from the main sights. From any entry point, you can see the church tower and waterfront promenade marking the Old Town: Just walk in that direction, and you're there.

Docking in Split: Cruise ships that dock in Split do so along a busy and very practical strip of land called Obala Kneza Domagoja, on the east side of the City Harbor. Also along here are docks for various passenger boats and car ferries to destinations throughout Croatia and Italy, the main bus station, the train station, and a wide range of services: travel agencies, ATMs, a post office, Internet cafés, shops, and cafés (see "Helpful Hints," later). On arrival, just walk around the harbor toward the big bell tower (about a 10-minute walk): Exit the ship, turn left, and walk (with the harbor on your left) straight into town.

Tendering in Split: Tenders arrive at the Obala Lazareta embankment, right in front of the Old Town—just a three-minute walk from Diocletian's Palace.

Missing the Boat: For information on what to do if you miss your boat at the end of your visit, see the sidebar near the end of this chapter.

Orientation to Split

(area code: 021)

Split sprawls, but almost everything of interest to travelers is around the City Harbor (Gradska Luka). At the top of this harbor is the Old Town (Stari Grad). Between the Old Town and the sea is the Riva, a waterfront pedestrian promenade lined with cafés and shaded by palm trees. The main ferry terminal (Trajektni Terminal, a.k.a. Trajektna Luka) juts into the harbor from the east side. Along the harborfront embankment between the ferry terminal and the Old Town are the long-distance bus station (Autobusni Kolodvor) and the forlorn little train station (Željeznička Stanica). West of the Old Town, poking into the Adriatic, is the lush and hilly Marjan peninsula.

Split's domino-shaped Old Town is made up of two square sections. The east half was once Diocletian's Palace, and the west half is the medieval town that sprang up next door. The shell of Diocletian's ruined palace provides a checkerboard street plan, with a gate at each end. But the streets built since are anything but straight, making the Old Town a delightfully convoluted maze (double-decker in some places). At the center of the former palace is a square called the Peristyle (Peristil), where you'll find the TI, cathedral, and highest concentration of Roman ruins.

Tourist Information

Split's TI is on the square called the Peristyle, in the very center of Diocletian's Palace (Easter-mid-Oct Mon-Sat 8:00-21:00, Sun 8:00-13:00; mid-Oct-Easter Mon-Fri 8:00-20:00, Sat 8:00-13:00, closed Sun; exact location might change due to restoration—ask around, tel. 021/345-606, www.visitsplit.com). Pick up the free town map, monthly *Visit Split* booklet (with information on museums, events, restaurants, and more), and other brochures.

The TI also sells the **Splitcard,** which includes free admission to several sights (including the City Museum, Ethnographic Museum, and cathedral), a 50 percent discount at other sights (including the Meštrović Gallery and Archaeological Museum), and minor discounts at other attractions, shops, and restaurants around town (35 kn/72 hours). This card might save busy sightseers some money—do the arithmetic.

Split Essentials

English	Croatian	Pronounced
Old Town	Stari Grad	STAH-ree grahd
City Harbor	Gradska Luka	GRAHD-skah LOO-kah
Harborfront promenade	Riva	REE-vah
Peristyle (old Roman square)	Peristil	PEH-ree-steel
Soccer team	Hajduk	HIGH-dook
Local sculptor	Ivan Meštrović	EE-vahn MESH-troh-veech
Adriatic Sea	Jadran	YAH-drahn

Helpful Hints

Internet Access: Internet cafés are plentiful in the Old Town; look for signs, especially around the Peristyle. Closer to the stations and ferry terminal is **Backpacker C@fé,** which has Internet access, coffee, and drinks, with outdoor seating, and used paperbacks for sale (30 kn/hour, daily July-Aug 6:00-23:00, shoulder season 6:30-22:00, even shorter hours off-season, near the beginning of Obala Kneza Domagoja, tel. 021/338-548).

Post Office: A modern little post office is next to the bus station (Mon-Fri 7:30-19:00, Sat 7:30-14:30, closed Sun, on Obala Kneza Domagoja).

Travel Agencies: Travel49, run by gregarious Josip, is a jack-of-all-trades agency buried deep in the Old Town. Josip offers walking tours (see "Tours in Split," later), bike tours, excursions, a room-booking service, bike and car rental, Internet access, luggage storage, and other services (May-Nov daily 8:00-22:00, shorter hours off-season, mornings only in winter, on Dioklecijanova 5, tel. 021/572-772, www.diocletianpalacetour.com). **Turistički Biro,** between the two halves of the Old Town on the Riva, sells guidebooks, maps, and tickets for excursions (mid-June-Sept Mon-Fri 8:00-21:00, Sat 8:00-20:00, closed Sun except mid-July-mid-Sept Sun 8:00-13:00; Oct-mid-June Mon-Fri 8:00-20:00, Sat 8:00-13:00, closed Sun; Riva 12, tel. & fax 021/347-100, turist.biro.split@st.t-com.hr).

Wine Shop: At **Vinoteka Bouquet,** at the west end of the Riva (near the restaurants and launderette on Šperun street), knowledgeable Denis can help you pick out a bottle of Croatian wine to suit your tastes (Mon-Fri 8:30-12:30 & 17:00-20:30,

Sat 9:00-13:30, closed Sun, Obala Hrvatskog Narodnog Preporoda 3, tel. 021/348-031).

Who's Hajduk?: You'll see the word *Hajduk* (HIGH-dook), and a distinctive red-and-white checkerboard circle design (or red-and-blue stripes), all over town. Hajduk Split is the fervently supported local soccer team, named for a band of highwaymen bandits who rebelled against Ottoman rule in the 17th-19th centuries. Most locals adore Hajduk as much as they loathe their bitter rivals, Dinamo Zagreb.

G'day, *Gospod*: You may notice a surprising concentration of Australians in Split. Many of them are actually Australian-born Croats, returning to the cosmopolitan capital city of their parents' Dalmatian homeland.

Getting Around Split

Most of what you'll want to see is within walking distance, but some sights (such as the Meštrović Gallery) are more easily reached by bus or taxi.

By Bus: Local buses, run by Promet, cost 10 kn per ride (or 9 kn if you buy a ticket from a newsstand or Promet kiosk, ask for a *putna karta;* zone I is fine for any ride within Split, but you need the 20-kn zone IV ticket for the ride to Trogir). For a round-trip within the city, buy a 16-kn transfer ticket, which works like two individual tickets (must buy at kiosk). Validate your ticket in the machine or with the driver as you board the bus. Suburban buses to towns near Split (such as Trogir) generally use the suburban bus station (Prigradski Autobusni Kolodvor), a 10-minute walk due north of the Old Town on Domovinskog rata. Bus information: www.promet-split.hr.

By Taxi: Taxis start at 20 kn, then cost around 10 kn per kilometer. Figure 50 kn for most rides within the city—but if going from one end of the Old Town to the other, it can be faster to walk. To call for a taxi, try Radio Taxi (tel. 021/970).

Tours in Split

Walking Tours—Various companies offer walking tours of Split's Old Town. The most established is **Unique Walking Tours,** part of Travel49. Their 1.5-hour tours depart from the Peristyle (80 kn, 20 percent discount if you buy tickets at Travel49 office and show this book; May-Oct daily at 10:30, 12:00, 14:00, and 19:00; April and Nov daily at 11:00 only; no tours Dec-March; see Travel49 listing earlier, under "Helpful Hints").

Local Guides—Consider hiring an insider to show you around. **Maja Benzon** is a smart, savvy guide who leads good walking tours through the Old Town (500 kn/up to 2 hours, 600 kn/3 hours, mobile 098-852-869, maja.benzon@gmail.com). You can also hire a guide through the **guide association,** which has an office at the Peristyle (525 kn/1.5-2 hours; June-Aug Mon-Fri 9:00-13:00 & 15:00-19:00, Sat 9:00-14:00, closed Sun; May and Sept Mon-Fri 9:00-17:00, Sat 9:00-15:00, closed Sun; Oct-April generally open mornings only but closed Sun; tel. 021/360-058, tel. & fax 021/346-267, mobile 098-361-936, www.guides.hr, info@guides.hr).

Self-Guided Walk of Diocletian's Palace

SPLIT

Split's top activity is visiting the remains of Roman Emperor Diocletian's enormous retirement palace (Dioklecijanova Palača), sitting on the harbor in the heart of the city. This monstrous complex was two impressive structures in one: luxurious villa and fortified Roman town. Since the ruins themselves are now integrated with the city's street plan, exploring them is free (though you'll pay to enter a few parts, such as the cellars and the cathedral/mausoleum). Fragments of the palace are poorly marked, and there are no good guidebooks or audioguides for tracking down the remains, making Split a good place to take a walking tour or hire a local guide (see "Tours in Split," earlier). This self-guided tour provides enough information for most visitors. To begin the tour, stand in front of the palace (at the east end of the Riva) to get oriented.

Background: Diocletian grew up just inland from Split, in the town of Salona (Solin in Croatian), which was then the capital

of the Roman province of Dalmatia. He worked his way up the Roman hierarchy and ruled as emperor for the unusually long tenure of 20 years (A.D. 284-305). Despite all of his achievements, Diocletian is best remembered for two questionable legacies: dividing the huge empire among four emperors (which helped administer it more efficiently, but began a splintering effect that arguably led to the empire's decline); and torturing and executing Christians, including thousands right here on the Dalmatian Coast.

As Diocletian grew older, he decided to return to his homeland for retirement. Since he was in poor health, the medicinal sulfur spring here was another plus. His massive palace took only 11 years to build—and this fast pace required a big push (more than 2,000 slaves died during construction). Huge sections of his palace still exist, modified by medieval and modern developers alike. To get a sense of the

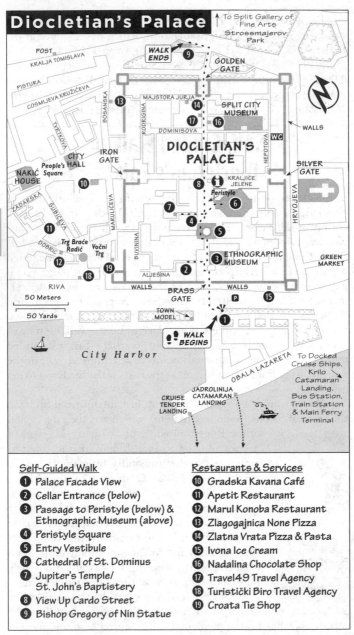

Diocletian's Palace

To Split Gallery of
Fine Arts
Strossmajerov
Park

POST
KRALJA TOMISLAVA

PISTURA
COSMIJEVA KRUŽIĆEVA

TVRTKOVA

BOSANSKA

**WALK
ENDS** ❾

GOLDEN
GATE

MAJSTORA JURJA

RODRIGINA

❶❹

DOMINISOVA

SPLIT CITY
MUSEUM

❶❻

WALLS

CITY
HALL

IRON
GATE

**DIOCLETIAN'S
PALACE**

NEPOTOVA

WC

SILVER
GATE

NAKIĆ
HOUSE

People's
Square

❶⓿

ZADARSKA

ŠUBIĆEVA

MARULIĆEVA

❽
❼

❹

KRALJICE
JELENE
ℹ

Peristyle
❻

HRVOJEVA

❶❶

❺

BUXININA

Trg Braće
Radić

Voćni
Trg

❶❷

❶⑨

ETHNOGRAPHIC
MUSEUM

❸

❷

GREEN
MARKET

DOBRIC

❶❽

ALJEŠINA

RIVA

50 Meters

WALLS

BRASS
GATE

WALLS

P

❶❺

50 Yards

TOWN
MODEL

**WALK
BEGINS** ❶

City Harbor

OBALA LAZARETA

To Docked
Cruise Ships,
Krilo
Catamaran
Landing,
Bus Station,
Train Station
& Main Ferry
Terminal

JADROLINIJA
CATAMARAN
LANDING

CRUISE
TENDER
LANDING

Self-Guided Walk

❶ Palace Facade View
❷ Cellar Entrance (below)
❸ Passage to Peristyle (below) &
   Ethnographic Museum (above)
❹ Peristyle Square
❺ Entry Vestibule
❻ Cathedral of St. Dominus
❼ Jupiter's Temple/
   St. John's Baptistery
❽ View Up Cardo Street
❾ Bishop Gregory of Nin Statue

Restaurants & Services

❶⓿ Gradska Kavana Café
❶❶ Apetit Restaurant
❶❷ Marul Konoba Restaurant
❶❸ Zlagogajnica None Pizza
❶❹ Zlatna Vrata Pizza & Pasta
❶❺ Ivona Ice Cream
❶❻ Nadalina Chocolate Shop
❶❼ Travel49 Travel Agency
❶❽ Turistički Biro Travel Agency
❶⑨ Croata Tie Shop

SPLIT

original palace, check out the big illustration posted across from the palace entry. Across the street at the end of the Riva, notice the big car-size model of today's Old Town, which is helpful for orientation. (Both the sign and the model are usually crowded with tour groups.)

Palace Facade

The "front" of today's Split—facing the harbor—was actually the back door of Diocletian's Palace. There was no embankment in front of the palace back then, so the water came right up to this door—sort of an emergency exit by boat. Looking out to the water, appreciate the palace's strategic location, in a place easy to fortify and to watch for enemies approaching either by land or by sea.

Visually trace the outline of the gigantic palace, which was more than 600 feet long on each side. On the corner to the right stands a big, rectangular guard tower (one of the original 16). To the left, the tower is gone and the corner is harder to pick out (look for the beginning of the newer-looking buildings). Mentally erase the ramshackle two-story buildings added 200 years ago, which obscure the grandness of the palace wall.

Halfway up the facade, notice the row of 42 arched window frames (mostly filled in today). Diocletian and his family lived in the seaside half of the palace. Imagine him strolling back and forth along this fine arcade, enjoying the views of his Adriatic homeland. The inland, non-view half of the palace was home to 700 servants, bodyguards, and soldiers.

• *Now go through the door in the middle of the palace (known as the "Brass Gate," located under the Substructure of Diocletian's Palace banner). Just inside the door and to the left is the entrance to...*

Diocletian's Cellars (Podromi)

Since the palace was built on land that sloped down to the sea, these chambers were built to level out a foundation for the massive

structure above (like a modern "daylight basement"). These cellars were filled with water from three different sources: a freshwater spring, a sulfur spring, and the sea. Later, medieval residents used them as a dump. Rediscovered only in the last century, the cellars enabled archaeologists to derive the floor plan of some of the palace's long-gone upper sections. Today, these underground chambers are used for art exhibits and a little strip of souvenir stands. But before you go shopping, explore the cellars at this end (25 kn, short and dry

10-kn guidebook, some posters inside explain the site; opens daily at 9:00 and closes June-Aug at 21:00, Sept at 20:00, May and Oct at 18:00, April at 17:00; Nov-March Mon-Sat 9:00-14:00, closed Sun).

⊙ **Self-Guided Tour:** Use the free map you get at the entry to navigate this labyrinthine complex of cellars. First visit the **western cellars** (to the left as you enter). Near the ticket-seller, notice the big **topographical map** of the Split area, clearly showing the city's easily defensible location—with a natural harbor sheltered by tall mountains. You'll see the former Roman city of Salona, Diocletian's birthplace, just inland.

Then head into the main part of the cellars by going through the door on the right, just past the ticket-seller. This takes you into the complex's vast, vaulted **main hall**—the biggest space in the cellars, with stout pillars to support everything upstairs. When those first villagers took refuge in the abandoned palace from the rampaging Slavs in 641, the elite lived upstairs, grabbing what was once the emperor's wing. They carved the rough holes you see in the ceiling to dump their garbage and sewage. Over the generations, the basement (where you're standing) filled up with layers of waste that solidified, ultimately becoming a once-stinky, then-precious bonanza for 19th- and 20th-century archaeologists. Today this hall is used for everything from flower and book shows to fashion catwalks.

Exit the main hall through either of the doors on the left, turn right down the narrow corridor, and then turn left at the end of the corridor. In this room you'll see a stone olive-oil press. Continue through a small room and into a round room, which has a headless, pawless black granite sphinx—one of 13 that Diocletian brought home from Egypt (only four survive, including a mostly intact one we'll see soon on the Peristyle). Look up to admire the circular brickwork. Then continue straight ahead into the long room, which displays two petrified beams. Looking just overhead, you'll see the holes that once held these beams to support floorboards, making this a two-story cellar.

Exit through the door at the far-right corner (near the mound of ancient garbage) to another round room, featuring a bust of Diocletian (or is it Sean Connery?). Continue straight ahead (near the public WCs), then turn left, left, and right into the second grand hall, with more beam holes and a giant replica of a golden Diocletian coin at the far end. Exiting this hall at the end opposite the coin, you'll find an unexcavated wing—a compost pile of ancient lifestyles, awaiting the tiny shovels and toothbrushes of future archaeologists. Here you'll also see original Roman sewer pipes—square outside and round inside—designed to fit into each other to create long pipes.

From here, head back out to the exit. If you'd like to see more cellars—mostly with their ceilings missing, so they're open to the air—cross over into the **eastern cellars** (same ticket). This section is less interesting than the western part, but worth a quick visit.

• *When you're finished, head back to the main gallery. Ignore the tacky made-in-Malaysia trinket shops as you head down the passage and up the stairs into the...*

Peristyle (Peristil)

This square was the centerpiece of Diocletian's Palace. As you walk up the stairs, the entry vestibule into the residence is above your

head, Diocletian's mausoleum (today's Cathedral of St. Dominus) is to your right, and the street to Jupiter's Temple is on your left. On this square, you'll find the TI (because the old structures on the square are being restored, its exact location might vary). Straight ahead, beyond the little chapel, is the narrow street to the former main entrance to the palace, the Golden Gate.

Go to the middle of the square and take it all in. The red granite pillars—which you'll see all over Diocletian's Palace—are from Egypt, where Diocletian spent many of his pre-retirement years. Imagine the pillars defining fine arcades—now obscured by medieval houses. (As the Peristyle is undergoing a lengthy restoration, you may notice that many of the ruins are lighter-colored than others, and scaffolding may block your view.) The black sphinx is the only one of Diocletian's collection of 13 that's still (mostly) intact.

• *Climb the stairs (above where you came in) into the domed, open-ceilinged...*

Entry Vestibule: Impressed? That's the idea. This was the grand entry to Diocletian's living quarters, meant to wow visitors. Emperors were believed to be gods. Diocletian called himself "Jovius"—the son of Jupiter, the most powerful of all gods. Four times a year (at the change of the seasons), Diocletian would stand here and overlook the Peristyle. His subjects would lie on the ground in worship, praising his name and kissing his scarlet robe.

Notice the four big niches at floor level, which once held statues of the four tetrarchs who ruled the unwieldy empire after Diocletian retired. The empty hole in the ceiling was once capped by a dome (long since collapsed), and the ceiling itself was covered with frescoes and mosaics.

In this grand space, you're likely to run into an all-male band of *klapa* singers, performing traditional a cappella harmonies. Just stand and enjoy a few glorious tunes—you'll rarely find a better group or acoustics. A 100-kn *klapa* CD is the perfect souvenir.

Wander out back to the harbor side through medieval buildings (some with seventh-century foundations), which evoke the way local villagers came in and took over the once-spacious and elegant palace. Back in this area, you'll find the beautifully restored home of the **Ethnographic Museum** (described later, under "Sights in Split").

• *Now go back into the Peristyle and turn right, climbing the steps to the...*

Cathedral of St. Dominus (Katedrala Sv. Duje)

The original octagonal structure was Diocletian's elaborate mausoleum, built in the fourth century. But after the fall of Rome,

it was converted into the town's cathedral. Construction of the bell tower began in the 13th century and took 300 years to complete. Before you go inside, notice the sarcophagi ringing the cathedral. In the late Middle Ages, this was prime post-mortem real estate, since being buried closer to a cathedral improved your chances of getting to heaven. On the 13th-century main doors, notice the 14 panels on each of the two wings—showing 28 scenes from the life of Christ.

Various parts of the cathedral are covered by separate tickets: 15 kn for the "treasury" (actually the fee to enter the cathedral), another 10 kn to climb the tower, and yet another 5 kn for the crypt below. All the sights are open similar hours, but can be closed unexpectedly for services (generally open daily in summer 7:00-19:00, often closed Sat afternoons for weddings and Sun mornings for Mass; in winter daily 7:00-12:00, maybe later on request; Kraj Sv. Duje 5, tel. 021/344-121).

Buy your treasury/cathedral ticket and step inside the oldest—and likely smallest—building used as a cathedral anywhere in Christendom. Imagine the place in pre-Christian times, with Diocletian's tomb in the center. The granite columns and the relief circling the base of the dome (about 50 feet up)—a ring of carvings heralding the greatness of the emperor—are the only surviving decor from those days. The small red-marble pillars around the top of the pulpit (near the entry) were scavenged from Diocletian's sarcophagus. These pillars are all that remain of Diocletian's remains.

Diocletian brutally persecuted his Christian subjects. Just before he moved to the Dalmatian Coast, he had Bishop Dominus of Salona killed, along with several thousand Christians. When Diocletian died, there were riots of happiness. In the seventh century, his mausoleum became a cathedral dedicated to the martyred bishop. The extension behind the altar was added in the ninth century. The sarcophagus of St. Dominus (to the right of the altar, with early-Christian carvings) was once the cathedral's high altar. To the left of today's main altar is the impressively detailed, Renaissance-era altar of St. Anastasius, who is lying on a millstone that is tied to his neck. On Diocletian's orders, this Christian martyr was drowned in A.D. 302. To the left of St. Anastasius' altar is the "new" altar of St. Dominus; his relics lie in the 18th-century Baroque silver reliquary, decorated with a relief showing him being beheaded. Posthumous poetic justice: Now Christian saints are entombed in Diocletian's mausoleum...and Diocletian is nowhere to be found.

For another 10 kn, you can climb 183 steep steps to the top of the 200-foot-tall **bell tower.** You'll be rewarded with sweeping views of Split, but it's not for claustrophobes or those scared of heights.

If you circle down and around the right side of the cathedral, you'll find the entrance to the **crypt** (separate 5-kn ticket). This musty, domed cellar (with eerie acoustics) was originally used to level the foundation of Diocletian's mausoleum. Later, Christians turned it into another chapel. The legend you'll likely hear about Diocletian torturing and murdering Christians in this very crypt, which began about the same time this became a church, is probably false.

Jupiter's Temple/St. John's Baptistery

Remember that Diocletian believed himself to be Jovius (that's Jupiter, Jr.). On exiting the mausoleum of Jovius, worshippers would look straight ahead to the temple of Jupiter. (Back then, all of these medieval buildings weren't cluttering up the view.) Make your way through the narrow alley (directly across from the cathedral entry), past another headless, pawless sphinx, to explore the small temple (5 kn, same hours as cathedral; if it's locked, go ask the guy at the cathedral to let you in).

About the time the mausoleum became a cathedral, this temple was converted into a baptistery. The big 12th-century baptismal font—large enough to immerse someone (as was the tradition in those days)—is decorated with the intricate, traditional *pleter* design also used around the border of Croatia's current passport stamp. On the font, notice the engraving: a bishop (on the left) and the king on his throne (on the right). At their feet (literally under the feet of the bishop) is a submissive commoner—neatly summing up the social structure

of the Middle Ages. Standing above the font is a statue of St. John the Baptist counting to four, done by the great Croatian sculptor Ivan Meštrović (see page 817). The half-barrel vaulted ceiling, completed later, is considered the best-preserved of its kind anywhere. Every face and each patterned box is different.

• *Back at the Peristyle, stand in front of the little chapel with your back to the entry vestibule. The little street just beyond the chapel (going left to right) connects the east and west gates. If you've had enough Roman history, head right (east) to go through the "Silver Gate" and find Split's busy, open-air Green Market. Or, head to the left (west), which takes you to the "Iron Gate" and People's Square (see "Sights in Split," later) and, beyond that, the fresh-and-smelly fish market. But if you want to see one last bit of Roman history, continue straight ahead up the...*

Cardo

A traditional Roman street plan has two roads: Cardo (the north-south axis) and Decumanus (the east-west axis). Split's Cardo street was the most important in Diocletian's Palace, connecting the main entry with the heart of the complex. As you walk, you'll pass several noteworthy sights: in the first building on the right, a bank with modern computer gear all around its exposed Roman ruins (look through window); at the first gate on the left, the courtyard of a Venetian merchant's palace (a reminder that Split was dominated by Venice from the 15th century on); on the right, an alley to the **City Museum** (described later, under "Sights in Split"); and, on the right, the **Nadalina** chocolate shop, a local artisan chocolatier selling mostly dark chocolate creations with some innovative Dalmatian flavors (30 kn/100 grams, 13-kn chocolate bars, Mon-Fri 9:00-21:00, Sat 9:00-12:00, closed Sun).

• *Before long, you'll pass through the...*

Golden Gate (Zlatna Vrata)

This great gate was the main entry of Diocletian's Palace. Its name wasn't literal—the "gold" instead suggests the importance of this gateway to Salona, the Roman provincial capital at the time. Standing inside the gate itself, you can appreciate the double-door design that kept the palace safe. Also notice how this ancient building is now being used in very different ways from its original purpose. Above, on the outer wall, you can see the bricked-in windows that contain part of a Dominican convent. At the top of the inner wall, notice somebody's garden terrace.

Go outside the gate, where you'll get a much clearer feel for the way the palace looked before so many other buildings were grafted on. Straight ahead from here is Salona (Solin), which was a major city of 60,000 (and Diocletian's hometown) before there was a Split. The big statue by Ivan Meštrović is **Bishop Gregory of Nin,** a 10th-century Croatian priest who tried to convince the Vatican to allow sermons during Mass to be said in Croatian, rather than Latin. People rub his toe for good luck (though only nonmaterial wishes are given serious consideration). The big building beyond the statue houses Split's new **Gallery of Fine Arts** (described later, under "Sights in Split").

• *Your tour is finished. Now enjoy the rest of Split.*

Sights in Split

In or near the Old Town

In addition to the palace, cellars, and cathedral described on my self-guided walk, you can also enjoy these attractions.

▲**People's Square (Narodni Trg)**—The lively square at the center of the Old Town is called by locals simply *Pjaca,* pronounced the same as the Italian *piazza* (PYAH-tsah). Stand in the center and

enjoy the bustle. Look around for a quick lesson in Dalmatian history. When Diocletian lived in his palace, a Roman village popped up here, just outside the wall. Face the former wall of Diocletian's Palace (behind and to the right of the 24-hour clock tower). This was the western entrance, or "Iron Gate." By the 14th century, a medieval town had developed, making this the main square of Split.

On the wall just to the right of the lane leading to the Peristyle, look for the life-size relief of **St. Anthony.** Notice the creepy "mini-me" clutching the saint's left leg—depicting the sculptor's donor, who didn't want his gift to be forgotten. Above this strange statue, notice the smaller, faded relief of a man and a woman arguing.

Turn around and face the square. On your left is the city's grand old café, **Gradska Kavana,** which has been the Old Town's venerable meeting point for generations. Today it's both a café and a restaurant with disappointing food but the best outdoor ambience in town (30-kn breakfasts, 50-75-kn pastas, 70-130-kn main courses, daily 7:00-24:00, Narodni trg 1, tel. 021/317-835).

Across the square, the white building jutting into the square was once the **City Hall** and now houses temporary exhibitions. The loggia is all that remains of the original Gothic building.

At the far end of the square is the out-of-place **Nakić House,** built in the early 20th-century Viennese Secession style—a reminder that Dalmatia was part of the Habsburg Empire, ruled by Vienna, from Napoleon's downfall through World War I.

The lane on the right side of the Nakić House leads to Split's **fish market** (Ribarnica), where you can see piles of the still-wriggling catch of the day. No flies? It's thanks to the sulfur spring in the nearby spa building (with the gray statues, on the corner). Just beyond the fish market is the pedestrian boulevard Marmontova.

Ethnographic Museum (Etnografski Muzej)—This museum uses well-presented temporary exhibits to show off the culture, costumes, furniture, tools, jewelry, weapons, and paintings of Dalmatia. It's all displayed in a gorgeously renovated early-medieval palace with a confusing tree-house floor plan. You'll find it in the upper level of the Old Town, behind Diocletian's entry vestibule. Check out the artsy "golden fleece" entry door. The ground floor sports the remains of a seventh-century church, and the exhibits usually include a good look at traditional folk dress. Your ticket also includes access to the roof of the vestibule (find the stairs at the far end of the museum); while it's not high enough to be thrilling, and you can't actually see down into the vestibule, it's a nice view over the rooftops of Split.

Cost and Hours: 10 kn, some English explanations; July-mid-Sept Mon-Fri 9:00-21:00, Sat 9:00-13:00, closed Sun; June Mon-Fri 9:00-14:00 & 17:00-20:00, Sat 9:00-13:00, closed Sun; mid-Sept-May Mon-Fri 9:00-14:00, Sat 9:00-13:00, closed Sun; Severova 7, tel. 021/344-164, www.etnografski-muzej -split.hr.

Split City Museum (Muzej Grada Splita)—This museum traces how the city grew over the centuries. It's a bit dull, but it can help you appreciate a little better the layers of history you're seeing in the streets. The ground floor displays Roman fragments (including coins from the days of Diocletian) and temporary exhibits. The upstairs focuses on the Middle Ages (find the terrace displaying carved stone monuments), and the top floor goes from the 16th century to the present (10 kn, some English descriptions, 75-kn guidebook is overkill; May-Sept Tue-Fri 9:00-21:00, Sat-Mon 9:00-16:00; Oct-April Tue-Fri 9:00-16:00, Sat-Sun 10:00-13:00, closed Mon; Papalićeva 1, tel. 021/360-171, www.mgst.net).

The 15th-century Papalić Palace, which houses the City Museum, is a sight all its own. At the end of the palace, near Cardo street, look up to see several typical Venetian-style Gothic-Renaissance windows. The stone posts sticking out of the wall next to them were used to hang curtains.

Radić Brothers Square (Trg Braće Radića)—Also known as Voćni Trg ("Fruit Square") for the produce that was once sold here, this little piazza is just off the Riva between the two halves of the Old Town. Overhead is a **Venetian citadel.** After Split became part of the Venetian Republic, there was a serious danger of attack by the Ottomans, so octagonal towers like this were built all along the coast. But this imposing tower had a second purpose: to encourage citizens of Split to forget about any plans of rebellion.

In the middle of the square is a studious sculpture by Ivan Meštrović of the 16th-century poet **Marko Marulić,** who is considered the father of the Croatian language. Marulić was the first to write literature in the Croatian vernacular, which before then had generally been considered a backward peasants' tongue.

On the downhill (harbor) side of the square is **Croata,** a necktie boutique that loves to explain how Croatian soldiers who fought with the French in the Thirty Years' War (1618-1648) had a distinctive way of tying their scarves. The French found it stylish, adopted it, and called it *à la Croate*—or eventually, *cravate*—thus creating the modern necktie that many people wear to work every day throughout the world. Croata's selection includes ties with traditional Croatian motifs, such as the checkerboard pattern from the flag or writing in the ninth-century Glagolitic alphabet. Though pricey, these ties make nice souvenirs (250-700 kn, Mon-Fri 8:00-20:30, Sat 8:00-13:00, closed Sun, shorter hours off-season). There's also a bigger, second location of this shop on the Peristyle.

Green Market—This lively open-air market bustles at the east end of Diocletian's Palace. Locals shop for produce and clothes here, and there are plenty of tourist souvenirs as well. Browse the wide selection of T-shirts, and ignore the creepy black-market tobacco salesmen who mutter at you: *"Cigaretta?"*

Split Gallery of Fine Arts (Galerija Umjetnina Split)—This collection, beautifully displayed in a finely restored old hospital just behind Diocletian's Palace, features mostly Croatian artwork from the 14th to the 21st centuries. It's basically a hodgepodge with few highlights—best reserved for art-lovers. Cross through the courtyard, climb up the stairs, and follow the one-way route through the chronologically displayed collection, which is heavy on the 20th century (20 kn, Tue-Sat 11:00-19:00, Sun 10:00-13:00, closed Mon, mod café, go straight out the Golden Gate and a bit to the left—behind the statue of Gregory of Nin—to Kralja Tomislava 15, tel. 021/350-110, www.galum.hr).

Archaeological Museum (Arheološki Muzej)—If you're intrigued by all the "big stuff" from Split's past (buildings and ruins), consider paying a visit to this collection of its "little stuff." A good exhibit of artifacts (mostly everyday domestic items) traces this region's history from its Illyrian beginnings chronologically through its notable Roman period (items from Split and Salona) to the Middle Ages. About a 10-minute walk north of the Old Town, it's worth the trip for archaeology fans (20 kn; June-Sept Mon-Sat 9:00-14:00 & 16:00-20:00, closed Sun; Oct-May Mon-Fri 9:00-14:00 & 16:00-20:00, Sat 9:00-14:00, closed Sun; Zrinsko Frankopanska 25, tel. 021/329-340, www.mdc.hr/split-arheoloski). Don't confuse this with the less-interesting Museum of Croatian Archaeological Monuments, on the way to the Ivan Meštrović Gallery.

Ivan Meštrović Sights, West of the Old Town

The excellent Meštrović Gallery and nearby Kaštelet Chapel just outside the Old Town can be reached by foot, bus, or taxi.

▲▲Meštrović Gallery (Galerija Meštrović)—Split's best art museum is dedicated to the sculptor Ivan Meštrović, the most important of all Croatian artists (see sidebar). Many of Meštrović's finest works are housed in this palace, designed by the sculptor himself to serve as his residence, studio, and exhibition space. If you have time, it's worth the 25-minute walk or short bus or taxi ride from the Old Town.

Cost and Hours: 30 kn, includes Kaštelet Chapel entry, free guide booklet, 80-kn guidebook is overkill for most visitors, pricey mobile-phone audioguides available; May-Sept Tue-Sun 9:00-19:00, closed Mon; Oct-April Tue-Sat 9:00-16:00, Sun 10:00-15:00, closed Mon; hours can be sporadic—call to confirm it's open before making the trip, Šetalište

Ivan Meštrović
(1883-1962)

Ivan Meštrović (EE-vahn MESH-troh-veech), who achieved international fame for his talents as a sculptor, was Croatia's answer to Rodin. You'll see Meštrović's works everywhere in the streets, squares, and museums of Croatia.

Meštrović came from humble beginnings. He grew up in a family of poor, nomadic farm workers just inland from Split. At an early age, his drawings and wooden carvings showed promise, and a rich family took him in and made sure he was properly trained. He eventually went off to school in Vienna, where he fell in with the Secession movement and found fame and fortune. He lived in Prague, Paris, and Switzerland, fully engaged in the flourishing European artistic culture at the turn of the 20th century (he counted Rodin among his friends). After World War I, Meštrović moved back to Croatia, and established an atelier (workshop) in Zagreb.

Later in life—like Diocletian before him—Meštrović returned to Split and built a huge seaside mansion (today's Meštrović Gallery). The years between the World Wars were Meštrović's happiest and most productive. It was during this time that he sculpted his most internationally famous works, a pair of giant Native American warriors on horseback in Chicago's Grant Park. But when World War II broke out, Meštrović—an outspoken supporter of the ideals of a united Yugoslavia—was briefly imprisoned by the anti-Yugoslav Ustaše (Croatia's Nazi puppet government). After his release, Meštrović fled to Italy, then the US, where he lectured at prominent universities such as Notre Dame and Syracuse. After the war, the Yugoslav dictator Tito invited Meštrović to return, but the very religious artist refused to cooperate with an atheist regime. (Meštrović was friends with the Archbishop Alojzije Stepinac, who was imprisoned by Tito.) Meštrović died in South Bend, Indiana.

Meštrović worked in wood, plaster, marble, and bronze, and dabbled in painting. His sculptures depict biblical, mythological, political, and everyday themes. Meštrović's figures typically have long, angular fingers, arms, and legs. Whether whimsical or emotional, Meštrović's expressive, elongated faces—often with a strong-profile nose—powerfully connect with the viewer.

Ivana Meštrovića 46, tel. 021/340-800, www.mdc.hr/mestrovic.

Getting There: To get to the gallery, you can take **bus** #12 from the little cul-de-sac at the west end of the Riva (departs hourly, get off at the stop in front of the gallery—just after your bus passes a museum prominently marked *Muzej Hrvatskih Arheoloških Spomenika*). Or you can **walk** about 25 minutes: Follow the harbor west of town toward the big marina, swing right with the road, and follow the park until you see the gallery on your right. A **taxi** from the west end of the Old Town to the gallery costs about 50 kn (much more from the east end of the Old Town).

◗ Self-Guided Tour: After buying your ticket (and asking about the time for your return bus to the Old Town), climb the stairs toward Meštrović's house, pausing in the **garden** to admire a smattering of sculptures (including several female nudes, Cyclops hurling a giant shot put, and an eagle).

Climbing another set of stairs, you reach the **Entrance Hall,** displaying sculptures mostly of Carrara marble, which was Michelangelo's favorite medium. Notice the black sculptures by the two staircases: on the left, representing birth, and on the right, representing death—Meštrović strove to capture the full range of human experience in his work.

Go to the left, and enter the **Dining Room** at the end of the main floor. It's decorated with portraits of Meštrović's wife, mother, and children. Meštrović often used his mother as a model for older women and his second wife Olga as a model for younger women. Also look for the self-portrait and two painted portraits of Meštrović (one as a young man, another shortly before his death). A painting of the *Last Supper* hangs in virtually every Dalmatian dining room. Meštrović's is no exception—he painted this version himself. At the end of the room are two giant caryatids carved from Dalmatian stone (embedded with fragments of seashells).

Now climb the stairs and go to the right, into the **Secession Room.** Some of these works—including the girl singing and the intimate portrait of a family—show the influence of Meštrović's contemporary, Rodin.

Pass through the room of drawings into the **Long Hall,** lined with life-size figures and a view terrace. The woman sitting with her knees apart and feet together is demonstrating a favorite pose of Meštrović's.

At the end of the hall is the **Study Room,** filled with miniature sculptures Meštrović created to prepare for larger-scale works. Notice the small study of *Job*, then go into the small side-room to see the much larger final version. One of Meštrović's most powerful works, *Job*—howling with an agony verging on insanity—was carved by the artist in exile, as his country was turned upside down by World War II. Meštrović sketched his inspiration for this piece (displayed on the wall) while he was imprisoned by the Ustaše.

Head down the stairs and turn left into the **Sacral Room.** Meštrović was very religious, and here you can see some of his

many works depicting biblical figures. The giant, wood-carved *Adam* and *Eve* dominate the room, but don't miss the smaller side-room, with another of the gallery's highlights: the quietly poignant *Roman Pietà*. Meštrović follows the classical pyramid form, with Joseph of Arimathea (top), Mary (left), and Mary Magdalene (right) surrounding the limp body of Christ. But the harmony is broken by the painful angles of the mourning faces. While this sculpture is plaster, Meštrović also completed a marble version for the campus of Notre Dame in the US.

▲**Kaštelet Chapel**—If you enjoy the gallery, don't miss the nearby Kaštelet Chapel ("Chapel of the Holy Cross"). Meštrović bought this 16th-century fortified palace to display his 28 wood reliefs of Jesus' life. Because he carved these over a nearly 30-year span (completing the last 12 when he was in the US), you can watch Meštrović's style change over time. (However, note that he didn't carve the reliefs in chronological order—ask for a booklet identifying the topic and year for each one.) While the earlier pieces are well-composed and powerful, the later ones seem more hastily done, as Meštrović rushed to complete his opus. Work clockwise around the room, tracing the life of Christ. Notice that some of the Passion scenes are out of order (a side-effect of Meštrović's nonlinear schedule). The beautiful *pietà* near the end still shows some of the original surface of the wood, demonstrating the skill required to create depth and emotion in just a few inches of medium. Dominating the chapel is an extremely powerful wooden crucifix, with Christ's arms, legs, fingers, and toes bent at unnatural angles—a typically expressionistic flair Meštrović used to exaggerate suffering.

Cost and Hours: The chapel is covered by the same 30-kn ticket as the gallery, and open the same hours.

Getting There: It's a five-minute walk past the gallery down Šetalište Ivana Meštrovića (on the left, in an olive grove).

Activities in Split

▲▲**Strolling the Riva (Obala Hrvatskog Narodnog Preporoda)**—The official name for this seaside pedestrian drag is the "Croatian National Revival Embankment," but locals just call it "Riva" (Italian for "harbor"). This is the town's promenade, an

SPLIT

integral part of Mediterranean culture. After dinner, Split residents collect their families and friends for a stroll on the Riva. It

offers some of the best people-watching in Croatia; make it a point to be here for an hour or two after dinner. At the west end of the Riva, the people-parade of Croatian culture turns right and heads away from the water, up Marmontova. The stinky smell that sometimes accompanies the stroll isn't from a sewer. It's sulfur—a reminder that the town's medicinal sulfur spas have attracted people here since the days of Diocletian.

The Riva recently underwent an extensive, costly, and controversial renovation. The old potholed pavement and scrubby gardens were torn up and replaced with a broad, sleek, carefully landscaped people zone. A clean, synchronized line of modern white lampposts and sun screens sashays down the promenade. But many locals miss the colorful quirks of the old version. For example, each café used to have its own tables and umbrellas; now they're forced to buy identical tables and chairs to make everything match. (In protest, some cafés have chosen to offer no outdoor seating at all.) Some locals think that the starkly modern strip is at odds with the rest of the higgledy-piggledy Old Town, while others see this as simply the early-21st century's contribution to the architectural hodgepodge that is Split.

Exploring Matejuška Fishermen's Port—While Split's harborfront Riva is where the beautiful people stroll, the city's fish-

ermen roots still thrive just to the west. The neighborhood called Matejuška—at the little harbor where the Varoš district hits the water (a five-minute walk beyond the end of the Riva, with the water on your left)—has long been Split's working fishermen's harbor. While the area has received a facelift to match the one along the Riva, it still retains its striped-collar character. You'll notice that the enclosed harbor area is filled with working fishing boats and colorful dinghies that bob in unison. Along the breakwater, notice the new fishermen's lockers, where people who earn their living from the Adriatic still keep their supplies. You'll see the most fisherman action here in the mornings.

The far side of the breakwater—all glitzy white marble—is

another world, with a pebbly beach, inviting plaza, and some of the best views looking back on the Riva. After its recent facelift, this jetty has become a popular open-air, after-hours hangout spot for local young people. Like Split itself, these two worlds—that of grizzled fishermen mending nets, and that of teenagers living it up—coexist more smoothly than anyone might have guessed.

Hiking the Marjan Peninsula—This huge, hilly, and relatively undeveloped spit of parkland is improbably located right next to Split's Old Town—it almost feels like a chunk of Dalmatian island wilderness, a stone's throw from the big city. With out-of-the-way beaches and miles of hiking trails, the Marjan (MAR-yahn) Peninsula is where Split goes to relax. Every local has their favorite hidden paths and beach coves on Marjan—ask around for tips.

From the Šperun neighborhood at the west end of the Old Town, you can hike as high (or as low) as you want; in fact, the best views are from the lowest viewpoint. If you're in great shape, figure about an hour hike up to the top viewpoint, then another 45 minutes back down.

No matter how high you want to go, start by climbing the stairs past the recommended Šperun restaurant, and continue straight up Senjska ulica. Following the stairs all the way up for about 10 to 15 steep minutes, you'll reach a spectacular view terrace (with sweeping views over Split's Old Town) next to a little café. If you like, you can continue higher; the views are good, but you can't really see the Old Town beyond here.

To keep ascending, curl around past the restaurant (following signs for *Crkva sv. Nikole* and *Sedlo*) and follow the steeply inclined pathway up, passing the fenced-in park on your right. Soon you'll reach the small chapel of St. Nicholas. Just behind it, look for the steps up and to the right, signed for *Marjanske Skale*. At the top of these stairs is Split's very humble zoo (10 kn for adults, 5 kn for kids, daily 8:00-18:00). From here, a broad path cuts through the woods, with smaller paths branching off downhill. For the highest viewpoint, follow signs for Sedlo and hike up the steps to the view terrace there. At top-of-the-world Sedlo, you enjoy 360-degree views of Split's urban sprawl, receding layers of jagged and majestic mountains, offshore islands, and the bay behind the Marjan Peninsula...but you can't see much of the Old Town.

It's easiest to go back down the way you came. But for a longer hike, you can continue down the stairs at the far end of the view terrace, and follow signs for *Crkva sv. Jere*. Ultimately this leads you along the length of the peninsula, mostly through trees (read: no views). Eventually you'll come to switchbacks that lead you back down to the main road running along the perimeter of Marjan; from here, you can turn left to get back to town, or right for an even longer walk around the far end of Marjan.

The peninsula also has a pair of good beaches (Ježinac and Bene) that are described next.

Hitting the Beach—Since it's more of a big city than a resort, Split's beaches aren't as scenic (and the waters not as clear) as those of small towns elsewhere along the coast. The beach that's most popular—and crowded—is **Bačvice,** in a sandy cove just a short walk east of the main ferry terminal. As it's very shallow, it's especially popular with kids. After dark, it becomes a hopping meat-market nightlife zone for older "kids." You'll find less crowded beaches just to the east of Bačvice.

Or head in the other direction to Marjan, the peninsular city park, which is ringed with several sunbathing beaches. Along the southern edge of Marjan, just below the Meštrović Gallery, is a rocky but more local-feeling and less crowded beach called **Ježinac** (Croatian for "sea urchin"...be sure to wear water shoes). **Bene Beach** is along the northern edge of Marjan—reachable on bus #12 (the same one that goes to the Meštrović Gallery), by bike, or by foot (about a 45-minute walk from the Old Town).

Near Split

Trogir—Of the many options near Split, the small town of Trogir is the most enticing (about a 30-minute drive away). This medieval-architecture-packed, made-for-tourists village is popular among yachters; the proud masts of tall ships line the harbor three deep. The main square is marked by the Cathedral of St. Lawrence, whose bell tower is a textbook lesson in Dalmatian architecture styles: straightforward Gothic at the bottom, Venetian Gothic in the middle, and Renaissance at the top. For me, Trogir is nothing to jump ship for, but it's an easy side-trip for those looking to get away from urban Split. (Note that Trogir is also easily reachable by public transport: At the bus station next to the cruise port, go to the ticket window and ask for the next bus to Trogir—25 kn, 2/hour, about a 30-minute trip; when returning, be sure to take a bus going to Split's main bus station near the cruise port, not the suburban bus station farther away.)

Eating in Split

Split's Old Town has oodles of atmosphere, but the street called Šperun, just a couple of blocks west of the Old Town, has several characteristic *konoba*s (traditional restaurants) with good prices (including my first two listings, below). Service in Split's restaurants tends to be a bit grouchy, and you may be unceremoniously turned away if they're very busy. All of these eateries are marked on the maps on pages 806 and 824.

Šperun Restaurant has a classy, cozy Old World ambience

and a passion for good Dalmatian food. Animated owner Zdravko Banović and his son Damir serve a mix of Croatian and "eclectic Mediterranean," specializing in seafood. A "buffet" table of *antipasti* (starters) in the lower dining room shows you what you're getting, so you can select your ideal meal (not self-service—order from the waiter). This place distinguishes itself by offering a warm welcome and good food for reasonable prices (35-70-kn pastas, 50-120-kn meat and seafood dishes, daily 9:00-23:00, air-con interior, a few sidewalk tables, reservations wise in summer, Šperun 3, tel. 021/346-999). Their annex across the street, **Bistrot Šperun Deva,** has a simpler and cheaper menu, and lots of outdoor seating (30-40-kn salads, 50-60-kn main courses, daily 8:00-23:00, Šperun 2).

Konoba Varoš, though bigger and more impersonal than Šperun, is beloved by natives and tourists alike for its great food. Serious waiters serve a wide range of Croatian cooking (including pastas, seafood, and meat dishes) under droopy fishnets in a slightly gloomy throwback interior (50-80-kn pastas, 60-110-kn main courses, daily 9:00-24:00, lots of groups, reservations smart—busiest 20:00-22:00, Ban Mladenova 7, tel. 021/396-138).

Black Cat Bistro, popular with expats, is an innovative eatery offering a range of eclectic flavors, including Tex-Mex, Indian, and Thai—and all are reasonably well-executed. The menu also features several hearty salads that go beyond the cabbage-and-lettuce rut. Choose between the inviting covered terrace out on a local-feeling lane, or the nondescript interior (45-65-kn salads and main courses, 30-35-kn sandwiches and wraps, Mon-Sat 8:00-23:00, closed Sun, corner of Petrova and Šegvića, tel. 021/490-284). It's about a five-minute walk beyond the Old Town: From the Green Market, walk up Kralja Zvonimira and take the first right down Petrova (just past the big, white building); you'll see the restaurant on your right just after the road curves to the left.

Konoba Matejuška offers charm, good food, and fair prices in a cozy, inviting, mellow, five-table cellar (30-55-kn starters, 50-150-kn main dishes, daily 7:30-9:30 & 13:00-16:00 & 19:00-23:00, below Villa Matejuška hotel at Tomića Stine 3, tel. 021/355-152).

Apetit is a new place serving up traditional, home-cooked Dalmatian cuisine in an appealingly modern, second-floor dining room. As there's no outdoor seating, this is a good option in bad weather (45-70-kn pastas, 60-110-kn main courses; 90-kn daily special in summer includes soup, salad, and main dish; daily 9:00-24:00, Šubićeva 5, tel. 021/332-549).

Marul Konoba offers traditional Dalmatian cuisine with delightful outdoor seating on a fine Old Town square, or in an atmospheric, oak-and-stone interior (45-65-kn pastas, 65-110-kn

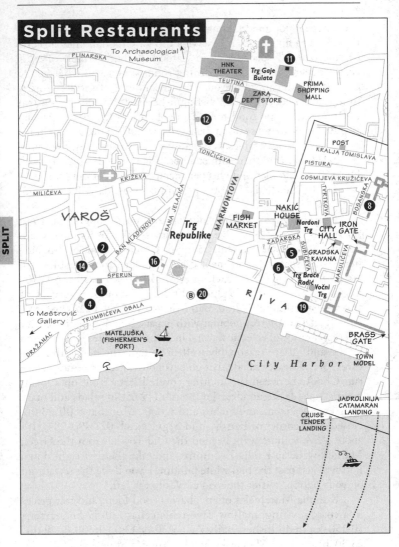

Split Restaurants

main courses, daily 8:00-24:00, Trg Braće Radića 2, tel. 021/ 339-068).

Maslina ("Olive"), an unpretentious family-run spot filled with locals, hides behind a shopping mall on the busy Marmontova pedestrian street. They serve a wide range of 40-70-kn pizzas and pastas, plus 65-110-kn meat and fish dishes (Tue-Sat 10:00-24:00, Sun-Mon 12:00-24:00, Teutina 1A, tel. 021/314-988, Pezo family). Approaching the top of Marmontova from the harbor, look for the low-profile wooden archway on the left beyond the café tables (just before the big Zara department store).

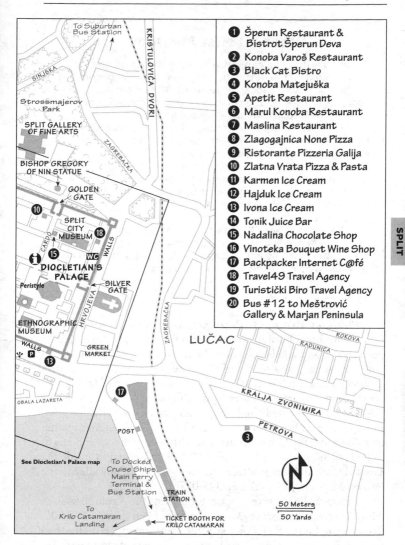

1. Šperun Restaurant & Bistrot Šperun Deva
2. Konoba Varoš Restaurant
3. Black Cat Bistro
4. Konoba Matejuška
5. Apetit Restaurant
6. Marul Konoba Restaurant
7. Maslina Restaurant
8. Zlagogajnica None Pizza
9. Ristorante Pizzeria Galija
10. Zlatna Vrata Pizza & Pasta
11. Karmen Ice Cream
12. Hajduk Ice Cream
13. Ivona Ice Cream
14. Tonik Juice Bar
15. Nadalina Chocolate Shop
16. Vinoteka Bouquet Wine Shop
17. Backpacker Internet C@fé
18. Travel49 Travel Agency
19. Turistički Biro Travel Agency
20. Bus #12 to Meštrović Gallery & Marjan Peninsula

SPLIT

Take-Away Pizza: **Zlagogajnica None** ("Grandma's") is a stand-up or take-away pizza joint handy for a quick bite in the Old Town. In addition to pizzas and bruschettas with various toppings, they serve up a pair of traditional pizza-like specialties (with crust on bottom and top, like a filled pizza): *viška pogača,* with tomatoes, onion, and anchovy; and *soparnik,* with a thin layer of spinach, onion, and olive oil. They can also make you a grilled sandwich—just point to what you want (10-30 kn, Mon-Sat 7:00-23:00, closed Sun, just outside Diocletian's Palace on the skinny street that runs along the wall at Bosanska 4, tel. 021/347-252).

What If I Miss My Boat?

Remember that you can get help from the cruise line's port agent (listed on the destination information sheet distributed on the ship) and the local TI (see page 802). If the port agent suggests a costly solution (such as a private car with a driver), you may want to instead consider public transit.

Your best option for getting to train-less **Dubrovnik** is by bus (almost hourly, less off-season, 4-5 hours, 105-155 kn). To reach **Venice,** you can take an overnight train (17 hours; departs Split after 21:00, arrives in Venice after 14:00, requires early-morning change in Zagreb and bus connection from Villach), or an overnight boat via Ancona, Italy (then train to Venice—almost hourly, 4.25-5.25 hours, most transfer in Bologna).

Reaching **Greece** is even trickier, as train and boat connections are overly long. Your best option is to consult a local **travel agent** (see listing on page 803). For additional advice on what to do if you miss the boat, see page 131.

Pizzerias: **Ristorante Pizzeria Galija,** at the west end of the Old Town, has a boisterous local following and good wood-fired pizza, pasta, and salads (35-50 kn, Mon-Sat 9:00-24:00, Sun 12:00-24:00, air-con, just a block off the pedestrian drag Marmontova at Tončićeva 12, tel. 021/347-932; the recommended Hajduk ice-cream shop is nearby). **Zlatna Vrata** ("Golden Gate"), right in the Old Town, offers wood-fired pizzas and pasta dishes. The food and interior are nothing special, but there's wonderful outdoor seating in a tingle-worthy Gothic courtyard with pointy arches and lots of pillars (40-60 kn, Mon-Sat 7:00-24:00, closed Sun, just inside the Golden Gate and—as you face outside—up the skinny alley to the left, on Majstora Jurja, tel. 021/345-015).

Gelato: Split has several spots for delicious ice cream *(sladoled).* Most ice-cream parlors *(kuća sladoleda)* are open daily 8:00-24:00. To my taste buds, the following three spots are much better than the other options in town. Locals swarm to a pair of places near Trg Gaje Bulata (the modern shopping square—with the big Prima mall and modern-looking church—at the top end of the Marmontova pedestrian drag, just beyond the northwest corner of the Old Town): **Karmen** (hides behind the building in the middle of the square, facing the modern church on Kačićeva) and **Hajduk** (named for Split's soccer team; ask them to dip your cone in milk chocolate for no extra charge; a block west from the top of Marmontova and around the corner from Pizzeria Galija at Matošićeva 4). More central, at the east end of the Riva, look for **Ivona** (near entrance to Diocletian's cellars at Kaštelanska cesta 65).

Smoothies and Fruit Juices: For a healthier energy boost, head for **Tonik Juice Bar,** run by Croat-Aussie Stefanie. You can select from the diverse smoothie menu (25-30 kn), or they'll custom-make a juice combo to your liking (15-40 kn). In summer, they also serve light meals (25-kn wraps and salads, 25-kn muesli for breakfast, June-Sept daily 7:00-23:00, shoulder season 8:00-21:00, less in winter, near the launderette and Šperun street restaurants at Ban Mladenova 5, mobile 098-641-376).

DUBROVNIK

Dubrovnik is a living fairy tale that shouldn't be missed. It feels like a small town today, but 500 years ago, Dubrovnik was a major maritime power, with the third-biggest navy in the Mediterranean. Still jutting confidently into the sea and ringed by thick medieval walls, Dubrovnik deserves its nickname: the Pearl of the Adriatic. Within the ramparts, the traffic-free Old Town is a fun jumble of quiet, cobbled back lanes; low-impact museums; narrow, steep alleys; and kid-friendly squares. After all these centuries, the buildings still hint at old-time wealth, and the central promenade (Stradun) remains the place to see and be seen. If I had to pick just one place to visit in Croatia, this would be it.

The city's charm is the sleepy result of its no-nonsense past. Busy merchants, the salt trade, and shipbuilding made Dubrovnik rich. But the city's most valued commodity was always its freedom—even today, you'll see the proud motto *Libertas* displayed all over town (see *"Libertas"* sidebar).

Dubrovnik flourished in the 15th and 16th centuries, but an earthquake destroyed nearly everything in 1667. Most of today's buildings in the Old Town are post-quake Baroque, although a few palaces, monasteries, and convents displaying a rich Gothic-Renaissance mix survive from Dubrovnik's earlier Golden Age.

Dubrovnik remained a big tourist draw through the Tito years, bringing in much-needed hard currency from Western visitors. Consequently, the city was never given the hard socialist patina of other Yugoslav cities (such as the nearby Montenegrin capital Podgorica, then known as "Titograd").

As Croatia violently separated from Yugoslavia in 1991, Dubrovnik became the only coastal city to be pulled into the fight-

Libertas

Libertas—liberty—has always been close to the heart of every Dubrovnik citizen. Dubrovnik was a proudly independent

republic for centuries, even as most of Croatia became Venetian and Hungarian. Dubrovnik believed so strongly in *libertas* that it was the first foreign state in 1776 to officially recognize an upstart, experimental republic called the United States of America.

In the Middle Ages, the city-state of Dubrovnik (then called Ragusa) bought its independence from whoever was strongest— Byzantium, Venice, Hungary, the Ottomans—sometimes paying off more than one at a time. Dubrovnik's ships flew whichever flags were necessary to stay free, earning the nickname "Town of Seven Flags." As time went on, Europe's big-league nations were glad to have a second major seafaring power in the Adriatic to balance the Venetian threat. A free Dubrovnik was more valuable than a pillaged, plundered Dubrovnik.

In 1808, Napoleon conquered the Adriatic and abolished the Republic of Dubrovnik. After Napoleon was defeated, the fate of the continent was decided at the Congress of Vienna. But Dubrovnik's delegate was denied a seat at the table. The more powerful nations, no longer concerned about Venice and fed up after years of being sweet-talked by Dubrovnik, were afraid that the delegate would play old alliances off each other to re-establish an independent Republic of Dubrovnik. Instead, the city became a part of the Habsburg Empire and entered a long period of decline.

Libertas still hasn't died in Dubrovnik. In the surreal days of the early 1990s, when Yugoslavia was reshuffling itself, a movement for the creation of a new Republic of Dubrovnik gained some momentum (led by a judge who, in earlier times, had convicted others for the same ideas). Another movement pushed for Dalmatia to secede as its own nation. But now that the dust has settled, today's locals are content and proud to be part of an independent Republic of Croatia.

ing (see "The Siege of Dubrovnik" sidebar). Imagine having your youthful memories of good times spent romping in the surrounding hills replaced by visions of tanks and warships shelling your hometown. The city was devastated, but Dubrovnik has been repaired with amazing speed. The only physical reminders of the war are lots of new, bright-orange roof tiles. Locals, relieved the fighting is over but forever hardened, are often willing to talk openly about

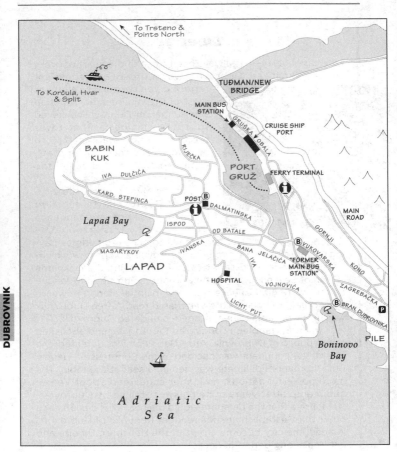

the experience with visitors—offering a rare opportunity to grasp the harsh realities of war from an eyewitness perspective.

Though the war killed tourism in the 1990s, today the crowds are most decidedly back. In fact, Dubrovnik's biggest downside is the overwhelming midday crush of multinational tourists who converge on the Old Town when their cruise ships dock. But locals—relieved that all these visitors are finally helping them get their economy back on track—appreciate that the numbers are about back to prewar levels. While Europeans and Australians have been flocking here for years, Americans have only just begun to rediscover Dubrovnik.

Planning Your Time

You have three good choices, which I'd suggest doing in this order:

• Walk around the **city walls** (allow about 1.5 hours). Upon

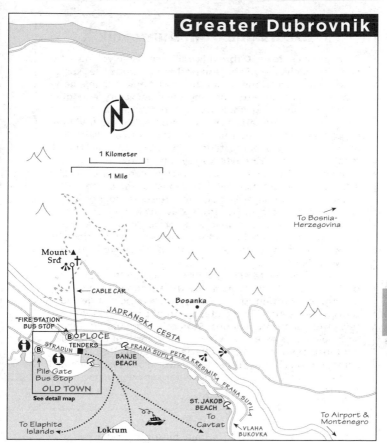

Greater Dubrovnik

N

1 Kilometer
1 Mile

To Bosnia-Herzegovina

Mount Srđ

CABLE CAR

Bosanka

JADRANSKA CESTA

"FIRE STATION" BUS STOP

PLOČE
TENDERS
STRADUN
FRANA SUPILA
BANJE BEACH
PETRA KREŠIMIRA FRANA SUPILA

Pile Gate Bus Stop
OLD TOWN
See detail map

ST. JAKOB BEACH
To Cavtat

To Elaphite Islands
Lokrum
VLAHA BUKOVKA

To Airport & Montenegro

DUBROVNIK

arrival, make a beeline to the walls before the crowds hit and it gets too hot. If there's already a long line, save the walls for later in the day, when the crowds subside (though afternoons can still be scorchingly hot).

• Follow my **self-guided walk** through the heart of town (allow about an hour). Dip into any **museums or churches** that appeal to you.

• In the afternoon, consider swimming or sunbathing at one of the **beaches** near the Old Town, or take a dip right below the city walls (see page 861).

Arrival in Dubrovnik

Arrival at a Glance: Cruise ships arriving in Dubrovnik either tender directly to the Old Port (right in the heart of the Old Town), or dock at Port Gruž (about two miles northwest of the

Excursions from Dubrovnik

Croatia's finest town, **Dubrovnik** will easily keep you busy for however much time you have in port. While cruise lines sometimes push excursions to nearby towns and villages, none of them comes close to matching the epic history, engaging sights, and fun-loving ambience of Dubrovnik itself.

Most cruise-line excursions hype a "Croatian village experience" where they shuttle passengers to a "rustic" (but made-for-tour-groups) restaurant in Dubrovnik's hinterland, most often in the **Konavle Valley** (about a half-hour drive south of the city). While these excursions can offer a glimpse into traditional Croatian lifestyles, most of the clichés you'll see here are kept on life-support for cruise-line tour groups.

Another typical offering is **Cavtat,** a bayfront resort town about a half-hour's drive south of Dubrovnik's Old Town. It's charming enough, but more convenient than exciting—its main appeal is its ability to handle the overflow from an overcrowded Dubrovnik.

A few more interesting sights line up on the road north of Dubrovnik: Plant-lovers enjoy the surprisingly engaging **Trsteno Arboretum,** punctuated by a classical-style fountain and aqueduct (30 minutes north of Dubrovnik). A small town with giant fortifications, **Ston** offers the opportunity to scramble up its extensive walls (1 hour north of Dubrovnik). And just beyond Ston, the **Pelješac Peninsula** produces some of Croatia's best-regarded wines. While this area could fill an enjoyable day, Dubrovnik is far superior to any of the alternatives.

Old Town—about a 10- to 15-minute bus or taxi ride).

Currency Reminder: Remember that Croatia officially uses its own currency, the kuna ($1 = about 5 kunas, abbreviated *kn*). Many merchants and sights here also accept euros, but many others do not—don't expect to be able to pay with euros everywhere. If you're riding the bus into town, be aware that drivers accept only kunas. Fortunately, there are ATMs and exchange desks at Port Gruž and throughout the Old Town. Consider getting a small amount of kunas for purchases and entry fees while you're in town.

Tendering to the Old Port

It couldn't be simpler: Tenders deposit cruise passengers at Dubrovnik's Old Port, which forms the "mouth" of the city's stoutly walled Old Town. Just walk straight ahead up the small pier and through the hole in the wall, then bear left, and you'll find

Services at (and near) Port Gruž

Several of these services are actually near the Jadrolinija office, a 5- to 10-minute walk from the cruise terminals. If you can wait to get to Dubrovnik, you'll find all the services you need there.

ATMs: A cash machine is in front of the Jadrolinija office. (You'll need the local currency, kunas, if you want to take the public bus into town.)

Internet Access: You can get online inside the Port Authority building, as well as in the Jadrolinija office building. For alternatives in the Old Town, see "Helpful Hints" on page 835.

Pharmacy: You'll find one across the street from the port terminal, next to the Dominican Monastery of the Holy Cross.

yourself right on Dubrovnik's main drag, the Stradun. Because the tenders put you right in the heart of town, this is a place where tendering might actually be better than docking—provided that you get your tender ticket as early as possible, and make it off the boat on one of the first tenders.

DUBROVNIK

Docking at Port Gruž

Port Gruž is a long harbor that sits on the other side of a ridge from the Old Town. Depending on where along the harbor your ship docks, you'll exit through one of two terminal buildings—either the larger Port Authority building, or at a smaller terminal a bit farther from town. Also along this harborfront are the docks for various passenger boats and car ferries to other points in Croatia. Services cluster near the office of the national ferry company, Jadrolinija, which is a 5- to 10-minute walk toward town from the cruise terminals (walk along the main portside road, Gruška obala, with the water on your right).

Tourist Information: A TI is across the street from the Jadrolinija ferry dock (July-mid-Sept daily 8:00-20:00; mid-Sept-Oct Mon-Fri 8:00-19:00, Sat-Sun 9:00-14:00; Nov-March Mon-Fri 9:00-18:00, Sat 9:00-14:00, closed Sun; April-May Mon-Fri 8:00-19:00, Sat 9:00-14:00, closed Sun; June Mon-Fri 8:00-20:00, Sat-Sun 9:00-14:00; Gruška obala, tel. 020/417-983).

Getting into Town

Your goal is to get from the cruise terminal to the Pile Gate (pronounced PEE-leh), which marks the western end of the Old Town (and is the starting point for my self-guided walk).

By Taxi

Taxis wait at the cruise terminal, charging about 80 kn or €10 for the ride to the Pile Gate. To hire a driver for a full day of sightseeing in the area, consider the options listed on page 840.

By Public Transportation

On the road in front of each cruise terminal, you'll find a city bus stop, where you can hop on a bus (#1, #1a, #1b, or #1c) to the Pile stop (8 kn if you buy ticket beforehand at a kiosk—ask for *autobusna karta,* ow-toh-BOOS-nah KAR-tah; or 10 kn if you buy one from the bus driver). Get out at Pile, the end of the line. For more details about Dubrovnik's public buses, see page 839.

Tour Options in Dubrovnik

For information on walking tours and local guides for hire, see "Tours in Dubrovnik" on page 839. Dubrovnik can also be a good place to hire a local driver to visit the surrounding area; I've listed some favorites on page 840.

Returning to Your Ship

If returning to Port Gruž, head back via the transportation hub just outside the Old Town's Pile Gate. Here you can hire a taxi to take you back to your ship, or you can ride bus #1, #1a, #1b, or #1c (the bus departs just across the little square from where it arrives; this stop is both the beginning and end of the line). If you miss the boat, see the sidebar at the end of this chapter.

Orientation to Dubrovnik

(area code: 020)

Nearly all of the sights worth seeing are in Dubrovnik's traffic-free, walled **Old Town** (Stari Grad) peninsula. The main pedestrian promenade through the middle of town is called the **Stradun;** from this artery, the Old Town climbs steeply uphill in both directions to the walls. The Old Town connects to the mainland through three gates: the **Pile Gate,** to the west; the **Ploče Gate,** to the east; and the smaller **Buža Gate,** at the top of the stepped lane called Boškovićeva. The **Old Port** (Gradska Luka), with leisure boats to nearby destinations, is at the east end of town. While greater Dubrovnik has about 50,000 people, the local population within the Old Town is just a few thousand in the winter—and even smaller in summer, when many residents move out to rent their apartments to tourists.

The **Pile** (PEE-leh) neighborhood, a pincushion of tourist services, is just outside the western end of the Old Town (through the Pile Gate). In front of the gate, you'll find a TI and Internet café (sharing an office), ATMs, a post office, taxis, buses (fanning out to all the outlying neighborhoods), a cheap Konzum grocery store, and the Atlas Travel Agency (described later, under "Helpful Hints"). This is also the starting point for my self-guided walk.

Tourist Information

Dubrovnik's TI has several branches (www.tzdubrovnik.hr), with hours that tend to fluctuate depending on demand. Plans to consolidate smaller TIs into one larger office just outside the Pile Gate (near the main bus stop) might lead to the closure of some of these branches. Until then, you'll find TIs at the following locations (though only the Old Town and Port Gruž TIs are likely to stay open through the winter):

• In the **Old Town,** a few steps off the main drag at Široka 1 (July-mid-Sept daily 8:00-22:00; mid-Sept-Oct Mon-Fri 8:00-19:00, Sat-Sun 9:00-14:00; Nov-March Mon-Sat 9:00-19:00, Sun 9:00-14:00; April-June Mon-Sat 9:00-21:00, Sun 9:00-14:00; tel. 020/323-587).

• In the **Pile** neighborhood just outside the Old Town, 100 yards up the street from the Pile Gate (July-mid-Sept daily 8:00-21:00; June and mid-Sept-Oct Mon-Fri 8:00-19:00, Sat 9:00-14:00, closed Sun; April-May Mon-Fri 8:00-15:00, Sat 9:00-14:00, closed Sun; likely closed Nov-March; Branitelja Dubrovnika 7, tel. 020/427-591; Internet access in the same office).

• At **Port Gruž,** across the street from the Jadrolinija ferry dock (see details on page 833).

All the TIs are government-run and legally can't sell you anything except an unhelpful "Dubrovnik Card"—but they can answer questions and give you a copy of the free town map and monthly information booklet *The Best in Dubrovnik Riviera,* which contains helpful maps, bus and ferry schedules, museum prices and hours, a current schedule of events and performances, specifics on side-trip destinations, and more.

Helpful Hints

Festivals: Dubrovnik is most crowded during its Summer Festival, a month and a half of theater and musical performances held annually from July 10 to August 25 (www.dubrovnik-festival .hr). This is quickly followed by the "Rachlin & Friends" classical music festival in September (www.julianrachlin.com).

Crowd-Beating Tips: Dubrovnik has been discovered—especially by cruise ships (800 of which visit each year). Cruise-ship crowds descend on the Old Town on most summer days, roughly between 8:30 and 14:00 (the streets are most crowded 9:00-13:00). In summer, try to avoid the big sights—especially

Dubrovnik at a Glance

▲▲▲**Stradun Stroll** Charming walk through Dubrovnik's vibrant Old Town, ideal for coffee, ice cream, and people-watching. **Hours:** Always open. See page 840.

▲▲▲**Town Walls** Scenic mile-long walk along top of 15th-century fortifications encircling the city. **Hours:** July-Aug daily 8:00-19:30, progressively shorter hours off-season until 10:00-15:00 in mid-Nov-mid-March. See page 847.

▲**Franciscan Monastery Museum** Tranquil cloister, medieval pharmacy-turned-museum, and a century-old pharmacy still serving residents today. **Hours:** Daily April-Oct 9:00-18:00, Nov-March 9:00-17:00. See page 851.

▲**Cathedral** Eighteenth-century Roman Baroque cathedral and treasury filled with unusual relics such as a swatch of Jesus' swaddling clothes. **Hours:** Church—daily 8:00-20:00, treasury—generally open same hours as church, both have shorter hours off-season. See page 852.

▲**Dominican Monastery Museum** Another relaxing cloister with precious paintings, altarpieces, and manuscripts. **Hours:** Daily May-Sept 9:00-18:00, Oct-April 9:00-17:00. See page 853.

▲**Synagogue Museum** Europe's second-oldest synagogue and Croatia's only Jewish museum, with 13th-century Torahs and Holocaust-era artifacts. **Hours:** May-mid-Nov daily 10:00-20:00; mid-Nov-April Mon-Fri 10:00-13:00, closed Sat-Sun. See page 855.

▲**Institute for the Restoration of Dubrovnik Photos** and videos of the recent war and an exhibit on restoration work. **Hours:** June-Sept Mon-Fri 10:00-14:00, closed Sat-Sun; rotating exhibits Oct-May. See page 856.

walking around the wall—during these peak times, and hit the beach or take a siesta midday, when the town is hottest and most crowded.

Wine Shops: D'vino Wine Bar, just a few steps off the main drag, is the handiest place in Dalmatia to taste and learn about Croatian wines. Run by Brit Rob and Aussie/Croat Sasha, this cozy bar (with a few outdoor tables) sells more than 75 wines by the glass and lots more by the bottle. The emphasis is on Croatian wines, but they also have vintages from Italy, France, Spain, the US, Australia, and South America. Each

▲**Serbian Orthodox Church and Icon Museum** Active church serving Dubrovnik's Serbian Orthodox community and museum with traditional religious icons. **Hours:** Church—daily May-Sept 8:00-20:00, Oct-April 8:00-15:00, short services daily at 8:30 and 19:00, longer liturgy Sun at 9:00; museum—May-Oct Mon-Sat 9:00-14:00, closed Sun; Nov-April Mon-Fri 9:00-14:00, closed Sat-Sun. See page 856.

▲**Rupe Granary and Ethnographic Museum** Good folk museum with tools, jewelry, clothing, and painted eggs above immense underground grain stores. **Hours:** Wed-Mon 9:00-16:00, closed Tue. See page 858.

▲**Mount Srđ** Napoleonic fortress capping the mountain above Dubrovnik, now hosting a modest museum to the recent war. **Hours:** Mountaintop—always open; museum—daily 10:00-18:30, maybe until 20:00 in summer. See page 859.

Rector's Palace Sparse antiques collection in the former home of rectors who ruled Dubrovnik in the Middle Ages. **Hours:** Daily May-Oct 9:00-18:00, Nov-April 9:00-16:00. See page 851.

Maritime Museum Contracts, maps, paintings, and models from Dubrovnik's days as a maritime power and shipbuilding center. **Hours:** Vary with demand, usually March-Oct Tue-Sun 9:00-18:00, closed Mon, shorter hours Nov-Feb. See page 855.

Aquarium Tanks of local sea life housed in huge, shady old fort. **Hours:** Daily July-Aug 9:00-21:00, progressively shorter hours off-season until 9:00-13:00 Nov-March. See page 855.

War Photo Limited Thought-provoking photographic look at contemporary warfare. **Hours:** June-Sept daily 9:00-21:00; May and Oct Tue-Sat 9:00-15:00, Sun 10:00-14:00, closed Mon; closed Nov-April. See page 856.

DUBROVNIK

wine is well-described on the menu, and the staff is happy to guide you through your options—just tell them what you like (18-80-kn glasses—most around 25-35 kn, 50-kn wine flights, daily June-Sept 12:00-24:00, Oct-May 17:00-24:00, Palmotićeva 4a, tel. 020/321-130). **Vinoteka Miličić** offers a nice variety of local wines and helpful advice for choosing one—though they do tend to push their own wines (daily 9:00-23:00 in peak season, shorter hours off-season, near the Pile end of the Stradun, tel. 020/321-777).

Internet Access: You'll see signs all over town for Internet cafés with similar rates (around 5 kn/10 minutes). In the Old Town, my favorite is the modern **Netcafé,** with several speedy terminals right on Prijeko street, the "restaurant row" (daily 9:00-24:00, Prijeko 21, tel. 020/321-025). In the Pile neighborhood, I use the **Dubrovnik Internet Centar** inside the Pile TI (May-Sept daily 8:00-24:00; Oct-April Mon-Sat 8:00-21:00, closed Sun; Branitelja Dubrovnika 7). The city has plans to provide free Wi-Fi throughout the Old Town—it might be worth giving this a shot (ask at a TI). Otherwise, Dubrovnik Internet Centar sells vouchers to get online at hotspots around the Old Town (including the Stradun and Old Port; 50 kn/1 day).

English Bookstore: The **Algoritam** shop, right on the Stradun, has a wide variety of guidebooks (including this one), nonfiction books about Croatia and the former Yugoslavia, novels, and magazines—all in English (July-Aug Mon-Sat 9:00-23:00, Sun 10:00-13:00 & 18:00-22:00; June and Sept Mon-Sat 9:00-21:00, Sun 10:00-13:00; Oct-May Mon-Fri 9:00-20:30, Sat 9:00-15:00, Sun 9:00-13:00; Placa 8).

Car Rental: The big international chains, such as **Avis** (tel. 020/313-633), have offices near the Port Gruž embankment where the big boats come in. In addition, the many travel agencies closer to the Old Town also have a line on rental cars. Figure €50-60 per day, including taxes, insurance, and unlimited mileage (at the bigger chains, there's usually no extra charge for drop-off elsewhere in Croatia). Be sure the agency knows if you're crossing a border (such as Bosnia-Herzegovina or Montenegro) to ensure you have the proper paperwork.

Travel Agency: The most established company is **Atlas,** with an office just outside the Pile Gate from the Old Town—though the location might change (June-Sept Mon-Sat 8:00-21:00, Sun 8:00-13:00; Oct-May Mon-Fri 8:00-20:00, Sat 8:00-15:00, closed Sun; down the little alley at Sv. Đurđa 4, otherwise look for signs to new location around the bus-stop area, tel. 020/442-574, fax 020/323-609, www.atlas-croatia.com, atlas.pile@atlas.hr). They also have an office at the ferry terminal building at Port Gruž (May-Sept only).

Best Views: Walking the **Old Town walls** late in the day, when the city is bathed in rich light, is a treat. The **Fort of St. Lawrence,** perched above the Pile neighborhood cove, has great views over the Old Town. A stroll up the road east of the city walls offers nice views back on the Old Town (best light early in the day).

Better yet, if you have a car, head south of the city in the morning for gorgeously lit Old Town views over your right shoulder; various turn-offs along this road are ideal photo stops. The best one, known locally as the **"panorama point,"** is where the road leading up and out of Dubrovnik meets the main road that passes above the town (look for the pull-out on the right, with tour buses). Even if you're heading north, in good weather it's worth a quick detour south for this view. For the highest vantage point without wings, head up to the fortress atop **Mount Srđ,** directly above the Old Town, which also houses a museum about the recent war (described later, under "Sights in Dubrovnik").

Getting Around Dubrovnik

If you're staying in or near the Old Town, everything is easily walkable.

By Bus: Libertas runs Dubrovnik's public buses. Tickets, which are good for an hour, are cheaper if you buy them in advance from a newsstand (8 kn, ask for *autobusna karta*, ow-toh-BOOS-nah KAR-tah) than if you buy them from the bus driver (10 kn). A 24-hour ticket costs 25 kn, and a ticket for 20 rides costs 120 kn (only sold at special bus-ticket kiosks, such as the one near the Pile Gate bus stop).

When you enter the bus, validate your ticket in the machine next to the driver (orange arrow in, white side up). Because most tourists can't figure out how to validate their tickets, it can take a long time to load the bus (which means drivers are understandably grumpy, and locals aren't shy about cutting in line).

All buses stop near the Old Town, just in front of the Pile Gate (buy tickets at the newsstand or bus-ticket kiosk right by the stop). You'll find bus schedules and a map in the TI booklet (for more information, visit www.libertasdubrovnik.hr).

By Taxi: Taxis start at 25 kn, then charge 8 kn per kilometer. The handiest taxi stand for the Old Town is just outside the Pile Gate. The biggest operation is Radio Taxi (tel. 020/970).

Tours in Dubrovnik

Walking Tours—Two companies—**Dubrovnik Walking Tours** and **Dubrovnik Walks**—offer similar one-hour walking tours of the Old Town daily at 10:00, and sometimes again in the afternoon (90 kn, also other departures and topics, most tours begin near the Pile Gate; look for fliers at TI or see www.dubrovnik -walking-tours.com or www.dubrovnikwalks.com). These tours are pricey and brief, touching lightly on the same basic information explained in this chapter.

Local Guide—For an in-depth look at the city, consider hiring your own local guide. **Štefica Curić** really knows her stuff and can give you an insider's look at the city (480 kn/2 hours, mobile

091-345-0133, dugacarapa@yahoo.com). If Štefica is busy, she can refer you to another good guide for the same price. The TI can also suggest guides.

Bus-plus-Walking Tours—Two big companies (**Atlas** and **Elite**) offer expensive tours of Dubrovnik (about 220 kn, 2 hours).

From Dubrovnik

Hire Your Own Driver—I enjoy renting my own car to see the sights around Dubrovnik (see "Helpful Hints," earlier). But if you're more comfortable having someone else do the driving, consider hiring a driver. While the drivers listed here are not official tour guides, they speak great English and offer ample commentary as you roll, and can help you craft a good day-long itinerary to Mostar, Montenegro, Korčula, or anywhere else near Dubrovnik (typically departing around 8:00 and returning in the early evening). Friendly **Pepo Klaić,** a veteran of the 1991 war, enjoys surprising my readers with worthwhile detours—go along with his suggestions (€250/day, €125 for half-day trip to nearer destinations, airport transfer for about 200 kn—cheaper than a taxi, these prices for up to 4 people—more expensive for bigger group, mobile 098-427-301, http://pepoklaic.pondi.hr, pepoklaic@yahoo.com). For €70, Pepo can drive you to the fortress at Mount Srđ up above the Old Town, with sweeping views of the entire area (about 1-1.5 hours round-trip). **Petar Vlašić** can do similar tours for similar prices, and specializes in wine tours to the Pelješac Peninsula, with stops at various wineries along the way (220-kn airport transfers, mobile 091-580-8721, www.dubrovnikrivieratours.com, meritum @du.t-com.hr). **Pero Carević** also drives travelers on excursions (similar prices, mobile 098-765-634, villa.ragusa@du.t-com.hr).

Self-Guided Walk in Dubrovnik

Running through the heart of Dubrovnik's Old Town is the 300-yard-long Stradun promenade—packed with people and lined with sights. This walk offers an ideal introduction to Dubrovnik's charms. It takes about a half-hour, not counting sightseeing stops.

• *Begin at the busy square in front of the west entrance to the Old Town, the Pile Gate.*

Pile Neighborhood

This bustling area is the nerve center of Dubrovnik's tourist industry—it's where the real world meets the fantasy of Dubrovnik. Near the modern, mirrors-and-TV-screens monument is a leafy café terrace. Wander over to the edge of the terrace and take in the imposing walls of the Pearl of the Adriatic. The huge, fortified peninsula just outside the city walls is the **Fort of St. Lawrence**

(Tvrđava Lovrijenac), Dubrovnik's oldest fortress and one of the top venues for the Dubrovnik Summer Festival. Shakespearean plays are often performed here, occasionally starring Goran Višnjić, the Croatian actor who became an American star on the TV show *ER*. You can climb this fortress for great views over the Old Town (20 kn, or covered by same ticket as Old Town walls on the same day).

• *Cross over the moat (now a shady park) to the round entrance tower in the Old Town Wall. This is the...*

Pile Gate (Gradska Vrata Pile)

Just before you enter the gate, notice the image above the entrance of **St. Blaise** (Sveti Vlaho in Croatian) cradling Dubrovnik in his

arm. You'll see a lot more of Blaise during your time here—we'll find out why later on this walk.

Inside the outer wall of the Pile Gate and to the left, a white **sign** shows where each bomb dropped on the Old Town in the recent war. Once inside town, you'll see virtually no signs of the war—demonstrating the townspeople's impressive resilience in rebuilding so well and so quickly.

Passing the rest of the way through the gate, you'll find a lively little square surrounded by landmarks. To the left, a steep stairway leads up to the imposing **Minčeta Tower.** This is a good starting point for Dubrovnik's best activity, walking around the top of the wall (described later, under "Sights in Dubrovnik").

Next to the stairway is the small **Church of St. Savior** (Crkva Svetog Spasa). Appreciative locals built this votive church to thank God after Dubrovnik made it through a 1520 earthquake. When the massive 1667 quake destroyed the city, this church was one of the only buildings left intact. And during the recent war, the church survived another close call when a shell exploded on the ground right in front of it (you can still see faint pockmarks from the shrapnel).

The giant, round structure in the middle of the square is **Onofrio's Big Fountain** (Velika Onofrijea Fontana). In the Middle Ages, Dubrovnik had a complicated aqueduct system that brought water from the mountains seven miles away. The water

DUBROVNIK

Dubrovnik's Old Town

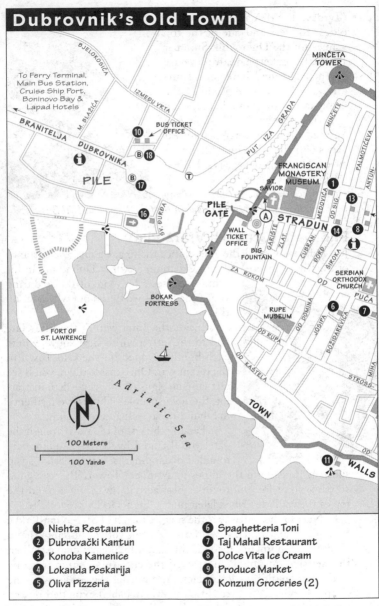

To Ferry Terminal,
Main Bus Station,
Cruise Ship Port,
Boninovo Bay &
Lapad Hotels

BJELOKOSIĆA

IZMEĐU VRTA

BRANITELJA

DUBROVNIKA

M. BLAŽIĆA

PILE

PUT IZA GRADA

MINČETA
TOWER

MINČETE

PALMOTIĆEVA

ANTUN-

BUS TICKET
OFFICE

FRANCISCAN
MONASTERY
MUSEUM

ST.
SAVIOR

PILE
GATE

WALL
TICKET
OFFICE

BIG
FOUNTAIN

STRADUN

MEDOVIĆA

OD SIG.

ČUBRAN.

ĐORĐ.

ŠIROKA

GARIŠTE

ZLAT.

ZA ROKOM

OD

SERBIAN
ORTHODOX
CHURCH

PUČA

SV. ĐURĐA

BOKAR
FORTRESS

FORT OF
ST. LAWRENCE

Adriatic Sea

100 Meters

100 Yards

N

RUPE
MUSEUM

OD DOMINA

OD RUPA

JOSIPA

BOŽIDAREVIĆA

OD KAŠTELA

TOWN

MIHA

STROSS-

OD

WALLS

DUBROVNIK

❶ Nishta Restaurant	❻	Spaghetteria Toni
❷ Dubrovački Kantun	❼	Taj Mahal Restaurant
❸ Konoba Kamenice	❽	Dolce Vita Ice Cream
❹ Lokanda Peskarija	❾	Produce Market
❺ Oliva Pizzeria	❿	Konzum Groceries (2)

Dubrovnik

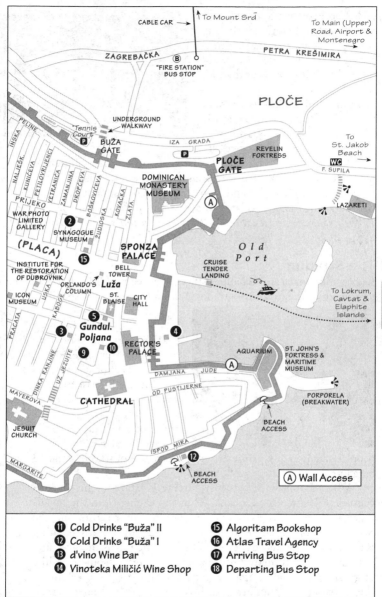

CABLE CAR → To Mount Srđ

To Main (Upper) Road, Airport & Montenegro

ZAGREBAČKA

PETRA KREŠIMIRA

(B) "FIRE STATION" BUS STOP

PLOČE

UNDERGROUND WALKWAY

"Tennis Court"

IZA GRADA

BUŽA GATE

REVELIN FORTRESS

To St. Jakob Beach →

PLOČE GATE

WC

F. SUPILA

DOMINICAN MONASTERY MUSEUM

LAZARETI

(A)

WAR PHOTO LIMITED GALLERY

PELINE

INSKA

NALJEŠK.

KUNIČEVA

PETILOVRIJENCI

VETRANIĆA

ZAMANJINA

DROPCEVA

BOŠKOVICEVA

ZLATA

KOVAČKA

ŽUDIOSKA

PRIJEKO

2 SYNAGOGUE MUSEUM

SPONZA PALACE

O l d   P o r t

(PLACA)

15

CRUISE TENDER LANDING

INSTITUTE FOR THE RESTORATION OF DUBROVNIK

BELL TOWER

Luža

ORLANDO'S COLUMN

ST. BLAISE

CITY HALL

ICON MUSEUM

USKA

KABOGE

5

Gundul. Poljana

4

To Lokrum, Cavtat & Elaphite Islands

PRACATA

3

10

RECTOR'S PALACE

AQUARIUM

ST. JOHN'S FORTRESS & MARITIME MUSEUM

(A)

DINKA RANJINE

IZ JEZUITE

9

DAMJANA   JUDE

MAYEROVA

PORPORELA (BREAKWATER)

OD PUSTIJERNE

CATHEDRAL

BEACH ACCESS

JESUIT CHURCH

MARGARITE

ISPOD MIRA

12

BEACH ACCESS

BEACH ACCESS

(A) Wall Access

DUBROVNIK

11 Cold Drinks "Buža" II
12 Cold Drinks "Buža" I
13 d'vino Wine Bar
14 Vinoteka Miličić Wine Shop
15 Algoritam Bookshop
16 Atlas Travel Agency
17 Arriving Bus Stop
18 Departing Bus Stop

ended up here, at the town's biggest fountain, before continuing
through the city. This plentiful
supply of water, large reserves of
salt (a key source of Dubrovnik's
wealth, from the nearby town
of Ston), and a massive granary
(now the Rupe Ethnographic
Museum) made little, independent Dubrovnik very siege-resistant.

The big building on the left just beyond the small Church of
St. Savior is the **Franciscan Monastery Museum.** This building,
with a delightful cloister and one of Europe's oldest pharmacies, is
worth touring (described later, under "Sights in Dubrovnik").
• *When you're finished taking in the sights on this square, continue
along...*

The Stradun

Dubrovnik's main promenade—officially called the Placa, but better known as the Stradun—is alive with locals and tourists alike.

This is the heartbeat of the
city: an Old World shopping
mall by day and sprawling
cocktail party after dark,
when everybody seems to
be doing the traditional
evening stroll—flirting,
ice-cream-licking, flaunt-
ing, and gawking. A coffee
and some of Europe's best
people-watching in a prime Stradun café is one of travel's great $3
bargains.

When Dubrovnik was just getting its start in the seventh
century, this street was a canal. Romans fleeing from the invading Slavs lived on the island of Ragusa (on your right), and the
Slavs settled on the shore. In the 11th century, the canal separating
Ragusa from the mainland was filled in, the towns merged, and
a unique Slavic-Roman culture and language blossomed. While
originally much more higgledy-piggledy, this street was rebuilt in
the current, more straightforward style after the 1667 earthquake.

During your time in Dubrovnik, you'll periodically hear
the rat-a-tat-tat of a drum echoing through the streets from the
Stradun. This means it's time to head for this main drag to get
a glimpse of the colorfully costumed "town guards" parading
through (and a cavalcade of tourists running alongside them, trying to snap a clear picture). You may also see some of these charac-

ters standing guard outside the town gates. It's all part of the local tourist board's efforts to make their town even more atmospheric.

• *Branching off from this promenade are several museums and other attractions—all described later, under "Sights in Dubrovnik." At the end of the Stradun is a passageway leading to the Ploče Gate. Just before this passage is the lively Luža Square. Its centerpiece is...*

Orlando's Column (Orlandov Stup)

Columns like this were typical of towns in northern Germany. Dubrovnik erected the column in 1417, soon after it had shifted allegiances from the oppressive Venetians to the Hungarians. By putting a northern European symbol in the middle of its most prominent square, Dubrovnik decisively distanced itself from Venice. Whenever a decision was made by the Republic, the town crier came to Orlando's Column and announced the news. The step he stood on indicated the importance of his message—the higher up, the more important the news. It was also used as the pillory, where people were publicly punished. The thin line on the top step in front of Orlando is exactly as long as the statue's forearm. This mark was Dubrovnik's standard measurement—not for a foot, but for an "elbow."

• *Now stand in front of Orlando's Column and orient yourself with a...*

Luža Square Spin-Tour

Orlando is looking toward the **Sponza Palace** (Sponza-Povijesni Arhiv). This building, from 1522, is the finest surviving example

of Dubrovnik's Golden Age in the 15th and 16th centuries. It's a combination of Renaissance (ground-floor arches) and Venetian Gothic (upstairs windows). Houses up and down the main promenade used to look like this, but after the 1667 earthquake, they were replaced with boring uniformity. This used to be the customs office *(dogana),* but now it's an exhaustive archive of the city's history, with temporary art exhibits and a war memorial. The poignant **Memorial Room of Dubrovnik Defenders** (on the left as you enter) has photos of dozens of people from Dubrovnik who were killed fighting Yugoslav forces in 1991. A TV screen and images near the ceiling show the devastation of the city. Though the English descriptions are slanted to the Croat perspective, by any measure it's compelling to look in the eyes of the brave young men who didn't start this war...but were willing to finish it (free, long hours daily in peak season, shorter hours off-season). Beyond the memorial room, the impressive **courtyard,** which generally displays temporary exhibits, is worth a peek (20 kn).

To the right of Sponza Palace is the town's **Bell Tower** (Gradski Zvonik). The original dated from 1444, but it was rebuilt when it started to lean in the 1920s. The big clock may be an octopus, but only one of its hands tells time. Below that, the circle shows the phase of the moon. At the bottom, the old-fashioned digital readout tells the hour (in Roman numerals) and the minutes (in five-minute increments). At the top of each hour (and again three minutes later), the time is clanged out on the bell up top by two bronze bell ringers, Maro and Baro. (If this all seems like a copy of the very similar clock on St. Mark's Square in Venice, locals are quick to point out that this clock predates that one by several decades.) The clock still has to be wound every two days. Notice the little window between the moon phase and the "digital" readout: The clock-winder opens this window to get some light. During the 1991-1992 siege, the clock-winder's house was destroyed—with the winding keys inside. For days, the clock bell didn't run. But then, miraculously, the keys were discovered lying in the street. The excited Dubrovnik citizens came together in this square and cheered as the clock was wound and the bell chimed, signaling to the soldiers surrounding the city that they hadn't won yet.

The big building to the right of the Bell Tower is the **City Hall** (Vijećnica). Next to that is **Onofrio's Little Fountain** (Mala Onofrijea Fontana), the little brother of the one at the other end of the Stradun. Beyond that is the **Gradska Kavana,** or "Town Café." This hangout—historically Dubrovnik's favorite spot for gossiping and people-watching—has pricey drinks and seating all the way through the wall to the Old Port. Just down the street from the Town Café is the Rector's Palace, and then the cathedral (for more on each, see "Sights in Dubrovnik").

Behind Orlando is **St. Blaise's Church** (Crkva Sv. Vlaha), dedicated to the patron saint of Dubrovnik. You'll see statues and paintings of St. Blaise all over town, always holding a model of the city in his left hand. According to legend, a millennium ago St. Blaise came to a local priest in a dream and warned him that the up-and-coming Venetians would soon attack the city. The priest alerted the authorities, who prepared for  war. Of course, the prediction came true. St. Blaise has been a Dubrovnik symbol—and locals have resented Venice—ever since.

• *Your tour is finished. From here, you've got plenty of sightseeing*

*options. As you face the Bell Tower, you can go up the street to the right
to reach the Rector's Palace and cathedral; you can walk through the
gate straight ahead to reach the Old Port; or you can head through the
gate and jog left to find the Dominican Monastery Museum. Even more
sights—including an old synagogue, an Orthodox church, two different
exhibits of war photography, and the medieval granary—are in the
steep streets between the Stradun and the walls.*

Sights in Dubrovnik

Nearly all of Dubrovnik's sights are inside the Old Town's walls.

Combo-Tickets: The Rector's Palace, Maritime Museum,
and Rupe Granary and Ethnographic Museum—which normally
cost 40 kn apiece—are covered by a combo-ticket (45 kn to visit
any two, 50 kn to visit all three, tickets sold at all three sights,
valid for three days). If you're visiting any one of these sights, you
might as well buy the three-sight ticket and poke into the others, since it costs just slightly more than an individual entry. The
TI's Dubrovnik Card—which covers the same three sights, plus
the City Walls and a few lesser attractions—won't save the casual
sightseer any money.

▲▲▲Town Walls (Gradske Zidine)

Dubrovnik's single best attraction is strolling the scenic mile-and-
a-quarter around the city walls. As you meander along this lofty
perch—with a sea of orange roofs on
one side, and the actual sea on the
other—you'll get your bearings and
snap pictures like mad of the ever-
changing views. Bring your map,
which you can use to pick out landmarks and get the lay of the land.

There have been walls here almost
as long as there's been a Dubrovnik.
As with virtually all fortifications on
the Croatian Coast, these walls were
beefed up in the 15th century, when
the Ottoman navy became a threat.
Around the perimeter are several substantial forts, with walls
rounded so that cannonballs would glance off harmlessly. These
stout forts intimidated would-be invaders during the Republic of
Dubrovnik's Golden Age, and protected local residents during the
1991-1992 siege.

Walking the walls also offers the best illustration of the
damage Dubrovnik sustained during the recent siege. It's easy
to see that nearly two-thirds of Dubrovnik's roofs were replaced

DUBROVNIK

The Siege of Dubrovnik

In June 1991, Croatia declared independence from Yugoslavia. Within weeks, the nations were at war. Though warfare raged in the Croatian interior, nobody expected that the bloodshed would reach Dubrovnik.

As refugees from Vukovar (in northeastern Croatia) arrived in Dubrovnik that fall, telling horrific stories of the warfare there, local residents began fearing the worst. Warplanes from the Serb-dominated Yugoslav National Army buzzed threateningly low over the town, as if to signal an impending attack.

Then, at 6:00 in the morning on October 1, 1991, Dubrovnik residents awoke to explosions on nearby hillsides. The first attacks were focused on Mount Srđ, high above the Old Town. First the giant cross was destroyed, then a communications tower (both have been rebuilt and are visible today). This first wave of attacks cleared the way for Yugoslav land troops— mostly Serbs and Montenegrins—who surrounded the city. The ragtag, newly formed Croatian army quickly dug in at the old Napoleonic-era fortress at the top of Mount Srđ, where just 25 or 30 soldiers fended off a Yugoslav takeover of this highly strategic position.

At first, the shelling targeted military positions on the outskirts of town. But soon, Yugoslav forces began bombing residential neighborhoods, then the Pearl of the Adriatic itself: Dubrovnik's Old Town. Defenseless townspeople took shelter in their cellars and sometimes even huddled together in the city wall's 15th-century forts. It was the first time in Dubrovnik's long history that the walls were actually used to defend against an attack.

Dubrovnik resisted the siege better than anyone expected. The Yugoslav forces were hoping that residents would flee the town, but the people of Dubrovnik stayed. Though severely outgunned and outnumbered, Dubrovnik's defenders managed to hold the fort atop Mount Srđ, while Yugoslav forces controlled the nearby mountaintops. All supplies had to be carried up to the fort by foot or by donkey. Dubrovnik wasn't prepared for war, so its citizens had to improvise their defense. Many brave young locals lost their lives when they slung old hunting rifles over their shoulders and, under cover of darkness, climbed the hills above Dubrovnik to meet Yugoslav soldiers face-to-face.

after the bombings (notice the new, bright-orange tiles—and how some buildings salvaged the old tiles, but have 20th-century ones underneath). Looking over this gorgeous panorama, ponder that the pristine-seeming Old Town was rebuilt using exactly the same materials and methods with which it was originally constructed.

The highest point is the empty Minčeta Tower, above the Pile

After eight months of bombing, Dubrovnik was liberated by the Croatian army, which attacked Yugoslav positions from the north. By the end of the siege, 100 civilians were dead, as well as more than 200 Dubrovnik citizens who lost their lives actively fighting for their hometown (much revered today as "Dubrovnik Defenders"). More than two-thirds of Dubrovnik's buildings had been damaged, and more than 30,000 people had to flee their homes—but the failed siege was finally over.

Why was Dubrovnik—so far from the rest of the fighting—dragged into the conflict? Yugoslavia wanted to catch the city and surrounding region off-guard, gaining a toehold on the southern Dalmatian Coast so it could push north to Split. They also hoped to ignite pro-Serb (and pro-Yugoslav) passions in the nearby Serb-dominated areas of Bosnia-Herzegovina and Montenegro. But perhaps most of all, Yugoslavia wanted to hit Croatia where it hurt—its proudest, most historic, and most beautiful city, the tourist capital of a nation dependent on tourism. (It seems their plan backfired. Locals now say, "When Yugoslavia attacked Dubrovnik, they lost the war"—because images of the historic city under siege swayed international public opinion *against* Yugoslavia.)

The war initially devastated the tourist industry. Now, to the casual observer, Dubrovnik seems virtually back to normal. Aside from a few pockmarks and bright, new roof tiles, there are scant reminders of what happened here nearly two decades ago. But even though the city itself has been repaired, the people of Dubrovnik are forever changed. Imagine living in an idyllic paradise, a place that attracted and awed visitors from around the world...and then watching it gradually blown to bits. It's understandable if Dubrovnik citizens are a little less in love with life than they once were.

Dubrovnik has various low-key attractions related to its recent war, including the Memorial Room of Dubrovnik Defenders in the Sponza Palace on Luža Square; the Institute for the Restoration of Dubrovnik, a few blocks away across the Stradun; and the museum in the ruined fortress atop Mount Srđ. Another sight, War Photo Limited, expands the scope to war photography from around the world. All of these sights are described in this chapter.

Gate at the west end of town. The tower rewards those who climb to its top with a fine view.

Posted signs send wall-walkers counterclockwise. Therefore, if you begin at the main Pile Gate entrance, you'll reach the Minčeta Tower last. Speed demons with no cameras can walk the walls in about an hour; strollers and shutterbugs should plan on longer. Because it can be very hot up top, with almost no shade, it's essential to bring sunscreen, a hat, and water. Take your time: There are several steep stretches, and you'll be climbing up and down the whole way around. A few shops and cafés along the top of the wall (mostly on the sea side) sell water and other drinks, but it's safest to bring what you'll need with you. Because your ticket is electronically scanned as you enter, you can't leave and re-enter the wall later.

Cost and Entrance: 70 kn to enter walls, also includes the St. Lawrence Fort outside the Pile Gate. The main entrance to the walls is just inside the Pile Gate: As you enter the Old Town through the gate, the stairs up to the top of the wall are directly to your left; but first, you have to buy your ticket at the office, tucked in the corner to your right. You can also buy tickets and enter the walls at two other points: near the Dominican Monastery north of the Ploče Gate, and by the Maritime Museum south of the Old Port.

Hours: July-Aug daily 8:00-19:30, progressively shorter hours off-season until mid-Nov-mid-March 10:00-15:00. Since the hours change with the season, confirm them by checking signs posted at the entrance (essential if you want to time your wall walk to avoid the worst crowds—explained below). Beware: The posted closing time indicates when the walls shut down, *not* the last entry—ascend at least an hour before this time if you want to make it all the way around. Attendants begin circling the walls about 30 minutes after the posted closing time to lock the gates. There's talk of eventually illuminating the walls at night, in which case the hours would be extended until after dark.

Audioguide: You can rent a 40-kn audioguide, separate from the admission fee, for a dryly narrated circular tour of the walls (look for vendors near the entry points). But I'd rather just enjoy the views and lazily pick out the landmarks with my map.

Crowd Control: Because this is Dubrovnik's top attraction, it's extremely crowded—particularly when cruise ships are in town. The walls are busiest in the morning, from about 8:30 until 11:00. There's generally an afternoon lull (11:00-15:00), but that's also the hottest time to be atop the walls. Crowds pick up again in the late afternoon (starting around 15:00), peaking about an hour before closing time (18:30 in high season). So the best strategy is this: Get to the walls as quickly as you can on arrival, in an attempt to beat the rush from your ship. If there's already a long line, consider waiting until mid-day (it'll be hot, but less crowded). If your ship arrives later in the day, consider tackling the walls close to closing time (carefully check the posted hours).

The "Other" Wall Climb: Your ticket for the Old Town Walls also includes the Fort of St. Lawrence just outside the Old Town (valid same day only; fort described on page 840). If you've already bought a 20-kn ticket there, show it when buying your main wall ticket and you'll pay only the difference.

Near the Pile Gate

This museum is just inside the Pile Gate.

▲**Franciscan Monastery Museum (Franjevački Samostan-Muzej)**—In the Middle Ages, Dubrovnik's monasteries flourished. While all you'll see here are a fine cloister and a one-room museum in the old pharmacy, it's a delightful space. Enter through the gap between the small church and the big monastery (30 kn, daily April-Oct 9:00-18:00, Nov-March 9:00-17:00, Placa 2, www .malabraca.hr). Just inside the door (before the ticket-seller), a century-old pharmacy still serves residents.

Explore the peaceful, sun-dappled **cloister.** Examine the capitals at the tops of the 60 Romanesque-Gothic double pillars. Each one is different. Notice that some of the portals inside the courtyard are made with a lighter-colored stone—these had to be repaired after being hit during the 1991-1992 siege. The damaged 19th-century frescoes along the tops of the walls depict the life of St. Francis, who supposedly visited Dubrovnik in the early 13th century.

In the far corner stands the monastery's original medieval **pharmacy.** Part of the Franciscans' mission was to contribute to the good health of the citizens, so they opened this pharmacy in 1317. The monastery has had a pharmacy in continual operation ever since. On display are jars, pots, and other medieval pharmacists' tools. The sick would come to get their medicine at the little window (on left side), which limited contact with the pharmacist and reduced the risk of passing on disease. Around the room, you'll also find some relics, old manuscripts, and a detailed painting of early 17th-century Dubrovnik.

Near Luža Square

These sights are at the far end of the Stradun (nearest the Old Port). As you stand on Luža Square facing the Bell Tower, the Rector's Palace and cathedral are up the wide street called Pred Dvorom to the right, and the Dominican Monastery Museum is through the gate by the Bell Tower and to the left.

Rector's Palace (Knežev Dvor)—In the Middle Ages, the Republic of Dubrovnik was ruled by a rector (similar to a Venetian doge), who was elected by the nobility. To prevent any one person from becoming too powerful, the rector's term was limited to one month. Most rectors were in their 50s—near the end of the average life span and when they were less likely to shake things up. During his term, a rector lived upstairs in this palace. Because it's been plundered twice, this empty-feeling museum isn't as interesting as most other European palaces—but it does offer a glimpse of Dubrovnik in its glory days (40 kn, covered by 45-kn or 50-kn combo-ticket, daily May-Oct 9:00-18:00, Nov-April 9:00-16:00, some posted English information, 6-kn English booklet is helpful, Pred Dvorom 3).

The **exterior** is decorated in the Gothic-Renaissance mix (with particularly finely carved capitals) that was so common in Dubrovnik before the 1667 earthquake.

Standing at the main door, you can generally get a free peek into the palace's impressive **courtyard**—a venue for the Summer Festival, hosting music groups ranging from the local symphony to the Vienna Boys' Choir. In the courtyard (and also visible from the door) is the only secular statue created during the centuries-long Republic. Dubrovnik republicans, mindful of the dangers of hero-worship, didn't believe that any one citizen should be singled out. They made only one exception—for Miho Pracat (a.k.a. Michaeli Prazatto), a rich citizen who donated vast sums to charity and willed a fleet of ships to the city. But notice that Pracat's statue is displayed in here, behind closed doors, not out in public.

The palace collection, which requires a ticket, is skippable. If you'd like to go **inside,** proceed to the ticket desk, then tour a few ground-floor exhibits. You'll see some old prison cells, which supposedly were placed within earshot of the rector's quarters, so he would hear the moans of the prisoners...and stay honest. Leaving the prison, you'll enter the courtyard described earlier, where you can get a better look at the Pracat statue.

On the mezzanine level (stairs near the main entrance), you'll find a decent display of furniture, a wimpy gun exhibit, a ho-hum coin collection, and an interesting painting of "Ragusa" in the early 17th century—back when it was still bisected by a canal.

Head back down to the courtyard and go to the upper floor (using the staircase across from mezzanine stairs, near the Pracat statue—notice the "hand" rails). Upstairs, you'll explore old apartments that serve as a painting gallery. The only vaguely authentic room is the red room in the corner, decorated more or less as it was in 1500, when it was the rector's office. Mihajlo Hamzić's exquisite *Baptism of Christ* painting, inspired by Italian painter Andrea Mantegna, is an early Renaissance work from the "Dubrovnik School."

▲**Cathedral (Katedrala)**—Dubrovnik's original 12th-century cathedral was funded largely by the English King Richard the Lionhearted. On his way back from the Third Crusade, Richard

was shipwrecked nearby. He promised God that if he survived, he'd build a church on the spot where he landed—which happened to be on Lokrum Island, just offshore. At Dubrovnik's request, Richard agreed to build his token of thanks inside the city instead. It was the finest Romanesque church on the Adriatic...before it was destroyed by the 1667 earthquake. This version is 18th-century Roman Baroque. Inside, you'll find a painting from the school of Titian *(Assumption of the Virgin)* over the stark contemporary altar, and a quirky treasury *(riznica)* packed with 187 relics (church: free, daily 8:00-20:00; treasury: 15 kn, generally open same hours as church; both have shorter hours off-season).

Examining the **treasury** collection, notice that there are three locks on the treasury door—the stuff in here was so valuable, three different VIPs (the rector, the bishop, and a local aristocrat) had to agree before it could be opened. On the table near the door are several of St. Blaise's body parts (pieces of his arm, skull, and leg—all encased in gold and silver). In the middle of the wall directly opposite the door, look for the crucifix with a piece of the True Cross. On a dig in Jerusalem, St. Helen (Emperor Constantine's mother) discovered what she believed to be the cross that Jesus was crucified on. It was brought to Constantinople, and the Byzantine czars doled out pieces of it to Balkan kings. Note the folding three-paneled altar painting (underneath the cross). Dubrovnik ambassadors packed this on road trips (such as their annual trip to pay off the Ottomans) so they could worship wherever they traveled. On the right side of the room, the silver casket supposedly holds the actual swaddling clothes of the Baby Jesus (or, as some locals call it somewhat less reverently, "Jesus' nappy"). Dubrovnik bishops secretly passed these clothes down from generation to generation... until a nun got wind of it and told the whole town. Pieces of the cloth were cut off to miraculously heal the sick, especially new mothers recovering from a difficult birth. No matter how often it was cut, the cloth always went back to its original form. Then someone tried to use it on the wife of a Bosnian king. Since she was Muslim, it couldn't help her, and it never worked again. True or not, this legend hints at the prickly relationships between faiths (not to mention the male chauvinism) here in the Balkans.

▲**Dominican Monastery Museum (Dominikanski Samostan-Muzej)**—You'll find many of Dubrovnik's art treasures—paintings, altarpieces, and manuscripts—gathered around the peaceful Dominican Monastery cloister inside the Ploče Gate (20

kn, art buffs enjoy the 50-kn English book, daily May-Sept 9:00-18:00, Oct-April 9:00-17:00). Historically, this was the church for wealthy people, while the Franciscan Church (down at the far end of the Stradun) was for poor people. Services were staggered by 15 minutes to allow servants to drop off their masters here, then rush down the Stradun for their own service.

Work your way clockwise around the cloister. The room in the far corner from the entry contains paintings from the **"Dubrovnik School,"** the Republic's circa-1500 answer to the art boom in Florence and Venice. Though the 1667 earthquake destroyed most of these paintings, about a dozen survive, and five of those are in this room. Don't miss the triptych by Nikola Božidarović with St. Blaise holding a detailed model of 16th-century Dubrovnik (left panel)—the most famous depiction of Dubrovnik's favorite saint. You'll also see reliquaries shaped like the hands and feet that they hold.

Continuing around the courtyard, duck into the next room. Here you'll see a painting by **Titian** depicting St. Blaise, Mary Magdalene, and the donor.

At the next corner of the courtyard is the entrance to the striking **church** at the heart of this still-active monastery. Step inside. The interior is decorated with modern stained glass, a fine 13th-century stone pulpit that survived the earthquake (reminding visitors of the intellectual approach to scripture that characterized the Dominicans), and a precious 14th-century Paolo Veneziano crucifix hanging above the high altar. The most memorable piece of art in the church is the *Miracle of St. Dominic,* showing the founder of the order bringing a child back to life (over the altar to the right, as you enter). It was painted in the Realist style (late 19th century) by Vlaho Bukovac.

Near the Old Port (Stara Luka)

The picturesque Old Port, carefully nestled behind St. John's Fort, faces away from what was Dubrovnik's biggest threat, the Venetians. At the port, you can watch cruise-ship passengers coming and going on their trans-

fer boats. The long seaside building across the bay on the left is the Lazareti, once the medieval quarantine house. In those days, all visitors were locked in here for 40 days before entering town. A bench-lined harborside walk leads around the fort to a breakwater, providing a peaceful perch. From the breakwater, rocky beaches curl around the outside of the wall.

Maritime Museum (Pomorski Muzej)—By the 15th century, when Venice's nautical dominance was on the wane, Dubrovnik emerged as a maritime power and the Mediterranean's leading shipbuilding center. The Dubrovnik-built "argosy" boat (from "Ragusa," an early name for the city) was the Cadillac of ships, frequently mentioned by Shakespeare. This small museum traces the history of Dubrovnik's most important industry with contracts, maps, paintings, and models—all well-described in English. The main floor takes you through the 18th century, and the easy-to-miss upstairs covers the 19th and 20th centuries. Boaters will find the museum particularly interesting (40 kn, covered by 45-kn or 50-kn combo-ticket, 5-kn English booklet, hours depend on demand—usually March-Oct Tue-Sun 9:00-18:00, closed Mon, shorter hours Nov-Feb, upstairs in St. John's Fort, at far/south end of Old Port, tel. 020/323-904).

Aquarium (Akvarij)—Dubrovnik's aquarium, housed in the cavernous St. John's Fort, is an old-school place, with 31 tanks on one floor. A visit here allows you a close look at the local marine life and provides a cool refuge from the midday heat (30 kn, kids-10 kn, English descriptions, daily July-Aug 9:00-21:00, progressively shorter hours off-season until 9:00-13:00 Nov-March, ground floor of St. John's Fort, enter from Old Port).

Between the Stradun and the Mainland

These two museums are a few steps off the main promenade toward the mainland.

▲**Synagogue Museum (Sinagoga-Muzej)**—When Jews were forced out of Spain in 1492, a steady stream of them passed through here en route to today's Turkey. Finding Dubrovnik to be a flourishing and relatively tolerant city, many stayed. Žudioska ulica ("Jewish Street"), just inside Ploče Gate, became the ghetto in 1546. It was walled at one end and had a gate (which would be locked at night) at the other end. Today, the same street is home to the second-oldest continuously functioning synagogue in Europe (after Prague's), which contains Croatia's only Jewish museum. The top floor houses the synagogue itself. Notice the lattice windows that separated the women from the men (in accordance with Orthodox Jewish tradition). Below that, a small museum with good English descriptions gives meaning to the various Torahs (including a 14th-century one from Spain) and other items—such as the written orders *(naredba)* from Nazi-era Yugoslavia, stating that Jews were to identify their shops as Jewish-owned and wear armbands. (The Ustaše—the Nazi puppet government in Croatia—interned and executed not only Jews and Roma/Gypsies, but also Serbs and other people they considered undesirable.) Of Croatia's 24,000 Jews, only 4,000 survived the Holocaust. Today Croatia has about 2,000 Jews, including 12 Jewish families who call Dubrovnik home (15 kn, 10-kn English booklet; May-mid-Nov daily 10:00-20:00; mid-Nov-April Mon-Fri 10:00-13:00, closed Sat-Sun; Žudioska ulica 5, tel. 020/321-028).

War Photo Limited—If the tragic story of wartime Dubrovnik has you in a pensive mood, drop by this gallery with images of warfare from around the world. The brainchild of Kiwi-turned-Croatian photojournalist Wade Goddard, this thought-provoking museum—with well-displayed exhibits on two floors—attempts to show the ugly reality of war through raw, often disturbing photographs taken in the field. A permanent exhibit depicts the wars in the former Yugoslavia through photography and video footage. Each summer, the gallery also houses two different temporary exhibits. Note that the focus is not solely on Dubrovnik, but on war anywhere and everywhere (30 kn; June-Sept daily 9:00-21:00; May and Oct Tue-Sat 9:00-15:00, Sun 10:00-14:00, closed Mon; closed Nov-April; Antuninska 6, tel. 020/322-166, www.war photoltd.com).

Between the Stradun and the Sea

▲**Institute for the Restoration of Dubrovnik (Zavod za Obnovu Dubrovnika)**—This small photo gallery is the closest thing Dubrovnik has to a museum about the eight-month siege of the city from late 1991 to mid-1992 (see "The Siege of Dubrovnik" sidebar, earlier). The front two rooms display images of bombed-out Dubrovnik, each one juxtaposed with an image of the same building after being restored. The back room offers rotating exhibits about efforts to restore Dubrovnik to its pre-siege glory. The photos are too few, but still illuminating. The highlight of the exhibit is a video showing a series of breathless news reports from a British journalist stationed here during the siege. As you watch shells devastating this glorious city, and look in the eyes of its desperate citizens at their darkest hour, you might just begin to grasp what went on here not so long ago (free; June-Sept Mon-Fri 10:00-14:00, closed Sat-Sun; Oct-May the same space is used for rotating exhibits on other topics; Zuzorić 6, tel. 020/324-060).

▲**Serbian Orthodox Church and Icon Museum (Srpska Pravoslavna Crkva i Muzej Ikona)**—Round out your look at Dubrovnik's faiths (Catholic, Jewish, and Orthodox) with a visit to this house of worship—one of the most convenient places in

The Serbian Orthodox Church

As you explore an Orthodox church, keep in mind that these churches carry on the earliest traditions of the Christian faith. Orthodox and Catholic Christianity came from the same roots, so the oldest surviving early-Christian churches (such as the stave churches of Norway) have many of the same features as today's Orthodox churches.

Notice that there are no pews. Worshippers stand through the service, as a sign of respect (though some older parishioners sit on the seats along the walls). Women stand on the left side, men on the right (equal distance from the altar—to represent that all are equal before God). The Orthodox Church uses essentially the same Bible as Catholics, but it's written in the Cyrillic alphabet, which you'll see displayed around any Orthodox church. Following Old Testament Judeo-Christian tradition, the Bible is kept on the altar behind the iconostasis, the big screen in the middle of the room covered with curtains and icons (golden paintings of saints), which separates the material world from the spiritual one. At certain times during the service, the curtains or doors are opened so the congregation can see the Holy Book.

Unlike many Catholic church decorations, Orthodox icons are not intended to be lifelike. Packed with intricate symbolism, and cast against a shimmering golden background, they're meant to remind viewers of the metaphysical nature of Jesus and the saints rather than their physical form, which is considered irrelevant. You'll almost never see a statue, which is thought to overemphasize the physical world...and, to Orthodox people, feels a little too close to violating the commandment, "Thou shalt not worship graven images." Orthodox services generally involve chanting (a dialogue that goes back and forth between the priest and the congregation), and the church is filled with the evocative aroma of incense.

The incense, chanting, icons, and standing up are all intended to heighten the experience of worship. While many Catholic and Protestant services tend to be more of a theoretical and rote consideration of religious issues (come on—don't tell me you've never dozed through the sermon), Orthodox services are about creating a religious experience. Each of these elements does its part to help the worshipper transcend the physical world and enter communion with the spiritual one.

Croatia to learn about Orthodox Christianity. Remember that people from the former Yugoslavia who follow the Orthodox faith are, by definition, ethnic Serbs. With all the (perhaps understandably) hard feelings about the recent war, this church serves as an important reminder that all Serbs aren't bloodthirsty killers.

Dubrovnik never had a very large Serb population (an Orthodox church wasn't even allowed inside the town walls until the mid-19th century). During the recent war, most Serbs fled, created new lives for themselves elsewhere, and saw little reason to return. But some old-timers remain, and Dubrovnik's dwindling, aging Orthodox population is still served by this church. The candles stuck in the sand and water (to prevent fire outbreaks) represent prayers: The ones at knee level are for the deceased, while the ones higher up are for the living. The gentleman selling candles encourages you to buy and light one, regardless of your faith, so long as you do so with the proper intentions and reverence (free entry, good 20-kn English book explains the church and the museum, daily May-Sept 8:00-20:00, Oct-April 8:00-15:00, short services daily at 8:30 and 19:00, longer liturgy Sundays at 9:00, Od Puča 8).

A few doors down, you'll find the **Icon Museum** (10 kn; May-Oct Mon-Sat 9:00-14:00, closed Sun; Nov-April Mon-Fri 9:00-14:00, closed Sat-Sun). This small collection features 78 different icons (stylized paintings of saints, generally on a golden background—a common feature of Orthodox churches) from the 15th through the 19th centuries, all identified in English. In the library—crammed with old shelves holding some 12,000 books—look for the astonishingly detailed calendar, with portraits of hundreds of saints. The gallery on the ground floor, run by Michael, sells original icons and reproductions (open longer hours than museum).

▲Rupe Granary and Ethnographic Museum (Etnografski Muzej Rupe)—This huge, 16th-century building was Dubrovnik's biggest granary. *Rupe* means "holes"—and it's worth the price of entry just to peer down into these cavernous underground grain stores, designed to maintain the perfect temperature to preserve the seeds (63 degrees Fahrenheit). When the grain had to be dried, it was moved upstairs—where today you'll find a surprisingly well-presented Ethnographic Museum, with tools, jewelry, clothing, instruments, painted eggs, and other folk artifacts from Dubrovnik's colorful history. Borrow the free English information guide at the entry (40 kn, covered by 45-kn or 50-kn combo-ticket,

Wed-Mon 9:00-16:00, closed Tue). The museum hides several blocks uphill from the main promenade, toward the sea (climb up Široka—the widest side street from the Stradun—which becomes Od Domina on the way to the museum).

Above Dubrovnik

▲**Mount Srđ**—After adding Dubrovnik to his holdings, Napoleon built a fortress atop the hill behind the Old Town to keep an eye on his new subjects (in

1810). During the city's 20th-century tourism heyday, a cable car was built to effortlessly whisk visitors to the top so they could enjoy the fine views from the fortress and the giant cross nearby. But when war broke out in the 1990s, Mount Srđ became a crucial link in the defense of Dubrovnik—the only high land that locals were able to hold. The fortress was shelled and damaged, and the cross and cable car were destroyed. Minefields and unexploded ordnance left the hilltop a dangerous no-man's land.

DUBROVNIK

More recently, the mountain's fortunes have reversed. The landmines have been cleared (see "Warning," next page), and in 2010, the cable car was rebuilt to once again connect Dubrovnik's Old Town to its mountaintop. Visitors head to the top both for the sweeping views and for a ragtag museum about the war. While the cable car is the easiest way to summit the mountain, you can, if

you're in great shape, hike up (see "Getting There," later).

The bird's-eye **view** is truly spectacular, looking straight down to the street plan of Dubrovnik's Old Town. From this lofty perch, you can see north to the Dalmatian islands (the Elaphite, Mljet, and beyond); south to Montenegro; and east into Bosnia-Herzegovina.

The **cross** was always an important symbol in this very Catholic town. After it was destroyed, a temporary wooden one was erected to encourage the townspeople who were waiting out the siege below. During a visit in 2003, Pope John Paul II blessed the rubble from the old cross; those fragments are now being used in the foundations of the city's newest churches.

The **fortress** houses a humble but interesting exhibit called "Dubrovnik During the Homeland War (1991-1995)." Photos, video clips, documents, and artifacts tell the story (with some English descriptions) of the overarching war with Yugoslavia and how the people defended this fortress. You'll see actual items used in the fighting: basic, rusty rifles that the Croatians used for their improvised defense, and mortar shells and other projectiles that Yugoslav forces hurled at the fortress and the city. Look for the wire-guided Russian rockets. After being launched at their target, the rockets would burrow into a wall, waiting to be detonated once their operators saw the opportunity for maximum destruction. The explanations are, perhaps understandably, slanted to the Croat perspective—with talk of "Serb-Montenegrin aggression" and statements such as, "This senseless attack...showed the full hate towards the Croatian people." Though the museum feels hastily assembled and a bit basic, it's fascinating to learn about this historical moment in a place that played such a major role in the events (15 kn, daily 10:00-18:30, maybe until 20:00 in summer).

After seeing the exhibit, climb up a few flights of stairs to the **rooftop** for the view. The giant communications tower overhead flew the Croatian flag during the war, to inspire the besieged residents below. At the other end of the fortress are the haunting remains of a simpler time: a badly damaged, light-up dance floor from the disco era, back when the fortress hosted not Napoleonic or Croatian soldiers, but a popular dance club for locals and tourists. You might see some charred trees around here—these were claimed not by the war, but more recently, by forest fires. (Fear of landmines and other explosives prevented locals from fighting the wildfires as aggressively as they might otherwise, making these fires more dangerous than ever.)

Warning: While this area has officially been cleared of landmines, nervous locals remind visitors that this was a war zone. Be sure to stay on clearly defined paths and roads.

Getting There: The newly rebuilt **cable car** is easily the best option for summiting Mount Srđ (73 kn round-trip, 44 kn one-way, daily 9:00-21:00, possibly shorter off-season). The lower station is just above the Buža Gate at the top of the Old Town (exit through gate and climb uphill one block, then look right).

You can also hire a **taxi,** but it's very expensive (figure €50-70 round-trip, including some waiting time at the top). Some cabbies will provide a little informal commentary during your visit. Or for €70, recommended driver Pepo Klaić will take you to the summit while sharing his firsthand experiences defending the fortress (listed on page 840).

Public **bus** #17 brings you from outside the Old Town's Ploče Gate most of the way up, but the frequency is limited (roughly every 2 hours, 25 minutes). From the bus stop, you'll still have to hike nearly a mile uphill, with almost no shade. For **hikers,** a switchback trail (used to supply the fortress during the siege) connects the Old Town to the mountaintop—but it's very steep and provides minimal shade. (If you're in great shape and it's not too hot, you could ride the cable car or bus up, then hike down.)

Activities in Dubrovnik

Swimming and Sunbathing—If the weather's good and you've had enough of museums, spend a sunny afternoon at the beach.

There are no sandy beaches on the mainland near Dubrovnik, but there are lots of suitable pebbly options, plus several concrete perches. The easiest and most atmospheric place to take a dip is right off the Old Town. From the Old Port and its breakwater, uneven steps clinging to the outside of the wall lead to a series of great sunbathing and swimming coves (and even a showerhead sticking out of the town wall). Other convenient public beaches include the delightful rocky beach that hangs onto the outside of the Old Town's wall (at the bar called Cold Drinks "Buža" I; for more on this bar, and how to find it, see "Drinks with a View," below), and Banje (just outside Ploče Gate, east of Old Town).

My favorite hidden beach—**St. Jakob**—takes a lot longer to reach, but if you're up for the hike, it's worth it to escape the crowds. Figure about a 25-minute walk (each way) from the Old

Town. Go through the Ploče Gate at the east end of the Old Town, and walk along the street called Frana Supila as it climbs uphill above the waterfront. At Hotel Argentina, take the right (downhill) fork and keep going on Vlaha Bukovca. Eventually you'll reach the small church of St. Jakob. You'll see the beach—in a cozy protected cove—far below. Curl around behind the church and keep an eye out for stairs going down on the right. Unfortunately, these stairs are effectively unmarked, so it might take some trial and error to find the right ones. (If you reach the rusted-white gateway of the old communist-era open-air theater, you've gone too far.) Hike down the very steep stairs to the gentle cove, which has rentable chairs and a small restaurant for drinks (and a WC). Enjoy the pebbly beach and faraway views of Dubrovnik's Old Town.

▲▲▲**Drinks with a View—Cold Drinks "Buža"** offers, without a doubt, the most scenic spot for a drink. Perched on a cliff above the sea, clinging like a barnacle to the outside of the city walls, this is a peaceful, shaded getaway from the bustle of the Old Town... the perfect place to watch cruise ships disappear into the horizon. *Buža* means "hole in the wall"—and that's exactly what you'll have to go through to get to this place. There are actually two different Bužas, with separate owners. My favorite is Buža II (which is actually the older and bigger of the pair). Filled with mellow tourists and bartenders pouring wine from tiny screw-top bottles into plastic cups, Buža II comes with castaway views and Frank Sinatra ambience. This is supposedly where Bill Gates hangs out when he visits Dubrovnik (25-40-kn drinks, summer daily 9:00-into the wee hours, closed mid-Nov-Jan). Buža I is more casual, plays hip rather than romantic music, and has concrete stairs leading down to a beach on the rocks below (18-45-kn drinks). If one Buža is full, check the other one.

Getting There: Both Bužas are high above the bustle of the main drag, along the seaward wall. To reach them from the cathedral area, hike up the grand staircase to St. Ignatius' Church, then go left to find the lane that runs along the inside of the wall. To find the classic Buža II, head right along the lane and look for the *Cold Drinks* sign pointing to a literal hole in the wall. For the hipper Buža I, go left along the same lane, and locate the hole in the wall with the *No Toples No Nudist* graffiti.

Shopping in Dubrovnik

Most souvenirs sold in Dubrovnik—from lavender sachets to plaster models of the Old Town—are pretty tacky. Whatever you buy, prices are much higher along the Stradun than on the side streets.

A classy alternative to the knickknacks is a type of local jewelry called *Konavoske puce* ("Konavle buttons"). Sold as earrings, pendants, and rings, these distinctive and fashionable filigree-style pieces consist of a sphere with several small posts. Though they're sold around town, it's least expensive to buy them on Od Puča street, which runs parallel to the Stradun two blocks toward the sea (near the Serbian Orthodox Church). The high concentration of jewelers  along this lane keeps prices reasonable. You'll find the "buttons" in various sizes, in both silver (affordable) and gold (pricey).

You'll also see lots of jewelry made from red coral, which can only be legally gathered in small amounts from two small islands in northern Dalmatia. If you see a particularly large chunk of coral, it's likely imported. To know what you're getting, shop at an actual jeweler instead of a souvenir shop.

Eating in Dubrovnik

In the Old Town

Nishta, featuring a short menu of delicious vegetarian fusion cuisine with Asian flair, offers a welcome change of pace from

the Dalmatian seafood-pasta-pizza rut. Busy Swiss owner/chef Gildas cooks, while his wife Ruža serves. This tiny place—which, in my experience, is the only reliably good eatery in town—has just a few indoor and outdoor tables. Even if you're not a vegetarian, it's worth a visit (55-80-kn main courses, Mon-Sat 12:00-15:00 & 18:00-22:00, closed Sun, on the restaurant-clogged Prijeko street—near the Pile Gate end of the street, mobile 098-186-7440).

Dubrovački Kantun ("Dubrovnik's Nook") serves up typical, traditional Dalmatian specialties in a cozy eight-table interior that's ideal on rainy days. For now, this is one of the Old Town's more reputable options for good food. Despite its lack of outdoor seating, I'd give it a serious look (hearty 25-kn soups, 65-70-kn pastas, 70-120-kn main courses, daily 12:00-16:00 & 18:00-24:00, near the corner of Boškovićeva and Prijeko, tel. 020/331-911, Andrej).

Konoba Kamenice, a no-frills fish restaurant, is a local institution offering inexpensive, fresh, and good meals on a charming market square, as central as can be in the Old Town. On the limited menu, the seafood dishes are excellent (try their octopus salad, even if you don't think you like octopus), while the few non-seafood dishes are uninspired. Some of the waitstaff are notorious for their playfully brusque service, but loyal patrons happily put up with it. Arrive early, or you'll have to wait (35-70-kn main courses, daily 8:00-23:00, until 22:00 off-season, Gundulićeva poljana 8, tel. 020/323-682).

Lokanda Peskarija enjoys an enticing setting, with a sea of tables facing the Old Port. Servings are hearty and come in a pot, "home-style." The 60-kn seafood risotto easily feeds two, and sharing is no problem. The menu's tiny—with only seafood options, and not much in the way of vegetables. Locals complain that the quality has taken a nosedive ever since the restaurant's following has grown and its idyllic setting expanded to the hilt.

But for reasonably priced seafood dishes on the water, this remains an acceptable option (most main courses 55-80 kn, daily 12:00-24:00, very limited indoor seating fills up fast, plenty of outdoor tables—which can also fill up, tel. 020/324-750, no reservations taken in summer). Notice that the tables farthest from the main restaurant have a different menu, focused on Balkan-style grilled meats; if that's what you want, skip this place and head for Taj Mahal instead (described later).

Pizza: Dubrovnik seems to have a pizzeria on every corner. Little separates the various options—just look for a menu and outdoor seating option that appeals to you. I've eaten well at **Oliva Pizzeria,** just behind St. Blaise's Church (35-65-kn pizzas, Lučarica 5, daily 10:00-24:00, tel. 020/324-594). Around the side is a handy take-out window for a bite on the go.

Pasta: **Spaghetteria Toni** is popular with natives and tourists. While nothing fancy, they offer good pastas at reasonable prices. Choose between the cozy 10-table interior, or the long alley filled with outdoor tables (45-80-kn pastas, 40-60-kn salads, daily in summer 11:00-23:00, closed Sun in winter, closed Jan, Nikole Božidarevića 14, tel. 020/323-134).

Bosnian Cuisine: For a break from Croatian fare, consider the grilled meats and other tasty Bosnian dishes at the misnamed **Taj Mahal.** Though the service can be lacking, the menu offers an enticing taste of the Turkish-flavored land to the east. Choose between the tight interior, which feels like a Bosnian tea house, or tables out on the alley (50-kn salads, 45-115-kn main courses, daily 10:00-24:00, Nikole Gučetića 2, tel. 020/323-221).

Ice Cream: Dubrovnik has lots of great *sladoled*, but locals swear by the stuff at **Dolce Vita** (daily 9:00-24:00, a half-block off the Stradun at Nalješkovićeva 1A, tel. 020/321-666).

The Old Town's "Restaurant Row," Prijeko Street: The street called Prijeko, a block toward the mainland from the Stradun promenade, is lined with outdoor, tourist-oriented eateries—each one with a huckster out front trying to lure in diners. (Many of them aggressively try to snare passersby down on the Stradun, as well.) Don't be sucked into this vortex of bad food at outlandish prices. The only place worth seeking out here is Nishta (described earlier); the rest are virtually guaranteed to disappoint. Still, it can be fun to take a stroll along here—the atmosphere is lively, and the sales pitches are entertainingly desperate.

Picnic Tips

Dubrovnik's lack of great restaurant options makes it a perfect place to picnic. You can shop for fresh fruits and veggies at the open-air produce market (each morning near the cathedral, on the square called Gundulićeva Poljana). Supplement your picnic with

> # What If I Miss My Boat?
>
> Remember that you can get help from the cruise line's port agent (listed on the destination information sheet distributed on the ship) and the local TI (see page 835). If the port agent suggests a costly solution (such as a private car with a driver), you may want to consider these options instead:
>
> To reach **Split** (possibly your ship's next stop, and home to the nearest train station), the bus is your best option (almost hourly, generally at the top of each hour, less off-season, 5 hours). Dubrovnik's long-distance bus terminal (*Autobusni Kolodvor*) is located near the port.
>
> Flying to **Italy** or **Greece** is the easiest option for both, though there are no direct flights to Venice or Athens, aside from the occasional charter flight from Dubrovnik to Athens. (You also won't find any direct boats, and the overland connections to both are overly long). Dubrovnik's small **airport** (Zračna Luka) is 13 miles south of the city. To get to the airport, you can take a Croatia Airlines bus (ask at the TI), or call a taxi at tel. 020/970.
>
> For a recommended local **travel agent**, see page 838. For more advice on what to do if you miss the boat, see page 131.

grub from the cheap **Konzum grocery store** (one location near the bus stop just outside Pile Gate: Mon-Sat 7:00-21:00, Sun 8:00-14:00; another on the market square near the produce-vendors: Mon-Sat 7:00-21:00, Sun 7:00-13:00). Good picnic spots include the shaded benches overlooking the Old Port; the Porporela breakwater (beyond the Old Port and fort—comes with a swimming area, sunny no-shade benches, and views of Lokrum Island); and the green, welcoming park in what was the moat just under the Pile Gate entry to the Old Town.

GREECE
Hellas / Ελλάς

GREECE

Hellas / Ελλάς

Slip that coaster under the rickety table leg, take a sip of wine, and watch the sun extinguish itself in the sea. You've arrived in Greece.

Greece offers sunshine, seafood, 6,000 islands, whitewashed houses with bright-blue shutters, and a relaxed lifestyle. As the cradle of Western civilization, it has some of the world's greatest ancient monuments. As a late bloomer in the modern age, it also retains echoes of a simpler, time-passed world. And contemporary Greece has one of Europe's fastest-changing cultural landscapes.

The ancient Greeks—who reached their apex in the city of Athens—have had an unmatched impact on European and American culture. For many travelers, coming to Athens is like a pilgrimage to the cradle of our civilization. Greece is the place that birthed the Olympics; the tall tales of Achilles, Odysseus, and the Trojan War; the rational philosophies of Socrates, Plato, and Aristotle; democracy, theater, mathematics...and the gyros sandwich.

You'll find two Greeces: the traditional/old/rural Greece, and the modern/young/urban one. On the islands, you'll still see men on donkeys and women at the well. In Athens and other cities, it's a concrete world of honking horns and buzzing mobile phones.

Tourism makes up 15 percent of the gross domestic product, and the people are welcoming and accommodating. Greeks pride themselves on a concept called *filotimo* ("love of honor"), roughly translated as openness, friendliness, and hospitality. It's easy to surrender to the Greek way of living.

You'll arrive at the Mediterranean's busiest passenger port: Piraeus, the port of Athens. While Piraeus itself is grimy and chaotic, it's just a quick bus, taxi, or Metro ride away from the glories of ancient Athens: the Acropolis, Parthenon, and Ancient Agora, with the characteristic Plaka neighborhood nearby.

This book also focuses on two of the most popular Greek islands: Mykonos is an adorable, windmill-topped fishing village slathered in white; cruisers enjoy its many beaches and side-tripping to the ancient ruins on nearby Delos. Santorini is the most geologically interesting of all the Greek islands, and arguably the most picturesque, with idyllic villages perched on the rim of a collapsed and flooded volcano crater.

I've also included brief coverage of a few other important Greek stops: Nafplio, a heavily fortified yet inviting city; Olympia (served by the port of Katakolo), where the world's favorite pastime was born; and the islands of Corfu, Crete (the port of Heraklion), and Rhodes.

Practicalities

This section covers just the basics on traveling in Greece.

Tourist Information: www.visitgreece.gr

Money: Greece uses the euro currency: 1 euro (€) = about $1.40.

Theft Alert: In Athens and any place with crowds, be wary of purse-snatchers and pickpockets, particularly at popular tourist sights and on public transportation. Keep your backpack in front of you on city buses.

Business Hours: Most shops catering to tourists are open long hours daily. Those for locals are more likely open Monday, Wednesday, and Saturday from 8:30 or 9:00 until early afternoon; Tuesday, Thursday, and Friday from 8:30 or 9:00 until late (roughly 20:00), but often with an afternoon break; and closed Sunday.

Internet Access: You'll find plenty of cafés that offer Wi-Fi to customers.

Sights: Some museums and sights are closed on Monday.

Buses: Greece's network of public buses, run by KTEL (ΚΤΕΛ in Greek), will get you most anywhere you want to go, but schedules are hard to nail down. Try this helpful, unofficial website in English: http://livingingreece.gr/2008/06/13/ktel-buses-of-greece. On the islands, bus tickets are sold in shops and at departure points.

Eating

Greek food is simple...and simply delicious.

A favorite Greek snack is souvlaki pita, a tasty shish kebab wrapped in flat bread. Souvlaki stands are all over Greece. Savory, flaky phyllo-dough pastries called *"pita"* (pies, not to be confused with pita bread) are another staple of Greek cuisine. These can be ordered as a starter in a restaurant or purchased from a bakery for a tasty bite on the run. The most common pies are *spanakopita* (spinach), *tiropita* (cheese), *kreato-pita* (lamb), and *meletzanitopita* (eggplant).

On the islands, eat fresh seafood. Don't miss the creamy yogurt with honey. Feta cheese salads and flaky, nut-and-honey baklava are two other tasty treats. Dunk your bread into *tzatziki*, the ubiquitous and refreshing cucumber-and-yogurt dip.

Mezedes are a great way to sample several tasty Greek dishes. This "small plates" approach is common and easy—instead of ordering a starter and a main dish per person, get two or three starters and one main dish to split.

Greece serves up a range of restaurant options: the *estiatorio*, a traditional Greek restaurant; the taverna, a rustic neighborhood spot with a smaller menu; the *mezedopolio*, an eatery specializing in small plates/appetizers; and the *ouzerie*, a bar that makes ouzo and often sells basic pub grub to go along with it. Wherever you eat, you are welcome to linger as long as you want—don't feel pressured to eat quickly and turn over the table.

Tipping: If you order your food at a counter, don't tip. At restaurants that have waitstaff, service is generally included, although it's common to round up the bill after a good meal, usually 5-10 percent.

Phoning

Use insertable phone cards (*telekarta*, or ΤΗΛΕΚΑΡΤΑ) for international and local calls from public pay phones; there are no coin phones. Buy the cards at TIs, tobacco shops, newsstand kiosks, post offices, and train stations. The other type of phone card, which has a scratch-to-reveal PIN code, doesn't always work from public phones.

Dialing: Greece has a direct-dial phone system (no area codes). To **call within Greece,** just dial the number. To **call to Greece,** dial the international access code (00 if calling from Europe, or 011 from North America), then 30 (Greece's country code), then the phone number. To **call home from Greece,** dial 00, 1, then your area code and phone number.

Directory Assistance: Tel. 11880 (Athens); tel. 132 (rest of Greece); 139 (international calls)

Emergency Telephone Numbers:
Police: Tel. 100

Tourist Police: Tel. 171 (English-speaking)

Ambulance or Fire: Tel. 176 or 199

Passport Problems: US Embassy in Athens (tel. 210-720-2419, after-hours emergency tel. 210-729-4301 or 210-729-4444); Canadian Embassy in Athens (tel. 210-727-3400).

ATHENS & the PORT of PIRAEUS

Democracy and mathematics. Medicine and literature. Theater and astronomy. Mythology and philosophy. All of these, and more, were first thought up by a bunch of tunic-clad Greeks in a small village huddled at the base of the Acropolis. During its Golden Age, Athens dominated ancient Greece, and later conquests by Alexander the Great spread its culture across the known world. The incredible advances in art, architecture, politics, science, and philosophy set the pace for all of Western civilization to follow.

A century and a half ago, Athens was a humble, forgotten city of about 8,000 people. Today it's the teeming home of nearly four million Greeks. The city is famous for its sheer size, noise, and pollution. The best advice to tourists has long been to see the big sights, then get out. But over the last decade or so, the city has made a concerted effort to curb pollution, clean up and pedestrianize the streets, spiff up the museums, and invest in one of Europe's better public transit systems. All of these urban upgrades reached a peak as Athens hosted the 2004 Olympic Games.

And yet, the conventional wisdom still holds true: Athens is a great city to see...but not to linger in. As everything worth a look is gathered around the Acropolis, it's made to order for a quick cruise visit.

Many cruises start or end in Athens. If that's the case for you, check the end of this chapter for airport information and recommended hotels.

Planning Your Time

Although Athens is a sprawling city, its main sights can be seen in a busy and well-organized day.

Excursions from Piraeus

Excursion choices from Piraeus swing from the ho-hum to the spectacular. Choose carefully before missing the magnificent Acropolis and the world-class museums of **Athens** itself—easily the best excursion from Piraeus.

Reconstructed for the 2004 Olympics, a 68,000-seat stadium sits at the center of the **Athens Olympic Sports Complex** (AOSC, better known by its Greek initials, OAKA). Your time is better spent elsewhere. (Note: Don't confuse this with the interesting ancient ruins of the 4th-century B.C. Panathenaic Stadium—which also hosted some events in the 2004 Olympiad, and sit just outside the Plaka neighborhood of downtown Athens; see page 965).

A 45-minute drive south of Piraeus, the Temple of Poseidon perches atop **Cape Sounion** with a knock-out view over the Aegean Sea, but it's not worth the drive if you're visiting other ancient sites.

Excursions to **Corinth** (1.25 hours west of Piraeus) focus on its ancient Greek and Roman ruins as well as the **Corinth Canal,** built by Greek engineers in the 19th century to connect the Gulf of Corinth with the Aegean Sea (severing the Peloponnesian Peninsula from the mainland). But Corinth's sights are trumped by those at Delphi.

The mountaintop palace/fortress at **Mycenae** (2 hours southwest of Piraeus) was the hub of a civilization that dominated Greece 1,000 years before its Golden Age. Its archaeological ruins, massive beehive tomb, and iconic Lion Gate are impressive attractions. These impossibly old ruins tickle the imaginations of armchair archaeologists, but are less visually striking than those in Athens or Delphi.

Overlooking the Gulf of Corinth, **Delphi** (2.5 hours northwest of Piraeus) is among the most spectacular of Greece's ancient sites. The Sanctuary of Apollo, home of the legendary fortune-telling oracle, is draped over a craggy mountainside, and next door is the great Archaeological Museum, where statues and treasures found on the site help bring the ruins to life. Though distant from Athens, Delphi's ruins rival those in the capital city; if you've already seen the Acropolis and other ancient biggies in Athens, Delphi might be worth the long bus trip to see.

ATHENS

First off, allow up to an hour and a half round-trip to get from the port to downtown Athens and back, whether by bus, Metro, or taxi. (The trip can be as quick as 20 minutes one-way by taxi, if the traffic doesn't slow you down.)

If your time in Athens is short, head straight for the Acropolis. With more time, I suggest doing the sights in this order, following my self-guided walks and tours:

• Take my **Athens City Walk** through the heart of town. Figure on two hours at a speedy pace. When finished, grab a souvlaki lunch near Monastiraki.

• Walk through the **Ancient Agora,** allowing up to two hours for my self-guided tour. If you're in a rush, just speed through here on your way up to the Acropolis.

• Tour the **Acropolis,** allowing two hours. The Acropolis is less crowded afternoons than mornings, but confirm carefully how late it's open—it closes at 15:00 in Oct-April.

• If time allows when you descend from the Acropolis, pay a visit to the nearby **Acropolis Museum** (closed Mon); allow 1.5 hours.

• If you have additional time—or if you skip one or more of the above sights—the **National Archaeological Museum** is well worth a visit, but is far from the other sights listed here (allow at least 2 hours to tour the collection, plus about 20 minutes each way by taxi from downtown).

If shopping interests you more than museums, see page 973.

Arrival at the Port of Piraeus

Arrival at a Glance: To reach central Athens, you can spring for a taxi (€15-20, 20-40 minutes); take public bus #040 (30-60 minutes); or ride the subway (walk 15-30 minutes—or ride a local bus—to the Metro station, then ride a train 20 minutes into town).

Port Overview

Piraeus, a city six miles southwest of central Athens, has been the port of Athens since ancient times. Today it's also the main hub for services to the Greek islands, making it the busiest passenger port in the Mediterranean. A staggering 13 million journeys begin or end here each year.

Piraeus' Great Harbor (Megas Limin) has 12 numbered docks, or "gates," which surround the harbor. Cruise ships dock at **Cruise Terminal A** (at Gate E11) or **Cruise Terminal B** (Gate E12) at the far-south end of the harbor. The two terminals are about a five-minute walk apart; north of these stretch 10 more "gates" with vessels heading to islands all over Greece and beyond.

As Piraeus is big, grimy, and of no sightseeing value, the best plan is to head for Athens as soon as you can. But if you wind up

Services at the Port of Piraeus

Here are the nearest locations of the following services at the port, though if you can wait until Athens, you'll find everything you need.

ATMs: There are ATMs in each cruise terminal building and at other locations around the port area.

Internet Access: There may be free Wi-Fi around the port, but it's not entirely reliable. If you walk around the port area, you'll see several Internet cafés.

Pharmacy: Several pharmacies are close to Cruise Terminal A on Sachtouri (ΣΑΧΤΟΥΡΗ) street. Pharmacy hours in Greece are usually Mon-Fri 8:00-14:30, also Tue and Thu-Fri 17:30-20:00. For 24-hour pharmacies, call 14944.

Baggage Storage: If Piraeus is your first or last stop, and you need a place to store bags, luggage lockers (€3) are at both the Metro and the suburban train stations. If you're in a pinch, various travel agencies closer to the port might be willing to store your bags for a fee.

with extra time here, you'll find that the northeast corner of the Great Harbor has the most activity: the Metro station and suburban train station (connected to the harbor by a modern pedestrian bridge) and—just down the street—Karaiskaki Square, which juts out into the harbor. Cheap eateries, flophouse hotels, and dozens of travel agencies round out the scene.

Tourist Information: Frustratingly, official tourist information is in short supply here. Both Athens and Piraeus sometimes run seasonal TI kiosks near the docks, but these tend to come and go. The port police (with several offices clearly marked in English) can be helpful. The port authority website is www.olp.gr.

Getting into Athens

By Taxi

Cabbies wait in front of each cruise terminal. The fair metered rate from either terminal into downtown is about €15-20, depending on traffic (includes legitimate €5.20 cruise terminal surcharge—you can try to avoid this by walking up to the main road and finding a taxi there). The trip can take anywhere from 20-40 minutes or more, depending on traffic. Some drivers offer a three-hour tour around the city center, including basic commentary and waiting time at the Acropolis (about €120). If this appeals to you, find a driver who speaks good English and would be fun to chat with.

ATHENS

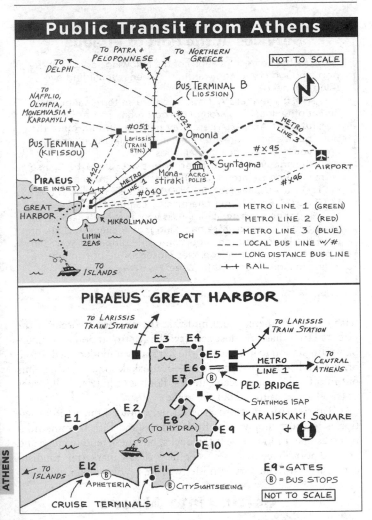

Public Transit from Athens

Piraeus' Great Harbor

E9 = GATES
Ⓑ = BUS STOPS

NOT TO SCALE

By Bus

Bus #040 goes from Piraeus' cruise-terminal area to Athens' main Syntagma Square (€1.20, 6-8/hour, 30-60 minutes depending on traffic). The bus leaves from the stop called Apheteria (ΑΦΕΤΗΡΙΑ, "starting point"), which is on the main road between the two cruise terminals. Several different bus lines stop here, so make sure you get on the right bus. To reach the bus stop from Cruise Terminal A, exit the terminal building, bear left and walk along the road up the low hill. When you reach the main road, turn right and walk along it to reach the Apheteria bus stop. From Cruise Terminal B, exit the building, and follow the road to the left of the pretty yellow church. You'll see the row of buses ahead.

By Hop-on, Hop-off Bus: CitySightseeing offers a hop-on, hop-off bus that includes a 70-minute itinerary around Piraeus and links to a separate 1.5-hour bus route around Athens (€22 for all-day tour; bus departs Piraeus at 8:30, 9:00, 9:30, 10:00, 11:30, 13:00, and 14:30; returns to Piraeus in the afternoon from "Melina Merkouri" stop across from Athens' Temple of Olympian Zeus at 10:45, 12:15, 13:45, 15:15, 16:45, and 20:00). The low-profile bus stop (a sign on a post) is about 300 yards past Cruise Terminal A on the main road, on the port side of the road.

By Metro

The Metro speedily connects Piraeus with downtown Athens' Monastiraki stop. The catch is that the Metro station is between gates E6 and E7, a 15- to 20-minute walk from Cruise Terminal A (5-10 minutes more from Cruise Terminal B).

The Metro station is a big yellow Neoclassical building with white trim, marked by a pedestrian bridge over the busy street (it's the only such bridge at Piraeus; the bus stop in front is named Stathmos ISAP/ΣΤΑΘΜΟΣ ΗΣΑΠ, and the station is sometimes labeled "Electric Railway Station" on maps). From here, Metro line 1/green links Piraeus with downtown Athens (covered by €1.40 transit ticket, good for 1.5 hours including transfers, train departs about every 10 minutes between 6:00-24:00). In about 20 minutes, the train reaches the city-center Monastiraki stop, near the Plaka and many recommended sights. (For Syntagma, at the start of my self-guided "Athens City Walk," ride the train one more stop to Omonia to transfer to line 2/red.) Warning: The Metro line between Piraeus and downtown Athens teems with pickpockets—watch your valuables and wear a money belt.

Getting from the Cruise Terminals to the Metro Station: You can take a **taxi** there (about €5-7), or catch public **bus** #843 from the Apheteria bus stop between the two terminals (bus stop described under "By Bus," earlier; buy €1.40 ticket from a kiosk to cover both the bus and the Metro ride and validate your ticket when you board, 6-10/hour Mon-Sat, 3-5/hour Sun). If you want to **walk** to the Metro, it'll take about 15-20 minutes from Terminal A and about 20-30 minutes from Terminal B. From **Cruise Terminal A,** exit the terminal building, keep left, and walk up the incline to the main road. At this road, head right to reach the Apheteria bus stop, and find bus #843; or, if you don't mind walking the whole way to the Metro, turn left onto the main road and simply follow it along the port. To reach the Metro from **Cruise Terminal B,** exit the building and follow the road to the left of the yellow church to reach the Apheteria stop (for bus #843), or continue walking on the same road around the port to the Metro station.

By Tour

For information on local tour options in Athens—including bus tours, walking tours, and a local guide for hire—see "Tours in Athens" on page 890.

Returning to Your Ship

If you're coming on bus #040 from Syntagma Square, get off at the Apheteria (ΑΦΕΤΗΡΙΑ) stop, right by the cruise terminals.

You can also return to Piraeus by Metro; take line 1/green toward Piraeus (the end of the line). Exit the Piraeus station out the side door, into a chaotic little square filled with vendors slinging knock-off designer bags. Head up the escalator and walk to the far end of the pedestrian bridge, then turn left and take the escalator back down to ground level. At the row of bus stops straight ahead, find the stop for bus #843. Your €1.40 Metro ticket will also cover you on this bus; just hop on and ride it to Apheteria (ΑΦΕΤΗΡΙΑ) bus stop, near both cruise terminals.

If you miss your boat, see the sidebar at the end of this chapter.

Orientation to Athens

Athens, while sprawling and congested, has a compact, pleasant tourist zone capped by the famous Acropolis—the world's top ancient site. In this historic town, you'll walk in the footsteps of the great minds who created democracy, philosophy, theater, and more...even when you're dodging motorcycles on "pedestrianized" streets. Romantics can't help but get goose bumps as they kick around the same pebbles that once stuck in Socrates' sandals, with the floodlit Parthenon forever floating ethereally overhead.

Many tourists visit Athens without ever venturing beyond the Plaka (Old Town) and ancient zone. With limited time, this is not a bad plan, as greater Athens offers few sights (other than the excellent National Archaeological Museum).

Because of its prominent position on the tourist trail, and the irrepressible Greek spirit of hospitality, the city is user-friendly. It seems that virtually all Athenians speak English, major landmarks are well-signed, and most street signs are in Greek followed by a transliteration in English (see sidebar on page 880).

Athens: A Verbal Map

Ninety-five percent of Athens is noisy, polluted modern sprawl, jammed with characterless concrete suburbs—poorly planned and hastily erected to house the area's rapidly expanding population. The construction of the Metro for the 2004 Olympics was, in many ways, the first time urban planners had ever attempted to tie

Athens Neighborhoods

NATIONAL ARCHAEOLOGICAL MUSEUM

OMONIA SQUARE

EXARCHIA

LYKAVITTOS HILL

←GAZI

ATHINAS

PANEPISTIMOU

Nat'l. LIBRARY

KOLONAKI

PSYRRI

ERMOU

SYNTAGMA

VASILISSIS SOFIAS

THISSIO

MONASTIRAKI

AGORA

SYNTAGMA SQUARE

PARLIAMENT

ACROPOLIS

APOSTOLOU PAVLOU

ADRIANOU

PLAKA

Nat'l. GARDEN

FILOPAPPOS HILL

DIONYSIOU AREOPAGITOU

ACROPOLIS MUSEUM

VASILISSIS AMALIAS

TEMPLE OF OLYMPIAN ZEUS

MAKRIGIANNI

SYNGROU

KOUKAKI

TO PIRAEUS + CRUISE PORT

NOT TO SCALE

DCH

the city together and treat it as a united entity.

But most visitors never see that part of Athens. In fact, you

can pretend that Athens is the same small, atmospheric village at the foot of the Acropolis as it was a century ago. Almost everything of importance to tourists is within a few blocks of the Acropolis. As you explore this city-within-a-city on foot, you'll realize just how small it is.

A good map is a necessity for enjoying Athens on foot. The fine map the TI gives out works great. Get a good map and use it.

Athens by Neighborhood

The Athens you'll be spending your time in includes the following districts:

The Plaka (PLAH-kah, Πλάκα in Greek): This neighborhood at the foot of the Acropolis is the core of the tourist's Athens. One of the only parts of town that's atmospheric and Old World-feeling, it's also the most crassly touristic. Its streets are lined with

ATHENS

Greek Words and English Spellings

Any given Greek name—for streets, sights, businesses, and more—can be transliterated many different ways in English. Throughout this book's Greek chapters, I've used the English spelling you're most likely to see locally, but you will definitely notice variations. If you see a name that looks (or sounds) similar to one in this book's Greece chapters, it's likely the same place. For example, the Ψυρή district might appear as Psyrri, Psyrrí, Psyri, Psirri, Psiri, and so on.

Most major streets in Athens are labeled in Greek in signs and on maps, followed by the transliteration in English. The word ΟΔΟΣ (odos) means "street," ΛΕΩΦ'ΟΡΟΣ (leoforos) is "avenue," and ΠΛΑΤΕΙΑ (plateia) is "square."

If a name used in this book appears locally only in Greek, I've included that spelling to aid with your navigation.

souvenir shops, tacky tavernas, a smattering of small museums, ancient Greek and Roman ruins, and pooped tourists. The Plaka's narrow, winding streets can be confusing at first, but you can't get too lost with a monument the size of the Acropolis looming overhead to keep you oriented. Think of the Plaka as Athens with training wheels for tourists. While some visitors are mesmerized by the Plaka, others find it obnoxious and enjoy venturing outside it for a change of scenery.

Monastiraki (mah-nah-stee-RAHee-kee, Μοναστηράκι): This area ("Little Monastery") borders the Plaka to the northwest, surrounding the square of the same name. It's known for its handy Metro stop (where line 1/green meets line 3/blue), seedy flea market, and souvlaki stands. The Ancient Agora is nearby (roughly between Monastiraki and Thissio).

Psyrri (psee-REE, Ψυρή): Formerly a dumpy ghetto just north of Monastiraki, Psyrri is emerging as a cutting-edge nightlife and dining district.

Syntagma (seen-DOG-mah, Σύνταγμα): Centered on Athens' main square, Syntagma ("Constitution") Square, this urban-feeling zone melts into the Plaka to the north and east. While the Plaka is dominated by tourist shops, Syntagma is where local urbanites do their shopping. Syntagma is bounded to the east by the Parliament building and the vast National Garden.

Thissio (thee-SEE-oh, Θησείο): West of the Ancient Agora, Thissio is an upscale, local-feeling residential neighborhood with piles of outdoor cafés and restaurants.

Gazi (GAH-zee, Γκάζι): At the western edge of the tourist's Athens (just beyond Thissio and Psyrri), Gazi is trendy, artsy, and gay-friendly.

Makrigianni (mah-kree-YAH-nee, Μακρυγιάννη) and **Koukaki** (koo-KAH-kee, Κουκάκι): Tucked just behind (south of) the Acropolis, these overlapping, nondescript urban neighborhoods have a lived-in charm of their own.

Kolonaki (koh-loh-NAH-kee, Κολωνάκι): Just north and east of the Parliament/Syntagma Square area, this upscale diplomatic quarter is home to several good museums and a yuppie dining zone.

Exarchia (ex-AR-kee-yah, Εξάρχεια): Just beyond Kolonaki is a rough-and-funky student zone. The origin of many of the protests that grabbed Greek headlines in 2010, it's a fascinating but not-for-everyone glimpse into an Athens that few tourists experience.

Tourist Information

The Greek National Tourist Organization (EOT), with its main branch near **Syntagma Square,** covers Athens and the rest of the country. Pick up their handy city map, the helpful *Athens Guide* booklet, and their slick, glossy book on Athens (all free). While their advice can be hit-or-miss, they do have stacks of informative handouts on museums, entertainment options, bus and train connections, and much more (Mon-Fri 9:00-19:00, Sat-Sun 10:00-16:00; from the top of Syntagma Square facing the Parliament, head right/south a few blocks along the busy avenue to Vasilissis Amalias 26; tel. 210-331-0392, www.gnto.gr, info@gnto.gr).

EOT also has an office at the **airport** (generally Mon-Fri 9:00-18:00, Sat-Sun 10:00-16:00 but depends on flight schedule, tel. 210-353-0448), plus a seasonal kiosk on Syntagma Square.

Helpful Website: While not officially part of the TI, **Matt Barrett's Athens Survival Guide** is a great resource for anyone visiting Greece (www.athensguide.com). Matt, who splits his time between North Carolina and Greece, splashes through his adopted hometown like a kid in a wading pool, enthusiastically sharing his discoveries and observations on his generous site. Matt covers emerging neighborhoods that few visitors venture into, and offers offbeat angles on the city and recommendations for vibrant, untouristy restaurants. He also blogs about his latest impressions on the city.

Helpful Hints

Theft Alert: Be wary of pickpockets, particularly in crowds, at the Monastiraki flea market, on major public transit routes (such as the Metro between the city and Piraeus), and at the port. The main streets through the Plaka—such as Adrianou and Pandrossou—attract as many pickpockets as tourists.

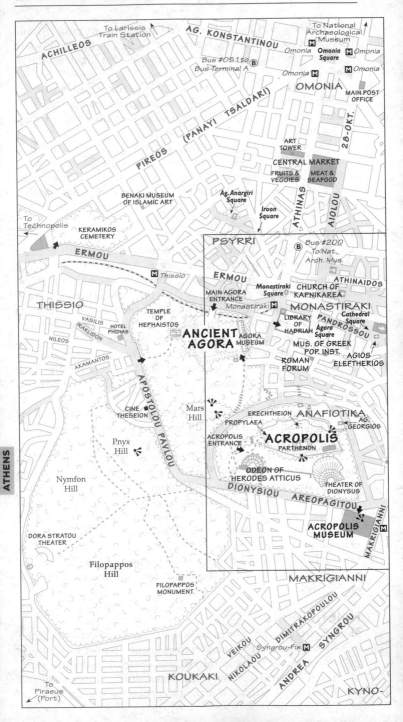

ATHENS

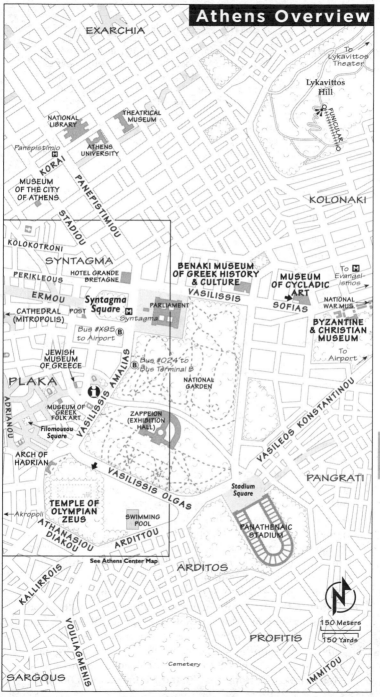

Athens Overview

EXARCHIA

To Lykavittos Theater

Lykavittos Hill

FUNICULAR

NATIONAL LIBRARY

THEATRICAL MUSEUM

Panepistimio

KORAI

ATHENS UNIVERSITY

PANEPISTIMIOU

KOLONAKI

MUSEUM OF THE CITY OF ATHENS

STADIOU

KOLOKOTRONI

SYNTAGMA

PERIKLEOUS

HOTEL GRANDE BRETAGNE

BENAKI MUSEUM OF GREEK HISTORY & CULTURE

VASILISSIS

MUSEUM OF CYCLADIC ART

To Evangel-ismos

ERMOU

Syntagma Square

PARLIAMENT

SOFIAS

NATIONAL WAR MUS

CATHEDRAL (MITROPOLIS)

POST

Syntagma

Bus #X95 to Airport

BYZANTINE & CHRISTIAN MUSEUM

JEWISH MUSEUM OF GREECE

VASILISSIS AMALIAS

Bus #024 to Bus Terminal B

To Airport

PLAKA

NATIONAL GARDEN

ADRIANOU

MUSEUM OF GREEK FOLK ART

ZAPPEION (EXHIBITION HALL)

VASILEOS KONSTANTINOU

Filomousou Square

ARCH OF HADRIAN

Akropoli

ATHANASIOU DIAKOU

TEMPLE OF OLYMPIAN ZEUS

VASILISSIS OLGAS

SWIMMING POOL

ARDITTOU

Stadium Square

PANGRATI

PANATHENAIC STADIUM

See Athens Center Map

ARDITOS

KALLIRROIS

150 Meters

150 Yards

PROFITIS

VOULIAGMENIS

Cemetery

IMMITOU

SARGOUS

ATHENS

Daily Reminder

Sunday: Most sights are open, but the Art Tower and Central Market are closed. The Monastiraki flea market is best to visit today. An elaborate changing of the guard—including a marching band—sometimes takes place at 11:00 in front of the Parliament building. Off-season (Nov-March), the Acropolis is free.

Monday: Many museums and galleries are closed, including the Acropolis Museum, Benaki Museum of Islamic Art, Museum of Greek Folk Art, Museum of Greek Popular Instruments, Art Tower, and National War Museum. The National Archaeological Museum opens at 13:30, and the Agora Museum opens at 13:00. Off-season (Nov-March), the Byzantine and Christian Museum is closed.

Tuesday: These sights are closed today: the Museum of Cycladic Art, Museum of Greek Folk Art Ceramics Collection, Museum of the City of Athens, Art Tower, and Benaki Museum of Greek History and Culture.

Wednesday: All major sights are open.

Thursday: All major sights are open.

Friday: All major sights are open.

Saturday: All major sights are open, except the Jewish Museum.

Traffic Alert: Streets that appear to be "traffic-free" often are shared by motorcycles or moped drivers gingerly easing their machines through crowds. Keep your wits about you, and don't step into a street—even those that feel pedestrian-friendly—without looking both ways.

Slippery Streets Alert: Athens (and other Greek towns) have some marble-like streets and red pavement tiles that become very slick when it rains. Watch your step.

Internet Access: Bits and Bytes, in the heart of the Plaka, has plenty of terminals, a peaceful folk/jazz ambience, and air-conditioning (€2 minimum, €2.50/hour, can burn your digital photos to a CD or DVD, open 24 hours daily, just off Agora Square at Kapnikareas 19, tel. 210-325-3142). At Syntagma Square, **Ivis Travel** has several Internet terminals (€2/30 minutes, €3/hour, €2 minimum, daily 8:00-22:00, upstairs at Mitropoleos 3—look for signs, tel. 210-324-3365).

Post Offices: The most convenient post office for travelers is at Syntagma Square (Mon-Fri 7:30-20:00, Sat 7:30-14:00, Sun 9:00-13:30, bottom of the square, at corner with Mitropoleos). Smaller neighborhood offices with shorter hours (generally Mon-Fri 7:30-14:00 or 14:30, closed Sat-Sun) are in Monastiraki (Mitropoleos 58) and Makrigianni (Dionysiou

Areopagitou 7).

Bookshops: Compendium Bookstore stocks mostly English-language books and has a secondhand section (Mon-Sat 9:00-17:00, until 20:30 on Tue and Thu-Fri, closed Sun; just southwest of Syntagma Square at the corner of Nikis and Nikodimou, Nikodimou 5, tel. 210-322-1248). **Eleftheroudakis** (ΕΛΕΥΘΕΡΟΥΔΑΚΗΣ) is Greece's answer to Barnes & Noble. Their main branch has a floor for travel guides and maps, and an entire floor for English books (Mon-Fri 9:00-21:00, Sat 9:00-18:00, closed Sun, 3 blocks north of Syntagma Square at Panepistimiou 17, tel. 210-325-8440, www.books.gr). Their smaller branch is in the tight streets southwest of Syntagma Square, near Compendium (same hours, Nikis 20, tel. 210-322-9388). For locations, see the map on page 977.

Getting Around Athens

Because Athens is such a huge city, you'll likely use public transportation to reach farther-flung destinations (such as the port of Piraeus, the airport, or the National Archaeological Museum).

For information on all of Athens' public transportation, see www.oasa.gr. Beware of pickpockets on the Metro and buses.

By Metro

The Metro is the most straightforward way to get around Athens. Just look for signs with a blue M in a green circle. The Metro is

slick, user-friendly, and new-feeling—mostly built, renovated, or expanded for the 2004 Olympics. Signs are in both Greek and English, as are announcements inside subway cars. Trains run about every five minutes (Sun-Thu 5:00-24:20, Fri-Sat 5:00-2:20 in the morning, www.amel.gr).

There are various types of tickets, which you can buy at machines or from ticket windows. The **basic ticket** (€1.40) is good for 1.5 hours, including transfers. If planning more than two rides in a day, consider the **24-hour ticket** (€4). Be sure to stamp your ticket in a validation machine, located near the ticket booth (24-hour tickets only need to be stamped the first time). Those riding without a ticket (or with an unstamped ticket) are subject to stiff fines. Note that even though the airport is on the Metro system, it's not covered by any of these tickets (you have to buy a separate €8 ticket—see page 978).

The three Metro lines are color-coded and numbered. Use the

Athens at a Glance

In the sight listings below, a page number directs you to a fuller description in this chapter; sights without page numbers are not described further and generally don't make the cut for a one-day visit.

▲▲▲**Acropolis** The most important ancient site in the Western world, where Athenians built their architectural masterpiece—the Parthenon. **Hours:** Daily May-Sept 8:00-20:00, Oct-April 8:00-15:00. See page 957.

▲▲▲**Acropolis Museum** Glassy modern temple for ancient art. **Hours:** Tue-Sun 8:00-20:00, closed Mon. See page 961.

▲▲▲**Ancient Agora** Social and commercial center of ancient Athens, with a well-preserved temple and intimate museum. **Hours:** Daily May-Sept 8:00-20:00, Oct-April 8:00-15:00, museum opens Mon at 13:00. See page 961.

▲▲▲**National Archaeological Museum** World's best collection of ancient Greek art, displayed chronologically from 7000 B.C. to A.D. 500. **Hours:** May-Sept Tue-Sun 8:00-20:00, Mon 13:30-20:00; Oct-April Tue-Sun 8:30-15:00, Mon 13:30-19:30. See page 967.

▲▲**"Acropolis Loop"** Traffic-free pedestrian walkways ringing the Acropolis with vendors, cafés, and special events. **Hours:** Always open. See page 957.

▲▲**Thissio and Psyrri** Vibrant nightlife neighborhoods near the center, great for eating, exploring, and escaping other tourists. **Hours:** Always open.

▲▲**Anafiotika** Delightful, village-like neighborhood draped across the hillside north of the Acropolis. **Hours:** Always open. See page 962.

▲▲**Temple of Olympian Zeus** Remains of the largest temple in ancient Greece. **Hours:** Daily 8:00-20:00, off-season until 17:00. See page 966.

▲▲**Benaki Museum of Greek History and Culture** Exquisite collection of artifacts from the ancient, Byzantine, Ottoman, and modern eras. **Hours:** Wed-Mon 9:00-17:00 except Thu until 24:00 and Sun until 15:00, closed Tue.

▲▲**Museum of Cycladic Art** World's largest compilation of Cycladic art, which looks surprisingly modern even though it's 4,000 years old. **Hours:** Mon and Wed-Sat 10:00-17:00, Thu until 20:00, Sun 11:00-17:00, closed Tue.

▲▲**Byzantine and Christian Museum** Fascinating look at the Byzantines, who borrowed from ancient Greece and Rome, then put their own stamp on a flourishing culture. **Hours:** April-Oct Tue-Sun 8:00-20:00, Mon 13:30-20:00; Nov-March Tue-Sun 8:30-15:00, closed Mon.

▲**Mars Hill** Historic spot—with a classic view of the Acropolis— where the Apostle Paul preached to the Athenians. **Hours:** Always open. See page 960.

▲**Gazi** Former depressed industrial zone, now the colorful and kinetic heart of Athens' gay community. **Hours:** Always open.

▲**Roman Forum and Tower of the Winds** Ancient Roman marketplace with wondrously intact tower. **Hours:** Daily 8:00-19:00, until 15:00 off-season. See page 962.

▲**Museum of Greek Popular Instruments** Musical instruments from the 18th century to today. **Hours:** Tue and Thu-Sun 10:00-14:00, Wed 12:00-18:00, closed Mon. See page 963.

▲**Jewish Museum of Greece** Triumphs—and persecutions—of Greek Jews since the second century B.C. **Hours:** Mon-Fri 9:00-14:30, Sun 10:00-14:00, closed Sat. See page 964.

▲**Syntagma Square** Athens' most famous public space with a popular changing-of-the-guard ceremony. **Hours:** Always open, guards change five minutes before the top of each hour. See page 964.

▲**Church of Kapnikarea** Small 11th-century Byzantine church with symbols of Greek Orthodox faith. **Hours:** Likely open daily 8:30-13:30 & 17:00-19:30. See page 965.

▲**Cathedral (Mitropolis)** Large, underwhelming head church of the Greek Orthodox faith. **Hours:** Generally open daily 8:00-13:00 & 16:30-20:00, no afternoon closure in summer. See page 965.

▲**Church of Agios Eleftherios** Tiny Byzantine church decorated with a millennia of Christian bric-a-brac. **Hours:** Likely open daily 8:30-13:30 & 17:00-19:30. See page 965.

▲**Panathenaic (a.k.a. "Olympic") Stadium** Gleaming marble stadium restored to its second-century A.D. condition. **Hours:** Daily 8:00-19:30. See page 965.

▲**Museum of the City of Athens** Models and exhibits about Athenian history, housed in a former royal residence. **Hours:** Mon and Wed-Fri 9:00-16:00, Sat-Sun 10:00-15:00, closed Tue.

Athens Transit

— METRO LINE 1 (GREEN)
— METRO LINE 2 (RED)
- - - METRO LINE 3 (BLUE)
- - - BUS LINE w/#
+++ RAIL
— COASTAL TRAM w/#

Kifissia
Irini
TRAINS TO ALL OVER GREECE
LINE 1 (GREEN)
BUS TERMINAL LIOSSION **B**
Agios Antonios
#024
TO PIRAEUS #X96
Victoria
Airport
Attiki
NATIONAL ARCHAEO-LOGICAL MUSEUM
LINE 3 (BLUE)
Larissa (TRAIN STN.)
Egaleo
Omonia
Kera-mikos
LYKAVITTOS HILL
BUS TERMINAL KIFISSOU **A**
#051
Evangelismos
Monastiraki Thissio
ACRO-POLIS
Syntagma
#X95
TO AIRPORT #X1
Akropoli
Syngrou-Fix
Piraeus
Neo Faliro
#040
Neos Kosmos
1 & 2
1
LINE 2 (RED)
CRUISE PORT
Nea Smyrni
Agios Dimitrios
N
2
SARONIC GULF
FERRIES & HYDROFOILS TO ISLANDS
TO VOULA
DCH
NOT TO SCALE

end-of-the-line stops to figure out which direction you need to go.

Line 1 (green) runs from the port of Piraeus in the southwest to Kifissia in the northern suburbs. Since this is an older line (officially called ISAP or "subway" rather than "Metro"), it's slower than the other two lines. Key stops include **Piraeus** (boats to the islands), **Thissio** (enjoyable neighborhood with good restaurants and nightlife), **Monastiraki** (city center), **Victoria** (10-minute walk from National Archaeological Museum), and **Irini** (Olympic Stadium). You can transfer to line 2 at Omonia, and to line 3 at Monastiraki. (Confusingly, on line 1, the Monastiraki stop is labeled "Monastirion.")

ΜΟΝΑΣΤΗΡΙΟΝ
Monastirion

Line 2 (red) runs from Agios Antonios in the northwest to Agios Dimitrios in the southeast. Important stops include **Larissa** (train station), **Syntagma** (city center), **Akropoli** (Acropolis and Makrigianni/Koukaki hotel neighborhood), and **Syngrou-Fix** (Makrigianni/Koukaki hotels). Transfer to line 1 at Omonia and to line 3 at Syntagma. Be aware that construction is currently under way to extend line 2 at both ends. When the work is com-

ATHENS

pleted (possibly in 2011), the end stations will be Anthoupoli in the northwest and Helliniko in the southeast.

Line 3 (blue) runs from Egaleo in the west to the airport in the east. Important stops are **Keramikos** (near Keramikos Cemetery and the lively Gazi district), **Monastiraki** (city center), **Syntagma** (city center), **Evangelismos** (Kolonaki neighborhood, with Byzantine and Christian Museum and National War Museum), and the **Airport** (requires a separate ticket). Transfer to line 1 at Monastiraki and to line 2 at Syntagma.

By Bus

Public buses help connect the dots between Metro stops. Buy the €1.20 tickets in advance, either from a special ticket kiosk or from one of the many regular newsstands that dot the streets. Tickets must be validated in the orange machines as you board. In general, I'd avoid buses—which are slow and overcrowded—with these exceptions: Bus **#200** whisks you from Athinas street near Monastiraki to the National Archaeological Museum. Bus **#040** goes from Piraeus' cruise-terminal area to Syntagma Square. Bus **#X95** zips between the airport and Syntagma Square, and bus **#X96** connects the airport with Piraeus—these airport express buses cost €5.

By Taxi

Despite the vulgar penchant cabbies here have for ripping off tourists, Athens is a great taxi town. Its yellow taxis are cheap and handy (€3 minimum charge covers most short rides in town; after that, it's €0.66/km, plus surcharges: €1 from Piraeus passenger ports and train and bus stations, €3.10 from the airport, €5.20 from cruise terminal at Piraeus). The €0.66 per kilometer day rate (tariff 1 on the meter) doubles between midnight and 5:00 in the morning (tariff 2). You'll also pay the double rate outside the city limits, and you're responsible for any tolls incurred by the driver (such as on the speedy road to the airport). Baggage costs €0.40 for each item over 10 kilograms (about 22 pounds).

In a semi-legal local custom, Athens' cabbies double up, picking up additional passengers headed the same way. Unfortunately, sharing the cab with strangers doesn't mean sharing the fare. The cabbie makes more and the passengers save nothing. Still, this makes it easier to find an available cab. You can simply hail any taxi, empty or not, and if your destination works for the cabbie, he'll welcome you in.

Hotels and restaurants can order you a cab, but there's a €2 surcharge to call for a taxi ("radio-taxi"). Note that cabbies may try to cheat you by saying the surcharge is €5. Hold firm, and they will docilely take the €2.

ATHENS

Tours in Athens

On Wheels

Bus Tours—Various companies offer half-day, bus-plus-walking tours of Athens for €52-54 (about 4 hours, including a guided visit to the Acropolis). Add a guided tour of the Acropolis Museum, and the price goes up to €67.

The most established operations include the well-regarded **Hop In** (modern comfy buses, narration usually English only, tel. 210-428-5500, www.hopin.com), **CHAT Tours** (tel. 210-323-0827, www.chatours.gr), **Key Tours** (tel. 210-923-3166, www.keytours.gr), and **GO Tours** (tel. 210-921-9555, www.gotours.com.gr).

Tourist Trains—Two different trains do a sightseeing circuit through Athens' tourist zone. As these goofy little trains can go where big buses can't, they can be useful for people with limited mobility. The **Sunshine Express** train runs about hourly; catch it on Aiolou street along the Hadrian's Library fence at Agora Square (€5, 40-minute loop, departs hourly; May-Sept Mon-Fri 11:30-14:30 & 17:00-24:00, Sat-Sun 11:00-24:00; Oct-April Sat-Sun only; www.sunshine-express.gr). The **Athens Happy Train** is similar, but offers hop-on, hop-off privileges at a few strategic stops (€6, full loop takes 1 hour, 2/hour, daily 9:00-24:00; catch it at the bottom of Syntagma Square, at Monastiraki Square, or just below the Acropolis; www.athenshappytrain.com).

By Foot

Rick Steves Free Audio Tours—I've produced free, self-guided audio versions of my tours of the major sights in Athens (download them at www.ricksteves.com/audioeurope, from iTunes, or through the Rick Steves Audio Europe smartphone app). These user-friendly, easy-to-follow, fun, and enlightening audio tours are available for the Acropolis, the Agora, the National Archaeological Museum, and my Athens City Walk. I created these tours because none of these sights offers good information on the spot, and quality local guides can be expensive, unreliable, and elusive. If you don't mind me in your ear, these audio tours are hard to beat: Nobody will stand you up, the quality is reliable, you can take the tour exactly when you like, and they're free.

Walking Tours—Athens Walking Tours offers two basic walks: the Acropolis and City Tour (€36 plus entry fees, daily at 9:30, 3 hours, departs from Syntagma Metro station, under hanging clock one level down) and Acropolis Museum tour (€29 plus entry fee, Tue-Sun at 13:45, 1.5 hours, meet inside museum, in front of cash desk). Those with energy can sign up for a combo version of these tours (€53, Tue-Sun at 9:30, 5.5 hours, reserve in advance, tel.

210-884-7269, mobile 694-585-9662, www.athenswalkingtours.gr, Despina).

Local Guide—A good private guide can bring Athens' sights to life. **Effie Perperi** is a fine choice (€50/hour, tel. 210-951-2566, mobile 697-739-6659, effieperperi@gmail.com).

Self-Guided Walks & Tours in Athens

Be prepared to do a lot of walking in Athens; its ancient neighborhoods aren't bus-friendly and some sights are a long walk from the nearest Metro station. What follows is a two-hour stroll through the Plaka—Athens' oldest neighborhood, plus guided tours of the Acropolis, the Ancient Agora, and the new Acropolis Museum.

Athens City Walk

From Syntagma Square to Monastiraki Square

Athens is a bustling metropolis of nearly four million people, home to one out of every three Greeks. Much of the city is unappealing, cheaply built, poorly zoned, 20th-century sprawl. But the heart and soul of Athens is engaging and refreshingly compact. This walk takes you through the striking contrasts of the city center, from chaotic, traffic-clogged urban zones; to sleepy streets packed with bearded priests shopping for a new robe or chalice; to peaceful back lanes—barely wide enough for a donkey—that twist their way up toward the Acropolis. Along the way, we'll learn about Athens' rich history, the intriguing tapestry of Orthodox churches that dot the city, and the way that locals live and shop.

The walk begins at Syntagma Square, meanders through the fascinating old Plaka district, and finishes at lively Monastiraki Square (near the Ancient Agora, markets, good restaurants, and a handy Metro stop). This sightseeing spine will help you get a once-over-lightly look at Athens, which you can use as a springboard for diving into the city's various colorful sights and neighborhoods.

Orientation

Churches: Athens' churches keep irregular hours, but they're generally open daily 8:30-13:30 & 17:00-19:30. If you want to buy candles at churches (as the locals do), be sure to have a few small coins.

Cathedral: Generally open daily 8:00-13:00 & 16:30-20:00, no afternoon closure in summer.

Temple of Olympian Zeus: €2, covered by Acropolis ticket, daily 8:00-20:00, until 17:00 off-season, Vasilissis Olgas 1, Metro line 2/red: Akropoli, tel. 210-922-6330, www.culture.gr.

Roman Forum: €2, covered by Acropolis ticket, daily 8:00-19:00, until 15:00 off-season, corner of Pelopida and Aiolou streets, Metro line 1/green or 3/blue: Monastiraki.

When to Go: Do this walk early in your visit, as it can help you get your bearings in this potentially confusing city. I'd suggest going in the morning, while all the churches are open (since many close for an afternoon break) and other sights—such as the Acropolis—are too crowded to enjoy.

Dress Code: Wearing shorts inside churches (especially the cathedral) is frowned upon, though usually tolerated.

Getting There: The walk begins at Syntagma Square, just northeast of the Plaka tourist zone. You can get here by Metro (line 2/red or line 3/blue to Syntagma stop). Conveniently, this is also where bus #040 from the cruise terminals at Piraeus stops.

Audioguide Tours: See "Rick Steves Free Audio Tours" on page 890.

Length of This Walk: Allow plenty of time. This three-part walk takes two hours without stops or detours. But if you explore and dip into sights here and there—pausing to ponder a dimly lit Orthodox church, or doing some window- (or actual) shopping—it can enjoyably eat up a half-day or more.

Starring: Athens' top squares, churches, and Roman ruins, connected by bustling urban streets that are alternately choked with cars and mopeds, or thronged by pedestrians, vendors, and fellow tourists.

The Walk Begins

This lengthy walk is thematically divided into three parts: The first part focuses on modern Athens, centered on Syntagma Square and the Ermou shopping street.
The second part focuses on Athens' Greek Orthodox faith, with visits to three different but equally interesting churches. And the third part is a wander through the charming old core of Athens, including the touristy Plaka and the mellow Greek-village-on-a-hillside of Anafiotika.

Part 1: Modern Athens

This part of our walk lets you feel the pulse of a European capital.

• *Start at Syntagma Square. From the leafy park at the center of the square, climb to the top of the stairs (in the middle of the square) and stand across the street from the big, Neoclassical Greek Parliament building.*

❶ Syntagma Square (Plateia Syntagmatos)

As you look at posh hotels and major banks, you are standing atop the city's central Metro stop, surrounded by buses, cars, and taxis.

Facing the Parliament building (east), get oriented to the square named for Greece's constitution (*syntagma;* seen-DOG-mah). From this point, sightseeing options spin off through the city like spokes on a wheel.

Fronting the square on the left (north) side are high-end hotels, including the opulent Hotel Grande Bretagne.

Directly to the left of the Parliament building is the head of Vasilissis Sofias avenue, lined with embassies and museums, including the Benaki Museum of Greek Culture and History, Museum of Cycladic Art, Byzantine and Christian Museum, and National War Museum. This boulevard leads to the ritzy Kolonaki quarter, with its funicular up to the top of Lykavittos Hill. Extending to the right of the Parliament building is the National Garden, Athens' "Central Park." Here you'll find the Zappeion mansion-turned-conference-hall (with a fine summer outdoor cinema nearby) and, beyond the greenery, the evocative, ancient Panathenaic Stadium.

On your right (south) is one of Athens' prime transit hubs, with stops for bus #X95 to the airport, bus #024 to Bus Terminal B/Liossion, and the Athens Coastal Tram. Beneath your feet is the Syntagma Metro station, the city's busiest. The TI is a few blocks away down busy Vasilissis Amalias street (beyond the tram terminus, not visible from here).

Behind you, at the west end of the square, stretches the traffic-free shopping street called Ermou, which heads to the Plaka neighborhood and Monastiraki Square. (We'll be heading that way soon.) Nearby is the terminus for one of Athens' two tourist trains (see page 890).

Take a moment to look at the square and modern Athens: People buzz about on their way to work, handing out leaflets, feeding pigeons, or just enjoying a park bench (and, perhaps, the free Wi-Fi the city provides here), shaded by a variety of trees. Plane trees (chosen for their resilience against pollution and the generous shade they provide) make Syntagma a breezy and restful spot. Breathe deep and ponder the fact that until 1990, Athens was the most polluted city in Europe. People advertising facial creams would put a mannequin outside on the street for three hours and film it turning black. The moral: You need our cream.

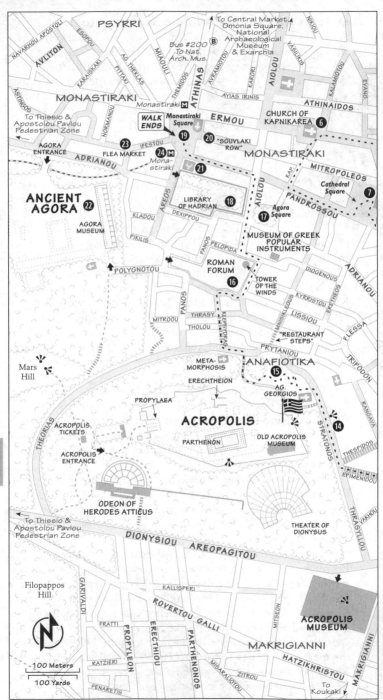

PSYRRI

To Central Market,
Omonia Square,
National
Archaeological
Museum
& Exarchia

Bus #200
To Nat.
Arch. Mus.

MONASTIRAKI

To Thissio &
Apostolou Pavlou
Pedestrian Zone

Monastiraki

ERMOU

CHURCH OF
KAPNIKAREA

WALK
ENDS

Monastiraki
Square

"SOUVLAKI
ROW"

MONASTIRAKI

FLEA MARKET

Monastiraki

MITROPOLEOS

Cathedral
Square

ANCIENT
AGORA

LIBRARY
OF HADRIAN

PANDROSSOU

AGORA
MUSEUM

Agora
Square

MUSEUM OF GREEK
POPULAR
INSTRUMENTS

ADRIANOU

POLYGNOTOU

ROMAN
FORUM

TOWER
OF THE
WINDS

Mars
Hill

"RESTAURANT
STEPS"

META-
MORPHOSIS

ANAFIOTIKA

ERECHTHEION

AG.
GEORGIOS

PROPYLAEA

ACROPOLIS
TICKETS

ACROPOLIS

ACROPOLIS
ENTRANCE

PARTHENON

OLD ACROPOLIS
MUSEUM

ODEON OF
HERODES ATTICUS

THEATER OF
DIONYSUS

To Thissio &
Apostolou Pavlou
Pedestrian Zone

DIONYSIOU AREOPAGITOU

Filopappos
Hill

ACROPOLIS
MUSEUM

MAKRIGIANNI

HATZIKHRISTOU

100 Meters

100 Yards

To
Koukaki

ATHENS

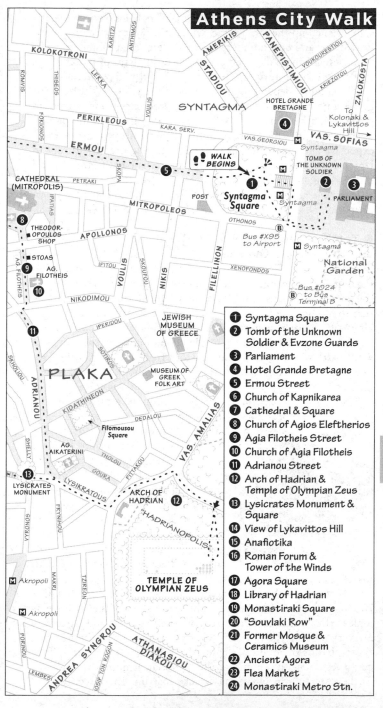

Athens City Walk

KOLOKOTRONI

SYNTAGMA

HOTEL GRANDE BRETAGNE

To Kolonaki & Lykavittos Hill

PERIKLEOUS

KARA. SERV.

VAS. SOFIAS

ERMOU

VAS. GEORGIOU

Syntagma

WALK BEGINS

TOMB OF THE UNKNOWN SOLDIER

CATHEDRAL (MITROPOLIS)

PETRAKI

POST

MITROPOLEOS

Syntagma Square

PARLIAMENT

OTHONOS

THEODOR-OPOULOS SHOP

APOLLONOS

Bus #X95 to Airport

Syntagma

STOAS

AG. FILOTHEIS

IPITOU

SKOUFOU

XENOFONDOS

National Garden

NIKODIMOU

VOULIS

NIKIS

Bus #024 to Bus Terminal B

IPERIDOU

JEWISH MUSEUM OF GREECE

ADRIANOU

PLAKA

SOTIROS

MUSEUM OF GREEK FOLK ART

KIDATHINEON

DEDALOU

SKOULOU

Filomousou Square

AG. AIKATERINI

THOLOU

PITTAKOU

VAS. AMALIAS

LYSICRATES MONUMENT

LYSIKRATOUS

GOURA

ARCH OF HADRIAN

SHELLY

FRYNIHOU

"HADRIANOPOLIS"

Akropoli

SONOROU

MAKRI

TZIREON

TEMPLE OF OLYMPIAN ZEUS

Akropoli

PORINOU

LEMBESI

ANDREA SYNGROU

ATHANASIOU DIAKOU

IOSIF TON ROGON

ATHENS

1. Syntagma Square
2. Tomb of the Unknown Soldier & Evzone Guards
3. Parliament
4. Hotel Grande Bretagne
5. Ermou Street
6. Church of Kapnikarea
7. Cathedral & Square
8. Church of Agios Eleftherios
9. Agia Filotheis Street
10. Church of Agia Filotheis
11. Adrianou Street
12. Arch of Hadrian & Temple of Olympian Zeus
13. Lysicrates Monument & Square
14. View of Lykavittos Hill
15. Anafiotika
16. Roman Forum & Tower of the Winds
17. Agora Square
18. Library of Hadrian
19. Monastiraki Square
20. "Souvlaki Row"
21. Former Mosque & Ceramics Museum
22. Ancient Agora
23. Flea Market
24. Monastiraki Metro Stn.

But over the last two decades, "green" policies have systematically cleaned up the air. Traffic, while still pretty extreme, is limited: Even- and odd-numbered license plates are prohibited in the center on alternate days. Check the license plates of passing cars (not taxis or motorcycles): The majority end with either an even or odd number, depending on the day of the week. Wealthy locals get around this restriction by owning two cars—one with even plates, the other with odd. While car traffic is down, motorcycle usage is up (since bikes are exempt). Central-heating fuel is more expensive and much cleaner these days (as required by European Union regulations), more of the city center is pedestrianized, and the city's public transport is top-notch.

• *Using the crosswalk (one on either side of Syntagma Square), cross the busy street. Directly in front of the Parliament you'll see the...*

❷ Tomb of the Unknown Soldier and the Evzone Guards

Standing amid pigeons and tourists in front of the imposing Parliament building, overlooking Syntagma Square, you're at the center of Athens' modern history. Above the simple marble-slab tomb—marked only with a cross—is a carved image of the Unknown Soldier, inspired by statues of ancient Greek warriors. Etched into the stone on each side of the tomb are the names of great battles in Greek military history from 1821 forward (practice your Greek alphabet by trying to read them: Cyprus, Korea, Rimini, Crete, and so on.)

The tomb is guarded by the much-photographed evzone, an elite infantry unit of the Greek army. The guard changes five minutes before the top of each hour, with a less elaborate crossing of the guard on the half-hour. They march with a slow-motion, high-stepping march to their new positions, then stand ramrod straight, where you can pose alongside them. A full changing-of-the-guard ceremony, complete with marching band, takes place most Sundays at 11:00.

These colorful characters are clad in traditional pleated kilts *(fustanella)*, white britches, and pom-pom shoes. (The outfits may look a little goofy to a non-Greek, but their mothers and girlfriends are very proud.) The uniforms were made famous by the Klephts, ragtag bands of mountain guerrilla fighters. After nearly four centuries under the thumb of the Ottoman Empire (from today's Turkey, starting in 1453), the Greeks rose up. The Greek War of

Independence (1821-1829) pitted the powerful Ottoman army against the lowly but wily Klephts. The Klephts reached back to their illustrious history, modeling their uniforms after those worn by soldiers from ancient Athens (the pom-poms date all the way back to the ancient Mycenaeans). The soldiers' winter skirts have 400 pleats...one for each year of Ottoman occupation (and don't you forget it). While considered heroes today for their courage and outrageous guerrilla tactics, the Klephts were once regarded as warlike bandits (their name shares a root with the English word "kleptomania").

As the Klephts and other Greeks fought for their independence, a number of farsighted Europeans (including the English poet Lord Byron)—inspired by the French Revolution and their own love of ancient Greek culture—came to their aid. In 1829, the rebels finally succeeded in driving their Ottoman rulers out of central Greece, and there was a movement to establish a modern democracy. However, the Greeks were unprepared to rule themselves, and so, after the Ottomans came...Otto.

• *For the rest of the story, take a step back for a view of the...*

❸ Parliament

The origins of this "palace of democracy" couldn't have been less democratic. The first independent Greek government, which

had its capital in Nafplio, was too weak to be viable. As was standard operating procedure at that time, the great European powers forced Greece to accept a king from established European royalty.

In 1832, Prince Otto of Bavaria became King Otto of Greece. A decade later, after the capital shifted to Athens, this royal palace was built to house King Otto and his wife, Queen Amalia. The atmosphere was tense. After fighting so fiercely for its independence from the Ottomans, the Greeks now chafed under royal rule from a dictatorial Bavarian monarch. The palace's over-the-top luxury only angered impoverished locals.

On September 3, 1843, angry rioters gathered in the square to protest, demanding a democratic constitution. King Otto stepped onto the balcony of this building, quieted the mob, and gave them what they wanted. The square was dubbed Syntagma (Constitution), and modern Athens was born. The former royal palace has been the home of the Greek Parliament since 1935. Today this is where 300 Greek parliamentarians (elected to four-year terms) tend to the business of the state—or, as more cynical locals would say, become corrupt and busily get themselves set up for their cushy, post-political lives.

• *Cross back to the heart of Syntagma Square, and focus on the grand building fronting its north side.*

❹ Hotel Grande Bretagne and Neoclassical Syntagma

Imagine the original Syntagma Square (which was on the outskirts of town in the early 19th century): a big front yard for the new royal

palace, with the country's influential families building mansions around it. Surviving examples include Hotel Grande Bretagne, the adjacent Hotel King George Palace, the Zappeion in the National Garden (not visible from here), and the stately architecture lining Vasilissis Sofias avenue behind the palace (now embassies and museums).

These grand buildings date from Athens' Otto-driven Neoclassical makeover. Eager to create a worthy capital for Greece, Otto imported teams of Bavarian architects to draft a plan of broad avenues and grand buildings in what they imagined to be the classical style. This "Neoclassical" look is symmetrical and geometrical, with pastel-colored buildings highlighted in white trim. The windows are rectangular, flanked by white Greek half-columns (pilasters), fronted by balconies, and topped with cornices. Many of the buildings themselves are also framed at the top with cornices. When you continue on this walk, notice not only the many Neoclassical buildings, but also the more modern buildings that try to match the same geometric lines.

Syntagma Square is also worth a footnote in American Cold War history. In December of 1944, Greek communists demonstrated here, inducing the US to come to the aid of the Greek government. This became the basis (in 1947) for the Truman Doctrine, which pledged US aid to countries fighting communism and helped shape American foreign policy for the next 50 years.

• *Head down to the bottom of Syntagma (directly across from the Parliament). Stroll down the traffic-free street near the McDonald's.*

❺ Ermou Street

The pedestrian mall called Ermou (AIR-moo) leads from Syntagma down through the Plaka to Monastiraki, then continues westward to the ancient Keramikos Cemetery and the Gazi district. Not long ago, this street epitomized all that was terrible about Athens:

ATHENS

lousy building codes, tacky neon signs, double-parked trucks, and noisy traffic. When Ermou was first pedestrianized in 2000, merchants were upset. Now they love the ambience created as countless locals stroll through what has become a people-friendly shopping zone.

This has traditionally been the street of women's shops. However, these days Ermou is dominated by high-class international chain stores, which appeal to young Athenians but turn off older natives, who lament the lack of local flavor. For authentic, hole-in-the-wall shopping, many Athenians prefer the streets just to the north, such as Perikleous, Lekka, and Kolokotroni. (For a self-guided shopping stroll in that area, see page 975.)

Even so, this people-crammed boulevard is a pleasant place for a wander. Do just that, proceeding gradually downhill and straight ahead for seven blocks. As you window-shop, notice that many of Ermou's department stores are housed in impressive Neoclassical mansions. Talented street performers (many of them former music professionals from Eastern Europe) provide an entertaining soundtrack. All of Athens walks along here: businesspeople, teenage girls with iPods, Orthodox priests, men twirling worry beads, activists gathering signatures, illegal vendors who sweep up their wares and scurry when they see police, cell-phone-toting shoppers, and, of course, tourists. Keep an eye out for vendors selling various snacks—including pretzel-like sesame rings called *koulouri* and slices of fresh coconut.

After six short blocks, on the right (at the intersection with Evangelistrias/Ευαγγελιστριασ), look for the little **book wagon** selling cheap lit. You'll likely see colorful, old-fashioned alphabet books (labeled ΑΛΦΑΒΗΤΑΡΙΟ, *Alphabetario*), which have been reprinted for nostalgic older Greeks. Remember that the English word "alphabet" comes from the first two Greek letters (alpha, beta).

Reaching the little church in the middle of the street (we'll visit it next, in Part 2 of this walk), look around you for **recycling bins.** Athens—long notorious for its grime and pollution—is striving to catch up to the green 21st century. While slow to adapt, Athenians are warming up to this new ethic.

Cap this first part of your walk (20 yards past the little church) by popping into the **shopping mall** on the right at Ermou 54. Enjoy the cool air along with the cool architecture. This slice of 19th-century Athenian elegance has been nicely preserved and earns its keep today as a place to shop.

Part 2: The Greek Orthodox Church

This part of our walk introduces you to the Orthodox faith of Greece, including stops at three different churches.

• *Stranded in the middle of both Ermou street and the commercial bustle of the 21st century is a little medieval church.*

❻ Church of Kapnikarea

After the ancient Golden Age, but before Otto and the Ottomans, Athens was part of the Byzantine Empire (A.D. 323-1453). In the 11th and 12th centuries, Athens boomed, and several Eastern Orthodox churches like this one were constructed.

The Church of Kapnikarea—named for the tax on the cloth merchants that once lined this square—is a classic 11th-century Byzantine church. Notice that Kapnikarea is square and topped with a central dome. Telltale signs of a Byzantine church include tall arches over the windows, stones surrounded by a frame of brick and mortar, and a domed cupola with a cross on top. The large white blocks are scavenged from other, earlier monuments (also typical of Byzantine churches from this era). Over the door is a mosaic of glass and gold leaf, which, though modern, is made in the traditional Byzantine style.

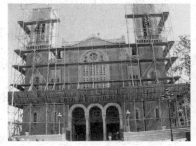

If the church is open, step inside. (If it's closed, don't fret—we'll be visiting a couple of similar churches later.) The church has no nave, just an entrance hall. Notice the symmetrical Greek-cross floor plan. It's decorated with standing candelabras, hanging lamps, tall arches, a wooden pulpit, and a few chairs. If you wish, you can do as the Greeks do and follow the standard candle-buying, icon-kissing ritual. The icon displayed closest to the door gets changed with the church calendar. You may notice lipstick smudges on the protective glass and a candle-recycling box behind the candelabra.

Look up into the central dome, lit with windows, which symbolizes heaven. Looking back down is the face of Jesus, the omnipotent *Pantocrator* (a Greek word meaning "Ruler of All") God blessing us on Earth. He holds a Bible in one hand and blesses us with the other. On the walls are iconic murals of saints. Notice the focus on the eyes, which are considered a mirror of the soul and a symbol of its purity.

• *When you leave the church, turn south toward the Acropolis and pro-*

ceed downhill on Kapnikareas street. Up ahead, catch a glimpse of the Acropolis. Go two blocks, to the traffic-free Pandrossou shopping street. Turn left and walk (passing the recommended Restaurant Hermion) up the pedestrian street to the cathedral.

❼ Cathedral (Mitropolis) and Cathedral Square (Plateia Mitropoleos)

Built in 1842, this "metropolitan church" (as the Greek Orthodox call their cathedrals) is the most important in Athens, which

makes it the head church of the Greek Orthodox faith. Unfortunately, it's unremarkable and oddly ramshackle inside and out...and has been decorated by scaffolding since the earthquake of 1989.

If it's open, head inside. Looking up (likely through more scaffolding), you'll notice balconies. Traditionally, women worshipped apart from men in the balconies upstairs. Women got the vote in Greece in 1954, and since about that time, they've been able to worship in the prime, ground-floor real estate alongside the men.

When you're back outside on the square, notice the statue facing the cathedral. This was erected by Athens' Jewish community as thanks to **Archbishop Damaskinos** (1891-1949), the rare Christian leader who stood up to the Nazis during the occupation of Greece. At great personal risk, Damaskinos formally spoke out against the Nazi occupiers on behalf of the Greek Jews he saw being deported to concentration camps. When a Nazi commander threatened to put Damaskinos before a firing squad, the archbishop defiantly countered that he should be hanged instead, in good Orthodox tradition. After the occupation, Damaskinos served as regent and then prime minister of Greece until the king returned from exile.

Here Damaskinos is depicted wearing the distinctive hat of an archbishop (a kind of fez with cloth hanging down the sides). He carries a staff and blesses with his right hand, making a traditional Orthodox sign of the cross, touching his thumb to his ring finger. This gesture forms the letters ICXC, the first and last letters of the Greek name for Jesus Christ (ΙΗΣΟΥΣ ΧΡΙΣΤΟΣ—

traditionally C was substituted for Σ). Make the gesture yourself with your right hand. Touch the tip of your thumb to the tip of your ring finger and check it out: Your pinkie forms the I, your slightly crossed index and middle fingers are the X, and your thumb and ring finger make a double-C. Jesus Christ, that's clever. If you were a priest, you'd make the sign of the cross three times, to symbolize the Father, the Son, and the Holy Spirit.

The double-headed eagle that hangs around Damaskinos' neck is an important symbol of the Orthodox faith. It evokes the Byzantine Empire, during which Orthodox Christianity was at its peak as the state religion. Appropriately, the eagle's twin heads have a double meaning: The Byzantine Emperor was both the secular and spiritual leader of his realm, which exerted its influence over both East and West. (Coincidentally, a similar symbol has been used by many other kingdoms and empires, including the Holy Roman Empire and the Austro-Hungarian Empire.)

At the far end of the square from the cathedral is another statue, of a warrior holding a sword. This is **Emperor Constantine XI Palaeologus** (1404-1453), the final ruler of the Byzantine Empire. He was killed defending Constantinople from the invading Ottomans, led by Mehmet the Conqueror. Considered the "last Greek king" and an unofficial saint, Constantine XI's death marked the ascension of the Ottomans as overlords of the Greeks for nearly four centuries. On his boots and above his head, you'll see the double-headed eagle again.

• The small church tucked behind the right side of the cathedral is the...

❽ Church of Agios Eleftherios

A favorite of local church connoisseurs, the 13th-century Church of Agios Eleftherios (St. Eleutherius) is sometimes referred to as "the old cathedral" and was used by the archbishops of Athens after the Ottomans evicted them from the church within the Parthenon. It's a jigsaw-puzzle hodge-podge of B.C. and A.D. adornments (and even tombstones) from earlier buildings. For example, the carved marble reliefs above the door were scavenged from the Ancient Agora in the 12th century. They are part of a calendar of ancient Athenian

festivals, thought to have been carved in the second century A.D. The frieze running along the top of the building depicts a B.C. procession.

Later, Christians added their own symbols to the same panels—making the church a treasure trove of medieval symbolism. There are different kinds of crosses (Maltese, Latin, double) as well as carved rosettes, stars, flowers, and griffins feeding on plants and snakes. Walk around the entire exterior. Then, step inside to sample unadorned 12th-century Orthodox simplicity.

• *Exit the church, go around its right side, then turn right. Look for a street sign that reads* ΑΓΙΑΣ ΦΙΛΟΘΕΗΣ, *and start up...*

❾ Agia Filotheis Street

This neighborhood is a hive of activity for Orthodox clerics. The priests dress all in black, wear beards, and don those fez-like hats. Despite their hermetic look, most priests are husbands, fathers, and well-educated pillars of the community, serving as counselors and spiritual guides to Athens' cosmopolitan populace.

Notice the stores. Just behind and facing the little church is the shop of the **Theodoropoulos** family—whose name strives to use every Greek character available (ΘΕΟΔΟΡΟΠΟΥΛΟΣ). They've been tailoring priestly robes since 1907.

This is just the first of many **religious objects stores** that line the street (most are open Mon, Wed, and Fri 8:30-15:00; Tue and Thu 8:30-14:00 & 17:30-20:30; closed Sat-Sun). Cross the busy Apollonos street and continue exploring the shops of Agia Filotheis street. The Orthodox religion comes with unique religious paraphernalia: icons, gold candelabras, hanging lamps, incense burners, oil lamps, chalices, various crosses, and gold objects worked in elaborate repoussé design.

Pop into the **stoas** (arcades) at #15 and #17 (on the left) to see workshops of local artisans who make these objects—painters creating or restoring icons in the traditional style, tailors making bishops' hats and robes, carvers making little devotional statuettes.

A few more steps up on the left, the ❿ **Church of Agia Filotheis** (named, like the street, for a patron of Athens—St. Philothei) is adjacent to an office building (at #19) that serves as the headquarters for the Greek Orthodox Church. Athenians come here to file the paperwork to make their marriages (and divorces) official.

Part 3: Athens' "Old Town" (The Plaka and Anafiotika)

This part of our walk explores the atmospheric, twisty lanes of old Athens. Remember, back before Athens became Greece's capital in the early 1800s, the city was a small town consisting of little more than what we'll see here.

• *Continue up Agia Filotheis street until you reach a tight five-way intersection. The street that runs ahead and to your right (labeled AΔPIANOY)—choked with souvenir stands and tourists—is our next destination. Look uphill and downhill along...*

⓫ Adrianou Street

This intersection may be the geographical (if not atmospheric) center of the neighborhood called the Plaka. Touristy Adrianou street is a main pedestrian drag that cuts through the Plaka, running roughly east-west from Monastiraki to here. Adrianou offers the full gauntlet of Greek souvenirs: worry beads, sea sponges, olive products, icons, carpets, jewelry, sandals, faux vases and Greek statues, profane and tacky T-shirts, and on and on. It also offers plenty of cafés for tourists seeking a place to sit and rest their weary feet.

• *Bear left onto Adrianou and walk uphill several blocks, following it as it curves to the right (south). Finally, the street dead-ends at a T-intersection with Lysikratous street. (There's a small square ahead on the left, with palm trees, the Byzantine church of Agia Aikaterini, and an excavated area showing the street level 2,000 years ago.)*

From here, you can turn right and take a few steps uphill to the Lysicrates Monument and Square (and skip ahead to the section on the Lysicrates Monument). But if you've got more time and stamina, it's worth a two-block walk to the left down Lysikratous street to reach the remains of the Arch of Hadrian.

⓬ "Hadrianopolis": Arch of Hadrian and Temple of Olympian Zeus

After the Romans conquered the Greeks, Roman emperor Hadrian (or Adrianou) became a major benefactor of the city of Athens. He built a triumphal arch, completed a temple beyond it (now ruined), and founded a library we'll see later. The area beyond the arch was known as Hadrianopolis, a planned neighborhood built by the emperor. The grand archway overlooks the bustling, modern Vasilissis Amalias avenue, facing the Plaka and Acropolis. (If you turned left and followed this road for 10 minutes, you'd pass the TI, then end up back on Syntagma Square—where we began this walk.)

Arch of Hadrian: The arch's once-brilliant-white Pentelic marble is stained by the exhaust fumes from some of Athens'

worst traffic. The arch is topped
with Corinthian columns, the Greek
style preferred by the Romans.
Hadrian built it in A.D. 132 to celebrate the completion of the Temple
of Olympian Zeus (which lies just
beyond—described next). Like a big
paifang gate marking the entrance to
a modern Chinatown, this arch represented the dividing line between
the ancient city and Hadrian's new
"Roman" city. An inscription on the
west side informs the reader, "This is

Athens, ancient city of Theseus," while the opposite frieze carries
the message, "This is the city of Hadrian, and not of Theseus." This
must have been a big deal for Hadrian, as the emperor himself
came here to celebrate the inauguration.

• *Look past the arch to see the huge (and I mean huge) Corinthian columns remaining from what was once a temple dedicated to the Olympian
Zeus. For a closer look, cross the busy boulevard (crosswalk to the right).
You can pretty much get the gist by looking through the fence. But if you
want to get close to those giant columns and wander the ruins, enter the
site (covered by Acropolis ticket). To reach the entrance (a five-minute
walk), curl around the left side of the arch, then turn right (following
the fence) up the intersecting street called Vasilissis Olgas. The entrance
to the temple is a few minutes' walk up, on the right-hand side.*

Temple of Olympian Zeus (Olympieion): This largest temple
in ancient Greece took almost 700 years to finish. It was begun late

in the sixth century B.C. during
the rule of the tyrant Peisistratos.
But the task proved beyond
him. The temple lay abandoned,
half-built, for centuries until the
Roman emperor Hadrian arrived
to finish the job in A.D. 131. When
completed, it was 360 feet by 145
feet, consisting of two rows of 20
columns on each of the long sides and three rows of eight columns
along each end. Although only 15 of the original 104 Corinthian
columns remain standing, their sheer size (a towering 56 feet high)
is enough to create a powerful impression of the temple's scale.
The fallen column—which resembles a tipped-over stack of bottle
caps—was toppled by a storm in 1852. The temple once housed a
suitably oversized statue of Zeus, head of the Greek gods who lived
on Mount Olympus, and an equally colossal statue of Hadrian.

• *Return to Lysikratous street and backtrack two blocks, continuing past the small square with the church you passed earlier. After another block, you'll run into another small, leafy square with the Acropolis rising behind it. In the square is an elegant, round, white, columned monument.*

⑬ Lysicrates Monument and Square

This elegant marble monument has Corinthian columns that support a dome with a (damaged) statue on top. A frieze runs along

the top, representing Dionysus turning pirates into dolphins. The monument is the sole survivor of many such monuments that once lined this ancient "Street of the Tripods." It was so called because the monuments came with bronze tripods that displayed grand ornamental pottery vases and cauldrons (like those you'll see in the museums) as trophies. These ancient "Oscars" were awarded to winners of choral and theatrical competitions staged at the Theater of

Dionysus on the southern side of the Acropolis. This now-lonely monument was erected in 334 B.C. by "Lysicrates of Kykyna, son of Lysitheides"—proud sponsor of the winning choral team that year. Excavations around the monument have uncovered the foundations of other monuments, which are now reburied under a layer of red sand and awaiting further study.

The square itself, shaded by trees, is a pleasant place to take a break before climbing the hill. Have a frappé or coffee at the café tables (€3.50), grab a cheap cold drink from the cooler in the hole-in-the-wall grocery store to the left, or just sit for free on the benches under the trees.

• Passing the monument on its left-hand side, head uphill toward the Acropolis, climbing the staircase called Epimenidou street. At the top of the stairs, turn right onto Stratonos street, which leads around the base of the Acropolis. As you walk along, the Acropolis and a row of olive trees are on your left. The sound of the crickets evokes for Athenians the black-and-white movies that were filmed in this area in the 1950s and '60s. To your right, you'll catch glimpses of another hill off in the distance.

⑭ View of Lykavittos Hill

This cone-shaped hill (sometimes spelled "Lycabettus") topped with a tiny white church is the highest in Athens, at just over 900 feet above sea level. The hill can be reached by a funicular, which leads up from the Kolonaki neighborhood to a restaurant and view terrace at the top. Although it looms high over the cityscape,

Lykavittos Hill will always be overshadowed by the hill you're climbing now.

• *At the small Church of St. George of the Rock (Agios Georgios), go uphill, along the left fork. As you immerse yourself in a maze of tiny, whitewashed houses, follow signs that point to the Acropolis (even if the path seems impossibly narrow). This charming "village" is a neighborhood called...*

⓰ Anafiotika

These lanes and homes were built by people from the tiny Cycladic island of Anafi, who came to Athens looking for work after

Greece gained its independence from the Ottomans. In this delightful spot, nestled beneath the walls of the Acropolis, the big city seems miles away. Keep following the *Acropolis* signs as you weave through narrow paths, lined with flowers and dotted with cats dozing peacefully in the sunshine (or slithering luxuriously past your legs). Though ancestors of the original islanders still live here, Anafiotika (literally "little Anafi") is slowly becoming a place for wealthy locals to keep an "island cottage" in the city. As you wander through the oleanders, notice the male fig trees—no fruit—that keep away flies and mosquitoes. Smell the chicken-manure fertilizer, peek into delicate little yards, and enjoy the blue doors and maroon shutters...it's a transplanted Cycladic world. Posters of Anafi hang here and there, evoking the sandy beaches of the ancestral home island.

• *You'll know you're on the right track when you see a religious building with the date 1874 on a wall plaque. Follow the narrow walkway a few more steps. Emerging from the maze of houses, you'll hit a fork at a wider, cobbled lane. Turn right (downhill) and continue down the steep incline. When you hit a wider road (Theorias), turn left and walk toward the small, Byzantine-style Church of the Metamorphosis. (Note: To walk to the Acropolis entry from here, you would continue along this road as it bends left around the hill. For more on the Acropolis, see the "Acropolis Tour" on page 928. For now, though, let's continue our walk.) Just before this church, turn right and go down the steep, narrow staircase (a lane called Klepsydras, labeled ΚΛΕΨΥΔΡΑΣ). Cross the street called Tholou and continue down Klepsydras. The lane gets even narrower (yes, keep going between the plants). Eventually you'll run into a railing overlooking some ruins.*

ATHENS

⑯ The Roman Forum and the Tower of the Winds

The rows of columns framing this rectangular former piazza were built by the Romans, who conquered Greece around 150 B.C. and stayed for centuries. This square—

sometimes called the "Roman Agora"—was the commercial center, or forum, of Roman Athens, with a colonnade providing shade for shoppers browsing the many stores that fronted it. Centuries later, the Ottomans made this their grand bazaar. The mosque survives (although its minaret, like all minarets in town, was torn down by the Greeks when they won their independence from the Ottomans in the 19th century).

Take a few steps to the right to see the octagonal, domed **Tower of the Winds** (a.k.a. "Bath-House of the Winds"). The

carved reliefs depict winds as winged humans who fly in, bringing the weather. Built in the first century B.C., this building was an ingenious combination of clock, weathervane, and guide to the planets. The beautifully carved reliefs are believed to represent the ancient Greek symbols for the eight winds. Even local guides don't know which is which, but the reliefs are still beautiful. As you walk down the hill (curving right, then left around the fence, always going downhill), you'll see reliefs depicting a boy with a harp, a boy with a basket of flowers (summer wind), a relief with a circle, and a guy blowing a conch shell—he's imitating Boreas, the howling winter wind from the north. The tower was once capped with a weathervane in the form of a bronze Triton (half-man, half-fish) that spun to indicate which wind was blessing or cursing the city at the moment. Bronze rods (no longer visible) protruded from the walls and acted as sundials to indicate the time. And when the sun wasn't shining, people told time using the tower's sophisticated water clock, powered by water piped in from springs on the Acropolis. Much later, under Ottoman rule, dervishes used the tower as a place for their whirling worship and prayer.

• *It's possible but unnecessary to enter the ruins: You've seen just about everything from this vantage point. If you do decide to enter the ruins, follow the spike-topped fence below the tower down Pelopida street and through an outdoor dining zone (where it curves and becomes*

Epameinonda) to reach the ticket office and entry gate, near the tallest standing colonnade (tower explained on a plaque inside; entry covered by Acropolis ticket). Don't confuse the Roman Forum with the older, more interesting Ancient Agora, which is near the end of this walk (see page 911).

Otherwise, from just below the Tower of the Winds, head down Aiolou street to...

⑰ Agora Square (Plateia Agoras)

This leafy, restaurant-filled square is the touristy epicenter of the Plaka. A handy Internet café is nearby (Bits and Bytes, see page

884), as well as a stop for one of the city's tourist trains (see page 890).

On the left side of the square, you'll see the second-century A.D. ruins of the ⑱ **Library of Hadrian.** Four lone columns sit atop the apse-like foundations of what was once a cultural center (library, lecture halls, garden, and art gallery), built by the Greek-loving Roman emperor for the Athenian citizens.

• *Continue downhill alongside the ruins to the next block, where Aiolou intersects with the claustrophobic Pandrossou market street (which we walked along earlier). Remember that this crowded lane is worked by expert pickpockets—be careful. Look to the right up Pandrossou: You may see merchants sitting in folding chairs with their backs to each other, competition having soured their personal relationships. Turn left on Pandrossou and wade through the knee-deep tacky tourist souvenirs. The second shop is dedicated to "The Round Goddess"—soccer. ("Soccer widows" are as prevalent in Greece as "football widows" in the US.) Continue until you spill out into Monastiraki Square.*

⑲ Monastiraki Square Spin-Tour

We've made it from Syntagma Square—the center of urban Athens—to the city's *other* main square, Monastiraki Square, the gateway to the touristy Old Town. To get oriented to Monastiraki Square, stand in the center, face the small church with the cross on top (which is north), and pan clockwise.

The name Monastiraki ("Little Monastery") refers to this square, the surrounding neighborhood, the flea-market action nearby...and the cute **Church of the Virgin** in the square's center (12th-century Byzantine, mostly restored with a much more modern bell tower).

Beyond that (straight ahead from the end of the square),

Athinas street heads north to the Central Market, Omonia Square, and (after about a mile) the National Archaeological Museum.

Just to the right (behind the little church) is the head of **Ermou street**—the bustling shopping drag we walked down earlier (though no longer traffic-free here). If you turned right and walked straight up Ermou, you'd be back at Syntagma Square in 10 minutes.

Next (on the right, in front of the little church) comes Mitropoleos street—Athens' ❷⓿ **"Souvlaki Row."** Clogged with outdoor tables, this atmospheric lane is home to a string of restaurants that serve sausage-shaped, skewered meat—grilled up spicy and tasty. The place on the corner—Bairaktaris (ΜΠΑΪΡΑΚΤΑΡΗΣ)—is the best-known, its walls lined with photos of famous politicians and artists who come here for souvlaki and pose with the owner. But the other two joints along here—Thanasis and Savas—have a better reputation for their souvlaki. You can sit at the tables, or, for a really cheap meal, order a souvlaki to go for less than €2. (For details, see "Eating in Athens," page 972.) A few blocks farther down Mitropoleos is the cathedral we visited earlier.

Continue spinning clockwise. Just past Pandrossou street (where you entered the square), you'll see a ❷⓵ **former mosque**

(look for the Arabic script under the portico and over the wooden door). Known as the Tzami (from the Turkish word for "mosque"), this was a place of worship from the 15th to 19th centuries. Today, it houses the Museum of Greek Folk Art's **ceramics collection** (see page 963). The mosque's front balcony (no ticket required) offers fine views over Monastiraki Square.

To the right of the mosque, behind the fence along Areos street, you might glimpse some huge Corinthian columns. This is the opposite end of the **Library of Hadrian** complex we saw earlier. Areos street stretches up toward the Acropolis. If you were to walk a block up this street, then turn right on Adrianou, you'd reach the ❷⓶ **Ancient Agora**—one of Athens' top ancient attractions (see the "Ancient Agora Tour" on the next page). Beyond the Agora are the delightful Thissio neighborhood, ancient Keramikos Cemetery, and Gazi district.

As you continue panning clockwise, next comes the pretty yellow building that houses the **Monastiraki Metro station**. This was Athens' original, British-built, 19th-century train station—

Neoclassical with a dash of Byzantium. This bustling Metro stop is the intersection of two lines: the old line 1 (green, with connections to the port of Piraeus, the Thissio neighborhood, and Victoria—near the National Archaeological Museum) and the modern line 3 (blue, with connections to Syntagma Square and the airport). The stands in front of the station sell seasonal fruit and are popular with local commuters.

Just past the station, Ifestou street leads downhill into the ㉓ **flea market** (antiques, jewelry, cheap clothing, and so on—for more details, see page 974). If locals need a screw for an old lamp, they know they'll find it here.

Keep panning clockwise. Just beyond busy Ermou street (to the left of Athinas street) is the happening **Psyrri** district. For years a run-down slum, this zone is being gentrified by twenty-somethings with a grungy sense of style. Packed with cutting-edge bars, restaurants, cafés, and nightclubs, it may seem foreboding and ramshackle, but is actually fun to explore.

㉔ Monastiraki Metro Station

Finish your walk by stepping into the Monastiraki Metro station and riding the escalator down to see an exposed bit of ancient Athens. Excavations for the Metro revealed an ancient aqueduct, which confined Athens' Eridanos River to a canal. The river had been a main axis of the town since the eighth century B.C. In the second century A.D., Hadrian and his engineers put a roof over it, turning it into a more efficient sewer. You're looking at Roman brick and classic Roman engineering. A cool mural shows the treasure trove archaeologists uncovered with the excavations.

This walk has taken us from ancient ruins to the Roman era, from medieval churches and mosques to the guerrilla fighters of Greek Independence, through the bustling bric-a-brac of the modern city, and finally to a place where Athens' infrastructure—both ancient and modern—mingles.

• *Our walk is over. If you're ready for a break, savor a spicy souvlaki on "Souvlaki Row."*

Ancient Agora Tour

While the Acropolis was the ceremonial showpiece, it was the Agora (Αγορά) that was the real heart of ancient Athens. For some 800 years, from its founding in the sixth century B.C. to its destruction by barbarians in A.D. 267, it was the hub of all commercial, political, and social life in Athens, as well as home to much of its religious life.

Agora means "gathering place," but you could call this space by any of the names we typically give to the busiest part of a city—

Acropolis Ticket

Your €12 Acropolis ticket gives you entry to six major ancient sites: the Acropolis, Ancient Agora, Roman Forum, Keramikos Cemetery, Temple of Olympian Zeus, and Theater of Dionysus. If you see only the Acropolis, you'll still pay €12—so the other sites are effectively free add-ons. (The other attractions do sell cheaper individual tickets—but as you're virtually guaranteed to visit the Acropolis sometime during your trip, these are pointless.) It's technically valid for four days, but there's no date printed on the ticket, so in practice you can use it anytime. The ticket is one long strip; perforated "coupons" are removed and used to enter the smaller sites. You can buy the ticket at any participating site. Only the Acropolis ticket is unique—the other stubs can be used as you like.

downtown, main square, forum, piazza, marketplace, commons, and so on. It was a lively place where the pace never let up— much like modern Athens.

Little survives from the classical Agora. Other than one very well-preserved temple and a rebuilt stoa, it's a field of humble ruins. But that makes it a quiet, uncrowded spot— nestled in the shadow of the Acropolis—to wander and get a feel for the ancients.

Orientation

Cost: €4 or covered by €12 Acropolis ticket (which you can buy here; see sidebar).

Hours: Daily May-Sept 8:00-20:00, Oct-April 8:00-15:00, last entry 30 minutes before closing. The Agora Museum inside has the same hours, except on Mon when it opens at 13:00.

Getting There: From Monastiraki (Metro line 1/green or line 3/blue), walk a block south (uphill, toward the Acropolis). Turn right on Adrianou street, and follow the pedestrian-only, café-lined street along the railroad tracks for about 200 yards.

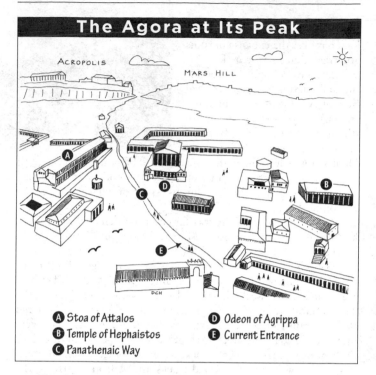

The Agora at Its Peak

ACROPOLIS

MARS HILL

Ⓐ Stoa of Attalos
Ⓑ Temple of Hephaistos
Ⓒ Panathenaic Way
Ⓓ Odeon of Agrippa
Ⓔ Current Entrance

ATHENS

The Agora entrance is on your left, across from a small yellow church. The entrance can be hard to spot: It's where a path crosses over the railroad tracks (look for a small, pale-yellow sign that says *Ministry of Culture—Ancient Agora*).

Compass Points: The Agora entrance is north; the Acropolis is south.

Information: Panels with printed descriptions of the ruins are scattered helpfully throughout the site. Tel. 210-321-0180, www.culture.gr.

Audioguide Tours: You can download a free audio version of this walk at www.ricksteves.com/audioeurope, from iTunes, or through the Rick Steves Audio Europe smartphone app.

Cuisine Art: Picnicking is not allowed in the Agora. Plenty of cafés and tavernas line busy Adrianou street near the Agora entrance.

Starring: A well-preserved temple, a rebuilt stoa, three monumental statues, and the ruins of the civilization that built the Western world.

The Tour Begins

Entering the site from the Adrianou street entrance, belly up to the illustration at the top of the ramp that shows Athens at its peak.

Face the Acropolis (to the south), look out over the expanse of ruins and trees, and get oriented.

The long column-lined building to the left is the reconstructed Stoa of Attalos (#13 on the illustration). To your right, atop a hill (the view is likely blocked by trees) is the well-preserved Temple of Hephaistos (#20). The pathway called the Panathenaic Way (#21) runs from the Agora's entrance up to the Acropolis. Directly ahead of you are three tall statue-columns—part of what was once the Odeon of Agrippa (#12).

In the distance, the Agora's far end is bordered by hills. From left to right are the Acropolis (#1), the Areopagus ("Hill of Ares," or Mars Hill, #2), and Pnyx Hill (#3).

Although the illustration implies that you're standing somewhere behind the Stoa Poikile ("Painted Stoa," #28), in fact you are located closer to the heart of the Agora, near the Altar of the Twelve Gods (#26). In ancient times, that altar was considered the geographical center of Athens, from which distances were measured. Today, the area north of the altar (and north of today's illustration) remains largely unexcavated and inaccessible to tourists, taken over by the railroad tracks and Adrianou street. The computer terminal (just to your right) is an impractical boondoggle that has never really worked—the result of corrupt cronyism that is so frustrating to Athenians. Someone made a fortune setting these things up.

This self-guided tour starts at the Stoa of Attalos (with its museum), then crosses the Agora to the Temple of Hephaistos, returning to the Panathenaic Way via three giant statues. Finally, we'll head up the Panathenaic Way toward the Acropolis.

• *Walk to the bottom of the ramp at your left for a better view. Find a shady spot to ponder...*

❶ The Agora at Its Peak, circa A.D. 150

What lies before you now is a maze of ruins—the remains of many centuries of buildings.

A millennium before the time of Socrates, during the Mycenaean Period (around 1400 B.C.), this area held the oldest cemetery in Athens. Later, the Agora was developed into an open marketplace—a rectangular area (about 100 yards by 200 yards), bordered by hills. Over time, that central square became surrounded by buildings, then filled in by more buildings. There were stoas like the (reconstructed) Stoa of Attalos (above on the

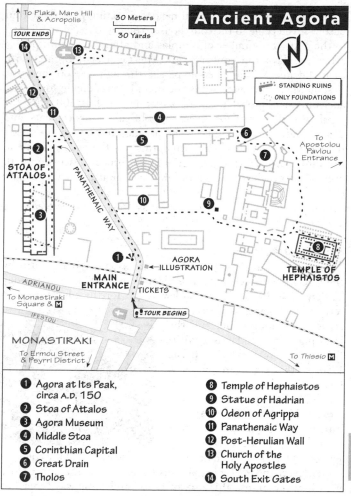

To Plaka, Mars Hill
& Acropolis

TOUR ENDS

30 Meters

30 Yards

Ancient Agora

STANDING RUINS

ONLY FOUNDATIONS

To
Apostolou
Pavlou
Entrance

STOA OF
ATTALOS

PANATHENAIC WAY

AGORA
ILLUSTRATION

MAIN
ENTRANCE

TICKETS

TOUR BEGINS

ADRIANOU

To Monastiraki
Square & M

IFESTOU

MONASTIRAKI

To Ermou Street
& Psyrri District

To Thissio M

TEMPLE OF
HEPHAISTOS

❶ Agora at Its Peak,
circa A.D. 150
❷ Stoa of Attalos
❸ Agora Museum
❹ Middle Stoa
❺ Corinthian Capital
❻ Great Drain
❼ Tholos

❽ Temple of Hephaistos
❾ Statue of Hadrian
❿ Odeon of Agrippa
⓫ Panathenaic Way
⓬ Post-Herulian Wall
⓭ Church of the
Holy Apostles
⓮ South Exit Gates

ATHENS

left), used for shops and offices; temples such as the Temple of
Hephaistos; and government buildings. Imagine the square framed
by these buildings—made of gleaming white marble, fronted with
columns, topped with red tile roofs. The square itself was studded with trees and dotted with statues, fountains, and altars.
Merchants sold goods from wooden market stalls.

The square buzzed with people—mostly men and lower-class
working women, as the place was considered a bit vulgar for genteel matrons. Both men and women would be dressed in simple
tunics (men's were knee-length, women's to the ankle). The Agora
was the place to shop—to buy groceries, clothes, dishes, or to get

your wagon wheel fixed. If you needed a zoning permit for your business, you came to the courthouse. You could make an offering to the gods at a number of temples and altars. At night, people attended plays and concerts, and the tavernas hummed with excited drinkers. Many people passed through here on their way to somewhere else, as this was the main intersection in town (and ancient Athens probably had a population of at least 100,000). The Agora was the center for speeches, political announcements, and demonstrations. On holidays, the parade ran down main street, the Panathenaic Way. At any time, this was the place to come to run into your friends, to engage in high-minded discussion with philosophers such as Socrates or Diogenes, or just to chat and hang out.

• *Now go to the long, intact, colonnaded building on your left (entrance at the south/far end), which is the....*

❷ Stoa of Attalos

This stoa—an ancient shopping mall—was originally built by the Greek-loving King Attalos II of Pergamon (in modern-day Turkey, 159-138 B.C.) as a thank-you gift for the education he'd

received in Athens. However, that structure is long gone, and the building we see today is a faithful reconstruction built in the 1950s by the American School of Classical Studies.

This is a typical two-story stoa. Like many of the Agora's buildings, it's made of white Pentelic marble. The portico is 381 feet by 64 feet, supported on the ground floor by 45 Doric columns (outer layer) and 22 Ionic columns (inner layer). The upper story uses Ionic columns. This mix of Doric and Ionic was typical of buildings from the period.

Stoas, with their covered walkways, provided protection from sun and rain for shoppers and businesspeople. This one likely served as a commercial mall. The ground floor was divided by

walls into 21 rooms that served as shops (it's now the museum). Upstairs were offices (which today house the American School of Classical Studies).

Like malls of today, the Agora's stoas were also social magnets. Imagine

ATHENS

ancient Greeks (their hard labor being done by slaves) lounging here, enjoying the shade of the portico. The pillars were designed to encourage people to lean against them (just as you may be doing right now)—with fluting starting only above six feet—for the comfort of philosophers.

• *The Stoa of Attalos houses the...*

❸ Agora Museum

The Agora is mostly ruins, but the excellent little museum displays some choice rubble that helps bring the place to life. Before entering, enjoy the arcade. Near the fifth column, find the impressive sculpted head of a bearded man with a full head of hair. This **Head of a Triton** (c. A.D. 150) comes from one of the statues that decorated the Odeon of Agrippa. Three of his fellow statues are still standing (we'll see them soon).

Walk halfway down the arcade and step inside the museum (included with your Agora ticket). The museum's modest but engaging collection fills a single long hall. Look in the corner for the 1952 photo showing this spot before the reconstruction. This well-described chronological stroll through art from 3200 B.C. gives you a glimpse of life in ancient Athens. Along the hall on the left, big panels show the Agora and Acropolis during each age, allowing you to follow their physical evolution.

The first few cases show off **jars** from various eras, including Neolithic (from the era when the Agora was first inhabited) and Geometric (with hash-mark designs). Much of this exhibit shows how pottery evolved over time. Usually painted red and black, pottery was a popular export product for the sea-trading Greeks. The earliest featured geometric patterns (eighth century B.C.), then a painted black silhouette on the natural orange clay, then a red figure on a black background.

In case 26 (on the right), look for the cute little baby's **commode,** with a photo showing how it was used. Nearby (case 69, on left) are Archaic-era statues with smiling faces.

Cases 30-32 (on right), with items from **early democracy,** are especially interesting. The "voting machine" (*kleroterion,* case 31) was used to choose council members. Citizens put their name in the slots, then black and white balls went into the tube to randomly select who would serve (much like your turn in jury duty). Below the machine are bronze ballots from the fourth century. The pottery shards with names painted on

The Agora in Action

Think of thousands of angry Athenian citizens assembled here, listening to speeches as they voted to ostracize a corrupt or tyrannical leader. Other than ostracisms, general assemblies were usually not held here, but rather on Pnyx Hill, which rises southwest of the Agora.

The roving philosopher **Socrates** (469-399 B.C.) spent much of his life simply hanging out in the Agora, questioning passersby, and urging people to "know thyself." Socrates discussed the meaning of piety, as recorded by Plato in the dialogue called the *Euthyphro*. "The lover of inquiry," said Socrates, "must follow his beloved wherever it may lead him." Shortly after, Socrates was tried and condemned to death here for "corrupting the youth"...by encouraging them to question Athenian piety.

Plato, Socrates' disciple and chronicler of his words, spent time teaching in the Agora, as did Plato's disciple **Aristotle.** (Their schools—Plato's Academy and Aristotle's Lyceum—were located elsewhere in Athens.)

The great statesman **Pericles** must have spent time here, since he oversaw the rebuilding program after the Persian invasion. (His famous Funeral Oration, however, was not given here.)

When Athens triumphed over Sparta in one battle during the Peloponnesian War (425 B.C.), **General Cleon** displayed the shields of captured prisoners in the Agora. This action mocked

them (*ostrakan*, case 30) were used as ballots in voting to ostracize someone accused of corruption or tyranny. Find the ones marked ΘEMISΘOKLES NEOKLEOS (item #37) and ARISSTEIΔES (item #17). During the Golden Age, Themistocles and Aristides were rivals (in both politics and romance) who served Athens honorably but were also exiled in political power struggles.

In case 32, see the *klepsydra* ("water thief")—a water clock used to time speeches at Council meetings. It took six minutes for the 1.7 gallons to drain. A gifted orator truly was good to the last drop...but not a second longer.

Across the hall (under the banner, between cases 68 and 67) is the so-called **Stele of Democracy** (c. 336 B.C.). This stone monument is inscribed with a decree outlawing tyranny. Above, a relief carving shows Lady Democracy crowning a man representing the

the Spartans for their surrender, since brave Spartans were always supposed to die with their shields on.

Diogenes the Cynic lived as a homeless person in the Agora and shocked the Athenians with his anti-materialist and free lifestyle. He lived in a wooden tub (in disregard for material comfort), masturbated openly (to prove how simply one's desires could be satisfied), and wandered the Agora with a lighted lamp in daylight (looking for one honest man in the corrupt city). According to legend, Alexander the Great was intrigued by this humble philosopher, who shunned materialism. One day he stood before him and said, "Diogenes, I will give you whatever you want. What would you like?" History's first hippie looked at the most powerful man on earth and replied, "Please get out of my sunshine."

The earliest Greek plays and concerts were performed here in the open air and, later, in theaters (including the Odeon of Agrippa). The playwright **Aristophanes** set scenes in the Agora, **Sophocles** spent time here, and all the major Greek plays would most likely have been performed here.

Imagine the buzz in the Agora at key points in Athens' history—as Athenians awaited the onslaught of the Persians and debated what to do, or as they greeted the coming of Alexander the Great, the conquering Romans, and the invasions of the Herulians and Slavs.

The **Apostle Paul** likely talked religion here in the Agora on his way to Corinth in A.D. 49 (Acts 17:17). He would have seen the various altars dedicated to pagan gods, which he decried from Mars Hill, overlooking the Agora.

Athenian people.

Next to that (in case 67) is a **bronze shield** captured from defeated Spartans in the tide-turning Battle of Sphacteria, which gave Athens the upper hand in the first phase of the Peloponnesian War. The next case over (case 66) displays herm heads. With news and directions attached, these functioned as signposts along roads.

In the middle of the room, find the case of **coins.** These drachms and tetradrachms feature Athena with her helmet. In Golden Age times, a drachm was roughly a day's wage. The ancients put coins like these in the mouth of a deceased person as payment for the underworld ferryman Charon to carry the soul safely across the River Styx. Coin #7, with the owl, was a four-drachm piece; that same owl is on Greece's €1 coin today.

For a reminder that the ancients weren't so different from us, look for the two **barbecue grills** (case 61, left; and case 42, right).

The exhibit winds up with **Roman sculpture heads** (cases 58 and 56, left), which show how the Romans were more honest than the Greeks when it came to portraying people with less-than-ideal features, and even more pottery items—including various toys (case 48, right).

• *Exiting the museum at the far end of the arcade (where there's a WC and a water fountain), backtrack to the southern end of the stoa (where you entered), then cross the main road and continue straight (west) along the lane, across the middle of the Agora. You're walking alongside the vast ruins (on your left) of what once was the...*

❹ Middle Stoa

Stretching clear across the Agora, this was part of a large complex of buildings that likely served as a big mall of shops and offices. It was a long, narrow rectangle (about 500 feet by 60 feet), similar to the reconstructed Stoa of Attalos you just left. You can still see the two lines of stubby column fragments that once supported the roof, a few stone steps, and (at the far end) some of the reddish foundation blocks. Constructed around 180 B.C., this stoa occupied what had been open space in the center of the Agora.

• *Midway down the lane (just before the wooden ramp), you'll come across a huge and frilly upper cap, or capital, of a column.*

❺ Corinthian Capital: The Center of the Agora

This capital (dating from the fourth century B.C.) once stood here atop a colossal column, one of a dozen columns that lined

the monumental entrance to the Odeon of Agrippa, a theater that extended northward from the Middle Stoa. (We'll learn more about the Odeon later on this tour.) The capital's elaborate acanthus-leaf decoration is an early example of the Corinthian order. The style was rarely used in Greek buildings but became wildly popular with the Romans.

From here, look back toward the entrance, overlooking what was once the vacant expanse at the center of the Agora. In 400 B.C., there was no Middle Stoa and no Odeon—this was all open space. As Athens grew, the space was increasingly filled in with shops and monuments. Now, imagine the place in its heyday (see the sidebar on page 918).

• *Continue westward (over a wooden bridge) across the Agora. Near the end of the Middle Stoa, you'll pass a gray well—still in its original spot and worn by the grooves of ropes. From here, look up at the Acropolis, where the towering but empty pedestal once sported the Monument of Agrippa, a grand statue with four horses. Mars Hill, likely lined with tourists, is where the Apostle Paul famously preached the Gospel (described on page 960). Below the Erechtheion are broken columns shoring up the side of the hill. These were rubble from the Mycenaean temples that were destroyed by the Persians. Past the well, jog to the right and cross the ditch over the wooden bridge. This ditch is part of the waterworks system known as the...*

❻ Great Drain

Dug in the fifth century B.C. and still functioning today, these ditches channel rainwater runoff from the southern hills through the Agora. Here at the southwest corner of the Agora, two main collection ditches meet and join. You can see exposed parts of the stone-lined ditch. The well we just passed was also part of this system.

• *Just over the wooden bridge is a 60-foot-across round footprint with a stubby column in its center. This is the...*

❼ Tholos

This rotunda-shaped building housed Athens' rulers. Built around 465 B.C., it was originally ringed with six Ionic columns that held up a conical roof. In the middle was an altar (marked today by the broken column).

The fundamental unit of Athenian democracy was the Assembly, made up of the thousands of adult male citizens who could vote. Athenian citizens were organized into 10 tribes; in order to prevent the people living in any one geographical area from becoming dominant, each tribe was composed of citizens from the city, the coast, and inland areas. Each man in the Assembly was considered to be from one of these tribes.

All of Athens' governing bodies met in the Agora. Though some Assembly meetings were held in the Agora's main square, the main assemblies were just uphill, on the slope of Pnyx Hill. The City Council also met in the Agora. The Council consisted of 500 men (50 from each of the 10 tribes) who were chosen from the Assembly by lottery to serve a one-year term. The Council proposed and debated legislation, but since Athens practiced direct (not representational) democracy, all laws eventually had to be approved by the whole Assembly. The Council chose 50 ministers who ran the day-to-day affairs.

As part of the civic center complex, the *tholos* served several functions. It was the headquarters, offices, and meeting hall for the 50 ministers. Many also lived and ate here, since the law required that at least a third of these ministers be on the premises at all times. The *tholos* housed the official weights and measures. Shoppers in the Agora could use these to check whether a butcher or tailor was shortchanging them. As the center of government, the *tholos* was also a kind of temple to the city. The altar in the middle held an eternal flame, representing the hearth of the extended "family" that was Athens.

• *Beyond and above the* tholos *is the hill-capping Temple of Hephaistos. To reach it, climb the stairs to the left and go through the trees, pausing along the way at a viewpoint with a chart.*

❽ Temple of Hephaistos (a.k.a. the Theseion or Theseum)

One of the best-preserved and most typical of all temples, this is textbook Golden Age architecture. Started in 450 B.C., it was built at Athens' peak as part of the massive reconstruction of the Agora after invading Persians destroyed the city (480 B.C.). But the temple wasn't completed and dedicated until 415 B.C., as work stalled when the Greeks started erecting the

great buildings of the Acropolis. Notice how the frieze around the outside of the building was only finished on the side facing the Agora (it's blank elsewhere).

As a classic "peripteral" or "peristyle" temple (like the Parthenon), the building is surrounded by columns—six on each end, 13 on the long sides (counting the corners twice). Also like the Parthenon, it's made of Pentelic marble in the Doric style, part of Pericles' vision of harking back to Athens' austere, solid roots. But the Temple of Hephaistos is only about half the size of the grand Parthenon and with fewer refinements (compared to the Parthenon's elaborate carvings and fancy math).

The temple's entrance was on the east end (the one facing the Agora). Priests would enter through the six columns here, into a covered portico (note the coffered ceiling). Next came a three-sided alcove called the *pronaos*, or "pre-temple." From there, you'd continue into the central hall *(cella)*, which once housed large bronze statues of Hephaistos, the blacksmith god, and Athena, patroness of Athens and of pottery. In ancient times, the temple was surrounded by metal-working and pottery shops, before the Romans replaced them with gardens, similar to today's. Behind the *cella* (the west end) is another three-sided alcove, matching the *pronaos.*

The carved reliefs (frieze and metopes) that run around the

upper part of the building are only partly done. Some panels may have been left unfinished, others may have once been decorated with painted (not sculpted) scenes, and a few panels have been removed and put in the Agora Museum.

At the end overlooking the Agora, look between the six columns and up at the frieze above the *pronaos* to find scenes of Theseus battling his enemies, trying to unite Athens. Theseus would go on to free Athens from the dominance of Crete by slaying the bull-headed Minotaur. To this day, Athenians call the temple the "Theseion" because the frieze decorations led them to mistakenly believe that it once held the remains of the mythical hero Theseus.

Walk around behind the temple, to the far (west) end. The

frieze above the three-sided alcove depicts the mythological battle between the Lapith tribe and centaurs during a wedding feast. Other scenes you'll see around the building (there are many interpretations) include Hercules (his labors and deification) and the birth of Erichthonios (one of Athens' first kings, who was born when spurned Hephaistos tried to rape Athena, spilled semen, and instead impregnated Gaia, the earth).

In A.D. 1300, the temple was converted into the Church of Agios Georgios, dedicated to Greece's patron saint, George, and given the vaulted ceiling that survives today. During the Ottoman occupation, the Turks kept the church open but permitted services to be held only once each year (on St. George's Day). Because it was continually in use, the temple-turned-church is remarkably well-preserved.

• *Note that there's a "back door" exit nearby for those wanting to take the smooth, paved walkway up to the Acropolis, rather than the rough climb above the Agora. (To find the exit, face the back of the temple, turn right, and follow the path to the green gate, which deposits you on the inviting, café-lined Apostolou Pavlou pedestrian drag. From here, you can turn left and walk up toward the Acropolis (see the "Acropolis Tour" on page 928).*

But there's still more to see in the Agora. Wind your way down the hill (east) and find the headless...

❾ Statue of Hadrian (second century A.D.)

The first Roman emperor to wear a beard (previously a Greek fashion), Hadrian (r. A.D. 117-138) was a Grecophile and benefactor of Athens. Get close to the statue and notice the insignia on the breastplate. There's Romulus and Remus, being suckled by the she-wolf who supports Athena on her back. This was Hadrian's vision—that by conquering Greece, Rome actually saved it. Hadrian was nicknamed Graecula ("The Little Greek") for his love of Greek philosophy, literature, and a handsome Greek teenager named Antinous.

Hadrian personally visited Athens, where he financed new construction, including Hadrian's Arch, the Library of Hadrian, the Temple of Olympian Zeus (which had been started by the Greeks), and a whole planned neighborhood called Hadrianopolis. (For more on these sights, see the "Athens City Walk" on page 891.) Hadrian's legacy endures. The main street through the Plaka is now called Adrianou—"Hadrian's" street.

• *Farther along, the lane passes three giants on four pedestals, which once guarded the...*

⑩ Odeon of Agrippa (a.k.a. the "Palace of the Giants")

This theater/concert hall, once fronted by a line of six fierce Triton statues (of which just three survived), was the centerpiece of the Agora during the Roman era.

A plaque explains the history of this building: During the Golden Age, this site was simply open space in the very center of the Agora. The *odeon* (a venue designed for musical performances) was built by the Roman general and governor Marcus Agrippa in the time of Caesar Augustus (around 15 B.C.), when Greece was a Roman-controlled province. For the theater-loving Greeks and their Greek-culture-loving masters, the *odeon* was a popular place. Two stories tall and built into the natural slope of the hill, it could seat more than a thousand people.

Back then, the entrance was on the south side (near the Middle Stoa), and these Triton statues didn't exist yet. Patrons entered from the south, walking through two rows of monumental columns, topped by Corinthian capitals. After the lobby, they emerged at the top row of a 20-tier, bowl-shaped auditorium, looking down on an orchestra and stage paved with multi-colored marble and decorated with statues. The sightlines were great because the roof, spanning 82 feet, had no internal support columns. One can only assume that, in its heyday, the *odeon* hosted plays by Aristophanes, Euripides, and Sophocles, plus lute concerts, poetry readings, and more lowbrow Roman-oriented entertainment.

Around A.D. 150, the famously unsupported roof collapsed. By then, Athens had a bigger, better performance venue (the Odeon of Herodes Atticus, on the other side of the Acropolis—described on page 932), so the Odeon of Agrippa was rebuilt at half the size as a 500-seat lecture hall. The new entrance was here on the north side, fronted by six colossal statues serving as pillars. Only two tritons (with fish tails), a giant (snake's tail), and an empty pedestal remain.

The building was burned to the ground in the Herulian invasion of A.D. 267 (explained later, under "Post-Herulian Wall"). Around A.D. 400, a large palace was built here, which also served as the university (or "gymnasium," which comes from the Greek word for "naked"—young men exercised in the buff during PE here). It lasted until the Constantinople-based Emperor Justinian closed all the pagan schools in A.D. 529. A plaque under the first statue gives more information.

• *Continue to the main road, where you'll see we've made a loop. Now turn right and start up toward the Acropolis on the...*

⓫ Panathenaic Way

The Panathenaic Way was Athens' main street. It started at the main city gate (the Dipylon Gate, near the Keramikos Cemetery),

cut diagonally through the Agora's main square, and wound up to the Acropolis— two-thirds of a mile in all. The Panathenaic Way was the primary north-south road, and here in the Agora it intersected with the main east-west road to the port of Piraeus. Though some stretches were paved, most of it (then as now) was just packed gravel. It was lined with important temples, businesses, and legal buildings.

During the Panathenaic Festival (July-August), this was the main parade route. Every year on Athena's birthday, Greeks celebrated by giving her statue a new dress, called a *peplos*. A wheeled float carrying the *peplos* was pushed up this street. Thousands participated—some dancing, some on horseback, others just walking—while spectators watched from wooden grandstands erected along the way. When the parade reached the Acropolis, the new dress was ceremonially presented to Athena and used to adorn her life-size statue at the Erechtheion. Every fourth year was a special celebration, when Athenians created an enormous

ATHENS

peplos for the 40-foot statue in the Parthenon. Today's tourists use the same path to connect the Agora and the Acropolis.

• *Continue up the Panathenaic Way, past the Stoa of Attalos. Along the left-hand side of the Panathenaic Way are several crude walls and column fragments.*

⓬ Post-Herulian Wall

This wall marks the beginning of the end of classical Athens.

In A.D. 267, the barbarian Herulians sailed down from the Black Sea and utterly devastated Athens. (The crumbling Roman Empire was helpless to protect its provinces.) The Herulians burned most of the Agora's buildings to the ground, leaving it in ashes.

As soon as the Herulians left, the surviving Athenians began hastily throwing up this wall—cobbled together from rubble—to keep future invaders at bay. They used anything they could find: rocks, broken columns, statues, frieze fragments, all thrown together without mortar to make a wall 30 feet high and 10 feet thick. Archaeologists recognize pieces scavenged from destroyed buildings, such as the Stoa of Attalos and the Odeon of Agrippa.

Up until this point, the Agora had always been rebuilt after invasions (such as the Persians in 480 B.C. and Romans in 89 B.C.); but after the Herulian invasion, the Agora never recovered as a public space. What remained suffered through a Slavic invasion in A.D. 580. By A.D. 700, it was a virtual ghost town, located outside the city walls, exposed to bandits and invaders. Only the hardiest of souls used it as a residence. (Looking up at the sheer face of the Acropolis, you may be able to make out other crude medieval dwellings—caves that pockmark the hillside.) Considering how accessible the Agora was over the centuries as a quarry for pre-cut stones, it's no wonder that so little of it survives today.

• *Next came the Christians. On the right is the...*

⓭ Church of the Holy Apostles

This charming little church with the lantern-like dome marks the Agora's revival. Built around A.D. 1000, it commemorates St. Paul's teaching in the Agora (see information about Mars Hill on page 960). Under protection from the

Christian rulers of Byzantium (in Constantinople, modern-day Istanbul), Athens—and the Agora—slowly recovered from centuries of invasions and neglect. The church was built on the ruins of an ancient nymphaeum, or temple atop a sacred spring, and became one of many Christian churches that served the booming populace of Byzantine Athens.

This church was the prototype for later Athenian churches: a Greek-cross floor plan with four equal arms, topped by a dome and featuring windows with tall horseshoe-shaped arches. (The narthex, or entrance, was added later, spoiling the four equal arms.) The church was built of large, rectangular dressed stone (ashlar) blocks, rather than small bricks. Ringing the eaves is a decorative pattern of bricks shaped into Arabic letters (Kufic script) added later, during the Ottoman occupation, when Christian churches like this were tolerated (but taxed) by the Muslim rulers.

Enter around the far side. It contains some interesting 18th-century Byzantine-style frescoes. The windows are in flower and diamond shapes. From the center, look up at Jesus as *Pantocrator* at the top of the dome, and see the icon on the altar and the faded frescoes on the walls. The uniform chipping on the surface of the frescoes was part of a process designed to rough it up so a new coat of whitewashing could adhere. Notice the remains of the marble altar screen with wide-open spaces—frames that once held icons.

• *End your tour by continuing up the Panathenaic Way to the south exit gates and looking back over the Agora and modern Athens.*

ATHENS

Legacy of the Agora

By the 18th century, the Agora had become a flourishing Turkish residential district. The Church of the Holy Apostles was only one of many churches serving the populace. In the early 20th century,

outdoor movies were shown in the Agora. In the 1930s, the American School of Classical Studies arrived, forced everyone out of their houses and businesses, and demolished buildings that had stood for centuries— all so they could dig here. The Church of the Holy Apostles was the only structure left standing, and it was heavily renovated by the American School to return it to its original state. Excavation in the Agora has continued nearly without pause for the past 70-some years.

Now that the ancient Agora has become a museum, the role of city center has shifted to Athens' many modern neighborhoods. Produce is bought and sold at the Central Market. The government center is at Syntagma Square. Multiple neighborhoods, like the Plaka, Psyrri, Thissio, and Gazi, harbor nightlife. Monastiraki and a dozen other squares have become the new social-center "agoras." And the Metro has replaced the Panathenaic Way as the main arterial.

• *Your tour is finished. There are three exits from the Agora: the gate you used to enter, at Adrianou street; the "back door" gate behind the Temple of Hephaistos; and the gate next to the Church of the Holy Apostles (**14**; where you are now). Keep your ticket if you want to return to the Agora later (note that the Acropolis ticket has one designated stub for the Acropolis, but all the others are interchangeable—so you can visit each covered sight once, or the same one several times).*

To head straight up to the Acropolis (to complete your own Panathenaic Festival), exit through the gate by the church, head straight up the hill, and follow the next section.

Acropolis Tour

Even in this age of superlatives, it's hard to overstate the historic and artistic importance of the Acropolis (Ακρόπολη). Crowned by the mighty Parthenon, the Acropolis ("high city") rises above the sprawl of modern Athens, a lasting testament to ancient Athens' glorious Golden Age in the fifth century B.C.

The Acropolis has been the heart of Athens since the beginning of recorded time (Neolithic era, 6800 B.C.). This limestone plateau, faced with sheer, 100-foot cliffs and fed by permanent springs, was a natural fortress. The Mycenaeans (c. 1400 B.C.) ruled the area from their palace on this hilltop, and Athena—the patron goddess of the city—was worshipped here from around 800 B.C. on.

But everything changed in 480 B.C., when Persia invaded Greece for the second time. As the Persians approached, the Athenians evacuated the city, abandoning it to be looted and vandalized. All of the temples atop the Acropolis were burned to the ground. The Athenians

Acropolis Overview

fought back at sea, winning an improbable naval victory at the Battle of Salamis. The Persians were driven out of Greece, and Athens found itself suddenly victorious. Cash poured into Athens from the other Greek city-states, which were eager to be allied with the winning side.

By 450 B.C., Athens was at the peak of its power and the treasury was flush with money...but in the city center, the Acropolis still lay empty, a vast blank canvas. Athens' leader at the time, Pericles, was ambitious and farsighted. He funneled Athens' newfound wealth into a massive rebuilding program. Led by the visionary architect/sculptor Pheidias, the Athenians transformed the Acropolis into a complex of supersized, ornate temples worthy of the city's protector, Athena.

The four major monuments—the Parthenon, Erechtheion, Propylaea, and Temple of Athena Nike—were built as a coherent ensemble (c. 450-400 B.C.). Unlike most ancient sites, which have layer upon layer of ruins from different periods, the Acropolis we see today was started and finished within two generations—a snapshot of the Golden Age set in stone.

For visitors with more time, this tour of the Acropolis can easily be preceded by the Ancient Agora Tour (see the previous section).

Orientation

Cost: €12 for Acropolis ticket (which also covers Ancient Agora, Roman Forum, Keramikos Cemetery, Temple of Olympian Zeus, and Theater of Dionysus—see sidebar on page 912); free for kids 18 and under, on Sun Nov-March, and on national holidays.

Hours: Daily May-Sept 8:00-20:00, Oct-April 8:00-15:00, last entry 30 minutes before closing.

When to Go: Get there early or late to avoid the crowds and mid-day heat. The place is miserably packed with tour groups from 10:00 to about 12:30 (when you might have to wait up to 45 minutes to get inside). On some days, as many as 6,000 cruise passengers converge on the Acropolis in a single morning. It's not the ticket-buying line that holds you up; instead, the worst lines are caused by the bottleneck of people trying to squeeze into the site through the Propylaea gate (so buying your ticket elsewhere doesn't ensure a speedy entry). Late in the day, as the sun goes down, the white Parthenon stone gleams a creamy golden brown, and what had been a tourist war zone is suddenly peaceful. On my last visit, I showed up late and had the place to myself in the cool of early evening.

Getting There: There's no way to reach the Acropolis without a lot of climbing (though people with disabilities can use an elevator—see below). Figure a 10- to 20-minute hike from the base of the Acropolis up to the hilltop archaeological site. There are multiple paths up to the Acropolis, but the only ticket office and site entrance are at the western end of the hill (to the right as you face the Acropolis from the Plaka).

If you're touring the Ancient Agora, you can hike directly up to the Acropolis entrance along the Panathenaic Way. The approach from the Dionysiou Areopagitou pedestrian zone behind (south of) the Acropolis is a bit less steep. From this walkway, various well-marked paths funnel visitors up to the entrance; the least steep one climbs up from the parking lot at the western end of the pedestrian zone. You can reach this path either by taxi or by tourist train (the Athens Happy Train—see page 890), but note that it still involves quite a bit of uphill hiking.

If you use a **wheelchair,** you can take the elevator that ascends the Acropolis (from the ticket booth, go around the left side of the hilltop). However, once up top, the site is not particularly level or well-paved, so you may need help navigating the

ATHENS

steep inclines and uneven terrain.

Information: Supplement this tour with the free information brochure (you may have to ask for it when you buy your ticket) and info plaques posted throughout. Tel. 210-321-4172, www.culture.gr.

Tours: At the entrance, you can hire your own **tour guide,** generally a professional archaeologist (around €90). You can download a free audio version of this walk at www.ricksteves.com/audioeurope, from iTunes, or through the Rick Steves Audio Europe smartphone app. The Acropolis is particularly suited to an audio tour, as it allows your eyes to enjoy the wonders of this sight while your ears learn its story.

Length of This Tour: Figure on two hours.

Baggage Check: Backpacks are allowed. Baby strollers are not. There's a checkroom just below the ticket booth near Mars Hill.

Services: There are WCs at the Acropolis ticket booth and more WCs and drinking fountains atop the Acropolis, in the former museum building (behind the Parthenon). Picnicking is not allowed on the premises. A post office and museum shop are near the ticket booth. A vending machine sells bottled water (just inside the ticket-check turnstile and to the right, €0.50, coins only).

Plan Ahead: Wear sensible shoes—Acropolis paths are steep and uneven. In summer, it gets very hot on top, so take a hat, sunscreen, sunglasses, and a bottle of water. Inside the turnstiles, there are no services except WCs and drinking fountains; pack whatever else you'll need (little snacks, guidebooks, camera batteries).

Starring: The Parthenon and other monuments from the Golden Age, plus great views of Athens and beyond.

ATHENS

The Tour Begins

• *Climb up to the Acropolis ticket booth and the site entrance, located at the west end of the hill.*

Near this entrance (below and toward the Ancient Agora) is the

huge, craggy boulder of **Mars Hill** (a.k.a. Areopagus). Consider climbing this rock for great views of the Acropolis' ancient entry gate (the Propylaea, described later) and the Ancient Agora. Mars Hill's bare, polished rock is extremely slippery—a metal staircase to the left helps somewhat. (For more on Mars Hill and its

The Acropolis

To Ancient Agora, Monastiraki & Plaka
Cliffs

Mars Hill

PROPYLAEA

1. Odeon of Herodes Atticus
2. Propylaea (Entrance Gate)
3. Temple of Athena Nike
4. Monument of Agrippa
5. Beulé Gate
6. Statue of Athena Promachos
7. Parthenon
8. Porch of the Caryatids
9. Erechtheion
10. Elevator & Column Drum Wall
11. Greek Flag & Views
12. Views to the South
13. Theater of Dionysus

BEULÉ GATE

TICKETS, WC & WATER

ACROPOLIS ENTRANCE

TEMPLE OF ATHENA NIKE

ODEON OF HERODES ATTICUS

STANDING RUINS
ORIGINAL FOOTPRINT

DIONYSIOU AREOPAGITOU

To Acropolis Museum

role in Christian history, see page 960.)

Before you show your ticket and enter the Acropolis site, make sure you have everything you'll need for your visit. Remember, after you enter the site, there are no services except WCs and water fountains.

• *Enter the site, and start climbing the paths that switchback up the hill, following signs on this one-way tourist route (bearing to the right). Before you reach the summit, peel off to the right for a bird's-eye view of the...*

Odeon of Herodes Atticus

This grand venue huddles under the Acropolis' majestic Propylaea entrance gate. While tourists call it a "theater," Greeks know it's technically an *odeon*, as it was used for musical rather than theatrical performances. (*Odeon* comes from the same root as the English "ode," from the Greek word for "song.")

A large 5,000-seat amphitheater built during Roman times, it's still used today for performances. From this perch you get a good look at the stage setup: a three-quarter-circle orchestra

ATHENS

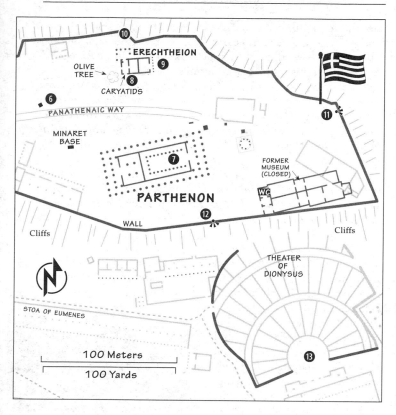

ERECHTHEION

OLIVE TREE →

CARYATIDS

PANATHENAIC WAY

MINARET BASE

PARTHENON

FORMER MUSEUM (CLOSED)

WC

WALL

Cliffs

Cliffs

THEATER OF DIONYSUS

STOA OF EUMENES

100 Meters

100 Yards

(where musicians and actors performed in Greek-style theater), the overgrown remnants of a raised stage (for actors in the Roman

tradition), and an intact stage wall for the backdrop. Originally, it had a wood-and-tile roof as well.

The *odeon* was built in A.D. 161 by Herodes Atticus, a wealthy landowner, in memory of his wife. Herodes Atticus was a Greek with Roman citizenship, a legendary orator, and a friend of Emperor Hadrian. This amphitheater is the most famous of the many impressive buildings he financed around the country.

Destroyed by the invading Herulians a century after it was built, the "Herodion" (as it's also called) was reconstructed in the 1950s to the spectacular state it's still in today. It's open to the public only during performances, such as the annual Athens & Epidavros Festival, which features an international lineup of dance, music,

ATHENS

and theater performed beneath the stars. If there's something on tonight, you may see a rehearsal from here. Athenians shudder when visitors—recalling the famous "Yanni Live at the Acropolis" concert—call this stately place "Yanni's Theater."

• *After climbing a few steps, you'll see two gates: On the right, steps lead down to the Theater of Dionysus (described on page 960); on the left is the actual entry uphill into the Acropolis. Stay left and continue up to reach the grand entrance gate of the Acropolis: the Propylaea. Stand at the foot of the (very) steep marble staircase, facing up toward the big Doric columns.*

As you face the Propylaea, to your left is a tall, gray stone pedestal with nothing on it: the Monument of Agrippa. On your right, atop the wall, is the Temple of Athena Nike. Behind you stands a doorway in a wall, known as the Beulé Gate.

The Propylaea

The entrance to the Acropolis couldn't be through just any old gate; it had to be the grandest gate ever built. Ancient visitors would stand here, catching their breath before the final push to the summit, and admire these gleaming columns and steep steps that almost fill your entire field of vision. Imagine the psychological impact this awe-inspiring, colonnaded entryway to the sacred rock must have had on ancient Athenians. Unlike today's path, the grand marble staircase didn't zigzag, but instead headed straight up. (A few original stairs survive under the wooden ramp.)

The Propylaea (pro-puh-LEE-ah) is U-shaped, with a large central hallway (the six Doric columns), flanked by side wings that reach out to embrace the visitor. The central building looked like a mini-Parthenon, with Doric columns topped by a triangular pediment. Originally, the Propylaea was painted bright colors and decorated with statues.

The left wing of the Propylaea was the Pinacoteca, or "painting gallery." In ancient times, this space contained artwork and housed visiting dignitaries and VIPs.

The buildings of the Acropolis were all built to complement each other. The Propylaea, constructed in five short years (437-432 B.C., just after the Parthenon was finished) was designed by Mnesicles, who also did the Erechtheion. The Propylaea gave the visitor a taste of the Parthenon to come. Both buildings are Doric (with Ionic touches) and are aligned east-west, with columns of similar width-to-height ratios.

ATHENS

• *Before ascending, notice the monuments flanking the entryway. To the right of the Propylaea, look up high atop the block wall to find the...*

Temple of Athena Nike

The Temple of Athena Nike (Greeks pronounce it "NEEK-ee") was started as the Propylaea was being finished (c. 427-421/415 B.C.). It was designed by Callicrates, one of the architects of the Parthenon. This little temple—nearly square, 11 feet tall, with four columns at both ends—had delightful proportions. Where the Parthenon and Propylaea are sturdy Doric, this temple pioneered the new style of Ionic, with elegant scroll-topped columns.

The Acropolis was mainly dedicated to the goddess Athena, patron of the city. At this temple, she was worshipped for bringing the Athenians victory ("Nike"). A statue of Athena inside the temple celebrated the turning-point victory over the Persians at the Battle of Plataea in 479 B.C. It was also meant to help ensure future victory over the Spartans in the ongoing Peloponnesian Wars. After the statue's wings were broken by Athenians wanting Athena to stay and protect their city, the place became known as the Temple of Wingless Athena.

The Temple of Athena Nike has undergone extensive restoration. From 2001 to 2010, it was completely disassembled, then cleaned, shored up, and pieced back together. This was the third time in its 2,500-year history that the temple had been entirely taken apart. The Ottomans pulled it down at the end of the 17th century and used the stone elsewhere, but Greeks reassembled the temple after regaining their independence. In 1935, it was taken apart for renovation and put back together in 1939. Unfortunately, that shoddy work did more harm than good—prompting the most recent restoration. Now it's been done the right way and should hold for another 2,500 years.

• *To the left (as you face the Propylaea) is the...*

Monument of Agrippa

This 25-foot-high pedestal, made of big blocks of gray marble with yellow veins, reaches as high up as the Temple of Athena Nike. The (now-empty) pedestal once held a bronze statue of the four-horse chariot driven by the winner of the race at the 178 B.C. Olympics.

Over the centuries, each ruler of Athens wanted to put his mark on the mighty Acropolis. When Rome occupied the city, Marc Antony placed

ATHENS

a statue of himself and his girlfriend Cleopatra atop the pedestal. After their defeat, the Roman general Agrippa (son-in-law of Augustus) replaced it with a statue of himself (in 27 B.C.).

• *Before entering, look downhill. Behind you is the...*

Beulé Gate

This ceremonial doorway was built by the Romans, who used the rubble from buildings that had recently been destroyed in the barbarian Herulian invasion of A.D. 267. (The gate's French name comes from the archaeologist who discovered it in 1852.) During Roman times, this gate was the official entrance to the Acropolis, making the Propylaea entry even grander.

• *Now climb the steps (or today's switchback ramps for tourists) and go...*

Inside the Propylaea

Imagine being part of the grand parade of the Panathenaic Festival, held every year (see page 925). The procession started at Athens' city gate (near the Keramikos Cemetery), passed through the Agora, then went around Mars Hill, through the central hall of the Propylaea, and up to the glorious buildings atop the summit of the Acropolis. Ancient Greeks approached the Propylaea by proceeding straight up a ramp in the middle, which narrowed as they ascended, funneling them into the central passageway. There were five doorways into the Propylaea, one between each of the six columns.

The Propylaea's central hall was once a roofed passageway. The marble-tile ceiling, now partially restored, was painted sky

blue and studded with stars. Floral designs decorated other parts of the building. The interior columns are Ionic, a bit thinner than the Doric columns of the exterior. You'll pass by some big column drums with square holes in the center, where iron pins once held the drums in place. (Greek columns were not usually made from a single piece of stone, but from sections—"column drums"—stacked on top of each other.)

• *Pass through the Propylaea. As you emerge out the other end, you're on top of the Acropolis. There it is—the Parthenon! Just like in the books. Stand and take it all in.*

ATHENS

The Acropolis

The "Acropolis rock" is a flat, slightly sloping limestone ridge covering seven acres, scattered with ruins. There's the Parthenon ahead to the right. To the left of that, with the six lady pillars (caryatids), is the Erechtheion. The Panathenaic Way ran between them. The processional street and the buildings were aligned east-west, like the hill.

Ancient visitors here would have come face-to-face with a welcoming 30-foot **Statue of Athena Promachos,** which stood

between the Propylaea and the Erechtheion. (Today there's just a field of rubble, with the statue's former location marked by three stones forming a low wall.) This was one of three statues of Athena on the Acropolis. The patron of the city was worshipped for her wisdom, purity, and strength; here she appeared in her role as "Frontline Soldier" *(promachos),* carrying a shield and spear. The statue was cast by Pheidias, the visionary sculptor/architect most responsible for the design of the Acropolis complex. The bronze statue was so tall that the shining tip of Athena's spear was visible from ships at Cape Sounion, 30 miles south. The statue disappeared in ancient times, and no one knows its fate.

Two important buildings, now entirely gone, flanked this statue and the Panathenaic Way. On the right was the Chalkotheke, a practical storage area for the most precious gifts brought to the temple—those made of copper and bronze. On the left stood the Arrephorion, a house where young virgins called *ergastinai* worked at looms to weave the *peplos,* the sacred dress given to Athena on her birthday.

• *Move a little closer for the classic view of the...*

Parthenon—The West End

The Parthenon is the hill's showstopper—the finest temple in the ancient world, standing on the highest point of the Acropolis, 490 feet above sea level. The Parthenon is now largely in ruins, partly from the ravages of time, but mostly from a freak accident in 1687, when it suffered bomb damage during a war.

It's impressive enough today, but imagine how awesome the Parthenon must have looked when it was completed nearly 2,500 years ago. This largest Doric temple in Greece is 228 feet long and 101 feet wide. At each end were eight fluted Doric columns, with 17 columns along each side (46 total), plus 19 inner columns in the Ionic style. The columns are 34 feet high and 6 feet in diameter.

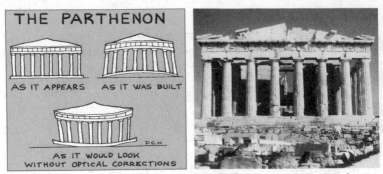

In its heyday, the temple was decorated with statues and carved reliefs, all painted in vivid colors. It's considered Greece's greatest Doric temple (though not its purest textbook example because it incorporates Ionic columns and sculpture).

The Parthenon served the cult of Virgin Athena, and functioned as both a temple (with a cult statue inside) and as the treasury of Athens (safeguarding the city's funds, which included the treasury of the Athenian League). You're looking at the west end—the classic view that greets visitors—but the building's main entrance was at the other end.

This large temple was completed in less than a decade (c. 450-440 B.C.), though the sculptural decoration took a few years more (finished c. 432). The project's overall "look" was supervised by the master sculptor-architect Pheidias; built by well-known architects Ictinus and Callicrates; and decorated with carved scenes from Greek mythology by sculptors Agoracritos and Alcamenes.

It's big, sure. But what makes the Parthenon truly exceptional is that the architects used a whole bagful of optical illusions to give the building an ever-so-subtle feeling of balance, strength, and harmonious beauty. Architects know that a long, flat baseline on a building looks to the human eye like it's sagging, and that parallel columns appear to bend away from each other. To create a building that looked harmonious, the Parthenon's ancient architects calculated bends in the construction. The base of the Parthenon actually arches several inches upward in the middle to counteract the "sagging" illusion (and to drain rainwater). Its columns tilt ever so slightly inward (one reason why the Parthenon has withstood earthquakes so well). If you extended all the columns upward several miles, they'd eventually touch. The corner columns are thicker to make them appear the same size as the rest; they're also spaced more closely. And the columns bulge imperceptibly halfway up ("entasis"), giving the subconscious impression of stout, barrel-chested men bearing the weight of the roof. For a building that seems at first to be all about right angles, the Parthenon is amazingly short on straight, structural lines.

ATHENS

All these clever refinements form a powerful subconscious impression on the viewer that brings an otherwise boring archi-

tectural box to life. It's amazing to think that all this was planned and implemented in stone so long ago.

The statues and carved reliefs that once decorated the outside of the Parthenon are now mostly fading or missing, but a few remain. Look up at the crossbeam atop the eight columns, decorated with panels of relief carvings called "metopes," depicting Athenians battling Amazons. Originally, there were 92 Doric-style metopes in high relief, mostly designed by Pheidias himself.

The crossbeams once supported a triangular pediment (now gone). This area was once filled in with statues, showing Athena with her olive tree competing with Poseidon and his trident to be Athens' patron god. Today just one statue remains (and it's a reconstruction).

Approach closer and look between the eight columns. Inside, there's another row of eight columns, supporting a covered entrance porch. Look up above the inner eight columns. Decorating those crossbeams are more relief carvings—the "frieze." Originally, a 525-foot-long frieze

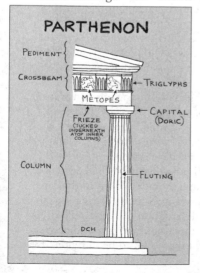

of panels circled the entire building. It showed the Panathenaic parade—dancing girls, men on horseback, sacrificial animals being led to the slaughter—while the gods looked on.

All of these sculptures—metopes, pediment, and frieze—were originally painted in bright colors. Today, most of the originals are in museums across Europe. In the early 1800s, the cream of the crop, the famous "Elgin Marbles," were taken by Lord Elgin to England, where they now sit in the British Museum. The Acropolis Museum (which stands at the base of the hill—you'll see it from a distance later on this tour) was built to house the fragments of the Parthenon sculpture that Athens still owns...and to try to entice the rest back from London.

• *Continue along the Panathenaic Way, walking along the long left (north) side of the Parthenon.*

Parthenon—The North Side

This view of the Parthenon gives a glimpse into how the temple was constructed and how it is being reconstructed today by modern archaeologists.

Looking between the columns, you can see remnants of the interior walls, built with thousands of rectangular blocks. The columns formed an open-air porch around the main building, which had an entry hall and *cella* (inner sanctum). Large roof tiles were fitted together atop wooden beams. These tiles were made of ultra-white, translucent Parian marble, and the interior glowed with the light that shone through it.

The Parthenon's columns are in the Doric style—stout, lightly fluted, with no base. The simple capital on top consists of a convex plate topped with a square slab. The capitals alone weigh 12 tons. The crossbeams consist of a lower half ("architrave") and upper half, its metopes interspersed with a pattern of grooves (called triglyphs).

The Parthenon (along with the other Acropolis buildings) was constructed from the very finest materials, including high-quality, white Pentelic marble from Penteliko Mountain, 16 miles away. Unlike the grand structures of the Egyptians (pyramids) and the Romans (Colosseum), the Parthenon was built not by slaves but by free men who drew a salary (though it's possible that slaves worked at the quarries).

Imagine the engineering problems of quarrying and transporting more than 100,000 tons of marble. Most likely, the column drums were cut at the quarry and rolled here. To hoist the drums in place, they used four-poster cranes (and Greek mathematics), centering the drums with a cedar peg in the middle. The drums were held together by metal pins that were coated in lead to prevent corrosion, then fitted into a square hole cut in the center of the drum. (The Ottomans scavenged much of this lead to make bullets, contributing to the destruction of the temple over the ages.) Because the Parthenon's dimensions are not mathematically precise (intentionally so), each piece had to be individually cut and sized to fit its exact place. The Parthenon's stones are so

ATHENS

Acropolis Now: The Renovation Project

The scaffolding, cranes, and modern construction materials you see here are part of an ongoing renovation project. The challenge is to save what's left of the Parthenon from the modern menaces of acid rain and pollution, which have already caused irreversible damage. Funded by Greece and the EU, the project began in 1984, which means that they've been at it more than twice as long as it took to build the Parthenon in the first place.

The project first involves cataloging every single stone of the Parthenon—blocks, drums, capitals, bits of rock, and pieces lying on the ground or in museums around the world. Next, archaeologists hope to put it back together, like a giant 70,000-piece jigsaw puzzle. Along the way, they're fixing previous restorations that were either inaccurate or problematic. For example, earlier restorers used uncoated iron and steel rods to hold things together. As weather fluctuations caused the metal to expand, the stone was damaged. This time around, restorers are using titanium instead of steel.

Whenever possible, the restorers use original materials. But you'll see big blocks of new marble lying on the ground—freshly cut from the same Pentelic quarries. The new marble is being used to replace damaged and missing marble. Many of the columns have lighter-colored "patches" where the restorers have added material. This looks like concrete or plaster, but it's actually new marble, cut to fit the exact hole. Though this newly cut marble looks much whiter, in time, it will age to the same color as the rest of the Parthenon.

When complete, the renovated Parthenon won't look like the pre-1687, undestroyed building—just a shored-up version of the ruin we see today. If you want to see the Parthenon temple in its heyday, there's a full-scale replica open to visitors...in Nashville, Tennessee.

well-crafted that they fit together within a thousandth of an inch. The total cost to build the Parthenon (in today's dollars) has been estimated at over a billion dollars.

• *Continue on to the...*

Parthenon—The East End (Entrance) and Interior

This end was the original entrance to the temple. Over the doorway, the triangular pediment depicted the central event in Athenian

history—the Birth of Athena, their patron goddess. Today, the pediment barely survives, and the original statues of the gods are in the British Museum. Originally, the gods were gathered at a banquet (see a copy of the reclining Dionysus at the far left—looking so drunk he's afraid to come down). Zeus got a headache and asked Hephaistos to relieve it. As the other gods looked on in astonishment, Hephaistos split Zeus' head open, and—at the peak of the pediment—out rose Athena. The now-missing statues were surprisingly realistic and three-dimensional, with perfect anatomy and bulging muscles showing through transparent robes.

Imagine this spot during the age of Pericles and Socrates. Stand back far enough to take it all in, mentally replace the 40-foot statue inside, and picture the place in all its glory, on the day of the Panathenaic parade. The parade has traveled through the Agora, ascended the Acropolis, passed through the Propylaea, and arrived here at the entrance of the Parthenon. People gather on the surrounding grass (the hard stone that you see today was once covered with earth and plants). Musicians play flutes and tambourines, girls dance, and men on horseback rein in their restless animals. On open-air altars, the priests offer a sacrifice of 100 oxen (a hecatomb—the ultimate sacrificial gift) to the goddess Athena.

Here at the Parthenon entrance, a select few are chosen to go inside. They proceed up the steps, entering through the majestic columns. First they enter a foyer called the *pronaos,* then continue into the main hall, the *cella*—100 feet long, 60 feet wide, and four stories tall. At the far end of the room is an enormous statue of Athena Parthenos ("Athena the Virgin"), standing 40 feet tall. The wooden core of the *chryselephantine* statue (from the Greek *chrysos,* "gold," and *elephantinos,* "ivory") was plated with ivory to represent her skin, and a ton of pure gold (a third of an inch thick) for her garments (or so say local guides). She was dressed as a warrior, wearing a helmet with her shield resting at her side. Her image was reflected in a pool in the center of the room. (The pool also served a practical purpose—the humidity helped preserve the ivory treasures.) In Athena's left hand was a spear propped on the ground. In her upturned right hand was a statuette of Nike—that is, she literally held Victory in the palm of her hand.

The statue was the work of the master Pheidias himself (447-438 B.C.). The statue was carried off to Constantinople in A.D. 426, where it subsequently vanished. A small-scale Roman copy is on display in Athens' National Archaeological Museum. Another famous *chryselephantine* statue by Pheidias—of a seated Zeus—was considered one of the Seven Wonders of the Ancient World.

The culmination of the Panathenaic parade was the presentation of a newly woven *peplos* to Athena, the patron of the city. Generally, the dress was intended for the life-size wooden statue of Athena kept at the Erechtheion (described later). But during the Grand Panathenaia (every four years), the Athenians presented a huge robe—big enough to cover a basketball court—to the 40-foot Virgin Athena in the Parthenon.

• *Behind you, the modern brown-brick building once housed the* **former Acropolis museum**—*its collection has been painstakingly moved into the modern Acropolis Museum down the hill. The old museum building may reopen someday as a coffee shop, but for now, it has just WCs and a drinking fountain alongside.*

Across the street from the Parthenon stands the Erechtheion, where the Panathenaic parade ended. There were three entrances to this building: the famous Porch of the Caryatids (the six ladies), the north porch (behind the Erechtheion), and the east end (to the right of the caryatids). Start by enjoying the...

Porch of the Caryatids

An inspired piece of architecture, this balcony has six beautiful maidens functioning as columns that support the roof. Each of

the lady-columns has a base beneath her feet, pleated robes as the fluting, and a fruit-basket hat as the capital. Both feminine and functional, they pose gracefully, exposing a hint of leg. It was the first time that the Greeks combined architectural elements and sculpture.

These are faithful copies of the originals, four of which are on display in the Acropolis Museum. The fifth was removed (c. 1805) by the sticky-fingered Lord Elgin, who shipped it to London. The sixth statue is in France. The caryatids were supposedly modeled on *Karyatides*—women from Karyai (modern Karyes, near Sparta on the Peloponnese), famous for their

After the Golden Age: The Acropolis Through History

Classical: The Parthenon and the rest of the Acropolis' buildings survived through classical times largely intact, despite Herulian looting (A.D. 267). As the Roman Empire declined, precious items were carried off, including the 40-foot Athena statue.

Christian: The Christian Emperor Theodosius II (a.k.a. Theodosius the Great) labored to outlaw pagan worship and close temples and other religious sites. After nearly a thousand years as Athena's temple, the Parthenon became a Christian church (fifth century A.D.). It remained Christian for the next thousand years, first as the Byzantine Orthodox Church of Holy Wisdom, then as a Roman Catholic cathedral (dedicated to Mary in 1204 by Frankish Crusaders). Throughout medieval times it was an important stop on the pilgrimage circuit.

After the Parthenon was converted into a church, the exterior was preserved, but pagan sculptures and decorations were removed (or renamed), and the interior was decorated with colorful Christian frescoes. The west end of the building became the main entrance, and the interior was reconfigured with an apse at the east end.

Muslim: In 1456, the Turks arrived, and converted the Parthenon into a mosque, adding a minaret. The Propylaea entry gate was used as a palace for the Turkish ruler of Athens. The Turks had no respect for the sacred history of the Acropolis—they even tore down stones just to get the lead clamps that held them in place, in order to make bullets. (The exasperated Greeks even offered them bullets to stop destroying the temple.) The Turks also used the Parthenon to store gunpowder, unfortunately

upright posture and noble character.

The Erechtheion was built by Mnesicles (c. 421-406 B.C.), the man who also did the Propylaea. Whereas the Propylaea and Parthenon are both sturdy Doric, the Erechtheion is elegant Ionic. In its day, it was a stunning white building (of Pentelic marble) with black trim and painted columns.

Near the porch (below, to the left) is an **olive tree,** a replacement for the one Athena planted here in her face-off with Poseidon (described later). Olive trees have been called "the gift of Athena to Athens." Greece has more than 100 million of these trees.

• *Walk around to the right and view the Erechtheion from the east end, with its six Ionic columns in a row.*

leading to the greatest catastrophe in the Acropolis' long history. It happened in...

1687: A Venetian army laid siege to the Acropolis. The Venetians didn't care about ancient architecture. As far as they were concerned, it was a lucky hit of mortar fire that triggered the massive explosion that ripped the center out of the Parthenon, rattled the Propylaea and the other buildings, and wiped out the Turkish defenders. Pieces of the Parthenon lay scattered on the ground, many of them gathered up as souvenirs by soldiers.

Lord Elgin: In 1801, Lord Elgin, the British Ambassador to the Ottomans in Constantinople, got "permission" from the sultan to gather sculptures from the Parthenon, buy them from locals, and

even saw them off the building (Greeks scoff at the idea that "permission" granted by an occupying power should carry any weight). He carted half of them to London, and the "Elgin Marbles" are displayed in the British Museum to this day, despite repeated requests for their return. Although a few original frieze, metope, and pediment carvings still adorn the Parthenon, most of the sculptures are on display in museums, including the Acropolis Museum.

From Independence to the Present: In the 19th century, newly independent Greece tore down the Parthenon's minaret and the other post-Classical buildings atop the Acropolis, turning it into an archaeological zone. Since then, the place has been excavated and there have been several renovation efforts. Today, the Acropolis still strikes wonder in the hearts of visitors, just as it has for centuries.

Erechtheion

Though overshadowed by the more impressive Parthenon, the Erechtheion (a.k.a. Erechtheum) was perhaps more prestigious. It stood on one of the oldest sites on the hill, where the Mycenaeans had built their palace. (The huge ruined stones scattered on the south side, facing the Parthenon, are all that's left of the Mycenaean palace.) Inside the Erechtheion was a life-size, olive-wood statue of Athena in her role of Athena Polias ("Protector of the City"). Pericles took the statue with him when the Athenians evacuated their city to avoid the invading Persians. Dating from about 900 B.C., this statue was much older and more venerable than either of Pheidias' colossal statues, supposedly having dropped from the sky as a gift from Athena.

This unique, two-story structure fits nicely into the slope of the hill. The east end (with the six Ionic columns) was the upper-level entrance. The lower entrance was on the north side (on the right), 10 feet lower, where you see six more Ionic columns. (These columns are the "face of the Acropolis" that Athenians see from the Plaka.) The Porch of the Caryatids (on the south side of the building, to the left) was yet another entrance. Looking inside the temple, you can make out that the inner worship hall, the *cella*, is divided in two by walls.

This complex layout accommodated the worship of various gods who had been venerated here since the beginning of time. Legend says this was the spot where Athena and Poseidon fought for naming rights to the city. Poseidon threw his trident, which opened a gash in the earth to bring forth water. It left a diagonal crack that you can still see in the pavement of the entrance farthest from the Parthenon (although lightning is a more likely culprit). But Athena won the contest by stabbing a rock with her spear, sprouting an olive tree near the Porch of the Caryatids. The twin *cellas* of the Erechtheion allowed the worship of both gods— Athena and Poseidon—side by side to show that they were still friends.

• *Look to the right (beyond the Plaka-facing porch). The modern* **elevator,** *useful during the Paralympics in 2004, carries people with disabilities up to the Acropolis. The north wall of the Acropolis has a retaining wall built from* **column drums.** *This is about all that remains of an earlier Parthenon that was destroyed after the Persian invasion of 480 B.C. The Persians razed the entire Acropolis, including an unfinished temple then under construction. When the Athenians rebuilt, this column from the old temple helped preserve the bitter memory of the Acropolis' destruction.*

Walk to the far end of the Acropolis. There you'll find an observation platform with a giant...

Greek Flag

The blue-and-white Greek flag's nine stripes symbolize (according to popular myth) the nine syllables of the Greek phrase for

"Freedom or Death." That phrase took on new meaning when the Nazis entered Athens in April of 1941. The evzone (elite member of a select infantry unit) who was guarding this flag was ordered by the Nazis to remove it. He calmly took it down, wrapped himself in it...and jumped to his death. About a month later, two heroic teenagers, Manolis Glezos and Apostolis Santas, scaled the wall, took down the Nazi flag, and raised the Greek flag. This was one of the first well-known acts of resistance against the Nazis, and the boys' bravery is honored by a plaque near the base of the steps. To this day, Greeks can see this flag from just about anywhere in Athens and think of their hard-won independence.

• *Walk out to the end of the rectangular promontory to see the...*

View of Athens

The Ancient Agora spreads below the Acropolis, and the sprawl of modern Athens whitewashes the surrounding hills. In 1830, Athens' population was about 5,000. By 1900, it was 600,000, and during the 1920s, with the influx of Greeks from Turkey, the population surged to 1.5 million. The city's expansion could barely keep up with its exploding population. With the boom times in the 1950s and 1980s, the city grew to nearly 4 million. Pan around. From this perch, you're looking at the homes of one out of every three Greeks.

Looking down on the **Plaka,** find (looking left to right) the Ancient Agora, with the Temple of Hephaistos. Next comes the Roman Forum (the four columns and palm trees) with its round, white, domed Temple of the Winds monument. The Anafiotika neighborhood clings to the Acropolis hillside directly below us. Beyond that, find the green and red dome of the cathedral.

Lykavittos Hill, Athens' highest point, is crowned with the Chapel of St. George (and an expensive view restaurant; cable car up the hill). Looking farther in the distance, you'll see white bits on the mountains behind— these are the **Pentelic quarries,** the source of the marble used to build (and now restore) the monuments of the Acropolis.

ATHENS

As you continue panning to the right, you'll spot the beige Neoclassical **Parliament** building, marking Syntagma Square; the **National Garden** is behind and to the right of it. In the garden is the yellow **Zappeion,** an exhibition hall. The green area in the far distance contains the 80,000-seat, marble **Panathenaic Stadium**—an ancient venue (on the site where Golden Age Athens held its games), which was rehabbed in 1896 to help revive the modern Olympics.

• *Complete your visual tour of Athens at the south edge of the Acropolis. To reach the viewpoint, walk back toward the Parthenon, then circle along its left side, by the cliff-top wall. Belly up to that wall for a....*

View from the South Side of the Acropolis

Look to the left. In the near distance are the huge columns of the **Temple of Olympian Zeus.** Begun in the sixth century B.C., it

wasn't finished until the time of the Roman emperor Hadrian, 700 years later. It was the biggest temple in all of Greece, with 104 Corinthian pillars, housing a 40-foot seated statue of Zeus, a replica of the famous one created by Pheidias in Olympia. This was part of "Hadrianopolis," a planned community in his day, complete with the triumphal **Arch of Hadrian** near the temple.

The **Theater of Dionysus**—which hosted great productions (including works by Sophocles) during the Golden Age—lies in ruins at your feet (a visit to these ruins is covered by your Acropolis ticket).

Beyond the theater is the wonderful **Acropolis Museum,** a black-and-gray modern glass building, with three rectangular floors stacked at irregular angles atop each other. The top floor—which houses replicas and some originals of the Parthenon's art—is angled to match the orientation of that great temple.

Looking right, you see **Filopappos Hill**—the green, tree-dotted hill topped with a marble monument to a popular Roman general in ancient times. This hill is where the Venetians launched the infamous mortar attack of 1687 that destroyed the Parthenon. Today, a theater here hosts popular folk-music performances.

Farther in the distance, you get a glimpse of the turquoise waters of the **Aegean** (the only island visible is Aegina). While the Persians were burning the Acropolis to the ground, the Athenians watched from their ships as they prepared to defeat them in the history-changing Battle of Salamis. In the distance, far to the right, is the port of Piraeus (the main departure point for boats to the islands).

• *Our tour is finished. Enjoy a few final moments with the Acropolis before you leave. If you're not yet ready to return to modern Athens, you can continue your sightseeing at several nearby sights.*

To reach the Theater of Dionysus ruins and the Acropolis Museum: Head left when you exit the Acropolis site, and walk down to the Dionysiou Areopagitou pedestrian boulevard. Turn left and follow this walkway along the base of the Acropolis. First you'll pass (on the left) the entrance to the Theater of Dionysus ruins, then (on the right) the Acropolis Museum (see the "Acropolis Museum Tour," next).

To reach the Ancient Agora: Turn right as you exit the Acropolis site, pass Mars Hill, and follow the Panathenaic Way down to the Ancient Agora (possible to enter through the "back door," facing the Acropolis).

Acropolis Museum Tour

Athens' Acropolis Museum (Μουσείο Ακρόπολης), opened in 2009, was custom-built to showcase artifacts from the Acropolis— the Parthenon sculptures, the original caryatids from the Erechtheion, and much more—complemented by modern exhibits about the Acropolis. The state-of-the-art building that houses the collection is the boldest symbol yet of today's Athens.

The museum also serves as a sort of 21st-century Trojan horse, intended to lure the famous Parthenon sculptures (the Elgin Marbles) away from London's British Museum and back to Athens. For years, the Greeks have asked for the Marbles back, and for years, the Brits have claimed that Greece can't give them a suitable home. Even now, with this ultramodern facility ready and waiting, Britain is reluctant to give in, for fear of setting a precedent...and getting "me, too" notices from Italy, Egypt, Iran, Iraq, and all the other nations who'd like to reclaim the missing pieces of their cultural heritage.

With or without the Elgin Marbles, this new museum has trumped the National Archaeological Museum as the most exciting museum in town, and is definitely worth your time.

Orientation

Cost: €5, free for kids 18 and under.

Hours: Tue-Sun 8:00-20:00, closed Mon, last entry 30 minutes before closing.

Getting There: It's the giant, can't-miss-it modern building facing the south side of the Acropolis from across the broad Dionysiou Areopagitou pedestrian drag. The museum is next to the Akropoli Metro stop (line 2/red).

Information: Museum archaeologists (with red badges) can answer questions, and a 13-minute video plays continuously in the atrium on Level Three. Tel. 210-924-1043, www.the acropolismuseum.gr.

Length of This Tour: Allow 1.5 hours.

Photography: Not allowed inside.

Services: A café and gift shop are on the ground floor (Level Zero); Level Two has a pricey but well-regarded restaurant, a bookstore, and great views.

Starring: Marble masterpieces from one of the most influential works of art in human history.

The Tour Begins

The striking, glassy building—designed by Swiss-born, New York-based architect Bernard Tschumi—gives a postmodern jolt to Athens' otherwise staid, mid-century-concrete cityscape, even as it echoes the ancient history all around it. Its two lower levels are aligned with the foundations of ancient ruins discovered beneath the building (which are exposed and still being excavated). The top floor sits askew, imitating the  orientation of the Parthenon. A long terrace extends over the main entry, with café tables stretching toward panoramic views of the Acropolis. The glass walls of the museum not only maximize the amount of natural light inside, but are also designed to "disappear," focusing attention away from the building and onto the statuary and views of the Acropolis itself.

Visitors enter into a grand lobby. The ground floor (Level Zero) has the ticket office, WCs, museum shop, and temporary exhibits. To proceed chronologically through the exhibits, you'd start with the Archaic collection on Level One, then go upstairs (to the top floor—Level Three) for the Parthenon section, then back down to Level One for Hellenistic and Roman sculpture. But for this tour, we'll do the small Hellenistic and Roman section as an out-of-chronological-sequence side-trip from the Archaic and Classical sections, and let the top-floor Parthenon sculptures be our finale.

• *After going through the turnstiles, head up the long, glass....*

Ramp

Pause to look through the glass floor at the ancient ruins being excavated beneath the museum. While the major buildings of

ancient Athens were at the Acropolis and Agora, this was a neighborhood of everyday houses and shops. Appropriately, the ramp is lined with artifacts that were found in the sanctuaries on the slopes leading up to the Parthenon. Many of these fifth-century B.C. artifacts owe their well-preserved state to having been buried with their owners.

Among the ramp's highlights is case #5, which takes you step-by-step through marriage rituals in ancient Athens. Freestanding cases mid-ramp give insight into the similarities between ancient Greek pagan worship rituals and later Christian styles. One has Christian-looking votives thanking the gods for prayers answered. On the right, just below the stairs, is an offering box (like you see in churches today); this one stood at the Sanctuary of Aphrodite. To assure a good marriage, you'd have been wise to pop in a silver drachm.

Level One

• *Climb the stairs at the top of the ramp toward a collection of statues.*

Pediment of the Hekatompedon (570 B.C.)

Throughout the centuries, three temples of Athena have occupied the spot where the Parthenon stands today. These statues once adorned the Hekatompedon, the first of those temples. On the left, Hercules fights a sea monster (Triton). In the center are the scant remains of two lions killing a bull. To the right, looking like the Three Musketeers, is a three-headed demon with a snake tail

holding the three elements (air, water, fire). They look more goofy than demonic. These so-called "Bluebeards" still have traces of the original paint.

• *Turn right and enter a gallery flooded with daylight.*

Kore and Kouros Statues

In this column-lined gallery stand several kore (female) and kouros (male) statues. They sport the characteristic stiff poses, braided hair, generic faces, and mysterious smiles of the Archaic era (c. 650-480 B.C.).

ATHENS

Acropolis Museum Level One

① Pediment of the Hekatompedon

② Kore & Kouros Statues

③ Pediment of the Old Temple

④ Pensive Athena Relief

⑤ Nike Adjusting Her Sandal Relief

⑥ Side-Trip to Hellenistic & Roman Art

⑦ Caryatids from the Erechtheion

⑧ Up to Parthenon Gallery

The men are generally naked, showing off buff and toned bodies. The bearded dudes are adults, while boys are beardless. Women are modestly clothed—except for Aphrodite. If you can find one naked breast in this gallery, it belongs to the goddess of love. The women pull up their robes as if readying to take a step. Before the coming of Golden Age realism, this was a crude way to suggest motion. These figures are almost always holding something. That's because the Greeks believed you shouldn't approach the gods without a gift of some kind. The equestrian statues represent the upper class, those wealthy elites who owned horses.

• *Halfway down the gallery, on the right against the interior wall, is the...*

Pediment of the Old Temple (Archaios Naos)

This decorated the short-lived temple to Athena that succeeded the Hekatompedon. The still-under-construction building was leveled by invading Persians in 480 B.C., paving the way for the Parthenon to be built. In the center, a large statue of Athena, dressed in an ankle-length cloak, strides forward, brandishing a snake as she attacks a giant, who sprawls backward onto his bum. These figures were part of a scene depicting the "Gods Versus Giants" battle atop the temple.

The glass case nearby displays fragments with burn marks, traces of the fire set by the Persians. The pesky Persians invaded Greece several times over a 50-year period (c. 499-449 B.C.). On the plus side, the wars forced Greeks to band together, and Athens emerged as a dominant naval power. Athenians rebuilt the Acropolis as a symbol of rebirth, with the Parthenon as its centerpiece. In just a few short decades, Greek society—and art— evolved rapidly and remarkably.

• *Continue down the gallery. Near the end, look for a well-preserved marble relief placed in front of a concrete pillar.*

Pensive Athena Relief (460 B.C.)

The goddess, dressed in a helmet and belted *peplos,* rests her forehead thoughtfully on her spear. While called "pensive," some think she was actually meant to be mourning the deaths of her citizens in the Persian War.

Enjoying the statuary in this hall, you can trace the evolution of Greek art from the static Archaic period to the mastery of the body as a living thing, free and full of movement, that we see in the Golden Age. In the Classical style of fifth-century B.C. Greece, the spine moves with the hips realistically.

• *Turn right and walk past a bank of elevators. Continue past an open gallery with some statuesque women (we'll visit them in a minute). After the second bank of elevators, look for a series of four squarish marble slabs on your left.*

Nike Adjusting Her Sandal Relief (c. 410 B.C.)

This relief originally decorated the Temple of Athena Nike (which stands near the entrance to the Acropolis). Nike figures had a better chance of survival through the ages than other statues, because anti-pagan Christian vandals mistook the winged Nikes for angels. Nearby is a display containing more chunks of the Temple of Athena Nike. You'll see toes gripping rocks, windblown robes, and realistically twisted bodies—exuberant, life-filled carvings signaling Athens' emergence from the Persian War.

• *Turn right and go up the long gallery for a...*

Side-Trip to Hellenistic and Roman Art

Before heading upstairs for the highlight of the collection, continue around on this floor to the small stretch of statues from the Hellenistic and Roman period. The head of Alexander the Great, on a square pillar in the center of the gallery, is a rare original, likely sculpted from life (336 B.C.). Alexander's upper lip curls, and his thick hair sprouts from the center of his forehead—immediately identifying this remarkable man. When he died in 323 B.C., this Macedonian had conquered Greece, embraced its customs, and

ATHENS

spread Greek culture throughout the Mediterranean world and as far east as India.

Nearby, find a model that shows the Acropolis as it looked in Roman times. The room also holds something that resembles a dirty soccer ball covered with graffiti. It's actually a spooky marble sphere etched with mysterious magic symbols (Roman, second or third century A.D.).

• *Now turn around, retracing your steps, and turn left at the bank of elevators. Around the corner, on their own, as if starring in their own revue on a beautifully lit stage, are the...*

Caryatids from the Erechtheion

Here stand four of the original six lady-columns that once supported the roof of the prestigious Erechtheion temple. (The six on the Acropolis today are copies; another original is in London's British Museum, and the last one is in France.) Despite their graceful appearance, these sculptures were fully functional structurally. Each has a fluted column for a leg, a capital-like hat, and buttressing locks of hair in the back. The caryatids were modeled on and named after the famously upright women of Karyai, near Sparta.

Time and the elements have ravaged these maidens. As recently as the 17th century (see the engravings), they had fragile arms holding baskets of flowers and jugs for ritual wine. Until the 1950s (before modern smog), their worn-down faces had crisp noses and mouths. In a half-century of Industrial Age pollution, they experienced more destruction than in the previous 2,000 years. But their future looks brighter now that they've been brought indoors out of the acidic air, cleaned up with a laser, and safely preserved for future generations. (For more on the caryatids in their original location, see page 943.)

There's a glass floor overhead, but you may not want to look up, out of respect for any female visitors wearing dresses above you.

• *Walk out of the Caryatid Gallery to the end of the building and ride the escalators up. Keep going up past Level Two, which has a restaurant and awesome view terrace. Head for the top floor—it's the reason you're here.*

Level Three

• *Before entering the actual Parthenon Gallery, sit in the atrium and enjoy the video on the Parthenon, which covers the temple's 2,500-year history, including a not-so-subtle jab at how Lord Elgin got the*

Marbles and made off with them to England. For more on Lord Elgin, see page 945.

Parthenon Models

Two models show how the west and east pediment statues (which are mostly fragments today) would have looked in their prime.

The east pediment (the model on the right) features Nike crowning newly born Athena with a wreath of olive branches. Zeus' head is split open, allowing Athena, the goddess of wisdom, to rise from his brain fully grown and fully armed, inaugurating the Golden Age of Athens. The other gods at this Olympian banquet—naked men and clothed women—are astounded by the amazing event. At the far left, Helios' four horses are doing their morning chore, dragging the sun out of the sea. And on the far right, the sun follows the horses back as it sets into the sea again.

The west pediment model (on the left) shows Athena and Poseidon competing for Athens' favor by giving gifts to the city. Poseidon spurts water (beneath him) and Athena presents an olive tree (behind). A big, heavenly audience looks on. Had Poseidon bested Athena, you'd be in Poseidonia today instead of Athens. Among the bystanders—tucked into the left corner of the pediment—are the mythical king of Athens and his daughters (Kekrops and Pandrosos). Passed over by Lord Elgin, their now headless and limbless statues are on display in the next room.

• *Leave the atrium and enter the huge gallery.*

The Parthenon Frieze

In the center of the room stands the museum's highlight—a life-size mock-up of the 525-foot frieze that once wrapped all the way around the outside of the Parthenon. The relief panels depict the annual parade, the Panathenaic procession, in which citizens climbed up the Acropolis to celebrate the birth of the city. Circle the perimeter and watch the parade unfold.

Men on horseback, chariots, musicians, children, and animals for sacrifice are all part of the grand parade, all heading in the same direction—uphill. Prance on. At the heart of the procession are maidens dressed in pleated robes. They shuffle along, carrying gifts for the gods, including incense burners, along with jugs of wine and bowls to pour out offerings. The procession culminates in the presentation of the *peplos* to Athena, as the gods look on.

Notice the details—for example, the muscles and veins in the horses' legs and the intricate folds in the cloaks and dresses. Some panels have holes drilled in them, where accessories such as gleaming bronze reins were fitted to heighten the festive look. Of course, all of these panels were originally painted in realistic colors. As you move along, notice that, despite the bustle of figures posed every which way, the frieze has one unifying element—all of the people's heads are at the same level, creating a single ribbon around the Parthenon.

Of the 525-foot-long frieze, the museum owns only 32 feet of original panels. These parts were already so acid-worn in 1801 that Lord Elgin didn't bother taking them. Filling in the gaps in this jigsaw puzzle are white plaster replicas of panels still in London's British Museum (marked BM), in Paris' Louvre, and in Copenhagen. Blank spaces represent the panels that were lost forever. Small 17th-century engravings show how the frieze looked before the 1687 explosion that devastated the Parthenon.

• *Now stroll through the gallery and look out the windows. Take a moment to...*

Ponder the Parthenon

There's the Parthenon itself, perched on the adjacent hilltop. The museum "disappears" around you, leaving you to enjoy the art and the temple it once decorated. The Parthenon is one of the most influential works humankind has ever created. For 2,500 years, it's inspired generations of architects, sculptors, painters, engineers, and visitors from around the globe. Here in the Acropolis Museum, you can experience the power of this cultural landmark. The people of Athens relish the Acropolis Museum. Local guides grow taller with every visit, knowing that Greece finally has a suitable place to preserve and share the best of its artistic heritage.

• *On your way down, stop by the restaurant on Level Two for its exterior terrace and the awesome view of the Acropolis. You're allowed to take photos here—and why not pay homage to Athena, too, while you're at it?*

Sights in Athens

While Athens has a world of interesting museums well worth knowing about on a longer visit (see the "Athens at a Glance" sidebar, earlier), for a one-day cruiser visit, I've listed just the main sights in the ancient center. These sights are all within easy walking distance of each other (except for the National Museum of Archeology). Don't let the length of my descriptions determine your sightseeing priorities. In this section, Athens' most important sights may have the shortest listings. These sights are covered in much more detail in one of the earlier walks or tours.

Note that many of Athens' top ancient sites are covered by the Acropolis ticket (see page 912).

The Acropolis and Nearby

▲▲▲**Acropolis**—The most important ancient site in the Western world, the Acropolis (which means "high city" in Greek) rises gleaming like a beacon above the gray concrete drudgery of modern Athens. This is where the Greeks built the mighty Parthenon—the most famous temple on the planet and an enduring symbol of ancient Athens' glorious Golden Age from nearly 2,500 years ago. For a self-guided tour, see page 928.

Cost and Hours: €12 for Acropolis ticket—see sidebar on page 912; free for kids 18 and under, on Sun Nov-March, and on all national holidays. Open daily May-Sept 8:00-20:00, Oct-April 8:00-15:00, last entry 30 minutes before closing. The main entrance is at the western end of the Acropolis. From the Ancient Agora in the Plaka, signs point uphill. Tel. 210-321-4172, www.culture.gr.

▲▲**"Acropolis Loop" (a.k.a. Dionysiou Areopagitou and Apostolou Pavlou)**—One of Athens' best attractions, this wide, well-manicured, delightfully traffic-free pedestrian boule-

vard circles the Acropolis. It's composed of two streets with tongue-twisting names—Dionysiou Areopagitou and Apostolou Pavlou (think of them as Dionysus Street and Apostle Paul's Street); for simplicity, I refer to them collectively as the "Acropolis Loop." One of the city's many big improvements made in preparation for its 2004 Olympics-hosting bid, this walkway immediately became a favorite local hangout, with vendors, al fresco cafés, and frequent special events enlivening its cobbles.

Dionysiou Areopagitou, wide and touristy, runs along the southern base of the Acropolis. It was named for Dionysus the Areopagite, a member of the ancient Roman-era senate that met atop Mars Hill (described next). The other section, **Apostolou Pavlou**—quieter, narrower, and tree-lined—curls around the western end of the Acropolis and the Ancient Agora. It feels more local and has the best concentration of outdoor eateries. This section was named for the Apostle Paul, who presented himself before Dionysus the Areopagite at Mars Hill.

Where Apostolou Pavlou meets the Thissio Metro stop, it flows into **Ermou** street—a similarly enjoyable, recently pedestrianized boulevard that continues westward to Keramikos Cemetery and the Gazi district's Technopolis.

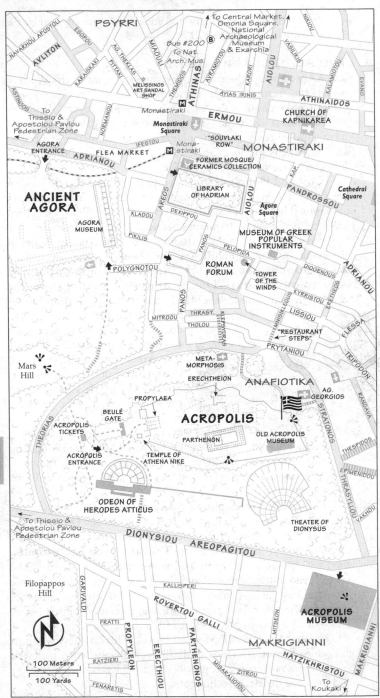

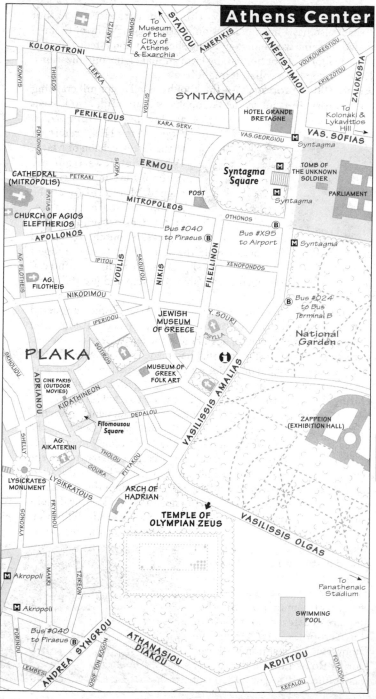

Athens Center

ATHENS

Stray cats are common in this warm part of Europe, but Athens also has a huge population of stray dogs. Many of them—including some who hang out along the Dionysiou Areopagitou—are cared for (but not housed) by local animal-rights organizations. Even if a dog has a collar, it might be a stray.

▲**Mars Hill (Areopagus)**—The knobby, windswept hill crawling with tourists in front of the Acropolis is Mars Hill, also known

as Areopagus (from *Areios Pagos,* "Ares Hill," referring to the Greek version of Mars). While the views from the Acropolis are more striking, rugged Mars Hill (near the Acropolis' main entrance, at the western end) makes a pleasant perch. As you're climbing Mars Hill, be warned: The stone stairs (and the top of the rock) have been polished to a slippery shine by history, and can be treacherous even when dry. Watch your step and use the metal staircase.

This hill has an interesting history. After Rome conquered Athens in 86 B.C., the Roman overlords wisely decided to extend citizenship to any free man born here. (The feisty Greeks were less likely to rise up against a state that had made them citizens.) While Rome called the shots on major issues, minor matters of local governance were determined on this hill by a gathering of leaders. During this time, the Apostle Paul—the first great Christian missionary and author of about half of the New Testament—preached to the Athenians here on Mars Hill. Paul looked out over the Agora and started talking about an altar he'd seen—presumably in the Agora (though archaeologists can't confirm)—to the "Unknown God." (A plaque embedded in the rock near the stairs contains the Greek text of Paul's speech.) Although the Athenians were famously open-minded, Paul encountered a skeptical audience and only netted a couple of converts (including Dionysus the Areopagite, a local judge and the namesake of the pedestrian

drag behind the Acropolis). Paul moved on to Corinth and a better reception.

Theater of Dionysus—The very scant remains of this theater are scattered southeast of the Acropolis, just above the Dionysiou Areopagitou walkway. During Roman times, the theater was connected to the Odeon of

Herodes Atticus (see page 932) by a long, covered stoa, creating an ensemble of inviting venues. But its illustrious history dates back well before that: It's fair to say that this is where our culture's great tradition of theater was born. During Athens' Golden Age, Sophocles and others watched their plays performed here. Originally just grass, with a circular dirt area as the stage, the theater was eventually expanded to accommodate 17,000—and stone seating was added—in 342-326 B.C., during the time of Alexander the Great. Later the Romans added a raised stage. Because the theater is included in your Acropolis ticket, consider an evocative stroll through its rubble. Plans are afoot to restore the theater to its former greatness.

Cost and Hours: May be closed for restoration. If open: €2, included in Acropolis ticket, same hours as Acropolis, main gate across from Acropolis Museum, tel. 210-322-4625.

▲▲▲**Acropolis Museum**—This museum is a modern-day temple to the Acropolis. Located at the foot of Athens' famous ancient

hill, it contains relics from the Acropolis, including statues of gods and goddesses, reliefs that once adorned the hilltop temples, and four of the six original caryatids (lady-columns) that once held up the roof of the prestigious Erechtheion temple. But the highlight is a life-size re-creation of the frieze that once wound all the way around the outside of the Parthenon, blending original pieces with copies of panels housed in the British Museum and other collections. For a self-guided tour, see page 949.

Cost and Hours: €5, free for kids 18 and under; open Tue-Sun 8:00-20:00, closed Mon, last entry 30 minutes before closing. The museum faces the south side of the Acropolis from across the broad Dionysus Areopagitou pedestrian drag, and is right at the Akropoli Metro stop (line 2/red). Tel. 210-924-1043, www.the acropolismuseum.gr.

▲▲▲**Ancient Agora: Athens' Market**—If the Acropolis was Golden Age Athens' "uptown," then the Ancient Agora was "downtown." Although literally and figuratively overshadowed by the impressive Acropolis, the Agora was for eight centuries the true meeting place of the city—a hive of commerce, politics, and everyday bustle.

Everybody who was anybody in ancient Athens spent time here, from Socrates and Plato to a visiting missionary named Paul. A visit here lets you ponder its sparse remains, wander through a modest museum in a rebuilt stoa (the Agora Museum), and admire its beautifully preserved Temple of Hephaistos. For a self-guided tour, see page 911.

Cost and Hours: Don't pay the €4 admission if you're also going to the Acropolis, as the Ancient Agora is included in the Acropolis ticket (see sidebar, on page 912). Open daily May-Sept 8:00-20:00, Oct-April 8:00-15:00, last entry 30 minutes before closing, Agora Museum opens at 13:00 on Mon, main entrance on Adrianou. From Monastiraki (Metro line 1/green or line 3/blue), walk a block south (uphill, toward the Acropolis). Tel. 210-321-0180, www.culture.gr.

The Plaka and Monastiraki

These sights are scattered around the super-central Plaka neighborhood. The first two sights are covered in more detail in the "Athens City Walk," on page 891.

▲▲**Anafiotika**—Clinging to the northern slope of the Acropolis (just above the Plaka), this improbable Greek-island-on-a-hillside feels a world apart from the endless sprawl of concrete and moped-choked streets that stretch from its base. For a break from the big city, escape here for an enjoyable stroll.

▲**Roman Forum (a.k.a. "Roman Agora") and Tower of the Winds**—

After the Romans conquered Athens in 86 B.C., they built their

version of an agora—the forum—on this spot. Today it's a pile of ruins, watched over by the marvelously intact Tower of the Winds. Panels circling the top of the tower depict the various winds that shape Greek weather. Nearby, a separate, fenced area of Roman ruins contains what's left of the Library of Hadrian.

Cost and Hours: €2, covered by Acropolis ticket, daily 8:00-19:00, until 15:00 off-season, corner of Pelopida and Aiolou streets, Metro lines 1/green and 3/blue: Monastiraki.

▲**Museum of Greek Popular Instruments**—Small but well-presented, this charming old place is one of the most entertaining museums in Athens. On its three floors, you can wander around listening (on headphones) to different instruments and styles of music. Examine instruments dating from the 18th century to today, including flutes, clarinets, bagpipes, drums, fiddles, violins, mandolins, bells, and even water whistles. Photos and paintings illustrate the instruments being played, and everything is described in English. This easily digestible collection is an enjoyable change of pace from more of the same old artifacts.

Cost and Hours: Free, Tue and Thu-Sun 10:00-14:00, Wed 12:00-18:00, closed Mon, near Roman Forum at Diogenous 1-3, Metro lines 1/green and 3/blue: Monastiraki, tel. 210-325-0198, www.culture.gr.

Museum of Greek Folk Art (Ceramics Collection)—Housed in the old mosque overlooking Monastiraki Square, this contains mostly pieces from the early 20th century, with an emphasis on traditional Greek and Cypriot workshops. Each item is accompanied by a brief description of the artist who crafted it. The mosque interior—with a rainbow-painted niche—is more interesting than the collection (€2, Wed-Mon 9:00-14:30, closed Tue, entrance along fence to right of mosque, Metro lines 1/green and 3/blue: Monastiraki, tel. 210-322-9031, www.culture.gr).

Museum of Greek Folk Art (Main Collection)—This dusty but well-presented little museum offers a classy break from the folk kitsch on sale throughout the Plaka. Five small floors display four centuries (17th-20th) of traditional artwork, all well-described in English. From the entry, turn right to find the elevator and head to the top floor. Then work your way down through each part of the collection. Wonderful folk costumes from each region fill the top floor, followed by jewelry and other silver and gold items. On the next floor down is a photo essay about Karpathos Island, called "Ethnographic Images of the Present." These vivid photos give you a fun trip to one of the country's most remote and traditional corners, with poetic descriptions: "In the coffee shop, there is room for everybody and everything: wise political words, incredible nautical tales, and memories." Continue down to the mezzanine, displaying Greek shadow puppets and ceramics. The ground floor holds a series of tapestries. While the collection can be a little difficult to appreciate, it offers a good look at Greek folk art.

Cost and Hours: €2, Tue-Sun 9:00-14:30, closed Mon, across from the Church of Metamorphosis at Kidathineon 17, Metro line 2/red: Akropoli or lines 2/red and 3/blue: Syntagma, tel. 210-322-9031, www.culture.gr.

ATHENS

▲**Jewish Museum of Greece**—Many Jewish communities trace their roots back to medieval Spain's Sephardic diaspora and, before that, to classical Greece. (Before the Nazis invaded, Greece had 78,000 Jews; more than 85 percent of them perished in the Holocaust.) This impressive collection of more than 8,000 Jewish artifacts—thoughtfully displayed on four floors of a modern building—traces the history of Greek Jews since the second century B.C. Downstairs from the entry, you can visit a replica synagogue with worship items. Then spiral up through the split-level space to see exhibits on Jewish holidays, history, Zionism, the Nazi occupation and Holocaust, traditional dress, everyday life, and the recollections of Greek Jews.

Cost and Hours: €6, borrow English descriptions in each room, Mon-Fri 9:00-14:30, Sun 10:00-14:00, closed Sat; Nikis 39, at the corner with Kidathineon, behind the Hard Rock Café—ring bell to get inside; Metro lines 2/red and 3/blue: Syntagma, tel. 210-322-5582, www.jewishmuseum.gr.

Syntagma

The Syntagma area borders the Plaka to the north and east. All of these sights are covered in detail in "Athens City Walk." I've listed only the essentials here.

▲**Syntagma Square (Plateia Syntagmatos)**—The "Times Square" of Athens is named for Greece's historic 1843 constitution, prompted by demonstrations right on this square. A major transit hub, the square is watched over by Neoclassical masterpieces such as the Hotel Grande Bretagne and the Parliament building.

Parliament—The former palace of King Otto, this is now a

house of democracy. In front, colorfully costumed evzone guards stand at attention at the Tomb of the Unknown Soldier and periodically do a ceremonial changing of the guard to the delight of tourists (guards change five minutes before the top of each hour, less elaborate crossing of the guard on the half-hour, full ceremony with marching band most Sundays at 11:00).

Ermou Street—This pedestrianized thoroughfare, connecting Syntagma Square with Monastiraki (and on to Thissio and Keramikos Cemetery), is packed with top-quality international shops. While most Athenians can't afford to shop here, it's enjoyable for people-watching and is refreshingly traffic-free in an otherwise congested area.

Southeast of Syntagma Square

▲**Panathenaic (a.k.a. "Olympic") Stadium**—In your travels through Greece, you'll see some ruined ancient stadiums (including the ones in Olympia and Delphi). Here's your chance to see one intact. This gleaming marble stadium has many names. Officially it's the Panathenaic Stadium, built in the fourth century B.C. to host the Panathenaic Games. Sometimes it's referred to as the Roman Stadium, because it was rebuilt by the great Roman benefactor Herodes Atticus in the second century A.D., using the same prized Pentelic marble that was used in the Parthenon. This magnificent white marble gives the place its most popular name: Kalimarmara ("Beautiful Marble") Stadium. It was restored to its Roman condition in preparation for the first modern Olympics in 1896. It saw Olympic action again in 2004, when it provided a grand finish for the marathon. In ancient times, 50,000 filled the stadium; today, 80,000 people can pack the stands.

Cost and Hours: €3, daily 8:00-19:30, located southeast of the Zappeion off Vasilissis Konstantinou, Metro line 2/red: Akropoli or line 3/blue: Evangelismos, tel. 210-325-1744.

Churches in the Plaka and Syntagma Area

All of these sights are covered in detail in the "Athens City Walk." Only the basics are listed here.

▲**Church of Kapnikarea**—Sitting unassumingly in the middle of Ermou street, this small, typical, 11th-century Byzantine church offers a convenient look at the Greek Orthodox faith (free, likely open daily 8:30-13:30 & 17:00-19:30).

▲**Cathedral (Mitropolis)**—Dating from the mid-19th century, this big but stark head church of Athens—and therefore of all of Greece—is covered in scaffolding inside and out (free, generally open daily 8:00-13:00 & 16:30-20:00, no afternoon closure in summer, Plateia Mitropoleos). The cathedral is the centerpiece of a reverent neighborhood, with a pair of statues out front honoring great heroes of the Church, surrounding streets lined with religious paraphernalia shops (and black-cloaked, long-bearded priests), and the cute little...

▲**Church of Agios Eleftherios**—This tiny church, huddled in the shadow of the cathedral, has a delightful hodgepodge of ancient and early Christian monuments embedded in its facade. Like so many Byzantine churches, it was partly built (in the 13th

century) with fragments of earlier buildings, monuments, and even tombstones.
Today it's a giant *Da Vinci Code*-style puzzle of millennia-old bits and pieces (free,
likely open daily 8:30-13:30 & 17:00-19:30,
Plateia Mitropoleos).

At the Edge of the Plaka, Along Vasilissis Amalias Avenue

These two sights, dating from Athens'
Roman period, overlook a busy highway
at the edge of the tourist zone (just a few steps up Dionysiou
Areopagitou from the Acropolis Museum and Metro line 2/red:
Akropoli, or a 10-minute walk south of Syntagma Square). Both
are described in greater detail in the "Athens City Walk."

▲**Arch of Hadrian**—This stoic triumphal arch marks the entrance
to what was once the proud "Hadrianopolis" development—a new
suburb of ancient Athens built by the Roman Emperor Hadrian
in the second century A.D. (free, always viewable). Just beyond the
arch is the...

▲▲**Temple of Olympian Zeus**—Started by an overambitious
tyrant in the sixth century B.C., this giant temple was not completed

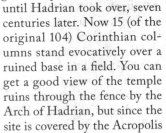

until Hadrian took over, seven
centuries later. Now 15 (of the
original 104) Corinthian columns stand evocatively over a
ruined base in a field. You can
get a good view of the temple
ruins through the fence by the
Arch of Hadrian, but since the
site is covered by the Acropolis
ticket, you can easily drop in for a closer look (otherwise €2,
daily 8:00-20:00, off-season until 17:00, tel. 210-922-6330, www
.culture.gr).

North of Monastiraki

Athinas street leads north from Monastiraki Square to Omonia
Square. Walking this grand street offers a great chance to feel
the pulse of modern, workaday Athens, with shops tumbling
onto broad sidewalks, striking squares, nine-to-fivers out having a smoke, and lots of urban energy. The first two sights are on
the way to Omonia Square (see map on page 882). Farther up the
street, past Omonia Square, is the superb National Archaeological
Museum.

Central Market—Take a vibrant, fragrant stroll through the modern-day version of the Ancient Agora. It's a living, breathing, smelly, and (for some) nauseating barrage on all the senses. You'll see dripping-fresh meat, livestock in all stages of dismemberment, still-wriggling fish, exotic nuts, and sticky figs. While it's not Europe's most colorful or appealing market, it offers a lively contrast to Athens' ancient sites.

The entire market square is a delight to explore, with colorful and dirt-cheap souvlaki shops and a carnival of people-watching. The best and cheapest selection of whatever's in season is at the fruit and vegetable stalls, which spread across Athinas street downhill to the west, flanked by shops selling feta from the barrel and a dozen different kinds of olives. Meat and fish markets are housed in the Neoclassical building to the east, behind a row of shops facing Athinas street that specialize in dried fruit and nuts. Try the roasted almonds and the delicious white figs from the island of Evia.

Cost and Hours: Free to enter, Mon-Sat 7:00-15:00, closed Sun, on Athinas between Sofokleous and Evripidou, between Metro lines 1/green and 2/red: Omonia and Metro lines 1/green and 3/blue: Monastiraki.

Art Tower—This contemporary gallery is worth seeking out for fans of cutting-edge art. Various temporary exhibits fill some of this skyscraper's eight stimulating floors; if it's open, just poke around. Located near the Central Market action, it's squeezed between produce stalls, overlooking the big, open square with the underground parking garage (free, Wed-Fri 15:00-20:00, Sat 12:00-16:00, closed Sun-Tue, Armodiou 10—look for ΑΡΜΟΔΙΟΥ 10, tel. 210-324-6100, www.artower.gr).

▲▲▲**National Archaeological Museum**—This museum is far and away the top ancient Greek art collection anywhere. Ancient

Greece set the tone for all Western art that followed, and this museum lets you trace its evolution—taking you in air-conditioned comfort from 7000 B.C. to A.D. 500 through beautifully displayed and described exhibits mostly on one floor. You'll see the rise and fall of Greece's various civilizations: the Minoans, Mycenaeans, those of Archaic Greece, the Classical Age and Alexander the Great, and the Romans who came from the west. You can also watch Greek sculpture evolve: from prehistoric Barbie dolls; to stiff Egyptian-style; to the *David*-like balance of the Golden Age; to wet T-shirt, buckin'-bronco Hellenistic; and finally, to the influence of the Romans. Walk once around fast for a time-lapse effect, then go around again for a closer look.

This museum is a great way to either start or finish your sightseeing through Greece. It's especially helpful for those traveling beyond Athens because it displays artifacts found elsewhere in Greece, including Mycenae, Epidavros, Santorini, and Olympia. In fact, the treasures displayed here are generally better than those remaining at the sites themselves. The sheer beauty of the statues, vases, and paintings helps bring the country's dusty ruins to life.

The collection is delightfully chronological. To sweep through Greek history, simply visit the numbered rooms in sequence. Essential stops (in this order) include stylized figurines of the Cycladic Islands, the golden artifacts of the Mycenaeans (including the so-called Mask of Agamemnon), and the stiff, stoic kouros statues of the Archaic age. Then comes the arrival of the Severe style (epitomized by the *Artemision Bronze*), where the art loosens up and comes to life. As Greece enters the Classical Period, look for the Bronze Statue of a Youth—balanced and lifelike. The dramatic *Statue of a Horse and Jockey* hints at the unbridled exuberance of Hellenism, which is taken to its extreme in the *Statue of a Fighting Gaul*. Rounding out the collection are Roman statuary and the Antikythera Mechanism, a crude computer from the first century B.C. Upstairs find colorful wall paintings from Thira (today's Santorini) and room upon room of ceramics.

Cost and Hours: €7; free for kids 18 and under, on the first Sun of each month, and all Sun Nov-March; May-Sept Tue-Sun 8:00-20:00, Mon 13:30-20:00; Oct-April Tue-Sun 8:30-15:00, Mon 13:30-19:30. While there are no audioguides, you can download a free audio version of my National Archaeological Museum Tour at www.ricksteves.com/audioeurope, from iTunes, or through the Rick Steves Audio Europe smartphone app. The museum is at 28 Oktovriou (a.k.a. Patission) #44. It's a 20-minute taxi ride from downtown (a steal at about €4). Or bus #200 can take you (and pickpockets) from Athinas street near Monastiraki to the museum. Tel. 210-821-7717, www.namuseum.gr.

Eating in Athens

In the Plaka

Taverna O Thespis is a rarity that feels like the good old days in the Plaka. It's tucked away above the crowds along the sleepy, stepped Thespidos lane, with tables cascading down a series of breezy terraces and the floodlit walls of the Acropolis towering overhead. Inside, two dining rooms feature murals of old Athens and Greek gods. Dine affordably on traditional specialties, such as the €12 *bekri meze* (pork with flavorful sauce). The menu is limited to the same old Greek standards you'll find elsewhere...but here, everything seems particularly well-executed (€5 starters, most main dishes €8-10, some seafood splurges, handy fixed-price meals for €14 or €17 including wine, daily 11:00-24:00, Thespidos 18, tel. 210-323-8242, Vlahos family).

Palia Taverna tou Psara ("The Old Tavern of Psaras") is a big, slick, pricey eatery that enjoys bragging about the many illustrious guests they've hosted since opening in 1898. It's the kind of place where a rowdy, rollicking group of a hundred can slam down a dish-'em-up Greek meal. If you don't want a main course (€10-23), you can order a good selection of their *mezedes* (€3-14). There's seating in two kitty-corner buildings, plus tables on the atmospheric street between them. The lower building features live folk music and an outdoor terrace with views over Athens' rooftops (daily 11:00-24:00, music generally Thu-Sat from 21:00, signposted off Tripodon at Eretheos 16, tel. 210-321-8734).

Restaurant Hermion is a dressy wicker indulgence in a quiet arcade off traffic-free (and loaded-with-tourists) Pandrossou. Choose between outdoor seating in an inviting courtyard and a cool air-conditioned interior. Under a canvas canopy surrounded by potted plants, you forget you're in a big city. The menu offers a wide range of €6-11 salads and lots of fish (€6-13 starters, €10-25 grilled meats, €17-30 fish dishes, daily 11:30-24:00; with your back to cathedral, leave the square downhill to the left, going 50 yards down Pandrossou to *Hermion* sign, then follow arcade passageway to Pandrossou 15; tel. 210-324-7148).

Sholarhio Ouzeri Kouklis, at the intersection of Tripodon and Epicharmou streets, serves only the small plates called *mezedes* (*meh-ZEH-dehs;* known internationally as *mezes*). While you could assemble a meal of these Greek "tapas" at nearly any restaurant, this one makes it their specialty. It's fun, inexpensive, and ideal for small groups wanting to try a variety of traditional *mezedes* and drink good, homemade booze on an airy perch at the top of the Plaka. Since 1935, the Kouklis family has been making ouzo liquor and running their restaurant—which maintains a 1930s atmosphere to this day. The waiter comes around with a big platter of dishes, and you choose what you like (€3-6/plate). Drinks are cheap, dessert is free, and the stress-free €14 meal deals are worth considering. As the plates are pretty big, this is most fun with a group of four or more. Many people sit on the street, waiting for a spot to open up on their lively front terrace, but you can also climb the spiral staircase to the often-empty upstairs area with its tiny romantic balconies for two. This place is in all the guidebooks— hardly a local scene, but still enjoyable (daily 11:00-2:00 in the morning, Tripodon 14, tel. 210-324-7605).

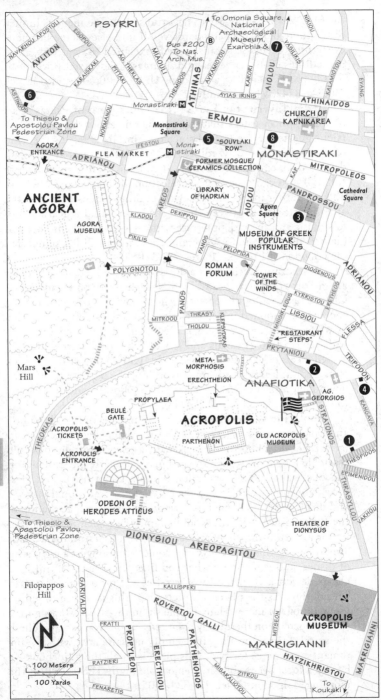

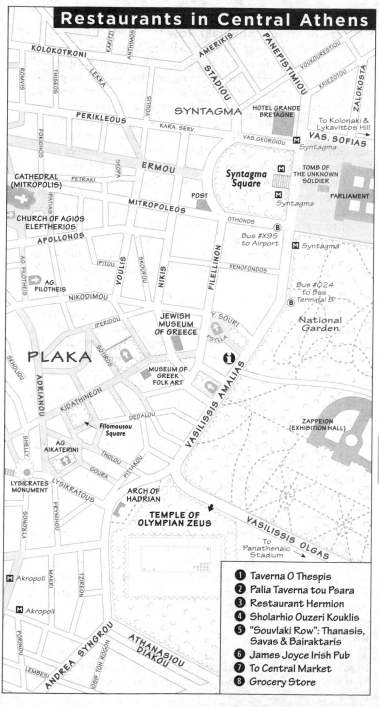

Restaurants in Central Athens

1. Taverna O Thespis
2. Palia Taverna tou Psara
3. Restaurant Hermion
4. Sholarhio Ouzeri Kouklis
5. "Souvlaki Row": Thanasis, Savas & Bairaktaris
6. James Joyce Irish Pub
7. To Central Market
8. Grocery Store

ATHENS

In Monastiraki

Eating Cheap on "Souvlaki Row"

Monastiraki Square (where it meets Mitropoleos street) is a popular place to head for fast food. This is souvlaki heaven, with several frantic restaurants—Thanasis, Savas, and Bairaktaris—spilling into the street and keeping hordes of hungry eaters happy. Souvlaki is grilled meat on a skewer, served on a plate or wrapped in pita bread to make a sandwich. These places also sell meat shaved from gyros, hearty Greek salads, wine, beer, and ouzo. Souvlaki goes well with *tzatziki,* the thick, garlicky yogurt-and-cucumber sauce. First decide whether you want your meal "to go" or at a table.

Take-Out: Gyros or a single souvlaki sandwich wrapped in a pita "to go" cost about €1.70—these places can fill and wrap a pita before you can blink. For these cheap carry-out prices, order and pay at the cashier, then take your receipt to the counter to claim your meal. It can be tricky to find a comfortable bench or other suitable perch in this crowded neighborhood—plan to munch as you walk (and watch out for the inevitable dribbles of souvlaki juice).

Table Service: The joints here on "Souvlaki Row" offer a good value if you're getting your food "to go." But you'll pay substantially more to sit and be waited on. Still, the ambience is lively, especially at the outdoor tables. A big plate of four souvlaki (plus pita bread, onions, and tomatoes) costs €9-10; a smaller helping of two souvlaki—plenty for most eaters—runs about €5-6.

Two popular options face each other across the street: **Thanasis** is famous for its special kebab, made from a traditional recipe that combines ground beef and lamb with Thanasis' secret blend of seasonings (daily 10:00-2:00 in the morning, Mitropoleos 69, tel. 210-324-4705). **Savas** is another old favorite with a similar menu and a little less character (daily 10:00-3:00 in the morning, Mitropoleos 86, tel. 210-324-5048). The dominant operation, **Bairaktaris,** offers lesser value.

Elsewhere in Monastiraki

The **James Joyce Irish Pub** offers an escape from Greece. Stepping inside, the complete Irish-pub menu (€8-12 main dishes), top Irish beers on tap, air-conditioned freshness, and rock 'n' roll ambience combine to transport you to Ireland (daily 12:00-2:00 in the morning, between the Thissio neighborhood and Ermou street at Astiggos 12, tel. 210-323-5055, Tom Cameron).

Picnics

To assemble a cheap meal of your own, head 500 yards north of Monastiraki (on Athinas) to the **Central Market.** There are no big supermarkets nearby, but the **Soros grocery store** stays open long hours and stocks enough for you to throw together a decent picnic (daily 8:00-22:00, near "Souvlaki Row" at Mitropoleos 78, tel. 210-322-6677).

In Makrigianni and Koukaki, Near the Acropolis Museum

New development in this area, including the Akropoli Metro stop, has brought with it a trendy and touristy row of restaurants, cafés, and ice-cream shops along pedestrian Makrigianni street facing the Acropolis Museum. The other pedestrian street, Dionysiou Areopagitou, also has plenty of tourist-friendly options between the museum and the Arch of Hadrian.

Mani Mani offers a touch of class for reasonable prices. The focus is on cuisine from the Mani Peninsula, so you'll find some pleasantly atypical options here—a nice change of pace from the same old standards. The decor, like the food, is thoughtfully updated Greek, with a soothing green-and-white color scheme. As it's all indoor seating, this is an especially good bad-weather option (€5-9 starters, €9-13 main dishes, Tue-Sat 13:00-17:30 & 20:00-24:00, Sun 13:00-17:30, closed Mon, reservations smart, look for low-profile green *MANH MANH* banner at Falirou 10 and go upstairs, tel. 210-921-8180).

Strofi Athenian Restaurant is my favorite place in town for white-tablecloth, elegantly modern, rooftop-Acropolis-view dining. A five-minute walk from the tourist crush, Niko Bletsos and his staff need to be as good as they are. While they have a fine air-conditioned interior, the breeze makes the rooftop comfortable even on hot evenings (€5-9 starters, €10-14 main dishes, daily 12:00-24:00, about 100 yards down Propyleon street off Dionysiou Areopagitou at Rovertou Galli 25, tel. 210-921-4130).

To Kati Allo Restaurant, under the far side of the Acropolis Museum, lacks tourists and is the quintessential neighborhood hole-in-the-wall. Run by English-speaking Kostas Bakatelos and his family, this place offers both sidewalk seating and (cooled-by-a-fan) inside tables. The menu, written on a blackboard, features a short list of cheap, fresh, and tasty local options (€6-8 main dishes, open daily, just off Makrigianni street at Hatzichristou 12, tel. 210-922-3071).

ATHENS

Shopping in Athens

While not quite a top shopping destination, Athens offers plenty of opportunities for visitors who want to pick up some good Greek souvenirs.

The main streets of the Plaka—especially **Adrianou** and **Pandrossou**—are crammed with crass tourist-trap shops, selling cheap plaster replicas of ancient artifacts, along with calendars, playing cards, postcards, and shockingly profane T-shirts. Competition is fierce between shops, so there's room to bargain, especially if you're buying several items.

The famous **Monastiraki flea market** stretches west of Monastiraki Square, along Ifestou street and its side streets. It's a fun place for tourists and pickpockets to browse, but it's not ideal for buying gifts for friends back home—unless they like junk. You'll see fake designer clothes, antiques, dusty books, and lots of stuff that might raise eyebrows at the airport (something going on every day, but best Sun 8:00-15:00, Metro line 1/green and line 3/blue: Monastiraki or line 1/green: Thissio).

For upscale shopping at mostly international chain stores, stroll the pedestrianized **Ermou street** between Syntagma Square and Monastiraki. Even fancier boutiques are in the swanky **Kolonaki** area.

For a self-guided walk of a more down-to-earth shopping area (which, thanks to its local flavor, might interest non-shoppers even more than shoppers), see the "Shop Like an Athenian" walk at the end of this section.

Most shops catering to tourists are open long hours daily. Those serving locals are more likely open Monday, Wednesday, and Saturday from 8:30 or 9:00 until early afternoon (between 14:30 and 16:00); Tuesday, Thursday, and Friday from 8:30 or 9:00 until late (roughly 20:00 or 21:00), but often with an afternoon break (around 14:00-17:00 or 18:00); and closed Sunday.

To find out how to get a VAT (Value-Added Tax) refund on your purchases, see page 127.

What and Where to Buy

Here are some of the more authentic items you can buy, along with good places to find them.

Jewelry—Serious buyers tell me that Athens is the best place in Greece to purchase jewelry, particularly at the shops along Adrianou. The choices are much better than you'll find elsewhere, and—if you know how to haggle—so are the prices. The best advice is to take your time, and don't be afraid to walk away. The sales staff gets paid on commission, and they hate to lose a potential customer. Most stores have similar selections, which they buy from factory wholesalers.

For something a bit more specialized (with very high prices), visit the sister shops of Byzantino and Olympico (both open daily 10:00-21:00, sometimes later in summer, tel. 210-324-6605, www .byzantino.com, run by Kosta). **Byzantino,** which made the jewelry worn by Greek dancers in the closing ceremonies of the 2000 Sydney Olympics, creates pricey handmade replicas of museum pieces (most cost hundreds of euros; Adrianou 120, plus another location nearby at the corner of Pandrossou and Eolou). **Olympico,** nearly next door, creates modern pieces in the Greek style, including some more affordable options (Adrianou 122).

Sandals—The place to buy real leather sandals is **Melissinos Art,** the famous "poet sandal-maker" of Athens. You'll find an assortment of styles for about €25 per pair. Prices depend on size and style: The more leather they use, the more you pay (daily 10:00-22:00, just off Monastiraki Square at the edge of Psyrri, Ag. Theklas 2, tel. 210-321-9247, www.melissinos-art.com). Stavros Melissinos—who's also a poet—ran this shop for decades. Now that he's retired, his son Pantelis (also a painter and playwright) has taken over the family business. When the Beatles came to his shop in 1968, Stavros was asked why he didn't ask for their autographs. He replied, "Why did they not ask for mine? I will be around long after the Beatles." He was right.

Carpets—The shops around the Plaka sell Persian-style carpets, but generally don't stock Greek ones. For Greek carpets, visit the **Institute of Social Protection and Solidarity Arts & Crafts Shop** (run by the Ministry of Health and Welfare). It has a good selection of colorful hand-knotted carpets, hand-woven kilims, needlepoint rugs, tablecloths, and cushion covers embroidered with folk designs. What's more, the profits go toward preservation of traditional handicrafts. The work is done by women who live in rural Greece and depend on this shop as their sole source of income (Tue-Fri 8:00-20:00, Mon and Sat 8:00-14:30, closed Sun, a block from the TI near Syntagma Square at Filellinon 14, tel. 210-325-0240).

Religious Items—For Greek Orthodox items, visit the shops near the cathedral, along Agia Filotheis street (described on page 903).

Worry Beads—Attentive travelers will notice Greeks (mostly men) constantly fidgeting with these strings of beads—endlessly flipping, spinning, and counting them. Loosely based on prayer beads, but today a secular hobby, worry beads make for a fun Greek souvenir. You'll see them sold all over central Athens.

Shop Like an Athenian: A Self-Guided Walk

While tourists and big-money Athenians strut their stuff on the upscale Ermou shopping street (described in "Athens City Walk"), many locals prefer the streets just to the north—including

Perikleous, Lekka, and Kolokotroni—for authentic, hole-in-the-wall shopping. Let's join them for this brief walk through some of central Athens' more colorful and totally untouristy neighborhoods.

Begin on Syntagma Square. At the bottom of the square, face the McDonald's. Exit the square on the street to the right, Karageorgi Servias (parallel to Ermou). About a block down this street, on the left, spot the several **chocolate shops.** Leonidas is a famous Belgian chocolatier with a Greek name (and origin). Beyond that are a pair of favorites: Aristokratikon (at #9, Mon-Fri 8:00-21:00, Sat 8:00-16:00, closed Sun) and Le Chocolat (at #3, daily 8:00-22:00). At Aristokratikon, you can point one-by-one at various treats to assemble a collection of top-notch candies: pistachio clusters, chocolate-dipped fruit, almond paste in white chocolate, and more (€35/kilogram, or about €4 for five pieces). Le Chocolat is a bit more genteel and stuffy-feeling. Notice the case of fancy desserts. Greeks bring these to a home when they're invited for a visit (instead of, say, a bottle of wine).

Passing Nikis street, continue along Karageorgi Servias. Notice that, while shopping malls are becoming as popular here as anywhere in Europe, many Greeks still prefer to do their shopping in more specialized, **hole-in-the-wall shops.** They explain that the items they can buy here are unique, with more personality than the cookie-cutter stuff sold at malls and department stores. For example, check out the make-your-own-jewelry shop on the left, at #11.

After another block, around Voulis street, the road's name changes to Perikleous. Keep walking along it. Ahead on the right, watch for the shop called ΖΟΥΛΟΒΙΤΣ **(Zoulovits)**—the Greek answer to Tiffany's (since 1948). Well-heeled Athenians buy high-class silver gifts here for weddings and christenings (for a baby, a silver cup with a blue or pink ribbon is a must; Mon-Fri 9:00-20:30, Sat 9:00-15:30, closed Sun, Perikleous 10, tel. 210-322-7694).

Turn right down **Lekka street,** in front of Zoulovits. Before Ermou was pedestrianized, Lekka was the main shopping drag. Along here are more silver and jewelry gift shops (cheaper alternatives to the "big Z" mentioned above). On the left, watch for some shopping galleries that burrow into the city block.

Soon Lekka hits **Kolokotroni street,** which is lined with more small shops (including some that specialize in engravings, old maps, and books). The traffic and noise along here will give you a new appreciation for the traffic-free shopping zones in the

ATHENS

Athens Shopping

To Central Market, Omonia Square, National Archaeological Museum & Exarchia

To Museum of the City of Athens

KOLOKOTRONI

SYNTAGMA

CHURCH OF KAPNIKAREA

To 8

ATHINAIDOS

PERIKLEOUS

WALK BEGINS

KARA SERV.

MONASTIRAKI

WALK ENDS

CATHEDRAL (MITROPOLIS)

ERMOU

Syntagma Square

PANDROSSOU

Cathedral Square

PETRAKI

POST

MITROPOLEOS

OTHONOS

100 Meters

100 Yards

CHURCH OF AGIOS ELEFTHERIOS

APOLLONOS

IPITOU

XENOFONDOS

AG. FILOTHEIS

NIKODIMOU

LISSIOU

IPERIDOU

JEWISH MUSEUM OF GREECE

ANAFIOTIKA

PLAKA

AG. GEORGIOS

ACROPOLIS

KIDATHINEON

Filomousou Square

DEDALOU

MUSEUM OF GREEK FOLK ART

PSYLLA

VAS. AMALIAS

① Chocolate Shops
② Zoulovits
③ Lekka Street
④ Kolokotroni Street
⑤ Kalamiotou Street
⑥ Bridal Shops
⑦ Byzantino & Olympico (Jewelry)
⑧ To Melissinos Art (Sandals)
⑨ Arts & Crafts (Carpets)
⑩ Compendium Bookstore
⑪ Eleftheroudakis Bookstores (2)

ATHENS

city center. Turn left and walk down Kolokotroni, watching (on the left) for a worry-bead shop—supplying the means of this very Greek nervous habit. Consider dropping in to peruse the many variations.

After a few blocks, turn left on traffic-free **Kalamiotou street,** and bear right at the fork. Soon after, cross Ermou street at the Byzantine Church of Kapnikarea. (This will look familiar if you've done the Athens walking tour.) Continue straight ahead past the church and one block down Kapnikareas.

When you reach the busy cross-street (Mitropoleos), you're

near three other favorite shops. Across Mitropoleos, notice the two shops flanking Kapnikareas. On the left corner, **To Κεντημα** (To Kentema) sells linens—specializing in white pieces that are given as a gift to a daughter or niece for her marriage. On the right corner, at #49, is **Selections ΧΥΤΗΡΟΓΛΟΥ** (Hitiroglou), selling Athens' best-quality fabric. And a few steps down the street to the right, at #74 (on the right-hand side), the shop called **Home Sweet Home** specializes in wedding gifts. Traditionally, weddings are held on the weekend. Three days beforehand, family and friends gather to make the couple's bed with brand-new bedding, then scatter cash across the top of it—sort of like a big, fat, Greek wedding shower.

Our shopping walk is finished. For more shopping, backtrack a block up to the Ermou pedestrian mall, or continue ahead one block (across Mitropoleos) to the tourist-trinket-heavy Pandrossou drag. Turn right on Pandrossou to head straight for Monastiraki Square, epicenter of the flea-market action.

Starting or Ending Your Cruise in Athens

If your cruise begins and/or ends in Athens, you'll want some extra time here; with an additional day you can see the National Archaeological Museum or visit the fun, thriving districts of Thissio, Psyrri, and Gazi. For a longer visit, pick up my *Rick Steves' Greece: Athens & the Peloponnese* guidebook.

Airport Connections

Eleftherios Venizelos International Airport, Athens' modern airport, is at Spata, 17 miles east of downtown (tel. 210-353-0000, www.aia.gr). This impressively slick, user-friendly airport has two sections: B gates (serving European/Schengen countries—no passport control) and A gates (serving other destinations, including the US). Both sections feed into the same main terminal building (with a common baggage claim, ATMs, shops, car-rental counters, information desks, and additional services). Upstairs, on the second floor (above entrance/exit #3), is a mini-museum of Greek artifacts.

Getting from the Airport to Downtown

By Metro: Line 3/blue zips you downtown in 45 minutes for €8 (2/hour, usually departs at :05 and :35 after the hour, daily 6:00-23:30; half-price for people under 18 or over 65, ticket good for 1.5 hours on other Athens transit). To catch this train from the airport arrivals hall, go through exit #3, cross the street, escalate to the skybridge, walk to the terminal to buy tickets, and follow signs down to the platforms (look for signs to *Metro*, not *suburban trains*). In downtown Athens, this train stops at Syntagma (transfer to line 2/red) and Monastiraki (transfer to line 1/green).

By Bus: Buses wait outside exit #5. Express bus #X95 operates 24 hours daily between the airport and Syntagma Square (3-5/hour, 3/hour at night, trip takes 1-1.5 hours depending on traffic). The downtown bus stop is on Othonos street, along the side of Syntagma Square (€5, tel. 185, www.oasa.gr).

By Taxi: A well-marked taxi stand outside exit #3 offers fixed-price transfers that include all fees (€40 to central Athens or to the port of Piraeus). If you arrange your own taxi (to or from the airport), figure around €30-40 total. Note that the cabbie will tack on several legitimate fees beyond what's on the meter, including the tolls to take the fast road, per-piece baggage charges, and a special airport fee (for details, see "Getting Around Athens—By Taxi" on page 889).

People on package trips are met at the airport by sign-waving cabbies who take them to their hotel and help get them settled in for about €75. Recently, private English-speaking cabbies have been providing this same service to anyone for about €55—though its value over simply catching a normal cab is questionable.

Getting from the Airport to Piraeus

A **taxi** from the airport directly to the cruise terminals costs about €40. **Express bus** #X96 connects the airport directly to Piraeus. Catch the bus in front of the arrivals hall outside exit #5. After your long ride to Piraeus, get off the bus right after you hit the port, at the Plateia Karaiskaki/ΠΛ. ΚΑΡΑΙΣΚΑΚΗ stop (look for gate E8); then cross the street and catch bus #843 going in the opposite direction, toward the cruise terminals, and get off at the Apheteria (ΑΦΕΤΗΡΙΑ) stop, which is between the terminals (€5, runs 24 hours daily, 2-6/hour depending on time of day, 1-1.5 hours depending on traffic). You can also get to Piraeus via a long **Metro** ride; take line 3/blue to Monastiraki and change to line 1/green toward Piraeus (€8, 2/hour, daily 6:00-23:30), then use the same ticket to ride bus #843 to the cruise terminals.

Hotels

If you need a hotel in Athens before or after your cruise, here are a few to consider in the Plaka and near the Acropolis.

In the Plaka

$$$ Hotel Plaka and **Hotel Hermes** are owned by the same company and have rooms at the same price. Hotel Plaka has a rooftop bar/terrace and 67 modern rooms (some with Acropolis views)

What If I Miss My Boat?

Remember that you can get help from the cruise line's port agent (listed on the destination information sheet distributed on the ship) and the local TI (for Athens, see page 881; for Piraeus, see page 875). If the port agent suggests a costly solution (such as a private car with a driver), you may want to consider public transit.

Frequent **ferries** from Piraeus serve most Greek islands. For **Mykonos** (3.5-5.5 hours), **Santorini** (5-9 hours), and other **Cycladic Islands,** try Blue Star Ferries (tel. 210-891-9010, www.bluestarferries.com), Hellenic Seaways (tel. 210-419-9000, www.hsw.gr), ANEK Lines (tel. 210-419-7420, www.anek.gr), Aegean Speed Lines (tel. 210-969-0950, www.aegeanspeedlines.gr), or SeaJets (tel. 210-412-1800, www.seajets.gr). To reach **Heraklion** (6-8 hours), the capital of Crete, the sleek Minoan Lines fleet (tel. 210-337-6910, www.minoan.gr) is better than ANEK Lines (listed above). To sail to **Rhodes** (13-21 hours), try Blue Star Ferries (listed above).

Buses serving the Peloponnese use the Athens bus station called Kifissou, or "Terminal A." This bus station is about three miles northwest of the city center. Buses leave from Terminal A to: **Nafplio** (hourly direct, 2.5 hours) and **Olympia,** near the port of **Katakolo** (2/day direct, 5 hours). Terminal A info: tel. 210-512-4910.

If you need to catch a **plane** to your next destination, see the information on Athens' airport earlier.

Any **travel agent** in Athens and Piraeus can help you. For more advice on what to do if you miss the boat, see page 131.

with updated bathrooms. The better-value Hotel Hermes has 45 even newer, nicer rooms on a quiet street closer to Syntagma and a little less convenient to the ancient sights (Sb-€69-99, Db-€89-135, Tb-€99-145, cheapest Nov-March, 10 percent discount when you reserve direct and show this book at check-in, check website for deals—mostly for longer stays, pay Wi-Fi). Hotel Plaka is at the corner of Mitropoleos and Kapnikarea (tel. 210-322-2096, fax 210-321-1800, www.plakahotel.gr, plaka@tourhotel.gr); Hotel Hermes is at Apollonos 19 (tel. 210-323-5514, fax 210-321-1800, www.hermeshotel.gr, hermes@tourhotel.gr).

$ Hotel Phaedra is simple but wonderfully located, overlooking a peaceful Plaka square with ancient ruins and a Byzantine church. The very institutional hallways lead to 21 nicely appointed rooms (Sb-€60, D-€65, twin Db-€70, Db with balcony-€80, T-€75, Tb-€90, 10 percent less off-season, breakfast-€5 extra, air-con, elevator, free Wi-Fi in lobby, 2 blocks from Hadrian's Arch at Cherefondos 16, at intersection with Adrianou, tel. 210-323-8461, fax 210-322-7795, www.hotelphaedra.com, info@hotelphaedra.com).

In Makrigianni and Koukaki, Behind the Acropolis

$$$ Hotel Acropolis Select has 72 rooms over a stylish lobby. Well-run by Kyriaki, it features a can-do staff and a generous breakfast. Their service ethic goes way beyond the norm—they've been known to send a guide on a motorbike to lead lost drivers to the hotel (Db-€80-120 depending on size and season, air-con, elevator, pay Internet access and pay Wi-Fi, Falirou 37-39, tel. 210-921-1611, fax 210-921-6938, www.acropoliselect.gr, selective@ath .forthnet.gr).

$$ Art Gallery Hotel is a comfy, cozy, well-run small hotel with 22 rooms near the top of a pleasant, pedestrian stair-step lane. The original artwork in the halls and rooms adds boutique-hotel charm (Sb-€40-70, Db-€60-90, Tb-€80-110, breakfast-€7, air-con, elevator, free Internet access and Wi-Fi, Erecthiou 5, tel. 210-923-8376, fax 210-923-3025, www.artgalleryhotel.gr, art galleryhotel@gmail.com). Say hello to the hotel's cats—Nelly, Sugar, and Artie.

$ Marble House Pension is a small, family-run place hiding at the end of a little cul-de-sac, a few minutes' walk past my other listings in this area. The 16 cozy rooms are simple but well cared for, and (true to its name) it's decorated with real marble. If you don't mind the dreary urban location, it's an excellent deal (Sb-€39, D-€45, Db-€49, Tb-€59, Qb-€65, cheaper late Oct-mid-March, breakfast-€5; air-con in some rooms-€9, ceiling fans in others; no elevator, free Internet access and Wi-Fi, 5-minute walk from Syngrou-Fix Metro at Zini 35a—from Zini street take the alley to the left of the tidy Catholic church, tel. 210-923-4058 or 210-922-8294, fax 210-922-6461, www.marblehouse.gr, info @marblehouse.gr).

ATHENS

MYKONOS

ΜΥΚΟΝΟΣ / Μυκονοσ

Mykonos (MEE-koh-nohs) is the very picture of the perfect Greek island town: a humble seafront village crouched behind a sandy harbor, thickly layered with blinding-white stucco, bright-blue trim, and bursting-purple bougainvilleas. (Thank goodness for all that color, since otherwise this island—one of Greece's driest—would be various shades of dull-brown.) On a ridge over town stretches a trademark row of five windmills, overlooking a tidy embankment so pretty they call it "Little Venice."

Mykonos' more recent status as a fashionable, jet-set destination and a mecca for gay holiday-makers also gives it a certain hip cachet. These days, weary fisherfolk and tacky trinket stalls share the lanes with top-end fashion boutiques. Prices are stunningly high here, and the island is crammed full of fellow vacationers, particularly in August (try to come in spring or fall, if you can). But the Mykonians have taken all of the changes in stride. Fishermen still hang out on the benches by the harbor—always wearing their traditional caps (Mykonian men are famous among Greeks for their baldness). The natives generally seem appreciative rather than corrupted by all the attention. On my last visit, I overheard a young tourist gushing to her mommy, "Boy, people sure are friendly here!"

While Mykonos has some museums, they merely provide an excuse to get out of the sun for a few minutes. The real attraction here is poking around the Old Town streets: shopping, dining, clubbing, or—best of all—simply strolling. The core of town is literally a maze, designed by the Mykonians centuries ago to discourage would-be invaders from finding their way. That tactic also works on today's tourists. But I can think of few places where

---

Excursions from Mykonos

Most excursions feature one or both of two main attractions: A guided walk around the town of **Mykonos;** and a tour of the ancient site of **Delos,** on a nearby island. Mykonos is beautiful, but there's not much to say about the place—it's simply a delight to wander. Delos, on the other hand, has a fascinating history that's best appreciated with the help of a good guide.

Other excursions may include side-trips to some of Mykonos' **beaches,** which you can easily reach on your own by taxi or bus. And many cruise lines offer an **"island highlights"** itinerary to various villages and countryside churches—but Mykonos town and the beaches are really the only things worth seeing on a short visit.

---

getting lost is so enjoyable.

If you manage to break free, wander up to the windmills for the view, or take a bus (or rent a scooter or ATV) to reach one of the many enticing sandy beaches around the island. Near Mykonos, accessible by an easy boat trip, is the island of Delos—one of the Greek islands' top ancient sites. Delos hosts the remains of what was one of the most important places in the ancient Greek world: the temples honoring the birthplace of the twin gods Apollo and Artemis (it later became a bustling shipping community). Delos was a pilgrimage site for believers who came from all over to worship this "birthplace of light." Judging by the present-day sun-worshippers who scramble for the best patch of sand on Mykonos each summer, things haven't changed much around here.

Planning Your Time

Mykonos is a delightful place to be on vacation, even if just for a few hours. Here are some good options for your time:

• Explore the Old Town lanes in Mykonos town. You can dip into the museums, but they're all skippable.

• Beach-lovers will want to head to any one of several fine beaches (described in this chapter, all within a 20-minute ride from Mykonos town). Allow a minimum of two hours, including transportation.

• Archaeologists and historians can take a boat to Delos (easy 30-minute boat trip each way). Figure about three hours total for the round-trip.

Crowd Warning: The island can be painfully crowded in peak season, roughly July through mid-September, peaking in August. During this time, the beaches (and everything else) are uncomfortably packed with people.

MYKONOS

Arrival in Mykonos

Cruise ships arriving at Mykonos either tender passengers directly to the heart of the Old Town or dock at the big New Port across the bay.

Tendering to the Old Town

If your cruise ship is tendered, you'll disembark at the pier extending out from the heart of town. Just walk down the pier and you're at the harbor (a public pay WC is on the right, along the water).

Docking at the New Port

Cruise ships dock at the New Port, across the bay from the Old Town, about a mile away. Many cruise lines offer a shuttle bus (often free) that zips you right to the Old Port. Or you can reach the Old Port by taxi (€5-6) or public bus (2/hour, €1.40). From there, it's an easy five-minute walk to the Old Town: Stroll past a stretch of beach, then down a cozy shop-lined lane to Taxi Square and the main harborfront.

If the line for the bus is just too long, and you're eager to stretch your legs, you could do the dreary 20- to 25-minute walk along the coast into town (turn right, follow the water, and just keep going—you can see the gaggle of white houses across the bay).

Orientation to Mykonos

Mykonos' main town is called Chora (or Hora, Χώρα; roughly, "Village"), and that's how you'll generally see it signed. For ease, I refer to it as "Mykonos town."

Mykonos town is the main point of entry for the island. The Old Town clusters around the south end of the Old Port (some inter-island boats depart from the north end of the Old Port). Arcing in front of the Old Town is the sandy harbor; at the east end is Taxi Square (a hub for taxis and other services) and, beyond that, the Remezzo bus station and the Old Port; at the west end of the harbor is the pier for Delos ferries and cruise-ship tenders, and beyond that, the Little Venice quarter and the windmill ridge. Squeezed between the harbor and the main road (passing above town on the gentle hill above) is a tight maze of whitewashed lanes.

While some streets have names, others don't, and in any case, locals never use those names—they just know where things are. If you can't find something, just ask.

Tourist Information

Though there is a TI building (at the corner of the Old Port), the space hasn't been occupied in a while. To fill the void, local hotels, travel agencies, and other friendly locals can answer basic questions. Look for the promotional but helpful red *Mykonos Guidebook* (free around town).

Getting Around Mykonos

Mykonos is a fun and easy island to explore, with several very different but equally inviting beach coves within a short drive.

By Taxi: The square at the southeast corner of the Old Port, nicknamed Taxi Square, is where you can catch a taxi to points around the island. Fares are reasonable; figure around €10 one-way to most beaches listed in this chapter (except Super Paradise, which is more like €15). Rather than paying the taxi to wait for you at the beach, hail or call a fresh one when you're ready to leave (tel. 22890-23700); you can also ask a taverna at the beach to call for you.

By Bus: Mykonos' bus network is well-designed for connecting travelers to its many fine beaches. Buses are frequent, though they might leave you a short walk from the beach itself. And since this is a party island, they run late into the night in peak season.

There are three bus stations in Mykonos town. For tourists, the most useful is the **Fabrika** station, with buses to nearby destinations, including the beaches I've described in this chapter. The Fabrika station is at the south end of town (away from the harbor), where several Old Town streets funnel gradually uphill to the main road that passes above. Two other stations are virtually next to each other at the northeast edge of the Old Town (from Taxi Square, head along the port with the water to your left): The **Old Port** station along the water is for buses to the New Port. The **Remezzo** station, a block uphill, serves buses to the eastern half of the island (the large town of Ano Mera, plus the smaller towns of Kalafati and Elia).

If you're taking a bus to beaches, here's how often they run: **Ornos/Ag. Ioannis** (1-2/hour), **Paradise** (2/hour), **Platis Gialos** (2/hour), and **Paraga** (hourly). Schedules are posted at stops. Rides cost €1.40; because tickets aren't always as readily sold at other points on the island, get a return ticket when buying your outbound ticket in Mykonos town.

By Motorized Scooter or All-Terrain Vehicle (ATV): On Greek islands, tourists are notorious for renting a scooter or ATV, overestimating their abilities to control a machine they've never driven before, and denting someone's fender or leaving a strip of knee or elbow skin on the pavement...or worse. That said, and keeping in mind the risks inherent in renting wheels here, it can be an affordable, efficient, and memorably fun way to connect distant beaches. If I were renting a scooter or ATV on a Greek isle, I'd do it here, where the roads are not too heavily trafficked (you'll pass more fellow scooters and ATVs than cars), and idyllic beaches are a short ride away.

Travel agencies all over town rent both types of wheels for reasonable all-day rates (€15-20/day for a scooter or ATV, ATVs with reverse gear cost about €5 more). Two people can ride one machine, but both should ask for helmets (while you'll see many riders without them, it's stupidly risky not to wear one, and most rental agencies are happy to loan you one). The paperwork is quick and casual (they'll take a credit-card imprint as a deposit, you'll fill up whatever gas you use before you return it, and insurance... what's that?). Once on the road, be especially careful around turns, where centrifugal forces make it suddenly more difficult to steer. Be aware that even distances that appear short can take time to reach on a slow-moving ATV; figure 15-20 minutes from Mykonos town to any of the beaches I list in this chapter (the farthest is Super Paradise). Note: You'll see ads for renting a "bike," but this refers to motorized scooters—the island is hilly and arid enough to make actual bicycling undesirable for all but the most serious cyclists.

By Car: You can also rent a car for as little as €40 per day, depending on demand; look for car-rental signs at several agencies around town.

Helpful Hints

Hours: I don't list specific hours for shops or restaurants, as these vary with demand. In peak season, they're open long hours daily, but when the tourists disappear, so do the opening hours.

English Bookstore: The **International Press Newsstand,** just off the harbor at the Taxi Square end, stocks a good selection of international (including English-language) paperbacks, magazines, and newspapers (daily, Kampani 5, tel. 22890-23316).

Services: You'll find travel agencies, ATMs, launderettes, Internet cafés, pay phones, and other helpful services scattered around the Old Town. For the highest concentration of services, head for the area around the Fabrika bus station, at the south end of the Old Town (near where it meets the main road; also pay WC, tattoo parlor).

Sights in Mykonos

▲▲**Old Town**—Mykonos' Old Town seems made for exploring. Each picture-perfect lane is slathered with a thick, bulbous layer

of stucco, giving the place a marshmallow-village vibe. All that white is the perfect contrast to the bright-blue sky and the vivid trim. Sometimes described as "Cubist" for its irregular jostle of angular rooflines, Mykonos' townscape is a photographer's delight. Enjoy getting lost, then found again. Try wandering aimlessly for a while—you'll be amazed at how quickly you find yourself going in circles. To get your bearings, look at a map and notice that three "main" roads (still barely wide enough for a moped) form a U-shaped circuit facing the harbor: Kouzi Georgouli, Enoplon Dynameon, and Matogianni.

Or just relax along the sandy **harbor.** The pier for excursion boats to Delos (described later) sticks straight out; nearby is an impossibly picturesque white chapel with sky-blue trim. Nurse an iced coffee or beer at a rustic café table and watch the tide of tourists wash over local village life. Glancing offshore, you'll see humble fishing boats bobbing in the foreground, with 2,000-passenger cruise ships looming in the distance. Along the sandy harbor, fisherfolk sort and clean their catch at the marble table (while

MYKONOS

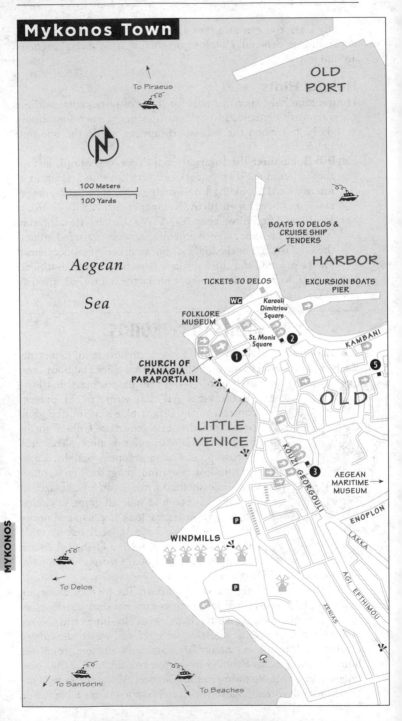

Mykonos Town

To Piraeus

N

100 Meters
100 Yards

Aegean

Sea

OLD
PORT

BOATS TO DELOS &
CRUISE SHIP
TENDERS

HARBOR

TICKETS TO DELOS

EXCURSION BOATS
PIER

WC

Karaoli
Dimitriou
Square

FOLKLORE
MUSEUM

St. Monis
Square

1

2

CHURCH OF
PANAGIA
PARAPORTIANI

KAMBANI

5

OLD

LITTLE
VENICE

KOUZI GEORGOULI

3

AEGEAN
MARITIME
MUSEUM

ENOPLON

LAKKA

P

WINDMILLS

P

AGL. EFTHIMOU

XENIAS

To Delos

To Santorini

To Beaches

MYKONOS

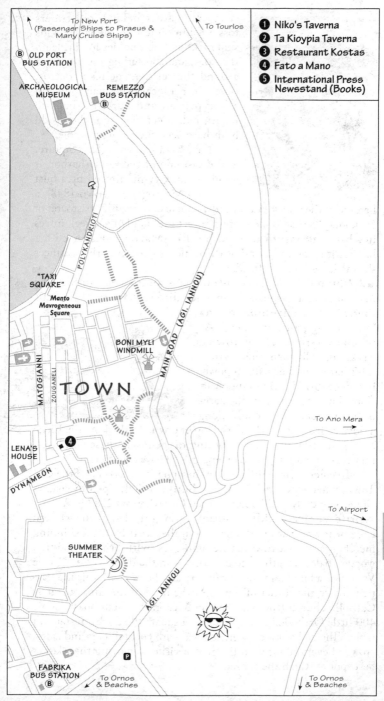

To New Port
(Passenger Ships to Piraeus &
Many Cruise Ships)

To Tourlos

1 Niko's Taverna
2 Ta Kioypia Taverna
3 Restaurant Kostas
4 Fato a Mano
5 International Press
Newsstand (Books)

B OLD PORT
BUS STATION

ARCHAEOLOGICAL
MUSEUM

REMEZZO
BUS STATION
B

POLYKANDRIOTI

"TAXI
SQUARE"

Manto
Mavrogeneous
Square

BONI MYLI
WINDMILL

MAIN ROAD (AGI. IANNOU)

MATOGIANNI

ZOUGANELI

T O W N

To Ano Mera

LENA'S
HOUSE

4

DYNAMEON

SUMMER
THEATER

AGI. IANNOU

To Airport

MYKONOS

P

FABRIKA
BUS STATION
B

To Ornos
& Beaches

To Ornos
& Beaches

stray cats gather below), old-timers toss a fishing line into the water, kids skip rocks and rent ponies for a ride on the sand, and shutterbug tourists flock around the resident pelican, Petros. (Ever since a local fisherman found an ailing pelican and nursed it back to health half a century ago, these odd birds have been the town's mascots.)

The piazza known as **Taxi Square,** at the east end of the sandy harbor, is a hub of activity monitored by a bust of Manto Mavrogenous (1796-1848), a heroine of the Greek War of Independence. A wealthy aristocrat of Mykonian heritage, she spent her fortune supplying Greek forces in a battle against their Turkish rulers. Mavrogenous ended her life destitute on the island of Paros, never regretting the sacrifices she made for Greece's freedom.

▲▲**Windmills**—Mykonos is infamous for its wind. In fact, the Mykonians have special names for different winds: "the bell-ringer," "the chair-thrower," and "the unseater of horsemen." As in many Greek island towns, Mykonos' old-fashioned windmills harnessed this natural power in order to grind grain to supply its ships. Five of them (plus the bases of two more) stand proudly along

a ridge called Kato Myloi at the top of town, overlooking the Little Venice area. While there's nothing to see inside these buildings, they make for a fine photo op and great views over town.

To enter a windmill, head to the opposite (east) end of the Old Town, where the **Boni Myli windmill** is briefly open to visitors (June-Sept daily 16:00-18:00, closed Oct-May, tel. 22890-22591).

▲**Little Venice (Mikri Venetia)**—Along the bay at the western edge of town, just below the windmills, wealthy local shipping merchants built a row of fine mansions, with brightly painted wooden balconies, that seem to rise from the deep. While "Little Venice" is a bit of a misnomer (where are the canals?), this is a particularly scenic corner of town. At the head of this area, a stately Catholic church (the only one on Mykonos, which boasts some 400 little Orthodox chapels) marks a square filled with restaurant tables. The embankment here is lined with cocktail bars and cafés, crowded every night with throngs of visitors enjoying the island's best spot to watch the sunset.

▲**Church of Panagia Paraportiani**—Huddled at the tip of land between Little Venice and the harbor, this unusual church

is a striking architectural oddity—a hodgepodge of five small chapels that gradually merged together, then were draped in a thick layer of whitewashed stucco. While it's a much-touted landmark (and one of the island's "most-photographed spots"), there's little to see beyond the initial, otherworldly appearance. One of the chapel interiors is open most days, where a local woman sells votive candles and fills the small space with the rich aroma of incense.

Archaeological Museum—Perched on a bluff at the south end of the Old Port, this museum displays artifacts from Rinia, which became the burial isle for Delos when residents of that sacred island's cemeteries were relocated by the Athenians in the sixth century B.C. (see sidebar on page 995). One room shows off intricately carved stone grave markers, called steles. The rest of the collection consists of sparsely described cases full of vases, jewelry, statue fragments, and other artifacts. There's relatively little to see, and it's difficult to appreciate—interesting only to armchair archaeologists (€2, Tue-Sun 8:30-15:00, closed Mon, tel. 22890-22325).

Aegean Maritime Museum—This tight but endearing collection traces the story of the local mercantile shipping industry. A desert isle of history in a sea of tourist kitsch, this little place takes its subject very seriously. In its four rooms, you'll find amphora jugs, model ships, a collection of stamps celebrating seafaring, and more. Don't miss the tranquil garden, which displays the actual, original lighthouse from the island's Cape Armenistis, as well as replicas of ancient sailors' gravestones. The good English descriptions offer a fine history lesson for those willing to read them (€4, April-Oct daily 10:30-13:00 & 18:30-21:00, closed Nov-March, Enoplon Dynameon 10, tel. 22890-22700).

Lena's House—Adjacent to the Maritime Museum (and part of the Folklore Museum), this is a typical middle-class Mykonian house dating from the late 19th century, complete with original furnishings and artwork (€2, April-Oct Mon-Sat 18:30-21:30, closed Sun and Nov-March, tel. 22890-22591).

Mykonos Folklore Museum—Housed in a typically Cycladic former sea captain's residence just up the bluff from the harbor, this museum displays a random mix of traditional folk items from around the island, as well as a typical kitchen and bedroom (free, April-Oct Mon-Sat 17:30-20:30, Sun 18:30-20:30, closed Nov-March, tel. 22890-22591).

Beaches

Mykonos' array of beaches rivals that of any Greek island. Each beach seems to specialize in a different niche: family-friendly or party; straight, gay, or mixed; nude or clothed; and so on. (Keep in mind that in Greece, even "family-friendly" beaches have topless sunbathers.) Get local advice to find the one that suits your beach-bum preferences, or choose from one of the options listed here (all of my suggestions are within a 15- to 20-minute bus or scooter/ATV ride from town).

To connect the beaches, you'll drive steeply up and down over the dusty, dirty, desolate spine of this arid island. You can also connect many of these beaches (including Psarou, Platis Gialos, Paradise, and Super Paradise) by regular shuttle boat.

All of these beaches have comfortable lounge chairs with umbrellas out on the sand. Figure around €10-15 for two chairs that share an umbrella (or half that for one chair). Just take a seat—they'll come by to collect money. Be warned that in peak season (July and especially Aug), all beaches are very crowded, and it can be difficult to find an available seat.

Mykonos' beaches are lined with cafés and tavernas, with typical Greek-island menus...sometimes utilitarian, sometimes surprisingly good. These can offer a welcome break from the sun.

Agios Ioannis—My favorite beach, this remote-feeling patch of sand tucked behind a mountain ridge best gives you the feeling

of being on a castaway isle. You'll enjoy views across to the important isle of Delos. From Mykonos town, go to Ornos, then head toward Kapari; on your way down the hill, turn off on the left at the low-profile beach signs (one directs you to Πύλη, one of the restaurants on the beach). You'll

drop down the road to an idyllic Robinson Crusoe spot where two restaurants (Puli and Hippie Fish) share a sandy beach. I ate well at **Puli** (Πύλη), with big portions and fresh, tasty Greek classics (daily, tel. 22890-26660).

For the even more secluded **Kapari** beach, continue down the road past the Agios Ioannis turnoff, then swing right at the white church.

Ornos—Easy to reach since it's in a sizable town in the middle of the island, this very family-friendly beach is also one of the more functional (and least memorable) of those I list. The whole place has an unpretentious charm.

Psarou and Platis Gialos—These two beaches, along the next cove to the east of Ornos, are much more densely developed. At

each one, a tight line of
hotels arcs along the top of
a crowded patch of sand.
Psarou is considered a
somewhat exclusive, favorite
retreat of celebrities, while
Platis Gialos feels more
geared toward families (the
far end from the bus stop/
parking is less claustrophobic).

Paradise—This famous "meat-market" beach is a magnet for
partiers in the Aegean, and even more of a destination than the
other beaches listed here. Located at the southern tip of the island,
Paradise (a.k.a. Kalamopodi) is presided over by hotels that run
party-oriented bars for young beachgoers—perfect if you want to
dance in the sand all night to the throbbing beat with like-minded
backpackers from around the world. As you approach, the last
stretch is through thick, high grasses, giving the place an air of
secrecy; then you'll pass long rows of lockers before popping out
at the party.

The next cove over hosts **Super Paradise** (Plintri) beach,
which has eclipsed the original as the premier party beach on the
island.

Eating in Mykonos

The twisting streets of the Old Town are lined with tourist-oriented restaurants. Don't look for good values here—Mykonos is

expensive. Little distinguishes one place
from another; simply choose the spot
with the menu and ambience that appeal
to you: with a sea view, out on a busy
pedestrian lane, or in a charming garden
courtyard.

Along the Harbor: While the many
tavernas and cafés that face the sandy
harbor are touristy and overpriced, it's
hard to argue with their appeal. Consider
enjoying an iced coffee or frappé—if not

a full meal—from this comfortable perch, which offers the best
people-watching (and sometimes cat- and pelican-watching) in
town.

Tavernas near St. Monis Square: Three rollicking tavernas
with huge outdoor terraces surround this stepped square with a
red-domed church, just a block above the harbor. Like the harborfront places, these are not necessarily the best values in town,

but the atmosphere is appealing (figure €4-8 starters, €8-20 main dishes, all open long hours daily). **Niko's Taverna** has an avid following (tel. 22890-24320), though locals prefer the food at **Ta Kioypia** (Τα Κιούπια, tel. 22890-22866).

Deeper in the Old Town: **Restaurant Kostas** has reasonable prices and unpretentious food on a charming little square facing a characteristic chapel (€4-10 starters, €9-20 main dishes, open daily, 5 Metropoleos, tel. 22890-23326). **Fato a Mano**—tucked away from the busiest part of the tourist zone, but still lively—offers a modern (rather than rustic) vibe and well-regarded food (€7-14 starters, €12-22 main dishes, daily 11:00-late, Meletopoulou Square, tel. 22890-26256).

Near Mykonos: Delos

Popular as Mykonos is today, centuries ago it was just another island, and the main attraction was next door: the island of Delos, worth ▲▲. In antiquity, Delos lived several lives: as one of the Mediterranean's most important religious sites, as the "Fort Knox" of Greek city-states, and as one of the ancient world's busiest commercial ports. Its importance ranked right up there with Athens, Delphi, or Olympia.

Today the island has no residents, and only ruins and a humble museum remain. Highlights of your visit include the much-photographed lion statues, some nice floor mosaics, and a windswept setting pockmarked with foundations that hint at Delos' glorious history.

Orientation to Delos

Cost: €5.

Hours: The site is closed (and boats do not run) on Mondays; on all other days, it's open from the arrival of the first boat to the departure of the last boat (for example, 9:30-15:00 in summer).

Warning: Delos is an uninhabited island with virtually no shade and only a small museum and café. Bring good shoes, sun protection, and plenty of water.

Getting There: Delos is reachable only by a 30-minute boat trip from Mykonos. Boats depart Mykonos from the pier extending straight out from the Old Town; you can buy the €15

The Rise and Fall of Delos

Delos enters history 3,000 years ago as a sacred place where a number of gods were worshipped. Blessed with a prime location (midway between the mainland of Greece and Asia Minor—today's Turkey—and in the center of the Greek islands), but cursed with no natural resources, the barren island survived as a religious destination for pilgrims bringing offerings to the gods.

According to myth, the philandering Zeus impregnated the mortal Leto. Zeus' furious wife Hera banished Leto from the earth, but Zeus implored his brother Poseidon to create a refuge for her by raising up the underwater world of "Invisible" (Greek *Adelos*) to create an island that was "Visible" *(Delos)*. Here, Leto gave birth to twins—Apollo (god of the sun) and Artemis (goddess of the moon). Their human followers built temples in their honor (ninth century B.C.), and pilgrims flocked here with offerings.

As Athens began to assert control over the Aegean (sixth century B.C.), it made sure that spiritually influential Delos stayed politically neutral. The Athenians ordered a "catharsis" (purification) of the island, removing dead bodies from the cemeteries. Later, they also decreed that no one could be born or die there—that is, there were to be no permanent residents. The Delians were relocated to an adjacent, larger island called Rinia. Ostensibly, this was to keep Delos pure for the gods, but in reality it removed any danger of rivals influencing the island's native population.

Because of its neutral status and central location, Delos was chosen in 478 B.C. as the natural meeting place for the powerful Delian League—an alliance of Greek city-states formed to battle the Persians and to promote trade. The combined wealth of the league was stored here in the fabulously rich bank of Delos. But all that changed in 454 B.C., when Pericles moved the treasury to Athens, and Delos reverted to being a pilgrimage site.

Centuries later, under the Romans, Delos' course changed dramatically once more. Thanks to its strategic location, the island was granted the right to operate as a free port (167 B.C.). Almost overnight, it became one of the biggest shipping centers in the known world, complete with a town of 30,000 inhabitants.

Then, in 88 B.C., soldiers from the Kingdom of Pontus, an enemy of Rome, attacked and looted the town, slaughtering 20,000 of its citizens. Delos never really recovered. Plagued by pirate attacks and shifting trade routes, Delos faded into history. Its once-great buildings were left to decay and waste away. In 1872, French archaeologists arrived (so far, scientists have excavated about one-fifth of the site), and Delos' cultural treasures were revealed to the modern world.

round-trip ticket at the little kiosk at the base of the pier. In peak season, boats go in each direction three times a day (Tue-Sun, generally departing Mykonos at 9:00, 10:00, and 11:00, and returning from Delos at 12:15, 13:30, and 15:00; no boats Mon); however, the specific times can change significantly depending on weather and cruise-ship arrivals and departures. This means you can have less than an hour to as much as six hours on the island.

Tours: Travel agencies in town sell package excursions that include the boat, museum entry, and a guided tour (ask at any travel agency). Local guides also meet arriving boats and show around small, impromptu groups (€10 for a one-hour quickie overview tour—you'll need more time to actually hike around the site and see the museum).

Length of This Tour: Most visitors find that two to three hours on the island is plenty to wander the site and see the museum.

Self-Guided Tour of Delos

• *From the boat dock, walk to the entrance, buy your ticket, pick up the helpful included map, and enter the gate.*

Pause and survey the site. The commercial harbor was to your right, and the sacred harbor to your left. Ahead and to the right are the foundations of shops and homes that once constituted one of the Aegean's finest cities. Standing above those ruins is Mount Kynthos, its hillsides littered with temple remains. The Agora of the Competaliasts—one of the main squares in town—is straight ahead (with the museum building poking up behind). The religious area (with the temples of Apollo) is ahead and to the left, at the end of the Sacred Way. And far to the left was the Sacred Lake (now a patch of trees), overlooked by the iconic row of lions.

• *Start by wandering through the long rows of foundations on your right. You can circle back to these at the end—after summiting the mountain and winding down past the theater—but it's a good idea to poke around now in case you run out of steam later.*

Residential and Commercial District: Most of these remains were either homes or shops. In the second century B.C. (when Delos was a bustling commercial port), the streets were lined with some 3,000 shops where you could buy just about anything, and the hillsides above were covered with the elaborate homes of wealthy merchants and shippers. Delos was considered to be the most important commer-

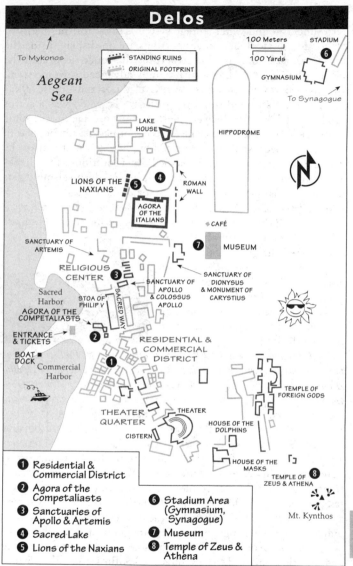

Delos

To Mykonos

Aegean Sea

STANDING RUINS
ORIGINAL FOOTPRINT

100 Meters
100 Yards

STADIUM **6**

GYMNASIUM

To Synagogue

LAKE HOUSE

HIPPODROME

LIONS OF THE NAXIANS **5** **4**

ROMAN WALL

AGORA OF THE ITALIANS

CAFÉ

SANCTUARY OF ARTEMIS

MUSEUM **7**

RELIGIOUS CENTER **3**

SANCTUARY OF APOLLO & COLOSSUS APOLLO

SANCTUARY OF DIONYSUS & MONUMENT OF CARYSTIUS

Sacred Harbor

STOA OF PHILIP V

AGORA OF THE COMPETALIASTS

ENTRANCE & TICKETS

BOAT DOCK

Commercial Harbor

2

1

RESIDENTIAL & COMMERCIAL DISTRICT

TEMPLE OF FOREIGN GODS

THEATER QUARTER

THEATER

CISTERN

HOUSE OF THE DOLPHINS

HOUSE OF THE MASKS

TEMPLE OF ZEUS & ATHENA **8**

Mt. Kynthos

1 Residential & Commercial District
2 Agora of the Competaliasts
3 Sanctuaries of Apollo & Artemis
4 Sacred Lake
5 Lions of the Naxians
6 Stadium Area (Gymnasium, Synagogue)
7 Museum
8 Temple of Zeus & Athena

MYKONOS

cial center in the known world. (One of its major commodities was human flesh—it was a major center in the ancient slave trade.) The city was cosmopolitan, with 30,000 residents and distinct ethnic groups, each with their own linguistic and cultural neighborhood (Greeks, Syrians, Beirutis, Italians, etc.). Remains of these same neighborhoods can still be seen today.

Poke into some of the **house foundations.** Homes were

generally organized around a central courtyard, above a giant cistern (underground water storage system). Look for fragments of elaborate mosaic floors (intact portions are on display inside the museum), as well as marble structures that once decorated the place. The city even had a surprisingly advanced sewer system. Because wood was rare on the arid Cycladic Islands, most buildings were constructed from dry-stone walls; wood was a status symbol, used only by the wealthiest to show off. Delos had some of the biggest homes of ancient Greece, not necessarily because of wealth, but because they could build big here without fear of the devastating earthquakes that plagued other locations. The Greeks attributed this to divine intervention, but modern seismologists have found that Delos sits away from major fault lines.

• *Now circle back to the agora that's near the boat dock. This is the...*

Agora of the Competaliasts: This was the main market square of the Roman merchants who worshipped the deities called *lares compitales,* who kept watch over the crossroads. This is not *the* agora, but one of many agoras (marketplaces) on Delos—a reminder that several different communities coexisted in this worldly trading city.

• *From this agora, the Sacred Way leads off to the left. Follow the same path ancient pilgrims walked as they approached the temples of Apollo. Along the left side of the road runs the long ledge of the pediment from the* **Stoa of Philip V** *(what we see here as the "bottom" actually ran along the top of the building). At the end of the Sacred Way is the...*

Religious Center: The **Sanctuary of Apollo,** and beyond that, the **Sanctuary of Artemis,** both consisted of several temples and other ceremonial buildings. Unfortunately, these once-great buildings are in near-total ruin. In its day, Apollo's sanctuary had three large, stern Doric temples lined with columns. The biggest temple was nearly 100 feet long. The nearby Porinos Naos served as the treasury of the Delian League. Other treasuries once held untold riches—offerings to the gods brought by devout pilgrims.

Next to one of the Apollo temple foundations is a giant marble pedestal that once held the **Colossus Apollo** statue. The 35-foot statue (seventh century B.C.) was a gift from the Naxians and was carved from a single block of marble. It's long gone now, but a few bits of its fingers are on display in the museum.

• *Beyond the Sanctuary, pass the foundations of the spacious* **Agora of the Italians** *on the way to the former...*

Sacred Lake: This was supposedly the source of Zeus' seed. When Leto was about to give birth to Zeus' children (according to the "Hymn to Delian Apollo," attributed to Homer), she cried

What If I Miss My Boat?

If your ship leaves Mykonos without you, remember that you can get help from the cruise line's port agent (listed on the destination information sheet distributed on the ship). If the port agent suggests a costly solution, you may want to consider public transit instead.

Mykonos has daily flights and ferries to **Athens.** Thanks to its worldwide popularity as a vacation spot, there are flights to many other European cities as well. Mykonos' small airport sits just two miles outside of town, easily connected by a short €5-10 taxi ride (www.mykonos-airport.com; airlines: www.olympicairlines.com, www.aegeanair.com).

Catamarans and ferries run to **Piraeus** (Athens' port): Daily, 3.5 hours on high-speed catamaran (Hellenic Seaways, tel. 210-419-9000, www.hsw.gr; or Aegean Speed Lines, tel. 210-969-0950, www.aegeanspeedlines.gr); or 5.5 hours on regular boat (Blue Star Ferries, tel. 210-891-9010, www.bluestarferries.com; or Hellenic Seaways); these boats leave from the New Port, about a mile north of town (buses—2/hour, €1.40, €5-6 taxi). If you need to get to another island, try the Flying Cat catamaran, which leaves from the Old Port from April through October daily at 14:55 (except the second Wed of each month) and heads for **Paros** (50 minutes), **Ios** (2 hours), **Santorini** (3 hours), and **Crete** (5 hours; operated by Hellenic Seaways, listed above).

Local **travel agents** can also be helpful—there are plenty in Mykonos. For more advice on what to do if you miss the boat, see page 131.

out: "Delos, if you would be willing to be the abode of my son Apollo and make him a rich temple, your people will be well-fed by strangers bringing offerings. For truly your own soil is not rich." The Sacred Lake was drained by French archaeologists to prevent the spread of bacterial disease.

• *Overlooking the lake are the famous...*

Lions of the Naxians: This row of seven sphinx-like lion statues (originally there were 12) is the main, iconic image of this

site. These are replicas, but five of the original statues (seventh century B.C.) are in the museum. One of the originals was stolen by the Venetians, "repaired" with an awkwardly too-big head, and still stands in front of Venice's Arsenal building.

• *Walk through the oval-shaped Sacred Lakebed and hike up toward the museum. Just before the museum, a path leads to the left far into the distance, where you could detour to find the remains of the gymnasium, stadium, and the Jewish synagogue. Delos'* **stadium** *was where Olympics-style games were held every five years. Like the more famous games at Olympia and Delphi, these were essentially religious festivals to the gods, particularly Dionysus. Pilgrims from across the Greek world gathered to celebrate with sports, song contests, theatrical performances, and general merrymaking.*

Make your way to the...

Museum: This scantily described collection includes statuary, vases, mosaic floors, and other items. Inside the door is a model of the site in its heyday. While most of the site's best pieces are in the National Archaeological Museum in Athens, a few highlights remain, including five of the original Lions of the Naxians (in a room of their own) and the fingers of Colossus Apollo.

For more body parts of other gods, exit the museum and go straight ahead to the **Monument of Carystius** (once part of the Sanctuary of Dionysus), with its large penis-on-a-pillar statues.

• *If you have the energy, turn left (with your back to the museum) and hike up the hill toward more remains of houses and temples. Hardy travelers can huff all the way up to...*

Mount Kynthos: At 370 feet, the island's highest point feels even taller on a hot day. To ancient Greeks, this conical peak looked like the spot from which Poseidon had pulled this mysterious isle up from the deep. Up here are the remains of the **Temple of Zeus and Athena.** As you observe the chain of islands dramatically swirling around Delos, you can understand why most experts believe that the Cycladic Islands got their name from the way they circle (or cycle around) this oh-so-important islet.

• *Head back downhill, toward the theater and harbor. On your way down, you'll pass the* **House of the Dolphins,** *with mosaics of cupids riding dolphins, and the* **House of the Masks,** *with a beautiful mosaic of a tambourine-playing Dionysus riding a leopard. As you return to the boat, you'll pass by the remains of a giant* **cistern** *and the 5,500-seat* **theater***...starring a 360-degree view of the Cycladic Islands.*

SANTORINI

ΣΑΝΤΟΡΊΝΗ / Σαντορίνη; a.k.a. Thira (ΘΗΡΑ / Θηρα)

If Santorini were only an island, it would already be one of the Mediterranean's most dramatic: a flooded caldera (collapsed volcanic crater) with a long, steep, multicolored arc of cliffs, thrusting up a thousand feet above sea level. Sometimes called "The Devil's Isle," this unique place has captured visitors' imaginations for millennia and might have inspired the tales of Atlantis. But the otherworldly appeal of Santorini (sahn-toh-REE-nee) doesn't end with its setting. Perched along the ridgeline is a gaggle of perfectly placed whitewashed villages, punctuated with azure domes, that make this, undeniably, one of Greece's most scenic spots. If this place didn't exist, some brilliant fantasy painter would have to conjure it up.

The island's main town, Fira (Φηρα, FEE-rah)—with Santorini's handiest services and best museum—is scenically situated, but is more functional than it is charming. Fira is not quite what you imagine when you think of "Santorini." If those chalk-white houses and vivid domes are what you came to see, don't linger in Fira—head to the northern tip of the island, to the town of Oia (Οια, EE-ah). Oia is the famous, idyllic white village smothering a steep cliff that tumbles down to the sea. Strolling through Oia is like spinning a postcard rack—it's tempting to see the town entirely through your camera's viewfinder.

Not surprisingly, Santorini is hugely popular and can be very crowded—and expensive—in peak season (roughly July through mid-September, peaking in the first half of August). Tourism—virtually the only surviving industry here—has made the island wealthy. It's one of the few places in Greece where the population isn't aging (as young people don't have to move away to find

Santorini Island

EXCURSION/
SHUTTLE BOAT
ROADS
TRAILS
BEACHES

TO
MYKONOS
& PIRAEUS

OIA

FINIKIA

RIVA

AEGEAN
SEA

THIRASIA

IMEROVIGLI
FIROSTEFANI

MANALOS

CABLE CAR

FIRA

NEA
KAMENI

OLD
PORT

MONOLITHOS

HOT
SPRINGS

SEA
DIAMOND
SHIPWRECK

PALEA
KAMENI

ATHINIOS
PORT

AIRPORT

AKROTIRI
TOWN

PIRGOS

KAMARI

ANCIENT
THIRA

EMPORIO

PERISSA

AKROTIRI
RUINS

TO
CRETE

3 KM
2 MILES

DCH

satisfying work). Fortunately, it's not difficult to break away from
the main tourist rut and discover some scenic lanes of your own. In
both Fira and Oia, the cliffside streets are strewn with countless
cafés, all of them touting "sunset views"...the end of the day is a
main attraction here.

Planning Your Time

Here are your top options:

• Go to Oia for classic Santorini views. You can take a bus,
taxi, or even a scenic five-mile hike to reach the town. Allow about
30 minutes each way to get there by bus or taxi; once there, plan on
at least another hour to stroll and snap photos.

• In Fira, visit the Museum of Prehistoric Thira (allow an hour)
and explore town, especially the steep lanes below the Orthodox
cathedral (allow an hour or more).

• Sun-worshippers head for the red- and black-sand beaches
(accessible by bus or taxi). Allow a half-day to all day.

• Sail from the Old Port out to the middle of the caldera (various options are offered by local travel agencies). Allow a half-day
to all day.

Excursions on Santorini

Remember, "Santorini" describes an archipelago of five islands. Most excursions are on the main island, Thira, and feature multiple stops. The prettiest town by far is **Oia**—be sure your excursion makes a stop there. The main town, **Fira,** is less interesting but has better museums (look for a tour of the excellent Museum of Prehistoric Thira, but skip the dull Archaeological Museum). Some excursions stop off at **Megalochori,** a traditional village that lacks the dramatic tumbling-down-a-cliff setting of the other two.

Other excursions can include various locations away from the main towns, including Santorini's red- and black-sand **beaches; archaeological sites** (such as Ancient Thira or, if it's open, Akrotiri); the panoramic mountain viewpoint at **Profitis Ilias;** and a countryside winery to learn more about Santorini's unique method of cultivating grapes. For something more volcanic, venture off the main island and head for the smaller, smoldering islets of **Nea Kameni** and **Palea Kameni,** including a dip in the natural hot-spring waters (local agencies sell similar, cheaper tours). Many of these places are described on page 1017.

Arrival in Santorini

On Your Own

Cruise ships generally anchor in the caldera below Fira, then tender passengers to the Old Port. Portside, you'll find some car-rental offices and companies selling boat excursions to the little volcanic islands in the middle of the caldera. From the port, there are three

different ways to reach Fira's town center on the cliff above: Take a cable car, hike up, or ride a donkey. The **cable car** is the easiest option (€4 each way, daily 7:00-21:00, every 20 minutes or more with demand, 3-minute ride to the top). But, because the cable car is small (six cars take six passengers each, maximum 36 people at a time), you might be in for a long wait if you arrive on a big ship with many passengers. **Hiking** up the 587 steps is very steep and demanding, and you'll share the steps with fragrant, messy donkeys. You can pay €5 to ride up on a **donkey,** but the stench and the bumpy ride make this far less romantic than it sounds.

Once at the **top** (the cable-car and donkey trail converge near the same point), you have several options for exploring the town: If

When Santorini Blew Its Top

Coming to Santorini—by boat or by plane—your eyes can't help but trace the telltale arc of the island, a sure sign that you're about to set foot on what was once a volatile volcano.

Situated atop an edgy stack of tectonic plates, Santorini was created by volcanic activity that lasted more than two million years. The island once had a tidy conical shape, but around 1630 B.C., it exploded in what geologists call the "Minoan eruption"—one of the largest in human history. It blew out 24 cubic miles of volcanic material—at least four times the amount ejected by the huge 1883 explosion of Krakatoa (in today's Indonesia).

It appears that the volcano gave Santorini's inhabitants ample warning before erupting  (via a major earthquake and later, an initial small eruption). No human skeletons and few valuable items from that time period have been found here— suggesting that islanders had time to pack up and evacuate. Good thing. Soon afterward, large amounts of ash and pumice blasted out of the crater, and superheated pyroclastic flows (à la Mount St. Helens) swept down the island's slopes. Eventually, the emptied-out volcano collapsed under its own weight, forming the flooded caldera (meaning "cauldron") that we see today.

The volcano's collapse displaced enough seawater to send a huge tsunami screaming south toward Crete, less than 70 miles away. Archaeologists speculate that the tsunami (and per-

you head straight up the stairs, you'll find (to the left) the Catholic cathedral and nearby folk museum, and (to the right) the less appealing of the town's two archaeological museums. If you turn right onto Gold Street (true to its name, lined with jewelry and tourist-trinket shops), you'll eventually reach the Orthodox cathedral, some recommended eateries, and Santorini's best museum (the Museum of Prehistoric Thira). Or, if you want to escape some of the crowds and browse the scenic veil of cafés that cascade down the cliff, head toward the water, go left down the stairs just past Kastro Café, turn off onto the road, and explore to your heart's content.

By Excursion

Note that cruise-ship excursions are more likely to tender passengers to the New Port at Athinios (about five miles south of Fira), where chartered buses wait to take you to your destination. From

haps earthquakes near the same time) caused severe hardship, eventually leading to the downfall of the Minoan civilization.

The volcano isn't done yet. Two little islets in the middle of the caldera emerged from the bay quite recently (by geological standards)—Palea Kameni ("Old Burnt Island") in 197 B.C., and Nea Kameni ("New Burnt Island") in A.D. 1707. To this day, these islets go through periods where they sputter and steam, and earthquakes continue to wrack the entire archipelago (including a devastating one in 1956). The last small eruption (on Nea Kameni) occurred in 1950, and steam and sulfur dioxide are sometimes emitted at the current active crater. Today, the hot springs on Palea Kameni are a popular tourist attraction.

Although the historic eruption devastated the island, it also created its remarkable shape and left behind a unique ecosys-

tem and agricultural tradition (see sidebar on page 1012). The volcanic soil was also the basis for a local industry. The upper layer of pumice and volcanic ash left by the eruption was quarried, pulverized, and mixed with lime to create a remarkably strong concrete (produced, until recently, in the big, deserted, blocky building on the cliff near Fira—visible from the bay below). Santorini is the country's sole source of this type of material.

Strolling on scenic, seismic Santorini, you're on special ground...carved out more than four millennia ago by one very big bang.

the Athinios port, a serpentine road climbs up the hill. Visible from the road above Athinios, the roped-off area in the bay is the site of the *Sea Diamond* shipwreck—a cruise ship that sank here in 2007; all but two of the 1,195 passengers were rescued.

After your excursion, the bus drops you off in Fira, where you can take the cable car (or donkey or hike) down to the return tenders below.

Orientation to Santorini

The five islands that make up Santorini (a Venetian bastardization of "Santa Irene," after a local church) are known to Greeks as Thira (Θηρα, THEE-rah). Most of the settlement is on the 15-mile-long main island, also called Thira. The west side of Thira is a sheer drop-off (into the mouth of the former volcano), while the east side tapers more gradually to the water (the former volcano's base).

SANTORINI

The primary tourist towns are on the steep, western side of Thira: The town of Fira is the island's capital and transportation hub, but the main attraction is Oia, a village six miles to the northwest. The relatively level east and south areas have the ancient sites and best beaches.

Getting Around Santorini

By Bus: In Fira, the bus station is a block off the main road, near the south end of town (just downhill from the Orthodox cathedral and Museum of Prehistoric Thira). Buy tickets and get information at the kiosk at the far end of the lot. In peak season, buses can be extremely crowded.

The most popular destinations from Fira by bus are: **Oia** (2/hour—generally departs at top and bottom of each hour, 25 minutes, €1.40), **Athinios** and the **New Port** (5-7/day, coordinated to meet boats, 20 minutes, €2), **Kamari** and its nearby beaches (2/hour, 10 minutes, €1.40), **Akrotiri** with its red-sand beaches and (likely closed) archaeological site (nearly hourly, 30 minutes, €1.70), **Perissa** with its black-sand beaches and access to the Ancient Thira archaeological site (2/hour, 30 minutes, €2), and the **airport** (10/day, 15 minutes, €1.40). Bus information: tel. 22860-25462, www.ktel-santorini.gr.

By Taxi: Just around the corner from Fira's bus station, along the main road, is a taxi stand (figure roughly €15 to Oia, €10 to Athinios port, €10 to Kamari's beaches, €15 to Akrotiri, and €15 to Perissa). You can also call for a taxi (tel. 22860-22555 or 22860-23951).

Fira

The island's main town, Fira, is a practical transit hub with an extraordinary setting. Sitting at a cliff-clinging café terrace and sipping an iced coffee gives you the chance to watch thousands of tourists flood into town each morning (via the cable car and donkey trail), then recede in the afternoon. All of this built-in business has made Fira a bit greedy; its so-called Gold Street, starting at the cable-car station,  is lined with aggressive jewelry salespeople and restaurants with great views, high prices, and low quality.

But if you can ignore the tackiness in this part of town, you'll

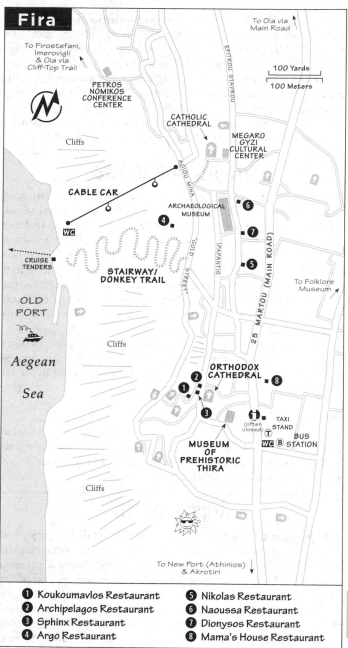

Fira

To Ola via Main Road

To Firostefani, Imerovigli & Oia via Cliff-Top Trail

PETROS NOMIKOS CONFERENCE CENTER

CATHOLIC CATHEDRAL

MEGARO GYZI CULTURAL CENTER

EPITROU STAVROU

Cliffs

100 Yards
100 Meters

CABLE CAR

AGIOU MINA

ARCHAEOLOGICAL MUSEUM

WC

CRUISE TENDERS

STAIRWAY/ DONKEY TRAIL

GOLD STREET

IPAPANTIS

25 MARTOU (MAIN ROAD)

To Folklore Museum

OLD PORT

Cliffs

Aegean Sea

ORTHODOX CATHEDRAL

MUSEUM OF PREHISTORIC THIRA

(often closed)

TAXI STAND

BUS STATION

WC

To New Port (Athinios) & Akrotiri

1. **Koukoumavlos Restaurant**
2. **Archipelagos Restaurant**
3. **Sphinx Restaurant**
4. **Argo Restaurant**
5. **Nikolas Restaurant**
6. **Naoussa Restaurant**
7. **Dionysos Restaurant**
8. **Mama's House Restaurant**

SANTORINI

discover that Fira has a charm of its own—particularly in the cozy labyrinth of streets that burrow between its main traffic street and the cliff edge, and on the steeply switchbacked lanes that zigzag down the side of the cliff. Fira also has a pair of cathedrals (Orthodox and Catholic), a variety of interesting museums (including the excellent Museum of Prehistoric Thira), and a handy array of services (Internet cafés, launderettes, and so on).

Remember that Fira is not the setting of all those famous Santorini photos—those are taken in Oia (described later).

Orientation to Fira

The core of Fira is squeezed between the cliff and the main road through town, called 25 Martou. This street—with a taxi stand, TI (if it's open), various scooter/ATV/car-rental places, Internet cafés, and other services—is busy and fairly dingy. The bus station is a block off this drag (around the corner from the TI and taxi stand). Most places of interest to visitors are in the cluster of narrow streets between the bus station (along the main road near the south end of town) and the cable-car station (along the cliff near the north end of town)—a distance you can easily cover in about a 10-minute walk.

If street names exist, locals completely ignore them. Making navigation even more confusing, it's a very vertical town—especially along the cliff. Use a map, and don't be afraid to ask for directions.

Tourist Information

Fira has the island's TI kiosk, but hours are sporadic and it's often closed (along the main road, about 50 yards toward the town center from the bus station). If it's not open, try asking at local travel agencies or other businesses for help.

Sights in Fira

▲▲**Museum of Prehistoric Thira**—This small but very good collection, while no competition for Greece's top archaeological museums, is Santorini's best. The manageable museum presents items from the ancient site at Akrotiri, at the southern end of the island. This settlement was the largest city outside Crete in the Minoan world, dating back to the earliest documented civilization on the Aegean (third to second millennium B.C.)—impossibly ancient, even to the ancients (for more on the Minoans, see page 1072). The people who lived here fled soon before Santorini blew its top (likely around 1630 B.C.—see sidebar, earlier), leaving behind intriguing artifacts of a civilization that disappeared from the earth not long after. While the Akrotiri site itself is indefinitely closed (see page 1017), its best selection of artifacts is viewable here. Everything is described in English and well-presented in modern, air-conditioned comfort.

Cost and Hours: €3; Easter-Oct Tue-Sun 8:00-20:00, Mon 13:30-20:00; Nov-Easter Tue-Sun 8:00-15:00, closed Mon; tel. 22860-23217.

⊙ Self-Guided Tour: The model of the Akrotiri site near the entrance puts the items in context. From here, follow the letters counterclockwise through the exhibit, starting with the Early Cycladic figures and vessels, dating from 2700-2300 B.C. The stiff figurines, with their arms crossed, perplex archaeologists, who speculate that they might represent the Mother Goddess worshipped here.

The majority of the museum's pieces date from the Late Cycladic Period (mid-17th century B.C.), when Akrotiri peaked just before its residents fled the erupting volcano. While they took valuable items (such as jewelry) with them, they left behind easily replaceable everyday objects and, of course, immovable items such as wall frescoes. These "left behind" items form the core of the collection.

Primitive cooking pots, clay ovens, and barbeque grills, along with bronze vases, daggers, tongs, and fishing hooks, offer clues about the mysterious Minoan lifestyle. The Minoans were traders

rather than warriors, so many items reflect their seafaring heritage. The stack of metal weights illustrates the evolution of standardization during early trading. Also look for the **three large containers,** each one marked differently to suggest their contents—for example, a vessel that held water was decorated with reeds (aquatic plants).

The museum's highlights are the vibrantly colorful, two-dimensional **wall frescoes.** In keeping with the artistic style of Crete (the home of the Minoans), men appear brown, and the women, white. (If you've been to the National Archaeological Museum in Athens, you might recognize this style of fresco from that museum's collection, which includes wall paintings of antelopes, swallows, and young men boxing, all from this same Akrotiri site. The

wall frescoes from the House of the Ladies show exquisitely dressed women. In one, an older woman leans over and appears to be touching the arm of another (now-missing) woman and holding a dress in her right hand. Farther along, you'll see a fragment of another wall fresco showing blue monkeys. Because monkeys are not indigenous to Greece, these images offer more evidence that the Minoans traveled far and wide, and interacted with exotic cultures.

Between these frescoes, the **vessels** from domestic life (such as beautiful vases decorated with dolphins and lilies) give us a glimpse of everyday life back then. Look for the ritual vessel shaped like a boar's head.

In the final display case (near the exit) is an exquisite miniature **golden ibex**—one of the few items of great value that was left behind by fleeing islanders.

Orthodox Cathedral of Candelmas (Panagia Ypapantis)—This modern cathedral, which caps Fira like a white crown, has a grandly painted interior that's worth a look. The cliff-hanging lanes just in front are some of Fira's most enjoyable (and least crowded) to explore.

Archaeological Museum—This museum pales in comparison to the Museum of Prehistoric Thira. Its dusty cases are crammed with sparsely described jugs, statues, and other artifacts from ancient Thira (in contrast to the older Minoan pieces from Akrotiri). Skip it unless you're an archaeologist (€3, Tue-Sun 8:30-15:00, closed Mon, just up the street from the top cable-car station).

Catholic Cathedral—Directly up the stairs from the top cable-car station, this cathedral is the heart of the island's Catholic community—a remnant of the island's past Venetian rule. Compare this rare Catholic cathedral to the giant Orthodox cathedral at the other end of town (described earlier): Inside this one are pews, few wall paintings, and none of the tall, skinny candles that are a mainstay of Orthodox worship. Next door is a Dominican monastery and church.

Megaro Gyzi Cultural Center—Hiding in the alleys behind the Catholic cathedral, this modest but endearing local history museum celebrates Santorini life. You'll see photographs of the town from the early to mid-20th century (including scenes before and after the devastating 1956 earthquake), an archive of historic manuscripts and documents, modern paintings of Santorini, and samples of the various types of volcanic rock found on the island. Find the circa-1870 clipping from a London newspaper article about "Santorin," complete with a picture of a smoldering islet in the caldera. Linger over the evocative etchings of traditional Santorini lifestyles (€3, May-Oct Mon-Sat 10:00-16:00, closed Sun and Nov-April, tel. 22860-23077, www.megarogyzi.gr).

Petros Nomikos Conference Center—This burnt-orange building, capping a cliff at the northern end of town, features replicas

of all the famous frescoes that have been excavated at the ancient Minoan site of Akrotiri. This made-for-tour-groups collection makes it easy to see the full sweep of Santorini's remarkable prehistoric art in one place. But, after all, these *are* copies—if you're already visiting Fira's Museum of Prehistoric Thira and the National Archaeological Museum in Athens, you'll be able to view the originals in person...making this collection pointless (€4, May-Oct daily 10:00-19:00, closed Nov-April, www.therafoundation.org).

Folklore Museum of Santorini—This collection of folkloric bits and pieces, housed in a restored 19th-century cave house in the Kodochori neighborhood (at the northeast edge of town), illuminates the way of life that has evolved on this chunk of volcanic rock. Exhibits include winemaking, traditional crafts, historical archives, and a small chapel (€3, April-Oct daily 10:00-1400 & 18:00-20:00, closed Nov-March, tel. 22860-22792).

Hike to Oia—With a few hours to spare, you can venture out on one of Greece's most scenic hikes. While the main road connecting Fira to Oia is drab and dusty, a wonderful cliff-top trail links the two towns, offering fantastic views most of the way. From Fira, head north through the adjoining villages of Firostefani and Imerovigli, then continue along the lip of the crater all the way to Oia. It's long (about five miles, plan on at least 3.5 hours one-way), fairly strenuous (with lots of ups and downs), and offers virtually no shade in hot weather, so don't attempt it unless you're in good shape and have the right gear (good shoes, water, food, sun protection). Get an early start. You can catch a bus or taxi back to Fira when you're done.

Eating in Fira

You have two choices: expensive with a view overlooking the caldera, or much cheaper at a more typical Greek taverna. In general, places that are closest to the cable car lure in cruise passengers with

Island Cuisine in a Desert

Santorini has an unusual approach to cuisine, dictated (like all facets of life here) by its volcanic geology. Most produce on the island is never watered...which is even more surprising when you think that Santorini—and the neighboring island of Anafi—are the only places in Europe technically classified as having a desert climate. But the island's very steep cliffs trap passing clouds, so most mornings, there's a fine layer of dew covering the ground—just enough to keep plants growing. Residents claim that this approach, along with the volcanic soil, makes their produce taste particularly sweet. Santorini specialties include grapes, tomatoes, eggplant, and cucumbers.

You'll find the predictable Greek classics on most menus, but also look for some local dishes. A Santorinian salad uses the island's cherry tomatoes and cucumbers; tomato croquettes are also popular. *Fava* is a chickpea spread similar to hummus. Because the main settlements of Santorini are perched on the tops of cliffs—with challenging access to the sea—fish isn't as integral to the cuisine as on other islands.

While Greece isn't particularly acclaimed for its wines, Santorini's are well-respected. The discovery of ancient grape seeds at Akrotiri proved that the winemaking tradition here dates back more than 3,500 years. Today, local grapes are mostly Assyrtiko, one of the best Greek varietals; they produce a dry white wine with citrus notes. The growing vines are twisted into a round basket shape called *ampelies*, with the grapes tucked inside to protect them from the strong sunlight and fierce winds. The shape also helps retain moisture from nighttime fog on this otherwise arid isle. Connoisseurs say that the *terroir* created by Santorini's porous volcanic soil gives the wine a special flavor. Two of the most renowned Santorini wines are Vinsanto (sweet dessert wine made from a blend of sun-dried grapes) and Nykteri (dry white wine produced in one day; the name means "night work"). Several shops in Fira or Oia have wine-tasting opportunities, and you can visit a countryside winery if you're interested.

great views, but—since they know cruisers are only in town for a few hours—have little incentive to put out good food. Natives and lingering travelers tend to dine at the places a 5- to 10-minute walk farther from the cable car.

With a Caldera View, Under the Orthodox Cathedral

The streets just under the Orthodox cathedral (the gigantic white-domed building at the south end of town) are lined with several expensive, trendy eateries with good food...you're paying a premium for the high-rent location (all open long hours daily, €10-15 starters, €20-30 main dishes). **Koukoumavlos** is particularly well-regarded (tel. 22860-23807); **Archipelagos** specializes in Greek standards and pasta (tel. 22860-23673); and **Sphinx** has a broader Mediterranean menu that includes quite a bit of Italian (tel. 22860-23823). The steep streets below these restaurants are filled mostly with hotels, but many turn their breakfast terraces into cafés; exploring this area to find your favorite perch for a cup of coffee is a fun activity.

Argo, which serves traditional Greek food specializing in fish, is also along the cliffs but a bit closer to the cable car. Reserve ahead for the upper deck, with the best caldera views (€4-12 starters, €10-18 main dishes, open long hours daily, along the donkey path just below "Gold Street," tel. 22860-22594).

In the Old Town

Deeper in the Old Town is a pedestrian street lined with several good choices (all open long hours daily). Like most Fira streets, it's nameless, located one block toward the cliff from the main road, a block north of the main square. Along here, the following three choices are most enticing: **Nikolas** oozes a family-run taverna vibe, with one big room crammed with tables overseen by the namesake patriarch; the menu consists of stick-to-your-ribs Greek classics (€3-5 starters, €7-14 main dishes, tel. 22860-24550). **Naoussa** is a family-friendly place churning out big plates of sloppy Greek food (€4-9 starters, €8-15 main dishes, tel. 22860-24869). **Dionysos** feels more trendy, with a vast terrace (€4-8 starters, €7-20 main dishes, tel. 22860-23845).

Mama's House, set a few steps down from the main road next to the taxi stand and TI, is another good budget choice with unpretentious Greek fare (€3-7 starters, €8-12 main dishes, daily 8:00-24:00, tel. 22860-21577).

Oia

Oia (remember, it's EE-ah, not OY-ah; sometimes spelled "Ia" in English) is the classic, too-pretty-to-be-true place you imagine when someone says "Greek islands." This idyllic ensemble of whitewashed houses and blue domes is delicately draped over a steep slope at the top of a cliff. And in their wisdom, the locals have positioned their town just right for enjoying a sunset over the caldera. On a blue-sky day or at sunset, there's no better place in Greece to go on a photo safari. In fact, if you can't snap a postcard-quality photo here, it's time to retire your camera.

Oia wasn't always this alluring. In fact, half a century ago it was in ruins—devastated by the earthquake on July 9, 1956. When rebuilding, natives seized the opportunity to make their town even more picture-perfect than before—and it paid off. While far from undiscovered, Oia is the kind of place that you don't mind sharing with boatloads of tourists. And if you break away from its main streets, you can find narrow, winding lanes that take you far from the crowds.

Getting There

To reach Oia from the island's transport hub at Fira, you'll have to take the bus (2/hour, generally departs Fira on the top and bottom of each hour, €1.40, 25 minutes) or a taxi (about €15 one-way).

Orientation to Oia

Oia lines up along its cliff. The main pedestrian drag, which traces the rim of the cliff, is called Nikolaou Nomikou. Oia's steep seaward side is smothered with accommodations and restaurants, while the flat landward side is more functional. The town is effectively traffic-free except for the main road, which sneaks up on Oia from behind, opening onto a parking lot and the town's bus stop. From here, just walk a few short, nondescript blocks toward the cliff and its million-dollar views.

Sights in Oia

▲▲▲**Oia Photo Safari**—The main sight here is the town itself, and the best advice is to just get lost with your camera cocked. Shoot the classic, blue-domed postcard views, but also wander around to find your own angle on the town. At the far tip of Oia, venture down, then up, to reach the old turret-like viewpoint, facing the windmills on the horizon and affording a breathtaking 360-degree view.

Why all the whitewash? For one thing, white reflects (rather than absorbs) the powerful heat of the sun. White is the color of lime—the mineral, not the fruit—mixed with water, which makes a good

Oia

To Tholos & Mavopetra Beach

To Fira and the Rest of Santorini

To Tholos & Mavopetra Beach

100 Yards
100 Meters

MAIN ROAD

AGIOS NIKOLAOS

BIG TOUR BUS PARKING LOT

BUS STOP **B** **WC**

PARKING LOT

STAIRWAY

ARMENI BEACH

Cliffs

Main Square

NOMIKOU (MAIN PEDESTRIAN DRAG)

POST

NIKALAOU

MARITIME MUSEUM

To Agios Ioannis & Amouda Port via Road

Cliffs

Aegean

Sea

TURRET VIEWPOINT

Cliffs

To Oia Town via Road

AMOUDA PORT

❶ Flora Café
❷ Floga Restaurant
❸ Kyprida Restaurant

antiseptic (islanders used it to paint their houses, so it would naturally disinfect the rainwater that was collected on rooftops). Later, white evolved into an aesthetic choice...and a patriotic one: During the 400-year Ottoman occupation, Greeks were not allowed to fly their blue-and-white flag. But here in Oia—with its white houses, blue domes, and the blue sea and sky—the whole village was one big, defiant banner for Greece.

The most interesting houses are the ones burrowed into the side of the rock wall. These "cliff houses," surrounded by air-filled pumice, are ideally insulated—staying cool in summer and warm in winter. While cliff houses were once the poorest dwellings in town, today only millionaires can afford to own them (and most are rented out as very pricey accommodations).

▲▲▲**Oia Sunset**—The best place on Santorini to enjoy the sunset, Oia becomes even more crowded when the sun goes down. Shutterbugs jockey for position on the town's best viewpoints, and all that white captures the swirling colors of the sky for a fleeting moment. Many travelers plan their day around being here at sunset.

Maritime Museum—Every Greek island seems to have its own maritime museum, and Oia hosts Santorini's. With two floors of old nautical objects and basic English labels, the collection includes roomfuls of old ship paintings, letters and documents, model ships, and well-endowed mastheads. It's the only museum in town, but it's nothing to jump ship for, unless you're a sailor or need a place to get out of the sun (€3, Wed-Mon 10:00-14:00 & 17:00-20:00, closed Tue, well-signposted a block off the main clifftop drag, tel. 22860-71156).

Eating in Oia

Dining with a view is a no-brainer here—it's worth the too-high prices to enjoy caldera views with your meal or drink. The cliffside places are pretty interchangeable, but if you can't make up your mind, consider one of these.

Flora Café is an affordable alternative to the budget-busting places along the cliff. Set along the main drag (at the Fira end of town), it offers a great view and serves up affordable, unpretentious fare in a casual pizzeria setting (€4-8 small dishes, €8-10 bigger meals, daily 9:00-late, tel. 22860-71424).

Floga dishes up traditional Greek food with a modern spin, a few steps below the main drag (and below Flora Café) at the Fira end of town (€8-12 starters, €11-19 main dishes, daily specials, open long hours daily, tel. 22860-71152).

Kyprida Restaurant, serving traditional Cypriot cuisine, is set a couple of blocks back from the cliff edge, but its top terrace still has a fine sunset view (€5-9 starters, €11-20 main dishes, daily 12:00-late, tel. 22860-71979).

More Sights on Santorini

The island of Santorini has several other worthwhile side-trips, doable by car, bus, or taxi.

Beaches—The volcanic composition of the island has created some unusual opportunities for beach bums. There are volcanic black-sand beaches near **Kamari** (tidy and more upscale-feeling) and **Perissa** (more popular with backpackers)—both on the east coast, but separated from each other by a mountain. Red-sand beaches are near the town of **Akrotiri** (facing away from the caldera along the southern arc of the island).

Ancient Sites—Santorini has two major archaeological sites: the Minoan site near Akrotiri (the town at the southern tip of the island) and the Archaic site at Ancient Thira (high on a bluff on the east coast, between Perissa and Kamari). As both of these (especially Akrotiri) have a history of unexpected closures, carefully confirm in town that they're open before making the trip there.

Near **Akrotiri** is the site of an important archaeological excavation from the Minoan period (whose citizens fled just before the massive 1630 B.C. eruption). But the site closed in 2005 after the roof of the visitor's center collapsed, killing one person. Authorities are implementing new safety measures and keep saying they might reopen it "next year" (year after year). Even if it's closed, you can still see the most interesting items discovered here—including some wonderful wall frescoes—on display at Fira's Museum of Prehistoric Thira (see page 1008).

The site at **Ancient Thira,** dramatically situated on a mountaintop between Perissa and Kamari, dates from a more recent civilization. It was settled post-volcano by Dorians from Sparta, likely in the ninth century B.C., and continued to thrive through the Hellenistic, Roman, and Byzantine periods. Open to visitors every day but Monday, this place is less distinctive than the Akrotiri site and is only worth a visit by archaeology completists. If you've toured other Greek ruins from this era—in Athens, Delphi, Olympia, Epidavros, etc.—you'll see nothing new here. You can reach the Ancient Thira site from Kamari, which has regular bus

SANTORINI

What If I Miss My Boat?

Remember that you can get help from the cruise line's port agent (listed on the destination information sheet distributed on the ship) and the local TI (see page 1008). If the port agent suggests a costly solution, you may want to consider public transit instead.

Because Santorini is a popular European getaway, many airlines fly here in the summer. Santorini's airport (a.k.a. Thira International Airport) sits along the flat area on the east (back) side of the island, about four miles from Fira (tel. 22860-28400, www.santoriniairport.com). It's connected to Fira by taxi (€10) or bus (10/day, 15 minutes, €1.40).

If you prefer boats, you could take a passenger ferry leaving from the New Port at Athinios, a 20-minute bus ride away from Fira. Santorini is connected daily to **Piraeus (Athens)** by a wide range of catamarans (5.25 hours; SeaJets, tel. 210-412-1800, www.seajets.gr; and Aegean Speed Lines, tel. 210-969-0950, www.aegeanspeedlines.gr) and slower ferries (8-9 hours; Blue Star Ferries, tel. 210-891-9800, www.bluestarferries.com; and ANEK Lines, tel. 210-419-7420, www.anek.gr). If you need to go to another island, the Flying Cat catamaran runs daily from April through October (except the second Wed of each month) to **Mykonos** (3 hours) and other Cycladic Islands, as well as to **Crete** (1.25 hours; Hellenic Seaways, tel. 210-419-9000, www.hsw.gr).

Any **travel agent** in Fira also should be able to help. For more advice on what to do if you miss the boat, see page 131.

excursions; hardy hikers could also huff up from Perissa on a very twisty serpentine path.

Volcanic Islets and Other Caldera Trips—A popular excursion is to sail from the Old Port below Fira out to the active volcanic islets in the middle of the caldera. The quickest trips include only a hike to the crater on **Nea Kameni** (€13); longer tours also include a visit to swim in the hot springs on **Palea Kameni** (€18), as well as other towns and villages (€25). Bus tours are also available. Various travel agencies around Santorini sell these trips— look for ads locally.

MORE PORTS IN GREECE

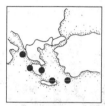

While your cruise ship can't stop at all of Greece's 6,000 islands—and I couldn't visit them all anyway—here's a brief overview of five other important Greek ports of call. In order from west to east, they are the verdant isle of Corfu; the ancient site of Olympia and its port of Katakolo; the chic, Italian-influenced city of Nafplio; the port of Heraklion, on Greece's southernmost island of Crete; and the faraway "crossroads" island of Rhodes, shaped by medieval Crusaders and Ottoman sultans.

Corfu

Less touristy and more real-feeling than its glamour-girl cousins Mykonos and Santorini, Corfu (in Greek: Κερκυρα/Kerkyra) is

a diamond in the rough. One of the Ionian islands, Corfu island is also one of Greece's northernmost, biggest, and greenest. Rather than an arid, desolate moonscape speckled with whitewashed houses and windmills, Corfu is hilly, thickly forested, and draped with villas that might look more at home in Venice or Croatia. As Europe's gateway to faraway, exotic Greece, Corfu was the likely inspiration for the island in Shakespeare's *The Tempest*. Its strategic location has made Corfu a bridge between the Greek world and various powers to the north: The Romans, Venetians, French, English, and Germans have all taken turns ruling the Ionian Islands, and only a two-mile-wide channel separates Corfu from Albania. These days Corfu's position attracts not sailors and invaders, but cruise ships seeking a day's rest midway between Venice and Santorini.

The island's main town, also called Corfu, is a fun-to-explore small city that squeezes a maze of Old World lanes between a pair of stout Venetian fortresses. Corfu's architecture is a hodgepodge of its past rulers: The grassy main square, called the Spianada, is lined with Venetian villas, English palaces, and a French colonnade, all of which lend it a certain faded elegance. The town's size (pop. 40,000) makes it feel lived-in—the many churches are alive with devout locals. The Corfiots go about their daily lives seemingly oblivious to the giant cruise ships that release thousands of daily visitors into their streets. Away from a few touristy main drags, shops and cafés outnumber trinket shops. And Corfu's museums—while still modest—are a notch above most islands' offerings.

To get out of town—on a local bus or taxi, with a rental car or hired driver, or on a shore excursion—head to Corfu island's many other enticing, some- times offbeat stopovers, from the escape-from-it-all villa of a reclusive Austrian empress (the Achilleion) to a series of enticing beaches and rocky coves (most famous is Paleokastritsa). Taken together, Corfu might not knock your socks off, but it'll give you a good picture of a real-world Greek island with a pervasive, gritty charm.

Planning Your Time

With a quick day in port, Corfu offers several options:

• Explore the **Old Town,** dipping into its small but good museums, visiting its busy churches, and hiking up to one or both fortresses. Allow anywhere from an hour (for a quick stroll through town) to all day.

• Tour the **Achilleion** (Austrian palace) and its gardens. Allow an hour or two for the visit, plus another half-hour each way to reach it from Corfu town.

• Hit the beach or climb the hills around **Paleokastritsa.** Allow a half-day to a full day.

You can reach the out-of-town destinations by public bus, but there can be long gaps in the schedule; fill those gaps with taxi rides. If you have a long day in port, you could rent a car or hire a driver to do everything—but it'll be a long and busy day.

Arrival at the Port of Corfu

Arrival at a Glance: Pay €1.20 for a bus or €10 for a taxi into town, or walk 20-25 minutes. Everything in Corfu town is walkable, and you can reach outlying sights by taxi or local bus.

Port Overview

Cruise ships dock at the New Port, about a mile west of the Old Town. It's an easy 300-yard walk from your ship to the terminal building, or you can take the free shuttle bus that zips arriving passengers this short distance.

Inside the terminal building, you'll find a **TI** kiosk (generally staffed when cruises arrive; pick up the free, excellent town map, with sight hours listed) and a **car-rental** office (varies by season, but in peak season figure roughly €60/day including insurance, €10 extra for 4x4 jeeps).

Getting into Town

You'll exit the terminal building and turn left into a long parking lot with rental cars and taxis, and beyond that, the public bus stop into town.

By Taxi

Taxi drivers prey on cruise passengers, demanding a no-meter €10 to the Old Town (more than double the fair metered rate; however, since all companies charge this same flat rate, there's little point trying to get them to use the meter). Many cabbies speak good English and will try to talk you into longer excursions to the Achilleion villa (about €20-25 one-way, or €100 round-trip including waiting time) or the picturesque Paleokastritsa bay (€40-45 one-way, €90 round-trip). A three- to four-hour deluxe tour to the island's highlights will run you around €150 (cabbies work on a €45 hourly rate). While this is handy, keep in mind that you can rent your own car for a fraction of the price (see car-rental information above).

By Public Transportation

At the far end of the taxi parking lot is the stop for the **public bus** to the Old Town (bus #2, but other numbers might make the run when a ship arrives—just ask "Old Town?"; buy €1.20 ticket on board, 2/hour, 5-minute trip to Spilia Gate). If you want to reach some of the outlying sights—such as the Achilleion or Paleokastritsa—ride this bus into town, then walk through the town center to the regional bus station (explained later).

To **walk** from the cruise terminal to the Old Town, simply follow the road with the water on your left, and you'll be there after about 20-25 minutes.

Arriving in Town, at the Spilia Gate

By taxi, bus, or foot, you'll wind up at the **Spilia Gate,** marking the entrance to the Old Town (ATM kiosk and taxi stand right out front).

Returning to Your Ship

From just outside the Spilia Gate, you have the same three options outlined above: Pay for a taxi, ride the bus, or walk.

Orientation to Corfu

Corfu town's Old Town is wedged between the new and old fortresses, facing the Old Port. If you venture to the south, you'll find that the Old Town ends abruptly, depositing you into a workaday New Town with cafés, shops, and offices. At the New Town park/square called Saroko, about a 20-minute walk from the Spilia Gate, is the main TI and the hub for buses to other points on the island (see "Getting Around Corfu Island," below).

Tourist Information

Corfu's helpful **TI** is in a green kiosk in the middle of Saroko Square (sporadic hours, but likely at least Mon-Fri 9:00-16:00, closed Sat-Sun, tel. 26610-48082, www.corfu.gr and www.zoom corfu.gr).

Getting Around Corfu Island

If you'd like to venture to the sights beyond Corfu town, you can ride a bus or take a taxi.

Two different sets of **buses** serve the island from Corfu town: blue local buses (including to the Achilleion) and green long-distance buses (including to Paleokastritsa). Both leave from near Saroko Square in the New Town: blue/local buses have a blue ticket office right on the square, and buses leave from nearby: Buses to the Achilleion depart from two blocks down Methodiou street, and green/long-distance buses depart from four blocks up Ioannou Theotoki street. Specifics for the Achilleion and Paleokastritsa are listed under "Elsewhere on Corfu," later; for full bus schedules, check www.terrakerkyra.gr. Note that bus routes make it difficult to connect quickly between outlying sights—you'll usually have to go back through Corfu town.

There's a **taxi** stand right in front of the Spilia Gate, and others around town. Corfu's taxi drivers take advantage of cruises by charging them inflated "flat rates" for popular trips. For example, the fair fare (on the meter) between Corfu town and the Achilleion should be about €15-20, but they'll tell you it's a flat rate of €25. If you feel feisty, you can try to talk them into using the meter, but they might refuse (official rates: €1.15 drop, €0.70/km in town, €1.20/km outside of town, €3.50 minimum, about €2 extra for calling a taxi and €2.60 extra for trips to or from the ports or airport).

Sights on Corfu

In the Old Town

Corfu's mazelike Old Town is enjoyable to explore. It's jammed onto a peninsula between two fortresses—each of which you

can climb for grand views over the rooftops. Nikiforou Theotoki street runs west to east, connecting the Spilia Gate (where buses and taxis from the cruise port arrive) with the Spianada (grassy main square). Along the way, it passes trinket shops and restaurants, as well as Iroon Square (with St. Spyridon Church).

Most visitors to Corfu stick to the souvenir-shop-lined main tourist streets. But if you get out of this rut, you'll discover that the town is big enough to reward those who poke around—especially some of the small neighborhood churches that cluster in the Campielo district, north of Nikiforou Theotoki.

I've listed the sights roughly in the order you'll reach them as you come from the Spilia Gate.

New Fortress (Neo Frourio)—The newer of Corfu's twin fortresses (from the late 16th and early 17th centuries), this is also the less interesting complex— but affords the best view in town. You'll hike up ramps and through tunnels to the imposing British Barracks, where (upstairs) you'll find a sparse ceramics collection and a rusty metal staircase leading up to the top terrace, with excellent views over the Old Town (€3, daily mid-April-early Oct 9:00-21:00, early

Oct-Nov 9:00-19:00, closed Dec-March, tel. 26610-27370).

▲**St. Spyridon Church**—One of Corfu's biggest churches, this sits between two bustling tourist streets. It offers an inviting opportunity to drop into a real, living community church. Stepping inside, you'll see a roughly even mix of tourists and locals. Sit and observe for a while. Worshippers come in to buy candles big and small (the largest are five feet tall and look like fluorescent light bulbs), which they light when saying a prayer. On the marble counter in front of the iconostasis (screen with icons), look for the small pads of paper, where locals write out prayer requests, then drop a coin in the box, put the paper in the basket, and light a candle. Step through the door in the right side of the iconostasis, into the tiny, evocative chapel. The silver coffin con-

tains the remains of St. Spyridon (A.D. 270-348), the town's patron saint, who fought against heresies in the early church. Stand to one side and watch the procession, as locals enter, cross themselves, and say a prayer. Some kneel at the casket, some kiss it, and others place fresh flowers or other items on it for a blessing. Meanwhile, tourists also step inside to survey the scene. It can be hard to tell who's who. On my last visit, I watched a woman standing for a long time staring intently at the relics, as if communing with the soul of St. Spyridon. Finally she said, in a thick, exasperated English accent, "I don't know who it is!"

If St. Spyridon is crowded, consider exploring the streets of the Campiello district to the north, where several other, smaller, less-touristed churches hide in a maze of streets. In this direction near the water is the Antivouniotissa Church and Byzantine Museum (described below).

Banknote Museum—This little collection, on Iroon Square in front of St. Spyridon, displays banknotes through history (free; April-Sept Wed and Fri 9:00-14:00 & 17:30-20:30, Thu and Sat-Sun 9:00-15:00; Oct-March Wed-Sun 8:00-15:00; closed Mon-Tue all year; tel. 26610-41552).

▲Antivouniotissa Church and Byzantine Museum—This late-15th-century Orthodox church has been converted into a fine venue for displaying Corfu's collection of Byzantine artwork, including a marvelous assortment of gilded icons (€2, Tue-Sun 8:30-15:00, possibly later in summer, closed Mon, Arseniou, tel. 26610-38313, www.antivouniotissamuseum.gr).

Theotoki Square—A few short blocks south of the main drag, this square features the Old Town Hall and Corfu's cathedral (with a stark interior and the remains of St. Theodora). There are no museums here, but it's a fine place to sit in the sun (on benches or at an outdoor café) and relax. If you see a commotion in front of the Old Town Hall, it's likely a wedding. After the couple leaves, the custodian sweeps the rice off the steps to the street below, where pigeons gorge themselves.

Spianada—The east end of Corfu's Old Town is filled with a broad expanse of grass, part of which was built by the British occupiers as a cricket pitch (and is still periodically used for matches today). This fine square is ringed with monumental buildings, including the Palace of Sts. Michael and George to the north and the Old Fortress to the east (both described

below). Running along the western side of the Spianada is a fine colonnade called the Liston, filled with inviting cafés. Built by a Parisian architect during a time of French occupation, this evokes a northern gentility.

▲Palace of Sts. Michael and George/Asian Art Museum— Holding court at the top of the Spianada, this strange hybrid is two

sights in one: A stately, British-built, early-19th-century mansion interior, and a well-explained collection of art from all over Asia. While strolling through grand rooms and peeking into sumptuously decorated throne rooms and halls with ceilings that drip with stucco, you'll see pieces of art

from China, Japan, Cambodia, India, Afghanistan, and Pakistan. Good English descriptions illuminate the small but well-presented exhibits. The main collection is upstairs, while temporary exhibits are on the ground floor (€3, ask for free audioguide that explains the building, Tue-Sun 8:00-20:00, Mon 13:30-20:00, Palea Anatora, tel. 26610-30443, www.culture.gr).

▲Old Fortress (Palaio Frourio)—The peninsula that jabs into the sea just east of the Old Town had been fortified for many

centuries, but the Venetians turned it into an imposing citadel in the mid-15th century—cutting it off from the mainland by digging a moat, and capping it with an ensemble of stout buildings. Today it features some underwhelming small

museums and offices for local agencies, and fine views across Old Town rooftops to the New Fortress. After buying your ticket and crossing the drawbridge, you'll reach the gatehouse, with the Byzantine Museum in the right side (featuring some nicely preserved mosaic floor fragments). Heading into the main part of the complex, swing around to the right to the Neoclassical Church of St. George, which looks like it could date from the Golden Age but was actually built during the British occupation. Then huff up (past the modern café) to the lighthouse at the very top of the rock, for great views (€4, daily April-Oct 8:00-20:00, Nov-March 8:30-15:00, last entry 30 minutes before closing, tel. 26610-27935).

▲**Archaeological Museum**—In this collection of Corfu's archaeological artifacts, the prize piece is the gigantic, 55-foot-long Gorgon pediment, which once topped the island's temple to Artemis (Archaic period, c. 590-580 B.C.). The carvings depict the grotesque Gorgon (a.k.a. Medusa) flanked by regal-looking giant cats, moments before she is beheaded by a very-small-in-comparison Perseus. More sculptures, vases, armor, and other ancient bits and pieces round out the collection (€3, Tue-Sun 8:30-15:00, closed Mon, possibly longer in summer, a short walk south along the coast to Vralia 1, tel. 26610-30680, www.culture.gr).

Sights South of the Old Town—For about 50 years (from the fall of Napoleon in 1814 until 1864), Corfu was a protectorate of the British Empire. Aside from the Spianada and palace in the heart of town, other remnants of that time still exist. Just west of the Archaeological Museum is a **British cemetery.** Farther to the south (about a mile from the Old Town center) are the manicured grounds of the estate called **Mon Repos,** featuring a Neoclassical mansion (housing both opulent furnishings and an archaeological museum) and the ruins of two ancient temples. This was the birthplace of Britain's Prince Philip (Queen Elizabeth's husband).

Just south of Mon Repos, at the far-south tip of the Kanoni Peninsula, is the picturesque so-called **"Mouse Island"** (Pontikonisi)—reachable by boat from the little Vlacherena monastery that sits on a spit just offshore.

Shopping—Aside from the typical Greek trinkets (e.g., jewelry and worry beads), Corfu is known for its kumquat brandy; you'll see orange bottles of this everywhere. Ecclesiastical shops, selling small icons and other religious items, cluster around St. Spyridon Church.

Elsewhere on Corfu

Corfu is a huge island (Greece's third largest), but on a brief visit, you'll have to limit your focus. Two nearby places might be worth a look. Cruise excursions generally feature bus tours that include one or both of these stops, then a drop-off (and sometimes a guided tour) in Corfu's Old Town.

▲**Achilleion**—Tucked into the Greek hillsides six miles south of Corfu town is an unlikely bit of Habsburg splendor. Empress

Elisabeth (1837-1898)—better known as Sisi—was the troubled and tragic Princess Di-like wife of Habsburg Emperor Franz Josef (who ruled the Austro-Hungarian Empire in the late 19th and early 20th centuries, when its territory covered much of Eastern Europe). Sisi struggled with courtly life and sought escape from the Vienna grind. She built an elegant yellow villa on a forested Corfu hillside, with terraced gardens and sculptures of figures from Greek mythology. After Sisi was assassinated, Germany's Kaiser Wilhelm II bought the place and used it to entertain foreign dignitaries. While this place barely cracks the "Top 10" of Habsburg sights, it's worth a look for its fine gardens—especially if you're a fan of palaces and Greece is handier to you than Austria.

Today visitors tour part of the palace, including Sisi's own private chapel, dining room, and grand staircase. Circle around outside the palace to reach the checkerboard terrace behind, lined with Greek statues. Peek into the top of the grand staircase, where you'll see a grandiose painting of Achilles, the great warrior for whom the palace was named. He holds Hector's helmet (and drags his vanquished rival's body behind

his chariot) as the terrified people of Troy watch from their fortified town in the background. In the lower part of the terrace, you'll see how Achilles met his end—a famous sculpture of the fallen warrior pulling an arrow from his vulnerable heel.

Cost and Hours: €7, €3 for the thorough and good audioguide, daily April-Oct 8:00-19:00, Nov-March 8:45-15:30, near village of Gastouri, tel. 26610-56245, www.corfu-casino.gr.

Getting There: Buses depart from Corfu's New Town (two blocks down Methodiou street from Saroko Square) six times a day to reach the palace (€1.30, 25-minute trip; schedule in 2010: Mon-Fri at 7:00, 10:00, 12:00, 14:00, 17:00, and 20:00; Sat the same except at 8:00 instead of 7:00; Sun at 9:00, 11:00, 14:00, 17:00, and 20:00). The same bus takes passengers back to Corfu about 25-30 minutes after this trip. Unfortunately, this leaves you with two or three hours at the palace—too much for most visitors (you can see the place in just an hour or so). The gardens are an enjoyable place to kill some time (bring a picnic). Or you can ride a taxi back to Corfu town (€15-20 is the fair metered rate, though most cabbies try to extort a "fixed rate" of €25; to call for a taxi at the Achilleion, dial 26610-33811, pay phone at café across the street from palace ticket office).

▲Paleokastritsa—This picturesque, very touristy resort village sits at a rocky harbor 14 miles northwest of Corfu town. Surrounded by cliffs and enveloped in grand scenery, it's one of the most popular spots on the island. Aside from relaxing on the beach, visitors here enjoy hiking up to the hilltop Theotokos Monastery, with a well-preserved, otherworldly Orthodox interior that hosts a small museum. The garden around the monastery, with views across the sea, is extremely photogenic.

Getting There: Green buses depart from the long-distance bus stop (near Ioannou Theotoki street) several times daily (€2.10, 45-minute trip; times in 2010: at 8:30, 10:00, 11:30, 14:15, 16:00, fewer on Sun, return bus departs from Paleokastritsa about 45 minutes later). A **taxi** costs around €35 one-way.

Olympia and the Port of Katakolo

A visit to Ancient Olympia (Αρχαία Ολυμπία)—most famous as the site of the original Olympic Games—offers one of your best opportunities for a hands-on antiquity experience. Line up at the original starting blocks in the 2,500-year-old Olympic Stadium. Visit the Temple of Zeus, former site of a gigantic statue of Zeus that was one of the Seven Wonders of the Ancient World. Ponder the temple's once-majestic columns—toppled like towers of checkers by an earthquake—which are as evocative as anything from ancient times. Take a close look at the Archaeological Museum's gold-medal-quality statues and artifacts. And don't forget to step back and enjoy the setting itself. Despite the crowds that pour through here, Olympia remains a magical place, with ruins nestled among lush, shady groves of pine trees.

Planning Your Time

Getting from Katakolo to Olympia takes 30 minutes (allow about 5 hours total, including lunch and transit time, once you leave your ship). Once at Olympia, focus on the two main sights:

Services in Katakolo

If you can't wait to get to Olympia for one of the following services, here are the nearest locations for each.

ATM: You'll find one on the main street at the far end of town (away from the dock).

Internet Access: Look for **Internet Service,** on the quiet street uphill and parallel to the main street (€2/30 minutes for Internet access or Wi-Fi, tel. 26210-41471, mobile 698-247-0148, kostadinoslagos@yahoo.com). Owner Kostadinos Lagos also rents **bikes** (€3/1 hour, €9/day). Some of the waterfront cafés also offer free Wi-Fi.

WCs: They are next to the beach in the public bath-house.

- The **Sanctuary of Olympia** (the archaeological site) takes about 1.5 hours to tour.
- To visit the adjacent **Archaeological Museum,** allow about an hour.

While you can see Olympia's sights in any order, I recommend walking the archaeological site first (while your energy is high), then touring the Archaeological Museum to reconstruct what you've seen. Unfortunately, Olympia (especially the Archaeological Museum) is most crowded between 10:00 and 13:00—just when you're in town—but keep in mind neither sight opens until 12:30 on Mondays.

Arrival at the Port of Katakolo

Arrival at a Glance: When the train is running, it's the easiest way to Ancient Olympia (45 minutes). However, if the train is not operating, you'll need to pay for a private bus service (€20 round-trip but must reserve in advance), a taxi (€80-100 round-trip), or renting your own car (€45 plus gas, 30-minute drive).

Port Overview

Cruise ships use the port of Katakolo (Κατάκολο; sometimes

called "Katakolon" in English), about 18 miles from Olympia. It's just a tiny fishing village-turned-tourist trap; the closest big city is Pyrgos, which has a TI and bus connections to the rest of Greece. Katakolo's main street—called Katakoloy Street—begins at the

dock. The town has blocks of tacky souvenir shops and waterfront cafés that exist primarily for cruisers.

Tourist Information: A TI is located in a small kiosk as you exit the cruise port, on the right (open only when ships arrive; Pyrgos TI tel. 26210-37111).

Getting to Olympia

Olympia is east of Katakolo, about a 30-minute drive from the port. Because the train connection is uncertain, a private bus is the cheapest and most dependable way to get to the archaeological site.

By Private Bus

Katakolon Express, a private bus service between Katakolo and Olympia, is designed for cruisers. The schedule varies, but it generally runs twice a day, giving you from three to seven hours at Olympia. The catch: You must reserve online at least one week prior to your arrival (€20 round-trip, mobile 697-725-7417, www .katakolon-express.com). They also offer guided minivan tours for small groups.

By Taxi

There are usually 50 hungry taxi drivers trying to get fares every time a ship docks. The rates are negotiable, but the going round-trip fare for a one-hour visit to the site runs €70-80, while a 2.5-hour visit costs €80-100. (Be aware that one hour isn't enough time to see the site and the museum.) Friendly George Letsios speaks good English and has a website where you can reserve a cab in advance (mobile 694-457-9917, www.taxikatakolon.gr, georgetaxi tours@gmail.com).

By Car

Driving from Katakolo to Olympia is easy—you don't even have to go through any towns. It takes about 30 minutes. But be aware that some car rental "deals" in Katakolo come with hidden costs. Avoid the sleazy agencies on the main street that advertise €40 rentals (they'll tack on insurance charges, gasoline, and even extra fees for air-conditioning). Try the Avis agency just uphill from the main street, marked with a large red billboard. They charge €45 plus gas for an air-conditioned, manual transmission Fiat (tel. 26210-42200, mobile 694-700-2290, www.katakolo-rentacar.com, helpful Kostas).

Driving to Olympia: It's best to get detailed directions from your rental agent, but here are the basics: Leave Katakolo on its main street and drive about 8 kilometers (5 miles) to the first village, Agios Ioannis. At the first stoplight, turn left onto a country road (following the blue *Ancient Olympia* sign). Follow the road as it winds up a hill and crosses some railroad tracks. At the first stop sign, you meet the main road (E55) to Olympia. Turn right and follow the modern highway to Ancient Olympia (Αρχαία Ολυμπία, well-marked with brown signs), bypassing the city of Pyrgos. Take the Olympia exit and follow the road, which becomes Olympia's main street and ends at the archaeological site.

Park for free at one of two lots: at the south end of town (closest to the site entrance), or at the east edge of town (closest to the Archaeological Museum). To reach the site from either parking lot, follow the signs, walking several hundred yards and crossing the Kladeos River.

By Train

In 2010, a train left Katakolo three times a day for Olympia; but as of 2011, that service is in flux due to the Greek financial crisis.

Check with the TI at the dock to see if the trains are still operating, but don't count on it. If the trains are running, you'll want to catch the first train in the morning—in 2010, it left at 9:22 and took 45 minutes. The train platform is a 10-minute walk from the cruise port (as you leave the port, turn right and follow the waterfront promenade to the tracks; buy your ticket on board).

The train leaves you at Olympia's station, a five-minute walk from the museum. With your back to the station, turn left at the street and walk until you reach a large parking lot. Look for a brown sign pointing to the museum and archaeological site.

By Tour

Hiring your own local guide for Olympia can be a good value—see page 1033.

Sights in Katakolo

If you find yourself with extra time in Katakolo, you have a few options.

For such a small town, it's surprising that Katakolo has two museums—both just a five-minute walk from the dock. However, due to the economic crisis, neither may be open (call 694-242-0157 or ask at the dockside TI to see if they are open). The **Museum of Ancient Greek Technology** is in the town park near the railroad tracks. It holds about 200 reconstructions of ancient Greek machines, covering the period from 2000 B.C. to A.D. 100. The nearby **Museum of Greek Musical Instruments,** which has about 40 instruments on display, is on the left side of the main street at the end of the retail strip.

Renata Beach is just a few steps from the dock on the left. There's a public bathhouse and a café. The water is fine, but this is a pebble beach, so bring beach shoes or flip-flops.

Returning to Your Ship

Drivers leaving Olympia take the highway in the direction of Pyrgos. As you bypass the city, watch carefully for the turnoff to Katakolo, marked in Greek (Κατάκολο) and in English. If you took the train, confirm departure times with the conductor (in 2010, the last train for Katakolo left Olympia at 15:41).

Orientation to Olympia

The Sanctuary of Olympia sits in the fertile valley of the Alphios River in the western Peloponnese, nine miles southeast of the

regional capital of Pyrgos. The archaeological site curves along the southeastern edge of the tidy modern village of Archaia (Ancient) Olympia. The town's layout is basically a low-lying, easy-to-manage grid, five streets wide by eight streets long. The main road (called Praxitelous Kondyli) runs from Pyrgos in the north and leads right into a parking lot (and bus stop) at the south end of town. From here, the museum and site are due east, over the Kladeos River.

Tourist Information

The **TI,** in the center of town on the main road next to the National Bank of Greece, is open only sporadically. A good (but unofficial) website is www.olympia-greece.org. It has information on both the sights and the town itself, including a map of the city.

Helpful Hints

Services: Olympia's main street has wide sidewalks, countless gift shops, and ample hotels, eateries, ATMs, and other tourist services. You'll also find a small grocery store here.

Taxis: There's a taxi stand in town where the main street meets a shady, angled side-street called Georgiou Douma. A one-way trip back to Katakolo costs around €40 (tel. 26240-22555).

Local Guide: Consider hiring **Niki Vlachou** to show you around the ruins and museums (reasonable and negotiable rates, contact for exact price, mobile 697-242-6085, niki@olympic tours.gr).

Self-Guided Tours in Olympia

A visit to Olympia has two parts: the site and the museum.

The Sanctuary of Olympia (The Site)

Olympia was the "Mecca" of ancient Greek religion—the location of its greatest sanctuary and one of its most important places of worship. In those times, people didn't live here—it was set aside as a monastery and pilgrimage site. The nearest city was 30 miles away. Ancient Greeks came here only every four years, during the religious festival that featured the Games. The heart of the sanctuary was a sacred enclosure called the Altis—a walled-off, rectangular area that housed two big temples, multiple altars, and statues to the gods.

Whereas Delphi served as a pilgrimage destination mostly for groups of wealthy people on a particular mission, every four years Olympia drew 40,000 ordinary folks for a Panhellenic party. As the site of the Olympic Games for more than a thousand years (c. 776 B.C.-A.D. 393), it was home to both temples and sports facilities.

Orientation to the Sanctuary of Olympia

Cost and Hours: €6, €9 combo-ticket includes Archaeological Museum; daily April-mid-Sept Tue-Sun 8:00-20:00, Mon 12:30-20:00; off-season hours vary but generally mid-Sept-March Tue-Sun 8:00-15:00, Mon 12:30-15:00; may stay open until 17:00 in early fall and late spring. Note that opening times can change without warning, and could be shortened due to budget cuts. Tel. 26240-22517, www.culture.gr.

Compass Points: As you walk from the entrance of the site

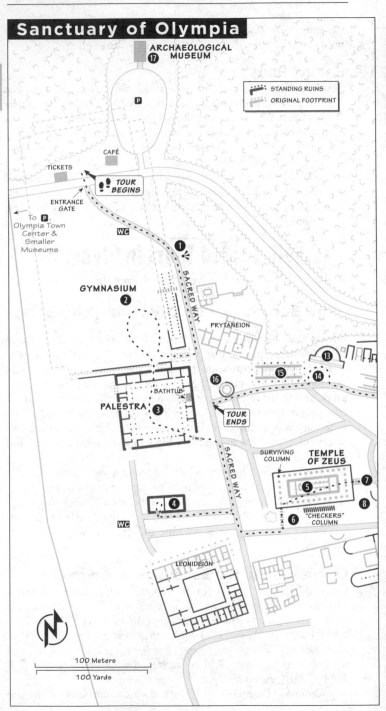

Sanctuary of Olympia

ARCHAEOLOGICAL MUSEUM 17

STANDING RUINS
ORIGINAL FOOTPRINT

P

CAFÉ

TICKETS

TOUR BEGINS

ENTRANCE GATE

To P
Olympia Town
Center &
Smaller
Museums

WC

SACRED WAY

1

GYMNASIUM 2

PRYTANEION

13

15   14

16

BATHTUB

PALESTRA 3

TOUR ENDS

SACRED WAY

SURVIVING COLUMN

TEMPLE OF ZEUS

4

5   7

8

WC

6   "CHECKERS" COLUMN

LEONIDEION

N

100 Meters

100 Yards

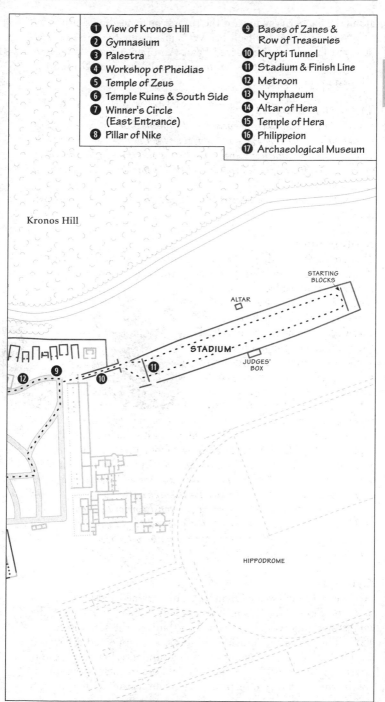

1 View of Kronos Hill
2 Gymnasium
3 Palestra
4 Workshop of Pheidias
5 Temple of Zeus
6 Temple Ruins & South Side
7 Winner's Circle (East Entrance)
8 Pillar of Nike
9 Bases of Zanes & Row of Treasuries
10 Krypti Tunnel
11 Stadium & Finish Line
12 Metroon
13 Nymphaeum
14 Altar of Hera
15 Temple of Hera
16 Philippeion
17 Archaeological Museum

Kronos Hill

STARTING BLOCKS

ALTAR

STADIUM

JUDGES' BOX

HIPPODROME

along the Sacred Way toward the ruins, you're heading south.

Services: The site itself has WCs just inside the entrance and near the far end of the Sacred Way. An open-air café is located between the site and the Archaeological Museum. No food is allowed inside the site.

The Tour Begins

• *Buy your tickets at the site entrance, then head through the gate. Walk straight ahead (passing WCs on the right), then bear left with the path. You'll pass an orientation board, then head south through the sanctuary down the main path, called the Sacred Way, which leads to the ancient world of Olympia.*

Walking south, look to your left (through the trees) to catch glimpses of....

Kronos Hill

This area was sacred, as it was considered to be the birthplace of Zeus. According to legend, it was on this hill that Kronos, Zeus' father, tried to eat baby Zeus. But pesky Zeus (aided by his mom, Rhea) escaped, and later overthrew Kronos and went on to lead the pantheon of gods. (Other versions of the myth place this event on Mt. Olympus, in northern Greece, where the gods eventually made their home.) The hill

was scorched by devastating wildfires in August of 2007—imagine how close the flames came to enveloping this ancient site. Locals replanted the hill, and it is beginning to look green again.

• *As you descend gradually down the Sacred Way, you enter a wide field scattered with ruins. The area to the left of the Sacred Way was the sacred enclosure. To the right was the area for the athletes.*

The first set of ruins on your right—consisting of two long rows of stubby columns—was once part of the gymnasium. (To explore the area more closely, look for the stairs down the path on the right, which lead farther into the ruins.)

Gymnasium

Athletes arriving for the Olympic Games trained and lived here in a complex of buildings similar to today's "Olympic Village." The largest building was the gymnasium (built in the second century B.C.). The truncated Doric columns once supported a covered arcade, one of four arcades that surrounded a big rectangular courtyard. Here athletes trained for field events such as the sprint, discus throw, and javelin throw. The courtyard (393 feet by 728

The Ancient Olympic Games

The Olympic Games were athletic contests held every four years as a way of honoring Zeus, the king of the gods. They were the culmination of a pilgrimage, as Greeks gathered to worship Zeus, the Games' patron.

The exact origins of the Games are lost in the mists of time, but they likely grew from a local religious festival first held at the Sanctuary of Olympia in about 1150 B.C. According to one legend, the festival was founded by Pelops, namesake of the Peloponnese; a rival legend credits Hercules. Sporting events became part of the festivities. A harmonious, healthy body was a "temple" that celebrated its creator by performing at its peak.

The first Olympic Games at which results were recorded are traditionally dated at 776 B.C. The Games grew rapidly, attracting athletes from throughout the Greek world to compete in an ever-growing number of events (eventually taking up to five days in all). They reached their height of popularity around 400 B.C. Of the four major Greek games (including those at Delphi, Corinth, and Nemea), Olympia was the first, biggest, and most prestigious.

Besides honoring Zeus and providing entertainment, the Games served a political purpose: to develop a Panhellenic ("all-Greek") identity among scattered city-states and far-flung colonies. Every four years, wars between bickering Greeks were halted with a one-month "sacred truce" so that athletes and fans could travel safely to Olympia. Leading citizens from all corners would assemble here, including many second- and third-generation Greeks who'd grown up in colonies in Italy, France, or Africa. Olympia was geographically central, and for the length of the festivities, it was also the symbolic heart of Greece.

This went on for 1,169 years, finally concluding in A.D. 393. Olympia today lives on in the spirit of the modern Olympic Games, revived in Athens in 1896. Every other year, athletes from around the world gather and—despite the politics that divide their countries—compete in contests that challenge the human spirit and foster a sense of common experience. Whether we're cheering on an American swimmer, a Chinese gymnast, or a Jamaican sprinter to go faster, longer, and better than any human has before, the  Games still bring the world together...just as they did in this tranquil pine grove so many centuries ago.

feet—about the size of six football fields, side by side) matched the length of the Olympic Stadium, so athletes could practice in a space similar to the one in which they would compete.

Because ancient Greeks believed that training the body was as important as training the mind, sports were a big part of every boy's education. Moreover, athletic training doubled as military training (a key element in citizenship)—so most towns had a gymnasium. The word "gymnasium" comes from the Greek *gymnos* ("naked"), which is how athletes trained and competed. Even today, the term "gymnasium" is used in many European countries (including Greece) to describe what Americans call high school.

Athletes arrived in Olympia a month early for the Games in order to practice and size up the competition. The Games were open to any free-born Greek male (both men and boys, who competed separately), but a good share of competitors were from aristocratic homes. Athletes trained hard. Beginning in childhood, they were given special diets and training regimens, often subsidized by their city. Many became professionals, touring the circuit of major festivals.

• *At the far end of the gymnasium ruins, you can walk directly into another twin row of (taller, more intact) columns. (You can also access this site from the Sacred Way, by taking the little wooden stairs farther down the path.) This is the...*

Palestra

Adjoining the gymnasium was this smaller but similar "wrestling school" (built around 300 B.C.). This square courtyard (216 feet on each side—about one acre), also surrounded by arcades, was

used by athletes to train for smaller-scale events: wrestling, boxing, long jump (performed while carrying weights, to build strength), and *pangration,* a kind of ancient "ultimate fighting" with only two rules: no biting and no eye-gouging.

Picture athletes in the courtyard working out. They were always naked, except for a layer of olive oil and dust for a bit of protection against scrapes and the sun. Sometimes they exercised in time with a flute player to coordinate their movements and to keep up the pace. Trainers and spectators could watch from the shade of the colonnades. Notice that the columns are smooth (missing their fluting) on the lower part of the inside face. This way, when it rained, athletes could exercise under the arcade (or take a breather by leaning up against a column) without scraping themselves on the grooves.

In the area nearest the Sacred Way, notice the benches where athletes were taught and people gathered for conversation. You can still see the bathtubs that athletes used to wash off their oil-dust coating. (They also used a stick-like tool to scrape off the oil.)

Besides being training facilities, palestras (found in almost any city) were also a kind of health club where men gathered to chat. Plato set his dialogue *Charmides* at a palestra in Athens, where Socrates goes to find his old friends.

• *Before you leave, there's a nice photo-op. Look back through the columns, across the Sacred Way, to the three surviving columns of the Philippeion (which we'll circle back to later).*

Continue (south) down the Sacred Way. Ahead on the right (set back from the path) is a ruined brick building. Climb the stairs at the far end and peek into the...

Workshop of Pheidias

In this building, the great sculptor Pheidias (c. 490-c. 430 B.C.) created the 40-foot statue of Zeus (c. 435 B.C.) that once stood in

the Temple of Zeus across the street. The workshop was built with the same dimensions as the temple's *cella* (inner room) so that Pheidias could create the statue with the setting in mind. Pheidias arrived here having recently completed his other masterpiece, the colossal Athena Parthenos for the

Parthenon in Athens. According to ancient accounts, his colossal Zeus outdid even that great work.

How do we know this building was Pheidias' place? Because archaeologists found sculptors' tools and molds for pouring metals, as well as a cup with Pheidias' name on it (all now displayed in the Archaeological Museum—see page 1051).

• *Farther south down the Sacred Way—but skippable—is a large, rubble-strewn, open field, with dozens of thigh-high Ionic capitals. This* *was the site of the massive **Leonideion,** a luxury, four-star hotel with 145 rooms (and private baths) built in the fourth century* B.C. *to house VIPs (dignitaries and famous athletes) during the Games.*

Now turn your attention to Olympia's main sight: the Temple of Zeus. It's located across the Sacred Way from Pheidias' workshop. All that remain are ruins, marked by a single standing column.

Temple of Zeus

The center of ancient Olympia—both physically and symbolically—was the massive Temple of Zeus, the King of the Gods

and patron of the Games. It was the first of the Golden Age temples, and one of the biggest (not much smaller than the Parthenon), and is the purest example of the Doric style.

The temple was built in the fifth century B.C. (470-457 B.C.), stood for a thousand years, and then crumbled into the evocative pile of ruins we see today, still lying where they fell in the sixth century A.D.

Mentally reconstruct the temple. It was huge—209 feet by 89 feet (about half an acre)—and stood six stories tall. The lone standing column is actually a reconstruction (of original pieces, cleaned and restacked), but it gives a sense of the scale: It's 34 feet tall, 7 feet thick, and weighs nine tons. This was one of 34 massive Doric columns that surrounded the temple (6 on each end, 13 along the sides)—making this a typical peripteral/peristyle temple, like Athens' Parthenon and Temple of Hephaistos (in the Ancient Agora).

The columns originally supported a triangular pediment at each end (now in the Archaeological Museum), carved with scenes of the *Battle of the Lapiths and Centaurs* (west end) and *Pelops and the Chariot Race* (east end, which was the main entrance).

• *Find the path that lets you get up close to the temple. As you approach the ruins, you're entering the Altis, or sacred enclosure. Wend your way through the...*

Temple Ruins: Walk between big gray blocks, two-ton column drums, and fallen 12-ton capitals. They're made not of marble but from local limestone. Look closely and you can see the seashell fossils in this porous (and not terribly

durable) sedimentary rock. Most of the temple was made of this cheaper local stone, then covered with a marble-powder stucco to make it glisten as brightly as if it were made of pure marble. The pediments and some other decoration were made of expensive white marble from the isle of Paros.

The olive trees mark the spot of the original tree (planted by Hercules, legends say) from which the winners' wreaths were made. Then as now, olives were vital to Greece, providing food, preservatives, fuel, perfumes...and lubrication for athletes.

• *If open, ascend a set of stairs (in the southwest corner, at the opposite end from the standing column, to the right) up onto what was once the south porch of the temple—the edge facing away from Kronos Hill.*

South Side: From here, you can look inside and make out the temple's layout, including the rectangular shape of the *cella*. This was the most sacred part of the temple, where Pheidias' statue of Zeus stood. Looking down to the ground along the south side, see five huge fallen columns, with their drums lined up in a row like dominos—or the vertebrae of dinosaurs.

• *Continue to the east end of the temple. From atop the temple's main stairs, look down on the courtyard below, the...*

Winner's Circle (East End): Here at the main entrance to the temple, winners of the Olympic Games were announced and crowned. As thousands gathered in the courtyard below, priests called the name of the winner, who scaled the steps against a backdrop of cheers from the crowd. The winner was crowned with a wreath of olive (not laurel) branches, awarded a statue in his honor—and nothing more. There were no awards for second and third place, and no gold, silver, or bronze medals—those are inventions of the modern Olympics. However, winners were usually showered with gifts and perks from their proud hometowns: free food for life, theater tickets, naming rights for gymnasiums, statues, pictures on ancient Wheaties boxes, and so on.

In the courtyard below, you can see pedestals that once held statues of winners, who were considered to be demi-gods. The inscriptions listed the winner's name, the date, the event won, his hometown, and the names of his proud parents.

A bit to the right stands the 29-foot-tall, white-marble, triangular **Pillar of Nike.** It's empty now, but it once held a famous statue of the goddess Nike (now in the Archaeological Museum—see page 1050). Nike was, of course, the personification of "Victory" (this particular statue commemorated the Messenian defeat of the Spartans in 425 B.C.). Overlooking this place, where athletic victories were celebrated, the statue must have been an inspiring sight.

The ruined building directly east of here was the Echo Hall, a long hall where winners were also announced as if into a microphone—the sound echoed seven times.

• *Descend the steps and turn left when you can (passing several of the inscribed pedestals mentioned earlier). Make your way north, until you bump into the low wall at the base of Kronos Hill. The foot of that hill is lined with a row of 16 pedestals, the...*

Bases of Zanes (Cheater Statues) and Row of Treasuries

At the Olympic Games, there were no losers...except quitters and cheaters.

These 16 pedestals once held bronze statues of Zeus (plural "Zanes"). The statues were paid for with fines levied on cheaters, whose names and ill deeds were inscribed in the bases. As people entered the stadium, they'd spit on the statues. Offenses ranged from doping (using forbidden herbs) or taking bribes, to failing to train in advance of the Games or quitting out of cowardice. Drinking animal blood—the Red Bull of the day—was forbidden. Official urine drinkers tested for this ancient equivalent of steroids.

Athletes took an oath not to cheat (at the Bouleuterion, along the south side of the Temple of Zeus) by stepping on castrated bulls' balls. As this was a religious event, and because physical training was a part of moral education, the oaths and personal honor were held sacred.

Just behind the statues (and a few feet higher in elevation) is a terrace with a row of treasuries. These small buildings housed expensive offerings to the gods. Many were sponsored by colonies as a way for Greeks living abroad to stay in touch with their cultural roots.

• *Turn right and pass under the arch of the...*

Krypti

Built around 200 B.C., this 100-foot-long tunnel, which once had a vaulted ceiling, was the athletes' entrance to the stadium. Along the walls are niches that functioned as equipment lockers. Just like today's NFL players, Olympia's athletes psyched themselves up for the big contest, shouting as they ran through this tunnel, then emerging into the stadium to the roar of the crowd.

• *On your mark, get set, go. Follow the Krypti as it leads into the...*

Stadium

Line up on that original marble-paved starting line from the ancient Olympic Games and imagine the scene. The place was

filled with 45,000 spectators—men, boys, and girls—who sat on the manmade banks on either side. One lone adult woman was allowed in: a priestess of the goddess Demeter Chamyne, who rose above the sea of testosterone from an altar on the north (left) bank (still visible today).

The stadium (built in the sixth century B.C.) held no seats except those for the judges, who sat in a special box (visible on the south bank, to your right). These Hellanodikai ("Judges of the Greeks") kept things on track. Elected from local noble families and carefully trained over 10 months for just a few days of Games, these referees were widely respected for their impartiality.

The stadium track is 192 meters (640 feet) from start to finish line. In fact, the Greek word *stadion* literally means a course that is 600 traditional Olympic feet long, supposedly first stepped off by the legendary hero Hercules. The line at the near (west) end marked the finish, where all races ended. (Some started at this end as well, depending on how many laps in the race, but most started at the far end.) The racers ran straight up and back on a

clay surface, not around the track. There were 20 starting blocks (all still visible today—count 'em), each with two grooves—one for each foot (athletes competed barefoot). They once had wooden starting gates (similar to those used in horse races today) to make sure no one could jump the gun.

The first Games featured just one event, a sprint race over one length of the stadium, or one *stadion*. (Imagine running this distance in 19.3 seconds, as Usain Bolt of Jamaica did at the 2008 Olympic Games.) Over time, more events were added. There were races of two *stadia* (that is, up and back, like today's 400-meter event), 24 *stadia* (similar to today's 5K race), and a race in which athletes competed in full armor, including shields.

At the height of the Games (c. 400 B.C.), there were 13 events (most held here in the stadium) over five days. Besides footraces, you'd see events such as the discus, javelin, boxing, wrestling, long jump, *pangration* (a wrestling/boxing/martial arts event), and the pentathlon. (In ancient times, there was no decathlon—that event is a modern invention.) South of the stadium was the hippodrome, or horse-racing track, where riding and chariot races took place. During the 2004 Games in Athens, the shot put competition was held in this stadium.

• *Backtrack through the tunnel and continue straight past the Zeus statues. You'll bump into some rectangular foundations, the ruins of the...*

Metroon (Temple of Gaia) and Site of the Altar of Zeus

The Metroon (mid-fourth century B.C.) was dedicated to the mother of the gods, worshipped by many names (Gaia, Ge, Ghea, Rhea, Kybele, and others). From here, you get nice views up to Kronos Hill.

Somewhere near here once stood the Altar of Zeus, though no one knows exactly where— nothing remains today. At this altar the ancient Olympians slaughtered and burned animals in sacrifice to the gods. For spe-
cial festivals, they'd sacrifice 100 cattle (a "hecatomb"), cook them on the altar, throw offerings into the flames, and feast on the flesh, leaving a pile of ashes 25 feet high.

In the middle of the wide path, under an olive tree, is a **sunken apse,** recently excavated by archaeologists. What you see are the foundations of a 4,000-year-old house, emphasizing that this site was important long before the Olympic Games and the Golden Age of ancient Greece.

• *Continuing on (westward), you'll find the ruins of a semi-circular structure built into the hillside, the...*

Nymphaeum

This was once a spectacular curved fountain, lined with two tiers of statues of emperors, some of which are now in the Archaeological

Museum. The fountain provided an oasis in the heat and also functioned as an aqueduct, channeling water throughout the sanctuary. It was built around A.D. 150 by the wealthy Roman Herodes Atticus (who also financed construction of the famous theater at the base of the Acropolis in Athens).

When the Romans conquered Greece in the second century B.C., they became fans of Greek culture, including the Olympics. The Romans repaired neglected buildings and built new structures, such as this one. But they also changed (some say perverted) the nature of the Games, transforming them from a Greek religious ritual to secular Roman spectacle. Rome opened up the Games to any citizen of the Empire, broadening their appeal at the cost of their Greek-ness.

Rome's notorious Emperor Nero—a big fan of the Olympics—attended the Games in the mid-first century A.D. He built a villa nearby, started music contests associated with the Games, and entered the competition himself as a charioteer. But when he fell off his chariot, Nero ordered the race stopped and proclaimed himself the winner.

• *In front of the Nymphaeum, between the Metroon and the Temple of Hera, are the rectangular foundations of what was once the...*

Altar of Hera

This humble site provides a bridge across millennia, linking the original Olympics to today's modern Games. Since 1936, this is

where athletes have lit the ceremonial Olympic torch (for both the summer and winter Games). A few months before the modern Games begin, local women dress up in priestess garb and parade here from the Temple of Hera. A curved, cauldron-

shaped mirror is used to focus the rays of the sun, igniting a flame. The women then carry the flame into the stadium, where runners light a torch and begin the long relay to the next city to host the

Games. From here, the relay will cover more than 1,500 miles to London for the 2012 Summer Games, and 1,000 miles to Sochi, Russia, for the 2014 Winter Games.

• *Continuing west, you'll come to the four standing Doric columns of the well-preserved...*

Temple of Hera

First built in 650 B.C., this is the oldest structure on the site and one of Greece's first monumental temples. The temple originally honored both Hera and her husband Zeus, before the Temple of Zeus was built.

The temple is long but not tall, giving it an intimate feel. It's 61.5 feet wide by 164 feet long and surrounded by columns (6 wide by 16 long)—both of which are a ratio of 3:8. That proportion was considered aesthetically harmonious as well as astronomically significant because the ancients synchronized the lunar and solar calendars by making the year three months longer every eight years.

The temple was originally made of wood. Over time, the wooden columns were replaced with stone columns, resulting in a virtual catalog of the various periods of the Doric style. The columns are made from the same shell-bearing limestone as most of the site's buildings, also originally covered in marble stucco.

Inside, a large statue of Hera once sat on a throne with Zeus standing beside her. Hera's priestesses wove a new dress for the statue every four years. The temple also housed a famous statue of Hermes and was topped with the Disk of the Sun (both are now in the Archaeological Museum—see page 1051).

Though women did not compete in the Olympics, girls and maidens competed in the Heraean Games, dedicated to Hera. The Heraean Games were also held every four years, though not in the same years as the Olympics. They were open only to unmarried virgins—no married women allowed—who raced on foot (running five-sixths of a *stadion*, or 160 meters/525 feet) and in chariots, wearing dresses with one breast exposed. Like the men, the winners received olive wreaths and fame, as well as a painted portrait displayed on a column of the Temple of Hera.

• *Continuing west, you'll reach a round-shaped temple with three Ionic columns (which we saw earlier), the...*

Philippeion

The construction of the Philippeion announced a new era in

Greece—the Hellenistic era. It was built by Philip of Macedon to mark his triumph over Greece. The Macedonians spoke Greek and had many similar customs, but they were a kingdom (not a democracy), and the Greeks viewed them as foreigners. Philip, the father of Alexander the Great, conquered Greece around 340 B.C., thus uniting the country—by force—while bringing its Classical Age to an end.

The temple—the first major building visitors saw upon entering the sacred site—originally had 18 Ionic columns of limestone and marble stucco (though today it appears dark, as the gleaming stucco is long gone). Inside stood statues of Philip and his family, including his son, the man who would bring Greece to its next phase of glory: Alexander the Great.

Just north of the Philippeion, bordering the Sacred Way and difficult to make out, are the scant remains of the Prytaneion, the building that once housed the eternal Olympic flame.

Olympia's Legacy

After the Classical Age, the Games continued, but not in their original form. First came Alexander and a new era of more secular values. Next came the Romans, who preserved the Games but also commercialized them and opened them up to non-Greeks. The Games went from being a somber celebration of Hellenic culture to being a bombastic spectacle. The lofty ideals for which the games were once known had evaporated—along with their prestige. As Rome/Greece's infrastructure decayed, so did the Games. A series of third-century earthquakes and the turmoil of the Herulian invasion (in A.D. 267) kept the crowds away. As Greece became Christian, the pagan sanctuary became politically incorrect.

The last ancient Games (the 293rd) were held in A.D. 393. A year later, they were abolished by the ultra-Christian emperor Theodosius I as part of a general purge of pagan festivals. The final blow was delivered in 426, when Theodosius II ordered the temples set ablaze. The remaining buildings were adopted by a small early Christian community, who turned Pheidias' workshop into their church. They were forced to abandon the area after a combination of earthquakes (in 522 and 551) and catastrophic floods and mudslides. Over the centuries, two rivers proceeded to bury the area under 25 feet of silt—thus preserving the remaining buildings until archaeologists rediscovered the site in 1766.

• *The Archaeological Museum is 200 yards to the north, and well-signed.*

Archaeological Museum

Many of Olympia's greatest works of art and artifacts have been removed from the site and are now displayed in this compact and manageable museum.

Orientation

Cost and Hours: €6, €9 combo-ticket includes archaeological site, same hours as the Sanctuary of Olympia, tel. 26240-22517, www.culture.gr.

Services: A museum shop, WCs, and café are to the right of the entrance.

The Tour Begins

Everything is well-described in English. This tour takes you past the highlights, but there's much more to see if you have time. As you enter, ask for the free booklet that includes a map of the museum (and the site).

• *In the entrance lobby, you'll encounter a...*

Model of the Site, Reconstructed: Looking at Olympia as it appeared in its Golden Age glory, you can see some of the artifacts that once decorated the site (and which now fill this museum). On the Temple of Zeus, notice the pediments, topped with statues and tripods. Southeast of the temple is the Pillar of Nike, topped with the statue of Nike. Find Pheidias' workshop and the Temple of Hera, topped with the Disk of the Sun. We'll see all of these items on this tour.

• *Continue straight ahead into the main hall. On the right wall are...*

Statues of Lapiths and Centaurs from the West Pediment of the Temple of Zeus: This 85-foot-long pediment stood over the back side of the temple (facing the Sacred Way). Study the scene: In the *Battle of the Lapiths and Centaurs*, the centaurs have crashed a human wedding party in order to carry off the women. See one dramatic scene of a woman and her horse-man abductor just left of center. The Lapith men fight back. In the center, a 10-foot-tall Apollo  stands calmly looking on. He puts his arm around the king's shoulder to assure him that they will drive off the centaurs.

• *On the opposite side of the hall are...*

Statues of Pelops from the East Pediment of the Temple

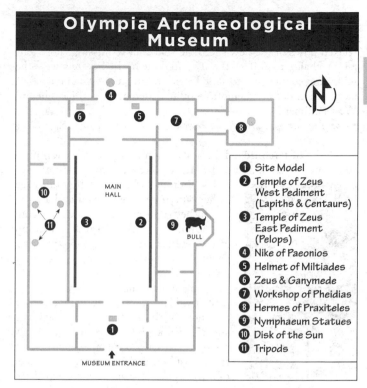

Olympia Archaeological Museum

MAIN HALL

BULL

MUSEUM ENTRANCE

1 Site Model
2 Temple of Zeus West Pediment (Lapiths & Centaurs)
3 Temple of Zeus East Pediment (Pelops)
4 Nike of Paeonios
5 Helmet of Miltiades
6 Zeus & Ganymede
7 Workshop of Pheidias
8 Hermes of Praxiteles
9 Nymphaeum Statues
10 Disk of the Sun
11 Tripods

of Zeus: This is what you would have seen above the temple's main entrance. Olympic victors stood beneath this pediment as

they received their olive wreaths. The statues tell the story of King Pelops, the legendary founder of the Games. A 10-foot-tall Zeus in the center is flanked by two competing chariot teams. Pelops (at Zeus' left hand, with the fragmented legs) prepares to race King Oenomaus (at Zeus' right) for the hand of the king's daughter Hippodamia (standing beside Pelops). The king, aware of a prophecy predicting that he would be murdered by his son-in-law, killed 13 previous suitors after defeating them in chariot races. But Pelops wins this race by sabotaging the king's wheels (that may be what the crouching figure is up to behind the king's chariot), causing the king to be dragged to his death by his horses (just like that chariot race in *Ben-Hur*). Pelops becomes king and goes on to unify the Peloponnesian people with a festival: the Olympic Games.

As some of the first sculpture of the Golden Age (made after the Persian invasion of 480 B.C.), this shows the realism and relaxed poses of the new age (note that they're missing those tell-tale Archaic-era smiles). But it's still done in the Severe style—the sculptural counterpart to stoic Doric architecture—with impassive faces and understated emotion, quite different from the exuberant West Pediment.

• *Continue straight ahead, where you'll see a statue rising and floating on her pedestal. She's the...*

Nike of Paeonios: This statue of Victory (c. 421 B.C.) once stood atop the triangular Pillar of Nike next to the Temple of

Zeus. Victory holds her billowing robe in her outstretched left hand and a palm leaf in her right as she floats down from Mt. Olympus to proclaim the triumph of the Messenians (the Greek-speaking people from southwest Peloponnese) over Sparta.

The statue, made of flawless pure-white marble from the island of Paros, was damaged in the earthquakes of A.D. 522 and 551. Today, her wings are completely missing, but they once stretched behind and above her, making the statue 10 feet tall. (She's about seven feet today.) With its triangular base, the whole monument to Victory would have been an imposing 36 feet tall, rising above the courtyard where Olympic winners were crowned.

• *In the glass case to the right as you face Nike are two bronze helmets. The green, battered one (#2) is the...*

Bronze Helmet of Miltiades (Hero of the Battle of Marathon): In September of 490 B.C., a huge force of invading Persians

faced off against the outnumbered Greeks on the flat plain of Marathon, north of Athens. While most of the Athenian generals wanted to wait for reinforcements, Miltiades convinced them to attack. The Greeks sprinted across the plain, into the very heart of the Persians—a bold move that surprised

and routed the enemy. According to legend, the good news was carried to Athens by a runner. He raced 26 miles from Marathon to Athens, announced "Hurray, we won!"...and dropped dead on the spot.

The legend inspired the 26-mile race called the marathon—but the marathon was not an Olympic event in ancient times. It was a creation for the first modern Games, revived in Athens in A.D. 1896.

• *A glass case to the left of Nike has the smaller-than-life-size...*

Statue of Zeus Carrying Off Ganymede: See Zeus' sly look as he carries off the beautiful Trojan boy Ganymede to be his cupbearer and lover. The terra-cotta statue was likely the central roof decoration (called an *akroterion*—see the nearby diagram) atop the Temple of Zeus.

• *Enter the room to the right as you face Nike.*

Workshop of Pheidias Room: The poster shows Pheidias' great statue of Zeus, and a model reconstructs the workshop where he created it. In the display case directly to the left as you enter, find exhibit #10, the clay cup of Pheidias. The inscription on it reads: "I belong to Pheidias." The adjacent case holds clay molds that were likely used for making the folds of Zeus' robe. The case in the opposite corner contains lead and bronze tools that would have been used by ancient sculptors.

• *The room hiding behind the Zeus poster contains...*

Hermes of Praxiteles: This seven-foot-tall statue (340-330 B.C.), discovered in the Temple of Hera, is possibly a rare original by the great sculptor Praxiteles. Though little is known of this

fourth-century sculptor, Praxiteles was recognized in his day as the master of realistic anatomy and the first to sculpt nude women. His works influenced generations of Greek and Roman sculptors, who made countless copies.

Hermes leans against a tree, relaxed. He carries a baby—the recently orphaned Dionysus—who reaches for a (missing) object that Hermes is using to distract him. Experts guess he was probably groping for a bunch of grapes, which would have hinted at Dionysus' future role as the debauched god of wine and hedonism.

Circle the statue and watch Hermes' face take on the many shades of thoughtfulness. From the front he appears serene. From the right (toward the baby), there's the hint of a smile, while from the left (toward his outstretched arm), he seems sad.

The statue has some of Praxiteles' textbook features. The body has the distinctive S-curve of Classical sculpture (head tilted one way, torso the other, legs another). He's leaning against a tree with his robe draped down. And the figure is interesting from all angles, not just the front. The famous Praxiteles could make hard, white, translucent marble appear as supple, sensual, and sexual as human flesh.

• *Consider detouring to see more statues, from the Roman Nymphaeum fountain. (If you're in a rush, skip this section and head for the Disk of the Sun.) To see the statues, backtrack into the Workshop of Pheidias Room, turn left, and proceed through the next room into the long hall.*

Nymphaeum Statues: The grand, semi-circular fountain near the Temple of Hera had two tiers of statues, including Roman

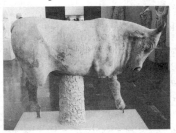

emperors and the family of the statue's benefactor, Herodes Atticus. Here you can see some of the surviving statues, as well as a sculpted bull (in the center of the room) that stood in the middle of the fountain. The bull's inscriptions explain the fountain's origins.

The next (smaller) room holds more Roman-era statues, from the Metroon and the Temple of Hera.

• *Head back to the Workshop of Pheidias Room, then backtrack past the helmets, Nike, and Zeus/Ganymede. Pass through the next room, and continue into the long hall with the large...*

Disk of the Sun: This terra-cotta disk—seven and a half feet across and once painted in bright colors—was the *akroterion* that perched atop the peak of the roof of the Temple of Hera. It stood as a symbol of how Hera's truth shines to earth.

• *The rest of this long room contains several...*

Tripods: These cauldrons-with-legs were used as gifts—to the gods and to victorious athletes. For religious rituals, tripods were used to pour liquid libations, to hold sacred objects, or to burn incense or sacrificial offerings. As ceremonial gifts to the gods, tripods were placed atop or around temples. And as gifts to athletes, they were a source of valuable bronze (which could easily be melted down into some other form), making for a nice "cash" prize.

Eating in Olympia

As no place in town really has an edge, you could simply window-shop to find the setting you like best. Along the main road, **Taverna Dionysos** (ΤΑΒΕΡΝΑ ΔΙΟΝΥΣΟΣ) is cozier than most, with indoor and outdoor seating (€2-5 starters, €6-9 main dishes, daily 11:00-23:00, tel. 26240-22932). More places cluster along the shady, angled side-street called Georgiou Douma; along here, **Taverna Gefsis Melathron** has the most charm and a good reputation (€3-5 starters, €5-9 main dishes, daily 11:00-23:00, until 22:00 off-season, Douma 3, tel. 26240-22916). Just above the main street is the more local-feeling **Anesi,** which specializes in grilled meats (€3 starters, €5-7 main dishes, open daily, corner of Avgerinou and Spiliopoulou, tel. 26240-22644). The **Europa Hotel** restaurant, on the hills overlooking Olympia, is a 20-minute uphill hike, or a five-minute taxi ride. Chef Alki practices his art on fresh products from the hotel's farm. The grilled meats and fish are savory and satisfying (€3-7 starters, €5-7 salads, €7-14 main dishes, vegetarian options, 1 Drouva Street, tel. 26240-22650).

Nafplio

The charming Peloponnesian port town of Nafplio (Ναύπλιο) is small, cozy, and strollable. Though it has plenty of tourism, Nafplio is both elegant and proud, loudly trumpeting its special footnotes in Greek history. Thanks to its highly strategic position—nestled under cliffs at the apex of a vast bay—it changed hands between the Ottomans and the Venetians time and again. But Nafplio ultimately distinguished itself in the 1820s by becoming the first capital of a newly independent Greece, headed by President Ioannis Kapodistrias. While those glory days have faded, the town retains a certain genteel panache. It's as chic as Athens, without all the graffiti.

Owing to its prestigious past, Nafplio's harbor is guarded by three castles: one on a small island (Bourtzi), another just above the Old Town (ancient Akronafplia), and a third capping a tall cliff above the city (Palamidi Fortress). If you're not up for the climb to Palamidi, explore Nafplio's narrow and atmospheric back streets, lined with elegant Venetian houses and Neoclassical mansions, and dip into its likeable museums.

Planning Your Time

Nafplio is light on sightseeing opportunities, but heavy on ambience.

• My **self-guided walk** offers the best overview of town. Allow 1.5 hours.

• The **Archaeological Museum** is Nafplio's best; allow about an hour.

• With more time, consider the arduous hike up to **Palamidi Fortress,** which takes 3-4 hours round-trip. Ideally, do the hike first thing in the morning, before the worst heat of the day (bring water and wear good shoes; to save time and sweat, you can also take a taxi there).

• Nafplio also serves as a launch pad for visiting two of the Peloponnese's best ancient sites (each a 45-minute drive away): the best-preserved ancient theater anywhere, at **Epidavros;** and the older-than-old hilltop fortress of **Mycenae.** Allow 5 hours total for either destination, including travel time from Nafplio via taxi.

Arrival in Nafplio

Tendering to the Old Town

It couldn't be easier: Tenders deposit cruise passengers at Nafplio's Old Town and the beginning of my self-guided walk. Just look for the obelisk in the square on the waterfront. Some smaller cruise ships actually dock along the waterfront.

Returning to Your Ship

From Syntagma Square, just head for the waterfront, looking for the square with the obelisk.

Orientation to Nafplio

Because everything of interest is concentrated in the peninsular Old Town, Nafplio feels smaller than its population of 15,000. The mostly traffic-free Old Town is squeezed between the hilltop Akronafplia fortress and the broad seafront walkways of Bouboulinas and Akti Miaouli; the core of this area has atmospherically tight pedestrian lanes, bursting with restaurants and shops. Syntagma Square (Plateia Syntagmatos) is the centerpiece of the Old Town. From here, traffic-free Vasileos Konstantinou—called "Big Street" (Megalos Dromos) by locals—runs east to Syngrou street, which separates the Old Town from the New Town.

Note that the town's name can be spelled a staggering number of different ways in English: Nafplio(n), Nauplio(n), Navplio(n), Naufplio(n), Nauvplio(n), and so on. This makes it tricky to look for information online (e.g., weather reports); try all the variations until you find one that works.

Tourist Information

Nafplio's clueless **TI** is just outside the New Town, a block away from the bus station (daily 9:00-13:00 & 16:00-20:00, in a dumpy building next to a fire station at 25 Martiou #4, tel. 27520-24444). Its guaranteed-job-security clerks are living proof that Greece needs to reform its civil-service system. If you visit, pick up the free town map and brochure...then get your questions answered elsewhere.

Helpful Hints

Bookshops: Conveniently located right on Syntagma Square, **Odyssey** sells international newspapers, maps, local guide-books, and paperbacks in English (daily 8:00-24:00, on Syntagma Square next to the National Bank building, tel. 27520-23430).

Internet Access: Posto, overlooking the big park just outside the Old Town, is probably Nafplio's most user-friendly Internet café (€2/hour, daily 8:00-1:00 in the morning, next to Goody's at Sidiras Merarchias 4).

Post Office: The post office is at the corner of Syngrou and Sidiras Merarchias (Mon-Fri 7:30-14:00, closed Sat-Sun).

Local Guide: Patti Staikou is a charming Nafplio native who enjoys sharing her town and nearby ancient sites with visitors (fair and negotiable prices for a 1-hour tour of Nafplio or 1.5-hour tours of Epidavros or Mycenae—she'll meet you there, mobile 697-778-3315, pstaikou@mail.gr).

Photography: Aris and Yiannis Karahalios at **Digital Photo Studio** can download your pictures to a CD (€5) or DVD (€8), and can even email a few of your favorites home (daily 9:00-22:30, Konstantinou 7, tel. 27520-28275).

Self-Guided Walk in Nafplio

This walk—which takes about an hour and a half—will give you a feel for Nafplio's pleasant Old Town.

• *We'll begin on the harborfront square opposite the fortified island, marked by a sturdy obelisk.*

Square of the Friends of the Greeks (Plateia Filellinon)

This space is named for the French soldiers who fell fighting for Greek independence in 1821. On the memorial **obelisk,** a classical-style medallion shows brothers in arms: Hellas and Gallia (Greeks and French). On the other side is the French inscription.

Face the **waterfront.** Nafplio has a busy cruise-ship business. Since they deepened the port a few years back, small ships

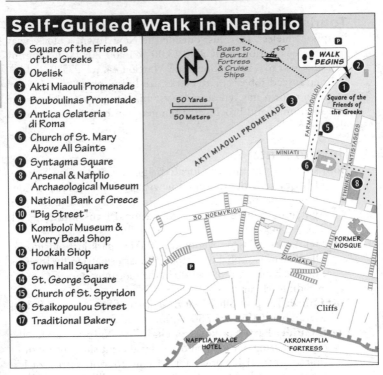

Self-Guided Walk in Nafplio

1. Square of the Friends of the Greeks
2. Obelisk
3. Akti Miaouli Promenade
4. Bouboulinas Promenade
5. Antica Gelateria di Roma
6. Church of St. Mary Above All Saints
7. Syntagma Square
8. Arsenal & Nafplio Archaeological Museum
9. National Bank of Greece
10. "Big Street"
11. Komboloï Museum & Worry Bead Shop
12. Hookah Shop
13. Town Hall Square
14. St. George Square
15. Church of St. Spyridon
16. Staikopoulou Street
17. Traditional Bakery

Boats to Bourtzi Fortress & Cruise Ships

WALK BEGINS

Square of the Friends of the Greeks

AKTI MIAOULI PROMENADE

FARMAKOPOULOU

MINIATI

ETHNIKIS ANTISTASEOS

30 NOEMVRIOU

ZIGOMALA

FORMER MOSQUE

Cliffs

NAFPLIA PALACE HOTEL

AKRONAFPLIA FORTRESS

50 Yards

50 Meters

can actually dock here, while tenders for bigger ships drop their passengers here. A goofy tourist train leaves from this parking lot (pricey at €4 for a 20-minute tour, doesn't even go to into the most charming center of town; departs every 30-45 minutes, sometimes with afternoon break).

Plenty of Nafplio bars, cafés, restaurants, and tavernas face the harbor. The embankment called **Akti Miaouli** (which covers all the vowels but one) promenades to the left with a long line of sedate al fresco tables filled by an older clientele. (Locals warn that these are the most expensive cafés in town, but well-heeled tourists don't mind shelling out an extra euro or two for the view.)

The **Bouboulinas** promenade heads in the other direction (to the right, as you face the water)—first passing fine fish tavernas (listed on page 1068) and then trendy bars. Late at night, forget about the fish—this is Nafplio's meat market, where hormone-oozing young Greeks hit the town. (The better-for-families hang-out is the kid-friendly Syntagma Square, which we'll visit later.)

From the harbor, you can also see the three Venetian forts of Nafplio. First, the mighty little fortress island just offshore, called **Bourtzi,** was built during the first Venetian occupation (15th century) to protect the harbor. Most of what you see today is an

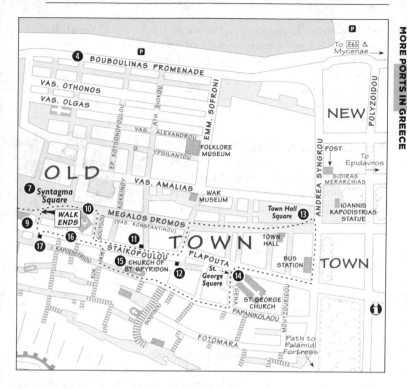

18th-century reconstruction from the second Venetian occupation.

A shuttle boat departs from here to visit the island. It's a fun little trip, but there's not much to see there beyond a pleasant city view (€4 round-trip, returns after 15 minutes, catch a later boat if you want to linger).

To see the other two forts, turn 180 degrees, putting your back to the water. Capping the hill high above is the Palamidi Fortress (highest, to the left); below it is Nafplio's ancient acropolis, the Akronafplia (lower, to the right). Locals claim that the **Palamidi Fortress,** built in just three

years (1711-1714), is the best-preserved Venetian fort in the Mediterranean. It can be reached by climbing nearly a thousand stone stairs... or by paying €7 for a taxi. While the commanding view is rewarding, the building

itself is a bulky, impressive, empty shell. The lower **Akronafplia Fortress** is built upon the remains of an ancient fort. The big stones at the base of its wall date from the third century B.C.

• *With your back to the water, walk up the street to the right of Hotel Grande Bretagne (Farmakopoulou). After a block, on the first corner (left), is a popular gelateria. Across the small square just beyond it (Komninou) is a church. First things first...*

Antica Gelateria di Roma

Greece has great honey-dripping desserts, but nobody does ice cream like the Italians. This popular, fun-loving, air-conditioned ice-cream parlor is run by Marcello and family, who offer a taste of Italy: gelato, fruit-based *sorbetto*, as well as other treats such as *biscotti*, *lemoncello*, and cappuccino. This is one holdover from the Venetian occupation that no local will complain about. (For more details, see page 1068.)

• *Just across the square stands the...*

Church of St. Mary Above All Saints

This church has a proud history: it originally dates from the 15th century; today's building is from the 18th century; and just a few years ago, they peeled back, then reapplied, all the plaster. The priest at this church is particularly active, keeping it open late

into the evening (long after many other Nafplio churches have closed). Outside the door he posts a daily message—a thought to ponder or a suggested prayer.

Step inside—it's generally open. The flat ceiling with the painted Trinity in three circular panels shows a Venetian influence—most Greek Orthodox churches of this period are domed. The more typical iconostasis, a wall of Greek Orthodox icons, separates worshippers from priests. If you're so moved, drop in a coin for a candle and light up a prayer.

• *Leaving the church through the door you came in, go right (around the corner of the church), and walk down the street with the church on your right. Go past the imposing Venetian arsenal, then stop to take in the big square you've suddenly landed in. If it's sunny, stand under the shady tree in the corner nearest where you entered. Survey this scene in a counterclockwise spin-tour, starting on your immediate right.*

Syntagma Square (Plateia Syntagmatos)

Like the main square in Athens, Nafplio's central plaza is "Constitution Square," celebrating the 1843 document that established a constitutional monarchy for Greece. Nafplio was one of the first towns liberated from the Ottoman Turks (1822), and it became the new country's first capital. The square is a delightful

mix of architecture revealing the many layers of local history.

The big building flying the Greek flag at the bottom of the square (on your right as you look into the square) was the Venetian **arsenal**. Of course, wherever Venice ruled, you'll find its symbol: the winged lion of its patron saint, Mark. The building is stout with heavily barred windows because it once stored gunpowder and weapons. Today, it houses the town's **Archaeological Museum,** which has reopened after a six-year renovation (museum described on page 1063).

Just to the left of the arsenal, a block farther inland, is a domed **mosque.** In 1825, with the Muslim Ottomans expelled, this building was taken over and renovated to house independent Greece's first parliament. Now it serves as a conference center.

The big **National Bank of Greece** (facing the long side of the square, opposite the cafés) could be described as "Neo-Minoan"— with its inverted Minoan-style columns (similar to those found in circa-1500 B.C. Minoan ruins on Crete) that taper toward the base, as if they were tree trunks stood on their heads. They are painted with the same color scheme found in Minoan frescoes.

Two small **monuments** stand in front of the bank: a Venetian winged lion from the old fortress; and a relief of an aristocratic

woman waving from a balcony—in 1833, she welcomed the newly-imported-from-Bavaria King Otto with his first waltz in Greece. (Otto spent just one year here before moving his capital to Athens.) The handy Odyssey book-

shop is just beyond the bank (see "Helpful Hints," earlier).

The second former **mosque** fronting this square (at the far end) was converted after independence into Greece's first primary school. Today it's a gallery and theater. The main drag through the Old Town is immediately opposite the arsenal, at the far end of the square.

• *Head across the square and walk down the pedestrian street opposite the arsenal.*

The Big Street (Megalos Dromos)

While Nafplio's main drag is named for King Constantine (Vasileos Konstantinou), locals know it as Megalos Dromos ("Big Street"). Strolling along here, you'll soon pass the quirky Lathos Bar ("Mistake Bar," #1 on left), run by an eccentric character. As you walk, you might notice that this town is something of a shoppers' paradise. Streets like this one are crammed with shops selling everything from the usual tacky tourist trinkets to expensive jewelry, all aimed at the fat wallets of Athenian out-of-towners.

• *You could continue along this shop-lined street. But instead, we'll take a more colorful route: Head up one block to the right and walk down the parallel street (turn right at the first corner up the narrow alley, then turn left onto Staikopoulou).*

Along this stretch of Staikopoulou are a pair of...

Uniquely Greek Shops

After about a block, on the left (at #25), is the **Komboloï Museum.** Owner Aris Evangelinos has a real passion for worry beads. If you're in the market for a set of beads, the ground-floor shop here features a remarkable selection—with beads from every material you can imagine (the cheapest, synthetic sets cost about €8; the priciest—which can cost hundreds of euros—are antique or made of amber). The upstairs "museum"—overpriced at €3—shows off a few small rooms of the owner's favorites from his vast collection, while a handful of English labels explain how variations on worry beads are used by many different faiths (shop—free, museum—€3; both open April-Sept daily 9:30-22:00; Oct-March Wed-Mon 9:30-20:30, closed Tue; Staikopoulou 25, tel. 27520-21618).

At the end of the block, look for a shop on the right (at #56) with a sign reading *ΕΡΓΑΣΤΗΡΙΟ ΚΟΜΠΟΛΟΓΙΟΥ* (Worry Bead Workshop) and, in English, oddly, "Laboratory." More than just another bead shop, this store also sells **hookahs** (water pipes) and the apple-flavored tobacco that smokers burn in them.

• *At the intersection next to the hookah*

shop, turn left and walk one block back down to the Big Street. Turn right onto the Big Street and follow it until you emerge into...

Town Hall Square

A statue of **King Otto** (ΟΘΩΝ) marks the one-time location of his palace. Otto, who had come from Bavarian royalty to rule Greece, decided to move the capital to Athens after just a year here in Nafplio. (An enthusiastic student of classical history, Otto was charmed by the idea of reviving the greatness of ancient Athens.) His palace here in Nafplio finally burned down in 1929.

Otto, looking plenty regal, gazes toward the New Town. Fifty yards in front of Otto (on the right) is the Neoclassical "first high school of Greece"—today's Town Hall. The monument in front celebrates a local hero from the war against the Ottomans.

• *At the far end of Town Hall Square, you hit the busy...*

Syngrou Street and the New Town

This thoroughfare separates the Old Town from the New. Out of respect for the three-story-tall Old Town, no new building is allowed to exceed that height—even in the New Town.

In the square across the street, the statue honors **Ioannis Kapodistrias,** the first president of Greece (back when Nafplio was the capital). He faces the Old Town...and Otto, who stepped in when the president's reign was cut tragically short. (We'll get the whole story later.)

Just behind Kapodistrias is a family-friendly **park.** If you want a cheap and fast meal, consider grabbing a bite at one of the family-filled gyros and souvlaki eateries surrounding the park (cheap €3 meals: order and pay at the bar, then find a bench in the park). Goody's (on the left, by the post office) is the Greek McDonald's—the local kids' favorite hamburger joint, found in towns all over Greece. The good Posto Internet café is two doors down from Goody's (see "Helpful Hints," earlier).

Without crossing Syngrou street, turn right. The commotion surrounds Nafplio's tiny but busy **bus station.** KTEL (or ΚΤΕΛ in Greek) is the national bus company; in the office here, you can buy tickets for bus trips, or use the ticket machine out front. The **TI**—which offers little help to visitors—is a block away from the bus station (see page 1055).

• *At the first corner, turn right on Plapouta street. Walk a block to...*

St. George Square

The focal point of the square, Nafplio's metropolitan church (equivalent to a Catholic "cathedral"), is dedicated to St. George and was the neighborhood church for King Otto. (Otto's palace was a block away—you can see Town Hall Square by looking down the small alley.) Step into the church's dark interior (noticing the clever system that prevents the doors from slamming) to see a gigantic chandelier hovering overhead.

• *Walk a block uphill (toward the fortress) and turn right on Papanikolaou street.*

Upper Streets of the Old Town

Strolling this quiet lane, note that the Neoclassical grid-planned town is to your right, while the higgledy-piggledy Ottoman town climbs the hillside (with winding and evocative lanes and stepped alleys) on your left.

Straight ahead (100 yards away) stands the white bell tower marking the **Church of St. Spyridon** and its square. Facing the square (on the left, hiding in a niche in the wall, near the steps) is the first of several 18th-century Turkish fountains we'll see. When the Ottomans controlled Greece, they still used the squiggly Arabic script you see here. It's likely a verse from the Quran, a

jaunty greeting, and/or a tribute to the person who paid for the fountain.

Continue straight along the side of the church to another Ottoman fountain (on the left)—with its characteristic cypress-tree-and-flowers decor.

Between here and the door of the church just ahead is the rough equivalent—to the Greeks—of Ford's Theater (where Lincoln was assassinated). Ioannis Kapodistrias was elected the first president of independent Greece in 1828. But just three years later, on October 9, 1831, he was shot and stabbed in this spot by Mani landowners who feared his promises of land reform. This led to chaos, less democratic idealism, and the arrival of Greece's imported Bavarian royalty (King Otto, whom we met earlier).

Pop into the church if it's open. Across from the church is a collapsing *hamam*, a Turkish bath from the 18th century.

• *At the next corner (Kokkinou street), turn right and climb down the slippery marble steps to Staikopoulou street (where we saw the hookah and worry bead shops earlier). This time we'll take it left, back to Syntagma Square.*

Staikopoulou Street

This bustling pedestrian drag is lined with grill restaurants (the harborfront is better for fish) and their happy hustlers, and another fine Ottoman fountain (on the right after a block). For a caloric finale, find the **traditional bakery** (on the left corner at #18, with

the ΠΑΡΑΔΟΣΙΑΚΑ ΓΛΥΚΑ sign, 10 yards before the tall skinny tree and the back of the National Bank). This place has been delighting locals with its *baklava* and *ekmek* (roughly, crème-topped *baklava*) since 1955. Choose a tasty Greek dessert from the display case, and enjoy it at the outdoor tables (for more details on this bakery, see page 1069).

A few steps down on the right takes you back to Syntagma Square.

• *Your walk is over. From here, you can enjoy the rest of the city, or you can head to any of Nafplio's three Venetian forts (see the next page).*

Sights in Nafplio

In the Old Town

▲▲**Nafplio Archaeological Museum**—Nafplio's top museum gives a concise overview of prehistoric Greece and the Mycenaean civilization. Visit here for a great warm-up before you go to Mycenae.

Recently renovated, the museum occupies the top two floors of the grand Venetian arsenal on the main square. Before touring the exhibits, climb the stairs to the second floor and watch one of two videos covering what you're about to see. If you have a choice, avoid the long, overly scholarly slideshow about regional archaeological digs; ask for the impressionistic video of schoolchildren learning about the discovery of the museum's priceless set of bronze armor.

After the film, go back downstairs and tour the exhibits, which are well-described in English. The collection runs in chronological order, with Stone Age tools suddenly giving way to dolphin frescoes inspired by the Minoan civilization on Crete. Eye-catching jewelry includes a bull-shaped crystal bead (look for the magnifying glass inside a glass case) and strings of gold beads.

The star of the museum stands in the center: the "Dendra Panoply," a 15th-century B.C. suit of bronze armor that was discovered in a Mycenaean chamber tomb. Also found at the site (and displayed here) is a helmet made from boar tusks. Experts consider this the oldest surviving suit of armor in all of Europe.

The second floor displays artifacts from the Age of Homer to the Roman occupation. Particularly striking are the ceremonial

terra-cotta masks along one wall, which look as if they belong in a circus. Check out the display of rare glasswork from the first century A.D.—somehow these pieces have survived two millennia without getting smashed.

Cost and Hours: €2; May-Sept Tue-Sun 8:00-20:00, Mon 13:30-20:00; Oct-April Tue-Sun 8:30-13:00, closed Mon; at the bottom of Syntagma Square, tel. 27520-27502, www.culture.gr.

Nafplio's Three Venetian Fortresses

In the days when Venice was the economic ruler of Europe (15th-18th centuries), the Venetians fortified Nafplio with a trio of stout fortresses. Today all three parts of the fortifications are open to visitors. These are listed in order from lowest to highest.

Bourtzi—While this heavily fortified island—just offshore from Nafplio's waterfront—looks strik-

ing, there's not much to do here. Still, it's a pleasant vantage point, offering fine views back on the city (boats depart from the bottom of the square called Plateia Filellinon, €4 round-trip, 4-person minimum, on island it's free to enter the fortress).

Akronafplia—Nafplio's ancient acropolis, capping the low hill just behind the Old Town, is fairly easy to reach (a manageable but sometimes-steep 10- to 15-minute uphill hike—from the Old Town). The earliest surviving parts of this fortress date back to the third century B.C., but the Venetians brought it up to then-modern standards in the 15th century. Up top, there's little to see aside from a few ruins (free to enter and explore anytime).

▲▲**Palamidi Fortress**—This imposing hilltop fortress, built between 1711 and 1714, is the best-preserved castle of its kind in

Greece. Palamidi towers over the Old Town, protected to the west by steep cliffs that plunge 650 feet to the sea. From its highest ramparts, you can spot several Aegean islands and look deep into the mountainous interior of the Peloponnesian Peninsula. These mighty outer walls enclose a series of interconnected bastions. Spend some time just poking around this sprawling complex, playing king- or queen-of-the-castle. Everything is well-marked with directional signs.

Cost and Hours: €4, daily April-Oct 8:30-19:15, Nov-March 8:30-15:00, tel. 27520-28036.

Getting There: If you're fit, you can reach the fortress the old-fashioned way: by **climbing** the strenuous, loooong flight of steps that lead up from the road to Akronafplia fortress (near the top end of Polyzoidou street, just outside the Old Town, roughly behind the TI). Alternatively, you can catch a **taxi** to the top for about €7 one-way.

Sights near Nafplio

Each of these ancient attractions is within a 45-minute taxi ride of Nafplio (in different directions), costing €25-35 round-trip. Joining a cruise line shore excursion can be an efficient way to see one or both of these.

▲▲▲**Epidavros**—This ancient site, 18 miles east of Nafplio, has an under-whelming museum, forgettable ruins... and the most magnificent theater of the ancient world. It was built nearly 2,500 years ago to seat 15,000. Today, it's kept busy reviving the greatest plays of antiquity. Try to see Epidavros either early or late in the day; the theater's marvelous acoustics are best enjoyed in near solitude.

▲▲▲**Mycenae**—This was the capital of the Mycenaeans, who won the Trojan War and dominated Greece 1,000 years before the

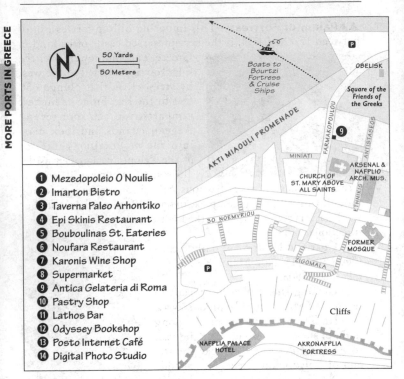

N

50 Yards
50 Meters

Boats to
Bourtzi
Fortress
& Cruise
Ships

OBELISK

Square of the
Friends of
the Greeks

AKTI MIAOULI PROMENADE

FARMAKOPOULOU

MINIATI

CHURCH OF
ST. MARY ABOVE
ALL SAINTS

ARSENAL &
NAFPLIO
ARCH. MUS.

ANTISTASEOS

ETHNIKIS

30 NOEMVRIOU

FORMER
MOSQUE

ZIGOMALA

Cliffs

NAFPLIA PALACE
HOTEL

AKRONAFPLIA
FORTRESS

1 Mezedopoleio O Noulis
2 Imarton Bistro
3 Taverna Paleo Arhontiko
4 Epi Skinis Restaurant
5 Bouboulinas St. Eateries
6 Noufara Restaurant
7 Karonis Wine Shop
8 Supermarket
9 Antica Gelateria di Roma
10 Pastry Shop
11 Lathos Bar
12 Odyssey Bookshop
13 Posto Internet Café
14 Digital Photo Studio

Acropolis and other Golden Age
Greek sights. The classical Greeks
marveled at the huge stones and
workmanship of the Mycenaean
ruins. Visitors today can still gape
at the Lion's Gate, peer into a
cool, ancient cistern, and explore
the giant *tholos* tomb called the
Treasury of Atreus. The tomb,

built in the 15th century B.C., stands like a huge stone igloo, with a
smooth subterranean dome 47 feet wide and 42 feet tall.

Eating in Nafplio

Mezedopoleio O Noulis—run by Noulis, the man with the
mighty moustache shown on the sign—serves up a fabulous range
of *mezedes* (appetizers). Three or four *mezedes* constitute a tasty meal
for two people. This place offers a rare chance to sample *saganaki
flambé* (fried cheese flambéed with Metaxa brandy, €7). As Noulis
likes to do it all himself, don't come here if you're in a hurry (€4-7
starters, €7 appetizer plate, €8-12 seafood and meat dishes; mid-

Nafplio Restaurants

May-Sept Mon-Sat 11:00-15:00 & 19:00-23:00, Oct-mid-May Mon-Sat 12:00-16:00, closed Sun year-round, Moutzouridou 21, tel. 27520-25541).

Imarton (ήμαρτον, "God Forbid Me") is a bright, tiny bistro with appealing traditional decor mingled with mod flair. Because the place is so small, dishes are prepared in advance and heated up when you order. They specialize in small plates rather than big dishes—mostly cheeses and a staggering variety of sausages. Their *soutzoukakia*—meatballs with spicy tomato sauce—are delicious (€3-6 small plates, €6-8 main dishes, €8-12 seafood items, late May-late Sept Tue-Sun 11:00-15:00 & 19:00-23:00, off-season Tue-Sun 12:00-16:00, closed Mon year-round, Plapouta 33).

Taverna Paleo Arhontiko ("Old Mansion") is a favorite town hangout. That's partly because of the food, and partly because there's live music every night from 22:00 in summer, and on Friday and Saturday nights in winter. It gets packed on weekends, when reservations are recommended (€3-5 appetizers, €6-12 main dishes, daily 12:00-16:00 & 19:00-24:00, at corner of Ypsilandou and Siokou, tel. 27520-22449).

Epi Skinis ("On Stage") is a new stage for former theater director Kouros Zachos and his wife Evangalia. The cozy dining room, decorated with playbills and other theater paraphernalia, feels a bit classier than the tavernas nearby. Theater-lovers in town to visit Epidavros might enjoy capping their day here (€3-8 starters, €8-17 main dishes, daily 12:00-1:00 in the morning, Amalias 19A, tel. 27520-21331).

Fish Restaurants on Bouboulinas: As you stroll the harborfront, the throbbing dance beats of the trendy café/bars gradually give way to the fishy aromas and aggressive come-ons of a string of seafood eateries. As these places are fairly interchangeable, you could just browse for what looks best to you (all open daily 12:00-24:00). Seafood here is typically priced by the kilogram or half-kilogram (figure about 250-300 grams for a typical portion—around €10-20 for a seafood entrée, or about €6-15 for a meat dish). These three are well-regarded: **Savouras** (ΣΑΒΟΥΡΑΣ, at #79), **Taberna Tou Stelara** (ΤΑΒΕΡΝΑ του Στελάρα, at #73), and **Arapakos** (ο Αραπάκοσ, at #81).

Italian on Syntagma Square: For a break from Greek food, **Noufara** offers Italian cuisine in a classy two-level interior or at a sea of white tables out on classy Syntagma Square. Heaters and fans allow this place's delightful outdoor seating to stay open in all sorts of weather (€4-6 starters, €6-12 pizzas and pastas, €8-18 main dishes, daily 10:00-2:00 in the morning, Syntagma Square 3, tel. 27520-23648).

Wine-Tasting: Dimitri Karonis specializes in Greek wines and ouzo, and gives a thorough and informative wine-tasting in the **Karonis Wine Shop** near Syntagma Square (Mon-Sat 8:30-14:30 & 18:00-21:30, closed Sun, Amalias 5, tel. 27520-24446)

Picnics: The **Carrefour Express** supermarket is the most convenient of several supermarkets in town (Mon-Fri 8:00-21:00, Sat 8:00-20:00, closed Sun, 100 yards from the post office at corner of Syngrou and Flessa, tel. 27520-25631).

Dessert

Antica Gelateria di Roma is the place to go for a mouthwatering array of *gelati* (dairy-based ice cream) and *sorbetti* (fruit-based sorbet) made fresh on the premises daily by Italian gelato master Marcello Raffo, his wife Monica, and his sister Claudia. According to their menu, gelato "is suggested for a balanced diet [for] children, athletes, pregnant women, and the elderly for a year round" (prices range from €1.50 to a small cone up to €4.50 for a big waffle cone). The Raffos also offer other Italian flavors, including *biscotti* cookies, the lemon liqueur *lemoncello,* the grape brandy *grappa,* and Italian-style cappuccino (daily 9:00-2:00 in the morning, Farmakopoulou 3, at corner with Kominou, tel. 27520-23520). Don't confuse this place with a different ice-cream parlor just up the street.

The best **sweets and pastries** in town are at the no-name shop at Staikopoulou 18 (with the ΠΑΡΑΔΟΣΙΑΚΑ ΓΛΥΚΑ sign). While English is limited, you can point to the dessert you'd like in the case inside, and they'll bring it out to you at a sidewalk table (treats for under €3, tel. 27520-26198).

Heraklion, Crete

Heraklion (ee-RAH-klee-oh; also spelled Iraklion or Iraklio; Ηράκλειον in Greek) is the main town of Crete—Greece's biggest, most populous island and the southernmost point in Europe. Crete (Κρήτη) is practically a mini-state of its own (in fact, from 1897 to 1913 it was an autonomous state within the Ottoman Empire). Historically, Crete was home to the Minoans—Europe's first advanced civilization, peaking around 1950 B.C., centuries before "the ancient Greeks" of Athens. The fascinating, colorful Minoan civilization left us with vivid frescoes hinting at a quirky and complicated society, and one of the most beloved myths of the

ancient world: the labyrinth, the minotaur, and the brave Athenian warrior Theseus.

Coming to Crete on a quick cruise visit provides, at best, a fleeting glimpse of its charms—but if a few hours is all you have, Crete can easily fill them. The port city of **Heraklion** itself (pop. 137,000) is an urban-feeling, workaday capital, lacking the storied charm of the "Greek isles." Its saving grace is its excellent museum of Minoan artifacts—easily Greece's best on the topic. Most cruisers opt to skip Heraklion entirely and head four miles inland to the ruins of **Knossos,** the palace from which the grand Minoan civilization was ruled.

If you have more time, the rest of Crete offers an engaging diversity of attractions: more Minoan ruins, scenic mountains, enticing beaches, characteristic rustic villages, and dramatic caves and gorges (including the famous Samaria Gorge).

Planning Your Time

Even on a short visit, with a shore excursion or a taxi, you can fit in both of the main sights near the cruise port. If you have more time, you can probably squeeze in both by public transportation.

• The ruins of **Knossos Palace** take you back to Minoan times. Allow 2 hours.

• The **Heraklion Archaeological Museum** displays artifacts from the Knossos site and other ancient settlements. Allow 1-2 hours, plus another hour or two if you want to explore downtown Heraklion before returning to your ship.

Arrival at the Port of Heraklion

Cruise ships dock at Heraklion's sprawling main port. Shuttle buses bring you to the terminal building, about a mile east of the city center. From here, you can catch a taxi or bus, or walk into town.

Getting into Town or to Knossos Palace

Taxis charge about €5 into the city center, or €10-15 one-way to Knossos (€50 round-trip to Knossos, including wait time). A taxi between Knossos and downtown Heraklion also costs about €10-15.

Bus #1 takes you downtown to Eleftherias Square, a crescent-shaped plaza just south of the Heraklion Archaeological Museum (4/hour, 15 minutes). Bus #2 goes to Knossos (2/hour, 30 minutes; tel. 28102-45020, www.ktelherlas.gr).

Walking into downtown takes about 20-25 minutes (partly uphill).

Orientation to Heraklion

Founded by Saracens, then expanded by crusading Venetians, the city of Heraklion today feels modern and bustling, with a low-rise Athenian ambience. The city cen-ter is a maze of six-story apartment buildings, with cafés, shops, and modern squares. The main part of town focuses on the Venetian-flavored Venizelos Square, whose trademark Morosini Fountain provides its nickname, "Fountain Square." While the streets around here can be fun to explore, from a sightseeing perspective there's just one game in town: the Heraklion Archaeological Museum, a five-minute walk east of Fountain Square.

The **TI** is across from the Heraklion Archaeological Museum, (Xanthoudidou 1, Mon-Sat 8:30-17:30, closed Sun, tel. 28102-28225). The city's municipal website has helpful travel information in English: www.heraklion.gr/en.

Sights in and near Heraklion

Because both of the sights here are tied to Crete's Minoan civilization, it's best to read the sidebar (next page) and both listings before visiting either of them.

▲▲▲Heraklion Archaeological Museum

One of Greece's top museums, this collection of Minoan artifacts is the perfect complement to the site of Knossos Palace. While the palace ruins feature replicas of the Minoans' sumptuous frescoes, here you'll see the originals, and many other artifacts—all well-lit and eloquently described. The full span of the museum covers some 5,500 years, but the prize pieces all relate to the Minoan civilization. The museum is in the midst of a perpetually delayed renovation, with much of its collection in mothballs, but the core of its collection (all that's worth seeing on a quick visit anyway) is on display in an annex down the street. If the museum seems closed, ask around to find the annex.

The main attraction is the remarkable display of Minoan **frescoes**. The frescoes are vivid, featuring primary colors of red, yellow, and blue, with thick black outlines. These are true frescoes, created by laying a coat of wet plaster on the walls and painting them before the plaster dried. The natural pigments interacted

with the plaster, creating a glowing translucent effect. *The Bull-Leaper* (c. 17th-15th centuries B.C.), illustrating the popular pastime of vaulting over a furious bull, demonstrates the grace of the easygoin' Minoan civilization. As in all Minoan frescoes, the women are pale-white (the figures flanking the bull), while men have an ochre skin tone (the leaper). Perhaps in Minoan society, women (who were held in high esteem) stayed indoors, while men toiled under the sun. Take a look at other frescoes. The blue monkeys (from an exotic, faraway land) hint at the Minoans' far-and-wide travel for trade. The woman with the dark hair, doe eyes, and blue shoulder tassels seemed like a chic sophisticate to the early-20th-century archaeologists who discovered her...and nicknamed her *La Parisienne* ("The Parisian"—see photo on page 1076). Notice her Egyptian-like profile and heavy "eyeliner"—maybe

The Minoans
(2000–1400 B.C.)

A safe, isolated location on the island of Crete, combined with impressive business savvy, enabled the so-called "Minoans" to dominate the pre-Greek world. Unlike most early peoples, they were traders, not fighters. Sailing from their home base on Crete with a large merchant fleet, they exported wine, olive oil, pottery, and well-crafted jewelry. They returned home with the wealth of the Mediterranean and built a lavish palace in Knossos, the capital.

From top to bottom, Minoan society was like one big transnational corporation: ruled by CEO kings, managed by CPA scholars, and blessed by bureaucrat priests. The only written records we have of their civilization are meticulous spreadsheets that show the micromanaged details of every business transaction (using the Linear A script). Thanks to their geographical remoteness and strong economy, the Minoans spent virtually nothing on their defense budget, and their cities and palaces had almost no fortifications.

No one knows where the Minoans originated, and their language has never been deciphered (not much literature survives), but they certainly were prosperous. Their palaces (at Knossos, Phaestus, and Akrotiri) were sprawling, serving as both corporate headquarters and as the center of cultural life. With tapered columns, airy porticos, and lively frescoes, the palaces exude an atmosphere of intimacy and coziness.

Even the poorest on Crete lived well, in multi-room apartments with indoor plumbing. Blessed with ample leisure time, the Minoans were avid sports fans. Surviving frescoes show athletes staring down a charging bull, then—shoop—at the last minute, somersaulting gracefully over the bull's horns, to land upright on their feet again.

Theirs was a delicate, sensual, happy-go-lucky society that apparently worshipped an easygoing Mother Earth and her all-girl pantheon of goddesses. The "Snake Goddess" was especially popular, shown as a bare-breasted, snake-handling woman. There was relative equality between rich and poor, as well as between the sexes. Though the king was a man, women could be priests and businesswomen, and they competed alongside men in boxing and bull-jumping. Minoan inheritance was probably matrilineal (meaning estates were handed down from mothers to daughters).

The colorful frescoes from Minoan palace walls are unique in the ancient world. Most early cultures painted and sculpted things with a particular function in mind: as propaganda for a king, to commemorate a famous battle, or to represent a god. But the Minoans were among the first to love beauty for its own sake. The frescoes are pure decoration, their creators delighting in everyday Minoans going about everyday life. Tanned, relaxed, good-looking men and women are shown dancing, fishing, or strolling with goddesses through a garden of exotic animals. The Minoans seemed more concerned with the good life than with the afterlife. Their love of beauty became part of the legacy of ancient Greece.

At their peak (c. 1500 B.C.), the Minoans dominated the Greek mainland and neighboring islands, where they built large palaces. Greek legend has it that "King Minos" demanded a yearly sacrifice of young Greeks to the dreadful Minotaur (half bull, half man), who lived in a labyrinth on the grounds of the palace in Knossos. However, the Minoans' domination was probably more cultural than political. The later Greeks would inherit the Minoans' business skills, social equality, love of art for art's sake, and faith in rational thought over brute military strength. Some scholars hail the Minoans as the first truly "European" civilization.

Precious little survives of this intriguing civilization. The scant remains of the Minoan palace at Knossos are easier to appreciate after visiting the excellent Heraklion Archaeological Museum (both described in this chapter). Perhaps the most interesting Minoan sight is the ruins of the Akrotiri settlement on the island of Santorini; while the site itself is currently closed, some of its best frescoes are in museums on Santorini (page 1008) and in Athens.

In about 1450 B.C., the Minoan civilization suddenly collapsed. Overnight, the great palaces became ghost towns, and no one knows why. Some think the atomic bomb-size eruption of the Santorini volcano (see page 1004) caused earthquakes and a tsunami that swept the Minoans into oblivion. Physically and economically weakened, they were easily overrun and absorbed by the warlike Mycenaeans from the mainland.

Though the Minoans are a very distant memory, their remarkable civilization provided a firm foundation for the Greek civilization that would become so influential worldwide.

Minoan artists were inspired by their neighbors (Egypt is just 400 miles across the sea). The *Prince of the Lilies*, with his pale hue, is likely actually a woman (he/she wears a headdress similar to the Snake Goddess) who was originally misidentified by archaeologists. Linger over all of these frescoes—the jug-carrying processional, the bluebird—and just bask in the colors.

Exploring the rest of the collection, pause at what catches your eye. The figure of the **Snake Goddess** holds a serpent in each hand; perhaps she was a guardian of the home, or maybe the snake (which sheds its skin periodically) symbolizes new life—combined with the ample bosom, an omen of fertility. Nearby, a collection of other clay goddess figurines line up to signal a touchdown.

The drinking vessel (rhyton) shaped like a **bull's head** boasts

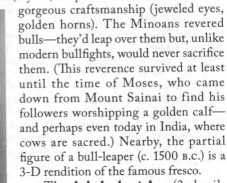

gorgeous craftsmanship (jeweled eyes, golden horns). The Minoans revered bulls—they'd leap over them but, unlike modern bullfights, would never sacrifice them. (This reverence survived at least until the time of Moses, who came down from Mount Sainai to find his followers worshipping a golden calf—and perhaps even today in India, where cows are sacred.) Nearby, the partial figure of a bull-leaper (c. 1500 B.C.) is a 3-D rendition of the famous fresco.

The **Arkalochori Axe** (2nd millennium B.C.) is a *labrys*, or double-headed axe—a symbol of the Minoan king and origin of the word "labyrinth"; this one is inscribed with iconography. The helmet fortified with pieces of boar tusk made its wearer appear very intimidating indeed.

The **Agia Triada sarcophagus** (c. 1400 B.C.) is covered with intricate frescoes that illustrate Minoan burial rituals—a bonanza for archaeologists struggling to understand that mysterious culture.

The clay **Phaistos Disc** (c. 1600-1450 B.C.) is inscribed with a spiral of hieroglyphic symbols—possibly a very early form of a printing press. (A replica of this disc is a popular Heraklion souvenir.)

Cost and Hours: €4; April-Oct Tue-Sun 8:00-20:00, Mon 13:30-20:00; Nov-March Tue-Sun 8:30-15:00 or maybe 17:00, Mon 12:00-17:00; Xanthoudidou 2, at the corner with Xatzidaki, tel. 28102-79086, www.culture.gr.

▲▲Knossos Palace

Knossos was the main palace of the Minoans, and provided a model for their many other villas around Crete (and on nearby islands). Rather than a "palace" in the monumental Versailles sense, Knossos was a vast (425 feet by 425 feet), mazelike series of interconnected rooms—likely the inspiration for the Minoan tales of the labyrinth. "Labyrinth" comes from the Greek *labrys*, a double-headed axe—you'll see this shape inscribed throughout the ruins.

Today's site has sprawling foundations punctuated with some early-20th-century reconstructions that strain to resurrect the majesty of the Minoans. But for the layperson, the site can be as underwhelming as its history is illustrious. Use your imagination (or team up with a good tour guide) to be impressed by the sheer age of this place. You're stepping on stones trod by sandal-clad feet 4,000 years ago.

The black-painted columns that taper at the bottom (the opposite of most Greek columns) were made of cypress trees that were felled and turned upside-down. Impressively advanced terra-cotta pipes carried drinking water into Knossos from miles away, and canals carried sewage away from the palace.

But Knossos' defining feature was its colorful frescoes, which celebrated life in landscapes and everyday scenes. Poke into some of the reconstructed rooms to see these colorful slices of Minoan life (here you'll see only replicas, but originals are displayed in the Heraklion Archaeological Museum).

At the center of the complex is the Throne Room, bathed in red-hued frescoes. The alabaster throne is flanked by fresco depictions of two griffins (mythical animals with a lion's body and an eagle's head and wings).

It was long after the peaceful Minoans (who never bothered to erect a wall around their palace) that the Venetians felt the need to fortify their settlements on Crete, and scavenged many of the pre-cut stones of Knossos to build a wall around Heraklion. The Knossos ruins were discovered in 1878, and the British archaeologist Arthur Evans began excavating Knossos in 1900. The rebuilt areas that visitors see today are based entirely on Evans' vision. Archaeologists debate how accurate his fanciful reconstructions are, and point out that they were designed not necessarily to be accurate, but to cheerlead for the glories of Minoan civilization. Excavations here coincided with the creation of the modern Greek nation, when other European countries were looking down their noses at Greece. The reconstruction emphasizes how sophisticated

this ancient society was (Look: Plumbing! Decoration!). One of its most famous frescoes, nicknamed *Le Parisienne* ("The Parisian"), was embraced partly for how it evoked the elegance of contemporary Europe.

Cost and Hours: €6, daily April-Sept 8:00-19:00, Oct 8:00-18:00, Nov-March 8:30-15:00, tel. 28102-31940, www.culture .gr. Guides wait out front, offering a one-hour tour for €10 (depart every 10 minutes or so); hiring your own private guide costs €100.

Rhodes

Rhodes (in Greek: Ρωδωσ/Rhodos, ROH-dohs), the largest of the Dodecanese Islands, sits at the sunny southeastern extreme of Greece, just 11 miles from Turkey. Compared to its glamorous Cycladic rivals, Santorini and Mykonos, Rhodes' charms are subtle but substantial—a foot wide and a mile deep. As the longtime bridge between the Aegean islands and Asia Minor, Rhodes is an exotic cultural cocktail of Greek and Turkish, with a dash of Crusaders from all

over Europe (see "Rhodes' History" sidebar). The island's main town, also called Rhodes, feels smaller than its population of 80,000. Its walled Old Town—with a bazaar-like atmosphere, a handful of intriguing sights, and very real-feeling back lanes, all lassoed by 3.5 miles of 40-foot-thick medieval walls—is a delight to explore. At the distant end of the island are the ruins of the

Lindos Acropolis, with fine views and a scattering of ancient columns.

Planning Your Time

As Greece's fourth-biggest island (pop. 120,000, nearly 50 miles long and 24 miles wide), Rhodes has far more to offer visitors than can be seen in a quick port visit. But even in just a few hours, you can get an enticing feel for its main town.

• In Rhodes' **Old Town,** explore the shopping streets and the back lanes (allow 1-2 hours), and dip into the Palace of the Grand Masters and the Archaeological Museum (allow an hour each).

• Many cruises offer a shore excursion to **Lindos Acropolis** (allow 3-4 hours total). But you'll spend more time getting there (45 minutes each way) than you will at the site (the hilltop acropolis can be seen in just 30-60 minutes, and the town of Lindos below is a quick walk-through).

Arrival at the Port of Rhodes

The cruise-ship harbor is conveniently located in front of the Old Town—you can see the formidable walls and towers from the ship.

Getting into Town

From your ship, you'll either walk or ride a free shuttle bus to the cruise terminal. From that terminal, head out to the main harbor-front road, turn right, and walk for about five minutes (passing a little pebbly beach on your right-hand side), then turn left through St. Mary's Gate into the city wall. (Travel agencies in front of this gateway rent cars and provide other services that can be useful to those arriving by cruise.)

Getting to Lindos Acropolis

With the cruise terminal so close to the town center, there's little need to hire a taxi or ride a bus on Rhodes, unless you're heading to the Lindos Acropolis (see "Getting There" details for Lindos Acropolis, later). Hiring a taxi for a four-hour tour around Rhodes town and the Lindos Acropolis costs about €140 (tel. 22410-69800).

Orientation to Rhodes

Rhodes' Old Town is divided into three sectors: The enjoyably touristy shopping drag, Sokratous street; the sightseeing spine along the northern edge of town, Ippoton, with Rhodes' two main sightseeing options (the Palace of the Grand Masters at the top,

Rhodes' History

Rhodes sightseeing is made more meaningful to visitors who can tease out its many strands of history. From the ancient Greeks, to a knightly order of Crusaders, to the Ottoman sultans, to a 20th-century tug-of-war among the Italians, Germans, British, and Greeks, Rhodes has long been a crossroads of history.

Because this eastern point is where the sun first shines on the Greek world each morning, the ancient Greeks believed Rhodes to be the home of the sun god, Helios. The local sandstone is embedded with seashells, leading the ancients to surmise that Helios had raised this place from the deep to create a home. In honor of their sun god, they erected here one of the seven wonders of the ancient world: the famous Colossus of Rhodes. Made of bronze and polished to a golden-like sheen, this 100-foot-tall statue of Helios took 12 years to build (in the late third century B.C.) but stood for only 56 years before it was toppled by an earthquake. After the Oracle of Delphi warned Rhodians that they had offended Helios, they decided not to rebuild it. While not a trace of the statue survives (modern bronze deer statues mark one possible location, overlooking the harbor), its legacy does—tales of the statue inspired the creators of the Statue of Liberty, which is of comparable size.

The 304 B.C. defeat of Rhodes' dangerous enemy Demetrius (which the Colossus was erected to celebrate) sparked a golden age for the island. For a time, Rhodes was a trading, naval, and cultural powerhouse. But as the Roman Empire leadership was being reshuffled, Rhodes backed Julius Caesar; after his assassination, its fortunes fell. Rhodes languished through Byzantine times.

Later, in the Middle Ages, Rhodes became a pawn of European power politics in the 14th century. As the nearest Greek island to the Holy Land, this became a logical stopping point

and the Archaeological Museum at the bottom); and the residential back streets in the southern quadrant of town.

To see it all, follow this route: After entering through St. Mary's Gate, turn right and stroll the narrow streets, passing first through the restaurant-crammed Marytron Square, then the wide Ippokratous Square (with its trademark fountain). From here, you can make a loop through town: Head straight up the main shopping street, Sokratous, then bear right at the minaret to find the Palace of the Grand Masters, and finally head back down Ippoton street (the Avenue of the

for passing Crusaders from all over Europe. In 1309, the Knights of St. John—an order of the Knights Hospitaller of Jerusalem—claimed Rhodes as their headquarters, and transformed it into a bustling European medieval burg, governed by their grand master. Rhodes became a magnet for knights coming from all over Europe, who gave the city a uniquely cosmopolitan appearance.

In 1552, Ottoman Sultan Süleyman the Magnificent kicked the knights off the island, adding it to his empire. (They fled to Malta, where they became the Knights of Malta—an order still in existence.) The Ottomans controlled Rhodes for centuries—erecting pointy minarets, building baths, and imbuing the place with an unmistakably Turkish aura that it retains today. Under the Ottomans, the population remained predominantly ethnic Greek, though there has also always been a large Jewish population here.

As the Ottoman Empire floundered in the early 20th century, Rhodes fell under Italian rule (in 1912). The occupying Italians tore down many of the Ottoman structures, rebuilt some of the earlier medieval ones (such as the Palace of the Grand Masters), and added an Italian layer to Rhodes' already eclectic mix. A few decades later, after Italy pulled out of World War II, British and German forces wrangled over who would control Rhodes and the Dodecanese Islands. Only after the dust settled, and Italy signed a 1947 peace treaty, did Rhodes officially become part of Greece for the first time since the Byzantine Empire.

Knights) to the Archaeological Museum—a few steps from where you began on Ippokratous Square.

The **TI** is just outside the city walls beyond Eleftherias Gate near the New Market (1 Etharhou Makariou, tel. 22410-44330). The city's official website has helpful tourist information in English: www.rhodes.gr/en.

Sights on Rhodes

Rhodes' Old Town

The major sights in the Old Town—including the Palace of the Grand Masters, the Archaeological Museum, and a few others—are covered by a €10 **combo-ticket,** which more than pays for itself even if you're visiting just the palace and the Archaeological

Museum (sold at participating museums).

Main Shopping Street (Sokratous)—The closest thing you'll find to a Turkish-style bazaar without setting foot in Turkey, Rhodes' Sokratous street is lined with hole-in-the-wall souvenir shops spilling out into the cobbles. While prices here are inflated, it's a fun place to shop for a Greek and/or Turkish souvenir. You'll

find the standard items: jewelry, worry beads, evil eyes, and so on.

This street also gives a glimpse of Rhodes' **Ottoman** past. The highly polished pebbles that pave the streets—typical in Turkish towns—can be slippery even when dry. At the top end of the street stands the bold minaret of the Mosque of Süleyman the Magnificent, built by that powerful sultan to celebrate his conquest of Rhodes in 1552. Nearby are an Ottoman library and baths complex.

▲▲Palace of the Grand Masters—This stout, intimidating palace, perched at the highest point in this hilly town, is—like everything else on Rhodes—layered with history. In the 14th century, the Knights of St. John added on

to an existing Byzantine fortress here to create a residence and political headquarters for their leader, the grand master. The building was destroyed during Ottoman times (in 1856) when artillery stored here accidentally exploded. When the Italians took over in the early 20th century, they elaborately restored it as an island retreat for their king, Victor Emmanuel III, and later for Mussolini. Their rebuild is a fanciful, over-the-top imagining of a medieval fortress that scarcely resembles its original self—but in some ways, that makes it even more interesting to tour.

The exhibit sprawls through imposing stone hallways on two floors, showing off both the building's fine interiors and a widely

ranging collection of artifacts. Most of the exhibits are corralled into two sections: ancient Rhodes, and Rhodes from the fourth century until the Ottomans. From the ancient Greek period, you'll see a sculpture of the head of Helios, the sun god, with radiating rays. Also from the ancient period come coins, sculptures, vases, and (in the cellar) pointy-based jugs called amphorae. The Byzantine era left behind sumptuous golden icons. But you can thank those Italian restorers for the most striking feature: the grand halls and rooms, fit for a king. Their best flourish—and the highlight of the entire sight—was their addition (mostly upstairs) of fantastically detailed floor mosaics, which they painstakingly transplanted here from their original homes on the isle of Kos (€6, €10 combo-ticket includes Archaeological Museum; May-Oct Tue-Sun 8:00-20:00, Mon 13:30-20:00; Nov-April Tue-Sun 8:30-15:00, closed Mon; Ippoton street, tel. 22410-25500, www.culture.gr).

▲**Avenue of the Knights**—This atmospheric cobbled lane, leading downhill from the palace (turn left as you exit the palace; street is officially named Ippoton), feels like a microcosm of medieval Europe. That's exactly what it was: The Knights of St. John were divided into seven separate language groups, each one assigned to defending a different section of the town wall. Each group lived in an inn that recreated the home they'd left behind. To this day, the Spanish order's inn still feels like a slice of Spain, the German order's inn resembles a German fort, and so on. While the Italian remodel in the early 20th century made the whole lane  more uniform, this is still the best place in town to time-travel to the Middle Ages.

▲**Archaeological Museum of Rhodes**—Housed in the sprawling former hospital of the Knights of St. John, this collection includes sculptures, vases and other pottery, tombstones, floor mosaics, and other artifacts. Upstairs are a pair of impressive statues  of Aphrodite. One small statue shows the goddess looking up, caught in a moment of vulnerable beauty as she washes her hair. Nicknamed the "Rhodes Venus," this is actually a replica of the third-century-B.C. original. Nearby is the life-size *Aphrodite Anadyomene* (literally "rising from the sea," c. 4th century B.C.). The sprawling complex of courtyards and gardens rivals the collection itself. One part of the building was used as a Turkish residence and retains many features of Ottoman dwellings of the era, such as the trademark long sofas for lounging (€6, same hours as the palace, Megalou Alexandrou Square, tel. 22410-75674, www.culture.gr).

Other Museums—Various other museums are scattered around the Old Town. The **Decorative Arts Collection,** near the Archaeological Museum, exhibits historical furnishings gathered from homes around the island (€2, closed Mon, Argyrokastrou square, tel. 22410-25500). Also nearby, the **Byzantine Museum** fills an old cathedral interior with frescoes, icons, and other ecclesiastical art (closed Mon). The **Epigraphical Collection,** sprawling through a different hospital complex, examines the development of inscriptions and writing (closed Mon). The **Municipal Gallery** collects 20th-century Greek artwork (€3, closed Sun-Mon, 2 Symis Square, tel. 22410-23766, www.mgamuseum.gr).

Wander the Back Streets—The southern half of the Old Town, while still hemmed in by the walls and within a literal stone's throw of the touristy bazaars, is a remarkably lived-in zone of Greek homes. While you'll find a few tavernas and hotels tucked in this area, workaday Rhodians definitely outnumber tourists here. Perhaps nowhere in Greece can such a short stroll away from the tourist zone reap such great rewards, immersing you immediately in a completely different world than the one you'll find in the main streets. Go for a stroll, peek down lanes and into family living rooms, and be generous with offering a cheery, *"Kali mera!"* (Good morning!).

▲Lindos Acropolis, South of Rhodes Town

The most popular side-trip from Rhodes is the ruined acropolis over the town of Lindos (Λίνδος, LEEN-dohs), 30 miles south of Rhodes town (about a 45-minute drive or bus ride). The town of Lindos—a whitewashed village huddled at the base of its acropolis-capped hill, with maze-like lanes crammed full of trinket stalls—is extremely touristy, and can be uncomfortably crowded during peak times. And, while the acropolis itself has its share of ruined columns and panoramic  views of Rhodes' coastline and hills, it doesn't break into the top 10 of best ancient Greek ruins.

From the town below, you can hike steeply up 278 tourist-clogged steps to the top, or you can pay €5 for a donkey to carry you up. At the top of the ramp, you'll pay €6 to enter the site (Sept-May Tue-Sun 8:00-18:40, shorter hours off-season, closed Mon, tel. 22410-75674).

Once at the top, you'll wander the remains of various structures. There was an important harbor beneath this strategic, easy-to-defend pinnacle even before the founding of Rhodes town

(which eventually superseded Lindos as the island's main settlement). The neat row of 20 columns at the bottom of the stairway survives from a stoa (covered walkway). The stairway leads up to the partially rebuilt Temple of Athena Lindia (from the fourth century B.C.). Worshippers did not actually enter this small building, which was reserved for priests; instead, they'd gather for worship and sacrifice at an altar out front. The large granite blocks scattered around the site were bases for statues. Long after the ancient Greeks, Rhodes' rulers modified this hilltop for their own purposes: Also at the site (near the base of the stairway), you'll see a Byzantine church and a fortress erected in the Middle Ages by

the Knights of St. John. As you pet an attention-starved kitten, survey the view of the town of Lindos, the surrounding bays and beaches, and the glimmering Aegean. The entirely enclosed bay with the little chapel is the Port of St. Paul, named for the apostle who came here as a missionary in A.D. 54.

Getting There: KTEL runs public buses between the Mandraki (MANΔPAKI) stop near the Rhodes TI and Lindos (hourly, 45 minutes, €4.60, tel. 22410-27706). A taxi from the cruise terminal in Rhodes costs about €50-60 one-way, or €115 round-trip including waiting time at the site.

TURKEY
Türkiye

TURKEY

Türkiye

Exotic, vibrant Turkey stands at the crossroads of continents. For thousands of years, the fortunes of the greatest empires of East and West have played out on this fertile peninsula. You'll walk in the footsteps of Roman emperors and Ottoman sultans as you explore some of the world's grandest monuments, their names etched in history: Hagia Sophia, Topkapı, Ephesus.

Today much of Turkey is scrambling into the modern Western world. The empires of the past have given way to a proud democracy with a secular government and a predominantly Muslim population. But the traditional way of life is richly dyed and woven into the land like a Turkish carpet. In the cities, you'll see women on hands and knees washing rugs in the streets, and in the villages, cars share the road with donkey carts.

Turkish culture is a feast for all the senses: Hear the wailing call to prayer echoing over rooftops as merchants invite you in for a look and a cup of tea. Inhale the apple-flavored smoke from a water pipe as you listen to the strains of exotic music. And enjoy meeting some of the planet's friendliest people, whether you're haggling for a carpet, learning about Islam from a peace-loving Muslim, or playing backgammon with a grizzled old Turk.

The main cruise destination in Turkey is Istanbul. As your cruise ship approaches, you'll be gradually swallowed up by this historic city prickly with minarets and studded with world-class monuments. Disembarking at the legendary Golden Horn, you're an easy walk or speedy tram ride from most of the city's top sights.

Another popular cruise-ship stop is Kuşadası, a straightforward port city offering ample carpet shops and—more importantly—access to the remarkable archaeological site at Ephesus, once one of the finest cities of the Roman world, and today one of the best ancient ruins anywhere.

Turkish Do's and Don'ts

Turkey gives Western visitors a refreshing dose of culture shock. Here are a few of the finer points to consider when interacting with your Turkish hosts:

- Don't signal to someone with your hands or your fingers, except when you're hailing a cab or trying to get your waiter's attention. In any other situation, it's considered rude.
- Don't get too close to people as you talk. Allow for plenty of personal space (an arm's length is fine). Especially when talking to someone of the opposite sex, keep your distance and don't touch them as you talk.
- Be careful with gestures: A "thumbs up" is—and means—OK. But putting your thumb between your index and middle finger and making a fist is equivalent to showing your middle finger in the US. (And you always thought Grandma was "stealing your nose.") Making a circle with your thumb and index finger while twisting your hand is a homophobic insult.
- Be aware of Turkish body language for "yes" and "no." A Turk nods her head down to say yes. She shakes it back and forth to say no, like Americans do. But she might also say no by tilting her head back. Learn the Turkish words for "yes" (evet; eh-veht) and "no" (hayır; hah-yur) to confirm.

Practicalities

This section covers just the basics on traveling in Turkey.

Tourist Information: www.tourismturkey.org

Money: Turkey uses its traditional currency, the lira: 1 Turkish lira (TL) = about $0.70. One lira is broken down into 100 *kuruş*. Prices are sometimes also listed in dollars or euros, especially in tourist areas.

Theft Alert: In Turkey, travelers are often pickpocketed. Thieves thrive on fresh-off-the-boat tourists, so leave behind any expensive-looking gear or fancy jewelry. Be careful on all public transportation and in crowds. Watch for distraction tactics such as dropped coins, "accidental" spills, kids who seem to be fighting for no reason, and locals who ask you for directions. Wear a money belt, sling your daypack across your front, and keep change in buttoned or front pockets.

Business Hours: Most shops are open daily 9:00-19:00; on Sundays, they open a little later.

Shopping Tip: If shopping for a Turkish souvenir at a touristy marketplace (such as Istanbul's famous Grand Bazaar, or a carpet shop in Kuşadası), be aware that the first price you're quoted is wildly inflated. Bargaining to reach a mutually agreed-upon price is expected. For more tips, see page 1180.

Internet Access: Internet cafés are easy to find in Istanbul (especially in the New District) and in Kuşadası.

Sights: On holidays, most museums and shops in Istanbul's tourist areas are open. Istanbul's Grand Bazaar is closed on Sundays.

Dress Code: As a sign of respect in mosques, cover your shoulders and knees; women should also wear head scarves (these are available at the door, but it can be more sanitary to bring your own).

Eating

Turkey's multiethnic cuisine reflects the rich cultural interaction of its ancestry: Turkish, Arab, Persian, and Greek. You'll find many similar foods in the countries that neighbor Turkey.

Restaurants in Turkey generally have a single menu and price list for both lunch and dinner. For the most part, once a restaurant is open, it serves meals nonstop until closing time.

"Self-servis" restaurants function like cafeterias. These are some of the best-value and most atmospheric places to eat. As you move through the line, point to what you'd like. Prices are set for full portions. If you ask for smaller portions, you'll pay the full price per item. If you're with a companion and want to sample several items, it's cheapest and simplest if you both order full portions at the counter and then split your order later when you sit down at your table.

For the traditional Turkish meat dish, look for a kebab restaurant *(kebab lokantası* or *kebabçı)*.  The meat is traditionally veal or a mix of lamb and veal, but more recently chicken *(tavuk)* and even fish have become popular. Kebabs have different names based on how they're cooked. A *şiş kebab* is any type of meat grilled on a skewer. A *döner kebab* is grilled, thinly sliced meat wrapped in pita or sandwich bread.

Seafood restaurants *(balık lokantası* or *balıkçı)* often offer a variety of small plates *(mezes)* and salads.

Dolma refers to stuffed vegetables such as bell peppers, tomatoes, eggplants, zucchinis, or grape leaves. *Börek* is a savory pastry made of phyllo dough. *Pide,* a Turkish-style pita bread, is topped with vegetables and cheese. Take a thin, flat *pide,* top it with meat, onions, and parsley, and you have *lahmacun.*

Cheap and filling, Turkish street food is easy to find. Common fare includes kebabs, sandwiches, *simit* (like sesame-covered bagels), and mussels *(midye tava)*. For a cheap picnic, buy a crunchy, freshly baked *simit*, and top it with tomatoes, cucumbers, and some *beyaz peynir*—white cheese made from cow's or sheep's milk—from a grocery.

Water: Do not drink tap water in Turkey. Bottled water is safe, cheap, and plentiful.

Tipping: If you order your food at a counter, don't tip, though it's nice to leave a lira or two on the table for the busser. At cafés and restaurants with table service, tip 10 percent.

Phoning

To make calls from public phones, use an insertable phone card (TT Smart Cards or Smart Telefon Kartı) or an international phone card (TT Kart). Buy them at post offices, Türk Telekom shops, most newsstands, and at food kiosks near phone booths. For tips on using these kinds of cards, see page 120.

Dialing: Turkish phone numbers have seven digits, preceded by a four-digit area code. Within an area code, just dial the local number; otherwise dial both the area code (which starts with a 0) and the local number. To **call to Turkey,** dial the international access code (00 from Europe, 011 from North America), then 90 (Turkey's country code), then the area code (without the initial 0) and local number. To **call home from Turkey,** dial 00, 1, then your area code and phone number.

Directory Assistance: Tel. 11811 (Turkish-language only); collect calls to the US: tel. 0800-314-0115 (Turkish-language only)

Emergency Telephone Numbers:

Police: Tel. 155

Emergency Medical Assistance: Tel. 112

Med-line Ambulance: Tel. 0212/444-1212

Passport Problems: US Consulate in Istanbul (24-hour emergency assistance tel. 0212/335-9000); Canadian Consulate in Istanbul (tel. 0212/251-9838).

ISTANBUL

Istanbul is the crossroads of civilizations, where Europe meets Asia, and where West meets East. Truly one of the world's great historic cities, Istanbul was once called Constantinople, named for the fourth-century Roman Emperor Constantine the Great. Over the centuries, the city has been the capital of two grand empires. The Byzantine Empire was born here in the fourth century A.D. and lasted until the 15th century, when the Ottoman Empire took over, ruling through the end of World War I. Even though Turkey isn't actually governed from Istanbul (Ankara, in the east, is the official capital), the city remains the historical, cultural, and financial center of the country.

Planning Your Time

This chapter focuses on the compact Sultanahmet district, in the center of the Old Town. From this area, Istanbul's top sights are all within walking distance. Read the list below and choose what appeals. If you'd like to do it all (and have about 10 hours), here's a good order to follow:

• The self-guided **Golden Horn Walk** begins near the cruise terminal (and takes 30-45 minutes); if you'd rather get to the major sights a.s.a.p., skip the walk and ride the tram to Sultanahmet.

• The self-guided **Historic Core of Istanbul Walk** takes you through Sultanahmet. Allow up to two hours, which includes visits to the Underground Cistern and Blue Mosque.

• The **Hagia Sophia** is a famous domed church-turned-mosque-turned-museum. Allow up to 1.5 hours for the self-guided tour.

Excursions from Istanbul

Most excursions offered in Istanbul are in the city itself. If you'd prefer to get out of town, consider a mini-cruise on the city's primary waterway. The 19-mile-long **Bosphorus Strait** curves like a snake as it connects the Black Sea in the north with the Sea of Marmara and—eventually—the Mediterranean in the south. Today Istanbul extends pretty much all the way up to the Black Sea, but a few neighborhoods in the north retain a village-like quality, where the men still fish for a living. A boat trip along the waterway (see page 1102) is the best way to appreciate the size and scale of Istanbul, but it's no substitute for experiencing the city itself.

• **Topkapı Palace,** where the sultans lived, is a huge complex. Allow up to two hours, or skip it if time is tight.

• The sprawling **Grand Bazaar** is a delightful place to wander, shop, and haggle. The Spice Market, a 15-minute walk away, is smaller and also fun. Take the self-guided Grand Bazaar and Spice Market Walk, allowing at least three hours (or more if you love to shop). Don't miss my shopping tips on page 1178.

If you end your day at the Spice Market, you're just an easy walk (or tram ride) across the Galata Bridge from where you started, near the cruise terminals.

Arrival at the Port of Istanbul

Arrival at a Glance: If you're in a hurry to get to the big sights in Sultanahmet, take a taxi (15-20 TL, or about $10-13) or tram (walk 5-10 minutes to the nearest tram stop, then ride straight into downtown). If you'd like to stretch your legs and get the lay of the land, consider walking five minutes to the Galata Bridge to do this chapter's self-guided Golden Horn Walk; after that, you can either walk or take a tram onward to Sultanahmet.

Port Overview

Istanbul is one of the most exciting cities to arrive in by cruise ship, with the minarets and palace towers of the old Ottoman capital growing ever taller as you approach. Ships dock right in the heart of town, near the mouth of the inlet called the Golden Horn, an easy walk or fast tram ride from most of the city's major sights.

The cruise port has a single, very long embankment served by two terminals. The majority of cruises send their passengers through the **Karaköy Terminal,** at the southwest end of the embankment, near the Galata Bridge. Some cruises disembark at the **Salıpazarı Terminal,** at the northeast end of the embankment (next to the Modern Arts Museum).

While both terminal buildings are humble and lack major services (the Karaköy terminal's TI is rarely open), the streets nearby have shops, cafés, and other resources, though no Internet cafés.

ATMs: If you're just arriving in Turkey and need local currency (Turkish lira, TL), head first to an ATM: From **Karaköy Terminal,** you'll find one directly in front of the terminal building, at the Garanti Bank; there's another down the street to the left, at DenizBank, and a cluster of four ATMs next to the Galata Bridge. Near **Salıpazarı Terminal,** just on the left as you exit the terminal, at the corner with the main road, is a small, freestanding VakifBank kiosk with an ATM; the TEB bank across the street also has a cash machine.

Getting to Sultanahmet

Most visitors head directly to the center of the Old Town, Sultanahmet, where the city's top landmarks and sights are concentrated—including Hagia Sophia, Topkapı Palace, and the Blue Mosque. The Grand Bazaar is nearby.

By Taxi

Taxi prices are particularly slippery in Istanbul. For tips on taking taxis in Istanbul—and getting a fair fare—see page 1099.

From **Karaköy Terminal,** the fair metered rate to the heart of the Sultanahmet sightseeing zone is about 15 TL (though some cabbies try to charge double or more). Taxis wait in front of the terminal, but if you walk just one or two blocks and find one on the street, you're less likely to be overcharged.

From **Salıpazarı Terminal,** the ride to Sultanahmet should cost about 20 TL. If taxis aren't waiting out front when your ship arrives, just start walking down the street (to the left) and flag one down; taxis also wait near the little park across the street from the mosque and fountain, about 10 minutes' walk from the terminal.

By Foot

From Karaköy Terminal

It takes just five minutes to walk from this terminal to the Galata Bridge: Exit the terminal, turn left, and walk about a block to the small park. Bear left diagonally through the middle of the park and walk along the waterfront (with the water on your left) past two blocks of restaurant and café terraces, and past the fishermen casting into the Horn. This chapter's self-guided "Golden Horn Walk" begins from the small square just next to the bridge. It takes you across the bridge, then left along the embankment to Sirkeci train station. From there, you can catch a tram or keep on hiking up to Sultanahmet (a fascinating 30-minute walk all the way from the cruise terminal to Sultanahmet).

From Salıpazarı Terminal

It's a dull 20-minute walk—mostly through industrial warehouse areas—from this terminal to the Galata Bridge: Exit the terminal and turn left onto the busy street called Meclis-i Mebusan Caddesi, and walk toward the big mosque. Keep going on this same street past the mosque and the decorative fountain, where the street changes names to Kemeraltı Caddesi. Continue following this street all the way to the Galata Bridge.

By Tram

Istanbul's handy tram is ideal for connecting most major points in town, including both cruise terminals (explained below). For details on riding Istanbul's user-friendly trams, see page 1100.

From Karaköy Terminal

First, walk to the Galata Bridge, following the instructions under "By Foot," previous page. Once at the Galata Bridge, stand with your back to the water, walk straight ahead up the small staircase, and look for the entrance to the pedestrian underpass marked *tramvay* and *İSKELE GİRİŞİ*. Going down these stairs, you'll find yourself in a confusing maze of hallways lined with shops. You're headed to the tram: At the first intersection, turn left, following signs for *tramvay (tram)*. Before surfacing to street level, you'll need to buy a card for the tram (there may be an automated machine upstairs at the platform itself). Once you buy your card, go up the stairs marked *tramvay*; you'll emerge in the middle of the bridge. Cross the tracks (looking carefully both ways) to the platform for trams headed toward Zeytinburnu (not toward Kabataş). Hop on the tram and ride it four stops to Sultanahmet, or—if you want to go straight to the Grand Bazaar—five stops to Çemberlitaş.

From Salıpazarı Terminal

It's about a 10-minute walk from the terminal to the nearest tram stop (called Tophane): Exit the terminal to the left, and walk along the busy street, past the mosque and the decorative fountain. Just after the fountain, use the crosswalk to reach the tram tracks in the middle of the busy street. Cross both sets of tracks to reach the far platform, for trams headed toward Zeytinburnu (not toward Kabataş). There's likely an automated machine for buying a transit card at the platform; if not—or if you need to break big bills to use

Istanbul Essentials

English	Turkish	Pronounced
Blue Mosque	*Sultanahmet Camii*	sool-tah-nah-meht jah-mee
Bosphorus Strait	*Boğaziçi*	boh-ahz-ee-chee
Burned Column (and major tram stop)	*Çemberlitaş*	chehm-behr-lee-tahsh
Divan Yolu (main street in Old Town)	*Divan Yolu*	dee-vahn yoh-loo
Galata Bridge	*Galata Köprüsü*	gah-lah-tah kohp-rew-sew
Galata Tower	*Galata Kulesi*	gah-lah-tah koo-leh-see
Golden Horn (inlet between Old Town and New District)	*Haliç*	hah-leech
Grand Bazaar	*Kapalı Çarşı*	kah-pah-luh chahr-shuh
Gülhane Park	*Gülhane Parkı*	gewl-hah-neh pahr-kuh
Hagia Sophia (church-and-mosque museum)	*Aya Sofya*	eye-ah soh-fee-yah
Hippodrome (ancient chariot racetrack)	*Hipodrom*	hee-poh-drohm
Historic Core of the Old Town	*Sultanahmet*	sool-tah-nah-meht

ISTANBUL

in the machines—go to a nearby shop or kiosk (you can cross the street to the small park, which is surrounded by shops).

By Tour

For information on local tour options in Istanbul—including hop-on, hop-off bus tours, Bosphorus cruises, and local guides for hire—see "Tours in Istanbul" on page 1102.

Returning to Your Ship

If you're coming on the tram to Karaköy Terminal, disembark at Karaköy and go down the stairs marked *TRAMVAY GİRİŞİ*. At the bottom of the stairs, turn right, then follow signs for *Karaköy İskelesi*. You'll pop out near the waterfront, and turn left to walk to the cruise terminal.

If you're heading for Salıpazarı Terminal, get off the tram at Tophane and walk 10 minutes from there (continue along the busy street in the direction the tram was going, and look for the terminal on your right, a few blocks after the mosque).

İstiklal Street (main street in New District)	İstiklal Caddesi	ees-teek-lahl jahd-deh-see
Mosque of Süleyman the Magnificent	Süleymaniye Camii	sew-lay-mah-nee-yeh jah-mee
New District	Pera, Beyoğlu	peh-rah, bay-yoh-loo
Rüstem Paşa Mosque	Rüstem Paşa Camii	rew-stehm pah-shah jah-mee
Sirkeci Train Station	Sirkeci Tren Garı	seer-keh-jee trehn gah-ruh
Spice Market	Mısır Çarşısı	muh-suhr chahr-shuh-shuh
Süleymaniye Neighborhood	Süleymaniye	sew-lay-mah-nee-yeh
Taksim Square (heart of New District)	Taksim Meydanı	tahk-seem may-dah-nuh
Topkapı Palace	Topkapı Sarayı	tohp-kah-puh sah-rah-yuh
Tünel (old-fashioned funicular in New District)	Tünel	tew-nehl
Underground Cistern	Yerebatan Sarayı	yeh-reh-bah-tahn sah-rah-yuh

ISTANBUL

Orientation to Istanbul

Istanbul: A Verbal Map

Istanbul, with almost 15 million people, sprawls over an enormous area on both banks of the **Bosphorus Strait** (Boğaziçi).

The Bosphorus runs north to south (from the Black Sea to the Sea of Marmara) through the middle of Istanbul, splitting the city in half and causing it to straddle two continents: Asia and Europe. Asian Istanbul (east of the Bosphorus) is mostly residential, while European Istanbul (west of the Bosphorus) is densely urban, containing all of the city's main attractions. Two suspension bridges—the Bosphorus Bridge and the Fatih Sultan Mehmet Bridge—span the Bosphorus Strait, connecting the two halves. Public ferries

ISTANBUL

Daily Reminder

Open Every Day: The Underground Cistern, Bosphorus cruise boats, Galata Tower, and most Turkish baths welcome tourists daily. Mosques are open daily, but close to tourists five times each day, when worshippers come to pray. For tips on visiting a mosque, see page 1098.

Sunday: The Grand Bazaar is closed.

Monday: Most of Istanbul's museums are closed today, including those operated by the Ministry of Culture—such as Hagia Sophia, the Istanbul Archaeological Museum, and the Turkish and Islamic Arts Museum. Dolmabahçe Palace, Istanbul Modern Arts Museum, and Pera Museum are also closed. Topkapı Palace is open (and crowded).

Tuesday: Topkapı Palace is closed, making Hagia Sophia very busy today.

Wednesday: Because Topkapı Palace is closed on Tuesday, it may be especially crowded first thing this morning.

Thursday: All sights are open except Dolmabahçe Palace. The Istanbul Modern Arts Museum is free today.

Friday: For Muslims, the Friday noon service is the week's most important. All mosques are closed as usual for the service, and very crowded before and after.

Saturday: Everything is open except the Quincentennial Museum of Turkish Jews.

Ramadan: During the Muslim holy month (Aug 1-29 in 2011, July 20-Aug 18 in 2012), a big, convivial, multi-generational festival breaks out each evening at sunset.

Religious Holidays: The Grand Bazaar and the Spice Market are closed on the first day of religious festivals (and often stay closed for the entire holiday). Museum hours are also readjusted for the first day of religious holidays: Most museums close in the morning, though a few close the entire day.

also link the banks, carrying millions of commuters each day.

A tapering inlet of the Bosphorus, called the **Golden Horn** (Haliç), runs roughly east to west, slicing through the middle of European Istanbul.

South of the Golden Horn is a peninsula known as the **Old Town**—the 3,000-year-old historical core of the city, surrounded by fragments of the original Byzantine wall. Near the tip of the Old Town peninsula is a compact and welcoming district called Sultanahmet, home to many of the city's most famous sights (Hagia Sophia, Blue Mosque, Topkapı Palace).

North of the Golden Horn is the modern, westward-looking, European-feeling **New District** (called "Pera" or "Beyoğlu" by locals), centered on Taksim Square and bisected by the main pedestrian drag called İstiklal Caddesi (a.k.a. İstiklal Street). The New District offers some interesting sights, good restaurants, and a 21st-century contrast to the Old Town.

Unlike many Western cities, Istanbul doesn't branch out from a main Town Hall or central square. In many parts of town, you may get lost if you're searching for a predictable, European-style square. (The Turkish word for "square"—*meydanı*—actually means something more like "area.") Instead, Istanbul is a cobbled-together collection of various landmarks and patches of land, all interconnected by twisty alleys. Sightseeing this decentralized, seemingly disorganized city can be intimidating for first-time visitors. But even though the city is an enormous metropolis, the tourist's Istanbul is compact and walkable, and an impressive public-transportation network efficiently connects the major sight-seeing zones (see "Getting Around Istanbul," page 1099).

For a full-color map of Istanbul, see the front of this book.

Tourist Information

Istanbul's state-run tourist offices, marked with an *i* sign in Istanbul, aren't particularly good sources of information. They suffer from long lines, offer little or no information, and usually have only colorful promotional booklets, brochures, and maps. The only reason to visit one is to pick up the good, free city map. The TI staff, many of whom are not fluent in English, will try to help you with your requests, but most likely with mixed results.

If you must visit a tourist office, try one of the locations listed below. (You may find a TI in the Karaköy cruise terminal, but it's rarely open.) The first two are in the Old Town and the last is at the airport (all have sporadic hours; generally daily 9:00-17:00):

• In the **Sultanahmet** neighborhood, in the center of the Old Town (Divan Yolu 3, at the bottom of the square called the Hippodrome, next to the tram tracks, tel. 0212/518-8754).

• At the **Sirkeci** train station, near the Golden Horn in the Old Town's Eminönü district (TI located by station entrance, in the left corner next to a ticket booth, tel. 0212/511-5888).

• At **Atatürk Airport**, Istanbul's main airport, nine miles outside the city center (at the International Arrivals desk inside the terminal, tel. 0212/465-3151).

Helpful Hints

Pharmacies: Pharmacies (*eczane;* edge-zah-neh) are generally open daily except Sunday (Mon-Sat 9:00-19:00). In every neighborhood, one pharmacy stays open late and on holidays for emergencies. These *nöbetçi eczane* (noh-bet-chee edge-zah-neh; "pharmacy on duty") are generally within walking distance or a 5- to 10-minute cab ride from wherever you are. The location of the nearest *nöbetçi eczane* is posted by the entrance to any pharmacy. When interpreting signs, note these translations: *bu gece* (tonight), *Pazar* (Sunday), and *gün/günü* (day). As in the rest of Europe, dates are listed day first, then month (e.g., 06/04 is April 6).

Street Safety: Be extremely cautious crossing streets that lack traffic lights. Look both ways, since many streets are one-way, and be careful of seemingly quiet bus, tram, or taxi lanes. Don't assume you have the right-of-way, even in a crosswalk. When crossing a street, keep your pace constant and don't stop suddenly. Drivers calculate your speed and won't hit you, provided you don't alter your route and pace. (Don't expect them to stop for you; they probably won't.)

Although it's technically illegal, cars park on sidewalks, especially in the Old Town. These parked cars, as well as free-standing merchandise kiosks and makeshift stands, can make sidewalks difficult to navigate. Try to stay by the side of the road, and pay attention to passing cars.

Public WCs: You'll generally pay 0.50 TL or less to use a public WC. Carry toilet paper or tissues with you, since some WCs are poorly supplied. Use the WCs in museums (likely free and better than public WCs), or walk into any sidewalk café or American fast-food joint as if you own the place and find the WC in the back.

In Turkey, plumbing isn't always up to modern standards. Rather than flush away soiled toilet paper, locals dispose of it in a designated trash can next to the toilet. It's culturally sensitive for visitors to do the same (especially if there's a sign requesting this).

Western-style toilets are the norm nowadays, but don't be surprised if you run across an "Oriental toilet," also known as a "Turkish toilet." This squat-and-aim system is basically a porcelain hole in the ground flanked by platforms for your feet.

Water: Remember, don't drink the tap water in Turkey. Bottled drinks and water served at better restaurants is fine.

Visiting a Mosque

At the Mosque: Touring some of Istanbul's many mosques (*camii* in Turkish; pronounced jah-mee) offers Westerners an essential opportunity to better understand the Muslim faith. But, just as touring a church in Christian Europe comes with a certain protocol, the following guidelines should be observed when visiting a mosque: Both men and women should have their shoes off, and knees and shoulders covered. At some major mosques (such as the Blue Mosque), you can borrow a sheet the mosque loans out for this purpose. Women should also cover their head with a scarf, as a sign of respect. Stay behind the cordoned-off area at the front of the mosque, which is reserved for worshippers. Be discreet when taking photos, and never photograph worshippers without first asking their permission.

When to Go: Specific "opening times" can vary greatly, but figure that most mosques are open to visitors from one hour after sunrise until about an hour before sunset, except during five daily services. The closure lasts from about 30 minutes before the service begins until after it ends (services last 15-30 minutes). If you are already inside when a service begins, you may be asked to leave so as not to disturb the congregation. If you're visiting a mosque on Friday, avoid the midday service, which is more heavily attended than others, and longer, because it includes a sermon.

Getting Around Istanbul

Even though Istanbul is a huge city, most of its tourist areas are easily walkable. You'll likely need public transportation only to connect sightseeing zones (for example, going from the Old Town to the New District across the Golden Horn). Fortunately, Istanbul has an impressively slick, modern, and user-friendly network of trams, funiculars, and Metro lines. Once you learn the system, it seems custom-made for tourists—the stops are located within a short walking distance of major attractions. Taxis and ferries round out your transportation options. (The city also has a bus system, but it's designed for commuters and useful only for reaching outlying areas not covered by tram—if you're headed anywhere off the city's tram line, it's worth the time savings to take a taxi instead of the bus.)

By Taxi

Taxis are an efficient, affordable way to get around town (2.50 TL drop fee, then roughly 1.60 TL/kilometer; no nighttime tariff). Figure about 5-10 TL for a short trip within the Old Town or New District.

All taxis are painted yellow, with their license plate number, name, and home office phone number displayed on the front doors. All have electronic meters, and the only way you can be cheated is if the driver takes a needlessly long route or claims you have to pay bogus "extra charges." (For example, if your cabbie claims that you owe him a 5-TL "nighttime charge" for a 15-TL

Paying for Public Transportation

Istanbul's public transportation is fairly easy to use, with one caveat: The payment system is constantly being tinkered with, so the following information may change by the time you visit. For the latest, check www.ricksteves.com/update.

A basic **single-ride card**—the simplest way to go—costs 1.75 TL per ride. (While the city hopes to begin charging 2.50 TL per ride, this plan has been so unpopular that it's unlikely to take effect before your visit.) **Multiple-ride** cards, which give you a cheaper per-ride rate, are also available (5 rides-12 TL). Cards are sold at major stops and most minor ones. These electronic cards, in theory, cover all forms of public transit. Be aware that the card system is new to Istanbul: When you visit, you may find that some forms of transit have switched to electronic cards, while others still use a plastic token (*jeton;* zheh-tohn). It's a good idea to have a transit card with you in case you find yourself at a stop without a card-vending machine. Whether you have a card or a token, to use it, simply insert it into the turnstile as you enter.

ride, politely refuse and pay what's on the meter.) Never go for an "off-meter" deal, because you'll always pay more than if you'd used the meter.

If a taxi's top light is on, it's available—just wave it down. Drivers usually flash their lights when they see you waiting by the side of the road to indicate that they will pick you up. Taxis can take up to four passengers. If you have difficulty hailing a cab off the street, ask someone where you can find a taxi stand. You can also call a taxi company, usually for no extra charge. Restaurants, museums, and even shopkeepers almost always have the phone number of a nearby taxi company—just ask.

To tip, simply round up the bill (generally 1-2 TL; for exceptional service, you could add a few liras more). If you need a receipt, ask: *"Fiş, lütfen"* (fish lewt-fehn; receipt, please).

By Tram, Light Rail, Funicular, and Metro

Istanbul's transit is convenient and inexpensive. Tram, light rail, funicular, and Metro lines intersect at central locations, and they all use the same cards and passes (in theory, at least—see sidebar). Transit system maps and timetables are available at www.istanbul ulasim.com.

By Tram: The seemingly made-for-tourists *tramvay* (trahm-vay) cuts a boomerang-shaped swath through the core of Istanbul's Old Town, then crosses the Golden Horn to the New District, where it continues along the Bosphorus. Destinations are posted

on the outside of the tram—
just hop on the one heading in
the direction you want to go.
Key tram stops include the following (from north to south):

• **Kabataş:** End of the
line in the New District, next
to the funicular up to Taksim
Square (described later) and a
few blocks from Dolmabahçe
Palace.

• **Tophane:** Near the Salıpazarı cruise terminal and the
Istanbul Modern Arts Museum.

• **Karaköy:** In the New District (directly across Galata Bridge
from the Old Town), near the Karaköy cruise terminal, the Galata
Tower, and the Tünel train up to İstiklal Street.

• **Eminönü:** On the Golden Horn in the Old Town, near the
Spice Market, Galata Bridge, and additional Bosphorus ferry terminals.

• **Sirkeci:** Sirkeci train station, near the Golden Horn and
several Bosphorus ferry terminals.

• **Gülhane:** At the side entrance to the Topkapı Palace
grounds, near the Istanbul Archaeological Museum.

• **Sultanahmet:** Dead-center in the Old Town, near Hagia
Sophia, the Blue Mosque, the
Hippodrome, and many recom-
mended restaurants.

• **Beyazıt** and **Çemberlitaş:**
Flanking the Grand Bazaar in
the Old Town.

There's also the **Nostalgic
Tram** that runs up and down
İstiklal Street, through the middle of the New District.

By Light Rail: West of the Grand Bazaar in the Old Town (at
the Yusufpaşa stop), the tram connects to a light-rail system that's
of little use to visitors, except that it's very handy for reaching the
airport (see page 1191).

By Funicular: An easy one-stop, two-minute underground
finiküler connects Taksim Square (and İstiklal Street) in the New
District with the Kabataş tram stop along the Bosphorus below.
At Kabataş, the tram and funicular stations are side by side; to find
the funicular station from Taksim Square, look for the combined
funicular/Metro entrance at the center of the square, right across
from the Marmara Hotel, and follow *Kabataş-Finiküler* signs.

A second underground funicular, called **Tünel,** connects the
Galata Bridge on the Golden Horn with İstiklal Street on the hill

above. This late-19th-century funicular is as historic as it is convenient. For details, see page 1175.

By Metro: The underground Metro—generally not useful for tourists—begins at Taksim Square and heads north into the business and residential Levent district. To find a Metro entrance, look for the big *M* signs.

By Ferry and Seabus

In this city where millions of people sail across the Bosphorus to work each day, the ferry system had better work well...and it does. In fact, locals much prefer ferries to avoid heavy traffic on the bridges over the Bosphorus, especially during rush hour. Ferries are convenient and inexpensive—just 1.75 TL one-way. (The Bosphorus cruise boats cost more.)

Tours in Istanbul

Hop-on, Hop-off Bus Tours—City Sightseeing's narrated double-decker bus tours enable you to hop off at any stop, tour a sight, and then catch a later bus to your next destination—but departures are so infrequent that this isn't really practical. The tour amounts to a pricey 90-minute ride in heavy traffic with useless multilingual commentary (a recorded voice occasionally interrupts the obnoxious loop of music to identify sights and to cross-promote other tours they run). The Old Town's single tram line will take you to any of these sights without the hassle, for a lot less money. The bus does, however, take you along the entire old city wall (quite impressive and hard to see otherwise, unless you catch a glimpse on your way from the airport), and offers views from the top deck, making it a convenient and scenic place to munch a kebab or picnic. (Thanks to a convertible roof, this still works in rainy or cold weather.) Pick up their brochure from their booth across from Hagia Sophia. The loop starts on the main street across from Hagia Sophia, but you can hop on at nearly any of the major sights along the route. Buses run year-round, with hourly departures in peak season (roughly mid-April-mid-Oct) and departures every two hours off-season (€20, 10 percent discount with this book, tel. 0212/234-7777, www .plantours.com).

▲▲▲Bosphorus Cruise—To get a feel for the famous Bosphorus Strait, consider a boat tour. You'll pass waterfront palaces, mansions, and mosques, and two continent-straddling suspension bridges. Various companies sell 10-TL cruise tickets on either side of the southern (Old Town) end of the Galata Bridge (behind bus stops to the west side, and next to Bosphorus ferry port on the east—look for *Bosphorus Tours* sign). These boats will take you as far as the second bridge (Fatih Sultan Mehmet Bridge) and back in

1.5 hours, with no stops and no narration. There's no set schedule for these private boats (at least, not one that's strictly adhered to). Boats depart as soon as they have enough people. Just buy your ticket and hop on.

The **Turyol** cruise company, on the west side of the bridge, next to the fish-sandwich boats and behind the bus stops, is one of many options (cruises generally run hourly Mon-Fri 12:00-18:00, Sat 12:00-19:00, Sun 11:00-19:30, less frequently mid-Sept-mid-June, tel. 0212/527-9952, ask for Mr. Ihsan or Mr. Şenol).

Local Guides—Lale and Tankut Aran, the co-authors of this chapter, own **SRM Travel,** which runs city tours, offers private guides, and helps develop custom itineraries for trips to Istanbul and the rest of Turkey. Mention this book to receive free travel consulting when you buy any travel service (tel. 0216/386-7623, www.srmtravel.com).

Readers have also had good experiences with the following guides: **Nilüfer İris** (especially good with senior travelers, mobile 0532/244-1395, tel. 0212/347-3854), **Attila Kılınç** (mobile 0532/294-7667, attguide@yahoo.com), **Nilay Çağlı Türkeli** (mobile 0532/720-8679, nilayturkeli@gmail.com), **Kağan Koşağan** of KSG Tours (tel. 0216/343-4215, www.tourguidesinturkey.com), **Dilek Arman** of Backpackers Travel (tel. 0212/638-6343, www.backpackerstravel.net), **Orçun Taran** (mobile 0532-256-9401, www.orcuntaran.com, taranorcun@gmail.com), **Pınar Çağlayan** (mobile 0538-315-5888, guidepinar@hotmail.com), and **Kürşat Taner Ünal** (ktanerunal@yahoo.com).

Bus Tours Beyond Istanbul—If you want to see much more of Turkey without having to figure out the long-distance bus system, consider the **Fez** bus, a hop-on, hop-off bus designed for backpackers (four itineraries ranging from 100 to 500 TL, mention this book for a 10 percent discount, tel. 0212/516-9024, www.feztravel.com).

Self-Guided Walks & Tours in Istanbul

The series of walks described below are designed to help you make the most of one (very busy) day in Istanbul. Each walk picks up more or less where the last one leaves off: The first takes you from the cruise ship terminal, across the Golden Horn to the base of the Old Town. The next takes you through the core of the Old Town, covering the Blue Mosque and other sights near the Hippodrome. Across the street, tour the Byzantine marvel of Hagia Sophia. From here you can head to the Grand Bazaar and follow the walk back to the Spice Market, near the Golden Horn waterfront, a pleasant walk (or short tram or taxi ride) from your ship. To get the most out of your day, keep up your pace and splice in a visit

Istanbul at a Glance

In the sight listings below, a page number directs you to a fuller description in this chapter; sights without page numbers are not described further and generally don't make the cut for a one-day visit.

▲▲▲**Hagia Sophia** Constantinople's Great Church, later converted to an Ottoman mosque, and now a museum. **Hours:** Tue-Sun 9:00-18:30, until 16:30 off-season, closed Mon. See page 1159.

▲▲▲**Blue Mosque** Ahmet I's 17th-century "so there!" response to Hagia Sophia, named for its brightly colored tiles. **Hours:** Generally open daily one hour after sunrise until one hour before sunset, closed to visitors five times a day for prayer. See page 1162.

▲▲▲**Topkapı Palace** Storied residence of the sultans, with endless museum exhibits, astonishing artifacts, and the famous Harem. **Hours:** Palace—late March-late Oct Wed-Mon 9:00-19:00, until 16:45 off-season, closed Tue. Harem—Wed-Mon 10:00-16:00, closed Tue. See page 1163.

▲▲▲**Grand Bazaar** World's oldest shopping mall, with more than 4,000 playfully pushy merchants. **Hours:** Mon-Sat 9:00-19:00, shops begin to close at 18:30, closed Sun and on the first day of most religious festivals. See page 1170.

▲▲▲**Mosque of Süleyman the Magnificent** The architect Sinan's 16th-century masterpiece, known for its serene interior and the tombs of Süleyman and his wife, Roxelana. **Hours:** Mosque—generally open daily one hour after sunrise until one hour before sunset, closed to visitors five times a day for prayer. Mausoleums—daily 9:00-17:00, until 18:00 in summer. See page 1170.

▲▲▲**Bosphorus Cruise** Boat ride on the Bosphorus Strait, offering a glimpse of untouristy Istanbul. **Hours:** Frequent departures all day long. See page 1102.

▲▲▲**İstiklal Street** Cosmopolitan pedestrian-only street in the New District, teeming with shops, eateries, and people. **Hours:** Always open. See page 1173.

▲▲**Underground Cistern** Vast sixth-century subterranean water reservoir built with recycled Roman columns. **Hours:** Daily 9:00-20:00, sometimes closes at 17:30 off-season. See page 1162.

▲▲**Turkish and Islamic Arts Museum** Carpets, calligraphy, ceramics, and other traditional art on display at the former İbrahim Paşa Palace. **Hours:** Tue-Sun 9:00-17:00, closed Mon. See page 1162.

▲▲**Istanbul Archaeological Museum** Complex covering Istanbul's ancient civilizations, including sumptuous tiles and highly decorated sarcophagi. **Hours:** Tue-Sun 9:00-16:45, closed Mon. See page 1169.

▲▲**Spice Market** Fragrant and colorful spices, dried fruit, and roasted nuts inside a 350-year-old market hall. **Hours:** Mon-Sat 8:00-19:30 (until 19:00 off-season), Sun 9:30-19:00. See page 1171.

▲▲**Galata Bridge** Restaurant-lined bridge spanning the Golden Horn, bristling with fishermen's poles and offering sweeping views of the Old Town. **Hours:** Always open. See page 1171.

▲▲**Chora Church** Modest church on the edge of the Old Town with some of the best Byzantine mosaics in captivity. **Hours:** Late March-late Oct Thu-Tue 9:00-19:00, until 17:00 off-season, closed Wed.

▲▲**Galata Tower** 14th-century stone Genoese tower with the city's best views. **Hours:** Daily 9:00-20:00. See page 1175.

▲**Hippodrome** Roman chariot racetrack-turned-square, linking Hagia Sophia and the Blue Mosque. **Hours:** Always open. See page 1162.

▲**Gülhane Park** Former imperial rose garden, now a grassy park. **Hours:** Always open. See page 1169.

▲**Rüstem Paşa Mosque** Small 16th-century mosque of Süleyman's Grand Vizier with extravagant tile decor. **Hours:** Generally open daily one hour after sunrise until one hour before sunset, closed to visitors five times a day for prayer. See page 1171.

▲**Taksim Square** Gateway to the pedestrianized İstiklal Street and heart of Istanbul's New District. **Hours:** Always open. See page 1173.

▲**Pera Museum** Compact New District collection of world-class Oriental paintings, Anatolian weights and measures, and Kütahya tiles. **Hours:** Tue-Sat 10:00-19:00, Sun 12:00-18:00, closed Mon. See page 1174.

ISTANBUL

to Topkapı Palace (immediately behind Hagia Sophia, described under "Sights in Istanbul").

Golden Horn Walk

From the Galata Bridge to Sirkeci Train Station

The famous Golden Horn—a strategic inlet branching off the Bosphorus Strait—defines Istanbul's Old Town peninsula. The city's fate has always been tied to this stretch of sea: The Golden Horn is Istanbul's highway, food source, and historic harbor all rolled into one. While much of the Old Town zone feels dedicated to tourists these days, a visit to the Golden Horn has you rubbing elbows with fishermen and commuters.

This walk offers a handy orientation to the city, since it affords a sweeping panorama of the Old Town peninsula. The walk is short (about a third of a mile), but allow around 45 minutes if you like to linger.

Getting to the Galata Bridge: The walk begins on the New District (north) end of the Galata Bridge, across the bridge from the Old Town. For instructions on getting here from your cruise ship, see page 1092.

The Walk Begins

• *Start at the Galata Bridge (at the east side of the north end—see map on facing page). If you wind up on the wrong side of the bridge, take the pedestrian underpass (with a WC) connecting the two sides. Position yourself on the riverbank, noticing the tulip shapes decorating the railing. With the water at your back, you're facing the neighborhood called...*

Karaköy

The New District covers the area from Karaköy to Taksim Square, a few blocks up the hill. In Byzantine times, this area was inhab-ited by the commercial colonies of Genoese and Venetian settlers. In the late Ottoman era, it was also a residential area for non-Muslims, including Jews, Catholics, and Eastern Orthodox Christians. Today, this part of the city is dominated by the famous Galata Tower (you can just see its cone-shaped top up the hill).

Karaköy is also Istanbul's main passenger port. As you turn and face the Old Town across the Golden Horn, you'll see public ferry and seabus docks along the embankment to your left. The port

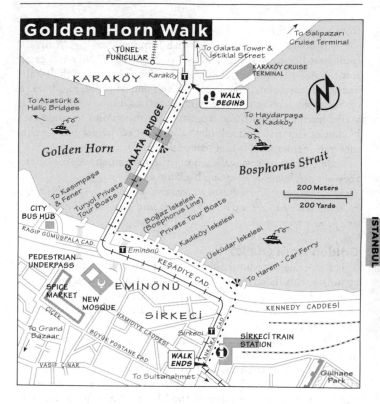

Golden Horn Walk

To Salıpazarı Cruise Terminal

TÜNEL FUNICULAR

To Galata Tower & İstiklal Street

KARAKÖY CRUISE TERMINAL

KARAKÖY — Karaköy

WALK BEGINS

To Atatürk & Haliç Bridges

To Haydarpaşa & Kadıköy

Golden Horn

GALATA BRIDGE

Bosphorus Strait

To Kasımpaşa & Fener

Turyol Private Tour Boats

200 Meters

200 Yards

CITY BUS HUB

RAGIP GÜMÜŞPALA CAD.

Boğaz İskelesi (Bosphorus Line)
Private Tour Boats

Kadıköy İskelesi

Üsküdar İskelesi

PEDESTRIAN UNDERPASS

Eminönü

REŞADİYE CAD.

To Harem - Car Ferry

SPICE MARKET

NEW MOSQUE

EMİNÖNÜ

SİRKECİ

KENNEDY CADDESİ

To Grand Bazaar

ÇİÇEK

HAMİDİYE CADDESİ

BÜYÜK POSTANE CAD.

Sirkeci — Sirkeci

ANKARA CAD.

SİRKECİ TRAIN STATION

VASIF ÇINAR

WALK ENDS

To Sultanahmet

Gülhane Park

ISTANBUL

is the scene of an extensive rebuilding project, as run-down buildings make way for art galleries and convention centers. A deluxe hotel is also planned. Locals grumble about political connections that made the project possible, but it's too late to go back now.

• *Notice that the bridge has two levels. We'll start by walking across the top level, then duck down to the lower level. Climb the stairs and wander across the bridge—dodging fishing poles as you walk.*

Fishermen

Enjoy the chorus line of fishing rods, dancing their little jig. While some of these intrepid folks are fishing for fun, others are

trying to land a little extra income. They catch mostly mackerel or anchovies—better than nothing, especially during the commercial fishing ban (no nets or sonar) that's in effect from June to September. During the ban, most of what you find in the market is either the expensive daily catch, imported frozen fish, or farm-raised fish.

Approach a fisherman and wish him well, saying *"Rastgele"* (pull your lips to your ears and say "rust-geh-leh"; "May you catch some"). Ask to see his catch of the day: *Bakabilir miyim?* (bah-kah-bee-leer mee-yeem; "May I see?"). Each one has a jar, jug, bucket, or Styrofoam cooler full of wriggling fish he'd love to show off. If you're having fun with the language, try this: Point to someone's bucket of tiny fish and ask playfully, *"Yem mi, yemek mi?"* (yehm mee yeh-mehk mee; "Is that bait or dinner?").

Be careful as you walk among the fishermen—occasionally they get careless as they swing back for a cast.

• *The part of the bridge between its two low-profile towers can be raised to let big ships pass. This is a good place to find a spot out of harm's way and ponder the famous...*

Golden Horn (Haliç)

This four-mile-long horn-shaped inlet glitters like precious metal at sunset. But its strategic value is also worth its weight in gold. Protected from the prevailing north winds, the Golden Horn has served as a natural harbor for centuries—the history of Istanbul is steeped in it.

This was once the main commercial port of Constantinople and a base for the Byzantine fleet. To block enemy fleets sailing into the heart of the city, and to more effectively levy taxes on ships, the Byzantines hung a massive chain across the entrance of the Horn (you can see some of the historic links in the Istanbul Archaeological Museum). The chain was breached only two times, by the Vikings (10th century) and by the Crusaders during the Fourth Crusade (1204).

In 1453, when the young Ottoman sultan Mehmet II set out to capture Constantinople, he knew it was crucial to gain control of the Horn. Rather than break the chain, he decided to bypass it altogether. His troops pulled their fleet of ships out of the waters of the Bosphorus, slid them on greased logs over the hills through what later became the New District, and launched them back into the Horn—all in just one night.

During Europe's Industrial Revolution, the Ottoman Empire was slow to adapt to a fast-changing world. It began the industrial race well after the West, then rushed to catch up, without much careful planning. The Horn became more and more polluted as industrial plants and shipyards were built along its banks.

In the 1980s, a clever Istanbul mayor with light blue eyes used a great gimmick to clean things up: He got people on board by saying his project would make the Horn as blue as his eyes. Factories were closed down and moved outside the city. Rotting buildings along the water with no historic significance were torn down, and empty space was converted into public parks. The area's entire infrastructure was renewed—a process that's ongoing.

• *Now look inland over the tram tracks and up the Golden Horn (with your back to the Bosphorus), to see the...*

Bridges over the Horn

Four bridges over the Golden Horn connect the Old Town to the New District. The first one you see is the low-lying Atatürk

Bridge, on floating platforms. Beyond that is the taller main highway bridge, called Haliç (hah-leech)—also the local name for the Golden Horn.

The old Galata Bridge was the first and, for decades, the only bridge spanning the Horn. It's the one you see in historic postcards from Istanbul. But the huge platforms it was built on blocked water circulation, worsening the Horn's pollution woes. So, in 1994, this historic bridge was replaced with the new Galata Bridge—the one you're standing on. A public outcry of nostalgia eventually compelled city leaders to reassemble the original bridge farther down the Horn (between the Atatürk and Haliç bridges—not visible from here).

• *Now take in the...*

Old Town Panorama

Use this sweeping vista of the Old Town to get your bearings. Straight ahead from the end of the bridge, you can see the main entrance to the famous **Spice Market** (stone-and-brick building with three small domes), which sells souvenirs, caviar, dried fruits, Turkish delight, "Turkish Viagra"...and, oh yeah, spices.

The handsome mosque just to the left of the Spice Market (partly obscured by the bridge tower) is the New Mosque of Mother Sultan, or simply **New Mosque.** Dating from the 17th century, it's one of the last examples of classical-style Ottoman mosques. After that time, mosques were built in an eclectic style, heavily influenced by Western architecture.

Behind the Spice Market, twisty streets lined with market stalls wind their way up the hill toward the famous **Grand Bazaar.** While the Spice Market and Grand Bazaar are increasingly deluged with tourists, this in-between zone sells more housewares and everyday textiles than souvenirs—meaning that it's packed tight with locals looking for a bargain, particularly on Saturdays. Thanks to these crowds—and a steady stream of delivery trucks and carts blocking the streets—it can take a half-hour to walk just these four blocks. This is the "real" Istanbul—gritty and authentic.

Farther to the right, past the open space and near the Golden Horn, you see the **Rüstem Paşa Mosque.** This tiny mosque, with its single dome and lone minaret, is dwarfed by the larger mosques around it. But a visit there offers a peek into a more intimate and cozy mosque, with some of the finest 16th-century Ottoman tiles around.

On the hillside just above the Rüstem Paşa Mosque is the 16th-century **Mosque of Süleyman the Magnificent,** with its handsome dome and four tall minarets. Elaborate and impressive, yet tastefully restrained, this mosque offers an insightful contrast to the over-the-top and more famous Blue Mosque.

To the left of Süleyman's mosque is the single, tall **Beyazıt Tower.** Sometimes referred to as the "fire tower," it marks the location of bustling Beyazıt Square and Istanbul University's main campus (next door to the Grand Bazaar).

Now look to your left. At the end of the Historical Peninsula, you can see the lush gardens marking the grounds of **Topkapı Palace.** Most of what you see from here is the palace's lower gardens, called Gülhane, now a public park. You can also see the tower marking the entrance to the Harem complex.

To the right of the palace (up the hill, above the modern buildings), notice the gorgeous dome and minarets of **Hagia Sophia**— once the greatest church in Byzantium, then a mosque, and today one of Istanbul's best museums. The famous **Blue Mosque,** which faces Hagia Sophia from across Sultanahmet Park, is not quite visible from here.

If you look far to the left, beyond the Topkapı Palace gardens, you can see the Bosphorus Strait and **Asian Istanbul** (the hilltop that bristles with TV towers, like a sea of giant minarets). The Bosphorus Bridge, an impressive suspension bridge, is also visible from here (unless it's really hazy).

• *Continue along the bridge to the second tower. Go inside the tower and take the stairs down...*

Under the Bridge

As you descend the stairs, look up for a fun view of dozens of fishing rods twitching along the railing of the bridge. As you walk down here, watch your head— sometimes an amateur fisherman carelessly lets his weight swing under. And keep an eye out for the flicker of a little silvery fish, thrashing through the air as he's reeled in by a happy predator.

Walk along the bridge (toward the Old Town), enjoying this "restaurant row." Passages lead to the other side of the bridge, which is lined with still more restaurants. As you walk, aggressive waiters will try to lure you into their restaurants. Even if you don't want a full meal, consider picking up a sandwich or having a drink at a café. The last restaurant, with dozens of simple brown tables, sells barbecued fish sandwiches to go—handy to eat as you walk (you'll smell the outdoor barbecue before you see it). If you cross under, you'll find a line of trendy teahouses and bars facing up the Golden Horn—great for backgammon, drinks, and sunsets. At the end of the bridge on the Old Town side, venerable "fish and bread" boats sell cheap fish sandwiches literally off the boat.

• *At the end of the bridge, turn left and continue along the...*

Commuter Ferry Terminals

This embankment bustles with thousands of commuters heading to and from work (during morning and evening rush hours) and shopping chores (especially Saturdays). Peek into the pedestrian underpass beneath the bridge for a taste of the shoulder-to-shoulder commute that many locals endure.

This area is also a hub for intercontinental traffic. Public fer-

ries carry millions of commuters every year between the European and Asian districts of Istanbul. Until the first bridge over the Bosphorus was built in the early 1970s, boats were the only way to cross from Europe to Asia. Locals still prefer the ferries, which are a convenient and cheap way to avoid the gridlock on the bridges.

Just beyond the first terminal (which serves public ferries that run up the Bosphorus) is the dock for **private tour boats** (look for the *Bosphorus Tours* sign). For only 10 TL (hawkers ask more), these boats take you as far as the second bridge on the Bosphorus and back again in 90 minutes (see page 1102).

• *When you spot the Harem ferry, it's time to head inland. For a nice panorama over the Galata Bridge and the New District, you could climb the pedestrian overpass. But for where we're going next, it's better to cross the street at the stoplight in order to stay on the proper side of the tram tracks.*

After you cross the street, you're in the Sirkeci neighborhood, and a few steps from the historic train station of the same name.

Sirkeci Train Station

This is a surprisingly low-profile train station for having once been

the terminal of the much-vaunted Orient Express. An old locomotive decorates the corner of the station, honoring this footnote in history. Pass the locomotive and turn left, finding your way to the station's main entrance (along the modern wall with the white doors, under the sign for *İstanbul Gar*). Once inside the door, a TI and well-signed ticket windows are to your left—and a statue of Atatürk is staring down at you from the head of the tracks.

Wander deeper into the station, past the ticket windows, and go left to find evidence of a more genteel, earlier age. Consider popping into the humble little **Railway Museum,** with its old photos and equipment (free, Tue-Sat 9:00-12:30 and 13:00-17:00, closed Sun-Mon). To the right of the museum is the old passenger waiting room, with wooden benches and stained-glass windows that recall the station's former glory.

The **Orient Express** train line began in the 1880s. You could board a train in Paris and step off into this very station three days later (after passing through Munich, Vienna, Budapest, and Bucharest). Traversing the mysterious East, and headed for the even more mysterious "Orient," passengers were advised to carry a gun. The train service was rerouted to avoid Germany during the Nazi years, and was temporarily disrupted during both World Wars, but otherwise ran until May of 1977. While this is the most famous route, almost any eastbound train from Western Europe could be called an "Orient Express." The train line was immortalized in literature and film—most famously by Agatha Christie, whose *Murder on the Orient Express* takes place on the Simplon Orient Express (Paris' Gare de Lyon station to Milan, Belgrade, Sofia, and Istanbul).

Though the Orient Express is now a private, once-a-year excursion, the Sirkeci station still serves trains bound for Europe, as well as suburban trains (it can get crowded at rush hour). Most of the travelers are urban workers, but you occasionally spot vagabonds or peasants fresh from the countryside, eyes wide as they first set foot in the big city.

• *Your walk is finished. To head up to Sultanahmet, you can take the tram (which departs from directly in front of the station) two stops uphill to the Sultanahmet stop, or follow the tram tracks on foot (10-15 minutes, passing the Grand Portal, described on page 1169).*

Historic Core of Istanbul Walk

Just like Rome, Istanbul's Old Town was built on seven hills. The district called Sultanahmet, on top of the first hill, is the historic core of the city. The Greek city of Byzantium was founded nearby, where Topkapı Palace stands today. Early Greek settlers—weary after their long journey—chose this highly strategic location, which could easily be fortified with walls on all sides. The site gave them control of all three surrounding bodies of water (the Bosphorus Strait, the Golden Horn, and the Sea of Marmara), and was convenient to the Greek colonies on the Black Sea.

Today, Sultanahmet is Istanbul's single best sightseeing zone for visitors, playing host to Istanbul's most important and impressive former church (Hagia Sophia) and mosque (the Blue Mosque), and its most significant Byzantine ruins (the Hippodrome and Underground Cistern).

Orientation

Length of This Walk: Allow about two hours, not including time for visiting Hagia Sophia. To shorten this walk, head straight to the Blue Mosque, then Hagia Sophia (or vice versa, depending on lines).

Getting There: If coming by tram, get off at the Sultanahmet stop, then walk to the park between the Blue Mosque and Hagia Sophia.

Hagia Sophia: 20 TL, Tue-Sun 9:00-18:30, until 16:30 off-season, last entry one hour before closing, closed Mon, Sultanahmet Meydanı, tel. 0212/528-4500.

Underground Cistern: 10 TL, daily 9:00-20:00, sometimes closes at 17:30 off-season, last entry 30 minutes before closing, Yerebatan Caddesi 13, tel. 0212/512-1570.

Blue Mosque: Free, generally open daily from one hour after sunrise until one hour before sunset, closed to visitors five times a day for prayer, Sultanahmet Meydanı.

The Walk Begins

• *Begin at the pond in Sultanahmet Park, sandwiched between Istanbul's two most famous sights: the Blue Mosque and Hagia Sophia.*

Sultanahmet Spin-Tour

With your back to the gray-colored Blue Mosque, face the orange Hagia Sophia (eye-ah soh-fee-yah). We'll take a slow spin clockwise to get the lay of the land. Behind Hagia Sophia, not visible from here, are the Topkapı Palace grounds, which also house the Istanbul Archaeological Museum. To reach the main palace

ISTANBUL

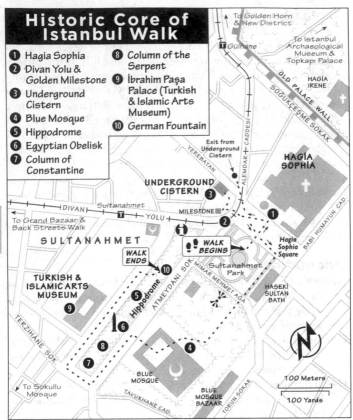

Historic Core of Istanbul Walk

1. Hagia Sophia
2. Divan Yolu & Golden Milestone
3. Underground Cistern
4. Blue Mosque
5. Hippodrome
6. Egyptian Obelisk
7. Column of Constantine
8. Column of the Serpent
9. İbrahim Paşa Palace (Turkish & Islamic Arts Museum)
10. German Fountain

entry, you'd walk along the front of Hagia Sophia to the right, then turn left at the first corner and walk along the side of the

church until you pass between the old walls through the Imperial Gate (palace described on page 1132).

Now turn 90 degrees to the right. The long terra-cotta-colored building with different-sized domes is the 16th-century **Haseki Sultan Bath,** now a government-owned emporium (see photo). Keep turning right, and at the other end of this lively park is the famous **Blue Mosque.** Just to its right (out of sight) is the long, narrow Byzantine square called the **Hippodrome** (the green-domed German Fountain you can see through the trees marks the near end of the Hippodrome—where we'll finish this walk). Keep turning until you are again facing Hagia Sophia.

Sultanahmet Park is a fine example of a city determined to be people-friendly. In spring it's a festival of tulips. If the fountain is on, notice that the arcs of water are designed to mimic the domes of Hagia Sophia. This is perhaps the best photo op for both Hagia Sophia and the Blue Mosque. The large cobbled street at the end of the park (near the Blue Mosque) turns into a parking lot during festivals and on some weekends.

• *Across the very broad street, two red Turkish flags mark the entrance to Hagia Sophia. Now, let's cross the street and go to church.*

Hagia Sophia

Hagia Sophia—the name means "divine wisdom"—served as the patriarchal church of Constantinople for centuries (similar to the Vatican in Rome). When an earlier church on this site was destroyed during the sixth-century Nika Revolt, the Byzantine Emperor Justinian seized the opportunity—and this prime real estate—to build the most spectacular church the world had ever seen. He hired a mathematician named Anthemius to engineer a building for the ages, with an enormous central dome unlike anything ever constructed. You could fit Paris' Notre-Dame Cathedral under Hagia Sophia's dome—or the Statue of Liberty, minus her torch. Nearly 1,500 years later, Hagia Sophia still dominates Istanbul's skyline.

When the Ottomans conquered Constantinople in 1453, Hagia Sophia (which they called Aya Sofya) was converted to a mosque,

and minarets were added to this otherwise very Byzantine-looking church. Because of its grand scale, grace, and beauty, Hagia Sophia's design influenced Ottoman architects for generations. That's why many mosques built after the Ottoman invasion—and long after the Byzantines became a distant memory—continued to incorporate many Byzantine elements.

You could tour Hagia Sophia now (using the "Hagia Sophia Tour," page 1126), or wait until the end of our orientation walk—we'll finish just up the street from here. (If you're visiting in peak season and the line is short, you'd be wise to pop in now—groups can inundate the place at a moment's notice.)

• *Leaving Hagia Sophia, turn right and walk to the busy street corner. (Hop-on, hop-off tour buses leave near here, at the little red tour kiosk; see page 1102 for listing.) Head across the tram tracks to the 30-foot–tall stone-and-brick tower that looks like a large chimney, with a fountain built into it.*

Divan Yolu and the Golden Milestone

The busy street with the trams is Divan Yolu (dee-vahn yoh-loo), the main thoroughfare through Sultanahmet. To the left (uphill),

it leads to the Grand Bazaar. To the right (downhill), it heads to the Galata Bridge and New District. Notice the dramatic boomerang-shaped swoop made by the street (and its tram tracks) as they pass Hagia Sophia. Since Istanbul's Old Town tram has only one line, it's remarkably user-friendly. If Istanbul is your jungle, consider this your vine. It swings to nearly all the places of tourist interest, and it can't get lost (trams run 6-8 times per hour).

Divan Yolu was also Constantinople's main transportation artery in Byzantine times, when it was named Mese ("Middle Way"). The road started right here, where the Golden Milestone (Miliarium Aureum) still stands (in a pit, to the left of the tower). Some 1,500 years ago, the Byzantines considered this point the center of the world. This ancient and once-gilded milestone showed the distances to key locations within the empire. Today it's a mere stub worn down by the centuries. Nothing remains of its decorative arches, or of the statues of Constantine and his mother, Helen, holding a cross that once adorned it.

• *Go downhill to the first corner and turn left. Across the street from the old yellow police building is the low-profile, red-and-white striped entrance to the...*

Underground Cistern

This vast underground reservoir dates back to Byzantine Emperor Justinian's reign in the sixth century A.D. Because it was built on the site of an earlier basilica, it's often called the "Basilica Cistern." Turks call it *yerebatan sarayı,* which means "sunken palace."

Buy your ticket and descend the stairs into the cistern. The visit is a level 15-minute, 400-yard underground stroll. (You'll exit up stairs through a different gate, a block down the street.) While your eyes adjust to the dimness, ponder the history of this spectacular site. The Byzantine Empire enjoyed a Golden Age under Emperor Justinian. Its currency was so strong that merchants in continental Europe and Asia demanded to be paid in Byzantine imperial coins. This enormous wealth can still be seen in the monuments and even the functional buildings (such as other cisterns) of that era. This massive reservoir—larger by far than any other in Constantinople—was built to meet the needs of a fast-growing capital city and to provide precious water in case of a shortage. The cistern covers an area about the size of two football fields—big enough to hold 27 million gallons of fresh water.

A forest of 336 columns supports the brick ceiling. Most of these were recycled from earlier Roman ruins in and around the city. Note the variety of capitals (tops of columns). Clay pipes and aqueducts carried water 12 miles to this cistern. (A half-mile-long chunk of the Valens Aqueduct still stands, spanning Atatürk Bulvarı, or Atatürk Boulevard, roughly a mile west of here.)

Gradually these pipes became clogged, and the cistern fell out of use. As time passed, neglect became ignorance, and people forgot it was even there. An Ottoman historian wrote that residents of this area were luckier than others, as they could easily drop a bucket into any garden well and collect apparently God-given water. (They didn't realize they were dipping their buckets into a Byzantine masterpiece.)

The platform you're walking on was constructed two decades ago to make the far reaches of the cistern more accessible to visitors. While water once filled this space halfway to the ceiling, today it's just a shallow pond, formed from rainwater that leaks in through cracks and compromised mortar in the ceiling. (Accumulated water is pumped out to prevent damage.) Before the walkway was built, the water was six feet deep, and the only way to see the cistern was to rent a boat and row in the dark—a perfectly evocative setting used for James Bond's adventures in *From Russia with Love*.

Walking toward the far end, notice that part of the cistern (which has suffered structural damage) is separated by a wall.

At the far end of the cistern, find the two recycled Medusa heads lying on the ground—one sideways and one upside-down—

squeezed under pillars. This fearsome mythological gorgon—with hair made of snakes and a gaze that could turn people to stone—was often carved by Greeks into tombstones or cemetery walls to scare off grave robbers. In Roman times, she became a protector of temples. When Christianity took hold, Medusa was a reminder of the not-so-distant Roman persecution of Christians—so it may be no coincidence that these pagan fragments were left here in a dark corner of the cistern, never to see daylight again. Another theory proposes that the architect simply needed a proper base to raise the two small columns to ceiling height...and the Medusas were a perfect fit.

On the way out, you'll see huge, blocky concrete columns built more recently to support the structure—quite a contrast to the ancient, graceful Roman columns.

• *Leaving the Underground Cistern, turn right and retrace your steps back up to the park where this walk began. Cross the park to find the towering Blue Mosque at the far end. Enjoy the view from the nice wooden benches. Read the next page or so while seated here.*

Blue Mosque

This famous and gorgeous mosque is one of the world's finest. It was built in just seven years (1609-1616) by the architect Mehmet Aga, who also rebuilt Kaaba (the holiest shrine of Islam—the giant black cube at the center of the mosque in the holy city of Mecca). Locals call it the Sultan Ahmet Mosque for the ruler who financed it, but travelers know it as the Blue Mosque because of the rich blue color of the handmade ceramic tiles that dominate the interior.

• *As you face the Blue Mosque, to your right (with the multitude of mini-domes and chimneys) is the madrassa, a school of theology. Facing the mosque, you can see it has...*

Six Minarets

Aside from its impressive scale and opulent interior, the Blue Mosque is unique because of its six minarets. According to Muslim tradition, the imam (the prayer leader) or the muezzin (a man chosen for his talent in correctly voicing the call to prayer) would climb to the top of a minaret five times each day to announce the call to prayer. On hearing this warbling chant, Muslims are to come to the mosque to pray. Today, an imam or muezzin still performs the call to prayer, but now it's amplified by loudspeakers at the top of the minarets.

A single minaret was adequate for its straightforward function, but mosques financed by sultans often wanted to show off with more. A story popular with tour guides is that Sultan Ahmet I asked the architect for a gold *(altın)* minaret—but the man thought he said "six" *(altı)*. In all likelihood, Ahmet probably requested the six minarets to flaunt his wealth. But at the time, the central mosque in the holy city of Mecca also had six. The clergy at Mecca feared that Ahmet's new mosque would upstage theirs—so the sultan built a seventh minaret at Mecca.

• *The walkway by the benches leads to the Blue Mosque. Through the gate at the end of the walkway, you enter the mosque's...*

Outer Courtyard

Straight ahead, a staircase leads up to the inner courtyard (described next). To the right of the staircase, notice the line of water taps used for ablution—the ritual cleansing of the body before worshipping, as directed by Islamic law. These are comparatively new, installed to replace the older fountain in the inner courtyard (which we'll see soon). To the left, another set of stairs leads to an entrance into the mosque designated for worshippers (you may exit through this gate when you leave the mosque).

• *Now take the stairs up into the...*

Inner Courtyard

The courtyard is surrounded by a portico, which provides shade and shelter. The shutters along the back wall open in summer for

ventilation. In the center of the courtyard is a fancy fountain, once used for ablutions but no longer functional. When the mosque fills up for special services, worshippers who can't fit inside pray in the large vaulted area in front of the mosque (on your left) and, if necessary, fill the rest of the courtyard. But today such jam-packed services are rare. Muslims are not required to actually go to the mosque five times each day; they can pray anywhere. The exception is the midday service on Friday, which the Quran dictates should be a time for all worshippers to come together in congregation—making mosques more crowded on Fridays.

• *Now go into the mosque. (For instructions and etiquette, see page 1098.) The main door on this west end is where visitors generally enter. (If this door is closed, you should be able to go around the corner on the right.) As you enter, take a plastic bag from the container and use it to carry your shoes, which you should remove before you step on the carpet. Entering the mosque is free, but you can make a donation as you exit.*

Interior

Stepping through the heavy leather drape into the interior, you'll understand why this is called the Blue Mosque. Let your eyes

adjust to the dim lighting as you breathe in the vast and intensely decorated interior.

Approach the wood railing to take a closer look at the apse (straight ahead from the main gate). The area beyond this barrier is reserved for worshippers, who fill the space at all times of day. The little shin-high wooden shelves are for storing worshippers' shoes.

On the far wall, look for the highly decorated marble niche with large candles on either side. This is the mihrab (meeh-rahb), which points southeast to Mecca, where all Muslims face when they worship. The surrounding wall is decorated with floral-designed stained-glass windows, many of them original.

On the right side of the apse is a staircase leading up to a platform with a cone on top. This is the *mimber* (meem-behr), similar to a pulpit in a Christian church. A *mimber* is symbolic of the growth of Islam—Muhammad had to stand higher and higher to talk to his growing following. It is used by the imam (prayer leader) to deliver a speech on Fridays, similar to a sermon in Christian services. As a sign of respect for Muhammad, the imam stands only halfway up the staircase.

Farther to the right, next to the main pillar, is a fancy marble platform elevated on columns. This is where the choir sings hymns a cappella (mainstream Islam uses no instruments) on important religious days.

Mosque services are segregated: The main hall is reserved for men, while women use the colonnaded area behind the barriers at the back, on both sides of the main entrance. Women can also use the upper galleries on crowded days. While many visitors think it is demeaning to women to make them stay in back, most Muslims feel it's respectful to women and more conducive to prayer. The men are better able to concentrate on God without the distraction of bent-over women in front of them, and the women feel more comfortable not having men behind them.

The huge dome—reaching a height of 141 feet and a diameter of 110 feet—is modeled after the one in Hagia Sophia, which was the first building to use pillars to support a giant central dome. As Turkish engineers improved on this concept over the years, they were able to create vast indoor spaces covered by cascading domes. The same fundamentals are still used today in many contemporary mosques.

Near the corners of the vast room, notice the giant pillars

paved with fluted marble panels. These "elephant feet" support the arches, dome, semi-domes, and cupolas. Since the weight is transferred mainly to these four pillars, thick, bulky walls aren't necessary. Like flying buttresses in a Gothic cathedral, this technique allowed the architect to fill the walls with decorative windows. Compare the Blue Mosque (with its 260 windows) with the gloomy interior of the much older (and bulkier) Hagia Sophia.

The low-hanging chandeliers were designed for oil lamps with floating wicks; they were designed to be raised and lowered to tend to the lamps (although now they hold electric bulbs). Years ago, a thick patchwork of handmade rugs covered the floor—these have been removed for preservation and replaced with the current machine-made carpeting. Notice that the carpets have lines to organize the worshippers—just like lined paper organizes words.

Islamic tradition forbids the portrayal of living beings in places of worship, which could distract people from worshipping Allah as the one God. As a result, the Muslim world excelled at non-figurative art. In this and other mosques, instead of paintings of saints and prophets, you'll see geometric designs and calligraphy.

Along with the painted floral and geometric patterns, more than 20,000 ceramic tiles were used extensively to decorate the mosque. Lower parts of the wall—up to the height of the marble application on the giant pillars—are paved with mostly blue, early-17th-century İznik tiles. İznik (a.k.a. Nicea, in ancient times) was the Ottoman Empire's tile-making center, and its tiles feature prominently in many museums around the world (including the Istanbul Archaeological Museum, nearby).

Artful Arabic calligraphy (*hat* in Turkish; pronounced "hot") is another form of mosque decoration. To make the words appear more beautiful, the *hattat* (hot-taht; calligrapher) takes liberties

with grammatical rules and often combines letters irregularly, making it difficult to read. Many of the examples of *hat* around the mosque are excerpts from the Quran or from the hadith (the collected teachings of the Prophet Muhammad). In a Christian church, you'd have God and Jesus front and center. Here, the two medallions high above the mihrab read *Muhammad* (left) and *Allah* (right).

The Blue Mosque represents the pinnacle of Ottoman architecture—and marks the beginning of the empire's decline. After its construction, the treasury was exhausted, and the Ottoman Empire entered a period of stagnation that eventually led to its collapse.

Never again could the empire afford a building of such splendor.

Additionally, the mosque's patron, Sultan Ahmet I, was too young and inexperienced to effectively wield his authority and became mired in bureaucracy and tradition. While a few of his successors (including his son, Murat IV) managed to temporarily revive the dying empire, Ahmet marked the beginning of a long string of incompetent sultans who would eventually rule over an empire known in the early 20th century as the "Sick Man of Europe."

• *Leave the mosque and return to the inner courtyard. With your back to the mosque, walk to the back of the courtyard. Before you exit, consider taking a seat on the marble steps and soaking up the view of the mosque and the people mingling about. The crowd is a fun mix of Turkish tourists, travelers from across the world, wide-eyed cruise groups, and pilgrims. Try out a little Turkish: You can say, "Nasılsınız?" (nah-suhl-suh-nuhz; "How are you?") and "Merhaba" (mehr-hah-bah; "Hello"). Every school kid knows how to say, "What is your name?" and "How old are you?"*

As you leave, turn around as you step out of the courtyard for one more glance at the graceful cascading-domes design (go halfway down the stairs and look back for a good photo op, with the domes nicely framed by the portal).

As you step outside the exterior gate, you enter a long, skinny square that was the ancient Hippodrome of Constantinople. The Egyptian Obelisk is directly ahead of you.

Hippodrome

Built in the fourth century A.D., the Hippodrome was Constantinople's primary venue for chariot races. But as the place where the people of the city gather, this racetrack has also been the scene of social and religious disputes, political clashes, and violent uprisings.

Chariot races were the most popular events in Constantinople, appealing to people from all walks of life. Winning teams became celebrities...at least until the next race. Between races, the masses were entertained by dancers, cheerleaders, musicians, acrobats, and performing animals.

The courtyard of the Blue Mosque marks the former site of the Hippodrome's *kathisma* (royal lodge). Supported by gorgeous marble columns, this grandstand was where the emperor and his family watched the races unfold. The lodge was connected to the Great Palace (on the site of today's Blue Mosque) for an easy escape in case the crowd got out of control.

Constantinople's social classes were identified by colors—Greens, Blues, Reds, and Whites—each with its favorite chariot team. Spectators at Hippodrome races, put on edge by social and economic gripes, often came to blows (something akin to today's soccer hooligans). Relations between the ruling and poor classes hit a low point in January of 532, when the Nika Revolt (named for the rebels' battle cry, *"Nika!"*—"Victory!") erupted at a chariot race. Emperor Justinian called in the Imperial Guard, who massacred some 30,000 protesters.

As big as today's gigantic football stadiums, the Hippodrome could seat 100,000 spectators. But when races went out of vogue, the once-proud structure became a makeshift quarry for builders scavenging pre-cut stones.

The Hippodrome was in ruins long before the Turks arrived. The Ottomans named it Atmeydanı ("horsetrack") and used it for horseback riding and archery training. Through the years, dirt dug up to make way for foundations of surrounding buildings was dumped here, so today's ground level is significantly higher than during Byzantine times. If you look down around the base of the monuments that are still standing, you'll see the original ground level. The last remaining stones of the Hippodrome's "bleachers" were used to build the Blue Mosque. Today, none of the original seating survives, and the ancient racetrack has been replaced by a modern road.

Every year during Ramadan, the Hippodrome attains a festive atmosphere in the evening, when Muslims break their fast at sunset.

• *In its Byzantine glory days, the Hippodrome was decorated with monuments from all over the world. The most famous one is right in the middle of the long square.*

Egyptian Obelisk

This ancient, pointy pillar was carved about 1,500 years before Christ to honor the Egyptian Pharaoh Thutmose III; its inscribed hieroglyphs commemorate his military achievements. The obelisk was brought here from the Temple of Karnak on the Upper Nile sometime in the fourth century A.D. What you see today is only the upper third of the original massive stone block (take a second to imagine its original height).

The most interesting part of the obelisk is its Byzantine base, which was cut out of local white marble and stands on four bronze feet. Reliefs on all four sides of the base depict Emperor Theodosius the Great and his family at the royal lodge, watching the Hippodrome races. On the side facing the Blue Mosque, the emperor gives an olive wreath to the winner, while his servant hands out a sack of coins. On the opposite side, envoys bow down before Theodosius in homage. At the bottom of the base (facing Hagia Sophia), find the relief showing the column as it lay horizontal, and how pulleys were used to raise it.

Throughout Asia Minor (Asian part of today's Turkey), the Latin and Greek languages coexisted during the early stages of the Byzantine Empire. At the obelisk's base, you'll see an inscription eulogizing the emperor, written in both Latin (on the side facing the Blue Mosque) and Greek (on the opposite side). Both inscriptions give basically the same information, but they differ when it comes to how long it took to raise the obelisk: The Latin version says 30 days, the Greek 32. This ancient typo perplexes archaeologists to this day.

• *The tall stone column that looks like a stone-paved obelisk, at the left end of the Hippodrome (with the Blue Mosque to your back), is the...*

Column of Constantine

Like the Egyptian Obelisk, this column went up in the fourth century A.D. But unlike its Egyptian sister, it was constructed here. In the early 10th century A.D., Emperor Constantine VII Porphyrogenitus sheeted the column with bronze panels. But as the city was looted during the Fourth Crusade (in the early 13th century), the panels were pulled down to make weapons. You can still see the holes where the panels were attached to the column.

• *Between the Column of Constantine and the Egyptian Obelisk is the bronze...*

Column of the Serpent

This was a victory monument dedicated to the gods by 31 Greek city-states to commemorate their victory against the Persians at Plataea (479 B.C.). It stood at the Temple of Apollo in Delphi for 800 years, until—like the Egyptian Obelisk—it was brought to Constantinople from Greece in the fourth century A.D. The names of the sponsoring cities are inscribed at the base (currently underground, buried by earth accumulated over the centuries).

Originally, this column showed three serpents twisted together, their heads supporting a golden trophy. The gold was gone even before the reign of Constantine the Great, but the heads survived until just 300 years ago—when they mysteriously vanished. Only the upper jaw of one snake still exists (on display in the Istanbul Archaeological Museum).

Other monuments that once decorated the Hippodrome are long gone, such as four famous cast-bronze horses from ancient Greece. During the Fourth Crusade, these were plundered and taken to Venice...where they're still on display at St. Mark's Basilica.

• *Across the Hippodrome from the Blue Mosque is the Turkish and Islamic Arts Museum, housed in the...*

İbrahim Paşa Palace

The palace—a gift from Sultan Süleyman the Magnificent to İbrahim Paşa in 1520—is one of the best examples of civil architecture in the city. The palace was once much bigger than what you see today—rivaling Topkapı Palace in both its size and its opulence. The only surviving bits are the reception hall and areas where guests were hosted, surrounding a small central courtyard. Looking at the facade, notice the Oriental-looking wooden balcony.

Through the years, the İbrahim Paşa Palace has been used as a palace school, a dormitory for single soldiers, and a prison. In 1983, it was restored and became the home of the **Turkish and Islamic Arts Museum,** with its collection of ceramics, glassware, calligraphy, and carpets (described on page 1162).

• *Our walk is nearly finished. Continue down to the north end of the Hippodrome (with the Blue Mosque on your right). You'll run into an octagonal pavilion with a green dome on dark pillars, the...*

German Fountain

This pavilion—which seems a little out of place surrounded by minarets and obelisks—would be more at home in Berlin. The fountain was a gift from the German government to commemorate Kaiser Wilhelm II's visit to Istanbul in 1898. It was constructed in pieces in Germany, then shipped to Istanbul in 1901 and reassembled on this location.

Kaiser Wilhelm II visited Istanbul three times to schmooze the sultan. By the early 20th century, it was obvious that a war between the great powers of Europe was imminent, and empires were choosing sides. Though the Ottoman Empire was in its waning days, it remained a formidable power in the east and a valuable ally for Germany. Sure enough, when World War I erupted in 1914, the Ottoman Empire joined the fray as Germany's unwilling ally. Less than four years later, the Ottomans had lost the war—and with it, what remained of their ailing empire. The last sultan was sent into exile with the establishment of the Turkish Republic in the 1920s.

• *We've come full circle—you're just up the street from Hagia Sophia (if you haven't yet, you can visit it with the self-guided tour, next). At the end of the Hippodrome, just before the street with the tram tracks (Divan Yolu), are a TI and some public WCs. Across the tracks are a pair of recommended local restaurants: Sultanahmet Köftecisi serves just meatballs, and the misnamed Pudding Shop (a.k.a. "Lale Restaurant") offers meat and veggie dishes,* döner kebab, *and sometimes fish in a cafeteria-style setting where you can see all of the choices (it may look crowded, but there's also seating upstairs). Just uphill from the restaurants on Divan Yolu is the Sultanahmet tram. Beyond that is a bustling commercial zone with more restaurants, a pharmacy, travel agencies, and banks (with ATMs). And farther up is the Grand Bazaar (from the Hippodrome, it's a 15-minute walk, or a quick ride on the tram from the Sultanahmet stop to the Çemberlitaş stop; to head straight there, skip to page 1140).*

Hagia Sophia Tour

For centuries, it was known as Megalo Ekklesia, the "Great Church" of Constantinople. The Greeks called it Hagia Sophia

(eye-ah soh-fee-yah), meaning "Divine Wisdom," an attribute of God. The Turkish version is Aya Sofya. But no matter what you call it, this place—first a church, then a mosque, and now a museum—is one of the most important and impressive structures on the planet.

Emperor Justinian built Hagia Sophia between A.D. 532 and 537. For 900 years, it served as the seat of the Orthodox Patriarch of Constantinople—the "eastern Vatican." Replete with shimmering mosaics and fine marble, Hagia Sophia was the single greatest architectural achievement of the Byzantine Empire.

When the Ottomans took Constantinople in 1453, Sultan

Mehmet the Conqueror—impressed with the Great Church's beauty—converted it into an imperial mosque. Hagia Sophia remained Istanbul's most important mosque for five centuries. In the early days of the Turkish Republic (1930s), Hagia Sophia was converted again, this time into a museum. It retains unique elements of both the Byzantine and Ottoman empires and their respective religions, Orthodox Christianity and Islam. In a sense, Hagia Sophia is Istanbul in architectural form: ancient, grand, gigantic, with some rough edges, but on the whole remarkably preserved—a fascinating, still-vigorous blend of East and West.

Orientation

Cost: 20 TL covers the entire museum, including the upper galleries (although in the future, each part may be covered by a different ticket—ask at the ticket office). Unless the other windows are closed, avoid the right-hand ticket window, which is reserved for tour guides with groups.

Hours: Tue-Sun 9:00-18:30 in summer, until 16:30 off-season; temporary exhibits and the upper galleries close 30 minutes earlier, closed Mon. Last entry one hour before closing.

When to Go: On Tuesdays in peak season, Topkapı Palace is closed, which means that Hagia Sophia gets more crowded.

Getting There: Hagia Sophia is in the Sultanahmet neighborhood in the heart of the Old Town, facing the Blue Mosque. The main entrance is at the southwest corner of the giant building, across the busy street with the tram tracks (Divan Yolu). If you arrive by tram, get off at the Sultanahmet stop, and walk a couple hundred yards downhill along Divan Yolu. Cross the wide street at the traffic light.

Getting In: Guided tours often bunch up at Hagia Sophia's security checkpoint and ticket-taker. Be patient—the logjam usually clears quickly.

Information: As you approach Hagia Sophia, loitering tour guides may offer to guide you around for a fee (generally 50 TL). Thanks to this self-guided tour, you won't need their help. And once inside, you'll find that most museum descriptions are in English. Tel. 0212/528-4500.

Length of This Tour: Allow at least an hour for the main floor. The upper galleries take about 30 minutes and can be skipped if you're pressed for time.

Security and Baggage: After buying your ticket, but before entering, you'll go through an airport-type security checkpoint. There is no bag check.

Services: The cafeteria is across from the main building entrance, to the left of the walkway that leads past ticket control. The WC is at the end of the walkway, past the cafeteria. There are two bookshops: one at the interior narthex, and the other at the exit, by the Vestibule of Guards.

Photography: Photography is allowed, but don't use your flash when taking pictures of icons, mosaic panels, or frescoes. English-language signs indicate where you should turn off your flash.

Starring: The finest house of worship in the Christian and Muslim worlds.

Background

Hagia Sophia was built over the remains of at least two earlier churches (described later). After the second of these churches was destroyed in the Nika riots in A.D.

532, Emperor Justinian I (r. 527-565) wasted no time, immediately putting his plan for Hagia Sophia into action. He asked for the near-impossible: a church with unbelievably grand proportions, a monument that would last for centuries and keep his name alive for future generations.

Justinian appointed two geometricians to do the job: Anthemius, from the Aegean town of Tralles, and his assistant, Isidore of Miletus. Both knew from the start that this would be a risky project. Making Justinian's vision a reality would involve enormous challenges. But they courageously went forward, creating a masterpiece unlike anything seen before.

More than 7,500 architects, stonemasons, bricklayers, plasterers, sculptors, painters, and mosaic artists worked around the clock for five years to complete Hagia Sophia—and drain the treasury—faster than even the emperor had anticipated. In December of 537, the Great Church of Constantinople held its first service in the presence of Emperor Justinian and the Patriarch of Constantinople.

The church was a huge success story for Justinian, who was understandably satisfied with his achievement. As the story goes, when he stepped inside the church, he exclaimed, "Solomon, I have surpassed you!" In the long history of the empire, the Byzantines would never again construct such a grand edifice, but its design would influence architects for centuries.

Hagia Sophia was a legend even before it was completed. People came from all over to watch the great dome slowly rise above the landscape of the city. It was the first thing that merchants saw from approaching ships and caravans. Hagia Sophia soon became a landmark, and it continues to hold a special place in the mystical skyline of Istanbul.

The structure served as a church for nearly a millennium. For a thousand years it stood as the greatest dome in the world, until the Renaissance, when Brunelleschi built his famous dome in Florence.

The day the Ottomans captured Constantinople in 1453, Hagia Sophia was converted into a mosque. Most of the functional elements that decorated the church were removed, and its figurative mosaics and frescoes were plastered over in accordance with Islamic custom. Today the interior holds elements mostly from the time when Hagia Sophia was used as a mosque (from 1453 until 1934, when it became a museum).

The Tour Begins

• *After you pass through security and ticket control, you'll see the official walkway leading straight ahead, toward the main entrance. Instead, we'll take a shortcut for a better entrance route: Turn right, cross the big paved path, and slip past the wooden kiosk toward the giant, ornate Rococo...*

Fountain

The Ottomans added this fountain in the mid-18th century. Across

from the fountain, notice the water taps in the portico by the side of the main building. When Hagia Sophia was a mosque, both of these were used for ablution (ritual cleansing before prayer) as part of Islamic tradition.

• *Enter the museum through its exit door at the far end of this courtyard (to the left). On the pillar before the door (to your right as you face the door, at the corner of the small museum bookstore), notice the Arabic translated into Turkish. According to Islamic tradition, in the seventh century, Muhammad himself predicted that Constantinople (which was Christian and ruled the Western world at that time) would be conquered, and he praised the commander and soldiers as "güzel" (elite or distinguished). Eight centuries later, his prediction came to pass. Now step into this historic place of worship through the...*

Vestibule of Guards

This entry is named for the imperial guards who waited here for the emperor while he was attending church services. Byzantine emperors used this entryway because of its proximity to the royal

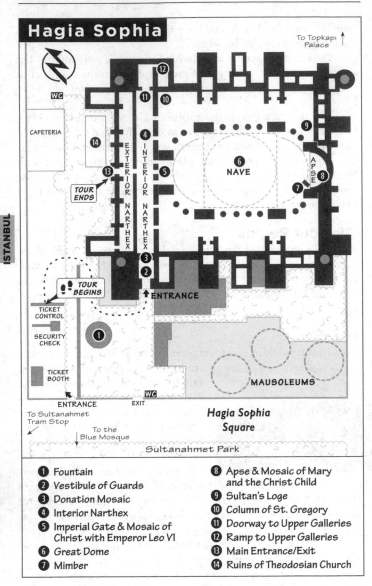

Hagia Sophia

To Topkapı Palace ↑

WC

CAFETERIA

⑭

EXTERIOR NARTHEX

INTERIOR NARTHEX

⑬

TOUR ENDS

④

⑤

⑪ ⑩

⑫

⑥ **NAVE**

⑨

A P S E ⑧

⑦

③

②

TOUR BEGINS

TICKET CONTROL

SECURITY CHECK

①

TICKET BOOTH

ENTRANCE ↑

ENTRANCE

WC EXIT

MAUSOLEUMS

To Sultanahmet Tram Stop

To the Blue Mosque

Hagia Sophia Square

Sultanahmet Park

ISTANBUL

- ① Fountain
- ② Vestibule of Guards
- ③ Donation Mosaic
- ④ Interior Narthex
- ⑤ Imperial Gate & Mosaic of Christ with Emperor Leo VI
- ⑥ Great Dome
- ⑦ Mimber
- ⑧ Apse & Mosaic of Mary and the Christ Child
- ⑨ Sultan's Loge
- ⑩ Column of St. Gregory
- ⑪ Doorway to Upper Galleries
- ⑫ Ramp to Upper Galleries
- ⑬ Main Entrance/Exit
- ⑭ Ruins of Theodosian Church

palace, which stood where the Blue Mosque is today.

Scholars believe that the entrance's imposing **bronze doors** were brought here sometime after Justinian (from an ancient temple in Antioch). At the top of the flat panel (about eye-level on the first door), you can see traces of the silver imperial monograms that were once affixed to the bronze sheeting. Notice that these doors can't open or close—they became stuck in place when the marble floor was renovated and raised.

Stepping inside the vestibule, look up: The vaulted ceiling is covered with original mosaics, dating back nearly 1,500 years to Justinian's time. The mosaics in his church—such as these—depicted geometric patterns rather than people, as was the fashion at the time. Later, figurative mosaics were also added.

• *Above the doorway into the church, notice the gorgeous...*

Donation Mosaic

The mosaic dates from the 11th-century reign of Basil II. Scenes such as this became common in later Orthodox churches, and usually depict the patron who funded the church's construction and to whom the church is dedicated. In the mosaic, you see Mary and the Christ child enthroned. Jesus holds the Gospels in his left hand and makes the three-fingered sign of the Trinity with his right hand. Two mighty Roman emperors flank the Holy Family: On the right, Constantine presents Mary and Christ with a model of his city, Constantinople (symbolized by city walls). On the left is Justinian, presenting a model of his greatest achievement, Hagia Sophia. Note the differences between this model and today's Hagia Sophia: Justinian's version had no minarets and no retaining or garden walls, and its dome was topped with a cross. It's fortunate that this mosaic has survived so beautifully intact, because many such mosaics were destroyed during the Iconoclast Era. If your neck is sore, or just for fun, turn 180 degrees, block the light with this book, and see the same mosaic more comfortably.

• *Now walk under the donation mosaic and straight into the...*

Interior Narthex

Hagia Sophia's interior narthex is an attractive space, with nine vaulted bays richly decorated with mosaics. The walls on either side are lined with inch-thick **marble panels,** which were glued to the wall with stucco and pinned with iron rods. In some parts of the building, such as the Vestibule of Guards, the iron rusted, and over time the marble pieces began to fall off (the Vestibule of Guards' walls are painted to replicate the original marble covering). But here in the interior narthex, which is more protected from the elements, after 15 centuries, the panels hang on.

On the narthex ceiling are original **Justinian mosaics** that survived the Iconoclast Era because they were non-figurative. The church's designer, Anthemius, sought to give the impression of movement. These mosaic pieces—interspersed with randomly placed bits of semiprecious stones—change from muted shades to brilliant reflection, depending on the direction of the light. Since services generally took place after sunset, the mosaic artists designed their work to be vivid even in flickering candlelight: simple polychrome crosses and starry shapes on a golden background.

Five doors on the left wall lead into the narrow, unadorned **exterior narthex.** Less splendid than the interior narthex, it holds a few uninteresting relics and the occasional temporary exhibit, along with the main visitors' entrance. We'll skip this for now.

At the far end of the interior narthex, notice the huge doorway leading to the ramp to the upper galleries. We'll go up this ramp later, after visiting the nave.

• *Just ahead of you, the central (and biggest) door to the nave is called the...*

Imperial Gate

This majestic doorway was reserved for the emperor—it was opened only for him. Notice the **metal hooks** attached to the top

of the doorway. The Ottomans added these to hold leather curtains—similar to those used in today's mosques—to protect worshippers from dust and to reduce the interruption of a giant door opening and closing.

Look at the panel glittering above the gate, the **Mosaic of Christ with Emperor Leo VI.** Despite being known as "Leo the Wise," the emperor is remembered more for his multiple marriages than for his intellect. His first three wives died without giving him a child, so he married his mistress—and the mother of his son—Zoe Carbonospina (meaning "Black Eyes"). This sparked a scandal:

The emperor was excommunicated by the patriarch and barred from attending the Christmas service in A.D. 906. In this scene, Leo seems to be asking for forgiveness—prostrating himself before Jesus, who blesses the emperor. The Greek reads, "May peace be with you. I

am the light of the earth." Mary and the Archangel Gabriel are portrayed in the roundels on either side of Jesus. Whitewashed over by the Ottomans, the mosaic was only rediscovered in 1933.

• *Now step through the Imperial Gate and into Hagia Sophia's...*

Nave

Overwhelming, unbelievable, fantastic: These are the words that fall from the open mouths of visitors to Hagia Sophia. Take a few steps into the grand space, close this book, shut your ears to the rumble of excited visitors, and just absorb the experience: You are in Hagia Sophia, the crowning achievement of the Byzantine Empire. Paris' Notre-Dame would fit within Hagia Sophia's great dome, and the Statue of Liberty could do jumping jacks here.

• *Take a few minutes to appreciate the feat of engineering that is Hagia Sophia. First, tune into the...*

Architecture

Hagia Sophia was designed as a classical basilica covered by a vast central dome. By definition, a "basilica" is characterized by a large, central open space, called a nave, flanked by rows of columns and narrow side aisles. It sounds simple, but even the two geometricians Justinian chose to build Hagia Sophia had doubts about whether the plan would work. Every so often, Anthemius would go to the emperor to tell him about potential risks. And every time, he got the same response: "Have faith in God." Anthemius was right to have worried. Despite his mastery of geometry, he made some miscalculations: A few decades after Hagia Sophia was completed, part of the gigantic dome collapsed. The dome was repaired using steeper angles than the original; even so, it would collapse and be rebuilt again in the 6th and 10th centuries.

The main dome—185 feet high and roughly 105 feet in diameter—appears to float on four great

arches. The secret is the clear glass windows at the base of the dome. The triangular pendentives in the corners gracefully connect the round dome to the rectangular building below, and the arches pass the dome's weight on to the massive piers at the corners.

Semi-domes at the ends extend the open space. Over 100 columns provide further support to the upper parts of the building. Many of these columns were brought here from other, even more ancient monuments and temples.

Hagia Sophia was a worthy attempt to create a vast indoor space, independent of the walls. But in practice, quite a bit of the dome's great weight is held up by the walls, which is why there aren't very many windows. The Byzantines built additional arches inside the walls to further help distribute the weight. These "hidden arches" are visible here and there, where the stucco layers have worn away.

As you look around, note the basic principle of Byzantine architecture: symmetry. All the architectural elements, including decorative pieces, are placed in a symmetrical fashion. If symmetry

demanded a window or door that would weaken a wall, then a false, painted-on one would be created in its place.

The artful use of light creates the interior's stunning effect. The windows at the base of the dome used clear glass, while other windows throughout the building used thin alabaster to further diffuse the light and create a more dramatic effect.

• *With the Imperial Gate directly behind you, face the apse and look up into the massive dome to see the...*

Dome Decorations

During the centuries that Hagia Sophia was used as a mosque, many of its original decorations—especially mosaics or frescoes depicting people—were covered over with whitewash and plaster. Ironically, in some cases, the plaster actually helped to preserve the artwork. For others, damage was inevitable, as the stucco absorbed the whitewash. In the 19th century, the sultan invited the Swiss-

born Fossati brothers to complete an extensive restoration of Hagia Sophia. They cleaned and catalogued many of the Byzantine figural mosaics before covering them up again.

At the base of the dome, between intersecting arches, are winged **seraphim.** Gold-leaf masks or medallions cover these angels' faces. The two nearest the apse are from the 14th century (the mask on the one to the left of the apse was removed in 2010, and the face is now revealed); the other two are replicas by the Fossati brothers.

The Ottoman additions that immediately draw your attention are Arabic calligraphy, especially the eight 24-foot-wide **medallions** suspended at the bases of the arches supporting the central and side domes. These huge, leather-wrapped wooden medallions were added in the 19th century and decorated by master Islamic calligraphers. In a church, you'd see paintings of Biblical figures and saints—however, in a mosque (which allows no depictions of people), you'll see ornately written names of leading Muslim figures. The two medallions on the arches flanking the apse are painted with the names of Allah (on the right) and Muhammad (on the left). The four at the center name the four caliphs, Muslim religious and social leaders who succeeded the Prophet Muhammad: Abu Bakr, Umar, Uthman, and Ali. The two medallions on the arches above the Imperial Gate bear the names of Muhammad's grandchildren and Ali's sons, who were assassinated.

• *Walk toward the front of the church. The heavy chandeliers hanging from the dome, additions from Ottoman times, held candlesticks, or glass oil lamps with floating wicks. The highly decorated staircase before you, set diagonally away from the wall, is the...*

Mimber

The *mimber* (meem-behr) is the pulpit in a mosque, used by the imam (cleric, like a priest or rabbi) to deliver his sermon on Fridays, or to talk to the public on special occasions. The imam stands halfway up the stairs as a sign of respect, reserving the uppermost step for the Prophet Muhammad.

• *Go beyond the* mimber *and face the...*

Apse

When Hagia Sophia (the original church, facing Jerusalem) was converted into a mosque, a small off-center niche was added in the apse's circular wall. Called the mihrab, this niche shows the precise direction to face during prayers (toward the holy city of Mecca, which is south of Jerusalem). The stately columns flanking the mihrab are actually huge candles—standard fixtures in royal mosques.

High above the mihrab, on the underside of the semi-dome, is a colorful **Mosaic of Mary and the Christ Child** on a gold background (to see better, raise this book to block the light). Christ is also dressed in gold. Part of the background is missing, but most of the scene is intact. This mosaic, the oldest one in Hagia Sophia, dates from the ninth century. It may have been the first figurative mosaic added after the Iconoclast Era, replacing a cross-design mosaic from the earlier period. The gold "clubs" on Mary's forehead and both shoulders stand for the Trinity. Notice also the red "spades" among the "clubs" on the pillows.

On the right end of the arch, just before the semi-dome (behind the large medallion), find the **Mosaic of Archangel Gabriel** with his wings sweeping down to the ground. On the opposite end of the arch, there was once a similar mosaic of the Archangel Michael.

To your left, by the side of the apse (the frilly gilded room under the big medallion), is the elevated prayer section for the sultans, or the **sultan's loge** (behind the gold-glazed metalwork). This area was added in the 19th century.

• *With your back to the apse, wander to the far-right corner of the nave. As you walk, notice the golden mosaics on the ceiling from Justinian's age. Past the large buttresses, separating the aisles from the nave, are rows of...*

Green Marble Columns

These columns carry the upper galleries and also provide support to the domes, easing the burden on the buttresses and the exterior walls. Notice the richly decorated white-marble capitals of these columns (with the joint monograms of Justinian and Theodora).

• *In the far corner (to your right, still facing the entry) is what looks like a five-foot-tall alabaster egg, but is actually an...*

Alabaster Urn

This is one of two Hellenistic-era **urns** (second century B.C., one on each side of the nave) that the sultan brought to Istanbul from Pergamon—the formidable ancient acropolis of north Aegean Turkey. Find the tap mounted in the side. Traditionally, Ottoman mosques had functional fountains inside, to provide drinking water for worshippers.

The two purple **porphyry columns** behind each urn are older than Hagia Sophia. Two columns stand at each corner—eight in all. Long ago, iron girdles were placed around the columns to prevent further damage (they already had cracks in them).

• *In the rear right-hand corner, about 10 yards beyond the alabaster urn, is the quirky and purportedly miraculous...*

Column of St. Gregory

This is the legendary "perspiring column," the Column of St.

Gregory, the miracle worker. For centuries, people believed this column "wept" holy water that could cure afflictions such as eye diseases and infertility.

How does it work? Put your thumb in the hole, and if it comes out feeling damp, your prayer will be answered. No? Try this. Put your thumb in the hole again, and this time, make a complete 360-degree circle with your hand, with your thumb still in the hole. The metal surrounding the hole has been polished by millions of hands over the years.

• *Walk through the door to the left of this column, leaving the nave and reentering the interior narthex. The huge door to your right leads to the...*

Upper Galleries

*The upper level of the church holds well-known mosaics, but if you're hoping to visit Topkapı Palace or linger in the Grand Bazaar, you may want to skip these galleries. Go through this door and follow the long, stone-paved **ramp up to the upper galleries** (watch your step, as the stones are smooth and uneven). Why a ramp, and not stairs? Because those of exalted rank were either carried by their servants, or rode up on horseback. As you step off the ramp, keep to the right and enter the well-lit...*

West Gallery

This gallery provides a direct view of the apse. Walk to the center of the gallery and look for a **green marble circle** in the floor right before the balustrade, with an ensemble of matching green columns on either side. This was the spot reserved for the empress' throne, directly across from the apse.

• *Turning left at the end of this gallery, you'll pass through the marble half wall—known as the Gate of Heaven and Hell—into the...*

South Gallery

This area originally was used for church council meetings. The

frescoes on the ceiling are copies of ancient designs, redone by the Fossati brothers during their 19th-century restoration.

Go to the first window on your right. To the right of the window is the *Deesis* **Mosaic,** one of the finest of

Hagia Sophia's Byzantine mosaics—though certainly not its best preserved. Dating from the 13th or 14th century, its theme—the Virgin Mary and John the Baptist asking Jesus for the salvation of souls—is common in Eastern Orthodox churches. Notice how Mary's and John's heads tilt slightly toward Christ. The workmanship is fascinating, especially the expression and detail in the faces. Get up close to examine how miniscule and finely cut the pieces are.

• *Walk to the far end of this gallery to see two more Byzantine mosaic panels, placed side by side.*

As you approach the end of the gallery, look for the 12th-century **Mosaic of the Virgin and Child with Emperor John Comnenus and Empress Irene.** Mary stands in the center, holding the Christ child in her arms. Christ's right hand extends in blessing, and he holds a scroll in his left hand. As in many such mosaics, the emperor offers Christ a bag of money (representing his patronage), and the empress presents a scroll. Their son Prince Alexius is portrayed to his mom's left on the adjoining pier—added to the scene only after he became co-emperor at age 17.

To the left is the 11th-century **Mosaic of Christ with Emperor Constantine IX Monomachus and Empress Zoe.** Constantine and Zoe are portrayed in ceremonial garments, flanking Christ on his throne. The inscription above the emperor's head reads, "Sovereign of Romans, Constantine Monomachus," while the empress is identified as "Zoe, the most pious Augusta."

Standard fare so far, but on closer examination, this mosaic gets quite interesting. If you look carefully, you can see that critical sections of text were erased and then restored (in what looks like a different font). Here's the story: Empress Zoe—the daughter of an emperor who had no male heirs—married Romanus Argyrus, but he was killed in his bath a few years later. Zoe then married her young lover, Michael IV, and, within a few years, he was dead, too. His nephew, Michael V, was named co-emperor and sent Zoe into exile. But the well-connected Zoe found a way back, had Michael V deposed, and at the age of 65 married a third time, to Constantine Monomachus.

That's three husbands in all—and a lot of extra work for the mosaic artists. So, instead of changing the image of Zoe's husband each time, they simply changed the title over his head. And Zoe's face, which was erased by Michael V, was restored to her youth-like appearance after she resumed her reign and married Constantine Monomachus.

• *Retrace your steps back down the ramp to the interior narthex, then turn right and exit the way others are entering. Just outside in a hole on your right are the remains of the earlier Theodosian Church.*

Previous Churches

At least two earlier churches have stood on this spot. No trace remains of the first church, where construction probably began in the fourth century A.D. as Constantine moved to strengthen his hold on the fledgling Byzantine Empire.

The next church, believed to have been built by Theodosius II, was grander in scale and more elaborate. But as fate would have it, this second church was also destroyed during a religious uprising—the Nika riots of 532 that caused the death of more than 30,000 people. Half of the city was reduced to ashes, including the church.

Some remains of the Theodosian Church are visible in the pit just outside the main entrance to Hagia Sophia. You can see part of the steps that led to the entrance portico, the bases of the columns that supported the entry porch, and fragments of marble blocks with carved designs of sheep. Other Theodosian Church artifacts, columns, and capitals are scattered nearby throughout Hagia Sophia's outdoor garden.

• *Your tour is finished. You're close to several other major sights, including the Blue Mosque, Hippodrome, and Underground Cistern (all described in the "Historic Core of Istanbul Walk," earlier). And directly behind Hagia Sophia is the wall of Topkapı Palace (described on page 1163).*

Grand Bazaar and Spice Market Walk

This walk has two parts: In the first, we'll tour the Grand Bazaar, the world's oldest shopping mall, and then we'll walk through the back streets of the Old Town, past the impressive Mosque of Süleyman the Magnificent, to the lively area around the Spice Market and the Eminönü waterfront. The Grand Bazaar is a labyrinthine warren of shops and pushy merchants—a unique Istanbul experience that shouldn't be missed, even if you're not a shopper. While parts of the bazaar and the Spice Market are overrun with international visitors, they also have many virtually tourist-free nooks and crannies that offer an insightful glimpse into the "real" Istanbul.

Orientation

Grand Bazaar: Mon-Sat 9:00-19:00, shops begin to close at 18:30, closed Sun and on the first day of most religious festivals, across the parking lot from the Çemberlitaş tram stop, behind the Nuruosmaniye Mosque.

Spice Market: Free to enter, Mon-Sat 8:00-19:30 (until 19:00 off-season), Sun 9:30-19:00, shops begin to close 30 minutes earlier, at the Old Town end of the Galata Bridge, near the Eminönü tram stop.

Rüstem Paşa Mosque: Free, generally open daily from one hour after sunrise until one hour before sunset, closed to visitors five times a day for prayer, on Hasırcılar Caddesi, Eminönü.

Getting There: It's behind the Nuruosmaniye Mosque, across the parking lot from the Çemberlitaş tram stop. From Sultanahmet (in the center of the Old Town), simply hop the tram to the next stop, or walk five gradually uphill blocks along the tram tracks.

Length of This Walk: Allow at least three hours at a fast pace; if you linger in the shops at the Grand Bazaar and Spice Market, it could fill an entire day.

Shopping Tips: This tour goes hand-in-hand with the "Shopping in Istanbul" section (page 1178). Consider reading that section beforehand, perhaps while nursing a cup of Turkish coffee in the bazaar (focus on the bargaining tips if you plan to buy anything). **Navigating the Bazaar:** The Grand Bazaar is a giant commercial complex with named "streets" *(caddesi)* and "alleys" *(sokak)*. But few of these streets and alleys are well-marked, or the signs are covered by merchandise, so relying

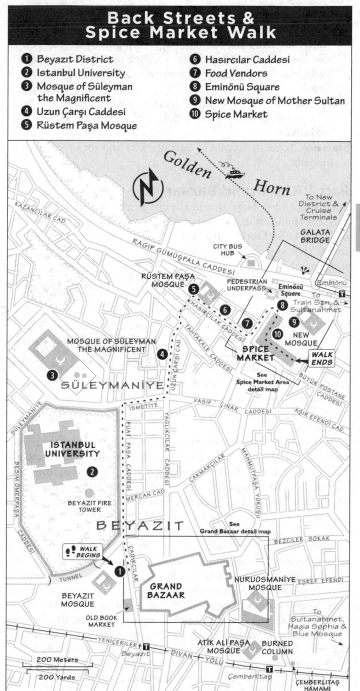

Back Streets & Spice Market Walk

1. Beyazıt District
2. Istanbul University
3. Mosque of Süleyman the Magnificent
4. Uzun Çarşı Caddesi
5. Rüstem Paşa Mosque
6. Hasırcılar Caddesi
7. Food Vendors
8. Eminönü Square
9. New Mosque of Mother Sultan
10. Spice Market

ISTANBUL

Golden Horn

KAZANCILAR CAD.

RAGIP GÜMÜŞPALA CADDESI

CITY BUS HUB

To New District & Cruise Terminals

GALATA BRIDGE

Eminönü

RÜSTEM PAŞA MOSQUE

PEDESTRIAN UNDERPASS

Eminönü Square

To Train Stn. & Sultanahmet

HASIRCILAR CADDESI

TAHTAKALE CADDESI

MOSQUE OF SÜLEYMAN THE MAGNIFICENT

UZUN ÇARŞI CAD.

NEW MOSQUE

SPICE MARKET

WALK ENDS

SÜLEYMANIYE

See Spice Market Area detail map

BÜYÜK POSTANE CADDESI

İSMETIYE

VASIF ÇINAR CADDESI

AŞIR EFENDI CAD.

FUAT PAŞA CADDESI

YAĞLIKÇILAR CADDESI

SÜLEYMANIYE

ISTANBUL UNIVERSITY

MERCAN CAD.

ÇAKMAKÇILAR

MAHMUTPAŞA YOKUŞU

BESIM ÖMERPAŞA CADDESI

BEYAZIT FIRE TOWER

See Grand Bazaar detail map

BEYAZIT

BEZCILER SOKAK

WALK BEGINS

ÇADIRCILAR

GRAND BAZAAR

NURUOSMANIYE MOSQUE

EŞREF EFENDI

TUNNEL

BEYAZIT MOSQUE

OLD BOOK MARKET

To Sultanahmet, Hagia Sophia & Blue Mosque

YENIÇERILER CADDESI

Beyazıt

DIVAN YOLU

ATIK ALI PAŞA MOSQUE

BURNED COLUMN

200 Meters

200 Yards

Çemberlitaş

ÇEMBERLITAŞ HAMAMI

on these names isn't always successful. Complicating matters is the bazaar's mazelike floor plan. To make things easier, navigate using the map on page 1144 and by asking people for help. (But be warned that asking a merchant for help may suck you into a lengthy conversation about the wonders of his wares.)

Pickpocket Alert: The Grand Bazaar probably contains the highest concentration of pickpockets in Istanbul. Watch your valuables.

Starring: Some of Istanbul's best markets and mosques...and its people.

Part 1: The Grand Bazaar

Sprawling over a huge area in the city center, Kapalı Çarşı (kah-pah-luh chahr-shuh; "Covered Market") was the first shopping mall ever built. During Byzantine times, this was the site of a bustling market; when the Ottomans arrived, it grew bigger and more diverse. The prime location attracted guilds, manufacturers, and traders, and it grew quickly— its separate chunks were eventually connected and roofed to form a single market hall. Before

long, the Grand Bazaar became the center for trade in the entire Ottoman Empire. At its prime, the market was locked down and guarded by more than a hundred soldiers every night, like a fortified castle.

The Grand Bazaar remained Turkey's commercial hub—for both locals and international traders—through the 1950s. Its 4,000 shops were bursting with everything you can imagine, from jewelry to silk clothing, and from traditional copperware to exotic Oriental imports. But then the Grand Bazaar was discovered by travelers seeking the ultimate "Oriental market" experience. Prodded by shopaholic tourists with fat wallets, prices and rents skyrocketed, and soon modest shopkeepers and manufacturers found themselves unable to compete with the big money circulating through the bazaar's lanes. These humble merchants moved outside the bazaar, displaced by souvenir and carpet shops.

Today's Grand Bazaar sells 10 times more jewelry than it used to. And, while tourists find it plenty atmospheric, locals now consider its flavor more Western than Oriental. And yet, even though the bazaar has lost some of its traditional ambience, enough artifacts remain to make it an irreplaceable Istanbul experience. This tour takes you through the schlocky tourist zones...but it also takes

ISTANBUL

you by the hand to the market's outer fringe, still frequented by more Turks than tourists.

• *Enter the Grand Bazaar through the* **Nuruosmaniye Gate**, *behind the Nuruosmaniye Mosque. As you walk through the gate, you're at the start of the bazaar's main street, called...*

Kalpakçılar Caddesi

Stepping through the door into air heated by thousands of watts of electric bulbs—and by bustling shoppers and merchants—you'll notice the temperature rise by several degrees. This scene is a little overwhelming at first sight. Welcome to the Grand Bizarre...er, Bazaar.

You're standing on the bazaar's main street, which leads straight from the Nuruosmaniye Mosque to the Beyazıt district, where we'll exit, though we'll take a very roundabout route along the way. This street, Kalpakçılar Caddesi (kahl-pahk-chuh-lahr jahd-deh-see), is "Hatmakers' Street." Historically, each street, alley, or corner of the bazaar was dedicated to a particular craft or item, and they still bear those names.

• *All those lightbulbs are illuminating...*

Jewelry Showcases

Today's high-traffic, high-rent Kalpakçılar Caddesi is dominated by these glittering displays, containing bigger-ticket items than the traditional hats. Turks love gold, not because they're vain or greedy, but because they're practical: Since local currency has a tendency to be devalued, people prefer to invest in something more tangible. Traditionally, Turks celebrating special occasions—such as a wedding or a boy's circumcision—receive gold as a gift. In fact, in the most traditional corners of Turkey, the groom's family still must present the bride's family with gold bracelets before the couple can marry.

Because all this gold is used primarily as an investment, and only secondarily as an accessory, it's most commonly sold in the form of simple 22-carat bracelets (24-carat is too soft to wear). If you see a woman whose arm is lined with five or six of these bracelets, she's not making a fashion statement—she's wearing her family's savings on her sleeve...literally. Recently, jewelers have started selling more elaborately decorated designer pieces. These are more expensive and less appealing to thrifty locals (since you're paying for the workmanship, not just the gold itself).

Instead, locals who want jewelry for fashion buy cheaper 14- or 18-carat bracelets. For tips on shopping for gold, see page 1183.

• *A few steps into the bazaar from the Nuruosmaniye Gate (after the fifth shop on the right), look for the entrance marked* Old Bazaar—Sandal Bedesteni *over the doorway, a little off the main street. Duck into the courtyard called...*

Sandal Bedesteni

The Grand Bazaar is made up of a series of *bedestens* (beh-dehs-tehns)—commercial complexes of related shops. The Sandal Bedesteni is one of the oldest, dating from the late 15th century. After the Ottomans arrived and took over a Byzantine market-place here, the bazaar grew organically—new buildings sporadi-

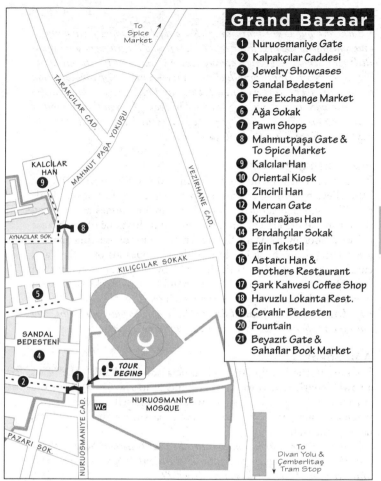

Grand Bazaar

1. Nuruosmaniye Gate
2. Kalpakçılar Caddesi
3. Jewelry Showcases
4. Sandal Bedesteni
5. Free Exchange Market
6. Ağa Sokak
7. Pawn Shops
8. Mahmutpaşa Gate & To Spice Market
9. Kalcılar Han
10. Oriental Kiosk
11. Zincirli Han
12. Mercan Gate
13. Kızlarağası Han
14. Perdahçılar Sokak
15. Eğin Tekstil
16. Astarcı Han & Brothers Restaurant
17. Şark Kahvesi Coffee Shop
18. Havuzlu Lokanta Rest.
19. Cevahir Bedesten
20. Fountain
21. Beyazıt Gate & Sahaflar Book Market

cally sprouted up, each one devoted to a particular trade or item. For the convenience of both the shopkeeper and the customer, shops dealing with similar items clustered together. These distinct units, many of which survive today, are called *bedesten* or *han*. The most traditional *bedestens* (like this one) have a central courtyard surrounded by shops and workshops on two floors. Later, developers roofed these commercial units and connected them with alleys, creating a unified central market hall. But if you pay attention, you'll notice that each part of the bazaar still has its own unique characteristics (and characters).

The Sandal Bedesteni once housed merchants of valuable fabrics (such as silk and velvet), turban-makers, and jewelers specializing in precious stones. Today it carries ordinary textile products and assorted tourist knockoffs.

• Backtrack out to the main drag (Kalpakçılar Caddesi), turn right, and continue to the first intersection, where you'll turn right on Sandal Bedesteni Sokak. Look high above, where signs point to various landmarks. Walk straight downhill on this alley—with a high concentration of souvenir shops, carpets, tiles, leather and kilim bags, and chandeliers—toward the intersecting arches. On the right, you'll pass another entrance to the Sandal Bedesteni we just visited. After that, take the next alley on the right. Walk 50 yards to the...

Free Exchange Market

You'll hear it before you see it. From about 10:00 until 17:00, the little alleys branching off this strip are squeezed full of hundreds of boisterous men shouting into their mobile phones and waving their arms. These are currency brokers, and this zone of the bazaar is like a poor man's Wall Street. In this humble setting, people are cutting deals involving hundreds of thousands of dollars and euros every minute. The Turkish lira is (by European standards) an unstable currency. So, in addition to gold, many Turks still invest in euros or dollars to shore up their savings.

• Backtrack to the alley called Sandal Bedesteni Sokak, turn right, and continue one block to where it intersects with the wider...

Ağa Sokak

Looking to the left up Ağa Sokak (aaa-aah soh-kahk—the "ğ" is a vowel lengthener, without any sound of its own), you'll see the entrance to Cevahir Bedesteni, where people sell antiques, semi-precious stones, and silver items. We'll pass through that *bedesten* later on the walk.

• Continue up the narrow alley called Sandal Bedesteni Sokak. Notice that the shops become less colorful and the clientele becomes more local. This section of the bazaar is mostly devoted to...

Pawn Shops

Many of these shops look empty, with signs on the windows and a few gold items and coins on display. This is where locals can exchange those "investment bracelets" and valuables for some hard cash. When these shops buy jewelry, they deduct whatever the seller paid for workmanship, charge a small commission, and pay for the actual value of the gold.

• Continue to the end of the alley, where it ends at Aynacılar Sokak (eye-nah-juh-lahr; "Mirror-Makers' Alley"). Looking to your right, you'll see another gate of the bazaar, named after the neighboring district.

Mahmutpaşa Gate

If you went through this exit and walked about 15 minutes down the hill, you'd reach the Spice Market. If time is short, you could skip the rest of the Grand Bazaar and head to the Spice Market from here (Spice Market described on page 1156). The area between here and there is a huge outdoor textile bazaar, with retail shops, wholesalers, and workshops.

• *Step outside the Mahmutpaşa Gate and walk a short distance down to a second gate, which opens onto Mahmutpaşa Yokuşu Sokak. Just beyond this second gate, on the left, is the entrance to...*

Kalcılar Han

Named after the traveling-salesman lodgers *(kalıcılar)* once accommodated here, this section of the bazaar is also known as the Gümüşçüler ("silversmith") Hanı, because it's a center for the production and sale of all sorts of handcrafted silver objects.

The Kalcılar Han, like others of its kind, resembles a factory. In each workshop, an artisan completes a different step of the production process. A single silver object goes from one workshop to another, just like in a factory production line, with artisans working together to create a finished piece.

As you walk the long entryway to the open courtyard, you're looking at a typical *han*—built on two floors around a central

courtyard. The first (ground) floor contained stables and storage, while travelers stayed in upper-floor rooms. Today, all the rooms on the upper floor are workshops.

To visit a silversmith, turn to your immediate right as you step into the courtyard, walk in, and take the stairs on the left (mind the low iron bar) to the upper floor. Turn right at the top and find the workshop of **Kapik Usta** at #10. Kapik Usta (kah-peek oos-tah; "Kapik the Master") is a master *sıvamacı* (suh-vah-mah-juh), a silversmith who uses molds. If he's not too busy, he may show you how he does it. Stay away from the lathe, and watch as Kapik transforms a flat piece of metal into a three-dimensional object.

Head to the opposite side of the *han* (by the stairs). At the workshop at #20, Master Zavel uses sand molds to shape melted silver. At #31 is **Barocco Silver,** owned by Kapik Usta's Armenian business partner, Aruş Usta (ah-roosh oos-tah; "Aruş the

Master"). He is a master *dövücü* (dew-vew-jew), a silversmith who uses a hammer to shape flat metal. Walk into his shop, where he works with his son, Dikran, who is also a master craftsman. For tips on buying silver, see page 1184.

• *Backtrack to the Mahmutpaşa Gate, step back inside the Grand Bazaar, and walk straight on Aynacılar Sokak until you hit the intersection marked by a charming little...*

Oriental Kiosk

This adorable structure, built as a teahouse in the 17th century, sells jewelry today. Notice the fountain next to the kiosk. The alley it's on is Acı Çeşme (ah-juh chesh-meh), which means "Bitter Fountain." Avoid the water here...just in case.

• *Turn right at the kiosk onto Acı Çeşme, and walk to the end of the alley. On your right just before the bazaar exit, marked by an arrow hanging from the vaulted ceiling, is the entrance to...*

Zincirli Han

Rough steps take you into Zincirli Han (zeen-jeer-lee hahn; "Chain Han"), which is surrounded mostly by jewelry shops, with some workshops on the upper floor. The shops here are less polished and fancy, and less aggressive, than those in the more touristy zones back in the heart of the bazaar.

At the far end of the courtyard, on the right (unmarked, at #13), is **Merim Kuyumculuk** (koo-yoom-joo-look; "jewelry"). Rather than selling lots of jewelry, this place focuses on production and wholesale—one of the few jewelers in the bazaar with its own workshop nearby.

To the left of Merim, fronting the courtyard, is **Osman's Carpet Shop.** Run by a hard-to-miss "professor of carpets" nicknamed Şişko (sheesh-koh; "Fatty"), this shop is regarded as *the* place to go to get a high-quality, expensive carpet and expert advice. Şişko—often assisted by son Nurullah or nephew Bilgin—won't hustle you or try to talk you into something, like the cheap carpet hawkers elsewhere in the bazaar. He prefers to equip cus-tomers with information to be sure they get the carpet that's right for them. This fifth-generation shop is hardly a secret—notice the celebrity photos, magazine clippings, and guidebook blurbs hanging on the wall. For tips on buying a carpet, see page 1180.

• *Leave Zincirli Han, head back to Acı Çeşme, turn right, and step outside the Grand Bazaar. The jewelry shop to your left just outside the*

Mercan Gate—with hundreds of 22-karat gold bracelets—will give you an idea what most jewelry around here looked like a decade or two ago, before fancier bracelets came into fashion.

Continue a few steps beyond the Mercan Gate, and go through the first building entrance to your left. You're now in...

Kızlarağası Han

The *kızlarağası* was the master of all eunuchs (castrated slaves who looked after the sultan's palace and harem). This humble courtyard is where you'll find middlemen who recycle secondhand gold and silver—or shavings and unwanted fragments from other workshops—and turn them into something usable.

Notice the low-profile teahouse in the center, serving simple glasses of tea to an almost exclusively local crowd.

Ayhan Usta (eye-hahn oos-tah; "Ayhan the Master") is one of the goldsmiths who works here (his shop is the third one on

the left as you enter, across from the teahouse). Ayhan speaks only Turkish, but if you peek into his shop and if he's up for visitors and not too busy, he'll motion you inside to watch him at work. Ayhan belongs to a dying breed. Not much gold production still takes place near the Grand Bazaar, and the few goldsmiths who remain may soon be moved to a plant outside the city.

• *Now go back in the Grand Bazaar, and take the first right as you step in. You'll walk down the big lane called...*

Perdahçılar Sokak

Perdahçılar Sokak (pehr-dah-chuh-lahr soh-kahk) was once the main clothing section of the bazaar; now it's a combination of carpet stores, souvenir shops, "genuine fake items" stands, and shops selling tourist knockoffs of traditional clothes—like fake pashminas or a tongue-in-cheek "one size fits all" belly-dancing outfit.

• *Continue to the T-junction, and turn right onto Yağlıkçılar Sokak (yaah-luhk-chuh-lahr soh-kahk), with items similar to what you've just seen. Walk all the way to the bazaar exit. To the right, just inside the exit door, notice the textile store called...*

Eğin Tekstil

This unassuming little shop provided many of the costumes for the 2004 movie *Troy*—about the ancient city-state near today's Truva, in northwestern Turkey. Go inside and say hello to owner Süleyman or his assistants, who'd be happy to tell you all about their shop's history...and, of course, what they're selling. Eğin Tekstil (eh-een tehks-teel) has been in the same family for five generations, nearly 150 years. In fact, Süleyman—who continues the family tradition even though he's actually a doctor by trade—still has the Ottoman deed to the store. Their specialty is the *peştemal* (pehsh-teh-mahl), the traditional wrap-around sheet for visits to a Turkish bath. This is one of the Grand Bazaar's few stores that actually has an annex behind the main shop built during Byzantine times, which is used for storage (the entrance is on the back wall).

• *Stepping outside the store, turn left and head back the way you came on Yağlıkçılar Sokak. After about 50 yards, on the right—marked with a sign for Brothers Restaurant—you'll see the entrance to...*

Astarcı Han

Go through the doorway, between shops and stands, into Astarcı Han (ahs-tahr-juh hahn; "Courtyard of the Cloth Lining"). Historically, this courtyard was home to textile workshops. A few still remain here: Notice the one in the right-hand corner as you enter (peek inside with a smile to see the textile-makers in action).

On the left as you enter the courtyard is the recommended **Brothers (Kardeşler) Restaurant.** This place specializes in southeastern Turkish cuisine (8-11-TL main courses, 10-20-TL specialty dishes, no alcohol, Mon-Sat 8:00-17:00, closed Sun). WCs are next to the restaurant. If you'd like a cup of Turkish coffee after (or instead of) a meal, the perfect spot is coming right up.

• *Exit Astarcı Han and turn right onto Yağlıkçılar Sokak, continuing in the same direction as before. After a few blocks, keep an eye out on the right-hand side for the tiny green box-like wooden balcony—used for the call to prayer, like a low-tech minaret—marking one of the bazaar's mosques (attached to the wall above the jewelry store); next to it are steps leading up to the mosque.*

Go 50 yards past the mosque on the right-hand corner to find a venerable tea and coffee house called...

Şark Kahvesi

Şark Kahvesi (shark kah-veh-see; "Oriental Coffee Shop") is an Istanbul institution and a good place to sample Turkish coffee. "Turkish coffee" refers not to a type of coffee, but to the way it's prepared: by adding grounds directly to cold water in a copper pot, then stirring until the water boils. Because it's unfiltered, the coffee never completely dissolves. The trick is to gently agitate your cup time and time again to remix the grounds with the water. Otherwise you'll drink weak coffee, and wind up with a thick layer of grounds at the bottom when you're done.

Locals prefer Turkish coffee (*kahve*; kah-veh) without sugar, but many first-timers—even coffee-loving ones—prefer to add sugar to make its powerful flavor a bit more palatable. Since the sugar is added while the coffee is being cooked, you have to ask for it when you place your order: *az şekerli* (ahz sheh-kehr-lee) will get you a little sugar, *orta şekerli* (ohr-tah sheh-kehr-lee) is a medium scoop, and just *şekerli* (sheh-kehr-lee) roughly translates as "tons of sugar—I hate the taste of real coffee."

• *Just past Şark Kahvesi on Yağlıkçılar Sokak, a lane on the right leads to the **Havuzlu Lokanta restaurant**, which serves a sped-up version of traditional Ottoman cuisine (4.50-TL salads and starters, 9-TL vegetarian dishes, 14-16-TL main courses, 1 TL extra for water and bread, Mon-Sat 12:00-17:30, closed Sun). Unless you're stopping for lunch, head left, down Zenneciler Sokak (zehn-neh-jee-lehr soh-kahk). After about 100 yards, you'll emerge into a courtyard we saw earlier from the other side...*

Cevahir Bedesten

Cevahir Bedesten (jeh-vah-heer beh-dehs-tehn) was built as a freestanding warehouse for merchants in the 15th century. It has been used for many purposes since, but the basic structure—with domed bays supported by eight massive pillars—is still intact. Entering the courtyard, you may notice it's taller than the rest of the bazaar, and, since it's devoted to big-ticket items, it's a bit quieter. Most merchants here are antique dealers, selling icons, metal objects, miniatures, coins, cameras, daggers, and so on; others here sell semiprecious stones, either by the piece or on chains. There are also a few silver shops and places where you can buy worry beads with semiprecious stones.

• *From the center of Cevahir Bedesten, turn 90 degrees to the right and leave through the door into the bustling alleys of the bazaar—this zone is packed with souvenir shops, as well as carpets and traditional metal items. Soon you'll run into the main street, Kalpakçılar Caddesi.*

*Turn right on Kalpakçılar Caddesi and walk about 200 yards to the gate leading to the Beyazıt (beh-yah-zuht) district. Halfway to the Beyazıt exit, keep an eye on your right, behind the **fountain**, for a stretch of shops selling leather, denim, and other textiles. At the end of Kalpakçılar Caddesi, you'll exit through the...*

Beyazıt Gate and Sahaflar Book Market

You may feel that you've only seen a small part of the very Grand Bazaar. You're right—there are another 4,000 shops we haven't passed on this tour. Entire trips, books, and lifetimes are devoted to the wonders of the Grand Bazaar.

But for now, let's look at one more interesting corner of the Grand Bazaar scene. As you exit through the Beyazıt Gate (with a tram stop 100 yards to your left), turn right and walk toward the crowded market area for textiles, clothes, and shoes—popular with local bargain-hunters. After about 20 yards, look on your left for steps leading to Sahaflar (sah-hahf-lahr), the old book market. For two centuries, this was a magnet for bibliophiles—even 20 years ago, you could find rare old collector's items with fancy illustrations. But today only a few shops sell those items (or handmade replicas of them), while most others carry textbooks, books that are hard to sell at a mainstream bookstore, and books on religious topics.

• *Our bazaar tour is finished. The second half of this walk takes you through the back streets of Istanbul's Old Town, past the Mosque of Süleyman the Magnificent and on to the Spice Market (near the waterfront and a short walk back to the cruise terminals), giving you a taste of the authentic city.*

If you'd prefer to skip the rest of this walk, you can go to Beyazıt Square and catch a tram back to the Sultanahmet stop (for the center of the Old Town), or to the Karaköy stop for your ship (see "Returning to Your Ship," page 1094).

Part 2: Back Streets and Spice Market

This next stretch—through the Beyazıt district, connecting the Grand Bazaar and the Mosque of Süleyman the Magnificent—involves about a half-mile of walking, with relatively little to see in between...but it's worth the trek.

Beyazıt District

Facing the book market, go right and walk a couple hundred yards through the outdoor textile market. At the end of the textile alley, you'll be facing the wall of Istanbul University's main campus (across the street). This area, called Beyazıt, is where the market crowds and the student population mix, giving it a special spice.

• *Continue straight down the busy street (Fuat Paşa Caddesi) with the university wall across the street on your left. Go a block or so along the right side of the road, then cross the street to the left side (along the wall). We'll continue about a quarter-mile straight downhill along this road.*

Notice that many stores along here sell **kitchen utensils.** This district was once Istanbul's coppersmith center. Even up until the early 1980s, many people still used copper utensils. But now that modern materials and methods have taken over, coppersmiths are mainly a thing of the past, and most of the utensils along here are made of steel, aluminum, or pressed copper or brass.

• *At the fenced gate in the wall, the landmark Beyazıt fire tower marks the grounds of...*

Istanbul University

This partly state-subsidized school (closed to tourists) is the city's biggest university, with thousands of students from all over Turkey.

This is the larger of Istanbul University's two main campuses.

• *After the shops end, the wall continues. Keep going until the end of the wall. If you can spare the time, consider making a detour to see the gigantic and freshly restored* **Mosque of Süleyman the Magnificent** *(300 yards uphill to your left, described on page 1170). Otherwise, turn right steeply downhill about 150 yards to the second street on your left (Uzun Çarşı Caddesi—look for a sycamore tree on the corner and a fast-food kiosk across the street). Turning downhill and left onto this street, you'll see the brick minaret of a 15th-century mosque straight ahead and, behind it, the minaret of our next stop—Rüstem Paşa Mosque.*

Uzun Çarşı Caddesi

As you walk straight ahead along this street—which soon becomes a narrow alley, near the brick minaret—you'll be jostled by shoppers and nudged by delivery trucks trying to sneak their way into the commercial sprawl. Shops on either side cater to locals: hardware stores, stationery shops, toy stores, quilt-makers, sportswear vendors, shoe stores, and so on. If you're looking for a traditional backgammon board—without all that shiny, fake mother-of-pearl and wood inlay that strain your eyes as you play—you'll find it here, and dirt cheap.

• *The alley runs directly into a two-story stone building with an arched entryway. Go through the humble doorway and take the stairs up into the courtyard of the...*

Rüstem Paşa Mosque

Built by Sinan in the 16th century, this mosque stands on an elevated platform, supported by vaults that house shops (which once provided income for the mosque's upkeep). Admire the giant portico that covers most of the mosque's courtyard, and notice that Rüstem Paşa seems to be missing one feature found at almost every mosque: a fountain for ablution. Because of the limited space in this courtyard, Sinan placed the fountain at street level (down the stairs across the courtyard from where you entered).

The mosque's facade is slathered in gorgeous 16th-century İznik tiles, but the interior is even more impressive. To enter, go around the left side to find the visitors' entrance. Inside, virtually every surface is covered with floral-designed tile panels. (Locals say that if the Blue Mosque is Istanbul's Notre-Dame, this tiny gem is its Sainte-Chapelle.)

• *Because the next alley we'll be using is always packed with people—especially on Saturdays—consider reading the following section before you start walking. Leave the mosque complex through the door you entered, passing some enticing tile souvenirs. Turn left and walk down...*

Hasırcılar Caddesi

Hasırcılar (hah-sur-juh-lahr) Caddesi ("Mat-Weavers' Alley") is a real-life market street—part of the commercial sprawl surrounding our next sight, the Spice Market.

As you walk, notice the porters and the carts squeezing their heavy, wide loads through the alley. You'll pass old *bedestens* (traditional commercial buildings) and stores, many of them family-owned for generations. If you had strolled this street a century ago, only the shoppers' clothes would have been different.

At the first corner on your left, notice the store selling hunting knives and rifles. Turkey has strong gun-control laws, but they don't extend to hunting rifles—you just need a hunting license to own one of these weapons.

One block before the Spice Market entrance, you'll smell the aroma of fresh-roasted coffee and spices. If you're in the market for spices, dried fruits, sweets, and nuts, start checking the prices along here—they're cheaper than in the high-rent Spice Market. Ask for a sample, and don't feel obligated to buy. While bargaining has become common in the Grand Bazaar, around here you'll generally pay what's on the price tag for food and spices—though souvenirs and exotic items (such as saffron and imported caviar) may be haggled over.

• *Half a block before the arched entry to the Spice Market (the big brick-and-stone building at the end of the alley), you'll be immersed in a lively bazaar of...*

Food Vendors

On your left, look for the thriving deli, **Namlı Şarküteri,** with the large containers of olives, pickled peppers, and hanging pastramis out front (get a sample inside). It's been here for over a century, selling a wide range of traditional cold *mezes* (appetizers): dry salted fish, spicy tomato and pepper pastes, pickles, *sucuk* (soo-jook; spicy veal sausage), Turkish pastrami, and a variety of white cheeses made from sheep's and cow's milk. They also make a high-cholesterol sandwich called *kumru* (koom-roo; meaning "dove"), stuffed with spicy sausages, salami, and smoked cow's tongue. Wander through to get a feeling for what locals buy at the grocery store, and say hello to Zeki, the guy who runs the place. Upstairs is an oasis of a cafeteria (air-con, bright, cheery, and fast).

A little farther ahead on the right, just before the Spice Market entrance, is one of the best coffee vendors in town: the venerable **Kurukahveci Mehmet Efendi Mahdumları** (say it three times fast). This is the locals' favorite place to get ground coffee. Remember that only sealed packets can be taken through US Customs, and pick up the leaflet with preparation instructions when you check out. There's often a long line of loyal customers waiting at the cashier. If you can't find it on the map, just follow your nose.

• *Just after the coffee shop is the Spice Market's Hasırcılar Gate. Rather than entering the market here, let's walk around the side of the L-shaped building to the main entrance, facing the Golden Horn. Turn left and continue along the street (following the Spice Market wall).*

Along this alley you'll spot several more shops displaying spices, dried fruits, and sweets, alongside butcher, fishmonger, and dairy shops. The Turks have a word for this vibrant scene: *pazar* (pah-zahr), which gave us the English word "bazaar."

The alley opens into the large **Eminönü Square,** with the Golden Horn (not quite visible from here) on the other side of the busy street.

Before or after you tour the Spice Market, consider these options. You could take a break, sitting with locals on the platforms by the side of the square, watching the people pass by. (If you've bought some munchies, here's a good place to picnic. You can get a beverage from a nearby store, or from the newsstand straight ahead.)

If you'd like a cup of coffee or tea, walk down the alley (bordering the square) to your immediate left as you face the Golden Horn. You'll soon come to **Ender Çikolata,** a chocolate and candy store (on the left). It has tables and chairs across the alley, where you can sit down and relax.

• *Continue around the corner of the Spice Market to the right to reach the main entrance.*

In Front of the Spice Market

The square in front of the Spice Market is dominated by the **New Mosque of Mother Sultan** (or simply "New Mosque")—one of the latest examples of classical, traditional-style Ottoman mosques.

This square was once a huge outdoor bazaar. You may still see a few makeshift stands with vendors hawking anything from clothes to fake jewelry to giant posters of pop stars. The vendors, who "forget" to pay taxes, are routinely rounded up by local police—so don't be surprised if you see a string of people running up the street with merchandise in their hands, chased by municipal inspectors.

Also notice the **pigeons.** Consider that most Turks believe it's good luck if a pigeon leaves its mark on you. Unless you're interested in putting this to the test, don't get too close to the buildings (where the birds are likely to be perched overhead, just waiting to bestow luck).

With the mosque on your left, you're facing the front of the Spice Market. Notice the outdoor plant and pet market to the left.

A WC is just around this corner, in the inner corner of the "L" formed by the Spice Market.

• *Now go through the main entrance into the...*

Spice Market

Built in the mid-17th century, this market hall was gradually taken over by merchants dealing in spices, herbs, medicinal plants,

and pharmaceuticals. While it's quite a touristy scene today, most stalls still sell much of the same products, and the air is heavy with the aroma of exotic spices. Locals call it the Mısır Carşışı (Egyptian Bazaar) because it was once funded by taxes paid by Egypt.

While smaller and less imposing than the Grand Bazaar, the Spice Market is more colorful, with the ambience of a true Oriental market. On either side of the long, vaulted central hall are a wide range of merchant stalls, most of them

with sacks and barrels out front showing off their wares. While merchants once sat quietly, cross-legged, next to their shops, today they engage in a never-ending game of one-upmanship, competing for the attention of passersby. If you're offered a sample of something (such as Turkish delight), feel free to accept—but be warned that it can be difficult to pry yourself away from the sales pitch that's sure to ensue. (To the left as you enter, note the staircase leading to the second floor. Upstairs is the recommended and historic **Pandelli Restaurant,** described on page 1189).

Aside from the spice shops, you'll also see stores slinging natural sponges, lentils and beans, dried vegetables, dried fruits (especially figs and apricots), pistachios and hazelnuts, and sweets of several different kinds—including, of course, Turkish delight. While most Westerners think of Turkish delight as being colored and fruit-flavored, locals prefer more adventurous varieties: with

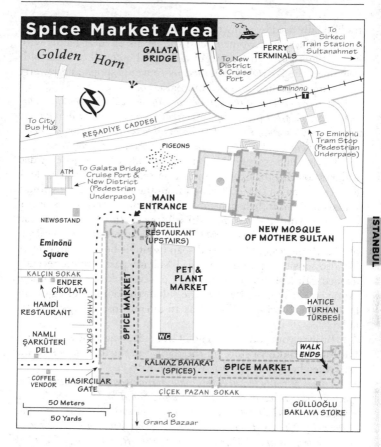

Spice Market Area

Golden Horn

GALATA BRIDGE

To New District & Cruise Port

FERRY TERMINALS

To Sirkeci Train Station & Sultanahmet

Eminönü T

To City Bus Hub

REŞADİYE CADDESİ

To Eminönü Tram Stop (Pedestrian Underpass)

PIGEONS

ATM

To Galata Bridge, Cruise Port & New District (Pedestrian Underpass)

MAIN ENTRANCE

NEWSSTAND

PANDELLI RESTAURANT (UPSTAIRS)

NEW MOSQUE OF MOTHER SULTAN

Eminönü Square

KALÇIN SOKAK

ENDER ÇİKOLATA

PET & PLANT MARKET

SPICE MARKET

TAHMİS SOKAK

HAMDİ RESTAURANT

HATICE TURHAN TÜRBESİ

NAMLI ŞARKÜTERİ DELI

WC

WALK ENDS

COFFEE VENDOR

HASIRCILAR GATE

KALMAZ BAHARAT (SPICES)

SPICE MARKET

ÇİÇEK PAZAN SOKAK

50 Meters

50 Yards

To Grand Bazaar

GÜLLÜOĞLU BAKLAVA STORE

ISTANBUL

double-roasted pistachios, or the kind with walnuts in grape or mulberry molasses called *sucuk* (soo-jook; also the name of the spicy veal sausage).

Look for the granddaddy of spices, **saffron.** Locals still use saffron (mostly in rice pilaf and dessert), though not as much as they used to. The best saffron is Spanish; the local kind—cheaper and not as dark-red—usually comes mixed with other herbs. The **caviar** you see isn't local; it's mostly from Iran or Russia. More authentic are the Turkish dried **apricots** and **figs.** Dried vegetables, eggplant, and green peppers hang from the walls. Cooks use these to make *dolma* (dohl-mah; "to stuff"), stuffing them with rice and raisins, or rice and meat. You'll also see lots of sacks full of green powder. This is **henna,** traditionally used by women as a hair dye and for skin care. In the countryside, young women stain the palms of their hands with henna the night before they get married. Lately all of these old-fashioned shops are being joined by souvenir shops and jewelry stores, making this a mini-Grand Bazaar of sorts.

• *Walk to the far end of the hall, at the intersection with the side wing of the Spice Market (to the left). Straight ahead is a gate leading to an always-busy street that heads five blocks up to the Grand Bazaar; to the right is the Hasırcılar Gate, leading to the alley we just came down.*

Go left and start walking down the side wing—less crowded and less colorful than the main concourse. After a few steps, look for a tiny shop on the left (second from the corner) called **Kalmaz Baharat.** *Baharat* (bah-hah-raht) means "spice," and this is one of the few remaining shops that still sells the exotic spices of the past. Adnan, the owner, has herbal teas, thick aromatic oils, natural-fiber bath gloves, and olive-oil soap (white is better than green). He also sells the aphrodisiac called "sultan's paste" (more recently dubbed "Turkish Viagra"). This mix of several kinds of herbs and exotic spices supposedly gave the sultan the oomph to enjoy his huge harem, and is still used as an all-purpose energy booster today.

Browse your way to the end of this side wing (notice the great **Güllüoğlu Baklava** store on the right, the third shop before the exit), then head back the way you came.

• *When you're ready to finish this walk, retrace your steps and leave the Spice Market through the main entrance. You'll be facing the Galata Bridge over the Golden Horn, with your cruise ship just past the far side of the bridge. To head back across the bridge on foot, walk to the pedestrian underpass ahead of you (a little to the left, with an ATM kiosk nearby) that will take you under the busy street to the Galata Bridge. (Notice the many restaurants on the lower level of the bridge; this area is described in the Golden Horn Walk, earlier.)*

To reach the Eminönü tram stop—where you can catch the tram to go to the center of the Old Town (Sultanahmet stop), or ride it one stop to the Karaköy cruise terminal (or two stops to the Salıpazarı terminal)—walk to the right between the New Mosque and the busy street. Where the mosque ends, you'll see the entrance to another pedestrian underpass. Halfway through the underpass, steps lead up to separate platforms: The first one is for the Old Town. The second platform—a little farther on—is for the New District (and your ship), across the Galata Bridge.

Alternatively, you can generally wave down a cab along the main street right in front of the Spice Market. Or, to walk up to Sultanahmet (about 15 minutes away), turn right, walk with the New Mosque on your left, go straight ahead five blocks to the Sirkeci train station, and follow the tram tracks uphill.

Sights in Istanbul

While Istanbul has many interesting sights well-worth knowing about on a longer visit (see the "Istanbul at a Glance" sidebar, page 1104), for a one-day cruiser visit, I've listed just the most important and central sights.

The sights listed in this section are arranged by neighborhood for handy sightseeing. Don't let the length of these descriptions determine your sightseeing priorities. In this section, Istanbul's most important sights have the shortest listings. These sights are covered in much more detail in one of the earlier walks or tours.

Ticket offices of the city's museums are in the process of being privatized. It's unclear what changes that could bring, but it may mean that opening times will differ from what I've listed here. If a sight is a must-see for you, check its hours in advance (on its website or a TI), and visit well before the closing times listed here.

In the Old Town
Istanbul's highest concentration of sights is in its Old Town, mostly in the Sultanahmet neighborhood.

In the Sultanahmet Area
Some of the following sights are linked by the "Historic Core of Istanbul Walk," which describes the Blue Mosque, the Hippodrome, and the Underground Cistern in greater detail (see page 1113).

▲▲▲**Hagia Sophia (Aya Sofya)**—It's been called the greatest house of worship in the Christian and Muslim worlds: Hagia Sophia (eye-ah soh-fee-yah), the Great Church of Constantinople. Built by the Byzantine Emperor Justinian in A.D. 537 on the grandest scale possible, it was later converted into a mosque by the conquering Ottomans, and now serves as Istanbul's most impressive museum. Hagia Sophia remains the high point of Byzantine architecture. Inside, restoration work attempts to do justice to the Christian and Islamic elements that meld peacefully under Hagia Sophia's soaring arches.

Cost and Hours: 20 TL, covers entire museum; Tue-Sun 9:00-18:30, until 16:30 off-season, temporary exhibits and upper galleries close 30 minutes earlier, closed Mon, last entry one hour before closing, in the heart of the Old Town at Sultanahmet Meydanı, tel. 0212/528-4500.

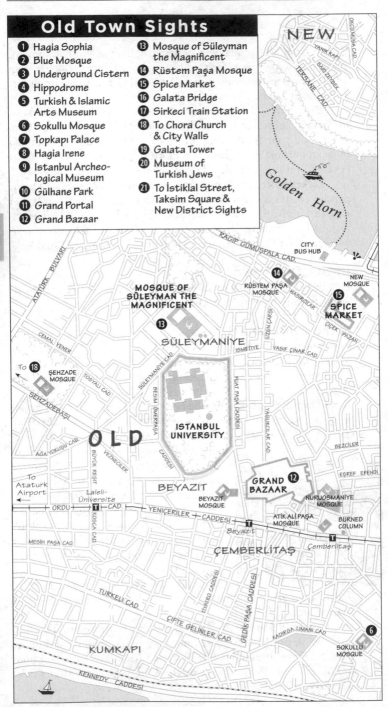

Old Town Sights

1. Hagia Sophia
2. Blue Mosque
3. Underground Cistern
4. Hippodrome
5. Turkish & Islamic Arts Museum
6. Sokullu Mosque
7. Topkapı Palace
8. Hagia Irene
9. Istanbul Archeological Museum
10. Gülhane Park
11. Grand Portal
12. Grand Bazaar
13. Mosque of Süleyman the Magnificent
14. Rüstem Paşa Mosque
15. Spice Market
16. Galata Bridge
17. Sirkeci Train Station
18. To Chora Church & City Walls
19. Galata Tower
20. Museum of Turkish Jews
21. To İstiklal Street, Taksim Square & New District Sights

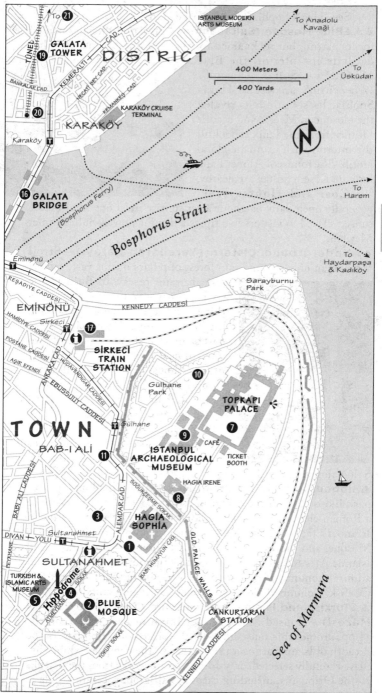

ISTANBUL

See "Hagia Sophia Tour" on page 1126.

▲▲▲Blue Mosque (Sultanahmet Camii)—Officially named for its patron, but nicknamed for the cool hues of the tiles that

decorate its interior, the Blue Mosque was Sultan Ahmet I's 17th-century answer to Hagia Sophia. Its six minarets rivaled the mosque in Mecca, and beautiful tiles from the İznik school fill the interior with exquisite floral motifs. The tombs of Ahmet I and his wife Kösem Sultan are nearby.

Cost and Hours: Free, generally open daily one hour after sunrise until one hour before sunset, closed to visitors five times a day for prayer, Sultanahmet Meydanı.

▲▲Underground Cistern (Yerebatan Sarayı)—Stroll through an underground rain forest of pillars in this vast, subter-

ranean water reservoir. Built in the sixth century A.D. to store water for a thirsty and fast-growing capital city, the 27-million-gallon-capacity cistern covers an area about the size of two football fields. Your visit to the dimly lit, cavernous chamber includes two stone Medusa heads recycled from earlier Roman structures.

Cost and Hours: 10 TL, daily 9:00-20:00, sometimes closes at 17:30 off-season, last entry 30 minutes before closing, Yerebatan Caddesi 13, Sultanahmet, tel. 0212/512-1570.

▲Hippodrome (Sultanahmet Meydanı)—This long, narrow park-like square in the center of Istanbul's Old Town was once a Roman chariot racetrack. Today it's the front yard for many of Istanbul's most famous sights, including Hagia Sophia, the Blue Mosque, and the İbrahim Paşa Palace (home to the Turkish and Islamic Arts Museum). Strolling the Hippodrome's length, you'll admire monuments that span the ages, including the Egyptian Obelisk, Column of Constantine, and German Fountain.

▲▲Turkish and Islamic Arts Museum (Türk-İslam Eserleri Müzesi)—Housed in the former İbrahim Paşa Palace on the Hippodrome, this museum's 40,000-piece collection covers the breadth of Islamic art over the centuries. The compact exhibit displays carefully selected, easy-to-appreciate works from the Selçuks to the Ottomans, including carpets, calligraphy, ceramics, glass, and art represented in wood, stone, and metal. The downstairs Ethnographic Department uses fascinating full-size reconstructions and models to show the development of the traditional Turkish home.

Cost and Hours: 10 TL, Tue-Sun 9:00-17:00, last entry at 16:30, closed Mon, no photography, Sultanahmet Meydanı—across from the Hippodrome's Egyptian Obelisk, Sultanahmet, tel. 0212/518-1805.

Topkapı Palace and Nearby

This walled zone, at the tip of the Old Town Peninsula, is a five-minute walk from the heart of the Sultanahmet district. On the sprawling grounds of the Topkapı Palace complex, you'll find the former residence of the sultans, one of Istanbul's top museums, and all the historical trappings of a once-thriving empire.

▲▲▲**Topkapı Palace (Topkapı Sarayı)**—For centuries, this was the palace where the great sultans hung their turbans. Topkapı

Palace stands on the ruins of Byzantium, the ancient Greek settlement at the eastern tip of the Old Town peninsula. After capturing Constantinople, Ottoman Sultan Mehmet the Conqueror chose this prime location—overlooking the Sea of Marmara, the Bosphorus, and the Golden Horn—as the administrative center of his empire. In the 1470s, he built a large complex with offices, military barracks, a council chamber, and a reception hall. A century later, Topkapı (tohp-kah-puh) became the sultan's residence when Süleyman the Magnificent turned it into a home. Topkapı efficiently served as the sole administrative palace for Ottoman sultans for more than 400 years, until a new European-style palace was built on the Bosphorus in the mid-19th century (Dolmabahçe Palace).

Originally known as the sultan's "New Palace," Topkapı was gradually enlarged over the centuries. Each reigning sultan contributed his own flourishes, according to the style of the era. In its many pavilions and courtyards you can see a 16th-century kitchen, 10,000 pieces of fine Chinese porcelain, traditional weapons, royal robes, ceremonial thrones, and Sultan Ahmet III's tulip garden. The Imperial Treasury is home to the famous jewel-encrusted Topkapı Dagger and the stunning 86-carat Spoonmaker's Diamond. A separate ticket covers the cloistered rooms of the famous Harem, where the sultan's wives and concubines lived.

Cost and Hours: Palace—20 TL, late March-late Oct Wed-Mon 9:00-19:00, until 16:45 off-season, closed Tue, exhibits begin to close one hour earlier; Harem—15 TL, Wed-Mon 10:00-16:00, closed Tue; audioguide-10 TL for whole palace except the Harem, 10 TL for Harem; between the Golden Horn and Sea of Marmara in the Sultanahmet district, a short walk from Hagia Sophia and the Sultanahmet tram stop. You can also take the tram to the Gülhane stop, go in the gate on the side wall of the Topkapı complex, and bear right up the hill. Tel. 0212/512-0480, www.topkapisarayi.gov.tr.

❍ Self-Guided Tour: The palace complex's main entry is near the back of Hagia Sophia, through the **Imperial Gate** in the outer wall. Mehmet the Conqueror (a.k.a. Mehmet II) built the gate when he chose this site as his administrative center in the 15th century—just above the entryway, notice his imperial signature, or *tuğra* (too-rah).

Going through the Imperial Gate, you find yourself in Topkapı's **First Courtyard.** This wide-open space was reserved for public officials, civil servants, and service personnel. It was also called the "Courtyard of Janissaries," for the royal soldiers who assembled here.

As you walk from the Imperial Gate toward the palace through the First Courtyard, notice the terra-cotta church on your left (not generally open to the public). **Hagia Irene** dates back to the reign of Justinian in the sixth century. Soon after Constantine split the Roman Empire between West and East—with the Eastern capital here, in Byzantium (renamed Constantinople)—Hagia Irene hosted the Second Ecumenical Council to set the course for the new church (in A.D. 381).

Past the Imperial Gate are the palace's ticket office and gift shop, and a WC. Just beyond the ticket window, in the wall, notice the little Executioner's Fountain—where the executioner washed his hands...and blade. With that cheerful thought, turn your attention to the **Gate of Salutation.** It dates from the mid-16th century, when the towers were used for defense as much as

Topkapı Palace

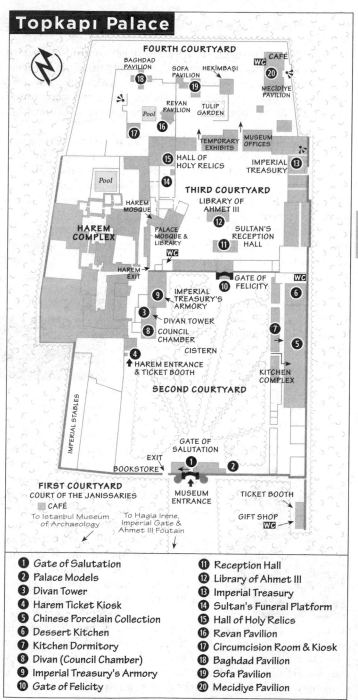

1. Gate of Salutation
2. Palace Models
3. Divan Tower
4. Harem Ticket Kiosk
5. Chinese Porcelain Collection
6. Dessert Kitchen
7. Kitchen Dormitory
8. Divan (Council Chamber)
9. Imperial Treasury's Armory
10. Gate of Felicity
11. Reception Hall
12. Library of Ahmet III
13. Imperial Treasury
14. Sultan's Funeral Platform
15. Hall of Holy Relics
16. Revan Pavilion
17. Circumcision Room & Kiosk
18. Baghdad Pavilion
19. Sofa Pavilion
20. Mecidiye Pavilion

for decoration, and was likely modeled after medieval European fortresses.

As you pass through security and ticket control, look up to see the ornate decorations on the underside of the large eave. Once through the gate, you're now in the palace complex's **Second Courtyard.** This was not a private garden, but a ceremonial courtyard—host to centuries of coronations, successions, and other major benchmarks.

To get your historical orientation, head around to the right side of the security checkpoint (with the gate at your back) to find two glass showcases with elaborate **models** of Topkapı Palace. Behind these, find the map showing the growing Ottoman Empire.

Along the right side of the Second Courtyard, marked by the domes and tall chimneys, are the palace workshops and **imperial kitchens,** which now house a porcelain and silver collection (possibly closed during your visit). To the left of the tall Divan Tower (at the far-left corner of the courtyard) is the **Divan**—the council chamber where the viziers (ministers) of the imperial council governed the Ottoman Empire for almost 400 years. Inside the council chamber (the larger room), the viziers would sit on the sofa according to their rank in the hierarchy. (This is why some people call sofas "divans.")

To the left of the Divan, just around the corner, is the ticket booth and entrance to the **Harem** (hah-rehm). (If there's a line

at the Harem entrance, you'd be wise to skip it now and return after you've seen the rest of the palace—keeping in mind the Harem's early closing time—and proceed now to the Gate of Felicity, described later.) The one-way route of the Harem includes about 20 rooms, including stunning tile work, the mother sultan's private apartments, wives' and concubines' courts, the sultan's own living quarters, and the grand reception hall, all well-described by audioguide.

The word "harem" refers to two things: the wives, favorites, and concubines of the sultan; and the part of the palace where they lived. Contrary to Western fantasy, the Harem was not the site of a round-the-clock mindless orgy, but a carefully administered social institution that ensured the longevity of the Ottoman Empire. Its primary role was to provide future heirs to the Ottoman throne, an essential responsibility that was too important to be left to coincidence. Thanks largely to the Harem, the Ottoman Empire was ruled by a single dynasty from start to finish, avoiding many of the squabbles and battles for succession that tainted other great empires.

The sultan was the head of the household, which he shared with his mother. The only men who could enter the Harem—other than the sultan and young princes—were the sultan's close relatives, the "black eunuchs" (enslaved and castrated North Africans who served the Harem) and, when necessary, doctors. The sultan could have up to four wives, with the first one being considered the senior, most influential wife. Also living in the Harem was a collection of several hundred concubines—female slaves who kept house.

Leaving the Harem, you'll find yourself in the Third Courtyard of the palace complex. To go back to where you started,

turn right and follow the wall to pass through the striking **Gate of Felicity.**

The gate leads to the **Third Courtyard** and, in it, the sultans' **Reception Hall,** a throne room designed to impress visitors. Go right into the throne room—admiring the gorgeous 16th-century throne—and out the other side. The gray-white marble building straight ahead is the 18th-century **Library of Ahmet III.** Indoor photography is not allowed in the other sights surrounding the Third Courtyard (Imperial Treasury, Sultans' Clothing Collection, and Hall of Muslim Relics—coming up next).

On your right, at the edge of the courtyard, is the impressive **Imperial Treasury.** Its four chambers display a sumptuous collection of the sultans' riches: imperial thrones, jewels, and more. The fourth room is the most spectacular, holding the famous Topkapı Dagger and the 86-carat pearl-shaped Spoonmaker's Diamond—one of the biggest diamonds in the world (they say a poor man found this diamond in the dirt in the 17th century and bartered it to a spoonmaker for wooden spoons).

Back outside, follow the portico to the right (notice the stairs, to your immediate right, leading down into the Fourth Courtyard and its Mecidiye Pavilion, with a restaurant, cafeteria, and WC). In front of the large hall at the end of the portico, look for the marble slab to the left of the door, next to the columns—the **Sultan's Funeral Platform.** According to Muslim tradition, after a dead body is washed and wrapped in a white shroud, it's laid on a slab for a final religious service—to honor and pray for the deceased.

Step into the **Hall of Holy Relics,** which shows off some of the most significant holy items of the Muslim faith. These relics were brought to Istanbul in the early 16th century, when their original locations—Egypt, Mecca, and Medina—were conquered by the Ottomans. As this is a very holy site for Muslims, you'll see many people praying with their hands open. Read the rules on the sign next to the entrance, and be respectful as you visit this exhibit. You'll see items related to the Kabaa (the holiest of Muslim shrines, the big black cube in the center of the mosque at Mecca), strangely well-preserved everyday items from the lives of religious figures (the footprint of Muhammad, Muhammad's sandals, Moses' staff, Abraham's granite cooking pot, David's sword, Joseph's turban), and relics from Muhammad, including hair from his beard and his sword and bow. In the room next to the tiled Fountain Room, an imam (cleric) reads verses from the Quran 24 hours a day—as imams have nonstop since the 16th century.

The last section of the palace, just through the portico described earlier, is the **Fourth Courtyard.** The most intimate and cozy of Topkapı's zones, it enjoys fine views over the Golden Horn and Bosphorus, and is dotted with several decorative pavilions.

Atop the marble staircase (to your left as you enter the Fourth Courtyard) is the **Revan Pavilion.** Step inside to take a look at the interior, which is typical of the style of the time: decorated with 17th-century İznik tiles, pillowed sofas, and mother-of-pearl and tortoiseshell inlays, and roofed with a central dome.

Outside the pavilion, past the pool, find the **Circumcision Room**—the highly decorated pavilion at the edge of the terrace  used for the ritual circumcision of heirs to the throne. Stroll along the pool and pop over to the left to the bronze-gilded **kiosk** with the perfect panorama of the Golden Horn and New District. With that grand view on your left, continue straight ahead to the Baghdad Pavilion, built by Sultan Murat IV to celebrate the conquest of Baghdad.

Down the stairs you'll pass the **Tulip Garden,** where Sultan Ahmet III grew rare bulbs in an unusual time of peace and prosperity for the Ottoman Empire. The first building on the left, just beyond the garden, is the late-17th-century **Sofa Pavilion.** Ahmet III would lounge on a sofa here and gaze at his tulips after a long night of worldly pleasures.

At the far end of the courtyard is the **Mecidiye Pavilion.** In addition to spectacular views, the pavilion hosts a pair of restaurants (one self-service, the other with table service) offering a convenient and scenic finish to your tour.

▲▲Istanbul Archaeological Museum (İstanbul Arkeoloji Müzesi)—In a city as richly layered with the remains of fallen  civilizations as Istanbul, this museum is a worthwhile stop. Although not as extensive as its more-established European counterparts (such as London's British Museum), the variety and quality of the Istanbul Archaeological Museum's collection rivals any, with intricately carved sarcophagi, an army of Greek and Roman sculptures, gorgeous İznik tiles, ancient Babylonian friezes, and an actual chunk of the chain that the Byzantines stretched across the Golden Horn. The complex consists of three separate museums (all covered by the same ticket). In the main building, the Museum of Archaeology houses a vast exhibit on the Greeks, the Romans, and other early civilizations of the Near East. The star attraction here is the elaborately decorated and remarkably well-preserved Alexander Sarcophagus. The other museums are small enough to merit at least a quick walk-through: The Museum of the Ancient Orient shows off striking fragments from the even-more-ancient civilizations of Mesopotamia and Anatolia (the Asian portion of modern-day Turkey, east of the Bosphorus Strait), such as the 13th-century B.C. Kadesh Treaty—the first written peace agreement in world history. And the Tiled Kiosk sparkles with a staggering array of sumptuous ceramics and tiles.

Cost and Hours: 10 TL includes all three sections; Tue-Sun 9:00-16:45, closed Mon; last entry at 16:00, Osman Hamdi Bey Yokuşu, Gülhane, Eminönü. Tel. 0212/520-7740, www.istanbul arkeoloji.gov.tr.

▲Gülhane Park—Originally Topkapı Palace's imperial garden, today it's Istanbul's oldest park and a welcoming swath of open green space within the bustling city. Located on the hillside below the palace, with terraces stretching to the shore below, Gülhane is a favorite weekend spot for locals. Come here to commune with Turks as they picnic with their families and enjoy a meander along the park's shady paths. On some summer weekends, the park hosts free concerts.

Grand Portal (Bab-ı Ali)—In the 19th century, this grand gate with its wavy roof and twin fountains was the entrance to the office of the Grand Vizier. The gate was called Bab-ı Ali because, historically, the word *bab* (door) was also used to refer to the authority of the state. Each Wednesday and Friday, commoners could enter here and tell their problems to public officials. It was here that all domestic and foreign affairs were discussed and presented to the

ISTANBUL

sultan for a final decision. The surrounding neighborhood (also known as Bab-ı Ali) was the center of the Turkish news media for about 50 years (until the 1990s). Now it's a dull administrative district. But you can still find the historic gate just outside the Topkapı Palace wall, near the Gülhane tram stop.

West of Sultanahmet: From the Grand Bazaar to the Golden Horn

Heading west from Sultanahmet, you enter an area that's more residential and less touristy, offering an opportunity to delve into the "real" Istanbul—rubbing elbows with locals at some of its best mosques and markets. While some attractions here—such as the Grand Bazaar—are tourist magnets, the lanes connecting them are filled mostly with residents. The following sights are linked by the "Grand Bazaar and Spice Market Walk," which describes these sights and the Rüstem Paşa Mosque in greater detail.

▲▲▲**Grand Bazaar (Kapalı Çarşı)**—Shop till you drop at the world's oldest market venue. Although many of its stalls have been

overtaken by souvenir shops, in many ways Istanbul's unique Grand Bazaar remains much as it was centuries ago: enchanting and perplexing visitors with its maze-like network of more than 4,000 colorful shops, fragrant eateries, and insistent shopkeepers. Despite the tourists and the knickknacks, the heart of the Grand Bazaar still beats, giving the observant visitor a glimpse of the living Istanbul.

Cost and Hours: Free, Mon-Sat 9:00-19:00, shops begin to close at 18:30, closed Sun and on the first day of most religious festivals, www.grandbazaaristanbul.org. It's across the parking lot from the Çemberlitaş tram stop, behind the Nuruosmaniye Mosque.

▲▲▲**Mosque of Süleyman the Magnificent (Süleymaniye**

Camii)—This soothing and restrained—but suitably magnificent—house of worship was built by the empire's greatest architect (Sinan) and dedicated to one of its greatest sultans. Although less colorful than the Blue Mosque, this mosque rivals it in size, scope, and beauty. Enjoy the numerous courtyards and tranquil interior, decorated in pastel hues and stained glass. Completed in 1557, the whole thing took just one decade to finish. Today the mosque is almost as clean and shiny as it was the day it opened, thanks to a three-year renovation completed in 2010. Out back are the elaborate tombs of Süleyman the Magnificent and his wife, Roxelana, as well as sweeping views of the city below.

Cost and Hours: Mosque—free, generally open daily one hour after sunrise until one hour before sunset, closed to visitors five times a day for prayer; mausoleums—free, daily 9:00-17:00, until 18:00 in summer. It's on Sıddık Sami Onar Caddesi, in the Süleymaniye district.

▲**Rüstem Paşa Mosque (Rüstem Paşa Camii)**—This small 16th-century mosque, designed by the prolific and talented architect Sinan, was built to honor Süleyman the Magnificent's Grand Vizier, Rüstem Paşa. Elevated one story above street level in a bustling market zone, its facade is studded with impressive İznik tiles—but the wall-to-wall decorations inside are even more breathtaking.

Cost and Hours: Free, generally open daily one hour after sunrise until one hour before sunset, closed to visitors five times a day for prayer, on Hasırcılar Caddesi, Eminönü.

▲▲**Spice Market (Mısır Çarşışı)**—This market was built about 350 years ago to promote the spice trade in Istanbul...and, aside from a few souvenir stands that have wriggled their way in, it still serves essentially the same purpose. Today the halls of the Spice Market are filled with equal numbers of locals and tourists. In addition to mounds of colorful spices (such as green henna and deep-red saffron), you can also get dried fruits (including apricots and figs), fresh roasted nuts, Turkish delight, supposed aphrodisiacs (Sultan's paste, or "Turkish Viagra"), imported caviar, and lots more.

Cost and Hours: Free to enter; Mon-Sat 8:00-19:30, until 19:00 off-season; Sun 9:30-19:00, shops begin to close 30 minutes earlier. It's right on Cami Meydanı Sokak along the Golden Horn, at the Old Town end of the Galata Bridge, near the Eminönü tram stop.

On the Golden Horn

The following sights are on the inlet called the Golden Horn, near the Spice Market. Known as Eminönü, this district is a major transit hub, where the tram, bus, seabus, and ferry systems link up—so it can be packed at rush hour. This area is covered by the "Golden Horn Walk" (page 1106).

▲▲**Galata Bridge (Galata Köprüsü)**—In 1994, this modern bridge replaced what had been the first and, for many years, only bridge spanning the Golden Horn. Now, lined with hundreds of fishermen dipping their hooks into the water below, the new Galata Bridge is an Istanbul fixture. A stroll across the Galata Bridge

ISTANBUL

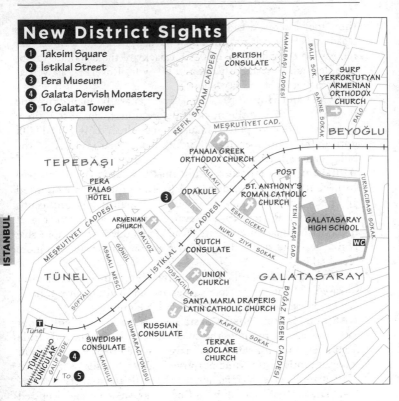

New District Sights

1. Taksim Square
2. İstiklal Street
3. Pera Museum
4. Galata Dervish Monastery
5. To Galata Tower

offers panoramic views of Istanbul's Old Town. Consider stopping for a drink or a meal at one of the many restaurants built into the bridge's lower level (tram stops: Eminönü on the Old Town end of the bridge, and Karaköy on the New District end).

Sirkeci Train Station (Sirkeci Tren Garı)—This 19th-century example of European-Orientalism architecture was the terminus of the Orient Express. The famous train, which traveled from Paris through "exotic" Eastern Europe to Istanbul, was immortalized by Agatha Christie in *Murder on the Orient Express*. Though trains still depart to Europe from here, today the station is used mostly by commuters. The modest Railway Museum inside the station is worth a look.

Cost and Hours: Railway Museum—free, Tue-Sat 9:00-12:30 & 13:00-17:00, closed Sun-Mon; near the ferry ports, tram stop: Sirkeci, tel. 0212/520-6575.

In the New District

The New District, which is across the Golden Horn from the Old Town, offers a modern, urban, and very European-flavored contrast to the historic creaks and quirks of the Old Town. These are

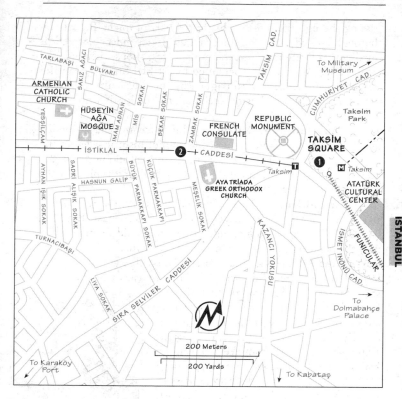

listed roughly in the order you'll reach them going from Taksim Square toward the Golden Horn.

Taksim Square
▲**Taksim Square (Taksim Meydanı)**—At the center of the New District is the busy, vibrant Taksim Square. Taksim is the gateway to Istanbul's main pedestrian thoroughfare, İstiklal Street, with its historic buildings and colorful shops. This enormous square is also the New District's "Grand Central Station," connecting to the rest of the city by bus, Metro, funicular, and Nostalgic Tram. To get there from the Old Town or from the cruise ship terminal, ride the tram to Kabataş (the end of the line) and follow the crowds directly into the funicular station (may require a token, rather than a transit card). Take the handy little one-stop funicular up to Taksim Square, and exit following signs for *İstiklal Caddesi*.

On or near İstiklal Street
▲▲▲**İstiklal Street (İstiklal Caddesi)**—Linking Taksim Square with the Tünel district (and, below that, the Galata district), İstiklal Street is urban Istanbul's main pedestrian drag,

passing through the most sophisticated part of town. The vibrant thoroughfare, whose name translates as "Independence Street," is lined with a lively mix of restaurants, cafés, shops, theaters, and art galleries. Visitors are enchanted by İstiklal Street's beautiful Art Nouveau facades and intrigued by the multicultural mix of tourists, international businesspeople, and the locals who throng its elegant sidewalks.

▲**Pera Museum (Pera Müzesi)**—This museum beautifully displays its modest but interesting collection of historic weights and measures, Kütahya tiles, and Oriental paintings and portraits. It's housed in a renovated late-19th-century building typical of the once high-end Pera neighborhood.

Cost and Hours: 7 TL, Tue-Sat 10:00-19:00, Sun 12:00-18:00, closed Mon, Meşrutiyet Caddesi 65, Tepebaşı, Beyoğlu, tel. 0212/334-9900. The museum's 4-TL audioguide, which covers only the paintings, is fast moving and worthwhile.

Pera Palas Hotel—Agatha Christie fans will want to visit this hotel down the street from the Pera Museum (just past the multi-story Hotel Pera Marmara). This historic landmark recently reopened after an extensive renovation (www.perapalas.com).

By the late 19th century, the Orient Express train service from Western Europe had become all the rage (for more, see page 1112). But Istanbul lacked a European-style hotel elegant enough to impress the posh passengers arriving on those trains. To satisfy upper-crust demand, the company that operated the Orient Express built the top-of-the-top Pera Palas Hotel in 1892. Allied forces used the hotel as a base during the occupation of Istanbul at the end of World War I. In World War II, it was a hotbed of spies and counterspies. The hotel's guest book reads like a history lesson: Atatürk, the Duke of Windsor, Yugoslav president Josip Broz Tito, Jackie Kennedy, Mata Hari, and Agatha Christie (who stayed here several times in the 1920s and 1930s while writing *Murder on the Orient Express*).

Some of Ataturk's personal belongings and medals are displayed in Room 101 (free—but attendants expect a tip, open to visitors daily 10:00-11:00 & 15:00-16:00).

In the Galata District

The old-feeling neighborhood climbing up a hill from the Golden Horn into the New District, called Galata, has a seedier, less modern-European ambience than Taksim Square or İstiklal Street. Running up and down the hill under Galata is the old-fashioned subterranean funicular called Tünel (the entrance at the top of the hill is at the end of İstiklal Street; down below, it's near the Karaköy tram stop and Galata Bridge). The sights below are listed in order from the top of the hill down to the waterfront.

▲▲**Galata Tower (Galata Kulesi)**—The most prominent feature of the New District skyline, the 205-foot-tall stone Galata

Tower was built by the Genoese in the mid-14th century and has been used over the centuries as a fire tower, a barracks, a dungeon, and even as a launch pad to test the possibility of human-powered flight.

In the Middle Ages, when Byzantines controlled the historic core of the city, this was the territory of Genoa (the Italian city once controlled much of the Mediterranean). This tower—sometimes called the "Genoese Tower"—was part of a mid-14th-century fortification. But, with a key location facing the Byzantine capital across the Golden Horn, the dramatic tower's purpose was likely as much to show off as to defend.

Today, the tower is a tourist attraction—offering visitors perhaps the best view of Istanbul. Climb the little staircase around behind the tower, take the elevator to the seventh-floor restaurant, and go to the observation terrace.

As you enjoy the view, ponder the attention-grabbing story of a 17th-century aviation pioneer, Hezarfen Ahmet Çelebi. According to legend, Hezarfen Ahmet was so inspired by the drawings and models of Leonardo da Vinci that he built his own set of artificial wings, which allowed him to hang-glide a few miles from the top of this tower, across the Bosphorus, to Asian Istanbul.

Cost and Hours: 10 TL, daily 9:00-20:00, Büyük Hendek Sokak, tel. 0212/293-8180.

Quincentennial Museum of Turkish Jews (500 Yıl Vakfı Türk Musevileri Müzesi)—In 1492, King Ferdinand and Queen Isabel of Spain ordered their Sephardic Jewish population to accept the Christian faith, or leave and "dare not return." The Ottoman sultan Beyazıt Han was the only monarch of the time who extended an invitation to take in these refugees. Turkey's Jewish people—many of whom can still trace their roots back to Spain—remain a vibrant part of the Turkish cultural mosaic. This museum, founded 500 years after the Spanish expulsion (hence the "quincentennial"), commemorates those first Sephardic Jews who found a new home here. Housed in an inactive early-19th-century synagogue (built on the remains of a much-older synagogue), the small museum displays items donated by the local Jewish community. Particularly interesting are the ethnographic section, showing scenes from daily life, and a chair used in the Jewish circumcision rite.

Cost and Hours: 7 TL, Mon-Thu 10:00-16:00, Sun and Fri 10:00-14:00, closed Sat and on Jewish holidays, Karaköy Meydanı, Perçemli Sokak, tel. 0212/292-6333, www.muze500.com.

Getting There: The museum is conveniently located in Karaköy, close to the New District end of the Galata Bridge. It's on a dead-end alley, Perçemli Sokak, near your cruise ship and a few hundred yards from the Karaköy tram stop. If you're coming across the Galata Bridge by tram from the Old Town, get off at Karaköy, then take the pedestrian underpass as if you're heading for Tünel; once you're up the steps, back on the street level, Perçemli Sokak is the alley on your right.

Along the Bosphorus, Between Galata and Beşiktaş

This area, stretching north along the Bosphorus from the Galata Bridge, has been enjoying a wave of renovation, yet still retains the charm of its genteel past. I've listed these sights in the order you reach them, coming from Galata.

Istanbul Modern Arts Museum (İstanbul Modern Sanat Müzesi)—The only museum in Istanbul dedicated to the works of contemporary Turkish artists, "Istanbul Modern" offers a look at Istanbul's current art scene and the upper crust of local society that it attracts. Located in a huge warehouse in the port area (and perhaps dwarfed by your cruise ship), the museum is a bright and user-friendly space, where you can see the well-described art of a hundred Turkish painters from the 20th century on one floor, with temporary exhibits downstairs.

Cost and Hours: 10 TL, free on Thu, open Tue-Sun 10:00-18:00, Thu until 20:00, closed Mon, last entry 30 minutes before closing, near your cruise ship at Meclis-I Mebusan Caddesi, Liman İşletmeleri Sahası, Antrepo 4, tram stop: Tophane, tel. 0212/334-7300, www.istanbulmodern.org.

▲Dolmabahçe Palace (Dolmabahçe Sarayı)—This palace was the last hurrah of the Ottoman Empire. By the late 19th century, the empire was called the "Sick Man of Europe," and other European emperors and kings derided its ineffective and back-ward-seeming sultan. In a last-ditch attempt to rejuvenate the declining image of his empire, Sultan Abdülmecit I built the ostentatious Dolmabahçe (dohl-mah-bah-cheh) Palace—with all the trappings of a European monarch—to replace the unmistakably Oriental-feeling Topkapı

Palace as the official residence of the sultan. (It didn't work—instead, Dolmabahçe was the final residence of the long line of Ottoman sultans, falling empty when the royal family was sent into exile in 1922.) Completed in 1853, the palace is a fusion of styles—from Turkish-Ottoman elements to the frilly Rococo that was all the rage in Europe at the time. Its construction drained the already dwindling treasury, and the empire actually had to take a foreign loan to complete Dolmabahçe. Today the building belongs to the Turkish Parliament, which uses it only for important occasions, such as the 2004 NATO summit.

Cost and Hours: Given your limited time, the palace is best enjoyed from the water, as its interior, while certainly impressive, doesn't stack up against the city's major sights. The palace is accessible only with a guided tour, available in English (20 TL for Selamlık section, 10 TL for Harem, 2-4/hour, one hour, late March-late Oct Tue-Wed and Fri-Sun 9:00-16:00, until 15:00 off-season, closed Mon and Thu, Dolmabahçe Caddesi, Beşiktaş, tram/funicular stop: Kabataş, tel. 0212/236-9000, ext. 1522, www.dolmabahcepalace.com).

Kadıköy: A Quick Trip to Asia

While virtually all of Istanbul's "sights" are on the European side, the city itself spills over the Bosphorus into Asia. Of Istanbul's 15 million residents, more than a third live in Asian Istanbul, a.k.a. Anadolu Yakası (ah-nah-doh-loo yah-kah-suh, "the Anatolian side").

There have long been small towns and villages in this area, but today it consists mostly of modern sprawl. Development boomed here after the first bridge over the Bosphorus opened in 1974 (though regular ferry service started in the 1850s). While European Istanbul has its old quarters and traditional living, the residents of Asian Istanbul generally choose to live on the Asian side for its modern infrastructure, bigger houses and condos, and the efficiencies of modern life. The people of Asian Istanbul tend to be more progressive and secular than their counterparts across the strait (for example, you'll see fewer women wearing head scarves, and it's a voting stronghold for the modern Social Democrat party). Each day, millions of people commute across the Bosphorus (mostly on ferries) from their homes in Asia to their jobs in Europe.

For the handiest intercontinental trip, ride the ferry from the Old Town to Kadıköy. A historic town known in ancient times as Chalcedon, Kadıköy pre-dates even the Byzantine Empire. Today's Kadıköy, with over a million people, is a modern commercial and residential district that grew up around the ferry landing.

Upon arrival in Kadıköy, you'll see it's well-designed to deal with hordes of commuters. Buses fan out from the ferry dock. Shops and restaurants fill the grid-planned commercial zone that stretches inland from the dock. Notice the shopping-mall ambience, youthful and Western energy of the crowds, and modern efficiency of the commerce.

As you step off the dock, walk about 100 yards to the right, to the traffic light (past the Atatürk statue at the center of the square). The Town Hall is right across from you, by the traffic light. Cross the street and walk straight (with the Town Hall on your right) by the side of the park, then cross a second street, which puts you in the market area.

Kadıköy Çarşışı (chahr-shuh-suh, market) is the historic core of the area—and it doesn't get more authentic than the surrounding neighborhood. Here in the market area, you can find everything from grocers and fishmongers to popular delis and specialty olive-oil stores. (Watch for a goose, the mascot of shopkeepers, waddling around loose.) The streets are lined with boutiques, bookstores, fast-food kiosks, grocery stores, and cafés, bars, and restaurants (which begin bustling in the late afternoon). Busy as it is throughout the day, it gets even more crowded at rush hour—commuters pause here to enjoy a drink or meal with their friends, or to do some last-minute shopping.

Getting There: From the Old Town side of the Golden Horn, near the Galata Bridge (at Eminönü), catch the boat to the Kadıköy dock (2/hour, 25-minute ride, 1.75 TL one-way). The boat ride itself is enjoyable—the views from the boat alone justify the trip.

Shopping in Istanbul

Shopping can provide a good break from Istanbul's mosques, museums, and monuments. And diving into the city's bustling, colorful marketplaces can be a culturally enlightening experience. For information on VAT refunds and customs, see page 127.

Where to Shop

Shopping in the Grand Bazaar and at other Old Town merchants (such as the craft market tucked behind the Blue Mosque) is lively, memorable, and fun, and prices can be low—but the quality is often questionable. Istanbul's residents prefer shopping at the more expensive but reliably good-quality stores elsewhere in town.

Dealing with Aggressive Merchants

Throughout the Grand Bazaar—and just about everywhere in the Old Town—you'll constantly be barraged by people selling  everything you can imagine. They may greet you enthusiastically, ask if you need help, or tell you about their cousin who just happens to live in your hometown. While not dangerous, the salesmen can be particularly aggressive, even intimidating, to single women. However, it can be fun if you loosen up and approach it with a sense of humor. The main rule of thumb: Don't feel compelled to look at or buy anything you don't want. These salesmen prey on Americans' gregariousness and tendency to respond politely to anyone who offers a friendly greeting. They often use surprising or attention-grabbing openers:

"Hello, Americans! Where are you from? I have a cousin there!"

"Are you lost? Can I help you find something?"

"Nice shoes! Are those Turkish shoes?"

"Would you like a cup of tea?"

The list is endless—collect your favorites.

If you're not interested, simply say a firm, "No, thanks!" and brush past them, ignoring any additional comments. This seems cold, but it's the only way to cover the market without constantly getting tied up in a conversation.

If, on the other hand, you're looking to chat, merchants can be very talkative—but be warned that a lengthy conversation may give them false hopes that you're looking to buy, and could make it even more difficult to extract yourself gracefully from the interaction.

What to Buy

Textiles

The cotton T-shirts you'll see around the Old Town and in the Grand Bazaar make decent souvenirs or gifts, but are usually low-quality—they'll likely fade and shrink after a few washes.

Many people associate Turkey with **pashminas**—high-quality shawls traditionally made with Himalayan goat wool. And, in fact, the Old Town is a pashmina paradise, with every color of the rainbow. But Turkey doesn't produce pashmina wool, so the ones you see here are imports. Still, they're practical and fun, and cheaper than the fakes sold in the US.

A *peştemal* (pehsh-teh-mahl) is a large, thin, cotton **bath towel** that Turks wrap around themselves at the baths; nowadays they're also used as curtains or tablecloths. Bathing Turks scrub

How to Get the Best Bargain

Many visitors to Istanbul are surprised to find that bargaining for a lower price is no longer common in much of the city. At modern stores or shopping malls, the posted prices are final. But in the tourist zones—such as the Grand Bazaar, Spice Market, and other shops around the Old Town—merchants know you're expecting to haggle...and they're happy to play along. (Local shoppers have less patience for this game. Notice that even in the Grand Bazaar, locals don't often haggle—if they think something is overpriced, they either ask for a discount or simply walk away.)

In the Old Town market areas where bargaining is common, you'll constantly be bombarded by sales pitches. If you aren't interested in what they're selling, try not to establish eye contact. Although this may feel rude, it's the best way to avoid unnecessary conversations and save your time and energy for the items you do want.

If you are interested in an item, don't make it obvious. Take your time, browse around, and pretend you might just wander off

away dead skin and dirt with *kese* (keh-seh)—simple rectangular **mittens** made out of raw silk or synthetic fabric. Look for these two authentically Turkish items at the Eğin Tekstil shop on Yağlıkçılar Street in the Grand Bazaar (see page 1149).

Turkey produces wonderful **silk,** but be careful: In the Grand Bazaar and other Old Town shops, scarves and other items billed as silk are often made of polyester or, at best, low-grade silk.

Carpets and Kilims

If you want to buy a Turkish carpet, it's worth knowing a bit about what you're looking for—if only to avoid advertising your inexperience. For example, folding a carpet to check the knots will not only give you away as a novice, but can actually ruin the carpet if it's silk. Rubbing a carpet with a piece of wet tissue to test its colorfastness is akin to licking a shirt before you buy it. And beware of shopkeepers who stress "authenticity" over quality. Authenticity is an important consideration when shopping for traditional wool-on-wool carpets. But for wool-on-cotton or silk-on-silk, it can actually be better to get a piece made with newer techniques, which produce tighter weaves, brighter and more durable colors, and more intricate patterns.

at any moment—feigned disinterest is part of the game. You're better off keeping a low profile—this isn't the time to show off your nicest clothes, jewelry, and wads of cash.

Merchandise often doesn't have price tags, because shop owners want you to ask—giving them an opening to launch into a sales pitch. Don't suggest a number; let them be the first to mention a price. When they do, assume it's elevated. Even if you counter with only half their original offer, you may find your price easily accepted—meaning you've already offered too much.

More likely, a spirited haggling war will ensue. If you don't like to bargain, you'll pay more than you should. Play along to get a lower price and a fun cultural interaction. These haggling sessions can drag on for some time, as you sip tea (usually apple-flavored) offered by shopkeepers who want to keep you around. When you start to walk away, that last price they call out is probably the best price you'll get.

There's room for bargaining even on fixed-price commodities, such as gold and silver, where you're being charged not only for the precious metal but also for the workmanship.

If you're haggling over something unique, be prepared to pay a premium. Shopkeepers already know that you won't be able to find it elsewhere.

Carpets can range in price from several hundred dollars to several thousand or more, depending on the age, size, quality, and uniqueness. Merchants will ship them home for you, though many tourists find it cheaper and more foolproof to carry them back (the carpets can be folded and tied tightly into a squarish bundle).

Wool-on-wool carpets, which are made of wool pile on a wool skeleton (formed by vertical warp and horizontal weft threads), are the most traditional kind of Turkish carpet. Although becoming less common, these are still woven in countryside villages. Each region has its own distinctive, centuries-old, design-and-color combination. In general, wool-on-wool carpets cost less than other Turkish rugs. The best way to gauge the authenticity of a wool-on-wool carpet is to look for the natural, less-vibrant colors that come from vegetable dyes made from local plants. Density—the number of knots per inch—is less important to the quality of a wool-on-wool carpet. Fewer knots don't signify a lower-quality wool rug, but they do mean that the rug is more likely to stretch over time.

Newer carpet styles, such as **wool-on-cotton** (wool pile on a cotton skeleton) and **silk-on-silk,** first appeared in the 19th century. The new materials allowed weavers to create more intricate floral and geometric patterns than traditional designs. (A weaver can fit more knots onto a cotton skeleton than onto a wool one.) Professional designers make these patterns with the exact thickness of the yarn in mind—so irregular hand-spun wool won't work. Wool-on-cotton and silk-on-silk carpets are colored with chemical dyes, which can be as good, or even better, than natural dyes. If someone tries to sell you a wool-on-cotton carpet by advertising that it's "made with hand-spun wool," "dyed with vegetable colors," or that it "features a traditional design, passed from mother to daughter," walk away. Unlike wool-on-wool carpets, density is important in assessing quality for wool-on-cotton and silk-on-silk carpets.

Kilims (kee-leem) feature a flat weave without the pile, similar to a Navajo rug. These also have traditional designs and natural colors. Used in the past as blankets and bedspreads, they're mainly popular now as decorative items (and can be used as wall hangings). Kilims are generally inexpensive, but old and rare pieces can cost several thousand dollars. For a wearable, affordable kilim, consider a vest made out of the material; you'll see these at the Grand Bazaar and elsewhere.

Osman's Carpet Shop, in Zincirli Han in the Grand Bazaar, is regarded as *the* place to go for expert advice—and high-quality (expensive) carpets. Osman, who's often assisted by son Nurullah or nephew Bilgin, won't hustle you. He prefers to equip customers with information to be sure they get the carpet that's right for them.

Punto of Istanbul, a couple of blocks away from the Grand Bazaar's Nuruosmaniye Gate, carries a wide variety of carpets—from simple kilims to fancy silk carpets—and has down-to-earth prices compared to most. Shop anonymously as you haggle, then, before you pay, show this book for an additional 10 percent discount from manager Metin (Nuru Osmaniye, Gazi Sinan Paşa Sokak, Vezirhan 17, tel. 0212/511-0854).

Tiles and Ceramics

A Turkish specialty is *çini* (chee-nee), which is usually translated in English as "**tile**" (or "quartz tile"). The word *çini* can be used to describe flat tiles used for architectural decoration, and also functional items such as bowls, vases, cups, and so on. While English-speakers might sometimes use the word "ceramic" to

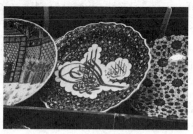

describe these functional items, *çini* technically has a higher quartz content than ceramic, and is therefore more difficult to work with. Strictly speaking, while "tiles" *(çini)* are very traditional in Turkey, "ceramics" *(seramik;* seh-rah-meek*)* don't have much of a history here—though you will find them sold in markets. You'll also see **pottery** *(çömlek;* chom-lehk*)*: simple, fired earthenware objects shaped on a wheel, usually without any design or glaze.

High-quality items are often too costly for regular stores to carry; only specialty stores are likely to have the best ceramics and tile. If you're looking for something simple, you'll find plenty of inexpensive, pretty pieces at souvenir stores all around the Old Town and Grand Bazaar.

ISTANBUL

Traditional Arts: *Hat* and *Tezhip*

Hat (pronounced "hot") is artful Arabic calligraphy. To make written words appear more beautiful, the calligrapher *(hattat;* hot-taht*)* bends grammatical rules and often combines letters irregularly. Over the centuries, this decorative art has reached a very sophisticated level of expression, almost like a painting. *Tezhip* (tehz-heep) is the illumination and embellishment of manuscripts, scrolls, and books with geometric or floral patterns.

If you're just curious, the **Traditional Turkish Handicrafts Center** in the Old Town, near Hagia Sophia, is a good place to visit. A small gallery shows works for sale, and you're welcome to watch classes in progress (Tue-Sun 8:30-19:00, closed Mon; kitchen serves basic meals, snacks, tea, and coffee; Caferiye Sokak, Soğukkuyu Çıkmazı 1, Sultanahmet, tel. 0212/513-3601). The Handicrafts Center is next door to the Yeşil Ev Hotel, in a historic madrassa between Hagia Sophia and the Blue Mosque. Each room around the madrassa's courtyard is assigned to a particular art and artist, such as *hat*, traditional doll-making, miniatures, embroidery, lace work, traditional book binding, glass, and porcelain.

For traditional dolls, visit the **doll shop** in the Handicrafts Center in the Old Town at Kabasakal Caddesi 5. The folk dolls made by Lütfiye Bakutan and Selma Yurtlu are masterpieces you can't find anywhere else. Look for Selma's unique wall-hangings featuring dolls playing flutes, praying, and more (daily April-Oct 9:00-18:00, until 17:00 in winter, Sultanahmet).

Gold

Gold is a good buy in Turkey. Prices change with the daily rate of gold; when you ask the price of a piece, the shopkeeper will weigh it for you. Simple bangles often cost little more than the gold itself.

Most mass-produced jewelry is made from molds with 14-carat gold, as it is harder and cheaper. Handmade items are the most expensive; in some pieces, the fine workmanship is more valuable than the gold. While the cheaper items cost around $14-20 per gram, the price can go as high as $35-50 per gram for finely crafted pieces. Precious and semiprecious stones are generally paired with 18-carat gold.

Silver

Silver jewelry, with or without semiprecious stones, is a good and affordable alternative to fancy gold jewelry. As with gold, silver pieces usually won't have a price tag, but are sold by weight. Look around a bit in the Grand Bazaar to get an idea of what's available and the range of prices. **Kalcılar Han** in the Grand Bazaar (see page 1147) is a production center for silver items, with shops on its lower and upper levels. Most of the silver you see in the Grand Bazaar shops is handcrafted on site.

You can also find **beads** to make your own jewelry. A few shops in the Grand Bazaar (in and near **Cevahir Bedesten,** see page 1151) carry silver jewelry and semiprecious stone beads.

Souvenirs and Trinkets

The Grand Bazaar is filled with stalls hawking endless mountains of junk, most of it imported. This stuff sells well, as it's cheap and

looks "Oriental." Those hats with tiny circular mirrors are common not because they're crafted by local artisans (they're made outside of Turkey), but because the merchants know tourists will buy them. Fortunately, the bazaar is also filled with plenty of affordable, authentically Turkish trinkets that make wonderful gifts.

You can't miss the **"evil eyes"** (*nazarlık;* nah-zahr-luhk)—blue-and-white glass beads that look like eyes. Traditionally thought to ward off negative energy from jealous eyes, these are a kind of good-luck charm popular among Turks. You'll see them on doorways, hanging down from rear-view mirrors, or anywhere else people want protection. Babies wear them, adults wear them, and teenage girls braid them in their hair. *Nazarlık*s are authentically and uniquely Turkish, which makes them good gifts. They come in various sizes—some with a metal frame, others on a hooked pin, still others embedded in tiles.

Small Turkish **tea glasses,** made of clear glass and shaped like a tulip blossom, are easy to find.

Machine-made textiles with traditional designs make good tablecloths, pillowcases, bedspreads, and sofa throws. Some are velvet, with silky-looking, colorful embroideries.

Coffee and pepper grinders don't break easily, since they're made of brass or wood.

The same goes for **backgammon sets** and **inlaid wooden boxes.** The best are inlaid with mother-of-pearl, while the cheapest are inlaid with plastic.

If you decide to buy a glass **water pipe** (*nargile;* nahr-gee-leh), get the kind that separates into parts and is easily reassembled.

Mined in central Turkey, **onyx** is plentiful, affordable, and popular in decorative objects such as vases and bowls, as well as chess sets (but not so common in jewelry).

Gifts for children are more limited. Consider Halloween **costumes.** You'll find tiny, colorful Turkish princess outfits for girls, with coins adorning the sleeves and trousers. Cheap knockoffs of **soccer jerseys** also abound.

Eating in Istanbul

In the Old Town's Sultanahmet Area

These restaurants—along with much of Istanbul's best sightseeing—are concentrated in the Sultanahmet area.

Balıkçı Sabahattin is the one Old Town seafood restaurant that locals cross the Bosphorus for. With white-tablecloth outdoor tables on a quiet street about three blocks below the Blue Mosque, it's known for its delicious hot and cold *mezes*—including herbed monkfish, rice pilaf with mussels, and grilled calamari (figure 60 TL per person for salad, *mezes*, and a glass of wine). If you still have room after the appetizers, try one of the fish dishes for 25-35 TL (daily 11:00-24:00, 5-TL per person cover charge, reservations recommended, Seyit Hasan Kuyu Sokak 1, Cankurtaran, tel. 0212/458-1824).

Rami's signature dish is "paper kebab," a vegetable and lamb stew that's wrapped and baked in oiled paper. You'll eat in a small, restored Ottoman house decorated with old furniture and paintings by the owner's father, the painter Rami Uluer (14-27-TL starters and salads, 29-33-TL main courses, daily 12:30-23:00, cash only, 15 percent service charge, behind the Blue Mosque at

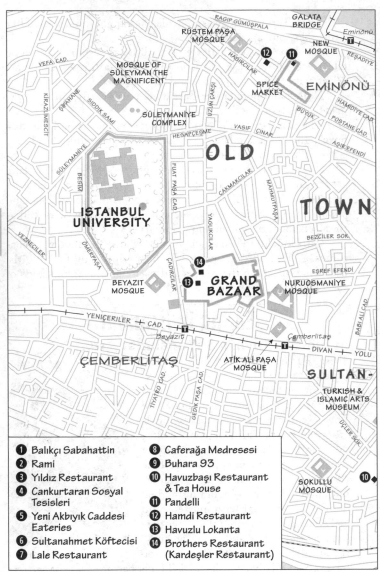

RAGIP GÜMÜŞPALA

GALATA
BRIDGE

Eminönü

RÜSTEM PAŞA
MOSQUE

HASIRCILAR

12

11

NEW
MOSQUE

REŞADIYE

VEFA CAD.

MOSQUE OF
SÜLEYMAN THE
MAGNIFICENT

SPICE
MARKET

EMINÖNÜ

HAMIDIYE CAD.

ŞIFAHANE

SIDDIK SAMI

UZUN ÇARŞI

POSTANE CAD.

KIRAZLIMESCIT

SÜLEYMANIYE
COMPLEX

HESAPÇEŞME

VASIF CINAR

BÜYÜK

AŞIR EFENDİ

SÜLEYMANIYE

FUAT PAŞA CAD.

OLD

BEŞIM

ISTANBUL
UNIVERSITY

ÇAKMAKÇILAR

MAHMUTPAŞA

TOWN

VEZNECİLER

ÖMERPAŞA

YAĞLIKÇILAR

BEZCİLER SOK.

YAĞLIKÇILAR

14

ÇADIRCILAR

EŞREF EFENDİ

BEYAZIT
MOSQUE

13

GRAND
BAZAAR

NURUOSMANİYE
MOSQUE

BABIALI CAD.

YENİÇERİLER ── CAD.

Beyazit

Çemberlitaş

DIVAN ── YOLU

ÇEMBERLİTAŞ

TİYATRO CAD.

GEDİK PAŞA CAD.

ATİK ALİ PAŞA
MOSQUE

SULTAN-

TURKISH &
ISLAMIC ARTS
MUSEUM

ÜÇLER SOK.

1 Balıkçı Sabahattin
2 Rami
3 Yıldız Restaurant
4 Cankurtaran Sosyal
Tesisleri
5 Yeni Akbıyık Caddesi
Eateries
6 Sultanahmet Köftecisi
7 Lale Restaurant

8 Caferağa Medresesi
9 Buhara 93
10 Havuzbaşı Restaurant
& Tea House
11 Pandelli
12 Hamdi Restaurant
13 Havuzlu Lokanta
14 Brothers Restaurant
(Kardeşler Restaurant)

SOKULLU
MOSQUE

10

Utangaç Sokak 4, tel. 0212/517-6593 or 0212/638-5321).

Yıldız Restaurant started off as a coffee shop run by Erol Taş, a popular actor in the 1970s and 1980s who always played the bad guy. Locals often call it by its old name, "Erol Taş Kıraathanesi" (Erol Taş coffee shop). Today, hardworking İsmet Yıldız runs the place as a simple restaurant and neighborhood café. Inside, the walls are covered with photos of famous Turkish actors and

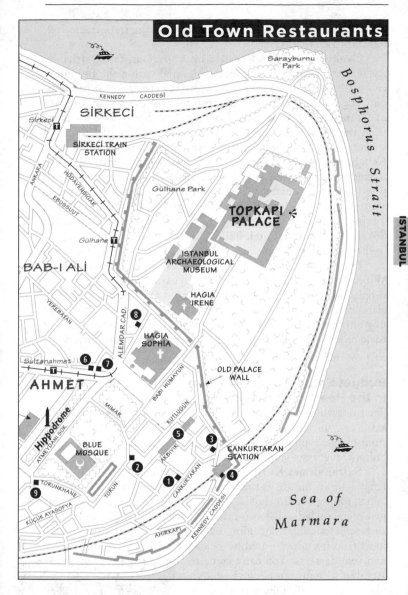

Old Town Restaurants

actresses; many were personal friends and clients of the iconic villain. There's a real neighborhood vibe here, with people reading newspapers, playing backgammon, and occasionally smoking water pipes. From time to time, famous actors drop in, and sometimes extras gather here for film-industry gossip (5-TL vegetable *mezes*, 10-15 TL seafood *mezes*, 5-10-TL salads, 12-20-TL main courses, daily 7:00-24:00, Cankurtaran Meydanı 18, Sultanahmet, a few blocks toward the Sea of Marmara by the train tracks, tel. 0212/518-1257).

Cankurtaran Sosyal Tesisleri is a spacious, family-friendly restaurant catering mostly to locals, located within the Byzantine city walls south of Cankurtaran Meydanı. You can eat inside or out. The tables outdoors have a great view of the Bosphorus, Sea of Marmara, and Asian side of Istanbul (the downside is the noise from the four-lane road on the other side of the wall). The food is remarkably good and inexpensive. Their speciality, Topkapı Kebab, is a mix of chicken, veal, mushrooms, and tomatoes topped with cheese. They also serve *künefe*, a delicious traditional shredded-wheat dessert (3-4 TL soups and starters, 4-8 TL hot starters, 8-10 TL kebabs, 12-15 TL seafood, 4-6 TL desserts, 9 TL breakfast plate, daily 8:30-23:00, no alcohol, Ahırkapı İskele Sokak 1, Cankurtaran, tel. 0212/458-5414). Their simple cafeteria in the garden serves only beverages.

On the Backpackers' Strip: **Yeni Akbıyık Caddesi** ("New White Moustache Street") is lined with casual restaurants serving simple food and beer to a United Nations of gregarious young travelers. Eateries usually open early in the morning to offer breakfast to youth hostelers. You'll find several small grocery stores selling basic food items and fruit on the same street (one block below the Blue Mosque, toward the Sea of Marmara).

Budget Eateries on Divan Yolu, in the Heart of Sultanahmet

The first two famous and very convenient restaurants stand side by side along the busy street called Divan Yolu, across the tram tracks from Hagia Sophia and the Hippodrome (just downhill from the Sultanahmet tram stop).

Sultanahmet Köftecisi ("Sultanahmet Meatballs") is so famous for its meatballs that it's inspired an epidemic of imitation joints, rolling out knockoff *köfte* throughout Turkey. The very limited menu includes just two main courses (10-TL *köfte* and 15-TL *şiş kebab*), four sides (including a tomato-and-onion salad and the local favorite, *piyaz*—a white-bean salad in olive oil for 5 TL), and two desserts. You can't come to Istanbul without sampling these *köfte* (daily 11:00-23:30, Divan Yolu 12, tel. 0212/520-0566).

Lale Restaurant is the **"Pudding Shop,"** where a generation of vagabond hippies started their long journey east on the "Freak Road" to Kathmandu in the 1960s. (Enjoy the hippie history shared on its wall full of clippings.)

Today, this much tamer but still tourist-friendly self-service cafeteria cranks out a selection of seasonal Turkish food and chicken and beef kebabs. Show this book to the cashier before you pay and receive a 10 percent discount (6-TL soups, salads, cold starters, and desserts; 8-TL vegetarian dishes, 12-14-TL main courses, daily 7:00-22:30, Divan Yolu 6, tel. 0212/522-2970).

Caferağa Medresesi, in an old madrassa (seminary) next to Hagia Sophia, serves basic food (mostly grilled meat and chicken) to students, amateur artists, and a handful of in-the-know locals. Drop in for a look, or stay for a cup of traditional Turkish coffee or a meal. The setting is casual and friendly, with tables in the atrium, which is filled with hundreds of tulips in the spring (5-6-TL soups, salads, sandwiches, and side dishes; 10-15-TL main courses; madrassa open 8:30-19:00, lunch served 11:00-16:00, drinks served until 19:00, Caferiye Sokak, Sogukkuyu Çıkmazı 1, tel. 0212/513-3601). The madrassa trains students in traditional Turkish arts and crafts, including tile painting, calligraphy, gold gilding, miniature painting, and the reed flute.

Budget Eateries Behind the Blue Mosque near the Top of the Hippodrome

These two popular budget options—friendly rivals facing each other across the street—are a few steps off the top of the Hippodrome and tucked behind the Blue Mosque. They distinguish themselves by remaining humble, affordable, and local-feeling, despite their prime location. To get here from the Hippodrome, face the Column of Constantine with the Blue Mosque on your left, then leave the Hippodrome on the street to the left, and hook downhill to the right...following the sounds of happy al fresco diners.

Buhara 93's affordable, down-to-earth food tastes like Grandma just cooked it: simple and tasty. Their *lavaş* (flat bread) is baked after you order and served right out of the wood-fired oven. This is also a fine place to sample *pide* (8-12-TL main dishes, daily 8:00-22:30, can be crowded at lunch and early dinner but no reservations needed, no alcohol, Nakilbend Caddesi 15, tel. 0212/516-9657).

Havuzbaşı Restaurant and Tea House is situated on a relaxed, idyllic outdoor patio just beyond the tourist crush below the Hippodrome. Stop by for dessert or coffee, hookahs (12.50 TL per group, free extra mouthpieces), backgammon, and non-alcoholic drinks (it's near a mosque). Fake dervishes whirl nightly at 21:00 from mid-May through August (Küçükayasofya Mahiye, Nakilbent Sokak 2, tel. 0212/638-8819).

In or near the Spice Market

Pandelli, on the Spice Market's second floor, is open for lunch only.

Started by Chef Pandelli in the 1930s, it still serves a mouthwatering traditional Turkish-Ottoman menu, including an especially good eggplant *börek*. Although the restaurant always appears to be overcrowded with businesspeople, they eat quickly, so you won't wait long for a table (12-35-TL starters, 18-40-TL main dishes, daily 11:30-19:00, go up tiled staircase just inside Spice Market's main entrance at Eminönü Mısır Çarşısı 1, tel. 0212/527-3909).

Hamdi Restaurant is a dressy white-tablecloth place with vested waiters, a bright glassed-in roof terrace, and great views of the city and over the water. Be warned that the service is slow. They serve a variety of traditional kebabs from southeast Turkey (upper Mesopotamia). Consider the various kebabs: pistachio lamb, grilled eggplant, plum lamb, or grilled garlic lamb. The delicious *beyti* (behy-tee) kebab—a mix of barbecued beef and lamb wrapped in thin filo bread—takes longer to make. The wheat pilaf, called *firik* (fee-reek), is also good. For dessert, try the pistachio *katmer* or the baklava (15-25-TL kebabs, 6-TL desserts, slow service, daily 11:30-23:30, next to Spice Market, Kalçın Sokak 17, tel. 0212/528-0390). Take the elevator to the crowded third-floor terrace—the views are best from the narrow balcony (if there's an empty table here, grab it).

Starting or Ending Your Cruise in Istanbul

If your cruise begins and/or ends in Istanbul, you'll want some extra time here; for most travelers, two days is a minimum to see the highlights of this gigantic, historical layer cake of a city. For a longer visit here, pick up the *Rick Steves' Istanbul* guidebook.

Atatürk Airport

Istanbul's main airport, Atatürk, is used for most international flights (except some flights from Europe, which use Sabiha Gökçen Airport—described in the sidebar). Located to the west of the city center on the European side, Atatürk Airport is a 30- to 60-minute taxi ride (depending on traffic) to either the Old Town or the New District (airport info tel. 0212/465-3000, www.ataturk airport.com).

Atatürk Airport's international and domestic terminals are located across from each other and connected by an indoor corridor on the upper level. Both terminals occupy two floors, with arrivals on the ground level and departures on the upper level. The arrivals level of the international terminal has a TI desk, where you can pick up a free map and brochures. Each terminal also has an airport information desk, a pharmacy, car-rental agen-

---

Flying in Turkey

Atatürk Airport is the hub for Turkish Airlines (www.thy.com), the country's major airline. Smaller, private carriers—which fly from Atatürk Airport to other major Turkish cities, such as Ankara, İzmir, and Trabzon—include Atlasjet Airlines (www.atlasjet.com), Pegasus Airlines (www.flypgs.com), and Onur Air (www.onurair.com.tr).

Istanbul's other airport, **Sabiha Gökçen Airport,** is on the Asian side. It's served mainly by budget airlines—but the added expense of getting across the Bosphorus Bridge to your Old Town or New District hotel might negate your savings (figure 85-100 TL for a taxi, 1-2.5 hours depending on traffic, www.sgairport.com).

For a domestic economy flight within Turkey, estimate 75-250 TL one-way (about $50-170). You can buy your ticket in Turkey from a local travel agent, or book online through the airline's website. Flights book up more quickly in high season (May-Sept).

---

cies, exchange offices, and ATMs (located mainly on the arrivals level).

Arriving at Atatürk Airport

When you arrive at the international terminal, signs and airport staff direct you to passport control. Before going through this checkpoint, you'll have to buy a visa (windows are next to passport control; $20 for Americans, $60 in US dollars for Canadians, exact change required; for more visa information, see page 44). After getting your visa, go through passport control, then baggage claim, then Customs and into the arrivals lounge.

From here, you have several options for getting to the Old Town or the New District: cheap public transportation (via light rail and tram, easiest for the Old Town), the airport shuttle bus (most convenient for the New District), or a taxi (priciest choice, but provides door-to-door service to your hotel). For more information on transportation within and from Istanbul, see www.turkeytravelplanner.com/go/Istanbul/Transport.

By Light Rail and Tram: Public transportation from the airport into Istanbul is inexpensive (3.50 TL to the Old Town, 5.25 TL to the New District) but involves at least one transfer, making it a hassle if you have a lot of luggage. From the international terminal's arrivals level, take the escalator (located midway along the terminal) to the light rail (*hafif raylı*) platform; trains leave from the airport station (called Havalimanı) every 5-15 minutes (6:00-24:00, www.istanbululasim.com). Take the light rail

What If I Miss My Boat?

Remember that you can get help from the cruise line's **port agent** (listed on the destination information sheet distributed on the ship) and the local TI (see page 1097). If the port agent suggests a costly solution (such as a private car with a driver), you may want to consider other options.

Frequent trains leave from both of Istanbul's main stations: Sirkeci (seer-keh-jee, on the Old Town side of the Golden Horn—just a few steps from the Galata Bridge), which serves trains to Europe, and Haydarpaşa (high-dar-pah-shah, on the Asian side of the city—reached by frequent ferries from Eminönü waterfront), which serves trains to Asian Turkey, including **Ephesus** (overnight train to Izmir via Eskişehir, then one-hour train to Selçuk).

Long-distance **buses**, which leave from the city's main bus terminal (otogar; oh-toh-gar), located in the Esenler (eh-sehn-lehr) district on the European side, are quite comfortable, and may also be helpful in a pinch.

If you need to catch a **plane** to your next destination, see the next page for information on Istanbul's two airports.

Any local **travel agent** also should be able to help. For more advice on what to do if you miss the boat, see page 131.

to Zeytinburnu, where you can catch the tram (look for signs to the tram, or ask). To reach the Old Town, take the tram to the Sultanahmet stop. To go all the way to the New District, stay on the tram and take it across the Golden Horn; get off at the Karaköy stop (near Tünel funicular and the cruise terminals). Remember that any time you change between the light rail, tram, Metro, or funicular, you'll need to pay for a new ride (1.75 TL/ride, buy cards at ticket booths at major stops, see sidebar on page 1100). The light rail is also handy for reaching the city's main bus terminal (Otogar).

By Airport Shuttle Bus: Airport shuttle buses are usually white, and are marked with *Havaş* (hah-vahsh) signs. As you exit the arrivals level, go past the taxi stand to the *Havaş* stop. Shuttles leave the airport every 30 minutes from 4:00 to 1:00 in the morning (10 TL, www.havas.com.tr). If you're heading to the Old Town, get off at *Aksaray* (ahk-sah-ray), then take a taxi or tram (described next) to the core of the Old Town.

Back to the Airport by Shuttle Bus: If you're heading from the Old Town to the airport, you'll probably notice that local travel agencies advertise shuttle-bus services for as little as €5 per person (get details at each agency). If you go this route, note that you may need to catch the bus at the travel agency; some buses don't pick up at hotels.

By Taxi: The taxi stand is right outside the arrivals (ground) level of the terminal. Airport cabs are yellow; as long as they're in the line, you know that they work for the official airport-taxi service. It's a 30-60-minute ride to your hotel in the Old Town or to the New District; expect to pay roughly 35-55 TL ($25-40). Up to four people can fit into a cab—share to save money. For taxi tips, see page 1099.

Departing from Atatürk Airport

To leave Turkey by air, enter the airport's international terminal after first going through a security checkpoint. Once inside, scan the screens for the check-in desk for your flight. After checking in, you'll go through passport control and a second security checkpoint to reach the gate area.

Hotels

If you need a hotel in Istanbul before or after your cruise, here are a few to consider.

$$$ Hotel Sultanhan SC is an elegant hotel just off Divan Yolu, close to the Grand Bazaar and within walking distance of the Blue Mosque and Hagia Sophia. Its 40 rooms—larger than the norm for most Old Town hotels—have been restored with considerable care, and the staff is especially attentive (Sb-€160-190, Db-€210-220, Tb-€250-280, room rates can vary—check website for specials, 10 percent off best Internet rate if you mention this book when you reserve and show it at check-in, air-con, elevator, free Wi-Fi, Piyer Loti Caddesi 15-17, tel. 0212/516-3232, fax 0212/516-5995, www.hotelsultanhan.com, info@hotelsultanhan .com, manager Enis Akça).

$$$ Aya Sofya Pensions SC is beautifully located on a quiet, traffic-free lane squeezed between Hagia Sophia and the Topkapı Palace wall. The pension consists of a whole street's worth of 19th-century Ottoman row houses, converted into 64 rooms for rent. Higher prices are for rooms with a view of Hagia Sophia (spring/summer: Sb-€120-140, Db-€170-200; winter: Sb-€70-85, Db-€90-110; request room with air-con in summer, lots of stairs and no elevator, all along Soğukçeşme Sokak, tel. 0212/513-3660, fax 0212/513-3669, www.ayasofyapensions.com, info@ayasofya konaklari.com).

$$ Ottoman Hotel Imperial SC is a freshly renovated, former Ottoman school and hospital right across the street from Hagia Sophia. Its 27 rooms—plus 25 more in a brand-new annex building—are comfortable and plush (Sb-€79-120, Db-€99-150, Tb-€129-180, "premium" rooms with Hagia Sophia view-€30 extra, 5 percent discount with this book, free airport pickup with 3-night stay, air-con, elevator, Internet access and free Wi-Fi, laundry service, Caferiye Sokak 6/1, tel. 0212/513-6151, fax 0212/512-7628, www.ottomanhotelimperial.com, info@ottomanhotel imperial.com).

$$ Amiral Palace Hotel SC is a charming boutique hotel near the heart of the Old Town. Modern and traditional elements mix in its 32 comfortable rooms, and its terrace has million-dollar views of the Sea of Marmara and islands (Sb-€65-120, Db-€75-140, Tb-€95-160, check website for specials and seasonal rates, 10 percent off best Internet rate if you mention this book when you reserve and show it at check-in, free airport pickup with 3-night stay, air-con, elevator, Wi-Fi, Bayramfırını Sokak 7, Cankurtaran, tel. 0212/458-6800, fax 0212/458-0666, www.amiralpalacehotel .com, info@amiralpalacehotel.com).

$ Sphendon Hotel SC, cute and new, has a tiny seaview terrace and a delightful patio out back where breakfast is served in the summer. Its 12 rooms are within walking distance of the heart of the Old Town (Sb-€60-90, Db-€70-110, lower prices in off-season, 5 percent cash discount, free airport pickup with 3-night stay, plus free airport drop-off with 5-night stay, air-con, Wi-Fi, Akbıyık Değirmeni Sokak 50, tel. 0212/518-5820, fax 0212/518-5825, www.hotelsphendon.com, owner Erdal Demirli).

EPHESUS
& the PORT of KUŞADASI

Efes

The port city of Kuşadası, Turkey's second-busiest cruise destination (after Istanbul), is at the heart of a seaside resort region. Virtually every visitor here does one of two things: Tour the remarkable ancient Roman ruins at nearby Ephesus (EFF-eh-suhs), or shop for a Turkish carpet and other souvenirs in Kuşadası (koo-shah-DAH-suh) itself.

With extra time, there are other options: The House of the Virgin Mary, in the hills above Ephesus, is where Mary supposedly spent the last several years of her life. The town of Selçuk (SELL-chuck) features the Ephesus Museum, with some of the best artifacts from the site, plus the ruined Basilica of St. John, where the apostle/evangelist is said to be entombed.

But Ephesus is truly the only must-see. The ruins of that grand metropolis rank among the top archaeological sites anywhere. Even those who don't like ruins are turned on by Ephesus' ancient landscape and visible history. While the shopping in Kuşadası is good, don't do it at the expense of missing Ephesus.

Planning Your Time

Even on a short visit (7-8 hours), you can fit in any or all of these options:

• Tour ancient **Ephesus;** allow 2-3 hours for a good look at the site, plus about 30-45 minutes each way to get there from the Kuşadası cruise port.

• Visit the nearby **House of the Virgin Mary;** allow 1 hour total round-trip from Ephesus.

• Visit the town of **Selçuk** (next to Ephesus), with three attractions: the Ephesus Museum (allow 1 hour), the Basilica of

Services near the Port of Kuşadası

You'll find everything you need in town, but if you want it now, here are the nearest locations:

ATMs: Cash machines are in the mall-like shopping zone right at the cruise terminal complex.

Internet Access: You can get online right in the terminal complex: Exit the terminal building, turn left, and look for the **Kuşadası Calling Station** (Internet terminals with English keyboards, Wi-Fi, cheap international calling cards). You can also get online inside the **Liman Hotel** (exit straight ahead, turn right at the TI; 3 lonely terminals in the lobby, €2/hour, also Wi-Fi, Kıbrıs Street, Buyral Road 4).

Pharmacy: Two pharmacies are within a few blocks of the cruise terminal. Head to Barbaros Boulevard (see "Shopping in Kuşadası," later); you'll find one pharmacy near the top of this boulevard (just before the intersection with Sağlik Caddesi) and another down Bahar Sokak (the second narrow street leading to the left as you head up Barbaros Boulevard—roughly across the boulevard from the upper corner of the old caravanserai).

St. John (allow 30 minutes), and—for shoppers—the Carpetium carpet shop (allow as much time as you like).

• Kuşadası itself offers little in the way of sightseeing, but its **bazaar** of shops and cafés is enjoyable to explore (an hour or more)—particularly if this is your only stop in Turkey.

While cruise lines (hungry for commissions) try to steer you into Kuşadası and its shops, it's more satisfying to linger at the outlying sights than to kill time back at the port. With a long enough stop at Kuşadası and your own taxi or driver, you can squeeze in all of the above and make it back to port for your ship's departure.

Arrival at the Port of Kuşadası

Arrival at a Glance: To reach Ephesus on your own, you can either take a taxi (efficient but expensive—120 TL/about $80 round-trip, 30 minutes each way) or ride in a shared minibus, called a dolmuş (dirt-cheap at 5.50 TL/about $3.50 per person, but requires a transfer plus a 15-minute walk).

Port Overview

Kuşadası, a city of about 65,000, is the primary port for accessing the ancient site of Ephesus. Cruise ships arrive at a pier right in the heart of town. You'll funnel into a gauntlet of local trinket and carpet shops and international chains (Starbucks, Burger King,

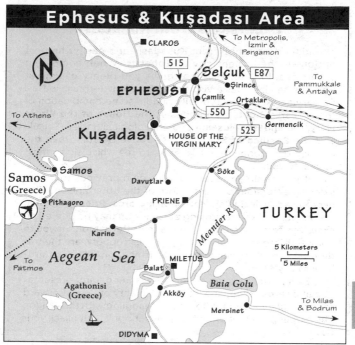

Ephesus & Kuşadası Area

and so on). As you exit the other end, the busy bazaar of more tourist-oriented shops is ahead and uphill. Tours, guides, and

taxis—eager to take arriving passengers to Ephesus—cluster near the cruise terminal.

Tourist Information: The TI is straight ahead as you exit the terminal complex, on the right-hand corner of the first intersection (Mon-Fri 8:00-12:00 & 13:30-17:30, closed Sat-Sun except on busy days mid-May-Sept).

Price Warning: The prices for just about everything in Kuşadası (not just big-ticket carpets, but also restaurants, taxis, and more) increase dramatically when the first cruise ship docks in the morning, then drop again when the last boat pulls out in the evening. In general, you can expect to pay a premium for the privilege of arriving by cruise ship. The farther you walk into town, the lower the prices drop.

Heat Warning: In the height of summer, Ephesus can be scorchingly hot, with little shade. Wear light colors and comfortable shoes. Bring water, a hat, sunscreen, and sunglasses.

Excursions from Kuşadası

The main destination from Kuşadası—and easily the best option—is the ancient city of **Ephesus.** When comparing excursions, look for one that gives you plenty of time at Ephesus and includes a visit to the excellent Terrace Houses. Cruise-line excursions typically bundle some combination of three nearby sights with Ephesus: the **House of the Virgin Mary,** the **Ephesus Museum** of archaeological finds in Selçuk, and the **Basilica of St. John** just above Selçuk. Read the detailed descriptions in this chapter to see which sights most appeal to you.

If you've already seen Ephesus on a previous trip, consider an excursion to one or more of the other ancient sites near Kuşadası, including **Metropolis, Claros, Priene, Didyma,** and **Miletus.** (If you're arriving at İzmir, you may be offered an excursion to the famous ancient site of **Pergamon.**) If you're not interested in ancient sites, your best options are the traditional Turkish-Greek village of **Şirince,** or Turkey's third-largest city, **İzmir.**

Every cruise excursion includes an engaging presentation at a **carpet shop,** and leaves you plenty of time afterward to linger, get your hopes up, and try haggling with the vendor. The carpet presentation can be fun, but don't let it hijack your day.

EPHESUS

Getting to Ephesus and Other Sights

The rich and complicated story of Ephesus is best explained by a local guide, and getting to the site by public transportation is time-consuming. For these reasons, taking a shore excursion to Ephesus or hiring your own local guide is worth considering. If you want to go to Ephesus on your own, follow this chapter's self-guided tour.

With a Private Guide

Hiring your own private guide for Ephesus is a great way to have an informative, well-organized visit. Local guides for hire wait at the two entrances to the Ephesus site, and some may even meet arriving cruise-ship passengers in Kuşadası. Because demand is high when cruisers hit town, the top guides book up early; to get the best-quality guides, make arrangements as far ahead as possible. The price for a guided tour varies based on demand, duration, specific destinations, the guide's level of expertise, and whether transportation is included; for a full-day tour, a couple will likely pay around $200-500. The companies and individuals listed below will charge fairly.

Two companies can help you find a guide for Ephesus: the İzmir-based **Melitour,** run by Mehlika Seval and Asli Kumari (mobile 0533-368-3113, www.melitour.com, melitour@yahoo.com); and the Istanbul-based **SRM Travel,** run by Lale and Tankut Aran (tel. 0216/386-7623, www.srmtravel.com).

Guides who can sometimes be booked independently are **Can Yiğit** (mobile 0532-426-6335, guidecan68@yahoo.com) and **Secil Gündoğdular** (mobile 0533-571-9148, secilgundogdular@hotmail .com).

By Taxi

A taxi stand is in front of the cruise terminal complex, just past the TI. If going to Ephesus, ask to be dropped off at the upper gate (the trip takes about 30 minutes each way). Here are the approximate fares:

- One-way to Ephesus: 80 TL
- Round-trip to Ephesus (with 2-3 hours of waiting time): 120 TL
- Round-trip to Ephesus (for 2-3 hours) plus 30 minutes at the House of the Virgin Mary: 160 TL
- Round-trip to Ephesus (for 2-3 hours) plus the House of the Virgin Mary (for 30 minutes) and an hour at Selçuk: 180 TL

The 180-TL fare (about $125) for a do-it-all day is reasonable, especially if you split the cost with other travelers (taxis fit up to four).

Cabbies may quote prices either in Turkish lira (TL) or in euros, and will generally accept either form of payment (roughly, 2 TL = €1). If the cabbie's initial estimate is much higher than the prices listed above, negotiate them down or ask the next guy. Also, be aware that cabbies tend to give better prices for package deals. If you end up taking different taxis for each segment of the Ephesus/Virgin Mary/Selçuk/port trip, your total price will likely be more than the round-trip fares listed above (for example, round-trip between Ephesus and the House of the Virgin Mary costs 70 TL, and one-way between Ephesus and Selçuk is 15 TL).

Remember that cabbies, unlike private guides, provide only transportation and no information.

By Public Transportation

To reach Ephesus from Kuşadası, you'll take a short ride within town on one *dolmuş* minibus, then switch to a different *dolmuş* for the longer ride to Ephesus (figure about 30-40 minutes total one-way), followed by a 15-minute walk to the site's entrance gate. If you want to connect to the House of the Virgin Mary or the sights in Selçuk, you may need to fill in the gaps with shorter taxi rides.

Step 1: From the Ship to Downtown Kuşadası

Exit the cruise terminal complex and go straight ahead. Bear left past the TI, and just beyond the taxi stand, wait along the street for a *dolmuş*—look for a boxed "D" on the sign at the curb. Take any minivan marked *Kadınlar Denizi* ("Ladies' Beach"). These come by every 10 minutes or so. When you get in, tell the driver you're going to Selçuk (SELL-chuck) and pay him 1.50 TL per person; after just a few minutes, he'll tell you where to change to the next *dolmuş*. (Your stop is after the yellow "taxi office" sign.)

Step 2: From Downtown Kuşadası to Ephesus' Lower Gate

When you leave the first *dolmuş*, walk across the street to the park (Salih Killi Dinlenme Parkı). At the corner, look for the Kuşadası-Selçuk *dolmuş*. The *dolmuş* leaves from here about every 20 minutes; don't be surprised if it waits to fill up before it takes off. Pay the driver 4 TL per person, and tell him you want to go to Efes (EH-fehs). The trip, passing resort beaches and water parks, takes about 25-30 minutes. The driver will let you off at a road branching to the right with an *Efes (Ephesus)* sign—listen for him to announce "Efes." This is also called "Efes Yolu," the road to Ephesus. (You'll catch the return *dolmuş* to Kuşadası at the same spot, but across the street—wave one down for a ride back to town.)

Walk up the slightly uphill road (branching off the main road) for about a half-mile (15 minutes). When the road forks to the right, keep going straight (even though the right fork is signed for Ephesus—that's for drivers). You'll pass (on your left) the ruins of the ancient stadium, which once held 20,000 spectators. Walk through the big bus parking lot to the ticket office.

Note: While most package excursions begin at the upper gate of Ephesus, then work their way downhill through the site, the *dolmuş* leaves you closer to the lower gate of Ephesus. This means that you'll see the sights going uphill (which helps you avoid the crowds, especially at the beginning of the day). If you want to begin at the upper gate instead, ride the *dolmuş* all the way into Selçuk, then hire a taxi to drive you to Ephesus' upper gate (15 TL).

Returning to Your Ship

If you're hiring a taxi or private guide, they'll get you back to the port.

If you're taking public transportation back from Ephesus, remember that the return *dolmuş* departs across the street from where you were first dropped off (opposite the road leading to Ephesus' lower gate). Wait by the roadside and flag down any passing *dolmuş* marked *Selçuk-Kuşadası* (you want to take a *dolmuş* going toward your right, as you face Ephesus). Pay 4 TL per person and ride into Kuşadası, where you can walk, taxi, or ride another *dolmuş* to your ship. If you're in a rush, hire a taxi back to Kuşadası (there are taxi stands at both Ephesus gates); to split the cost, try to team up with other travelers returning to your ship.

If you have extra time to spend in Kuşadası, you can linger in the bustling **shopping** zone that sprawls in front of the cruise terminal. For pointers, see the next section.

If you want to hit the **beach,** just walk along the coastal road (with the sea on your left) for about 10 minutes from the cruise terminal.

Better yet, if you have enough time, go for a **stroll** through the hilly upper streets above the main port and shopping area of Kuşadası. Away from the tourist zone, you'll catch a glimpse of real-world Turkey.

Shopping in Kuşadası

EPHESUS

While there's not much sightseeing in Kuşadası, it's an entertaining place to buy some souvenirs.

The fun (if touristy) Kuşadası **bazaar** is pleasant to explore even if you're not shopping. From the cruise terminal, go straight ahead past the TI and taxi stand, then turn left and pass the old stone caravanserai (inn) on the right (now a carpet shop, hotel, and restaurant—peek inside to see the courtyard, with pointed arches). The bazaar is just beyond the caravanserai on the right, along the pedestrianized Barbaros Boulevard and intersecting alleys. Many of the same items sold in Istanbul are available here, at similar prices—carpets, leather, tiles, silver and gold jewelry, and so on (for more on these items, see page 1179). Salespeople here can be extremely aggressive, especially toward single women. Avoid eye contact, and ignore attention-grabbing sales pitches; even saying "No, thanks" elicits a lengthy conversation. If buying anything, it's expected that you'll try to haggle down the price (for bargaining tips, see page 1180). The prices are more down-to-earth the farther you get from the main drag.

Buying a Turkish Carpet in Kuşadası

People back home—not to mention your cruise director—will rave to you that shopping for a carpet is a "quintessential Turkish experience." There's no doubt that high-quality Turkish carpets are impressive works of art created by master craftspeople, and many are museum-worthy. But buying a good carpet for a good price is next to impossible on a short port visit. The carpet industry in Kuşadası is a finely tuned machine, calibrated expressly for the tourist trade—and the cruise lines are their eager partner. Wrapped up in the $3,000 price of your carpet is several hundred dollars in kickbacks for your cruise line.

First, realize that an authentic, high-quality carpet will cost you many thousands of dollars (though smaller ones can be more affordable). As with any big purchase, do some homework before you get serious about buying. Research from home, and visit Turkish carpet importers in your area to educate yourself about how much various carpets are worth. (For starters, see the carpet explanation on page 1180.) Ideally, once in Turkey, you'd shop for your carpet at a small-town cooperative, the best place to buy as directly as possible from the person who made it. To get the best deal, you'd select a rug you like, already knowing roughly what it's worth, and confidently haggle to an agreeable price without middlemen and mark-ups getting in the way. Unfortunately, this isn't feasible on a short visit, especially by cruise ship.

When you arrive at Kuşadası, your cruise line will hand out a list of "authorized" or "recommended" carpet shops. This list offers peace of mind, and does provide some measure of consumer protection. But it also gives you the false impression that the cruise line has already done the hard work of comparison shopping and quality control for you. In fact, the list primarily consists of carpet shops willing to pay commissions to the cruise line. At the beginning of each season, some carpet shops pay cruise lines a small fortune for the privilege of being "recommended."

Most excursions from Kuşadası include a stop for a carpet-weaving demonstration. The best of these are enjoyable and truly educational cultural experiences. You'll be invited into a comfortable carpet sales hall and offered tea and snacks. Your articulate host will poetically describe both the art and technique of carpet-weaving, stressing the painstaking work involved ("A poor village woman toiled for two years at her loom to create this masterpiece..."). After a demonstration of how silk is teased from silkworms and a good look at the weaving process, you'll be taken into the showroom and educated on the various types and qualities of carpets. You'll take your shoes off and walk across a carpet to feel the pile under your toes. Shop assistants will unroll carpet after carpet, dizzying you with gorgeous patterns unlike any you've seen at big-box furniture stores back home. And then it's time for the hard sell, when the carpet you fall in love with drops 20 percent in price after the first bargaining exchange, and you think: Maybe I can get a good deal here. Don't count on getting unbiased advice from your shore excursion's local guide, who likely gets a cut of your purchase.

When you're back on the ship, the cruise line encourages you to "register" your carpet with them to activate the "shopper's guarantee," or to drop a copy of your carpet receipt into a raffle for a prize. The real motive is to discover which carpet shops made sales, and for how much, generating further commissions for the cruise line.

Ultimately the carpet shop may hand over as much as 60 or 70 percent of the sales price to the cruise line...a huge expense that they pass on to cruise passengers in the form of dramatic markups.

I wish I could tell you that there's one spunky carpet shop in Kuşadası that sidesteps this whole mess and sells its wares directly to the cruise passenger without the huge mark-up. But in truth, there's effectively no way to avoid this racket in the port.

But there is an alternative in the small town of Selçuk, near the site at Ephesus. **Carpetium** is across the street from the road leading up to Ephesus' lower gate, on the main highway that connects Kuşadası to Selçuk (you can stop off here if you're going to the site by taxi or *dolmuş*, or with a private guide/driver). It carries a wide variety of carpets—from simple kilims to fancy silk carpets—and has down-to-earth prices compared to shops around the cruise port. Shop anonymously as you haggle; then, before you pay, show this book for an additional 10 percent discount from manager Varol. If you make any purchase, they'll cover your ride back to the cruise port (Kuşadası 1. km Caddesi, Selçuk, tel. 0232/892-4316).

Ultimately, locals explain, it's a toss-up whether you pay less in Turkey or at a good importer back home. But for many travelers, buying a Turkish carpet in Turkey is worth the premium. If that's your preference, be a smart consumer and equip yourself with good information.

Arrival at the Port of İzmir

While Kuşadası is the primary port of entry for this part of Turkey, some cruises call instead at the large city of İzmir, about an hour north of Ephesus (and 1.5 hours north of Kuşadası).

Because of the greater distance and complexity of reaching Ephesus by public transportation, if you are arriving in İzmir, the cruise line's shore excursion to Ephesus is probably your best option (or hire your own guide and driver, through the companies described on page 1198). Cabbies charge about 300 TL for the round-trip taxi ride from İzmir to Ephesus, including wait time.

If you'd rather take public transportation to Ephesus, here's the complicated scoop: From İzmir's cruise port, take a taxi to the main bus station, or *otogar* (25 TL, 30-minute ride). Then catch a public bus toward Kuşadası (15 TL, 4/hour). Rather than riding the bus all the way to Kuşadası, hop off after about an hour—just after you leave the town of Selçuk, at the road to Ephesus (ask the driver to let you off at "Efes" or "Efes Yolu"). You'll get off along a country road; walk up the intersecting road for about 15 minutes to Ephesus' lower gate (see the instructions on page 1200).

Near Kuşadası: Ephesus

Ephesus—one of the most important cities of the Roman Empire—is among the world's best ancient sites. Whether you're strolling its broad boulevards, appreciating the pillared facade of the famous Library of Celsus, peeling back the layers of dust to understand the everyday lifestyles of the rich and Roman at the Terrace Houses, or testing the acoustics in the theater where gladiators once tussled, Ephesus is a perfect place to time-travel back to the grandeur of Rome.

Orientation to Ephesus

Cost: 20 TL for site entry, plus another 15 TL for the Terrace Houses.

Hours: Daily mid-March-late Oct 8:00-18:30, off-season until 16:30.

Getting There: There are two entrance gates to the site, about 1.5 miles apart. I've oriented this tour the way most visitors see Ephesus, beginning at the upper gate and working down to the lower gate. Cruise-line excursions take this approach to the site, and it's how you'll likely do it if you're riding a taxi to Ephesus. But if you are relying on public transportation (*dolmuş* minivan taxis) to reach Ephesus, you'll begin at the lower gate. In that case, you can either hire a taxi (15 TL) to bring you around to the upper gate, or simply see the site uphill...and hold this book upside-down.

Audioguide: It costs 10 TL to rent a decent audioguide, with 1.5 hours of commentary on the main site, plus 20 minutes on the Terrace Houses. The 20-TL (or €10) deposit will be refunded when you return the audioguide at the other end of the site.

Local Guide: Private guides, hoping you'll hire them for a tour,

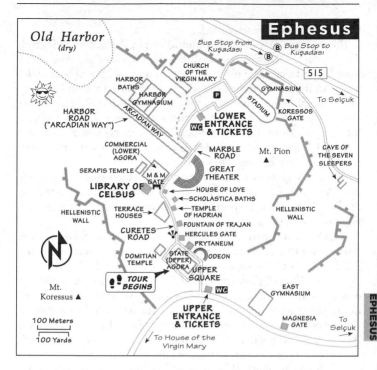

hang out at each entrance. These guides charge about 60-70 TL per hour; a typical tour of the site takes about two hours and costs 120 TL. Negotiate a good price, and don't be afraid to talk to a few different guides to decide who you like best.

Services: You'll find bathrooms and basic snack stands at each entrance gate.

Be Prepared: If it's hot, remember to wear light clothes and bring sunglasses and water (but remember not to drink Turkish tap water). Even with a hat, sunscreen is essential, as sunlight reflects off the marble. Wear durable shoes to traverse the uneven, sometimes steep terrain.

Background

At its peak, Ephesus was one of the grandest cities of the ancient world, ranking among the four leading centers of the Roman Empire (along with Alexandria, Antioch, and Rome itself). With a staggering quarter of a million residents, Ephesus was the second-biggest city on the planet (after Rome). The Ephesus we see today reflects the many civilizations—Greek, Persian, Roman, and Christian—that passed through Asia Minor (today's Turkey) in the days before the Ottomans. Julius Caesar, Anthony and Cleopatra, St. Paul, and possibly St. John and even the Virgin Mary have all walked these same marble roads.

The area was first settled around 1000 B.C. According to legend, the Oracle of Delphi prophesied that the Greek prince Androklos would found a city at a place revealed to him by "a wild boar and a fish." Androklos set sail to the west, and eventually found his way to the beach where the Cayster (a.k.a. Meander) River met the Aegean Sea. While Androklos grilled his dinner at a campfire, a fish jumped out of the pan, knocked some embers into a bush, and ignited it—flushing out a boar. Androklos tracked the boar into the valley where he would found Ephesus.

The city grew as a seaport and the worship center of the goddess Artemis. By 500 B.C., it was a bustling cultural capital on the Mediterranean. It sported the enormous Temple of Artemis, famous in its day and now in ruins.

Ephesus was part of the sophisticated Ionian world of western Asia Minor that inspired the rise of Golden Age Greece across the pond. The Ephesians spoke Greek (but with an Ionian dialect), produced "Greek" philosophers such as Heraclitus (who said the only constant is change), and popularized the style of Greek columns called Ionic (topped with scroll-like capitals). From time to time over the centuries, more warlike people—Lydians, Persians, Athenians, Alexander the Great, and Romans—overran Ephesus, but everyday life went on unchanged in this cosmopolitan city.

Oddly, the physical location of ancient Ephesus has moved over time. The sandy composition of the valley's soil and the constant movement of alluvial sands has made this an ever-changing landscape. The Meander River (whose circuitous course gave us the word) had a tendency to shift its path over time. When the river's access to the sea silted up in the third century B.C., the Ephesians relocated their city to the valley where the ruins now sit.

It was under Roman rule that Ephesus reached its peak. In A.D. 27, Emperor Augustus made the city the capital of the Roman province of Asia (roughly today's Turkish west coast). The harbor at Ephesus bustled with trade (including the slave trade) throughout the vast Roman Empire. By A.D. 100, it had become a city of marble buildings and grand monuments, with an  infrastructure that could support hundreds of thousands of togaed citizens. The ruins you'll see today date largely from the city's Roman heyday in the first and second centuries A.D.

Ephesus' prominence attracted some of the earliest followers of Christ. St. Paul came to Ephesus (about A.D. 52), where

The Ephesian Artemis

Throughout its history, the area around Ephesus has had a deep connection to various incarnations of a life-giving female deity: first a Hittite mother-goddess called Kubaba, then an Anatolian one named Cybele. During the Greek period, the cult of the goddess Artemis (daughter of Zeus, twin sister of Apollo) caught on here. This Greek virgin goddess was associated with childbirth and chastity, the moon and the wilderness, and the hunt and wild animals. The Romans later worshipped her as Diana.

The Ephesian version of Artemis took on characteristics of previous local mother-goddesses. According to tradition, Artemis was born in May, when Ephesians celebrated a festival of roses (and the month when we celebrate Mother's Day). They'd sacrifice bulls at the Temple of Artemis, cut off the testicles, and drape them over the statue of Artemis to celebrate her fertility. Many depictions of Artemis (including the famous statue in the Ephesus Museum in Selçuk) show her covered with these bulbous shapes. Another interpretation: These are not bulls' balls, but the many breasts of a life-sustaining mother-goddess. Or perhaps they are eggs, signifying her potent fertility.

In the sixth century B.C., locals built a spectacular Temple of Artemis, one of the Seven Wonders of the Ancient World. Only a single pillar of that temple survives today, on the other side of the hill from the archaeological site at Ephesus (see page 1223). Through Roman times, devotees of Artemis worshipped her using small carved statues.

Some historians believe that it's no coincidence that this ancient site so connected with the cult of a mother-goddess was later believed to be the final earthly home of the Virgin Mary (see "House of the Virgin Mary," page 1219).

EPHESUS

he conducted missionary work and wrote his First Epistle to the Corinthians ("Love is patient, love is kind. It does not envy, it does not boast, it is not proud"). St. John also may have come to Ephesus (about A.D. 90), having been charged with spreading Christianity in the Roman province of Asia. And even the Virgin Mary supposedly retired to Ephesus (brought by John).

As the Roman Empire fell, so fell Ephesus. In A.D. 263, invading barbarians looted the city, and it never really recovered. Ephesus limped along under the wing of the Byzantine Empire—

the Christian empire ruled from Constantinople (today's Istanbul). By the seventh century A.D., that same old problem—the silting up of the harbor inlet—finally closed Ephesus' harbor for good. The city was relocated once again, this time to the area around today's town of Selçuk. The marshy ground bred mosquito-borne malaria that decimated the population. The impressive buildings were scavenged for their conveniently pre-cut stones. Earthquakes further leveled the monuments. History forgot Ephesus until the 1860s, when a series of British, German, and Austrian archaeologists rediscovered and excavated the site (many of its treasures are now on display in Vienna's Ephesus Museum, and others are in the British Museum in London). Although only 15 percent of the site has been unearthed, it is still the largest excavated area in the world.

Self-Guided Tour of Ephesus

The excavated area of Ephesus basically represents the city center—the "downtown" of the ancient metropolis. Beginning at the upper gate and working downhill, you'll pass through the government center, residential neighborhood, shopping area, and theater and nightlife district. Along the way, you'll walk three different roads: the Curetes (Priests') Road, connecting the upper gate to the Library of Celsus; the Marble Road, between the library and the Great Theater; and the Harbor Road, connecting the theater to the harbor (and, along the way, the lower gate).

• *Just inside the upper gate is a large, rectangular space ringed with the ruins of various buildings. Take a little time to explore this area.*

Upper Square

Near the entrance, look for the large stack of terra cotta **pipes.** Ephesus had one of the ancient world's most sophisticated public waterworks systems. Runoff from the surrounding hills flowed across a network of four major aqueducts before being funneled into these clay pipes, which fed the city's fountains and the homes of the wealthy.

The double-row of pillars in the middle of the field marks the footprint of the **basilica.** It has the typical basilica floor plan—a large central hall or nave, flanked by two narrower side aisles. The columns are Ionic—slender, fluted, and topped with (mostly missing) scroll-like capitals. While today the word "basilica" signifies a church, back then it was a place where goods were traded, a sort of ancient stock exchange.

Next to the basilica was the **State Agora** (or Upper Agora). An agora was an open-air courtyard surrounded by covered arcades that housed shops. Here shoppers could get out of the sun and rain, catch up with their neighbors, and talk politics. This agora—525 feet long and 240 feet wide—originally had a temple to the goddess Isis in the center.

Tucked into the hillside, the largest structure you see (with

semicircular rows of seats) is the **Odeon** (c. A.D. 150). This indoor theater, once topped with a wooden roof, seated 1,500. Compared with the huge open-air theater we'll see later, this was an intimate venue for plays and concerts. It also served as the meeting place (bouleuterion) for

the city council. According to records, every Thursday at 11:00, 450 aristocrats would hash out the civic business of Ephesus.

The two standing pillars next to the Odeon are what's left of the **Prytaneion.** One of the city's top spiritual sites, this was

where the "eternal flame" was kept (in the rectangular pit). Just as Rome had its eternal flame tended by Vestal Virgins, Ephesus chose honored citizens to make sure this fire always flickered, to guarantee the city's continued prosperity.

The Prytaneion is also where visiting dignitaries were welcomed.

On the hill high above (not visible from here) is the **Cave of the Seven Sleepers.** According to local legend, in the third century—when Christianity was still outlawed in Rome—seven young worshippers fell asleep while they hid in a cave to avoid mandatory worship of the pagan gods. They finally awoke more than a century later, after Christianity had become the state religion. The church built over their tombs is a popular pilgrimage site. (The legend is also told in the Quran—sura 18—and Muslim pilgrims come here to honor the sacrifices made by Christian believers.)

• *The group of ruins clustered around the bottom of this area marks the site of...*

Domitian Square

The centerpiece of this quarter was the **Temple of Domitian,** dedicated to the first century A.D. Roman emperor. Though little remains today, the temple was large—two stories tall (as the ruin suggests) and covering the area of a football field.

Resting on the ground across from the temple site, look for the **Nike frieze,** which once topped a gate. This depicts the Greek goddess Nike giving the wreath of victory to the Romans. Look closely under her right heel—is that a swoosh I see?

Flanking the ramp roughly between Domitian Square and the main road are two **pillars** with directional aids: one, facing the square with the marketplace, is a statue of Hermes (god of merchants); the other, facing a pharmacy, is a carving of Asklepios (symbolizing medicine). Cosmopolitan Ephesus was filled with traders and merchants who spoke a Babel of languages, so these pictograms helped arriving sailors find their way.

Partway down the road, on the right, you'll pass between the pillars of the **Hercules Gate;** notice the lion's skin wrapped around the god's body). This gate narrowed the road so that wheeled traffic couldn't pass—creating a pedestrian zone.

• *Heading downhill, pause to appreciate the remarkable panorama spreading before you.*

Curetes Road

This road gives you a small glimpse of the epic scale of Ephesus at its peak. Mentally replace the tourists with toga-clad ancients to easily imagine the Roman metropolis. Statues, bubbling fountains, arches, and shops lined the street. Columns supported a covered sidewalk for pedestrians, while chariots, wagons, and men on horseback traveled the road. In the shade of the arcades, people could hang out and play games

such as backgammon (game boards were inscribed in the stone, including one that's now in the Ephesus Museum in Selçuk). The buildings on either side of the street had shops below, and homes above. The street takes its name from the *curetes*, a committee of six officers who made decisions about city administration.

On the right, with the huge reservoir basin (66 x 33 feet) topped by a pediment on stilts, is the **Fountain of Trajan.** Beneath the pediment once stood a gigantic statue of the powerful emperor proudly gazing over the pond. While the wealthy had indoor plumbing, fountains like this were the sole source of water for everyone else.

• *You're approaching the famous facade of the Library of Celsus. Before you get there, visit the sights on either side of the road. On the left is the modern building housing the excavation of the Terrace Houses (explained later). On the right is a series of open-air building ruins.*

Buildings along Curetes Road

On the right, across from the top of the Terrace Houses building, is the **Scholastica Baths** complex. Like all Roman baths, this was divided into rooms with special purposes: a changing room, a cooling-off room (frigidarium), a warm room (tepidarium), a hot steam room (caldarium), and so on. The tradition of large public baths in Mediterranean lands has continued through the centuries—from Romans to Byzantines to Ottomans to today's Turks.

Down Curetes Road from the baths, on the right, are the Corinthian columns and lone surviving curved arch once believed to be the ruins of the **Temple of Hadrian.** (More recently, archaeologists have said, "Hmmm...maybe not.") Regardless of the building's purpose, it features detailed reliefs. The central relief over the door likely depicts the snake-headed Medusa. Another shows the legend of Ephesus' founding, with

Androklos stalking the wild boar (originals are in the Ephesus Museum in Selçuk).

• *From the main drag, go in the little doorway by the audioguide marker #143.*

Find your way to the U-shaped **latrine** room, with marble seating surrounding an open-air courtyard with a fountain. Few Ephesians could afford private bathrooms, so most people took care of business at a public latrine like this one. Visiting the loo evolved into a social event, and this room had seats for a rollicking party of 40. A wooden roof once topped the seating area. A constantly flushing stream of water ran beneath the seats, whisking waste immediately to a sewer; along the floor was a second stream with clean water for washing.

Near the very bottom of Curetes Road was the so-called **House of Love,** with Four Seasons mosaics on the floors. While tour guides love to spin titillating tales about how this was a popular brothel, most historians believe it was simply a residential home.

• *Across the street from these buildings is a separate sight, which requires its own ticket. It's well worth the extra 15 TL to visit the...*

Terrace Houses

This modern complex—protecting seven three-story homes, each with its own courtyard and elaborate decorations—presents a vivid

picture of the lifestyle of upper-class Ephesians. Covered in 1999, and opened to visitors in 2006, the Terrace Houses offer an unparalleled opportunity to see how the ancients lived and to watch ongoing excavations. Visitors follow a one-way route through the complex, appreciating the carefully restored mosaic floors and frescoed walls. (Because of ongoing excavations, your route may differ from the description below.)

The first (and biggest) unit you'll enter has the features typical of all upper-class Roman homes: living rooms and dining rooms on the ground floor, bedrooms upstairs, and an open-air courtyard in the center. This allowed air to circulate, while the lack of windows on the outer walls kept out dust, noise, and sun—a system still used in homes wealthy and poor in hot climates around the world. Beneath the courtyard floor is a cistern that collected rainwater to supply the house. Although most of the walls as seen today are rough brick (stripped of their original decoration), they once were covered with marble or frescoes (mostly depicting scenes from mythology). Keep an eye out for surviving water pipes in the passages. While ordinary Roman citizens used shared bathing and latrine facilities (like the complex you saw across the street), the wealthy could afford private plumbing. There were two systems of pipes in these homes: one for water, and one (under the floors and between walls) to carry hot air to heat the home.

The Marble Hall was the dining room, where homeowners entertained casual guests. This one had all marble floors and walls; archaeologists have identified some 120,000 fragments, which they are trying to piece back together (you may see workers actually sorting the marble). In the middle of the room, a gurgling pool provided both decoration and a soothing soundtrack. The huge vaulted hall of the Official Guest Room is even more impressive, with a big decorative pool and a restored ceiling.

Continuing upstairs to the bedrooms, you'll have a good view

down into the courtyard of the next house. Up above was a small storage room that held amphorae (pointy-bottomed clay jugs) containing the household supplies of wine, olive oil, and so on. The amphorae were partially buried in soil or sand to keep their contents cool. On the walls, you can see several faint, overlapping layers of frescoes (successive waves of earthquakes and fires over the generations forced homeowners to periodically redecorate). Look for the replica of a list of household expenses—a sort of "shopping list" offering a fascinating glimpse of daily life here.

Continuing up the stairs, keep an eye out for even more beautifully preserved frescoes and mosaics: a lion, Dionysus (god of wine), Medusa (though evil, she protected this house), the philosopher Socrates, Eros (a.k.a. Cupid), Apollo (god of art) and the nine Muses (guardians of artistic inspiration), a fish and a duck (in the kitchen), and so on.

Look for the small bathroom. Like the large latrine across the street, this one was also communal, with two side-by-side seats (even in a wealthy household, pooping was a social event) and a constantly flowing channel of clean water at one's feet for washing.

From the very top of the complex, look down to a particularly well-preserved mosaic floor, with the sea god Triton on the right, and a Nereid (protector of sailors), riding a seahorse, on the left.

• *Leaving the Terrace Houses, head back to the main road and turn left to face the...*

Library of Celsus

One of the most iconic Roman-ruin images in the world, this structure epitomizes Ephesus at its peak. It was the third-largest library of the ancient world (behind the collections in Alexandria and Pergamon), with some 12,000 volumes. Its namesake was a well-read governor of this province, whose son built the library as a mausoleum in his honor in A.D. 123. The ruined library was restored to its current appearance in the 1970s.

The library's facade—two monumental stories tall—features a distinctive grid of columns and recessed niches. Those Corinthian columns (topped with leafy capitals) on the ground floor are 40 feet tall. There were three grand doorways, each matched by windows above. The four statues in the niches represent the traits of Celsus: wisdom, knowledge, intelligence, and valor. An optical illusion causes this grand facade to seem even bigger—the outer columns are actually smaller than the central ones, making the facade appear to bulge in the middle.

Begin climbing the steps to the library. On the second step from the top, on the right side, look for the metal box that protects an image of a menorah lightly carved into the step. Ephesus had a large Jewish population that was on relatively good terms with the Romans (since, unlike Christians, the Jews never attempted to convert pagans to their own faith).

Step into the small interior, and picture it in its prime. The walls and floors were once gleaming marble (which covered the restored brick understructure we see today). Light poured in through the big east-facing windows, which caught the morning sun. The niches that you see once held scrolls. A three-foot-wide gap between the inner and outer walls helped to circulate air to preserve the delicate documents.

The earliest scrolls were made of Egyptian papyrus (a plant material). But as the collection at Pergamon grew, rivaling the library in Alexandria, the Egyptians jealously refused to export any papyrus. As always limited only by their ingenuity, the Romans simply invented a different material: parchment, made of dried-out animal skin. (This library's collection included both types of scrolls.) Eventually the sheets of parchment, rather than being rolled, were stacked and bound at one end—creating the book format that you're holding right now.

Back outside, notice the triple-arched **gate** next to the library. This area was part of a larger library complex that included a lecture hall (now destroyed). The gate (rebuilt in 1989) is inscribed in bronze letters with two names: Mazaeus and Mithridates. These were slaves who, freed by their master Emperor Augustus, became wealthy enough to build this gate in appreciation of their liberty.

• *Go through the gate to the beginning of the Marble Road. Note: Depending on ongoing excavations, you may be able to actually walk down the Marble Road, or (especially on weekdays) you may be detoured through the Commercial Agora to the Harbor Road—in which case, you can backtrack up Harbor Road to reach the Great Theater ruins.*

Marble Road

Not much survives along this road, which ran alongside the com-
mercial marketplace. True to its name, the road itself was paved with marble, which is still very slippery when wet. Notice the ruts in the pavement, worn from centuries of chariot and wagon wheels.

Keep an eye out for a **carving** in the middle of this road (face the gate of Mazaeus and Mithridates and look on the ground to the left). Local guides love to explain that this carving might be a form of early advertising. It depicts a foot (meaning "turn here"), two fingers
(pointing the way), a woman's head (indicating a brothel), and a heart. The message was clear even to illiterate sailors just arriving in town: "Yoo-hoo, sailor! Turn here, and walk this way for lovely ladies offering true love."
• *On the left side of the road (with the gate at your back), trace the faint, rectangular outline of the...*

Commercial Agora

This large marketplace was the main supermarket and shopping

mall of Ephesus. Like all ago-
ras, this was an open courtyard (360 feet square) surrounded by columns that supported a por-
tico to shade businesses. From the array of shops stocked with goods brought in from the nearby harbor, Ephesians could buy anything they wanted. Engraved marble slabs out front pictured what each shop sold: a cleaver for the butcher, an olive branch for the oil vendor, a fish for the fish-monger, and so on. In the center of the courtyard stood a sundial (now displayed in the Ephesus Museum in Selçuk), used to deter-mine the opening and closing times of the shops. The agora dou-bled as a site for local festivities ranging from sporting events to cockfights to performances (there was a viewing terrace between the Marble Road and the agora, not far from the Great Theater).

• *The primary surviving landmark along this road is the...*

Great Theater (a.k.a. Greco-Roman Theater)

It's huge. The theater held about 25,000 spectators (possibly the largest anywhere). Since a Roman theater was typically designed

to accommodate 10 percent of its city's population, experts guess that ancient Ephesus had 250,000 residents.

Although the theater is partly ruined, the acoustics are still so good that performers don't need microphones to be heard (as tour guides and would-be divas love to demonstrate to the delight of sightseers).

Check out the 66 rows, divided into the classes of Roman society. The lower level was reserved for VIPs and the emperor's box. Many seats here were covered in marble, with comfy seatbacks. The middle level held Roman citizens (most middle-class Ephesians). The upper level was bleacher seating for the lower classes—free men and women, and foreigners.

The ancient Greeks built the theater in the third century B.C. When the Romans came, they enlarged and modified it for their particular brand of entertainment, raising the stage and adding a backdrop. They enlarged the stage wall (to 60 feet high) to improve acoustics and framed the stage area with pillars, creating a proscenium. Notice the wall around the orchestra (in front of the stage). When the theater hosted gladiator fights, this wall protected spectators from the action. In modern times, the theater is still a popular venue, presenting concerts by everyone from Sting to Pavarotti to Diana Ross. (These have been suspended in recent years, while the theater is retrofitted to prevent vibrations from damaging the structure.)

This theater played a role in the dramatic story of the Apostle Paul, who lived in Ephesus about A.D. 52-54. Paul strongly denounced the worship of false idols. But remember that the cult of the goddess Artemis was big business in Ephesus. Artemis idol-carvers didn't like Paul's interference one bit. According to the Bible (Acts 19), they stirred up an angry mob and snatched some of Paul's Christian companions. Shouting "Artemis is great," the rabble-rousers dragged the captured Christians to this theater. Paul wanted to save them, but cooler-headed colleagues held him back. Fortunately, the enraged crowd inside calmed down and spared the Christians from harm.

• *Standing with your back to the theater, you're looking down the...*

Harbor Road (a.k.a. Arcadian Way)

Most visitors entered Ephesus on this road, which links the city and the harbor. It made a powerful first impression: marble-paved, 35 feet wide, lined with covered sidewalks, and lit with 50 street-lamps (a luxury rare in the ancient world). Like the Strip in today's Las Vegas, this was the city's glitzy main drag. The shops along the way sold a dazzling array of goods from around the known world. Notice that, while the functional Marble Road is rutted with tracks from cart wheels, this showcase boulevard is in great condition (no carts allowed). Ceremonial processions traveled this route, and it was also the place in town to promenade—just as families around the Mediterranean still enjoy an evening stroll.

Far on the horizon—a third of a mile away—lay the original harbor, an inlet of the distant sea. There you can see ruins of the giant **Harbor Gymnasium** and **Harbor Baths** (558 x 525 x 92 feet), which encouraged arriving visitors to scrub up before entering town. This harbor gradually silted up over the centuries—first becoming marshland, and then solid ground—leaving today's waterfront five miles away. Trade dried up, too, and the city declined. By the year 1500, Ephesus disappeared completely from history. Fortunately for us, archaeologists re-opened this cultural time capsule and brought the treasures of Ephesus back to life.

• *Your visit to ancient Ephesus is over. But there are a few other interesting sights nearby. If you're ready to leave, walk down the Harbor Road a short distance, and look for the row of trees on your right. This marks the path to the lower gate, where taxis and tour buses await to take you back to Kuşadası, to the House of the Virgin Mary, or the nearby town of Selçuk.*

Before departing, consider visiting...

More Sights at Ephesus

From the lower gate, you're about halfway to the scant remains of the **stadium** (not excavated, so there's little to see—ahead and on the right, with your back to the gate). Sports were very important to Ephesian life. Major athletic events filled this stadium; smaller ones took place in the agora and various gymnasiums. Fans revered successful athletes and openly bet on the outcome of contests.

Off to the left as you face the gate, in the middle of a field, are the remains of the **Church of the Virgin Mary,** also known as the "Double Church." This is where (in A.D.

Mary in Ephesus?

When Jesus saw his mother and the disciple whom he loved standing nearby, he said to his mother, "Woman, behold, your son!" Then he said to the disciple, "Behold, your mother!" And from that hour the disciple took her to his own home.

John 19:26-27

Christian belief is split on where Mary lived late in life: Jerusalem or Ephesus? Adherents of the Ephesus tradition think she may have come here with the Apostle John, to whom Jesus had entrusted his mother (see biblical passage above). Believers offer these details: After Jesus' death, the Apostle John was sent to convert the pagans of Rome's province of Asia. He came to its capital, Ephesus—and, because of Jesus' commission, he likely would have brought Mary. To avoid antagonizing the local population of pagan Artemis-worshippers, Mary lived in a house on Mount Koressos, high above the city. After 11 years, Mary was taken up into heaven (the Assumption).

Another piece of evidence that Mary lived here, say the faithful, is the existence of the Church of the Virgin Mary in the city of Ephesus (whose ruins can still be seen; see page 1217). During the early years of Christianity, such churches were only dedicated to people who lived or died in the immediate area.

During Byzantine times (fifth and sixth centuries), Mary's house was converted into a chapel but sustained damage in various earthquakes. The house—and the specifics of the story surrounding it—gradually crumbled over the centuries. And yet, a ragtag band of local Christians still venerated this place. For

431) the Council of Ephesus decreed that Mary was to be known as "Mother of God," because Church doctrine believes that Jesus and God are one.

Ephesus Connections

By Taxi: From the lower gate, it costs a hefty 70 TL round-trip to reach the House of the **Virgin Mary,** including 30 minutes of waiting time (15 minutes each way—try to share the taxi with others wanting to make this trip; does not include 12.50 TL per person entry fee). From the upper gate, the same trip is about 60 TL. From either gate into **Selçuk** is 15 TL one-way, and returning to **Kuşadası's** cruise port costs about 60 TL. The taxi trip between the upper and lower **gates** is about 15 TL.

By *Dolmuş:* Remember, if you're taking the *dolmuş* back to **Kuşadası,** you can catch it either in Selçuk (if you're going there to see the Ephesus Museum) or along the main road below the lower

reasons that even they were unsure of, every 10 years they would visit the site on August 15—the Assumption of Mary.

In the early 1800s, a nun named Anne Catherine Emmerich—who lived halfway across Europe in Germany, and never set foot in Turkey—had a vision of Mary's house on the slopes of this distant mountain. Decades later, the remains of the house were discovered by priests familiar with Emmerich's visions and the tradition of local reverence for the site. Catholic officials eventually determined that this was the final residence of the Virgin Mary and, in the late 19th century, declared it a place of pilgrimage. The house was restored and opened to visitors in 1951; since then, three sitting popes (Paul VI, John Paul II, and Benedict XVI) have visited here.

Doubters question this entire account. For one thing, biblical scholars believe that John the Apostle, John the Evangelist (who wrote the gospel), and John the Prophet (a.k.a. John of Patmos, who wrote the Book of Revelation) were most likely three different people, whom early church fathers mistakenly amalgamated into a single person. Based on hard historical evidence, only John the Prophet is certain to have spent time in Ephesus. And even if the various Johns were one and the same, the Bible isn't entirely explicit about precisely who became Mary's caretaker—that person is identified only as "the disciple whom [Jesus] loved." And the only gospel to relate this story at all was the one attributed to—guess who?—John. Is the story possible? Yes. Probable? No.

But if you do believe that this really was Mary's final home, it's comforting to imagine that, after a tumultuous life, she was able to retire in such a tranquil setting.

gate (a 15-minute walk from the lower gate). There is no *dolmuş* from the upper gate (to Kuşadası, Selçuk, or anywhere else). Note also that there is no public transportation from Ephesus to the House of the Virgin Mary—only taxis.

House of the Virgin Mary

According to many observant Christians, the hillside of Mount Koressos above the ancient city of Ephesus is where the Virgin Mary, mother of Jesus Christ, spent the last 11 years of her life. (For the whole story, see the sidebar above.) While the House of the Virgin Mary is a major Catholic pilgrimage site, Muslims also consider this a special place and appreciate Mary as the mother of a great prophet. They refer to her as "Mother Mary" and to the site as Meryemana (Mother Mary's House).

The experience of visiting the house is powerful to some, underwhelming to others. After twisting up a high road above Ephesus, you'll pay 12.50 TL per person to enter the parking lot (same hours as the Ephesus site). Leave your taxi and walk through the beautiful **garden,** on a path

lined with olive trees. You'll pass a large hole in the ground, which may have been a cistern (see the water pipes buried in the ground) or a baptistery. Then you reach an outdoor amphitheater, where priests celebrate outdoor Mass.

The stone **house** itself—a rebuilt shrine on the original foundations—is small and humble. The earlier structure was likely a typical Roman house—two stories, made of stone, and with four or five rooms. The red line on the outside wall marks the house's first foundation. Inside, devoted visitors shuffle through and say a prayer. The house has two rooms open to sightseers: a living room (large) and bedroom (small).

Down the hill in front is a wall of spouting **fountains.** The natural spring water is blessed as holy water, which the faithful believe has healing powers. The wishing wall nearby is full of tissues and notes with requests for the Virgin Mary.

Selçuk

The sleepy town of Selçuk is the modern-day descendant of Ephesus. It's an unexceptional but pleasant small Turkish town with a pair of important sights: the Ephesus Museum (collecting artifacts from the ancient site nearby), in the center of town, and the foundations of the Basilica of St. John, on a hilltop a short walk from downtown.

Selçuk's **TI** is in front of the museum (Mon-Fri 8:30-12:00 & 13:00-17:30, closed Sat-Sun, shorter hours off-season, tel. 232/892-6328). **Taxis** wait nearby (the ride between Selçuk and Kuşadası should be about 50 TL—if your cabbie says it's more, try talking him down).

Sights in Selçuk

Ephesus Museum

There's no actual museum at the ancient site of Ephesus, so if you want to see some of the artifacts found there, this is your best opportunity. While not critical, a visit here rounds out your understanding of Ephesus.

Cost and Hours: 5 TL, same hours as Ephesus site.

Self-Guided Tour: The U-shaped museum has six rooms.

Room 1 displays findings from the Terrace Houses, including some original frescoes and mosaics, as well as medical tools,

cosmetics, and jewelry. In the middle of the room is an ivory frieze, reassembled from tiny fragments, showing war preparations under Emperor Trajan (second century A.D.). The statue in the niche depicts Artemis as a hunter. While Roman-era iconography depicts "Diana" (as they called her) this way, we'll see the more local interpretation of her later.

In Room 2, you'll see various statues that filled the niches at some of the fountains at Ephesus, including the Fountain of Trajan. The backgammon boards carved into the marble show that this game, invented by the Persians and still popular among Turks today, was adopted and enjoyed by Romans.

Room 3 is the Eros (Cupid) Room—many items here (frescoes, statues, and so on) are decorated with the lovesick little cherub.

From here you can poke into the courtyard at the center of the museum to see the sundial that originally sat in Ephesus' marketplace. The courtyard also contains sarcophagi from excavated cemeteries.

Room 4 collects tomb findings from different historical periods. Look for the

diagram explaining nine different historical burial methods. This collection of tomb pottery, weapons, and glass dates from a time when you *could* take it with you—which made these graves a big target for looters and tomb raiders. To the left of the stairs, notice the display with five pre-Greek/pre-Roman depictions of the mother-goddess (the prototype for Artemis-Diana, and arguably even Mary); for more on this evolution, see page 1207.

Speaking of the mother-goddess, Room 5 shows off the collection's highlight (on the left)—a larger-than-life, first-century A.D. statue of Artemis (from the Prytaneion, the "eternal flame" temple at Ephesus). Whether the bulbous orbs hanging from her torso are eggs, breasts, or bull testicles, they certainly represent fertility. Notice how she is surrounded by the wild animals she's thought

to rule over. Her headdress resembles the Temple of Artemis (a model of that temple is in the middle of the room). Across the room is a smaller, later (second century A.D.) statue of Artemis, which has similar themes (many breasts, wild animals)—but adds a new one, the signs of the zodiac around her neck.

Finally, in Room 6, you'll see exhibits about the emperors, who were venerated as gods. The original frieze from the so-called Temple of Hadrian, with Androklos chasing the boar of the Ephesian founding legend, is preserved here, along with the head and forearm of a 23-foot-tall statue of Domitian (from his namesake temple near the upper gate), and busts of various other emperors.

Basilica of St. John

This ruined basilica, perched on a hill over Selçuk, is a pilgrimage site for Christians. While there's little to actually see here (aside from some broken walls), it's very historic and an easy walk from the town center, affording fine views over the valley below. From here, you also get your best look at the once famous, now under-whelming ruins of the Temple of Artemis.

The Basilica of St. John—the last great monument of ancient Ephesus—was built on the supposed tomb of the Apostle John. Although skeptical historians dispute accounts of John's life in Ephesus, here's the story: John, one of Jesus' disciples, is said to have come to Ephesus in about A.D. 90 to preach the gospel. When John died about A.D. 100, he was buried at this hilltop location. (For more on the biblical John—or Johns—see the "Mary in Ephesus?" sidebar, earlier.)

Some 400 years later, the Byzantine (and Christian) Emperor Justinian built this church to venerate St. John. The church was 360 feet long (about the size of Westminster Abbey) and had six domes. In the center—beneath the central dome—was John's tomb.

The basilica was constructed largely from stones scavenged from Ephesus and from a pagan structure that preceded it—the

---

What If I Miss My Boat?

Remember that you can get help from the cruise line's port agent (listed on the destination information sheet distributed on the ship) and the local TI (see page 1197). If the port agent suggests a costly solution (such as a private car with a driver), you may want to consider public transit.

If your next stop is **Istanbul,** all connections are through the city of İzmir, about an hour and a half north of Kuşadası; a train runs several times daily from Selçuk to İzmir's airport (station name: A. Menderes) and to İzmir (station name: Basmane). From İzmir, you can continue by train (there's an overnight connection from İzmir to Istanbul, with a change in Eskişehir) or plane (İzmir and Istanbul are connected by frequent flights).

If you're heading for the **Greek islands,** your gateway will be the island of Samos, which is connected to Kuşadası by a daily ferry. From Samos, boats go to Piraeus (Athens) as well as various Greek islands.

If you're in a hurry to reach **Athens,** consider flying instead (via İzmir).

Any **travel agent** can help you. For more advice on what to do if you miss the boat, see page 131.

Temple of Artemis at the foot of the hill. Because Muslims were pushing into the area at the time, the basilica's builders also erected a castle nearby, with walls extending down to encompass the basilica. Ultimately the walls failed to protect the hilltop; the Muslims took over and converted the basilica into a mosque, before it was damaged by an earthquake and fell into disrepair.

Today visitors can pay 5 TL to walk through the rubble (open same hours as Ephesus site). The supposed site of St. John's tomb is marked by a marble slab and four pillars, representing the four Evangelists. You'll also see the baptistery's plunge pool and (in the little chapel in the left transept) some frescoes of Jesus, Mary, and St. John.

From the viewpoint terrace in front of the basilica ruins, in one glimpse, you can take in the full 3,000-year sweep of this region's spiritual history: the Christian basilica ruins; the more recent Muslim **İsabey Mosque** complex at the foot of the hill; and the pagan temple ruins in the distance.

Those ruins—the **Temple of Artemis**—first put Ephesus on the tourist map. Today the site is marked by a lone rebuilt pillar, one of the 127 that once supported a huge structure, completed in Greek times (about 550 B.C.). The ancients considered the fabled temple one of the Seven Wonders of the World. Financed by the famously wealthy King Croesus, the marble temple rose five stories

high and was about three times as big as Athens' Parthenon—
making it the ancient Greeks' all-around largest building. A giant
statue of Artemis presided over an opulent interior adorned with
marble, paintings, gold, and silver—drawing pilgrims and tourists from throughout the ancient world. In 356 B.C., the temple
was burned by a man named Herostratus, who was desperate to
become famous at any cost (a motive still called "Herostratic fame"
today). The Ephesians rebuilt and enlarged it, then had to rebuild
it once more after the Goths trashed it. When the first Christian
missionaries (including St. John) came here in the first century
A.D., they met resistance from locals who were still worshipping
Artemis.

But soon Christians had the upper hand in Ephesus. In A.D.
401, the temple was destroyed for good by order of Christian
authorities intent on stamping out paganism. The structure lay buried for 17 centuries, until archaeologists came prospecting. Their
goal was not so much the city of Ephesus as it was this legendary
structure—the place where, for centuries, the faithful worshipped
the goddess Artemis.

APPENDIX

Contents

Tourist Information

Tourist Information Offices

In the US

Tourist offices in the US are a wealth of information. Before your trip, scan the websites of the countries you'll be visiting or contact them to briefly describe your trip and request information. They'll mail you a general interest brochure, and you can download many other brochures free of charge.

Spain: tel. 212/265-8822, www.spain.info
France: tel. 514/288-1904, www.franceguide.com
Italy: tel. 212/245-5618, www.italiantourism.com
Croatia: tel. 800-829-4416, http://us.croatia.hr
Greece: tel. 212/421-5777, www.visitgreece.gr
Turkey: tel. 212/687-2194, www.tourismturkey.org

In Europe

A good first stop in a new town can be the tourist information office (abbreviated **TI** in this book). TIs are good places to get a city map, advice on public transportation (including bus and train

European Calling Chart

Just smile and dial, using this key:
AC = Area Code, LN = Local Number.

European Country	Calling long distance within ...	Calling from the US or Canada to ...	Calling from a European country to ...
Austria	AC + LN	011 + 43 + AC (without the initial zero) + LN	00 + 43 + AC (without the initial zero) + LN
Belgium	LN	011 + 32 + LN (without initial zero)	00 + 32 + LN (without initial zero)
Bosnia-Herzegovina	AC + LN	011 + 387 + AC (without initial zero) + LN	00 + 387 + AC (without initial zero) + LN
Britain	AC + LN	011 + 44 + AC (without initial zero) + LN	00 + 44 + AC (without initial zero) + LN
Croatia	AC + LN	011 + 385 + AC (without initial zero) + LN	00 + 385 + AC (without initial zero) + LN
Czech Republic	LN	011 + 420 + LN	00 + 420 + LN
Denmark	LN	011 + 45 + LN	00 + 45 + LN
Estonia	LN	011 + 372 + LN	00 + 372 + LN
Finland	AC + LN	011 + 358 + AC (without initial zero) + LN	999 (or other 900 number) + 358 + AC (without initial zero) + LN
France	LN	011 + 33 + LN (without initial zero)	00 + 33 + LN (without initial zero)
Germany	AC + LN	011 + 49 + AC (without initial zero) + LN	00 + 49 + AC (without initial zero) + LN
Gibraltar	LN	011 + 350 + LN	00 + 350 + LN
Greece	LN	011 + 30 + LN	00 + 30 + LN
Hungary	06 + AC + LN	011 + 36 + AC + LN	00 + 36 + AC + LN
Ireland	AC + LN	011 + 353 + AC (without initial zero) + LN	00 + 353 + AC (without initial zero) + LN

European Country	Calling long distance within ...	Calling from the US or Canada to ...	Calling from a European country to ...
Italy	LN	011 + 39 + LN	00 + 39 + LN
Montenegro	AC + LN	011 + 382 + AC (without initial zero) + LN	00 + 382 + AC (without initial zero) + LN
Morocco	LN	011 + 212 + LN (without initial zero)	00 + 212 + LN (without initial zero)
Netherlands	AC + LN	011 + 31 + AC (without initial zero) + LN	00 + 31 + AC (without initial zero) + LN
Norway	LN	011 + 47 + LN	00 + 47 + LN
Poland	LN	011 + 48 + LN (without initial zero)	00 + 48 + LN (without initial zero)
Portugal	LN	011 + 351 + LN	00 + 351 + LN
Slovakia	AC + LN	011 + 421 + AC (without initial zero) + LN	00 + 421 + AC (without initial zero) + LN
Slovenia	AC + LN	011 + 386 + AC (without initial zero) + LN	00 + 386 + AC (without initial zero) + LN
Spain	LN	011 + 34 + LN	00 + 34 + LN
Sweden	AC + LN	011 + 46 + AC (without initial zero) + LN	00 + 46 + AC (without initial zero) + LN
Switzerland	LN	011 + 41 + LN (without initial zero)	00 + 41 + LN (without initial zero)
Turkey	AC (if there's no initial zero, add one) + LN	011 + 90 + AC (without initial zero) + LN	00 + 90 + AC (without initial zero) + LN

APPENDIX

- The instructions above apply whether you're calling a land line or mobile phone.
- The international access codes (the first numbers you dial when making an international call) are 011 if you're calling from the US or Canada, or 00 if you're calling from virtually anywhere in Europe (except Finland, where it's 999 or another 900 number, depending on the phone service you're using).
- To call the US or Canada from Europe, dial 00, then 1 (the country code for the US and Canada), then the area code and number. In short, 00 + 1 + AC + LN = Hi, Mom!

schedules), walking-tour schedules, and information on special events. Many TIs have information on the entire country or at least the region, so try to pick up maps for destinations you'll be visiting later in your trip.

Be wary of the travel agencies or special information services that masquerade as TIs but serve fancy hotels and tour companies. They're in the business of selling things you don't need.

Travel Advisories

For up-to-date information on health and security abroad, check these helpful resources before leaving on your cruise.

US Department of State: tel. 202/647-5225, www.travel.state .gov

Canadian Department of Foreign Affairs: Canadian tel. 800-267-6788, www.dfait-maeci.gc.ca

US Centers for Disease Control and Prevention: tel. 800-CDC-INFO (800-232-4636), www.cdc.gov/travel

Telephoning

Smart travelers use the telephone to get tourist information, reserve restaurants, confirm tour times, and phone home. For details on your options for making calls—both from a cruise ship and from mobile phones—see page 82. For more in-depth information, see www.ricksteves.com/phoning.

For useful phone numbers such as emergency services, embassies and consulates, and directory assistance, see the country-overview chapters earlier in this book.

How to Dial

Calling from the US to Europe, or vice versa, is simple—once you break the code. The European calling chart on the previous page will walk you through it.

No matter where you're calling from, to dial internationally you must first dial the international access code of the place you're calling from (to "get out" of the domestic phone system), and then the country code of the place you're trying to reach.

The US and Canada have the same international access code: 011. Virtually all of Europe, including Turkey, has its own shared international access code: 00. (You might see a + in front of a European number; that's a reminder to dial the access code of the place you're calling from.)

Each country has its own country code; you'll see those listed in the European calling chart. Specific dialing instructions for each country are also included in each country-overview chapter in this book.

Transportaton

While in port, you're likely to use public transportation to get around (and, in some cases, to get to) the cities you're here to see.

Taxis

Taxis are underrated, scenic time-savers that zip you effortlessly from the cruise terminal to any sight in town, or between sights. Especially for couples and small groups who value their time, a taxi ride can be a good investment. Unfortunately, many predatory taxi drivers prey on cruisers who are in town just for the day by charging them inflated fares for short rides. Prepare yourself by reading the "Taxi Tips" on page 114.

City Transit

Shrink and tame big cities by mastering their subway and bus systems. Europe's public-transit systems are so good that many Europeans go through life never learning to drive. With a map, anyone can decipher the code to cheap and easy urban transportation.

Subway Basics

Most of Europe's big cities are blessed with an excellent subway system, often linked effortlessly with suburban trains. Learning a city's network of underground trains is a key to efficient sightseeing. European subways go by many names, but "Metro" is the most common term.

   Plan your route. Figure out your route before you enter the station so you can march confidently to the correct train. Get a good subway map (often included on free city maps, or ask for one at the station) and consult it often. In the stations, maps are usually posted prominently. A typical subway map is a spaghetti-like tangle of intersecting, colorful lines. Some cities, like Rome, have just two lines, while Barcelona has eight. Individual lines are color-coded, numbered, and/or lettered; their end points are also indicated. These end points—while probably places you will never go to—are important, since they tell you which direction the train is moving in and appear (usually) as the name listed on the front of the train. Figure out the line you need, the end point of the direction you want to go, and (if necessary) where to transfer to another line.

   Validate your ticket. You may need to insert your ticket into a slot in the turnstile (then retrieve it) in order to validate it. If you have an all-day or multi-day ticket, you may only need to validate it the first time you use it, or not at all (ask when you buy it).

   Get off at the right place. Once on the train, follow along with each stop on your map (some people count stops). Sometimes the driver or an automated voice announces the upcoming stop—but don't count on this cue, as a foreign name spoken by a native speaker over a crackly loudspeaker can be difficult to understand. As you pull into each station, its name will be posted prominently on the platform or along the wall.

Transfer. Changing from one subway line to another can be as easy as walking a few steps away to an adjacent platform—or a bewildering wander via a labyrinth of stairs and long passageways. Fortunately, most subway systems are clearly signed—just follow along (or ask a local for help).

Exit the station. When you arrive at your destination station, follow exit signs up to the main ticketing area, where you'll usually find a posted map of the surrounding neighborhood to help you get your bearings. Individual exits are signposted by street name or nearby landmarks. Bigger stations have multiple exits. Choosing the right exit will help you avoid extra walking and crossing busy streets.

Bus Basics

Getting around town on the city bus system has some advantages over subways. Buses are often a better bet for shorter distances. Some buses go where the subway can't. Since you're not underground, it's easier to stay oriented and get the lay of the land. In fact, some public bus routes are downright scenic—Rome's cute *elettrico* minibus #116 winds you through the medieval core of the city for €1. The obvious disadvantage of buses is that they're affected by traffic, so avoid them during rush hour.

Plan your route. Tourist maps often indicate bus lines and stops. If yours doesn't, ask for a specific bus map at the TI. Many bus stops have timetables and route maps posted.

Validate your ticket. Tickets are checked on European buses in a variety of ways. Usually you enter at the front of the bus and show your ticket to the driver, or validate it by sticking it in an automated box. In some cases, you buy your ticket directly from the driver; other times, you'll buy your ticket at a kiosk or automated machine near the bus stop.

Trains

If you venture beyond your port city, European trains generally go where you need them to go and are fast, frequent, and affordable. "Point-to-point" or buy-as-you-go tickets can be your best bet for short travel distances anywhere. (If you're doing a substantial amount of pre- or post-cruise travel on your own, a railpass can be a good value.) You can buy train tickets either from home, or once you get to Europe. If your travel plans are set, and you don't want to risk a specific train journey selling out, it can be smart to get your tickets before your trip. For links to the websites for many European national rail companies, see www.railfaneurope .net; for additional details on buying tickets on European sites and complete railpass information, see www.ricksteves.com/rail. For train schedules, consult Germany's excellent all-Europe site: http: //bahn.hafas.de/bin/query.exe/en.

If you want to be more flexible, you can keep your options open by buying tickets in Europe. Nearly every station has old-fashioned ticket windows staffed by human beings, usually marked by long lines. Bridge any communication gap by writing out your plan: destination city, date (European-style: day/month/year), time (if you want to reserve a specific train), number of people, and first or second class.

To get tickets faster, savvy travelers figure out how to use automated ticket machines: Choose English, follow the step-by-step instructions, and swipe your credit card. Some machines accept cash. It's often possible to buy tickets on board the train, but expect to pay an additional fee for the convenience.

Seat reservations guarantee you a place to sit on the train, and can be optional or required depending on the route and train. Reservations are required for any train marked with an "R" in the schedule. Note that seat reservations are already included with many tickets, especially for the fastest trains (such as France's TGV, Eurostar Italia in Italy, or AVE in Spain). But for many trains (local, regional, interregional, and many EuroCity and InterCity trains), reservations are not necessary and not worth the trouble and expense unless you're traveling during a busy holiday period.

Be aware that many cities have more than one train station. Ask for help and pay attention. Making your way through stations and onto trains is largely a matter of asking questions, letting people help you, and assuming things are logical. I always ask someone on the platform if the train is going where I think it is (point to the train or track and ask, *"Roma?"*).

Buses

In most countries, trains are faster, more comfortable, and have more extensive schedules than buses. But in some countries—especially Greece, Turkey, and parts of Croatia and Spain—buses are often the better (or only) option. Use buses mainly to pick up where Europe's great train system leaves off.

Resources

Resources from Rick Steves

Rick Steves' Mediterranean Cruise Ports is one of many books in my series on European travel, which includes country guidebooks,

city guidebooks (including Rome, Venice, Florence, Istanbul, Athens, and more), Snapshot Guides (excerpted chapters from my country guides), Pocket Guides (full-color little books on big cities), and my budget-travel skills handbook, *Rick Steves' Europe Through the Back Door*. My phrase books—for Spanish, French, Italian, German, and Portuguese—are practical and budget-oriented. My other books include *Europe 101* (a crash course on art and history) and *Travel as a Political Act* (a travelogue sprinkled with tips for bringing home a global perspective).

Video: My public television series, *Rick Steves' Europe,* covers European destinations in 100 shows. To watch episodes, visit www.hulu.com/rick-steves-europe; for scripts and other details, see www.ricksteves.com/tv.

Audio: My weekly public radio show, *Travel with Rick Steves,* features interviews with travel experts from around the world. I've also produced free self-guided audio tours of the top sights

in many European cities, including Florence, Rome, Venice, and Athens. All of this audio content is available for free at Rick Steves Audio Europe, an extensive online library organized by destination. Choose whatever interests you, and download it to your iPod, smartphone, or computer at www.ricksteves .com or iTunes. Rick Steves Audio Europe is also available as a free app for your iPhone or Android.

Maps

The black-and-white maps in this book, designed by my well-traveled staff, are concise and simple. The maps are intended to help you locate recommended places and get to local TIs, where you can pick up more in-depth maps of cities and regions (usually free). Better maps are sold at newsstands and bookstores, though you likely won't need them for a brief port visit. Before you buy a map, look at it to be sure it has the level of detail you want.

Begin Your Trip at www.ricksteves.com

At our travel website, you'll find a wealth of free information on European destinations, including fresh monthly news and helpful tips from thousands of fellow travelers. You'll also find my latest guidebook updates (www.ricksteves.com/update) and my travel blog. You can even follow me on Facebook and Twitter.

Our **online Travel Store** offers travel bags and accessories specially designed by me to help you travel smarter and lighter. These include my popular carry-on bags (roll-aboard and rucksack versions), money belts, totes, toiletries kits, adapters, other accessories, and a wide selection of guidebooks, planning maps, and DVDs.

Rick Steves' Europe Through the Back Door travel company leads free-spirited, small-group **tours** to dozens of Europe's top destinations. Several of our shorter tours (such as Rome, Istanbul, Barcelona-Madrid, the Heart of Portugal, and Athens & the Heart of Greece) are great ways to extend your European adventure before or after a cruise. For all the details, and to get our Tour Catalog and a free Rick Steves Tour Experience DVD (filmed on location during an actual tour), visit www.ricksteves.com or call us at 425/608-4217.

Other Resources

For most travelers, this book has more than enough information. But if you're heading beyond my recommended destinations, $40 for extra maps and books can be money well-spent. There's a staggering array of websites, guidebooks, and other useful resources for people interested in cruising. Every avid cruiser has their favorite go-to site for tips and information, but my list below will help you get started with some of the best-regarded.

Books

For reviews of various cruise lines and ships, refer to my list on page 17. For more destination-specific information, the following books are worthwhile, though are not updated annually; check the publication date before you buy. The Rough Guide and Lonely Planet series, which individually cover various countries and cities included in this book, are both quite good. If choosing between these two titles, I'd buy the one that was published most recently. Lonely Planet's fat, far-ranging *Mediterranean Europe* overview book gives you little to go on for each destination, but their country- and city-specific guides are more thorough.

The colorful Eyewitness series, which focuses mainly on sights, is fun for their great graphics and photos, but relatively skimpy on content, and they weigh a ton. You can buy them in Europe (no more expensive than in the US) or simply borrow a book for a minute from other travelers at certain sights to make sure you're aware of that place's highlights. The tall, green Michelin guides to Italy and Rome include great maps and lots of solid, encyclopedic coverage of sights, customs, and culture (sold in English in some parts of Europe). The Cadogan guides offer a thoughtful look at the rich and confusing local culture, as does the Culture Shock series.

Beyond the guidebook format, look for the well-written history of the cruise industry, *Devils on the Deep Blue Sea* (by Kristoffer Garin). There's also a variety of tell-all type books offering behind-the-scenes intrigue from a life working on cruise ships. More titillating than well-written, these are good vacation reads to enjoy poolside. They include *Cruise Confidential* (by Brian David Bruns) and *The Truth about Cruise Ships* (by Jay Herring).

Holidays and Festivals

Europe celebrates many holidays, which close sights and bring crowds.

Note that the following list (for 2012) isn't complete. Your best source for general information is the TI in each town. Before your trip, you can check with the national tourist offices of the countries you'll be visiting, listed at the beginning of this chapter. It's worth a quick look at websites of your must-see sights to turn up possible holiday closures.

Jan 1	New Year's Day
Jan 6	Epiphany
April 6	Good Friday
April 8, 9	Easter Sunday, Monday
May 1	Labor Day
May 17	Ascension
May 27	Pentecost
May 28	Whitmonday
June 7	Corpus Christi
Aug 15	Assumption
Nov 1	All Saint's Day
Nov 11	Armistice Day/St. Martin's Day
Dec 25	Christmas Day
Dec 31	New Year's Eve

Conversions and Climate

Numbers and Stumblers

- Europeans write a few of their numbers differently than we do. 1 = 1, 4 = 4, 7 = 7.
- In Europe, dates appear as day/month/year, so Christmas is 25/12/12.
- Commas are decimal points and decimals commas. A dollar and a half is 1,50, and there are 5.280 feet in a mile.
- When pointing, use your whole hand, palm down.
- When counting with fingers, start with your thumb. If you hold up your first finger to request one item, you'll probably get two.
- What Americans call the second floor of a building is the first floor in Europe.
- On escalators and moving sidewalks, Europeans keep the left "lane" open for passing. Keep to the right.

Metric Conversions (approximate)

A kilogram is 2.2 pounds, and 1 liter is about a quart, or almost four to a gallon. A kilometer is six-tenths of a mile. I figure kilometers to miles by cutting them in half and adding back 10 percent of the original (120 km: 60 + 12 = 72 miles, 300 km: 150 + 30 = 180 miles).

1 foot = 0.3 meter	1 square yard = 0.8 square meter
1 yard = 0.9 meter	1 square mile = 2.6 square kilometers
1 mile = 1.6 kilometers	1 ounce = 28 grams
1 centimeter = 0.4 inch	1 quart = 0.95 liter
1 meter = 39.4 inches	1 kilogram = 2.2 pounds
1 kilometer = 0.62 mile	32°F = 0°C

Clothing Sizes

For US-to-European clothing size conversions, see page 126.

Climate

First line, average daily high temperature; second line, average daily low; third line, average days without rain. For more detailed weather statistics for European destinations (as well as the rest of the world), check www.worldclimate.com.

	J	F	M	A	M	J	J	A	S	O	N	D
SPAIN												
Barcelona												
	55°	57°	60°	65°	71°	78°	82°	82°	77°	69°	62°	56°
	43°	45°	48°	52°	57°	65°	69°	69°	66°	58°	51°	46°
	26	23	23	21	23	24	27	25	23	22	24	25
FRANCE												
Nice												
	50°	53°	59°	64°	71°	79°	84°	83°	77°	68°	58°	52°
	35°	36°	41°	46°	52°	58°	63°	63°	58°	51°	43°	37°
	23	22	24	23	23	26	29	26	24	23	21	21
ITALY												
Florence												
	40°	46°	56°	65°	74°	80°	84°	82°	75°	63°	51°	43°
	32°	35°	43°	49°	57°	63°	67°	66°	61°	52°	43°	35°
	25	21	24	22	23	21	25	24	25	23	20	24
Rome												
	52°	55°	59°	66°	74°	82°	87°	86°	79°	71°	61°	55°
	40°	42°	45°	50°	56°	63°	67°	67°	62°	55°	49°	44°
	13	19	23	24	26	26	30	29	25	23	19	21
Naples												
	54°	55°	60°	64°	72°	79°	85°	85°	80°	71°	62°	56°
	40°	41°	44°	48°	55°	62°	66°	66°	61°	55°	47°	42°
	20	19	22	18	25	27	29	28	23	23	17	20

APPENDIX

J	F	M	A	M	J	J	A	S	O	N	D

ITALY
Venice

42°	46°	53°	62°	70°	76°	81°	80°	75°	65°	53°	46°
33°	35°	41°	49°	56°	63°	66°	65°	61°	53°	44°	37°
25	21	24	21	23	22	24	24	25	24	21	23

CROATIA
Dubrovnik

53°	55°	58°	63°	70°	78°	83°	82°	77°	69°	62°	56°
42°	43°	57°	52°	58°	65°	69°	69°	64°	57°	51°	46°
13	13	11	10	10	6	4	3	7	11	16	15

GREECE
Athens

56°	57°	60°	66°	75°	83°	88°	88°	82°	73°	66°	59°
44°	45°	47°	53°	60°	68°	73°	72°	67°	59°	53°	48°
24	22	26	27	28	28	30	30	28	27	24	24

TURKEY
Istanbul

48°	49°	53°	63°	70°	79°	82°	82°	77°	68°	60°	52°
35°	36°	39°	45°	53°	60°	65°	66°	60°	53°	45°	39°
13	14	17	21	23	24	27	27	23	20	16	13

APPENDIX

Temperature Conversion:
Fahrenheit and Celsius

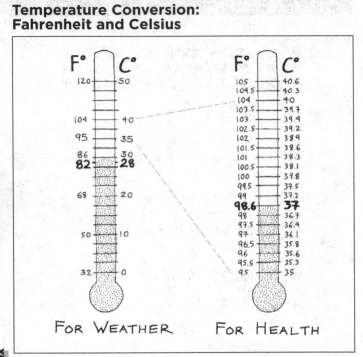

FOR WEATHER   FOR HEALTH

Europe takes its temperature using the Celsius scale, while we opt for Fahrenheit. For a rough conversion from Celsius to Fahrenheit, double the number and add 30. For weather, remember that 28°C is 82°F—perfect. For health, 37°C is just right.

Spanish Survival Phrases

Spanish has a guttural sound similar to the J in Baja California. In the phonetics, the symbol for this clearing-your-throat sound is the italicized *h*.

Good day.	Buenos días.	bway-nohs dee-ahs
Do you speak English?	¿Habla Usted inglés?	ah-blah oo-stehd een-glays
Yes. / No.	Sí. / No.	see / noh
I (don't) understand.	(No) comprendo.	(noh) kohm-prehn-doh
Please.	Por favor.	por fah-bor
Thank you.	Gracias.	grah-thee-ahs
I'm sorry.	Lo siento.	loh see-ehn-toh
Excuse me.	Perdóneme.	pehr-doh-nay-may
(No) problem.	(No) problema.	(noh) proh-blay-mah
Good.	Bueno.	bway-noh
Goodbye.	Adiós.	ah-dee-ohs
one / two	uno / dos	oo-noh / dohs
three / four	tres / cuatro	trays / kwah-troh
five / six	cinco / seis	theen-koh / says
seven / eight	siete / ocho	see-eh-tay / oh-choh
nine / ten	nueve / diez	nway-bay / dee-ayth
How much is it?	¿Cuánto cuesta?	kwahn-toh kway-stah
Write it?	¿Me lo escribe?	may loh ay-skree-bay
Is it free?	¿Es gratis?	ays grah-tees
Is it included?	¿Está incluido?	ay-stah een-kloo-ee-doh
Where can I buy / find...?	¿Dónde puedo comprar / encontrar...?	dohn-day pway-doh kohm-prar / ayn-kohn-trar
I'd like / We'd like...	Quiero / Queremos...	kee-ehr-oh / kehr-ay-mohs
...a room.	...una habitación.	oo-nah ah-bee-tah-thee-ohn
...a ticket to ___.	...un billete para ___.	oon bee-yeh-tay pah-rah
Is it possible?	¿Es posible?	ays poh-see-blay
Where is...?	¿Dónde está...?	dohn-day ay-stah
...the train station	...la estación de trenes	lah ay-stah-thee-ohn day tray-nays
...the bus station	...la estación de autobuses	lah ay-stah-thee-ohn day ow-toh-boo-says
...the tourist information office	...la oficina de turismo	lah oh-fee-thee-nah day too-rees-moh
Where are the toilets?	¿Dónde están los servicios?	dohn-day ay-stahn lohs sehr-bee-thee-ohs
men	hombres, caballeros	ohm-brays, kah-bah-yay-rohs
women	mujeres, damas	moo-heh-rays, dah-mahs
left / right	izquierda / derecha	eeth-kee-ehr-dah / day-ray-chah
straight	derecho	day-ray-choh
When do you open / close?	¿A qué hora abren / cierran?	ah kay oh-rah ah-brehn / thee-ay-rahn
At what time?	¿A qué hora?	ah kay oh-rah
Just a moment.	Un momento.	oon moh-mehn-toh
now / soon / later	ahora / pronto / más tarde	ah-oh-rah / prohn-toh / mahs tar-day
today / tomorrow	hoy / mañana	oy / mahn-yah-nah

In a Spanish Restaurant

I'd like / We'd like...	Quiero / Queremos...	kee-**ehr**-oh / kehr-**ay**-mohs
...to reserve...	...reservar...	ray-sehr-**bar**
...a table for one / two.	...una mesa para uno / dos.	oo-nah **may**-sah **pah**-rah **oo**-noh / dohs
Non-smoking.	No fumador.	noh foo-mah-**dohr**
Is this table free?	¿Está esta mesa libre?	ay-**stah** ay-stah **may**-sah **lee**-bray
The menu (in English), please.	La carta (en inglés), por favor.	lah **kar**-tah (ayn een-**glays**) por fah-**bor**
service (not) included	servicio (no) incluido	sehr-**bee**-thee-oh (noh) een-kloo-**ee**-doh
cover charge	precio de entrada	**pray**-thee-oh day ayn-**trah**-dah
to go	para llevar	**pah**-rah yay-**bar**
with / without	con / sin	kohn / seen
and / or	y / o	ee / oh
menu (of the day)	menú (del día)	may-**noo** (dayl **dee**-ah)
specialty of the house	especialidad de la casa	ay-spay-thee-ah-lee-**dahd** day lah **kah**-sah
tourist menu	menú turístico	meh-**noo** too-ree-stee-koh
combination plate	plato combinado	**plah**-toh kohm-bee-**nah**-doh
appetizers	tapas	**tah**-pahs
bread	pan	pahn
cheese	queso	**kay**-soh
sandwich	bocadillo	boh-kah-**dee**-yoh
soup	sopa	**soh**-pah
salad	ensalada	ayn-sah-**lah**-dah
meat	carne	**kar**-nay
poultry	aves	**ah**-bays
fish	pescado	pay-**skah**-doh
seafood	marisco	mah-**ree**-skoh
fruit	fruta	**froo**-tah
vegetables	verduras	behr-**doo**-rahs
dessert	postres	**poh**-strays
tap water	agua del grifo	**ah**-gwah dayl **gree**-foh
mineral water	agua mineral	**ah**-gwah mee-nay-**rahl**
milk	leche	**lay**-chay
(orange) juice	zumo (de naranja)	**thoo**-moh (day nah-**rahn**-hah)
coffee	café	kah-**feh**
tea	té	tay
wine	vino	**bee**-noh
red / white	tinto / blanco	**teen**-toh / **blahn**-koh
glass / bottle	vaso / botella	**bah**-soh / boh-**tay**-yah
beer	cerveza	thehr-**bay**-thah
Cheers!	¡Salud!	sah-**lood**
More. / Another.	Más. / Otro.	mahs / **oh**-troh
The same.	El mismo.	ehl **mees**-moh
The bill, please.	La cuenta, por favor.	lah **kwayn**-tah por fah-**bor**
tip	propina	proh-**pee**-nah
Delicious!	¡Delicioso!	day-lee-thee-**oh**-soh

For hundreds more pages of survival phrases for your trip to Spain, check out *Rick Steves' Spanish Phrase Book*.

French Survival Phrases

When using the phonetics, try to nasalize the n sound.

Good day.	**Bonjour.**	boh<u>n</u>-zhoor
Mrs. / Mr.	**Madame / Monsieur**	mah-dahm / muhs-yur
Do you speak English?	**Parlez-vous anglais?**	par-lay-voo ah<u>n</u>-glay
Yes. / No.	**Oui. / Non.**	wee / noh<u>n</u>
I understand.	**Je comprends.**	zhuh koh<u>n</u>-prah<u>n</u>
I don't understand.	**Je ne comprends pas.**	zhuh nuh koh<u>n</u>-prah<u>n</u> pah
Please.	**S'il vous plaît.**	see voo play
Thank you.	**Merci.**	mehr-see
I'm sorry.	**Désolé.**	day-zoh-lay
Excuse me.	**Pardon.**	par-doh<u>n</u>
(No) problem.	**(Pas de) problème.**	(pah duh) proh-blehm
It's good.	**C'est bon.**	say boh<u>n</u>
Goodbye.	**Au revoir.**	oh vwahr
one / two	**un / deux**	uh<u>n</u> / duh
three / four	**trois / quatre**	twah / kah-truh
five / six	**cinq / six**	sa<u>n</u>k / sees
seven / eight	**sept / huit**	seht / weet
nine / ten	**neuf / dix**	nuhf / dees
How much is it?	**Combien?**	koh<u>n</u>-bee-a<u>n</u>
Write it?	**Ecrivez?**	ay-kree-vay
Is it free?	**C'est gratuit?**	say grah-twee
Included?	**Inclus?**	a<u>n</u>-klew
Where can I buy / find...?	**Où puis-je acheter / trouver...?**	oo pwee-zhuh ah-shuh-tay / troo-vay
I'd like / We'd like...	**Je voudrais / Nous voudrions...**	zhuh voo-dray / noo voo-dree-oh<u>n</u>
...a room.	**...une chambre.**	ewn shah<u>n</u>-bruh
...a ticket to ___.	**...un billet pour ___.**	uh<u>n</u> bee-yay poor
Is it possible?	**C'est possible?**	say poh-see-bluh
Where is...?	**Où est...?**	oo ay
...the train station	**...la gare**	lah gar
...the bus station	**...la gare routière**	lah gar root-yehr
...tourist information	**...l'office du tourisme**	loh-fees dew too-reez-muh
Where are the toilets?	**Où sont les toilettes?**	oo soh<u>n</u> lay twah-leht
men	**hommes**	ohm
women	**dames**	dahm
left / right	**à gauche / à droite**	ah gohsh / ah dwaht
straight	**tout droit**	too dwah
When does this open / close?	**Ça ouvre / ferme à quelle heure?**	sah oo-vruh / fehrm ah kehl ur
At what time?	**À quelle heure?**	ah kehl ur
Just a moment.	**Un moment.**	uh<u>n</u> moh-mah<u>n</u>
now / soon / later	**maintenant / bientôt / plus tard**	ma<u>n</u>-tuh-nah<u>n</u> / bee-a<u>n</u>-toh / plew tar
today / tomorrow	**aujourd'hui / demain**	oh-zhoor-dwee / duh-ma<u>n</u>

APPENDIX

In a French Restaurant

I'd like / We'd like...	**Je voudrais / Nous voudrions...**	zhuh voo-dray / noo voo-dree-ohn
...to reserve...	**...réserver...**	ray-zehr-vay
...a table for one / two.	**...une table pour un / deux.**	ewn tah-bluh poor uhn / duh
Non-smoking.	**Non fumeur.**	nohn few-mur
Is this seat free?	**C'est libre?**	say lee-bruh
The menu (in English), please.	**La carte (en anglais), s'il vous plaît.**	lah kart (ahn ahn-glay) see voo play
service (not) included	**service (non) compris**	sehr-vees (nohn) kohn-pree
to go	**à emporter**	ah ahn-por-tay
with / without	**avec / sans**	ah-vehk / sahn
and / or	**et / ou**	ay / oo
special of the day	**plat du jour**	plah dew zhoor
specialty of the house	**spécialité de la maison**	spay-see-ah-lee-tay duh lah may-zohn
appetizers	**hors-d'oeuvre**	or-duh-vruh
first course (soup, salad)	**entrée**	ahn-tray
main course (meat, fish)	**plat principal**	plah pran-see-pahl
bread	**pain**	pan
cheese	**fromage**	froh-mahzh
sandwich	**sandwich**	sahnd-weech
soup	**soupe**	soop
salad	**salade**	sah-lahd
meat	**viande**	vee-ahnd
chicken	**poulet**	poo-lay
fish	**poisson**	pwah-sohn
seafood	**fruits de mer**	frwee duh mehr
fruit	**fruit**	frwee
vegetables	**légumes**	lay-gewm
dessert	**dessert**	duh-sehr
mineral water	**eau minérale**	oh mee-nay-rahl
tap water	**l'eau du robinet**	loh dew roh-bee-nay
milk	**lait**	lay
(orange) juice	**jus (d'orange)**	zhew (doh-rahnzh)
coffee	**café**	kah-fay
tea	**thé**	tay
wine	**vin**	van
red / white	**rouge / blanc**	roozh / blahn
glass / bottle	**verre / bouteille**	vehr / boo-teh-ee
beer	**bière**	bee-ehr
Cheers!	**Santé!**	sahn-tay
More. / Another.	**Plus. / Un autre.**	plew / uhn oh-truh
The same.	**La même chose.**	lah mehm shohz
The bill, please.	**L'addition, s'il vous plaît.**	lah-dee-see-ohn see voo play
tip	**pourboire**	poor-bwar
Delicious!	**Délicieux!**	day-lee-see-uh

For more user-friendly French phrases, check out *Rick Steves' French Phrase Book and Dictionary* or *Rick Steves' French, Italian & German Phrase Book*.

Italian Survival Phrases

Good day.	**Buon giorno.**	bwohn JOR-noh
Do you speak English?	**Parla inglese?**	PAR-lah een-GLAY-zay
Yes. / No.	**Sì. / No.**	see / noh
I (don't) understand.	**(Non) capisco.**	(nohn) kah-PEES-koh
Please.	**Per favore.**	pehr fah-VOH-ray
Thank you.	**Grazie.**	GRAHT-seeay
You're welcome.	**Prego.**	PRAY-go
I'm sorry.	**Mi dispiace.**	mee dee-speeAH-chay
Excuse me.	**Mi scusi.**	mee SKOO-zee
(No) problem.	**(Non) c'è un problema.**	(nohn) cheh oon proh-BLAY-mah
Good.	**Va bene.**	vah BEHN-ay
Goodbye.	**Arrivederci.**	ah-ree-vay-DEHR-chee
one / two	**uno / due**	OO-noh / DOO-ay
three / four	**tre / quattro**	tray / KWAH-troh
five / six	**cinque / sei**	CHEENG-kway / SEHee
seven / eight	**sette / otto**	SEHT-tay / OT-toh
nine / ten	**nove / dieci**	NOV-ay / deeAY-chee
How much is it?	**Quanto costa?**	KWAHN-toh KOS-tah
Write it?	**Me lo scrive?**	may loh SKREE-vay
Is it free?	**È gratis?**	eh GRAH-tees
Is it included?	**È incluso?**	eh een-KLOO-zoh
Where can I buy / find...?	**Dove posso comprare / trovare...?**	DOH-vay POS-soh kohm-PRAH-ray / troh-VAH-ray
I'd like / We'd like...	**Vorrei / Vorremmo...**	vor-REHee / vor-RAY-moh
...a room.	**...una camera.**	OO-nah KAH-meh-rah
...a ticket to ___.	**...un biglietto per ___.**	oon beel-YEHT-toh pehr
Is it possible?	**È possibile?**	eh poh-SEE-bee-lay
Where is...?	**Dov'è...?**	DOH-veh
...the train station	**...la stazione**	lah staht-seeOH-nay
...the bus station	**...la stazione degli autobus**	lah staht-seeOH-nay DAYL-yee OW-toh-boos
...tourist information	**...informazioni per turisti**	een-for-maht-seeOH-nee pehr too-REE-stee
...the toilet	**...la toilette**	lah twah-LEHT-tay
men	**uomini, signori**	WOH-mee-nee, seen-YOH-ree
women	**donne, signore**	DON-nay, seen-YOH-ray
left / right	**sinistra / destra**	see-NEE-strah / DEHS-trah
straight	**sempre diritto**	SEHM-pray dee-REE-toh
When do you open / close?	**A che ora aprite / chiudete?**	ah kay OH-rah ah-PREE-tay / keeoo-DAY-tay
At what time?	**A che ora?**	ah kay OH-rah
Just a moment.	**Un momento.**	oon moh-MAYN-toh
now / soon / later	**adesso / presto / tardi**	ah-DEHS-soh / PREHS-toh / TAR-dee
today / tomorrow	**oggi / domani**	OH-jee / doh-MAH-nee

In an Italian Restaurant

I'd like...	Vorrei...	vor-REHee
We'd like...	Vorremmo...	vor-RAY-moh
...to reserve...	...prenotare...	pray-noh-TAH-ray
...a table for one / two.	...un tavolo per uno / due.	oon TAH-voh-loh pehr OO-noh / DOO-ay
Non-smoking.	Non fumare.	nohn foo-MAH-ray
Is this seat free?	È libero questo posto?	eh LEE-bay-roh KWEHS-toh POH-stoh
The menu (in English), please.	Il menù (in inglese), per favore.	eel may-NOO (een een-GLAY-zay) pehr fah-VOH-ray
service (not) included	servizio (non) incluso	sehr-VEET-seeoh (nohn) een-KLOO-zoh
cover charge	pane e coperto	PAH-nay ay koh-PEHR-toh
to go	da portar via	dah POR-tar VEE-ah
with / without	con / senza	kohn / SEHN-sah
and / or	e / o	ay / oh
menu (of the day)	menù (del giorno)	may-NOO (dayl JOR-noh)
specialty of the house	specialità della casa	spay-chah-lee-TAH DEHL-lah KAH-zah
first course (pasta, soup)	primo piatto	PREE-moh peeAH-toh
main course (meat, fish)	secondo piatto	say-KOHN-doh peeAH-toh
side dishes	contorni	kohn-TOR-nee
bread	pane	PAH-nay
cheese	formaggio	for-MAH-joh
sandwich	panino	pah-NEE-noh
soup	minestra, zuppa	mee-NEHS-trah, TSOO-pah
salad	insalata	een-sah-LAH-tah
meat	carne	KAR-nay
chicken	pollo	POH-loh
fish	pesce	PEH-shay
seafood	frutti di mare	FROO-tee dee MAH-ray
fruit / vegetables	frutta / legumi	FROO-tah / lay-GOO-mee
dessert	dolci	DOHL-chee
tap water	acqua del rubinetto	AH-kwah dayl roo-bee-NAY-toh
mineral water	acqua minerale	AH-kwah mee-nay-RAH-lay
milk	latte	LAH-tay
(orange) juice	succo (d'arancia)	SOO-koh (dah-RAHN-chah)
coffee / tea	caffè / tè	kah-FEH / teh
wine	vino	VEE-noh
red / white	rosso / bianco	ROH-soh / beeAHN-koh
glass / bottle	bicchiere / bottiglia	bee-keeAY-ray / boh-TEEL-yah
beer	birra	BEE-rah
Cheers!	Cin cin!	cheen cheen
More. / Another.	Ancora un po.' / Un altro.	ahn-KOH-rah oon poh / oon AHL-troh
The same.	Lo stesso.	loh STEHS-soh
The bill, please.	Il conto, per favore.	eel KOHN-toh pehr fah-VOH-ray
tip	mancia	MAHN-chah
Delicious!	Delizioso!	day-leet-seeOH-zoh

For more user-friendly Italian phrases, check out *Rick Steves' Italian Phrase Book & Dictionary* or *Rick Steves' French, Italian, and German Phrase Book*.

Croatian Survival Phrases

When using the phonetics, pronounce ī / Ī as the long I sound in "light."

English	Croatian	Phonetics
Hello. (formal)	**Dobar dan.**	DOH-bahr dahn
Hi. / Bye. (informal)	**Bog.**	bohg
Do you speak English?	**Govorite li engleski?**	GOH-voh-ree-teh lee EHN-glehs-kee
Yes. / No.	**Da. / Ne.**	dah / neh
I (don't) understand.	**(Ne) razumijem.**	(neh) rah-ZOO-mee-yehm
Please. / You're welcome.	**Molim.**	MOH-leem
Thank you (very much).	**Hvala (ljepa).**	HVAH-lah (LYEH-pah)
Excuse me. / I'm sorry.	**Oprostite.**	oh-PROH-stee-teh
problem	**problem**	proh-BLEHM
No problem.	**Nema problema.**	NEH-mah proh-BLEH-mah
Good.	**Dobro.**	DOH-broh
Goodbye.	**Do viđenja.**	doh veed-JAY-neeah
one / two	**jedan / dva**	YEH-dahn / dvah
three / four	**tri / četiri**	tree / CHEH-teh-ree
five / six	**pet / šest**	peht / shehst
seven / eight	**sedam / osam**	SEH-dahm / OH-sahm
nine / ten	**devet / deset**	DEH-veht / DEH-seht
hundred / thousand	**sto / tisuća**	stoh / TEE-soo-chah
How much?	**Koliko?**	KOH-lee-koh
local currency	**kuna**	KOO-nah
Write it?	**Napišite?**	nah-PEESH-ee-teh
Is it free?	**Da li je besplatno?**	dah lee yeh BEH-splaht-noh
Is it included?	**Da li je uključeno?**	dah lee yeh OOK-lyoo-cheh-noh
Where can I find / buy...?	**Gdje mogu pronaći / kupiti...?**	guh-DYEH MOH-goo PROH-nah-chee / KOO-pee-tee
I'd like / We'd like...	**Želio bih / Željeli bismo...**	ZHEH-lee-oh beeh / ZHEH-lyeh-lee BEES-moh
...a room.	**...sobu.**	SOH-boo
...a ticket to ___.	**...kartu do ___.**	KAR-too doh
Is it possible?	**Da li je moguće?**	dah lee yeh MOH-goo-cheh
Where is...?	**Gdje je...?**	guh-DYEH yeh
...the train station	**...željeznička stanica**	ZHEH-lyehz-neech-kah STAH-neet-sah
...the bus station	**...autobusna stanica**	OW-toh-boos-nah STAH-neet-sah
...the tourist information office	**...turističko informativni centar**	TOO-ree-steech-koh EEN-for-mah-teev-nee TSEHN-tahr
...the toilet	**...vece (WC)**	VEHT-SEH
men	**muški**	MOOSH-kee
women	**ženski**	ZHEHN-skee
left / right	**lijevo / desno**	LEE-yeh-voh / DEHS-noh
straight	**ravno**	RAHV-noh
At what time...	**U koliko sati...**	oo KOH-lee-koh SAH-tee
...does this open / close?	**...otvara / zatvara?**	OHT-vah-rah / ZAHT-vah-rah
(Just) a moment.	**(Samo) trenutak.**	(SAH-moh) treh-NOO-tahk
now / soon / later	**sada / uskoro / kasnije**	SAH-dah / OOS-koh-roh / KAHS-nee-yeh
today / tomorrow	**danas / sutra**	DAH-nahs / SOO-trah

In a Croatian Restaurant

I'd like to reserve...	**Rezervirao bih...**	reh-zehr-VEER-ow beeh
We'd like to reserve...	**Rezervirali bismo...**	reh-zehr-VEE-rah-lee BEES-moh
...a table for one / two.	**...stol za jednog / dva.**	stohl zah YEHD-nog / dvah
Non-smoking.	**Za nepušače.**	zah NEH-poo-shah-cheh
Is this table free?	**Da li je ovaj stol slobodan?**	dah lee yeh OH-vī stohl SLOH-boh-dahn
Can I help you?	**Izvolite?**	EEZ-voh-lee-teh
The menu (in English), please.	**Jelovnik (na engleskom), molim.**	yeh-LOHV-neek (nah EHN-glehs-kohm) MOH-leem
service (not) included	**posluga (nije) uključena**	POH-sloo-gah (NEE-yeh) OOK-lyoo-cheh-nah
cover charge	**couvert**	KOO-vehr
"to go"	**za ponjeti**	zah POHN-yeh-tee
with / without	**sa / bez**	sah / behz
and / or	**i / ili**	ee / EE-lee
fixed-price meal (of the day)	**(dnevni) meni**	(duh-NEHV-nee) MEH-nee
specialty of the house	**specijalitet kuće**	speht-see-yah-LEE-teht KOO-cheh
half portion	**pola porcije**	POH-lah PORT-see-yeh
daily special	**jelo dana**	YEH-loh DAH-nah
fixed-price meal for tourists	**turistički meni**	TOO-ree-steech-kee MEH-nee
appetizers	**predjela**	PREHD-yeh-lah
bread	**kruh**	krooh
cheese	**sir**	seer
sandwich	**sendvič**	SEND-veech
soup	**juha**	YOO-hah
salad	**salata**	sah-LAH-tah
meat	**meso**	MAY-soh
poultry	**perad**	PEH-rahd
fish	**riba**	REE-bah
seafood	**morska hrana**	MOHR-skah HRAH-nah
fruit	**voće**	VOH-cheh
vegetables	**povrće**	POH-vur-cheh
dessert	**desert**	deh-SAYRT
(tap) water	**voda (od slavine)**	VOH-dah (ohd SLAH-vee-neh)
mineral water	**mineralna voda**	MEE-neh-rahl-nah VOH-dah
milk	**mlijeko**	mlee-YEH-koh
(orange) juice	**sok (od naranče)**	sohk (ohd NAH-rahn-cheh)
coffee	**kava**	KAH-vah
tea	**čaj**	chī
wine	**vino**	VEE-noh
red / white	**crno / bijelo**	TSEHR-noh / bee-YEH-loh
sweet / dry / semi-dry	**slatko / suho / polusuho**	SLAHT-koh / SOO-hoh / POH-loo-soo-hoh
glass / bottle	**čaša / boca**	CHAH-shah / BOHT-sah
beer	**pivo**	PEE-voh
Cheers!	**Živjeli!**	ZHEE-vyeh-lee
More. / Another.	**Još. / Još jedno.**	yohsh / yohsh YEHD-noh
The same.	**Isto.**	EES-toh
Bill, please.	**Račun, molim.**	RAH-choon MOH-leem
tip	**napojnica**	NAH-poy-neet-sah
Delicious!	**Izvrsno!**	EEZ-vur-snoh

Greek Survival Phrases

Knowing a few phrases of Greek can help if you're traveling off the beaten path. Just learning the pleasantries (such as please and thank you) will improve your connections with locals, even in the bigger cities.

Because Greek words can be transliterated differently in English, I've also included the Greek spellings. Note that in Greek, a semicolon is used the same way we use a question mark.

Hello. (formal)	**Gia sas.** Γειά σας.	yah sahs
Hi. / Bye. (informal)	**Gia.** Γειά.	yah
Good morning.	**Kali mera.** Καλή μέρα.	kah-**lee meh**-rah
Good afternoon.	**Kali spera.** Καλή σπέρα.	kah-**lee speh**-rah
Do you speak English?	**Milate anglika?** Μιλάτε αγγλικά;	mee-**lah**-teh ahn-glee-**kah**
Yes. / No.	**Ne. / Ohi.** Ναι. / Όχι.	neh / **oh**-hee
I understand.	**Katalaveno.** Καταλαβαίνω.	kah-tah-lah-**veh**-noh
I don't understand.	**Den katalaveno.** Δεν καταλαβαίνω.	dehn kah-tah-lah-**veh**-noh
Please. (Also: You're welcome.)	**Parakalo.** Παρακαλώ.	pah-rah-kah-**loh**
Thank you (very much).	**Efharisto (poli).** Ευχαριστώ (πολύ).	ehf-hah-ree-**stoh** (poh-**lee**)
Excuse me. (Also: I'm sorry.)	**Sygnomi.** Συγνώμη.	seeg-**noh**-mee
(No) problem.	**(Kanena) problima.** (Κανένα) πρόβλημα.	(kah-**neh**-nah) **prohv**-lee-mah
Good.	**Orea.** Ωραία.	oh-**reh**-ah
Goodbye.	**Antio.** Αντίο.	ahd-**yoh** (think "adieu")
Good night.	**Kali nikta.** Καλή νύχτα.	kah-**lee neek**-tah
one / two	**ena / dio** ένα / δύο	**eh**-nah / **dee**-oh
three / four	**tria / tessera** τρία /τέσσερα	**tree**-ah / **teh**-seh-rah
five / six	**pente / exi** πέντε / έξι	**peh**-deh / **ehk**-see
seven / eight	**efta / ohto** εφτά / οχτώ	ehf-**tah** / oh-**toh**
nine / ten	**ennia / deka** εννιά / δέκα	ehn-**yah** / **deh**-kah
hundred / thousand	**ekato / hilia** εκατό / χίλια	eh-kah-**toh** / **heel**-yah
How much?	**Poso kani?** Πόσο κάνει;	**poh**-soh **kah**-nee
euro	**evro** ευρώ	ev-**roh**
Write it?	**Grapsete to?** Γράπσετε το;	**grahp**-seh-teh toh

Is it free?	Ine dorean? Είναι δωρεάν;	ee-neh doh-ree-**ahn**
Is it included?	Perilamvanete? Περιλαμβάνεται;	peh-ree-lahm-**vah**-neh-teh
Where can I find / buy...?	Pou boro na vro / agoraso...? Που μπορώ να βρω / αγοράσω...;	poo boh-**roh** nah vroh / ah-goh-**rah**-soh
I'd like / We'd like...	Tha ithela / Tha thelame... Θα ήθελα / Θα θέλαμε...	thah **ee**-theh-lah / thah **theh**-lah-meh
...a room.	...ena dhomatio. ...ένα δωμάτιο.	eh-nah doh-**mah**-tee-oh
...a ticket to ___.	...ena isitirio gia ___. ...ένα εισιτήριο για ___.	eh-nah ee-see-**tee**-ree-oh yah ___
Is it possible?	Ginete? Γίνεται;	yee-neh-teh
Where is...?	Pou ine...? Που είναι...;	poo ee-neh
...the bus station	...o stathmos ton leoforion ...ο σταθμός των λεωφορίων	oh **stahth**-mohs tohn leh-oh-foh-**ree**-ohn
...the train station	...o stathmos tou trenou ...ο σταθμός του τρένου	oh **stahth**-mohs too **treh**-noo
...the tourist information office	...to grafeio enimerosis touriston ...το γραφείο ενημέρωσης τουριστών	too grah-**fee**-oh eh-nee-**meh**-roh-sis too-ree-**stohn**
...the toilet	...toualeta ...τουαλέτα	twah-**leh**-tah
men	andres άντρες	**ahn**-drehs
women	gynekes γυναικες	yee-**neh**-kehs
left / right	dexia / aristera δεξιά / αριστερά	dehk-see-**ah** / ah-ree-steh-**rah**
straight	efthia ευθεία	ehf-**thee**-ah
At what time...	Ti ora... Τι ώρα...	tee **oh**-rah
...does this open / close?	...anigete / klinete? ...ανοίγετε / κλείνετε;	ah-**nee**-yeh-teh / **klee**-neh-teh
Just a moment.	Ena lepto. Ένα λεπτό.	eh-nah lep-**toh**
now / soon / later	tora / se ligo / argotera τώρα / σε λίγο / αργότερα	toh-rah / seh **lee**-goh / ar-**goh**-teh-rah
today / tomorrow	simera / avrio σήμερα / αύριο	see-meh-rah / **ahv**-ree-oh

In a Greek Restaurant

I'd like to reserve...	**Tha ithela na kliso...** Θα ήθελα να κλείσω...	thah **ee**-theh-lah nah **klee**-soh
We'd like to reserve...	**Tha thelame na klisoume...** Θα θέλαμε να κλείσουμε...	thah **theh**-lah-meh nah **klee**-soo-meh
...a table for one / two.	**...ena trapezi gia enan / dio.** ...ένα τραπέζι για έναν / δύο.	eh-nah trah-**peh**-zee yah eh-nahn / **dee**-oh
non-smoking	**mi kapnizon** μη καπνίζων	mee kahp-**nee**-zohn
Is this table free?	**Ine eleftero afto to trapezi?** Είναι ελέυθερο αυτό το τραπέζι;	ee-neh eh-**lef**-teh-roh ahf-**toh** toh trah-**peh**-zee
The menu (in English), please.	**Ton katalogo (sta anglika) parakalo.** Τον κατάλογο (στα αγγλικά) παρακαλώ.	tohn kah-**tah**-loh-goh (stah ahn-glee-**kah**) pah-rah-kah-**loh**
service (not) included	**to servis (den) perilamvanete** το σέρβις (δεν) περιλαμβάνεται	toh **sehr**-vees (dehn) peh-ree-lahm-**vah**-neh-teh
cover charge	**kouver** κουβέρ	koo-**vehr**
"to go"	**gia exo** για έξω	yah **ehk**-soh
with / without	**me / horis** με / χωρίς	meh / hoh-**rees**
and / or	**ke / i** και / ή	keh / ee
fixed-price meal	**menu** μενού	meh-**noo**
specialty of the house	**i specialite tou magaziou** η σπεσιαλιτέ του μαγαζιού	ee speh-see-ah-lee-**teh** too mah-gah-zee-**oo**
half-portion	**misi merida** μισή μερίδα	mee-**see** meh-**ree**-dah
daily special	**to piato tis meras** το πιάτο της μέρας	toh pee-**ah**-toh tees meh-rahs
appetizers	**proto piato** πρώτο πιάτο	**proh**-toh pee-**ah**-toh
bread	**psomi** ψωμί	psoh-**mee**
cheese	**tiri** τυρί	tee-**ree**
sandwich	**sandwich** or **toast** σάντουιτς, τόστ	"sandwich," "toast"
soup	**soupa** σούπα	**soo**-pah
salad	**salata** σαλάτα	sah-**lah**-tah
meat	**kreas** κρέας	**kray**-ahs

poultry / chicken	poulerika / kotopoulo	poo-leh-ree-**kah** / koh-**toh**-poo-loh
	πουλερικα / κοτόπουλο	
fish /seafood	psari / psarika	psah-ree / psah-ree-**kah**
	ψάρι / ψαρικά	
shellfish	thalassina	thah-lah-see-**nah**
	θαλασσινά	
fruit	frouta	froo-tah
	φρούτα	
vegetables	lahanika	lah-hah-nee-**kah**
	λαχανικά	
dessert	gliko	lee-**koh**
	γλυκό	
(tap) water	nero (tis vrisis)	neh-**roh** (tees **vree**-sees)
	νερο (της βρύσης)	
mineral water	metalliko nero	meh-tah-lee-**koh** neh-**roh**
	μεταλλικό νερό	
milk	gala	**gah**-lah
	γάλα	
(orange) juice	himos (portokali)	hee-**mohs** (por-toh-**kah**-lee)
	χυμός (πορτοκάλι)	
coffee	kafes	kah-**fehs**
	καφές	
tea	tsai	**chah**-ee
	τσάι	
wine (spoken)	krasi	krah-**see**
	κρασί	
wine (printed on label)	inos	**ee**-nohs
	οίνος	
red / white	kokkino / aspro	**koh**-kee-noh / **ah**-sproh
	κόκκινο / άσπρο	
sweet / dry / semi-dry	gliko / ksiro / imixiro	lee-**koh** / ksee-**roh** / ee-**meek**-see-roh
	γλυκό / ξηρό / ημίξηρο	
glass / bottle	potiri / boukali	poh-**tee**-ree / boo-**kah**-lee
	ποτήρι /μπουκάλι	
beer	bira	**bee**-rah
	μπύρα	
Here you are. (when given food)	Oriste.	oh-**ree**-steh
	Ορίστε.	
Enjoy your meal!	Kali orexi!	kah-**lee oh**-rehk-see
	Καλή όρεξη!	
(To your) health! (like "Cheers!")	(Stin i) gia mas!	(stee nee) yah mahs
	(Στην υ) γειά μας!	
Another.	Allo ena.	**ah**-loh **eh**-nah
	Άλλο ένα.	
Bill, please.	Ton logariasmo parakalo.	tohn loh-gah-ree-ahs-**moh** pah-rah-kah-**loh**
	Τον λογαριασμό παρακαλώ.	
tip	bourbouar	boor-boo-**ar**
	μπουρμπουάρ	
Very good!	Poli oreo!	poh-**lee** oh-**ray**-oh
	Πολύ ωραίο!	
Delicious!	Poli nostimo!	poh-**lee nohs**-tee-moh
	Πολύ νόστιμο!	

Turkish Survival Phrases

When using the phonetics, pronounce "ī" as the long "i" sound in "light"; "ew" as "oo" (with your lips pursed); and "g" as the hard "g" in "go."

Hello.	**Merhaba.**	mehr-hah-bah
Good day.	**İyi günler.**	ee-yee gewn-lehr
Good morning.	**Günaydın.**	gew-nī-duhn
Good evening.	**İyi akşamlar.**	ee-yee ahk-shahm-lahr
How are you? *	**Nasılsınız?**	nah-suhl-suh-nuhz
Do you speak English?	**İngilizce biliyormusunuz?**	een-gee-leez-jeh bee-lee-yohr-moo-soo-nooz
Yes. / No.	**Evet. / Hayır.**	eh-veht / hah-yur
I understand.	**Anlıyorum.**	ahn-luh-yoh-room
I don't understand.	**Anlamıyorum.**	ahn-lah-muh-yoh-room
Please.	**Lütfen.**	lewt-fehn
Thank you (very much).	**Teşekkür (ederim).**	teh-shehk-kewr (eh-deh-reem)
I'm sorry.	**Üzgünüm.**	ewz-gew-newm
Excuse me. (to pass)	**Afedersiniz. / Pardon.**	ah-feh-dehr-see-neez / pahr-dohn
No problem.	**Sorun yok.**	soh-roon yohk
There is a problem.	**Sorun var.**	soh-roon vahr
Good.	**İyi.**	ee-yee
Goodbye. (said by person leaving)	**Hoşçakal.**	hohsh-chah-kahl
Goodbye. (said by person staying)	**Güle güle.**	gew-leh gew-leh
one / two	**bir / iki**	beer / ee-kee
three / four	**üç / dört**	ewch / dirt
five / six	**beş / altı**	behsh / ahl-tuh
seven / eight	**yedi / sekiz**	yeh-dee / seh-keez
nine / ten	**dokuz / on**	doh-kooz / ohn
How much is it?	**Ne kadar?**	neh kah-dahr
Write it?	**Yazarmısınız?**	yah-zahr-muh-suh-nuhz
Is it free?	**Ücretsizmi?**	ewj-reht-seez-mee
Is it included?	**Dahilmi?**	dah-heel-mee
Where can I find...?	**Nerede bulurum...?**	neh-reh-deh boo-loo-room
Where can I buy...?	**Nereden alabilirim...?**	neh-reh-dehn ah-lah-bee-lee-reem
I'd like / We'd like...	**İstiyorum / İstiyoruz...**	ees-tee-yoh-room / ees-tee-yoh-rooz
...a room.	**...oda.**	oh-dah
...a ticket to ___.	**...___'ya bilet.**	___ yah bee-leht
Is it possible?	**Olasımı?**	oh-lah-suh-muh
Where is...?	**...nerede?**	neh-reh-deh
...the train station	**Tren istasyonu...**	trehn ees-tahs-yoh-noo
...the bus station	**Otobüs durağı...**	oh-toh-bews doo-rah-uh
...the tourist information office	**Turizm enformasyon bürosu...**	too-reezm ehn-fohr-mahs-yohn bew-roh-soo
...the toilet	**Tuvalet...**	too-vah-leht
men / women	**bay / bayan**	bī / bah-yahn
left / right	**sol / sağ**	sohl / saah
straight	**doğru**	doh-roo
What time does this open / close?	**Ne zaman açılıyor / kapanıyor?**	neh zah-mahn ah-chuh-luh-yohr / kah-pah-nuh-yohr
At what time?	**Ne zaman?**	neh zah-mahn
Just a moment.	**Bir saniye.**	beer sah-nee-yeh
now / soon / later	**şimdi / birazdan / sonra**	sheem-dee / bee-rahz-dahn / sohn-rah
today / tomorrow	**bugün / yarın**	boo-gewn / yah-ruhn

* People will answer you by saying, "Teşekkür ederim" (Thank you very much).

In a Turkish Restaurant

English	Turkish	Pronunciation
restaurant	lokanta / restaurant	loh-kahn-tah / rehs-toh-rahnt
I'd like / We'd like to make a reservation.	Rezervasyon yapmak istiyorum / istiyoruz.	reh-zehr-vahs-yohn yahp-mahk ee-stee-yoh-room / ees-tee-yoh-rooz
One / Two persons.	Bir / İki kişilik.	beer / ee-kee kee-shee-leek
Non-smoking.	Sigarasız.	see-gah-rah-suhz
Is this table free?	Bu masa boşmu?	boo mah-sah bohsh-moo
The menu (in English), please.	(İngilizce) menü lütfen.	een-ghee-leez-jeh meh-new lewt-fehn
tax included	KDV hariç	kah-deh-veh hah-reech
tax not included	KDV değil	kah-deh-veh deh-eel
service included	servis hariç	sehr-vees hah-reech
service not included	servis değil	sehr-vees deh-eel
"to go"	Paket	pah-keht
and / or	ve / veya	veh / veh-yah
menu	menü	meh-new
daily menu / meal of the day	günün menüsü / günün yemeği	gew-newn meh-new-sew / gew-newn yeh-meh-ee
portion / half-portion	porsiyon / yarım porsiyon	pohr-see-yohn / yah-ruhm pohr-see-yohn
daily special	günün spesyali	gew-newn spehs-yah-lee
appetizers	meze	meh-zeh
bread	ekmek	ehk-mehk
cheese	peynir	peh-neer
sandwich	sandöviç	sahn-doh-veech
soup	çorba	chohr-bah
salad	salata	sah-lah-tah
meat	et	eht
poultry	tavuk	tah-vook
fish	balık	bah-luhk
seafood	deniz ürünleri	deh-neez ew-rewn-leh-ree
fruit	meyve	mey-veh
vegetables	sebze	sehb-zeh
dessert	tatlı	taht-luh
water	su	soo
milk	süt	sewt
orange juice	portakal suyu	pohr-tah-kahl soo-yoo
coffee	kahve	kahh-veh
tea	çay	chī
wine	şarap	shah-rahp
red / white	kırmızı / beyaz	kuhr-muh-zuh / beh-yahz
beer	bira	bee-rah
glass / bottle	bardak / şişe	bahr-dahk / shee-sheh
big / small	büyük / küçük	bew-yewk / kew-chewk
Cheers!	Şerefe!	sheh-reh-feh
more / another	biraz daha / bir tane daha	bee-rahz dah-hah / beer tah-neh dah-hah
The same.	Aynısından.	ī-nuh-suhn-dahn
Bill, please.	Hesap, lütfen.	heh-sahp lewt-fehn
tip	bahşiş	bah-sheesh
Delicious!	Nefis!	neh-fees

INDEX

INDEX

INDEX

MAP INDEX

Audio Europe

RICK STEVES AUDIO EUROPE

Rick's free app and podcasts

The FREE **Rick Steves Audio Europe**™ app for iPhone, iPad and iPod Touch gives you 29 self-guided audio tours of Europe's top museums, sights and historic walks—plus more than 200 tracks filled with cultural insights and sightseeing tips from Rick's radio interviews—all organized into geographic-specific playlists.

Let **Rick Steves Audio Europe**™ amplify your guidebook.

With Rick whispering in your ear, Europe gets even better.

Thanks Facebook fans for submitting photos while on location! From top: John Kuijper in Florence, Brenda Mamer with her mother in Rome, Angel Capobianco in London, and Alyssa Passey with her friend in Paris.

Find out more at ricksteves.com

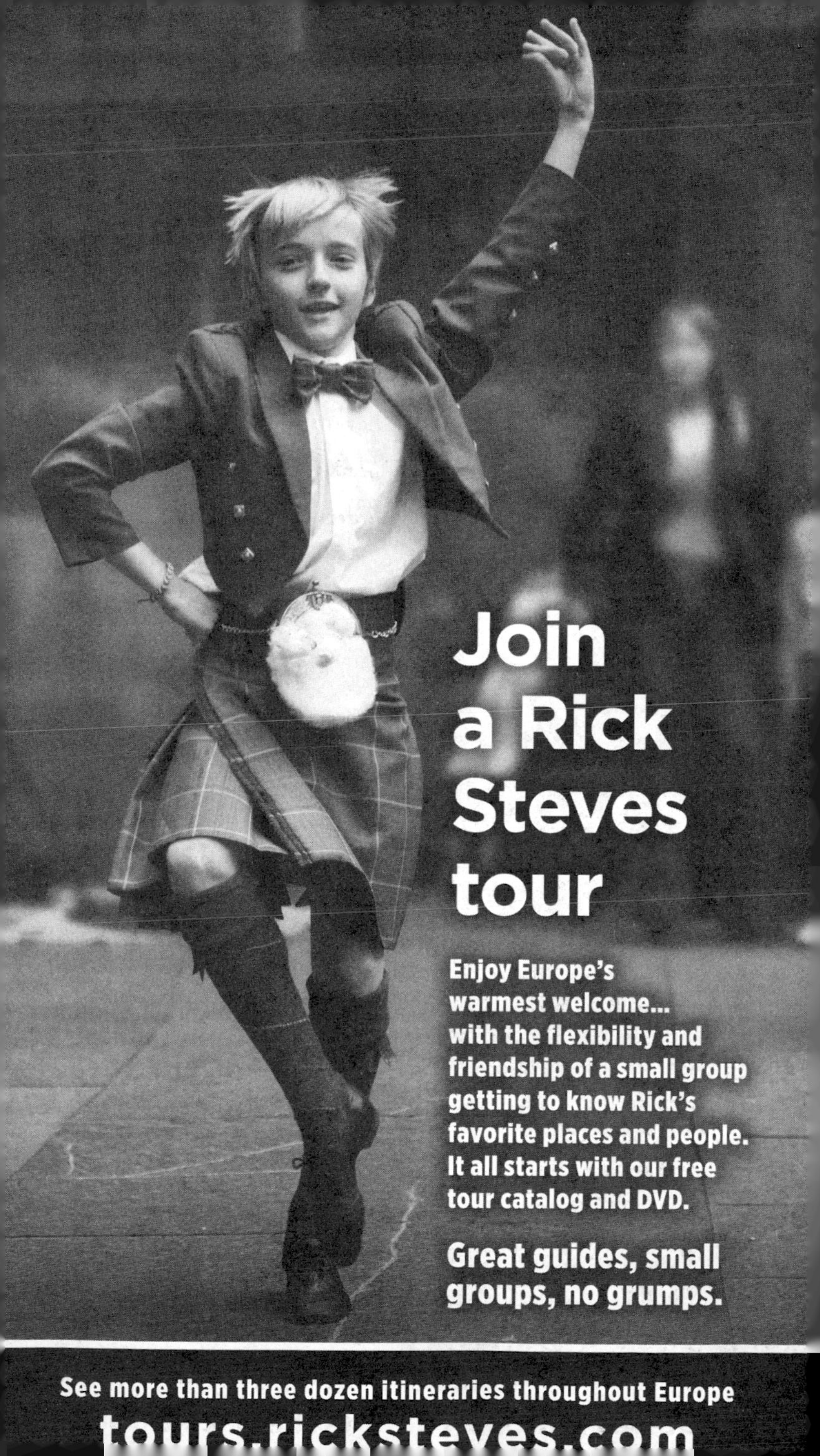

Join
a Rick
Steves
tour

**Enjoy Europe's
warmest welcome...
with the flexibility and
friendship of a small group
getting to know Rick's
favorite places and people.
It all starts with our free
tour catalog and DVD.**

**Great guides, small
groups, no grumps.**

Rick Steves

EUROPE GUIDES

Best of Europe
Eastern Europe
Europe Through the Back Door
Mediterranean Cruise Ports

COUNTRY GUIDES

Croatia & Slovenia
England
France
Germany
Great Britain
Ireland
Italy
Portugal
Scandinavia
Spain
Switzerland

CITY & REGIONAL GUIDES

Amsterdam, Bruges & Brussels
Athens & the Peloponnese
Budapest
Florence & Tuscany
Istanbul
London
Paris
Prague & the Czech Republic
Provence & the French Riviera
Rome
Venice
Vienna, Salzburg & Tirol

SNAPSHOT GUIDES

Barcelona
Berlin
Bruges & Brussels
Copenhagen & the Best of Denmark
Dublin
Dubrovnik
Hill Towns of Central Italy
Italy's Cinque Terre
Krakow, Warsaw & Gdansk
Lisbon
Madrid & Toledo
Munich, Bavaria & Salzburg
Naples & the Amalfi Coast
Northern Ireland
Norway
Scotland
Sevilla, Granada & Southern Spain
Stockholm

POCKET GUIDES

London
Paris
Rome

TRAVEL CULTURE

Europe 101
European Christmas
Postcards from Europe
Travel as a Political Act

Rick Steves guidebooks are published by Avalon Travel,
a member of the Perseus Books Group.

NOW AVAILABLE: eBOOKS, APPS & BLU-RAY

eBOOKS

Most guides are available as eBooks from Amazon, Barnes & Noble, Borders, Apple, and Sony. Free apps for eBook reading are available in the Apple App Store and Android Market, and eBook readers such as Kindle, Nook, and Kobo all have free apps that work on smartphones.

RICK STEVES' EUROPE DVDs

10 New Shows 2011–2012
Austria & the Alps
Eastern Europe
England & Wales
European Christmas
European Travel Skills & Specials
France
Germany, BeNeLux & More
Greece & Turkey
Iran
Ireland & Scotland
Italy's Cities
Italy's Countryside
Scandinavia
Spain
Travel Extras

BLU-RAY

Celtic Charms
Eastern Europe Favorites
European Christmas
Italy Through the Back Door
Mediterranean Mosaic
Surprising Cities of Europe

PHRASE BOOKS & DICTIONARIES

French
French, Italian & German
German
Italian
Portuguese
Spanish

JOURNALS

Rick Steves' Pocket Travel Journal
Rick Steves' Travel Journal

APPS

Select Rick Steves guides are available as apps in the Apple App Store.

PLANNING MAPS

Britain, Ireland & London
Europe
France & Paris
Germany, Austria & Switzerland
Ireland
Italy
Spain & Portugal

Rick Steves books and DVDs are available at bookstores and through online booksellers.

Credits

Contributors

Steve Smith

Steve manages tour planning for Rick Steves' Europe Through the Back Door and co-authors the France guidebooks with Rick (as well as this book's coverage of Provence and the French Riviera). Fluent in French, he's lived in France on several occasions starting when he was seven, and has traveled there annually since 1986.

Lale Surmen Aran & Tankut Aran

Istanbul-based Lale and Tankut are co-authors of *Rick Steves' Istanbul* (and this book's Istanbul chapter) and lead tours for Turkish and American groups, including Rick Steves' Europe Through the Back Door. They have a passion for unusual travel destinations, and with each trip, they say they become new souls, enriched and enlightened.

Gene Openshaw

Gene is a writer, composer, and lecturer on art and history. Specializing in writing walking tours of Europe's cultural sights (including many featured in this book), Gene has co-authored 10 of Rick's books. Gene lives near Seattle with his daughter, and roots for the Mariners in good times and bad.

Acknowledgments

This book would not have been possible without the help of our cruising friends. Special thanks to Todd and Carla Hoover, cruisers extraordinaire, and to Sheri Smith at Elizabeth Holmes Travel (www.elizabethholmes.com). Applause for Vanessa Bloy at Windstar Cruises, Paul Allen and John Primeau at Holland America Line, and Courtney Recht at Norwegian Cruise Line. And high fives for Ben Curtis, Sheryl Harris, Paul and Bev Hoerlein, Jenn Schutte, Lisa Friend, and Noelle Kenney.

Images

Location	Photographer
Introduction: Istanbul Waterfront	Cameron Hewitt
Part I	
Full-page image: Toulon, French Riviera	Cameron Hewitt
Choosing a Cruise: Istanbul	Cameron Hewitt
Booking a Cruise: Cannes	Cameron Hewitt
Part II	
Aboard Ship	Cameron Hewitt
Before Your Cruise: Civitavecchia	Cameron Hewitt
On the Ship: View from the Ship	Cameron Hewitt
In Port: Departing the Ship	Cameron Hewitt
Part III	
Monaco Port	Cameron Hewitt
Mediterranean Cruise Ports:	
Civitavecchia Port	Cameron Hewitt
Full page image:	
Block of Discord, Barcelona	Robyn Cronin
Barcelona's Montjuic	David C. Hoerlein
Full-page image: Nice, France	Cameron Hewitt
Pont du Gard Aqueduct	Rick Steves
Cannes, France	Steve Smith
Full-page image:	
Michelangelo's *David,* Florence	Rick Steves
Livorno Port	Cameron Hewitt
Piazzo Navona, Rome	Rick Steves
Naples and Mt. Vesuvius	David C. Hoerlein
Church of San Giorgio Maggiore, Venice	David C. Hoerlein
Full-page image: Dubrovnik, Croatia	Cameron Hewitt
Riva Promenade and Old Town, Split	Cameron Hewitt
View of Old Town, Dubrovnik	Cameron Hewitt
Athens, Greece	Cameron Hewitt
Mykonos	Cameron Hewitt
Santorini	Cameron Hewitt
Corfu	Cameron Hewitt
Hagia Sofia, Istanbul	Carol Ries
Istanbul Docks	Cameron Hewitt
Library of Celsus, Ephesus	Cameron Hewitt

Rick Steves' Guidebooks

Country Guides

Rick Steves' Best of Europe

Rick Steves' Croatia & Slovenia

Rick Steves' Eastern Europe

Rick Steves' England

Rick Steves' France

Rick Steves' Germany

Rick Steves' Great Britain

Rick Steves' Ireland

Rick Steves' Italy

Rick Steves' Portugal

Rick Steves' Scandinavia

Rick Steves' Spain

Rick Steves' Switzerland

City and Regional Guides

Rick Steves' Amsterdam, Bruges & Brussels

Rick Steves' Budapest

Rick Steves' Florence & Tuscany

Rick Steves' Greece: Athens & the Peloponnese

Rick Steves' Istanbul

Rick Steves' London

Rick Steves' Paris

Rick Steves' Prague & the Czech Republic

Rick Steves' Provence & the French Riviera

Rick Steves' Rome

Rick Steves' Venice

Rick Steves' Vienna, Salzburg & Tirol

Rick Steves' Phrase Books

French

French/Italian/German

German

Italian

Portuguese

Spanish

Snapshot Guides

Excerpted chapters from country guides, such as *Rick Steves' Snapshot Barcelona, Rick Steves' Snapshot Scotland,* and *Rick Steves' Snapshot Hill Towns of Central Italy.*

Pocket Guides (new in 2011)

Condensed, pocket-size, full-color guides to Europe's top cities: Rome, Paris, London, and more.

Other Books

Rick Steves' Europe 101: History and Art for the Traveler

Rick Steves' Europe Through the Back Door

Rick Steves' European Christmas

Rick Steves' Mediterranean Cruise Ports

Rick Steves' Postcards from Europe

Rick Steves' Travel as a Political Act

ABOUT THE AUTHOR

RICK STEVES

Since 1973, Rick Steves has spent 100 days every year exploring Europe. Rick produces a public television series (*Rick Steves' Europe*), a public radio show (*Travel with Rick Steves*), and an app and podcast (*Rick Steves Audio Europe*); writes a bestselling series of guidebooks and a nationally syndicated newspaper column; organizes guided tours that take over ten thousand travelers to Europe annually; and offers an information-packed website (www.ricksteves.com). With the help of his hardworking staff of 80 at Europe Through the Back Door—in Edmonds, Washington, just north of Seattle—Rick's mission is to make European travel fun, affordable, and culturally enlightening for Americans.

Writer and Researcher
CAMERON HEWITT

Cameron Hewitt is a writer and editor for Rick Steves' guidebooks. His favorite area is Central and Eastern Europe, where he co-authors Rick's books on Eastern Europe, Croatia & Slovenia, and Budapest. For this book, Cameron cruised the Mediterranean to research and write the port arrival instructions and cruising-specific travel skills. While on board, he climbed the rock wall, played a round of bingo, aced the "name that TV theme song" contest in the piano lounge, battled the dreaded cruise-ship virus, and went back for thirds at the midnight buffet...but refused to join the conga line. When he's not traveling, Cameron lives in Seattle with his wife Shawna.

Avalon Travel
a member of the Perseus Books Group
1700 Fourth Street
Berkeley, CA 94710

Printed in the U.S.A. by Worzalla.
Second printing October 2011.
ISBN 978-1-59880-836-0
ISSN 2160-6471

For the latest on Rick's lectures, guidebooks, tours, public radio show, and public television series, contact Europe Through the Back Door, Box 2009, Edmonds, WA 98020, tel. 425/771-8303, fax 425/771-0833, www.ricksteves.com, rick@ricksteves.com.

Europe Through the Back Door Managing Editor: Risa Laib
ETBD Editors: Jennifer Madison Davis, Tom Griffin, Cathy Lu, Suzanne Kotz, Cathy McDonald, Gretchen Strauch, Elizabeth Wang
Writing and Research: Cameron Hewitt
Avalon Travel Senior Editor and Series Manager: Madhu Prasher
Avalon Travel Project Editor: Kelly Lydick
Copy Editor: Judith Brown
Proofreader: Noël Chrisman
Indexer: Stephen Callahan
Production and Typesetting: McGuire Barber Design
Cover Design: Kimberly Glyder Design
Graphic Content Director: Laura VanDeventer
Maps & Graphics: David C. Hoerlein, Laura VanDeventer, Lauren Mills, Barb Geisler, Mike Morgenfeld, Brice Ticen, Kat Bennett
Photography: Cameron Hewitt, Rick Steves, Robyn Cronin, Laura VanDeventer, David C. Hoerlein, Rich Earl, Steve Smith, Dorian Yates, Gene Openshaw, Jennifer Hauseman, Bruce VanDeventer, Dominic Bonuccelli, Anne Jenkins, Mike Potter, Ben Cameron, Les Wahlstrom, Gretchen Strauch, Rhonda Pelikan, Tom Griffin, David Willet, Carol Ries, Mary Ann Cameron, Tankut Aran
Cover Photo: Bodrum © Cameron Hewitt